W9-CQM-762
Uberti...Reaching Back Through Time
No one dreams of the Old West without conjuring up images of six-shooters and lever-action rifles. Relive the old days with an Uberti .45 Top Break like Jesse James carried, a formidable Walker black powder revolver, or a Henry lever-action, just like the one used by Sitting Bull at the Little Big Horn.
Whether you're just out target shooting or headed into the high country after big game, with an Uberti you're holding history in your hands.
A. Uberti
History Repeats Itself
To request a FREE 68 minute DVD catalog, visit FreeDVD.uberti.com.
Imported by Stoeger Industries® Part of the Benelli USA® family (301) 283-6300

FEDERAL PREMIUM®
AMMUNITION
VITAL-SHOK™

Every shot counts™

NEW!
from
BURRIS
Laser Scope
BURRIS
4X-12X-42mm with XTR Ballistic Mil-Dot
4X-12X-42mm with Ballistic Plex
XTR Ballistic Mil-Dot
Ballistic Plex
Euro Diamond
2.5X-10X LRS
Euro Diamond
1X-4X LRS
3P#4 LRS
XTS-2575
XTS-2575
Spotting Scope
Euro Diamond
8X-42mm
10X-42mm
12X-50mm
Digital Dimmer
switch
XTS-235
Xtreme Tactical SpeedDot
Signature Select
8X-32mm
10X-32mm
1" Xtreme Tactical Rings
FastFire
Red Dot Reflex Sight
XTB Weaver-Style
Solid Steel Bases
Tripod with
Micro Adjust Window Mount
Euro Diamond
Heavy Duty
Tripod
30mm & 1" Picatinni Ring Tops

GUN TRADER'S GUIDE 30th Edition

This year's *Gun Trader's Guide* marks its 30th Edition and the 54th anniversary of the release of the first edition in 1953. *Gun Trader's* was the brainchild of author, photographer and firearms dealer Paul Wahl. In 1952, inspired by his experiences in the firearms business (Wahl Arms Incorporated), Wahl contracted with Greenburg Publishing in New York City to produce "an illustrated handbook for shooters, collectors and dealers." The result was a small size, hardback book with a modest selection of illustrations that listed collectable firearms and current (1950s) values.

A second, revised and enlarged edition, also a hard cover, was produced in 1957 and the third was released by Chilton House and Modern Guide Publications as a magazine format in 1962. Three years later, Wahl signed on with Shooter's Bible Inc. (now Stoeger Publishing) in Hackensack, New Jersey and released the fourth edition in the now familiar large size soft cover format.

Between 1980 and 1985, Paul Wahl suffered a string of family and personal illnesses that forced his retirement as editor of the *Gun Trader's Guide*. The task of revising the *Guide* fell to John E. Traister and the task is currently accomplished by editor Stephen D. Carpenteri. Paul Wahl died in 1993 but his legacy continues in the annual editions of *Gun Trader's Guide*.

The first *Gun Trader's Guide* was released during the final year of full-scale combat during the Korean War. For our 30th Edition, we have chosen to honor the American fighting men who served in that bloody conflict. Our cover showcases the primary military firearms carried by American soldiers, sailors, airmen and Marines who fought to preserve freedom in Korea.

At the end of World War II, the United States found itself with vast stores of unused military equipment, all of which it no longer needed. In the rush to demobilize and bring home as many veterans as possible, thousands of commands simply walked away and abandoned their equipment. Materiel stockpiled overseas was given away, stolen or left to rot.

Despite wastage, the military still retained huge stocks of weapons. Even with the first indications of a

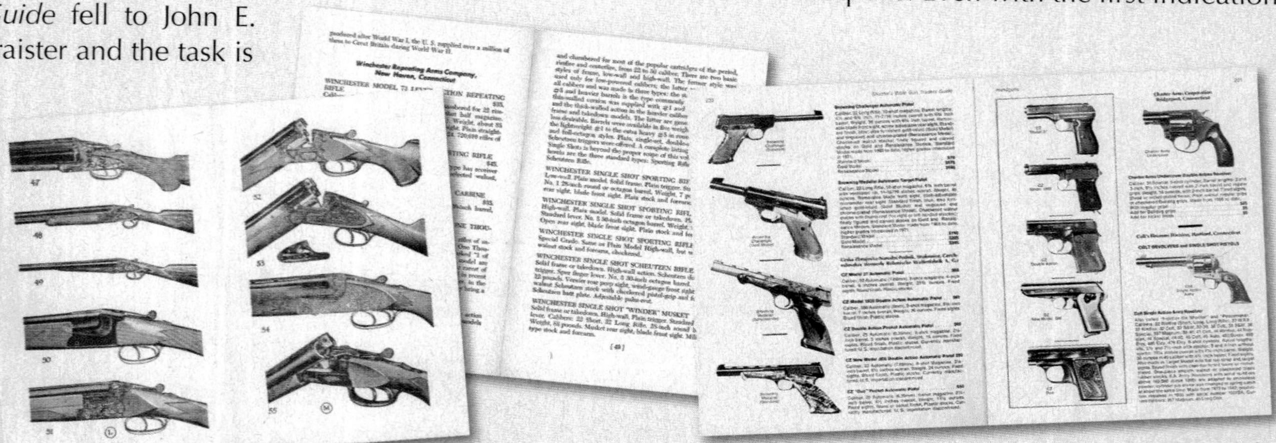

Opposite page (top): **The first edition of *Gun Trader's Guide,* printed by Greenburg in 1953, was an 8¼" x 5½" hardback book.**

Opposite page (bottom): **The first and sixth editions of *Gun Trader's* used engravings of guns taken from old manufacturer's catalogs.**

This page: **Later editions, printed in 1968 and 1973, were large format paperbacks with artwork covers.**

"cold war" looming between the Western democracies and an aggressive Soviet Union, American military leaders had no plans to develop new military small arms. When open warfare flared on the Korean Peninsula, for the most part American fighting men made do with the same arsenal with which they fought World War II.

The primary infantry weapon used by American GIs during the Korean War was the U.S. Rifle Caliber .30 M1. The "Garand," named after its inventor, Springfield Armory firearms designer John C. Garand, was the world's first semi-automatic rifle to be generally issued to infantry. Placed in service beginning in 1936, it was intended to replace the Army's famous 1903 Springfield bolt-action rifle and was subsequently issued to the other services. The first production model was tested and proof-fired on July 21, 1937.

The new rifle weighed approximately 9 pounds, 10 ounces unloaded and was 43.6 inches in length. It was gas-operated with a clip-charged, fixed magazine. The clip loading system was an eight-round *en bloc* clip that was top-loaded, along with its sheet-steel clip, directly into the fixed magazine. When the last cartridge was fired, the clip was ejected and the bolt locked open. The M1 was chambered for the Army's standard .30-06 Springfield cartridge giving the M1 a maximum effective range of about 600 yards.

The first production M1s were fitted with what proved to be an unreliable gas system that employed a muzzle extension gas trap. This was soon replaced by a drilled gas port and most of the early rifles were refitted. Today, unmodified, muzzle extension gas-trap Garands are highly prized collector's items.

Springfield Armory produced modest quantities of the new rifle throughout the late 1930s. Following the outbreak of war in Europe in 1939, however, military planners acted to increase stocks and awarded a production contract to the Winchester Repeating Arms which began deliveries in 1941. Later contracts were awarded to Harrington & Richardson and International Harvester. During the Second World War and later during the Korean War, more than 5.5 million Garands were produced.

Also issued to Americans and their UN allies fighting in Korea was the U.S. Carbine, Caliber .30, M1, a lightweight semi-automatic weapon. Before the US entry into World War II, ordnance planners sought a secondary firearm for the Army. Soldiers assigned to rear areas, airborne troops and frontline troops

"This is a book which the compiler often wished someone would produce."

Paul Wahl, 1953

required to carry extra gear, such as artillerymen and engineers, needed a lightweight weapon that would be handier than the Garand, but with greater range, accuracy and stopping power than the M1911A1 pistol. Submachine guns such as the Thompson were powerful enough at close range but were expensive and difficult to maintain.

Late in 1937, the Chief of Infantry called for the development of such a semi-automatic rifle and the Ordnance Department, working with Winchester Repeating Arms, developed a new cartridge firing a 110-grain bullet with a muzzle velocity of 2000 feet-per-second. The new round, designated the Cartridge, Caliber .30SL, M1, possessed about two times more muzzle energy than the standard .45 ACP pistol cartridge but almost three times less than that of the Army's .30-06 rifle cartridge.

Following a series of tests in September 1941, a rifle design submitted by Winchester was chosen. The M1 Carbine was approved on October 22, 1941 and Winchester received a contract for 900,000 rifles.

The resulting M1 Carbine was a gas operated, rotating bolt magazine fed, semi-automatic weapon with low recoil and a relatively high rate of fire using large-capacity (15-round), detachable magazines. At 5.47 pounds, the M1 Carbine weighed half as much as the M1 Garand with a handy overall length of 35.6 inches. The safety on early issue carbines was a cross-bolt push-button but was later replaced by the lever-type switch. Early model M1 carbines had a flip-up peep-hole rear sights which were replaced on later models by a sight with an adjustable diopter. During World War II, M1 Carbines were issued without a bayonet, but a bayonet and attachment were fitted to all Carbines issued in Korea.

Between 1941 and the end of World War II, more than 6 million M1 Carbines were produced by 10 different government contractors, including Inland Manufacturing, Underwood-Elliot-Fisher Co., Saginaw Steering Gear Division of the General Motors, National Postal Meter Co., Quality Hardware & Machine Co., International Business Machines (IBM), Standard Products Co. and Rock-Ola Co. After 1944, only Winchester and Inland continued to manufacture M1s. During the War, Inland produced the U.S. Carbine, Caliber .30, M1A1 with a metal-frame folding buttstock to reduce the size for airborne troops.

In October 1944, a fully automatic version of the carbine was adopted with a 30-round magazine. Designated the M2, it was designed for both semi- and fully-automatic fire, with a fire mode selector located on the left side of the receiver.

Members of the American armed forces received two campaign decorations for service in Korea, the United States medal at left and a medal awarded by the United Nations with a bar reading "Korea."

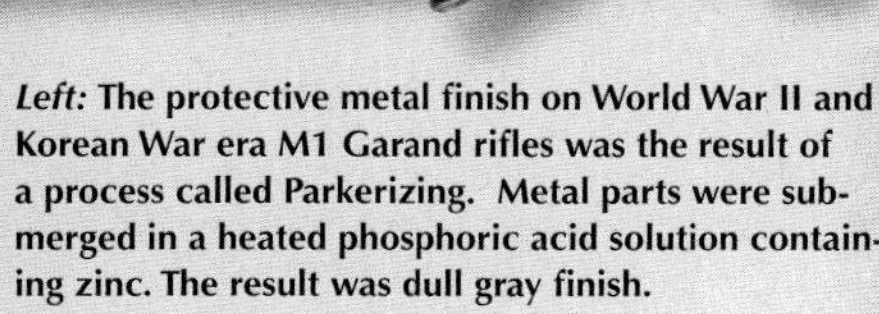

Left: The protective metal finish on World War II and Korean War era M1 Garand rifles was the result of a process called Parkerizing. Metal parts were submerged in a heated phosphoric acid solution containing zinc. The result was dull gray finish.

Right: Riflemen of the 1st Marine Division fire their M1s at attacking Chinese infantry near the Chosen Reservoir on November 27, 1950.

The standard personal defense weapon carried by officers and enlisted specialists of all services during World War II and Korea was the M1911A1 .45 cal. Pistol. Its predecessor, the Model 1911 pistol, had been adopted in 1911 in response to arguments that the Army .38 caliber revolver lacked sufficient stopping power. After a series of competitions and tests, a pistol based on a John M. Browning design was selected. The powerful Colt design was the United States' first military semi-automatic sidearm.

Battlefield experience in the First World War led to minor changes including extending the tang of grip safety, adding a raised and knurled mainspring housing and machining a clearance cut on the receiver. Designated the 1911A1, it weighed 3 pounds loaded, was 8.63 inches long and fired the potent .45 ACP cartridge at 830 feet per second. Its magazine capacity was 7 rounds.

All told, nearly two million M1911A1s were produced for the armed forces during World War II. Colt's wartime production was augmented by several manufacturers including Remington Rand, Ithaca, Union Switch and Signal Co. and Singer.

Most Garands and Carbines that saw service during World War II or Korea were refurbished sometime during their career. Damaged or abused rifles and carbines were disassembled, cleaned, repaired, restocked and returned to service. As a result, it is probable that most of the "all original matching parts" rifles found in the gun collecting market have been reassembled at some time or other by collectors. This is relatively easy to achieve since only the receivers were serial numbered. Parts were simply stamped with a manufacturer's ID code.

M1 Garands and Carbines remained in service until the late 1950s when they were replaced by the M14 and M16 rifles. Thousands were shipped to allies worldwide during World War II and Korea and as Cold War military aid to Great Britain, France, Belgian, Nationalist China, the Philippines, Norway, Denmark, Italy, South Korea, Israel and even the Japanese Defense Forces to name a few.

In recent years, the Garand and M1 Carbines, always popular with target shooters and "plinkers," have become highly collectible. It is not unusual for a good condition, World War II period Garand or Carbine, particularly one with rare manufacturer's marks or intact inspector's marks on the stock, to sell for $1000 to $1400 or more. Inland paratrooper carbines with folding stocks command premium prices (though any buyer should be aware that these rare stocks have been reproduced) as do M1C sniper versions. A basic World War II 1911A1 in top condition can sell for as much as $2,000.

Harris Andrews
Managing Editor, Stoeger Publishing

Gunners of Battery A, 17th Field Artillery Battalion, fire their 8-inch howitzer against Chinese forces near Chorwon, Korea on June 10, 1951.

Colt Model 1911 Semi-Automatic Pistol

Adopted by the U.S. Ordnance Department in 1911, the Colt semi-automatic pistol was originally manufactured by Colt and the government's Springfield Armory. In 1917, with the US entry into World War I, the government contracted with Colt for one million pistols and contracts were signed for the production of a total of two million more pistols with Remington-UMC, North American Arms, Savage, Winchester, National Cash Register Co., Burroughs Adding Machine, Lamston Monotype, and Caron Bros. A total of 629,000 pistols were completed by the war's end in1918. Production was resumed in 1924 with a series of design modifications introduced during the inter-war period resulting in the Model 1911 A1. From the onset of World War II until its end in 1945 Colt, Remington UMC, Remington-Rand, Ithaca, Singer, and Union Switch and Signal Company manufactured nearly 2 million M1911A1s.

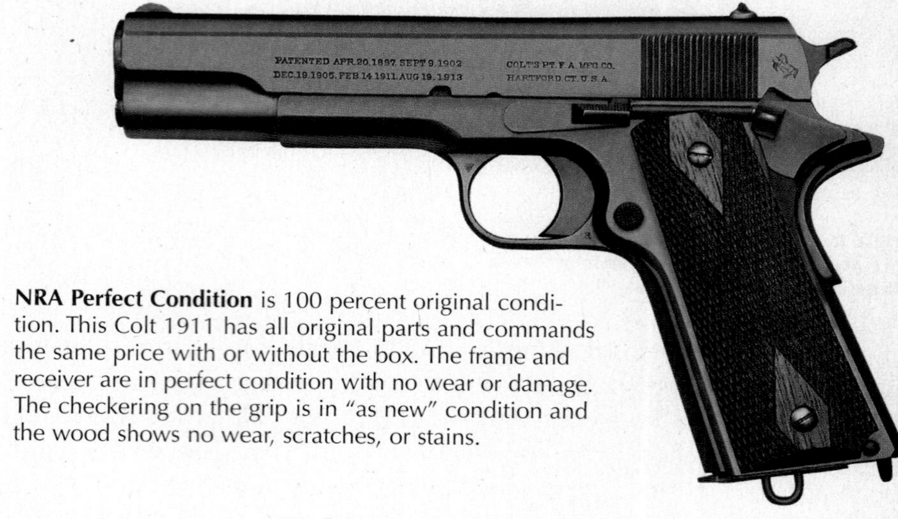

NRA Perfect Condition is 100 percent original condition. This Colt 1911 has all original parts and commands the same price with or without the box. The frame and receiver are in perfect condition with no wear or damage. The checkering on the grip is in "as new" condition and the wood shows no wear, scratches, or stains.

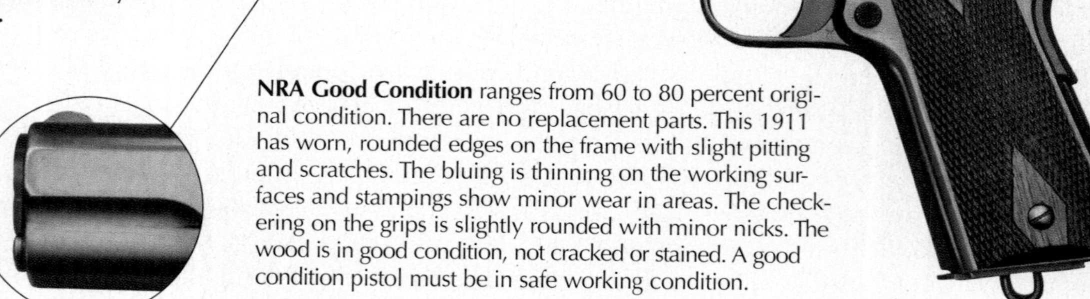

NRA Good Condition ranges from 60 to 80 percent original condition. There are no replacement parts. This 1911 has worn, rounded edges on the frame with slight pitting and scratches. The bluing is thinning on the working surfaces and stampings show minor wear in areas. The checkering on the grips is slightly rounded with minor nicks. The wood is in good condition, not cracked or stained. A good condition pistol must be in safe working condition.

NRA Fair Condition ranges from 20 to 60 percent original condition. This Model 1911 is in well-worn condition with the frame retaining only 40 percent of its original finish. Some major and minor parts have been replaced and scratches and pitting from rust and corrosion are evident on the frame and slide. Serial numbers and other markings are shallow and difficult to identify. While the grips on this pistol are not badly scratched or soiled, they show worn checkering and several large and small dents. The gun must function and shoot properly.

Winchester Model 94

Winchester produced approximately 2,550,000 Model 94 lever action rifles between 1894 and 1962. The Model 94 was manufactured in both rifle and carbine versions with several configurations that included pistol- and straight-grip stocks, various grades of wood, and several different barrel lengths and magazine capacities. Crescent and shotgun style buttstocks and takedown barrels were also offered. The Model 94 was produced in 25-35, 30, 30-30, 32-40 and 38-55 calibers.

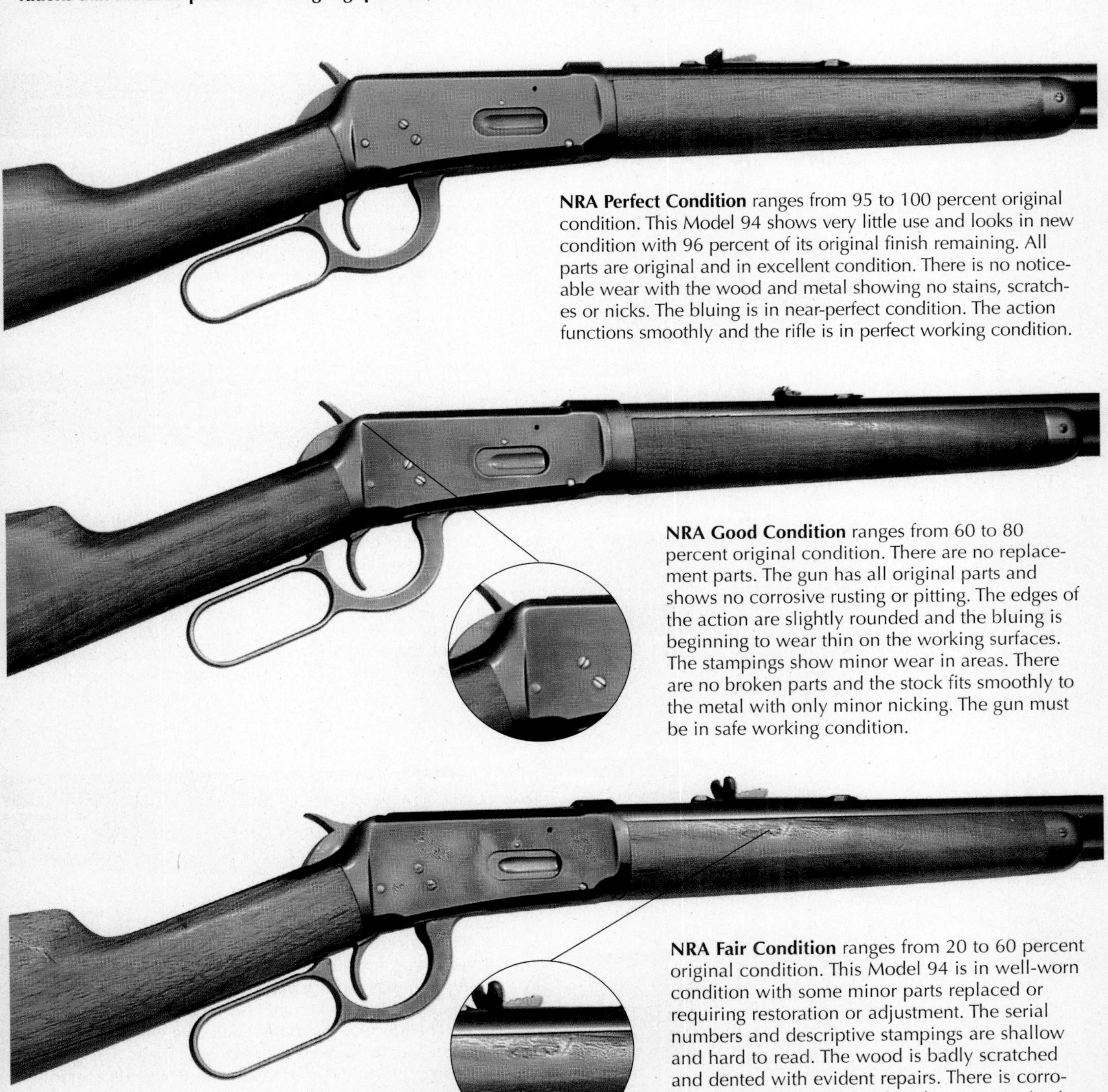

NRA Perfect Condition ranges from 95 to 100 percent original condition. This Model 94 shows very little use and looks in new condition with 96 percent of its original finish remaining. All parts are original and in excellent condition. There is no noticeable wear with the wood and metal showing no stains, scratches or nicks. The bluing is in near-perfect condition. The action functions smoothly and the rifle is in perfect working condition.

NRA Good Condition ranges from 60 to 80 percent original condition. There are no replacement parts. The gun has all original parts and shows no corrosive rusting or pitting. The edges of the action are slightly rounded and the bluing is beginning to wear thin on the working surfaces. The stampings show minor wear in areas. There are no broken parts and the stock fits smoothly to the metal with only minor nicking. The gun must be in safe working condition.

NRA Fair Condition ranges from 20 to 60 percent original condition. This Model 94 is in well-worn condition with some minor parts replaced or requiring restoration or adjustment. The serial numbers and descriptive stampings are shallow and hard to read. The wood is badly scratched and dented with evident repairs. There is corrosive pitting and scratches but the gun remains in safe firing condition.

Winchester Model 12

When introduced in 1912, the hammerless Model 12 slide-action shotgun was offered only in 20-guage with a 2½-inch chamber. In 1914 12- and 16-guage versions were introduced followed by a 28-guage in 1937. The Model 12 was available with various chokes and with walnut, straight or pistol grip stock and forearm. Winchester sold more than 1,900,000 Model 1912s during the shotgun's 51-year history.

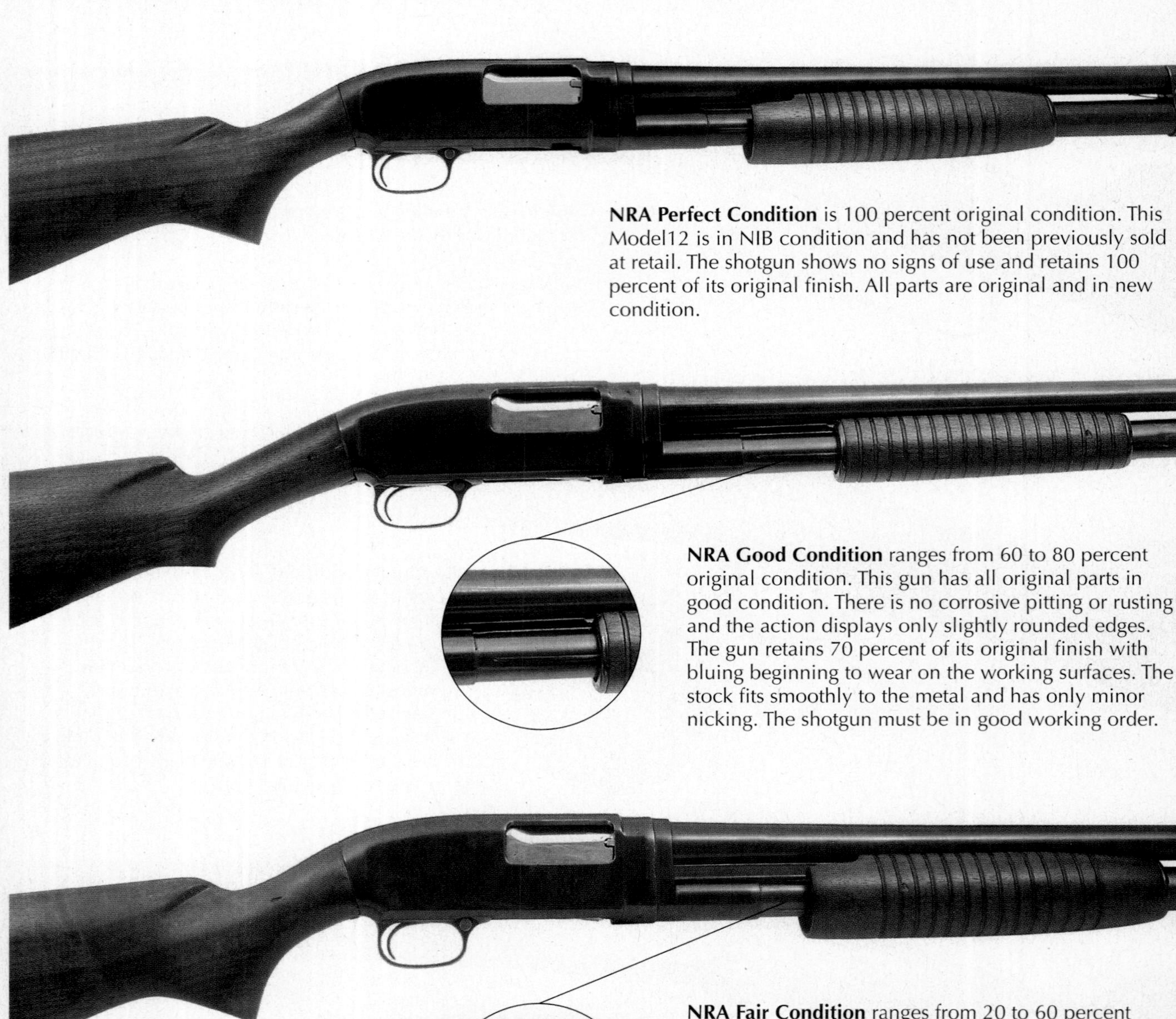

NRA Perfect Condition is 100 percent original condition. This Model12 is in NIB condition and has not been previously sold at retail. The shotgun shows no signs of use and retains 100 percent of its original finish. All parts are original and in new condition.

NRA Good Condition ranges from 60 to 80 percent original condition. This gun has all original parts in good condition. There is no corrosive pitting or rusting and the action displays only slightly rounded edges. The gun retains 70 percent of its original finish with bluing beginning to wear on the working surfaces. The stock fits smoothly to the metal and has only minor nicking. The shotgun must be in good working order.

NRA Fair Condition ranges from 20 to 60 percent original condition. Showing a well-worn condition, this gun may require minor parts to be replaced or adjusted. The serial numbers and descriptive stamping are shallow and difficult to read. The wood is badly scratched and dented with evident repairs. Corrosive pitting and scratches in the metal, while considerable, do not render the gun unsafe.

30th Edition
Completely Revised and Updated

Gun Trader's Guide

STOEGER PUBLISHING COMPANY
Accokeek, Maryland

STOEGER PUBLISHING COMPANY
is a division of Benelli U.S.A.

Benelli U.S.A.
Vice President and General Manager: Stephen Otway
Vice President of Marketing and Communications: Stephen McKelvain

Stoeger Publishing Company
President: Jeffrey K. Reh
Publisher: Jennifer Thomas
Managing Editor: Harris J. Andrews
Creative Director: Cynthia T. Richardson
Graphic Designer: Williams Graves
Special Accounts Manager: Julie Brownlee
Publishing Assistant: Stacy Logue
Proofreader: Stacy Logue

Editor of Gun Trader's Guide: Stephen D. Carpenteri

ISBN-10: 0-88317-344-1 BK0702
ISBN-13: 978-0-88317-344-2
ISSN: 0883-4431
Library of Congress Control number: 85641040

Manufactured in the United States of America

Distributed to the book trade and to the sporting goods trade by:
Stoeger Industries, Stoeger Publishing Company
17603 Indian Head Highway, Suite 200
Accokeek, Maryland 20607-2501

Front Cover: Our cover this year showcases the primary U.S. military small arms of the Korean War. Featured are the U.S. Rifle Caliber .30 M1 (top), the U.S. Carbine, Caliber .30, M1, (center) and the .45 caliber Model 1911A1 pistol.

Special thanks to: : Steve Claggett and Kenneth L. Smith-Christmas for their assistance in preparing our Korean War tribute cover.

OTHER PUBLICATIONS:

Shooter's Bible
"The World's Standard Firearms Reference Book"

Hunting & Shooting
The Bowhunter's Guide
Elk Hunter's Bible
Deer Rifles & Cartridges
High Performance
Muzzleloading
Big Game Rifles
High Power Rifle Accuracy: Before You Shoot
Hunt Club Management Guide
The Hunter's Journal
Hunting Tough Bucks
Hunting Whitetails East & West
Hunting the Whitetail Rut
Modern Shotgunning
The Pocket DEER Hunting Guide
Shotgunning for Deer
Successful Gun Trading
Sure-Fire Whitetail Tactics
Taxidermy Guide
Trailing the Hunter's Moon
Whitetail Strategies: The Ultimate Guide

Firearms
Antique Guns: A Collector's Guide
Beretta Pistols The Ultimate Guide
Guns & Ammo: The Shooter's Guide to Classic firearms
Gunsmithing Made Easy
How to Buy & Sell Used Guns
Model 1911: Automatic Pistol
Modern Beretta Firearms

Reloading
The Handloader's Manual of Cartridge Conversions 3rd Ed.

Fishing
Big Bass Zone
Catfishing: Beyond the Basics
The Crappie Book
Fishing Made Easy
Fishing Online: 1,000 Best Web Sites
Flyfishing for Trout A-Z
Out There Fishing
The Pocket FISHING Basics Guide
Practical Bowfishing
Walleye Pro's Notebook

Cooking Game
The Complete Book of Dutch Oven Cooking
Dress `Em Out
Wild About Freshwater Fish
Wild About Game Birds
Wild About Seafood
Wild About Venison
Wild About Waterfowl
World's Best Catfish Cookbook

Nature
The Pocket DISASTER Survival Guide
The Pocket FIRST-AID Field Guide
The Pocket OUTDOOR Survival Guide
U.S. Guide to Venomous Snakes and Their Mimics

Fiction
The Hunt
Wounded Moon

Nonfiction
Escape In Iraq: The Thomas Hamill Story

Special thanks to the National Rifle Association, for access to their image archives.

Introduction

This 30th edition of Stoeger's *Gun Trader's Guide* is designed to provide the professional and amateur gun enthusiast with more specifications and photographs of collectible firearms than ever before. In the past 50 years, the *Gun Trader's Guide* has grown to over 550 pages and now lists more than 6,000 firearms and variations.

The first edition of the *Gun Trader's Guide* contained some 1,360 listings accompanied by 100 illustrations. Now, after 29 revisions, the book has evolved into one of the most complete catalogs of the most popular rifles, shotguns and handguns of the late 19th and 20th centuries.

The current edition of the *Gun Trader's Guide* has been expanded to include more listings than ever before, with nearly 2,750 illustrations. Hundreds of thousands of gun buffs have made the *Gun Trader's Guide* their primary reference for identification and comparison of sporting, military and law enforcement firearms, including rare and unusual collectibles and commemoratives.

The format of the *Gun Trader's Guide* is simple and straightforward, listing thousands of firearms manufactured since the late 1800s in the United States and abroad. Most entries include complete specifications including model number and name, caliber/gauge, barrel length, overall length, weight, distinguishing features, variations and the dates of manufacture (when they can be accurately determined) and date of discontinuation. Many illustrative photos accompany the text to help the reader with identifications and comparisons. Also new with this edition, first/last entries are listed at the top of the page for additional ease in finding a particular manufacturer.

SIMPLIFIED STRUCTURE

Production data includes:

- Specifications
- Variations of different models
- Dates of manufacture
- Current values
- Tabbed sections for user friendly reference
- Complete index of all firearms

The *Gun Trader's Guide* is revised annually to ensure that its wealth of information is both current and detailed. The principal features that contribute to the unique nature of this firearms reference guide include the extensive pictorial format and accompanying comprehensive specifications. It provides a convenient procedure for identifying vintage firearms while simultaneously determining and verifying their current value.

Values shown are based on national averages obtained by conferring with hundreds of gun dealers, traders, collectors and auctioneers, not by applying an arbitrary mathematical formula that could produce unrealistic figures. The values listed accurately reflect the average of prices being charged nationwide at the time of publication.

In some rare cases, however, like with the Winchester Model 1873 "One of One Thousand" rifle or the Parker AA1 Special shotgun in 28 gauge, where very little trading took place, active gun collectors were consulted to obtain current market values.

ORGANIZATION OF LISTINGS

In the early editions of the *Gun Trader's Guide,* firearms were frequently organized chronologically by date of production within manufacturers' listings because firearms aficionados know that many gun-making companies used the date that a particular model was introduced as the model number. For example, the Colt U.S. Model 1911 semi-automatic pistol was introduced in 1911; the French Model 1936 military rifle was introduced in 1936; and the Remington Model 32 shotgun debuted in 1932. However, during the first quarter of the 20th century, gunmakers began assigning names and numbers that did not relate to the year the gun was introduced. As these recent models and their variations multiplied through the years, it became increasingly difficult to track them by date, especially for the less-experienced collector.

Also, some Winchester and Remington firearms are grouped differently in this edition. For example, The Winchester Model 1894, in its many variations, was produced beginning in 1894 and later manufactured as the "Model 94" by U.S. Repeating Arms Co. (Collectors note: this Model 1894, et al, the famed Model 70 Winchester and the Model 1300 pump shotgun, all Winchester standards, were discontinued in 2006.) In general, Winchester used the year of introduction to name its firearms; that is, Model 1890, 1892, 1894, 1895, etc. Shortly after World War I, Winchester dropped the first two digits and listed the models as 90, 92, 94, 95, etc. Later, guns were given model numbers that had no relation to the date of manufacture. Marlin and several other manufacturers used a similar approach in handling model designations.

As a result, Winchester rifles are grouped alphanumerically in two different groups: Early Winchesters, manufactured before 1920 under the 4-digit model/date designations; and those manufactured after 1920 with their revised model format designations. If any difficulty is encountered in locating a particular model, the different models and their variations are cross-referenced in the index.

Past readers have reported difficulty in finding certain Remington rifles. In this edition, Remington rifles have been grouped according to action type: That is, single-shot rifles, slide actions, autoloaders, etc. Our surveys revealed this to be the easiest way to locate a specific firearm. Again, use the index if difficulty in finding a particular model is encountered.

In researching data for this edition, we found that not all manufacturers' records were available and some information was unobtainable by press time. For example, many early firearms production records were destroyed in a fire that ravaged the Winchester plant. Some manufacturers' records have simply been lost, or were simply not maintained accurately. These circumstances resulted in some minor deviations in the presentation format of certain model listings. For example, production dates may not be listed when manufacturing records are unclear or unavailable. As an alternative, approximate dates of manufacture may be listed to reflect the availability of guns from a manufacturer or distributor. These figures may represent disposition dates indicating when that particular model was shipped to a distributor or importer. Frequently, especially with foreign manufacturers, production records are unavailable. Therefore, availability information is often based on importation records that reflect domestic distribution only.

This is simply to advise the reader of the procedure and policy used regarding these published dates and further establish the distinction between "production dates," which are based on manufacturers' records and "availability dates," which are based on distribution records in the absence of recorded production data.

To further ensure that we have the most accurate information available, we encourage and solicit the users of the *Gun Trader's Guide* to communicate with our research staff at the Stoeger offices (address below) and forward any verifiable information they may have, especially in relation to older, out-of-production models.

CAUTION TO READERS

To comply with ever-changing Federal regulations, all manufacturers who produce firearms intended for disposition to the general public and designed to accept large capacity ammunition feeding devices are required to redesign those models to limit their capacities to 10 rounds or less, or discontinue production or importation. This amendment to the Gun Control Act of 1968 prohibits the manufacture, transfer or possession of all such devices manufactured after October 13, 1994. The grandfather clause of this amendment exempts all such devices lawfully possessed at the time the legislation became law. These pre-ban arms (manufactured before October 13, 1994) may therefore be bought, sold or traded without any additional restrictions imposed by this law.

All post-ban feeding devices must meet the new requirements. For the purposes of this book, models previously designed to accept high capacity feeding devices will be listed at their original specifications and capacities if only the feeding device was modified to reduce that capacity.

Regarding shotguns, the reader should be aware that shotgun barrels must be 18 inches or longer except when used by military or law enforcement personnel. A special permit from the Bureau of Alcohol, Tobacco and Firearms is required for all others.

Because state laws vary and may change annually, it is in the collector's best interest to inquire about the legality of ownership, concealment or display of firearms in his town or county. Firearms restrictions are not universal and ignorance of the law is no defense! Protect yourself by knowing which guns you may own, purchase and transport under the laws of your state.

ACKNOWLEDGEMENTS
The publisher wishes to express special thanks to the many collectors, dealers, manufacturers, shooting editors and other industry professionals who provided product information and willingly shared their knowledge in making this the best *Gun Trader's Guide* ever.

Also, our appreciation is extended to the firearm firms and distributors' public relations and production personnel, and all the research personnel who we work with throughout the year. We are especially grateful to everyone for their assistance and cooperation in compiling information for the *Gun Trader's Guide* and for allowing us to reproduce photographs and illustrations of their collectible firearms.

Finally, our thanks to all the dedicated readers who take the time to write us with comments, suggestions and queries about various firearms. We appreciate your input and encourage you to continue. We value your input!

Readers may send comments or suggestions to:
Managing Editor
Gun Trader's Guide
Stoeger Publishing Company
17603 Indian Head Highway
Suite 200
Accokeek, MD 20607-2501

How To Use This Guide

Are you planning on buying or selling a used rifle, shotgun or handgun? Perhaps you just want to establish the value of a favorite gun in your collection. No matter what your interest in collectible modern firearms, today's enthusiast inevitably turns to the *Gun Trader's Guide* to determine specifications, date of manufacture and the updated value of a specific firearm.

Opening the book, the collector asks himself two questions: "How much is my used gun worth?" and "How was that price determined?"

Gun prices contained in this book are "retail;" that is, the price the average U.S. consumer may expect to pay for a similar item. However, many variables must be considered when buying or selling any used gun. Scarcity, demand, geographical location, the buyer's position and the gun's condition govern the selling price of a particular gun. Sentiment often shades the value of a particular gun in the seller's mind, but the market value of Grandpa's old .30/30 can not be logically catalogued nor effectively marketed (except possibly to someone else in the family!).

TEST SALE

To illustrate how the price of a particular gun may fluctuate, let us consider the popular Winchester Model 94 (discontinued in 2006 after 110 years of continuous production) and see what its value might be.

The model 1894 (or Model 94) is a lever-action, solid-frame repeater. Round or octagon barrels of 26 inches were standard when the rifle was first introduced in 1894. However, half-octagon barrels were available for a slight increase in price. Various magazine lengths were also available.

Fancy-grade versions in all Model 94 calibers were available with 26-inch round, nickel steel barrels. This grade featured a checkered fancy walnut pistol grip stock and forearm, and was available with either shotgun or rifle-type butt plates.

In addition, Winchester produced this model in carbine-style with a saddle ring on the left side of the receiver. The carbine had a 20-inch round barrel and full or half magazine. Some carbines were supplied with standard-grade barrels while others were made of nickel steel. Trapper models were also available with shortened 14-, 16- or 18-inch barrels.

In later years, the Rifle and Trapper models were discontinued and only the carbine remained. Eventually, the saddle ring was eliminated from this model and the carbine butt stock was replaced with a shotgun-type butt stock and shortened forend.

After World War II, the finish on Winchester Model 94 carbines changed to strictly hot caustic bluing; thus, pre-war models usually demand a premium over post-war models.

Then, in 1964, beginning with serial number 2,700,000, the action on the Winchester Model 94 was redesigned for easier manufacture. Many collectors and firearms enthusiasts considered this (and other) design changes to be inferior to former models. Therefore, the term "pre-64" has become the watchword for collectors when it comes to setting values on Winchester-made firearms. This will likely be the case in the future as the now-discontinued models 70, 94 and 1300 Winchester guns reach the collectible market.

Whether this evaluation is correct or not is not the issue. The justification for a price increase of pre-1964 models was that they were no longer available. This diminished availability placed them immediately in the "scarce" class and made them increasingly more desirable to collectors.

Shortly after the 1964 transition, Winchester began producing Model 94 commemorative models in great numbers, adding to the confusion of the concept of "limited production." Increased availability adversely affected the annual appreciation and price stability of these commemorative models. The negative response generated by this marketing practice was increased when the Winchester company was sold in the 1980s. The name of this long-established American firearms manufacturer was changed to U.S. Repeating Arms Company, which manufactured the Model 94 in both standard, carbine and big bore models until 2006. Later, the Angle-Eject model was introduced, a design change that allowed for the mounting of scope sights directly above the action.

With the above facts in mind, let's explore the *Gun Trader's Guide* to establish the approximate value of your particular Model 94. We will assume that you recently inherited the rifle, which has Winchester Model 94 inscribed on the barrel. Turn to the Rifle Section of the book and look under the W listings until you find Winchester. (The Contents section will also indicate where the Winchester Rifle section begins.) The Index (at the back of the book) is another possible means of locating your rifle.

The listings in the *Gun Trader's Guide* are arranged within each manufacturer's entry, first by model numbers in consecutive numerical order followed by model names in alphabetical order. At first glance, you see that there are two model designations that may apply: the original designation (Model 1894) or the revised, shorter designation (Model 94). Which of these designations applies to your recently acquired Winchester?

The first step in the process is to try to match the appearance of your model with an illustration in the book. The photos may all look alike at first glance, but close evaluation and careful attention to detail will enable you to eliminate models that are not applicable. Further examination of your gun might reveal a curved or crescent-shaped butt plate. By careful observation of your gun's characteristics and close visual comparison of the photographic examples, you may logically conclude that your gun is the Winchester Model 94 Lever Action Rifle. (Please note that the guns shown in the *Gun Trader's Guide* are not always shown in proportion to one another; that is, a carbine barrel might not appear to be shorter than a rifle barrel.)

You have now tentatively determined your model, but, to be sure, you should read through the specifications for that model and establish that the barrel on the pictured rifle is 26 inches long; round, octagonal or half-octagonal.

Upon measuring, you find that the barrel on your rifle is approximately 26 inches, perhaps a trifle under; and it is round. Additionally, your rifle is marked .38-55 (the caliber designation). The caliber offerings listed in the specifications include .38-55, so you are further convinced that this is your gun. You may read on to determine that this rifle was manufactured from 1894 to 1937. After that date, only the shorter-barreled carbine was offered by Winchester, and then only in .25-35, .30-30 and .32 Special.

At this point, you know you have a Winchester Model 94 rifle manufactured before World War II. You read the value and take the rifle to your dealer to initiate a sale. Here is a look at some of the scenarios you may encounter:

SCENARIO I

If the rifle is truly in excellent condition, that is, if it retains at least 95 percent of its original finish on both the metal and wood and has a perfect bore, then the gun does in fact have a collectible value as noted. However, keep in mind that the dealer is in business to make a profit. If he pays you the full value of the gun, he will have to charge more than this when he sells it in order to make a reasonable profit. If more than the fair market value is charged, the gun will not sell or someone will pay more for the gun than it is actually worth.

Therefore, expect a reputable dealer to offer you less than the published, maximum value for the gun in its present condition. The exact amount will vary for a variety of reasons. For example, if the dealer already has a dozen or so of the same model on his shelf and they do not sell well, his offer will be considerably lower. On the other hand, if the dealer does not have any of this model in stock and knows several collectors who want it, chances are his offer will be considerably higher.

SCENARIO II

Perhaps you overlooked the true state of the rifle's condition. Suppose the gun's finish is apparently flawless but not much of the original bluing remains. There are several shiny, bare-metal spots mixed with a brown patina over the remaining metal. Also, much of the original varnish on the wood has been worn off from extended use. Consequently, the rifle is not in "excellent" condition, and is worth proportionately less than the value shown in this book.

SCENARIO III

Your Winchester Model 94 rifle looks nearly new, as if it were just out of the box, and the rifle works perfectly. Therefore, you are convinced that

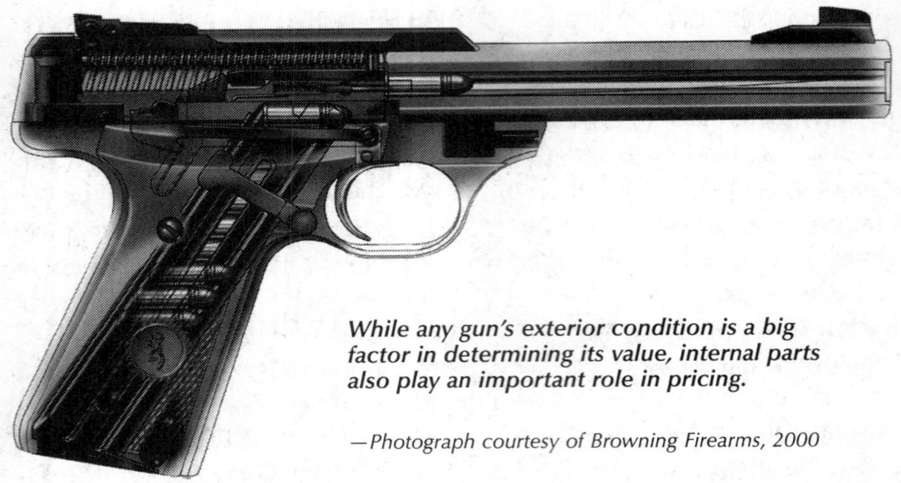

While any gun's exterior condition is a big factor in determining its value, internal parts also play an important role in pricing.

—Photograph courtesy of Browning Firearms, 2000

the dealer should pay you the full value of the gun (less a reasonable profit of 25 to 35 percent). When the dealer offers you about half what you expect, you are shocked!

Although the rifle looks new to you, the experienced dealer has detected that the gun has been refinished. Perhaps you did not notice the rounding of the formerly sharp edges on the receiver, or the slight funneling of some screw holes — all dead giveaways that the rifle has been refinished. If so, your rifle is not in "excellent" condition as you originally assumed, and is therefore worth less than "book" value.

A knowledgeable gun dealer will check each firearm to determine that it functions properly, and the condition of interior parts may also be a factor in determining the value of any firearm. Even when a collectible firearm has been expertly refinished to Excellent condition, a rule of thumb is to deduct 50 percent from the value listed in this book. If the job is poorly done, deduct 80 percent or more.

Now, if you are somewhat of an expert and know for certain that your rifle has never been refinished or otherwise repaired or damaged, there is still at least 95 percent of its original finish left, and you believe you have a firearm worth full book value, understand that a dealer will still only offer you from 25 percent to 50 percent less for it due to profit margins, over-stocked goods, etc.

OTHER OPTIONS

One alternative is to advertise your gun in a local newspaper and sell the firearm directly to a private collector. Many collectors have a special interest in certain models, manufacturers or product lines and will happily pay full price for a hard-to-find piece. However, this approach may prove both frustrating and expensive. In addition, there may be federal and local restrictions on the sale of firearms in your area, so check with the local police chief or sheriff before you proceed.

If you experience such complications, chances are the next time you have a firearm to sell you will be more than happy to take it to a dealer and let him make his fair share of profit!

STANDARDS OF CONDITION

The condition of a firearm is an important factor in determining its value. In some rare and unusual models, a variation in condition from "Excellent" to "Very Good" can mean a value difference of several thousand dollars. Therefore, you must be able to determine the gun's condition before you can accurately evaluate the value of the firearm.

Several sets of standards are available, but the National Rifle Association Standards of Condition of Modern Firearms are probably the most popular. In recent years, condition has been established by the percentage of original finish remaining on the wood and metal of the firearm.

Here's a look at how these standards are applied:

EXCELLENT

For the purpose of assigning comparative values as a basis for trading, firearms listed in this book are assumed to be in Excellent condition if they have 95 percent or more remaining original finish, no noticeable marring of wood or metal, and the bore has no pits or rust.

To the novice, this translates to a practically new gun, almost as though you had just removed the firearm from its shipping box. The trained eye, however, will see the difference between "new" or "mint" condition and merely "excellent."

VERY GOOD

Any other defects, no matter how minor, diminish the value of a firearm below those listed in this book. For example, if more than 5 percent of the original finish is gone and there are minor surface dents or scratches, regardless of how small, the gun is no longer in Excellent condition. Instead, it is considered to be in Very Good condition provided the gun is in perfect working order. Despite the minor defects, the gun will still look relatively new to the untrained buyer.

GOOD

If the gun is in perfect working condition and functions properly but has minor wear on working surfaces (perhaps some bad scratches on the wood or metal), the gun is considered to be in Good condition, one grade below Very Good, according to NRA standards. Again, the price shown in this book for that particular firearm must be reduced to reflect its true value.

The two remaining NRA conditions fall under the headings of Fair and Poor. These guns normally have little value unless they are of historical importance or an aficionado simply must have them to complete his collection. The value of such guns is then determined by the price the buyer is willing to pay.

Previous editions of the *Gun Trader's Guide* offered multiplication factors to use for firearms in other than Excellent condition. These factors are listed below, but be aware that the figures given are not etched in stone. Instead, they are simply another rough means of establishing the value of a particular firearm.

For guns in other than Excellent condition, multiply the price shown in this book for the model in question by the following factors:

Multiplication Factors for Guns Not in Excellent Condition:

CONDITION X	FACTOR
Mint or New (NiB)	1.25
Excellent (Ex)	1.00
Very Good	.85
Good (Gd)	.68
Fair	.45
Poor	.15

PARTING THOUGHTS

Remember, the word "guide" in *Gun Trader's Guide* should be taken literally. This book is meant to be a reference only and is not the gospel of the collectible trade. We sincerely hope, however, that you find this publication useful when you decide to buy or sell a used, collectible firearm. Study all available references, manufacturers' histories and visit state and regional auction houses and dealers to develop an accurate assessment of your firearm's true value.

Also, keep in mind that gun values vary from region to region. For this reason, we recommend that you attend gun shows and auctions to develop a better understanding of gun values and pricing in your part of the country. And, whenever you travel, check the prices of guns you're familiar with to determine their value in other parts of the country. The difference can be surprising!

Finally, beware of guns that have been refinished or refurbished, either by amateurs or even expert gunsmiths. A century-old gun that looks brand new has probably been refinished and will actually be worth far less than a time-worn original. Every new screw, pin or spring added to an original firearm diminishes its value — the worn, even pitted original parts of a firearm enhance its value far more than their modern replacements. Refinishing a gun may improve its looks and satisfy the final owner, but it will lose collectible value that will never be recovered.

NATIONAL RIFLE ASSOCIATION STANDARDS OF CONDITION

- **New:** Not previously sold at retail. In same condition as current factory production.
- **New, discontinued:** Same as New, but a discontinued model.
- **Perfect:** In new condition in every respect, sometimes referred to as mint.
- **Excellent:** New condition. Used very little, no noticeable marring of wood or metal, bluing perfect (except at muzzle or sharp edges).
- **Very Good:** In perfect working condition, no appreciable wear on working surfaces. No broken parts, no corrosion or pitting, only minor surface dents or scratches.
- **Good:** In safe working condition, minor wear on working surfaces. No broken parts, no corrosion or pitting that will interfere with proper functioning.
- **Fair:** In safe working condition but well worn, perhaps requiring replacement of minor parts or other adjustments that should be reported by the seller. No rust, but may have corrosion pits that do not render the gun unsafe or inoperable.
- **Poor:** Badly worn, rusty and battered, perhaps requiring major adjustment or repairs to return to operating condition.

Contents

Colt Model 1911

RIFLES

Winchester Model 94 Traditional

SHOTGUNS

Winchester Model 12 Standard

30th Edition
GUN TRADER'S GUIDE

Handguns

NOTE: *Abbreviations used throughout the Handgun section: DA = Double Action; SA = Single Action; LR = LR; WMR = Winchester Magnum Rimfire; Adj. = Adjustable; Avail. = Available; Bbl., = Barrel; Disc. = Discontinued; TT = Target Trigger; TH = Target Hammer.*

Accu-Tek Model AT .380

Accu-Tek Model BL-9

Accu-Tek HC-380SS

AA ARMS — Monroe, North Carolina

AP-9 SERIES

Semiautomatic recoil-operated pistol w/polymer integral grip/frame design. Fires from a closed bolt. Caliber: 9mm Parabellum. 10- or 20*-round magazine, 3- , 5- or 11-inch bbl., 11.8 inches overall w/5-inch bbl., Weight: 3.5 lbs. Fixed blade, protected post front sight adjustable for elevation, winged square notched rear. Matte phosphate/blue or nickel finish. Checkered polymer grip/frame. Made from 1988-99.

AP9 model
(pre-94 w/ventilated bbl., shroud . . NiB $458 Ex $355 Gd $235
AP9 Mini model
(post-94 w/o bbl., shroud). . . . . . . NiB $227 Ex $226 Gd $149
AP9 Target model
(pre-94 w/11-inch bbl.) . . . . NiB $453 Ex $380 Gd $267
Nickel finish, add. $25

ACCU-TEK — Chino, California

MODEL AT-9 AUTO PISTOL

Caliber: 9mm Para. 8-round magazine, Double action only. 3.2-inch bbl., 6.25 inches overall. Weight: 28 oz. Fixed blade front sight, adj. rear w/3-dot system. Firing pin block with no external safety. Stainless or black over stainless finish. Checkered black nylon grips. Announced 1992, but made from 1995-99.

Satin stainless model . . . . NiB $285 Ex $224 Gd $147
Matte black stainless . . . . NiB $256 Ex $208 Gd $158

MODEL AT-25 AUTO PISTOL

Similar to Model AT380 except chambered .25 ACP w/7-round magazine, Made from 1992-96.

Lightweight w/aluminum frame. . . . . NiB $169 Ex $144 Gd $92
Bright stainless (disc. 1991). . . . . . . NiB $173 Ex $150 Gd $107
Satin stainless model . . . . NiB $177 Ex $144 Gd $104
Matte black stainless . . . . NiB $170 Ex $139 Gd $98

MODEL AT-32 AUTO PISTOL

Similar to Model AT-.380 except chambered .32 ACP. Made from 1990 -2003.

Lightweight w/aluminum
Frame (disc. 1991). . . . . NiB $144 Ex $118 Gd $85
Satin stainless model . . . . NiB $195 Ex $169 Gd $118
Matte black stainless . . . . NiB $195 Ex $169 Gd $118

MODEL AT-40 DA AUTO PISTOL

Caliber: .40 S&W. Seven-round magazine, 3.2-inch bbl., 6.25 inches overall. Weight: 28 oz. Fixed blade front sight, adj. rear w/3-dot system. Firing pin block with no external safety. Stainless or black over stainless finish. Checkered black nylon grips. Announced 1992, but made from 1995-96.

Satin stainless model . . . . NiB $285 Ex $218 Gd $156
Matte black stainless . . . . NiB $285 Ex $218 Gd $156

MODEL AT-380 AUTO PISTOL

Caliber: .380 ACP. Five-round magazine, 2.75-inch bbl., 5.6 inches overall. Weight: 20 oz. External hammer w/slide safety. Grooved black composition grips. Alloy or stainless frame w/steel slide. Black, satin aluminum or stainless finish. Made from 1992-2003.

Standard alloy frame (disc. 1992) . . . NiB $176 Ex $144 Gd $93
Satin stainless model . . . . NiB $271 Ex $221 Gd $159
Matte black stainless . . . . NiB $271 Ex $221 Gd $159

MODELS BL-9, BL 380 .... NiB $195 Ex $159 Gd $113
Ultra compact DAO semiautomatic pistols. Calibers: .380 ACP, 9mm Para. 5-round magazine, 3-inch bbl., 5.6 inches overall. Weight: 24 oz. Fixed sights. Carbon steel frame and slide w/black finish. Polymer grips. Made 1997 to date.

MODELS CP-9, CP-40, CP-45
Compact, double action only, semiautomatic pistols. Calibers: 9mm Parabellum, .40 S&W, .45 ACP, 8-, 7- or 6-round magazine, 3.2-inch bbl., 6.25 inches overall. Weight: 28 oz. Fixed blade front sight, adj. rear w/3-dot system. Firing-pin block with no external safety. Stainless or black over stainless finish. Checkered black nylon grips. Made1997-2002 (CP-9), 1999 (CP-40), 1996 (CP-45.
Black stainless model. . . . . NiB $244 Ex $187 Gd $135
Satin stainless model . . . . NiB $244 Ex $187 Gd $135

MODEL HC-380SS AUTO PISTOL . . . . NiB $274 Ex $223 Gd $172
Caliber: .380 ACP. 13-round magazine, 2.75-inch bbl., 6 inches overall. Weight: 28 oz. External hammer w/slide safety. Checkered black composition grips. Stainless finish. Made 1993 to date.

ACTION ARMS — Philadelphia, Pennsylvania

See also listings under CZ pistols. Action Arms stopped importing firearms in 1994.

AT-84 DA AUTOMATIC PISTOL . . . NiB $594 Ex $522 Gd $471
Caliber: 9mm Para. 15-round magazine, 4.75-inch bbl., 8 inches overall. Weight: 35 oz. Fixed front sight, drift-adj. rear. Checkered walnut grips. Blued finish. Made in Switzerland from 1987-89.

AT-84P DA AUTO PISTOL . . . . NiB $713 Ex $574 Gd $383
Compact version of the Model AT-84. Only a few prototypes were manufactured in 1985. No resale value established.

AT-88P DA AUTO PISTOL . . . . NiB $675 Ex $546 Gd $382
Compact version of the AT-88S w/3.7-inch bbl. Only a few prototypes of this model were manufactured in 1985. Note: The AT-88 pistol series was later manufactured by Sphinx-Muller as the AT-2000 series.

AT-88S DA AUTOMATIC PISTOL. . . NiB $599 Ex $496 Gd $337
Calibers: 9mm Para. or .41 Action Express, 10-round magazine, 4.6-inch bbl., 8.1 inches overall. Weight: 35.3 oz. Fixed blade front sight, adj. rear. Checkered walnut grips. Imported from 1989-91.

ADVANTAGE ARMS — St. Paul, Minnesota

MODEL 422 . . . . NiB $190 Ex $149 Gd $97
Hammerless, top-break, 4-bbl., derringer w/rotating firing pin. Calibers: .22 LR and .22 Mag., 4-round capacity, 2.5 inch bbl., 4.5 inches overall. Weight: 15 oz. Fixed sights. Walnut grips. Blued, nickel or PDQ matte black finish. Made from 1985-87.

S. A. ALKARTASUNA FABRICA DE ARMAS — Guernica, Spain

"RUBY" AUTOMATIC PISTOL. . . . . NiB $288 Ex $268 Gd $164
Caliber: .32 Automatic (7.65mm). Nine-round magazine, 3.63-inch bbl., 6.38 inches overall. Weight: About 34 oz. Fixed sights. Blued finish. Checkered wood or hard rubber grips. Made from 1917-22. Note: Mfd. by a number of Spanish firms, the Ruby was a secondary standard service pistol of the French Army in World Wars I and II. Specimens made by Alkartasuna bear the "Alkar" trademark.

Action Arms AT-84 with Prototype of Model AT-84P in background

AMERICAN ARMS — Kansas City, Missouri

Importer of Spanish and Italian shotguns, pistols, and rifles. Acquired by Trisatan Arms, Ltd., in 2000.

BISLEY SA REVOLVER . . . . NiB $471 Ex $383 Gd $291
Uberti reproduction of Colt's Bisley. Caliber: .45 LC. Six-round cylinder, 4.75-, 5.5- or 7.7-inch bbl., Case-hardened steel frame. Fixed blade front sight, grooved top strap rear. Hammer block safety. Imported from 1997-98

CX-22 DA AUTOMATIC PISTOL
Similar to Model PX-.22 except w/8-round magazine, 3.33-inch bbl., 6.5 inches overall. Weight: 22 oz. Made from 1990 to 1995.
Standard w/chrome
Slide (disc. 1990). . . . . NiB $224 Ex $178 Gd $121
Classic model . . . . NiB $204 Ex $167 Gd $120

EP-380 DA AUTOMATIC PISTOL . . . . NiB $493 Ex $464 Gd $432
Caliber: .380 Automatic. Seven-round magazine, 3.5-inch bbl., 6.5 inches overall. Weight: 25 oz. Fixed front sight, square notch adj. rear. Stainless finish. Checkered wood grips. Made from 1989-91.

ESCORT DA AUTO PISTOL . . . . NiB $295 Ex $223 Gd $130
Caliber: .380 ACP. 7-round magazine, 3.38-inch bbl., 6.13 inches overall. Weight: 19 ounces. Fixed, low-profile sights. Stainless steel frame, slide, and trigger. Nickel-steel bbl., Soft polymer grips. Loaded chamber indicator. Made from 1995-97.

MATEBA AUTO REVOLVER
Unique combination action design allows both slide and cylinder to recoil together causing cylinder to rotate. Single or double action. Caliber: .357 Mag. Six-round cylinder, 4- or 6-inch bbl., 8.77 inches overall w/4-inch bbl., Weight: 2.75 lbs. Steel/alloy frame. Ramped blade front sight, adjustable rear. Blue finish. Smooth walnut grips. Imported from 1997-99.
Mateba model (w/4-inch bbl.). . . . NiB $1132 Ex $919 Gd $648
Mateba model (w/6-inch bbl.). . . . NiB $1197 Ex $971 Gd $683

P-98 DA AUTOMATIC PISTOL . . . . NiB $210 Ex $179 Gd $138
Caliber: .22 LR. Eight-round magazine, 5-inch bbl., 8.25 inches overall. Weight: 25 oz. Fixed front sight, square notch adj. rear. Blued finish. Serrated black polymer grips. Made from 1989-96.

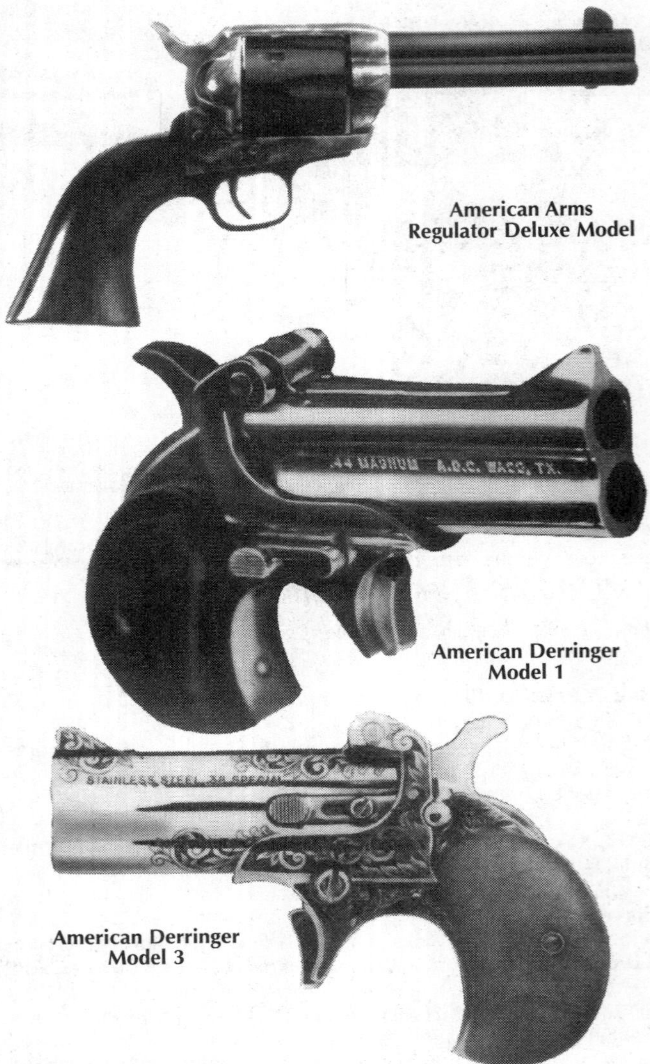

American Arms
Regulator Deluxe Model

American Derringer
Model 1

American Derringer
Model 3

PK-22 DA
AUTOMATIC PISTOL . . . . NiB $185 Ex $159 Gd $133
Caliber: .22 LR. Eight-round magazine, 3.33-inch bbl., 6.33 inches overall. Weight: 22 oz. Fixed front sight, V-notch rear. Blued finish. Checkered black polymer grips. Made from 1989-96.

PX-22 DA AUTOMATIC PISTOL . . . NiB $185 Ex $159 Gd $133
Caliber: .22 LR. Seven-round magazine, 2.75-inch bbl., 5.33 inches overall. Weight: 15 oz. Fixed front sight, V-notch rear. Blued finish. Checkered black polymer grips. Made from 1989-96.

PX-25 DA AUTOMATIC PISTOL . . . NiB $195 Ex $159 Gd $144
Same general specifications as the Model PX-22 except chambered for .25 ACP. Made from 1991-92.

REGULATOR SA REVOLVER
Similar in appearance to the Colt Single-Action Army. Calibers: .357 Mag., .44-.40, .45 Long Colt. Six-round cylinder, 4.75- or 7.5-inch bbl., blade front sight, fixed rear. Brass trigger guard/backstrap on Standard model. Casehardened steel on Deluxe model. Made from 1992 to date.
Standard model . . . . NiB $354 Ex $281 Gd $184
Standard combo set
(45 LC/.45 ACP & .44-.40/.44 Spec.). . . . NiB $379 Ex $302 Gd $220
Deluxe model . . . . .NiB $346 Ex $281 Gd $199
Deluxe combo set (.45 LC/.45
ACP & .44-40/.44 Spec.) . . . . NiB $400 Ex $348 Gd $204
Stainless steel . . . . NiB $378 Ex $307 Gd $217

BUCKHORN SA REVOLVER
Similar to Regulator model except chambered .44 Mag. w/4.75-, 6- or 7.7-inch bbl., Fixed or adjustable sights. Hammer block safety. Imported 1993-96.
Buckhorn model (standard sights) . . NiB $359 Ex $287 Gd $204
W/adjustable sights, add $15

SABRE DA AUTOMATIC PISTOL
Calibers: 9mm Para., .40 S&W. Eight-round magazine (9mm), 9-round (.40 S&W), 3.75-inch bbl., 6.9 inches overall. Weight: 26 oz. Fixed blade front sight, square, notch adj. rear. Black polymer grips. Blued or stainless finish. Advertised 1991 but not imported.
Blued finish . . . . NiB $427 Ex $345 Gd $243
Stainless steel . . . . NiB $464 Ex $366 Gd $265

SPECTRE DA AUTO PISTOL
Blowback action, fires closed bolt. Calibers: 9mm Para., .40 S&W, .45 ACP. 30-round magazine, 6-inch bbl., 13.75 inches overall. Weight: 4 lbs. 8 oz. Adj. post front sight, fixed U-notch rear. Black nylon grips. Matte black finish. Imported 1990-94.
9mm Para. NiB $579 Ex $472 Gd $425
.40 S&W (disc. 1991) . . . . NiB $446 Ex $364 Gd $259
.45 ACP . . . . NiB $504 Ex $415 Gd $302

WOODMASTER SA AUTO PISTOL. . . . . . NiB $240 Ex $195 Gd $138
Caliber: .22 LR. 10-round magazine, 5.88-inch bbl., 10.5 inches overall. Weight: 31 oz. Fixed front sight, square-notch adj. rear. Blued finish. Checkered wood grips. Disc. 1989.

454 SSA REVOLVER. . . . . NiB $949 Ex $759 Gd $563
Umberti SSA chambered 454. Six-round cylinder, 6-inch solid raised rib or 7.7-inch top-ported bbl., satin nickel finish. Hammer block safety. Imported from 1996-97.

AMERICAN DERRINGER CORPORATION — Waco, Texas

MODEL 1, STAINLESS
Single-action pocket pistol similar to the Remington O/U derringer. Two-shot capacity. More than 60 calibers from .22 LR to .45-70. Three-inch bbl., 4.82 inches overall, weight: 15 oz. Automatic bbl., selection. Satin or high-polished stainless steel. Rosewood grips. Made from 1980 to date.
.45 Colt, .44-40 Win., .44
Special, .410 . . . . NiB $433 Ex $388 Gd $320
.45-70, .44 Mag., 41 Mag.,
.30-30 Win., .223 Rem. . . . . NiB $519 Ex $503 Gd $397
.357 Max., .357 Mag., .45 Win.
Mag., 9mm Para. . . . . NiB $382 Ex $358 Gd $270
.38 Special, .38 Super, .32 Mag.,
.22 LR, .22 WRM. . . . . NiB $366 Ex $339 Gd $218

MODEL 2 STEEL "PEN" PISTOL
Calibers: .22 LR, .25 Auto, .32 Auto (7.65mm). single-shot. Two-inch bbl., 5.6 inches overall (4.2 inches in pistol format). Weight: 5 oz. Stainless finish. Made from 1993-94.
.22 LR . . . . NiB $188 Ex $153 Gd $112
.25 Auto. . . . . NiB $193 Ex $158 Gd $117
.32 Auto. . . . . NiB $219 Ex $168 Gd $127

MODEL 3 STAINLESS STEEL . . . . NiB $112 Ex $93 Gd $66
Single-shot. Calibers: .32 Mag. or .38 Special. 2.5-inch bbl., 4.9 inches overall. Weight: 8.5 oz. Rosewood grips. Made from 1984-95.

MODEL 4 DOUBLE DERRINGER
Calibers: .357 Mag., .357 Max., .44 Mag., .45 LC, .45 ACP (upper bbl., and 3-inch .410 shotshell (lower bbl.). 4.1-inch bbl, 6 inches overall. Weight: 16.5 oz. Stainless steel. Staghorn grips. Made from 1984 to date.
.357 Mag., .357 Max . . . . NiB $465 Ex $409 Gd $288
.44 Mag., .45 LC, .45 ACP . . . . NiB $557 Ex $498 Gd $338
Engraved, add $125

MODEL 6
Caliber: .22 Mag., .357 Mag., .45 LC, .45 ACP or .45 LC/.410 or .45 Colt. Bbl.: 6 inches, 8.2 inches overall. Weight: .22 oz. Satin or high-polished stainless steel w/rosewood grips. Made from 1986 to date.
.22 Magnum . . . . NiB $481 Ex $372 Gd $307
.357, .45 ACP, .45 LC. . . . . NiB $481 Ex $372 Gd $318
.45/LC/.410 O/U. . . . . NiB $491 Ex $379 Gd $338
Engraved, add $125

MODEL 7
Same general specifications as the Model 1 except high-strength aircraft aluminum is used to replace some of the stainless steel parts, which reduces its weight to 7.5 oz. Made from 1986 to date.
.22 LR, .22 WMR. . . . . NiB $415 Ex $182 Gd $131
Calibers .32, .38 and .44 . . . . NiB $539 Ex $488 Gd $427

MODEL 10
Same general specifications as the Model 7 except chambered for .38 Special, .45 ACP or .45 Long Colt.
.38 Special or .45 ACP. . . . . NiB $361 Ex $304 Gd $253
.45 Long Colt. . . . . NiB $412 Ex $304 Gd $253
Model 11 . . . . NiB $222 Ex $182 Gd $131
Same general specifications as Model 7 except with a matte gray finish only, weight: 11 oz. Made from 1980 to date.

25 AUTOMATIC PISTOL
Calibers: .25 ACP or .250 Mag. Bbl.: 2.1 inches, 4.4 inches overall. Weight: 15.5 oz. Smooth rosewood grips. Limited production.
.25 ACP blued
(est. production 50). . . . . NiB $575 Ex $442 Gd $340
.25 ACP stainless
(est. production 400). . . . . NiB $442 Ex $350 Gd $289
.250 Mag. stainless
(est. production 100). . . . . NiB $605 Ex $544 Gd $417

MODEL 38 DA DERRINGER
Hammerless, double action, double bbl (o/u). Calibers: .22 LR, .38 Special, 9mm Para., .357 Mag., .40 S&W. Three-inch bbl., weight: 14.5 oz. Made from 1990 to date.
.22 LR or .38 Special. . . . . NiB $478 Ex $441 Gd $392
9mm Para. NiB $270 Ex $223 Gd $160
.357 Mag. NiB $518 Ex $488 Gd $422
.40 S&W . . . . NiB $321 Ex $264 Gd $190

ALASKAN SURVIVAL MODEL. . . . . NiB $518 Ex $477 Gd $340
Same general specifications as the Model 4 except upper bbl., chambered for .45-70 or 3-inch .410 and .45 Colt lower bbl. Also available in .45 Auto, .45 Colt, .44 Special, .357 Mag. and .357 Max. Made from 1985 to date.

COP DA DERRINGER . . . . NiB $276 Ex $313 Gd $213
Hammerless, double-action, four-bbl., derringer. Caliber: .357 Mag. 3.15-inch bbl., 5.5 inches overall. Weight: 16 oz. Blade front sight, open notched rear. Rosewood grips. Intro. 1990 but only limited production occurred.

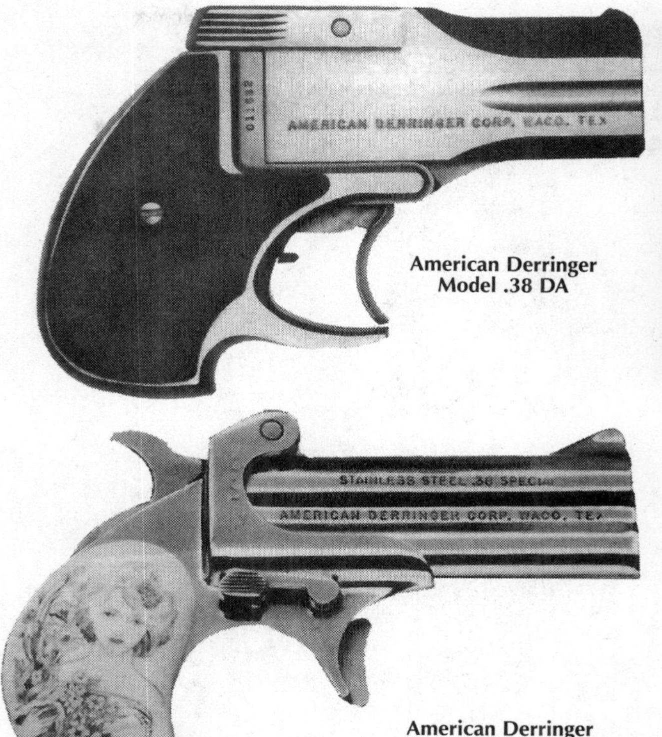

American Derringer Model .38 DA

American Derringer Lady Derringer

LADY DERRINGER
Same general specifications as Model 1 except w/custom-tuned action fitted w/scrimshawed synthetic ivory grips. Calibers: .32 H&R Mag., .32 Special, .38 Special (additional calibers on request). Deluxe Grade engraved and highly polished w/French fitted jewelry box. Made from 1991 to date. Deluxe and Engraved models disc. 1994.
Lady Derringer . . . . NiB $393 Ex $363 Gd $322
Deluxe. . . . . NiB $408 Ex $379 Gd $337
Engraved . . . . NiB $971 Ex $900 Gd $849

MINI-COP DA DERRINGER . . . . . . NiB $288 Ex $227 Gd $166
Same general specifications as the American Derringer Cop except chambered for .22 Magnum. Made from 1990-95.

SEMMERLING LM-4
Manually operated repeater. Calibers: .45 ACP or 9mm. Five-round (.45 ACP) or 7-round magazine (9mm)., 3.6-inch bbl., 5.2 inches overall. Weight: 24 oz. Made from 1997 to date. Limited availability.
Blued finish . . . . NiB $2701 Ex $2192 Gd $1541
Stainless steel . . . . NiB $3536 Ex $2860 Gd $1995

TEXAS COMMEMORATIVE
Same general specifications as Model 1 except w/solid brass frame, stainless bbls. and rosewood grips. Calibers: .22 LR, .32 Mag., .38 Special, .44-40 Win. or .45 Colt. Made from 1991 to date.
.38 Special . . . . NiB $399 Ex $358 Gd $282
.44-40 or .45 Colt . . . . NiB $486 Ex $435 Gd $409

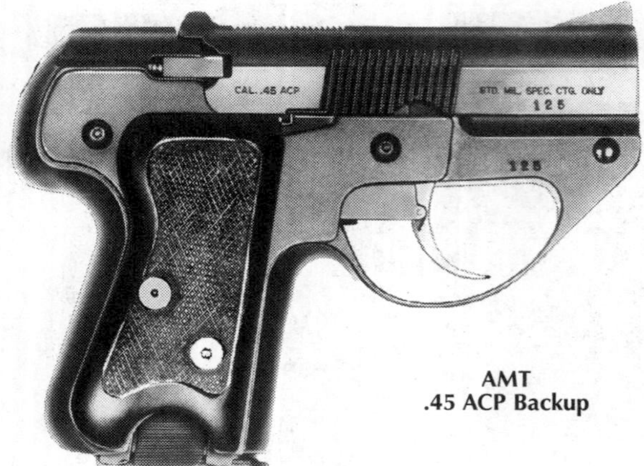

AMT
.45 ACP Backup

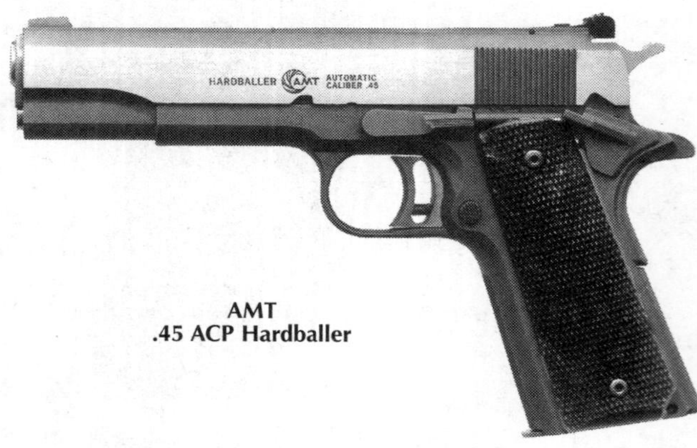

AMT
.45 ACP Hardballer

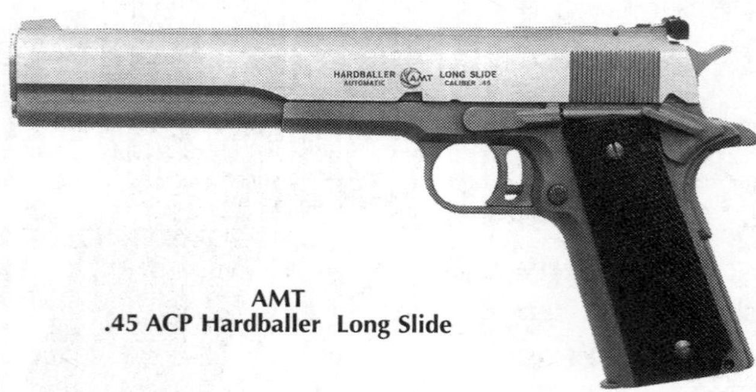

AMT
.45 ACP Hardballer Long Slide

AMERICAN FIREARMS MFG. CO., INC. — San Antonio, Texas

25 AUTO PISTOL
Caliber: .25 Auto. 8-round magazine, 2.1-inch bbl., 4.4 inches overall. Weight: 14.5 oz. Fixed sights. Stainless or blued ordnance steel. Smooth walnut grips. Made from 1966-74.
Stainless steel model . . . . NiB $245 Ex $203 Gd $148
Blued steel model . . . . NiB $189 Ex $165 Gd $127

380 AUTO PISTOL. . . . . NiB $760 Ex $708 Gd $631
Caliber: .380 Auto. 8-round magazine, 3.5-inch bbl., 5.5 inches overall. Weight: 20 oz. Stainless steel. Smooth walnut grips. Made from 1972-74.

AMT (ARCADIA MACHINE & TOOL) — Irwindale, California (Previously Irwindale Arms, Inc.)

NOTE: *The AMT Backup II automatic pistol was introduced in 1993 as a continuation of the original .380 backup with the traditional double action function and a redesigned double safety.*

45 ACP HARDBALLER
Caliber: .45 ACP. Seven-round magazine, 5-inch bbl., 8.5 inches overall. Weight: 39 oz. Adj. or fixed sights. Serrated matte slide rib w/loaded chamber indicator. Extended combat safety, adj. trigger and long grip safety. Wraparound Neoprene grips. Stainless steel. Made 1978-2001.
.45 ACP Hardballer . . . . NiB $493 Ex $339 Gd $215
Long slide conversion kit
(disc. 1997), add $300

45 ACP HARDBALLER LONG SLIDE
Similar to the standard AMT Hardballer except w/2-inch-longer bbl. and slide. Also chambered for .400 Cor-Bon. Made from 1980-2001
.45 ACP long slide . . . . NiB $467 Ex $389 Gd $261
.400 Cor-Bon long slide
(Intro.1998). . . . . NiB $447 Ex $364 Gd $257
5-inch conversion kit
(disc. 1997), add $300

1911 GOVERNMENT MODEL
AUTO PISTOL . . . . NiB $360 Ex $308 Gd $231
Caliber: .45 ACP. Seven-round magazine, 5-inch bbl., 8.5 inches overall. Weight: 38 ounces. Fixed sights. Wraparound Neoprene grip. Made from 1979 to date.

AUTOMAG II
AUTOMATIC PISTOL . . . . NiB $437 Ex $313 Gd $200
Caliber: .22 Mag. Seven- or 9-round magazine, bbl., lengths: 3.38-4.5-, 6-inch. Weight: 32 oz. Fully adj. Millett sights. Stainless finish. Smooth black composition grips. Made from 1986-2001.

AUTOMAG III
AUTOMATIC PISTOL . . . . NiB $569 Ex $491 Gd $388
Calibers: .30 M1 and 9mm Win. Mag. Eight-round magazine., 6.38-inch bbl., 10.5 inches overall. Weight: 43 ounces. Millet adj. sights. Stainless finish. Carbon fiber grips. Made from 1992-2001.

AUTOMAG IV
AUTOMATIC PISTOL . . . . NiB $573 Ex $481 Gd $388
Calibers: 10mm Mag., .45 Win. Mag. 8- or 7-round magazine, 6.5- or 8.63-inch bbl., 10.5 inches overall. Weight: 46 oz. Millet adj. sights. Stainless finish. Carbon fiber grips. Made from 1992-2001.

AUTOMAG V
AUTOMATIC PISTOL . . . . NiB $928 Ex $798 Gd $720
Caliber: .50 A.E. Five-round magazine, 7-inch bbl., 10.5 inches overall. Weight: 46 oz. Custom adj. sights. Stainless finish. Carbon fiber grips. Made from 1994-95.

BACKUP AUTOMATIC PISTOL
Caliber: .22LR, .380 ACP. Eight-round (.22LR) or 5-round (.380 ACP) magazine, 2.5-inch bbl., 5 inches overall. Weight: 18 oz. Open sights. Carbon fiber or walnut grips. Stainless steel finish. Made from 1990-98.
.22 LR (disc. 1987) . . . . NiB $331 Ex $213 Gd $156
.380 ACP (disc. 2000) . . . . NiB $279 Ex $202 Gd $146

BACKUP II
AUTOMATIC PISTOL . . . . NiB $287 Ex $215 Gd $173
Caliber: .380 ACP, 5-round magazine, 2.5-inch bbl., 5 inches overall. Weight: 18 oz. Open sights. Stainless steel finish. Carbon-fiber grips. Made from 1993-98.

BACKUP DAO AUTO PISTOL
Calibers: .380 ACP, .38 Super, 9mm Para., .40 Cor-Bon, .40 S&W, .45 ACP. Six-round (.380, .38 Super 9mm) or 5-round (.40 Cor-Bon, .40 S&W, .45 ACP) magazine, 2.5-inch bbl., 5.75-inches overall. Weight: 18 oz. (.380 ACP) or 23 oz. Open fixed sights. Stainless steel finish. Carbon fiber grips. Made from 1992 to date.
.380 ACP . . . . NiB $248 Ex $196 Gd $155
.38 Super, 9mm . . . . NiB $273 Ex $212 Gd $140
.40 Cor-Bon, .40 S&W,
.45 ACP . . . . NiB $267 Ex $217 Gd $153

BULL'S EYE
TARGET MODEL . . . . NiB $432 Ex $372 Gd $326
Caliber: .40 S&W. Eight-round magazine, 5-inch bbl., 8.5 inches overall. Weight: 38 oz. Millet adjustable sights. Wide adj. trigger. Wraparound Neoprene grips. Made from 1990-92.

JAVELINA . . . . NiB $602 Ex $499 Gd $385
Caliber: 10mm. Eight-round magazine, 7-inch bbl., 10.5 inches overall. Weight: 48 oz. Long grip safety, beveled magazine well, wide adj. trigger. Millet adj. sights. Wraparound Neoprene grips. Stainless finish. Made from 1991-93.

LIGHTNING AUTO PISTOL
Caliber: .22 LR. 10-round magazine, 5-, 6.5-, 8.5-, 10-inch bbl., 10.75 inches overall (6.5-inch bbl.). Weight: 45 oz. (6.5-inch bbl.). Millett adj. sights. Checkered rubber grips. Stainless finish. Made from 1984-87.
Standard model . . . . NiB $382 Ex $278 Gd $176
Bull's-Eye model . . . . NiB $452 Ex $382 Gd $316

ON DUTY DA PISTOL
Calibers: .40 S&W, 9mm Para., .45 ACP. 15-round (9mm), 13-shot (.40 S&W) or 9-round (.45 ACP) magazine, 4.5-inch bbl., 7.75 inches overall. Weight: 32 oz. Hard anodized aluminum frame. Stainless steel slide and bbl., Carbon fiber grips. Made from 1991-94.
9mm or .40 S&W . . . . NiB $419 Ex $326 Gd $279
.45 ACP . . . . NiB $460 Ex $382 Gd $228

SKIPPER AUTO PISTOL . . . . NiB $408 Ex $310 Gd $279
Calibers: .40 S&W and .45 ACP. Seven-round magazine, 4.25-inch bbl., 7.5 inches overall. Weight: 33 oz. Millet adj. sights. Walnut grips. Matte finish stainless steel. Made from 1990-92.

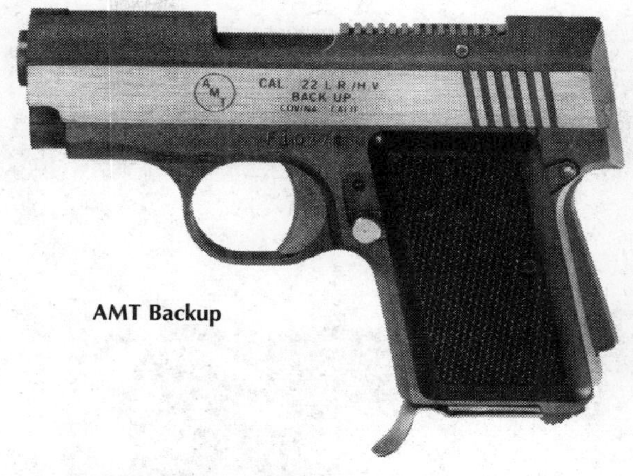

AMT Backup

AMT Backup DAO

AMT Bull's Eye Target

AMT Skipper

ANSCHUTZ PISTOLS — Ulm, Germany Mfd. by J.G. Anschutz GmbH Jagd und Sportwaffenfabrik

Currently imported by Accuracy International, Boseman, MT and AcuSport Corporation, Bellefontaine, OH

MODEL 64P
Calibers: .22 LR or .22 Magnum. Five- or 4-round magazine, 10-inch bbl., 64MS action w/two-stage trigger. Target sights optional. Rynite black synthetic stock. Imported from 1998 to date.
.22 LR . . . . NiB $512 Ex $400 Gd $342
.22 Mag. . . . . NiB $544 Ex $529 Gd $472
W/tangent sights, add $80

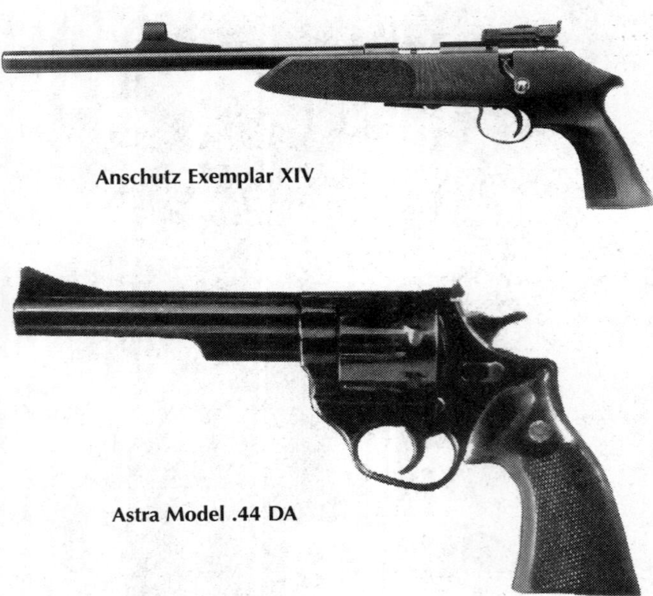

Anschutz Exemplar XIV

Astra Model .44 DA

EXEMPLAR (1416P/1451P) BOLT-ACTION PISTOL
Caliber: .22 LR, single-shot or 5-round clip. Seven- or 10-inch bbl., 19 inches overall (10-inch bbl.). Weight: 3.33 lbs. Match 64 action. Slide safety. Hooded ramp post front sight, adjustable open notched rear. European walnut contoured grip. Exemplar made from 1987-95 and 1400 series made from 1997 to date. Note: The .22 WMR chambering was also advertised but never manufactured.
Exemplar w/7- or 10-inch bbl. . . . . NiB $432 Ex $390 Gd $333
Left-hand model (disc. 1997). . . . . NiB $451 Ex $499 Gd $416
Model 1451P (single-shot). . . . . . . NiB $453 Ex $369 Gd $261
Model 1416P (5-round repeater) . . . NiB $441 Ex $359 Gd $254

EXEMPLAR HORNET . . . . NiB $910 Ex $713 Gd $614
Based on the Anschutz Match 54 action, tapped and grooved for scope mounting with no open sights. Caliber: .22 Hornet, 5-round magazine, 10-inch bbl., 20 inches overall. Weight: 4.35 lbs. Checkered European walnut grip. Winged safety. Made from 1990 to 1995.
EXEMPLAR XIV . . . . NiB $551 Ex $499 Gd $416
Same general specifications as the standard Exemplar bolt-action pistol except with 14-inch bbl., weight: 4.15 lbs. Made from 1989-95.

ARMSCOR (Arms Corp.) — Manila, Philippines

Currently imported by K.B.I., Harrisburg, PA. (Imported 1991-95 by Ruko Products, Inc., Buffalo NY. Previously by Armscor Precision, San Mateo, CA.)

MODEL M1911-A-1
AUTOMATIC PISTOL . . . . NiB $422 Ex $381 Gd $238
Caliber: .45 ACP. Eight-round magazine, 5-inch bbl., 8.75 inches overall. Weight: 38 oz. Blade front sight, drift adjustable rear w/3-dot system. Skeletonized tactical hammer and trigger. Extended slide release and beavertail grip safety. Parker-ized finish. Checkered composition or wood stocks. Imported from1996-97.

MODEL M1911-A-1
COMMANDER . . . . NiB $435 Ex $330 Gd $260
Caliber: .45 ACP. Similar to M1911-A-1 except with Commander configuration and 4-inch bbl. Rear slide serrations only. Imported in 2001.
Two-tone finish . . . . add $50
Stainless . . . . add $100

MODEL M1911-A-1 COMBAT. . . . . NiB $460 Ex $355 Gd $285
Caliber: .45 ACP. Similar to M1911-A-1 except with Combat configuration. Bbl.:3.5 inches. Checkered hardwood grips. Weight: 2.16 pounds.
Two-tone finish . . . . add $50
Stainless . . . . add $100

MODEL M1911-A-1
MEDALLION SERIES . . . . $580 Ex $410 Gd $320
Caliber: 9mm Para., .40 S&W, .45ACP. Standard or Tactical, blue finish standard. Bbl.: 5 inches. Custom model with match barrel, checkered wood Pachmayr grips. Imported.
Two-tone finish (Tactical) . . . . add $225
Chrome (Tactical) . . . . add $250

MODEL200DC/TC
DA REVOLVER . . . . .NiB $184 Ex $164 Gd $138
Caliber: .38 Special. Six-round cylinder, 2.5-, 4-, or 6-inch bbl.; 7.3, 8.8, or 11.3 inches overall. Weight: 22, 28, or 34 oz. Ramp front and fixed rear sights. Checkered mahogany or rubber grips. Imported from 1996 to date.

MODEL202A REVOLVER . . . . .NiB $206 Ex $151 Gd $106
Caliber: .38 Special. Similar to Model 200 (DC) revolver except does not have barrel shroud. Imported.

MODEL206 REVOLVER . . . . .NiB $227 Ex $167 Gd $122
Caliber: .38 Special. Similar to Model 200 (DC) revolver except has a 2-7/8-inch bbl. Weight: 24 ounces. Imported.

MODEL210 REVOLVER . . . . .NiB $222 Ex $167 Gd $117
Caliber: .38 Special. Similar to Model 200 (DC) except has a 4-inch ventilated rib bbl., adjustable rear sight. Weight: 28 ounces. Imported.

ASAI AG — Advanced Small Arms Industries Solothurn, Switzerland

Currently imported by Magnum Research Inc., Minneapolis, MN.

See listings under Magnum Research Pistols

ASTRA PISTOLS — Guernica, Spain Manufactured by Unceta y Compania

Currently imported by E.A.A. Corporation, Sharpes, FL.

MODEL 357 DA REVOLVER . . . . . . NiB $277 Ex $241 Gd $206
Caliber: .357 Magnum. Six-round cylinder. 3-, 4-, 6-, 8.5-inch bbl., 11.25 inches overall (with 6-inch bbl.). Weight: 42 oz. (with 6-inch bbl.). Ramp front sight, adj. rear sight. Blued finish. Checkered wood grips. Imported from 1972-88.

MODEL 44 DA REVOLVER
Similar to Astra ..357 except chambered for .44 Magnum. Six- or 8.5-inch bbl., 11.5 inches overall (6-inch bbl.). Weight: 44 oz. (6-inch bbl.). Imported from 1980-93.
Blued finish (disc. 1987) . . . . NiB $311 Ex $265 Gd $239
Stainless finish (disc. 1993) . . . . . . NiB $316 Ex $265 Gd $239

MODEL 41 DA REVOLVER . . . . . . .NiB $299 Ex $258 Gd $176
Same general specifications as Model 44 except in .41 Mag. Imported from 1980-85.

MODEL 45 DA REVOLVER . . . . NiB $314 Ex $263 Gd $237
Similar to Astra .357 except chambered for .45 Colt or .45 ACP. Six- or 8.5-inch bbl., 11.5 inches overall (with 6-inch bbl.). Weight: 44 oz. (6-inch bbl.). Imported from 1980-87.

MODEL 200 FIRECAT
VEST POCKET AUTO PISTOL . . . . .NiB $273 Ex $222 Gd $207
Caliber: .25 Automatic (6.35mm). Six-round magazine, 2.25-inch bbl., 4.38 inches overall. Weight: 11.75 oz. Fixed sights. Blued finish. Plastic grips. Made 1920 to date. U.S. importation disc. in 1968.

MODEL 202 FIRECAT
VEST POCKET AUTO PISTOL . . . . . NiB $514 Ex $438 Gd $387
Same general specifications as the Model 200 except chromed and engraved w/pearl grips. U.S. importation disc. 1968.

MODEL 400 AUTO PISTOL. . . . . . . NiB $438 Ex $397 Gd $183
Caliber: 9mm Bayard Long (.38 ACP, 9mm Browning Long, 9mm Glisenti, 9mm Para. and 9mm Steyr cartridges may be used interchangeably in this pistol because of its chamber design). Nine-round magazine., 6-inch bbl., 10 inches overall. Weight: 35 oz. Fixed sights. Blued finish. Plastic grips. Made 1922-45. Note: This pistol, as well as Astra Models 600 and 3000, is a modification of the Browning Model 1912.

MODEL 600 MIL./POLICE-TYPE
AUTO PISTOL . . . . NiB $433 Ex $356 Gd $224
Calibers: .32 Automatic (7.65mm), 9mm Para. Magazine: 10-round (.32 cal.) or 8-round (9mm)., 5.25-inch bbl., 8 inches overall. Weight: About 33 oz. Fixed sights. Blued finish. Checkered wood or plastic grips. Made from 1944-45.

MODEL 800 CONDOR
MILITARY AUTO PISTOL. . . . . . . NiB $1572 Ex $1190 Gd $807
Similar to Models 400 and 600 except has an external hammer. Caliber: 9mm Para. Eight-round magazine, 5.25-inch bbl., 8.25 inches overall. Weight: 32.5 oz. Fixed sights. Blued finish. Plastic grips. Imported from 1958-65.

MODEL 2000 CAMPER
AUTOMATIC PISTOL . . . . NiB $395 Ex $283 Gd $191
Same as Model 2000 Cub except chambered for .22 Short only, has 4-inch bbl., overall length, 6.25 inches, weight: 11.5 oz. Imported from 1955-60.

MODEL 2000 CUB
POCKET AUTO PISTOL. . . . . NiB $271 Ex $210 Gd $138
Calibers: .22 Short, .25 Auto. Six-round magazine, 2.25-inch bbl., 4.5 inches overall. Weight: About 11 oz. Fixed sights. Blued or chromed finish. Plastic grips. Made 1954 to date. U.S. importation disc. 1968.

MODEL 3000
POCKET AUTO PISTOL. . . . . NiB $540 Ex $520 Gd $259
Calibers: .22 LR, .32 Automatic (7.65mm), .380 Auto (9mm Short). Ten-round magazine (.22 cal.), 7-round (.32 cal.), 6-round (.380 cal.). Four-inch bbl., 6.38 inches overall. Weight: About 22 oz. Fixed sights. Blued finish. Plastic grips. Made from 1947-56.

MODEL 3003
POCKET AUTO PISTOL. . . . . NiB $1089 Ex $732 Gd $559
Same general specifications as the Model 3000 except chromed and engraved w/pearl grips. Disc. 1956.

Astra Model 3003 Pocket

Astra Model 4000 Falcon

MODEL 4000
ALCON AUTO PISTOL . . . . NiB $547 Ex $445 Gd $282
Similar to Model 3000 except has an external hammer. Calibers: .22 LR, .32 Automatic (7.65mm), .380 Auto (9mm Short). Ten-round magazine (.22 LR), 8-round (.32 Auto), 7-round (.380 Auto), 3.66-inch bbl., 6.5-inches overall. Weight: 20 oz. (.22 cal.) or 24.75 oz. (.32 and .380). Fixed sights. Blued finish. Plastic grips. Made from 1956-71.

MODEL A-60 DA
AUTOMATIC PISTOL . . . . NiB $439 Ex $388 Gd $255
Similar to the Constable except in .380 only, w/13-round magazine and slide-mounted ambidextrous safety. Blued finish only. Imported from 1980-91.

MODEL A-70 COMPACT AUTO PISTOL
Calibers: 9mm Para., .40 S&W. Eight-round (9mm) or 7-round (.40 S&W) magazine., 3.5-inch bbl., 6.5 inches overall. Blued, nickel or stainless finish. Weight: 29.3 oz. Imported from 1992-96.
Blued finish . . . . NiB $298 Ex $273 Gd $191
Nickel finish . . . . NiB $329 Ex $304 Gd $222
Stainless finish. . . . . NiB $390 Ex $350 Gd $298

MODEL A-75 DECOCKER AUTO PISTOL
Similar to the Model 70 except in 9mm, .40 S&W and .45 ACP w/decocking system and contoured pebble-textured grips. Imported from 1993-97.
Blued finish, 9mm or .40 S&W . . . . NiB $304 Ex $273 Gd $207
Nickel finish, 9mm or .40 S&W. . . . NiB $319 Ex $273 Gd $191
Stainless, 9mm or .40 S&W. . . . . . . NiB $309 Ex $273 Gd $202
Blued finish, .45 ACP. . . . . NiB $335 Ex $274 Gd $182
Nickel finish, .45 ACP . . . . NiB $359 Ex $294 Gd $182
Stainless, .45 ACP . . . . NiB $401 Ex $350 Gd $248

MODEL A-75 ULTRALIGHT . . . . . . NiB $332 Ex $286 Gd $199
Similar to the standard Model 75 except 9mm only w/24-oz. alloy

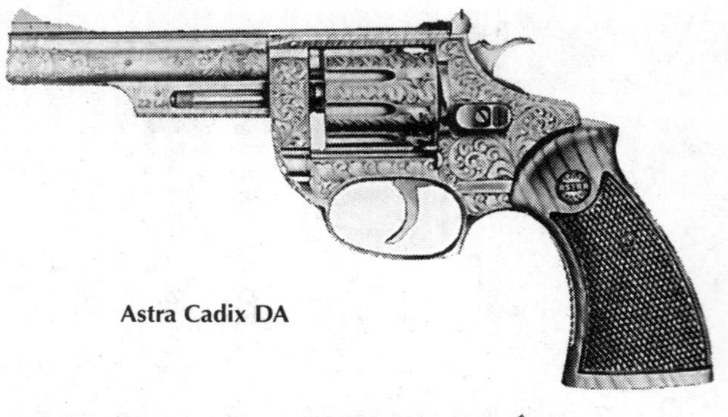
Astra Cadix DA

Astra Constable DA

Auto-Ordnance 1927 A-5 w/drum magazine

MODEL A-80 AUTO PISTOL . . . . . . NiB $404 Ex $353 Gd $241
Calibers: 9mm Para., .38 Super, .45 ACP. 15-round magazine or 9-round (.45 ACP). Bbl.: 3.75 inches., 7 inches overall. Weight: 36 oz. Imported from 1982-89.

MODEL A-90 DA AUTOMATIC PISTOL . . . . .NiB $438 Ex $361 Gd $254
Calibers: 9mm Para., .45 ACP. 15-round (9mm) or 9-round (.45 ACP) magazine, 3.75-inch bbl., 7 inches overall. Weight: about 40 oz. Fixed sights. Blued finish. Checkered plastic grips. Imported from 1985-90.

MODEL A-100 DA AUTO PISTOL
Same general specifications as the Model A-90 except selective double action chambered for 9mm Para., .40 S&W or .45 ACP. Imported from 1991-97.
Blued finish . . . . NiB $412 Ex $361 Gd $259
Nickel finish . . . . NiB $438 Ex $374 Gd $244
For night sights, add $85

CADIX DA REVOLVER
Calibers: .22 LR, .38 Special. Nine-round (.22 LR) or 5-round (.38 cal.) cylinder. Four- or 6-inch bbl., Weight: About 27 oz. (6-inch bbl.). Ramp front sight, adj. rear sight. Blued finish. Plastic grips. Imported from 1960-68.
Standard model . . . . NiB $222 Ex $191 Gd $125
Lightly engraved model . . . . NiB $342 Ex $278 Gd $196
Heavily engraved model (shown) . . . . . NiB $658 Ex $532 Gd $371

CONSTABLE DA AUTO PISTOL
Calibers: .22 LR, .32 Automatic (7.65mm), .380 Auto (9mm Short). Magazine capacity: 10-round (.22 LR), 8-round (.32), 7-round (.380). 3.5-inch bbl., 6.5 inches overall. Weight: about 24 oz. Blade front sight, windage adj. rear. Blued or chromed finish. Imported from 1965-92.
Stainless finish . . . . NiB $377 Ex $306 Gd $217
Blued finish . . . . NiB $326 Ex $266 Gd $189
Chrome finish (disc. 1990) . . . . NiB $345 Ex $281 Gd $199

AUTAUGA ARMS — Prattville, Alabama

MODEL 32 (MK II) DAO AUTOMATIC PISTOL . . . . NiB $361 Ex $259 Gd $203
Caliber: .32 ACP. Six-round magazine, 2-inch bbl., weight: 11.36 oz.. Double action only. Stainless steel. Black polymer grips. Made from 1997 to date.

AUTO-ORDNANCE CORPORATION — West Hurley, New York

1911 A1 GOVERNMENT AUTO PISTOL
Copy of Colt 1911 A1 semiautomatic pistol. Calibers: 9mm Para., .38 Super, 10mm, .45 ACP. 9-round (9mm, .38 Super) or 7-round 10mm, .45 ACP) magazine. Five-inch bbl., 8.5 inches overall. Weight: 39 oz. Fixed blade front sight, rear adj. Blued, satin nickel or Duo-Tone finish. Checkered plastic grips. Made from 1983-99.
.45 ACP caliber . . . . NiB $396 Ex $330 Gd $248
9mm, 10mm, .38 Super. . . . . NiB $405 Ex $340 Gd $234

1911A1 .40 S&W PISTOL . . . . NiB $396 Ex $330 Gd $248
Similar to the Model 1911 A1 except has 4.5-inch bbl., w/7.75-inch overall length. Eight-round magazine, weight: 37 oz. Blade front and adj. rear sights w/3-dot system. Checkered black rubber wrap-around grips. Made from 1991-99.

1911 "THE GENERAL". . . . . NiB $417 Ex $355 Gd $233
Caliber: .45 ACP. Seven-round magazine, 4.5-inch bbl., 7.75 inches overall. Weight: 37 oz. Blued nonglare finish. Made from 1992-99.

1927 A-5 SEMIAUTOMATIC PISTOL
Similar to Thompson Model 1928A submachine gun except has no provision for automatic firing and does not have detachable butt-stock. Caliber: .45 ACP, 5-, 15-, 20- and 30-round detachable box magazines. 30-round drum also available. 13-inch finned bbl., 26 inches overall. Weight: About 6.75 lbs. Adj. rear sight, blade front. Blued finish. Walnut grips. Made from 1977-94.
W/box magazine . . . . NiB $922 Ex $743 Gd $518
W/drum magazine (illustrated) . . . NiB $1254 Ex $1011 Gd $701

ZG-51 PIT BULL AUTOMATIC PISTOL . . . . NiB $422 Ex $345 Gd $248
Caliber: .45 ACP. Seven-round magazine, 3.5-inch bbl., 7 inches overall. Weight: 32 oz. Fixed front sight, square-notch rear. Blued finish. Checkered plastic grips. Made from 1991-99.

LES BAER — Hillsdale, Illinois

1911 CONCEPT SERIES AUTOMATIC PISTOL

Similar to Government 1911 built on steel or alloy full-size or compact frame. Caliber: .45 ACP. Seven-round magazine, 4.25- or 5-inch bbl. Weight: 34 to 37 oz. Adjustable low mount combat or BoMar target sights. Blued, matte black, Two-Tone or stainless finish. Checkered wood grips. Made from 1996 to date.

Concept models I & II . . . . .NiB $1193 Ex $965 Gd $673
Concept models III, IV & VII. . . . NiB $1308 Ex $1057 Gd $735
Concept models V, VI & VIII . . . . NiB $1369 Ex $1097 Gd $763
Concept models IX & X. . . . . NiB $1372 Ex $1108 Gd $770

1911 PREMIER SERIES AUTOMATIC PISTOL

Similar to the Concept series except also chambered for .38 Super, 9x23 Win., .400 Cor-Bon and .45 ACP. 5- or 6-inch bbl. Weight: 37 to .40 oz. Made from 1996 to date.

Premier II
(9x23 w/5-inch bbl.) . . . . NiB $1456 Ex $1177 Gd $820
Premier II (.400
Cor-Bon w/5-inch bbl.) . . . . NiB $1329 Ex $1075 Gd $751
Premier II (.45 ACP
w/5-inch bbl.) . . . . NiB $1239 Ex $1003 Gd $702
Premier II (.45 ACP
S/S w/5-inch bbl.) . . . . NiB $1367 Ex $1105 Gd $771
Premier II (.45/.400
combo w/5-inch bbl.) . . . . NiB $1527 Ex $1233 Gd $858
Premier II (.38
Super w/6-inch bbl.) . . . . NiB $1711 Ex $1381 Gd $959
Premier II (.400
Cor-Bon w/6-inch bbl.) . . . . NiB $1545 Ex $1248 Gd $868
Premier II (.45 ACP
w/6-inch bbl.) . . . . NiB $1456 Ex $1177 Gd $820

S.R.P. AUTOMATIC PISTOL

Similar to F.B.I. Contract "Swift Response Pistol" built on a (customer-supplied) Para-Ordance over-sized frame or a 1911 full-size or compact frame. Caliber: .45 ACP. Seven-round magazine, 5-inch bbl., weight: 37 oz. Ramp front and fixed rear sights, w/Tritium Sight insert.

SRP 1911Government
or Commanche model. . . . . NiB $2099 Ex $1692 Gd $1172
SRP P-12 model. . . . . NiB $2392 Ex $1926 Gd $1331
SRP P-13 model. . . . . NiB $2169 Ex $1748 Gd $1209
SRP P-14 model. . . . . NiB $2042 Ex $1646 Gd $1140

1911 ULTIMATE MASTER COMBAT SERIES AUTOMATIC PISTOL

Model 1911 in Combat Competition configuration. Calibers: .38 Super, 9x23 Win., .400 Cor-Bon and .45 ACP. Five- or 6-inch NM bbl., weight: 37 to 40 oz. Made from 1996 to date.

Ultimate MC (.38 or 9x23
w/5-inch bbl.) . . . . NiB $2179 Ex $1758 Gd $1219
Ultimate MC (.400 Cor-Bon
w/5-inch bbl.) . . . . NiB $2009 Ex $1620 Gd $1123
Ultimate MC (.45 ACP
w/5-inch bbl.) . . . . NiB $1914 Ex $1544 Gd $1071
Ultimate MC (.38 or 9x23
w/6-inch bbl.) . . . . NiB $2236 Ex $1804 Gd $1251
Ultimate MC (.400 Cor-Bon
w/6-inch bbl.) . . . . NiB $2083 Ex $1681 Gd $1167
Ultimate MC (.45 ACP
w/6-inch bbl.) . . . . NiB $1971 Ex $1590 Gd $1102
Ultimate "Steel Special"
(.38 Super Bianchi SPS). . . . . . . NiB $2481 Ex $1998 Gd $1380
Ultimate "PARA" (.38, 9x23
or .45 IPSC comp) . . . . NiB $2519 Ex $2028 Gd $1400
W/Triple-Port Compensator, add. $95

Auto-Ordnance ZG-51 Pit Bull

1911 CUSTOM CARRY SERIES AUTOMATIC PISTOL

Model 1911 in Combat Carry configuration built on steel or alloy full-size or compact frame. 4.5- or 5-inch NM bbl., chambered for .45 ACP. Weight: 34 to 37 oz.

Custom carry (steel frame
w/4.24- or 5-inch bbl.) . . . . NiB $1400 Ex $1132 Gd $789
Custom carry (alloy frame
w/4.24-inch bbl.). . . . . NiB $1623 Ex $1311 Gd $911

BAUER FIREARMS CORPORATION — Fraser, MI

.25 AUTOMATIC PISTOL. . . . . NiB $168 Ex $148 Gd $107

Stainless steel. Caliber: .25 Automatic. Six-round magazine, 2.13-inch bbl., 4 inches overall. Weight: 10 oz. Fixed sights. Checkered walnut or simulated pearl grips. Made from 1972-84.

BAYARD PISTOLS — Herstal, Belgium Mfd. by Anciens Etablissements Pieper

MODEL 1908
POCKET AUTOMATIC PISTOL . . . . NiB $381 Ex $279 Gd $151

Calibers: .25 Automatic (6.35mm). .32 Automatic (7.65mm), .380 Automatic (9mm Short). Six-round magazine, 2.25-inch bbl., 4.88 inches overall. Weight: About 16 oz. Fixed sights. Blued finish. Hard rubber grips. Intro. 1908. Disc. 1923.

MODEL 1923 POCKET
.25 AUTOMATIC PISTOL. . . . . NiB $381 Ex $320 Gd $177

Caliber: .25 Automatic (6.35mm). 2.13-inch bbl., 4.31 inches overall. Weight: 12 oz. Fixed sights. Blued finish. Checkered hard-rubber grips. Intro. 1923. Disc. 1930.

MODEL 1923 POCKET
AUTOMATIC PISTOL . . . . NiB $389 Ex $320 Gd $177

Calibers: .32 Automatic (7.65mm), .380 Automatic (9mm Short). Six-round magazine, 3.31-inch bbl., 5.5 inches overall. Weight: About 19 oz. Fixed sights. Blued finish. Checkered hard-rubber grips. Intro. 1923. Disc. 1940.

MODEL 1930 POCKET
.25 AUTOMATIC PISTOL. . . . . NiB $381 Ex $279 Gd $146

This is a modification of the Model 1923, which it closely resembles.

BEEMAN PRECISION ARMS, INC. — Santa Rosa, CA

P08 AUTOMATIC PISTOL . . . . NiB $435 Ex $369 Gd $205

Caliber: .22 LR. 10-round magazine, 3.8-inch bbl., 7.8 inches overall. Weight: 25 oz. Fixed sights. Blued finish. Checkered hardwood grips. Imported from 1969-91.

Benelli MP90S

Benelli MP95E

Beretta Model 21

MINI P08 AUTOMATIC PISTOL . . . NiB $404 Ex $328 Gd $232
Caliber: Same general specifications as P08 except shorter 3.5-inch bbl., 7.4 inches overall. Weight: 20 oz. Imported from 1986-91.

SP METALLIC SILHOUETTE PISTOLS
Caliber: .22 LR. Single-shot. Bbl. lengths: 6-, 8-, 10- or 15-inches. Adj. rear sight. Receiver contoured for scope mount. Walnut target grips w/adj. palm rest. Models SP made 1985-86 and SPX 1993-94.
SP Standard W/8-or 10-inch bbl.. . . NiB $270 Ex $220 Gd $157
SP Standard W/12-inch bbl. . . . . . . NiB $315 Ex $254 Gd $180
SP Standard W/15-inch bbl. . . . . . . NiB $333 Ex $271 Gd $191
SP Deluxe W/8-or 10-inch bbl. . . . . NiB $321 Ex $261 Gd $184
SP Deluxe W/12-inch bbl. . . . . NiB $340 Ex $276 Gd $194
SP Deluxe W/15-inch bbl. . . . . NiB $359 Ex $291 Gd $205
SPX Standard W/10-inch bbl. . . . . . NiB $662 Ex $533 Gd $372
SPX Deluxe W/10-inch bbl. . . . . NiB $891 Ex $721 Gd $501

BEHOLLA PISTOL — Suhl, Germany Mfd. by both Becker and Holländer and Stenda-Werke GmbH

POCKET AUTOMATIC PISTOL . . . . NiB $245 Ex $200 Gd $128
Caliber: .32 Automatic (7.65mm). Seven-round magazine, 2.9-inch bbl., 5.5 inches overall. Weight: 22 oz. Fixed sights. Blued finish. Serrated wood or hard rubber grips. Made by Becker and Hollander 1915-1920, by Stenda-Werke circa 1920-25. Note: Essentially the same pistol was manufactured concurrently w/the Stenda version as the "Leonhardt" by H. M. Gering and as the "Menta" by August Menz.

BENELLI PISTOLS — Urbino, Italy *Imported by Benelli USA*

MP90S WORLD CUP TARGET PISTOL
Semiautomatic blowback action. Calibers: .22 Short, .22LR, .32 W.C. Five-round magazine, 4.33-inch fixed bbl. 6.75 inches overall. Weight: 36 oz. Post front sight, adjustable rear. Blue finish. Anatomic shelf-style grip. Imported from 1992 to 2001.
MP90S (.22 LR) . . . . NiB $1329 Ex $1140 Gd $625
MP90S (.22 Short, disc. 1995). . . . NiB $1121 Ex $909 Gd $637
MP90S (.32 WC) . . . . NiB $1378 Ex $1105 Gd $777
W/conversion kit, add $550

MP95E SPORT TARGET PISTOL
Similar to the MP90S except with 5- or 9-round magazine, 4.25- inch bbl., Blue or chrome finish. Checkered target grip. Imported from1994 to date.
Blue MP95 (.22 LR) . . . . NiB $751 Ex $622 Gd $390
Blue MP95 (.32 WC) . . . . NiB $739 Ex $596 Gd $415
Chrome, add $85

BERETTA USA CORP. — Accokeek, Maryland

Beretta firearms are manufactured by Fabbrica D'Armi Pietro Beretta S. p. A. in the Gardone Val Trompia (Brescia), Italy. This prestigious firm has been in business since 1526. In 1977, Beretta U.S.A. Corp., a manufacturing and importing facility, opened in Accokeek, MD. (Previously imported by Garcia Corp., J.L. Galef & Son, Inc. and Berben Corporation.) Note: Beretta also owns additional firearms manufacturing companies including: Benelli, Franchi, Sako, Stoeger, Tikka and Uberti.

MODEL 20 DA AUTO PISTOL. . . . . NiB $180 Ex $159 Gd $108
Caliber: .25 ACP. Eight-round magazine, 2.5-inch bbl., 4.9 inches overall. Weight: 10.9 oz. Plastic or walnut grips. Fixed sights. Made from 1984-85.

MODEL 21 DA AUTO PISTOL
Calibers: .22 LR and .25 ACP. Seven-round (.22 LR) or 8-round (..25 ACP) magazine, 2.5-inch bbl., 4.9 inches overall. Weight: About 12 oz. Blade front sight, V-notch rear. Walnut grips. Made from 1985 to date. Model 21EL disc. 2000.
Blued finish . . . . NiB $215 Ex $165 Gd $123
Nickel finish (.22 LR only). . . . . NiB $253 Ex $206 Gd $145
Model 21EL engraved model . . . . . . NiB $333 Ex $270 Gd $190

MODEL 70
AUTOMATIC PISTOL . . . . NiB $250 Ex $203 Gd $144
Improved version of Model 1935. Steel or lightweight alloy. Calibers: .32 Auto (7.65mm), .380 Auto (9mm Short). Eight-round (.32) or 7-round (.380) magazine, 3.5-inch bbl., 6.5 inches overall. Weight: Steel, 22.25 oz.; alloy, 16 oz. Fixed sights. Blued finish. Checkered plastic grips. Made 1959-85. Note: Formerly marketed in U.S. as "Puma" (alloy model in .32) and "Cougar" (steel model in .380). Disc.

MODEL 70S. . . . . NiB $263 Ex $232 Gd $150
Similar to Model 70T except chambered for .22 Auto and .380 Auto. Longer bbl. guide and safety lever blocking hammer. Front blade and rear sight fixed on breechblock. Weight: 1 lb., 7 oz. Made from 1977-85.

MODEL 70T
AUTOMATIC PISTOL . . . . NiB $299 Ex $273 Gd $170
Similar to Model 70. Caliber: .32 Automatic (7.65mm). Nine-round magazine, 6-inch bbl., 9.5 inches overall. Weight: 19 oz. adj. rear sight, blade front sight. Blued finish. Checkered plastic grips. Intro. in 1959. Disc.

MODEL 71
AUTOMATIC PISTOL . . . . NiB $243 Ex $217 Gd $145
Same general specifications as alloy Model 70. Caliber: .22 LR. Six-inch bbl., 8-round magazine, Adj. rear sight frame. Single action. Made from 1959-89. Note: Formerly marketed in U.S. as the "Jaguar Plinker."

MODEL 72 . . . . NiB $243 Ex $217 Gd $140
Same as Model 71 except has 6-inch bbl., weight: 18 oz. Intro. in 1959. Disc. Note: Formerly marketed in U.S as "Jaguar Plinker."

MODEL 76
AUTO TARGET PISTOL
Caliber: .22 LR. 10-round magazine, 6-inch bbl., 8.8 inches overall. Weight: 33 oz. adj. rear sight, front sight w/interchangeable blades. Blued finish. Checkered plastic or wood grips. Made from 1966-85. Note: Formerly marketed in the U.S. as the "Sable."
Model 76 w/plastic grips. . . . . NiB $399 Ex $323 Gd $226
Model 76W w/wood grips. . . . . NiB $463 Ex $374 Gd $261

MODEL 81 DA AUTO PISTOL. . . . . NiB $338 Ex $276 Gd $184
Caliber: .32 Automatic (7.65mm). 12-round magazine, 3.8-inch bbl., 6.8 inches overall. Weight: 23.5 oz. Fixed sights. Blued finish. Plastic grips. Made principally for the European market 1975-84, w/similar variations as implemented on the Model 84.

MODEL 82 DA AUTO PISTOL. . . . . NiB $322 Ex $261 Gd $184
Caliber: .32 ACP. Similar to the Model 81 except with a slimmer-profile frame designed to accept a single column 9-round magazine. Matte black finish. Importation disc. 1984.

MODEL 84 DA AUTO PISTOL. . . . . NiB $328 Ex $282 Gd $178
Same as Model 81 except made in caliber .380 Automatic w/13-round magazine, 3.82-inch bbl., 6.8 inches overall. Weight: 23 oz. Fixed front and rear sights. Made from 1975-82.

MODEL 84B DA AUTO PISTOL . . . NiB $323 Ex $276 Gd $194
Improved version of Model 84 w/strengthened frame and slide, and firing-pin block safety added. Ambidextrous reversible magazine release. Blued or nickel finish. Checkered black plastic or wood grips. Other specifications same. Made circa 1982-84.

MODEL 84(BB) DA AUTO PISTOL
Improved version of Model 84B w/further-strengthened slide, frame and recoil spring. Caliber: .380 ACP. 13-round magazine, 3.82-inch bbl., 6.8 inches overall. Weight: 23 oz. Checkered black plastic or wood grips. Blued or nickel finish. Notched rear and blade front sight. Made circa 1984-94.
Blued w/plastic grips. . . . . NiB $470 Ex $382 Gd $260
Blued w/wood grips . . . . NiB $489 Ex $398 Gd $280
Nickel finish w/wood grips . . . . NiB $535 Ex $444 Gd $305

MODEL 84
CHEETAH SEMI-AUTO PISTOL
Similar to the Model 84 BB except with required design changes as mandated by regulation, including reduced magazine capacity (10-round magazine) and marked as 9mm short (.380) as a marketing strategy to counter increased availability of 9mm chamberings from other manufacturers. Made from 1994 to date.
Blued w/plastic grips. . . . . NiB $450 Ex $367 Gd $260
Blued w/wood grips . . . . NiB $489 Ex $398 Gd $280
Nickel finish w/wood grips . . . . NiB $527 Ex $429 Gd $302

Beretta Model 71

Beretta Model 72

Beretta Model 84

Beretta Model 84
Cheetah (Nickel finish)

Beretta Model 85

Beretta Model 85BB

Beretta Model 86 Cheetah

MODEL 85
DA AUTO PISTOL . . . . NiB $480 Ex $382 Gd $228
Similar to the Model 84 except designed with a slimmer-profile frame to accept a single column 8-round magazine, no ambidextrous magazine release. Matte black finish. Weight: 21.8 oz. Introduced in 1977 following the Model 84.

MODEL 85B DA AUTO PISTOL . . . NiB $485 Ex $392 Gd $259
Improved version of the Model 85. Imported from 1982-85.

MODEL 85BB DA PISTOL
Improved version of the Model 85B w/strengthened frame and slide. Caliber: .380 ACP. Eight-round magazine, 3.82 inch bbl., 6.8 inches overall. Weight: 21.8 oz. Blued or nickel finish. Checkered black plastic or wood grips. Imported from 1985-94.

Blued finish
w/plastic grips. . . . . NiB $416 Ex $339 Gd $240
Blued finish
w/wood grips . . . . NiB $462 Ex $375 Gd $265
Nickel finish
w/wood grips . . . . NiB $513 Ex $416 Gd $293

MODEL 85 CHEETAH
SEMI-AUTO PISTOL
Similar to the Model 85 BB except with required design changes as mandated by regulation and marked as 9mm short (.380) as a marketing strategy to counter increased availability of 9mm chamberings from other manufacturers. Made from 1994 to date.
Blued finish
w/plastic grips. . . . . NiB $416 Ex $339 Gd $228
Blued finish
w/wood grips . . . . NiB $469 Ex $385 Gd $278
Nickel finish
w/wood grips . . . . NiB $513 Ex $427 Gd $309

MODEL 85F
DA PISTOL
Similar to the Model 85BB except has re-contoured trigger guard and manual ambidextrous safety w/decocking device. Bruniton finish. Imported in 1990.
Matte black Bruniton
finish w/plastic grips. . . . . NiB $420 Ex $343 Gd $230
Matte black Bruniton
finish w/wood grips. . . . . NiB $486 Ex $400 Gd $289

MODEL 86 CHEETAH
DA AUTO PISTOL . . . . NiB $534 Ex $425 Gd $230
Caliber: .380 auto. Eight-round magazine, 4.4- inch bbl., 7.3 inches overall. Weight: 23.3 oz. Bruniton finish w/wood grips. Made from 1986-89. (Reintroduced 1990 in the Cheetah series.)

MODEL 87 CHEETAH
AUTOMATIC PISTOL
Similar to the Model 85 except in .22 LR w/8- or 10- round magazine (Target) and optional extended 6-inch bbl. (Target in single action). Overall length: 6.8 to 8.8 inches. Weight: 20.1 oz. to 29.4 oz (Target). Checkered wood grips. Made from 1987 to date.
Blued finish
(double-action) . . . . NiB $534 Ex $425 Gd $230
Target model
(single action) . . . . NiB $484 Ex $400 Gd $286

MODEL 89
GOLD STANDARD TARGET
AUTOMATIC PISTOL . . . . NiB $687 Ex $563 Gd $373
Caliber: .22 LR. Eight-round magazine, 6-inch bbl., 9.5 inches overall. Weight: 41 oz. Adj. target sights. Blued finish. Target-style walnut grips. Made from 1988 to date.

MODEL 90
DA AUTO PISTOL. . . . . NiB $300 Ex $221 Gd $151
Caliber: .32 Auto (7.65mm). Eight-round magazine, 3.63-inch bbl., 6.63 inches overall. Weight: 19.5 oz. Fixed sights. Blued finish. Checkered plastic grips. Made from 1969-83.

MODEL 92 DA AUTO
PISTOL (1ST SERIES) . . . . NiB $702 Ex $597 Gd $314
Caliber: 9mm Para. 15-round magazine, 4.9-inch bbl., 8.5 inches overall. Weight: 33.5 oz. Fixed sights. Blued finish. Plastic grips. Initial production of 5,000 made in 1976.

MODEL 92D DA AUTO PISTOL
Same general specifications as Model 92F except DA only w/bobbed hammer and 3-dot sight. Made from 1992 to date.
Model 92D . . . . NiB $499 Ex $396 Gd $308
With Tritium
sight system add $80

MODEL 92F COMPACT
DA AUTOMATIC PISTOL . . . . NiB $627 Ex $514 Gd $236
Caliber: 9mm Para. 12-round magazine, 4.3-inch bbl., 7.8 inches overall. Weight: 31.5 oz. Wood grips. Square-notched rear sight, blade front integral w/slide. Made from 1986-93.

MODEL 92F COMPACT L TYPE M DA AUTOMATIC PISTOL
Same general specifications as the original 92F Compact except 8-round magazine, Weight: 30.9 oz. Bruniton matte finish. Made from 1998 to date.
Model 92F
Compact L Type M. . . . . NiB $629 Ex $516 Gd $238
Model 92F
Compact L Type M Inox. . . . . NiB $629 Ex $516 Gd $238
W/Tritium
sight system, add $80

MODEL 92F DA AUTOMATIC PISTOL
Same general specifications as Model 92 except w/slide-mounted safety and repositioned magazine release. Replaced Model 92SB. Blued or stainless finish. Made from 1985 to date.
Blued finish . . . . NiB $629 Ex $516 Gd $248
Stainless finish. . . . . NiB $629 Ex $516 Gd $248
Model 92F-EL gold. . . . . NiB $762 Ex $634 Gd $472

MODEL 92FS DA AUTOMATIC PISTOL
Calibers: 9mm, 9mmx19 and .40 S&W. 15- round magazine, 4.9-inch bbl., 8.5 inches overall. Weight: 34.4 to 35.3 oz. Ambidextrous safety/decock lever. Chrome-lined bore w/combat trigger guard. Bruniton finish w/plastic grips or Inox finish w/rubber grips. Made from 1991 to date.
Model 92FS . . . . NiB $681 Ex $547 Gd $325
Model 92FS, Inox . . . . NiB $706 Ex $603 Gd $325
Model 92FS — Brigadier
(Made 1999 to date) . . . . NiB $589 Ex $480 Gd $340
Model 92FS —
Brigadier Inox . . . . NiB $706 Ex $603 Gd $330
Model 92FS — Centurion
(Made 1992 to date) . . . . NiB $706 Ex $603 Gd $330
Model 92FS — 470th Anniver.
(Made 1999) . . . . NiB $2249 Ex $2001 Gd $1203

MODEL 92S DA AUTO
PISTOL (2ND SERIES) . . . . NiB $718 Ex $613 Gd $306
Revised version of Model 92 w/ambidextrous slide-mounted safety modification intended for both commercial and military production. Evolved to Model 92S-1 for U.S. Military trials. Made from 1980-85.

MODEL 92SB DA
AUTO PISTOL (3RD SERIES) . . . . . . NiB $734 Ex $641 Gd $343
Same general specifications as standard Model 92 except has slide-mounted safety and repositioned magazine release. Made from 1981-85.

MODEL 92 SB-F
DA AUTO PISTOL . . . . NiB $713 Ex $610 Gd $301
Caliber: 9mm Para. 15-round magazine, bbl.: 4.9 inches, 8.5 inches overall. Weight: 34 oz. Plastic or Beretta Model 92 SB-F DA Auto Pistol wood grips. Square-notched rear sight, blade front sight integral w/slide. This model, also called Model 92S-1, is the standard-issue sidearm for the U.S. Armed Forces. Made from 1985 to date.

Beretta Model 90

Beretta Model 92F

Beretta Model 92
Compact L Type M

Beretta Model 92FS
Brigadier Inox

Beretta Model 96

Beretta Model 949 Olimpionico

Beretta Model 950BS Jetfire

MODEL 96 DA AUTO PISTOL
Same general specifications as Model 92F except in .40 S&W. 10-round magazine (9-round in Compact model). Made from 1992 to date.
Model 96 D (DA only). . . . . NiB $450 Ex $365 Gd $256
Model 96 Centurion (compact) . . . . NiB $498 Ex $396 Gd $257
W/Tritium sights, add $80
W/Tritium sights system, add $95

MODEL 101 . . . . NiB $275 Ex $245 Gd $147
Same as Model 70T except caliber .22 LR, has 10-round magazine, Intro. in 1959. Disc.

MODEL 318 (1934) AUTO PISTOL . NiB $301 Ex $265 Gd $152
Caliber: .25 Automatic (6.35mm). Eight-round magazine, 2.5-inch bbl., 4.5 inches overall. Weight: 14 oz. Fixed sights. Blued finish. Plastic grips. Made from 1934 to c. 1939.

MODEL 949
OLIMPIONICO AUTO PISTOL . . . . NiB $715 Ex $601 Gd $241
Calibers: .22 Short, .22 LR. Five-round magazine, 8.75-inch bbl., 12.5 inches overall. Weight: 38 oz. Target sights. Adj. bbl., weight. Muzzle brake. Checkered walnut grips w/thumbrest. Made from 1959-64.

MODEL 950B AUTO PISTOL. . . . . . . NiB $178 Ex $139 Gd $87
Same general specifications as Model 950CC except caliber .25 Auto, has 7-round magazine, Made from 1959 to date. Note: Formerly marketed in the U.S. as "Jetfire."

MODEL 950BS JETFIRE SA PISTOL
Calibers: .25 ACP or .22 Short (disc.1992). Seven- or 8-round magazine, 2.4- or 4- inch bbl., 4.5 to 4.7 inches overall. Weight: 9.9 oz. Fixed blade front and V-notch rear sights. Matte Blue or Inox (Stainless) finish. Checkered black plastic grips. Made from 1987 to date.
Blued finish . . . . NiB $176 Ex $142 Gd $103
Nickel finish . . . . NiB $227 Ex $185 Gd $130
Inox finish . . . . NiB $201 Ex $164 Gd $106
W/4-inch bbl.,
(.22 Short) . . . . NiB $209 Ex $169 Gd $120

MODEL 950CC
AUTO PISTOL . . . . NiB $154 Ex $133 Gd $87
Caliber: .22 Short. Six-round magazine, hinged 2.38-inch bbl., 4.75 inches overall. Weight: 11 oz. Fixed sights. Blued finish. Plastic grips. Made from 1959 to date. Note: Formerly marketed in the U.S. as "Minx M2."

MODEL 950CC
SPECIAL AUTO PISTOL. . . . . NiB $154 Ex $133 Gd $87
Same general specifications as Model 950CC Auto except has 4-inch bbl. Made from 1959 to date. Note: Formerly marketed in the U.S. as "Minx M4."

MODEL 951 (1951)
MILITARY AUTO PISTOL . . . . NiB $309 Ex $257 Gd $180
Caliber: 9mm Para. Eight-round magazine, 4.5-inch bbl., 8 inches overall. Weight: 31 oz. Fixed sights. Blued finish. Plastic grips. Made from 1952 to date. Note: This is the standard pistol of the Italian Armed Forces, also used by Egyptian and Israeli armies and by the police in Nigeria. Egyptian and Israeli models usually command a premium. Formerly marketed in the U.S. as the "Brigadier."

MODEL 1915
AUTO PISTOL . . . . NiB $1030 Ex $773 Gd $361
Calibers: 9mm Glisenti and .32 ACP (7.65mm). Eight-round magazine, 4-inch bbl., 6.7 inches overall (9mm), 5.7 inches (.32 ACP). Weight: 30 oz. (9mm), 20 oz. (.32 ACP). Fixed sights. Blued finish. Wood grips. Made 1915-1922. An improved postwar 1915/1919 version in caliber .32 ACP was later offered for sale in 1922 as the Model 1922.

MODEL 1923 AUTO PISTOL. . . . . NiB $1082 Ex $927 Gd $309
Caliber: 9mm Glisenti (Luger). Eight-round magazine, 4-inch bbl., 6.5 inches overall. Weight: 30 oz. Fixed sights. Blued finish. Plastic grips. Made circa 1923-36.

MODEL 1934 AUTO PISTOL
Caliber: .380 Automatic (9mm Short). Seven-round magazine, 3.38-inch bbl., 5.88 inches overall. Weight: 24 oz. Fixed sights. Blued finish. Plastic grips. Official pistol of the Italian Armed Forces. Wartime pieces not as well made and finished as commercial models. Made from 1934-59.
Commercial model . . . . NiB $412 Ex $361 Gd $220
War model. . . . . NiB $386 Ex $356 Gd $211

MODEL 1935 AUTO PISTOL

Caliber: .32 ACP (7.65mm). Eight-round magazine, 3.5-inch bbl., 5.75 inches overall. Weight: 24 oz. Fixed sights. Blued finish. Plastic grips. A roughly-finished version of this pistol was produced during WW II. Made from 1935-1959.

Commercial model . . . . **NiB $388 Ex $352 Gd $208**
War model. . . . . **NiB $337 Ex $285 Gd $182**

MODEL 3032 DA SEMIAUTOMATIC TOMCAT

Caliber: .32 ACP. Seven-round magazine, 2.45-inch bbl., 5 inches overall. Weight: 14.5 oz. Fixed sights. Blued or stainless finish. Made from 1996 to date.

Matte blue. . . . . **NiB $294 Ex $227 Gd $145**
Polished blue. . . . . **NiB $341 Ex $286 Gd $215**
Stainless. . . . . **NiB $363 Ex $301 Gd $219**

MODEL 8000/8040/8045 COUGAR DA PISTOL

Calibers: 9mm, .40 S&W and .45 Auto. Eight- or 10- shot magazine, 3.6 to 3.7- inch bbl., 7- to 7.2 inches overall. Weight: 32 to 32.6 oz. Short recoil action w/rotating barrel. Fixed sights w/3-dot Tritium system. Textured black composition grips. Matte black Bruniton finish w/alloy frame. Made from 1994 to date.

8000 Cougar D
(9mm DAO). . . . . **NiB $653 Ex $596 Gd $344**
8000 Cougar F
(9mm DA) . . . . **NiB $653 Ex $596 Gd $344**
8040 Cougar D
(.40 S&W DAO). . . . . **NiB $653 Ex $596 Gd $344**
8040 Cougar F
(.40 S&W DA) . . . . **NiB $653 Ex $596 Gd $344**
8045 Cougar D
(.45 Auto DAO). . . . . **NiB $674 Ex $601 Gd $354**
8045 Cougar F
(.45 Auto DA) . . . . **NiB $674 Ex $601 Gd $354**

MODEL 8000/8040/8045 MINI COUGAR DA PISTOL

Calibers: 9mm, .40 S&W and .45 Auto. Six- 8- or 10-round magazine, 3.6- to 3.7- inch bbl., 7 inches overall. Weight: 27.4 to 30.4 oz. Fixed sights w/3-dot Tritium system. Ambidextrous safety/decocker lever. Matte black Bruniton finish w/anodized aluminum alloy frame. Made from 1998 to date.

8000 Mini
Cougar D (9mm DAO) . . . . **NiB $681 Ex $547 Gd $289**
8000 Mini
Cougar F (9mm DA) . . . . **NiB $701 Ex $567 Gd $299**
8040 Mini
Cougar D (.40 S&W DAO) . . . . **NiB $701 Ex $567 Gd $299**
8040 Mini
Cougar F (.40 S&W DA) . . . . **NiB $701 Ex $567 Gd $299**
8045 Mini
Cougar D (.45 Auto DAO). . . . . **NiB $691 Ex $557 Gd $274**
8045 Mini
Cougar F (.45 Auto DA). . . . . **NiB $701 Ex $567 Gd $299**

MODEL 9000S SUBCOMPACT PISTOL SERIES

Calibers: 9mm, .40 S&W. 10-round magazine, 3.5- inch bbl., 6.6 inches overall. Weight: 25.7 to 27.5 oz. Single/double and double-action only. Front and rear dovetail sights w/3- dot system. Chrome-plated barrel w/Techno-polymer frame. Geometric locking system w/tilt barrel. Made from 1999 to date.

Type D (9mm) . . . .**NiB $536 Ex $457 Gd $296**
Type D (.40 S&W) . . . . **NiB $550 Ex $447 Gd $297**
Type F (9mm). . . . . **NiB $576 Ex $477 Gd $303**
Type F (.40 S&W). . . . . **NiB $586 Ex $492 Gd $312**

Beretta
Model 3032 Tomcat

Beretta
Model 8000 Cougar D

Beretta
Model 8000 Cougar F

Beretta
Model 8040 Mini Cougar D

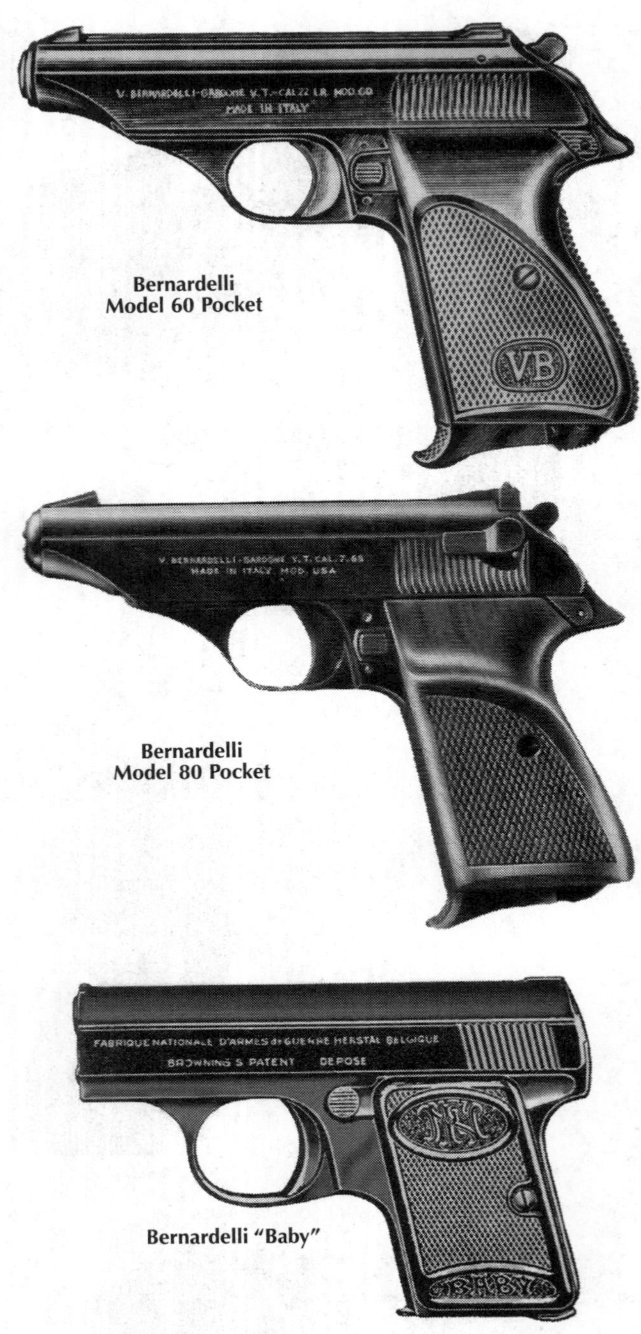
Bernardelli Model 60 Pocket

Bernardelli Model 80 Pocket

Bernardelli "Baby"

VINCENZO BERNARDELLI, S.P.A. Gardone V. T. (Brescia), Italy

Currently imported by Armsport, Inc., Miami, FL

MODEL 60 POCKET AUTOMATIC PISTOL .... NiB $245 Ex $219 Gd $152
Calibers: .22 LR, .32 Auto (7.65mm), .380 Auto (9mm Short). Eight-round magazine (.22 and .32), 7-round (.380). 3.5-inch bbl., 6.5 inches overall. Weight: About 25 oz. Fixed sights. Blued finish. Bakelite grips. Made from 1959-90.

MODEL 68 AUTOMATIC PISTOL . . . NiB $159 Ex $139 Gd $97
Caliber: 6.35. Five- and 8-round magazine, 2.13-inch bbl., 4.13 inches overall. Weight: 10 oz. Fixed sights. Blued or chrome finish. Bakelite or pearl grips. This model, like its .22-caliber counterpart, was known as the "Baby" Bernardelli. Disc. 1970.

MODEL 69 AUTOMATIC TARGET PISTOL .... NiB $624 Ex $521 Gd $341
Caliber: .22 LR. 10-round magazine, 5.9-inch bbl., 9 inches overall. Weight: 2.2 lbs. Fully adj. target sights. Blued finish. Stippled right- or left-hand wraparound walnut grips. Made from 1987 to date. Note: This was previously Model 100.

MODEL 80 AUTOMATIC PISTOL .... NiB $206 Ex $180 Gd $118
Calibers: .22 LR, .32 ACP (7.65mm), .380 Auto (9mm Short). Magazine capacity: 10-round (.22), 8-round (.32), 7-round (.380). 3.5-inch bbl., 6.5 inches overall. Weight: 25.6 oz. adj. rear sight, white dot front sight. Blued finish. Plastic thumbrest grips. Note: Model 80 is a modification of Model 60 designed to conform w/U.S. import regulations. Made from 1968-88.

MODEL 90 SPORT TARGET .... NiB $306 Ex $231 Gd $128
Same as Model 80 except has 6-inch bbl., 9 inches overall, weight: 26.8 oz. Made from 1968-90.

MODEL 100 TARGET AUTOMATIC PISTOL .... NiB $435 Ex $363 Gd $244
Caliber: .22 LR. 10-round magazine, 5.9-inch bbl., 9 inches overall. Weight: 37.75 oz. Adj. rear sight, interchangeable front sights. Blued finish. Checkered walnut thumbrest grips. Made from 1969-86. Note: Formerly Model 69.

MODEL AMR AUTO PISTOL...... NiB $435 Ex $363 Gd $234
Simlar to Model USA except with 6-inch bbl. and target sights. Imported from 1992-94.

"BABY" AUTOMATIC PISTOL..... NiB $273 Ex $196 Gd $119
Calibers: .22 Short, .22 Long. Five-round magazine, 2.13-inch bbl., 4.13 inches overall. Weight: 9 oz. Fixed sights. Blued finish. Bakelite grips. Made from 1949-68.

MODEL P010 AUTOMATIC PISTOL .... NiB $737 Ex $634 Gd $402
Caliber: .22 LR. Five- and 10-round magazine, 5.9-inch bbl. w/7.5-inch sight radius. Weight: 40 oz. Interchangeable front sight, adj. rear. Blued finish. Textured walnut grips. Made from 1988-92 and 1995-97.

P018 COMPACT MODEL .... NiB $534 Ex $508 Gd $266
Slightly smaller version of the Model P018 standard DA automatic except has 14-round magazine and 4-inch bbl., 7.68 inches overall. Weight: 33 oz. Walnut grips only. Imported from 1987-96.

P018 DOUBLE-ACTION AUTOMATIC PISTOL
Caliber: 9mm Para. 16-round magazine, 4.75-inch bbl., 8.5 inches overall. Weight: 36 oz. Fixed combat sights. Blued finish. Checkered plastic or walnut grips. Imported from 1987-96.
W/plastic grips .... NiB $534 Ex $446 Gd $271
W/walnut grips .... NiB $563 Ex $461 Gd $322

P-ONE DA AUTO PISTOL
Caliber: 9mm Parabellum or .40 S&W. 10- or 16-round magazine, 4.8-inch bbl., 8.35 inches overall. Weight: 34 oz. Blade front sight, adjustable rear w/3-dot system. Matte black or chrome finish. Checkered walnut or black plastic grips. Imported from 1993-97.
Model P-One blue finish . . . . NiB $632 Ex $535 Gd $323
Model P-One chrome finish . . . . . . NiB $664 Ex $545 Gd $391
W/walnut grips, add $35

P-ONE PRACTICAL VB AUTO PISTOL
Similar to Model P One except chambered for 9x21mm w/2-, 4- or 6-port compensating system for IPSC competition. Imported from 1993-97.
Model P One
Practical (2 port) . . . . NiB $1094 Ex $1017 Gd $744
Model P One
Practical (4 port) . . . . NiB $1201 Ex $1001 Gd $721
Model P One
Practical (6 port) . . . . NiB $1617 Ex $1321 Gd $942
W/chrome finish, add $60

SPORTER AUTOMATIC PISTOL . . . . . NiB $335 Ex $304 Gd $201
Caliber .22 LR. Eight-round magazine, bbl., lengths: 6-, 8- and 10-inch, 13 inches overall (10-inch bbl.). weight: About 30 oz. (10-inch bbl.) Target sights. Blued finish. Walnut grips. Made from 1949-68.

MODEL USA AUTO PISTOL
Single-action, blowback. Calibers: .22 LR, .32 ACP, .380 ACP. Seven-round magazine or 10-round magazine (.22 LR). 3.5-inch bbl., 6.5 inches overall. Weight: 26.5 oz. Ramped front sight, adjustable rear. Blue or chrome finish. Checkered black bakelite grips w/thumbrest. Imported from 1991-97.
Model USA blue finish . . . . NiB $412 Ex $325 Gd $236
Model USA chrome finish . . . . NiB $501 Ex $418 Gd $310

VEST POCKET
AUTOMATIC PISTOL . . . . NiB $276 Ex $220 Gd $148
Caliber: .25 Auto (6.35mm). Five- or 8-round magazine, 2.13-inch bbl., 4.13 inches overall. Weight: 9 oz. Fixed sights. Blued finish. Bakelite grips. Made from 1945-68.

Bernardelli P010

Bernardelli P018

BERSA PISTOLS — Argentina

Currently imported by Eagle Imports, Wanamassa, NJ (Previously by Interarms & Outdoor Sports)

MODEL 83 DA AUTO PISTOL
Similar to the Model 23 except for the following specifications: Caliber: .380 ACP. Seven-round magazine, 3.5-inch bbl., Front blade sight integral on slide, square-notch rear adj. for windage. Blued or satin nickel finish. Custom wood grips. Imported from 1988-94.
Blued finish . . . . NiB $259 Ex $203 Gd $172
Satin nickel . . . . NiB $319 Ex $269 Gd $206

MODEL 85 DA AUTO PISTOL
Same general specifications as Model 83 except 13-round magazine, Imported from 1988-94.
Blued finish . . . . NiB $310 Ex $269 Gd $162
Satin nickel . . . . NiB $412 Ex $344 Gd $258

MODEL 86 DA AUTO PISTOL
Same general specifications as Model 85 except available in matte blued finish and w/Neoprene grips. Imported from 1992-94.
Matte blued finish . . . . NiB $344 Ex $293 Gd $185
Nickel finish . . . . NiB $416 Ex $336 Gd $246

Bersa Model 85

Bersa Model 383

Bersa Thunder .380

Bersa Thunder .380 Deluxe

MODEL 95 DA AUTOMATIC PISTOL
Caliber: .380 ACP. Seven-round magazine, 3.5-inch bbl., weight: 23 oz. Wraparound rubber grips. Blade front and rear notch sights. Imported from 1995 to date.
Blued finish . . . . NiB $295 Ex $188 Gd $132
Nickel finish . . . . NiB $277 Ex $211 Gd $155

MODEL 97 AUTO PISTOL. . . . . NiB $352 Ex $307 Gd $194
Caliber: .380 ACP. Seven-round magazine, 3.3-inch bbl., 6.5 inches overall. Weight: 28 oz. Intro. 1982. Disc.

MODEL 223
Same general specifications as Model 383 except in .22 LR w/10-round magazine capacity. Disc. 1987.
Double-action . . . . NiB $223 Ex $191 Gd $131
Single-action . . . . NiB $213 Ex $181 Gd $128

MODEL 224
Caliber: .22 LR. 10-round magazine, 4-inch bbl., weight: 26 oz. Front blade sight, square-notched rear adj. for windage. Blued finish. Checkered nylon or custom wood grips. Made 1984. SA. disc. 1986.
Double-action . . . . NiB $223 Ex $192 Gd $131
Single-action . . . . NiB $127 Ex $190 Gd $124

MODEL 226
Same general specifications as Model 224 but w/6-inch bbl. Disc. 1987.
Double-action . . . . NiB $223 Ex $191 Gd $131
Single-action . . . . NiB $313 Ex $181 Gd $128

MODEL 383 AUTO PISTOL
Caliber: .380 Auto. Seven-round magazine, 3.5-inch bbl. Front blade sight integral on slide, square-notched rear sight adj. for windage. Custom wood grips on double-action, nylon grips on single action. Blued or satin nickel finish. Made 1984. SA. disc. 1989.
Double-action . . . . NiB $140 Ex $115 Gd $69
Single-action . . . . NiB $180 Ex $141 Gd $94
Satin nickel . . . . NiB $224 Ex $182 Gd $108

MODEL 622 AUTO PISTOL. . . . . . . NiB $177 Ex $145 Gd $105
Caliber: .22 LR. Seven-round magazine, 4- or 6-inch bbl., 7 or 9 inches overall. Weight: 2.25 lbs. Blade front sight, square-notch rear adj. for windage. Blued finish. Nylon grips. Made from 1982-87.

MODEL 644 AUTO PISTOL . . . . NiB $254 Ex$219 Gd $142
Caliber: .22 LR. 10-round magazine, 3.5-inch bbl., weight: 26.5 oz. 6.5 inches overall. Adj. rear sight, blade front. Contoured black nylon grips. Made from 1980-88.

THUNDER 9 AUTO PISTOL . . . . . . NiB $260 Ex $219 Gd $142
Caliber: 9mm Para. 15-round magazine, 4-inch bbl., 7.38 inches overall. Weight: 30 oz. Blade front sight, adj. rear w/3-dot system. Ambidextrous safety and decocking device. Matte blued finish. Checkered black polymer grips. Made from 1993-96.

THUNDER .22 AUTO PISTOL (MODEL 23)
Caliber: .22 LR, 10-round magazine, 3.5-inch bbl., 6.63 inches overall. Weight: 24.5 oz. Notched-bar dovetailed rear, blade integral w/slide front. Black polymer grips. Made from 1989 to date.
Blued finish . . . . NiB $254 Ex $219 Gd $132
Nickel finish . . . . NiB $267 Ex $219 Gd $154

THUNDER .380 AUTO PISTOL
Caliber: .380 ACP. Seven-round magazine, 3.5-inch bbl., 6.63 inches overall. Weight: 25.75 oz. Notched-bar dovetailed rear, blade integral w/slide front. Blued, satin nickel, or Duo-Tone finish. Made from 1995 to date.

Blued finish . . . . NiB $250 Ex $266 Gd $138
Satin nickel finish . . . . NiB $290 Ex $240 Gd $177
Duo-Tone finish. . . . . NiB $277 Ex $230 Gd $170

THUNDER .380 PLUS AUTO PISTOL
Same general specifications as standard Thunder .380 except has 10-round magazine and weight: 26 oz. Made from 1995-97.

Matte finish . . . . NiB $257 Ex $210 Gd $150
Satin nickel finish . . . . NiB $308 Ex $250 Gd $177
Duo-Tone finish. . . . . NiB $289 Ex $235 Gd $167

BROLIN ARMS — La Verne, California

"LEGEND SERIES" SA AUTOMATIC PISTOL
Caliber: .45 ACP. Seven-round magazine, 4- or 5-inch bbl., weight: 32-36 oz. Walnut grips. Single action, full size, compact, or full size frame compact slide. Matte blued finish. Lowered and flared ejection port. Made from 1995-98.

Model L45 . . . . NiB $476 Ex $415 Gd $272
Model L45C. . . . . NiB $492 Ex $431 Gd $298
Model L45T . . . . NiB $502 Ex $442 Gd $308

"PATRIOT SERIES" SA AUTOMATIC PISTOL
Caliber: .45 ACP. Seven-round magazine, 3.25- and 4-inch bbl., weight: 33-37 oz. Wood grips. Fixed rear sights. Made from 1996-97.

Model P45 . . . . NiB $646 Ex $533 Gd $355
Model P45C (disc. 1997). . . . . NiB $671 Ex $681 Gd $610
Model P45T (disc. 1997) . . . . NiB $681 Ex $559 Gd $335

"PRO-STOCK AND PRO-COMP" SA PISTOL
Caliber: .45 ACP. Eight-round magazine, 4- or 5-inch bbl., weight: 37 oz. Single action, blued or two-tone finish. Wood grips. Bomar adjustable sights. Made from 1996-97.

Model Pro comp . . . . NiB $754 Ex $616 Gd $436
Model Pro stock . . . . NiB $677 Ex $565 Gd $392

TAC SERIES
Caliber: .45 ACP. Eight-round magazine, 5-inch bbl., 8.5 inches overall. Weight: 37 oz. Low profile combat or Tritium sights. Beavertail grip safety. Matte blue, chrome or two-tone finish. Checkered wood or contoured black rubber grips. Made from 1997-98.

Model TAC 11 service . . . . NiB $667 Ex $570 Gd $361
Model TAC 11 compact. . . . . NiB $677 Ex $566 Gd $361
W/Tritium sights, add $95

BANTAM MODEL . . . . NiB $410 Ex $295 Gd $210
Caliber: 9mmPara., .40 S&W. Single or double-action, super compact size, concealed hammer, all steel construction; 3-dot sights; royal blue or matte finish. Manufactured 1999 only.

BRONCO PISTOL — Eibar, Spain
Manufactured by Echave y Arizmendi

MODEL 1918 POCKET
AUTOMATIC PISTOL . . . . NiB $209 Ex $184 Gd $97
Caliber: .32 ACP (7.65mm). Six-round magazine 2.5-inch bbl., 5 inches overall. Weight: 20 oz. Fixed sights. Blued finish. Hard rubber grips. Made circa 1918-.25.

Browning
Model 25 Automatic

SEMIAUTOMATIC PISTOL . . . . NiB $194 Ex $148 Gd $121
Caliber: .25 ACP, 6-round magazine, 2.13-inch bbl., 4.13 inches overall. Weight: 11 oz. Fixed sights. Blued finish. Hard rubber grips. Made from 1919-35.

BROWNING PISTOLS — Morgan, Utah

The following Browning pistols have been manufactured by Fabrique Nationale d'Armes de Guerre (now Fabrique Nationale Herstal) of Herstal, Belgium, by Arms Technology Inc. of Salt Lake City and by J. P. Sauer & Sohn of Eckernforde, W. Germany. (See also FN Browning and J.P. Sauer & Sohn listings.)

.25 AUTOMATIC PISTOL
Same general specifications as FN Browning Baby (see separate listing). Standard Model, blued finish, hard rubber grips. Light Model, nickel-plated, Nacrolac pearl grips. Renaissance Engraved Model, nickel-plated, Nacrolac pearl grips. Made by FN from 1955-69.

Standard model . . . . NiB $547 Ex $495 Gd $248
Lightweight model. . . . . NiB $557 Ex $495 Gd $248
Renaissance model . . . . NiB $1055 Ex $823 Gd $463

.32 AND .380 AUTOMATIC PISTOL, 1955 TYPE
Same general specifications as FN Browning .32 (7.65mm) and .380 Pocket Auto. Standard Model, Renaissance Engraved Model as furnished in .25 Automatic. Made by FN from 1955-69.

Standard model (.32 ACP) . . . . NiB $488 Ex $402 Gd $279
Standard model (.380 ACP) . . . . NiB $418 Ex $351 Gd $248
Renaissance model . . . . NiB $1120 Ex $876 Gd $644

.380 AUTOMATIC PISTOL, 1971 TYPE
Same as .380 Automatic, 1955 Type except has longer slide, 4.44-inch bbl., is 7.06 inches overall, weight: 23 oz. Rear sight adj. for windage and elevation, plastic thumbrest grips. Made from 1971-75.

Standard model. . . . . NiB $457 Ex $359 Gd $256
Renaissance model . . . . NiB $1056 Ex $850 Gd $567

BDA DA AUTOMATIC PISTOL
Similar to SIG-Sauer P220. Calibers: 9mm Para., .38 Super Auto, .45 Auto. Nine-round magazine (9mm and .38), 7-round (.45 cal), 4.4-inch bbl., 7.8 inches overall. Weight: 29.3 oz. Fixed sights. Blued finish. Plastic grips. Made from 1977-79 by J. P. Sauer.

Browning
BDA .380 Nickel Finish

Browning
Buck Mark 22 Field (5.5)

Browning
Buck Mark 22 Bullseye

Browning
Buck Mark 22 Plus

Browning
BDM 9mm DA

BDA .380 DA AUTOMATIC PISTOL

Caliber: .380 Auto. 10- or 13-round magazine, bbl. length: 3.81 inches., 6.75 inches overall. Weight: 23 oz. Fixed blade front sight, square-notch drift-adj. rear sight. Blued or nickel finish. Smooth walnut grips. Made from 1982-97 by Beretta.

Blued finish ....NiB $503 Ex $395 Gd $246
Nickel finish .... NiB $489 Ex $406 Gd $298

BDM SERIES AUTOMATIC PISTOLS

Calibers: 9mm Para., 10-round magazine, 4.73-inch bbl., 7.85 inches overall. Weight: 31 oz., windage adjustable sights w/3-dot system. Low profile removable blade front sights. Matte blued, Bi-Tone or silver chrome finish. Selectable shooting mode and decocking safety lever. Made from 1991-98.

BDM Standard................. NiB $540 Ex $342 Gd $315
BDM Practical................. NiB $548 Ex $447 Gd $318
BDM-D Silver Chrome .... NiB $554 Ex $452 Gd $322

BUCK MARK .22 AUTOMATIC PISTOL

Caliber: .22 LR. 10-round magazine, 5.5- inch bbl., 9.5 inches overall. Weight: 32 oz. Black molded grips. Adj. rear sight. Blued or nickel finish. Made from 1985 to date.

Blued finish .... NiB $243 Ex $202 Gd $125
Nickel finish .... NiB $304 Ex $254 Gd $190

BUCK MARK .22 BULLSEYE PISTOL

Same general specifications as the standard Buck Mark 22 except w/7.25-inch fluted barrel, 11.83 inches overall. Weight: 36 oz. Adjustable target trigger. Undercut post front sight, click-adjustable Pro-Target rear. Laminated, Rosewood, black rubber or composite grips. Made from 1996 to date.

Standard model (composite grips).. NiB $361 Ex $299 Gd $211
Target model .... NiB $438 Ex $335 Gd $211

BUCK MARK .22
BULLSEYE TARGET .... NiB $448 Ex $345 Gd $221

Caliber: .22 LR. 10-round magazine, 7.25- inch fluted bbl., 11.83 inches overall. Weight: 31 oz. Rosewood wrap-around finger groove grips w/matte blued finish. Made from 1996 to date.

BUCK MARK .22 FIELD
(5.5) AUTO PISTOL............. NiB $376 Ex $288 Gd $195

Calibers: .22 LR. 10-round magazine, 5.5- inch bbl., 9.58 inches overall. Weight: 35.5 oz. Standard sights. Matte Blue finish. Made from 1991 to date.

BUCK MARK .22 MICRO AUTOMATIC PISTOL

Same general specifications as standard Buck Mark .22 except w/4-inch bbl., 8 inches overall. Weight: 32 oz. Molded composite grips. Ramp front sight, Pro Target rear sight. Made from 1992 to date.

Blued finish .... NiB $292 Ex $235 Gd $127
Nickel finish .... NiB $312 Ex $279 Gd $203

Browning
Buck Mark .22 Silhouette

Browning
Buck Mark .22 Target (5.5)

BUCK MARK .22 MICRO PLUS AUTO PISTOL
Same specifications as the Buck Mark .22 Micro except ambidextrous, laminated wood grips. Made from 1996 to date.
Blued finish . . . . **NiB $292 Ex $235 Gd $132**
Nickel finish . . . . **NiB $325 Ex $276 Gd $211**

BUCK MARK .22 PLUS AUTOMATIC PISTOL
Same general specifications as standard Buck Mark .22 except for black molded, impregnated hardwood grips. Made from 1987 to date.
Blued finish . . . . **NiB $292 Ex $235 Gd $122**
Nickel finish . . . . **NiB $331 Ex $280 Gd $217**

BUCK MARK .22 TARGET (5.5) AUTO PISTOL
Caliber: .22 LR. 10-round magazine, 5.5- inch bbl., 9.6 inches overall. Weight: 35.5 oz. Pro target sights. Wrap-around walnut or contoured finger groove grips. Made from 1990 to date.
Matte blue finish . . . . **NiB $391 Ex $319 Gd $185**
Nickel finish (1994 to date). . . . . . . **NiB $470 Ex $393 Gd $297**
Gold finish (1991-99) . . . . **NiB $512 Ex $432 Gd $330**

BUCK MARK .22 SILHOUETTE . . . . NiB $406 Ex $319 Gd $169
Same general specifications as standard Buck Mark .22 except for 9.88-inch bbl. Weight: 53 oz. Target sights mounted on full-length scope base, and laminated hardwood grips and forend. Made from 1987 to date.

BUCK MARK .22
UNLIMITED SILHOUETTE . . . . NiB $473 Ex $375 Gd $241
Same general specifications as standard Buck Mark .22 Silhouette except w/14-inch bbl., 18.69 inches overall. Weight: 64 oz. Interchangeable post front sight and Pro Target rear. Nickel finish. Made from 1992 to date.

Browning
Buck Mark .22 Micro Plus

BUCK MARK .22
VARMINT AUTO PISTOL. . . . . NiB $359 Ex $298 Gd $200
Same general specifications as standard Buck Mark .22 except for 9.88-inch bbl. Weight: 48 oz. No sights, full-length scope base, and laminated hardwood grips. Made from 1987 to date.

Browning Challenger
Standard Model

CHALLENGER AUTOMATIC PISTOL
Caliber: .22 LR. 10-round magazine, bbl. lengths: 4.5 and 6.75-inches. 11.44 inches overall (with 6.75-inch bbl.). Weight: 38 oz. (6.75-inch bbl.). Removable blade front sight, screw adj. rear. Standard finish, blued, also furnished gold inlaid (Gold model) and engraved and chrome-plated (Renaissance model). Checkered walnut grips. Finely figured and carved grips on Gold and Renaissance models. Standard made by FN 1962-75, higher grades. Intro. 1971. Disc.
Standard model . . . . **NiB $431 Ex $369 Gd $251**
Gold model . . . . **NiB $1548 Ex $1342 Gd $630**
Renaissance model . . . . **NiB $1548 Ex $1342 Gd $630**

Browning Challenger
Renaissance Model

CHALLENGER II
AUTOMATIC PISTOL . . . . NiB $246 Ex $215 Gd $132
Same general specifications as Challenger Standard model w/6.75-inch bbl. except changed grip angle and impregnated hardwood grips. Original Challenger design modified for lower production costs. Made by ATI from 1976-83.

Browning
Challenger III Sporter .22

Browning
Hi-Power Mark III

Browning
9mm Hi-Power w/Molded Grips

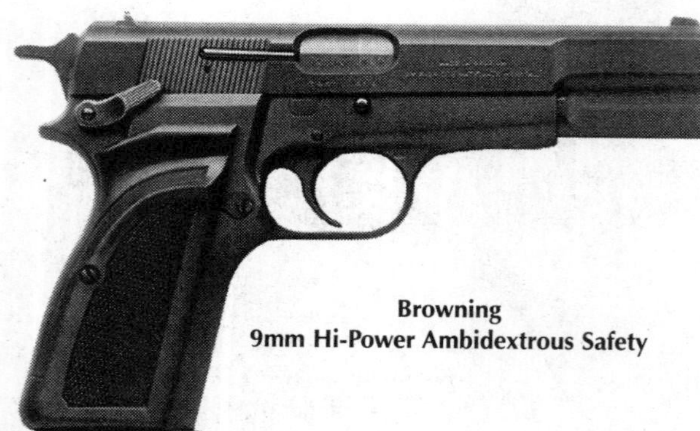
Browning
9mm Hi-Power Ambidextrous Safety

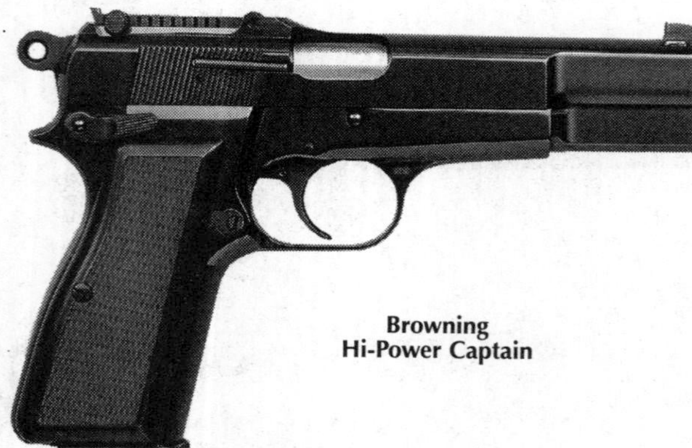
Browning
Hi-Power Captain

CHALLENGER III AUTOMATIC PISTOL . . . . NiB $243 Ex $212 Gd $129
Same general description as Challenger II except has 5.5 inch bull bbl., alloy frame and new sight system. Weight: 35 oz. Made from 1982-84. Sporter Model w/6.75-inch bbl.. Made from 1984-86.

HI-POWER AUTOMATIC PISTOL
Same general specifications as FN Browning Model 1935 except chambered for 9mm Para., .30 Luger and .40 S&W. 10- or 13-round magazine, 4.63-inch bbl., 7.75 inches overall. Weight: 32 oz. (9mm) or 35 oz. (.40 S&W). Fixed sights, also available w/rear sight adj. for windage and elevation, and ramp front sight. Ambidextrous safety added after 1989. Standard model blued, chrome-plated or Bi-Tone finish. Checkered walnut, contour-molded Polyamide or wraparound rubber grips. Renaissance Engraved model chrome-plated, w/Nacrolac pearl grips. Made by FN from 1955 to date.

Standard model, fixed sights, 9mm . . . . NiB $780 Ex $646 Gd $481
Standard model, fixed sights, .40 S&W (intro. 1986). . . . . NiB $790 Ex $764 Gd $584
Standard model, .30 Luger (1986-89). . . . . NiB $764 Ex $659 Gd $455
Renaissance model, fixed sights. . . . . NiB $1477 Ex $1016 Gd $602
W/adjustable rear sight, add $50
W/ambidextrous safety, add $95
W/moulded grips, deduct $40
W/tangent rear sight (1965-78), add* $295
W/T-Slot grip & tangent sight (1965-78), add* $595
***Check FN agent to certify value**

HI-POWER CAPITAN AUTOMATIC . . . . NiB $683 Ex $570 Gd $390
Similar to the standard Hi-Power except fitted w/adj. 500-meter tangent rear sight and rounded serrated hammer. Made from 1993-2000.

HI-POWER MARK III AUTOMATIC PISTOL . . . . NiB $606 Ex $457 Gd $359
Calibers: 9mm and .40 S&W. 10-round magazine, 4.75-inch bbl., 7.75 inches overall. Weight: 32 oz. Fixed sights with molded grips. Durable non-glare matte blue finish. Made from 1985 to date.

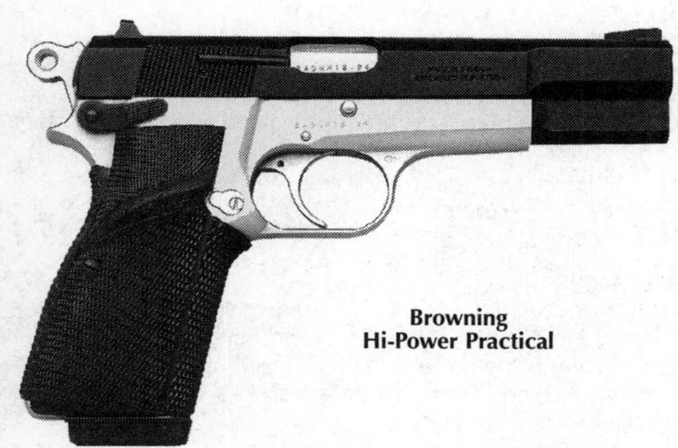

Browning
Hi-Power Practical

Browning
Hi-Power Silver Chrome

HI-POWER PRACTICAL AUTOMATIC PISTOL
Similar to the standard Hi-Power except has silver-chromed frame and blued slide w/Commander-style hammer. Made from 1991 to date.
W/fixed sights . . . . NiB $637 Ex $498 Gd $359
W/adj. sights . . . . NiB $670 Ex $558 Gd $415

HI-POWER SILVER CHROME
AUTOMATIC PISTOL . . . . NiB $766 Ex $616 Gd $374
Calibers: 9mm and .40 S&W. 10-round magazine, 4.75-inch bbl., 7.75 inches overall. Weight: 36 oz. Adjustable sights with Pachmayer grips. Silver-chromed finish. Made from 1991 to date.

HI-POWER 9MM CLASSIC
Limited Edition 9mm Hi-Power, w/silver-gray finish, high-grade engraving and finely-checkered walnut grips w/double border. Proposed production of the Classic was 5000 w/less than half that number produced. Gold Classic limited to 500 w/two-thirds proposed production in circulation. Made from 1985-86.
Gold classic. . . . . NiB $2658 Ex $2144 Gd $1487
Standard classic. . . . . NiB $1370 Ex $1114 Gd $786

Browning
Hi-Power 9mm Classic

INTERNATIONAL
MEDALIST AUTOMATIC
TARGET PISTOL . . . . NiB $927 Ex $782 Gd $463
Modification of Medalist to conform w/International Shooting Union rules. 5.9-inch bbl., Smaller grip with no forearm. Weight: 42 oz. Made from 1970-73.

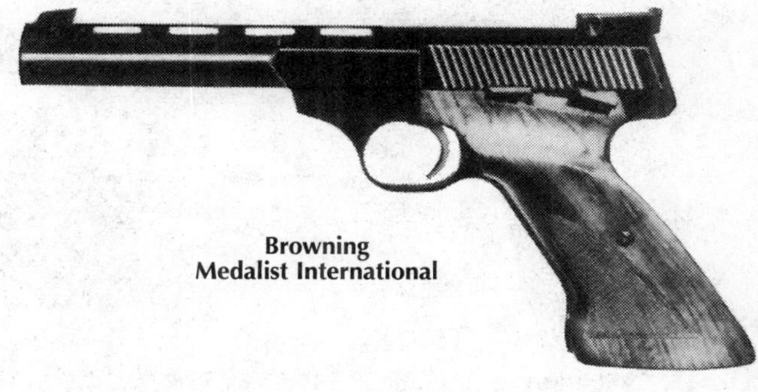

Browning
Medalist International

MEDALIST AUTOMATIC TARGET PISTOL
Caliber: .22 LR. 10-round magazine, 6.75-inch bbl. w/vent rib, 11.94 inches overall. Weight: 46 oz. Removable blade front sight, click-adj. micrometer rear. Standard finish, blued also furnished gold-inlaid (Gold Model) and engraved and chrome-plated (Renaissance Model). Checkered walnut grips w/thumbrest (for right- or left-handed shooter). Finely figured and carved grips on Gold and Renaissance Models. Made by FN from 1962-75. Higher grades. Intro. 1971.
Standard model . . . . NiB $937 Ex $782 Gd $524
Gold model . . . . NiB $2078 Ex $1769 Gd $977
Renaissance model . . . . NiB $2530 Ex $2088 Gd $1338

NOMAD
AUTOMATIC PISTOL . . . . NiB $352 Ex $300 Gd $197
Caliber: .22 LR. 10-round magazine, bbl. lengths: 4.5 and 6.75-inches, 8.94 inches overall (4.5-inch bbl.). Weight: 34 oz. (with 4.5-inch bbl.). Removable blade front sight, screw adj. rear. Blued finish. Plastic grips. Made by FN from 1962-74.

Browning
Medalist Automatic Target Pistol

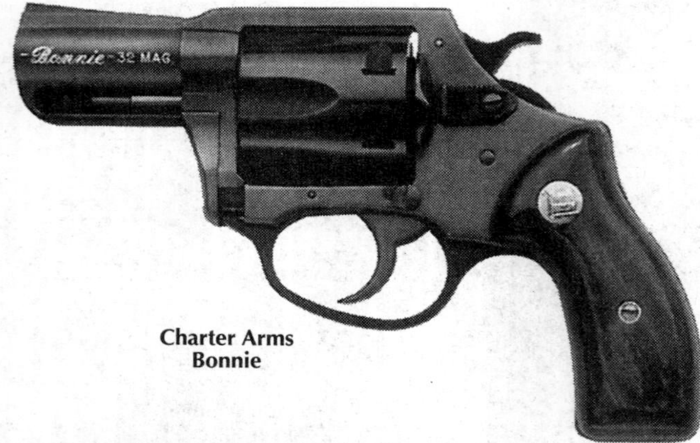

Charter Arms Bonnie

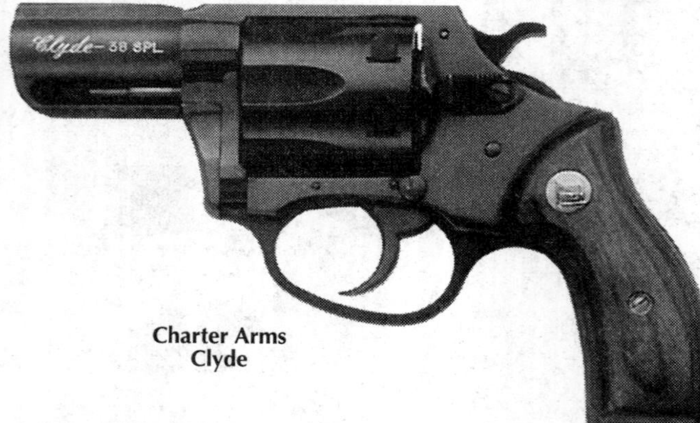

Charter Arms Clyde

RENAISSANCE 9MM, .25 AUTO AND .380 AUTO (1955) ENGRAVED MODELS, CASED SET . . . . NiB $4786 Ex $3860 Gd $2675
One pistol of each of the three models in a special walnut carrying case, all chrome-plated w/Nacrolac pearl grips. Made by FN from 1955-69.

BRYCO ARMS INC. — Irvine, California Distributed by Jennings Firearms. Inc. Carson City, NV

MODELS J22, J25 AUTO PISTOL
Calibers: .22 LR, .25 ACP. Six-round magazine, 2.5-inch bbl., about 5 inches overall. Weight: 13 oz. Fixed sights. Chrome, satin nickel or black Teflon finish. Walnut, grooved black Cycolac or resin-impregnated wood grips. Made from 1981 to date.
Model J-22 (disc. 1985). . . . . NiB $98 Ex $81 Gd $60
Model J-25 (disc. 1995). . . . . NiB $83 Ex $71 Gd $56

MODELS M25, M32, M38 AUTO PISTOL
Calibers: .25 ACP, .32 ACP, .380 ACP. Six-round magazine, 2.81-inch bbl., 5.31 inches overall. Weight: 11oz. to 15 oz. Fixed sights. Chrome, satin nickel or black Teflon finish. Walnut, grooved, black Cycolac or resin-impregnated wood grips. Made from 1988-2000.
Model M25 (disc.). . . . . NiB $82 Ex $67 Gd $57
Model M32 . . . . NiB $112 Ex $92 Gd $68
Model M38 . . . . NiB $124 Ex $103 Gd $72

MODEL M48 AUTO PISTOL . . . . NiB $102 Ex $91 Gd $66
Calibers: .22 LR, .32 ACP, .380 ACP. Seven-round magazine, 4-inch bbl., 6.69 inches overall. Weight: 20 oz. Fixed sights. Chrome, satin nickel or black Teflon finish. Smooth wood or black Teflon grips. Made from 1989-95.

MODEL M58 AUTO PISTOL . . . . NiB $102 Ex $91 Gd $66
Caliber: .380 ACP. 10-round magazine, 3.75-inch bbl., 5.5 inches overall. Weight: 30 oz. Fixed sights. Chrome, satin nickel, blued or black Teflon finish. Smooth wood or black Teflon grips. Made from 1993-95.

MODEL M59 AUTO PISTOL . . . . NiB $112 Ex $102 Gd $66
Caliber: 9mm Para. 10-round magazine, 4-inch bbl., 6.5 inches overall. Weight: 33 oz. Fixed sights. Chrome, satin nickel, blued or black Teflon finish. Smooth wood or black Teflon grips. Made from 1994-96.

MODEL NINE SA AUTO PISTOL . . . . NiB $137 Ex $117 Gd $76
Similar to Bryco/Jennings Model M59 except w/redesigned slide w/loaded chamber indicator and frame mounted ejector. Weight: 30 oz. Made from 1997 to date.

MODEL T-.22 TARGET PISTOL . . . . NiB $130 Ex $107 Gd $77
Similar to Bryco/Jennings Model M48 except chambered for .22 LR only, w/target configuration sights and redesigned slide w/loaded chamber indicator and hold open. Made from 1997 to date.

BUDISCHOWSKY PISTOL — Mt. Clemens, Michigan, Mfd. by Norton Armament Corporation

TP-70 DA AUTOMATIC PISTOL
Calibers: .22 LR, .25 Auto. Six-round magazine, 2.6-inch bbl., 4.65 inches overall. Weight: 12.3 oz. Fixed sights. Stainless steel. Plastic grips. Made from 1973-77.
.22 LR . . . . NiB $370 Ex $313 Gd $237
.25 Auto. . . . . NiB $359 Ex $288 Gd $206

CALICO LIGHT WEAPONS SYSTEMS — Bakersfield, California

MODEL 110 AUTO PISTOL. . . . . . . NiB $695 Ex $627 Gd $466
Caliber: .22 LR. 100-round magazine, 6-inch bbl., 17.9 inches overall. Weight: 3.75 lbs. Adj. post front sight, fixed U-notch rear. Black finish aluminum frame. Molded composition grip. Made from 1986-94.

MODEL M-950 AUTO PISTOL . . . . NiB $515 Ex $438 Gd $319
Caliber 9mm Para. 50- or 100-round magazine, 7.5-inch bbl., 14 inches overall. Weight: 2.25 lbs. Adj. post front sight, fixed U-notch rear. Glass-filled polymer grip. Made from 1989-94.

CHARTER ARMS CORPORATION — Stratford, Connecticut

MODEL 40 AUTOMATIC PISTOL . . . . . NiB $295 Ex $270 Gd $152
Caliber: .22 RF. Eight-round magazine, 3.3-inch bbl., 6.3 inches overall. Weight: 21.5 oz. Fixed sights. Checkered walnut grips. Stainless steel finish. Made from 1985-86.

MODEL 79K
DA AUTOMATIC PISTOL . . . . NiB $358 Ex $333 Gd $221
Calibers: .380 or .32 Auto. Seven-round magazine, 3.6-inch bbl., 6.5 inches overall. Weight: 24.5 oz. Fixed sights. Checkered walnut grips. Stainless steel finish. Made from 1985-86.

BONNIE AND CLYDE SET. . . . . NiB $465 Ex $404 Gd $272
Matching pair of shrouded 2.5-inch bbl., revolvers chambered for .32 Magnum and .38 Special. Blued finish w/scrolled name on bbls.. Made from 1989-90.

BULLDOG .44 DA REVOLVER
Caliber: .44 Special. Five-round cylinder, 2.5- or 3-inch bbl., 7 or 7.5 inches overall. Weight: 19 or 19.5 oz. Fixed sights. Blued, nickel-plated or stainless finish. Checkered walnut Bulldog or square buttgrips. Made from 1973-96.
Blued finish/
Pocket Hammer (2.5-inch) . . . . NiB $244 Ex $214 Gd $107
Blued finish/
Bulldog grips (3-inch disc. 1988) . . . . NiB $224 Ex $179 Gd $127
Electroless nickel. . . . . NiB $251 Ex $204 Gd $144
Stainless steel/
Bulldog grips (disc. 1992) . . . . NiB $214 Ex $173 Gd $117
Neoprene grips/
Pocket Hammer. . . . . NiB $219 Ex $178 Gd $126

BULLDOG .357 DA REVOLVER . . . NiB $204 Ex $168 Gd $107
Caliber: .357 Magnum. Five-round cylinder, 6-inch bbl., 11 inches overall. Weight: 25 oz. Fixed sights. Blued finish. Square, checkered walnut grips. Made from 1977-96.

BULLDOG NEW POLICE DA REVOLVER
Same general specifications as Bulldog Police except chambered for .44 Special. Five-round cylinder, 2.5- or 3.5-inch bbl. Made from 1990-92.
Blued finish . . . . NiB $253 Ex $192 Gd $140
Stainless finish (2.5-inch bbl. only). . . . . NiB $193 Ex $158 Gd $107

BULLDOG POLICE DA REVOLVER
Caliber: .38 Special or .32 H&R Magnum. Six-round cylinder, 4-inch bbl., 8.5 inches overall. Weight: 20.5 oz. Adj. rear sight, ramp front. Blued or stainless finish. Square checkered walnut grips. Made from 1976-93. Shroud dropped on new model.
Blued finish . . . . NiB $227 Ex $183 Gd $130
Stainless finish. . . . . NiB $217 Ex $178 Gd $119
.32 H&R Magnum (disc.1992). . . . . NiB $232 Ex $186 Gd $130

BULLDOG PUG DA REVOLVER
Caliber: .44 Special. Five-round cylinder, 2.5 inch bbl., 7.25 inches overall. Weight: 20 oz. Blued or stainless finish. Fixed ramp front sight, fixed square-notch rear. Checkered Neoprene or walnut grips. Made from 1988-93.
Blued finish . . . . NiB $247 Ex $217 Gd $146
Stainless finish. . . . . NiB $247 Ex $217 Gd $146

BULLDOG TARGET DA REVOLVER
Calibers: .357 Magnum, .44 Special (latter intro. in 1977). Four-inch bbl., 8.5 inches overall. Weight: 20.5 oz. in .357. Adj. rear sight, ramp front. Blued finish. Square checkered walnut grips. Made from 1976-92.
Blued finish (disc.1989). . . . . NiB $212 Ex $170 Gd $121
Stainless steel . . . . NiB $247 Ex $171 Gd $105

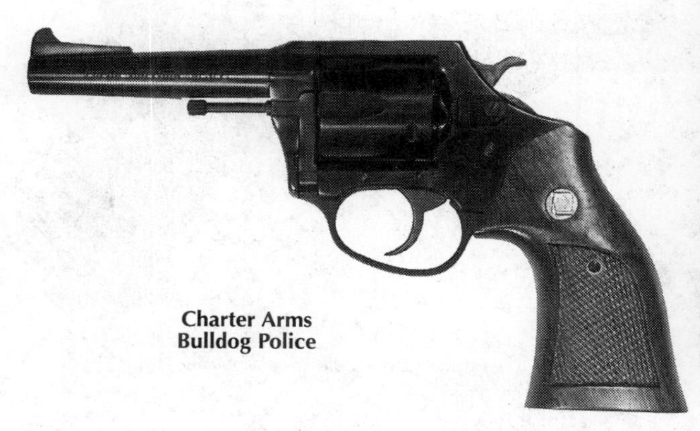

Charter Arms
Bulldog Police

Charter Arms
Bulldog Police

Charter Arms
Bulldog Target

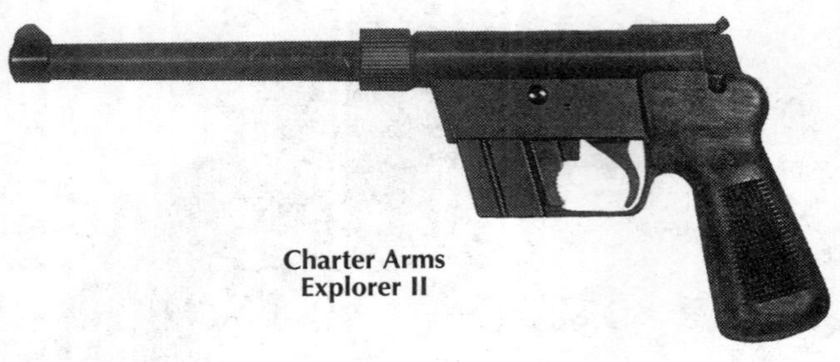

Charter Arms
Explorer II

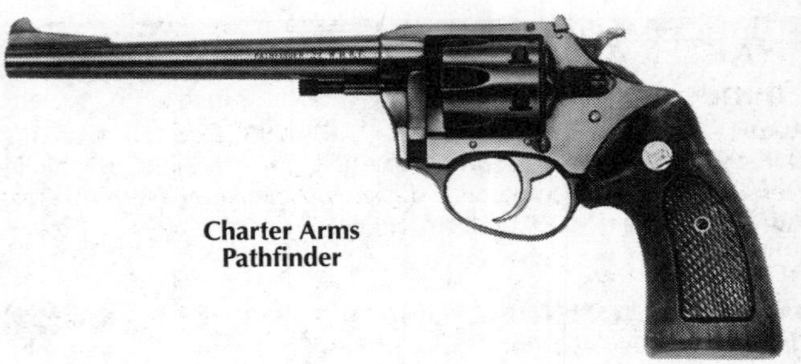

Charter Arms
Pathfinder

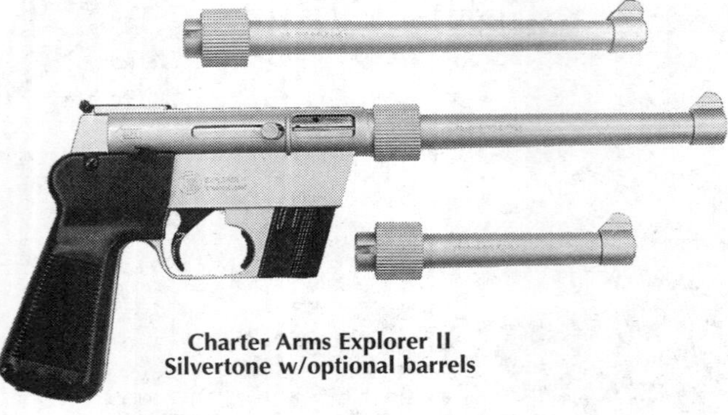

Charter Arms Explorer II
Silvertone w/optional barrels

Charter Arms Police Undercover
.32 H&R Magnum

Charter Arms Undercover
.32 S&W Long

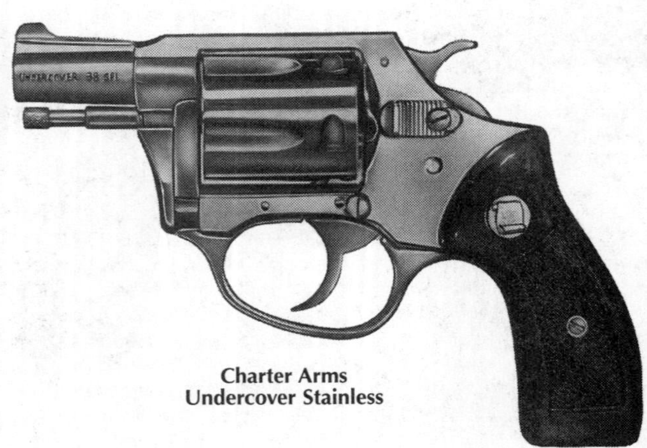

Charter Arms
Undercover Stainless

BULLDOG TRACKER
DA REVOLVER. . . . . NiB $203 Ex $168 Gd $107
Caliber: .357 Mag. Five-round cylinder, 2.5-, 4- or 6-inch bbl., 11 inches overall (6-inch bbl.). Weight: 21 oz. (2.5-inch bbl.). Adj. rear sight, ramp front. Checkered walnut grips. Blued finish. 4- or 6-inch bbl., Disc.1986. Reintroduced 1989-92. See illustration previous page.

EXPLORER II SEMIAUTO SURVIVAL PISTOL
Caliber: .22 RF. Eight-round magazine, 6-, 8- or 10-inch bbl., 13.5 inches overall (6-inch bbl.). Weight: 28 oz. finishes: Black, heat cured, semigloss textured enamel or silvertone anticorrosion. Disc. 1987.
Standard model . . . . NiB $107 Ex $97 Gd $66
Silvertone (w/optional
6- or 10-inch bbl.) . . . . NiB $129 Ex $116 Gd $76

OFF-DUTY DA REVOLVER
Calibers: .22 LR or .38 Special. Six-round (.22 LR) or 5-round (.38 Spec.) cylinder. Two-inch bbl., 6.25 inches overall. Weight: 16 oz. Fixed rear sight, Partridge-type front sight. Plain walnut grips. Matte black, nickel or stainless steel finish. Made from 1992-96.
Matte black finish . . . . NiB $188 Ex $163 Gd $102
Nickel finish . . . . NiB $219 Ex $169 Gd $117
Stainless steel . . . . NiB $208 Ex $171 Gd $117

PATHFINDER DA REVOLVER
Calibers: .22 LR, .22 WMR. Six-round cylinder, bbl. lengths: 2-, 3-, 6-inches, 7.13 inches overall (in 3-inch bbl.), and regular grips. Weight: 18.5 oz. (3-inch bbl.). Adj. rear sight, ramp front. Blued or stainless finish. Plain walnut regular, checkered Bulldog or square buttgrips. Made 1970 to date. Note: Originally designated "Pocket Target," name was changed in 1971 to "Pathfinder." Grips changed in 1984. Disc. 1993.
Blued finish . . . . NiB $203 Ex $168 Gd $107
Stainless finish. . . . . NiB $203 Ex $168 Gd $107

CHARTER ARMS PIT BULL DA REVOLVER
Calibers: 9mm, .357 Magnum, .38 Special. Five-round cylinder, 2.5-, 3.5- or 4-inch bbl., 7 inches overall (2.5-inch bbl.). Weight: 21.5 to 25 oz. All stainless steel frame. Fixed ramp front sight, fixed square-notch rear. Checkered Neoprene grips. Blued or stainless finish. Made from 1989-93.
Blued finish . . . . NiB $252 Ex $200 Gd $119
Stainless finish . . . . NiB $262 Ex $211 Gd $119

CHARTER ARMS UNDERCOVER DA REVOLVER
Caliber: .38 Special. Five-round cylinder,. bbl., lengths: 2-, 3-, 4-inches, 6.25 inches overall (2-inch bbl.), and regular grips. Weight: 16 oz. (2-inch bbl.). Fixed sights. Plain walnut, checkered Bulldog or square buttgrips. Made from 1965-96.
Blued or nickel-plated finish . . . . . . NiB $193 Ex $163 Gd $102
Stainless finish . . . . NiB $279 Ex $214 Gd $127

CHARTER ARMS UNDERCOVER
Same general specifications as standard Undercover except chambered for .32 H&R Magnum or .32 S&W Long, has 6-round cylinder and 2.5-inch bbl.
.32 H&R Magnum (blued) . . . . NiB $193 Ex $163 Gd $102
.32 H&R Magnum nickel . . . . NiB $193 Ex $163 Gd $102
.32 H&R Magnum (stainless) . . . . . . NiB $282 Ex $216 Gd $170
.32 S&W Long (blued) disc. 1989 . . . . . NiB $282 Ex $216 Gd $170

CHARTER ARMS UNDERCOVER POCKET POLICE DA REVOLVER
Same general specifications as standard Undercover except has 6-round cylinder and pocket-type hammer. Blued or stainless steel finish. Made from 1969-81.
Blued finish . . . . NiB $175 Ex $160 Gd $109
Stainless steel . . . . NiB $231 Ex $192 Gd $143

CHARTER ARMS UNDERCOVER POLICE DA REVOLVER
Same general specifications as standard Undercover except has 6-round cylinder. Made from 1984-89. Reintroduced 1993.
Blued, .38 Special . . . . NiB $229 Ex $198 Gd $122
Stainless, .38 Special . . . . NiB $228 Ex $188 Gd $137
.32 H&R Magnum . . . . NiB $210 Ex $175 Gd $127

CHARTER ARMS UNDER-
COVERETTE DA REVOLVER . . . . . . NiB $176 Ex $161 Gd $110
Same as Undercover model w/2-inch bbl. except caliber .32 S&W Long, 6-round cylinder, blued finish only. Weight: 16.5 oz. Made from 1972-83.

CIMARRON F.A. CO. — Fredricksburg, Texas

CIMARRON EL PISTOLERO
SINGLE-ACTION REVOLVER . . . . . NiB $446 Ex $352 Gd $224
Calibers: .357 Mag., .45 Colt. Six-round cylinder, 4.75- 5.5- or 7.5-inch bbl., polished brass backstrap and triggerguard. Otherwise, same as Colt Single-Action Army revolver w/parts being interchangeable. Made from 1997-98.

COLT MANUFACTURING CO., INC. — Hartford, Connecticut

Previously Colt Industries, Firearms Division. Production of some Colt handguns spans the period before World War II to the postwar years. Values shown for these models are for earlier production. Those manufactured c. 1946 and later generally are less desirable to collectors and values are approximately 30 percent lower.

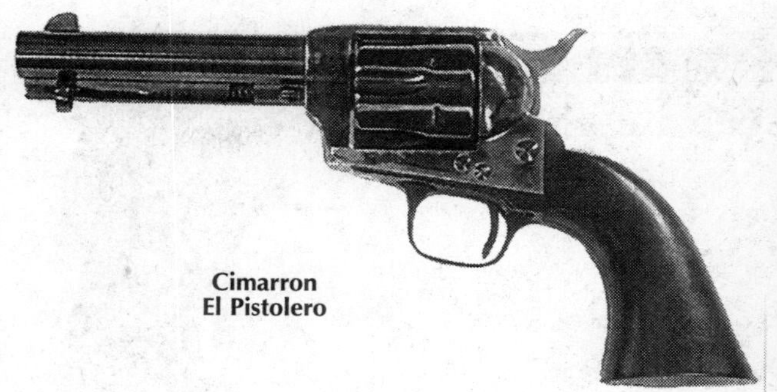

Cimarron El Pistolero

NOTE: *For ease in finding a particular firearm, Colt handguns are grouped into three sections: Automatic Pistols, Single-Shot Pistols, Derringers and Revolvers. For a complete listing, please refer to the Index.*

AUTOMATIC PISTOLS

COLT MODEL 1900 .38 AUTOMATIC PISTOL
Caliber: .38 ACP (modern high-velocity cartridges should not be used in this pistol). Seven-round magazine, 6-inch bbl., 9 inches overall. Weight: 35 oz. Fixed sights. Blued finish. Hard rubber and plain or checkered walnut grips. Sharp-spur hammer. Combination rear sight and safety unique to the Model 1900 (early production). In mid-1901 a solid rear sight was dovetailed into the slide. (SN range 1-4274) Made from 1900-03. Note: 250 models were sold to the military (50 Navy and 200 Army).
Early commercial model
(w/sight/safety) . . . . NiB $7033 Ex $5148 Gd $1926
Late commercial model
(W/dovetailed sight) . . . . NiB $6070 Ex $4093 Gd $2805
Army Model w/U.S. inspector
marks (1st Series - SN 90-150
w/inspector mark J.T.T) . . . . NiB $16,380 Ex $10,920 Gd $8719
(2nd Series - SN 1600-1750
w/inspector mark R.A.C.) . . . . NiB $10,237 Ex $8190 Gd $5569
Navy model (Also marked
w/USN-I.D. number) . . . . NiB $18,018 Ex $11,953 Gd $8982

COLT MODEL 1902 MILITARY .38 AUTOMATIC PISTOL
Caliber: .38 ACP (modern high-velocity cartridges should not be used in this pistol). Eight-round magazine, 6-inch bbl., 9 inches overall. Weight: 37 oz. Fixed sights w/blade front and V-notch rear. Blued finish. Checkered hard rubber grips. Round back hammer, changed to spur type in 1908. No safety but fitted w/standard military swivel. About 18,000 produced with split SN ranges. The government contract series (15,001-15,200) and the commercial sales series (15,000 receding to 11,000) and (30,200-47,266). Made from 1902-29.
Early military model (w/front
slide serrations) . . . . NiB $3698 Ex $3438 Gd $3230
Late military model (w/rear
slide serrations) . . . . NiB $2937 Ex $2398 Gd $2190
Marked "U.S. Army" (SN 15,001-
15,200) . . . . NiB $9015 Ex $6935 Gd $4595

COLT MODEL 1902 SPORTING
.38 AUTOMATIC PISTOL. . . . . . NiB $3775 Ex $2475 Gd $1071
Caliber: .38 ACP (modern high-velocity cartridges should not be used in this pistol). Seven-round magazine, 6-inch bbl., 9 inches overall. Weight: 35 oz. Fixed sights w/blade front and V-notch rear. Blued finish. Checkered hard rubber grips. Round back hammer was standard but some spur hammers were installed during late production. No safety and w/o swivel as found on military model. Total production about 7,500 w/split SN ranges (4275-10,999) and (30,000-30,190) Made from 1902-08.

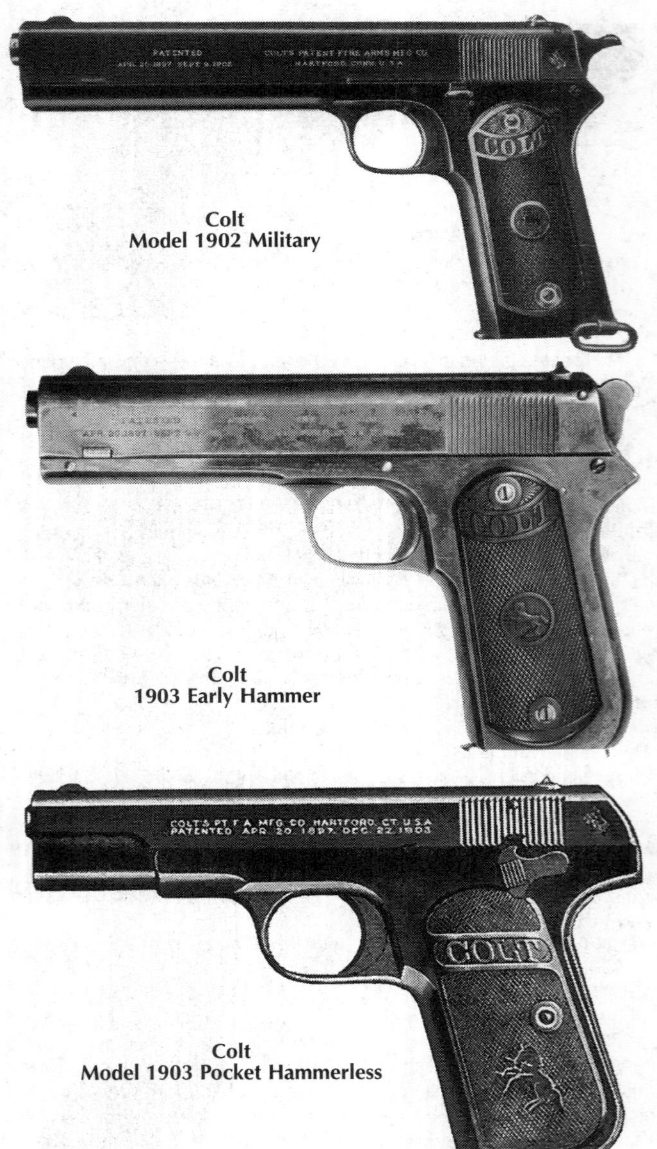

Colt
Model 1902 Military

Colt
1903 Early Hammer

Colt
Model 1903 Pocket Hammerless

MODEL 1903 POCKET .32 AUTOMATIC PISTOL FIRST ISSUE - COMMERCIAL SERIES

Caliber: .32 Auto. Eight-round magazine, 4-inch bbl., 7 inches overall. Weight: 23 oz. Fixed sights. Blued or nickel finish. Checkered hard rubber grips. Hammerless (concealed hammer). Slide lock and grip safeties. Fitted w/barrel bushing but early models have no magazine safety. Total production of the Model 1903 reached 572,215. The First Issue production occurred 1903-08 (SN range 1-72,000).

Blued finish . . . . NiB $980 Ex $673 Gd $507
Nickel finish . . . . NiB $1083 Ex $694 Gd $522

MODEL 1903 POCKET .32 AUTOMATIC PISTOL SECOND ISSUE - COMMERCIAL SERIES

Same as First Issue but with 3.75-inch bbl. and small extractor. Production occurred 1908-10 (SN range 72,001 -105,050).

Blued finish . . . . NiB $713 Ex $541 Gd $401
Nickel finish . . . . NiB $736 Ex $599 Gd $432

MODEL 1903 POCKET .32 AUTOMATIC PISTOL, THIRD ISSUE - COMMERCIAL SERIES

Caliber: .32 Auto. Similar to Second Issue w/3.75-inch bbl. except with integral barrel bushing and locking lug at muzzle end of bbl. Production occurred 1910-26 (SN range 105,051-468,096).

Blued finish . . . . NiB $607 Ex $472 Gd $322
Nickel finish . . . . NiB $647 Ex $497 Gd $297

MODEL 1903 POCKET .32 AUTOMATIC PISTOL FOURTH ISSUE - COMMERCIAL SERIES

Caliber: .32 Auto. Similar to Third Issue except a slide lock safety change was made when a Tansley-style disconnector was added on all pistols above SN 468,097, which prevents firing of cartridge in chamber when the magazine is removed. Blued or nickel finish. Checkered walnut grips. These design changes were initiated 1926-.45 (SN range 105,051-554,446).

Blued finish . . . . NiB $603 Ex $492 Gd $350
Nickel finish . . . . NiB $666 Ex $542 Gd $384

MODEL 1903 POCKET (HAMMER) .38 AUTOMATIC PISTOL

Caliber: .38 ACP (modern high-velocity cartridges should not be used in this pistol). Similar to Model 1902 Sporting .38 but w/shorter frame, slide and 4.5-inch bbl. Overall dimension reduced to 7.5 inches. Weight: 31 oz. Fixed sights w/blade front and V-notch rear. Blued finish. Checkered hard rubber grips. Round back hammer, changed to spur type in 1908. No safety. (SN range 16,001-47,226 with some numbers above 30,200 assigned to 1902 Military). Made from 1903-1929.

Early model
(round hammer) . . . . NiB $2270 Ex $1980 Gd $995
Late model
(spur hammer). . . . . NiB $1835 Ex $1245 Gd $745

MODEL 1903 POCKET HAMMERLESS (CONCEALED HAMMER) .32 AUTOMATIC PISTOL - MILITARY

Caliber: .32 ACP. Eight-round magazine, Similar to Model 1903 Pocket .32 except concealed hammer and equipped w/magazine safety. Parkerized or blued finish. (SN range with "M" prefix M1-M200,000) Made from 1941-.45.

Blued service model (marked
"U.S. Property") . . . . NiB $1570 Ex $1085 Gd $785
Parkerized service model (marked
"U.S. Property") . . . . NiB $1560 Ex $585 Gd $735
Blued documented
Officer's model . . . . NiB $3521 Ex $3746 Gd $1646
Parkerized documented
Officer's model . . . . NiB $2465 Ex $2140 Gd $1540

MODEL 1905 .45 AUTOMATIC PISTOL

Caliber: .45 (Rimless) Automatic. Seven-round magazine, 5-inch bbl., 8 inches overall. Weight: 32.5 oz. Fixed sights w/blade front and V-notch rear. Blued finish. Checkered walnut, hard rubber or pearl grips. Predecessor to Model 1911 Auto Pistol and contributory to the development of the .45 ACP cartridge. (SN range 1-6100) Made from 1905-11.

Commercial model . . . . NiB $5607 Ex $3357 Gd $1607
W/slotted backstrap
(500 produced) . . . . NiB $8380 Ex $7630 Gd $6130
W/shoulder stock/holster . . . . $7500 to $10,000

MODEL 1905 .45 (1907)
CONTRACT PISTOL . . . . NiB $12,000 Ex $9500 Gd $6250

Variation of the Model 1905 produced to U.S. Military specifications, including loaded chamber indicator, grip safety and lanyard loop. Only 201 were produced, but 200 were delivered and may be identified by the chief inspector's initials "K.M." (SN range 1-201) Made from 1907-08.

MODEL 1908 POCKET .25 HAMMERLESS AUTO PISTOL
Caliber: .25 Auto. Six-round magazine, 2-inch bbl., 4.5 inches overall. Weight: 13 oz. Flat-top front, square-notch rear sight in groove. Blued, nickel or Parkerized finish. Checkered hard rubber grips on early models, checkered walnut on later type, special pearl grips illustrated. Both a grip safety and slide lock safety are included on all models. The Tansley-style safety disconnector was added in 1916 at pistol No. 141000. (SN range 1-409,061) Made from 1908-41.
Blued finish . . . . NiB $1004 Ex $796 Gd $640
Nickel finish . . . . NiB $1056 Ex $900 Gd $744
Marked "U.S. Property" (w/blued finish) . . . . NiB $3368 Ex $1784 Gd $1398
Marked "U.S. Property" (w/parkerized finish) . . . . NiB $2741 Ex $2231 Gd $1555

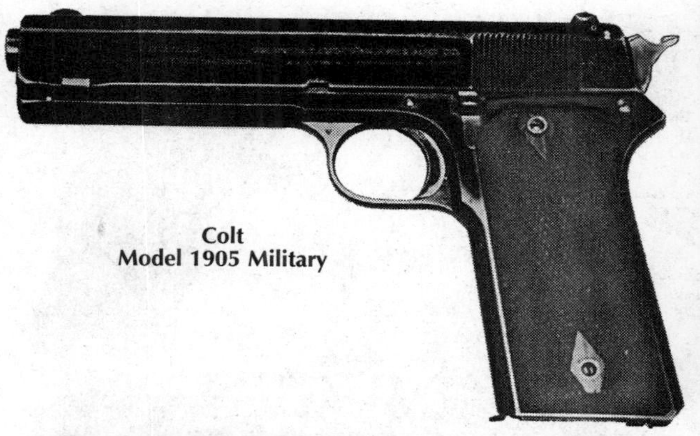
Colt
Model 1905 Military

MODEL 1908 POCKET .380 AUTOMATIC PISTOL
Similar to Pocket .32 Auto w/3.75-inch bbl. except chambered for .380 Auto w/seven-round magazine. Weight: 23 oz. Blue, nickel or Parkerized finish. (SN range 1-138,009) Made from 1908-45.
First Issue (made 1908-11, w/bbl., lock and bushing, w/SN 1-6,250) . . . . . NiB $952 Ex $744 Gd $380
Second Issue (made 1911-28, w/o bbl., lock and bushing, w/SN 6,251-92,893) . . . . NiB $900 Ex $588 Gd $328
Third Issue (made 1928-45, w/safety disconnector, w/SN 92,894-138,009) . . . . NiB $620 Ex $510 Gd $416
Parkerized service model (Marked "U.S. Property" made 1942-45, w/SN "M" prefix.) . . . . . NiB $2467 Ex $1843 Gd $1583
Documented officer's model (service model w/military assignment papers) . . . . NiB $2958 Ex $2398 Gd $1682

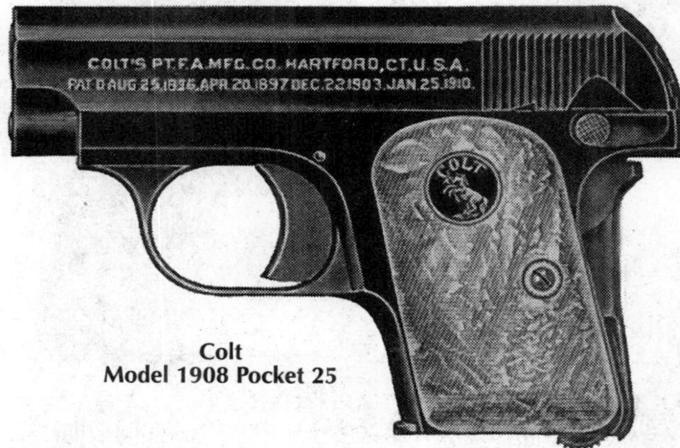

Colt
Model 1908 Pocket 25

NOTE: *During both World Wars, Colt licensed other firms to make these pistols under government contract, including Ithaca Gun Co., North American Arms Co., Ltd. (Canada), Remington-Rand Co., Remington-UMC, Singer Sewing Machine Co., and Union Switch & Signal Co. M1911 also produced at Springfield Armory.*

MODEL 1911 AUTOMATIC PISTOL
Caliber: .45 Auto. Seven-round magazine, 5-inch bbl., 8.5 inches overall. Weight: 39 oz. Fixed sights. Blued finish on Commercial model. Parkerized or similar finish on most military pistols. Checkered walnut grips (early production), plastic grips (later production). Checkered, arched mainspring housing and longer grip safety spur adopted in 1923 (on M1911A1).
Model 1911 commercial (C-series) . . . . NiB $1880 Ex $1528 Gd $1079
Model 1911A1 commercial (Pre-WWII) . . . . NiB $3770 Ex $3043 Gd $2113

Colt
Model 1911

U.S. GOVERNMENT MODEL 1911
Colt manufacture. . . . . NiB $1415 Ex $1207 Gd $879
North American manufacture . . . . NiB $25,868 Ex $20,693 Gd $14,071
Remington-UMC manufacture. . . . . NiB $2371 Ex $1923 Gd $1349
Springfield manufacture . . . . . . NiB $2333 Ex $1892 Gd $1329
Navy Model M1911 type. . . . . . NiB $3055 Ex $2469 Gd $1720

U.S. GOVERNMENT MODEL 1911A1
Singer manufacture . . . . . NiB $25,936 Ex $20,748 Gd $14,109
Colt, Ithaca, Remington-Rand manufacture. . . . . NiB $1017 Ex $829 Gd $588
Union Switch & Signal manufacture . . . . NiB $1519 Ex $1234 Gd $870

Colt
1991 A1

Colt Cadet .22

Colt All American Model 2000

MODEL M1991 A1 SEMIAUTO PISTOL
Reissue of Model 1911A1 (see above) w/a continuation of the original serial number range 1945. Caliber: .45 ACP. Seven-round magazine, 5-inch bbl., 8.5 inches overall. Weight: 39 oz. Fixed blade front sight, square notch rear. Parkerized finish. Black composition grips. Made from 1991 to date. (Commander and Compact variations intro. 1993).
Standard model. . . . . NiB $959 Ex $902 Gd $699
Commander w/4.5-inch bbl., ... NiB $699 Ex $637 Gd $397
Compact w/3.5-inch bbl., (six-round). . . . . NiB $803 Ex $699 Gd $543

.22 CADET AUTOMATIC PISTOL . . . . . NiB $259 Ex $211 Gd $150
Caliber: 22 LR. 10-round magazine, 4.5-inch vent rib bbl., 8.63 inches overall. Weight: 33.5 oz. Blade front sight, dovetailed rear. Stainless finish. Textured black polymer grips w/Colt medallion. Made 1993-95. Note: The Cadet Model name was disc. under litigation but the manufacturer continued to produce this pistol configuration as the Model "Colt 22". For this reason the "Cadet" model will command slight premiums.

.22 SPORT AUTOMATIC PISTOL . . . . . NiB $435 Ex $331 Gd $180
Same specifications as Cadet Model except renamed Colt .22 w/composition monogrip or wraparound black rubber grip. Made from 1995-98.

.22 TARGET PISTOL. . . . . NiB $329 Ex $282 Gd $152
Similar to Colt 22 Sport Model except w/6-inch vent rib bbl., 10.12 inches overall. Weight: 40.5 oz. Partridge style front sight, adjustable white outline rear on full length grooved rib. Made from 1995 to date.

ACE AUTOMATIC PISTOL
Caliber: .22 LR (regular or high speed). 10-round magazine. Built on the same frame as the Government Model .45 Auto w/same safety features, etc. Hand-honed action, target bbl., adj. rear sight. 4.75-inch bbl., 8.25. inches overall. Weight: 38 oz. Made from 1930-.40.
Commercial model . . . . NiB $2053 Ex $1646 Gd $1133
Service model (1938-42). . . . . . NiB $2891 Ex $2320 Gd $1590

ALL AMERICAN
MODEL 2000 DA PISTOL . . . . NiB $830 Ex $726 Gd $466
Hammerless semiautomatic w/blued slide and polymer or alloy receiver fitted w/roller-bearing trigger. Caliber: 9mm Para. 15-round magazine, 4.5-inch bbl., 7.5 inches overall. Weight: 29 oz. (Polymer) or 33 oz (Alloy). Fixed blade front sight, square-notch rear w/3-dot system. Matte blued slide w/black polymer or anodized aluminum receiver. Made from 1992-94.

AUTOMATIC .25 PISTOL
As a result of the 1968 Firearms Act restricting the importation of the Colt Pocket Junior that was produced in Spain, Firearms International was contracted by Colt to manufacture a similar blowback action with the same exposed hammer configuration. Both the U.S. and Spanish-made. .25 automatics were recalled to correct an action malfunction. Returned firearms were fitted with a rebounding firing pin to prevent accidental discharges. Caliber: .25 ACP. Six-round magazine, 2.25-inch bbl., 4.5 inches overall. Weight: 12.5 oz. Integral blade front, square-notch rear sight groove. Blued finish. Checkered wood grips w/Colt medallion. Made from 1970-75.
Model as issued. . . . . NiB $339 Ex $287 Gd $131
Model recalled
& refitted. . . . . NiB $349 Ex $287 Gd $131

CHALLENGER
AUTOMATIC PISTOL . . . . NiB $545 Ex $441 Gd $238
Same basic design as Woodsman Target, Third Issue but lacks some of the refinements. Fixed sights. Magazine catch on butt as in old Woodsman. Does not stay open on last shot. Lacks magazine safety. 4.5- or 6-inch bbl., 9 to 10.5 inches overall. Weight: 30 oz. (4.5-inch bbl.) or 31.5 oz. (6-inch bbl.) Blued finish. Checkered plastic grips. Made from 1950-55.

COMBAT COMMANDER AUTOMATIC PISTOL
Same as Lightweight Commander except has steel frame w/blued or nickel-plated finish. Weight: 36 oz. Made from 1950-76.
9mm Para. . . . . NiB $688 Ex $559 Gd $394
.38 Super, .45 ACP. . . . . NiB $794 Ex $644 Gd $453

COMMANDER LIGHTWEIGHT AUTOMATIC PISTOL
Same basic design as Government Model except w/shorter 4.25-inch bbl., and a special lightweight "Coltalloy" receiver and mainspring housing. Calibers: .45 Auto, .38 Super Auto, 9mm Para. Seven-round magazine (.45 cal.), nine-round (.38 Auto and 9mm), 8 inches overall. Weight: 26.5 oz. Fixed sights. Round spur hammer. Improved safety lock. Blued finish. Checkered plastic or walnut grips. Made from 1950-76.
9mm Para. . . . . NiB $679 Ex $553 Gd $392
.38 Super, .45 ACP. . . . . NiB $731 Ex $595 Gd $425

CONVERSION
UNIT—.22-.45. . . . . NiB $2925 Ex $2365 Gd $1649
Converts Service Ace .22 to National Match .45 Auto. Unit consists of match-grade slide assembly and bbl., bushing, recoil spring, recoil spring guide and plug, magazine and slide stop. Made from 1938-42.

CONVERSION
UNIT — .45-.22 . . . . NiB $553 Ex $455 Gd $330
Converts Government Model .45 Auto to a .22 LR target pistol. Unit consists of slide assembly, bbl., floating chamber (as in Service Ace), bushing, ejector, recoil spring, recoil spring guide and plug, magazine and slide stop. The component parts differ and are not interchangable between post war, series 70, series 80, ACE I and ACE II units. Made from 1938 to date.

DELTA ELITE SEMIAUTO PISTOL
Caliber: 10 mm. Five-inch bbl., 8.5 inches overall. Eight-round magazine, Weight: 38 oz. Checkered Neoprene combat grips w/Delta medallion. Three-dot, high-profile front and rear combat sights. Blued or stainless finish. Made from 1987-96.
First Edition
(500 Ltd. edition). . . . . NiB $1231 Ex $1038 Gd $700
Blued finish . . . . NiB $683 Ex $559 Gd $401
Matte stainless finish . . . . NiB $709 Ex $580 Gd $415
Ultra stainless finish . . . . NiB $813 Ex $663 Gd $472

DELTA GOLD CUP SEMIAUTO PISTOL
Same general specifications as Delta Elite except in match configuration w/Accro adjustable rear sight. Made from 1989-93 and 1995-96.
Blued finish (disc. 1991) . . . . NiB $778 Ex $634 Gd $451
Stainless steel finish. . . . . NiB $993 Ex $842 Gd $686

GOLD CUP MARK III
NATIONAL MATCH . . . . NiB $1163 Ex $950 Gd $664
Similar to Gold Cup National Match .45 Auto except chambered for .38 Special Mid Range. Five-round magazine, Made from 1961-74.

GOLD CUP NATIONAL
MATCH .45 AUTO. . . . . NiB $1059 Ex $903 Gd $547
Match version of Government Model .45 Auto w/same general specifications except: match grade bbl., w/new design bushing, flat mainspring housing, long wide trigger w/adj. stop, hand-fitted slide w/improved ejection port, adj. rear sight, target front sight, checkered walnut grips w/gold medallions. Weight: 37 oz. Made from 1957-70.

GOVERNMENT MODEL 1911/1911A1
See Colt Model 1911.

HUNTSMAN . . . . NiB $510 Ex $406 Gd $302
Same specifications as the Challenger. Made from 1955-76.

MK I & IL/SERIES '90 DOUBLE
EAGLE COMBAT COMMANDER . . . . . NiB $632 Ex $513 Gd $361
Calibers: .40 S&W, .45 ACP. Seven-round magazine, 4.25-inch bbl., 7.75 inches overall. Weight: 36 oz. Fixed blade front sight, square-notch rear. Checkered Xenoy grips. Stainless finish. Made from 1992-96.

MK IL/SERIES '90 DOUBLE EAGLE DA SEMIAUTO PISTOL
Calibers: .38 Super, 9mm, .40 S&W, 10mm, .45 ACP. Seven-round magazine. Five-inch bbl., 8.5 inches overall. Weight: 39 oz. Fixed or Accro adj. sights. Matte stainless finish. Checkered Xenoy grips. Made from 1991-96.
.38 Super, 9mm, .40
S&W (fixed sights). . . . . NiB $672 Ex $546 Gd $384
.45 ACP (adjustable sights) . . . . NiB $668 Ex $544 Gd $386
.45 ACP (fixed sights) . . . . NiB $642 Ex $507 Gd $371
10mm (adjustable sights). . . . . NiB $662 Ex $539 Gd $383
10mm (fixed sights). . . . . NiB $636 Ex $518 Gd $368

MK IL/SERIES '90 DOUBLE
EAGLE OFFICER'S ACP . . . . NiB $668 Ex $546 Gd $386
Same general specifications as Double Eagle Combat Commander except chambered for .45 ACP only, 3.5-inch bbl., 7.25 inches overall. Weight: 35 oz. Also available in lightweight (25 oz.) w/blued finish (same price). Made from 1990-93.

MK IV/SERIES '70 COMBAT COMMANDER
Same general specifications as the Lightweight Commander except made from 1970-83.
Blued finish . . . . NiB $645 Ex $523 Gd $362
Nickel finish . . . . NiB $712 Ex $488 Gd $392

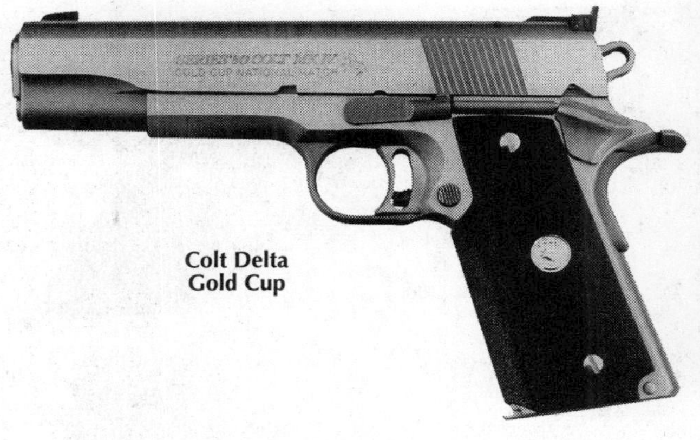
Colt Delta
Gold Cup

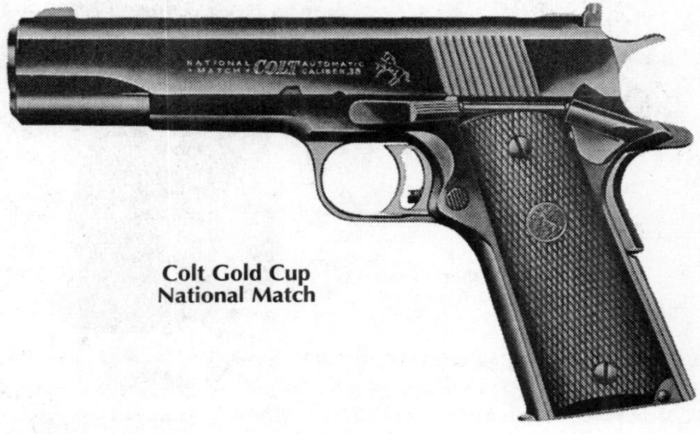
Colt Gold Cup
National Match

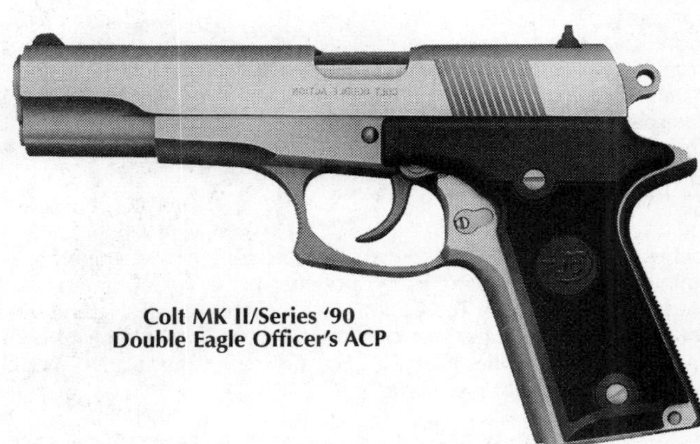
Colt MK II/Series '90
Double Eagle Officer's ACP

MK IV/SERIES '70 GOLD CUP
NATIONAL MATCH .45 AUTO . . . NiB $1043 Ex $866 Gd $679
Match version of MK IV/Series '70 Government Model. Caliber: .45 Auto only. Flat mainspring housing. Accurizor bbl., and bushing. Solid rib, Colt-Elliason adj. rear sight undercut front sight. Adj. trigger, target hammer. 8.75 inches overall. Weight: 38.5 oz. Blued finish. Checkered walnut grips. Made from 1970-84.

MK IV/SERIES '70 GOV'T.
AUTO PISTOL . . . . NiB $882 Ex $674 Gd $414
Calibers: .45 Auto, .38 Super Auto, 9mm Para. Seven-round magazine in .45, 9-round in .38 and 9mm. Five-inch bbl., 8.38 inches overall. Weight: 38 oz., (.45); 39 oz. in .38 and 9mm. Fixed rear sight and ramp front sight. Blued or nickel-plated finish. Checkered walnut grips. Made from 1970-84.

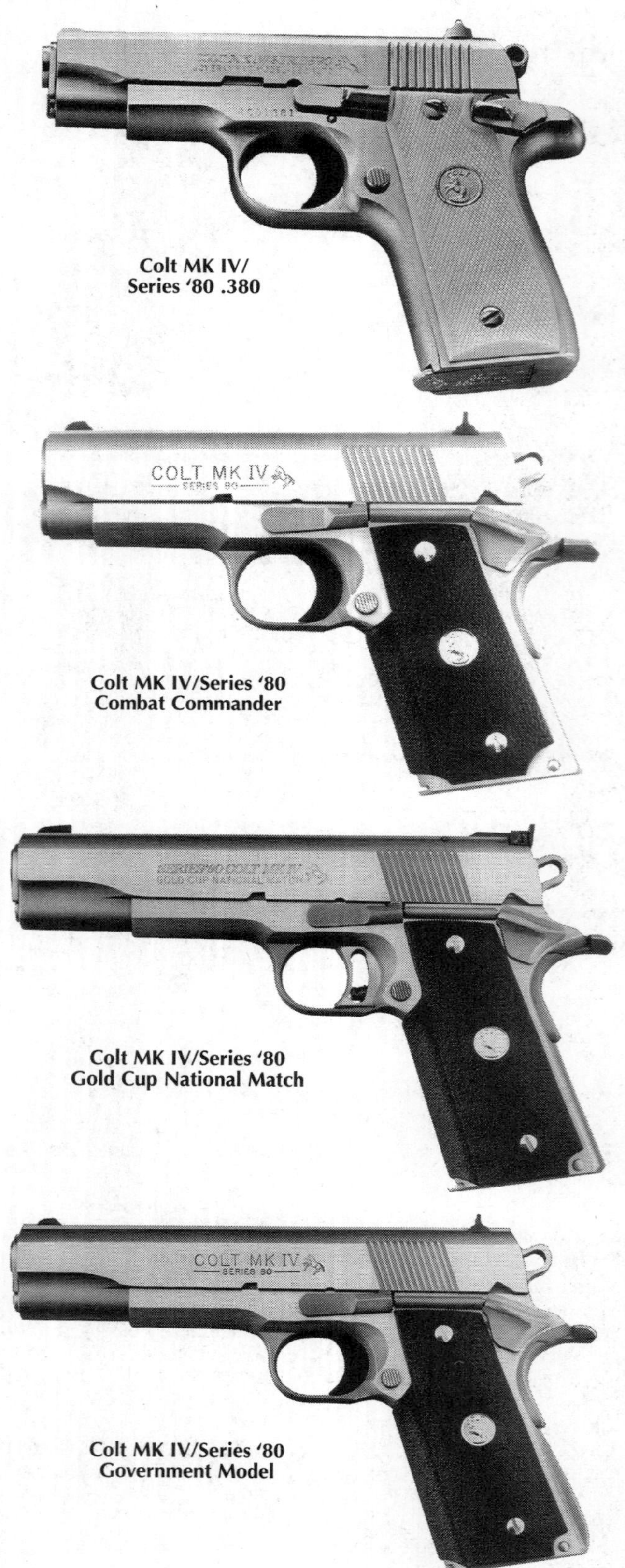

Colt MK IV/ Series '80 .380

Colt MK IV/Series '80 Combat Commander

Colt MK IV/Series '80 Gold Cup National Match

Colt MK IV/Series '80 Government Model

MK IV/SERIES '80 .380 AUTOMATIC PISTOL
Caliber: .380 ACP, 3.29-inch bbl., 6.15 inches overall. Weight: 21.8 oz. Composition grips. Fixed sights. Made since 1984 to date.

Blued finish (disc.1997) . . . . **NiB $479 Ex $344 Gd $240**
Bright nickel (disc.1995) . . . . **NiB $552 Ex $411 Gd $261**
Satin nickel Coltguard (disc.1989) . . . . **NiB $531 Ex $375 Gd $255**
Stainless finish . . . . **NiB $536 Ex $385 Gd $271**

MK IV/SERIES '80 COMBAT COMMANDER
Updated version of the MK IV/Series '70 w/same general specifications. Blued, two-tone or stainless steel w/"pebbled" black Neoprene wraparound grips. Made since 1979.

Blued finish (disc.1996) . . . . **NiB $632 Ex $533 Gd $356**
Satin nickel (disc.1987) . . . . **NiB $673 Ex $558 Gd $381**
Stainless finish . . . . **NiB $694 Ex $548 Gd $404**
Two-tone finish . . . . **NiB $719 Ex $569 Gd $408**

MK IV/SERIES '80 COMBAT ELITE
Same general specifications as MK IV/Series '80 Combat Commander except w/Elite enhancements. Calibers: .38 Super, .40 S&W, .45 ACP. Stainless frame w/blued steel slide. Accro adj. sights and beavertail grip safety. Made from 1992-96.

.38 Super, .45 ACP . . . . **NiB $813 Ex $699 Gd $397**
.40 S&W . . . . **NiB $782 Ex $680 Gd $366**

MK IV/SERIES '80 GOLD CUP NATIONAL MATCH
Same general specifications as Match '70 version except w/additional finishes and "pebbled" wraparound Neoprene grips. Made from 1983-96.

Blued finish . . . . **NiB $968 Ex $786 Gd $422**
Bright blued finish . . . . **NiB $1009 Ex $720 Gd $495**
Stainless finish . . . . **NiB $807 Ex $661 Gd $432**

MK IV/SERIES '80 GOVERNMENT MODEL
Same general specifications as Government Model Series '70 except also chambered in .40 S&W, w/"pebbled" wraparound Neoprene grips, blued or stainless finish. Made since 1983.

Blued finish . . . . **NiB $786 Ex $576 Gd $368**
Bright blued finish . . . . **NiB $857 Ex $602 Gd $497**
Bright stainless finish . . . . **NiB $781 Ex $675 Gd $371**
Matte stainless finish . . . . **NiB $776 Ex $570 Gd $381**

MK IV/SERIES '80 LIGHT-WEIGHT COMMANDER . . . . **NiB $664 Ex $512 Gd $357**
Updated version of the MK IV/Series '70 w/same general specifications.

MK IV/SERIES '80 MUSTANG .380 AUTOMATIC
Caliber: .380 ACP. Five- or 6-round magazine, 2.75-inch bbl., 5.5 inches overall. Weight: 18.5 oz. Blued, nickel or stainless finish. Black composition grips. Made from 1986-97.

Blued finish . . . . **NiB $461 Ex $362 Gd $263**
Nickel finish (disc.1994) . . . . **NiB $518 Ex $362 Gd $271**
Satin nickel Coltguard (disc.1988) . . . . **NiB $508 Ex $342 Gd $262**
Stainless finish . . . . **NiB $528 Ex $362 Gd $271**

MK IV/SERIES '80 MUSTANG PLUS II

Caliber: .380 ACP, 7-round magazine, 2.75-inch bbl., 5.5 inches overall. Weight: 20 oz. Blued or stainless finish w/checkered black composition grips. Made from 1988-96.

Blued finish . . . . NiB $472 Ex $373 Gd $277
Stainless finish. . . . . NiB $528 Ex $372 Gd $262

MK IV/SERIES '80 MUSTANG POCKETLITE

Same general specifications as the Mustang 30 except weight: 12.5 oz. w/aluminum alloy receiver. Blued, chrome or stainless finish. Optional wood grain grips. Made since 1988.

Blued finish . . . . NiB $474 Ex $375 Gd $276
Lady Elite
(two-tone) finish . . . . NiB $499 Ex $453 Gd $312
Stainless finish. . . . . NiB $530 Ex $374 Gd $284
Teflon/stainless finish . . . . NiB $557 Ex $370 Gd $271

MK IV/SERIES '80 OFFICER'S ACP AUTOMATIC PISTOL

Calibers: .40 S&W and .45 ACP, 3.63-inch bbl., 7.25 inches overall. Weight: 34 oz. Made from 1984-97. .40 S&W, disc.1992.

Blued finish
(disc.1996). . . . . NiB $585 Ex $482 Gd $342
Matte finish . . . . NiB $562 Ex $457 Gd $334
Satin nickel finish . . . . NiB $648 Ex $525 Gd $363
Stainless steel . . . . NiB $610 Ex $496 Gd $352

MK IV/SERIES '80
SA LIGHTWEIGHT CONCEALED
CARRY OFFICER . . . . NiB $657 Ex $535 Gd $371

Caliber: .45 ACP. Seven-round magazine, 4.25-inch bbl., 7.75 inches overall. Weight: 35 oz. Aluminum alloy receiver w/stainless slide. Dovetailed low-profile sights w/3-dot system. Matte stainless finish w/blued receiver. Wraparound black rubber grip w/finger grooves. Made since 1998.

MK IV/SERIES '90 DEFENDER
SA LIGHTWEIGHT . . . . NiB $647 Ex $523 Gd $355

Caliber: .45 ACP. Seven-round magazine, 3-inch bbl., 6.75 inches over-all. Weight: 22.5 oz. Aluminum alloy receiver w/stainless slide. Dovetailed low-profile sights w/3-dot system. Matte stainless finish w/Nickel-Teflon receiver. Wraparound black rubber grip w/finger grooves. Made since 1998.

MK IV/SERIES 90
PONY DAO PISTOL . . . . NiB $538 Ex $446 Gd $307

Caliber: .380 ACP. Six-round magazine, 2.75-inch bbl., 5.5 inches overall. Weight: 19 oz. Ramp front sight, dovetailed rear. Stainless finish. Checkered black composition grips. Made since 1997.

MK IV/SERIES 90
PONY POCKETLITE. . . . . NiB $518 Ex $430 Gd $293

Similar to standard weight Pony Model except w/aluminum frame. Brushed stainless and Teflon finish. Made from 1997 to date.

NATIONAL MATCH AUTOMATIC PISTOL

Identical to the Government Model .45 Auto but w/hand-honed action, match-grade bbl., adj. rear and ramp front sights or fixed sights. Made from 1932-40.

W/adjustable
sights . . . . NiB $2943 Ex $2373 Gd $1667
W/fixed sights . . . . NiB $2141 Ex $1702 Gd $1205

NRA CENTENNIAL
.45 GOLD CUP
NATIONAL MATCH . . . . NiB $1530 Ex $1264 Gd $890

Only 2500 produced in 1971.

Colt MK IV/Series '80 Mustang Plus II

Colt MK IV/Series '80 Mustang Pocketlite

Colt MK IV/Series '80 Officer's ACP

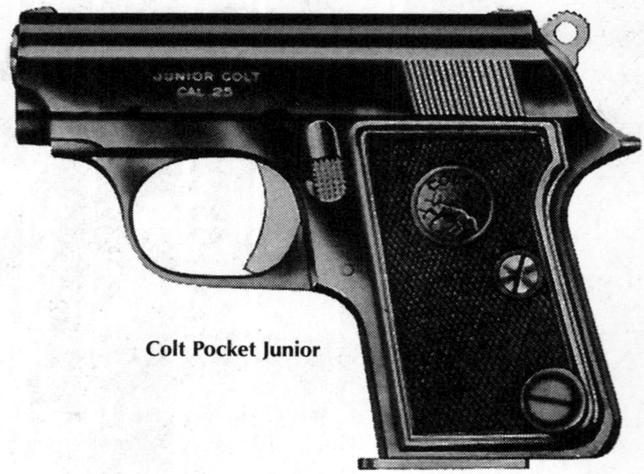

Colt Pocket Junior

POCKET JUNIOR MODEL
AUTOMATIC PISTOL . . . . NiB $414 Ex $320 Gd $206
Made in Spain by Unceta y Cia (Astra). Calibers: .22 Short, .25 Auto. Six-round magazine, 2.25 inch bbl., 4.75 inches overall. Weight: 12 oz. Fixed sights. Checkered walnut grips. Note: In 1980, this model was subject to recall to correct an action malfunction. Returned firearms were fitted with a rebounding firing pin to prevent accidental discharges. Made from 1958-68.

SUPER .38
AUTOMATIC PISTOL
Identical to Government Model .45 Auto except for caliber and magazine capacity. Caliber: .38 Automatic. Nine-round magazine, Made from 1928-70.
Pre-war . . . . NiB $2912 Ex $2354 Gd $1752
Post-war. NiB $1151 Ex $638 Gd $370

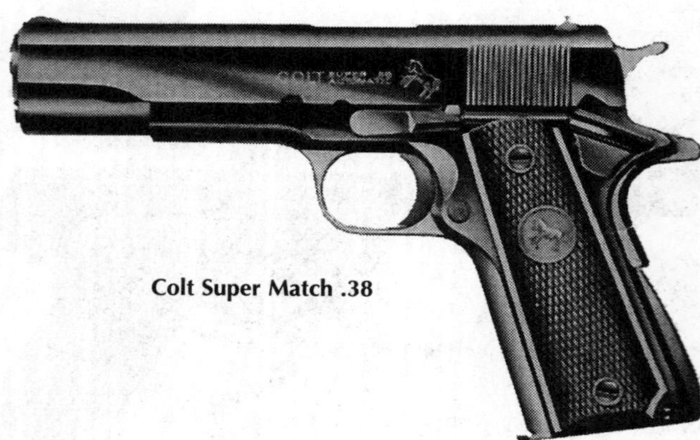
Colt Super Match .38

SUPER MATCH .38
AUTOMATIC PISTOL
Identical to Super .38 Auto but w/hand-honed action, match grade bbl., adjustable rear sight and ramp front sight or fixed sights. Made from 1933-46.
W/adjustable sights . . . . NiB $7049 Ex $5577 Gd $3910
W/fixed sights . . . . NiB $4771 Ex $3857 Gd $2676

TARGETSMAN. . . . . NiB $749 Ex $687 Gd $333
Similar to Woodsman Target but has "economy" adj. rear sight, lacks automatic slide stop. Made from 1959-76.

Colt Targetsman

WOODSMAN MATCH TARGET
AUTOMATIC PISTOL
FIRST ISSUE. . . . . NiB $1537 Ex $1485 Gd $861
Same basic design as other Woodsman models. Caliber: .22 LR. 10-round magazine, 6.5-inch bbl., slightly tapered w/flat sides, 11 inches overall. Weight: 36 oz. Adjustable rear sight. Blued finish. Checkered walnut one-piece grip w/extended sides. Made from 1938-42.

WOODSMAN MATCH
TARGET AUTO PISTOL,
SECOND ISSUE. . . . . NiB $959 Ex $782 Gd $512
Same basic design as Woodsman Target Third Issue. Caliber: .22 LR (reg. or high speed). 10-round magazine, Six-inch flat-sided heavy bbl., 10.5 inches overall. Weight: 40 oz. Click adj. rear sight, ramp front. Blued finish. Checkered plastic or walnut grips. Made from 1948-76.

WOODSMAN
MATCH TARGET "4 1/2"
AUTOMATIC PISTOL . . . . NiB $907 Ex $585 Gd $439
Same as Match Target second issue except w/4.5-inch bbl., 9 inches overall. Weight: 36 oz. Made from 1950-76.

Colt Woodsman
Match Target First Issue

WOODSMAN SPORT MODEL
AUTOMATIC PISTOL,
FIRST ISSUE. . . . . NiB $995 Ex $813 Gd $553
Caliber: .22 LR (reg. or high speed). Same as Woodsman Target second issue except has 4.5-inch bbl., adjustable rear sight w/fixed or adjustable front sight. Weight: 27 oz., 8.5 inches overall. Made from 1933-48.

WOODSMAN SPORT
MODEL AUTOMATIC
PISTOL, SECOND ISSUE . . . . NiB $995 Ex $813 Gd $553
Same as Woodsman Target third Issue but w/4.5-inch bbl., 9 inches overall. Weight: 30 oz. Made from 1948-76.

WOODSMAN TARGET MODEL AUTOMATIC, FIRST ISSUE . . . . NiB $813 Ex $761 Gd $397
Caliber: .22 LR (reg. velocity). 10-round magazine, 6.5-inch bbl., 10.5 inches overall. Weight: 28 oz. Adjustable sights. Blued finish. Checkered walnut grips. Made 1915-.32. Note: The mainspring housing of this model is not strong enough to permit safe use of high-speed cartridges. Change to a new heat-treated mainspring housing was made at pistol No. 83,790. Many of the old models were converted by installation of new housings. The new housing may be distinguished from the earlier type by the checkering in the curve under the breech. The new housing is grooved straight across, while the old type bears a diagonally-checkered oval.

WOODSMAN TARGET MODEL AUTOMATIC, SECOND ISSUE . . . . NiB $736 Ex $580 Gd $372
Caliber: .22 LR (reg. or high speed). Same as original model except has heavier bbl., and high-speed mainspring housing. (See note under Woodsman, First Issue). Weight: 29 oz. Made from 1932-48.

WOODSMAN TARGET MODEL AUTOMATIC, THIRD ISSUE . . . . . . NiB $586 Ex $461 Gd $279
Same basic design as previous Woodsman pistols but w/longer grip, magazine catch on left side, larger thumb safety, slide stop, slide stays open on last shot, magazine disconnector thumbrest grips. Caliber: .22 LR (reg. or high speed). 10-round magazine, 6-inch bbl., 10.5 inches overall. Weight: 32 oz. Click adjustable rear sight, ramp front sight. Blued finish. Checkered plastic or walnut grips. Made from 1948-76.

WORLD WAR I 50TH ANNIVERSARY COMMEMORATIVE SERIES
Limited production replica of Model 1911 .45 Auto engraved w/battle scenes, commemorating Battles at Chateau Thierry, Belleau Wood Second Battle of the Marne, Meuse Argonne. In special presentation display cases. Production: 7,400 Standard model, 75 Deluxe, 25 Special Deluxe grade. Match numbered sets offered. Made in 1967, 68, 69. Values indicated are for commemoratives in new condition.
Standard grade . . . . NiB $1022 Ex $834 Gd $593
Deluxe grade. . . . . NiB $2053 Ex $1664 Gd $1167
Special Deluxe grade. . . . . NiB $3960 Ex $3182 Gd $2210

WORLD WAR II COMMEMORATIVE .45 AUTO . . . . NiB $1057 Ex $901 Gd $709
Limited production replica of Model 1911A1 .45 Auto engraved w/respective names of locations where historic engagements occurred during WW II, as well as specific issue and theater identification. European model has oak leaf motif on slide, palm leaf design frames the Pacific issue. Cased. 11,500 of each model were produced. Made in 1970. Value listed is for gun in new condition.

WORLD WAR II 50TH ANNIVERSARY COMMEMORATIVE. . . . . NiB $2347 Ex $1983 Gd $1490
Same general specifications as the Colt World War II Commemorative .45 Auto except slightly different scroll engraving, 24-karat gold-plate trigger, hammer, slide stop, magazine catch, magazine catch lock, safety lock and four grip screws. Made in 1995 only.

WORLD WAR II D-DAY INVASION COMMEMORATIVE . . . . NiB $1427 Ex $1354 Gd $968
High-luster and highly decorated version of the Colt Model 1911A1. Caliber: .45 ACP. Same general specifications as the Colt Model 1911 except for 24-karat gold-plated hammer, trigger, slide stop, magazine catch, magazine catch screw, safety lock and four grip screws. Also has scrolls and inscription on slide. Made in 1991 only.

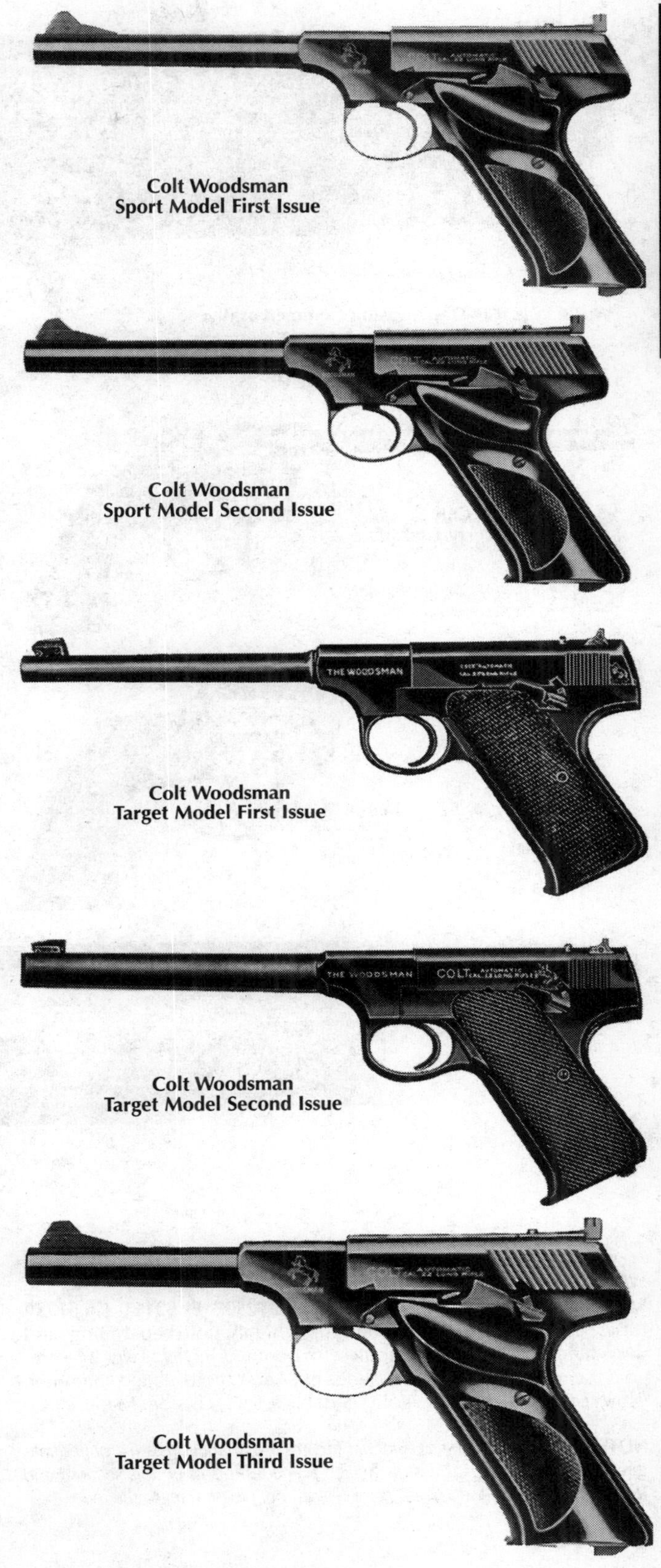

Colt Woodsman Sport Model First Issue

Colt Woodsman Sport Model Second Issue

Colt Woodsman Target Model First Issue

Colt Woodsman Target Model Second Issue

Colt Woodsman Target Model Third Issue

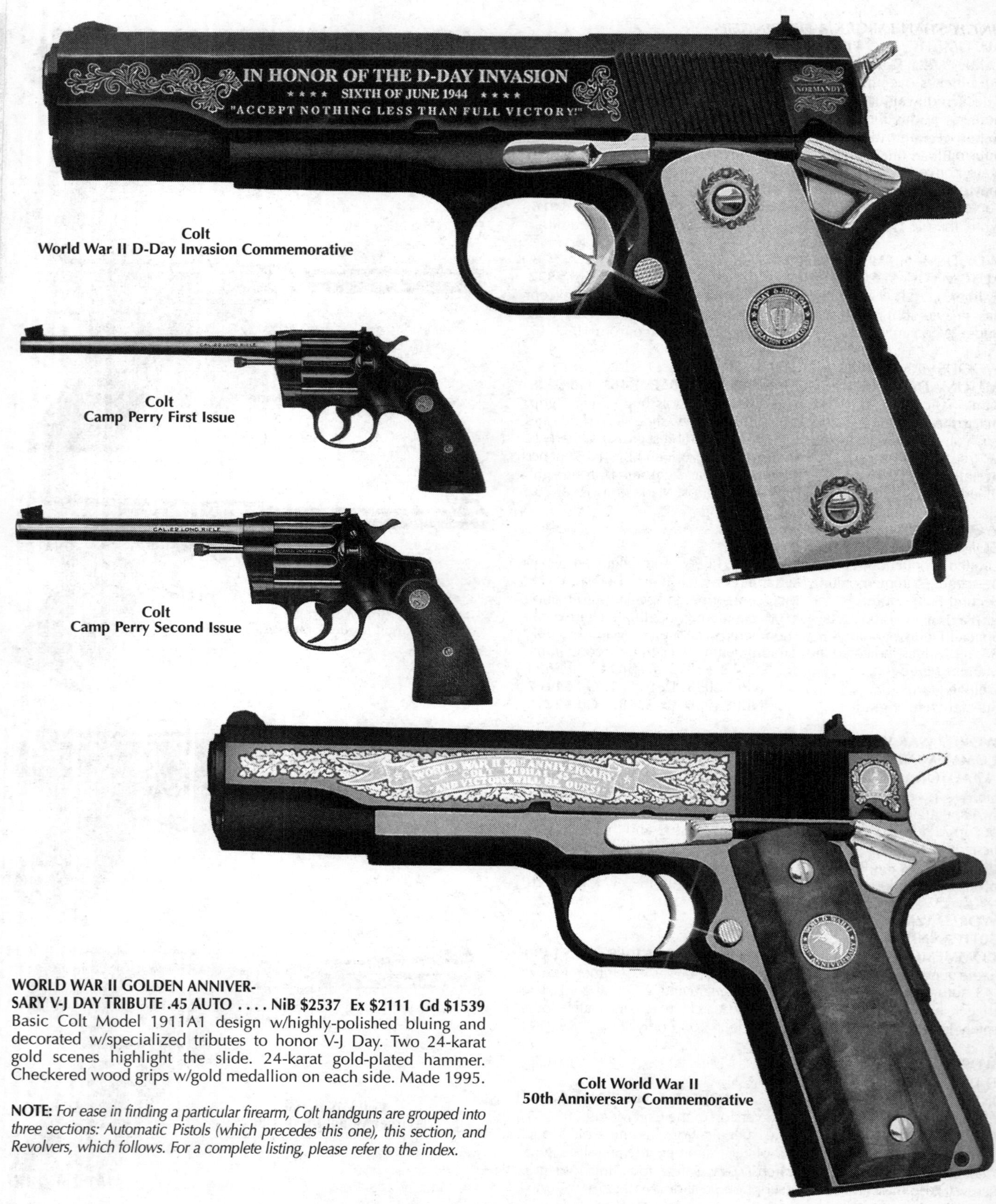
IN HONOR OF THE D-DAY INVASION
★★★★ SIXTH OF JUNE 1944 ★★★★
"ACCEPT NOTHING LESS THAN FULL VICTORY!"
NORMANDY

Colt
World War II D-Day Invasion Commemorative

Colt
Camp Perry First Issue

Colt
Camp Perry Second Issue

WORLD WAR II GOLDEN ANNIVERSARY V-J DAY TRIBUTE .45 AUTO . . . . NiB $2537 Ex $2111 Gd $1539
Basic Colt Model 1911A1 design w/highly-polished bluing and decorated w/specialized tributes to honor V-J Day. Two 24-karat gold scenes highlight the slide. 24-karat gold-plated hammer. Checkered wood grips w/gold medallion on each side. Made 1995.

NOTE: *For ease in finding a particular firearm, Colt handguns are grouped into three sections: Automatic Pistols (which precedes this one), this section, and Revolvers, which follows. For a complete listing, please refer to the index.*

Colt World War II
50th Anniversary Commemorative

SINGLE-SHOT PISTOLS & DERRINGERS

CAMP PERRY MODEL SINGLE-SHOT PISTOL, FIRST ISSUE . . . NiB $1770 Ex $1443 Gd $1002
Built on Officers' Model frame. Caliber: .22 LR (embedded head chamber for high-speed cartridges after 1930). 10 inch bbl., 13.75 inches overall. Weight: 34.5 oz. Adj. target sights. Hand-finished action. Blued finish. Checkered walnut grips. Made from 1926-34.

CAMP PERRY MODEL SECOND ISSUE. . . . . NiB $1542 Ex $1282 Gd $918
Same general specifications as First Issue except has shorter hammer fall and 8-inch bbl., 12 inches overall. Weight: 34 oz. Made from 1934-41 (about 440 produced).

CIVIL WAR CENTENNIAL MODEL PISTOL
Single-shot replica of Colt Model 1860 Army Revolver. Caliber: .22 Short. Six-inch bbl., weight: 22 oz. Blued finish w/gold-plated frame, grip frame, and trigger guard, walnut grips. Cased. 24,114 were produced. Made in 1961.
Single pistol. . . . . NiB $290 Ex $239 Gd $174
Pair w/consecutive serial numbers . . . . NiB $632 Ex $504 Gd $354

DERRINGER NO. 4
Replica of derringer No. 3 (1872 Thuer Model). Single-shot w/sideswing bbl., Caliber: .22 Short, 2.5-inch bbl., 4.9 inches overall. Weight: 7.75 oz. Fixed sights. Gold-plated frame w/blued bbl., and walnut grips or completely nickel- or gold-plated w/simulated ivory or pearl grips. Made from 1959-63. 112,000 total production. (SN w/D or N suffix)
Single pistol (gun only) . . . . NiB $154 Ex $128 Gd $95
Single pistol (cased w/accessories) . . . . NiB $416 Ex $312 Gd $182

DERRINGER NO. 4 COMMEMORATIVE MODELS
Limited production version of .22 derringers issued, w/appropriate inscription, to commemorate historical events. Additionally, non-firing models (w/unnotched bbls.) were furnished in books, picture frames and encased in plexiglass as singles or in cased pairs.
No. 4 Presentation Derringers (Non-firing w/accessories) . . . . NiB $4100
Ltd. Ed. Book Series (W/nickel-plated derringers) . . . . NiB $394
1st Presentation Series (Leatherette covered metal case) . . . . NiB $368
2nd Presentation Series (Single wooden case) . . . . NiB $264
2nd Presentation Series (Paired wooden case) . . . . NiB $394
1961 Issue Geneseo, Illinois, 125th Anniversary (104 produced). . . . . NiB $753
1962 Issue Fort McPherson, Nebraska, Centennial (300 produced) . . . . NiB $472

LORD AND LADY DERRINGERS (NO. 5)
Same as Derringer No. 4. Lord model with blued bbl., w/gold-plated frame and walnut grips. Lady model is gold-plated w/simulated pearl grips. Furnished in cased pairs. Made from 1970-72. (SN w/Der sufix)
Lord derringer, pair in case. . . . . . . NiB $503 Ex $411 Gd $295
Lady derringer, pair in case. . . . . . . NiB $515 Ex $412 Gd $302
Lord and Lady derringers, one each, in case. . . . . NiB $534 Ex $437 Gd $312

ROCK ISLAND ARSENAL CENTENNIAL PISTOL . . . . NiB $456 Ex $451 Gd $264
Limited production (550 pieces) version of Civil War Centennial Model single-shot .22 pistol, made exclusively for Cherry's Sporting Goods, Geneseo, Illinois, to commemorate the centennial of the Rock Island Arsenal in Illinois. Cased. Made in 1962.

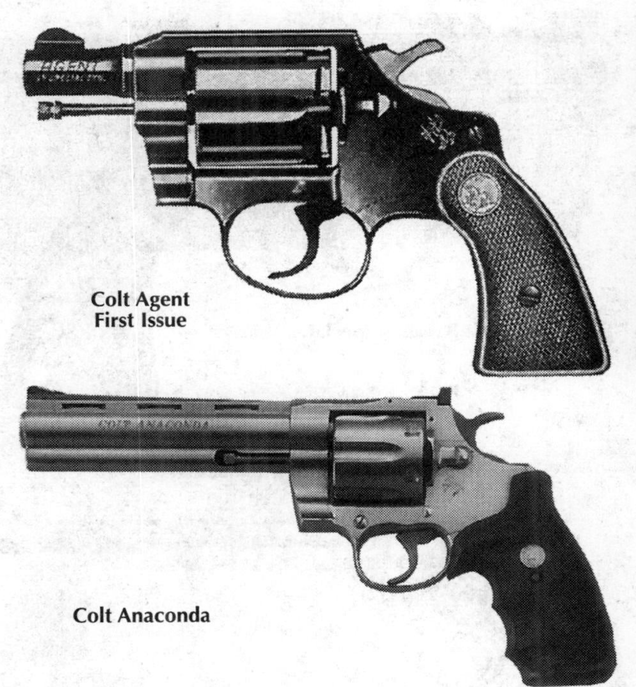

Colt Agent First Issue

Colt Anaconda

NOTE: *This section of Colt handguns contains only revolvers. For automatic pistols or single-shot pistols and derringers, please see the two sections that precede this. For a complete listing, please refer to the Index.*

REVOLVERS

.38 DS II REVOLVER . . . . NiB $481 Ex $386 Gd $273
Caliber: .38 Special. Six-round cylinder, 2-inch bbl., 7 inches overall. Weight: 21 oz. Ramp front sight, fixed notch rear. Satin stainless finish. Black rubber combat grip w/finger grooves. Made from 1997 to date.

AGENT DA REVOLVER, FIRST ISSUE. NiB $487 Ex $435 Gd $284
Same as Cobra, first issue except has short-grip frame .38 Special only, weight: 14 oz. Made from 1955-72.

AGENT (LW) DA REVOLVER, SECOND ISSUE. . . . . NiB $456 Ex $425 Gd $253
Same as Colt Agent, first issue except has shrouded ejector rod and alloy frame. Made from 1973-86.

ANACONDA DA REVOLVER
Calibers: .44 Mag., .45 Colt., bbl. lengths: 4, 6 or 8 inches; 11.63 inches overall (with 6-inch bbl.). Weight: 53 oz. (6-inch bbl.). Adj. white outline rear sight, red insert ramp-style front. Matte stainless or Realtree gray camo finish. Black Neoprene combat grips w/finger grooves. Made since 1990.
Matte stainless . . . . NiB $722 Ex $561 Gd $358
Realtree gray camo finish (disc. 1996) . . . . NiB $774 Ex $592 Gd $384
Custom model (.44 Mag. w/ported bbl.). . . . . NiB $975 Ex $689 Gd $377
First Edition model (Ltd. Edition 1000). . . . . NiB $1050 Ex $842 Gd $478
Hunter model (.44 Mag. w/2x scope). . . . . NiB $1211 Ex $203 Gd $618

Colt Banker's Special

Colt Bisley

Colt Buntline Special .45

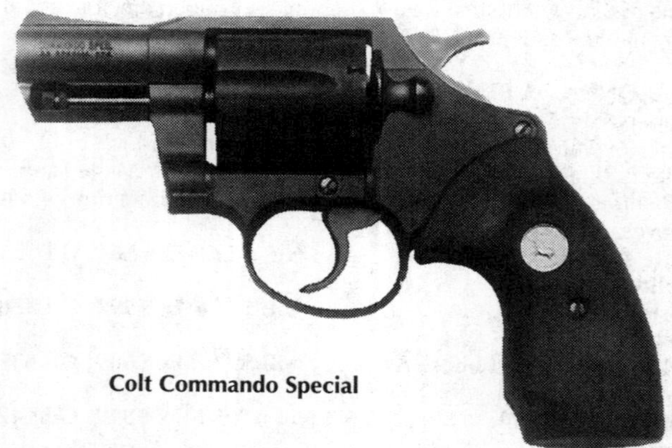
Colt Commando Special

ANACONDA TITANIUM DA REVOLVER
Same general specifications as the standard Anaconda except chambered .44 Mag. only w/titanium-plated finish, gold-plated trigger, hammer and cylinder release. Limited edition of 1,000 distributed by American Historical Foundation w/personalized inscription. Made in 1996.
One of 1000 . . . . NiB $2553 Ex $2060 Gd $1430
Presentation case, add. $200

ARMY SPECIAL DA REVOLVER . . . . . . NiB $809 Ex $731 Gd $471
.41-caliber frame. Calibers: .32-20, .38 Special (.41 Colt). Six-round cylinder, right revolution. Bbl., lengths: 4-, 4.5, 5-, and 6-inches, 9.25 inches overall (4-inch bbl.). Weight: 32 oz. (4-inch bbl.). Fixed sights. Blued or nickel-plated finish. Hard rubber grips. Made 1908-27. Note: This model has a somewhat heavier frame than the New Navy, which it replaced. Serial numbers begin w/300,000. The heavy .38 Special High Velocity loads should not be used in .38 Special arms of this model.

BANKER'S SPECIAL DA REVOLVER
This is the Police Positive w/a 2-inch bbl., otherwise specifications same as that model, rounded butt intro. in 1933. Calibers: .22 LR (embedded head-cylinder for high speed cartridges intro. 1933), .38 New Police. 6.5 inches overall. Weight: 23 oz. (.22 LR), 19 oz. (.38). Made from 1926-.40.
.38 caliber . . . . NiB $1187 Ex $966 Gd $181
.22 caliber . . . . NiB $2211 Ex $1834 Gd $1288

BISLEY MODEL SA REVOLVER
Variation of the Single-Action Army, developed for target shooting w/modified grips, trigger and hammer. Calibers: General specifications same as SA Army. Target Model made w/flat-topped frame and target sights. Made from 1894-1915.
Standard model . . . . NiB $8299 Ex $6662 Gd $4567
Target model (flat-top) . . . . . . NiB $12,251 Ex $9845 Gd $6767

BUNTLINE SPECIAL .45 . . . . NiB $1298 Ex $1068 Gd $750
Same as standard SA Army except has 12-inch bbl., caliber .45 Long Colt. Made from 1957-75.

COBRA DA REVOLVER,
ROUND BUTT, FIRST ISSUE . . . . . . NiB $514 Ex $420 Gd $301
Lightweight Detective Special w/same general specifications as that model except w/Colt-alloy frame. Two-inch bbl., calibers: .38 Special, .38 New Police, .32 New Police. Weight: 15 oz., (.38 cal.). Blued finish. Checkered plastic or walnut grips. Made from 1951-73.

COBRA DA REVOLVER,
SECOND ISSUE. . . . . NiB $514 Ex $420 Gd $254
Lightweight version of Detective Special, Second Issue has aluminum alloy frame. 16.5 oz. Made from 1973-81.

COBRA DA REVOLVER
SQUARE BUTT . . . . NiB $488 Ex $384 Gd $254
Lightweight Police Positive Special w/same general specifications except has Colt-alloy frame, 4-inch bbl., Calibers: .38 Special, .38 New Police, .32 New Police. Weight: 17 oz. in .38 caliber. Blued finish. Checkered plastic or walnut grips. Made from 1951-73.

COMMANDO SPECIAL
DA REVOLVER. . . . . NiB $490 Ex $384 Gd $280
Caliber: .38 Special. Six-round cylinder, 2-inch bbl., 6.88 inches overall. Weight: 21.5 oz. Fixed sights. Low-luster blued finish. Made from 1982-86.

DETECTIVE SPECIAL DA REVOLVER, FIRST ISSUE
Similar to Police Positive Special w/2-inch bbl., otherwise specifications same as that model, rounded butt intro. 1933. .38 Special only in pre-war issue. Blued or nickel-plated finish. Weight: 17 oz. 6.75 inches overall. Made from 1926-46.
Blued finish . . . . NiB $519 Ex $415 Gd $311
Nickel finish . . . . NiB $910 Ex $749 Gd $566

Colt Cobra
Round Butt First Issue

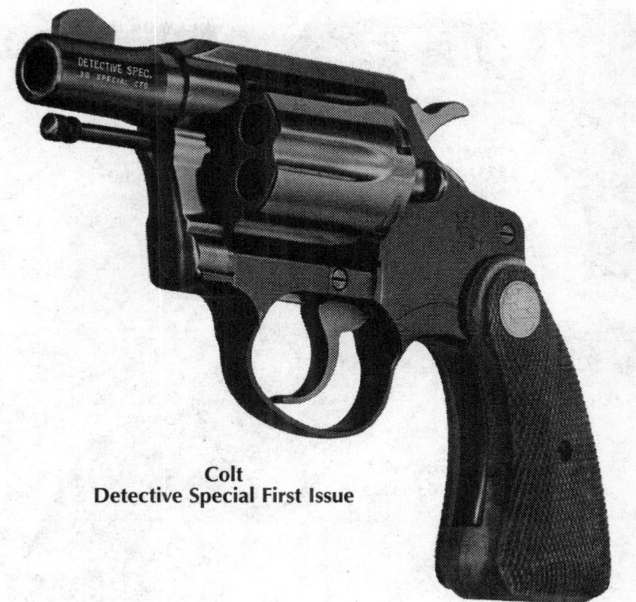

Colt
Detective Special First Issue

DETECTIVE SPECIAL DA REVOLVER, 2ND ISSUE
Similar to Detective special first issue except w/2- or 3-inch bbl., and also chambered .32 New Police, .38 New Police. Wood, plastic or over-sized grips. Made from 1947-72.
Blued finish . . . . NiB $512 Ex $420 Gd $304
Nickel finish . . . . NiB $570 Ex $467 Gd $324
W/three-inch bbl., add $95

DETECTIVE SPECIAL DA REVOLVER, 3RD ISSUE
"D" frame, shrouded ejector rod. Caliber: .38 Special. Six-round cylinder, 2-inch bbl., 6.88 inches overall. Weight: 21.5 oz. Fixed rear sight, ramp front. Blued or nickel-plated finish. Checkered walnut wraparound grips. Made from 1973-84.
Blued finish . . . . NiB $513 Ex $409 Gd $305
Nickel finish . . . . NiB $523 Ex $430 Gd $310
W/three-inch bbl., add $75

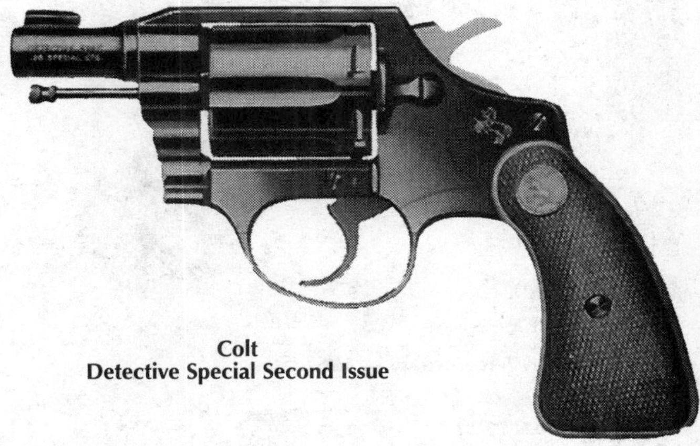
Colt
Detective Special Second Issue

DETECTIVE SPECIAL DA REVOLVER, 4TH ISSUE
Similar to Detective Special, Third Issue except w/alloy frame. Blued or chrome finish. Wraparound black neoprene grips w/Colt medallion. Made from 1993-95.
Blued finish . . . . NiB $487 Ex $456 Gd $305
Chrome finish . . . . NiB $492 Ex $409 Gd $282
DAO model (bobbed hammer) . . . . NiB $523 Ex $430 Gd $310

DIAMONDBACK DA REVOLVER
"D" frame, shrouded ejector rod. Calibers: .22 LR, .22 WRF, .38 Special. Six-round cylinder, 2.5-, 4- or 6-inch bbl., w/vent rib, 9 inches overall (with 4-inch bbl). Weight: 31.75 oz. (.22 cal., 4-inch bbl.), 28.5 oz. (.38 cal.). Ramp front sight, adj. rear. Blued or nickel finish. Checkered walnut grips. Made from 1966-84.
Blued finish . . . . NiB $732 Ex $628 Gd $316
Nickel finish . . . . NiB $663 Ex $519 Gd $363
.22 Mag. model . . . . NiB $696 Ex $545 Gd $377
W/2.5-inch bbl., add $75

DA ARMY (1878) REVOLVER. . . . NiB $5621 Ex $5101 Gd $2760
Also called DA Frontier. Similar in appearance to the smaller Lightning Model but has heavier frame of different shape, round disc on left side of frame, lanyard loop in butt. Calibers: .38-40, .44-40, .45 Colt. Six-round cylinder, bbl. lengths: 3.5- and 4-inches (w/o ejector), 4.75-, 5.5- and 7.5-inches w/ejector. 12.5 inches overall (7.5-inch bbl.). Weight: 39 oz. (.45 cal., 7.5-inch bbl.). Fixed sights. Hard rubber bird's-head grips. Blued or nickel finish. Made from 1878-1905.

Colt
Diamondback

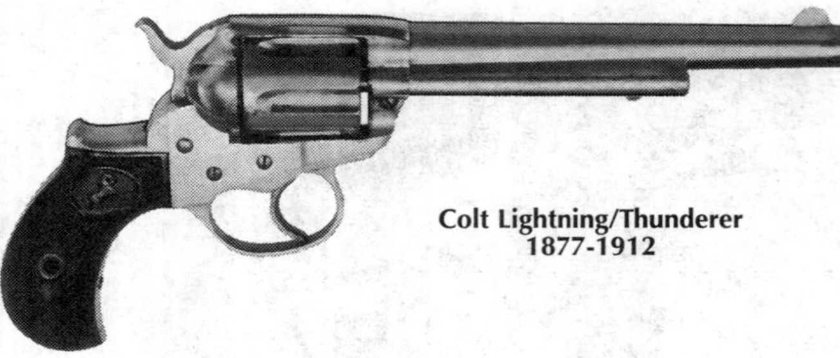

Colt Lightning/Thunderer
1877-1912

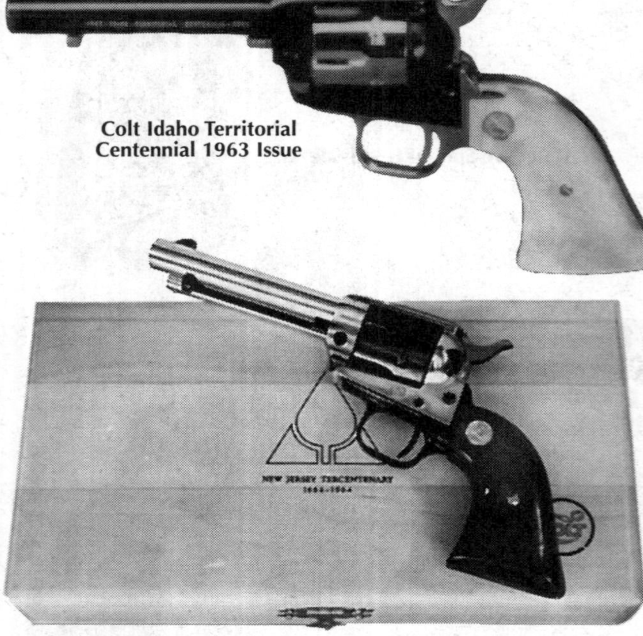

Colt Idaho Territorial
Centennial 1963 Issue

Colt New Jersey Tercentenary — 1964 issue

Colt General Hood
Centennial 1964 issue

FRONTIER SCOUT REVOLVER

SA Army replica, scale. Calibers: .22 Short, Long, LR or .22 WMR (interchangeable cylinder available). Six-round cylinder, 4.75-inch bbl., 9.9 inches overall. Weight: 24 oz. Fixed sights. Plastic grips. Originally made w/bright alloy frame. Since 1959 w/steel frame and blued finish or all-nickel finish w/composition, wood or Staglite grips. Made from 1958-71.

Blued finish, plastic grips. . . . . NiB $409 Ex $332 Gd $228
Nickel finish, wood grips. . . . . NiB $457 Ex $379 Gd $259
Buntline model, add $60
Extra interchangeable cylinder, add $75

FRONTIER SCOUT REVOLVER COMMEMORATIVE MODELS

Limited production versions of Frontier Scout issued, w/appropriate inscription, to commemorate historical events. Cased. Note: Values indicated are for commemoratives in new condition.

1961 ISSUES
Kansas Statehood Centennial (6201 produced). . . . . NiB $507
Pony Express Centennial (1007 produced). . . . . NiB $549

1962 ISSUES
Columbus, Ohio, Sesquicentennial (200 produced) . . . . NiB $689
Fort Findlay, Ohio, Sesquicentennial (130 produced) . . . . NiB $835
Fort Findlay Cased Pair, .22 Long Rifle and .22 Magnum (20 produced) . . . . NiB $3270
New Mexico Golden Anniversary . . . . NiB $593
West Virginia Statehood Centennial (3452 produced) . . . . NiB $507

1963 ISSUES
Arizona Territorial Centennial (5355 produced). . . . . NiB $497
Battle of Gettysburg Centennial (1019 produced). . . . . NiB $507
Carolina Charter Tercentenary (300 produced). . . . . NiB $497
Fort Stephenson, Ohio, Sesquicentennial (200 produced). . . . . NiB $959
General John Hunt Morgan Indiana Raid . . . . NiB $768
Idaho Territorial Centennial (902 produced) . . . . NiB $493

1964 ISSUES
California Gold Rush (500 produced) . . . . NiB $518
Chamizal Treaty (450 produced) . . . . NiB $523
General Hood Centennial (1503 produced) . . . . NiB $507
Montana Territorial Centennial (2300 produced) . . . . NiB $497
Nevada "Battle Born" (981 produced) . . . . NiB $507
Nevada Statehood Centennial (3984 produced) . . . . NiB $472
New Jersey Tercentenary (1001 produced) . . . . NiB $487
St. Louis Bicentennial (802 produced) . . . . NiB $507
Wyoming Diamond Jubilee (2357 produced) . . . . NiB $497

1965 ISSUES
Appomattox Centennial (1001 produced) . . . . NiB $497
Forty-Niner Miner (500 produced) . . . . NiB $507
General Meade Campaign (1197 produced) . . . . NiB $507
Kansas Cowtown Series—Wichita 500 produced) . . . . NiB $497
Old Fort Des Moines Reconstruction (700 produced) . . . . NiB $518
Oregon Trail (1995 produced) . . . . NiB $507
St. Augustine Quadricentennial (500 produced) . . . . NiB $518

1966 ISSUES

Colorado Gold Rush (1350 produced) . . . . NiB $481
Dakota Territory (1000 produced) . . . . NiB $497
Indiana Sesquicentennial (1500 produced) . . . . NiB $492
Kansas Cowtown Series—Abilene (500 produced) . . . . NiB $497
Kansas Cowtown Series—Dodge City (500 produced) . . . . NiB $507
Oklahoma Territory (1343 produced) . . . . NiB $497

1967 ISSUES

Alamo (4500 produced) . . . . NiB $507
Kansas Cowtown Series—Coffeyville (500 produced). . . . . NiB $497
Kansas Trail Series—Chisholm Trail (500 produced). . . . . NiB $507
Lawman Series— Bat Masterson (3000 produced). . . . . NiB $518

1968 ISSUES

Kansas Trail Series—Santa Fe Trail (501 produced). . . . . NiB $497
Kansas Trail Series—Pawnee Trail (501 produced). . . . . NiB $487
Lawman Series—Pat Garrett (3000 produced). . . . . NiB $528
Nebraska Centennial (7001 produced). . . . . NiB $492

1969 ISSUES

Alabama Sesquicentennial (3001 produced) . . . . NiB $492
Arkansas Territory Sesquicentennial (3500 produced) . . . . NiB $487
California Bicentennial (5000 produced). . . . . NiB $471
General Nathan Bedford Forrest (3000 produced) . . . . NiB $497
Golden Spike (11,000 produced). . . . . NiB $518
Kansas Trail Series—Shawnee Trail (501 produced) . . . . NiB $492
Lawman Series—Wild Bill Hickock (3000 produced) . . . . NiB $528

1970 ISSUES

Kansas Fort Series—Fort Larned (500 produced) . . . . NiB $497
Kansas Fort Series—Fort Hays (500 produced) . . . . NiB $497
Kansas Fort Series—Fort Riley (500 produced). . . . . NiB $497
Lawman Series—Wyatt Earp (3000 produced). . . . . NiB $601
Maine Sesquicentennial (3000 produced). . . . . NiB $487
Missouri Sesquicentennial (3000 produced) . . . . NiB $492

1971 ISSUES

Kansas Fort Series—Fort Scott (500 produced) . . . . . . NiB $497

1972 ISSUES

Florida Territory Sesquicentennial (2001 produced) . . . NiB $492

1973 ISSUES Arizona ranger (3001 produced) . . . . NiB $683 Ex $596 Gd $318

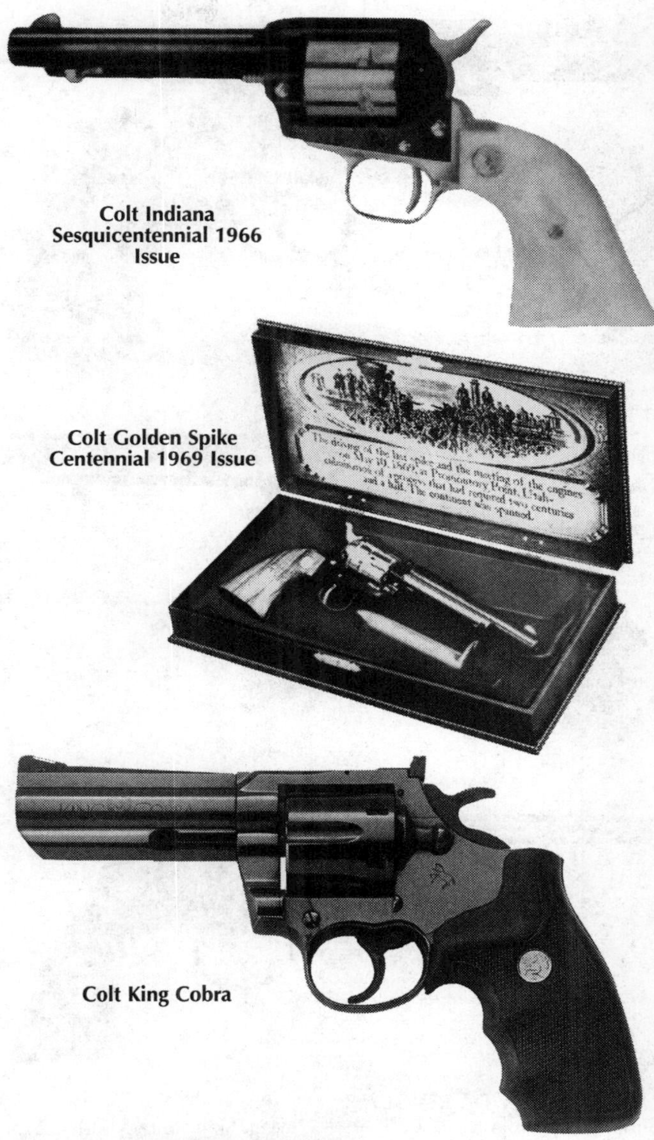

Colt Indiana Sesquicentennial 1966 Issue

Colt Golden Spike Centennial 1969 Issue

Colt King Cobra

COLT KING COBRA REVOLVER

Caliber: .357 Mag., bbl. lengths: 2.5-, 4-, 6- or 8-inches, 9 inches overall (with 4-inch bbl.). Weight: 42 oz., average. Matte stainless steel finish. Black Neoprene combat grips. Made 1986 to date. 2.5-inch bbl. and "Ultimate" bright or blued finish. Made from 1988-92.

Matte stainless. . . . . NiB $496 Ex $402 Gd $289
Ultimate bright stainless . . . . NiB $538 Ex $429 Gd $312
Blued. . . . . NiB $476 Ex $424 Gd $268

LAWMAN MK III DA REVOLVER

"J" frame, shrouded ejector rod on 2-inch bbl., only. Caliber: .357 Magnum. Six-round cylinder, bbl. lengths: 2-, 4-inch. 9.38 inches overall (w/4-inch bbl.), Weight: (with 4-inch bbl.), 35 oz. Fixed rear sight, ramp front. Service trigger and hammer or target trigger and wide-spur hammer. Blued or nickel-plated finish. Checkered walnut service or target grips. Made from 1969-1982.

Blued finish . . . . NiB $455 Ex $361 Gd $221
Nickel finish . . . . NiB $476 Ex $377 Gd $237

Colt Lawman MK V

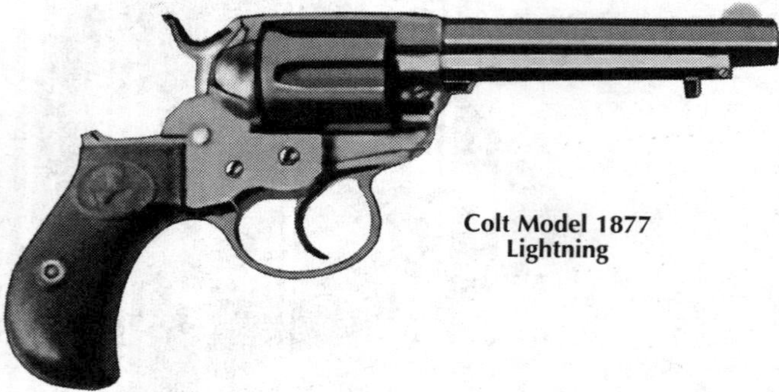
Colt Model 1877 Lightning

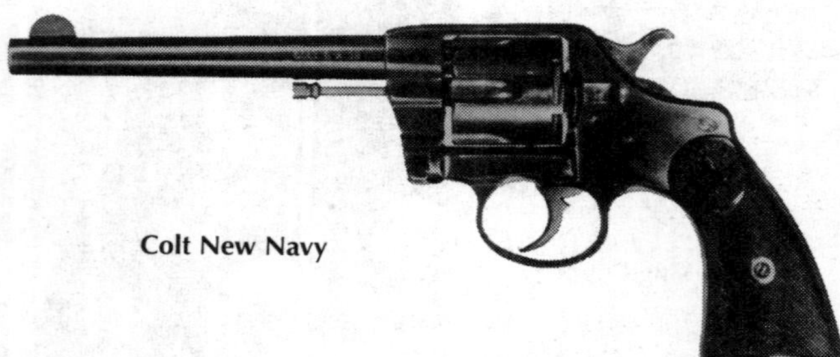
Colt New Navy

LAWMAN MK V DA REVOLVER
Similar to Trooper MK V. Caliber: .357 Mag. Six-round cylinder, 2- or 4-inch bbl., 9.38 inches overall (4-inch bbl.). Weight: 35 oz. (4-inch bbl.). Fixed sights. Checkered walnut grips. Made from 1983-85.
Blued finish . . . . NiB $319 Ex $271 Gd $189
Nickel finish . . . . NiB $350 Ex $284 Gd $201

MAGNUM CARRY DA REVOLVER . . . . NiB $456 Ex $343 Gd $274
Similar to Model DS II except chambered for .357 Magnum. Made from 1998 to date.

MARINE CORPS MODEL (1905) DA REVOLVER
General specifications same as New Navy Second Issue except has round butt, was supplied only in .38 caliber (.38 Short & Long Colt, .38 Special) w/6-inch bbl. (SN range 10,001-10,926) Made from 1905-09.
Marine Corps model . . . . NiB $3018 Ex $2446 Gd $1692
Marked "USMC" . . . . NiB $3954 Ex $3330 Gd $2316

METROPOLITAN MK III DA REVOLVER . . . . NiB $482 Ex $383 Gd $278
Same as Official Police MK III except has 4-inch bbl. w/service or target grips. Weight: 36 oz. Made from 1969-72.

MODEL 1877 LIGHTNING REVOLVER . . . . . . NiB $1905 Ex $1542 Gd $1078
Also called Thunderer Model. Calibers: .38 and .41 centerfire. Six-round cylinder, bbl. lengths: 2.5-, 3.5-, 4.5- and 6-inch without ejector, 4.5- and 6-inch w/ejector, 8.5 inches overall (3.5-inch bbl.). Weight: 23 oz. (.38 cal., with 3.5-inch bbl.) Fixed sights. Blued or nickel finish. Hard rubber bird's-head grips. Made from 1877-09.

NEW FRONTIER BUNTLINE SPECIAL
Same as New Frontier SA Army except has 12-inch bbl.,
Second generation (1962-75) . . . NiB $1380 Ex $1121 Gd $790
Third generation (1976-92) . . . . . . NiB $1158 Ex $944 Gd $669

NEW FRONTIER SA ARMY REVOLVER
Same as SA Army except has flat-top frame, adj. target rear sight, ramp front sight, smooth walnut grips. 5.5- or 7.5-inch bbl., Calibers: .357 Magnum, .44 Special, .45 Colt. Made from 1961-92.
Second generation (1961-75) . . . NiB $1365 Ex $1105 Gd $741
Third generation (1976-92) . . . . . . NiB $1157 Ex $949 Gd $689

NEW FRONTIER SA .22 REVOLVER . . . . . . NiB $406 Ex $302 Gd $188
Same as Peacemaker .22 except has flat-top frame, adj. rear sight, ramp front sight. Made from 1971-76; reintro. 1982-86.

NEW NAVY (1889) DA, FIRST ISSUE
Also called New Army. Calibers: .38 Short & Long Colt, .41 Short & Long Colt. Six-round cylinder, left revolution. Bbl. lengths: 3-, 4.5- and 6-inches, 11.25 inches overall (with 6-inch bbl.). Weight: 32 oz. with 6-inch bbl. Fixed sights, knife-blade and V-notch. Blued or nickel-plated finish. Walnut or hard rubber grips. Made 1889-94. Note: This model, which was adopted by both the Army and Navy, was Colt's first revolver of the solid frame, swing-out cylinder type. It lacks the cylinder-locking notches found on later models made on this .41 frame; ratchet on the back of the cylinder is held in place by a double projection on the hand.
First issue. . . . . NiB $1913 Ex $1560 Gd $1096
First issue w/3-inch bbl. . . . . . . NiB $2670 Ex $2162 Gd $1513
Navy contract, marked "U.S.N.(SN 1-1500). . . . . NiB $3508 Ex $2833 Gd $1970

NEW NAVY (1892) DA, SECOND ISSUE
Also called New Army. General specifications same as First Issue except has double cylinder notches and double locking bolt. Calibers: .38 Special added in 1904 and .32-20 in 1905. Made 1892-07. Note: The heavy .38 Special High Velocity loads should not be used in .38 Special arms of this model.
Second issue . . . . NiB $1666 Ex $1365 Gd $958
Second issue w/3-inch bbl. . . . . NiB $2418 Ex $1962 Gd $1380
Navy contract, marked "U.S.N". . . . . . NiB $2736 Ex $2217 Gd $1553

NEW POCKET DA REVOLVER . . . . NiB $710 Ex $581 Gd $416
Caliber: .32 Short & Long Colt. Six-round cylinder. bbl. lengths: 2.5, 3.5- and 6-inches. 7.5 inches overall w/3.5-inch bbl., Weight: 16 oz., with 3.5-inch bbl. Fixed sights, knife-blade and V-notch. Blued or nickel finish. Rubber grips. Made from 1893-05.

NEW POLICE DA REVOLVER . . . . . NiB $612 Ex $550 Gd $378
Built on New Pocket frame but w/larger grip. Calibers: .32 Colt New Police, .32 Short & Long Colt. Bbl. lengths: 2.5-, 4- and 6-inches, 8.5 inches overall (with 4-inch bbl.). Weight: 17 oz., with 4-inch bbl. Fixed knife-blade front sight, V-notch rear. Blued or nickel finish. Rubber grips. Made from 1896-05.

NEW POLICE TARGET DA REVOLVER . . . . . NiB $1505 Ex $1349 Gd $829
Target version of the New Police w/same general specifications. Target sights. Six-inch bbl., blued finish only. Made from 1896-05.

NEW SERVICE DA REVOLVER
Calibers: .38 Special, .357 Magnum (intro. 1936), .38-40, .44-40, .44 Russian, .44 Special, .45 Auto, .45 Colt, .450 Eley, .455 Eley, .476 Eley. Six-round cylinder, bbl. lengths: 4-, 5- and 6-inch in .38 Special and .357 Magnum, 4.5-, 5.5- and 7.5 inches in other calibers; 9.75 inches overall (with 4.5-inch bbl.). Weight: 39 oz. (.45 cal. with 4.5-inch bbl.). Fixed sights. Blued or nickel finish. Checkered walnut grips. Made 1898-42. Note: More than 500,000 of this model in caliber .45 Auto (designated "Model 1917 Revolver") were purchased by the U.S. Gov't. during WW I. These arms were later sold as surplus to National Rifle Association members through the Director of Civilian Marksmanship. Price was $16.15 plus packing charge. Supply exhausted during the early 1930s.
Commercial model . . . . NiB $1776 Ex $1439 Gd $1008
Magnum . . . . NiB $1164 Ex $950 Gd $675
1917 Army. . . . . NiB $1126 Ex $629 Gd $655

NEW SERVICE TARGET . . . . NiB $1266 Ex $1127 Gd $716
Target version of the New Service. Calibers: Originally chambered for .44 Russian, .450 Eley, .455 Eley and .476 Eley, later models in .44 Special, .45 Colt and .45 Auto. Six- or 7.5-inch bbl., 12.75 inches overall (7.5-inch bbl.). Adj. target sights. Hand-finished action. With blued finish. Checkered walnut grips. Made 1900-40.

OFFICERS' MODEL MATCH . . . . . . NiB $796 Ex $666 Gd $380
Same general design as Officers' Model revolvers. Has tapered heavy bbl., wide hammer spur, Adjustable rear sight ramp front sight, large target grips of checkered walnut. Calibers: .22 LR, .38 Special. Six-inch bbl., 11.25 inches overall. Weight: 43 oz. (in .22 cal.), 39 oz. (.38 cal.). Blued finish. Made from 1953-70.

OFFICERS' MODEL SPECIAL. . . . . . NiB $840 Ex $580 Gd $372
Target version of Officers' Model Second Issue w/similar characters except w/heavier, nontapered bbl. redesigned hammer. Ramp front sight, Colt Officers' Model Special "Coltmaster" rear sight adj. for windage and elevation. Calibers: .22 LR, .38 Special. Six-inch bbl. 11.25 inches overall. Weight: 39 oz. (in .38 cal.), 43 oz., (.22 cal.). Blued finish. Checkered plastic grips. Made from 1949-53.

OFFICERS' MODEL TARGET DA REVOLVER, FIRST ISSUE . . . . NiB $1278 Ex $1038 Gd $732
Caliber: .38 Special. Six-inch bbl., hand-finished action, adj. target sights. Checkered with walnut grips. General specifications same as New Navy, Second Issue. Made from 1904-08.

OFFICERS' MODEL TARGET, SECOND ISSUE
Calibers: .22 LR (intro. 1930, embedded head-cylinder for high-speed cartridges after 1932), .32 Police Positive (made 1932-1942), .38 Special. Six-round cylinder, bbl. lengths: 4-, 4.5-, 5-, 6- and 7.5-inch (in .38 Special) or 6-inch only (.22 LR and .32 PP), 11.25 inches overall (6-inch bbl. in .38 Special). Adj. target sights. Blued finish. Checkered walnut grips. Hand-finished action. General features same as Army Special and Official Police of same date. Made from 1908-49 (w/exceptions noted).
Second issue (.38 caliber) . . . . NiB $1072 Ex $864 Gd $609
Second issue (.32 caliber) . . . . . . NiB $1660 Ex $1342 Gd $924
Second issue (.22 caliber) . . . . NiB $1174 Ex $952 Gd $669
W/shorter bbls. (4-, 4.5- or 5-inches), add 40%

OFFICIAL POLICE DA REVOLVER
Calibers: .22 LR (intro. 1930, embedded head-cylinder for high-speed cartridges after 1932), .32-20 (disc. 1942), .38 Special, .41 Long Colt (disc. 1930). Six-round cylinder, bbl. lengths: 4-, 5-, and 6-inch or 2-inch and 6-inch heavy bbl. in .38 Special only; .22 LR w/4- and 6-inch bbls. only; 11.25 inches overall. Weight: 36 oz. (standard 6-inch bbl.) in .38 Special. Fixed sights. Blued or nickel-plated finish. Checkered walnut grips on all revolvers of this model except some of postwar production had checkered plastic grips. Made 1927-69. Note: This model is a refined version of the Army Special, which it replaced in 1928 at about serial number 520,000. The Commando .38 Special was a wartime adaptation of the Official Police made to government specifications. Commando can be identified by its sandblasted blued finish. Serial numbers start w/number 1-50,000 (1942-45).
Commercial model (pre-war) . . . . . NiB $580 Ex $476 Gd $343
Commercial model (post-war). . . . . NiB $516 Ex $424 Gd $308
Commando model. . . . . NiB $612 Ex $502 Gd $361

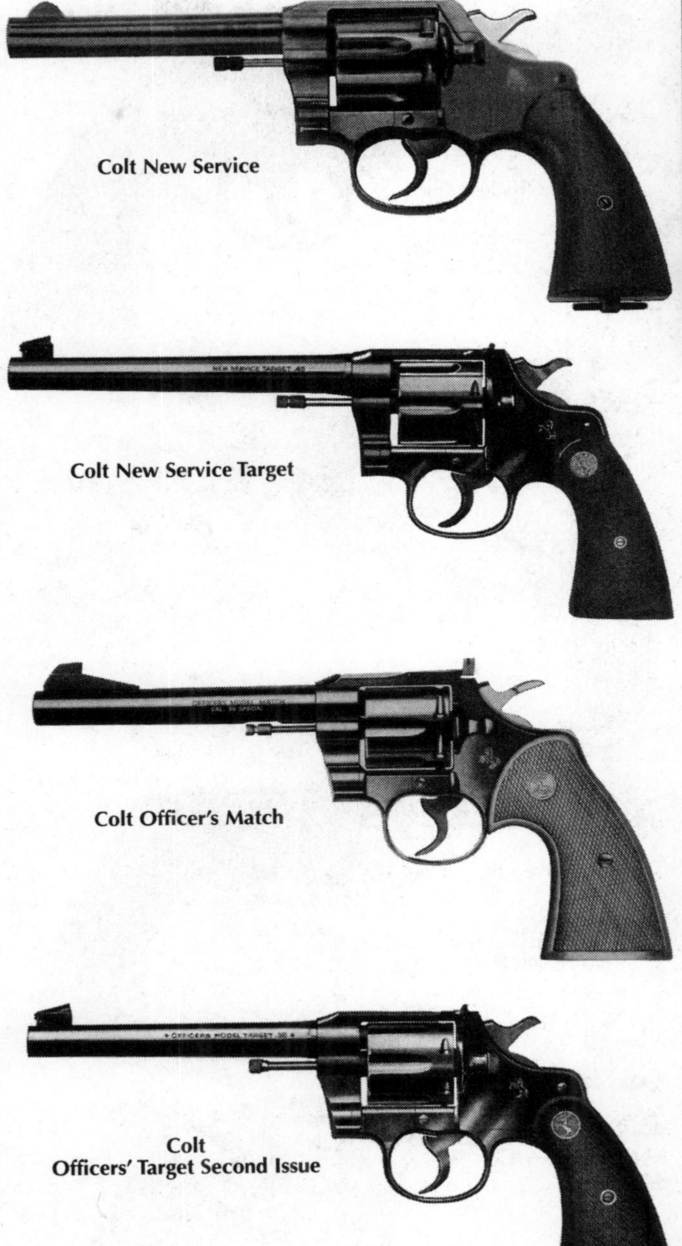

Colt New Service

Colt New Service Target

Colt Officer's Match

Colt Officers' Target Second Issue

Colt Official Police

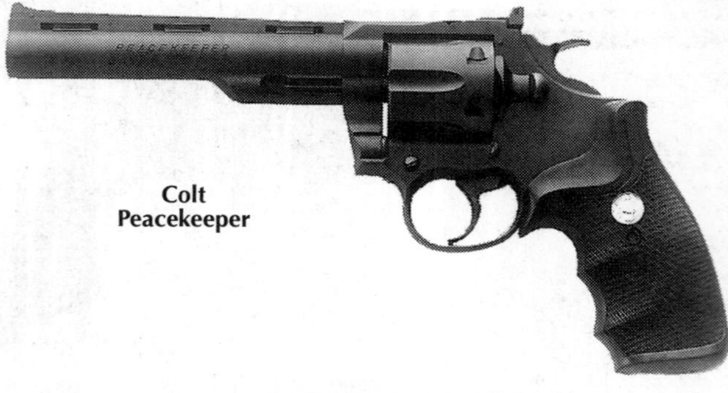

Colt
Peacekeeper

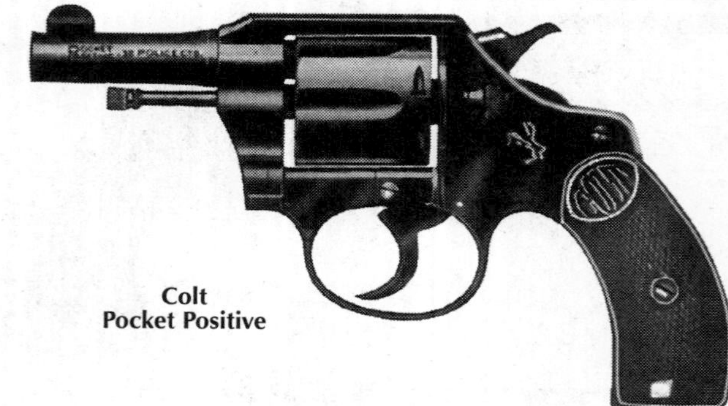

Colt
Pocket Positive

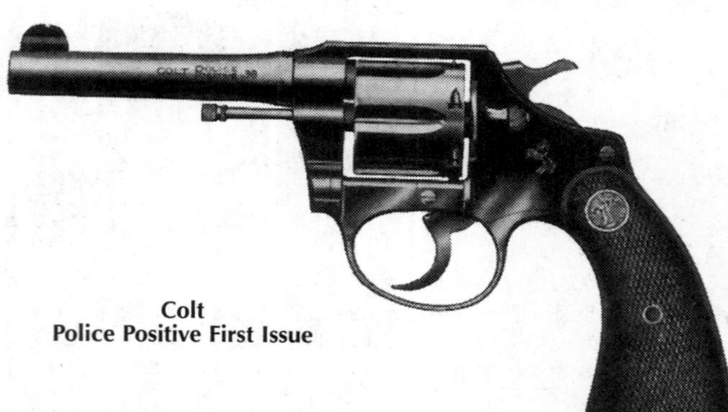

Colt
Police Positive First Issue

OFFICIAL POLICE MK III DA REVOLVER . . . . NiB $284 Ex $232 Gd $164
"J" frame, without shrouded ejector rod. Caliber: .38 Special. Six-round cylinder. bbl., lengths: 4-, 5-, 6-inches, 9.25 inches overall w/4-inch bbl., weight: 34 oz. (4-inch bbl.). Fixed rear sight, ramp front. Service trigger and hammer or target trigger and wide-spur hammer. Blued or nickel-plated finish. Checkered walnut service grips. Made from 1969-75.

PEACEKEEPER DA REVOLVER . . . . . NiB $456 Ex $383 Gd $191
Caliber: .357 Mag. Six-round cylinder, 4- or 6-inch bbl., 11.25 inches overall (6-inch bbl.). Weight: 46 oz. (with 6-inch bbl.). Adj. white outline rear sight, red insert ramp-style front. Non-reflective matte blued finish. Made from 1985-89.

PEACEMAKER .22 SECOND AMENDMENT COMMEMORATIVE. . . . . NiB $617 Ex $513 Gd $253
Caliber: .22, revolver w/7.5-inch bbl., nickel-plated frame, bbl. ejector rod assembly, hammer and trigger, blued cylinder, backstrap and trigger guard. Black pearlite grips. bbl., inscribed "The Right to Keep and Bear Arms." Presentation case. Limited edition of 3000 issued in 1977. Top value is for revolver in new condition.

PEACEMAKER .22 SA REVOLVER . . NiB $407 Ex $303 Gd $251
Calibers: .22 LR and .22 WMR. Furnished w/cylinder for each caliber, 6-round. Bbl.: 4.38-, 6- or 7.5-inches, 11.25 inches overall (with 6-inch bbl.). Weight: 30.5 oz. (with 6-inch bbl.). Fixed sights. Black composite grips. Made from 1971-76.

POCKET POSITIVE DA REVOLVER. . . . . NiB $591 Ex $529 Gd $357
General specifications same as New Pocket except this model has positive lock feature (see Police Positive). Calibers: .32 Short & Long Colt (disc. 1914), .32 Colt New Police (.32 S&W Short & Long). Fixed sights, flat top and square notch. Blue or nickel finish. Made from 1905-40.
Blue finish . . . . NiB $559 Ex $456 Gd $325
Nickel finish . . . . NiB $663 Ex $539 Gd $391

POLICE POSITIVE DA, FIRST ISSUE
Improved version of the New Police w/the "Positive Lock," which prevents the firing pin coming in contact w/the cartridge except when the trigger is pulled. Calibers: .32 Short & Long Colt (disc. 1915), .32 Colt New Police (.32 S&W Short & Long), .38 New Police (.38 S&W). Six-round cylinder, bbl. lengths: 2.5- (.32 cal. only), 4- 5- and 6-inches; 8.5 inches overall (with 4-inch bbl.). Weight 20 oz. (with 4-inch bbl.). Fixed sights. Blued or nickel finish. Rubber or checkered walnut grips. Made from 1905-47.
Blue finish . . . . NiB $496 Ex $404 Gd $288
Nickel finish . . . . NiB $560 Ex $456 Gd $323

POLICE POSITIVE DA, SECOND ISSUE
Same as Detective Special second issue except has 4-inch bbl., 9 inches overall, weight: 26.5 oz. Intro. in 1977. Note: Original Police Positive (First Issue) has a shorter frame, is not chambered for .38 Special.
Blue finish . . . . NiB $482 Ex $394 Gd $280
Nickel finish . . . . NiB $554 Ex $451 Gd $320

POLICE POSITIVE SPECIAL DA REVOLVER . . . . NiB $554 Ex $451 Gd $320
Based on the Police Positive w/frame lengthened to permit longer cylinder. Calibers: .32-20 (disc. 1942), .38 Special, .32 New Police and .38 New Police (intro. 1946). Six-round cylinder; bbl. lengths: 4-(only length in current production), 5- and 6-inch; 8.75 inches overall (with 4-inch bbl.). Weight: 23 oz. (with 4-inch bbl. in .38 Special). Fixed sights. Checkered grips of hard rubber, plastic or walnut. Made from 1907-73.

COLT POLICE POSITIVE TARGET DA REVOLVER. . . . . NiB $840 Ex $685 Gd $487
Target version of the Police Positive. Calibers: .22 LR (intro. 1910, embedded-head cylinder for high-speed cartridges after 1932), .22 WRF (1910-35), .32 Short & Long Colt, (1915), .32 New Police (.32 S&W Short & Long). Six-inch bbl., blued finish only, 10.5 inches overall. Weight: 26 oz. in .22 cal. Adj. target sights. Checkered walnut grips. Made from 1905-40.

Colt SA Army

Colt
Police Positive Target

Colt Python

PYTHON DA REVOLVER

"I" frame, shrouded ejector rod. Calibers: .357 Magnum, .38 Special. Six-round cylinder, 2.5-, 4-, 6- or 8-inch vent rib bbl., 11.25 inches overall (with 6-inch bbl.). Weight: 44 oz. (6-inch bbl.). Adj. rear sight, ramp front. Blued, nickel or stainless finish. Checkered walnut target grips. Made from 1955 to date. Ultimate stainless finish made from 1985 to date.

Blued finish . . . . NiB $1002 Ex $877 Gd $383
Royal blued finish . . . . NiB $700 Ex $585 Gd $437
Nickel finish . . . . NiB $688 Ex $575 Gd $430
Stainless finish . . . . NiB $768 Ex $674 Gd $475
Ultimate stainless finish . . . . NiB $1037 Ex $881 Gd $439
Hunter model (w/2x scope) . . . . NiB $1576 Ex $1399 Gd $853
Silhouette model (w/2x scope) . . . . NiB $1634 Ex $1450 Gd $801

SHOOTING MASTER DA REVOLVER

Deluxe target arm based on the New Service model. Calibers: Originally made only in .38 Special, .44 Special, .45 Auto and .45 Colt added in 1933, .357 Magnum in 1936. Six-inch bbl., 11.25 inches overall. Weight: 44 oz., in (.38 cal.), adj. target sights. Hand-finished action. Blued finish. Checkered walnut grips. Rounded butt. Made from 1932-41.

Shooting Master .38 Special . . . . NiB $1425 Ex $1269 Gd $853
Shooting Master .357 Mag. . . . . NiB $1472 Ex $1196 Gd $842
Shooting Master .44 Special, .45 ACP, .45LC. . . . . NiB $3930 Ex $3618 Gd $2162

SA ARMY REVOLVER

Also called Frontier Six-Shooter and Peacemaker. Available in more than 30 calibers including: .22 Rimfire (Short, Long, LR), .22 WRF, .32 Rimfire, .32 Colt, .32 S&W, .32-20, .38 Colt, .38 S&W, .38 Special, .357 Magnum, .38-40, .41 Colt, .44 Rimfire, .44 Russian, .44 Special, .44-40, .45 Colt, .45 Auto, .450 Boxer, 450 Eley, .455 Eley, .476 Eley. Six-round cylinder. Bbl. lengths: 4.75, 5 .5 and 7.5 inches w/ejector or 3 and 4 inches w/o ejector. 10.25 inches overall (with 4.75-inch bbl.). Weight: 36 oz. (.45 cal. w/4.75-inch bbl.). Fixed sights. Also made in Target Model w/flat top-strap and target sights. Blued finish w/casehardened frame or nickel-plated. One-piece smooth walnut or checkered black rubber grips. Note: S.A. Army Revolvers w/serial numbers above 165,000 (circa 1896) are adapted to smokeless powder and cylinder pin screw was changed to spring catch at about the same time. The "First Generation" of SA Colts included both blackpowder and smokeless configurations and were manufactured from 1873 to 1940. Production resumed in 1955 w/serial number 1001SA and continued through 1975 to complete the second series, which is referred to as the "Second Generation." In 1976, the "Third Generation" of production began and continues to to date. However, several serial number rollovers occurred at 99,999. For example, in 1978 the "SA" suffix became an "SA" prefix and again in 1993, when the serial number SA99,999 was reached, the serialization format was changed again to include both an "S" prefix and an "A" suffix. Although the term "Fourth Generation" is frequently associated with this rollover, no series change actually occurred, therefore, the current production is still a "Third Generation" series. Current calibers: .357 Magnum, .44 Special, .45 Long Colt.

Pinched frame (1873 only) . . . . NiB $82,616 Ex $66,092 Gd $ 44,943
Early commercial (1873-77) . . . . NiB $42,576 Ex $34,060 Gd $23,161
Early military (1873-77) . . . . NiB $48,750 Ex $39,000 Gd $26,520
Large bore rimfire (1875-80) . . . . NiB $39,650 Ex $31,720 Gd $21,570
Small bore rimfire (1875-80) . . . . NiB $30,550 Ex $24,440 Gd $16,619
Frontier six-shooter, .44-40 (1878-82) . . . . NiB $46,216 Ex $36,972 Gd $25,141
Storekeeper's model, no ejector (1883-98) . . . . NiB $48,750 Ex $39,000 Gd $26,520
Sheriff's model (1883-98) . . . . NiB $46,150 Ex $36,920 Gd $25,106
Target model, flat top strap, target sights . . . . NiB $25,350 Ex $20,280 Gd $13,790
U.S. Cavalry model, .45 (1873-92) . . . . NiB $44,850 Ex $35,880 Gd $24,398

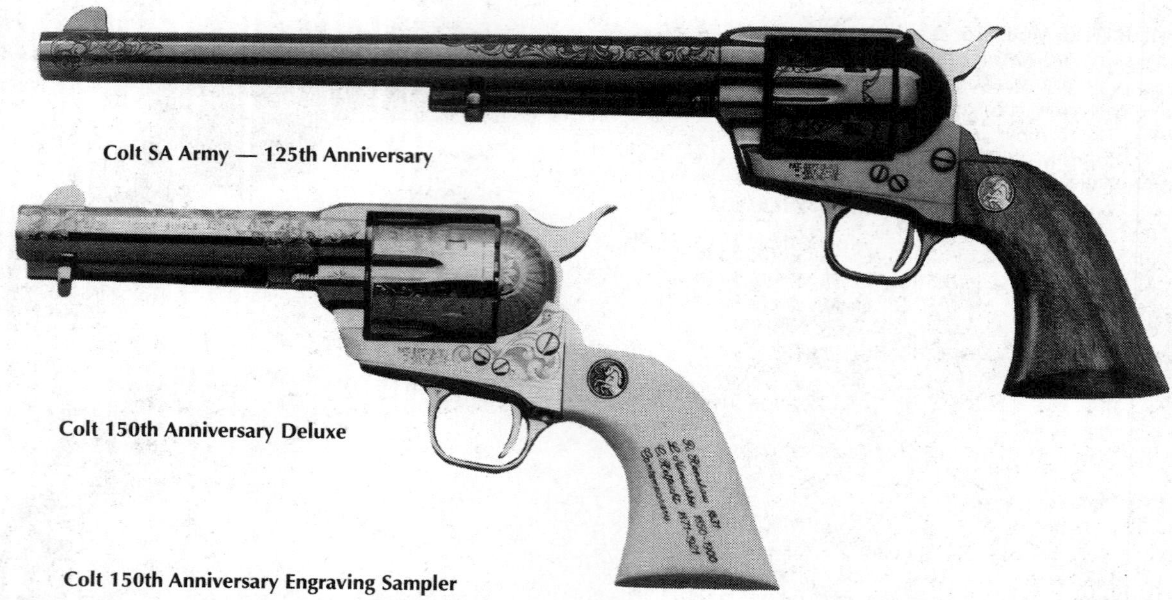

Colt SA Army — 125th Anniversary

Colt 150th Anniversary Deluxe

Colt 150th Anniversary Engraving Sampler

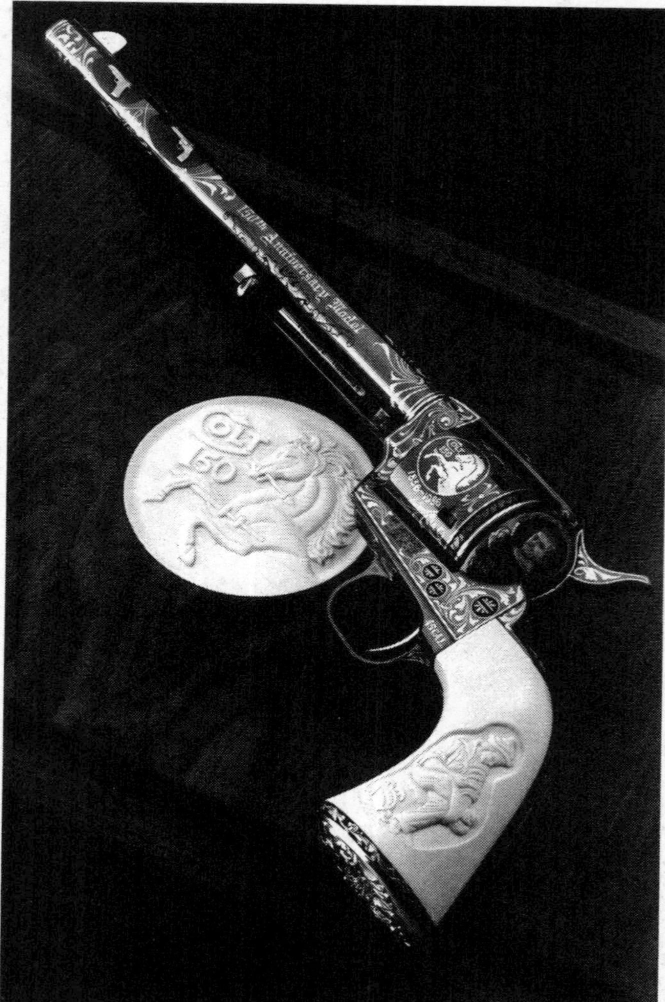

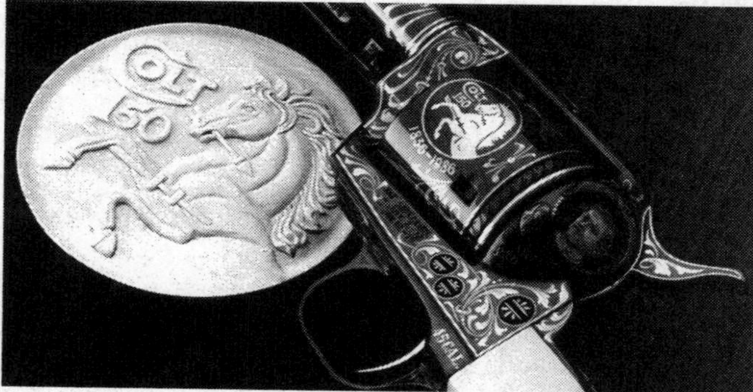

In the previous section the GTG deviates from the observed practice of listing only the value of firearms produced after 1900. This deliberate departure from the standard format is intended to provide a general reference and establish proper orientation for the reader, because the Colt SSA had its origins in the last quarter of the 19th century. Consequently, antique firearms produced prior to 1898 have been listed as a preface and introduction to the first series of production (what is now recognized as "1st Generation") in order to systematically demonstrate the progressive and sequential development of the multi-generation Colt SAA. Therefore, the previous general values have been provided to establish a point of reference to allow a more comprehensive examination of the evolution of the Colt SAA. However, please note that the following values apply only to original models, not to similar S.A.A. revolvers of more recent manufacture.

Standard model, pre-war
(1st generation) . . . . $12,950 to $65,000
Standard model (1955-75)
(2nd generation) . . . . NiB $2418 Ex $1969 Gd $1395
Standard model (1976 to date) . . . NiB $1190 Ex $977 Gd $705

SA ARMY — 125TH ANNIVERSARY. . . NiB $1906 Ex $1557 Gd $1111
Limited production deluxe version of SA Army issued in commemoration of Colt's 125th Anniversary. Caliber: .45 Long Colt., 7.5-inch bbl., cold-plated frame trigger, hammer, cylinder pin, ejector rod tip, and grip medallion. Presentation case w/anniversary medallion. Serial numbers "50AM." 7368 were made in 1961.

SA ARMY COMMEMORATIVE MODELS
Limited production versions of SA Army .45 issued, w/appropriate inscription to commemorate historical events. Cased. Note: Values indicated are for commemorative revolvers in new condition.

1963 ISSUES
Arizona Territorial Centennial (1280 produced) . . . . NiB $1613
West Virginia Statehood Centennial (600 produced) . . . . NiB $1535

1964 ISSUES
Chamizal Treaty (50 produced) . . . . NiB $1638
Colonel Sam Colt Sesquicentennial Presentation (4750 produced) . . . . NiB $1613
Deluxe Presentation (200 produced) . . . . NiB $2874
Special Deluxe Presentation (50 produced) . . . . NiB $4482
Montana Territorial Centennial (851 produced) . . . . NiB $1613
Nevada "Battle Born" (100 produced) . . . . NiB $1685
Nevada Statehood Centennial (1877 produced) . . . . NiB $1582
New Jersey Tercentenary (250 produced) . . . . NiB $1570
Pony Express Presentation (1004 produced) . . . . NiB $1685
St. Louis Bicentennial (450 produced) . . . . NiB $1613
Wyatt Earp Buntline (150 produced) . . . . NiB $2851

1965 ISSUES
Appomattox Centennial (500 produced) . . . . NiB $1643
Old Fort Des Moines Reconstruction (200 produced) . . . . NiB $1565

1966 ISSUES
Abercrombie & Fitch Trailblazer —Chicago (100 produced) . . . . NiB $1452
Abercrombie & Fitch Trailblazer —New York (200 produced) . . . . NiB $1427
Abercrombie & Fitch Trailblazer —San Francisco (100 produced) . . . . NiB $1452
California Gold Rush (130 produced) . . . . NiB $1643
General Meade (200 produced) . . . . NiB $1643
Pony Express Four Square (4 guns) . . . . NiB $6667

1967 ISSUES
Alamo (1000 produced) . . . . NiB $1634
Lawman Series—Bat Masterson (500 produced) . . . . NiB $1809

1968 ISSUES
Lawman Series—Pat Garrett (500 produced) . . . . NiB $1634

1969 ISSUES
Lawman Series—Wild Bill Hickok (500 produced) . . . . NiB $1634

1970 ISSUES
Lawman Series—Wyatt Earp (501 produced) . . . . NiB $2855

Colt SA Army Flat Top

Missouri Sesquicentennial (501 produced) . . . . NiB $1634
Texas Ranger (1000 produced) . . . . NiB $2539

1971 ISSUES
NRA Centennial, .357 or .45 (5001 produced) . . . . NiB $1634

1975 ISSUES
Peacemaker Centennial .45 (1501 produced) . . . . NiB $1659
Peacemaker Centennial .44-40 (1501 produced) . . . . NiB $1762
Peacemaker Centennial Cased Pair (501 produced) . . . . NiB $3313

1979 ISSUES
Ned Buntline .45 (3000 produced) . . . . NiB $1222

1986 ISSUES
Colt 150th Anniversary (standard) . . . . NiB $1912
Colt 150th Anniversay (engraved) . . . . NiB $2951

COLT SA COWBOY REVOLVER . . . . NiB $548
SSA variant designed for "Cowboy Action Shooting." Caliber: .45 Colt. Six-round cylinder, 5.5-inch bbl., 11 inches overall. Weight: 42 oz. Blade front sight, fixed V-notch rear. Blued finish w/color casehardened frame. Smooth walnut grips. Made from 1999 to date.

SA SHERIFF'S MODEL .45
Limited edition replica of Storekeeper's Model in caliber .45 Colt, made exclusively for Centennial Arms Corp. Chicago, Illinois. Numbered "1SM." Blued finish w/casehardened frame or nickel-plated. Walnut grips. Made in 1961.
Blued finish (478 produced) . . . NiB $2899 Ex $2360 Gd $1670
Nickel finish (25 produced). . . . NiB $6768 Ex $5446 Gd $3777

THREE-FIFTY-SEVEN DA REVOLVER
Heavy frame. Caliber: .357 Magnum. Six-shot cylinder, 4 or 6-inch bbl. Quickdraw ramp front sight, Accro rear sight. Blued finish. Checkered walnut grips. 9.25 or 11.25 inches overall. Weight: 36 oz. (4-inch bbl.), 39 oz. (6 inch bbl.). Made from 1953-61.
W/standard hammer and service grips . . . . NiB $634 Ex $522 Gd $379
W/wide-spur hammer and target grips . . . . NiB $672 Ex $553 Gd $399

TROOPER DA REVOLVER
Same specifications as Officers' Model Match except has 4-inch bbl. w/quick-draw ramp front sight, weight: 34 oz. in .38 caliber. Made from 1953-69.
W/standard hammer and service grips . . . . NiB $489 Ex $402 Gd $292
W/wide-spur hammer and target grips . . . . NiB $552 Ex $454 Gd $327

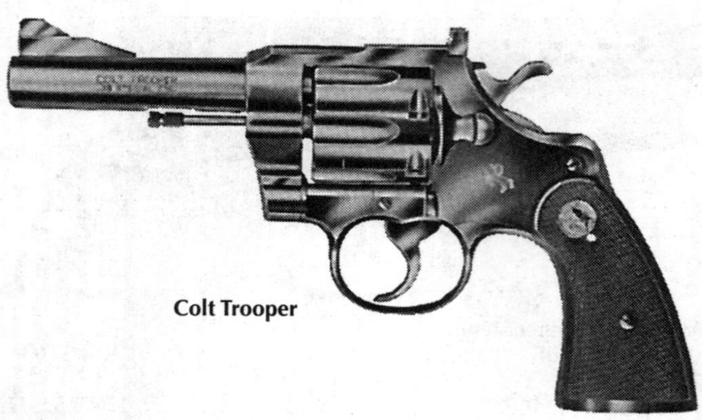
Colt Trooper

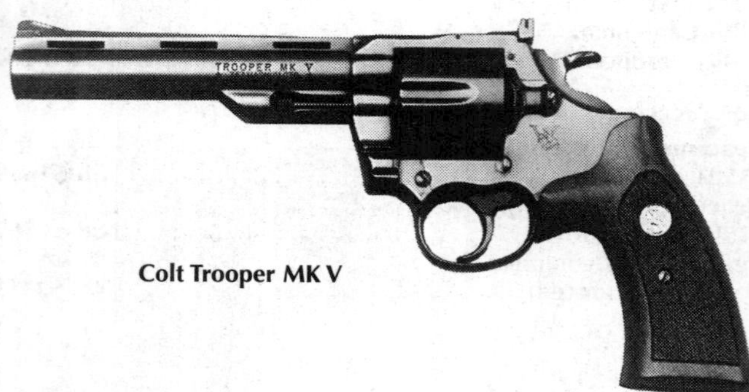
Colt Trooper MK V

Colt U.S. Bicentennial Commemorative Set

TROOPER MK III DA REVOLVER
"J"frame, shrouded ejector rod. Calibers: .22 LR, .22 Magnum, .38 Special, .357 Magnum. Six-round cylinder. bbl. lengths: 4-, 6-inches. 9.5 inches overall (with 4-inch bbl.). Weight: 39 oz. (4-inch bbl.). Adj. rear sight, ramp front. Target trigger and hammer. Blued or nickel-plated finish. Checkered walnut target grips. Made from 1969-78.
Blued finish . . . . NiB $460 Ex $388 Gd $182
Nickel finish . . . . NiB $506 Ex $413 Gd $182

TROOPER MK V REVOLVER
Re-engineered Mark III for smoother, faster action. Caliber: .357 Magnum. Six-round cylinder, bbl. lengths: 4-, 6-, 8-inch w/vent rib. Adj. rear sight, ramp front, red insert. Checkered walnut grips. Made from 1982-86.
Blued finish . . . . NiB $491 Ex $423 Gd $310
Nickel finish . . . . NiB $542 Ex $465 Gd $285

VIPER DA REVOLVER . . . . NiB $491 Ex $439 Gd $307
Same as Cobra, Second Issue except has 4-inch bbl., 9 inches overall, weight: 20 oz. Made from 1977-84.

U.S. BICENTENNIAL
COMMEMORATIVE SET. . . . . NiB $2643
Replica Colt 3rd Model Dragoon revolver w/accessories, Colt SA Army revolver, and Colt Python revolver. Matching roll-engraved unfluted cylinders, blued finish and rosewood grips w/Great Seal of the United States silver medallion. Dragoon revolver has silver grip frame. Serial numbers 0001 to 1776. All revolvers in set have same number. Deluxe drawer-style presentation case of walnut w/book compartment containing a reproduction of "Armsmear." Issued in 1976. Value is for revolvers in new condition.

COONAN ARMS, INC. — Maplewood, Minnesota *(formerly St. Paul, Minnesota)*

MODEL .357 MAGNUM AUTO PISTOL
Caliber: .357 Mag. Seven-round magazine, 5- or 6-inch bbl., 8.3 inches overall (with 5-inch bbl.). Weight: 42 oz. Front ramp interchangeable sight, fixed rear sight, adj. for windage. Black walnut grips. Made from 1983-99.
Model A Std. grade w/o grip
safety (disc. 1991). . . . . NiB $863 Ex $703 Gd $497
Model B Std. grade w/5-inch bbl., ... NiB $639 Ex $522 Gd $374
Model B Std. grade w/6-inch bbl., ... NiB $671 Ex $548 Gd $392
Model B w/5-inch
compensated bbl., (Classic). . . . . NiB $1166 Ex $946 Gd $666
Model B w/6-inch
compensated bbl. NiB $919 Ex $745 Gd $522

.357 MAGNUM CADET COMPACT
Similar to the standard .357 Magnum model except w/3.9-inch bbl., on compact frame. Six-round (Cadet), 7- or 8-round magazine (Cadet II). Weight: 39 oz., 7.8 inches overall. Made from 1993-99.
Cadet model . . . . NiB $727 Ex $589 Gd $413
Cadet II model. . . . . NiB $847 Ex $687 Gd $398

CZ PISTOLS — Uhersky Brod (formerly Strakonice), Czechoslovakia Mfd. by Ceska Zbrojovka-Nardoni Podnik (formerly Bohmische Waffenfabrik A. G.)

Currently imported by CZ-USA, Kansas City, KS. Previously by Magnum Research and Action Arms. Vintage importation is by Century International Arms. Also, see Dan Wesson Firearms listings.

CZ P-01 . . . . NiB $604 Ex $359 Gd $274
Caliber: 9mm Para. Based on CZ-75 design but with improved metals, aluminum alloy frame, hammer forged bbl. (3.8 inches), checkered rubber grips, matte black polycoat finish. Imported.

CZ 40 . . . . NiB $459 Ex $334 Gd $289
Caliber: .40 S&W. M1911-style frame, CZ-75B operating mechanism; single or double-action; black polycoat finish. Fixed sights; 10-round mag.

MODEL 27 AUTO PISTOL . . . . .NiB $605 Ex $502 Gd $307
Caliber: .32 Automatic (7.65mm). Eight-round magazine, 4-inch bbl., 6 inches overall. Weight: 23.5 oz. Fixed sights. Blued finish. Plastic grips. Made from 1927-51. Note: After the German occupation (March 1939), Models 27 and 38 were marked w/manufacturer code "fnh." Designation of Model 38 was changed to "Pistole 39(t)."

MODEL .38 AUTO PISTOL (VZ SERIES)
Caliber: .380 Automatic (9mm). Nine-round magazine, 3.75-inch bbl., 7 inches overall. Weight: 26 oz. Fixed sights. Blued finish. Plastic grips. After 1939 designated as T39. Made from 1938-45.
CZ DAO model . . . . NiB $478 Ex $400 Gd $300
CZ SA/DA model. . . . . NiB $1365 Ex $1075 Gd $752

MODEL 50 DA AUTO PISTOL. . . . . NiB $197 Ex $162 Gd $118
Similar to Walther Model PP except w/frame-mounted safety and trigger guard not hinged. Caliber: .32 ACP (7.65mm), 8-round magazine, 3.13-inch bbl., 6.5 inches overall. Weight: 24.5 oz. Fixed sights. Blued finished. Intro. in 1950. disc. Note: "VZ50" is the official designation of this pistol used by the Czech National Police ("New Model .006" was the export designation but very few were released).

MODEL 52 SA AUTO PISTOL . . . . . . NiB $206 Ex $175 Gd $109
Roller-locking breech system. Calibers: 7.62mm or 9mm Para. Eight-round magazine, 4.7-inch bbl., 8.1 inches overall. Weight: 31 oz. Fixed sights. Blued finish. Grooved composition grips. Made from 1952-56.

MODEL 70 DA AUTO PISTOL. . . . . . NiB $458 Ex $375 Gd $268
Similar to Model 50 but redesigned to improve function and dependability. Made from 1962-83.

MODEL 75 DA/DAO AUTOMATIC PISTOL
Calibers: 9mm Para. or .40 S&W w/selective action mode. 10-, 13- or 15-round magazine, 3.9-inch bbl., (Compact) or 4.75-inch bbl., (Standard), 8 inches overall (Standard). Weight: 35 oz. Fixed sights. Blued, nickel, Two-Tone or black polymer finish. Checkered wood or high-impact plastic grips. Made from 1994 to date.
Black polymer finish . . . . NiB $420 Ex $344 Gd $247
High-polish blued finish . . . . NiB $484 Ex $395 Gd $282
Matte blued finish . . . . NiB $446 Ex $364 Gd $260
Nickel finish . . . . NiB $472 Ex $385 Gd $275
Two-tone finish . . . . NiB $458 Ex $375 Gd $268
W/.22 Kadet conversion, add $250
Compact model, add $35

82 DA AUTO PISTOL . . . . NiB $349 Ex $323 Gd $200
Similar to the standard CZ 83 model except chambered in 9x18 Makarov. This model currently is the Czech military sidearm.

83 DA AUTOMATIC PISTOL
Calibers: .32 ACP, .380 ACP. 15-round (.32 ACP) or 13-round (.380 ACP) magazine, 3.75-inch bbl., 6.75 inches overall. Weight: 26.5 oz. Fixed sights. Blued (standard); chrome and nickel (optional special edition) w/brushed, matte or polished finish. Checkered black plastic grips. Made from 1985 to date.
Standard finish. . . . . NiB $380 Ex $308 Gd $194
Special edition. . . . . NiB $520 Ex $423 Gd $297
Engraved . . . . NiB $1149 Ex $934 Gd $661

CZ Model 75 Compact

CZ Model 75 Kadet

CZ Model 83

CZ Model 85 Combat

CZ Model 97B

CZ Model 100

Daewoo DH40

85 COMBAT DA AUTOMATIC PISTOL
Similar to the standard CZ 85 model except w/13-round magazine, combat-style hammer, fully adj. rear sight and walnut grips. Made from 1986 to date.
Black polymer finish . . . . **NiB $509 Ex $447 Gd $272**
High-polished blued finish . . . . **NiB $549 Ex $447 Gd $317**
Matte blued finish . . . . **NiB $549 Ex $447 Gd $317**

MODEL 97B DA AUTOLOADING PISTOL . . . . **NiB $581 Ex $514 Gd $323**
Similar to the CZ Model 75 except chambered for the .45 ACP cartridge. 10-round magazine, Frame-mounted thumb safety that allows single-action, cocked-and-locked carry. Made from 1997 to date.

MODEL 100 DA AUTOMATIC PISTOL . . . . **NiB $416 Ex $359 Gd $225**
Caliber: 9mm, .40 S&W. 10-round magazine, 3.8-inch bbl., Weight: 25 oz. Polymer grips w/fixed low-profile sights. Made from 1996 to date.

MODEL 1945 DA POCKET AUTO PISTOL . . . . **NiB $271 Ex $224 Gd $163**
Caliber: .25 Auto (6.35mm). Eight-round magazine, 2.5-inch bbl., 5 inches overall. Weight: 15 oz. Fixed sights. Blued finish. Plastic grips. Intro. 1945. disc.

DUO POCKET AUTO PISTOL . . . . **NiB $265 Ex $234 Gd $157**
Caliber: .25 Automatic (6.35mm). Six-round magazine, 2.13 inch bbl., 4.5 inches overall. Weight: 14-.5 oz. Fixed sights. Blued or nickel finish. Plastic grips. Made circa 1926-60.

DAEWOO PISTOLS — Seoul, Korea
Mfd. by Daewoo Precision Industries Ltd.

Imported by Daewoo Precision Industries, Southhampton, PA, Previously by Nationwide Sports Distributors and KBI, Inc.

DH40 AUTO PISTOL . . . . **NiB $443 Ex $385 Gd $254**
Caliber: .40 S&W. 12-round magazine, 4.25-inch bbl., 7 inches overall. Weight: 28 oz. Blade front sight, dovetailed rear w/3-dot system. Blued finish. Checkered composition grips. DH/DP series feature a patented "fastfire" action w/5-6 lb. trigger pull. Made from 1994-96.

DH45 AUTO PISTOL . . . . **NiB $687 Ex $565 Gd $399**
Caliber: .45 ACP. 13-round magazine, 5-inch bbl., 8.1 inches overall. Weight: 35 oz. Blade front sight, dovetailed rear w/3-dot system. Blued finish. Checkered composition grips. Announced 1994, but not imported.

DP51 AUTO PISTOL . . . . **NiB $417 Ex $341 Gd $244**
Caliber: 9mm Para. 13-round magazine, 4.1-inch bbl., 7.5 inches overall. Weight: 28 oz. Blade front and square-notch rear sights. Matte black finish. Checkered composition grips. Made from 1991-96.

DP52 AUTO PISTOL . . . . **NiB $376 Ex $330 Gd $213**
Caliber: .22 LR. 10-round magazine, 3.8-inch bbl., 6.7 inches overall. Weight: 23 oz. Blade front sight, dovetailed rear w/3-dot system. Blued finish. Checkered wood grips. Made from 1994-96.

DAKOTA/E.M.F. CO. — Santa Ana, California

MODEL 1873 SA REVOLVER
Calibers: .22 LR, .22 Mag., .357 Mag., .45 Long Colt, .30 M1 carbine, .38-40, .32-20, .44-40. Bbl. lengths: 3.5, 4.75, 5.5, 7.5 inches. Blued or nickel finish. Engraved models avail.
Standard model . . . . NiB $371 Ex $295 Gd $252
W/extra cylinder . . . . NiB $731 Ex $618 Gd $473

MODEL 1875 OUTLAW
SA REVOLVER . . . . NiB $477 Ex $392 Gd $283
Calibers: .45 Long Colt, .357 Mag., .44-40. 7.5-inch bbl. Casehardened frame, blued finish. Walnut grips. This is an exact replica of the Remington Number 3 revolver produced 1875-89.

MODEL 1890 REMINGTON POLICE
Calibers: .357 Mag., .44-40, .45 Long Colt, 5.75-inch bbl., blued or nickel finish. Similar to Outlaw w/lanyard ring and no bbl. web .
Standard model . . . . NiB $503 Ex $412 Gd $296
Nickel model . . . . NiB $592 Ex $483 Gd $345
Engraved model . . . . NiB $681 Ex $555 Gd $394

BISLEY SA REVOLVER
Calibers: .44-40, .45 Long Colt, .357 Mag, 5.5- or 7.5-inch bbl., disc. 1992. Reintroduced 1994.
Standard model . . . . NiB $407 Ex $351 Gd $249
Target model . . . . NiB $453 Ex $371 Gd $254

HARTFORD SA REVOLVER
Calibers: .22 LR, .32-20, .357 Mag., .38-40, .44-40, .44 Special, .45 Long Colt. These are exact replicas of the original Colts w/steel backstraps, trigger guards and forged frames. Blued or nickel finish. Imported from 1990 to date.
Standard model . . . . NiB $407 Ex $330 Gd $234
Engraved model . . . . NiB $686 Ex $560 Gd $399
Hartford Artillery,
U.S. Cavalry models . . . . NiB $453 Ex $371 Gd $244

SHERIFF'S MODEL
SA REVOLVER . . . . NiB $443 Ex $356 Gd $254
Calibers: .32-20, .357 Mag., .38-40, .44 Special, .44-40, .45 LC. 3.5-inch bbl. Reintroduced 1994.

TARGET SA REVOLVER . . . . NiB $443 Ex $320 Gd $239
Calibers: .45 Long Colt, .357 Mag., .22 LR; 5.5- or 7.5-inch bbl. Polished, blued finish, casehardened frame. Walnut grips. Ramp front, blade target sight, adj. rear sight.

CHARLES DALY HANDGUNS — Currently imported by K.B.I., Harrisburg, PA.

MODEL M1911-A1 FIELD FS AUTOMATIC PISTOL
Caliber: .45 ACP. Eight- or 10-round magazine (Hi-Cap), 5-inch bbl., 8.75 inches overall. Weight: 38 oz. Blade front sight, drift adjustable rear w/3-dot system. Skeletonized tactical hammer and trigger. Extended slide release and beavertail grip safety. Matte blue, stainless or Duo finish. Checkered composition or wood stocks. Imported from 1996 to date.
Matte blue (Field FS) . . . . NiB $494 Ex $432 Gd $279
Stainless (Empire FS) . . . . NiB $647 Ex $534 Gd $356
Duo (Superior FS) . . . . NiB $528 Ex $432 Gd $310
W/.22 conversion kit, add $200

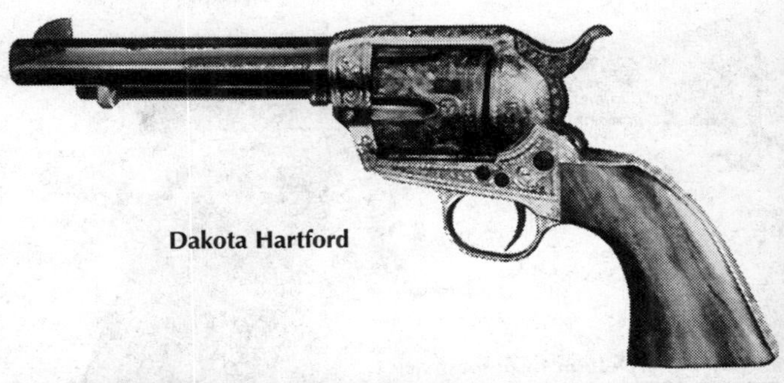
Dakota Hartford

DAVIS INDUSTRIES, INC. — Chino, California

MODEL D DERRINGER
Single-action double derringer. Calibers: .22 LR, .22 Mag., .25 ACP, .32 Auto, .32 H&R Mag., 9mm, .38 Special. Two-round capacity, 2.4-inch or 2.75-inch bbl., 4 inches overall (2.4-inch bbl.). Weight: 9 to 11.5 oz. Laminated wood grips. Black Teflon or chrome finish. Made from 1987 to date.
.22 LR or .25 ACP . . . . NiB $102 Ex $87 Gd $68
.22 Mag., .32 H&R Mag., .38 Spec. . . . . NiB 118 Ex $102 Gd $78
.32 Auto. . . . . NiB $116 Ex $97 Gd $75
9mm Para. . . . . NiB $134 Ex $113 Gd $85

LONG BORE DERRINGER. . . . . NiB $122 Ex $102 Gd $78
Similar to Model D except in calibers .22 Mag., .32 H&R Mag., .38 Special, 9mm Para. 3.75-inch bbl., weight: 16 oz. Made from 1995 to date.

MODEL P-.32 . . . . NiB $109 Ex $92 Gd $71
Caliber: .32 Auto. Six-round magazine, 2.8-inch bbl., 5.4 inches overall. Weight: 22 oz. Black Teflon or chrome finish. Laminated wood grips. Made from 1987 to date.

MODEL P-.380 . . . . NiB $113 Ex $102 Gd $77
Caliber: .380 Auto. Five-round magazine, 2.8-inch bbl., 5.4 inches overall. Weight: 22 oz. Black Teflon or chrome finish. Made from 1990 to date.

DESERT INDUSTRIES, INC. — Las Vegas, Nevada (Previously Steel City Arms, Inc.)

DOUBLE DEUCE DA PISTOL . . . . . NiB $397 Ex $341 Gd $244
Caliber: .22 LR. Six-round magazine, 2.5-inch bbl., 5.5 inches overall. Weight: 15 oz. Matte-finish stainless steel. Rosewood grips.

TWO-BIT SPECIAL PISTOL . . . . NiB $397 Ex $341 Gd $234
Similar to the Double Deuce model except chambered in .25 ACP w/5-shot magazine,

(NEW) DETONICS MFG. CORP — Phoenix, Arizona (Previously Detonics Firearms Industries, Bellevue, WA)

COMBAT MASTER
Calibers: .45 ACP, .451 Detonics Mag. Six-round magazine, 3.5-inch bbl., 6.75 inches overall. Combat-type w/fixed or adjustable sights. Checkered walnut grip. Stainless steel construction. Disc. 1992.
MK I matte stainless,
fixed sights, (disc. 1981) . . . . NiB $584 Ex $502 Gd $349
MK II stainless steel finish, (disc. 1979) NiB $584 Ex $502 Gd $349

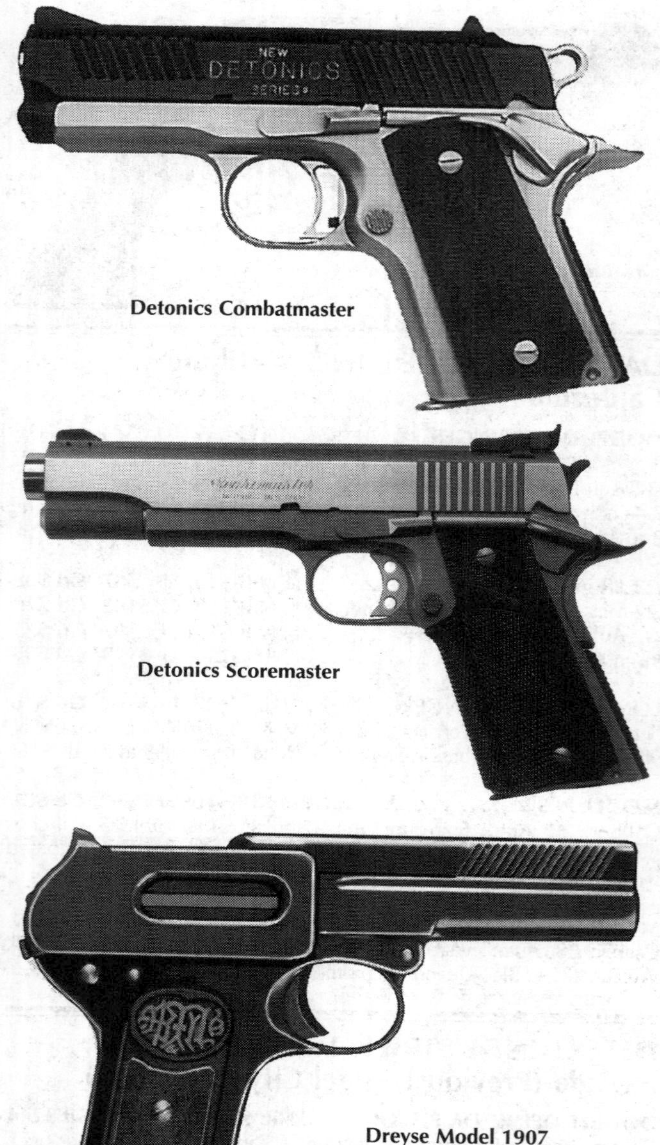

Detonics Combatmaster

Detonics Scoremaster

Dreyse Model 1907

MK III chrome, (disc. 1980) .... **NiB $518 Ex $422 Gd $300**
MK IV polished blued, adj. sights, (disc. 1981) .... **NiB $569 Ex $463 Gd $328**
MK V matte stainless, fixed sights, (disc. 1985) .... **NiB $728 Ex $593 Gd $419**
MK VI polished ptainless, adj. sights, (disc. 1989).............. **NiB $785 Ex $638 Gd $451**
MK VI in .451 Magnum, (disc. 1986) .... **NiB $1151 Ex $944 Gd $667**
MK VII matte stainless steel, no sights, (disc. 1985) .... **NiB $1007 Ex $815 Gd $570**
MK VII in .451 Magnum, (disc. 1980) .... **NiB $1348 Ex $1094 Gd $770**

POCKET 9 .... **NiB $631 Ex $504 Gd $389**
Calibers: 9mm Para., .380. Six-round magazine, three-inch bbl., 5.88 inches overall. Fixed sights. Double- and single-action trigger mechanism. Disc. 1986.

SCOREMASTER .... **NiB $1087 Ex $929 Gd $776**
Calibers: .45 ACP, .451 Detonics Mag. Seven-round magazine. Five- or 6-inch heavyweight match bbl., 8.75 inches overall. Weight: 47 oz. Stainless steel construction, self-centering bbl., system. Disc. 1992.

SERVICE MASTER .... **NiB $900 Ex $747 Gd $492**
Caliber: .45 ACP. Seven-round magazine, 4.25-inch bbl., weight: 39 oz. Interchangeable front sight, Millett rear sight. Disc. 1986.

SERVICE MASTER II............ **NiB $1012 Ex $834 Gd $553**
Same general specifications as standard Service Master except comes in polished stainless steel w/self-centering bbl., system. Disc. 1992.

DOWNSIZER CORPORATION — Santee, California

MODEL WSP DAO PISTOL .... **NiB $461 Ex $344 Gd $242**
Single-round, tip-up pistol. Calibers: .22 Mag., .32 Mag., .380 ACP. 9mm Parabellum, .357 Mag., .40 S&W, .45 ACP. Six-round cylinder, 2.10-inch bbl. w/o extractor, 3.25 inches overall. Weight: 11 oz. No sights. Stainless finish. Synthetic grips. Made from 1994 to date.

DREYSE PISTOLS — Sommerda, Germany Mfd. by Rheinische Metallwaren und Maschinenfabrik ("Rheinmetall")

MODEL 1907 AUTOMATIC PISTOL .... **NiB $283 Ex $217 Gd $155**
Caliber: .32 Auto (7.65mm). Eight-round magazine, 3.5-inch bbl., 6.25 inches overall. Weight: About 24 oz. Fixed sights. Blued finish. Hard rubber grips. Made circa 1907-14.

VEST POCKET AUTOMATIC PISTOL .... **NiB $365 Ex $274 Gd $187**
Conventional Browning type. Caliber: .25 Auto (6.35mm). Six-round magazine, 2-inch bbl., 4.5 inches overall. Weight: About 14 oz. Fixed sights. Blued finish. Hard rubber grips. Made circa 1909-14.

DWM PISTOL — Berlin, Germany Mfd. by Deutsche Waffen-und-Munitionsfabriken

POCKET AUTOMATIC PISTOL .... **NiB $821 Ex $668 Gd $472**
Similar to the FN Browning Model 1910. Caliber: .32 Automatic (7.65mm). 3.5-inch bbl., 6 inches overall. Weight: About 21 oz. Blued finish. Hard rubber grips. Made circa 1921-31.

ED BROWN — Perry, Montana

"CLASS A LTD" SA AUTOMATIC PISTOL .... **NiB $2446 Ex $2058 Gd $964**
Caliber: .38 Super, 9mm, 9x23, .45 ACP. Seven-round magazine, 4.25- or 5-inch bbl., weight: 34-39 oz. Rubber checkered or optional Hogue exotic wood grip. M1911 style single action pistol. Fixed front and rear Novak Lo-mount or fully adjustable sights.

"CLASSIC CUSTOM" SA AUTOMATIC PISTOL . . . . NiB $2962 Ex $2447 Gd $1263
Caliber: .45 ACP. Seven-round magazine, 4.25- or 5-inch bbl., weight: 39 oz. Exotic Hogue wood grip w/modified ramp or post front and rear adjustable sights.

"SPECIAL FORCES" SA AUTOMATIC PISTOL . . . . NiB $1317 Ex $1126 Gd $776
Caliber: .45 ACP. Seven-round magazine, 4.25- or 5-inch bbl., weight: 34-39 oz. Rubber checkered, optional exotic wood grips. Single action M1911 style pistol.

ENFIELD REVOLVER — Enfield Lock, Middlesex, England Manufactured by Royal Small Arms Factory

(BRITISH SERVICE) NO. 2 MK 1 REVOLVER . . . . NiB $280 Ex $239 Gd $177
Webley pattern. Hinged frame. Double action. Caliber: .380 British Service (.38 S&W w/200-grain bullet). Six-round cylinder, 5-inch bbl., 10.5 inches overall. Weight: About 27.5 oz. Fixed sights. Blued finish. Vulcanite grips. First issued in 1932, this was the standard revolver of the British Army in WW II. Now obsolete. Note: This model also produced w/spurless hammer as No. 2 Mk 1* and Mk 1**.

ENTREPRISE ARMS — Irwindale, California

"ELITE" SA AUTOMATIC PISTOL . . . . NiB $704 Ex $642 Gd $575
Single action M1911 style pistol. Caliber: .45 ACP. 10-round magazine, 3.25-, 4.25-, 5-inch bbl., (models P325, P425, P500). Weight: 36-40 oz. Ultraslim checkered grips, Tactical 2 high profile sights w/3-dot system. Lightweight adjustable trigger. Blued or matte black oxide finish. Made from 1997 to date.

"MEDALIST" SA AUTOMATIC PISTOL
Similar to Elite model except machined to match tolerances and target configuration. Caliber: .45 ACP, .40 S&W. 10-round magazine, 5-inch compensated bbl. w/dovetail front and fully adjustable rear Bo-Mar sights. Weight: 40 oz. Made from 1997 to date.
.40 S&W model . . . . NiB $1099 Ex $894 Gd $632
.45 ACP model . . . . NiB $965 Ex $786 Gd $557

"TACTICAL" SA AUTOMATIC PISTOL
Similar to Elite model except in combat carry configuration. Dehorned frame and slide w/ambidextrous safety. Caliber: .45 ACP. 10-round magazine, 3.25-, 4.25-, 5-inch bbl., weight: 36-40 oz. Tactical 2 Ghost Ring or Novak Lo-mount sights.
Tactical 2 ghost ring sights . . . . NiB $1058 Ex $955 Gd $620
Novak Lo-Mount . . . . NiB $923 Ex $759 Gd $550
Tactical plus model . . . . NiB $991 Ex $816 Gd $589

BOXER SA AUTOMATIC PISTOL . . . . NiB $1352 Ex $1141 Gd $785
Similar to Medalist model except w/profiled slide configuration and fully adjustable target sights. weight: 42 oz. Made from 1997 to date.

"TSM" SA AUTOMATIC PISTOL
Similar to Elite model except in IPSC configuration. Caliber: .45 ACP, .40 S&W. 10-round magazine, 5-inch compensated bbl., w/dovetail front and fully adjustable rear Bo-Mar sights. Weight: 40 oz. Made from 1997 to date.
TSM I model . . . . NiB $2201 Ex $1995 Gd $865
TSM II model . . . . NiB $2298 Ex $1866 Gd $1314
TSM III model . . . . NiB $2523 Ex $2046 Gd $1437

Enfield
(British Service)No. 2 MK 1 Revolver

Erma
Model ER-772 Match Revolver

ERMA-WERKE — Dachau, Germany

MODEL ER-772 MATCH REVOLVER . . . . NiB $1247 Ex $1015 Gd $624
Caliber: .22 LR. Six-round cylinder, 6-inch bbl., 12 inches overall. Weight: 47.25 oz. Adjustable micrometer rear sight and front sight blade. Adjustable trigger. Interchangeable walnut sporter or match grips. Polished blued finish. Made from 1991-94.

MODEL ER-773 MATCH REVOLVER . . . . NiB $1045 Ex $942 Gd $555
Same general specifications as Model 772 except chambered for .32 S&W. Made from 1991-95.

MODEL ER-777 MATCH REVOLVER . . . . NiB $983 Ex $881 Gd $546
Caliber: .357 Magnum. Six-round cylinder. 4- or 5.5-inch bbl., 9.7 to 11.3 inches overall. Weight: 43.7 oz. (with 5.5-inch bbl.). Micrometer adj. rear sight. Checkered walnut sporter or match-style grip (interchangeable). Made from 1991-95.

MODEL ESP-85A COMPETITION PISTOL
Calibers: .22 LR and .32 S&W Wadcutter. Eight- or 5-round magazine, 6-inch bbl., 10 inches overall. Weight: 40 oz. Adj. rear sight, blade front sight. Checkered walnut grip w/thumbrest. Made from 1991-97.
Match model . . . . NiB $1377 Ex $1048 Gd $681
Chrome match . . . . NiB $1489 Ex $1258 Gd $964
Sporting model . . . . NiB $1199 Ex $981 Gd $703
Conversion unit .22 LR . . . . NiB $1106 Ex $906 Gd $651
Conversion unit .32 S&W . . . . . . NiB $1206 Ex $1066 Gd $706

European American Armory
Big Bore Bounty Hunter

MODEL KGP68
AUTOMATIC PISTOL . . . . NiB $505 Ex $454 Gd $299
Luger type. Calibers: .32 Auto (7.65mm), .380 Auto (9mm Short). Six-round magazine (.32 Auto), 5-round (.380 Auto), 4-inch bbl., 7.38 inches overall. Weight: 22.5 oz. Fixed sights. Blued finish. Checkered walnut grips. Made from 1968-93.

MODEL KGP69
AUTOMATIC PISTOL . . . . NiB $505 Ex $454 Gd $233
Luger type. Caliber: .22 LR. Eight-round magazine, 4-inch bbl., 7.75 inches overall. Weight: 29 oz. fixed sights. Blued finish. Checkered walnut grips. Imported from 1969-93.

Erma-Werke
Model KGP69

EUROPEAN AMERICAN ARMORY — Hialeah, Florida

See also listings under Astra Pistols.

EUROPEAN MODEL AUTO PISTOL
Calibers: .32 ACP (SA only), .380 ACP (SA or DA), 3.85-inch bbl., 7.38 overall, 7-round magazine, Weight: 26 oz. Blade front sight, drift-adj. rear. Blued, chrome, blue/chrome, blue/gold, Duo-Tone or Wonder finish. Imported 1991 to date.
Blued .32 caliber (disc. 1995) . . . . NiB $187 Ex $155 Gd $115
Blue/chrome .32 caliber
(disc. 1995) . . . . NiB $213 Ex $176 Gd $129
Chrome .32 caliber
(Disc. 1995). . . . . NiB $230 Ex $191 Gd $132
Blued .380 caliber . . . . NiB $204 Ex $161 Gd $118
Blue/chrome .380 caliber
(disc. 1993) . . . . NiB $213 Ex $186 Gd $129
DA .380 caliber (disc. 1994) . . . . . . NiB $232 Ex $201 Gd $149
Lady .380 caliber (disc. 1995). . . . . NiB $277 Ex $227 Gd $174
Wonder finish .380 caliber . . . . NiB $204 Ex $171 Gd $118

BIG BORE BOUNTY HUNTER SA REVOLVER
Calibers: .357 Mag., .41 Mag., .44-40, .44 Mag., .45 Colt. Bbl., lengths: 4.63, 5.5, 7.5 inches. Blade front and grooved topstrap rear sights. Blued or chrome finish w/color casehardened or gold-plated frame. Smooth walnut grips. Imported 1992 to date.
Blued finish . . . . NiB $287 Ex $237 Gd $174
Blued w/color-
casehardened frame . . . . NiB $361 Ex $300 Gd $193
Blued w/gold-plated frame . . . . . . NiB $340 Ex $280 Gd $203
Chrome finish . . . . NiB $377 Ex $315 Gd $237
Gold-plated frame, add $100

Model ESP-85A
Competition Pistol

BOUNTY HUNTER SA REVOLVER

Calibers: .22 LR, .22 Mag. Bbl. lengths: 4.75, 6 or 9 inches. Blade front and dovetailed rear sights. Blued finish or blued w/gold-plated frame. European hardwood grips. Imported from 1991 to date.

Blued finish (4.75-inch bbl.) . . . . NiB $104 Ex $87 Gd $66
Blued .22 LR/.22 WRF combo (4.75-inch bbl.) . . . . NiB $123 Ex $103 Gd $76
Blued .22 LR/.22 WRF combo (6-inch bbl.) . . . . NiB $129 Ex $108 Gd $80
Blued .22 LR/.22 WRF combo (9-inch bbl.) . . . . NiB $136 Ex $113 Gd $83

EA22 TARGET . . . . NiB $391 Ex $319 Gd $226

Caliber: .22 LR. 12-round magazine, 6-inch bbl., 9.10 inches overall. Weight: 40 oz. Ramp front sight, fully adj. rear. Blued finish. Checkered walnut grips w/thumbrest. Made from 1991-94.

FAB 92 AUTO PISTOL

Similar to the Witness model except chambered in 9mm only w/slide-mounted safety and no cock-and-lock provision. Imported from 1992-95.

FAB 92 standard . . . . NiB $372 Ex $316 Gd $206
FAB 92 compact . . . . NiB $372 Ex $316 Gd $206

STANDARD GRADE REVOLVER

Calibers: .22 LR, .22 WRF, .32 H&R Mag., .38 Special. Two-, 4- or 6-inch bbl., blade front sight, fixed or adj. rear. Blued finish. European hardwood grips w/finger grooves. Imported 1991 to date.

.22 LR (4-inch bbl.) . . . . NiB $193 Ex $159 Gd $115
.22 LR (6-inch bbl.) . . . . NiB $206 Ex $169 Gd $122
.22 LR combo (4-inch bbl.) . . . . NiB $270 Ex $220 Gd $157
.22 LR combo (6-inch bbl.) . . . . NiB $306 Ex $250 Gd $177
.32 H&R, .38 Special (2-inch bbl.) . NiB $199 Ex $164 Gd $118
.38 Special (4-inch bbl.) . . . . NiB $213 Ex $174 Gd $125
.357 Mag . . . . NiB $230 Ex $194 Gd $133

TACTICAL GRADE REVOLVER

Similar to the Standard model except chambered in .38 Special only. Two- or 4-inch bbl., fixed sights. Available w/compensator. Imported from 1991-93.

Tactical revolver . . . . NiB $245 Ex $215 Gd $143
Tactical revolver w/compensator . . . . . NiB $336 Ex $281 Gd $197

WINDICATOR TARGET REVOLVER . . . . . . NiB $463 Ex $361 Gd $234

Calibers: .22 LR, .38 Special, .357 Magnum. Eight-round cylinder in .22 LR, 6-round in .38 Special and .357 Magnum. Six-inch bbl. w/bbl. weights. 11.8 inches overall. Weight: 50.2 oz. Interchangeable blade front sight, fully adj. rear. Walnut competition-style grips. Imported from 1991-93.

WITNESS DA AUTO PISTOL

Similar to the Brno CZ-75 w/a cocked-and-locked system. Double or single action. Calibers: 9mm Para. .38 Super, .40 S&W, 10mm; .41 AE and .45 ACP. 16-round magazine (9mm), 12 shot (.38 Super/.40 S&W), or 10-round (10mm/.45 ACP), 4.75-inch bbl., 8.10 inches overall. Weight: 35.33 oz. Blade front sight, rear sight adj. for windage w/3-dot sighting system. Steel or polymer frame. Blued, satin chrome, blue/chrome, stainless or Wonder finish. Checkered rubber grips. EA Series imported 1991 to date.

9mm blue . . . . NiB $387 Ex $316 Gd $224
9mm chrome or blue/chrome . . . . NiB $400 Ex $326 Gd $231
9mm stainless . . . . NiB $457 Ex $372 Gd $263
9mm Wonder finish . . . . NiB $412 Ex $336 Gd $238
.38 Super and .40 S&W blued . . . . NiB $406 Ex $331 Gd $235
.38 Super and .40 S&W chrome or blue/chrome . . . . NiB $449 Ex $366 Gd $260
.38 Super and .40 S&W stainless . . . . NiB $475 Ex $387 Gd $274
.38 Super and .40 S&W Wonder finish . . . . NiB $437 Ex $356 Gd $253
10mm, .41 AE and .45 ACP blued . . . . NiB $500 Ex $407 Gd $288

European American Armory Windicator Target

European American Armory Witness

10mm, .41 AE and .45 ACP chrome or blue/chrome . . . . NiB $511 Ex $423 Gd $298
10mm, .41 AE and .45 ACP stainless . . . . . . NiB $577 Ex $468 Gd $330
10mm, .41 AE and .45 ACP Wonder finish . . . . NiB $526 Ex $428 Gd $302

COMPACT WITNESS DA AUTO PISTOL (L SERIES)

Similar to the standard Witness series except more compact w/ 3.625-inch bbl., and polymer or steel frame. Weight: 30 oz. Matte blued or Wonder finish. EA Compact series imported 1999 to date.

9mm blue . . . . NiB $402 Ex $341 Gd $239
9mm Wonder finish . . . . NiB $423 Ex $366 Gd $249
.38 Super and .40 S&W blued . . . . NiB $412 Ex $336 Gd $240
.38 Super and .40 S&W Wonder finish . . . . NiB $437 Ex $356 Gd $253
10mm, .41 AE and .45 ACP blued . . . . NiB $502 Ex $407 Gd $288
10mm, .41 AE and .45 ACP Wonder fin. . . . NiB $528 Ex $430 Gd $304
W/ported bbl., add $30

WITNESS CARRY COMP

Double/Single action. Calibers: .38 Super, 9mm Parabellum, .40 S&W, 10mm, .45 ACP. 10-, 12- or 16-round magazine, 4.25-inch bbl., w/1-inch compensator. Weight: 33 oz., 8.10 inches overall. Black rubber grips. Post front sight, drift adjustable rear w/3-dot system. Matte blue, Duo-Tone or Wonder finish. Imported 1992 to date.

9mm, .40 S&W . . . . NiB $468 Ex $402 Gd $239
.38 Super, 10mm, .45 ACP. . . . . NiB $412 Ex $336 Gd $240
W/Duo-Tone finish (disc.), add $25
W/Wonder finish, add $10

Feather Guardian Angel Derringer

FEG Mark II AP-.22

WITNESS LIMITED
CLASS AUTO PISTOL . . . . NiB $927 Ex $784 Gd $464
Single action. Calibers: .38 Super, 9mm Parabellum, .40 S&W, .45 ACP. 10-round magazine, 4.75-inch bbl., Weight: 37 oz. Checkered competition-style walnut grips. Long slide w/post front sight, fully adj. rear. Matte blue finish. Imported 1994 to date.

WITNESS SUBCOMPACT DA AUTO PISTOL
Calibers: 9mm Para., .40 S&W, 41 AK, .45 ACP. 13-round magazine in 9mm, 9-round in .40 S&W, 3.66-inch bbl., 7.25 inches overall. Weight: 30 oz. Blade front sight, rear sight adj. for windage. Blued, satin chrome or blue/chrome finish. Imported from 1995-97.
9mm blue . . . . NiB $371 Ex $346 Gd $320
9mm chrome or blue/chrome . . . . . NiB $416 Ex $341 Gd $245
.40 S&W blue . . . . NiB $416 Ex $341 Gd $245
.40 S&W chrome or blue/chrome . . NiB $454 Ex $371 Gd $265
.41 AE blue . . . . NiB $487 Ex $397 Gd $283
.41 AE chrome or blue/chrome . . . . NiB $518 Ex $422 Gd $300
.45 ACP blued . . . . NiB $499 Ex $407 Gd $290
.45 ACP chrome or blue/chrome . . . NiB $473 Ex $407 Gd $295

WITNESS TARGET PISTOLS
Similar to standard Witness model except fitted w/2- or 3-port compensator, competition frame and S/A target trigger. Calibers: 9mm Para., 9x21, .40 S&W, 10mm and .45 ACP, 5.25-inch match bbl., 10.5 inches overall. Weight: 38 oz. Square post front sight, fully adj. rear or drilled and tapped for scope. Blued or hard chrome finish. Low-profile competition grips. Imported 1992 to date.
Silver Team (blued w/2-port
compensator). . . . . NiB $933 Ex $755 Gd $526
Gold Team (chrome
w/3-port compensator) . . . . NiB $1877 Ex $1483 Gd $1061

FAS PISTOLS — Malino, Italy Currently imported by Nygord Precision Products *(Previously by Beeman Precision Arms and Osborne's, Cheboygan, MI)*

601 SEMIAUTOMATIC MATCH TARGET PISTOL
Caliber: .22 Short. Five-round top-loading magazine, 5.6-inch ported and ventilated bbl., 11 inches overall. Weight: 41.5 oz. Removable, adj. trigger group. Blade front sight, open-notch fully adj. rear. Stippled walnut wraparound or adj. target grips.
Right-hand model . . . . NiB $973 Ex $788 Gd $552
Left-hand model . . . . NiB $1094 Ex $941 Gd $559

602 SEMIAUTOMATIC MATCH TARGET PISTOL
Similar to Model FAS 601 except chambered for .22 LR. Weight: 37 oz.
Right-hand model . . . . NiB $941 Ex $661 Gd $508
Left-hand model . . . . NiB $962 Ex $661 Gd $533

603 SEMIAUTOMATIC
MATCH TARGET PISTOL. . . . . NiB $1047 Ex $945 Gd $563
Similar to Model FAS 601 except chambered for .32 S&W (wadcutter).

607 SEMIAUTOMATIC
MATCH TARGET PISTOL. . . . . NiB $1047 Ex $945 Gd $602
Similar to Model FAS 601 except chambered for .22 LR, w/removable bbl. weights. Imported 1995 to date.

FEATHER INDUSTRIES, INC. — Boulder, Colorado

GUARDIAN ANGEL DERRINGER
Double-action over/under derringer w/interchangeable drop-in loading blocks. Calibers: .22 LR, .22 WMR, 9mm, .38 Spec. Two-round capacity, 2-inch bbl., 5 inches overall. weight: 12 oz. Stainless steel. Checkered black grip. Made from 1988-95.
.22 LR, .22 WMR. . . . . NiB $205 Ex $103 Gd $72
9mm, .38 Special (disc. 1989). . . . . . NiB $143 Ex $108 Gd $77

FEG (FEGYVERGYAN) PISTOLS — Budapest, Soroksariut, Hungary *(Currently imported by KBI, Inc. and Century International Arms (Previously by Interarms)*

MARK II AP-.22 DA AUTOMATIC PISTOL . . . . NiB $282 Ex $246 Gd $164
Caliber: .22 LR. Eight-round magazine, 3.4-inch bbl., Weight: 23 oz. Drift-adj. sights. Double action, all-steel pistol. Imported 1997 to date.

MARK II AP-.380 DA AUTOMATIC PISTOL . . . NiB $282 Ex $246 Gd $175
Caliber: .380. Seven-round magazine, 3.9-inch bbl., weight 27 oz. Drift-adj. sights. Double action, all-steel pistol. Imported 1997 to date.

MARK II APK-.380 DA
AUTOMATIC PISTOL. NiB $282 Ex $246 Gd $175
Caliber: .380. Seven-round magazine, 3.4-inch bbl., weight: 25 oz. Drift-adj. sights. Double action, all-steel pistol. Imported 1997 to date.

MODEL GKK-9 (92C) AUTO PISTOL . . . . NiB $365 Ex $330 Gd $207
Improved version of the double-action FEG Model MBK. Caliber: 9mm Para. 14-round magazine, 4-inch bbl., 7.4 inches overall. Weight: 34 oz. Blade front sight, rear sight adj. for windage. Checkered wood grips. Blued finish. Imported from 1992-93.

MODEL GKK-.45 AUTO PISTOL
Improved version of the double-action FEG Model MBK. Caliber: .45 ACP. Eight-round magazine, 4.1-inch bbl., 7.75 inches overall. Weight: 36 oz. Blade front sight, rear sight adj. for windage w/3-dot system. Checkered walnut grips. Blued or chrome finish. Imported from 1993-96.
Blued model (disc. 1994). . . . . NiB $346 Ex $284 Gd $204
Chrome model. . . . . NiB $340 Ex $304 Gd $197

MODEL MBK-9HP
AUTO PISTOL. . . . . NiB $281 Ex $255 Gd $128
Similar to the double-action Browning Hi-Power. Caliber: 9mm Para. 14-round magazine, 4.6-inch bbl., 8 inches overall. Weight: 36 oz. Blade front sight, rear sight adj. for windage. Checkered wood grips. Blued finish. Imported from 1992-93.

MODEL PJK-9HP AUTO PISTOL
Similar to the single-action Browning Hi-Power. Caliber: 9mm Para. 13-round magazine, 4.75-inch bbl., 8 inches overall. Weight: 21 oz. Blade front sight, rear sight adj. for windage w/3-dot system. Checkered walnut or rubber grips. Blued or chrome finish. Imported 1992 to date.
Blued model . . . . NiB $282 Ex $232 Gd $169
Chrome model. . . . . NiB $288 Ex $262 Gd $186

MODEL PSP-.25 AUTO PISTOL
Similar to the Browning .25. Caliber: .25 ACP. Six-round magazine, 2.1-inch bbl., 4.1 inches overall. Weight: 9.5 oz. Fixed sights. Checkered composition grips. Blued or chrome finish.
Blued model . . . . NiB $281 Ex $205 Gd $159
Chrome model. . . . . NiB $281 Ex $205 Gd $159

MODEL SMC-.22 AUTO PISTOL . . . NiB $269 Ex $220 Gd $158
Same general specifications as FEG Model SMC-.380 except in .22 LR. Eight-round magazine, 3.5-inch bbl., 6.1 inches overall. Weight: 18.5 oz. Blade front sight, rear sight adj. for windage. Checkered composition grips w/thumbrest. Blued finish.

MODEL SMC-.380 AUTO PISTOL . . . NiB $235 Ex $210 Gd $143
Similar to the Walther DA PPK w/alloy frame. Caliber: .380 ACP. Six-round magazine, 3.5-inch bbl., 6.1 inches overall. Weight: 18.5 oz. Blade front sight, rear sight adj. for windage. Checkered composition grips w/ thumbrest. Blued finish. Imported 1993 to date.

MODEL SMC-918 AUTO PISTOL. . . . NiB $240 Ex $210 Gd $153
Same general specifications as FEG Model SMC-.380 except chambered in 9x18mm Makarov. Imported from 1994-97.

FIALA OUTFITTERS, INC. — New York

REPEATING PISTOL. . . . . NiB $536 Ex $460 Gd $256
Despite its appearance, which closely resembles that of the early Colt Woodsman and High-Standard, this arm is not an automatic pistol. It is hand-operated by moving the slide to eject, cock and load. Caliber: .22 LR. 10-round magazine, bbl. lengths: 3-, 7.5- and 20-inch. 11.25 inches overall (with 7.5-inch bbl.). Weight: 31 oz. (with 7.5-inch bbl.). Target sights. Blued finish. Plain wood grips. Shoulder stock was originally supplied for use w/20-inch bbl. Made from 1920-23. Value shown is for pistol w/one bbl. and no shoulder stock.

F.I.E. CORPORATION — Hialeah, Florida

The F.I.E Corporation became QFI *(Quality Firearms Corp.) of Opa Locka, Fl., about 1990, when most of F.I.E's models were discontinued.*

FEG Model PJK-9HP

F.I.E. Model A27BW

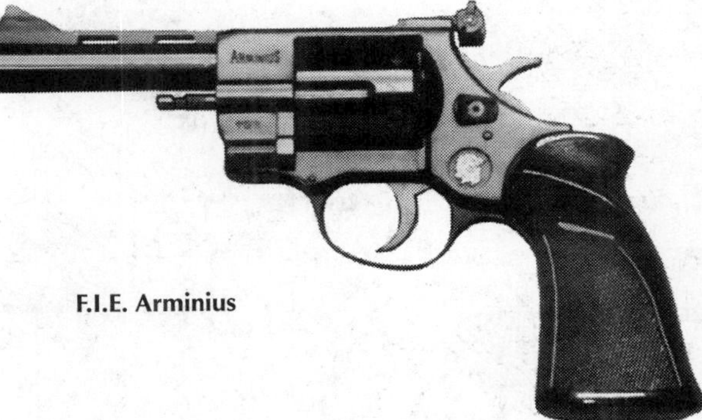
F.I.E. Arminius

MODEL A27BW "THE
BEST" SEMIAUTO . . . . NiB $151 Ex $131 Gd $95
Caliber: .25 ACP. Six-round magazine, 2.5-inch bbl., 6.75 inches overall. Weight: 13 oz. Fixed sights. Checkered walnut grip. Discontinued in 1990.

ARMINIUS DA STANDARD REVOLVER
Calibers: .22 LR, .22 combo w/interchangeable cylinder, .32 S&W, .38 Special, .357 Magnum. Six, 7 or 8 rounds depending on caliber. Swing-out cylinder. bbl., lengths: 2-, 3-, 4, 6-inch. Vent rib on calibers other than .22, 11 inches overall (with 6-inch bbl.). Weight: 26 to 30 oz. Fixed or micro-adj. sights. Checkered plastic or walnut grips. Blued finish. Made in Germany. Disc.
.22 LR . . . . NiB $106 Ex $94 Gd $72
.22 Combo. NiB $174 Ex $148 Gd $97
.32 S&W . . . . NiB $182 Ex $142 Gd $101
.38 Special. . . . . NiB $135 Ex $157 Gd $112
.357 Magnum . . . . NiB $214 Ex $179 Gd $133

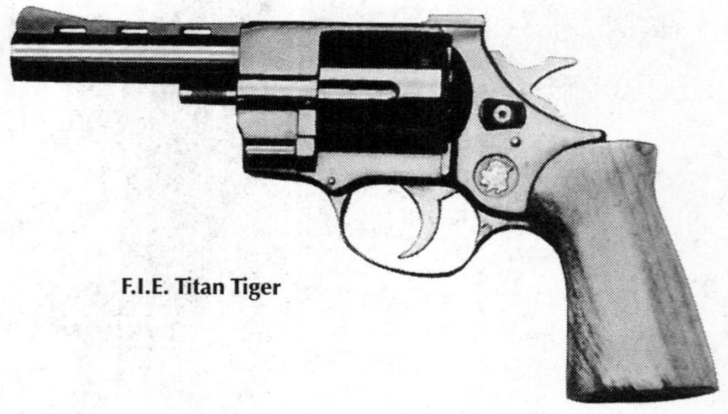

F.I.E. Titan Tiger

F.I.E. Titan II

F.I.E. Model TZ75

BUFFALO SCOUT SA REVOLVER
Calibers: .22 LR, .22 WRF, .22 combo w/interchangeable cylinder. 4.75-inch bbl., 10 inches overall. Weight: 32 oz. Adjustable sights. Blued or chrome finish. Smooth walnut or black checkered nylon grips. Made in Italy. Disc.
Blued standard. NiB $94 Ex $74 Gd $54
Blued convertible . . . . NiB $114 Ex $94 Gd $70
Chrome standard. . . . . NiB $101 Ex $84 Gd $53
Chrome convertible. . . . . NiB $135 Ex $114 Gd $86

HOMBRE SA REVOLVER . . . . NiB $245 Ex $205 Gd $133
Calibers: .357 Magnum, .44 Magnum, .45 Colt. Six-round cylinder. bbl. lengths: 6 or 7.5 inches, 11 inches overall (with - inch bbl.). Weight: 45 oz. (6-inch bbl.). Fixed sights. Blued bbl., w/color-casehardened receiver. Smooth walnut grips. Made from 1979-90.

SUPER TITAN II
Caliber: .32 ACP or .380 ACP, 3.25-inch bbl., weight: 28 oz. Blued or chrome finish. Disc. 1990.
.32 ACP in blue . . . . NiB $243 Ex $213 Gd $126
.32 ACP in chrome . . . . NiB $222 Ex $182 Gd $131
.380 ACP in blue . . . . NiB $228 Ex $187 Gd $135
.380 ACP in chrome . . . . NiB $247 Ex $207 Gd $145

TEXAS RANGER
SINGLE-ACTION REVOLVER
Calibers: .22 LR, .22 WRF, .22 combo w/interchangeable cylinder. bbl., lengths: 4.75-, 6.5-, 9-inch. 10 inches overall (with 4.75-inch bbl.). Weight: 32 oz. (with 4.75-inch bbl.). Fixed sights. Blued finish. Smooth walnut grips. Made from 1983-90.
Standard . . . . NiB $104 Ex $93 Gd $63
Convertible . . . . NiB $161 Ex $137 Gd $108

LITTLE RANGER SA REVOLVER
Same as the Texas Ranger except w/3.25-inch bbl. and bird's-head grips. Made from 1986-90.
Standard . . . . NiB $101 Ex $90 Gd $70
Convertible . . . . NiB $164 Ex $139 Gd $109

TITAN TIGER DOUBLE-
ACTION REVOLVER . . . . NiB $154 Ex $133 Gd $89
Caliber: .38 Special. Six-round cylinder, 2- or 4-inch bbl., 8.25 inches overall (with 4-inch bbl.). Weight: 30 oz. (4-inch bbl.). Fixed sights. Blued finish. Checkered plastic or walnut grips. Made in the U.S. Disc. 1990.

TITAN II SEMIAUTOMATIC
Caiibers: .22 LR, .32 ACP, .380 ACP. 10-round magazine, integral tapered post front sight, windage-adjustable rear sight. European walnut grips. Blued or chrome finish. Disc. 1990.
.22 LR in blue . . . . NiB $152 Ex $126 Gd $75
.32 ACP in blued . . . . NiB $191 Ex $157 Gd $113
.32 ACP in
chrome . . . . NiB $243 Ex $203 Gd $152
.380 ACP in blue . . . . NiB $224 Ex $184 Gd $133
.380 ACP in
chrome . . . . NiB $249 Ex $204 Gd $147

MODEL TZ75 DA SEMIAUTOMATIC
Double action. Caliber: 9mm. 15-round magazine, 4.5-inch bbl., 8.25 inches overall. Weight: 35 oz. Ramp front sight, windage-adjustable rear sight. European walnut or black rubber grips. Imported from 1988-90.
Blued finish . . . . NiB $418 Ex $367 Gd $260
Satin chrome . . . . NiB $491 Ex $398 Gd $282

YELLOW ROSE SA REVOLVER
Same general specifications as the Buffalo Scout except in .22 combo w/interchangeable cylinder and plated in 24-karat gold. Limited Edition w/scrimshawed ivory polymer grips and American walnut presentation case. Made from 1987-90.
Yellow Rose
.22 combo . . . . NiB $155 Ex $134 Gd $119
Yellow Rose
Limited Edition . . . . NiB $277 Ex $236 Gd $175

FIREARMS INTERNATIONAL CORP. — Washington, D.C.

MODEL D
AUTOMATIC PISTOL . . . . NiB $262 Ex $215 Gd $155
Caliber: .380 Automatic. Six-round magazine, 3.3-inch bbl., 6.13 inches overall. Weight: 19.5 oz. Blade front sight, windage-adjustable rear sight. Blued, chromed, or military finish. Checkered walnut grips. Made from 1974-77.

REGENT DA
REVOLVER. NiB $140 Ex $117 Gd $97
Calibers: .22 LR, .32 S&W Long. Eight-round cylinder (.22 LR), or 7-round (.32 S&W). Bbl. lengths: 3-, 4-, 6-inches (.22 LR) or 2.5-, 4-inches (.32 S&W). Weight: 28 oz.(with 4-inch bbl.). Fixed sights. Blued finish. Plastic grips. Made from 1966-72.

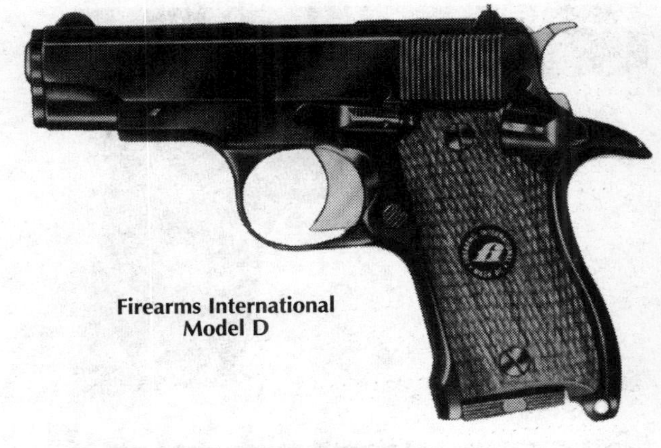
Firearms International Model D

Firearms International Regent

FN BROWNING PISTOLS — Liege, Belgium Mfd. by Fabrique Nationale Herstal

See also Browning Pistols.

6.35MM POCKET AUTO PISTOL
(See FN Browning Baby Auto Pistol)

MODEL 1900 POCKET
AUTO PISTOL . . . . NiB $559 Ex $461 Gd $250
Caliber: .32 Automatic (7.65mm). Seven-round magazine, 4-inch bbl., 6.75 inches overall. Weight: 22 oz. Fixed sights. Blued finish. Hard rubber grips. Made from 1899-10.

MODEL 1903 MILITARY AUTO PISTOL
Caliber: 9mm Browning Long. Seven-round magazine, 5-inch bbl., 8 inches overall. Weight: 32 oz. Fixed sights. Blued finish. Hard rubber grips. Note: Aside from size, this pistol is of the same basic design as the Colt Pocket .32 and .380 Automatic pistols. Made from 1903-39.
Model 190
Standard . . . . NiB $551 Ex $449 Gd $319
Model 1903
(w/slotted backstrap). . . . . NiB $808 Ex $655 Gd $459
Model 1903 (w/slotted
backstrap, shoulder stock
and extended magazine) . . . . . . NiB $3205 Ex $2604 Gd $1797

MODEL 1910
POCKET AUTO PISTOL . . . . NiB $393 Ex $368 Gd $249
Calibers: .32 Auto (7.65mm), .380 Auto (9mm). Seven-round magazine (.32 cal.), or 6-round (.380 cal.), 3.5-inch bbl., 6 inches overall. Weight: 20.5 oz. Fixed sights. Blued finish. Hard rubber grips. Made from 1910-54.

MODEL 1922 (10/.22)
POLICE/MILITARY AUTO
Calibers: .32 Auto (7.65mm), .380 Auto (9mm). Nine-round magazine (.32 cal.), or 8-round (.380 cal.), 4.5-inch bbl., 7 inches overall. Weight: 25 oz. Fixed sights. Blued finish. Hard rubber grips. Made from 1922-59.
Model 1910
commercial . . . . NiB $449 Ex $372 Gd $243
Model 191
Military contract . . . . NiB $548 Ex $446 Gd $316
Model 1910 (w/Nazi
proofs 1940-44), add 25%

FN Browning 6.35mm Pocket

FN Browning 1900 Pocket

FN Browning 1910 Pocket

FN Browning 1922 Police/Military

FN Browning 1935 Military Hi-Power

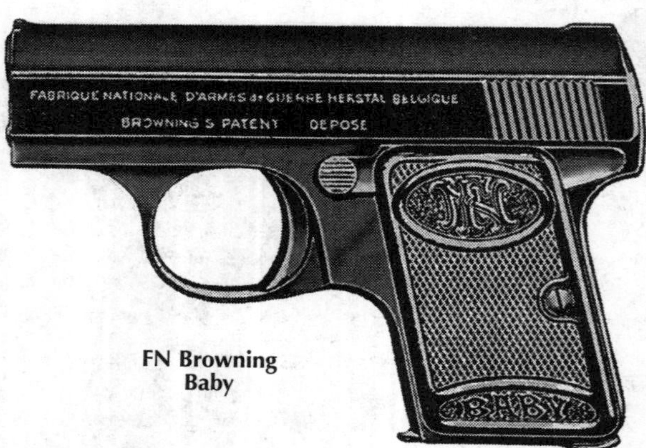

FN Browning Baby

MODEL 1935 MILITARY HI-POWER PISTOL

Variation of the Browning-Colt .45 Auto design. Caliber: 9mm Para.13-round magazine, 4.63-inch bbl., 7.75 inches overall. Weight: About 35 oz. Adjustable rear sight and fixed front, or both fixed. Blued finish (Canadian manufacture Parkerized). Checkered walnut or plastic grips. Note: Above specifications in general apply to both the original FN production and the pistols made by John Inglis Company of Canada for the Chinese government. A smaller version, w/shorter bbl. and slide and 10-round magazine, was made by FN for the Belgian and Rumanian Governments about 1937-1940. Both types were made at the FN plant during the German occupation of Belgium.

Pre-war commercial (w/fixed sights). . . . . NiB $1086 Ex $880 Gd $674
Pre-war commercial
(w/tangent sight only). . . . . NiB $1962 Ex $1292 Gd $674
Pre-war commercial
(w/tangent sight, slotted backstrap) . . . NiB $2914 Ex $2554 Gd $1369
Pre-war Belgian military contract. . . . . . . NiB $1162 Ex $972 Gd $662
Pre-war Foreign military contract. . . . . NiB $2132 Ex $1721 Gd $1196
War production (w/fixed sights) . . . . NiB $806 Ex $653 Gd $467
War production (w/tangent sight only). . NiB $1357 Ex $1101 Gd $773
War production
(w/tangent sight and slotted backstrap) . . . NiB $3370 Ex $2686 Gd $1846
Post-war/pre-BAC (w/fixed sights) . . . . NiB $678 Ex $550 Gd $387
Post-war/pre-BAC (w/tangent sight only) . . NiB $749 Ex $606 Gd $425
Post-war/pre-BAC
(w/tangent sight, slotted backstrap) . . . . NiB $1330 Ex $1074 Gd $746
Inglis manufacture
Canadian military (w/fixed sights) . . . . NiB $967 Ex $735 Gd $452
Canadian military
(w/fixed sight, slotted) . . . . NiB $1804 Ex $1455 Gd $1011
Canadian military
(w/tangent sight, slotted) . . . . NiB $1477 Ex $1195 Gd $834
Canadian military
(marked w/Inglis logo) . . . . NiB $2565 Ex $2080 Gd $1435
Chinese military contract
(w/tangent sight, slotted) . . . . NiB $3314 Ex $2670 Gd $1846
Canadian military
(w/fixed sight, slotted backstrap) . . . . . NiB $1810 Ex $1462 Gd $1017
Canadian military
(marked w/Inglis logo) . . . . NiB $2565 Ex $2080 Gd $1435
W/issue wooden holster, add $400

BABY AUTO PISTOL . . . . NiB $559 Ex $497 Gd $353

Caliber: .25 Automatic (6.35mm). Six-round magazine, 2.13-inch bbl., 4 inches overall. Weight: 10 oz. Fixed sights. Blued finish. Hard rubber grips. Made from 1931-83.

FOREHAND & WADSWORTH — Worcester, Massachusetts

REVOLVERS

See listings of comparable Harrington & Richardson and Iver Johnson revolvers for values.

FORT WORTH FIREARMS — Fort Worth, TX

MATCH MASTER STANDARD. . . . . NiB $369 Ex $244 Gd $219

Semi-automatic. Caliber: .22LR. Equipped with 3 7/8-, 4 1/2-, 5 1/2-, 7 1/2- or 10-inch bull bbl., double extractors, includes upper push button and standard magazine release, angled grip, low profile frame. Made from 1995-2000.

≈

MATCH MASTER DOVETAIL .... **NiB $470 Ex $395 Gd $305**
Similar to Match Master except has 3 7/8-, 4 1/2-, or 5 1/2-inch bbl. with dovetail rib.

MATCH MASTER DELUXE .... **NiB $530 Ex $425 Gd $330**
Similar to Match master Standard except has Weaver rib on bbl.
W/10-inch bbl. .... **Add $100**

SPORT KING .... **NiB $530 Ex $280 Gd $255**
Semi-automatic. Caliber: .22 LR. Equipped with 4 1/2- or 5 1/2-inch bbl., blued finish, military grips, drift sights, 10 round magazine. Made from 1995-2000.

CITATION .... **NiB $393 Ex $298 Gd $253**
Semi-automatic. Caliber: .22 LR. Equipped with 5 1/2-inch bull bbl. or 7 1/2-inch fluted bbl., military grips, 10-round magazine.

TROPHY .... **NiB $398 Ex $313 Gd $248**
Semi-automatic. Caliber: .22 LR. Equipped with 5 1/2- or 7 1/2-inch bull bbl. blued finish, military grips, 10-round magazine.
W/LH action (5 1/2-inch bbl. only) .... **Add $50**

VICTOR .... **NiB $458 Ex $368 Gd $278**
Semi-automatic. Caliber: .22LR. Equipped with 3 7/8-, 4 1/2- (VR or Weaver rib), 8- (Weaver rib) or 10-inch (Weaver rib) bbls.; blued finish, military grips, 10-round magazine.
W/4 1/2- or 4 1/2-inch Weaver rib bbls. .... **Add $80**
W/8- or 10-inch Weaver rib bbls. .... **Add $175**

OLYMPIC .... **NiB $607 Ex $492 Gd $382**
Semi-automatic. Caliber: .22 LR or Short. Equipped with 6 1/2-inch fluted bbl., blued finish, military grips, 10-round magazine.

SHARPSHOOTER .... **NiB $376 Ex $316 Gd $241**
Semi-automatic. Caliber: .22 LR. Equipped with 5 1/2-inch bull bbl.,blued finish, military grips, 10-round magazine.

LE FRANCAIS PISTOLS — St. Etienne, France Produced bv Manufacture Francaise d'Armes et Cycles

ARMY MODEL AUTOMATIC PISTOL .... **NiB $1641 Ex $1224 Gd $808**
Similar in operation to the Le Francais .25 Automatics. Caliber: 9mm Browning Long. Eight-round magazine, 5-inch bbl., 7.75 inches overall. Weight: About 34 oz. Fixed sights. Blued finish. Checkered walnut grips. Made from 1928-38.

POLICEMAN MODEL AUTOMATIC PISTOL .... **NiB $927 Ex $876 Gd $365**
DA. Hinged bbl., Caliber: .25 Automatic (6.35mm). Seven-round magazine, 3.5-inch bbl., 6 inches overall. Weight: About 12 oz. Fixed sights. Blued finish. Hard rubber grips. Introduced in 1914. disc.

STAFF OFFICER MODEL AUTOMATIC PISTOL .... **NiB $314 Ex $269 Gd $187**
Caliber: .25 Automatic. Similar to the "Policeman" model except does not have cocking-piece head, barrel, is about an inch shorter and weight is an ounce less. Introduced in 1914. disc.

FREEDOM ARMS — Freedom, Wyoming

MODEL 1997 PREMIER GRADE SA REVOLVER
Calibers: .357 Mag., .41 Mag. or .45 LC. Five- or 6-round cylinder, 4.25, 5, 5.5, 6 or 7.5-inch bbl., removable front blade with adjustable or fixed rear sight. Hardwood or black Micarta grips. Satin stainless finish. Made from 1997 to date.
Premier grade 97 .... **NiB $1776 Ex $1339 Gd $798**
For extra cylinder, add **$200**
For fixed sights, deduct **$75**

MODEL FA-.44 (83-44) SA REVOLVER
Similar to Model 454 Casull except chambered in .44 Mag. Made from 1988 to date.
Field grade .... **NiB $1440 Ex $1088 Gd $847**
Premier grade .... **NiB $1774 Ex $1311 Gd $796**
Silhouette class (w/10-inch bbl.) . **NiB $1445 Ex $1105 Gd $858**
Silhouette pac (10-inch bbl., access.) .... **NiB $1440 Ex $1100 Gd $847**
For fixed sights, deduct **$95**

MODEL FA-.45 (83-45) SA REVOLVER
Similar to Model 454 Casull except chambered in .45 Long Colt. Made from 1988-90.
Field grade .... **NiB $1294 Ex $985 Gd $624**
Premier grade .... **NiB $1159 Ex $939 Gd $656**
For fixed sights, deduct **$95**

MODEL FA-252 (83-22) SA REVOLVER
Calibers: .22 LR w/optional .22 Mag. cylinder. Bbl. lengths: 5.13 and 7.5 (Varmint Class), 10 inches (Silhouette Class). Adjustable express or competition silhouette sights. Brushed or matte stainless finish. Black Micarta (Silhouette) or black and green laminated hardwood grips (Varmint). Made from 1991 to date.
Silhouette class .... **NiB $1958 Ex $1646 Gd $693**
Silhouette class w/extra .22 Mag. cyl .... **NiB $1523 Ex $1234 Gd $863**
Varmint class .... **NiB $1166 Ex $946 Gd $666**
Varmint class w/extra .22 Mag. cyl .... **NiB $1457 Ex $1180 Gd $826**

MODEL FA-353 (83-357) SA REVOLVER
Caliber: .357 Mag., bbl. lengths: 4.75, 6, 7.5 or 9 inches. Removable blade front sight, adjustable rear. Brushed or matte stainless finish. Pachmayr Presentation or impregnated hardwood grips.
Field grade .... **NiB $1028 Ex $834 Gd $587**
Premier grade .... **NiB $1650 Ex $1544 Gd $694**
Silhouette class (w/9-inch bbl.) .... **NiB $1049 Ex $852 Gd $602**

MODEL FA-454AS (83-454) REVOLVER
Caliber: .454 Casull (w/optional .45 ACP, .45 LC, .45 Win. Mag. cylinders). Five-round cylinder, bbl. lengths: 4.75, 6, 7.5 or 10 inches. Adjustable express or competition silhouette sights. Pachmayr presentation or impregnated hardwood grips. Brushed or matte stainless steel finish.
Field grade .... **NiB $1651 Ex $1237 Gd $593**
Premier grade .... **NiB $2117 Ex $1781 Gd $700**
Silhouette class (w/10-inch bbl.) . **NiB $1059 Ex $859 Gd $604**
For extra cylinder, add **$250**

MODEL FA-454FS REVOLVER
Same general specifications as Model FA-454AS except w/fixed sight.
Field grade .... **NiB $1681 Ex $1468 Gd $902**
Premier grade .... **NiB $1717 Ex $1494 Gd $902**

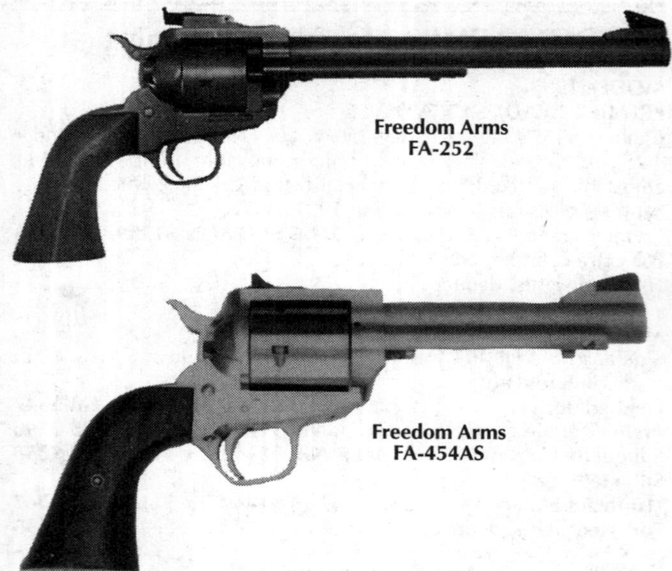

Freedom Arms
FA-252

Freedom Arms
FA-454AS

MODEL FA-454 GAS REVOLVER . . . . . . NiB $1681 Ex $1468 Gd $902
Field Grade version of Model FA-454AS except not made w/12-inch bbl., Matte stainless finish, Pachmayr presentation grips. Adj. Sights or fixed sight on 4.75-inch bbl.

MODEL FA-555 REVOLVER
Similar to Model .454 Casull except chambered in .50 AK. Made from 1994 to date.
Field grade . . . . NiB $1492 Ex $1101 Gd $848
Premier grade . . . . NiB $1855 Ex $1365 Gd $1005

MODEL FA-BG-22LR
MINI-REVOLVER . . . . NiB $200 Ex $155 Gd $120
Caliber: .22 LR. Three-inch tapered bbl., partial high-gloss stainless steel finish. Disc. 1987.

MODEL FA-BG-22M
MINI-REVOLVER . . . . NiB $224 Ex $172 Gd $131
Same general specifications as model FA-BG-22LR except in caliber .22 WMR. Disc. 1987.

MODEL FA-BG-22P
MINI-REVOLVER . . . . NiB $224 Ex $183 Gd $121
Same general specifications as Model FA-BG-22LR except in .22 percussion. Disc. 1987.

MODEL FA-L-22LR MINI-REVOLVER . . . NiB $181 Ex $170 Gd $93
Caliber: .22 LR, 1.75-inch contoured bbl., partial high-gloss stainless steel finish. Bird's-head-type grips. Disc. 1987.

MODEL FA-L-22M
MINI-REVOLVER . . . . NiB $191 Ex $160 Gd $119
Same general specifications as Model FA-L-22LR except in caliber .22 WMR. Disc. 1987.

MODEL FA-L-22P MINI-REVOLVER . . . NiB $208 Ex $147 Gd $111
Same general specifications as Model FA-L-22LR except in .22 percussion. Disc. 1987.

MODEL FA-S-22LR MINI-REVOLVER . . . NiB $181 Ex $170 Gd $93
Caliber: .22 LR. One-inch contoured bbl., partial high-gloss stainless steel finish. Disc. 1988.

MODEL FA-S-22M MINI-REVOLVER. . . NiB $183 Ex $162 Gd $121
Same general specifications as Model FA-S-22LR except in caliber .22 WMR. Disc. 1988.

MODEL FA-S-22P MINI-REVOLVER . . . NiB $183 Ex $162 Gd $118
Same general specifications as Model FA-S-22LR except in .22 percussion. Disc. 1988.

FRENCH MILITARY PISTOLS — Cholet, France

Manufactured originally by Société Alsacienne de Constructions Mécaniques (S.A.C.M.). Currently made by Manufacture d'Armes Automatiques, Lotissement Industriel des Pontots, Bayonne

MODEL 1935A AUTOMATIC PISTOL. . . . . . NiB $307 Ex $256 Gd $129
Caliber: 7.65mm Long. Eight-round magazine, 4.3-inch bbl., 7.6 inches overall. Weight: 26 oz. Two-lug locking system similar to the Colt U.S. M1911A1. Fixed sights. Blued finish. Checkered grips. Made 1935-45. Note: This pistol was used by French troops during WW II and in Indo-China 1945-54.

MODEL 1935S AUTOMATIC PISTOL . . . . NiB $366 Ex $336 Gd $188
Similar to Model 1935A except shorter (4.1-inch bbl., and 7.4 inches overall) and heavier (28 oz.). Single-step lug locking system.

MODEL 1950 AUTOMATIC PISTOL . . . . NiB $450 Ex $366 Gd $260
Caliber: 9mm Para. Nine-round magazine, 4.4-inch bbl., 7.6 inches overall. Weight: 30 oz. Fixed sights, tapered post front and U-notched rear. Similar in design and function to the U.S. .45 service automatic except no bbl., bushing.

MODEL MAB F1 AUTOMATIC PISTOL. . . . . NiB $613 Ex $562 Gd $256
Similar to Model MAB P-15 except w/6-inch bbl. and 9.6 inches overall. Adjustable target-style sights. Parkerized finish.

MODEL MAB P-8 AUTOMATIC PISTOL. . . . . NiB $543 Ex $445 Gd $319
Similar to Model MAB P-15 except w/8-round magazine,

MODEL MAB P-15 AUTOMATIC PISTOL. . . . NiB $613 Ex $562 Gd $358
Caliber: 9mm Para. 15-round magazine, 4.5-inch bbl., 7.9 inches overall. Weight: 38 oz. Fixed sights, tapered post front and U-notched rear.

FROMMER PISTOLS — Budapest, Hungary
Mfd. by Fémáru-Fegyver-és Gépgyár R.T.

LILLIPUT POCKET
AUTOMATIC PISTOL . . . . NiB $448 Ex $346 Gd $193
Caliber: .25 Automatic (6.35mm). Six-round magazine, 2.14-inch bbl., 4.33 inches overall. Weight: 10.13 oz. Fixed sights. Blued finish. Hard rubber grips. Made during early 1920s. Note: Although similar in appearance to the Stop and Baby, this pistol is designed for blowback operation.

STOP POCKET AUTOMATIC PISTOL . . NiB $342 Ex $293 Gd $140
Locked-breech action, outside hammer. Calibers: .32 Automatic (7.65mm), .380 Auto (9mm short). Seven-round (.32 cal.) or 6-round (.380 cal.) magazine, 3.88-inch bbl., 6.5 inches overall. Weight: About 21 oz. Fixed sights. Blued finish. Hard rubber grips. Made from 1912-20.

BABY POCKET AUTOMATIC PISTOL . . NiB $284 Ex $248 Gd $131
Similar to Stop model except has 2-inch bbl., 4.75 inches overall. Weight 17.5 oz. Magazine capacity is one round less than Stop Model. Intro. shortly after WW I.

Galena Industries Inc., — Sturgis, South Dakota

Galena Industries purchased the rights to use the AMT trademark in 1998. Many, but not all, original AMT designs were included in the transaction.

AMT BACKUP . . . . NiB $358 Ex $263 Gd $218
Caliber: .380 (small frame, 2.5-inch bbl. only), .38 Super, .357 Sig, .40 S&W, .400 CorBon, .45 ACP, 9mm; magazine capacity: 5 or 6 rounds. Double action, 3-inch bbl., weight: 18 oz. (in .380), or 23 oz.
.38 Super, .357 Sig, .400 CorBon. . . . . Add $50

AUTOMAG II SEMI AUTO . . . . NiB $488 Ex $359 Gd $282
Caliber: .22 WMR, 9-round magazine (except 7-round in 3.38-inch bbl.); 3.38- 4.5- or 6-inch bbls.; weight: About 32 oz.

AUTOMAG III . . . . NiB $591 Ex $462 Gd $359
Similar to Automag II except chambered for the .30 Carbine cartridge, 6.38-inch bbl., stainless steel finish, weight: About 43 oz.

AUTOMAG IV . . . . NiB $76 Ex $521 Gd $418
Caliber: .45 Winchester Magnum; 7-round magazine, 6.5-inch bbl., weight: 46 oz.

AUTOMAG .440 CORBON . . . . NiB $995 Ex $842 Gd $583
Semiautomatic, 7.5-inch bbl., 5-round magazine, checkered walnut grips, matte black finish, weight: 46 oz. Intro. in 2000.

GALENA HARDBALLER. . . . . NiB $508 Ex $385 Gd $307
Based on the Colt Model 1911 frame. Caliber: .45 ACP, .40 S&W, .400 CorBon, 7-round magazine capacity, 5-inch bbl., weight: About 38 oz.

GALENA LONGSLIDE . . . . NiB $591 Ex $462 Gd $359
Similar to Hardballer model except caliber: .45 ACP, 7-inch bbl., 7-round magazine capacity, stainless steel finish, weight: About 46 ounces.

GALENA ACCELERATOR . . . . NiB $618 Ex $490 Gd $361
Similar to Hardballer model except caliber: .400 CorBon, 7-inch bbl., 7-round magazine capacity, stainless steel finish, weight: About 46 ounces.

GALENA COMMANDO . . . . NiB $488 Ex $359 Gd $282
Similar to Hardballer model except caliber: .40 S&W, 4-inch bbl., 8-round magazine capacity, stainless steel finish, weight: About 38 ounces.

GALESI PISTOLS — Collebeato (Brescia), Italy Mfd. by Industria Armi Galesi

MODEL 6
POCKET AUTOMATIC PISTOL . . . . NiB $189 Ex $148 Gd $108
Calibers: .22 Long, .25 Automatic (6.35mm). Six-round magazine, 2.25-inch bbl., 4.38 inches overall. Weight: About 11 oz. Fixed sights. Blued finish. Plastic grips. Made from 1930 to date.

MODEL 9 POCKET
AUTOMATIC PISTOL
Calibers: .22 LR, .32 Auto (7.65mm), .380 Auto (9mm Short). Eight-round magazine, 3.25-inch bbl., 5.88 inches overall. Weight: About 21 oz. Fixed sights. Blued finish. Plastic grips. Made from 1930 to date.

Galesi
Model 6 Pocket

AUTOMATIC PISTOL
Note: Specifications vary, but those shown for .32 Automatic are common.
.22 LR or
.380 Auto. . . . . NiB $219 Ex $178 Gd $117
.32 Auto. . . . . NiB $188 Ex $168 Gd $101

GLISENTI PISTOL — Carcina (Brescia), Italy Mfd. by Societa Siderurgica Glisenti

MODEL 1910 ITALIAN
SERVICE AUTOMATIC. . . . . NiB $876 Ex $748 Gd $417
Caliber: 9mm Glisenti. Seven-round magazine, 4-inch bbl., 8.5 inches overall. Weight: About 32 oz. Fixed sights. Blued finish. Hard rubber or plastic grips. Adopted 1910 and used through WWII.

GLOCK, INC. — Smyrna, Georgia

NOTE: *Models: 17, 19, 20, 21, 22, 23, 24, 31, 32, 33, 34 and 35 were fitted with a redesigned grip-frame in 1998. Models: 26, 27, 29, 30 and all "C" guns (compensated models) retained the original frame design.*

MODEL 17 DA
AUTOMATIC PISTOL
Caliber: 9mm Parabellum. 10-, 17- or 19-round magazine, 4.5-inch bbl., 7.2 inches overall. Weight: 22 oz. w/o magazine, Polymer frame, steel bbl., slide and springs. Fixed or adj. rear sights. Matte, nonglare finish. Made of only 35 components, including three internal safety devices. Imported from 1983 to date.
Model 17 (w/fixed sights) . . . . NiB $555 Ex $483 Gd $305
Model 17C (compensated bbl.) . . . . NiB $713 Ex $606 Gd $330
W/adjustable sights, add $30
W/Meprolight sights, add $80
W/Trijicon sights, add $105

MODEL 17L
COMPETITION
Same general specifications as Model 17 except weight: 23.35 oz. with 6-inch bbl. 8.85 inches overall. Imported from 1988 to date.
Model 1 L7 (w/fixed sights) . . . . . . .NiB $727 Ex $620 Gd $370
W/ported bbl., (early production), add $35
W/adjustable sights, add $30

Glock Model 19 Compact

Glock Model 30

MODEL 19 COMPACT

Same general specifications as Model 17 except smaller version with 4-inch bbl., 6.85 inches overall and weight: 21 oz. Imported from 1988 to date.

Model 19 (w/fixed sights) . . . . NiB $560 Ex $488 Gd $310
Model 19C (compensated bbl.). . . . . NiB $571 Ex $468 Gd $335
W/adjustable sights, add $30
W/Meprolight sights, add $80
W/Trijicon sights, add $105

MODEL 20 DA AUTO PISTOL

Caliber: 10mm. 15-round, hammerless, 4.6-inch bbl., 7.59 inches overall. Weight: 26.3 oz. Fixed or adj. sights. Matte, non-glare finish. Made from 1991 to date.

Model 20 (w/fixed sights) . . . . NiB $781 Ex $679 Gd $322
Model 19C (compensated bbl.) . . . . NiB $746 Ex $621 Gd $437
W/adjustable sights, add $30
W/Meprolight sights, add $80
W/Trijicon sights, add $105

MODEL 21 AUTOMATIC PISTOL

Same general specifications as Model 17 except chambered in .45 ACP. 13-round magazine, 7.59 inches overall. Weight: 25.2 oz. Imported from 1991 to date.

Model 21 (w/fixed sights) . . . . NiB $680 Ex $555 Gd $366
Model 21C (compensated bbl.) . . . . NiB $733 Ex $599 Gd $425
W/adjustable sights, add $30
W/Meprolight sights, add $80
W/Trijicon sights, add $105

MODEL .22 AUTOMATIC PISTOL

Same general specifications as Model 17 except chambered for .40 S&W. 15-round magazine, 7.4 inches overall. Imported from 1992 to date.

Model .22 (w/fixed sights). . . . . NiB $704 Ex $555 Gd $351
Model 22C
(compensated bbl.) . . . . NiB $653 Ex $532 Gd $377
W/adjustable sights, add $30
W/Meprolight sights, add $80
W/Trijicon sights, add $105

MODEL 23 AUTOMATIC PISTOL

Same general specifications as Model 19 except chambered for .40 S&W. 13-round magazine, 6.97 inches overall. Imported from 1992 to date.

Model 23 (w/fixed sights) . . . . NiB $569 Ex $497 Gd $344
Model 23C (compensated bbl.) . . . . NiB $606 Ex $497 Gd $359
W/adjustable sights, add $30
W/Meprolight sights, add $80
W/Trijicon sights, add $105

MODEL 24 AUTOMATIC PISTOL

Caliber: .40 S&W, 10- and 15-round magazines (the latter for law enforcement and military use only), 8.85 inches overall. Weight: 26.5 oz. Manual trigger safety; passive firing block and drop safety. Made from 1995 to date.

Model 24 (w/fixed sights) . . . . NiB $742 Ex $599 Gd $370
Model 24C (compensated bbl.) . . . . NiB $730 Ex $596 Gd $426
W/adjustable sights, add $30

MODEL 26 DA AUTOMATIC PISTOL

Caliber: 9mm, 10-round magazine, 3.47-inch bbl., 6.3 inches overall. Weight: 19.77 oz. Imported from 1995 to date.

Model 26 (w/fixed sights) . . . . NiB $525 Ex $493 Gd $366
Model 26C (compensated bbl.) . . . . NiB $609 Ex $499 Gd $358
W/adjustable sights, add $30

MODEL 27 DA AUTO PISTOL

Similar to the Glock Model .22 except subcompact. Caliber: .40 S&W, 10-round magazine, 3.5-inch bbl., Weight: 21.7 oz. Polymer stocks, fixed or fully adjustable sights. Imported from 1995 to date.

Model 27 (w/fixed sights) . . . . NiB $553 Ex $481 Gd $354
W/adjustable sights, add $30
W/Meprolight sights, add $80
W/Trijicon sights, add $105

MODEL 28 COMPACT (LAW ENFORCEMENT ONLY)

Same general specifications as Model .25 except smfrom aller version. .380 ACP with 3.5-inch bbl., weight: 20 oz. Imported 1999 to date.

MODEL 29 DA AUTO PISTOL

Similar to the Glock Model 20 except subcompact. Caliber: 10mm. 10-round magazine, 3.8-inch bbl., weight: 27.1 oz. Polymer stocks, fixed or fully adjustable sights. Imported from 1997 to date.

Model 29 (w/fixed sights) . . . . NiB $660 Ex $563 Gd $369
W/adjustable sights, add $30
W/Meprolight sights, add $80
W/Trijicon sights, add $100

MODEL 30 DA AUTO PISTOL

Similar to the Glock Model 21 except subcompact. Caliber: .45 ACP. 10-round magazine, 3.8-inch bbl., weight: 26.5 oz. Polymer stocks, fixed or fully adjustable sights. Imported from 1997 to date.

Model 30 (w/fixed sights) . . . . NiB $660 Ex $563 Gd $369
W/adjustable sights, add $30
W/Meprolight sights, add $80
W/Trijicon sights, add $105

MODEL 31 DA AUTOMATIC PISTOL
Caliber: .357 Sig., safe action system. 10- 15- or 17-round magazine, 4.49-inch bbl., weight: 23.28 oz. Safe Action trigger system w/3 safeties. Imported from 1998 to date.
Model 31
(w/fixed sights) . . . . NiB $546 Ex $474 Gd $347
Model 31C
(compensated bbl.) . . . . NiB $605 Ex $499 Gd $363
W/adjustable sights, add $30
W/Meprolight sights, add $80
W/Trijicon sights, add $105

MODEL .32 DA AUTOMATIC PISTOL
Caliber: .357 Sig., safe action system. 10- 13- or 15-round magazine, 4.02-inch bbl., weight: 21.52 oz. Imported from 1998 to date.
Model .32
(w/fixed sights) . . . . NiB $543 Ex $471 Gd $344
Model 32C. NiB $561 Ex $456 Gd $323
W/adjustable sights, add $30
W/Meprolight sights, add $80
W/Trijicon Sights, add $105

MODEL 33 DA AUTOMATIC PISTOL
Caliber: .357 Sig., safe action system. Nine- or 11-round magazine, 3.46-inch bbl. Weight: 19.75 oz. Imported from 1998 to date.
Model 33
(w/fixed sights) . . . . NiB $545 Ex $473 Gd $346
W/adjustable sights, add $30
W/Meprolight sights, add $80
W/Trijicon sights, add $105

MODEL 34 AUTO PISTOL. . . . . NiB $733 Ex $631 Gd $396
Similar to Model 17 except w/redesigned grip-frame and extended slide-stop lever and magazine release. 10-, 17- or 19-round magazine, 5.32- inch bbl. Weight: 22.9 oz. Fixed or adjustable sights. Imported from 1998 to date.

MODEL 35 AUTO PISTOL. . . . . NiB $733 Ex $662 Gd $396
Similar to Model 34 except .40 S&W. Imported from 1998 to date.

MODEL 36 DA AUTOMATIC PISTOL
Caliber: .45 ACP., safe action system. Six-round magazine, 3.78-inch bbl., weight: 20.11 oz. Safe Action trigger system w/3 safeties. Imported from 1999 to date.
Model 36
(w/fixed sights) . . . . NiB $660 Ex $563 Gd $369
W/adjustable sights, add $30
W/Meprolight sights, add $80
W/Trijicon sights, add $105

DESERT STORM
COMMEMORATIVE. . . . . NiB $1100 Ex $916 Gd $595
Same specifications as Model 17 except "Operation Desert Storm, January 16-February 27, 1991" engraved on side of slide w/list of coalition forces. Limited issue of 1,000 guns. Made in 1991.

GREAT WESTERN ARMS CO. — North Hollywood, California

NOTE: *Values shown are for improved late model revolvers early Great Westerns are variable in quality and should be evaluated accordingly. It should also be noted that, beginning about July 1956, these revolvers were offered in kit form. Values of guns assembled from these kits will, in general, be of less value than factory-completed weapons.*

Grendel Model P-12

DOUBLE BARREL DERRINGER . . . . NiB $335 Ex $309 Gd $183
Replica of Remington Double Derringer. Caliber: .38 S&W. Double bbls. (superposed), 3-inch bbl. Overall length: 5 inches. Fixed sights. Blued finish. Checkered black plastic grips. Made from 1953-62.

SA FRONTIER REVOLVER . . . . NiB $539 Ex $488 Gd $284
Replica of the Colt Single Action Army Revolver. Calibers: .22 LR, .357 Magnum, .38 Special, .44 Special, .44 Magnum .45 Colt. Six-round cylinder, bbl. lengths: 4.75-, 5.5 and 7.5-inches. Weight: 40 oz. in .22 cal. w/5.5-inch bbl. Overall length: 11.13 inches w/5.5-inch bbl. Fixed sights. Blued finish. Imitation stag grips. Made from 1951-1962.

GRENDEL, INC. — Rockledge, Florida

MODEL P-10 AUTOMATIC PISTOL
Hammerless, blow-back action. DAO with no external safety. Caliber: .380 ACP. 10-round box magazine integrated in grip. Three-inch bbl., 5.3 inches overall. Weight: 15 oz. Matte blue, nickel or green Teflon finish. Made from 1988-91.
Blued finish . . . . NiB $163 Ex $148 Gd $107
Nickel finish . . . . NiB $204 Ex $173 Gd $129
Teflon finish. . . . . NiB $214 Ex $178 Gd $132
W/compensated bbl., add $45

MODEL P-12 DA AUTOMATIC PISTOL
Caliber: .380 ACP. 11-round Zytel magazine, 3-inch bbl., 5.3 inches overall. Weight: 13 oz. Fixed sights. Polymer DuPont ST-800 grip. Made from 1991-95.
Standard model . . . . NiB $178 Ex $153 Gd $107
Electroless nickel. . . . . NiB $225 Ex $188 Gd $141

MODEL P-30 AUTOMATIC PISTOL
Caliber: .22 WMR. 30-round magazine, 5-or 8-inch bbl., 8.5 inches overall w/5-inch bbl., weight: 21 oz. Blade front sight, fixed rear sight. Made from 1991-95.
W/5-inch bbl.,. . . . . NiB $270 Ex $229 Gd $203
W/8-inch bbl.,. . . . . NiB $270 Ex $229 Gd $203

MODEL P-31
AUTOMATIC PISTOL . . . . NiB $382 Ex $346 Gd $219
Caliber: .22 WMR. 30-round Zytel magazine, 11-inch bbl., 17.3 inches overall. Weight: 48 oz. Adjustable blade front sight, fixed rear. Checkered black polymer DuPont ST-800 grip and forend. Made from 1991-95.

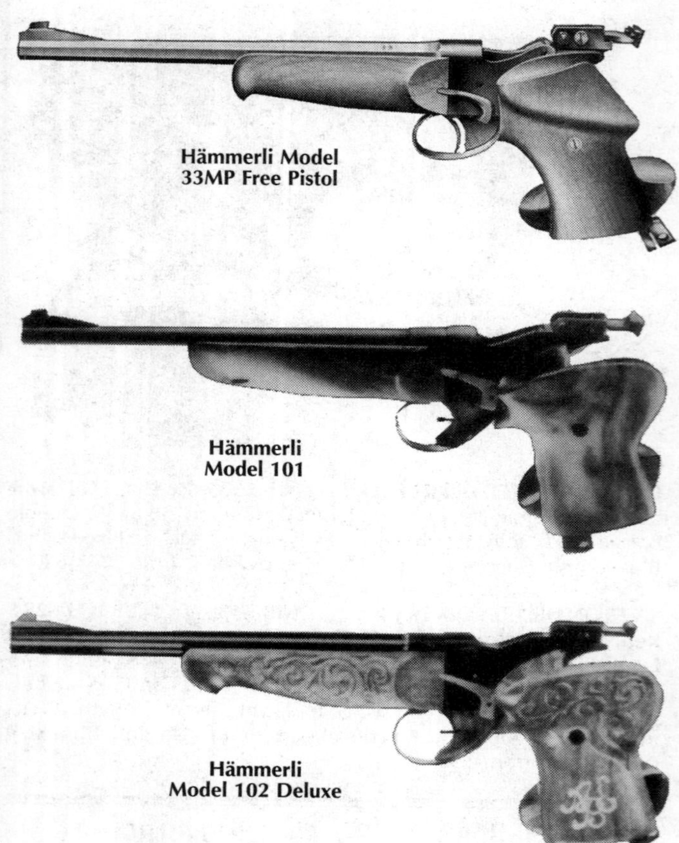

Hämmerli Model 33MP Free Pistol

Hämmerli Model 101

Hämmerli Model 102 Deluxe

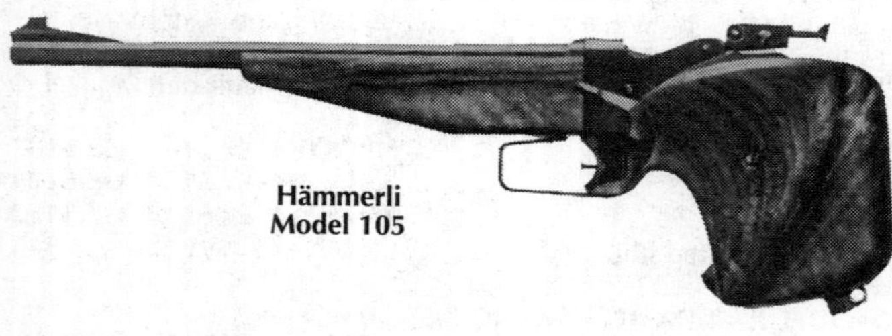

Hämmerli Model 105

GUNSITE — Paulden, Arizona

"ADVANCED TACTICAL" SA AUTO PISTOL
Manufactured w/Colt 1991 or Springfield 1991 parts. Caliber: .45 ACP. Eight-round magazine, 3.5-, 4.25-, 5-inch bbl. Weight: 32-38 oz. Checkered or laser-engraved walnut grips. Fixed or Novak Lo-mount sights.
Stainless finish . . . . NiB $1100 Ex $897 Gd $638
Blued finish . . . . NiB $972 Ex $795 Gd $568

"CUSTOM CARRY" SA AUTO PISTOL
Caliber: .45 ACP. Eight-round magazine, 3.5-, 4.25-, 5-inch bbl., Weight: 32-38 oz. Checkered or laser-engraved walnut grips. Fixed Novak Lo-mount sights. Single action, manufactured based on enhanced colt models.
Stainless finish . . . . NiB $1140 Ex $939 Gd $660
Blued finish . . . . NiB $1102 Ex $899 Gd $640

H&R 1871, INC. — Gardner, Massachusetts

NOTE: *In 1991, H&R 1871, Inc. was formed from the residual of the parent company, Harrington & Richardson, and then took over the New England Firearms facility. H&R 1871 produced firearms under both their logo and the NEF brand name until 1999, when the Marlin Firearms Company acquired the assets of H&R 1871. See listings under Harrington & Richardson, Inc.*

HÄMMERLI AG JAGD-UND SPORTWAFFE FABRIK — Lenzburg, Switzerland

Currently imported by Sigarms, Inc., Exeter, NH. Previously by Hammerli, USA; Beeman Precision Arms & Mandall Shooting Supplies.

MODEL 33MP FREE PISTOL . . . . . NiB $1022 Ex $816 Gd $532
System Martini single-shot action, set trigger. Caliber: .22 LR. 11.5-inch octagon bbl., 16.5 inches overall. Weight: 46 oz. Micrometer rear sight, interchangeable front sights. Blued finish. Walnut grips, forearm. Imported from 1933-49.

MODEL 100 FREE PISTOL
Same general specifications as Model 33MP. Improved action and sights, redesigned stock. Standard model has plain grips and forearm, deluxe model has carved grips and forearm. Imported from 1950-56.
Standard model . . . . NiB $878 Ex $734 Gd $517
Deluxe model . . . . NiB $1074 Ex $847 Gd $569

MODEL 101 . . . . NiB $956 Ex $740 Gd $565
Similar to Model 100 except has heavy round bbl. w/matte finish, improved action and sights, adj. grips. Weight: About 49 oz. Imported from 1956-60.

MODEL 102
Same as Model 101 except bbl., has highly polished blued finish. Deluxe model (illustrated) has carved grips and forearm. Made from 1956-60.
Standard model . . . . NiB $956 Ex $730 Gd $565
Deluxe model . . . . NiB $1070 Ex $843 Gd $565

MODEL 103 . . . . NiB $1005 Ex $845 Gd $500
Same as Model 101 except has lighter octagon bbl. (as in Model 100) w/highly polished blued finish, grips and forearm of select French walnut. Weight: About 46 oz. Imported from 1956-60.

MODEL 104 . . . . NiB $833 Ex $730 Gd $410
Similar to Model 102 except has lighter round bbl., improved action redesigned grips and forearm. Weight: 46 oz. Imported from 1961-65.

MODEL 105 . . . . NiB $1013 Ex $786 Gd $462
Similar to Model 103 except has improved action, redesigned grips and forearm. Imported from 1961-65.

MODEL 106 . . . . NiB $987 Ex $761 Gd $441
Similar to Model 104 except has improved trigger and grips. Made from 1966-71.

MODEL 107
Similar to Model 105 except has improved trigger and stock. Deluxe model (illustrated) has engraved receiver and bbl., carved grips and forearm. Imported from 1966-71.
Standard model . . . . NiB $1076 Ex $849 Gd $447
Deluxe model . . . . NiB $1416 Ex $1076 Gd $519

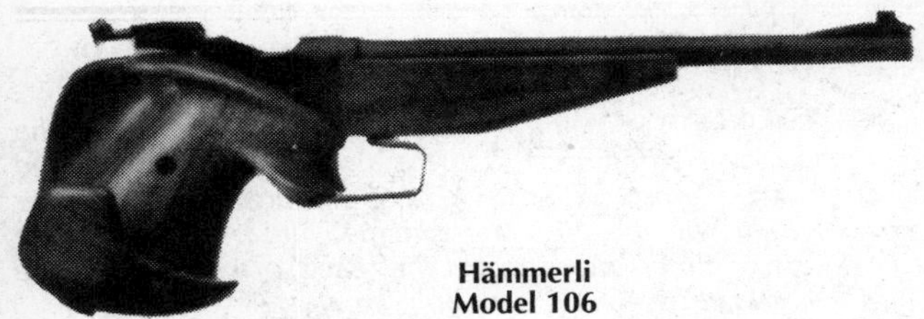
Hämmerli
Model 106

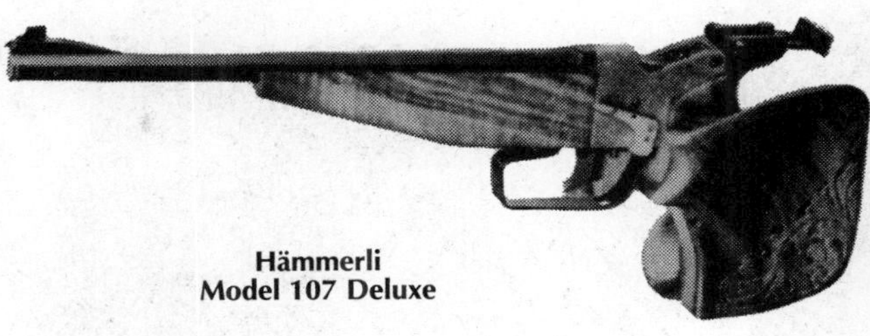
Hämmerli
Model 107 Deluxe

MODEL 120 HEAVY BARREL
Same as Models 120-1 and 120-2 except has 5.7-inch heavy bbl., weight: 41 oz. Available w/standard or adj. grips. Imported from 1972 to date.
W/standard grips. . . . . NiB $663 Ex $601 Gd $354
W/adj. grips. . . . . NiB $714 Ex $560 Gd $354

MODEL 120-1 SINGLE-SHOT FREE PISTOL . . . . NiB $663 Ex $601 Gd $354
Side lever-operated bolt action. Adj. single-stage or two-stage trigger. Caliber: .22 LR, 9.9-inch bbl., 14.75 inches overall. Weight: 44 oz. Micrometer rear sight, front sight on high ramp. Blued finish bbl., and receiver, lever and grip frame anodized aluminum. Checkered walnut thumbrest grips. Imported from 1972 to date.

MODEL 120-2 . . . . NiB $663 Ex $601 Gd $354
Same as Model 120-1 except has hand-contoured grips w/adj. palm rest (available for right or left hand). Imported from 1972 to date.

MODELS 150/151 FREE PISTOLS
Improved Martini-type action w/lateral-action cocking lever. Set trigger adj. for weight, length and angle of pull. Caliber: .22 LR, 11.3-inch round free-floating bbl., 15.4 inches overall. Weight: 43 oz. (w/extra weights, 49.5 oz.). Micrometer rear sight, front sight on high ramp. Blued finish. Select walnut forearm and grips w/adj. palm shelf. Imported from 1972-93.
Model 150 (disc. 1989) . . . . NiB $1986 Ex $1621 Gd $956
Model 151 (disc. 1993) . . . . NiB $1986 Ex $1621 Gd $956

MODEL 152 ELECTRONIC PISTOL
Same general specifications as Model 150 except w/electronic trigger. Made from 1990-92
Right hand . . . . NiB $2141 Ex $1734 Gd $1106
Left hand . . . . NiB $2012 Ex $1638 Gd $1160

MODELS 160/162 FREE PISTOLS
Caliber: .22 LR. Single-shot. 11.31-inch bbl., 17.5 inches overall. Weight: 46.9 oz. Interchangeable front sight blades, fully adj. match rear. Match-style stippled walnut grips w/adj. palm shelf and polycarbon fiber forend. Imported from 1993-2002.
Model 160 w/mechanical set trigger (disc. 2000) . . . . NiB $1785 Ex $1599 Gd $904
Model 162 w/electronic trigger. . . . . NiB $1914 Ex $1548 Gd $1078

MODEL 208 STANDARD AUTO PISTOL . . . . NiB $1728 Ex $1419 Gd $904
Caliber: .22 LR. Eight-round magazine, 5.9-inch bbl., 10 inches overall. Weight: 35 oz. (bbl. weight adds 3 oz.). Micrometer rear sight, ramp front. Blued finish. Checkered walnut grips w/adj. heel plate. Imported from 1966-88.

MODEL 208S TARGET PISTOL . . . . . NiB $1882 Ex $1419 Gd $775
Caliber: .22 LR. Eight-round magazine, 6-inch bbl., 10.2 inches overall. Weight: 37.3 oz. Micrometer rear sight, ramp front sight. Blued finish. Stippled walnut grips w/adj. heel plate. Imported from 1990 to date.

MODEL 211 . . . . NiB $1672 Ex $1390 Gd $788
Same as Model 208 except has standardd. thumbrest grips. Imported from 1966-91.

Hämmerli
Model 120 Heavy Barrel

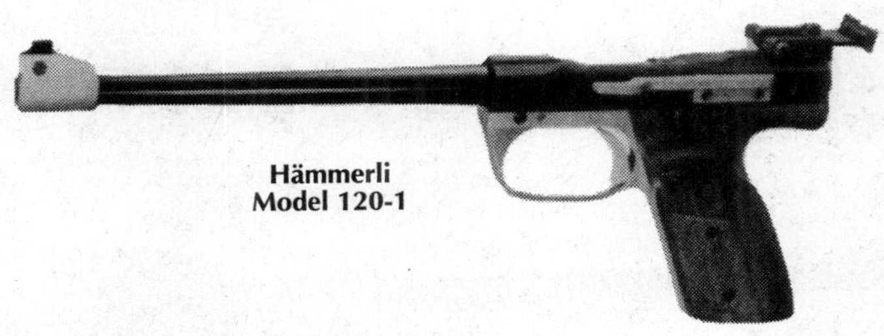
Hämmerli
Model 120-1

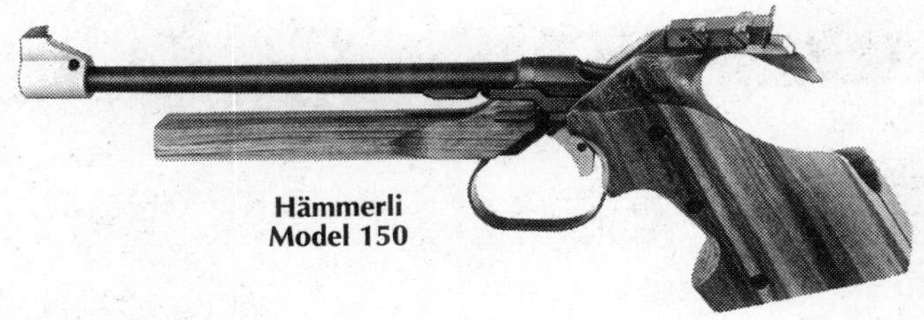
Hämmerli
Model 150

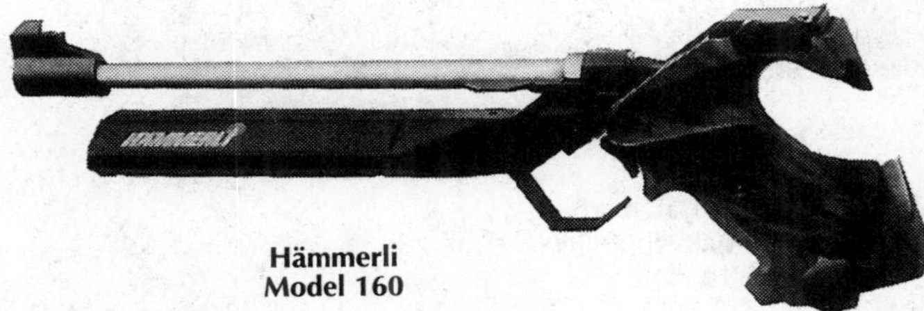

Hämmerli
Model 160

Hämmerli
Model 208

Hämmerli
Model 232 Rapid Fire

Hämmerli
Model 215

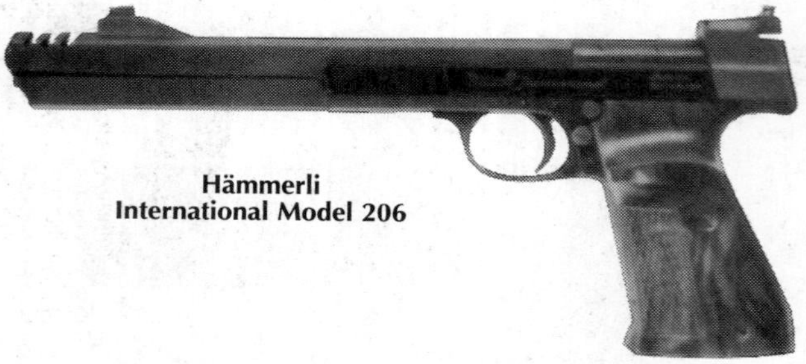

Hämmerli
International Model 206

Hämmerli
International Model 207

Hämmerli
International Model 210

MODEL 212
HUNTER'S PISTOL . . . . NiB $1363 Ex $1188 Gd $745
Caliber: .22 LR, 4.88-inch bbl., 8.5 inches overall. Weight: 31 oz. Blade front sight, square-notched fully adj. rear. Blued finish. Checkered walnut grips. Imported from 1984-93.

MODEL 215 . . . . NiB $1513 Ex $1157 Gd $658
Similar to the Model 208 except w/heavier bbl. and fewer deluxe features. Imported from 1990-93.

MODEL 230-1 RAPID FIRE
AUTO PISTOL . . . . NiB $1513 Ex $1235 Gd $745
Caliber: .22 Short. Five-round magazine, 6.3-inch bbl., 11.6 inches overall. Weight: 44 oz. Micrometer rear sight, post front. Blued finish. Smooth walnut thumbrest grips. Imported from 1970-83.

MODEL 230-2 RAPID FIRE
AUTO PISTOL . . . . NiB $806 Ex $724 Gd $714
Same as Model 230-1 except has checkered walnut grips w/adj. heel plate. Imported from 1970-83.

MODEL 232 RAPID FIRE
AUTO PISTOL . . . . NiB $1497 Ex $1219 Gd $729
Caliber: .22 Short. Six-round magazine, 5.1-inch ported bbl., 10.5 inches overall. Weight: 44 oz. Fully adj. target sights. Blued finish. Stippled walnut wraparound target grips. Imported from 1984-93.

INTERNATIONAL MODEL 206
AUTO PISTOL . . . . NiB $740 Ex $689 Gd $385
Calibers: .22 Short, .22 LR. Six-round (.22 Short) or 8-round (.22 LR) magazine, 7.1-inch bbl. w/muzzle brake, 12.5 inches overall. Weight: 33 oz. (.22 Short), 39 oz. (.22 LR) (supplementary weights add 5 and 8 oz.). Micrometer rear sight, ramp front. Blued finish. Standard thumbrest grips. Imported from 1962-69.

INTERNATIONAL MODEL 207
AUTO PISTOL . . . . NiB $792 Ex $714 Gd $431
Same as Model 206 except has grips w/adj. heel plate, weight: 2 oz. more. Made from 1962-69.

INTERNATIONAL MODEL 209
AUTO PISTOL . . . . NiB $871 Ex $778 Gd $547
Caliber: .22 Short. Five-round mag., 4.75-inch bbl., w/muzzle brake and gas-escape holes, 11 inches overall. Weight: 39 oz. (interchangeable front weight adds 4 oz.). Micrometer rear sight, post front. Blued finish. Standard thumbrest grips of checkered walnut. Imported from 1966-70.

INTERNATIONAL MODEL 210 . . . . NiB $871 Ex $783 Gd $588
Same as Model 209 except has grips w/adj. heel plate, is 0.8-inch longer and weighs 1 ounce more. Made from 1966-70.

MODEL 280 TARGET PISTOL
Carbon-reinforced synthetic frame and bbl., housing. Calibers: .22 LR, .32 S&W Long WC. Six-round (.22 LR) or 5-round (.32 S&W) magazine, 4.5-inch bbl. w/interchangeable metal or carbon fiber counterweights. 11.88 inches overall. Weight: 39 oz. Micro-adj. match sights w/interchangeable elements. Imported from 1988 to date.
.22 LR . . . . NiB $1574 Ex $1240 Gd $573
.32 S&W Long WC . . . . NiB $1736 Ex $1428 Gd $1035
.22/.32 Conversion kit, add $800

VIRGINIAN SA REVOLVER . . . . NiB $591 Ex $555 Gd $227
Similar to Colt Single-Action Army except has base pin safety system (SWISSAFE). Calibers: .357 Magnum, .45 Colt. Six-round cylinder. 4.63-, 5.5- or 7.5-inch bbl., 11 inches overall (with 5.5-inch bbl.). Weight: 40 oz. (with 5.5-inch bbl.). Fixed sights. Blued bbl. and cylinder, casehardened frame, chrome-plated grip frame and trigger guard. One-piece smooth walnut stock. Imported from 1973-76 by Interarms, Alexandria, Va.

WALTHER OLYMPIA MODEL 200 AUTOMATIC PISTOL, 1952-TYPE. . . . NiB $737 Ex $680 Gd $450
Similar to 1936 Walther Olympia Funfkampf model. Calibers: .22 Short, .22 LR. Six-round (.22 Short) or 10-round (.22 LR) magazine, 7.5-inch bbl., 10.7 inches overall. Weight: 27.7 oz. (.22 Short, light alloy breechblock), 30.3 oz. (.22 LR). Supplementary weights provided. Adj. target sights. Blued finish. Checkered walnut thumbrest grips. Imported from 1952-58.

WALTHER OLYMPIA MODEL 200,1958-TYPE . . . NiB $793 Ex $680 Gd $484
Same as Model 200 1952 type except has muzzle brake, 8-round magazine (.22 LR). 11.6 inches overall. Weight: 30 oz. (.22 Short), 33 oz. (.22 LR). Imported 1958-63.

WALTHER OLYMPIA MODEL 201 . . . . NiB $737 Ex $670 Gd $454
Same as Model 200,1952-Type except has 9.5-inch bbl. Imported from 1955-57.

WALTHER OLYMPIA MODEL 202 . . . . NiB $789 Ex $680 Gd $520
Same as Model 201 except has grips w/adjustable heel plate. Imported from 1955-57.

WALTHER OLYMPIA MODEL 203
Same as corresponding Model 200 (1955 type lacks muzzle brake) except has grips w/adjustable heel plate. Imported from 1955-63.
1955 type . . . . NiB $793 Ex $680 Gd $520
1958 type . . . . NiB $850 Ex $737 Gd $541

WALTHER OLYMPIA MODEL 204
American model. Same as corresponding Model 200 (1956-Type lacks muzzle brake) except in .22 LR only, has slide stop and micrometer rear sight. Imported from 1956-63.
1956-type . . . . NiB $827 Ex $714 Gd $565
1958-type . . . . NiB $884 Ex $771 Gd $570

WALTHER OLYMPIA MODEL 205
American model. Same as Model 204 except has grips w/adjustable heel plate. Imported from 1956-63.

Hämmerli-Walther Olympia Model 203 1958-Type

Hämmerli-Walther Olympia Model 205

SIG-Hämmerli Model P240 Target

1956-type . . . . NiB $893 Ex $780 Gd $579
1958-type . . . . NiB $950 Ex $837 Gd $610

MODEL P240 TARGET AUTO PISTOL
Calibers: .32 S&W Long (wadcutter), .38 Special (wadcutter). Five-round magazine, 5.9-inch bbl., 10 inches overall. Weight: 41 oz. Micrometer rear sight, post front. Blued finish/smooth walnut thumbrest grips. Accessory .22 LR conversion unit available. Imported from 1975-86.
.32 S&W Long . . . . NiB $1600 Ex $1343 Gd $7102
.38 Special. . . . . NiB $2264 Ex $1827 Gd $1269
.22 LR conversion unit, add . . . . NiB $606 Ex $550 Gd $380

Harrington & Richardson SL .32

HARRINGTON & RICHARDSON, INC. — Gardner, Massachusetts Now H&R 1871, Inc., Gardner, Mass.

Formerly Harrington & Richardson Arms Co. of Worcester, Mass. One of the oldest and most distinguished manufacturers of handguns, rifles and shotguns, H&R suspended operations on January 24, 1986. In 1987, New England Firearms was established as an independent company producing selected H&R models under the NEF logo. In 1991, H&R 1871, Inc., was formed from the residual of the parent company and then took over the New England Firearms facility. H&R 1871 produced firearms under both its logo and the NEF brand name until 1999, when the Marlin Firearms Company acquired the assets of H&R 1871.

NOTE: *For ease in finding a particular firearm, H&R handguns are grouped into Automatic/Single-Shot Pistols, followed by Revolvers. For a complete listing, please refer to the index.*

Harrington & Richardson USRA Model Single-Shot Target Pistol

AUTOMATIC/SINGLE-SHOT PISTOLS

SL .25 PISTOL . . . . NiB $422 Ex $377 Gd $208
Modified Webley & Scott design. Caliber: .25 Auto. Six-round magazine, 2-inch bbl., 4.5 inches overall. Weight: 12 oz. Fixed sights. Blued finish. Black hard rubber grips. Made from 1912-16.

SL .32 PISTOL . . . . NiB $377 Ex $361 Gd $193
Modified Webley & Scott design. Caliber: .32 Auto. Eight-round magazine, 3.5-inch bbl., 6.5 inches overall. Weight: About 20 oz. Fixed sights. Blued finish. Black hard rubber grips. Made from 1916-24.

USRA MODEL SINGLE-SHOT TARGET PISTOL . . . . NiB $499 Ex $473 Gd $269
Hinged frame. Caliber: .22 LR, bbl. lengths: 7-, 8- and 10-inch. Weight: 31 oz. w/10-inch bbl., Adj. target sights. Blued finish. Checkered walnut grips. Made from 1928-41.

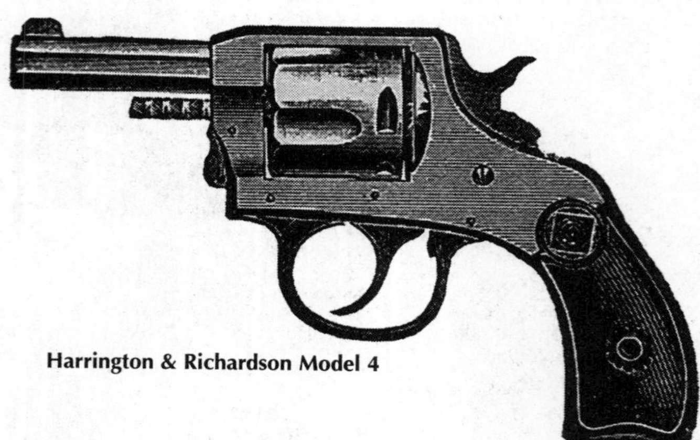
Harrington & Richardson Model 4

REVOLVERS

MODEL 4 (1904) DA . . . . NiB $118 Ex $108 Gd $57
Solid frame. Calibers: .32 S&W Long, .38 S&W. Six-round cylinder (.32 cal.), or 5-round (.38 cal.), bbl. Lengths: 2.5-, 4.5- and 6-inch. Weight: About 16 oz. (in .32 cal.) Fixed sights. Blued or nickel finish. Hard rubber grips. Disc. prior to 1942.

MODEL 5 (1905) DA. . . . . NiB $118 Ex $108 Gd $62
Solid frame. Caliber: .32 S&W. Five-round cylinder, bbl., lengths: 2.5-,4.5- and 6-inch. Weight: About 11 oz. Fixed sights. Blued or nickel finish. Hard rubber grips. Disc. prior to 1942.

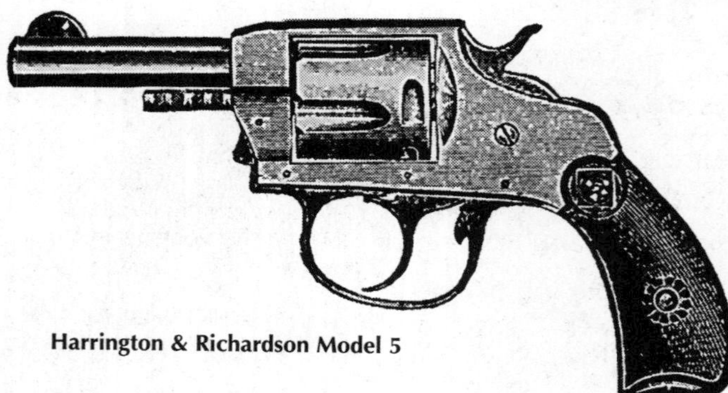
Harrington & Richardson Model 5

MODEL 6 (1906) DA. . . . . NiB $118 Ex $108 Gd $62
Solid frame. Caliber: .22 LR. Seven-round cylinder, bbl. lengths: 2.5, 4.5- and 6-inches. Weight: About 10 oz. Fixed sights. Blued or nickel finish. Hard rubber grips. Disc. prior to 1942.

.22 SPECIAL DA. . . . . NiB $189 Ex $164 Gd $92
Heavy hinged frame. Calibers: .22 LR, .22 Mag. Nine-round cylinder, 6-inch bbl., weight: 23 oz. Fixed sights, front gold-plated. Blued finish. Checkered walnut grips. Recessed safety cylinder on later models for high-speed ammunition. Disc. prior to 1942.

MODEL 199 SPORTSMAN SA REVOLVER . . . . **NiB $309 Ex $269 Gd $141**
Hinged frame. Caliber: .22 LR. Nine-round cylinder, 6-inch bbl., 11 inches overall. Weight: 30 oz. Adj. target sights. Blued finish. Checkered walnut grips. Disc. 1951.

MODEL 504 DA . . . . **NiB $188 Ex $168 Gd $122**
Caliber: .32 H&R Magnum. Five-round cylinder, 4- or 6-inch bbl., (square butt), 3- or 4-inch bbl., round butt. Made from 1984-86.

MODEL 532 DA . . . . **NiB $120 Ex $110 Gd $69**
Caliber: .32 H&R Magnum. Five-round cylinder, 2.5- or 4-inch bbl., weight: Approx. 20 and 25 oz. respectively. Fixed sights. American walnut grips. Lustre blued finish. Made from 1984-86.

MODEL 586 DA . . . . **NiB $198 Ex $178 Gd $122**
Caliber: .32 H&R Magnum. Five-round cylinder. bbl. lengths: 4.5, 5.5, 7.5, 10 inches. Weight: 30 oz. average. Adj. rear sight, blade front. Walnut finished hardwood grips. Made from 1984-86.

MODEL 603 TARGET . . . . **NiB $188 Ex $142 Gd $102**
Similar to Model 903 except in .22 WMR. Six-round capacity w/unfluted cylinder. Made from 1980-83.

MODEL 604 TARGET . . . . **NiB $193 Ex $153 Gd $102**
Similar to Model 603 except w/6-inch bull bbl., weight: 38 oz. Made from 1980-83.

MODEL 622/623 DA . . . . **NiB $136 Ex $116 Gd $70**
Solid frame. Caliber: .22 Short, Long, LR, 6-round cylinder. bbl., lengths: 2.5-, 4-, 6-inches. Weight: 26 oz. (with 4-inch bbl.). Fixed sights. Blued finish. Plastic grips. Made from 1957-86. Note: Model 623 is same except chrome or nickel finish.

MODEL 632/633 GUARDSMAN DA REVOLVER . . . . **NiB $125 Ex $101 Gd $66**
Solid Frame. Caliber: .32 S&W Long. Six-round cylinder, bbl., lengths: 2.5- or 4-inch. Weight: 19 oz. (with 2.5-inch bbl.). Fixed sights. Blued or chrome finish. Checkered Tenite grips (round butt on 2.5-inch, square butt on 4-inch). Made from 1953-86. Note: Model 633 is the same except for chrome or nickel finish.

MODEL 649/650 DA . . . . **NiB $164 Ex $143 Gd $83**
Solid frame. Side loading and ejection. Convertible model w/two 6-round cylinders. Calibers: .22 LR, .22 WMR. 5.5-inch bbl., Weight: 32 oz. Adj. rear sight, blade front. Blued finish. One-piece, Western-style walnut grip. Made from 1976-86. Note: Model 650 is same except nickel finish.

MODEL 666 DA . . . . **NiB $121 Ex $91 Gd $55**
Solid frame. Convertible model w/two 6-round cylinders. Calibers: .22 LR, .22 WMR. Six-inch bbl., weight: 28 oz. Fixed sights. Blued finish. Plastic grips. Made from 1976-78.

MODEL 676 DA . . . . **NiB $162 Ex $141 Gd $65**
Solid frame. Side loading and ejection. Convertible model w/two 6-round cylinders. Calibers: .22 LR, .22 WMR, bbl. lengths: 4.5, 5.5, 7.5, 12-inches. Weight: 32 oz. (with 5.5-inch bbl.). Adj. rear sight, blade front. Blued finish, color-casehardened frame. One-piece, Western-style walnut grip. Made from 1976-1980.

MODEL 686 DA . . . . **NiB $208 Ex $185 Gd $111**
Caliber: .22 LR and .22 WMR. Six-round magazine, 4.5, 5.5, 7.5, 10 or 12-inch bbl. Adj. rear sight, ramp and blade front. Blued, color-casehardened frame. Weight: 31 oz. (with 4.5-inch bbl.). Made from 1980-86.

Harrington & Richardson Model 6

Harrington & Richardson .22 Special

Harrington & Richardson Model 199 Sportsman

Harrington & Richardson Model 632

Harrington & Richardson Model 622

Harrington & Richardson Model 649

Harrington & Richardson Model 650

Harrington & Richardson Model 686

Harrington & Richardson Model 733

Harrington & Richardson Model 666

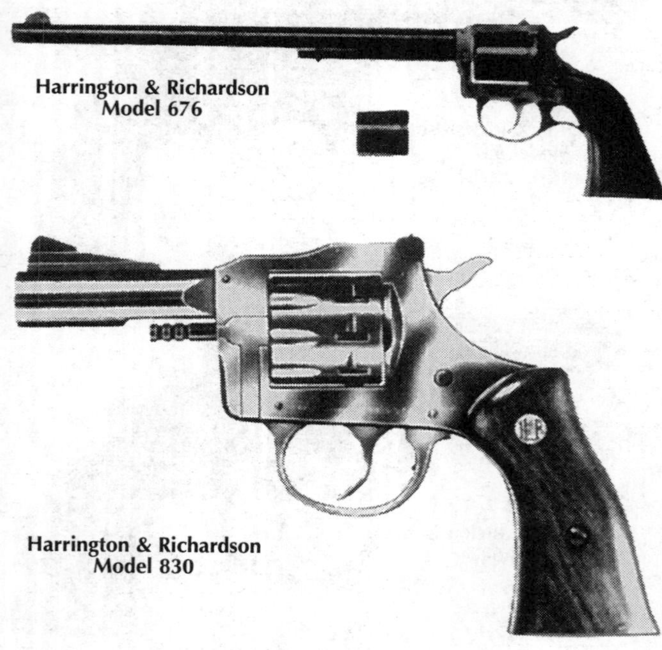

Harrington & Richardson Model 676

Harrington & Richardson Model 830

MODEL 732/733 DA. . . . . NiB $147 Ex $119 Gd $73
Solid frame, swing-out 6-round cylinder. Calibers: .32 S&W, .32 S&W Long. bbl., lengths: 2.5 and 4-inch. Weight: 26 oz. (with 4-inch bbl.). Fixed sights (windage adj. rear on 4-inch bbl. model). Blued finish. Plastic grips. Made from 1958-86. Note: Model 733 is the same except with nickel finish.

MODEL 826 DA . . . . NiB $150 Ex $124 Gd $78
Caliber: .22 WMR. Six-round magazine, 3-inch bull bbl., ramp and blade front sight, adj. rear. American walnut grips. Weight: 28 oz. Made from 1981-83.

MODEL 829/830 DA
Same as Model 826 except in .22 LR caliber. Nine round capacity. Made from 1981-83.
Model 829, blued . . . . NiB $150 Ex $129 Gd $83
Model 830, nickel . . . . NiB $155 Ex $134 Gd $88

MODEL 832,1833 DA
Same as Model 826 except in .32 SW Long. Blued or nickel finish. Made from 1981-83.
Model 832, blued . . . . NiB $168 Ex $143 Gd $88
Model 833, nickel . . . . NiB $165 Ex $149 Gd $93

MODEL 900/901 DA. . . . . NiB $109 Ex $104 Gd $63
Solid frame, snap-out cylinder. Calibers: .22 Short, Long, LR. Nine-round cylinder, bbl. lengths: 2.5, 4, and 6-inches. Weight: 26 oz. (with 6-inch bbl.). Fixed sights. Blued finish. Cycolac grips. Made from 1962-73. Note: Model 901 (disc. in 1963) is the same except has chrome finish and white Tenite grips.

MODEL 903 TARGET. . . . . NiB $172 Ex $157 Gd $101
Caliber: .22 LR. Nine round capacity. SA/DA, 6-inch target-weight flat-side bbl., swing-out cylinder. Weight: 35 oz. Blade front sight, adj. rear. American walnut grips. Made from 1980-83.

MODEL 904 TARGET. . . . . NiB $172 Ex $154 Gd $101
Similar to Model 903 except 4 or 6-inch bull bbl. Weight: 32 oz. with 4-inch bbl. Made from 1980-86.

Harrington & Richardson
Model 900

Harrington & Richardson
Model 925

MODEL 905
TARGET . . . . NiB $207 Ex $167 Gd $124
Same as Model 904 except w/4-inch bbl. only. Nickel finish. Made from 1981-83.

MODEL 922
DA REVOLVER
FIRST ISSUE. . . . . NiB $235 Ex $187 Gd $136
Solid frame. Caliber: .22 LR. Nine-round cylinder, 10-inch octagon bbl., (early model) or 6-inches, round bbl. (later production). Weight: 26 oz. (with 6-inch bbl.). Fixed sights. Blued finish. Checkered walnut grips. Safety cylinder on later models. Disc. prior to 1942.

MODEL 922/923
DA REVOLVER,
SECOND ISSUE. . . . . NiB $118 Ex $98 Gd $74
Solid frame. Caliber: .22 LR. Nine-round cylinder, bbl. lengths: 2.5, 4, and 6-inches. Weight: 24 oz. (with 4-inch bbl.). Fixed sights. Blued finish. Plastic grips. Made 1950-86. Note: Second Issue Model 922 has a different frame from that of the First Issue. Model 923 is same as Model 922, Second Issue except for nickel finish.

MODEL 925
DEFENDER . . . . NiB $162 Ex $134 Gd $99
DA. Hinged frame. Caliber: .38 S&W. Five-round cylinder, 2.5-inch bbl., weight: 22 oz. Adj. rear sight, fixed front. Blued finish. One-piece wraparound grip. Made from 1964-78.

MODEL 926 DA . . . . NiB $162 Ex $134 Gd $99
Hinged frame. Calibers: .22 LR, .38 S&W. Nine-round (.22 LR) or 5-round (.38) cylinder, 4-inch bbl., weight: 31 oz. Adj. rear sight, fixed front. Blued finish. Checkered walnut grips. Made from 1968-78.

Harrington & Richardson
Model 903

Harrington & Richardson
Model 905

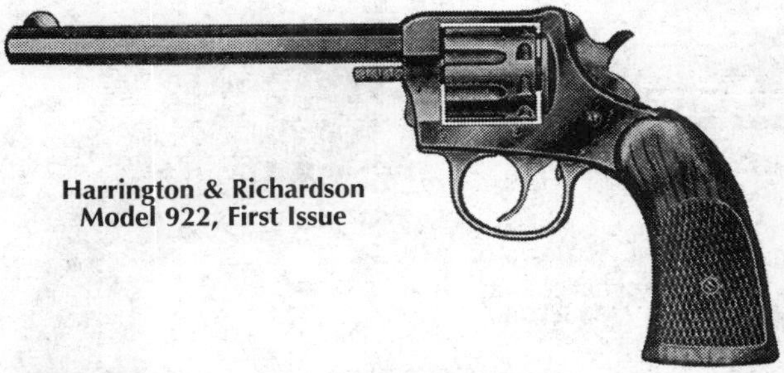

Harrington & Richardson
Model 922, First Issue

Harrington & Richardson
Model 922, Second Issue

Harrington & Richardson
Model 926

Harrington & Richardson
Model 939

Harrington & Richardson
Model 929

Harrington & Richardson
Model 949

Harrington & Richardson
Model 950

Harrington & Richardson
Model 999, First Issue

Harrington & Richardson
Model 999, Second Issue

MODEL 929/930
SIDEKICK DA REVOLVER. . . . . NiB $135 Ex $113 Gd $84
Caliber: .22 LR. Solid frame, swing-out 9-round cylinder, bbl. lengths: 2.5-, 4-, 6-inches. Weight: 24 oz. (with 4-inch bbl.). Fixed sights. Blued finish. Checkered plastic grips. Made from 1956-86. Note: Model 930 is same except with nickel finish.

MODEL 939/940
ULTRA SIDEKICK
DA REVOLVER. . . . . NiB $172 Ex $138 Gd $103
Solid frame, swing-out 9-round cylinder. Safety lock. Calibers: .22 Short, Long, LR. Flat-side 6-inch bbl. w/vent rib. Weight: 33 oz. Adj. rear sight, ramp front. Blued finish. Checkered walnut grips. Made 1958-86, reintroduced by H&R 1871 in 1992. Note: Model 940 is same except has round bbl.

MODEL 949/950
FORTY-NINER
DA REVOLVER. . . . . NiB $159 Ex $128 Gd $92
Solid frame. Side loading and ejection. Calibers: .22 Short, Long, LR. Nine-round cylinder, 5.5- or 7.5 inch bbl., weight: 31 to 38 oz. Adj. rear sight, blade front. Blued or nickel finish. One-piece, Western-style walnut grip. Made 1960-86, reintroduced by H&R 1871 in 1992-99. Note: Model 950 is same except has nickel finish.

MODEL 976 DA . . . . NiB $133 Ex $108 Gd $82
Same as Model 949 except has color-casehardened frame, 7.5-inch bbl. Weight: 36 oz. Intro. 1977. Disc.

HARRINGTON & RICHARDSON
MODEL 999 SPORTSMAN
DA REVOLVER, FIRST ISSUE. . . . . . NiB $230 Ex $189 Gd $123
Hinged frame. Calibers: .22 LR, .22 Mag. Same specifications as Model 199 Sportsman Single Action. Disc. before 1942.

MODEL 999 SPORTSMAN
DA REVOLVER
SECOND ISSUE. . . . . NiB $247 Ex $201 Gd $130
Hinged frame. Caliber: .22 LR. Nine-round cylinder, 6-inch bbl. w/vent rib. Weight: 30 oz. Adj. sights. Blued finish. Checkered walnut grips. Made from 1950-86.

(NEW) MODEL 999
SPORTSMAN
DA REVOLVER. . . . . NiB $245 Ex $201 Gd $146
Hinged frame. Caliber: .22 Short, Long, LR. Nine-round cylinder. Six-inch bbl. w/vent rib. Weight: 30 oz. Blade front sight adj. for elevation, square-notched rear adj. for windage. Blued finish. Checkered hardwood grips. Reintroduced by H&R 1871 in 1992.

AMERICAN DA .... NiB $114 Ex $94 Gd $70
Solid frame. Calibers: .32 S&W Long, .38 S&W. Six-round (.32 cal.) or 5-round (.38 cal.) cylinder, bbl. lengths: 2.5-,4.5- and 6-inches. Weight: About 16 oz. Fixed sights. Blued or nickel finish. Hard rubber grips. Disc. prior to 1942.

AUTOMATIC EJECTING DA REVOLVER..... NiB $191 Ex $156 Gd $110
Hinged frame. Calibers: .32 S&W Long, .38 S&W. Six-round (.32 cal.) or 5-round (.38 cal.) cylinder, bbl. lengths: 3.25-, 4-, 5- and 6-inches. Weight: 16 oz. (.32 cal.), 15 oz. (.38 cal.). Fixed sights. Blued or nickel finish. Black hard rubber grips. Disc. prior to 1942.

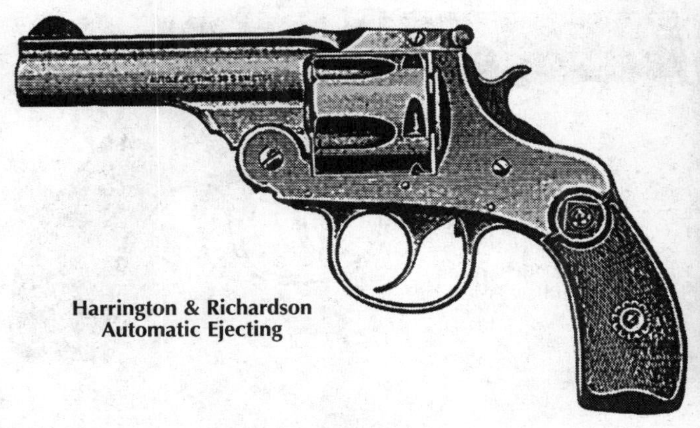

Harrington & Richardson
Automatic Ejecting

BOBBY DA .... NiB $329 Ex $273 Gd $181
Hinged frame. Calibers: .32 S&W, .38 S&W. Six-round cylinder (.32 cal.) or 5-round (.38 cal.). Four-inch bbl., 9 inches overall. Weight: 23 oz. Fixed sights. Blued finish. Checkered walnut grips. Disc. 1946. Note: Originally designed and produced for use by London's bobbies.

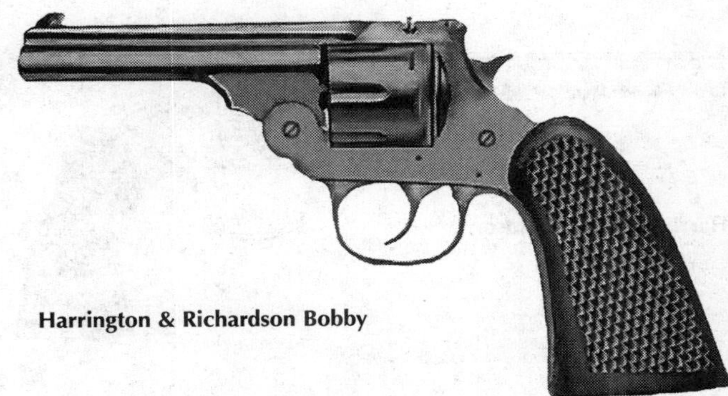

Harrington & Richardson Bobby

DEFENDER .38 DA .... NiB $168 Ex $137 Gd $96
Hinged frame. Based on the Sportsman design. Caliber: .38 S&W. Bbl. lengths: 4- and 6-inches, 9 inches overall (with 4-inch bbl.). Weight: 25 oz. with 4-inch bbl. Fixed sights. Blued finish. Black plastic grips. Disc. 1946. Note: This model was manufactured during WW II as an arm for plant guards, auxiliary police, etc.

EXPERT MODEL DA .... NiB $212 Ex $173 Gd $124
Same specifications as .22 Special except has 10-inch bbl., weight: 28 oz. Disc. prior to 1942.

HAMMERLESS DA, LARGE FRAME....... NiB $145 Ex $120 Gd $104
Hinged frame. Calibers: .32 S&W Long 38 S&W. Six-round (.32 cal.), or 5-round (.38 cal.) cylinder, bbl. lengths: 3.25, 4, and 6-inches. Weight: About 17 oz. Fixed sights. Blued or nickel finish. Hard rubber grips. Disc. prior to 1942.

Harrington & Richardson
Defender .38

HAMMERLESS DA, SMALL FRAME........ NiB $145 Ex $120 Gd $87
Hinged frame. Calibers: .22 LR, .32 S&W. Seven-round (.22 cal.) or 5-round (.32 cal.) cylinder, bbl. lengths: 2, 3, 4, 5 and 6-inches. Weight: About 13 oz. Fixed sights. Blued or nickel finish. Hard rubber grips. Disc. prior to 1942.

HUNTER MODEL DA .... NiB $161 Ex $131 Gd $89
Solid frame. Caliber: .22 LR. Nine-round cylinder, 10-inch octagon bbl., weight: 26 oz. Fixed sights. Blued finish. Checkered walnut grips. Safety cylinder on later models. Note: An earlier Hunter Model was built on the smaller 7-round frame. Disc. prior to 1942.

NEW DEFENDER DA............ NiB $285 Ex $229 Gd $168
Hinged frame. Caliber: .22 LR. Nine-round cylinder, 2-inch bbl., 6.25 inches overall. Weight: 23 oz. Adj. sights. Blued finish. Checkered walnut grips, round butt. Note: Basically, this is the Sportsman DA w/a short bbl., Disc. prior to 1942.

PREMIER DA .... NiB $124 E $109 Gd $78
Small hinged frame. Calibers: .22 LR, .32 S&W. Seven-round (.22 LR) or 5-round (.32) cylinder. Bbl. Lengths: 2, 3, 4, 5, and 6-inches. Weight: 13 oz. (in .22 LR), 12 oz. (in .32 S&W). Fixed sights. Blued or nickel finish. Black hard rubber grips. Disc. prior to 1942.

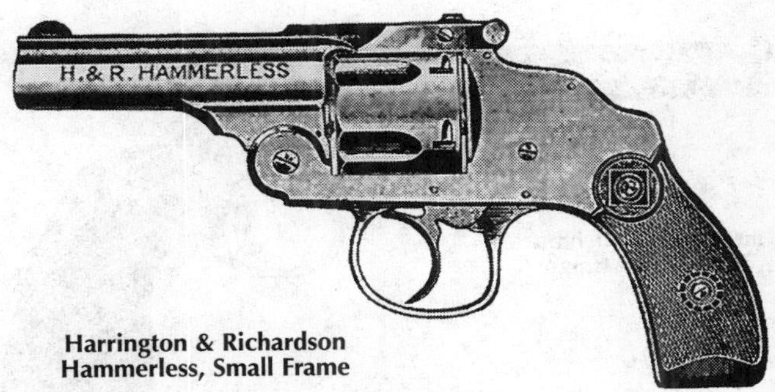

Harrington & Richardson
Hammerless, Small Frame

MODEL STR 022 BLANK REVOLVER .... NiB $99 Ex $83 Gd $62
Caliber: .22 RF blanks. Nine-round cylinder, 2.5-inch bbl. Weight: 19 oz. Satin blued finish.

MODEL STR 032 BLANK REVOLVER .... NiB $113 Ex $93 Gd $69
Same general specifications as STR 022 except chambered for .32 S&W blank cartridges.

Harrington & Richardson Premier

Harrington & Richardson Vest Pocket

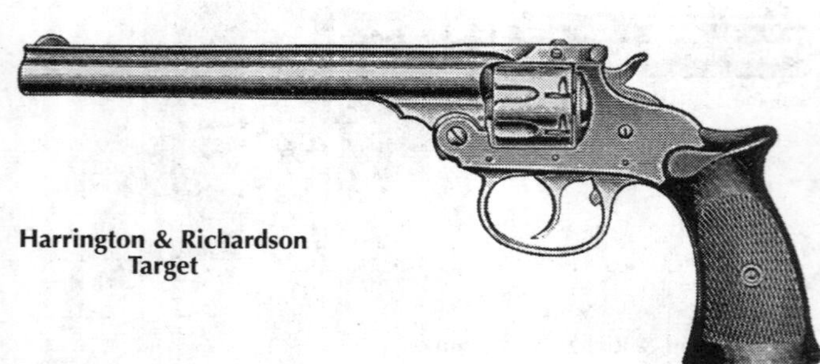
Harrington & Richardson Target

Harrington & Richardson Young American

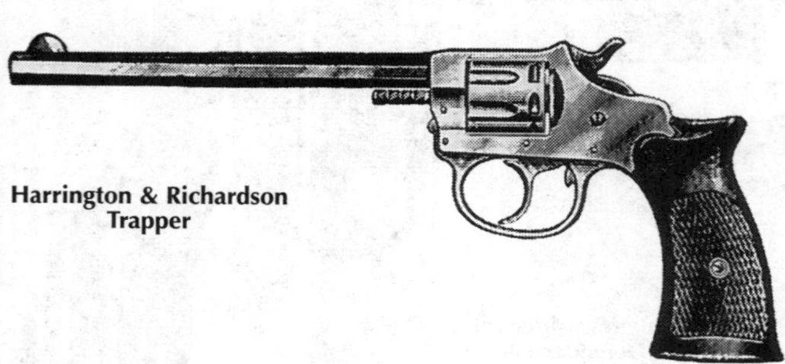
Harrington & Richardson Trapper

Harrington & Richardson Ultra Sportsmen

TARGET MODEL DA . . . . NiB $185 Ex $152 Gd $109
Small hinged frame. Calibers: .22 LR, .22 W.R.F. Seven-round cylinder, 6-inch bbl., weight: 16 oz. Fixed sights. Blued finish. Checkered walnut grips. Disc. prior to 1942.

TRAPPER MODEL DA . . . . NiB $172 Ex $141 Gd $101
Solid frame. Caliber: .22 LR. Seven-round cylinder, 6-inch octagon bbl., weight: 12.5 oz. Fixed sights. Blued finish. Checkered walnut grips. Safety cylinder on later models. Disc. prior to 1942.

ULTRA SPORTSMAN. . . . . NiB $252 Ex $203 Gd $152
SA. Hinged frame. Caliber: .22 LR. Nine-round cylinder, 6-inch bbl., weight: 30 oz. Adj. target sights. Blued finish. Checkered walnut grips. This model has short action, wide hammer spur, cylinder is length of a .22 LR cartridge. Disc. prior to 1942.

VEST POCKET DA . . . . NiB $114 Ex $94 Gd $70
Solid frame. Spurless hammer. Calibers: .22 Rimfire, .32 S&W. Seven-round (.22 cal.) or 5-round (.32 cal.) cylinder, 1.13-inch bbl., weight: About 9 oz. Blued or nickel finish. Hard rubber grips. Disc. prior to 1942.

YOUNG AMERICA DA . . . . NiB $114 Ex $94 Gd $70
Solid frame. Calibers: .22 Long, .32 S&W. Seven-round (.22 cal.) or 5-round (.32 cal.) cylinder. Bbl. lengths: 2-, 4.5- and 6-inches. Weight: About 9 oz. Fixed sights. Blued or nickel finish. Hard rubber grips. Disc. prior to 1942.

HARTFORD ARMS & EQUIPMENT CO. — Hartford, Connecticut

Hartford pistols were the forebearer of the original High Standard line. High Standard Mfg. Corp. acquired Hartford Arms & Equipment Co. in 1932. The High Standard Model B is essentially the same as the Hartford Automatic.

AUTOMATIC TARGET PISTOL. . . . . NiB $703 Ex $577 Gd $399
Caliber. .22 LR. 10-round magazine, 6.75-inch bbl., 10.75 inches overall. Weight: 31 oz. Target sights. Blued finish. Black rubber grips. This gun closely resembles the early Colt Woodsman and High Standard pistols. Made from 1929-30.

REPEATING PISTOL. . . . . NiB $546 Ex $445 Gd $316
Same general design as the automatic pistol of this manufacture, but this model is a hand-operated repeating pistol on the order of the Fiala. Made from 1929-30.

SINGLE-SHOT TARGET PISTOL. . . . NiB $538 Ex $435 Gd $297
Similar in appearance to the Hartford Automatic. Caliber: .22 LR, 6.75-inch bbl., 10.75 inches overall. Weight: 38 oz. Target sights. Mottled frame and slide, blued bbl., Black rubber or walnut grips. Made from 1929-30.

HASKELL MANUFACTURING — Lima, Ohio

See listings under Hi-Point.

HAWES FIREARMS — Van Nuys, California

DEPUTY MARSHAL SA REVOLVER
Calibers: .22 LR, also .22 WMR in two-cylinder combination. Six-round cylinder, 5.5-inch bbl., 11 inches overall. Weight: 34 oz. Adj. rear sight, blade front. Blued finish. Plastic or walnut grips. Imported from 1973-81.
.22 LR (plastic grips) . . . . NiB $105 Ex $86 Gd $65
Combination, .22 LR/.22 WMR (plastic). . . . . NiB $111 Ex $91 Gd $67
Walnut grips, add. $10

DEPUTY DENVER MARSHAL
Same as Deputy Marshal SA except has brass frame. Imported from 1973-81.
.22 LR (plastic grips). . . . . NiB $111 Ex $91 Gd $67
Combination, .22 LR/.22 WMR (plastic). . . . . NiB $111 Ex $91 Gd $67
Walnut grips add $10

DEPUTY MONTANA MARSHAL
Same as Deputy Marshal except has brass grip frame. Walnut grips only. Imported from 1973-81.
.22 LR . . . . NiB $142 Ex $117 Gd $86
Combination, .22 LR/.22 WMR . . . . . NiB $168 Ex $137 Gd $99

DEPUTY SILVER CITY MARSHAL
Same as Deputy Marshal except has chrome-plated frame, brass grip frame, blued cylinder and bbl., Imported from 1973-81.
.22 LR (plastic grips). . . . . NiB $117 Ex $100 Gd $66
Combination, .22 LR/.22 WMR (plastic). . . . NiB $137 Ex $117 Gd $86
Walnut grips add $10

DEPUTY TEXAS MARSHAL
Same as Deputy Marshal except has chrome finish. Imported from 1973-81.
.22 LR (plastic grips). . . . . NiB $122 Ex $107 Gd $81
Combination, .22 LR/.22 WMR (plastic). . . . NiB $153 Ex $132 Gd $91
Walnut grips add. $10

FAVORITE SINGLE-SHOT TARGET PISTOL. . NiB $165 Ex $110 Gd $70
Replica of Stevens No. 35. Tip-up action. Caliber: .22 LR. Eight-inch bbl., 12 inches overall. Weight: 24 oz. Target sights. Chrome-plated frame. Blued bbl., Plastic or rosewood grips (add $5). Imported from1972-76.

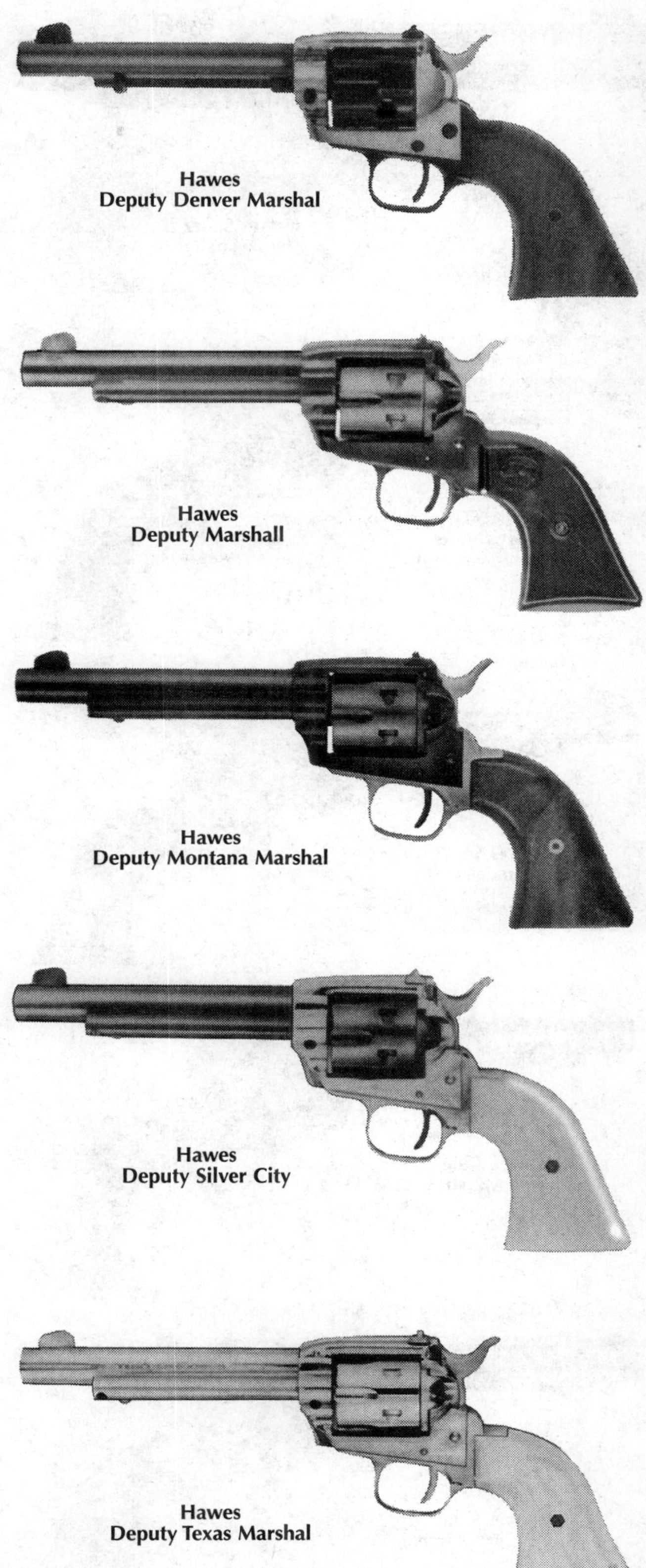

Hawes
Deputy Denver Marshal

Hawes
Deputy Marshall

Hawes
Deputy Montana Marshal

Hawes
Deputy Silver City

Hawes
Deputy Texas Marshal

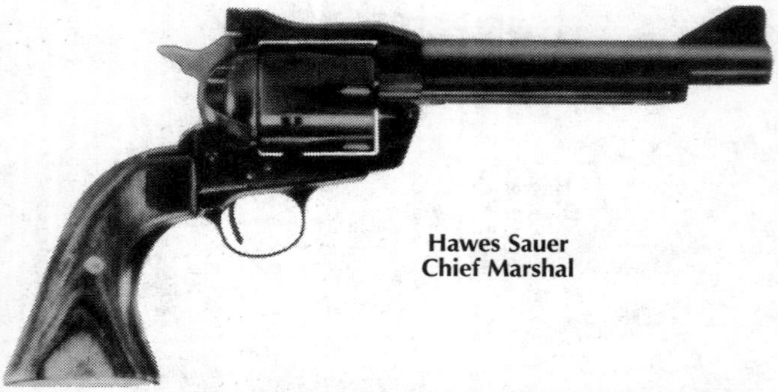

Hawes Sauer
Chief Marshal

Hawes Sauer
Texas Marshal

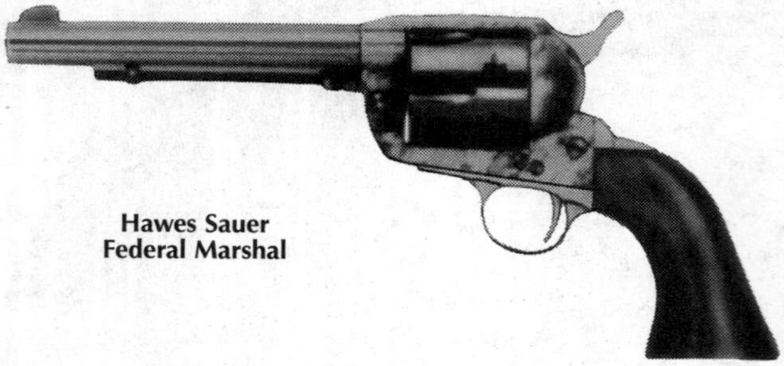

Hawes Sauer
Federal Marshal

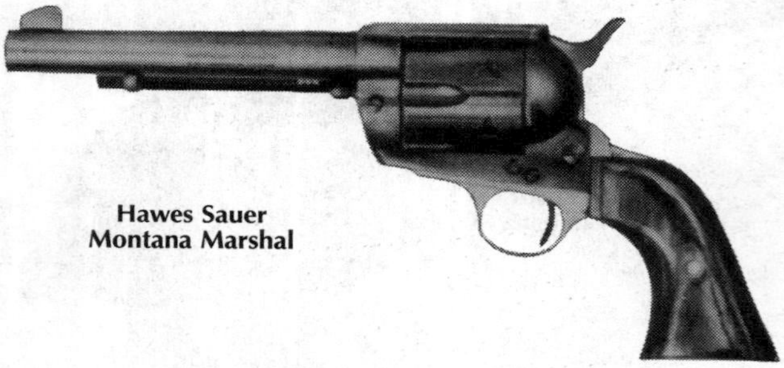

Hawes Sauer
Montana Marshal

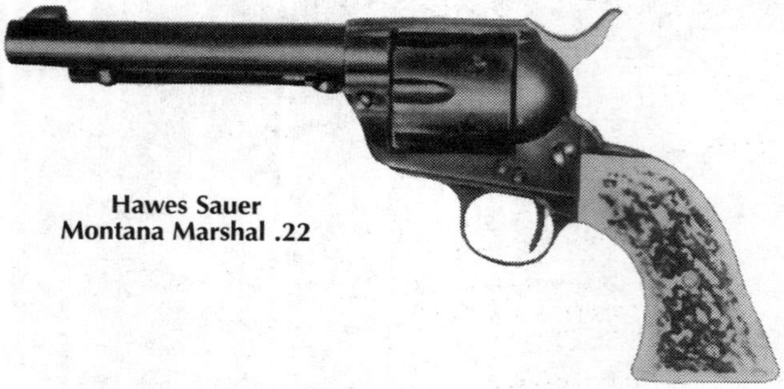

Hawes Sauer
Montana Marshal .22

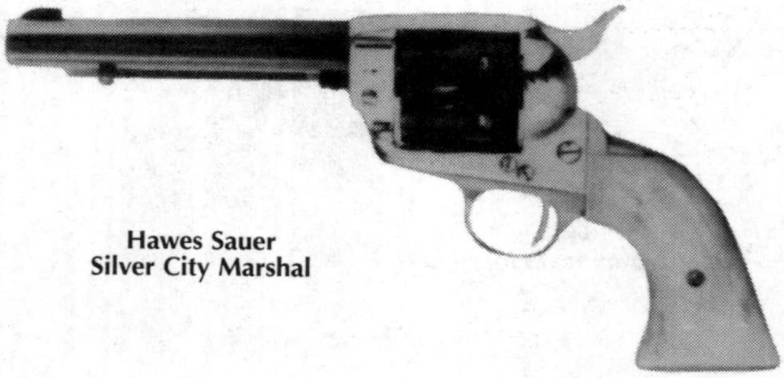

Hawes Sauer
Silver City Marshal

SAUER CHIEF MARSHAL SA TARGET REVOLVER

Same as Western Marshal except has adjustable rear sight and front sight, oversized rosewood grips. Not made in .22 caliber. Imported from 1973-81.

.357 Magnum or .45 Colt . . . . NiB $287 Ex $236 Gd $171
.44 Magnum . . . . NiB $319 Ex $261 Gd $188
Combination .357 Magnum
and 9mm Para.
.45 Colt and .45 Auto . . . . NiB $318 Ex $272 Gd $159
Combination
.44 Magnum and .44-40 . . . . NiB $312 Ex $261 Gd $185

SAUER FEDERAL MARSHAL

Same as Western Marshal except has color-casehardened frame, brass grip frame, one-piece walnut grip. Not made in .22 caliber. Imported from 1973-81.

.357 Magnum or .45 Colt . . . . NiB $272 Ex $221 Gd $159
.44 Magnum . . . . NiB $307 Ex $241 Gd $167
Combination
.357 Magnum and 9mm Para.,
.45 Colt and .45 Auto . . . . NiB $318 Ex $273 Gd $160
Combination .44 Magnum and .44-40 . . . . NiB $313 Ex $262 Gd $186

SAUER MONTANA MARSHAL

Same as Western Marshal except has brass grip frame. Imported from 1973-81.

.357 Magnum or .45 Colt . . . . NiB $287 Ex $236 Gd $171
.44 Magnum . . . . NiB $319 Ex $261 Gd $188
Combination .357 Magnum and 9mm Para.,
.45 Colt and .45 Auto . . . . NiB $341 Ex $280 Gd $201
Combination .44 Magnum and .44-40 . . . . NiB $354 Ex $290 Gd $208
.22 LR . . . . NiB $280 Ex $230 Gd $167
Combination .22 LR and .22 WMR . . . . NiB $299 Ex $245 Gd $177

SAUER SILVER CITY MARSHAL

Same as Western Marshal except has nickel plated frame, brass grip frame, blued cylinder and barrel, pearlite grips. Imported from 1973-81.

.44 Magnum . . . . NiB $344 Ex $283 Gd $204
Combination .357 Magnum and 9mm Para.
.45 Colt and .45 Auto . . . . NiB $318 Ex $247 Gd $165
Combination .44 Magnum and .44-40 . . . . NiB $344 Ex $258 Gd $191

SAUER TEXAS MARSHAL

Same as Western Marshal except nickel plated, has pearlite grips. Imported from 1973-81.

.357 Magnum or .45 Colt . . . . NiB $320 Ex $262 Gd $189
.44 Magnum . . . . NiB $339 Ex $278 Gd $199
Combination .357 Magnum and 9mm Para.,
.45 Colt and .45 Auto . . . . NiB $364 Ex $298 Gd $214
Combination .44 Magnum and .44-40 . . . . NiB $384 Ex $313 Gd $224
.22 LR . . . . NiB $282 Ex $232 Gd $169
Combination .22 LR and .22 WMR . . . . NiB $312 Ex $242 Gd $171

SAUER WESTERN MARSHAL SA REVOLVER
Calibers: .22 LR (disc.), .357 Magnum, .44 Magnum, .45 Auto. Also in two-cylinder combinations: .22 WMR (disc.), 9mm Para., .44-40, .45 Auto. Six-round cylinder, bbl. lengths: 5.5-inch (disc.), 6-inch, 11.75 inches overall (with 6-inch bbl.). Weight: 46 oz. Fixed sights. Blued finish. Originally furnished w/simulated stag plastic grips. Recent production has smooth rosewood grips. Made from 1968 by J. P. Sauer & Sohn, Eckernforde, Germany. Imported from 1973-81.
.357 Magnum or .45 Colt . . . . NiB $292 Ex $237 Gd $172
.44 Magnum . . . . NiB $327 Ex $272 Gd $192
Combination .357 Magnum and 9mm Para.,
.45 Colt and .45 Auto . . . . NiB $308 Ex $252 Gd $186
Combination .44 Magnum
and .44-40. NiB $339 Ex $278 Gd $199
.22 LR . . . . NiB $237 Ex $186 Gd $146
Combination .22 LR
and .22 WMR . . . . NiB $257 Ex $222 Gd $166

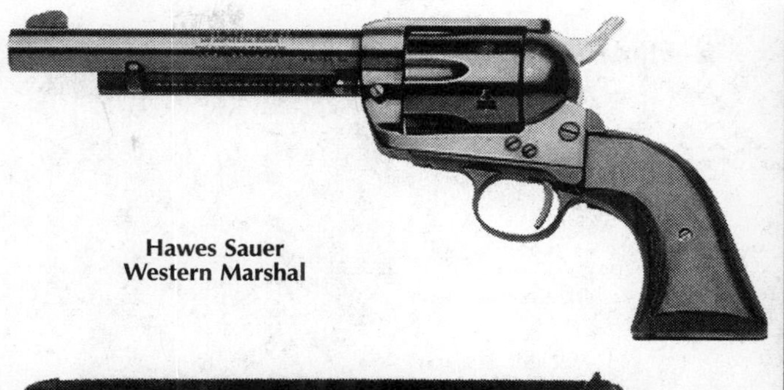
Hawes Sauer Western Marshal

HECKLER & KOCH — Oberndorf/Neckar, West Germany, and Chantilly, Virginia

MODEL HK4 DA AUTO PISTOL
Calibers: .380 Automatic (9mm Short), .22 LR, .25 Automatic (6.35mm), .32 Automatic (7.65mm) w/conversion kits. Seven-round magazine (.380 Auto), 8-round in other calibers, 3.4-inch bbl., 6.19 inches overall. Weight: 18 oz. Fixed sights. Blued finish. Plastic grip. Disc. 1984.
.22 LR or .380 Automatic . . . . . . NiB $443 Ex $350 Gd $2242
.25 ACP or .32 ACP Automatic . . . . NiB $443 Ex $350 Gd $242
.380 Automatic w/.22
conversion unit . . . . NiB $555 Ex $453 Gd $323
.380 Automatic w/.22, .25, .32
conversion units . . . . NiB $757 Ex $617 Gd $438

Heckler & Koch Model HK4

MODEL MARK 23
DA AUTO PISTOL . . . . NiB $2252 Ex $1726 Gd $1195
Short-recoil semiautomatic pistol w/polymer frame and steel slide. Caliber: .45 ACP. 10-round magazine, 5.87-inch bbl., 9.65 inches overall. Weight: 43 oz. Seven interchangeable rear sight adjustment units w/3-dot system. Developed primarily in response to specifications by the Special Operations Command (SOCOM) for a Special Operations Forces Offensive Handgun Weapon System. Imported from 1996 to date.

Heckler & Koch Mark 23

MODEL P7K3 DA
AUTO PISTOL
Caliber: .380 ACP. Eight-round magazine, 3.8 inch-bbl., 6.3 inches overall. Weight: About 26 oz. Adj. rear sight. Imported from 1988-94.
P7K3 in .380 Cal. . . . . NiB $903 Ex $743 Gd $516
.22 LR conversion kit. . . . . NiB $671 Ex $578 Gd $403
.32 ACP conversion kit . . . . NiB $357 Ex $305 Gd $213

MODEL P7M8 . . . . NiB $940 Ex $754 Gd $538
Squeeze-cock SA semiautomatic pistol. Caliber: 9mm Para. Eight-round magazine, 4.13-inch bbl., 6.73 inches overall. Weight: 29.9 oz. Matte black or nickel finish. Adjustable rear sight. Imported from 1985 to date.

MODEL P7M10
Caliber: .40 S&W. Nine-round magazine, 4.2-inch bbl., 6.9 inches overall. Weight: 43 oz. Fixed front sight blade, adj. rear w/3-dot system. Imported from 1992-94.
Blued finish . . . . NiB $1103 Ex $851 Gd $609
Nickel finish . . . . NiB $1113 Ex $861 Gd $519

Heckler & Koch Model P7K3

Heckler & Koch
Model P7M13

Heckler & Koch USP45

Heckler & Koch
Model P7 (PSP)

Heckler & Koch
Model P9S DA

MODEL P7M13 . . . . NiB $983 Ex $782 Gd $561
Caliber: 9mm. 13-round magazine, 4.13-inch bbl., 6.65 inches overall. Weight: 34.42 oz. Matte black finish. Adj. rear sight. Imported 1985-94.

MODEL P7(PSP)
AUTO PISTOL . . . . NiB $820 Ex $667 Gd $471
Caliber: 9mm Para. Eight-round magazine, 4.13-inch bbl., 6.54 inches overall. DA. Weight: About 33.5 oz. Blued finish. Imported 1983-85 and again in 1990 with limited availability.

MODEL P9S
DA AUTOMATIC PISTOL
Calibers: 9mm Para., .45 Automatic. Nine-round (9mm) or 7-round (.45 Auto) magazine. Four-inch bbl., 7.63 inches overall. Weight: 32 ounces. Fixed sights. Blued finish. Contoured plastic grips. This model disc. 1986.
9mm . . . . NiB $800 Ex $615 Gd $446
.45 Automatic . . . . NiB $816 Ex $672 Gd $461

MODEL P9S TARGET COMPETITION KIT
Same as Model P9S Target except comes w/extra 5.5-inch bbl. and bbl. weights. Also available w/walnut competition grip.
W/standard grip . . . . NiB $1222 Ex $944 Gd $696
W/competition grip. . . . . NiB $1293 Ex $1047 Gd $734

MODEL SP89. . . . . NiB $3898 Ex $3125 Gd $2147
Semiautomatic, recoil-operated, delayed roller-locked bolt system. Caliber: 9mm Para. 15-round magazine, 4.5-inch bbl., 13 inches overall. Weight: 68 oz. Hooded front sight, adj. rotary-aperture rear. Imported 1989-93.

MODEL USP
AUTO PISTOL
Polymer integral grip/frame design w/recoil reduction system. Calibers: 9mm Para., .40 S&W or .45 ACP. 15-round (9mm) or 13-round (.40 S&W and .45ACP) magazine, 4.13- or 4.25-inch bbl., 6.88 to 7.87 inches overall. Weight: 26.5-30.4 oz. Blade front sight, adj. rear w/3-dot system. Matte black or stainless finish. Stippled black polymer grip. Available in SA/DA or DAO. Imported 1993 to date.
Matte
Black finish . . . . NiB $713 Ex $549 Gd $394
Stainless. NiB $656 Ex $533 Gd $377
W/Tritium sights, add $95
W/ambidextrous decocking lever, add $20

Heckler & Koch Model USP45
Compact 50th Anniversary

Heckler & Koch
Model USP9 Compact (Stainless)

MODEL USP9 COMPACT
Caliber: 9mm. 10-round magazine, 4.25-inch bbl., 7.64 inches overall. Weight: 25.5 oz. Short recoil w/modified Browning action. 3-dot sighting system. Polymer frame w/integral grips. Imported from 1997 to date.
Blued finish . . . . NiB $663 Ex $550 Gd $385
Stainless finish . . . . NiB $699 Ex $575 Gd $405
W/ambidextrous
decocking lever, add $15

MODEL USP40 COMPACT
Caliber: .40 S&W. 10-round magazine, 3.58- inch bbl., 6.81 inches overall. Weight: 27 oz. Short recoil w/modified Browning action. 3-dot sighting system. Polymer frame w/integral grips. Imported from 1997 to date.
Blued finish . . . . NiB $714 Ex $586 Gd $390
Stainless finish . . . . NiB $761 Ex $611 Gd $405
W/ambidextrous
decocking lever, add $15

MODEL USP45 COMPACT
Caliber: .45 ACP. Eight-round magazine, 3.8- inch bbl., 7.09 inches overall. Weight: 28 oz. Short recoil w/modified Browning action. 3-dot sighting system. Polymer frame w/integral grips. Imported from 1998 to date.
Blued finish . . . . NiB $714 Ex $586 Gd $390
Stainless finish . . . . NiB $761 Ex $611 Gd $405
W/ambidextrous
decocking lever, add $15
50th Anniversary
(1 of 1,000) . . . . NiB $1347 Ex $1091 Gd $663

Heckler & Koch
Model USP357 Compact

MODEL
USP EXPERT . . . . NiB $1410 Ex $1070 Gd $792
Caliber: .45 ACP. 10-round magazine, 6.2- inch bbl., 9.65 inches overall. Weight: 30 oz. Adjustable 3-dot target sights. Short recoil modified Browning action w/recoil reduction system. Reinforced polymer frame w/integral grips and match-grade slide. Imported from 1999 to date.

Heckler & Koch
Model USP Expert

MODEL USP
TACTICAL . . . . NiB $1128 Ex $886 Gd $603
SOCOM Enhanced version of the USP Standard Model, w/4.92-inch threaded bbl. Chambered for .45 ACP only. Imported from 1998 to date.

Heckler & Koch
Model USP Tactical

Heckler & Koch Model VP 7OZ

Heritage Rough Rider

Heritage Sentry

MODEL VP 70Z AUTO PISTOL . . . . NiB $607 Ex $479 Gd $350
Caliber: 9mm Para. 18-round magazine, 4.5-inch bbl., 8 inches overall. Weight: 32.5 oz. DA Fixed sights. Blued slide, plastic receiver and grip. Disc. 1986.

HELWAN PISTOLS

See listings under Interarms.

HERITAGE MANUFACTURING — Opa Locka, Florida

MODEL HA25 AUTO PISTOL
Caliber: .25 ACP. Six-round magazine, 2.5-inch bbl., 4.63 inches overall. Weight: 12 oz. Fixed sights. Blued or chrome finish. Made from 1993 to date.
Blued . . . . NiB $139 Ex $113 Gd $82
Chrome . . . . NiB $144 Ex $118 Gd $87

ROUGH RIDER SA REVOLVER
Calibers: .22 LR, .22 Mag. Six-round cylinder. bbl. lengths: 2.75, 3.75, 4.75, 6.5 or 9 inches. Weight: 31-38 oz. Blade front sight, fixed rear. High-polished blued finish w/gold accents. Smooth walnut grips. Made from 1993 to date.
.22 LR . . . . NiB $128 Ex $103 Gd $82
.22 LR/.22 WRF combo . . . . NiB $159 Ex $128 Gd $97

SENTRY DA REVOLVER
Calibers: .22 LR, .22 Mag., .32 Mag., 9mm or .38 Special. Six- or 8-round (rimfire) cylinder, 2- or 4-inch bbl., 6.25 inches overall (2-inch bbl.). Ramp front sight, fixed rear. Blued or nickel finish. Checkered polymer grips. Made from 1993-97.
Blued . . . . NiB $130 Ex $108 Gd $79
Nickel . . . . NiB $143 Ex $118 Gd $87

STEALTH DA AUTO PISTOL . . . . . . NiB $295 Ex $243 Gd $177
Calibers: 9mm, .40 S&W. 10-round magazine, 3.9-inch bbl., weight: 20.2 oz. Gas-delayed blowback, double action only. Ambidextrous trigger safety. Blade front sight, drift-adj. rear. Black chrome or stainless slide. Black polymer grip frame. Made from 1996 to date.

HI-POINT FIREARMS — Mansfield, Ohio

MODEL JS-9MM AUTO PISTOL . . . . NiB $137 Ex $112 Gd $76
Caliber: 9mm Para. Eight-round magazine, 4.5-inch bbl., 7.75 inches overall. Weight: 39 oz. Fixed low-profile sights w/3-dot system. Matte blue, matte black or chrome finish. Checkered synthetic grips. Made from 1990-98.

MODEL JS-9MM COMPETITION PISTOL (STALLARD). . . . . NiB $127 Ex $107 Gd $76
Similar to standard JS-9 except w/4-inch compensated bbl. w/ shortened slide and adj. sights. 10-round magazine, 7.25 inches overall. Weight: 30 oz. Made from 1998 to date.

MODEL JS-9MM/C-9MM COMPACT PISTOL (BEEMILLER) . . . . NiB $128 Ex $107 Gd $75
Similar to standard JS-9 except w/3.5-inch bbl. and shortened slide w/alloy or polymer frame. 6.72 inches overall. Weight: 29 oz. or 32 oz. Three-dot-style sights. Made from 1993 to date.

MODEL CF-.380 POLYMER . . . . NiB $88 Ex $68 Gd $48
Caliber: .380 ACP. Eight-round magazine, 3.5-inch bbl., 6.72 inches overall. Weight: 32 oz. Three-dot sights. Made from 1994 to date.

MODEL JS-.40/JC-.40 AUTO PISTOL (IBERIA) . . . . NiB $156 Ex $127 Gd $91
Similar to Model JS-9mm except in caliber .40 S&W.

MODEL JS-.45/JH-.45 AUTO PISTOL (HASKELL) . . . . NiB $173 Ex $137 Gd $97
Similar to Model JS-9mm except in caliber .45 ACP w/7-round magazine and two-tone Polymer finish.

J. C. HIGGINS

See Sears, Roebuck & Company

HIGH STANDARD SPORTING FIREARMS — East Hartford, Connecticut Formerly High Standard Mfg. Co., Hamden, Connecticut

A long-standing producer of sporting arms, High Standard disc. its operations in 1984. See new High Standard models under separate entry, HIGH STANDARD MFG. CO., INC.

NOTE: *For ease in finding a particular firearm, High Standard handguns are grouped into three sections: Automatic pistols (below), derringers and revolvers. For a complete listing, please refer to the Index.*

High Standard Model A

High Standard Model B

High Standard Model D

High Standard Dura-Matic

AUTOMATIC PISTOLS

MODEL A
HAMMERLESS . . . . NiB $817 Ex $659 Gd $465
Caliber: .22 LR. 10-round magazine, bbl. lengths: 4.5-, 6.75-inch. 11.5 inches overall (6.75-inch bbl.). Weight: 36 oz. (in 6.75-inch bbl.). Adj. target sights. Blued finish. Checkered walnut grips. Made from 1938-42.

MODEL B
AUTOMATIC PISTOL . . . . NiB $494 Ex $407 Gd $331
Original Standard pistol. Hammerless. Caliber: .22 LR. 10-round magazine, bbl. lengths: 4.5-, 6.75-inch, 10.75 inches overall (with 6.75-inch bbl.). Weight: 33 oz. (6.75-inch bbl.). Fixed sights. Blued finish. Hard rubber grips. Made from 1932-42.

MODEL C
AUTOMATIC PISTOL . . . . NiB $978 Ex $779 Gd $524
Same as Model B except in .22 Short. Made from 1935-42.

MODEL D
AUTOMATIC PISTOL . . . . NiB $889 Ex $723 Gd $511
Same general specifications as Model A but heavier bbl., weight: 40 oz. (6.75-inch bbl.). Made from 1937-42.

DURA-MATIC
AUTOMATIC PISTOL . . . . NiB $356 Ex $294 Gd $214
Takedown. Caliber: .22 LR. 10-round magazine, 4.5 or 6.5 inch interchangeable bbl., 10.88 inches overall (6.5-inch bbl.). Weight: 35 oz. (in 6.5-inch bbl.). Fixed sights. Blued finish. Checkered grips. Made from 1952-70.

MODEL E
AUTOMATIC PISTOL . . . . NiB $1798 Ex $1401 Gd $1100
Same general specifications as Model A but w/extra heavy bbl. and thumbrest grips. Weight: 42 oz. (6.75-inch bbl.). Made from 1937-42.

FIELD-KING
AUTOMATIC PISTOL
FIRST MODEL
Same general specifications as Sport-King but w/heavier bbl. and target sights. Late model 6.75-inch bbls. have recoil stabilizer and lever take-down feature. Weight: 43 oz. (6.75-inch bbl.). Made from 1951-58.
W/one bbl. NiB $698 Ex $596 Gd $382
W/both bbls. . . . . NiB $766 Ex $669 Gd $492

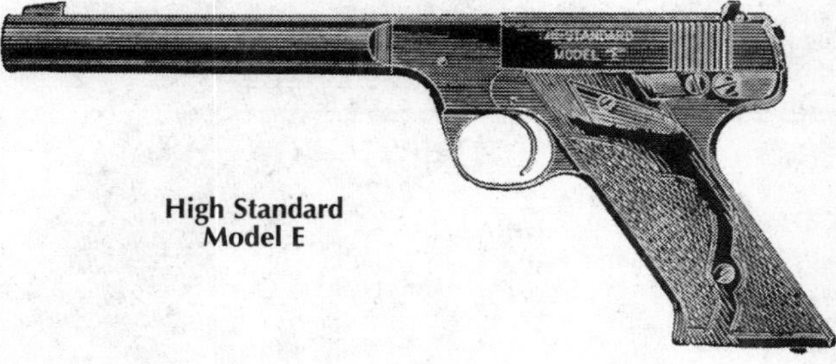

High Standard Model E

FIELD-KING AUTOMATIC PISTOL
SECOND MODEL
Same general specifications as First Model Field-King but w/button take-down and marked FK 100 or FK 101.
W/one bbl. NiB $679 Ex $552 Gd $271
W/both bbls. . . . . NiB $813 Ex $679 Gd $455

High Standard
G-.380

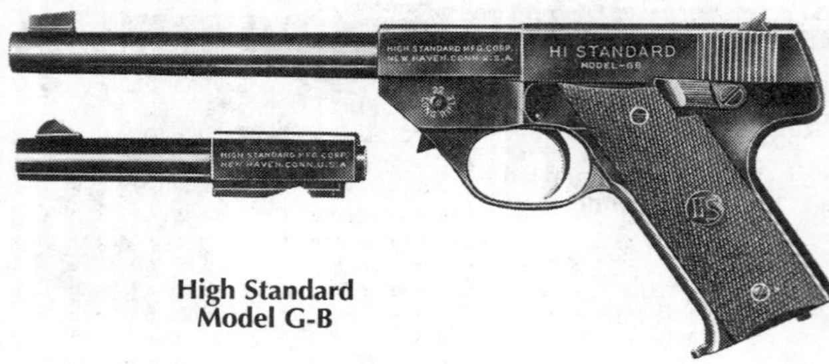

High Standard
Model G-B

High Standard
Model G-E

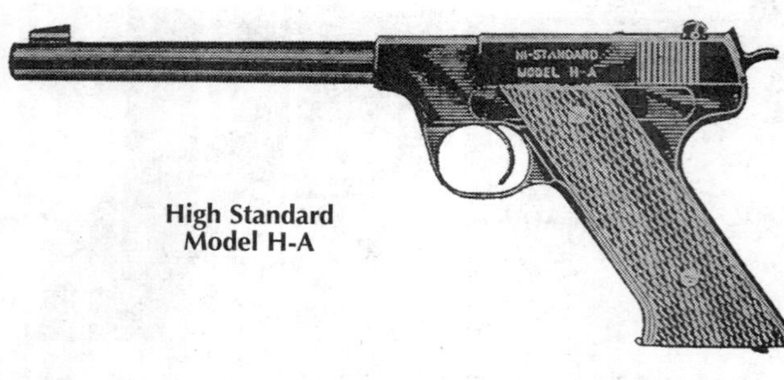

High Standard
Model H-A

High Standard
Model H-B

FLITE-KING AUTOMATIC PISTOL — FIRST MODEL
Same general specifications as Sport-King except in .22. Short w/aluminum alloy frame and slide and marked FK 100 or FK 101. Weight: 26 oz. (6.5-inch bbl.). Made from 1953-58.
W/one bbl. NiB $543 Ex $442 Gd $313
W/both bbls. . . . . NiB $645 Ex $524 Gd $378

FLITE-KING AUTOMATIC PISTOL — SECOND MODEL
Same as Flite-King—First Model except w/steel frame and marked in the 102 or 103 series. Made from 1958-66.
Model 102 . . . . NiB $628 Ex $462 Gd $340
Model 103 . . . . NiB $583 Ex $442 Gd $319

MODEL G-.380
AUTOMATIC PISTOL . . . . NiB $619 Ex $539 Gd $375
Lever takedown. Visible hammer. Thumb safety. Caliber: .380 Automatic. Six-round magazine, 5-inch bbl., weight: 40 oz. Fixed sights. Blued finish. Checkered plastic grips. Made from 1943-50.

MODEL G-B AUTOMATIC PISTOL
Lever takedown. Hammerless. Interchangeable bbls. Caliber: .22 LR. 10-round magazine, bbl. lengths: 4.5, 6.75 inches, 10.75 inches overall (with 6.75-inch bbl.). Weight: 36 oz. (with 6.75-inch bbl.). Fixed sights. Blued finish. Checkered plastic grips. Made from 1948-51.
W/one bbl. NiB $600 Ex $462 Gd $340
W/both bbls. . . . . NiB $619 Ex $539 Gd $376

MODEL G-D AUTOMATIC PISTOL
Lever takedown. Hammerless. Interchangeable bbls. Caliber: .22 LR. 10-round magazine, bbl. lengths: 4.5, 6.75 inches. 11.5 inches overall (with 6.75-inch bbl.). Weight: 41 oz. (6.75-inch bbl.). Target sights. Blued finish. Checkered walnut grips. Made from 1948-51.
W/one bbl. NiB $988 Ex $767 Gd $566
W/both bbls. . . . . NiB $1125 Ex $895 Gd $648

MODEL G-E AUTOMATIC PISTOL
Same general specifications as Model G-D but w/extra heavy bbl. and thumbrest grips. Weight: 44 oz. (with 6.75-inch bbl.). Made from 1949-51.
W/one bbl. . . . . NiB $1430 Ex $1220 Gd $947
W/both bbls. . . . . NiB $1707 Ex $1367 Gd $1089

MODEL H-A
AUTOMATIC PISTOL . . . . NiB $1339 Ex $1193 Gd $827
Same as Model A but w/visible hammer, no thumb safety. Made from 1939-42.

MODEL H-B
AUTOMATIC PISTOL . . . . NiB $701 Ex $555 Gd $399
Same as Model B but w/visible hammer, no thumb safety. Made from 1940-42.

MODEL H-D
AUTOMATIC PISTOL . . . . NiB $1253 Ex $1063 Gd $744
Same as Model D but w/visible hammer, no thumb safety. Made from 1939-42.

MODEL H-DM
AUTOMATIC PISTOL . . . . NiB $718 Ex $601 Gd $453
Also called H-D Military. Same as Model H-D but w/thumb safety. Made from 1941-51.

MODEL H-E
AUTOMATIC PISTOL . . . . NiB $2591 Ex $2041 Gd $1119
Same as Model E but w/visible hammer, no thumb safety. Made from 1939-42.

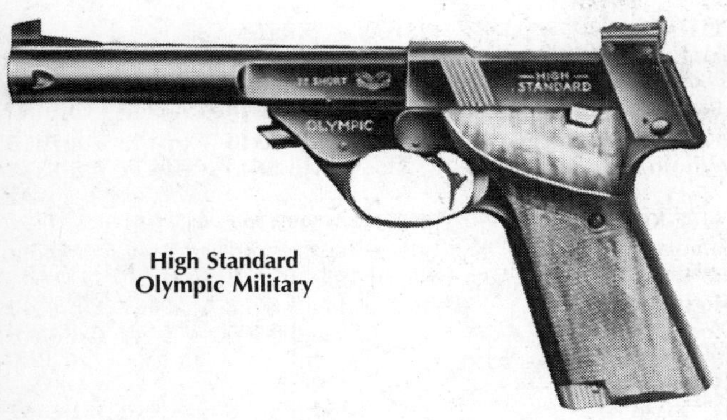

High Standard
Olympic Military

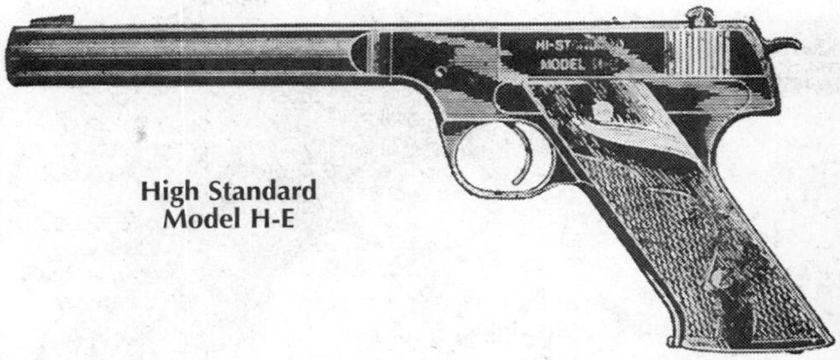

OLYMPIC AUTOMATIC PISTOL FIRST MODEL (G-O)
Same general specifications as Model G-E but in .22 Short w/light alloy slide. Made from 1950-51.
W/one bbl. . . . . NiB $1228 Ex $1093 Gd $588
W/both bbls. . . . . NiB $1816 Ex $1467 Gd $1023

OLYMPIC AUTOMATIC SECOND MODEL
Same general specifications as Supermatic but in .22 Short w/light alloy slide. Weight: 39 oz. (6.75-inch bbl.). Made from 1951-58.
W/one bbl. . . . . NiB $1144 Ex $1017 Gd $692
W/both bbls. . . . . NiB $1440 Ex $1178 Gd $869

OLYMPIC AUTOMATIC PISTOL THIRD MODEL . . . . NiB $1142 Ex $929 Gd $682
Same as Supermatic Trophy w/bull bbl. except in .22 Short. Made from 1963-66.

OLYMPIC COMMEMORATIVE
Limited edition of Supermatic Trophy Military issued to commemorate the only American-made rimfire target pistol ever to win an Olympic gold medal. Highly engraved w/Olympic rings inlaid in gold. Deluxe presentation case. Two versions issued: In 1972 (.22 LR) and 1980 (.22 Short).
1972 issue . . . . NiB $6300 Ex $5250 Gd $3463
1980 issue . . . . NiB $2138 Ex $1789 Gd $1164

OLYMPIC I.S.U . . . . NiB $954 Ex $775 Gd $546
Same as Supermatic Citation except caliber .22 Short, 6.75- or 8-inch tapered bbl. w/stabilizer, detachable weights. Made from 1958-77. Eight-inch bbl. disc. in 1966.

OLYMPIC I.S.U. MILITARY . . . . . NiB $2159 Ex $1109 Gd $660
Same as Olympic I.S.U. except has military grip and bracket rear sight. Intro. in 1965. Disc.

OLYMPIC MILITARY . . . . NiB $1102 Ex $907 Gd $711
Same as Olympic — Third Model except has military grip and bracket rear sight. Made in 1965.

PLINKER . . . . NiB $347 Ex $282 Gd $200
Similar to Dura-Matic with same general specifications. Made from 1971-73.

SHARPSHOOTER AUTOMATIC PISTOL . . . . NiB $764 Ex $632 Gd $447
Takedown. Hammerless. Caliber: .22 LR. 10-round magazine, 5.5-inch bull bbl., 9 inches overall. Weight: 42 oz. Micrometer rear sight, blade front sight. Blued finish. Plastic grips. Made from 1971-83.

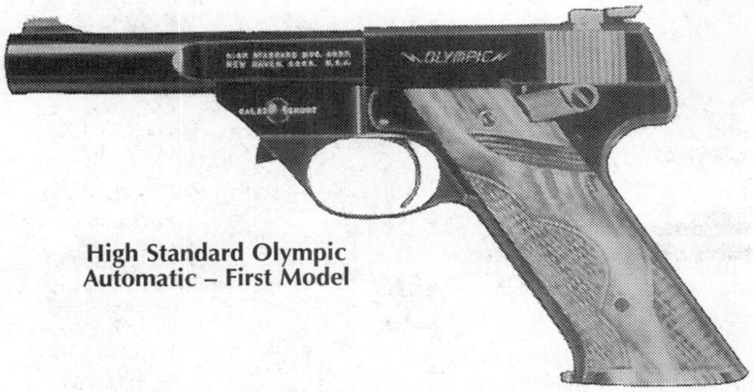

High Standard
Model H-E

High Standard Olympic
Automatic – First Model

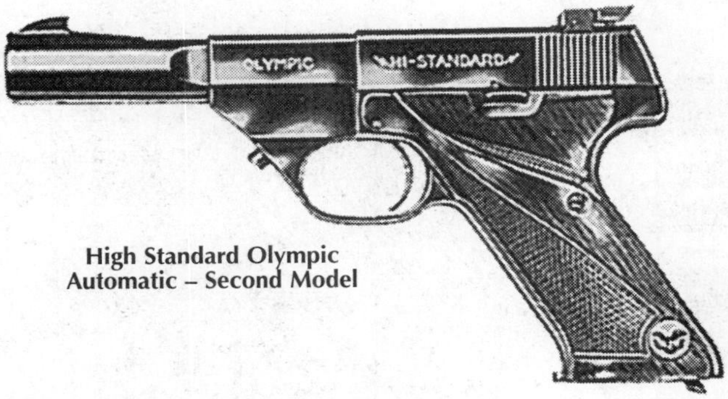

High Standard Olympic
Automatic – Second Model

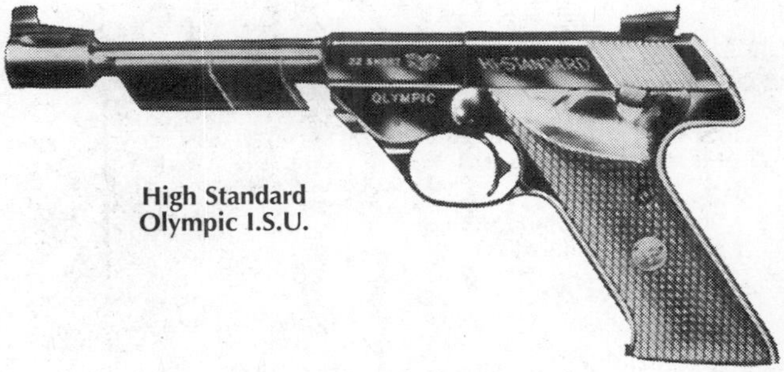

High Standard
Olympic I.S.U.

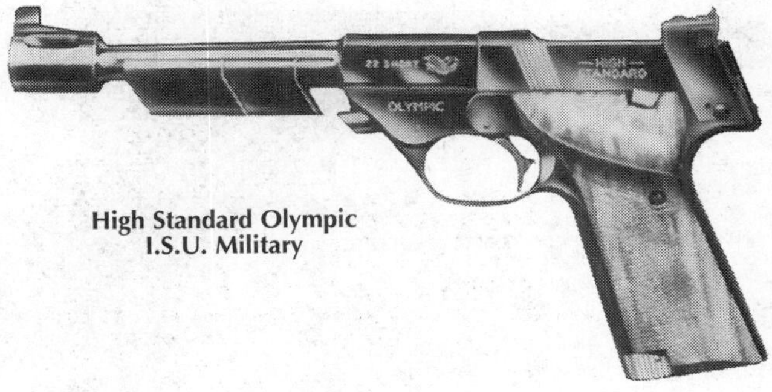

High Standard Olympic
I.S.U. Military

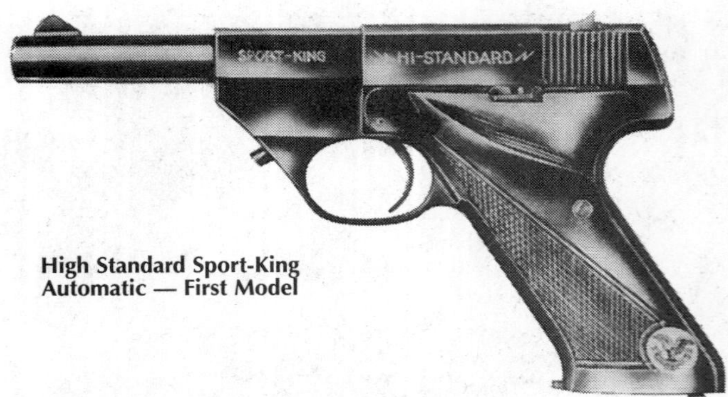

High Standard Sport-King Automatic — First Model

SPORT-KING AUTOMATIC PISTOL FIRST MODEL

Takedown. Hammerless. Interchangeable barrels. Caliber: .22 LR. 10-round magazine, barrel lengths: 4.5-, 6.75-inches. 11.5 inches overall (with 6.75-inch barrel). Weight: 39 oz. (with 6.75-inch barrel). Fixed sights. Blued finish. Checkered plastic thumbrest grips. Made from 1951-58. Note: 1951-54 production has lever takedown as in "G" series. Later version (illustrated at left) has push-button takedown.

W/one bbl. . . . . NiB $397 Ex $327 Gd $237
W/both bbls. . . . . NiB $480 Ex $393 Gd $281

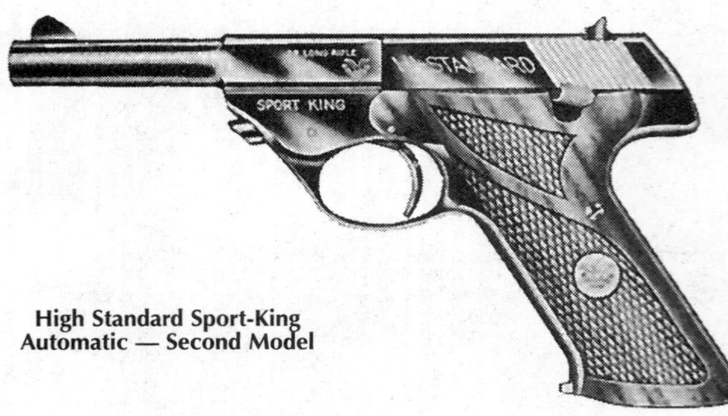

High Standard Sport-King Automatic — Second Model

SPORT-KING AUTOMATIC PISTOL SECOND MODEL . . . . NiB $425 Ex $349 Gd $252

Caliber: .22 LR. 10-round magazine, 4.5- or 6.75 inch interchangeable bbl. 11.25 inches overall (with 6.75-inch barrel). Weight: 42 oz. (with 6.75-inch barrel). Fixed sights. Blued finish. Checkered grips. Made from 1958-70.

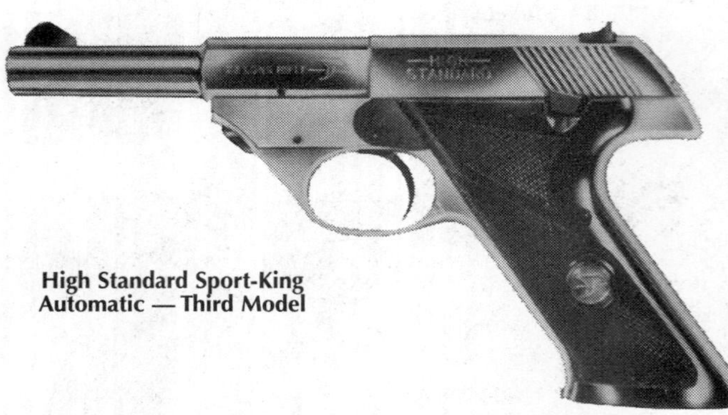
High Standard Sport-King Automatic — Third Model

SPORT-KING AUTOMATIC PISTOL THIRD MODEL . . . . NiB $384 Ex $316 Gd 228

Similar to Sport-King — Second Model with same general specifications for weight and length. Blued or nickel finish. Introduced in 1974. Disc.

SPORT-KING LIGHTWEIGHT

Same as standard Sport-King except lightweight has forged aluminum alloy frame. Weight: 30 oz. with 6.75-inch barrel Made from 1954-65.

W/one bbl. . . . . NiB $405 Ex $299 Gd $208
W/both bbls. . . . . NiB $481 Ex $403 Gd $236

High Standard Supermatic

SUPERMATIC AUTOMATIC PISTOL

Takedown. Hammerless. Interchangeable bbls. Caliber: .22 LR. 10-round magazine, barrel lengths: 4.5-, 6.75-inches. Late model 6.75-inch barrel have recoil stabilizer feature. Weight: 43 oz. (with 6.75-inch barrel) 11.5 inches overall (with 6.75-inch barrel). Target sights. Elevated serrated rib between sights. Adjustable barrel weights add 2 or 3 oz. Blued finish. Checkered plastic thumbrest grips. Made from 1951-58.

W/one bbl. . . . . NiB $767 Ex $624 Gd $443
W/both bbls. . . . . NiB $927 Ex $753 Gd $531

SUPERMATIC CITATION

Same as Supermatic Tournament except 6.75-, 8- or 10-inch tapered bbl. with stabilizer and two removable weights. Also furnished with Tournament's 5.5-inch bull barrel, adjustable trigger pull, recoil-proof click-adjustable rear sight (barrel-mounted on 8- and 10-inch barrels), checkered walnut thumbrest grips on bull barrel model. Currently manufactured with only bull barrel. Made from 1958-66.

With 5.5-inch bull bbl. . . . . NiB $727 Ex $573 Gd $315
With 6.75-inch tapered bbl. . . . . NiB $727 Ex $573 Gd $315
With 8-inch tapered bbl. . . . . NiB $964 Ex $774 Gd $563
With 10-inch tapered bbl. . . . . NiB $1172 Ex $993 Gd $761

High Standard Victor
Solid Rib Barrel

High Standard
Supermatic Citation Bull Barrel

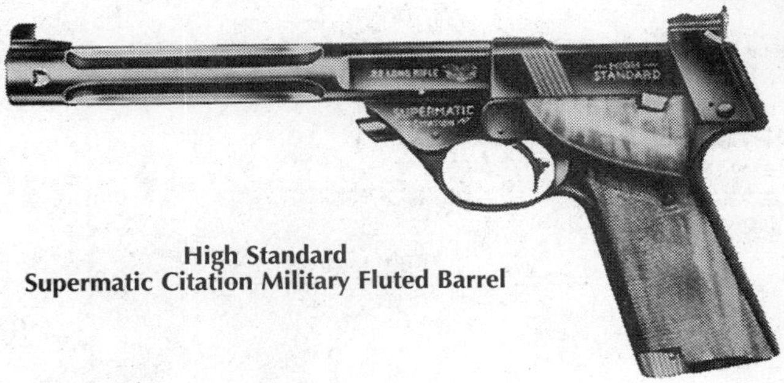

High Standard
Supermatic Citation Military Fluted Barrel

High Standard
Supermatic Tournament Bull Barrel

High Standard
Supermatic Tournament Military Tapered Barrel

High Standard
Supermatic Trophy Bull Barrel

SUPERMATIC CITATION MILITARY
Same as Supermatic Citation except has military grip and bracket rear sight as in Supermatic Trophy. Made from 1965-73.
W/bull bbl. . . . . NiB $662 Ex $540 Gd $388
W/fluted bbl. . . . . NiB $897 Ex $748 Gd $558

SUPERMATIC TOURNAMENT . . . . NiB $671 Ex $594 Gd $305
Takedown. Caliber: .22 LR. 10-round magazine, interchangeable 5.5-inch bull or 6.75-inch heavy tapered bbl., notched and drilled for stabilizer and weights. 10 inches overall (with 5.5-inch bbl.). Weight: 44 oz. (5.5-inch bbl.). Click adj. rear sight, undercut ramp front. Blued finish. Checkered grips. Made from 1958-66.

SUPERMATIC TOURNAMENT MILITARY . . . . NiB $661 Ex $537 Gd $377
Same as Supermatic Tournament except has military grip. Made 1965-71.

SUPERMATIC TROPHY
Same as Supermatic Citation except with 5.5-inch bull bbl., or 7.25-inch fluted bbl., w/detachable stabilizer and weights, extra magazine, High-luster blued finish, checkered walnut thumbrest grips. Made from 1963-66.
W/bull bbl. . . . . NiB $1202 Ex $996 Gd $537
W/fluted bbl. . . . . NiB $1233 Ex $1011 Gd $563

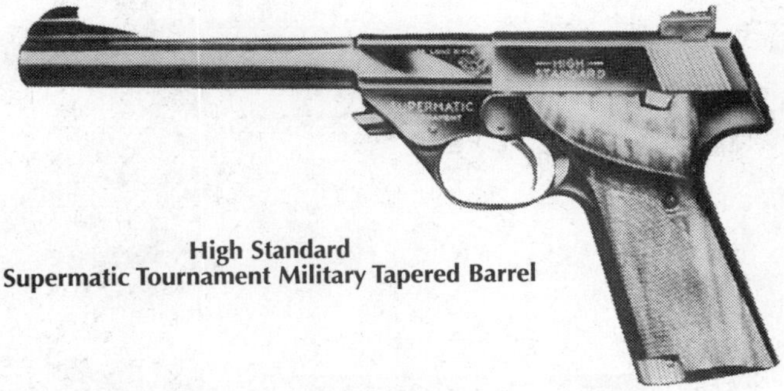

SUPERMATIC TROPHY MILITARY
Same as Supermatic Trophy except has military grip and bracket rear sight. Made from 1965-84.
W/bull bbl. NiB $998 Ex $896 Gd $489
W/fluted bbl. . . . . NiB $488 Ex $895 Gd $509

VICTOR AUTOMATIC . . . . NiB $865 Ex $690 Gd $458
Takedown. Caliber: .22 LR. 10-round magazine, 4.5-inch solid or vent rib and 5.5-inch vent rib, interchangeable bbl., 9.75 inches overall (with 5.5-inch bbl.). Weight: 52 oz. (with 5.5-inch bbl.). Rib mounted target sights. Blued finish. Checkered walnut thumbrest grips. Standard or military grip configuration. Made from 1972-84 (standard-grip model, 1974-75).

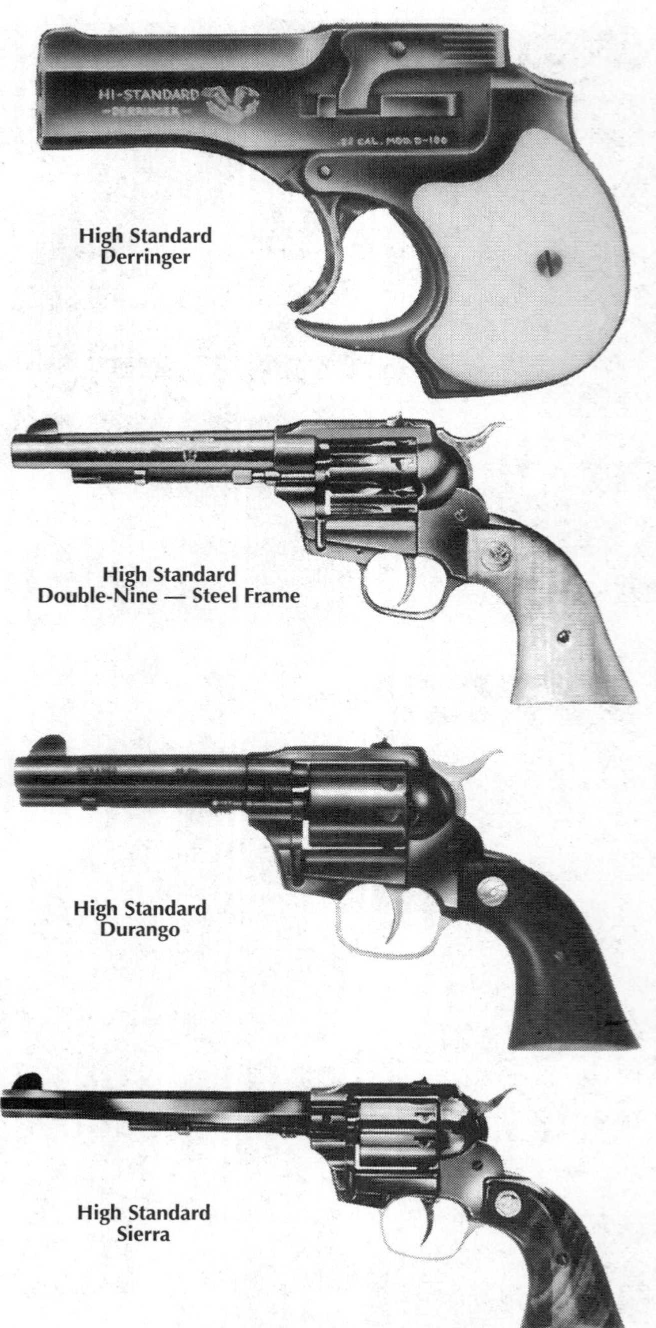

High Standard Derringer

High Standard Double-Nine — Steel Frame

High Standard Durango

High Standard Sierra

NOTE: *High Standard automatic pistols can be found in the preceding section, while revolvers immediately follow this derringer listing.*

DERRINGERS

DERRINGER

Hammerless, double action, two-round, double bbl. (over/under). Calibers: .22 Short, Long, LR or .22 Magnum Rimfire, 3.5-inch bbls., 5 inches overall. Weight: 11 oz. Standard model has blued or nickel finish w/plastic grips. Presentation model is goldplated in walnut case. Standard model made from 1963 (.22 S-L-LR) and 1964 (.22 MRF) to 1984. Gold model, made from 1965-83.

Gold Presentation One Derringer.................... NiB $749 Ex $606 Gd $425
Silver Presentation One Derringer.................... NiB $716 Ex $581 Gd $408
Presentation Set, matched pair, consecutive numbers (1965 only)................ NiB $1347 Ex $1091 Gd $763
Standard model (blue)........... NiB $282 Ex $233 Gd $168
Standard model (nickel) .... NiB $308 Ex $252 Gd $181
Standard model (Electroless nickel).............. NiB $323 Ex $266 Gd $192
Standard model (blue)........... NiB $285 Ex $235 Gd $171

REVOLVERS

NOTE: *Only High Standard revolvers can be found in this section. See the preceding sections for automatic pistols and derringers. For a complete listing of High Standard handguns, please refer to the Index.*

CAMP GUN................... NiB $288 Ex $237 Gd $171
Same as Sentinel Mark I/Mark IV except has 6-inch bbl., adj. rear sight, target-style checkered walnut grips. Caliber: .22 LR or .22 WMR. Made from 1976-83.

DOUBLE-NINE DA REVOLVER —ALUMINUM FRAME
Western-style version of Sentinel. Blued or nickel finish w/simulated ivory, ebony or stag grips, 5.5-inch bbl., 11 inches overall. Weight: 27.25 oz. Made from 1959-71.
Blue model .... NiB $247 Ex $201 Gd $129
Nickel model.................. NiB $258 Ex $211 Gd $137

DOUBLE-NINE—STEEL FRAME
Similar to Double-Nine—Aluminum Frame, w/same general specifications except w/steel frame and has extra cylinder for .22 WMR, walnut grips. Intro. in 1971. Disc.
Blue model .... NiB $308 Ex $252 Gd $182
Nickel model.................. NiB $321 Ex $261 Gd $188

DOUBLE-NINE DELUXE .... NiB $317 Ex $261 Gd $187
Same as Double-Nine — Steel Frame except has adj. target rear sight. Intro. in 1971. Disc.

DURANGO
Similar to Double-Nine—Steel Frame except .22 LR only, available w/4.5- or 5.5-inch bbl. Made from 1971-73.
Blue model .... NiB $208 Ex $171 Gd $124
Nickel model.................. NiB $221 Ex $180 Gd $129

HIGH SIERRA DA REVOLVER
Similar to Double-Nine—Steel Frame except has 7-inch octagon bbl., w/gold-plated grip frame, fixed or adj. sights. Made from 1973-1983.
W/fixed sights .... NiB $378 Ex $309 Gd $220
W/adj. sights.................. NiB $398 Ex $327 Gd $236

HOMBRE
Similar to Double-Nine—Steel Frame except .22 LR only, lacks single-action type ejector rod and tube, has 4.5-inch bbl. Made from 1971-73.
Blue model .... NiB $202 Ex $168 Gd $122
Nickel model.................. NiB $221 Ex $180 Gd $132

KIT GUN DA REVOLVER......... NiB $234 Ex $193 Gd $133
Solid frame, swing-out cylinder. Caliber: .22 LR. Nine-round cylinder, 4-inch bbl., 9 inches overall. Weight: 19 oz. Adj. rear sight, ramp front. Blued finish. Checkered walnut grips. Made from 1970-73.

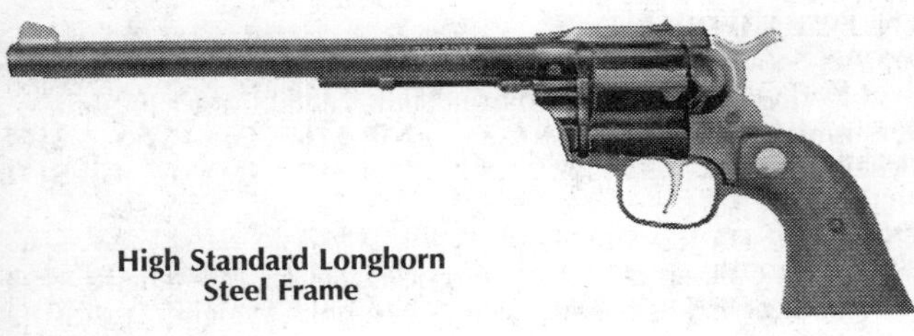
High Standard Longhorn Steel Frame

High Standard Kit Gun

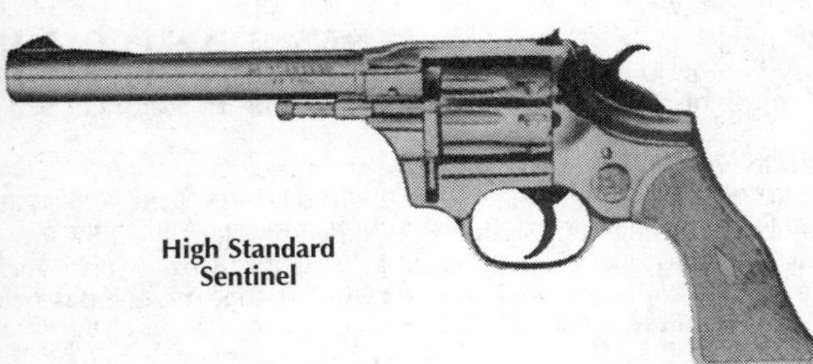
High Standard Sentinel

High Standard Longhorn Aluminum Frame

LONGHORN ALUMINUM FRAME

Similar to Double-Nine—Aluminum Frame except has Longhorn hammer spur, 4.5-, 5.5- or 9.5-inch bbl., Walnut, simulated pearl or simulated stag grips. Blued finish. Made from 1960-1971.

W/4.5- or 5.5-inch bbl. . . . . NiB $270 Ex $223 Gd $162
W/9.5-inch bbl . . . . NiB $294 Ex $239 Gd $170

LONGHORN STEEL FRAME

Similar to Double-Nine — Steel Frame except has 9.5-inch bbl. w/fixed or adj. sights. Made from 1971-1983

W/fixed sights . . . . NiB $289 Ex $239 Gd $175
W/adj. sights . . . . NiB $427 Ex $359 Gd $262

NATCHEZ . . . . NiB $280 Ex $234 Gd $175

Similar to Double-Nine — Aluminum Frame except 4.5-inch bbl., 10 inches overall, weight: 25.25 oz., blued finish, simulated ivory bird's-head grips. Made 1961-66.

POSSE . . . . NiB $195 Ex $160 Gd $116

Similar to Double-Nine — Aluminum Frame except 3.5-inch bbl., 9 inches overall, weight: 23.25 oz. Blued finish, brass-grip frame and trigger guard, walnut grips. Made from 1961-66.

High Standard Natchez

SENTINEL DA REVOLVER

Solid frame, swing-out cylinder. Caliber: .22 LR. Nine-round cylinder, 3- 4- or 6-inch bbl. Nine inches overall (with 4-inch-bbl.). Weight: 19 oz. (with 4-inch bbl.). Fixed sights. Aluminum frame. Blued or nickel finish. Checkered grips. Made from 1955-56.

Blue model . . . . NiB $171 Ex $142 Gd $105
Blue/green model . . . . NiB $165 Ex $155 Gd $127
Gold model . . . . NiB $349 Ex $318 Gd $195
Nickel model. . . . . NiB $182 Ex $167 Gd $116
Pink model . . . . NiB $363 Ex $327 Gd $193

SENTINEL DELUXE

Same as Sentinel except w/4- or 6-inch bbl., wide trigger, drift-adj. rear sight, two-piece square-butt grips. Made from 1957-74. Note: Designated Sentinel after 1971.

Blue model . . . . NiB $167 Ex $152 Gd $116
Nickel model . . . . NiB $193 Ex $177 Gd $126

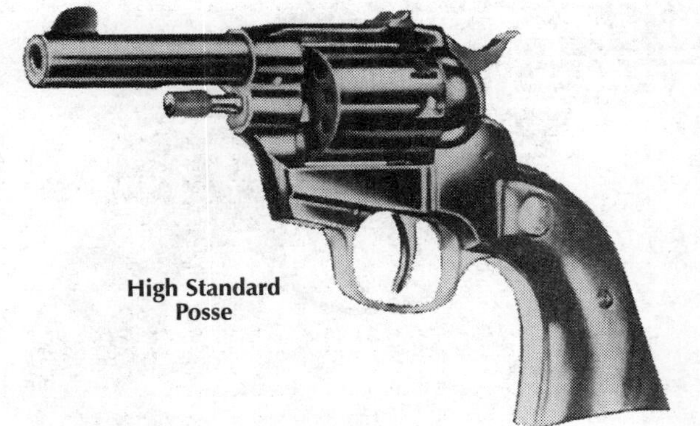
High Standard Posse

High Standard Sentinel I

High Standard Sentinel Mark II

High Standard Sentinel Mark III

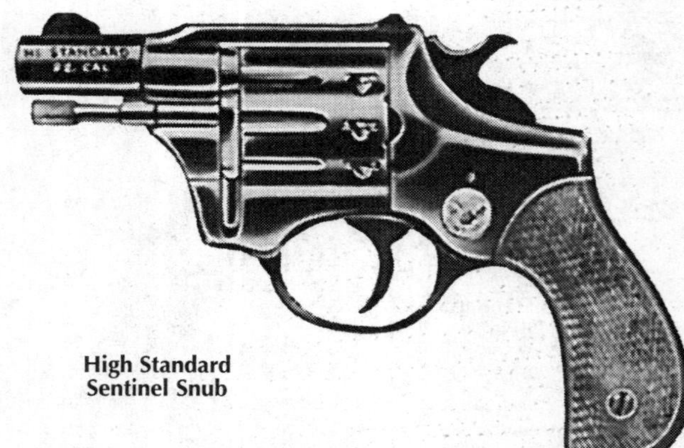

High Standard Sentinel Snub

SENTINEL IMPERIAL
Same as Sentinel except has onyx-black or nickel finish, two-piece checkered walnut grips, ramp front sight. Made from 1962-65.
Blue model . . . . NiB $167 Ex $152 Gd $106
Nickel model . . . . NiB $177 Ex $167 Gd $116

SENTINEL 1 DA REVOLVER
Steel frame. Caliber: .22 LR. Nine-round cylinder, bbl. lengths: 2-, 3-, 4-inch, 6.88 inches overall (with 2-inch bbl.). Weight: 21.5 oz. (2-inch bbl.). Ramp front sight, fixed or adj. rear. Blued or nickel finish. Smooth walnut grips. Made from 1974-83.
Blue model . . . . NiB $265 Ex $218 Gd $157
Nickel model . . . . NiB $330 Ex $269 Gd $192
W/adj. sights . . . . NiB $356 Ex $290 Gd $205

SENTINEL MARK II
DA REVOLVER . . . . NiB $310 Ex $284 Gd $171
Caliber: .357 Magnum. Six-round cylinder, bbl. lengths: 2.5-, 4-, 6-inch, 9 inches overall w/4-inch bbl., weight: 38 oz. (with 4-inch bbl.). Fixed sights. Blued finish. Walnut service or combat-style grips. Made from 1974-76.

SENTINEL MARK III . . . . NiB $345 Ex $282 Gd $202
Same as Sentinel Mark II except has ramp front and adj. rear sights. Weight: 40 oz. (with 4-inch bbl.). Blued finish. Made from 1974-76.

SENTINEL MARK IV
Same as Sentinel Mark I except in .22 WMR. Made from 1974-83.
Blue model . . . . NiB $319 Ex $262 Gd $188
Nickel model . . . . NiB $345 Ex $282 Gd $202
W/adj. sights . . . . NiB $378 Ex $308 Gd $220

SENTINEL SNUB
Same as Sentinel Deluxe except w/2.75-inch bbl., (7.25 inches overall, weight: 15 oz.), checkered bird's head-type grips. Made from 1957-74.
Blued finish . . . . NiB $172 Ex $167 Gd $116
Nickel finish . . . . NiB $183 Ex $177 Gd $126

HIGH STANDARD MFG. CO., INC. — Houston, Texas Distributed from Hartford, Connecticut

10X AUTOMATIC PISTOL . . . . NiB $997 Ex $791 Gd $482
Caliber: .22 LR. 10-round magazine, 5.5-inch bbl., 9.5 inches overall. Weight: 45 oz. Checkered walnut grips. Blued finish. Made from 1994 to date.

OLYMPIC I.S.U. AUTOMATIC PISTOL
Same specifications as the 1958 I.S.U. issue. See listing under previous High Standard Section.
Olympic I.S.U. model . . . . NiB $608 Ex $505 Gd $248
Olympic I.S.U. military model. . . . . NiB $552 Ex $455 Gd $248
Military model . . . . NiB $474 Ex $387 Gd $277

SPORT KING AUTO PISTOL . . . . NiB $374 Ex $307 Gd $221
Caliber: .22 LR. 10-round magazine, 4.5- or 6.75-inch bbl., 8.5 or 10.75 inches overall. Weight: 44 oz. (with 4.5-inch bbl.), 46 oz. (with 6.75-inch bbl.). Fixed sights, slide mounted. Checkered walnut grips. Parkerized finish. Advertised in 1996 to date. No resale value established.

SUPERMATIC CITATION AUTO PISTOL
Caliber: .22 LR. 10-round magazine, 5.5- or 7.75-inch bbl., 9.5 or 11.75 inches overall. Weight: 44 oz. (with 5.5-inch bbl.), 46 oz. (with 7.75-inch bbl.). Frame-mounted, micro-adj. rear sight, undercut ram.

front sight. Blued or Parkerized finish. Made from 1994 to date.
Supermatic Citation model . . . . NiB $465 Ex $373 Gd $229
.22 Short conversion . . . . NiB $368 Ex $306 Gd $218

CITATION MS AUTO PISTOL . . . . . NiB $687 Ex $606 Gd $349
Similar to the Supermatic Citation except has 10-inch bbl., 14 inches overall. Weight: 49 oz. Made from 1994 to date.

SUPERMATIC TOURNAMENT. . . . . NiB $418 Ex $342 Gd $245
Caliber: .22 LR. 10-round magazine, bbl. lengths: 4.5, 5.5, or 6.75 inches, overall length: 8.5, 9.5 or 10.75 inches. Weight: 43, 44 or 45 oz. depending on bbl. length. Micro-adj. rear sight, undercut ramp front sight. Checkered walnut grips. Parkerized finish. Made from 1994 to date.

SUPERMATIC TROPHY
Caliber: .22 LR. 10-round magazine, 5.5 or 7.25-inch bbl., 9.5 or 11.25 inches overall. Weight: 44 oz. (with 5.5-inch bbl.). Micro-adj. rear sight, undercut ramp front sight. Checkered walnut grips w/thumbrest. Blued or Parkerized finish. Made from 1994 to date.
Supermatic Trophy. . . . . NiB $482 Ex $393 Gd $280
.22 Short Conversion. . . . . NiB $368 Ex $306 Gd $218

VICTOR AUTOMATIC
Caliber: .22 LR.10-round magazine, 4.5- or 5.5-inch ribbed bbl., 8.5 or 9.5 inches overall. Weight: 45 oz. (with 4.5-inch bbl.), 46 oz. (with 5.5-inch bbl.). Micro-adj. rear sight, post front. Checkered walnut grips. Blued or Parkerized finish. Made from 1994 to date.
Victor Model . . . . NiB $550 Ex $452 Gd $246
.22 Short conversion . . . . NiB $348 Ex $306 Gd $218

HOPKINS & ALLEN ARMS CO. — Norwich, Connecticut

HOPKINS & ALLEN REVOLVERS
See listings of comparable Harrington & Richardson and Iver Johnson models for values.

INGRAM — Mfd. by Military Armament Corp.

See listings under M.A.C. (Military Armament Corp.)

Note: *Military Armament Corp. ceased production of the select-fire automatic, M10 (9mm & .45 ACP) and M11 (.380 ACP) in 1977. Commercial production resumed on semiautomatic versions under the M.A.C. banner until 1982.*

INTERARMS — Alexandria, Virginia

See also Bersa Pistol.

HELWAN BRIGADIER
AUTO PISTOL . . . . NiB $221 Ex $174 Gd $113
Caliber: 9mm Para. Eight-round magazine, 4.25-inch bbl., 8 inches overall. Weight: 32 oz. Blade front sight, dovetailed rear. Blued finish. Grooved plastic grips. Imported from 1987-95.

VIRGINIAN DRAGOON SA REVOLVER
Calibers: .357 Magnum, .44 Magnum, .45 Colt. Six-round cylinder. Bbls.: 5- (not available in .44 Magnum), 6-, 7.5-, 8.38-inch (latter only in .44 Magnum w/adj. sights), 11.88 inches overall with (6-inch bbl.). Weight: 48 oz. (with 6-inch bbl.). Fixed sights or micrometer rear and ramp front sights. Blued finish w/color-casetreated frame. Smooth walnut grips. SWISSAFE base pin safety system.

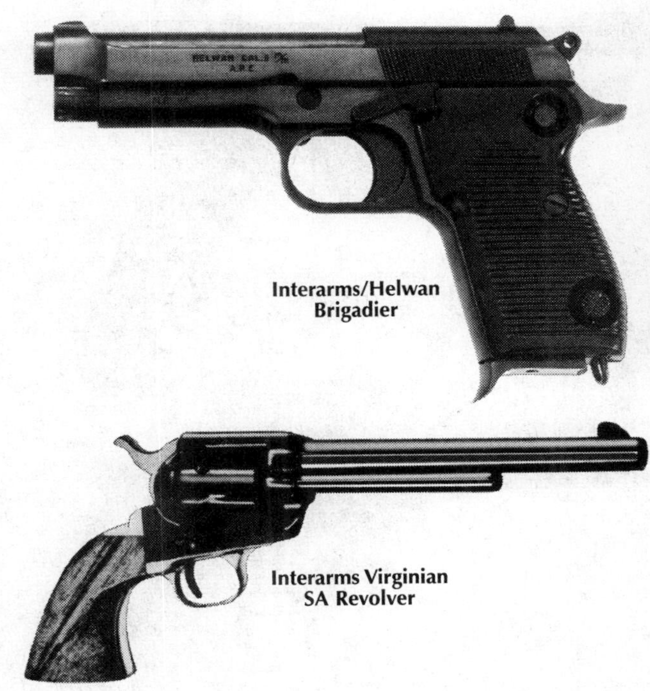
Interarms/Helwan Brigadier

Interarms Virginian SA Revolver

Manufactured by Interarms Industries Inc., Midland, VA. 1977-84.
Standard Dragoon . . . . NiB $284 Ex $253 Gd $186
Engraved Dragoon . . . . NiB $586 Ex $509 Gd $355
Deputy model . . . . NiB $278 Ex $242 Gd $181
Stainless. . . . . NiB $284 Ex $253 Gd $227

VIRGINIAN REVOLVER
SILHOUETTE MODEL . . . . NiB $399 Ex $250 Gd $244
Same general specifications as regular model except designed in stainless steel w/untapered bull bbl., lengths of 7.5, 8.38 and 10.5 inches. Made from 1985-86.

VIRGINIAN SA REVOLVER . . . . . . NiB $539 Ex $437 Gd $307
Similar to Colt Single-Action Army except has base pin safety system. Imported from 1973-76. (See also listing under Hämmerli.)

INTRATEC U.S.A., INC. — Miami, Florida

CATEGORY 9 DAO
SEMIAUTOMATIC. . . . . NiB $239 Ex $203 Gd $121
Blowback action w/polymer frame. Caliber: 9mm Par Eight-round magazine, 3-inch bbl., 7.7 inches overall. Weight: 18 oz. Textured black polymer grips. Matte black finish. Made from 1993 to date.

CATEGORY 40
DAO SEMIAUTOMATIC . . . . NiB $237 Ex $193 Gd $137
Locking-breech action w/polymer frame. Caliber: .40 S&W. Seven-round magazine, 3.25-inch bbl., 8 inches overall. Weight: 21 oz. Textured black polymer grips. Matte black finish. Made from 1994 to date.

CATEGORY 45
DAO SEMIAUTOMATIC . . . . NiB $255 Ex $214 Gd $151
Locking-breech action w/polymer frame. Caliber: .45 ACP. Six-round magazine, 3.25-inch bbl., 8 inches overall. Weight: 21 oz. Textured black polymer grips. Matte black finish. Made from 1994 to date.

Japanese
Model 14 (1925)

Japanese
Model 26 DAO Revolver

**MODEL PROTEC .22
DA SEMIAUTOMATIC**
Caliber: .25 ACP. 10-round magazine, 2.5-inch bbl., 5 inches overall. Weight: 14 oz. Wraparound composition grips. Black Teflon, satin grey or Tec-Kote finish. Advertised in 1992.
ProTec .22 standard . . . . NiB $130 Ex $99 Gd $48
ProTec .22 w/satin or Tec-Kote . . . . NiB $135 Ex $104 Gd $53

MODEL PROTEC .25 DA SEMIAUTOMATIC
Caliber: .25 ACP. Eight-round magazine, 2.5-inch bbl., 5 inches overall. Weight: 14 oz. Fixed sights. Wraparound composition grips. Black Teflon, satin grey or Tec-Kote finish. Made from 1991 to date. Note: Formerly Model Tec-.25.
ProTec .25 standard. . . . . NiB $108 Ex $88 Gd $60
ProTec .25 w/satin or Tec-Kote . . . . . . NiB $114 Ex $94 Gd $93

MODEL TEC-9 SEMIAUTOMATIC
Caliber: 9mm Para. 20- or 36-round magazine, 5-inch bbl., weight: 50-51 oz. Open fixed front sight, adj. rear. Military nonglare blued or stainless finish.
Tec-9 w/blued finish . . . . NiB $275 Ex $224 Gd $159
Tec-9 w/nickel finish. . . . . NiB $274 Ex $224 Gd $160
Tec 9S w/stainless finish . . . . NiB $358 Ex $291 Gd $203

MODEL TEC-9M SEMIAUTOMATIC
Same specifications as Model Tec-9 except has 3-inch bbl. without shroud and 20-round magazine, blued or stainless finish.
Tec-9M w/blued finish. . . . . NiB $239 Ex $203 Gd $146
Tec-9MS w/stainless finish. . . . . NiB $327 Ex $265 Gd $188

MODEL TEC-22T SEMIAUTOMATIC
Caliber: .22 LR. 10/.22-type 30-round magazine, 4-inch bbl., 11.19 inches overall. Weight: 30 oz. Protected post front sight, adj. rear sight. Matte black or Tec-Kote finish. Made from 1989 to date.
Tec-22T standard. . . . . NiB $186 Ex $155 Gd $114
Tec-22TK Tec-Kote . . . . NiB $221 Ex $181 Gd $129

**MODEL TEC
DOUBLE DERRINGER. . . . . NiB $137 Ex $114 Gd $83**
Calibers: .22 WRF, .32 H&R Mag., .38 Special. Two-round capacity, 3-inch bbl., 4.63 inches overall. Weight: 13 oz. Fixed sights. Matte black finish. Made from 1986-88.

ISRAEL ARMS — Kfar Sabs, Israel

Imported by Israel Arms International, Houston TX

**MODEL BUL-M5 LOCKED
BREECH (2000) AUTO PISTOL . . . . NiB $446 Ex $312 Gd $276**
Similar to the M1911 U.S. Government model. Caliber: .45 ACP. Seven-round magazine, 5-inch bbl., 8.5 inches overall. Weight: 38 oz. Blade front and fixed, low-profile rear sights.

KAREEN MK II (1500) AUTO PISTOL
Single-action only. Caliber: 9mm Para. 10-round magazine, 4.75-inch bbl., 8 inches overall. Weight: 33.6 oz. Blade front sight, rear adjustable for windage. Textured black composition or rubberized grips. Blued, two-tone, matte black finish. Imported from 1996 to date.
Blued or matte black finish . . . . . . NiB $446 Ex $353 Gd $260
Two-tone finish . . . . NiB $655 Ex $516 Gd $383
Meprolite sights, add. $40

**KAREEN MK II COMPACT
(1501) AUTO PISTOL . . . . NiB $436 Ex $369 Gd $271**
Similar to standard Kareen MKII except w/3.85-inch bbl., 7.1 inches overall. Weight: 32 oz. Imported 1997 to date.

GOLAN MODEL (2500) AUTO PISTOL
Single or double action. Caliber: 9mm Para., .40 S&W. 10-round magazine, 3.85-inch bbl., 7.1 inches overall. Weight: 34 oz. Steel slide and alloy frame w/ambidextrous safety and decocking lever. Matte black finish. Imported from 1997 to date.
9mm Para. NiB $883 Ex $715 Gd $501
.40 S&W . . . . NiB $722 Ex $587 Gd $414

**GAL MODEL
(5000) AUTO PISTOL . . . . NiB $392 Ex $311 Gd $221**
Caliber: .45 ACP. Eight-round magazine, 4.25-inch bbl., 7.25 inches overall. Weight: 42 oz. Low profile 3-dot sights. Combat-style black rubber grips. Imported from 1997 to date.

JAPANESE MILITARY PISTOLS — Tokyo, Japan Manufactured by Government Plant

**MODEL 14 (1925)
AUTOMATIC PISTOL . . . . NiB $675 Ex $547 Gd $384**
Modification of the Nambu Model 1914, changes chiefly intended to simplify mass production. Standard round trigger guard or oversized guard for use w/gloves. Caliber: 8mm Nambu. Eight-round magazine, 4.75-inch bbl., 9 inches overall. Weight: About 29 oz. Fixed sights. Blued finish. Grooved wood grips. Intro. 1925 and mfd. through WW II.

MODEL 26 DAO REVOLVER . . . . . NiB $603 Ex $418 Gd $285
Top-break frame. Caliber: 9mm. Six-round cylinder w/automatic extractor/ejector, 4.7-inch bbl., adopted by the Japanese Army from 1893 to 1914, replaced by the Model 14 Automatic Pistol but remained in service through World War II.

MODEL 94 (1934)
AUTOMATIC PISTOL . . . . NiB $304 Ex $232 Gd $155
Poorly designed and constructed, this pistol is unsafe and can be fired merely by applying pressure on the sear, which is exposed on the left side. Caliber: 8mm Nambu. Six-round magazine, 3.13-inch bbl., 7.13 inches overall. Weight: About 27 oz. Fixed sights. Blued finish. Hard rubber or wood grips. Intro. in 1934, principally for export to Latin American countries, production continued thru WW II.

Japanese Model 94 (1934)

NAMBU MODEL
1914 AUTOMATIC PISTOL . . . . . NiB $1709 Ex $1503 Gd $761
Original Japanese service pistol, resembles Luger in appearance and Glisenti in operation. Caliber: 8mm Nambu. Seven-round magazine, 4.5-inch bbl., 9 inches overall. Weight: About 30 oz. Fixed front sight, adj. rear sight. Blued finish. Checkered wood grips. Made from 1914-1925.

JENNINGS FIREARMS INC. — Currently Mfd. by Bryco Arms, Irvine, California Previously by Calwestco, Inc. & B.L. Jennings

See additional listings under Bryco Arms.

MODEL J AUTO PISTOL
Calibers: .22 LR, .25 ACP. Six-round magazine, 2.5-inch bbl., about 5 inches overall. Weight: 13 oz. Fixed sights. Chrome, satin nickel or black Teflon finish. Walnut, grooved black Cycolac or resin-impregnated wood grips. Made from 1981-85 under Jennings and Calwestco logos; from 1985 to date by Bryco Arms.
Model J-22. . . . . NiB $89 Ex $75 Gd $53
Model J-25. . . . . NiB $84 Ex $68 Gd $48

Jennings Model J Auto Pistol

IVER JOHNSON ARMS, INC. — Jacksonville, Arkansas

Operation of this company dates back to 1871, when Iver Johnson and Martin Bye partnered to manufacture metallic cartridge revolvers. Johnson became the sole owner and changed the name to Iver Johnson's Arms & Cycle Works, which it was known as for almost 100 years. Modern management shortened the name, and after several owner changes the firm was moved from Massachusetts, its original base, to Jacksonville, Arkansas. In 1987, the American Military Arms Corporation (AMAC) acquired the operation, which subsequently ceased in 1993.

NOTE: *For ease in finding a particular firearm, Iver Johnson handguns are divided into two sections: Automatic Pistols (below) and Revolvers, which follow. For the complete handgun listing, please refer to the Index.*

AUTOMATIC PISTOLS

9MM DA AUTOMATIC . . . . NiB $407 Ex $331 Gd $234
Caliber: 9mm. Six-round magazine, 3-inch bbl., 6.5 inches overall. Weight: 26 oz. Blade front sight, adj. rear. Smooth hardwood grip. Blued or matte blued finish. Intro. 1986.

COMPACT .25 ACP . . . . NiB $195 Ex $164 Gd $112
Bernardelli V/P design. Caliber: .25 ACP. Five-round magazine, 2.13-inch bbl., 4.13 inches overall. Weight: 9.3 oz. Fixed sights. Checkered composition grips. Blued slide, matte blued frame and color-casehardened trigger. Made from 1991-93.

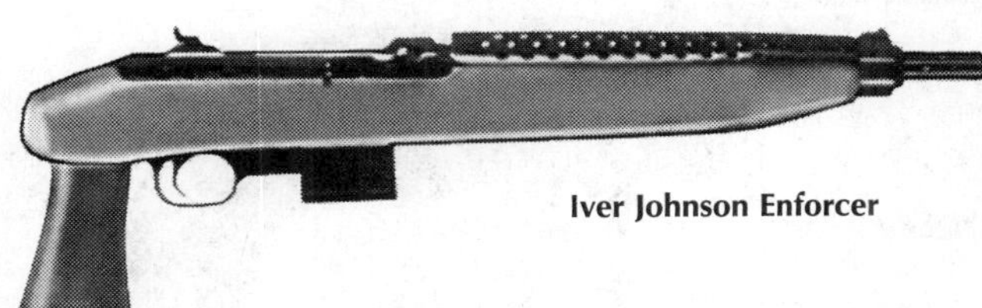
Iver Johnson Enforcer

ENFORCER . . . . NiB $503 Ex $395 Gd $286
Semiautomatic. Caliber: .30 U.S. Carbine. Five-, 15-, or 30-round magazine, 9.5- inch bbl., weight: 5.5 lbs. Adj. sights. Walnut stock. Made from mid-1980s-1993.

PP30 SUPER
ENFORCER AUTOMATIC . . . . NiB $473 Ex $380 Gd $246
Caliber: .30 U.S. Carbine. Fifteen- or 30-round magazine, 9.5-inch bbl., 17 inches overall. Weight: 4 pounds. Adj. peep rear sight, blade front. American walnut stock. Made from 1984-86.

PONY AUTOMATIC PISTOL
Caliber: .380 Auto. Six-round magazine, 3.1-inch bbl., 6.1 inches overall. Blue, matte blue, nickel finish or stainless. Weight: 20 oz. Wooden grips. Smallest of the locked breech automatics. Made from 1982-88. Reintroduced from 1990-93.
Blue or matte
blue model . . . . NiB $347 Ex $295 Gd $212
Nickel model. . . . . NiB $398 Ex $306 Gd $213
Deluxe model . . . . NiB $424 Ex $347 Gd $254

Iver Johnson
Model TP

Iver Johnson
Model 57A Target

Iver Johnson
Model 55 Target

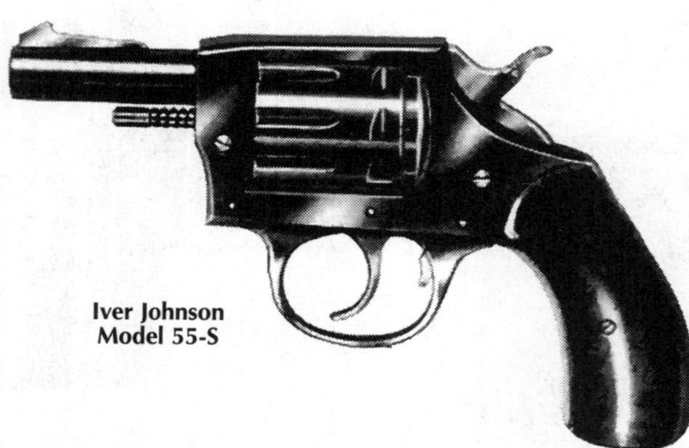
Iver Johnson
Model 55-S

Iver Johnson
Model 56 Blank Revolver

MODEL TP-22 DA AUTOMATIC. . . . . NiB $165 Ex $124 Gd $83
Calibers: .22 LR, Seven-round magazine, 2.85-inch bbl., 5.39 inches overall. Blued finish. Weight: 14.46 oz. Made from 1982-93.

MODEL TP25 DA POCKET PISTOL . . . . NiB $201 Ex $165 Gd $119
Double-action automatic. Caliber: .25 ACP. Seven-round magazine, 3-inch bbl., 5.5 inches overall. Weight: 12 oz. Black plastic grips and blued finish. Made from 1982-93.

TRAILSMAN AUTOMATIC PISTOL
Caliber: .22 LR. 10-round magazine, 4.5 or 6-inch bbl., 8.75 inches overall (with 4.5-inch bbl.). Weight: 46 oz. Fixed target-type sights. Checkered composition grips. Made from 1984-90.
Standard model . . . . NiB $237 Ex $196 Gd $140
Deluxe model . . . . NiB $276 Ex $226 Gd $162

REVOLVERS

MODEL 55 TARGET DA REVOLVER . . . . NiB $155 Ex $124 Gd $83
Solid frame. Caliber: .22 LR. Eight-round cylinder, bbl. lengths: 4.5-, 6-inches. 10.75 inches overall (with 6-inch bbl.). Weight: 30.5 oz. (with 6-inch bbl.). Fixed sights. Blued finish. Walnut grips. Note: Original model designation was 55; changed to 55A when loading gate was added in 1961. Made from 1955-77.

MODEL 55-S REVOLVER. . . . . NiB $165 Ex $124 Gd $83
Same general specifications as the Model 55 except for 2.5-inch bbl. and small, molded pocket-size grip.

MODEL 56 BLANK REVOLVER . . . . NiB $100 Ex $84 Gd $62
Solid frame. Caliber: .22 blanks only. Eight-round cylinder, 2.5-inch solid bbl., 6.75 inches overall. Weight: 10 oz.

MODEL 57A TARGET DA REVOLVER. . . . . NiB $134 Ex $119 Gd $83
Solid frame. Caliber: .22 LR. Eight-round cylinder, bbl. lengths: 4.5, and 6-inches. 10.75 inches overall. Weight: 30.5 oz. with 6-inch bbl. Adj. sights. Blued finish. Walnut grips. Note: Original model designation was 57, changed to 57A when loading gate was added in 1961. Made from 1956-75.

MODEL 66 TRAILSMAN DA REVOLVER. . . . . NiB $124 Ex $93 Gd $72
Hinged frame. Rebounding hammer. Caliber: .22 LR. Eight-round cylinder, 6-inch bbl., 11 inches overall. Weight: 34 oz. Adj. sights. Blued finish. Walnut grips. Made from 1958-75.

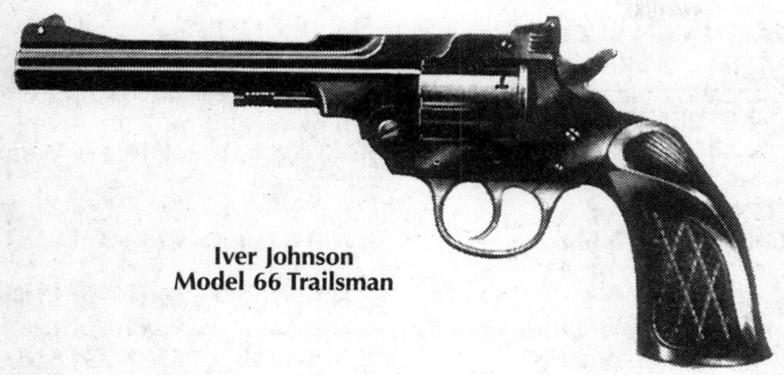
Iver Johnson
Model 66 Trailsman

Iver Johnson
Model 67 Viking

MODEL 67 VIKING DA REVOLVER . . . . NiB $163 Ex $134 Gd $98
Hinged frame. Caliber: .22 LR. Eight-round cylinder, bbl. lengths: 4.5- and 6-inches, 11 inches overall (with 6-inch bbl.). Weight: 34 oz. (with 6-inch bbl.). Adj. sights. Walnut grips w/thumbrest. Made from 1964-75.

MODEL 67S VIKING SNUB REVOLVER . . . . NiB $165 Ex $124 Gd $83
DA. Hinged frame. Calibers: .22 LR, .32 S&W Short and Long, .38 S&W. Eight-round cylinder in .22, 5-round in .32 and .38 calibers; 2.75-inch bbl. Weight: 25 oz. Adj. sights. Tenite grips. Made from 1964-75.

MODEL 1900 DA REVOLVER . . . . . . NiB $135 Ex $114 Gd $68
Solid frame. Calibers: .22 LR, .32 S&W, .32 S&W Long, .38 S&W. Seven-round cylinder in .22 cal.,or 6-round (.32 S&W), 5-round (.32 S&W Long, .38 S&W); bbl. lengths: 2.5-, 4.5- and 6-inches. Weight: 12 oz. (in .32 S&W w/2.5-inch bbl.). Fixed sights. Blued or nickel finish. Hard rubber grips. Made from 1900-47.

MODEL 1900 TARGET DA REVOLVER. . . . . NiB $196 Ex $160 Gd $114
Solid frame. Caliber: .22 LR. Seven-round cylinder, bbl. lengths: 6- and 9.5-inches. Fixed sights. Blued finish. Checkered walnut grips. (This earlier model does not have counterbored chambers as in the Target Sealed 8. Made from 1925-42.)

AMERICAN BULLDOG DA REVOLVER
Solid frame. Calibers: .22 LR, .22 WMR, .38 Special. Six-round cylinder in .22, 5-round in .38. Bbl. lengths: 2.5-, 4-inch. 9 inches overall (with 4-inch bbl.). Weight: 30 oz. (with 4-inch bbl.). Adj. sights. Blued or nickel finish. Plastic grips. Made from 1974-76.
.38 Special. . . . . NiB $186 Ex $155 Gd $103
Other calibers . . . . NiB $165 Ex $124 Gd $83

ARMSWORTH MODEL 855 SA. . . . NiB $256 Ex $189 Gd $142
Hinged frame. Caliber: .22 LR. Eight-round cylinder, 6-inch bbl., 10.75 inches overall. Weight: 30 oz. Adj. sights. Blued finish. Checkered walnut one-piece grip. Adj. finger rest. Made from 1955-57.

CADET DA REVOLVER . . . . NiB $163 Ex $139 Gd $88
Solid frame. Calibers: .22 LR, .22 WMR, .32 S&W Long, .38 S&W, .38 Special. Six- or 8-round cylinder in .22, 5-round in other calibers, 2.5-inch bbl., 7 inches overall. Weight: 22 oz. Fixed sights. Blued finish or nickel finish. Plastic grips. Note: Loading gate added in 1961, .22 cylinder capacity changed from 8 to 6 rounds in 1975. Made from 1955-77.

CATTLEMAN SA REVOLVER
Patterned after the Colt Army SA revolver. Calibers: .357 Magnum, .44 Magnum, .45 Colt. Six-round cylinder. Bbl. lengths: 4.75-, 5.5- (not available in .44), 6- (.44 only), 7.25-inch. Weight: About 41 oz. Fixed sights. Blued bbl., and cylinder color-casehardened frame, brass grip frame. One-piece walnut grip. Made by Aldo Uberti, Brescia, Italy, from 1973-78.
.44 Magnum . . . . NiB $282 Ex $231 Gd $154
Other calibers . . . . NiB $252 Ex $209 Gd $138

Iver Johnson
Model 67S Viking Snub

Iver Johnson
Model 1900 Target

Iver Johnson
Cadet

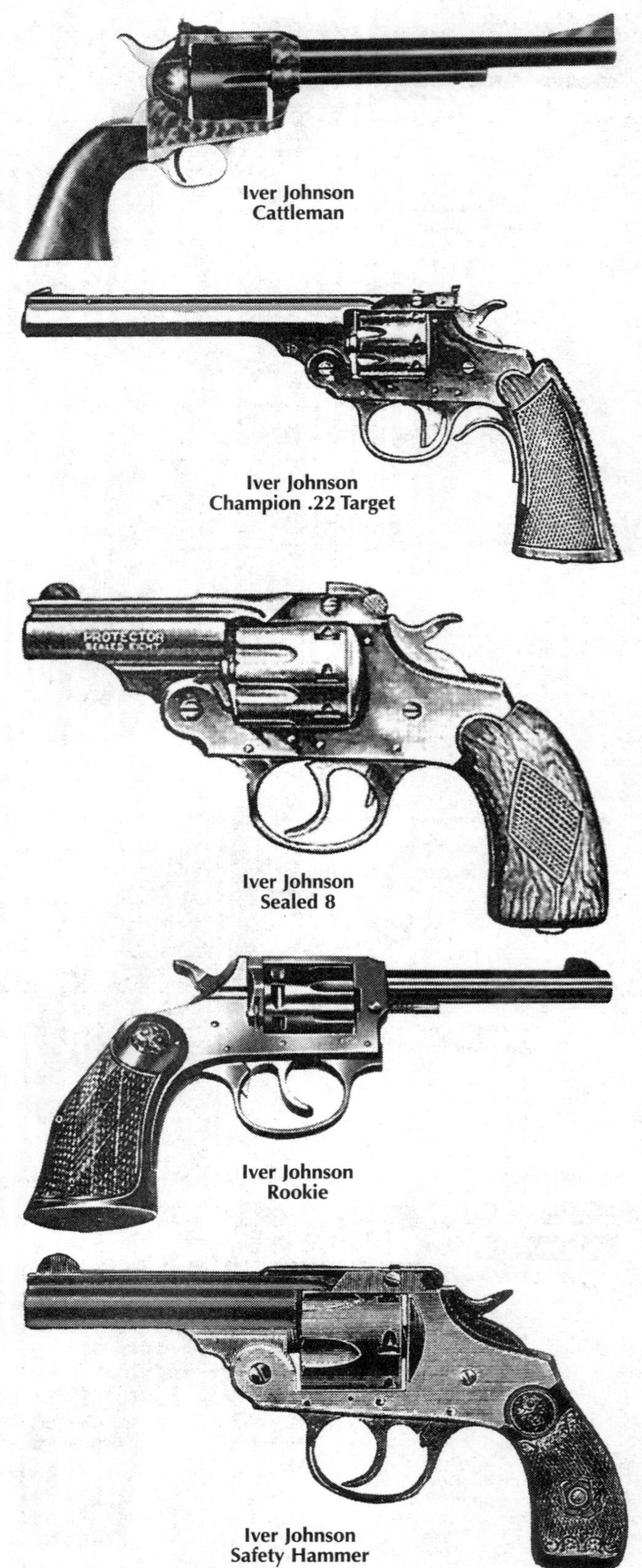
Iver Johnson Cattleman

Iver Johnson Champion .22 Target

Iver Johnson Sealed 8

Iver Johnson Rookie

Iver Johnson Safety Hammer

CATTLEMAN BUCKHORN SA REVOLVER
Same as standard Cattleman except has adj. rear and ramp front sights. Bbl. lengths: 4.75- (.44 only), 5.75- (not available in .44), 6- (.44 only), 7.5- or 12-inches bbl., weight: About 44 oz. Made from 1973-78.

.357 Magnum or .45 Colt w/12-inch bbl. . . . . NiB $339 Ex $257 Gd $184
.357 Magnum or .45 Colt w/5.75- or 7.5-inch bbl. . . . . . NiB $287 Ex $231 Gd $164
.44 Magnum, w/12-inch bbl. . . . . . NiB $416 Ex $339 Gd $240
.44 Magnum, other bbls. . . . . NiB $339 Ex $287 Gd $205

CATTLEMAN BUNTLINE SA REVOLVER
Same as Cattleman Buckhorn except has 18-inch bbl., walnut shoulder stock w/brass fittings. Weight: About 56 oz. Made from 1973-78.

.44 Magnum . . . . NiB $534 Ex $436 Gd $309
Other calibers . . . . NiB $483 Ex $394 Gd $281

CATTLEMAN TRAIL BLAZER. . . . . NiB $213 Ex $171 Gd $120
Similar to Cattleman Buckhorn except .22 caliber has interchangeable .22 LR and .22 WMR cylinders, 5.5- or 6.5-inch bbl., weight: About 40 oz. Made from 1973-78.

CHAMPION .22 TARGET SA . . . . NiB $259 Ex $212 Gd $151
Hinged frame. Caliber: .22 LR. Eight-round cylinder. Single action. Counterbored chambers as in Sealed 8 model, 6-inch bbl., 10.75 inches overall. Weight: 28 oz. Adj. target sights. Blued finish. Checkered walnut grips, adj. finger rest. Made from 1938-48.

DELUXE TARGET . . . . NiB $258 Ex $212 Gd $160
Same as Sportsman except has adj. sights. Made from 1975-76.

PROTECTOR SEALED 8 DA REVOLVER. . . . . NiB $202 Ex $151 Gd $114
Hinged frame. Caliber: .22 LR. Eight-round cylinder, 2.5-inch bbl., 7.25 inches overall. Weight: 20 oz. Fixed sights. Blued finish. Checkered walnut grips. Made from 1933-49.

ROOKIE DA REVOLVER. . . . . NiB $125 Ex $104 Gd $84
Solid frame. Caliber: .38 Special. Five-round cylinder, 4-inch bbl., 9-inches overall. Weight: 30 oz. Fixed sights. Blued or nickel finish. Plastic grips. Made from 1975-77.

SAFETY HAMMER DA REVOLVER. . . . . NiB $166 Ex $135 Gd $94
Hinged frame. Calibers: .22 LR, .32 S&W, .32 S&W Long, .38 S&W. Seven-round cylinder in .22 cal.,or 6-round (.32 S&W Long), 5-round (.32 S&W, .38 S&W). bbl. lengths: 2, 3, 3.25, 4, 5 or 6 inches. Weight w/4-inch bbl.: 15 oz. (.22, .32 S&W), 19.5 oz. (.32 S&W Long) or 19 oz. (.38 S&W). Fixed sights. Blued or nickel finish. Hard rubber, round butt grips or square butt, rubber or walnut grips available. Note: .32 S&W Long and .38 S&W models built on heavy frame. Made from 1892-1950.

SAFETY HAMMERLESS DA REVOLVER. . . . . NiB $176 Ex $148 Gd $99
Similar to the Safety Hammer Model except w/shrouded hammerless frame. Made from 1895-1950.

SIDEWINDER DA REVOLVER . . . . NiB $165 Ex $150 Gd $93
Solid frame. Caliber: .22 LR. Six- or 8-round cylinder, bbl. lengths: 4.75, 6 inches; 11.25 inches overall (with 6-inch bbl.). Weight: 31 oz. (with 6-inch bbl.). Fixed sights. Blued or nickel finish w/plastic staghorn grips or color-casehardened frame w/walnut grips. Note: Cylinder capacity changed from 8 to 6 rounds in 1975. Intro. 1961. Disc.

SIDEWINDER "S" . . . . NiB $175 Ex $150 Gd $108
Same as Sidewinder except has interchangeable cylinders in .22 LR and .22 WMR, adj. sights. Intro. 1974. Disc.

SPORTSMAN DA REVOLVER . . . . NiB $154 Ex $124 Gd $93
Solid frame. Caliber: .22 LR. Six-round cylinder. Bbl. lengths: 4.75-, 6-inches, 10.75 inches overall (with 6-inch bbl.). Weight: 30.5 oz. (with 6-inch bbl.). Fixed sights. Blued finish. Plastic grips. Made from 1974-76.

SUPERSHOT 9 DA REVOLVER . . . . NiB $170 Ex $145 Gd $88
Same as Supershot Sealed 8 except has nine non-counterbored chambers. Made from 1929-49.

SUPERSHOT .22 DA REVOLVER . . . . NiB $122 Ex $102 Gd $71
Hinged frame. Caliber: .22 LR. Seven-round cylinder, 6-inch bbl. Fixed sights. Blued finish. Checkered walnut grips. This earlier model does not have counterbored chambers as in the Supershot Sealed 8. Made from 1929-49.

SUPERSHOT MODEL 844 DA . . . . . NiB $201 Ex $160 Gd $113
Hinged frame. Caliber: .22 LR. Eight-round cylinder, bbl. lengths: 4.5- or 6-inch, 9.25 inches overall (with 4.5-inch bbl.). Weight: 27 oz. (4.5-inch bbl.). Adj. sights. Blued finish. Checkered walnut one-piece grip. Made from 1955-56.

SUPERSHOT SEALED 8 DA REVOLVER . . . . NiB $201 Ex $160 Gd $114
Hinged frame. Caliber: .22 LR. Eight-round cylinder, 6-inch bbl., 10.75 inches overall. Weight: 24 oz. Adj. target sights. Blued finish. Checkered walnut grips. Postwar model does not have adj. finger rest as earlier version. Made from 1931-57.

SWING-OUT DA REVOLVER
Calibers: .22 LR, .22 WMR, .32 S&W Long, .38 Special. Six-round cylinder in .22, 5-round in .32 and .38. Two, 3-, 4-inch plain bbl., or 4- 6-inch vent rib bbl., 8.75 inches overall (with 4-inch bbl.). Fixed or adj. sights. Blued or nickel finish. Walnut grips. Made in 1977.
W/plain barrel, fixed sights . . . . NiB $177 Ex $147 Gd $105
W/vent rib, adj. sights . . . . NiB $167 Ex $198 Gd $126

TARGET 9 DA REVOLVER . . . . NiB $209 Ex $172 Gd $126
Same as Target Sealed 8 except has nine non-counterbored chambers. Made from 1929-46.

TARGET SEALED 8 DA REVOLVER . . . . NiB $198 Ex $153 Gd $121
Solid frame. Caliber: .22 LR. Eight-round cylinder, bbl. lengths: 6- and 10-inches. 10.75 inches overall (with 6-inch bbl.). Weight: 24 oz. (with 6-inch bbl.). Fixed sights. Blued finish. Checkered walnut grips. Made from 1931-57.

TRIGGER-COCKING SA TARGET . . . . NiB $271 Ex $220 Gd $163
Hinged frame. First pull on trigger cocks hammer, second pull releases hammer. Caliber: .22 LR. Eight-round cylinder, counterbored chambers, 6-inch bbl., 10.75 inches overall. Weight: 24 oz. Adj. target sights. Blued finish. Checkered walnut grips. Made from 1940-47.

Iver Johnson Sidewinder

Iver Johnson Supershot Sealed 8

Iver Johnson Target Sealed 8

Kahr Model K9

KAHR ARMS — Pearl River, New York and Worchester, MA

MODEL K9 DAO AUTO PISTOL
Caliber: 9mm Para. Seven-round magazine, 3.5-inch bbl., 6 inches overall. Weight: 24 oz. Fixed sights. Matte black, electroless nickel, Birdsong Black-T or matte stainless finish. Wraparound textured polymer or hardwood grips. Made from 1994 to date.
Duo-Tone finish . . . . NiB $727 Ex $594 Gd $418
Matte black finish . . . . NiB $605 Ex $477 Gd $338
Electroless nickel finish . . . . NiB $631 Ex $513 Gd $361
Black-T finish . . . . NiB $856 Ex $639 Gd $480
Matte stainless finish . . . . NiB $586 Ex $477 Gd $337
Lady K9 model . . . . NiB $567 Ex $461 Gd $326
Elite model . . . . NiB $599 Ex $487 Gd $344
Tritium Night Sights, add $90

Kel-Tec Model P-11

Kimber Model Classic .45

MODEL K40 DAO AUTO PISTOL
Similar to Model K9 except chambered .40 S&W w/5- or 6-round magazine, Weight: 26 oz. Made from 1997 to date.
Matte black finish . . . . NiB $555 Ex $451 Gd $317
Electroless nickel finish . . . . NiB $660 Ex $538 Gd $381
Black-T finish. . . . . NiB $696 Ex $558 Gd $382
Matte stainless finish . . . . NiB $581 Ex $467 Gd $320
Covert model
(shorter grip-frame) . . . . NiB $550 Ex $441 Gd $301
Elite model . . . . NiB $625 Ex $513 Gd $370
Tritium Night Sights, add. $90

MODEL MK9 DAO AUTO PISTOL
Similar to Model K9 except w/Micro-Compact frame. Six- or 7-round magazine, 3- inch bbl., 5.5 inches overall. Weight: 22 oz. Stainless or Duo-Tone finish. Made from 1998 to date.
Duo-Tone finish . . . . NiB $755 Ex $617 Gd $441
Matte stainless
finish . . . . NiB $630 Ex $518 Gd $364
Elite model . . . . NiB $632 Ex $518 Gd $364
Tritium Night
Sights, add $90

KBI, INC — Harrisburg, Pennsylvania

MODEL PSP-.25 AUTO PISTOL. . . . NiB $258 Ex $201 Gd $134
Caliber: .25 ACP. Six-round magazine, 2.13-inch bbl., 4.13 inches overall. Weight: 9.5 oz. All-steel construction w/dual safety system. Made from 1994 to date.

KEL-TEC CNC INDUSTRIES, INC. — Cocoa, Florida

MODEL P-11 DAO PISTOL
Caliber: 9mm Parabellum or .40 S&W. 10-round magazine, 3.1-inch bbl., 5.6 inches overall. Weight: 14 oz. Blade front sight, drift adjustable rear. Aluminum frame w/steel slide. Checkered black, gray, or green polymer grips. Matte blue, nickel, stainless steel or Parkerized finish. Made from 1995 to date.
9mm . . . . NiB $294 Ex $243 Gd $180
.40 S&W . . . . NiB $296 Ex $238 Gd $164
Parkerized finish, add $40
Nickel finish, add (disc. 1995). $30
Stainless finish, add
(1996 to date) $55
Tritium Night Sights, add. $80
.40 cal. conversion kit, add $175

KIMBER MANUFACTURING, INC. — Yonkers, New York (Formerly Kimber of America, Inc.)

MODEL CLASSIC .45
Similar to Government 1911 built on steel, polymer or alloy full-size or compact frame. Caliber: .45 ACP. Seven-, 8-, 10- or 14-round magazine, 4- or 5-inch bbl., 7.7 or 8.75 inches overall. Weight: 28 oz. (Compact LW), 34 oz. (Compact or Polymer) or .38 oz. (Custom FS). McCormick low-profile combat or Kimber adj. target sights. Blued, matte black oxide or stainless finish. Checkered custom wood or black synthetic grips. Made from 1994 to date.
Custom (matte black) . . . . NiB $653 Ex $550 Gd $359
Custom Royal (polished blue) . . . . . NiB $711 Ex $576 Gd $403
Custom stainless (satin stainless) . . . NiB $673 Ex $545 Gd $382
Custom Target (matte black) . . . . . . NiB $685 Ex $555 Gd $388
Target Gold Match
(polished blue). . . . . NiB $948 Ex $729 Gd $540
Target stainless Match
(polished stainless) . . . . NiB $764 Ex $866 Gd $603
Polymer (matte black) . . . . NiB $774 Ex $629 Gd $443
Polymer Stainless
(satin stainless slide) . . . . NiB $926 Ex $745 Gd $526
Polymer Target
(matte black slide). . . . . NiB $868 Ex $704 Gd $495
Compact (matte black) . . . . NiB $613 Ex $498 Gd $352
Compact stainless (satin stainless) . . . . . . NiB $678 Ex $550 Gd $386
Compact LW (matte
black w/alloy frame) . . . . NiB $678 Ex $534 Gd $380

KORTH PISTOLS — Ratzeburg, Germany

Currently imported by Keng's Firearms Specialty, Inc. Previously by Beeman Precision Arms; Osborne's and Mandall Shooting Supply

REVOLVERS COMBAT, SPORT, TARGET
Calibers: .357 Mag. and .22 LR w/interchangeable combination cylinders of .357 Mag./9mm Para. or .22 LR/.22 WMR also .22 Jet, .32 S&W and .32 H&R Mag. Bbls: 2.5-, 3-, 4-inch (combat) and 5.25- or 6-inch (target). Weight: 33 to 42 oz. Blued, stainless, matte silver or polished silver finish. Checkered walnut grips. Imported 1967 to date.
Standard rimfire model . . . . NiB $3354 Ex $2665 Gd $1810
Standard centerfire model. . . . . NiB $3401 Ex $2680 Gd $1851
ISU Match Target model . . . . . . NiB $4127 Ex $3365 Gd $2263
Custom stainless finish, add. $450
Matte silver finish, add $650
Polished silver finish, add $950

SEMIAUTOMATIC PISTOL
Calibers: 30 Luger, 9mm Para., .357 SIG, .40 S&W, 9x21mm. 10- or 14-round magazine, 4- or 5-inch bbl., all-steel construction, recoil-operated. Ramp front sight, adj. rear. Blued, stainless, matte silver or polished silver finish. Checkered walnut grips. Imported from 1988 to date.
Standard model . . . . NiB $5009 Ex $4012 Gd $2781
Matte silver finish, add $650
Polished silver finish, add $950

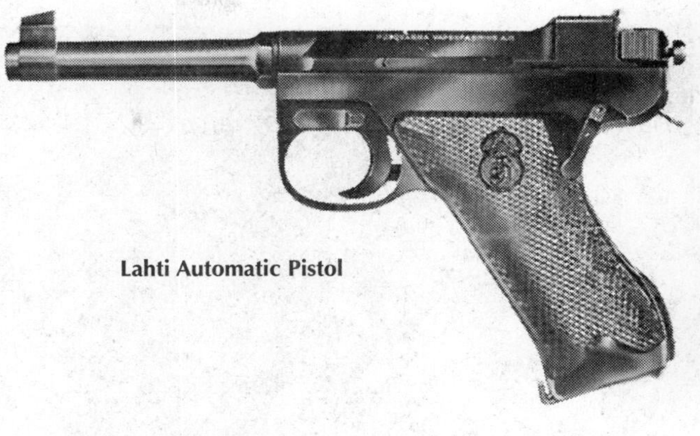

Lahti Automatic Pistol

LAHTI PISTOLS — Mfd. by Husqvarna Vapenfabriks A. B. Huskvarna, Sweden, and Valtion Kivaar Tedhas ("VKT") Jyväskyla, Finland

AUTOMATIC PISTOL
Caliber: 9mm Para. Eight-round magazine, 4.75-inch bbl., weight: About 46 oz. Fixed sights. Blued finish. Plastic grips. Specifications given are those of the Swedish Model 40 but also apply in general to the Finnish Model L-35, which differs only slightly. A considerable number of Swedish Lahti pistols were imported and sold in the U.S. The Finnish model, somewhat better made, is rare. Finnish Model L-35 adopted 1935. Swedish Model 40 adopted 1940 and mfd. through 1944.
Finnish L-35 model . . . . NiB $2457 Ex $1932 Gd $1309
Swedish 40 model . . . . NiB $546 Ex $422 Gd $278

L.A.R. Mark I Grizzly

L.A.R. MANUFACTURING, INC. — West Jordan, Utah

MARK I GRIZZLY WIN. MAG. AUTOMATIC PISTOL
Calibers: .357 Mag., .45 ACP, .45 Win. Mag. Seven-round magazine, 6.5-inch bbl., 10.5 inches overall. Weight: 48 oz. Fully adj. sights. Checkered rubber combat-style grips. Blued finish. Made from 1983 to date. 8- or 10-inch bbl., Made from 1987-99.
.357 Mag. (6.5 inch barrel) . . . . . . NiB $1164 Ex $888 Gd $687
.45 Win. Mag.(6.5 inch barrel) . . . NiB $1022 Ex $832 Gd $574
8-inch barrel . . . . NiB $1301 Ex $1095 Gd $812
10-inch barrel . . . . NiB $1378 Ex $1121 Gd $801

MARK IV GRIZZLY
AUTOMATIC PISTOL . . . . NiB $1094 Ex $909 Gd $625
Same general specifications as the L.A.R. Mark I except chambered for .44 Magnum, has 5.5- or 6.5-inch bbl., beavertail grip safety, matte blued finish. Made from 1991-99.

MARK V AUTO PISTOL . . . . NiB $980 Ex $774 Gd $568
Similar to the Mark I except chambered in 50 Action Express. Six-round magazine, 5.4- or 6.5-inch bbl., 10.6 inches overall (with 5.4-inch bbl.). Weight: 56 oz. Checkered walnut grips. Made from 1993-99.

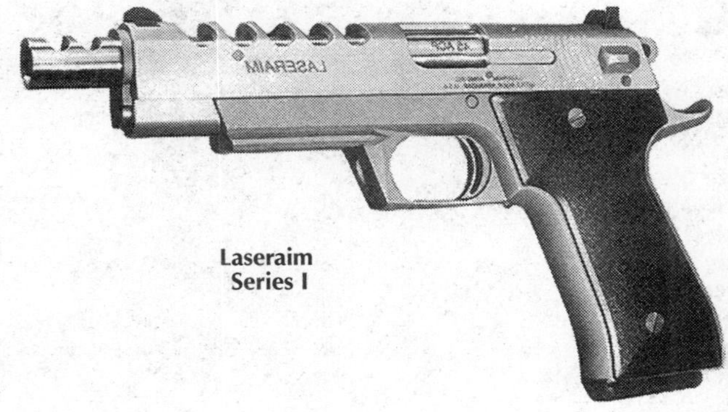

Laseraim Series I

LASERAIM TECHNOLOGIES INC. Little Rock, Arkansas

SERIES I SA AUTO PISTOL
Calibers: .40 S&W, .45 ACP, 10mm. Seven or 8- round magazine, 3.875- or 5.5-inch dual-port compensated bbl., 8.75 or 10.5 inches overall. Weight: 46 or 52 oz. Fixed sights w/Laseraim or adjustable Millet sights. Textured black composition grips. Extended slide release, ambidextrous safety and beveled magazine well. Stainless or matte black Teflon finish. Made from 1993 to date.
Series I w/adjustable sights . . . . . . NiB $458 Ex $356 Gd $254
Series I w/fixed sights . . . . NiB $417 Ex $324 Gd $244
Series I w/fixed sights (HotDot) . . . NiB $560 Ex $458 Gd $325
Series I Dream Team (RedDot) . . . . NiB $817 Ex $668 Gd $460
Series I Illusion (Laseraim) . . . . NiB $878 Ex $684 Gd $470

Laseraim Series II

Laseraim Series III
w/LA93 Illusion III Scope

Llama Model IIIA
Deluxe Chrome Engraved First Issue

Llama Model IIIA
Deluxe Blue Engraved Second Issue

SERIES II SA AUTO PISTOL
Similar to Series I except w/stainless finish and no bbl., compensator. Made from 1993-96.
Series II w/adjustable sights . . . . . . NiB $387 Ex $325 Gd $233
Series II w/fixed sights. . . . . NiB $364 Ex $297 Gd $215
Series II Dream Team. . . . . NiB $680 Ex $547 Gd $386
Series II Illusion. . . . . NiB $718 Ex $577 Gd $406

SERIES III SA AUTO PISTOL
Similar to Series II except w/serrated slide and 5-inch compensated bbl., only. Made from 1994 to date.
Series III w/
adjustable sights . . . . NiB $599 Ex $488 Gd $346
Series III w/fixed sights . . . . NiB $548 Ex $447 Gd $318

VELOCITY SERIES SA AUTO PISTOL
Similar to Series I except chambered for .357 Sig. or .400 Cor-Bon, 3.875-inch unported bbl., (compact) or 5.5-inch dual-port compensated bbl. Made from 1997 to date. See illustration previous page.
Compact model (unported) . . . . . . NiB $379 Ex $311 Gd $219
Government model (ported) . . . . . NiB $442 Ex $359 Gd $253
W/wireless laser
(HotDot), add $150

LIGNOSE PISTOLS — Suhl, Germany Aktien-Gesellschaft "Lignose" Abteilung

The following Lignose pistols were manufactured from 1920 to the mid-1930s. They were also marketed under the Bergmann name.

EINHAND MODEL 2A
POCKET AUTO PISTOL . . . . NiB $334 Ex $303 Gd $130
As the name implies, this pistol is designed for one-hand operation, pressure on a "trigger" at the front of the guard retracts the slide. Caliber: .25 Auto. (6.35 mm). Six-round magazine, 2-inch bbl., 4.75 inches overall. Weight: About 14 oz. Blued finish. Hard rubber grips.

MODEL 2 POCKET
AUTO PISTOL . . . . NiB $365 Ex $283 Gd $212
Conventional Browning type. Same general specifications as Einhand Model 2A but lacks the one-hand operation.

EINHAND MODEL
3A POCKET AUTO PISTOL . . . . NiB $428 Ex $336 Gd $239
Same as the Model 2A except has longer grip, 9-round magazine, weight: About 16 oz.

LLAMA HANDGUNS — Mfd. by Gabilondo y Cia, Vitoria, Spain (Imported by S.G.S., Wanamassa, New Jersey)

NOTE: *For ease in finding a particular Llama handgun, the listings are divided into two groupings: Automatic Pistols (below) and Revolvers, which follow. For a complete listing of Llama handguns, please refer to the index.*

AUTOMATIC PISTOLS

MODEL IIIA
AUTOMATIC PISTOL . . . . NiB $242 Ex $217 Gd $161
Caliber: .380 Auto. Seven-round magazine, 3.69-inch bbl., 6.5 inches overall. Weight: 23 oz. Adj. target sights. Blued finish. Plastic grips. Intro. 1951. Disc.

MODELS IIIA, XA, XV DELUXE
Same as standard Model IIIA, XA and XV except engraved w/blued or chrome finish and simulated pearl grips. Disc. 1984.
Chrome-engraved finish. . . . . NiB $357 Ex $293 Gd $211
Blue-engraved finish . . . . NiB $325 Ex $267 Gd $194

MODEL VIII
AUTOMATIC PISTOL . . . . NiB $400 Ex $283 Gd $221
Caliber: .38 Super. Nine-round magazine, 5-inch bbl., 8.5 inches overall. Weight: 40 oz. Fixed sights. Blued finish. Wood grips. Intro. in 1952. Disc.

MODELS VIII, IXA, XI DELUXE
Same as standard Models VIII, IXA and XI except finish (chrome engraved or blued engraved) and simulated pearl grips. Disc. 1984.
Chrome-engraved finish. . . . . NiB $452 Ex $369 Gd $263
Blue-engraved finish . . . . NiB $486 Ex $395 Gd $281

MODEL IXA AUTOMATIC PISTOL . . . . NiB $344 Ex $267 Gd $181
Same as model VIII except .45 Auto, 7-round magazine,

MODEL XA AUTOMATIC PISTOL. . . . . NiB $240 Ex $210 Gd $129
Same as model IIIA except .32 Auto, 8-round magazine,

MODEL XI AUTOMATIC PISTOL . . . . . NiB $338 Ex $276 Gd $196
Same as model VIII except 9mm Para.

MODEL XV AUTOMATIC PISTOL. . . . . NiB $281 Ex $230 Gd $153
Same as model XA except .22 LR.

MODELS BE-IIIA, BE-XA, BE-XV . . . . . . NiB $375 Ex $303 Gd $212
Same as models IIIA, XA and XV except w/blued-engraved finish. Made from 1977-84.

MODELS BE-VIII,
BE-IXA, BE-XI DELUXE . . . . NiB $438 Ex $356 Gd $252
Same as models VIII, IXA and XI except w/blued-engraved finish. Made from 1977-84.

MODELS C-IIIA, C-XA, C-XV . . . . . NiB $423 Ex $336 Gd $229
Same as models IIIA, XA and XV except in satin chrome.

MODELS C-VIII, C-IXA, C-XI . . . . . NiB $423 Ex $336 Gd $229
Same as models VIII, IXA and XI except in satin chrome.

MODELS CE-IIIA,
CE-XA, CE-XV . . . . NiB $463 Ex $397 Gd $275
Same as models IIIA, XA and XV except w/chrome engraved finish. Made from 1977-84.

MODELS CE-VIII,
CE-IXA, CE-XI . . . . NiB $433 Ex $336 Gd $270
Same as models VIII, IXA and XI, w/except chrome engraved finish. Made from 1977-84.

COMPACT FRAME
AUTO PISTOL . . . . NiB $438 Ex $341 Gd $234
Calibers: 9mm Para., .38 Super, .45 Auto. Seven-, 8- or 9-round magazine, 5-inch bbl., 7.88 inches overall. Weight: 34 oz. Blued, satin-chrome or Duo-Tone finishes. Made from 1990 to date. Duo-Tone disc. 1993.

DUO-TONE LARGE
FRAME AUTO PISTOL . . . . NiB $412 Ex $346 Gd $239
Caliber: .45 ACP. Seven-round magazine, 5-inch bbl., 8.5 inches overall. Weight: 36 oz. Adj. rear sight. Blued finished w/satin chrome. Polymer black grips. Made from 1990-93.

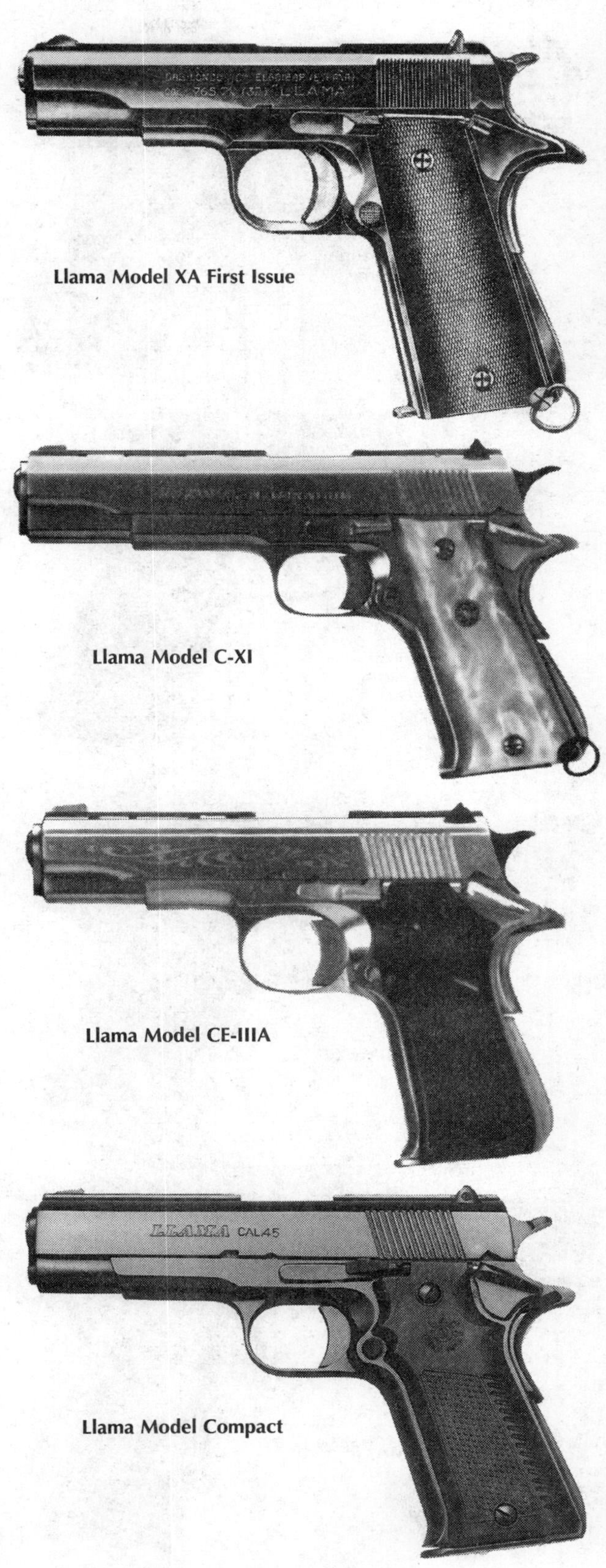

Llama Model XA First Issue

Llama Model C-XI

Llama Model CE-IIIA

Llama Model Compact

Llama Duo-Tone Large Frame

Llama M-82 DA Auto

Llama MINI-MAX II

Llama MAX-I

DUO-TONE SMALL FRAME AUTO PISTOL . . . . NiB $375 Ex $283 Gd $191
Calibers: .22 LR, .32 and .380 Auto. Seven- or 8-round magazine, 3.69 inch bbl., 6.5 inches overall. Weight: 23 oz. Square-notch rear sight, Partridge-type front. Blued finish w/chrome. Made from 1990-93.

MODEL G-IIIA DELUXE . . . . NiB $1132 Ex $917 Gd $638
Same as Model IIIA except gold damascened w/simulated pearl grips. Disc. 1982.

LARGE-FRAME AUTOMATIC PISTOL (IXA)
Caliber: .45 Auto. Seven-round magazine, 5-inch bbl., weight: 2 lbs., 8 oz. Adj. rear sight, Partridge-type front. Walnut grips or teakwood on satin chrome model. Later models w/polymer grips. Made from 1984 to date.
Blued finish . . . . NiB $370 Ex $263 Gd $181
Satin chrome finish . . . . NiB $416 Ex $334 Gd $232

M-82 DA AUTOMATIC PISTOL. . . . . NiB $744 Ex $591 Gd $382
Caliber: 9mm Para. 15-round magazine, 4.25-inch bbl., 8 inches overall. Weight: 39 oz. Drift-adj. rear sight. Matte blued finish. Matte black polymer grips. Made from 1988-93.

M-87 COMPETITION PISTOL . . . . NiB $1101 Ex $888 Gd $616
Caliber: 9mm Para. 15-round magazine, 5.5-inch bbl., 9.5 inches overall. Weight: 40 oz. Low-profile combat sights. Satin nickel finish. Matte black grip panels. Built-in ported compensator to minimize recoil and muzzle rise. Made from 1989-93.

MICRO-MAX SA AUTOMATIC PISTOL
Caliber: .380 ACP. Seven-round magazine, 3.125-inch bbl., weight: 23 oz. Blade front sight, drift adjustable rear w/3-dot system. Matte blue or satin chrome finish. Checkered polymer grips. Imported from 1997 to date.
Matte blue finish . . . . NiB $289 Ex $238 Gd $173
Satin chrome finish . . . . NiB $327 Ex $266 Gd $195

MINI-MAX SA AUTOMATIC PISTOL
Calibers: 9mm, .40 S&W or .45 ACP. Six- or 8-round magazine, 3.5-inch bbl., 8.3 inches overall. Weight: 35 oz. Blade front sight, drift adjustable rear w/3-dot system. Matte blue, Duo-Tone or satin chrome finish. Checkered polymer grips. Imported from 1996 to date.
Duo-Tone finish . . . . NiB $332 Ex $281 Gd $189
Matte blue finish . . . . NiB $295 Ex $255 Gd $169
Satin chrome finish . . . . NiB $357 Ex $281 Gd $199
Stainless (disc.) . . . . NiB $377 Ex $306 Gd $220

MINI-MAX II SA AUTOMATIC PISTOL
Cal: .45 ACP only. 10-round mag., 3.625 inch bbl., 7.375 inch overall. Wt: 37 oz. Blade front sight, drift adj. rear w/3-dot system. Shortened barrel and grip. Matte and Satin Chrome finish. Imp. 1998.
Matte blue finish . . . . NiB $447 Ex $364 Gd $256
Satin chrome finish . . . . NiB $482 Ex $389 Gd $277

MAX-I SA AUTOMATIC PISTOL
Calibers: 9mm or .45 ACP. 7- or 9-round magazine, 4.25- to 5.125 inch bbl., weight: 34 or 36 oz. Blade front sight, drift adj. rear w/3-dot system. Matte blue, Duo-Tone or satin chrome finish. Checkered black rubber grips. Imported from 1995 to date.
Duo-Tone finish . . . . NiB $290 Ex $239 Gd $168
Matte blue finish . . . . NiB $290 Ex $239 Gd $158
Satin chrome finish . . . . NiB $326 Ex $260 Gd $168

MAX-II SA AUTOMATIC PISTOL
Same as the MAX-I with 4.25 bbl. except w/10-round mag. Weight: 39 oz. Matte blue or satin chrome finish. Imported from 1996 to date.
Matte blue finish . . . . NiB $280 Ex $229 Gd $165
Satin chrome finish . . . . NiB $316 Ex $260 Gd $173

OMNI 45 DOUBLE-ACTION AUTOMATIC PISTOL . . . . NiB $438 Ex $356 Gd $244
Caliber: .45 Auto. Seven-round magazine, 4.25-inch bbl., 7.75 inches overall. Weight: 40 oz. Adj. rear sight, ramp front. Highly polished deep blued finish. Made from 1984-86.

OMNI 9MM DOUBLE-ACTION AUTOMATIC . . . . NiB $477 Ex $387 Gd $273
Same general specifications as .45 Omni except chambered for 9mm w/13-round magazine. Made from 1983-86.

SINGLE-ACTION AUTOMATIC PISTOL . . . . NiB $448 Ex $356 Gd $242
Calibers: .38 Super, 9mm, .45 Auto. Nine-round magazine (7-round for .45 Auto), 5-inch bbl., 8.5 inches overall. Weight: 2 lbs., 8 oz. Intro. in 1981.

SMALL-FRAME AUTOMATIC PISTOL
Calibers: .380 Auto (7-round magazine), .22 RF (8-round magazine), 3.69-inch bbl., weight: 23 oz. Partridge-blade front sight, adj. rear. Blued or satin-chrome finish.
Blued finish . . . . NiB $361 Ex $285 Gd $193
Satin-chrome finish . . . . NiB $423 Ex $336 Gd $234

REVOLVERS

MARTIAL DOUBLE-ACTION REVOLVER . . . . NiB $273 Ex $227 Gd $156
Calibers: .22 LR, .38 Special. Six-round cylinder, bbl. lengths: 4-inch (.38 Special only) or 6-inch; 11.25 inches overall (w/6-inch bbl.). Weight: About 36 oz. w/6-inch bbl. Target sights. Blued finish. Checkered walnut grips. Made from 1969-76.

MARTIAL DOUBLE-ACTION DELUXE
Same as standard Martial except w/satin chrome, chrome-engraved, blued engraved or gold damascened finish. Simulated pearl grips. Made from 1969-78.
Satin-chrome finish . . . . NiB $336 Ex $280 Gd $178
Chrome-engraved finish. . . . . NiB $392 Ex $321 Gd $219
Blue-engraved finish . . . . NiB $382 Ex $311 Gd $219
Gold-damascened finish . . . . . . NiB $1577 Ex $1288 Gd $970

COMANCHE I DOUBLE-ACTION REVOLVER. . . . . NiB $288 Ex $237 Gd $176
Same general specifications as Martial .22. Made from 1977-83.

COMANCHE II . . . . NiB $273 Ex $227 Gd $156
Same general specifications as Martial .38. Made from 1977-83.

COMANCHE III DOUBLE-ACTION REVOLVER. . . . . NiB $288 Ex $237 Gd $161
Caliber: .357 Magnum. Six-round cylinder, 4-inch bbl., 9.25 inches overall. Weight: 36 oz. Adj. rear sight, ramp front. Blued finish. Checkered walnut grips. Made from 1975-95. Note: Prior to 1977, this model was designated "Comanche."

COMANCHE III CHROME. NiB $368 Ex $283 Gd $203
Same gen. specifications as Comanche III except has satin chrome finish, 4- or 6-inch bbl. Made from 1979-92.

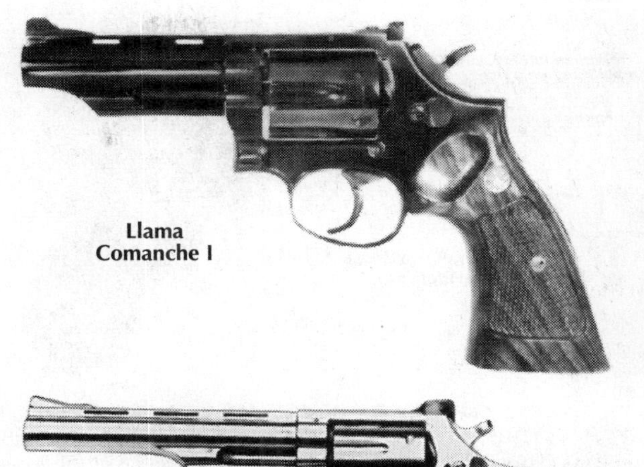

Llama
Comanche I

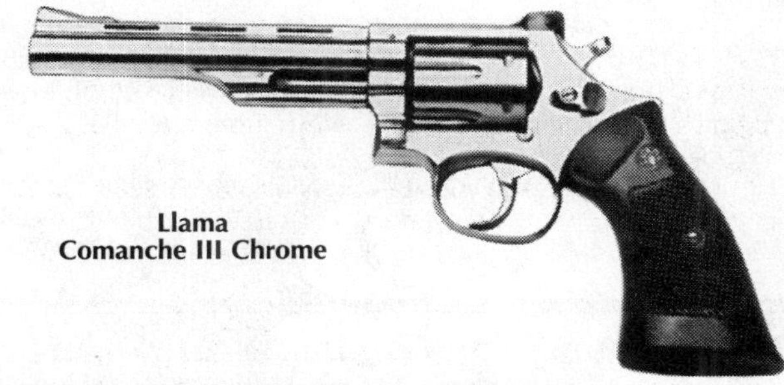

Llama
Comanche III Chrome

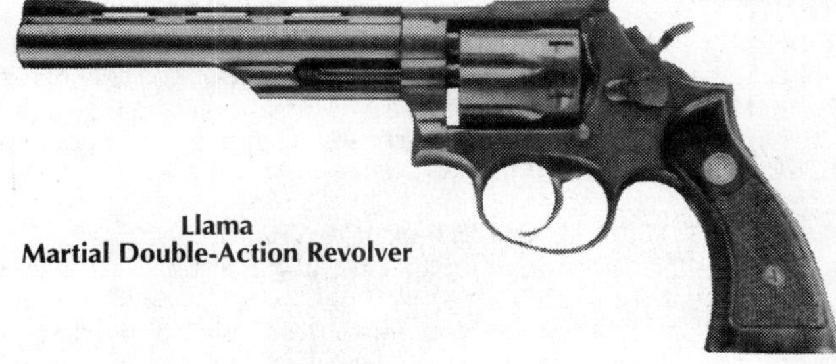

Llama
Martial Double-Action Revolver

Llama
Martial Deluxe Gold-Damascened

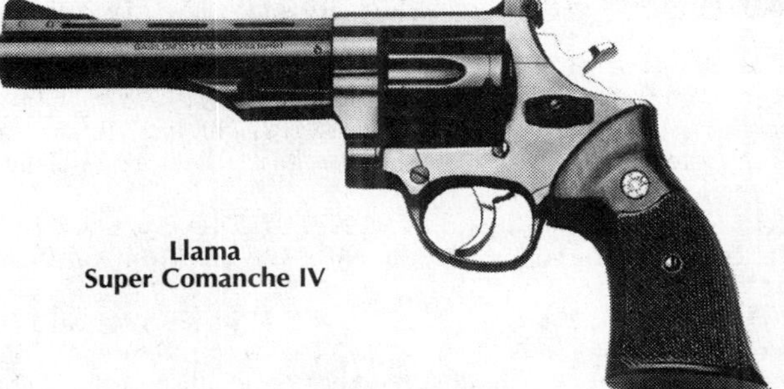

Llama
Super Comanche IV

Luger 1900
American Eagle

SUPER COMANCHE IV DA REVOLVER . . . NiB $375 Ex $308 Gd $217
Caliber: .44 Magnum. Six-round cylinder, 6-inch bbl., 11.75 inches overall. Weight: 50 oz. Adj. rear sight, ramp front. Polished deep blued finish. Checkered walnut grips. Made from 1980-93.

SUPER COMANCHE V DA REVOLVER . . . . NiB $359 Ex $288 Gd $209
Caliber: .357 Mag. Six-round cylinder, 4-, 6- or 8.5-inch bbl., weight: 48 ozs. Ramped front blade sight, click-adj. Rear. Made from 1980-89.

LORCIN Engineering Co., Inc. — Mira Loma, California

MODEL L-22 SEMIAUTOMATIC PISTOL . . . . . NiB $94 Ex $79 Gd $60
Caliber: 22 LR. Nine-round magazine, 2.5-inch bbl., 5.25 inches overall. Weight: 16 oz. Blade front sight, fixed notch rear w/3-dot system. Black Teflon or chrome finish. Black, pink or pearl composition grips. Made from 1990-98.

MODEL L-25, LT-.25 SEMIAUTOMATIC PISTOL
Caliber: 25 ACP. Seven-round magazine, 2.4-inch bbl., 4.8 inches overall. Weight: 12 oz. (LT-25) or 14.5 oz. (L-25). Blade front sight, fixed rear. Black Teflon or chrome finish. Black, pink or pearl composition grips. Made from 1989-98.
Model L-25 . . . . NiB $82 Ex $69 Gd $53
Model LT-25. . . . . NiB $94 Ex $79 Gd $60
Model Lady Lorcin. . . . . NiB $101 Ex $84 Gd $63

MODEL L-32 SEMIAUTOMATIC PISTOL . . . . NiB $101 Ex $84 Gd $63
Caliber: 32 ACP. Seven-round magazine, 3.5-inch bbl., 6.6 inches overall. Weight: 27 oz. Blade front sight, fixed notch rear. Black Teflon or chrome finish. Black composition grips. Made from 1992-98.

MODEL L-380 SEMIAUTOMATIC PISTOL
Caliber: .380 ACP. Seven- or 10-round magazine, 3.5-inch bbl., 6.6 inches overall. Weight: 23 oz. Blade front sight, fixed notch rear. Matte Black finish. Grooved black composition grips. Made from 1994-98.
Model L9MM (7-round). . . . . NiB $109 Ex $90 Gd $68
Model L9MM (10-round). . . . . NiB $140 Ex $116 Gd $85

MODEL L9MM SEMIAUTOMATIC PISTOL
Caliber: 9mm Parabellum. 10- or 13-round magazine, 4.5-inch bbl., 7.5 inches overall. Weight: 31 oz. Blade front sight, fixed notch rear w/3-dot system. Black Teflon or chrome finish. Black composition grips. Made from 1992-98.
Model L-380 (10-round) . . . . NiB $152 Ex $126 Gd $90
Model L-380 (13-round) . . . . NiB $184 Ex $154 Gd $103

O/U DERRINGER . . . . NiB $114 Ex $94 Gd $70
Caliber: .38 Special/.357 Mag., .45LC. Two-round derringer. 3.5-inch bbls. 6.5 inches overall. Weight: 12 oz. Blade front sight, fixed notch rear. Stainless finish. Black composition grips. Made from 1996-98.

LUGER PISTOLS

Mfd. by Deutsche Waffen und Munitionsfabriken (DWM), Berlin, Germany. Previously by Koniglich Gewehrfabrik Erfurt, Heinrich Krieghoff Waffenfabrik, Mauser-Werke, Simson & Co., Vickers Ltd., Waffenfabrik, Bern.

1900 AMERICAN EAGLE . . . . NiB $3128 Ex $1776 Gd $944
Caliber: 7.65 mm. Eight-round magazine; thin, 4.75-inch; tapered bbl.; 9.5 inches overall. Weight: 32 oz. Fixed rear sight, dovetailed front sight. Grip safety. Checkered walnut grips. Early-style toggle, narrow trigger, wide guard, no stock lug. American Eagle over chamber. Estimated 8000 production.

1900 COMMERCIAL . . . . NiB $3180 Ex $2660 Gd $1438
Same specifications as Luger 1900 American Eagle except DWM on early-style toggle, no chamber markings. Estimated 8000 production.

1900 SWISS. . . . . NiB $3960 Ex $3180 Gd $1464
Same specifications as Luger 1900 American Eagle except Swiss cross in sunburst over chamber. Estimated 9000 production.

1902 AMERICAN EAGLE . . . . . . NiB $8935 Ex $6855 Gd $3735
Caliber: 9mm Para. Eight-round magazine, 4-inch heavy tapered bbl., 8.75 inches overall. Weight: 30 oz. Fixed rear sight, dovetailed front sight. Grip safety. Checkered walnut grips. American Eagle over chamber, DWM on early-style toggle, narrow trigger, wide guard, no stock lug. Estimated 700 production.

1902 CARBINE . . . . NiB $13,338 Ex $10,670 Gd $7255
Caliber: 7.65mm. Eight-round magazine, 11.75-inch tapered bbl., 16.5 inches overall. Weight: 46 oz. Adj. 4-position rear sight, long ramp front sight. Grip safety. Checkered walnut grips and forearm. DWM on early-style toggle, narrow trigger, wide guard, no chamber markings, stock lug. Estimated 3200 production.
Model 1902 carbine (gun only). . . . . NiB $8993 Ex $6795 Gd $4621
Model 1902 carbine
(gun only, American Eagle). . . . . NiB $11,926 Ex $9542 Gd $6488
W/issued stock and matching numbers, add $4550
W/original stock and non-matching numbers, add $2550

1902 CARTRIDGE COUNTER . . . . NiB $27,040 Ex $17,160 Gd $8996
Caliber: 9mm Para. Eight-round magazine, Heavy, tapered 4-inch bbl., 8.75 inches overall. Weight: 30 oz. Fixed rear sight, dovetailed front sight. Grip safety. Checkered walnut grips. DWM on dished toggle w/lock, American Eagle over chamber when marked. No stock lug. Estimated production unknown.

1902 COMMERCIAL . . . . NiB $9011 Ex $7326 Gd $3788
Same basic specifications as Luger 1902 Cartridge Counter except DWM on early-style toggle, narrow trigger, wide guard, no chamber markings, no stock lug. Estimated 400 production.

1902 AMERICAN EAGLE . . . . . . NiB $9572 Ex $7326 Gd $3956
Same basic specifications as Luger 1902 Commercial except American Eagle over chamber, DWM on early-style toggle, narrow trigger, wide guard, no stock lug. Estimated 700 production.

1902 AMERICAN EAGLE
CARTRIDGE COUNTER . . . . NiB $26,936 Ex $17,160 Gd $9048
Same basic specifications as Luger 1902 Cartridge Counter except American Eagle over chamber, DWM on early-style toggle, narrow trigger, wide guard, no stock lug. Estimated 700 production.

1904 GL "BABY" . . . . Nib $195,000 Ex $156,000 Gd $106,080
Caliber: 9mm Para. Seven-round magazine, 3.25-inch bbl., 7.75 inches overall. Weight: Approx. 20 oz. Serial number 10077B. "GL" marked on rear of toggle. Georg Luger's personal sidearm. Only one made in 1904.

1904 NAVAL (REWORKED) . . . . . . Nib $13,056 Ex $10,444 Gd $7102
Caliber: 9mm Para. Eight-round magazine, bbl., length altered to 4 inches., 8.75 inches overall. Weight: 30 oz. Adj. two-position rear sight, dovetailed front sight. Thumb lever safety. Checkered walnut grips. Heavy tapered bbl., DWM on new-style toggle w/lock, 1902 over chamber. W/or without grip safety and stock lug. Estimated 800 production.

1906 (11.35). . . . . Nib $117,000 Ex $93,600 Gd $63,648
Caliber: .45 ACP. Six-round magazine, 5-inch bbl., 9.75 inches overall. Weight: 36 oz. Fixed rear sight, dovetailed front sight. Grip safety. Checkered walnut grips. GL monogram on rear toggle link, larger frame w/altered trigger guard and trigger, no proofs, no markings over chamber. No stock lug. Estimated production is 2. Note: This version of the Luger pistol is the most valuable next to the "GL" Baby Luger.

1906 AMERICAN EAGLE (7.65). . . . . Nib $3012 Ex $2180 Gd $1088
Caliber: 7.65mm. Eight-round magazine, thin 4.75-inch tapered bbl., 9.5 inches overall. Weight: 32 oz. Fixed rear sight, dovetailed front sight. Grip safety. Checkered walnut grips. DWM on new-style toggle, American Eagle over chamber. No stock lug. Estimated 8000 production.

1906 AMERICAN EAGLE (9MM) . . . . . . Nib $2882 Ex $2331 Gd $1343
Same basic specifications as the 7.65mm 1906 except in 9mm Para. w/4-inch barrel, 8.75 inches overall, weight: 30 ounces. Estimated 3500 production.

1906 BERN (7.65MM) . . . . Nib $2606 Ex $2294 Gd $1472
Same basic specifications as the 7.65mm 1906 American Eagle except checkered walnut grips w/.38-inch borders, Swiss Cross on new-style toggle, Swiss proofs, no markings over chamber, no stock lug. Estimated 17,874 production.

1906 BRAZILIAN (7.65MM) . . . . Nib $2685 Ex $1957 Gd $813
Same general specifications as the 7.65mm 1906 American Eagle except w/Brazilian proofs, no markings over chamber, no stock lug. Estimated 4500 produced.

1906 BRAZILIAN (9MM). . . . . . Nib $2621 Ex $2113 Gd $1464
Same basic specifications as the 9mm 1906 American Eagle except w/Brazilian proofs, no markings over chamber, no stock lug. Production unknown, but less than 4000 is estimated by collectors.

1906 COMMERCIAL . . . . Nib $2997 Ex $2009 Gd $1333
Calibers: 7.65mm 9mm. Same specifications as the 1906 American Eagle versions (above) except no chamber markings and no stock lug. Estimated production: 6000 (7.65mm) and 3500 (9mm).

1906 DUTCH . . . . Nib $1960 Ex $1582 Gd $1099
Caliber: 9mm Para. Same specifications as the 9mm 1906 American Eagle except tapered bbl., w/proofs, no markings over chamber, no stock lug. Estimated 3000 production.

1906 LOEWE AND COMPANY. . . . . . . Nib $4741 Ex $3817 Gd $2636
Caliber: 7.65mm. Eight-round magazine, 6-inch tapered bbl., 10.75 inches overall. Weight: 35 oz. Adj. two-position rear sight, dovetailed front sight. Grip safety. Checkered walnut grips. Loewe & Company over chamber, Naval proofs, DWM on new-style toggle, no stock lug. Estimated production unknown.

1906 NAVAL
Caliber: 9mm Para. Eight-round magazine, 6-inch tapered bbl., 10.75 inches overall. Weight: 35 oz. Adj. two-position rear sight, dovetailed front sight. Grip safety and thumb safety w/lower marking (1st issue), higher marking (2nd issue). Checkered walnut grips. No chamber markings, DWM on new-style toggle w/o lock, but w/stock lug. Est. production: 9000 (lst issue); 2,000 (2nd issue).
First issue . . . . Nib $3952 Ex $3152 Gd $1352
Second issue . . . . Nib $4152 Ex $3552 Gd $1352

1906 NAVAL COMMERCIAL. . . . . Nib $3930 Ex $3130 Gd $1330
Same as the 1906 Naval except lower marking on thumb safety, no chamber markings. DWM on new-style toggle, w/stock lug and commercial proofs. Estimated 3000 production.

1906 PORTUGUESE ARMY . . . . . Nib $1881 Ex $1481 Gd $581
Same specifications as the 7.65mm 1906 American Eagle except w/Portuguese proofs, crown and crest over chamber. No stock lug. Estimated 3500 production.

1906 PORTUGUESE NAVAL . . . . Nib $9560 Ex $6060 Gd $2060
Same as the 9mm 1906 American Eagle except w/Portuguese proofs, crown and anchor over chamber, no stock lug.

1906 RUSSIAN . . . . Nib $15,000 Ex $9950 Gd $5500
Same general specifications as the 9mm 1906 American Eagle except thumb safety has markings concealed in up position, DWM on new-style toggle, DWM bbl., proofs, crossed rifles over chamber. Estimated production unknown.

1906 SWISS. . . . . Nib $2485 Ex $1815 Gd $1285
Same general specifications as the 7.65mm 1906 American Eagle Luger except Swiss Cross in sunburst over chamber, no stock lug. Estimated 10,300 production.

1906 SWISS (REWORK). . . . . . . Nib $2472 Ex $1822 Gd $1272
Same basic specifications as the 7.65mm 1906 Swiss except in bbl. lengths of 3.63, 4 and 4.75 inches, overall length 8.38 inches (with 4-inch bbl.). Weight 32 oz. (with 4-inch bbl.). DWM on new-style toggle, bbl., w/serial number and proof marks, Swiss Cross in sunburst or shield over chamber, no stock lug. Estimated production unknown.

1906 SWISS POLICE . . . . Nib $2472 Ex $1822 Gd $1272
Same general specifications as the 7.65mm 1906 Swiss except DWM on new-style toggle, Swiss Cross in matted field over chamber, no stock lug. Estimated 10,300 production.

1908 BULGARIAN. . . . . Nib $2572 Ex $1872 Gd $822
Caliber: 9mm Para. Eight-round magazine, 4-inch tapered bbl., 8.75 inches overall. Weight: 30 oz. Fixed rear sight dovetailed front sight. Thumb safety w/lower marking concealed. Checkered walnut grips. DWM chamber marking, no proofs, crown over shield on new-style toggle lanyard loop, no stock lug. Estimated production unknown.

1908 COMMERCIAL . . . . Nib $1243 Ex $843 Gd $543
Same basic specifications as the 1908 Bulgarian except higher marking on thumb safety. No chamber markings, commercial proofs, DWM on new-style toggle, no stock lug. Estimated 4000 production.

1908 ERFURT MILITARY . . . . Nib $1262 Ex $1038 Gd $752
Caliber: 9mm Para. Eight-round magazine, 4-inch tapered bbl., 8.75 inches overall. Weight: 30 oz. Fixed rear sight dovetailed front sight. Thumb safety w/higher marking concealed. Checkered walnut grips. Serial number and proof marks on barrel, crown and Erfurt on new-style toggle, dated chamber, but no stock lug. Estimated production unknown.

Luger 1923 Stoeger

1908 MILITARY
Same general specifications as the 9mm 1908 Erfurt Military Luger except first and second issue have thumb safety w/higher marking concealed, serial number on bbl., no chamber markings, proofs on frame, DWM on new-style toggle but no stock lug. Estimated production: 10,000 (first issue) and 5000 (second issue). Third issue has serial number and proof marks on barrel, dates over chamber, DWM on new-style toggle but no stock lug. Estimated 3000 production.
First issue.................... Nib $1296 Ex $860 Gd $568
Second issue .... Nib $1296 Ex $828 Gd $474
Third issue................... Nib $1608 Ex $1036 Gd $672

1908 NAVAL .... Nib $4209 Ex $3399 Gd $2341
Same basic specifications as the 9mm 1908 military Lugers except w/6-inch bbl, adj. two-position rear sight, no chamber markings, DWM on new-style toggle, w/stock lug. Estimated 26,000 production.

1908 NAVAL
(COMMERCIAL) .... Nib $4797 Ex $3237 Gd $1677
Same specifications as the 1908 Naval Luger except no chamber markings or date. Commercial proofs, DWM on new-style toggle, w/stock lug. Estimated 1900 produced.

1914 ERFURT ARTILLERY ...... Nib $2678 Ex $1898 Gd $936
Caliber: 9mm Para. Eight-shot magazine, 8-inch tapered bbl., 12.75 inches overall. Weight: 40 oz. Artillery rear sight, Dovetailed front sight. Thumb safety w/higher marking concealed. Checkered walnut grips. Serial number and proof marks on barrel, crown and Erfurt on new-style toggle, dated chamber, w/stock lug. Estimated production unknown.

1914 ERFURT MILITARY .... Nib $1294 Ex $878 Gd $566
Same specifications as the 1914 Erfurt Artillery except w/4-inch bbl., and corresponding length, weight, etc.; fixed rear sight. Estimated 3000 production.

1914 NAVAL .... Nib $3455 Ex $2415 Gd $1115
Same specifications as 9mm 1914 Lugers except has 6-inch bbl. w/corresponding length and weight, adj. two-position rear sight. Dated chamber, DWM on new-style toggle, w/stock lug. Estimated 40,000 produced.

1914-1918 DWM ARTILLERY ...... Nib $2354 Ex $1938 Gd $976
Caliber: 9mm Para. Eight-shot magazine, 8-inch tapered bbl., 12.75 inches overall. Weight: 40 oz. Artillery rear sight, dovetailed front sight. Thumb safety w/higher marking concealed. Checkered walnut grips. Serial number and proof marks on barrel, DWM on new-style toggle, dated chamber, w/stock lug. Estimated 3000 production.

1914-1918 DWM MILITARY .....Nib $1764 Ex $882 Gd $570
Same specifications as the 9mm 1914-1918 DWM Artillery except w/4-inch tapered bbl., and corresponding length, weight, etc., and fixed rear sight. Production unknown.

1920 CARBINE
Caliber: 7.65mm. Eight-round magazine, 11.75-inch tapered bbl., 15.75 inches overall. Weight: 44 oz. Four-position rear sight, long ramp front sight. Grip (or thumb) safety. Checkered walnut grips and forearm. Serial numbers and proof marks on barrel, no chamber markings, various proofs, DWM on new-style toggle, w/stock lug. Estimated production unknown.
Model 1920 Carbine
(gun only) .... Nib $5706 Ex $4978 Gd $2690
Model 1920 Carbine
(W/shoulder stock), add $2500

1920 NAVY CARBINE .... Nib $3806 Ex $3064 Gd $2116
Caliber: 7.65mm. Eight-round magazine, 11.75-inch tapered bbl., 15.75 inches overall. Two-position sliding rear sight. Naval military proofs and no forearm. Production unknown.

1920 COMMERCIAL .... Nib $902 Ex $696 Gd $408
Calibers: 7.65mm, 9mm Para. Eight-round magazine, 3.63-, 3.75-, 4-, 4.75-, 6-, 8-, 10-, 12-, 16-, 18- or 20-inch tapered bbl., overall length: 8.375 to 24.75 inches. Weight: 30 oz. (with 3.63-inch bbl.). Varying rear sight configurations, dovetailed front sight. Thumb safety. Checkered walnut grips. Serial numbers and proof marks on barrel, no chamber markings, various proofs, DWM or crown over Erfurt on new-style toggle, w/stock lug. Production not documented.

1920 DWM OR ERFURT MILITARY ...... Nib $986 Ex $778 Gd $544
Caliber: 9mm Para. Eight-round magazine, 4-inch tapered barrel, 8.75 inches overall. Weight: 30 oz. Fixed rear sight dovetailed front sight. Thumb safety. Checkered walnut grips. Serial numbers and proof marks on barrel, dated chamber, various proofs, DWM or crown over Erfurt on new-style toggle, w/stock lug. Esimated 3000 production.

1920 POLICE................ Nib $1286 Ex $1011 Gd $704
Same specifications as 9mm 1920 DWM w/some dated chambers, various proofs, DWM or crown over Erfurt on new-style toggle, identifying marks on grip frame, w/stock lug. Estimated 3000 production.

1923 COMMERICAL .... Nib $894 Ex $582 Gd $332
Calibers: 7.65mm and 9mm Para. Eight-round magazine, 3.63, 3.75, 4, 6, 8, 12 or 16-inch tapered bbl., overall length: 8.38 inches (with 3.63-inch bbl.). Weight: 30 oz. (with 3.63-inch bbl.). Various rear sight configurations, dovetailed front sight. Thumb lever safety. Checkered walnut grips. DWM on new-style toggle, serial number and proofs on barrel, no chamber markings, w/stock lug. Estimated 15,000 production.

1923 DUTCH COMMERICAL......... Nib $1728 Ex $1520 Gd $688
Same basic specifications as 1923 Commercial Luger w/same caliber offerings, but only 3.63 or 4-inch bbl. Fixed rear sight, thumb lever safety w/arrow markings. Production unknown.

1923 KRIEGHOFF COMMERCIAL ..... Nib $1780 Ex $1416 Gd $865
Same specifications as 1923 Commercial Luger, w/same caliber offerings but bbl., lengths of 3.63, 4, 6, and 8 inches. "K" marked on new-style toggle. Serial number, proofs and Germany on barrel. No chamber markings, but w/ stock lug. Production unknown.

1923 SAFE AND LOADED...... Nib $1570 Ex $1102 Gd $582
Same caliber offerings, bbl., lengths and specifications as the 1923 Commercial except thumb lever safety, safe markings, w/stock lug. Estimated 10,000 production.

1923 STOEGER
Same general specifications as the 1923 Commercial Luger with the same caliber offerings and bbl., lengths of 3.75, 4, 6, 8 and up to 24 inches. Thumb lever safety. DWM on new-style toggle, serial number and/or proof marks on barrel. American Eagle over chamber but no stock lug. Estimated production less than 1000 (also see Stoeger listings). Note: Qualified appraisals should be obtained on all Stoeger Lugers with bbl. lengths over 8 inches to ensure accurate values.
3.75-, 4-, or 6-inch bbl. . . . . Nib $2921 Ex $2350 Gd $1570
8-inch bbl. . . . . Nib $3913 Ex $3143 Gd $2163

1926 "BABY" PROTOTYPE . . Nib $110,500 Ex $88,400 Gd $60,112
Calibers: 7.65mm Browning and 9mm Browning (short). Five-round magazine, 2.31-inch bbl., about 6.25 inches overall. Small-sized-frame and toggle assembly. Prototype for a Luger "pocket pistol," but never manufactured commercially. Checkered walnut grips, slotted for safety. Only four known to exist, but as many as a dozen could have been made.

1929 SWISS . . . . Nib $1861 Ex $1185 Gd $691
Caliber: 7.65mm. Eight-round magazine, 4.75-inch tapered bbl., 9.5 inches overall. Weight: 32 oz. Fixed rear sight, dovetailed front sight. Long grip safety and thumb lever w/S markings. Stepped receiver and straight grip frame. Checkered plastic grips. Swiss Cross in shield on new-style toggle. Serial numbers and proofs on barrel, no markings over chamber and no stock lug. Estimated 1900 production.

1934 KRIEGHOFF COMMERCIAL (SIDE FRAME). . . . . Nib $2920 Ex $2244 Gd $892
Caliber: 7.65mm or 9mm Para. Eight-round magazine, bbl. lengths: 4, 6, and 8 inches, overall length: 8.75 (with 4-inch bbl.). Weight: 30 oz. (with 4-inch bbl.). Various rear sight configurations w/dovetailed front sight. Thumb lever safety. Checkered brown plastic grips. Anchor w/H K Krieghoff Suhl on new-style toggle, but no chamber markings. Tapered bbl., w/serial number and proofs; w/stock lug. Estimated 1700 production.

1934 KRIEGHOFF S
Caliber: 9mm Para. Eight-round magazine, 4-inch tapered bbl., 8.75 inches overall. Weight: 30 oz. Fixed rear sight, dovetailed front sight. Thumb lever safety. Anchor w/H K Krieghoff Suhl on new-style toggle, S dated chamber, bbl., proofs and stock lug. Early model: Checkered walnut or plastic grips. Estimated 2500 production. Late model: Checkered brown plastic grips. Estimated 1200 production.
Early model . . . . Nib $3579 Ex $2878 Gd $1981
Late model. . . . . Nib $2601 Ex $2093 Gd $1444

1934 BYF . . . . Nib $1292 Ex $980 Gd $564
Caliber: 9mm Para. Eight-round magazine, 4-inch tapered bbl., 8.75 inches overall. Weight: 30 oz. Fixed rear sight, dovetailed front sight. Thumb lever safety. Checkered walnut or plastic grips. byf on new-style toggle, serial number and proofs on bbl., 41-42 dated chamber and w/stock lug. Estimated 3000 productlon.

1934 MAUSER S/42 K . . . . Nib $4752 Ex $4024 Gd $1632
Caliber: 9mm Para. Eight-round magazine, 4-inch tapered bbl., 8.75 inches overall. Weight: 30 oz. Fixed rear sight dovetailed front sight. Thumb lever safety. Checkered walnut or plastic grips. 42 on new-style toggle, serial number and proofs on barrel, 1939-.40 dated chamber markings and w/stock lug. Estimated 10,000 production.

1934 MAUSER S/42 (DATED) . . . . . Nib $1074 Ex $840 Gd $450
Same specifications as Luger 1934 Mauser 42 except 41 dated chamber markings and w/stock lug. Production unknown.

Luger S42

1934 MAUSER BANNER (MILITARY) . . . . . Nib $2757 Ex $1925 Gd $1041
Same specifications as Luger 1934 Mauser 42 except Mauser in banner on new-style toggle, tapered bbl., w/serial number and proofs usually, dated chamber markings and w/stock lug. Production unknown.

1934 MAUSER COMMERCIAL . . . . Nib $1593 Ex $1123 Gd $657
Same specifications as Luger 1934 Mauser 42 except checkered walnut grips. Mauser in banner on new-style toggle, tapered bbl., usually w/serial number and proofs, no chamber markings, but w/ stock lug. Production unknown.

1934 MAUSER DUTCH . . . . Nib $2966 Ex $1822 Gd $574
Same specifications as Luger 1934 Mauser 42 except checkered walnut grips. Mauser in banner on new-style toggle, tapered bbl., w/caliber, 1940 dated chamber markings and w/stock lug. Production unknown.

1934 MAUSER LATVIAN . . . . . . Nib $3019 Ex $2072 Gd $1822
Caliber: 7.65mm. Eight-round magazine, 4-inch tapered bbl., 8.75 inches overall. Weight: 30 oz. Fixed square-notched rear sight, dovetailed Partridge front sight. Thumb lever safety. Checkered walnut stocks. Mauser in banner on new-style toggle,1937 dated chamber markings and w/stock lug. Production unknown.

1934 MAUSER (OBERNDORF) . . . . Nib $2980 Ex $2394 Gd $1645
Same as 1934 Mauser 42 except checkered walnut grips. Oberndorf 1934 on new-style toggle, tapered bbl., w/proofs and caliber, Mauser banner over chamber and w/stock lug (also see Mauser).

1934 SIMSON-S TOGGLE . . . . . . Nib $1963 Ex $1391 Gd $611
Same as 1934 Mauser 42 except checkered walnut grips, S on new-style toggle, tapered bbl., w/serial number and proofs, no chamber markings; w/stock lug. Estimated 10,000 production.

42 MAUSER BANNER (BYF) . . . . . Nib $1287 Ex $975 Gd $559
Same specifications as Luger 1934 Mauser 42 except weight: 32 oz. Mauser in banner on new-style toggle, tapered bbl., w/serial number and proofs usually, dated chamber markings and w/stock lug. Estimated 3,500 production.

ABERCROMBIE AND FITCH . . . . Nib $6040 Ex $4584 Gd $1048
Calibers: 7.65mm and 9mm Para. Eight-round magazine, 4.75-inch tapered bbl., 9.5 inches overall. Weight: 32 oz. Fixed rear sight, dovetailed front sight. Grip safety. Checkered walnut grips. DWM on new-style toggle Abercrombie & Fitch markings on barrel, Swiss Cross in sunburst over chamber, no stock lug. Est. 100 production.

Luna Model 200
Free Pistol

DUTCH ROYAL AIR FORCE .... Nib $2955 Ex $1811 Gd $563
Caliber: 9mm Para. Eight-round magazine, 4-inch tapered bbl., 8.75 inches overall. Weight: 30 oz. Fixed rear sight dovetailed front sight. Grip safety and thumb safety w/markings and arrow. Checkered walnut grips. DWM on new-style toggle, bbl., dated w/serial number and proofs, no markings over chamber, no stock lug. Estimated 4000 production.

DWM (G DATE).............. Nib $1412 Ex $970 Gd $502
Caliber: 9mm Para. Eight-round magazine, 4-inch tapered bbl., 8.75 inches overall. Weight: 30 oz. Fixed rear sight, dovetailed front sight. Thumb lever safety. Checkered walnut grips. DWM on new-style toggle, serial number and proofs on barrel, G (1935 date) over chamber and w/stock lug. Production unknown.

DWM AND ERFURT .... Nib $1198 Ex $965 Gd $667
Caliber: 9mm Para. Eight-round magazine, 4- or 6-inch tapered bbl., overall length: 8.75 or 10.75 inches. Weight: 30 or 38 oz. Fixed rear sight, dovetailed front sight. Thumb safety. Checkered walnut grips. Serial numbers and proof marks on barrel, double dated chamber, various proofs, DWM or crown over Erfurt on new-style toggle and w/stock lug. Production unknown.

KRIEGHOFF 36 .... Nib $3163 Ex $2550 Gd $1743
Caliber: 9mm Para. Eight-round magazine, 4-inch tapered bbl., 8.75 inches overall. Weight: 30 oz. Fixed rear sight, dovetailed front sight. Thumb lever safety. Checkered brown plastic grips. Anchor w/H K Krieghoff Suhl on new-style toggle, 36 dated chamber, serial number and proofs on barrel and w/stock lug. Estimated 700 production.

KRIEGHOFF-DATED
1936-1945................. Nib $3239 Ex $2657 Gd $1097
Same specifications as Luger Krieghoff 36 except 1936-45 dated chamber, bbl. proofs. Est. 8600 production.

KRIEGHOFF (GRIP SAFETY) ... Nib $4812 Ex $3853 Gd $2650
Same specifications as Luger Krieghoff 36 except grip safety and thumb lever safety. No chamber markings, tapered bbl., w/serial number, proofs and caliber, no stock lug. Production unknown.

MAUSER BANNER
(GRIP SAFETY).............. Nib $2744 Ex $1912 Gd $1028
Caliber: 7.65mm. Eight-round magazine, 4.75-inch tapered bbl., 9.5 inches overall. Weight: 30 oz. Fixed rear sight, dovetailed front sight. Grip safety and thumb lever safety. Checkered walnut grips. Mauser in banner on new-style toggle, serial number and proofs on barrel, 1939 dated chamber markings, but no stock lug. Production unknown.

MAUSER BANNER 42 (DATED).... Nib $1589 Ex $1121 Gd $653
Caliber: 9mm Para. Eight-round magazine, 4-inch tapered bbl., 8.75 inches overall. Weight: 30 oz. Fixed rear sight, dovetailed front sight. Thumb lever safety. Checkered walnut or plastic grips. Mauser in banner on new-style toggle serial number and proofs on bbl., (usually) 1942 dated chamber markings and stock lug. Production unknown.

MAUSER BANNER
(SWISS PROOF)............. Nib $3353 Ex $2625 Gd $1377
Same specifications as Luger Mauser Banner 42 except checkered walnut grips and 1939 dated chamber.

MAUSER FREISE............. Nib $4702 Ex $3778 Gd $2568
Same specifications as Mauser Banner 42 except checkered walnut grips, tapered bbl. w/proofs on sight block and Freise above chamber. Production unknown.

S/42
Caliber: 9mm Para. Eight-round magazine, 4-inch tapered barrel. 8.75 inches overall. Weight: 30 oz. Fixed rear sight, dovetailed front sight. Thumb lever safety. Checkered walnut grips. S/42 on new-style toggle, serial number and proofs on barrel and w/stock lug. Dated Model: Has dated chamber; estimated 3000 production. G Date: Has G (1935 date) over chamber; estimated 3000 production. K Date: Has K (1934 date) over chamber; production unknown.
Dated model .... Nib $1061 Ex $827 Gd $437
G date model................. Nib $1159 Ex $931 Gd $640
K date model .... Nib $2481 Ex $2008 Gd $1388

RUSSIAN
COMMERCIAL.............. Nib $2840 Ex $2280 Gd $1564
Caliber: 7.65mm. Eight-round magazine, 3.63-inch tapered bbl., 8.38 inches overall. Weight: 30 oz. Fixed rear sight, dovetailed front sight. Thumb lever safety. Checkered walnut grips. DWM on new-style toggle, Russian proofs on barrel, no chamber markings but w/stock lug. Production unknown.

SIMSON AND COMPANY
Calibers: 7.65mm and 9mm Para. Eight-round magazine, Weight: 32 oz. Fixed rear sight, dovetailed front sight. Thumb lever safety. Checkered walnut grips. Simson & Company Suhl on new-style toggle, serial number and proofs on barrel, date over chamber and w/stock lug. Estimated 10,000 production.
Simson and Company (9mm w/1925 date)........... Nib $2660 Ex $2140 Gd $762
Simson and Company (undated).................... Nib $1541 Ex $865 Gd $501
Simson and Company (S code)..................... Nib $1960 Ex $1388 Gd $608

VICKERS-DUTCH .... Nib $2960 Ex $2128 Gd $880
Caliber: 9mm Para. Eight-round magazine, 4-inch tapered bbl., 8.75 inches overall. Weight: 30 oz. Fixed rear sight, dovetailed front sight. Grip safety and thumb lever w/arrow markings. Checkered walnut grips (coarse). Vickers LTD on new-style toggle, no chamber markings, dated barrel but no stock lug. Estimated 10,000 production.

LUNA FREE PISTOL — Zella-Mehlis, Germany Originally mfd. by Ernst Friedr. Buchel and later by Udo Anschutz

MODEL 200 FREE PISTOL....... Nib $1192 Ex 1078 Gd $672
Single-shot. System Aydt action. Set trigger. Caliber: .22 LR. Eleven-inch bbl., weight: 40 oz. Target sights. Blued finish. Checkered and carved walnut grip and forearm; improved design w/adj. hand base on later models of Udo Anschutz manufacture. Made prior to WWII.

M.A.C. (Military Armament Corp.) — Stephensville, Texas, Dist. by Defense Systems International, Marietta, Georgia. Previously by Cobray, SWD and RPB Industries

INGRAM MODEL 10 AUTO PISTOL
Select fire (NFA-Title II-Class III) SMG based on Ingram M10 blowback system using an open bolt design with or without telescoping stock. Calibers: 9mm or .45 ACP. Cyclic rate: 750 RPM (9mm) or 900 RPM (.45 ACP). 32- or 30-round magazine, 5.75-inch threaded bbl. (to accept muzzle brake) bbl. extension or suppressor, 10.5 inches overall w/o stock or 10.6 (w/telescoped stock) and 21.5 (w/extended stock). Weight: 6.25 pounds. Front protected post sight, fixed aperture rear sight. Garand-style safety in trigger guard.
9mm model . . . . Nib $921 Ex $843 Gd $609
.45 ACP model. . . . . Nib $921 Ex $843 Gd $609
W/bbl. extension, add $195
W/suppressor, add. $495

INGRAM MODEL 10A1S SEMIAUTOMATIC
Similar to the Model 10 except (Class I) semiautomatic w/closed bolt design to implement an interchangable component system to easily convert to fire 9mm and .45 ACP.
9mm model . . . . Nib $330 Ex $310 Gd $231
.45 ACP model. . . . . Nib $330 Ex $314 Gd $231
W/bbl. extension, add $150
W/fake suppressor, add. $195

INGRAM MODEL 11 SEMIAUTOMATIC
Similar to the Model 10A1 except (Class I) semiautomatic chambered .380 ACP.
.380 ACP model. . . . . Nib $699 Ex $642 Gd $522
W/bbl. extension, add $150
W/fake suppressor, add. $195

MAGNUM RESEARCH INC. — Minneapolis, Minnesota

BABY EAGLE SEMIAUTOMATIC . . . . Nib $459 Ex $391 Gd $245
DA. Calibers: 9mm, .40 S&W, .41 AE. 15-shot magazine (9mm), 9-round magazine (.40 S&W), 10-round magazine (.41 AE), 4.75-inch bbl., 8.15 inches overall. Weight: 35.4 oz. Combat sights. Matte blued finish. Imported from 1991-96 and 1999 to date.

DESERT EAGLE MK VII SEMIAUTOMATIC
Gas-operated. Calibers: .357 Mag., .41 Mag., .44 Mag., .50 Action Express (AE). Eight- or 9-round magazine, 6-inch w/standard bbl., or 10- and 14-inch w/polygonal bbl., 10.6 inches overall (with 6-inch bbl.). Weight: 52 oz. (w/alum. alloy frame) to 67 oz. (w/steel frame). Fixed or adj. combat sights. Combat-type trigger guard. finish: Military black oxide, nickel, chrome, stainless or blued. Wraparound rubber grips. Made by Israel Military Industries from 1984-95.
.357 standard (steel) or alloy (6-inch bbl.) . . . Nib $936 Ex $728 Gd $463
.357 stainless steel (6-inch bbl.) . . . . . Nib $994 Ex $806 Gd $565
.41 Mag. standard (steel) or alloy
6-inch bbl.) . . . . Nib $930 Ex $754 Gd $529
.41 Mag. stainless steel (6-inch bbl.). . . Nib $898 Ex $728 Gd $512
.44 Mag. standard (steel) or alloy
(6-inch bbl.) . . . . Nib $878 Ex $712 Gd $501
.44 Mag. stainless steel (6-inch bbl.). . . Nib $960 Ex $779 Gd $548
.50 AE Magnum standard . . . . Nib $1032 Ex $836 Gd $586
Add for 10-inch bbl. . . . . Nib $143 Ex $118 Gd $86
Add for 14-inch bbl. . . . . Nib $174 Ex $143 Gd $103

Magnum Research Model Desert Eagle Mark XIX (Shown w/Optional Leupold Scope

Magnum Research Model One Pro .45

MODEL DESERT EAGLE MARK XIX SEMI-AUTOMATIC PISTOL
Interchangeable component system based on .50-caliber frame. Calibers: .357 Mag., .44 Mag., .50 AE. Nine-, 8-, 7-round magazine, 6- or 10-inch bbl. w/dovetail design and cross slots to accept scope rings. Weight: 70.5 oz. (6-inch bbl.) or 79 oz. 10.75 or 14.75 inches overall. Sights: Post front and adjustable rear. Blue, chrome or nickel finish; available brushed, matte or polished. Hogue soft rubber grips. Made from 1995 to date.
.357 Mag. (W/6-inch bbl.). . . . . Nib $1125 Ex $969 Gd $475
.44 Mag. (W/6-inch bbl.) . . . . Nib $1053 Ex $855 Gd $600
.50 AE (W/6-inch bbl.) . . . . Nib $1093 Ex $886 Gd $621
W/10-inch bbl., add $50
Two caliber conversion (bbl., bolt & mag.), add $395
XIX Platform System
3 caliber-conversion w/6 bbls.) . . . . Nib $2918 Ex $2357 Gd $1627
XIX6 System (two caliber-conversion
w/2 6-inch bbls.) . . . . Nib $1956 Ex $1568 Gd $1085
XIX10 System
(two cal.-conv. w/ two 10 inch bbls.) . . . . . . Nib $2113 Ex $1703 Gd $1179
Custom shop finish, add 15%
24K gold finish, add. 35%

(ASAI) MODEL ONE PRO .45 PISTOL
Calibers: .45 ACP or .400 COR-BON, 3.75- inch bbl., 7.04 or 7.83 (IPSC Model) inches overall. Weight: 23.5 (alloy frame) or 31.1 oz. 10-round magazine. Short recoil action. SA or DA mode w/de-cocking lever. Steel or alloy grip-frame. Textured black polymer grips. Imported from 1998 to date.
Model 1P45 . . . . Nib $617 Ex $492 Gd $344
Model 1C45/400 (compensator kit), add $175
Model 1C400NC (400 conversion kit), add $125

Magnum Research SSP-91 Lone Eagle Pistol (w/Optional Leupold Scope)

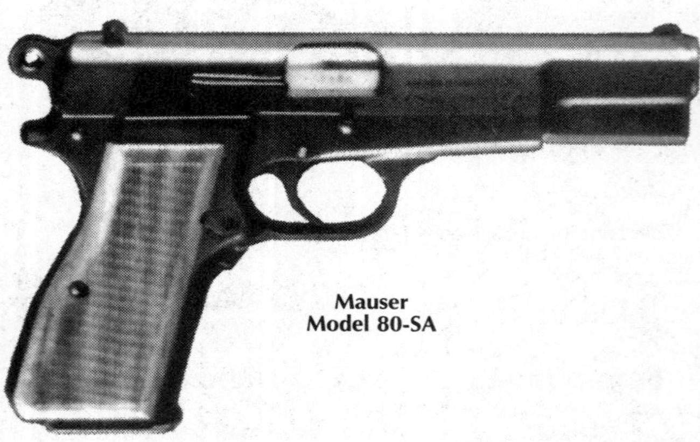
Mauser Model 80-SA

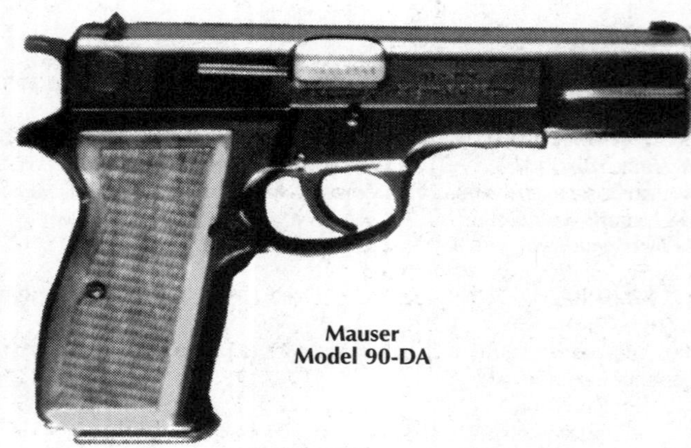
Mauser Model 90-DA

MOUNTAIN EAGLE SEMIAUTOMATIC

Caliber: .22 LR. 15-round polycarbonate resin magazine, 6.5-inch injection-molded polymer and steel bbl., 10.6 inches overall. Weight: 21 oz. Ramp blade front sight, adj. rear. Injection-molded, checkered and textured grip. Matte black finish. Made from 1992-96.

Mountain Eagle (standard, 6.5-inch bbl.) . . NiB $206 Ex $169 Gd $121
Mountain Eagle (compact 4.5-inch bbl.). . . NiB $194 Ex $158 Gd $114

SSP-91 LONE EAGLE PISTOL

Single-shot action w/interchangeable rotating breech bbl., assembly. Calibers: .22 LR, .22 Mag., .22 Hornet, .22-250, .223 Rem., .243 Win., 6mm BR, 7mm-08, 7mm BR, .30-06, .30-30, .308 Win., .35 Rem., .357 Mag., .44 Mag., .444 Marlin. 14-inch interchangeable bbl. assembly, 15 inches overall. Weight: 4.5 lbs. Black or chrome finish. Made from 1991 to date.

SSP-91 S/S pistol (complete gun w/black finish) . . . . . . NiB $452 Ex $385 Gd $249
SSP-91 S/S pistol (complete gun w/chrome finish) . . NiB $638 Ex $551 Gd $440
Extra 14-inch bbl., action w/black finish. . . . . . NiB $709 Ex $646 Gd $564
Extra 14-inch bbl., action w/chrome finish. . . . NiB $803 Ex $729 Gd $634
Ambidextrous stock assembly . . . . NiB $105 Ex $85 Gd $60
W/muzzle brake, add $65
W/open sights, add. $30

MAUSER PISTOLS — Oberndorf, Germany Waffenfabrik Mauser of Mauser-Werke A.G.

MODEL 80-SA AUTOMATIC . . . . . . NiB $496 Ex $366 Gd $226

Caliber: 9mm Para. 13-round magazine, 4.66-inch bbl., 8 inches overall. Weight: 31.5 oz. Blued finish. Hardwood grips. Made from 1991-94.

MODEL 90 DA AUTOMATIC . . . . . NiB $491 Ex $366 Gd $226

Caliber: 9mm Para. 14-round magazine, 4.66-inch bbl., 8 inches overall. Weight: 35 oz. Blued finish. Hardwood grips. Made from 1991-94.

MODEL 90 DAC COMPACT . . . . . . NiB $496 Ex $366 Gd $226

Caliber: 9mm Para. 14-round magazine, 4.13-inch bbl., 7.4 inches overall. Weight: 33.25 oz. Blued finish. Hardwood grips. Made from 1991-94.

MODEL 1898 (1896) MILITARY AUTO PISTOL

Caliber: 7.63mm Mauser, but also chambered for 9mm Mauser and 9mm Para. w/the latter being identified by a large red "9" in the grips. 10-round box magazine, 5.25-inch bbl., 12 inches overall. Weight: 45 oz. Adj. rear sight. Blued finish. Walnut grips. Made from 1897-1939. Note: Specialist collectors recognize a number of variations at significantly higher values. Price here is for more common commercial and military types with original finish.

Commercial model (pre-war) . . . . NiB $3446 Ex $2666 Gd $1028
Commercial model (wartime) . . . . NiB $1923 Ex $1455 Gd $571
Red 9 Commercial model (fixed sight) . . . . . NiB $1195 Ex $925 Gd $467
Red 9 WWI Contract (tangent sight). . . . . . . NiB $2079 Ex $1507 Gd $717
W/stock sssembly (matching SN), add $550

MODEL HSC DA AUTO PISTOL

Calibers: .32 Auto (7.65mm), .380 Auto (9mm Short). Eight-round (.32) or 7-round (.380) magazine, 3.4-inch bbl., 6.4 inches overall. Weight: 23.6 oz. Fixed sights. Blued or nickel finish. Checkered walnut grips. Made from 1938-45 and from 1968-96.

Commercial model (low grip screw). . . . . . NiB $4216 Ex $3176 Gd $1980
Commercial model (wartime) . . . . NiB $442 Ex $364 Gd $2013
Nazi military model (pre-war). . . . . NiB $810 Ex $602 Gd $238
Nazi military model (wartime) . . . . NiB $493 Ex $389 Gd $212
French production (postwar) . . . . NiB $415 Ex $327 Gd $177
Mauser production (postwar) . . . . NiB $389 Ex $332 Gd $181
Recent importation (Armes De Chasse) . . . . . . NiB $519 Ex $467 Gd $275
Recent importation (Interarms). . . . . NiB $363 Ex $311 Gd $181
Recent importation (European Amer. Arms) . . . NiB $304 Ex $262 Gd $158
Recent importation (Gamga, USA) . . . . NiB $436 Ex $368 Gd $254
American Eagle model (1 of 5000) . . . . NiB $484 Ex $392 Gd $276

LUGER LANGE PISTOL 08

Caliber: 9mm Para. Eight-inch bbl., Checkered grips. Blued finish. Accessorized w/walnut shoulder stock, front sight tool, spare magazine, leather case. Currently in production. Commemorative version made in limited quantities w/ivory grips and 14-carat gold monogram plate.

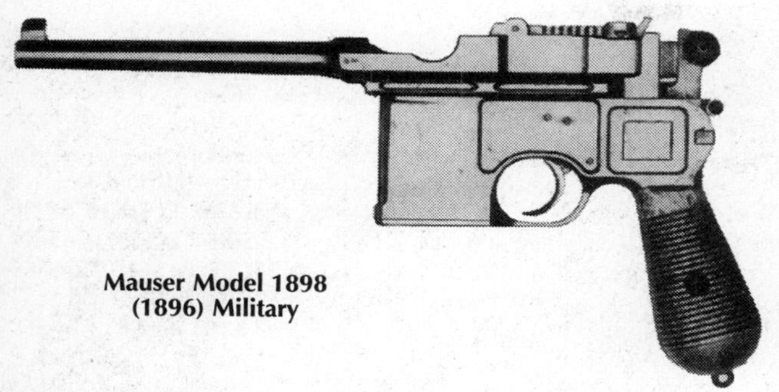

Mauser Model 1898 (1896) Military

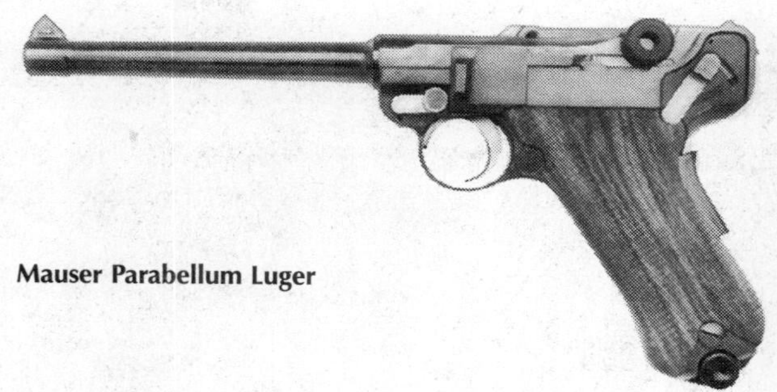

Mauser Parabellum Luger

Commemorative model (100 produced) . . . NiB $2684 Ex $2165 Gd $1501
Commemorative matched pair . . . . NiB $5322 Ex $4283 Gd $2954
Cartridge counter model. . . . . NiB $3473 Ex $2768 Gd $1935
Carbine model (w/matching buttstock) . NiB $6440 Ex $5178 Gd $3564

PARABELLUM LUGER AUTO PISTOL
Current commercial model. Swiss pattern with grip safety. Calibers: 7.65mm Luger, 9mm Para. Eight-round magazine, bbl. lengths: 4-, 6-inch, 8.75 inches overall (with 4-inch bbl.). Weight: 30 oz. (with 4-inch bbl.). Fixed sights. Blued finish. Checkered walnut grips. Made from 1970 to date. Note: Pistols of this model sold in the U.S. have the American Eagle stamped on the receiver.
Standard model (blue). . . . . NiB $1119 Ex $864 Gd $649

POCKET MODEL 1910 AUTO PISTOL
Caliber: .25 Auto (6.35mm). Nine-round magazine, 3.1-inch bbl., 5.4 inches overall. Weight: 15 oz. Fixed sights. Blued finish. Checkered walnut or hard rubber grips. Made from 1910-34.
Model 1910 (standard) . . . . NiB $471 Ex $341 Gd $175
Model 1910 (w/side latch) . . . . NiB $491 Ex $398 Gd $280

POCKET MODEL 1914 AUTOMATIC. . . . . . . NiB $471 Ex $341 Gd $180
Similar to Pocket Model 1910. Caliber: .32 Auto (7.65mm). Eight-round magazine, 3.4-inch bbl., 6 inches overall. Weight: 21 oz. Fixed sights. Blued finish. Checkered walnut or hard rubber grips. Made 1914-34

POCKET MODEL 1934 . . . . NiB $497 Ex $367 Gd $185
Similar to Pocket Models 1910 and 1914 in the respective calibers. Chief difference is in the more streamlined, one-piece grips. Made from 1934-39.

WTP MODEL I AUTO PISTOL. . . . . NiB $548 Ex $371 Gd $179
"Westentaschen-Pistole" (Vest Pocket Pistol). Caliber: .25 Automatic (6.35mm). Six-round magazine, 2.5-inch bbl., 4 inches overall. Weight: 11.5 oz. Blued finish. Hard rubber grips. Made from 1922-37.

WTP MODEL II AUTO PISTOL . . . . NiB $711 Ex $581 Gd $243
Similar to Model I but smaller and lighter. Caliber: .25 Automatic (6.35mm). Six-round magazine, 2-inch bbl., 4 inches overall. Weight: 9.5 oz. Blued finish. Hard rubber grips. Made from 1938-40.

MERWIN HULBERT & CO., — New York, NY

FIRST MODEL
FRONTIER ARMY . . . . NiB $3696 Ex $1928 Gd $836
Single action, .44 caliber, 7.5-inch bbl. Square butt, open top, scoop flutes on cylinder, two screws above trigger guard

SECOND MODEL
FRONTIER ARMY . . . . NiB $5269 Ex $1837 Gd $1005
Similar to First Model except has only one screw above trigger guard.

SECOND MODEL
POCKET ARMY . . . . NiB $5280 Ex $1380 Gd $912
Similar to Second Model except has bird's-head butt instead of square butt, 3.5- or 7-inch (scarce) bbl. Some models may be marked "Pocket Army."

THIRD MODEL
FRONTIER ARMY . . . . NiB $5280 Ex $1380 Gd $912
Caliber: .44, 7-inch round bbl. with no rib, single action. Square butt, top strap, usually has conventional fluting on cylinder but some have scoop flutes.

THIRD MODEL
FRONTIER ARMY . . . . NiB $5020 Ex $1224 Gd $860
Similar to Third Model Frontier Army SA except is double action.

THIRD MODEL POCKET ARMY .NiB $5020 Ex $1224 Gd $860
Caliber: .44, 3.5- or 7.5-inch bbl. with no rib. Single action, bird's-head butt, top strap.

THIRD MODEL POCKET ARMY . NiB $4760 Ex $1120 Gd $808
Similar to Third Model Pocket Army SA except is double action.

FOURTH MODEL FRONTIER ARMY . . NiB $6840 Ex $3720 Gd $1900
Caliber: .44, 3.5- 5- or 7-inch unique ribbed bbl. Single action, square butt, top strap, conventional flutes on cylinder.

FOURTH MODEL FRONTIER ARMY
Similar to Fourth Model Frontier Army SA except is double action.
. . . . . .NiB $6340 Ex $3200 Gd $1796

(The following handguns are foreign copies of Merwin Hulbert Co. guns and may be marked as such, or as "Sistema Merwin Hulbert," but rarely with the original Hopkins & Allen markings. These guns will usually bring half or less of a comparable genuine Merwin Hulbert product.)

FIRST POCKET MODEL. . . . . NiB $1609 Ex $617 Gd $383
Caliber: .38 Special, 5-round cylinder (w/cylinder pin exposed at front of frame), single action. Spur trigger; round loading hole in recoil shield, no loading gate.

SECOND POCKET MODEL . . . . . NiB $1452 Ex. $539 Gd $357
Similar to First Pocket Model except has sliding loading gate.

THIRD POCKET MODEL . . . . .NiB $1345 Ex $509 Gd $337
Similar to First Pocket Model except has enclosed cylinder pin.

THIRD POCKET
MODEL W/TRIGGER GUARD. . . . NiB $1345 Ex $535 Gd $363
Similar to First Pocket Model except w/conventional trigger guard.

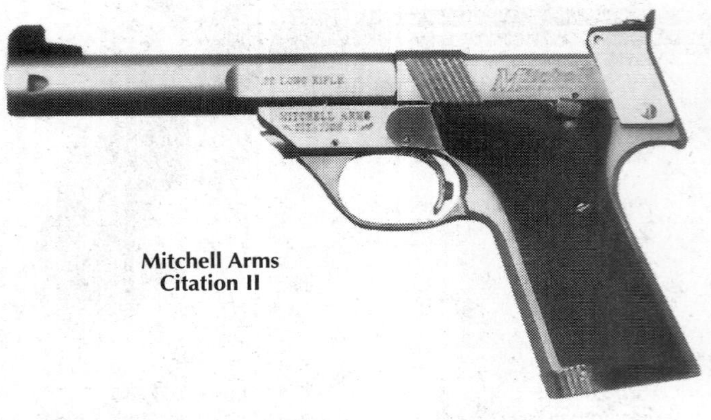
Mitchell Arms
Citation II

Mitchell Arms
Sharpshooter II

MEDIUM FRAME
POCKET MODEL.............. NiB $1038 Ex $472 Gd $332
Caliber: .38 Spec., 5-round cylinder, DA, may have hammer spur.

MEDIUM FRAME
POCKET MODEL 32 .... Nib $1194 Ex $514 Gd $358
Similar to Medium Frame Pocket Model except .32 caliber, 7-round cylinder, double action.

TIP-UP MODEL 22 .... NiB $1194 Ex $680 Gd $410
Similar to S&W Model One except .22 caliber, 7-round cylinder, spur trigger. Scarce.

MITCHELL ARMS, INC. — Santa Ana, California

MODEL 1911 GOLD SIGNATURE
Caliber: .45 ACP. Eight-round mag, 5-inch bbl., 8.75 inches overall. Weight: 39 oz. Interchangeable blade front sight, drift-adj. combat or fully adj. rear. Smooth or checkered walnut grips. Made from 1994-96.
Blued model w/fixed sights....... NiB $639 Ex $567 Gd $374
Blued model w/adj. sights........ NiB $659 Ex $578 Gd $384
Stainless model w/fixed sights..... NiB $814 Ex $697 Gd $595
Stainless model w/adj. sights...... NiB $845 Ex $722 Gd $620

ALPHA MODEL AUTO PISTOL
Dual action w/interchangeable trigger modules. Caliber: .45 ACP. Eight-round magazine, 5-inch bbl., 8.75 inches overall. Weight: 39 oz. Interchangeable blade front sight, drift-adj. rear. Smooth or checkered walnut grips. Blued or stainless finish. Made from 1994 to date. Advertised 1995, but not manufactured.
Blued model w/fixed sights................ NiB $940 Ex $762 Gd $534
Blued model w/adj. sights................. NiB $974 Ex $789 Gd $553
Stainless model w/fixed sights............. NiB $974 Ex $789 Gd $553
Stainless model w/adj. sights............. NiB $1005 Ex $814 Gd $569

AMERICAN EAGLE PISTOL .... NiB $627 Ex $508 Gd $356
Stainless-steel re-creation of the American Eagle Parabellum auto pistol. Caliber: 9mm Para. Seven-round magazine, 4-inch bbl., 9.6 inches overall. Weight: 26.6 oz. Blade front sight, fixed rear. Stainless finish. Checkered walnut grips. Made from 1993-94.

CITATION II AUTO PISTOL ...... NiB $430 Ex $328 Gd $200
Re-creation of the High Standard Supermatic Citation Military. Caliber: .22 LR. 10-round magazine, 5.5-inch bull bbl. or 7.25 fluted bbl., 9.75 inches overall (5.5-inch bbl.). Weight: 44.5 oz. Ramp front sight, slide-mounted micro-adj. rear. Satin blued or stainless finish. Checkered walnut grips w/thumbrest. Made from 1992-96.

OLYMPIC L.S.U.
AUTO PISTOL................. NiB $876 Ex $596 Gd $316
Similar to the Citation II model except chambered in .22 Short, 6.75-inch round tapered bbl. w/stabilizer and removable counterweights. Made from 1992-96.

SHARPSHOOTER I
AUTO PISTOL..................... NiB $354 Ex $314 Gd $201
Re-creation of the High Standard Sharpshooter. Caliber: .22 LR. 10-round magazine, 5-inch bull bbl., 10.25 inches overall. Weight: 42 oz. Ramp front sight, slide-mounted micro-adj. rear. Satin blued or stainless finish. Checkered walnut grips w/thumbrest. Made from 1992-96.

MODEL SA SPORT KING II....... NiB $296 Ex $241 Gd $171
Caliber: .22 LR. 10-round magazine, 4.5- or 6.75-inch bbl., 9 or 11.25 inches overall. Weight: 39 or 42 oz. Checkered walnut or black plastic grips. Blade front sight and drift adjustable rear. Made from 1993-94.

SA ARMY REVOLVER
Calibers: .357 Mag., .44 Mag., .45 Colt/.45 ACP. Six-round cylinder. bbl., lengths: 4.75, 5.5, 7.5 inches, weight: 40-43 oz. Blade front sight, grooved top strap or adj. rear. Blued or nickel finish w/colorcasehardened frame. Brass or steel backstrap/trigger guard. Smooth one-piece walnut grips. Imported from 1987-94 and 1997 to date.
Standard model w/blued finish.......... NiB $406 Ex $331 Gd $235
Standard model w/nickel finish.......... NiB $444 Ex $362 Gd $255
Standard model w/stainless backstrap ..... NiB $477 Ex $387 Gd $273
.45 Combo w/blued finish .... NiB $536 Ex $455 Gd $306
.45 Combo w/nickel finish .... NiB $577 Ex $467 Gd $327

TROPHY II
AUTO PISTOL................. NiB $465 Ex $389 Gd $205
Similar to the Citation II model except w/gold-plated trigger and gold-filled markings. Made from 1992-96.

VICTOR II AUTO PISTOL . . . . NiB $547 Ex $446 Gd $317
Re-creation of the High Standard Victor w/full-length vent rib. Caliber: .22 LR. 10-round magazine, 4.5- or 5.5-inch bbl., 9.75 inches overall (with 5.5-inch bbl.). Weight: 52 oz. (with 5.5-inch bbl.). Rib-mounted target sights. Satin blued or stainless finish. Checkered walnut grips w/thumbrest. Made from 1992-96.

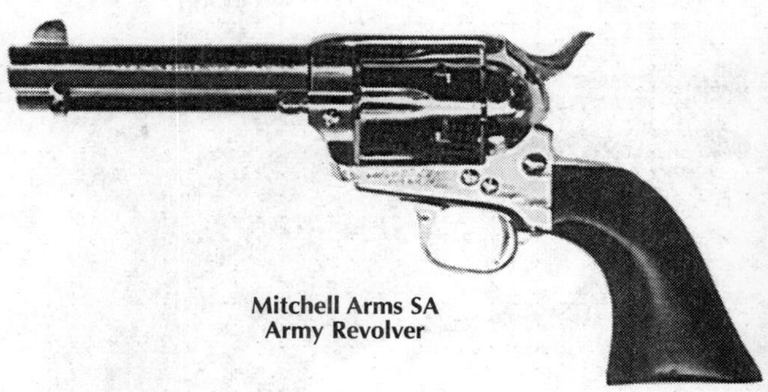
Mitchell Arms SA Army Revolver

GUARDIAN ANGEL
DERRINGER . . . . NiB $145 Ex $120 Gd $87
Hammerless, double-action O/U derringer w/interchangeable drop-in breech block. Calibers: .22 LR, .22 WRM. Two-round capacity. Two-inch bbl., 5 inches overall. Weight: 12 oz. Blue, nickel or gold finish. Blade front and fixed rear sights. Checkered black grips. Made from 1996-97.

GUARDIAN II . . . . NiB $265 Ex $216 Gd $154
Caliber: .38 Special, Six-round cylinder, 2-, 4- or 6-inch bbl., 8.5 inches overall (with 4-inch bbl.). Weight: 32 oz (with 4-inch bbl.). Blade ramp front and fixed rear sights. Checkered combat or target grips. Blued finish. Made in 1995.

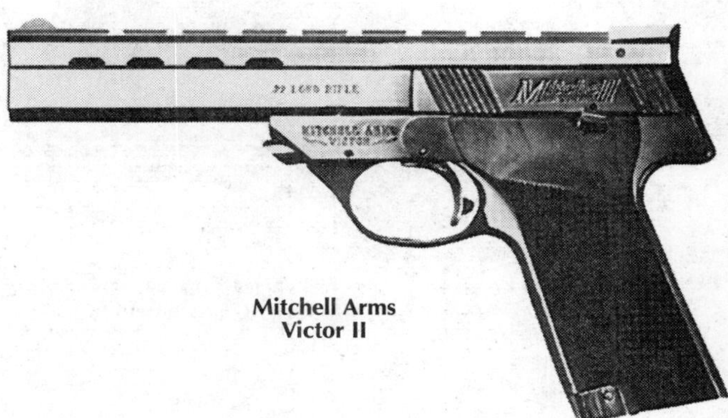
Mitchell Arms Victor II

GUARDIAN III . . . . NiB $302 Ex $251 Gd $165
Same specifications as Guardian II model except w/adjustable rear sights. Made in 1995.

TITAN II DA . . . . NiB $338 Ex $272 Gd $195
Caliber: .357 Mag. Six-round cylinder. 2-, 4- or 6-inch bbl., 7.75 inches overall (with 4-inch bbl.). Weight: 38 oz (with 4-inch bbl.). Blade front and fixed rear sights. Crane mounted cylinder release. Blued or stainless finish. Made in 1995.

TITAN III DA . . . . NiB $379 Ex $302 Gd $311
Same specification as the Titan II except w/adjustable rear sight. Made in 1995.

MKE PISTOL — Ankara, Turkey
Mfd. by Makina ve Kimya Endüstrisi Kurumu

KIRIKKALE DA
AUTOMATIC PISTOL . . . . NiB $399 Ex $328 Gd $200
Similar to Walther PP. Calibers: .32 Auto (7.65mm), .380 Auto (9mm Short). Seven-round magazine, 3.9-inch bbl., 6.7 inches overall. Weight: 24 oz. Fixed sights. Blued finish. Checkered plastic grips. Made from 1948-88. Note: This is a Turkish Army standard service pistol.

MKE Kirikkale

MOA CORPORATION — Dayton, Ohio

MAXIMUM SINGLE-SHOT PISTOL
Calibers: .22 Hornet to .454 Casull Mag. Armoloy, Chromoloy or stainless falling block action fitted w/blued or stainless 8.75-, 10- or 14-inch Douglas bbl., weight: 60-68 oz. Smooth walnut grips. Made from 1986 to date.

Chromoloy receiver
(blued bbl.) . . . . NiB $867 Ex $751 Gd $406
Armoloy receiver (blued bbl.) . . . . . NiB $878 Ex $781 Gd $429
Stainless receiver (blued bbl.) . . . . . NiB $981 Ex $884 Gd $639
W/stainless bbl., add $95
W/extra bbl., add $250

MOA Maximum Carbine Pistol

MAXIMUM CARBINE PISTOL
Similar to Maximum Pistol except w/18-inch bbl. Made from 1986-88 and from 1994 to date.

MOA Maximum (blued bbl.) . . . . . . NiB $894 Ex $716 Gd $492
MOA Maximum (stainless bbl.) . . . . NiB $966 Ex $790 Gd $548

Mossberg Brownie "Pepperbox" Pistol

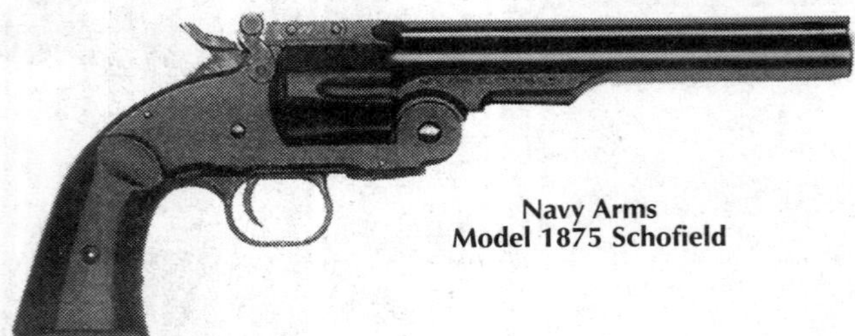

Navy Arms Model 1875 Schofield

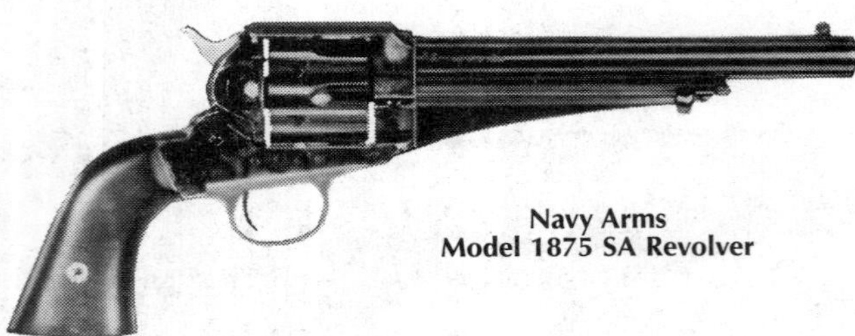

Navy Arms Model 1875 SA Revolver

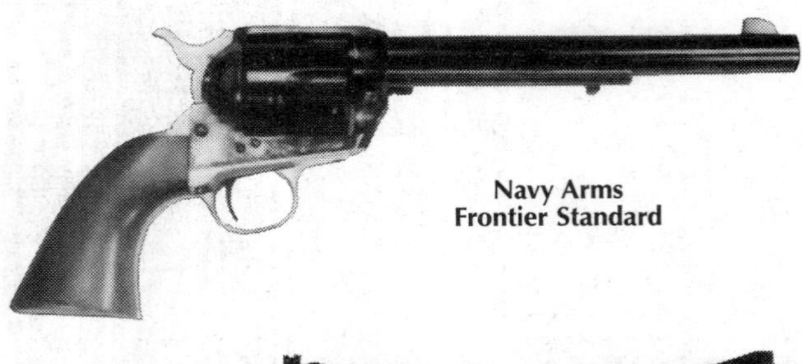

Navy Arms Frontier Standard

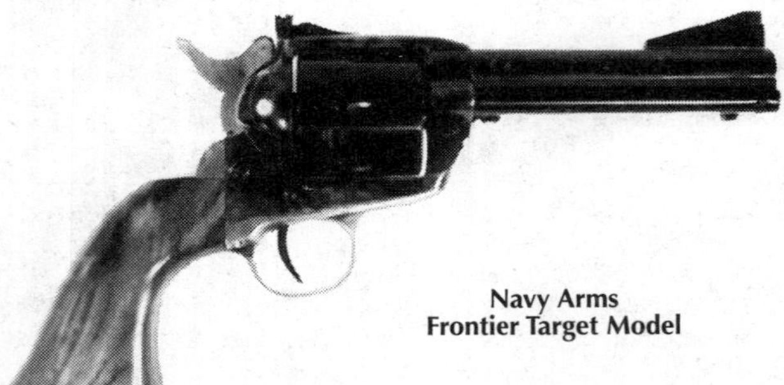

Navy Arms Frontier Target Model

O.F. MOSSBERG & SONS, INC. — North Haven, Connecticut

BROWNIE "PEPPERBOX" PISTOL. . . . . . . NiB $385 Ex $334 Gd $201
Hammerless, top-break, double-action, four bbls. w/revolving firing pin. Caliber: .22 LR, 2.5-inch bbls., weight: 14 oz. Blued finish. Serrated grips. Approximately 37,000 made from 1919-.32.

NAMBU PISTOLS

See Listings under Japanese Military Pistols.

NAVY ARMS COMPANY — Martinsburg, West Virginia

MODEL 1873 SA REVOLVER
Calibers: .44-40, .45 Colt. Six-round cylinder, bbl. lengths: 3, 4.75, 5.5, 7.5 inches, 10.75 inches overall (with 5.5-inch bbl.). Weight: 36 oz. Blade front sight, grooved topstrap rear. Blued w/color-case-hardened frame or nickel finish. Smooth walnut grips. Made from 1991 to date.
Blued finish w/brass backstrap . . . . . NiB $385 Ex $318 Gd $14
U.S. Artillery model w/5-inch bbl. . . . NiB $416 Ex $339 Gd $240
U.S. Cavalry model w/7-inch bbl. . . NiB $448 Ex $365 Gd $258
Bisley model . . . . NiB $385 Ex $334 Gd $184
Sheriff's model (disc. 1998) . . . . NiB $380 Ex $308 Gd $184

MODEL 1875 SCHOFIELD REVOLVER
Replica of S&W Model 3, top-break single-action w/auto ejector. Calibers: .44-40 or .45 LC. Six-round cylinder, 5- or 7-inch bbl., 10.75 or 12.75 inches overall. Weight: 39 oz. Blade front sight, square-notched rear. Polished blued finish. Smooth walnut grips. Made from 1994 to date.
Cavalry model (7-inch bbl.) . . . . . . NiB $655 Ex $578 Gd $2894
Deluxe Cavalry model
(engraved) . . . . NiB $1532 Ex $1235 Gd $839
Wells Fargo model (5-inch bbl.) . . . NiB $671 Ex $547 Gd $381
Deluxe Wells Fargo
model (engraved). . . . . NiB $1506 Ex $1210 Gd $839
Hideout model (3.5-inch bbl.) . . . . . NiB $639 Ex $526 Gd $370

MODEL 1875 SA REVOLVER. . . . . . NiB $410 Ex $334 Gd $237
Replica of Remington Model 1875. Calibers: .357 Magnum, .44-40, .45 Colt. Six-round cylinder, 7.5-inch bbl., 13.5 inches overall. Weight: About 48 oz. Fixed sights. Blued or nickel finish. Smooth walnut grips. Made in Italy c.1955-1980. Note: Originally marketed in the U.S. as Replica Arms Model 1875 (that firm was acquired by Navy Arms Co).

FRONTIER SA REVOLVER . . . . NiB $325 Ex $265 Gd $189
Calibers: .22 LR, .22 WMR, .357 Mag., .45 Colt. Six-round cylinder, bbl. lengths: 4.5-, 5.5-, 7.5-inches, 10.25 inches overall (with 4.5-inch bbl.). Weight: About 36 oz. (with 4.5-inch bbl.). Fixed sights. Blued bbl., and cylinder, color-casehardened frame, brass grip frame. One-piece smooth walnut grip. Imported from 1975-79.

FRONTIER TARGET MODEL . . . . . . NiB $350 Ex $285 Gd $203
Same as standard Frontier except has adj. rear sight and ramp front sight. Imported from 1975-79.

BUNTLINE FRONTIER. . . . . NiB $513 Ex $416 Gd $293
Same as Target Frontier except has detachable shoulder stock and 16.5-inch bbl. Calibers: .357 Magnum and .45 Colt only. Made from 1975-79.

LUGER (STANDARD) AUTOMATIC . . . . . . NiB $179 Ex $147 Gd $106
Caliber: .22 LR, standard or high velocity. 10-round magazine, bbl. length: 4.5 inches, 8.9 inches overall. Weight: 1 lb., 13.5 oz. Square blade front sight w/square notch, stationary rear sight. Walnut checkered grips. Non-reflecting black finish. Made from 1986-88.

ROLLING BLOCK
SINGLE-SHOT PISTOL . . . . NiB $373 Ex $315 Gd $196
Calibers: .22 LR, .22 Hornet, .357 Magnum. Eight-inch bbl., 12 inches overall. Weight: About 40 oz. Adjustable sights. Blued bbl., color-casehardened frame, brass trigger guard. Smooth walnut grip and forearm. Imported from 1965-80.

TT-OLYMPIA PISTOL. . . . . NiB $277 Ex $252 Gd $174
Reproduction of the Walther Olympia Target Pistol. Caliber: .22 LR. Eight inches overall 4.6-inch bbl., weight: 28 oz. Blade front sight, adj. rear. Blued finish. Checkered hardwood grips. Imported from 1992-94.

NEW ENGLAND FIREARMS — Gardner, Massachusetts

In 1987, New England Firearms was established as an independent company producing select H&R models under the NEF logo. In 1991, H&R 1871, Inc. was formed from the residual of the parent company and took over the New England Firearms facility. H&R 1871 produced firearms under both their logo and the NEF brand name until 1999, when the Marlin Firearms Company acquired the assets of H&R 1871.

MODEL R73 REVOLVER . . . . NiB $145 Ex $114 Gd $78
Caliber: .32 H&R Mag. Five-round cylinder, 2.5- or 4-inch bbl., 8.5 inches overall (with 4-inch bbl.). Weight: 26 oz. (with 4 inch bbl.). Fixed or adjustable sights. Blued or nickel finish. Walnut-finish hardwood grips. Made from 1988-99.

MODEL R92 REVOLVER . . . . NiB $145 Ex $114 Gd $78
Same general specifications as Model R73 except chambered for .22 LR. Nine-round cylinder. Weight: 28 oz. w/4 inch bbl., Made from 1988-99.

MODEL 832 STARTER PISTOL . . . . . . NiB $108 Ex $89 Gd $65
Calibers: .22 Blank, .32 Blank. Nine- and 5-round cylinders, respectively. Push-pin swing-out cylinder. Solid wood grips w/NEF medallion insert.

ULTRA REVOLVER. . . . . NiB $177 Ex $145 Gd $104
Calibers: .22 LR, .22 Mag. Nine-round cylinder in .22 LR, 6-round cylinder in .22 Mag., 4- or 6-inch ribbed bull bbl., 10.75 inches overall (with 6-inch bbl.). Weight: 36 oz. (with 6-inch bbl.). Blade front sight, adj. square-notched rear. Blued or nickel finish. Walnut-finish hardwood grips. Made from 1989-99.

LADY ULTRA REVOLVER. . . . . NiB $170 Ex $134 Gd $88
Same basic specifications as the Ultra except in .32 H&R Mag. w/5-round cylinder and 3-inch ribbed bull bbl., 7.5 inches overall. Weight: 31 oz. Made from 1992 -99.

NORTH AMERICAN ARMS — Provo, Utah

MODEL 22LR . . . . NiB $175 Ex $143 Gd $103
Same as Model 22S except chambered for .22 LR., is 3.88-inches overall, weight: 4.5 oz. Made from 1976 to date.

MODEL 22S MINI REVOLVER. . . . . NiB $188 Ex $154 Gd $110
Single-Action. Caliber: .22 Short. Five-round cylinder, 1.13-inch bbl., 3.5-inches overall. Weight: 4 oz. Fixed sights. Stainless steel. Plastic grips. Made from 1975 to date.

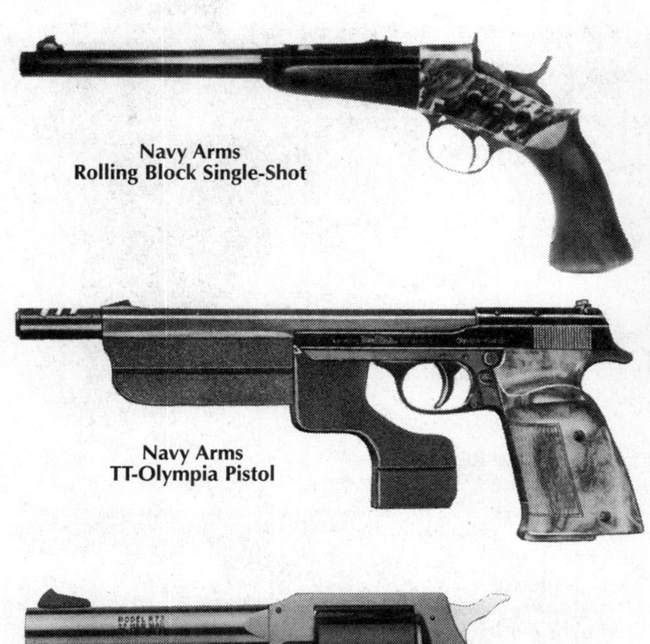

Navy Arms
Rolling Block Single-Shot

Navy Arms
TT-Olympia Pistol

New England Firearms
Model R73 Revolver

New England Firearms
Model 832 Starter Pistol

MODEL 450 MAGNUM EXPRESS
Single-Action. Calibers: .450 Magnum Express, .45 Win. Mag. Five-round cylinder, 7.5- or 10.5-inch bbl., matte or polished stainless steel finish. Walnut grips. Presentation case. Disc. 1986.
Matte stainless model . . . . NiB $1281 Ex $1026 Gd $771
Polished stainless model . . . . . . NiB $1487 Ex $1181 Gd $926
W/10-inch bbl., add $250
W/combo cylinder, add. $225

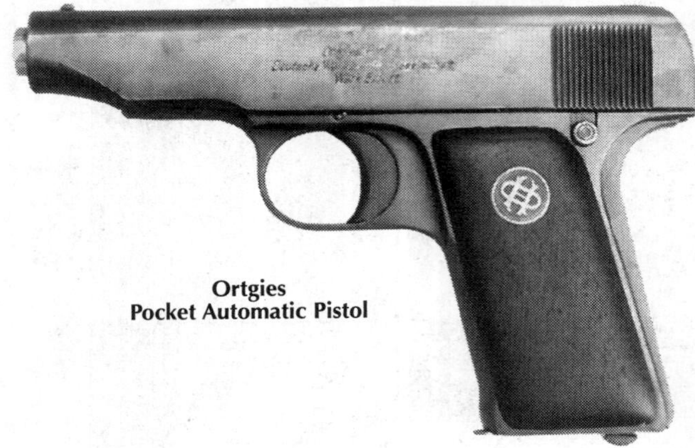

Ortgies
Pocket Automatic Pistol

BLACK WIDOW REVOLVER
SA. Calibers: .22 LR., .22 WMR. Five-round cylinder, 2-inch heavy vent bbl., 5.88-inches overall. Weight: 8.8 oz. Fixed or adj. sights. Full-size black rubber grips. Stainless steel brush finish. Made from 1990 to date.

Adj. sight model . . . . NiB $277 Ex $235 Gd $143
Adj. sight combo model . . . . NiB $317 Ex $261 Gd $189
Fixed sight model . . . . NiB $226 Ex $184 Gd $129
Fixed sight combo model. . . . . NiB $306 Ex $256 Gd $192

GUARDIAN DAO PISTOL. . . . . NiB $380 Ex $309 Gd $314
Caliber: .32 ACP. Six-round magazine, 2-inch bbl., 4.4 inches overall. Weight: 13.5 oz. Fixed sights. Black synthetic grips. Stainless steel. Made from 1997 to date.

MINI-MASTER TARGET REVOLVER
SA. Calibers: .22 LR., .22 WMR. Five-round cylinder, 4-inch heavy vent rib bbl., 7.75-inches overall. Weight: 10.75 oz. Fixed or adj. sights. Black rubber grips. Stainless steel brush finish. Made from 1990 to date.

Adj. sight model . . . . NiB $266 Ex $220 Gd $189
Adj. sight combo model . . . . NiB $374 Ex $310 Gd $228
Fixed sight model . . . . NiB $265 Ex $215 Gd $152
Fixed sight combo model. . . . . NiB $341 Ex $284 Gd $211

NORWEGIAN MILITARY PISTOLS Mfd. by Kongsberg Vaapenfabrikk, Government Arsenal at Kongsberg, Norway

MODEL 1914
AUTOMATIC PISTOL . . . . NiB $432 Ex $349 Gd $243
Similar to Colt Model 1911 .45 Automatic w/same general specifications except has lengthened slide stop. Made 1919-46.

NORWEGIAN
MODEL 1912 . . . . NiB $2728 Ex $2193 Gd $1508
Same as the model 1914 except has conventional slide stop. Only 500 were made.

OLYMPIC ARMS, INC. Olympia, Washington

OA-93 AR SEMIAUTOMATIC PISTOL
AR-15 style receiver with no buffer tube or charging handle. Caliber: .223 Rem. or 7.62x39mm. Five-, 20- or 30-round detachable magazine, 6-, 9- or 14-inch stainless steel bbl., 15.75 inches overall w/6-inch bbl., weight: 4 lbs., 3 oz. Flattop upper with no open sights. Vortex flash suppressor. A2 stowaway pistol grip and forward pistol grip. Made 1993-94. Note: All post-ban versions of OA-93 style weapons are classified by BATF as "Any Other Weapon" and must be transferred by a Class III dealer. Values listed here are for limited-production, pre-ban guns.

Model OA-93
(.223 Rem.) . . . . NiB $3598 Ex $2884 Gd $2629
Model OA-93
(7.62x39mm). . . . . NiB $4414 Ex $4210 Gd $3904

OA-96 AR SEMI-
AUTOMATIC PISTOL . . . . NiB $907 Ex $815 Gd $729
Similar to Model OA-93 AR except w/6.5-inch bbl. only chambered for .223 Rem. Additional compliance modifications include a fixed (nonremovable) well-style magazine and no forward pistol grip. Made from 1996 to date.

ORTGIES PISTOLS — Erfurt, Germany Manufactured by Deutsche Werke A.G.

POCKET AUTO-
MATIC PISTOL . . . . NiB $322 Ex $271 Gd $200
Calibers: .32 Auto (7.65mm), .380 Auto (9mm). Seven-round magazine (.380 cal.), 8-round (.32 cal.), 3.25-inch bbl., 6.5-inches overall. Weight: 22 oz. Fixed sights. Blued finish. Plain walnut grips. Made in 1920's.

VEST POCKET
AUTOMATIC PISTOL . . . . NiB $296 Ex $240 Gd $169
Caliber: .25 Auto (6.35mm). Six-round magazine, 2.75-inch bbl., 5.19 inches overall. Weight: 13.5 oz. Fixed sights. Blued finish. Plain walnut grips. Made in 1920's.

PARA-ORDNANCE MFG. INC. — Toronto, Canada

LIMITED EDITION SERIES
Custom-tuned and fully accessorized "Limited Edition" versions of standard "P" Models. Enhanced-grip frame and serrated slide fitted w/match-grade bbl., and full-length recoil spring guide system. Beavertail grip safety and skeletonized hammer. Ambidextrous safety and trigger-stop adjustment. Fully adjustable or contoured low-mount sights. For pricing see individual models.

MODEL P-10 SA
AUTO PISTOL
Super compact. Calibers: .40 S&W, .45 ACP. 10-round magazine, 3-inch bbl., weight: 24 oz. (alloy frame) or 31 oz. (steel frame). Ramp front sight and drift adjustable rear w/3-dot system. Steel or alloy frame. Matte black, Duo-Tone or stainless finish. Made from 1997 to date.

Alloy model. . . . . NiB $686 Ex $557 Gd $377
Duo-Tone model . . . . NiB $680 Ex $552 Gd $403
Stainless steel model . . . . NiB $769 Ex $634 Gd $461
Steel model . . . . NiB $664 Ex $542 Gd $385
Limited model (tuned & accessorized), add $125

P-12 COMPACT AUTO PISTOL
Calibers: .45 ACP. 11-round magazine, 3.5-inch bbl., 7-inches overall. Weight: 24 oz. (alloy frame). Blade front sight, adj. rear w/3-dot system. Textured composition grips. Matte black alloy or steel finish. Made from 1990 to date.

Made from 1990 to date.
Model P1245 (alloy) . . . . NiB $705 Ex $573 Gd $424
Model P1245C (steel) . . . . NiB $833 Ex $675 Gd $473
Limited model (tuned & accessorized), add $125

P-13 AUTO PISTOL
Same general specifications as Model P-12 except w/12-round magazine, 4.5-inch bbl., 8-inches overall. Weight: 25 oz. (alloy frame). Blade front sight, adj. rear w/3-dot system. Textured composition grips. Matte black alloy or steel finish. Made from 1990 to date.
Model P1345 (alloy) . . . . NiB $830 Ex $608 Gd $402
Model P1345C (steel) . . . . NiB $841 Ex $682 Gd $477
Limited model
(tuned & accessorized), add $125

P-14 AUTO PISTOL
Caliber: .45 ACP. 13-round magazine, 5-inch bbl., 8.5 inches overall. Weight: 28 oz. Alloy frame. Blade front sight, adj. rear w/3-dot system. Textured composition grips. Matte black alloy or steel finish. Made from 1990 to date.
Model P1445 (alloy) . . . . NiB $686 Ex $557 Gd $377
Model P1445C (steel) . . . . NiB $755 Ex $614 Gd $434
Limited model (tuned
& accessorized), add $125

MODEL P-15 AUTO PISTOL
Caliber: .40 S&W. 10-round magazine, 4.25-inch bbl., 7.75 inches overall. Weight: 28 to 36 oz. Steel, alloy or stainless receiver. Matte black, Duotone or stainless finish. Made from 1996-99.
Model P1540 (alloy) . . . . NiB $686 Ex $557 Gd $490
Model P1540C (steel) . . . . NiB $651 Ex $531 Gd $378
Duotone stainless model . . . . NiB $726 Ex $598 Gd $435
Stainless model . . . . NiB $767 Ex $634 Gd $464

MODEL P-16 SA AUTO PISTOL
Caliber: .40 S&W. 10- or 16-round magazine, 5-inch bbl., 8.5 inches overall. Weight: 40 oz. Ramp front sight and drift adjustable rear w/3-dot system. Carbon steel or stainless frame. Matte black, Duotone or stainless finish. Made from 1997 to date.
Blue steel model . . . . NiB $701 Ex $572 Gd $402
Duotone model . . . . NiB $722 Ex $593 Gd $428

Stainless model . . . . NiB $840 Ex $722 Gd $408
Limited model (tuned
& accessorized), add $125

MODEL P-18 SA AUTO PISTOL
Caliber: 9mm Parabellum. 10- or 18-round magazine, 5-inch bbl., 8.5 inches overall. Weight: 40 oz. Dovetailed front sight and fully adjustable rear. Bright stainless finish. Made from 1998 to date.
Stainless model . . . . NiB $789 Ex $634 Gd $505
Limited model (tuned
& accessorized), add $125

PHOENIX ARMS — Ontario, California

MODEL HP22/HP25
SA AUTO PISTOLS. . . . . NiB $134 Ex $82 Gd $54
Caliber: .22 LR, .25 ACP. 10-round magazine, 3-inch bbl., 5.5 inches overall. Weight: 20 oz. Checkered synthetic grips. Blade front sight, adjustable rear. Blue, chrome or nickel finish. Made from 1994 to date.

Para-Ordnance
P-12 Compact

Para-Ordnance
P-14 Auto Pistol

MODEL HP
RANGE-MASTER TARGET SA
AUTO PISTOL . . . . NiB $144 Ex $115 Gd $84
Similar to Model HP .22 except w/5.5-inch target bbl. and extended magazine, Ramp front sight, adjustable notch rear on vent rib. Checkered synthetic grips. Blue or satin nickel finish. Made from 1998 to date.

MODEL HP
RANGE-MASTER DELUXE TARGET
SA AUTO PISTOL . . . . NiB $245 Ex $148 Gd $107
Similar to Model HP Rangemaster Target model except w/dual-2000 laser sight and custom wood grips. Made from 1998 to date.

"RAVEN" SA
AUTO PISTOL . . . . NiB $83 Ex $64 Gd $49
Caliber: .25 ACP. Six-round magazine, 2.5 inch bbl., 4.75 inches overall. Weight: 15 oz. Ivory, pink pearl, or black slotted stocks. Fixed sights. Blue, chrome or nickel finish. Made from 1993 to date.

Plainfield Model 71

Plainfield Model 72

Radom P-35

PLAINFIELD MACHINE COMPANY — Dunellen, New Jersey

This firm disc. operation about 1982.

MODEL 71 AUTOMATIC PISTOL

Calibers: .22 LR, .25 Automatic w/conversion kit available. 10-round magazine (.22 LR) or 8-round (.25 Auto), 2.5-inch bbl., 5.13 inches overall. Weight: 25 oz. Fixed sights. Stainless steel frame/slide. Checkered walnut grips. Made from 1970-82.

.22 LR or .25 Auto only . . . . NiB $174 Ex $153 Gd $108
W/conversion kit. . . . . NiB $205 Ex $174 Gd $113

MODEL 72 AUTOMATIC PISTOL

Same as Model 71 except has aluminum slide, 3.5-inch bbl., 6 inches overall. Made from 1970-82

.22 LR or .25 Auto only . . . . NiB $184 Ex $159 Gd $955
W/conversion kit. . . . . NiB $199 Ex $1564 Gd $118

PROFESSIONAL ORDNANCE, INC. — Lake Havasu City, Arizona

MODEL CARBON-15 TYPE 20
SEMIAUTOMATIC PISTOL . . . . NiB $870 Ex $793 Gd $535

Similar to Carbon-15 Type 97 except w/unfluted barrel. Weight: 40 oz. Matte black finish. Made from 1999 to date.

MODEL CARBON-15 TYPE 97
SEMIAUTOMATIC PISTOL . . . . NiB $947 Ex $896 Gd $561

AR-15 operating system w/recoil reduction system. Caliber: .223 Rem. 10-round magazine, 7.25-inch fluted bbl., 20 inches overall. Weight: 46 oz. Ghost ring sights. Carbon-fiber upper and lower receivers w/Chromoly bolt carrier. Matte black finish. Checkered composition grip. Made from 1996 to date.

RADOM PISTOL — Radom, Poland Manufactured by the Polish Arsenal

P-35 AUTOMATIC PISTOL

Variation of the Colt Government Model .45 Auto. Caliber: 9mm Para. Eight-round magazine, 4.75-inch bbl., 7.75 inches overall. Weight: 29 oz. Fixed sights. Blued finish. Plastic grips. Made from 1935 thru WWII.

Commercial model
(Polish Eagle). . . . . NiB $2410 Ex $1660 Gd $523
Nazi military model
(W/slotted backstrap) . . . . NiB $936 Ex $736 Gd $232
Nazi military model
(W/takedown lever). . . . . NiB $576 Ex $401 Gd $217
Nazi military model
(No takedown lever or slot). . . . . . . NiB $411 Ex $329 Gd $208
Nazi military model (Parkerized) . . . . NiB $1070 Ex $864 Gd $246

RANDALL FIREARMS COMPANY — Sun Valley, California

The short-lived Randall firearms Company (1982 to 1984) was a leader in the production of stainless steel semi-autimatic handguns, particularly in left-handed configurations. Prices shown are for production models. Add 50% for prototype models (t-prefix on serial numbers) and $125 for guns with serial numbers below 2000. Scare models (C311, C332, etc., made in lots of four pieces or less) valued substantially higher to avid collectors.

MODEL A111 . . . . NiB $1030 Ex $855 Gd $580

Caliber: .45 Auto. Barrel: 5 inches. Round-slide top; right-hand model. Sights: Fixed. Total production: 3,431 pieces.

MODEL A112 . . . . NiB $1305 Ex $905 Gd $705

Calibers: 9mm. Barrel: 5 inches. Round-slide top; right-hand model. Sights: Fixed.

MODEL A121 . . . . NiB $1080 Ex $880 Gd $755

Caliber: .45 Auto. Barrel: 5 inches. Flat-slide top; right-hand model. Sights: Fixed.

MODEL A211 .... NiB $1156 Ex $931 Gd $756
Caliber: .45 Auto. Barrel: 4.25 inches. Round-slide top; right-hand model. Sights: Fixed.

MODEL A232 .... NiB $2170 Ex $1920 Gd $1445
Caliber: 9mm. Barrel: 4.25 inches. Flat-slide top; right-hand model. Sights: Fixed.

MODEL A331 .... NiB $1760 Ex $1510 Gd $1185
Caliber: .45 Auto. Barrel: 4.25 inches. Flat-slide top; right-hand model. Sights: Fixed.

MODEL B111 .... NiB $1890 Ex $1535 Gd $1260
Caliber: .45 Auto. Barrel: 5 inches. Round-slide top; left-hand model. Sights: Fixed. Toatal production: 297 pieces

MODEL B131 .... NiB $2135 Ex $1760 Gd $1385
Caliber: .45 Auto. Barrel: 5 inches. Flat-slide top; left-hand model. Sights: Millet. Total production: 225 pieces.

MODEL B311 .... NiB $2185 Ex $1835 Gd $1460
Caliber: .45 Auto. Barrel: 4.25 inches. Round-slide top; left-hand model. Sights: Fixed. Total production: 52 pieces.

MODEL B312 LEMAY .... NiB $4070 Ex $3270 Gd $2670
Caliber: 9mm. Barrel: 4.25 inches. Round-slide top; left-hand model. Sights: Fixed. Total production: 9 pieces.

MODEL B331 .... NiB $2516 Ex $2166 Gd $1691
Caliber: .45 Auto. Barrel: 4.25 inches. Flat-slide top; left-hand model. Sights: Millet. Total production: 45 pieces.

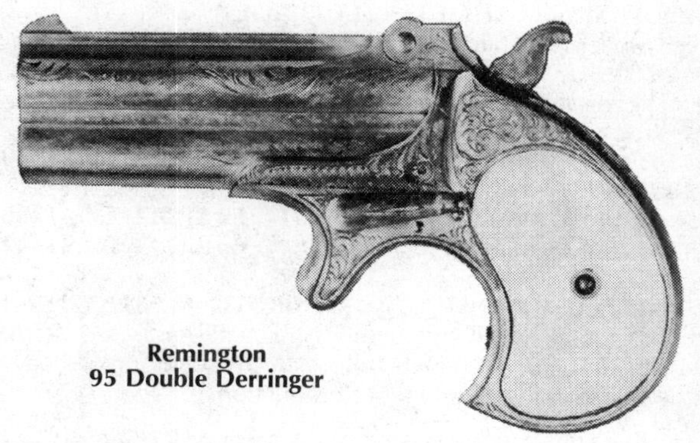

Remington
95 Double Derringer

Record-Match
Model 200 Free Pistol

RECORD-MATCH PISTOLS — Zella-Mehlis, Germany, Manufactured by Udo Anschütz

MODEL 200 FREE PISTOL .... NiB $1080 Ex $1023 Gd $781
Basically the same as Model 210 except w/different stock design and conventional set trigger, spur trigger guard. Made prior to WW II.

MODEL 210 FREE PISTOL...... NiB $1425 Ex $1363 Gd $787
System Martini action, set trigger w/button release. Caliber: .22 LR. Single-shot, 11-inch bbl., weight: 46 oz. Target sights micrometer rear. Blued finish. Carved and checkered walnut forearm and stock w/adj. hand base. Also made w/dual action (Model 210A); weight 35 oz. Made prior to WWII.

REISING ARMS CO. — Hartford, Connecticut

TARGET AUTOMATIC PISTOL..... NiB $521 Ex $392 Gd $212
Hinged frame. Outside hammer. Caliber: .22 LR. 12-round magazine, 6.5-inch bbl., fixed sights. Blued finish. Hard rubber grips. Made from 1921-24.

REMINGTON ARMS COMPANY — Ilion, New York

MODEL 51 AUTOMATIC PISTOL
Calibers: .32 Auto, .380 Auto. Seven-round magazine, 3.5-inch bbl., 6.63 inches overall. Weight: 21 oz. Fixed sights. Blued finish. Hard rubber grips. Made from 1918-34.
.32 ACP .... NiB $835 Ex $707 Gd $408
.380 ACP .... NiB $732 Ex $604 Gd $346

MODEL 95 DOUBLE DERRINGER
SA. Caliber: 41 Short Rimfire. Three-inch double bbls. (superposed), 4.88 inches overall. Early models have long hammer spur and two-armed extractor, but later guns have short hammer spur and sliding extractor (a few have no extractor). Fixed blade front sight and grooved rear. finish: Blued, blued w/nickel-plated frame or fully nickel-plated; also w/factory engraving. Grips: Walnut, checkered hard rubber, pearl, ivory. Weight: 11 oz. Made 1866-1935. Approximately 150,000 were manufactured. Note: During the 70 years of its production, serial numbering of this model was repeated two or three times. Therefore, aside from hammer and extractor differences between the earlier and later models, the best clue to the age of a Double Derringer is the stamping of the company's name on the top of the bbl., or side rib. Prior to 1888, derringers were stamped "E. Remington & Sons, Ilion, N.Y." on one side rib and "Elliot's Patent Dec. 12, 1865" on the other (Type I-early & mid-production) and on the top rib (Type I-late production). In 1888-1911, "Remington Arms Co., Ilion, N.Y." and patent date were stamped on the top rib (Type II) and from 1912-35 "Remington Arms - U.M.C. Co., Ilion, N.Y." and patent date were stamped on the top rib.
Model 95 (Early Type I,
w/o extractor) .... NiB $2115 Ex $2063 Gd $776
Model 95 (Mid Type I,
w/extractor) .... NiB $2269 Ex $2115 Gd $874
Model 95 (Late Type I,
w/extractor) .... NiB $2321 Ex $2115 Gd $879
Model 95 (Type II
produced 1988-11) .... NiB $1904 Ex $1492 Gd $668
Model 95 (Type III,
produced 1912-35) .... NiB $946 Ex $777 Gd $548
Factory-engraved model w/ivory
or pearl grips, add 35%

NEW MODEL SINGLE-SHOT TARGET PISTOL
Also called Model 1901 Target. Rolling-block action. Calibers: .22 Short & Long, .25 Stevens, .32 S&W, .44 S&W Russian. 10-inch half-octagon bbl., 14 inches overall. Weight: 45 oz. (.22 cal.). Target sights. Blued finish. Checkered walnut grips and forearm. Made from 1901-09.
Model 1901 (.22 caliber)..... NiB $2635 Ex $2340 Gd $1040
Model 1901
(.25 Stevens, .32 S&W) .... NiB $2314 Ex $1862 Gd $1286
Model 1901 (.44 Russian) ..... NiB $2841 Ex $2583 Gd $1141

MODEL XP-100 CUSTOM PISTOL .... NiB $535 Ex $432 Gd $241
Bolt-action, single-shot, long-range pistol. Calibers: .223 Rem., 7mm-08 or .35 Rem. 14.5-inch bbl., standard contour or heavy. Weight: About 4.25 lbs. Currently in production.

MODEL XP-100 SILHOUETTE..... NiB $585 Ex $473 Gd $330
Same general specifications as Model XP-100 except chambered for 7mm BR Rem. and 35 Rem. 14.75-inch bbl., weight: 4.13 lbs. Made from 1987-92.

MODEL XP-100
SINGLE-SHOT PISTOL. ....NiB $469 Ex $382 Gd $272
Bolt action. Caliber: 221 Rem. Fireball. 10.5-inch vent rib bbl., 16.75 inches overall. Weight: 3.75 lbs. Adj. rear sight, blade front, receiver drilled and tapped for scope mounts. Blued finish. One-piece brown nylon stock. Made from 1963-88.

MODEL XP-100
VARMINT SPECIAL .... NiB $547 Ex $444 Gd $253
Bolt-action, single-shot, long-range pistol. Calibers: .223 Rem., 7mm BR. 14.5-inch bbl., 21.25 inches overall. Weight: About 4.25 lbs. One-piece Du Pont nylon stock w/universal grips. Made from 1986-92.

MODEL XP-100R
CUSTOM REPEATER
Same general specifications as Model XP-100 Custom except 4- or 5- round repeater chambered for .22-250, .223 Rem., .250 Savage, 7mm-08 Rem., .308 Win., .35 Rem. and .350 Rem. Mag. Kevlar-reinforced synthetic or fiberglass stock w/blind magazine and sling swivel studs. Made from 1992-94 and from 1998 to date.
Model XP-100R (fiberglass stock) .... NiB $726 Ex $591 Gd $418
Model XP-100R KS (kevlar stock) .... NiB $663 Ex $616 Gd $410

NOTE: *The following Remington derringers were produced from the mid-1860s through the mid-1930s. The Zig-Zag model is reputed to be the first cartridge handgun ever produced at the Remington plant. Few if any Remington derringers exiswt in "new" or "in box" condition, therefore, guns in 90-percent condition command top price.*

ZIG-ZAG DERRINGER........ NiB $2800 Ex $1800 Gd $1000
Caliber: .22S, L, LR. Six shot, six-barrel (rotating) cluster. 3-inch bbl., blued, ring trigger. Two-piece rubber grips. Fewer than 1,000 pieces produced from 1861-1863.

ELIOT'S FIVE-SHOT
DERRINGER ....NiB $1795 Ex $900 $725
Caliber: .22S, L, LR. Five shot, five-barrel fixed cluster. 3-inch bbl., ring trigger, blue and/or nickel finish. Two-piece rubber, walnut, ivory or pearl grips.

ELIOT'S FOUR-SHOT
DERRINGER ....NiB $1595 Ex $975 $795
Caliber: .32. Four shot, four-barrel fixed cluster. 3-3/8 inch bbl., ring trigger, blue and/or nickel finish. Two-piece rubber, walnut, ivory or pearl grips. Approx. 25,000 pieces (.22 and .32) produced.

VEST POCKET DERRINGER ....NiB $1395 Ex $875 $700
Caliber: .22, .30, .32, .41 rimfire . Two shot, various bbl. lengths, blue or nickel finish. Two-piece walnut grips. Spur trigger. Made from 1865-88.

OVER AND UNDER DERRINGER . . .NiB $2600 Ex $1575 $900
Caliber: .41 rimfire. Two shot, 3-inch super imposed bbl., spur trigger, blue and/or nickel finish. Two-piece rubber, walnut, ivory or pearl grips. Oscillating firing pin. Produced 1866-1934. Also known as Double Derringer or Model 95. Type 1 and variatitons bear maker's name, patent data stamped between the barrels, with or without extractor. Types Two and Three marked "Remington Arms Company, Ilion, NY. Type Four marked on top of barrel, "Remington Arms-U.M.C. Co. Ilion, NY."

MODEL 1866
ROLLING BLOCK PISTOL ....NiB $6250 Ex $4100 $3000
Caliber: .50 rimfire. Single-shot, 8-1/2 inch round, blue finish. Walnut grip and forearm. Spur trigger. Made from 1866-67. Mistakenly designated as Model 1865 Navy. Top values are for military-marked, pristine pieces. Very few of these guns remain in original condition.

MODEL 1870 NAVY
ROLLING BLOCK PISTOL ....NiB $3475 Ex $2100 $1775
Caliber: .50 centerfire. Single shot, 7-inch round bbl. Standard trigger with trigger guard, walnut grip and forearm. Approx. 6,400 pieces made from 1870-75. Modified for the Navy from Model 1866. Higher values are for 8--inch commercial version without proof marks.

RIDER'S
MAGAZINE PISTOL ....NiB $2500 Ex $1750 $1225
Caliber: .32. Five shot, 3-inch octagon bbl. blued (add 50 percent for case-hardened receiver). Walnut, rosewood, ivory or pearl grips. Spur trigger. Made from 1871-88.

ELIOT'S
SINGLE-SHOT DERRINGER ....NiB $1650 Ex $1000 $825
Caliber: .41 rimfire. Single-shot, 2-1/2-inch round bbl., blue and/or nickel finish. Also known as "Mississippi Derringer." Two-piece walnut grips. Spur trigger. Approx. 10,000 made from 1867-88.

MODEL 1890
SINGLE-ACTION REVOLVER ......NiB $9000 Ex $6250 $3900
Caliber: .41 centerfire . Six shot, 5-3/4 or 7-1/2-inch round bbl., blue or nickel finish. Standard trigger with trigger guard. Two-piece ivory or pearl grips with Remington monogram. nickel finish valued about 15 percent less.

MODEL 51
SEMI-AUTO PISTOL ....NiB $610 Ex $375 $250
Caliber: .32 or .380 ACP. Eight shot, (7 in magazine).Two-piece hard rubber grips with company name, flat black finish. Approx. 65,000 pieces made from 1918-26, with another 11 pieces made from spare parts from 1927-34.

MODEL 1911
REMINGTON UMC ....NiB $4750 Ex $2500 $1375
Caliber: .45 ACP. WWII military contract production. Blued finish. Approx. 21,500 made from 1918-19, with serial numbers 1 to 21,676.

MODEL 1911A1
REMINGTON RAND ....NiB $750 Ex $425 $315
Caliber: .45 ACP. Parkerized finish. Two-piece walnut grips. Made from 1943-45 by Remington Rand Co., not Remington Arms Co.

RG REVOLVERS — Mfg. By Rohm Gmbh, Germany *(Imported by R.G. Industries, Miami, Florida)*

MODEL 23. NiB $113 Ex $98 Gd $68
SA/DA. 6-round magazine, swing-out cylinder. Caliber: .22 LR. 1.75- or 3.38-inch bbl., Overall length: 5.13 and 7.5 inches. Weight: 16-17 oz. Fixed sights. Blued or nickel finish. Disc. 1986.

MODEL 38S
SA/DA. Caliber: .38 Special. Six-round magazine, swing-out cylinder. Three- or 4-inch bbl., overall length: 8.25 and 9.25 inches. Weight: 32-34 oz. Windage-adj. rear sight. Blued finish. Disc. 1986.
W/plastic grips . . . . NiB $149 Ex $123 Gd $89
W/wood grips . . . . NiB $168 Ex $138 Gd $100

ROSSI REVOLVERS — Sáo Leopoldo, Brazil Manufactured by Amadeo Rossi S.A. *(Imported by Interarms, Alexandria, Virginia)*

MODEL 31 DA REVOLVER . . . . NiB $138 Ex $123 Gd $88
Caliber: .38 Special. Five-round cylinder, 4-inch bbl., weight: 20 oz. Blued or nickel finish. Disc. 1985.

MODEL 51 DA REVOLVER . . . . NiB $143 Ex $128 Gd $98
Caliber: .22 LR. Six-round cylinder, 6-inch bbl., weight: 28 oz. Blued finish. Disc. 1985.

MODEL 68 . . . . NiB $183 Ex $153 Gd $88
Caliber: .38 Special. Five-round magazine, 2- or 3-inch bbl., overall length: 6.5 and 7.5 inches. Weight: 21-23 oz. Blued finish. Nickel finish available w/3-inch bbl. Disc. 1998.

MODEL 84 DA REVOLVER . . . . NiB $210 Ex $170 Gd $140
Caliber: .38 Special. Six-round cylinder, 3-inch bbl., 8 inches overall. Weight: 27.5 oz. Stainless steel finish. Imported from 1984-86.

MODEL 85 DA REVOLVER . . . . NiB $226 Ex $185 Gd $132
Same as Model 84 except has vent rib. Imported from 1985-86.

MODEL 88 DA REVOLVER
Caliber: .38 Special. Five-round cylinder, 2- or 3-inch bbl., weight: 21 oz. Stainless steel finish. Imported from 1988-98.
Model 88 (disc.) . . . . NiB $215 Ex $165 Gd $130
Model 88 Lady Rossi
(round butt) . . . . NiB $239 Ex $195 Gd $139

MODEL 88/2 DA REVOLVER. . . . . . NiB $201 Ex $165 Gd $119
Caliber: .38 Special. Five-round cylinder, 2- or 3-inch bbl., 6.5 inches overall. Weight: 21 oz. Stainless steel finish. Imported from 1985-87.

MODEL 89 DA REVOLVER . . . . NiB $195 Ex $155 Gd $135
Caliber: .32 S&W. Six-round cylinder, 3-inch bbl., 7.5 inches overall. Weight: 17 oz. Stainless steel finish. Imported from 1989-90.

MODEL 94 DA REVOLVER . . . . . . .NiB $188 Ex $168 Gd $122
Caliber: .38 Special. Six-round cylinder, 3-inch bbl., 8 inches overall. Weight: 29 oz. Imported from 1985-88.

MODEL 95 (951) REVOLVER . . . . . NiB $217 Ex $178 Gd $129
Caliber: .38 Special. Six-round magazine, 3-inch bbl., 8 inches overall. Weight: 27.5 oz. Vent rib. Blued finish. Imported from 1985-90.

MODEL 351/352 REVOLVERS
Caliber: .38 Special. Five-round cylinder, 2-inch bbl., 6.87 inches overall. Weight: 22 oz. Ramp front and rear adjustable sights. Stainless or matte blued finish. Imported from 1999 to date.
Model 351 (matte blue finish) . . . . . NiB $280 Ex $229 Gd $158
Model 352 (stainless finish) . . . . NiB $229 Ex $188 Gd $136

MODEL 461/462 REVOLVERS
Caliber: .357 Magnum. Six-round cylinder, 2-inch heavy bbl., 6.87 inches overall. Weight: 26 oz. Rubber grips w/ serrated ramp front sight. Stainless or matte blued finish. Imported 1999 to date.
Model 461 (matte blue finish) . . . . . NiB $280 Ex $229 Gd $158
Model 462 (stainless finish) . . . . NiB $312 Ex $262 Gd $195

MODEL 511 DA REVOLVER . . . . . . NiB $219 Ex $188 Gd $141
Similar to the Model 51 except in stainless steel. Imported from 1986-1990.

MODEL 515 DA REVOLVER . . . . . . NiB $235 Ex $193 Gd $139
Calibers: .22 LR, .22 Mag. Six-round cylinder, 4-inch bbl., 9 inches overall. Weight: 30 oz. Red ramp front sight, adj. square-notched rear. Stainless finish. Checkered hardwood grips. Imported from 1992 to date.

MODEL 518 DA REVOLVER . . . . . . NiB $223 Ex $183 Gd $133
Similar to the Model 515 except in caliber .22 LR. Imported from 1993 to date.

MODEL 677 DA REVOLVER . . . . . . NiB $245 Ex $203 Gd $149
Caliber: .357 Mag. Six-round cylinder, 2-inch bbl., 6.87 inches overall. Weight: 26 oz. Serrated front ramp sight, channel rear. Matte blue finish. Contoured rubber grips. Imported from 1997 to date.

MODEL 720 DA REVOLVER . . . . . . NiB $248 Ex $203 Gd $146
Caliber: .44 Special. Five-round cylinder, 3-inch bbl., 8 inches overall. Weight: 27.5 oz. Red ramp front sight, adj. square-notched rear. Stainless finish. Checkered Neoprene combat-style grips. Imported from 1992 to date.

MODEL 841 DA REVOLVER . . . . . . NiB $235 Ex $193 Gd $139
Same general specifications as Model 84 except has 4-inch bbl., (9 inches overall), weight: 30 oz. Imported from 1985-86.

MODEL 851 DA REVOLVER . . . . . . NiB $233 Ex $193 Gd $142
Same general specifications as Model 85 except w/3-or 4-inch bbl., 8 inches overall (with 3-inch bbl.). Weight: 27.5 oz. (with 3-inch bbl.). Red ramp front sight, adj. square-notched rear. Stainless finish. Checkered hardwood grips. Imported from 1991 to date.

MODEL 877 DA REVOLVER . . . . . . NiB $253 Ex $214 Gd $160
Same general specifications as Model 677 except stainless steel. Made from 1996 to date.

MODEL 941 DA REVOLVER . . . . . . NiB $216 Ex $178 Gd $129
Caliber: .38 Special. Six-round cylinder, 4-inch bbl., 9 inches overall. Weight: 30 oz. Blued finish. Imported from 1985-86.

MODEL 951 DA REVOLVER . . . . . . NiB $239 Ex $198 Gd $146
Previous designation M95 w/same general specifications.

MODEL 971 DA REVOLVER
Caliber: .357 Magnum. Six-round cylinder, 2.5-, 4- or 6-inch bbl., 9 inches overall (with 4-inch bbl.). Weight: 36 oz. (with 4-inch bbl.). Blade front sight, adj. square-notched rear. Blued or stainless finish. Checkered hardwood grips. Imported from 1990 to date.
Blued finish . . . . NiB $225 Ex $183 Gd $132
Stainless finish. . . . . NiB $235 Ex $193 Gd $139
W/compensated bbl., add $15

Ruger Mark I Target W/5.5-inch Untapered Bull Barrel

Ruger Mark II

Ruger Mark II .22/.45

MODEL 971 VRC
DA REVOLVER. . . . . NiB $299 Ex $246 Gd $160
Same general specifications as Model 971 stainless except w/ventilated rib and compensated bbl. Made 1996 to date.

CYCLOPS DA REVOLVER . . . . NiB $422 Ex $338 Gd $254
Caliber: .357 Mag. Six-round cylinder, 6- or 8-inch compensated slab-sided bbl., 11.75 or 13.75 inches overall. Weight: 44 oz. or 51 oz. Undercut blade front sight, fully adjustable rear. B-Square scope mount and rings. Stainless steel finish. Checkered rubber grips. Made from 1997 to date.

DA REVOLVER. . . . . NiB $184 Ex $152 Gd $112
Calibers: .22 LR, .32 S&W Long, .38 Special. Five-round (.38) or 6-round cylinder (other calibers), bbl. lengths: 3-, 6-inches. Weight: 22 oz. (3-inch bbl.). Adj. Rear sight, ramp front. Blued or nickel finish. Wood or plastic grips. Imported from 1965-91.

SPORTSMAN'S .22 . . . . NiB $250 Ex $205 Gd $148
Caliber: .22 LR. Six-round magazine, 4-inch bbl., 9 inches overall. Weight: 30 oz. Stainless steel finish. Disc. 1991.

RUBY PISTOL
Manufactured by Gabilondo y Urresti, Eibar, Spain, and others

7.65MM
AUTOMATIC PISTOL. . . . . NiB $303 Ex $237 Gd $104
Secondary standard service pistol of the French Army in world wars I and II. Essentially the same as the Alkartasuna (see separate listing). Other manufacturers: Armenia Elgoibarresa y Cia., Eceolaza y Vicinai y Cia., Hijos de Angel Echeverria y Cia., Bruno Salaverria y Cia., Zulaika y Cia., all of Eibar, Spain-Gabilondo y Cia., Elgoibar Spain; Ruby Arms Company, Guernica, Spain. Made from 1914-.22.

RUGER HANDGUNS — Southport, Connecticut
Manufactured by Sturm, Ruger & Co.

Rugers made in 1976 are designated "Liberty" in honor of the U.S. Bicentennial and bring a premium of approximately 25 percent in value over regular models.
NOTE: *For ease in finding a particular Ruger handgun, the listings are divided into two groups: Automatic/Single-Shot Pistols (below) and Revolvers, which follow. For a complete listing, please refer to the index.*

AUTOMATIC/SINGLE-SHOT PISTOLS

HAWKEYE SINGLE-SHOT PISTOL . . . . . NiB $1396 Ex $1190 Gd $675
Built on a SA revolver frame w/cylinder replaced by a swing-out breechblock and fitted w/a bbl., w/integral chamber. Caliber: .256 Magnum. 8.5-inch bbl., 14.5 inches overall. Weight: 45 oz. Blued finish. Ramp front sight, click adj. rear. Smooth walnut grips. Made from 1963-65 (3300 produced).

MARK I TARGET MODEL AUTOMATIC PISTOL
Caliber: .22 LR. 10-round magazine, 5.25- and 6.88-inch heavy tapered or 5.5-inch untapered bull bbl., 10.88 inches overall (with 6.88-inch bbl.). Weight: 42 oz. (in 5.5- or 6.88-inch bbl.). Undercut target front sight, adj. rear. Blued finish. Hard rubber grips or checkered walnut thumbrest grips. Made from 1951-81.
Standard . . . . NiB $290 Ex $239 Gd $167
W/red medallion . . . . NiB $548 Ex $471 Gd $316
Walnut grips, add $15

MARK II AUTOMATIC PISTOL
Caliber: .22 LR, standard or high velocity 10-round magazine, 4.75- or 6-inch tapered bbl., 8.31 inches overall (with 4.75-inch bbl.). Weight: 36 oz. Fixed front sight, square notch rear. Blued or stainless finish. Made from 1982 to date.
Blued. . . . . NiB $316 Ex $280 Gd $157
Stainless . . . . NiB $363 Ex $311 Gd $141
Bright stainless (ltd.
prod. 5,000 in 1982). . . . . NiB $542 Ex $440 Gd $310

MARK II .22/.45 AUTOMATIC PISTOL

Same general specifications as Ruger Mark II .22 LR except w/blued or stainless receiver and bbl., in four lengths: 4-inch tapered w/adj. sights (P4), 4.75-inch tapered w/fixed sights (KP4), 5.25-inch tapered w/adj. sights (KP 514) and 5.5-inch bull (KP 512). Fitted w/Zytel grip frame of the same design as the Model 1911 45 ACP. Made from 1993 to date.

Model KP4 (4.75-inch bbl.). . . . . NiB $252 Ex $227 Gd $149
Model KP512, KP514
(w/5.5- or 5.25-inch bbl.) . . . . NiB $305 Ex $274 Gd $216
Model P4, P512
(Blued w/4- or 5.5-inch bbl.) . . . . NiB $243 Ex $201 Gd $146

MARK II BULL BARREL MODEL

Same as standard Mark II except for bull bbl. (5.5- or 10-inch). Weight: About 2.75 lbs.

Blued finish . . . . NiB $269 Ex $222 Gd $161
Stainless finish (intro. 1985) . . . . . . NiB $355 Ex $290 Gd $208

MARK II GOVERNMENT MODEL AUTO PISTOL

Civilian version of the Mark II used by U.S. Armed Forces. Caliber: .22LR. 10-round magazine, 6.88-inch bull bbl., 11.13 inches overall. Weight: 44 oz. Blued or stainless finish. Made from 1986 to date.

Blued model (MK687G commercial) . . . . . NiB $381 Ex $317 Gd $180
Stainless steel model
(KMK678G commercial) . . . . NiB $371 Ex $304 Gd $218
W/U.S. markings (military model) . . . . NiB $602 Ex $551 Gd $376

MARK II TARGET MODEL

Caliber: .22 LR. 10-round magazine, 4-, 5.5- and 10-inch bull bbl. or 5.25- and 6.88-inch heavy tappered bbl., weight: 38 oz. to 52 oz. 11.13 inches overall (with 6.88-inch bbl.). Made from 1982 to date.

Blued . . . . NiB $319 Ex $280 Gd $165
Stainless steel . . . . NiB $386 Ex $314 Gd $144

MODEL P-85 AUTOMATIC PISTOL

Caliber: 9mm. DA, recoil-operated. 15-round capacity, 4.5 inch bbl., 7.84 inches overall. Weight: 32 oz. Fixed rear sight, square-post front. Available w/decocking levers, ambidextrous safety or in DA only. Blued or stainless finish. Made from 1987-92.

Blued finish . . . . NiB $380 Ex $339 Gd $241
Stainless steel finish. . . . . NiB $395 Ex $349 Gd $323

MODEL P-89 AUTOMATIC PISTOL

Caliber: 9mm. DA w/slide-mounted safety levers. 15-round magazine, 4.5-inch bbl., 7.84 inches overall. Weight: 32 oz. Square-post front sight, adj. rear w/3-dot system. Blued or stainless steel finish. Grooved black Xenoy grips. Made from 1992 to date.

P-89 blued. . . . . NiB $428 Ex $377 Gd $243
P-89 stainless . . . . NiB $475 Ex $408 Gd $346

MODEL P-89 DAC/DAO AUTO PISTOLS

Similar to the standard Model P-89 except the P-89 DAC has ambidextrous decocking levers. The P-89 DAO operates in double-action-only mode. Made from 1991 to date.

P-89 DAC blued. . . . . NiB $428 Ex $372 Gd $243
P-89 DAC/DAO stainless . . . . NiB $475 Ex $394 Gd $294

MODEL P-90, KP90 DA AUTOMATIC PISTOL

Caliber: .45 ACP. Seven-round magazine, 4.5-inch bbl., 7.88 inches overall. Weight: 33.5 oz. Square-post front sight adj. square-notched rear w/3-dot system. Grooved black Xenoy composition grips. Blued or stainless finish. DAC model has ambidextrous decocking levers. Made from 1991 to date.

Model P-90 blued . . . . NiB $475 Ex $397 Gd $243
Model P-90 DAC (decockers) . . . . . NiB $485 Ex $408 Gd $253
Model KP-90 DAC stainless. . . . . . . NiB $485 Ex $415 Gd $356
Model KP-90 DAC (decockers) . . . . NiB $490 Ex $418 Gd $361

Ruger P-89 DAC/DAO

Ruger P-90

Ruger P-93 Compact

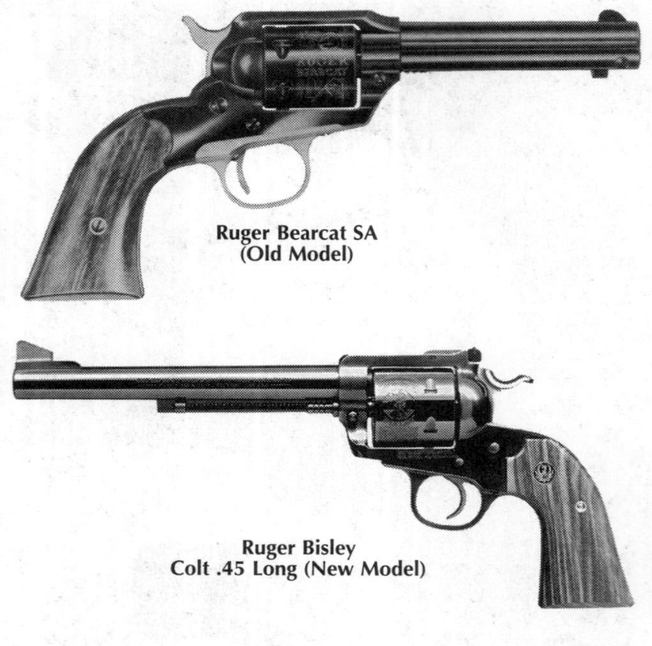
Ruger Bearcat SA (Old Model)

Ruger P-97

Ruger Bisley Colt .45 Long (New Model)

Ruger Bisley Single-Six Small Frame

Ruger Blackhawk

Ruger Blackhawk SA .44

MODEL P-91 DA AUTOMATIC PISTOL
Same general specifications as the Model P-90 except chambered for .40 S&W w/12-round double-column magazine, Made from 1992-94.
Model P-91 Standard . . . . NiB $434 Ex $382 Gd $325
Model P-91 DAC (decockers) . . . . . NiB $449 Ex $367 Gd $302
Model P-91 DAO (DA only) . . . . . . NiB $455 Ex $372 Gd $302

MODEL P-93 COMPACT AUTO PISTOL
Similar to the standard Model P-89 except w/3.9-inch bbl., (7.3 inches overall) and weight: 31 oz. Stainless steel finish. Made from 1993 to date.
Model P-93 DAC (decocker) (disc. 1994) . . . . . NiB $505 Ex $423 Gd $294
Model P-93 DAO (DA only) . . . . NiB $485 Ex $392 Gd $284

MODEL P-94 AUTOMATIC PISTOL
Similar to the Model P-91 except w/4.25-inch bbl., Calibers: 9mm or .40 S&W. Blued or stainless steel finish. Made from 1994 to date.
Model KP-94 DAC (S/S decocker) . . . . NiB $505 Ex $409 Gd $372
Model KP-94 DAO (S/S dble. action only) . . . . NiB $480 Ex $413 Gd $367
Model P-94 DAC (Blued decocker) . . . . NiB $454 Ex $366 Gd $330
Model P-94 DAO (blued dble. action only) . . . NiB $444 Ex $350 Gd $310

MODEL P-95 AUTOMATIC PISTOL
Caliber: 9mm Parabellum. 10-round magazine, 3.9-inch bbl., 7.3 inches overall. Weight: 27 oz. Square-post front sight, drift adjustable rear w/3-dot system. Molded polymer grip-frame fitted w/stainless or chrome-moly slide. Ambidextrous decocking levers (P-95D) or double action only (DAO). Matte black or stainless finish. Made from 1997 to date.
P-95 blued . . . . NiB $391 Ex $324 Gd $201
P-95 stainless . . . . NiB $427 Ex $350 Gd $206

MODEL P-97 AUTOMATIC PISTOL
Caliber: .45 ACP. Eight-round magazine, 4.5- inch bbl., 7.25 inches overall. Weight: 30.5 oz. Square-post front sight adj. square-notched rear w/3-dot system. Grooved black Xenoy composition grips. Blued or stainless finish. DAC model has ambidextrous decocking levers. Made from 1999 to date.
Model KP-97
DAO stainless . . . . NiB $445 Ex $362 Gd $244
Model KP-97
DAC (decockers) . . . . NiB $445 Ex $362 Gd $244

STANDARD MODEL AUTOMATIC PISTOL
Caliber: .22 LR. Nine-round magazine, 4.75- or 6-inch bbl., 8.75 inches overall (with 4.75-inch bbl.). Weight: 36 oz. (with 4.75 inch bbl.). Fixed sights. Blued finish. Hard rubber or checkered walnut grips.

Made from 1949 to date. Note: After the death of Alexander Sturm in 1951, the color of the eagle on the grip medallion was changed from red to black as a memorial. Known as the "Red Eagle Automatic," this early type is now a collector's item. Made from 1951-81.
W/red eagle medallion . . . . NiB $587 Ex $484 Gd $283
W/black eagle medallion. . . . . NiB $239 Ex $218 Gd $141
Walnut grips, add $15

NOTE: *This section contains only Ruger revolvers. Automatic and single-shot pistols may be found on the preceding pages. For a complete listing of Ruger handguns, please refer to the index.*

REVOLVERS

BEARCAT SA (OLD MODEL)
Aluminum frame. Caliber: .22 LR. Six-round cylinder, 4-inch bbl., 8.88 inches overall. Weight: 17 oz. Fixed sights. Blued finish. Smooth walnut grips. Made from 1958-73.

BEARCAT, SUPER (OLD MODEL) . . . . NiB $396 Ex $335 Gd $232
Same general specifications as Bearcat except has steel frame. Weight: 25 oz. Made from 1971-73.

NEW MODEL BEARCAT REVOLVER
Same general specifications as Super Bearcat except all steel frame and trigger guard. Interlocked mechanism and transfer bar. Calibers: .22 LR and .22WMR. Interchangeable 6-round cylinders (disc. 1996). Smooth walnut stocks w/Ruger medallion. Made from 1994 to date.
Convertible model (disc.
1996 after factory recall) . . . . NiB $396 Ex $319 Gd $242
Standard model (.22 LR only) . . . . NiB $355 Ex $293 Gd $190

BISLEY SA REVOLVER, LARGE FRAME
Calibers: .357 Mag., .41 Mag. .44 Mag., .45 Long Colt. 7.5-inch bbl., 13 inches overall. Weight: 48 oz. Non-fluted or fluted cylinder, no engraving. Ramp front sight, adj. rear. Satin blued or stainless. Made from 1986 to date.
Blued finish . . . . NiB $473 Ex $385 Gd $225
Vaquero/Bisley (blued w/case colored fr.) . . . . NiB $473 Ex $385 Gd $225
Vaquero/Bisley (stainless steel) . . . NiB $465 Ex $370 Gd $236
W/ivory grips, add. $35

BISLEY SINGLE-SIX REVOLVER, SMALL FRAME
Calibers: .22 LR and .32 Mag. Six-round cylinder, 6.5-inch bbl., 11.5 inches overall. Weight: 41 oz. Fixed rear sight, blade front. Blue finish. Goncalo Alves grips. Made from 1986 to date.
.22 caliber . . . . NiB $385 Ex $297 Gd $194
.32 H&R Mag. . . . . NiB $437 Ex $349 Gd $308

BLACKHAWK SA CONVERTIBLE (OLD MODEL)
Same as Blackhawk except has extra cylinder. Caliber combinations: .357 Magnum and 9mm Para., .45 Colt and .45 Automatic. Made from 1967-72.
.357/9mm combo (early w/o prefix SN) . . . NiB $452 Ex $400 Gd $241
.357/9mm combo (late w/prefix SN) . . . . . NiB $446 Ex $364 Gd $260
.45 LC/.45 ACP combo
(1967-85 & 1999 to date) . . . . NiB $555 Ex $503 Gd $339

BLACKHAWK SA REVOLVER (OLD MODEL)
Calibers: .30 Carbine, .357 Magnum, .41 Magnum, .45 Colt. Six-round cylinder, bbl. lengths: 4.63-inch (.357, .41, .45 caliber), 6.5-inch (.357, .41 caliber), 7.5-inch (.30, .45 caliber). 10.13 inches overall (.357 Mag. w/4.63-inch bbl.). Weight: 38 oz. (.357 w/4.63-inch bbl.). Ramp front sight, adj. rear. Blued finish. Checkered hard rubber or smooth walnut grips. Made from 1956-73.
.30 Carbine, .357 Mag. . . . . NiB $452 Ex $400 Gd $241
.41 Mag. . . . . NiB $452 Ex $349 Gd $241
.45 Colt . . . . NiB $473 Ex $411 Gd $246

Ruger GP-100 DA Revolver

Ruger New Model Blackhawk Convertible

Ruger Blackhawk High-Gloss Stainless (New Model) .357 Magnum

BLACKHAWK SA "FLAT-TOP" REVOLVER (OLD MODEL)
Similar to standard Blackhawk except w/"Flat Top" cylinder strap. Calibers: .357 or .44 Magnum. Six-round fluted cylinder, 4.625-, 6.5-, 7.5- or 10-inch bbl., adj. rear sight, ramp front. Blued finish. Black rubber or smooth walnut grips. Made from 1956-63.
.357 Mag. (w/4.625-inch bbl.) . . . . NiB $555 Ex $493 Gd $272
.357 Mag. (w/6.5-inch bbl.) . . . . NiB $761 Ex $607 Gd $349
.357 Mag. (w/10-inch bbl.). . . . . NiB $1280 Ex $1126 Gd $662
.44 Mag. (w/fluted cylinder/ 4.625-inch bbl.) . . NiB $759 Ex $605 Gd $347
.44 Mag. (w/fluted cylinder/ 6.5-inch bbl.). . . . NiB $811 Ex $656 Gd $398
.44 Mag. (w/fluted cylinder/ 10-inch bbl.) . . NiB $1268 Ex $1126 Gd $662

GP-100 DA REVOLVER
Caliber: .357 Magnum. Three- to 4-inch heavy bbl., or 6-inch standard or heavy bbl., Overall length: 9.38 or 11.38 inches. Cushioned grip panels. Made from 1986 to date.
Blued finish . . . . NiB $450 Ex $362 Gd $229
Stainless steel finish. . . . . NiB $476 Ex $373 Gd $270

NEW MODEL BLACKHAWK CONVERTIBLE
Same as New Model Blackhawk except has extra cylinder. Blued finish only. Caliber combinations: .357 Magnum/9mm Para., .44 Magnum/.44-40, .45 Colt/.45 ACP. (Limited Edition Buckeye Special .32-20/.32 H&R Mag. or .38-40/10mm). Made from 1973 to date.

Ruger Single-Six SSM
(New Model)

Ruger Redhawk

Ruger Super Blackhawk
(New Model)

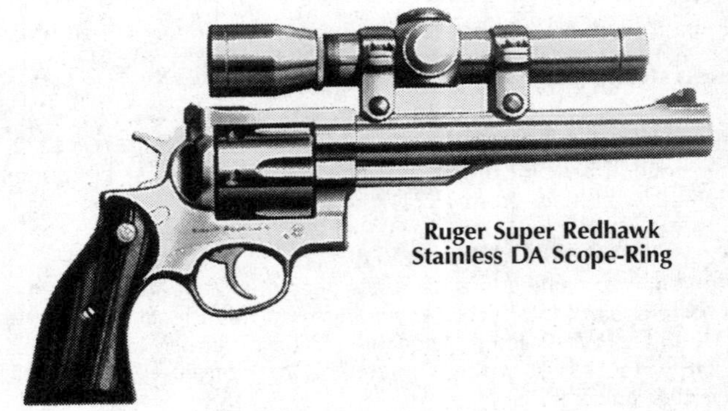

Ruger Super Redhawk
Stainless DA Scope-Ring

Ruger Super Single-Six
Convertible (New Model)

Ruger Police Service-Six
Stainless Steel

.32-20/.32 H&R Mag. (1989-90) .... NiB $419 Ex $342 Gd $203
.38-40/10mm (1990-91) .... NiB $392 Ex $321 Gd $231
.357/9mm combo .... NiB $419 Ex $342 Gd $202
.44/.44-40 combo (disc.1982) .... NiB $456 Ex $373 Gd $266
.45 LC/.45 ACP combo (disc. 1985) ...... NiB $424 Ex $347 Gd $248

NEW MODEL BLACKHAWK SA REVOLVER

Interlocked mechanism. Calibers: .30 Carbine, .357 Magnum, .357 Maximum, .41 Magnum, .44 Magnum, .44 Special, .45 Colt. Six-round cylinder, bbl. lengths: 4.63-inch (.357, .41, .45 Colt); 5.5 inch (.44 Mag., .44 Spec.); 6.5-inch (.357, .41, .45 Long Colt); 7.5-inch (.30, .45, .44 Special, .44 Mag.); 10.5-inch in .44 Mag; 10.38 inches overall (.357 Mag. w/4.63-inch bbl.). Weight: 40 oz. (.357 w/4.63-inch bbl.). Adj. rear sight, ramp front. Blued finish or stainless steel; latter only in .357 or .45 LC. Smooth walnut grips. Made from 1973 to date.

Blued finish........................ NiB $398 Ex $290 Gd $177
High-gloss stainless (.357 Mag., .45 LC) . . . NiB $392 Ex $321 Gd $231
Satin stainless (.357 Mag., .45 LC) .... NiB $379 Ex $311 Gd $223
.357 Maximum SRM (1984-85).......... NiB $419 Ex $342 Gd $218

NEW MODEL SINGLE-SIX SSM REVOLVER............ NiB $345 Ex $319 Gd $190

Same general specifications as standard Single-Six except chambered for .32 H&R Magnum cartridge. Bbl. lengths: 4.63, 5.5, 6.5 or 9.5 inches.

NEW MODEL SUPER BLACKHAWK SA REVOLVER

Interlocked mechanism. Caliber: .44 Magnum. Six-round cylinder, 5.5-inch, 7.5-inch and 10.5-inch bull bbl. 13.38 inches overall. Weight: 48 oz. Adj. rear sight, ramp front. Blued and stainless steel finish. Smooth walnut grips. Made 1973 to date, 5.5-inch bbl. made from 1987 to date.

Blued finish .... NiB $422 Ex $345 Gd $232
High-gloss stainless
(1994-96)..................... NiB $416 Ex $340 Gd $243
Satin stainless steel .... NiB $403 Ex $329 Gd $236

POLICE SERVICE-SIX

Same general specifications as Speed-Six except has square butt. Stainless steel models and 9mm Para. caliber available w/only 4-inch bbl., Made from 1971-88.

.38 Special, blued finish . . . . NiB $289 Ex $259 Gd $207
.38 Special, stainless steel . . . . NiB $310 Ex $274 Gd $248
.357 Magnum or 9mm Para.,
blued finish . . . . NiB $289 Ex $259 Gd $207
.357 Magnum, stainless steel. . . . . . NiB $315 Ex $279 Gd $248

REDHAWK DA REVOLVER

Calibers: .357 Mag., .41 Mag., .45 LC, .44 Mag. Six-round cylinder, 5.5- and 7.5-inch bbl., 11 and 13 inches overall, respectively. Weight: About 52 oz. Adj. rear sight, interchangeable front sights. Stainless finish. Made from 1979 to date; .357 Mag. disc. 1986. Alloy steel model w/blued finish intro. in 1986 in .41 Mag. and .44 Mag. calibers.

Blued finish . . . . NiB $542 Ex $378 Gd $233
Stainless steel . . . . NiB $578 Ex $465 Gd $383

SUPER REDHAWK STAINLESS DA SCOPE-RING REVOLVER

Calibers: .44 Mag., .454 Casull and .45 LC. Six-round cylinder, 7.5- to 9.5- inch bbl., 13 to 15 inches overall. Weight: 53 to 58 oz. Integral scope mounting system w/stainless rings. Adjustable rear sight. Cushioned grip panels. Made from 1987 to date.

Model .44 Mag. 7.5- inch
bbl., stainless. . . . . NiB $614 Ex $511 Gd $383
Model .44 Mag. 9.5- inch
bbl., stainless. . . . . NiB $614 Ex $511 Gd $383
Model .454 Casull & 45 LC
Stainless/target gray stainless . . . . . NiB $707 Ex $584 Gd $455

SECURITY-SIX DA REVOLVER

Caliber: .357 Magnum, handles .38 Special. Six-round cylinder, bbl. lengths: 2.25-, 4-, 6-inch, 9.25 inches overall (with 4-inch bbl.). Weight: 33.5 oz. (with 4-inch bbl.). Adj. rear sight, ramp front. Blued finish or stainless steel. Square butt. Checkered walnut grips. Made from 1971-85.

Blued finish . . . . NiB $298 Ex $247 Gd $181
Stainless steel . . . . NiB $344 Ex $283 Gd $206

SINGLE-SIX SA REVOLVER (OLD MODEL)

Calibers: .22 LR, .22 WMR. Six-round cylinder. bbl., lengths: 4.63, 5.5, 6.5, 9.5 inches, 10.88 inches overall (with 5.5-inch bbl.). Weight: About 35 oz. Fixed sights. Blued finish. Checkered hard rubber or smooth walnut grips. Made 1953-73. Note: Pre-1956 model w/flat loading gate is worth about twice as much as later version.

Standard . . . . NiB $339 Ex $262 Gd $148
Convertible (w/two cylinders,
.22 LR/.22 WMR). . . . . NiB $500 Ex $449 Gd $243

SINGLE-SIX — LIGHTWEIGHT. . . . NiB $552 Ex $449 Gd $217

Same general specifications as Single-Six except has 4.75-inch bbl., lightweight alloy cylinder and frame, 10 inches overall length, weight: 23 oz. Made in 1956.

SP101 DA REVOLVER

Calibers: .22 LR, .32 Mag., 9mm, .38 Special+P, .357 Mag. Five- or 6-round cylinder, 2.25-, 3.06- or 4-inch bbl., weight: 25-34 oz. Stainless steel finish. Cushioned grips. Made from 1988 to date.

Standard model . . . . .NiB $434 Ex $289 Gd $284
DAO model (DA only,
spurless hammer) . . . . NiB $413 Ex $325 Gd $284

SPEED-SIX DA REVOLVER

Calibers: .38 Special, .357 Magnum, 9mm Para. Six-round cylinder, 2.75-, 4-inch bbl., (9mm available only w/2.75-inch bbl.). 7.75 inches overall (2.75-inch bbl.). Weight: 31 oz. (with 2.75-inch bbl.).

Ruger
Super Redhawk Stainless

Ruger
Single-Six

Ruger
Single-Six Lightweight

Ruger
Super Single-Six Convertible

Ruger Single-Six Fixed Sight

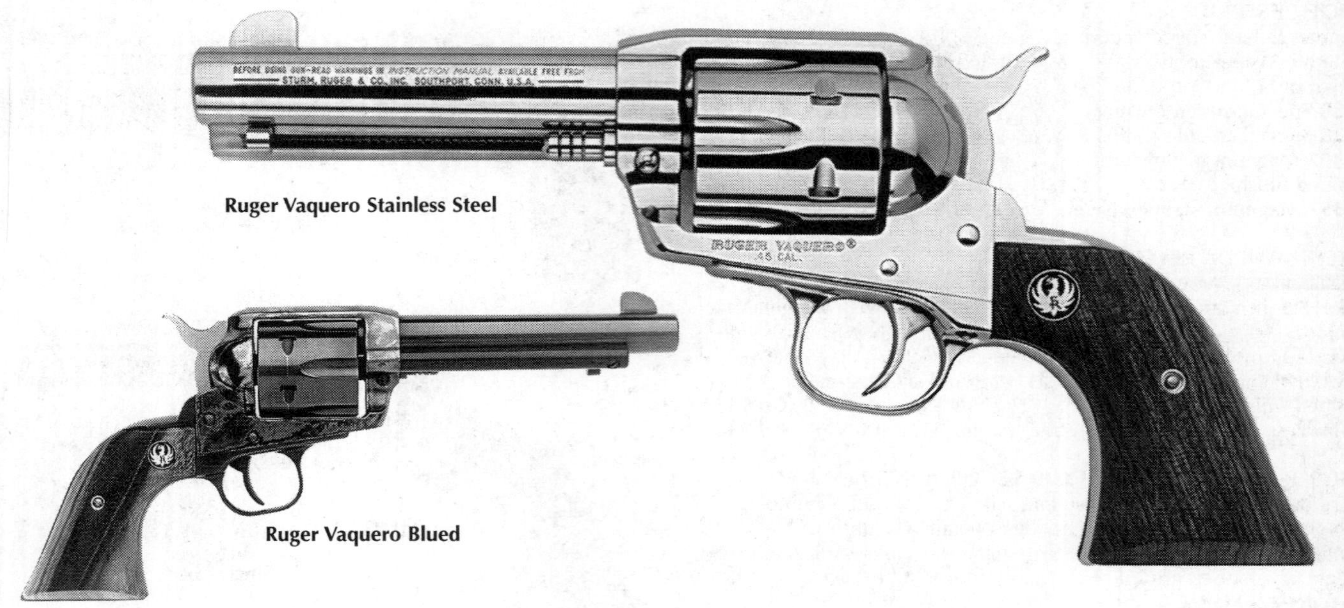

Ruger Vaquero Stainless Steel

Ruger Vaquero Blued

Fixed sights. Blued or stainless steel finish; latter available in .38 Special (with 2.75 inch bbl.), .357 Magnum and 9mm w/either bbl., Round butt. Checkered walnut grips. Made from 1973-87.

.38 Special, blued finish . . . . NiB $267 Ex $238 Gd $188
.38 Special, stainless steel . . . . NiB $318 Ex $279 Gd $152
.357 Magnum or 9mm Para.,
blued finish . . . . NiB $336 Ex $284 Gd $215
.357 Magnum or 9mm Para.,
stainless steel. . . . . NiB $336 Ex $284 Gd $215

SUPER BLACKHAWK
SA .44 MAGNUM REVOLVER (OLD MODEL)

SA w/heavy frame and unfluted cylinder. Caliber: .44 Magnum. Six-round cylinder. 6.5- or 7.5-inch bbl., Adj. rear sight, ramp front. Steel or brass grip frame w/square-back trigger guard. Smooth walnut grips. Blued finish. Made from 1956-73.

W/6.5-inch bbl., ... NiB $435 Ex $342 Gd $213
W/7.5-inch bbl., ... NiB $435 Ex $342 Gd $213
W/brass gripframe . . . . NiB $941 Ex $762 Gd $533

VAQUERO SA REVOLVER

Calibers: .357 Mag., .44-40, .44 Magnum, .45 Colt. Six-round cylinder. Bbl. lengths: 4.625, 5.5, 7.5 inches, 13.63 inches overall (with 7.5-inch bbl.). Weight: 41 oz. (with 7.5-inch bbl.). Blade front sight, grooved topstrap rear. Blued w/color casehardened frame or polished stainless finish. Smooth rosewood grips w/Ruger medallion. Made from 1993 to date.

Blued w/color-case
hardened frame . . . . NiB $471 Ex $368 Gd $316
Stainless finish . . . . NiB $471 Ex $368 Gd $316
W/ivory grips, add. $41

RUSSIAN SERVICE PISTOLS Mfd. by Government plants at Tula and elsewhere

Tokarev-type pistols have also been made in Hungary, Poland, Yugoslavia, People's Republic of China, N. Korea.

MODEL 30 TOKAREV
SERVICE AUTOMATIC

Modified Colt-Browning type. Caliber: 7.62mm Russian Auto (also uses 7.63mm Mauser Auto cartridge). Eight-round magazine, 4.5-inch bbl., 7.75 inches overall. Weight: About 29 oz. Fixed sights. Made from 1930 to mid-1950s. Note: A slightly modified version w/improved locking system and different disconnector was adopted in 1933.

Standard Service Model TT30 . . . . . NiB $365 Ex $330 Gd $202
Standard Service Model TT33 . . . . . NiB $365 Ex $330 Gd $202
Recent imports (distinguished
by importer marks) . . . . NiB $172 Ex $141 Gd $90

MODEL PM
MAKAROV AUTO PISTOL. . . . . NiB $493 Ex $442 Gd $228

Double-action, blowback design. Caliber: 9mm Makarov. Eight-round magazine, 3.8-inch bbl., 6.4 inches overall. Weight: 26 oz. Blade front sight, square-notched rear. Checkered composition grips.

Standard Service Model PM
(Pistole Makarov). . . . . NiB $512 Ex $416 Gd $294
Recent imports (distinguished
by importer marks) . . . . NiB $214 Ex $175 Gd $126

SAKO HANDGUNS — Riihimaki, Finland Manufactured by Oy Sako Ab

.22-.32 OLYMPIC
PISTOL (TRIACE)

Calibers: .22 LR, .22 Short, .32 S&W Long. Five-round magazine, 6- or 8.85- (.22 Short) inch bbl., weight: About 46 oz. (.22 LR); 44 oz. (.22 Short); 48 oz. (.32). Steel frame. ABS plastic, anatomically designed grip. Non-reflecting matte black upper surface and chromium-plated slide. Equipped w/carrying case and tool set. Limited importation from 1983-89.

Sako .22 or .32
Single pistol. . . . . NiB $1392 Ex $1239 Gd $729
Sako Triace, triple-barrel set
w/wooden grip . . . . NiB $2622 Ex $2316 Gd $1296

SAUER HANDGUNS
Mfd. through WW II by J. P. Sauer & Sohn, Suhl, Germany. Now mfd. by J. P. Sauer & Sohn, GmbH, Eckernförde, West Germany

See also listings under Sig Sauer.

MODEL 1913 POCKET
AUTOMATIC PISTOL . . . . NiB $324 Ex $253 Gd $171
Caliber: .32 Automatic (7.65mm). Seven-round magazine, 3-inch bbl., 5.88 inches overall. Weight: 22 oz. Fixed sights. Blued finish. Black hard rubber grips. Made from 1913-30.

MODEL 1930 POCKET AUTOMATIC PISTOL
Authority Model (Behorden Model). Successor to Model 1913, has improved grip and safety. Caliber: .32 Auto (7.65mm). Seven-round magazine, 3-inch bbl., 5.75 inches overall. Weight: 22 oz. Fixed sights. Blued finish. Black hard rubber grips. Made from 1930-38. Note: Some pistols made w/indicator pin showing when cocked. Also mfd. w/dual slide and receiver; this type weight: about 7 oz. less than the standard model.
Steel model . . . . NiB $355 Ex $258 Gd $171
Dural (alloy) model . . . . NiB $1613 Ex $1300 Gd $917

MODEL 38H DA AUTOMATIC PISTOL
Calibers: .25 Auto (6.35mm), .32 Auto (7.65mm), .380 Auto (9mm). Specifications shown are for .32 Auto model. Seven-round magazine, 3.25-inch bbl., 6.25 inches overall. Weight: 20 oz. Fixed sights. Blued finish. Black plastic grips. Also made in dual model weighing about 6 oz. less. Made 1938-1945. Note: This pistol, designated Model .38, was mfd. during WW II for military use. Wartime models are inferior in design to earlier production, as some lack safety lever.
.22 caliber . . . . NiB $431 Ex $329 Gd $151
.32 ACP . . . . NiB $433 Ex $361 Gd $219
.32 ACP (w/Nazi proofs) . . . . NiB $534 Ex $433 Gd $304
.380 ACP . . . . NiB $3590 Ex $2817 Gd $1358

POCKET .25 (1913)
AUTOMATIC PISTOL . . . . NiB $391 Ex $268 Gd $171
Smaller version of Model 1913, issued about same time as .32 caliber model. Caliber: .25 Auto (6.35mm). Seven-round magazine, 2.5-inch bbl., 4.25 inches overall. Weight: 14.5 oz. Fixed sights. Blued finish. Black hard rubber grips. Made from 1913-30.

SINGLE-ACTION REVOLVERS
See listings under Hawes.

SAVAGE ARMS CO. — Utica, New York

MODEL 101 SA
SINGLE-SHOT PISTOL . . . . NiB $176 Ex $145 Gd $84
Barrel integral w/swing-out cylinder. Calibers: .22 Short, Long, LR. 5.5-inch bbl. Weight: 20 oz. Blade front sight, slotted rear, adj. for windage. Blued finish. Grips of compressed, impregnated wood. Made from 1960-68.

MODEL 501/502F "STRIKER" SERIES PISTOLS
Calibers: .22 LR., and .22 WMR. 5- or 10- round magazine, 10-inch bbl., 19 inches overall. Weight: 4 lbs. Drilled and tapped sights for scope mount (installed). Ambidextrous rear grip. Made from 2000 to date.
Model 501F, .22 LR . . . . NiB $212 Ex $191 Gd $151
Model 502F, .22 WMR. . . . . NiB $232 Ex $207 Gd $156

MODEL 510/516 "STRIKER" SERIES PISTOLS
Calibers: 223 Rem., .22-250 Rem., .243 Win., 7mm-08 Rem., .260 Rem., and .308 Win. Three-round magazine, 14-inch bbl., .22.5 inches overall. Drilled and tapped for scope mounts. Left hand bolt with right hand ejection. Stainless steel finish. Made from 1998 to date.

Sako Model .22-.32 Olympic

Sauer 1930 Pocket

Savage Model 101

Model 510F . . . . NiB $421 Ex $370 Gd $212
Model 516FSAK. . . . . NiB $512 Ex $426 Gd $360
Model 516FSS . . . . NiB $416 Ex $370 Gd $354
Model 516BSAK . . . . NiB $512 Ex $426 Gd $370
Model 516BSS. . . . . NiB $574 Ex $467 Gd $385

MODEL 1907 AUTOMATIC PISTOL
Caliber: .32 ACP, 10-round magazine, 3.25-inch bbl., 6.5 inches overall. Weight: 19 oz. Checkered hard rubber or steel grips marked "Savage Quality," circling an Indian-head logo. Optional pearl grips. Blue, nickel, silver or gold finish. Made from 1908-20.
Blued model (.32 ACP). . . . . NiB $461 Ex $334 Gd $145
Blued model (.380 ACP) . . . . NiB $589 Ex $487 Gd $232
W/ optional nickel,
silver or gold finish, add. . . . . $750-$1200
W/optional pearl grips, add . . . . $225-$950

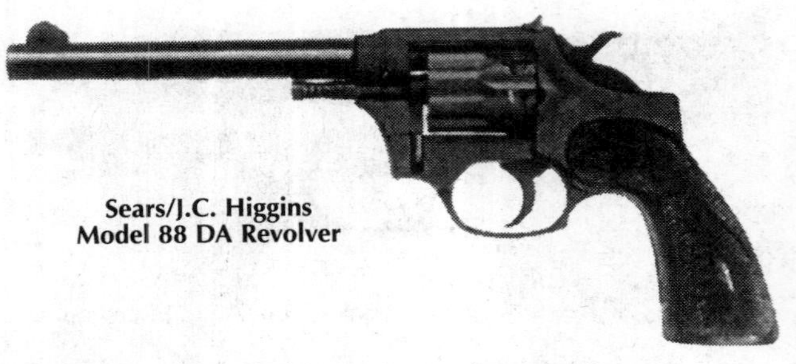

Sears/J.C. Higgins Model 88 DA Revolver

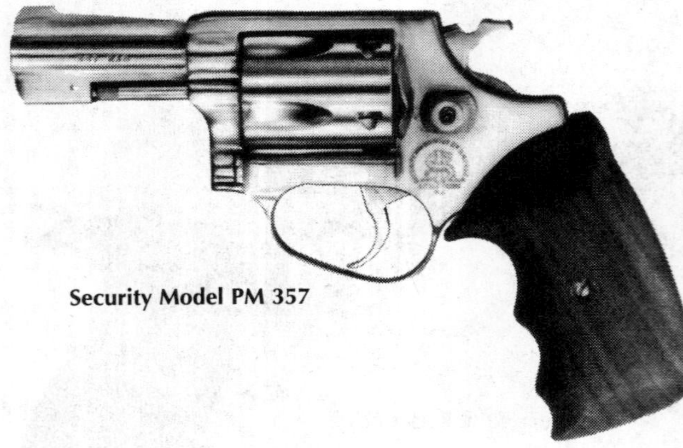

Security Model PM 357

Security Model PPM 357

Security Model PSS38

MODEL 1910 AUTOMATIC PISTOL
Calibers: .32 Auto, .380 Auto. 10-round magazine (.32 cal.), 9-round (.380 cal.). 3.75-inch bbl., (.32 cal.), 4.25-inch (.380 cal.). 6.5 inches overall (.32 cal.), 7 inches (.380 cal.). Weight: About 23 oz. Fixed sights. Blued finish. Hard rubber grips. Made in hammerless type w/grip safety or w/exposed hammer spur. Made from 1910-17.
.32 ACP . . . . NiB $340 Ex $289 Gd $197
.380 ACP . . . . NiB $515 Ex $424 Gd $291

MODEL 1915 AUTOMATIC PISTOL
Same general specifications as the Savage Model 1907 except the Model 1915 is hammerless and has a grip safety. It is also chambered for both the .32 and .380 ACP. Made froim 1915-17.
.32 ACP . . . . NiB $571 Ex $491 Gd $265
.380 ACP . . . . NiB $705 Ex $571 Gd $400

U.S. ARMY TEST MODEL 1910 . NiB $7735 Ex $5695 Gd $2635
Caliber: .45 ACP, Seven-round magazine w/exposed hammer. An enlarged version of the Model 1910 manufactured for military trials between 1907 and 1911. Note: Most "Trial Pistols" were refurbished and resold as commercial models. Values are for original Government Test Issue models.

MODEL 1917 AUTOMATIC PISTOL
Same specifications as 1910 Model except has spur-type hammer and redesigned, heavier grip. Made from 1917-28.
.32 ACP . . . . NiB $334 Ex $283 Gd $140
.380 ACP . . . . NiB $691 Ex $614 Gd $283

SEARS, ROEBUCK & COMPANY — Chicago, Illinois

J.C. HIGGINS MODEL 80
AUTO PISTOL . . . . NiB $198 Ex $147 Gd $117
Caliber: .22 LR. 10-round magazine, 4.5- or 6.5-inch interchangeable bbl., 10.88 inches overall (with 6.5-inch bbl.). Weight: 41 oz. (with 6.5-inch bbl.). Fixed Partridge sights. Blued finish. Checkered grips w/thumbrest.

J.C. HIGGINS MODEL 88
DA REVOLVER. . . . . NiB $137 Ex $112 Gd $81
Caliber: .22 LR. Nine-round cylinder, 4- or 6-inch bbl., 9.5 inches (with 4-inch bbl.). Weight: 23 oz. (with 4-inch bbl.). Fixed sights. Blued or nickel finish. Checkered plastic grips.

J.C. HIGGINS RANGER
DA REVOLVER. . . . . NiB $163 Ex $132 Gd $91
Caliber: .22 LR. Nine-round cylinder, 5.5-inch bbl., 10.75 inches overall. Weight: 28 oz. Fixed sights. Blued or chrome finish. Checkered plastic grips.

SECURITY INDUSTRIES OF AMERICA — Little Ferry, New Jersey

MODEL PM 357 DA REVOLVER . . . . . . NiB $253 Ex $202 Gd $151
Caliber: .357 Magnum. Five-round cylinder, 2.5-inch bbl., 7.5 inches overall. Weight: 21 oz. Fixed sights. Stainless steel. Walnut grips. Made from 1975-78.

MODEL PPM357 DA REVOLVER . . . . . NiB $253 Ex $202 Gd $151
Caliber: .357 Magnum. Five-round cylinder, 2-inch bbl., 6.13 inches overall. Weight: 18 oz. Fixed sights. Stainless steel. Walnut grips. Made from 1976-78. Note: Spurless hammer (illustrated) was disc. in 1977; this model has the same conventional hammer as other Security revolvers.

MODEL PSS 38
DA REVOLVER.................. NiB $200 Ex $175 Gd $134
Caliber: .38 Special. Five-round cylinder, 2-inch bbl., 6.5 inches overall. Weight: 18 oz. Fixed sights. Stainless steel. Walnut grips. Intro. 1973. disc.

R. F. SEDGLEY. INC. — Philadelphia, Pennsylvania

BABY HAMMERLESS
EJECTOR REVOLVER .... NiB $614 Ex $502 Gd $247
DA. Solid frame. Folding trigger. Caliber: .22 Long. Six-round cylinder, 4 inches overall. Weight: 6 oz. Fixed sights. Blued or nickel finish. Rubber grips. Made circa 1930-39.

L. W. SEECAMP, INC. — Milford, Connecticut

MODEL LWS .25
DAO PISTOL.................. NiB $448 Ex $371 Gd $264
Caliber: .25 ACP. Seven-round magazine, 2-inch bbl., 4.125 inches overall. Weight: 12 oz. Checkered black polycarbonate grips. Matte stainless finish. No sights. Made from 1981-85.

MODEL LWS .32 DAO PISTOL
Caliber: .32 ACP. Six-round magazine, 2-inch bbl., 4.25 inches overall. Weight: 12.9 oz. Ribbed sighting plane with no sights. Checkered black Lexon grips. Stainless steel. Made from 1985 to date. Limited production results in inflated resale values.
Matte stainless finish............ NiB $630 Ex $579 Gd $447
Polished stainless finish.......... NiB $646 Ex $590 Gd $452

SHERIDAN PRODUCTS, INC. — Racine, Wisconsin

KNOCKABOUT
SINGLE-SHOT PISTOL .... NiB $122 Ex $112 Gd $60
Tip-up type. Caliber: .22 LR, Long, Short; 5-inch bbl., 6.75 inches overall. Weight: 24 oz. Fixed sights. Checkered plastic grips. Blued finish. Made from 1953-60.

SIG PISTOLS — Neuhausen am Rheinfall, Switzerland, Mfd. by SIG Schweizerische Industrie-Gesellschaft

See also listings under SIG-Sauer.

MODEL P210-1
AUTOMATIC PISTOL .... NiB $2134 Ex $1799 Gd $1083
Calibers: .22 LR, 7.65mm Luger, 9mm Para. Eight-round magazine, 4.75-inch bbl., 8.5 inches overall. Weight: 33 oz. (.22 cal.) or 35 oz. (7.65mm, 9mm). Fixed sights. Polished blued finish. Checkered wood grips. Made from 1949-86.

MODEL P210-2.............. NiB $1616 Ex $1384 Gd $843
Same as Model P210-1 except has sandblasted finish, plastic grips. Not avail. in .22 LR. Disc. 1987.

MODEL P210-5
TARGET PISTOL .... NiB $2129 Ex $1876 Gd $1080
Same as Model P210-2 except has 6-inch bbl., micrometer adj. rear sight, target front sight, adj. trigger stop, 9.7 inches overall. Weight: About 38.3 oz. Disc. 1997.

SIG
Model P210-1

SIG
Model P210-6 Target Pistol

MODEL P210-6 TARGET PISTOL ...... NiB $2004 Ex $1618 Gd $974
Same as Model P210-2 except has micrometer adj. rear sight, target front sight, adj. trigger stop. Weight: About 37 oz. Disc. 1987.

P210 .22 CONVERSION UNIT .... NiB $814 Ex $651 Gd $455
Converts P210 pistol to .22 LR. Consists of bbl., w/recoil spring, slide and magazine,

SIG SAUER HANDGUNS Mfd. by J. P. Sauer & Sohn of West Germany, SIG of Switzerland, and other manufacturers

MODEL P220 DA/DAO AUTOMATIC PISTOL
Calibers: 22LR, 7.65mm, 9mm Para., .38 Super, .45 Automatic. Seven-round in .45, 9-round in other calibers, 4.4-inch bbl., 8 inches overall. Weight: 26.5 oz.(9mm). Fixed sights. Blue, electroless nickel, K-Kote, Duo/nickel or Ilaflon finish. Alloy frame. Checkered plastic grips. Imported from 1976 to date. Note: Also sold in U.S. as Browning BDA.
Blue finish .... NiB $746 Ex $633 Gd $416
Duo/nickel finish............... NiB $787 Ex $628 Gd $462
Nickel finish .... NiB $818 Ex $725 Gd $489
K-Kote finish .... NiB $787 Ex $628 Gd $410
Ilaflon finish .... NiB $787 Ex $628 Gd $462
.22 conversion kit, add $680
W/Siglite sights, add $92

MODEL P220 SPORT AUTOMATIC .... NiB $1292 Ex $1060 Gd $854
Similar to Model P220 except .45 ACP only w/4.5-inch compensated bbl., 10-round magazine, adj. target sights. Weight: 46.1 oz. Stainless finish. Made from 1999 to date.

SIG Sauer P220

SIG Sauer P225

SIG Sauer P230

MODEL P225 DA AUTOMATIC

Caliber: 9mm Para. Eight-round magazine, 3.85-inch bbl., 7 inches overall. Weight: 26.1 oz. Blue, nickel, K-Kote, Duo/nickel or Ilaflon finish.

Blued finish . . . . NiB $582 Ex $504 Gd $401
Duo/nickel finish. . . . . NiB $628 Ex $551 Gd $448
Nickel finish . . . . NiB $654 Ex $577 Gd $454
K-Kote finish . . . . NiB $654 Ex $577 Gd $474
W/Siglite sights, add $105

MODEL P226 DA/DAO AUTOMATIC

Caliber: .357 SIG, 9mm Para., .40 S&W, 10- or 15-round magazine, 4.4-inch bbl., 7.75 inches overall. Weight: 29.5 oz. Alloy frame. Blue, electroless nickel, K-Kote, Duo/nickel or Nitron finish. Imported from 1983 to date.

Blued finish . . . . NiB $815 Ex $681 Gd $413
Duo/nickel finish. . . . . NiB $856 Ex $764 Gd $439
Nickel finish . . . . NiB $762 Ex $619 Gd $438
K-Kote finish . . . . NiB $729 Ex $654 Gd $421
Nitron finish
(Blacken stainless) . . . . NiB $736 Ex $599 Gd $424
W/Siglite sights, add $85

MODEL P228 DA AUTOMATIC

Same general specifications as Model P226 except w/3.86-inch bbl., 7.13 inches overall. 10- or 13-round magazine, Imported from 1990-97.

Blued finish . . . . NiB $748 Ex $645 Gd $413
Duo/nickel finish. . . . . NiB $790 Ex $687 Gd $456
Electroless nickel finish . . . . NiB $820 Ex $717 Gd $486
K-Kote finish . . . . NiB $795 Ex $692 Gd $460
For Siglite nite sights, add $102

MODEL P229 DA/DAO AUTOMATIC

Same general specifications as Model P228 except w/3.86-inch bbl., 10- or 12-round magazine, weight: 32.5 oz. Nitron or Satin Nickel finish. Imported from 1991 to date.

Nitron finish
(Blackened stainless) . . . . NiB $800 Ex $697 Gd $413
Satin nickel finish . . . . NiB $841 Ex $738 Gd $455
For Siglite nite sights, add $100

MODEL P229
SPORT AUTOMATIC . . . . NiB $1278 Ex $1021 Gd $840

Similar to Model P229 except .357 SIG only w/4.5-inch compensated bbl., adj. target sights. Weight: 43.6 oz. Stainless finish. Made from 1998 to date.

MODEL P230 DA AUTOMATIC PISTOL

Calibers: .22 LR, .32 Auto (7.65mm), .380 Auto (9mm Short), 9mm Ultra. 10-round magazine in .22, 8-round in .32, 7-round in 9mm; 3.6-inch bbl., 6.6 inches overall. Weight: 18.2 oz. or 22.4 oz. (steel frame). Fixed sights. Blued or stainless finish. Plastic grips. Imported from 1976-96.

Blued finish . . . . NiB $477 Ex $374 Gd $260
Stainless finish (P230SL) . . . . NiB $533 Ex $451 Gd $430

MODEL P232 DA/DAO AUTOMATIC PISTOL

Caliber: .380 ACP. Seven-round magazine, 3.6-inch bbl., 6.6 inches overall. Weight: 16.2 oz. or 22.4 oz. (steel frame). Double/single action or double action only. Blade front and notch rear drift adjustable sights. Alloy or steel frame. Automatic firing pin lock and heelmounted magazine release. Blue, Duo or stainless finish. Stippled black composite stocks. Imported 1997 to date.

Blued finish . . . . NiB $502 Ex $441 Gd $263
Duo finish . . . . NiB $523 Ex $461 Gd $283
Stainless finish. . . . . NiB $539 Ex $482 Gd $410
For Siglite nite sights, add $40

MODEL P239 DA/DAO AUTOMATIC PISTOL

Caliber: .357 SIG, 9mm Parabellum or .40 S&W. Seven- or 8-round magazine, 3.6-inch bbl., 6.6 inches overall. Weight: 28.2 oz. Double/single action or double action only. Blade front and notch rear adjustable sights. Alloy frame w/stainless slide. Ambidextrous frame- mounted magazine release. Matte black or Duo finish. Stippled black composite stocks. Made from 1996 to date.

Matte black finish . . . . NiB $554 Ex $492 Gd $266
DAO finish. . . . . NiB $593 Ex $482 Gd $340
For Siglite nite sights, add $100

SMITH & WESSON, INC. — Springfield, Massachusetts

NOTE: *For ease in locating a particular S&W handgun, the listings are divided into two groupings: Automatic/Single-Shot Pistols (below) and Revolvers (page 155). For a complete handgun listing, please refer to the index.*

AUTOMATIC/SINGLE-SHOT PISTOLS

.32 AUTOMATIC PISTOL...... NiB $2964 Ex $2243 Gd $1625
Caliber: .32 Automatic. Same general specifications as .35 caliber model, but barrel is fastened to the receiver instead of hinged. Made from 1924-37.

MODEL .22 SPORT SERIES
Caliber: .22 LR. 10-round magazine, 4-, 5.5- or 7-inch standard (A-series) or bull bbl., (S-series). Single action. Eight, 9.5 or 11 inches overall. Weight: 28 oz. to 33 oz. Partridge front sight, fully adjustable rear. Alloy frame w/stainless slide. Blued finish. Black polymer or Dymondwood grips. Made from 1997 to date.
Model 22A (w/4-inch bbl.) .... NiB $246 Ex $221 Gd $142
Model 22A (w/5.5-inch bbl.)...... NiB $276 Ex $250 Gd $172
Model 22A (w/7-inch bbl.) .... NiB $315 Ex $290 Gd $212
Model 22S (w/5.5-inch bbl.) ...... NiB $349 Ex $324 Gd $246
Model 22S (w/7-inch bbl.) .... NiB $291 Ex $231 Gd $167
W/bull bbl., add $40
W/Dymondwood grips, add $75

35 (1913) AUTOMATIC PISTOL ... NiB $237 Ex $708 Gd $425
Caliber: 35 S&W Auto. Seven-round magazine, 3.5-inch bbl., (hinged to frame). 6.5 inches overall. Weight: 25 oz. Fixed sights. Blued or nickel finish. Plain walnut grips. Made from 1913-21.

MODEL 39 9MM DA AUTO PISTOL
Calibers: 9mm Para. Eight-round magazine, 4-inch barrel. Overall length: 7.44-inches. Steel or alloy frames. Weight: 26.5 oz. (w/alloy frame). Click adjustable rear sight, ramp front. Blued or nickel finish. Checkered walnut grips. Made 1954-82. Note: Between 1954 and 1966, 927 pistols were produced w/steel instead of alloy. In 1970, Model 39-1 w/alloy frame and steel slide. In 1971, Model 39-2 was introduced as an improved version of the original Model 39 w/modified extractor.
Model 39 (early production) 1954-70
First series (SN range 1000-2600) ..... NiB $1552 Ex $1357 Gd $714
9mm blue(w/steel frame & slide,
produced 1966) .... NiB $1306 Ex $1074 Gd $667
9mm blue (w/alloy frame) .... NiB $454 Ex $371 Gd $264
Nickel finish, add $35
Models 39-1, 39-2 (late production)
1970-82 9mm blue (w/alloy frame) ...... NiB $407 Ex $293 Gd $242
Nickel finish, add $35

MODEL 41 .22 AUTOMATIC PISTOL
Caliber: .22 LR, .22 Short (not interchangeably). 10-round magazine, bbl. lengths: 5-, 5.5-, 7.75-inches; latter has detachable muzzle brake, 12 inches overall (with 7.75-inch bbl.). Weight: 43.5 oz. (with 7.75-inch bbl.). Click adj. rear sight, undercut Partridge front. Blued finish. Checkered walnut grips w/thumbrest. 1957 to date.
.22 LR model................. NiB $746 Ex $592 Gd $298
.22 Short model
(w/counter-
weights & muzzle brake) ...... NiB $1191 Ex $965 Gd $677
W/extended sight, add $95
W/muzzle brake, add $45

Smith & Wesson
Model 22A Sport Series

Smith & Wesson
Model 22S Sport Series
w/Dymondwood Grips

Smith & Wesson
Model 41 .22

MODEL 46 .22 AUTO PISTOL..... NiB $504 Ex $386 Gd $247
Caliber: .22 LR. 10-round magazine, bbl. lengths: 5-, 5.5-, 7-inches. 10.56 inches overall (with 7-inch bbl.). Weight: 42 oz. (with 7-inch bbl.). Click adj. rear sight, undercut Partridge front. Blued finish. Molded nylon grips w/thumbrest. Only 4,000 produced. Made from 1959-68.

MODEL 52 .38 MASTER AUTO
Caliber: .38 Special (midrange wadcutter only). Five-round magazine, 5-inch bbl., overall length: 8.63 inches. Weight: 41 oz. Micrometer click rear sight, Partridge front on ramp base. Blued finish. Checkered walnut grips. Made from 1961-94.
Model 52 (1961-63) .... NiB $956 Ex $851 Gd $462
Model 52-1 (1963-71).......... NiB $750 Ex $621 Gd $359
Model 52-2 (1971-93).......... NiB $750 Ex $621 Gd $359
Model 52-A USA Marksman
(fewer than 100 mfg.) .... NiB $3160 Ex $2696 Gd $1821

Smith & Wesson
Model 46

Smith & Wesson
Model 52

Smith & Wesson
Model 59

Smith & Wesson
Model 422

Smith & Wesson
Model 439

MODEL 59
9MM DA AUTO
Similar specifications as Model 39 except has 14-round staggered column magazine, checkered nylon grips. Made from 1971-82.
Model 59, blue . . . . NiB $437 Ex $390 Gd $261
Model 59, nickel . . . . NiB $474 Ex $421 Gd $272
Model 59
(early production
w/smooth grip frame) . . . . NiB $626 Ex $509 Gd $361

MODEL 61
ESCORT POCKET AUTOMATIC PISTOL
Caliber: .22 LR. Five-round magazine, 2.13-inch bbl., 4.69 inches overall. Weight: 14 oz. Fixed sights. Blued or nickel finish. Checkered plastic grips. Made from 1970-73.
Model 61, blue . . . . NiB $285 Ex $244 Gd $141
Model 61, nickel . . . . NiB $311 Ex $265 Gd $141

MODEL 410
AUTO PISTOL . . . . NiB $508 Ex $377 Gd $217
Caliber: .40 S&W. Double action. 10-round magazine, 4-inch bbl., 7.5 inches overall. Weight: 28.5 oz. Alloy frame w/steel slide. Post front sight, fixed rear w/3-dot system. Matte blue finish. Checkered synthetic grips w/straight backstrap. Made from 1996 to date.

MODEL 411
AUTO PISTOL . . . . NiB $490 Ex $423 Gd $320
Similar to S&W Model 915 except in caliber .40 S&W. 11-round magazine, made from 1994-96.

MODEL 422 SA
AUTO PISTOL
Caliber: .22 LR. 10-round magazine, 4.5- or 6-inch bbl., 7.5 inches overall (with 4.5-inch bbl.). Weight: 22-23.5 oz. Fixed or adjustable sights. Checkered plastic or walnut grips. Blued finish. Made from 1987-96.
Standard model . . . . NiB $221 Ex $184 Gd $133
Target model . . . . NiB $263 Ex $210 Gd $138

MODEL 439
9MM AUTOMATIC
DA. Caliber: 9mm Para. Two 8-round magazines, 4-inch bbl., 7.44 inches overall. Alloy frame. Weight: 30 oz. Serrated ramp square front sight, square notch rear. Checkered walnut grips. Blued or nickel finish. Made from 1979-88.
Model 439, blue . . . . NiB $429 Ex $356 Gd $248
Model 439, nickel . . . . NiB $464 Ex $391 Gd $331
W/adjustable sights, add $24

Smith & Wesson
Model 645

Smith & Wesson
Model 459

MODEL 457
COMPACT AUTO PISTOL . . . . NiB $521 Ex $386 Gd $226
Caliber: .45 ACP. Double action. Seven-round magazine, 3.75-inch bbl., 7.25 inches overall. Weight: 29 oz. Alloy frame w/steel slide. Post front sight, fixed rear w/3-dot system. Bobbed hammer. Matte blue finish. Wraparound synthetic grip w/straight backstrap. Made from 1996 to date.

MODEL 459 DA AUTOMATIC
Caliber: 9mm Para. Two 14-round magazines, 4-inch bbl., 7.44 inches overall. Alloy frame. Weight: 28 oz. Blued or nickel finish. Made from 1979-87.
Model 459, blue . . . . NiB $463 Ex $396 Gd $288
Model 459, nickel . . . . NiB $509 Ex $443 Gd $319
FBI Model (brushed finish) . . . . NiB $717 Ex $666 Gd $388

MODEL 469
(MINI) AUTOMATIC . . . . NiB $423 Ex $371 Gd $268
DA. Caliber: 9mm Para. Two 12-round magazines, 3.5-inch bbl., 6.88 inches overall. Weight: 26 oz. Yellow ramp front sight, dovetail mounted square-notch rear. Sandblasted blued finish. Optional ambidextrous safety. Made from 1982-88.

Smith & Wesson
Model 469

MODEL 539 DA AUTOMATIC
Similar to Model 439 except w/steel frame. Caliber: 9mm Para. Two 8-round magazines, 4-inch bbl., 7.44 inches overall. Weight: 36 oz. Blued or nickel finish. Made from 1980-83.
Model 539, blue . . . . NiB $504 Ex $448 Gd $350
Model 539, nickel . . . . NiB $541 Ex $484 Gd $376
W/adjustable sights, add $30

MODEL 559 DA AUTOMATIC
Similar to Model 459 except w/steel frame. Caliber: 9mm Para. Two 14-round magazines, 4-inch bbl., 7.44 inches overall. Weight: 39.5 oz. Blued or nickel finish. (3750 produced) Made from 1980-83.
Model 559, blue . . . . NiB $541 Ex $489 Gd $298
Model 559, nickel . . . . NiB $571 Ex $525 Gd $329
W/adjustable sights, add $30

MODEL 622 SA AUTO PISTOL
Same general specifications as Model 422 except w/stainless finish. Made from 1989-96.
Standard model . . . . NiB $259 Ex $212 Gd $197
Target model . . . . NiB $315 Ex $264 Gd $212

MODEL 639 AUTOMATIC . . . . . . NiB $475 Ex $351 Gd $325
Caliber: 9mm Para. Two 12-round magazines, 3.5-inch bbl., 6.9 inches overall. Weight: 36 oz. Stainless. Made from 1982-88.

Smith & Wesson
Model 639

Smith & Wesson
Model 659

Smith & Wesson
Model 745

Smith & Wesson
Model 1026

MODEL 645 DA AUTOMATIC

Caliber: .45 ACP. Eight-round. 5-inch bbl., overall length: 8.5 inches. Weight: Approx. 38 oz. Red ramp front, fixed rear sights. Stainless. Made from 1986-88.

Model 645 (w/fixed sights) . . . . NiB $529 Ex $416 Gd $349
Model 645 (w/adjustable sights) . . . NiB $555 Ex $442 Gd $365

MODEL 659 9MM AUTOMATIC

DA. Similar to S&W Model 459 except weight: 39.5 oz. and finish is satin stainless steel finish. Made from 1983-88.

Model 659 (w/fixed sights) . . . . NiB $498 Ex $385 Gd $349
Model 659 (w/adjustable sights). . . . . NiB $524 Ex $411 Gd $375

MODEL 669 AUTOMATIC. . . . . NiB $478 Ex $354 Gd $253

Caliber: 9mm. 12-round magazine, 3.5 inch bbl., 6.9 inches overall. Weight: 26 oz. Serrated ramp front sight w/red bar, fixed rear. Non-glare stainless steel finish. Made from 1986-88.

MODEL 745 AUTOMATIC PISTOL

Caliber: .45 ACP. Eight-round magazine, 5-inch bbl., 8.63 inches overall. Weight: 38.75 oz. Fixed sights. Blued slide, stainless frame. Checkered walnut grips. Similar to the model 645, but w/o DA capability. Made from 1987-90.

W/standard competition features . . . . NiB $634 Ex $495 Gd $387
IPSC Commemorative (first 5,000) . . . . NiB $743 Ex $603 Gd $424

MODEL 908/909/910 AUTO PISTOLS

Caliber: 9mm Parabellum. Double action. Eight-round (Model 908), 9-round (Model 909) or 10-round (Model 910) magazine; 3.5- or 4-inch bbl.; 6.83 or 7.38 inches overall. Weight: 26 oz. to 28.5 oz. Post front sight, fixed rear w/3-dot system. Matte blue steel slide w/alloy frame. Delrin synthetic wrap-around grip w/straight backstrap. Made from 1994 to date.

Model 908. NiB $474 Ex $356 Gd $217
Model 909 (disc 1996) . . . . NiB $408 Ex $320 Gd $217
Model 910 . . . . NiB $474 Ex $356 Gd $217

MODEL 915 AUTO PISTOL . . . . . . NiB $395 Ex $298 Gd $215

DA. Caliber: 9mm Para. 15-round magazine, 4-inch bbl., 7.5 inches overall. Weight: 28.5 oz. Post front sight, fixed square-notched rear w/3-dot system. Xenoy wraparound grip. Blued steel slide and alloy frame. Made from 1992-94.

MODEL 1000 SERIES DA AUTO

Caliber: 10mm. Nine-round magazine, 4.25- or 5-inch bbl., 7.88 or 8.63 inches overall. Weight: About 38 oz. Post front sight, adj. or fixed square-notched rear w/3-dot system. One-piece Xenoy wraparound grips. Stainless slide and frame. Made from 1990-94.

Model 1006 (fixed sights, 5 inch bbl.) . . . . NiB $697 Ex $584 Gd $455
Model 1006 (Adj. sights, 5 inch bbl.) . . . . . NiB $725 Ex $612 Gd $483
Model 1026 (fixed sights, 5 inch bbl., decocking lever) . . . . NiB $692 Ex $585 Gd $455
Model 1066 (fixed sights, 4.25 inch bbl.) . . . . NiB $671 Ex $573 Gd $450
Model 1076 (fixed sights, 4.25 inch bbl., frame-mounted decocking lever, straight backstrap). NiB $707 Ex $589 Gd $455
Model 1076 (same as above w/Tritium night sight) . . . . NiB $749 Ex $630 Gd $496
Model 1086 (same as model 1076 in DA only) . . . . NiB $775 Ex $573 Gd $450

MODEL 2206 SA AUTOMATIC PISTOL

Similar to Model 422 except w/stainless-steel slide and frame, weight: 35-39 oz. Partridge front sight on adj. sight model; post w/white dot on fixed sight model. Plastic grips. Made from 1990-96.

Standard model . . . . NiB $331 Ex $264 Gd $212
Target model . . . . NiB $403 Ex $315 Gd $269

MODEL 2213
SPORTSMAN AUTO . . . . NiB $293 Ex $236 Gd $195

Caliber: .22 LR. Eight-round magazine, 3-inch bbl., 6.13 inches overall. Weight: 18 oz. Partridge front sight, fixed square-notched rear w/3-dot system. Black synthetic molded grips. Stainless steel slide w/alloy frame. Made from 1992-99.

MODEL 2214
SPORTSMAN AUTO . . . . NiB $267 Ex $221 Gd $164

Same general specifications as Model 2214 except w/blued slide and matte black alloy frame. Made from 1990-99.

MODEL 3904/3906 DA AUTO PISTOL

Caliber: 9mm. Eight-round magazine, 4-inch bbl., 7.5 inches overall. Weight: 25.5 oz. (Model 3904) or 34 oz. (Model 3906). Fixed or adj. sights. Delrin one-piece wraparound checkered grips. Alloy frame w/blued carbon steel slide (Model 3904) or satin stainless (Model 3906). Made from 1989-91.

Model 3904 w/adjustable sights . . . . NiB $529 Ex $462 Gd $380
Model 3904 w/fixed sights . . . . NiB $508 Ex $442 Gd $333
Model 3904 w/Novak LC sight . . . . NiB $534 Ex $426 Gd $302
Model 3906 w/adjustable sights . . . . NiB $599 Ex $522 Gd $450
Model 3906 w/Novak LC sight . . . . NiB $570 Ex $493 Gd $421

Smith & Wesson Model 3906

MODEL 3913/3914 DA AUTOMATIC

Caliber: 9mm Parabellum (Luger). Eight-round magazine, 3.5-inch bbl., 6.88 inches overall. Weight: 25 oz. Post front sight, fixed or adj. square-notched rear. One-piece Xenoy wraparound grips w/straight backstrap. Alloy frame w/stainless or blued slide. Made from 1990 to date.

Model 3913 stainless . . . . NiB $683 Ex $529 Gd $441
Model 3913LS Lady Smith stainless w/contoured trigger guard . . . . NiB $699 Ex $544 Gd $441
Model 3913TSW (intro. 1998) . . . . NiB $683 Ex $539 Gd $441
Model 3914 blued compact (disc 1995) . . . . NiB $526 Ex $432 Gd $327

MODEL 3953/3954 DA AUTO PISTOL

Same general specifications as Model 3913/3914 except double action only. Made from 1991 to date.

Model 3953 stainless, double action only . . . . NiB $683 Ex $539 Gd $441
Model 3954 blued, double action only (disc. 1992) . . . . NiB $505 Ex $438 Gd $335

Smith & Wesson Model 3953

MODEL 4000 SERIES DA AUTO

Caliber: .40 S&W. 11-round magazine, 4-inch bbl., 7.88 inches overall. Weight: 28-30 oz. w/alloy frame or 36 oz. w/stainless frame. Post front sight, adj. or fixed square-notched rear w/2 white dots. Straight backstrap. One-piece Xenoy wraparound grips. Blued or stainless finish. Made between 1990-93.

Model 4003 stainless w/alloy frame . . . . . . NiB $650 Ex $557 Gd $454
Model 4003 TSW w/ S&W Tactical options . . . . NiB $812 Ex $715 Gd $421
Model 4004 blued w/alloy frame . . . . NiB $594 Ex $485 Gd $345
Model 4006 stainless frame, fixed sights. NiB $603 Ex $521 Gd $335
Model 4006 stainless frame, Adj. sights . . . . NiB $722 Ex $608 Gd $459
Model 4006 TSW w/ S&W Tactical options . . . . NiB $817 Ex $714 Gd $421
Model 4013 stainless frame, fixed sights . . . . NiB $663 Ex $550 Gd $344
Model 4013 TSW w/ S&W Tactical options . . . . NiB $802 Ex $647 Gd $483
Model 4014 blued, fixed sights (disc. 1993). . . . . NiB $572 Ex $485 Gd $330
Model 4026 w/decocking Lever (disc. 1994) . . . . NiB $686 Ex $586 Gd $459
Model 4043 DA only, stainless w/alloy frame . . . . NiB $812 Ex $709 Gd $421
Model 4044 DA only, blued w/alloy frame . . . . NiB $603 Ex $521 Gd $351
Model 4046 DA only, stainless frame, fixed sights. . . . . NiB $730 Ex $610 Gd $466
Model 4046 TSW w/ S&W Tactical options . . . . NiB $834 Ex $725 Gd $416
Model 4046 DA only, stainless frame, Tritium night sight . . . . NiB $971 Ex $864 Gd $589

Smith & Wesson Model 4013

Smith & Wesson Model 4046

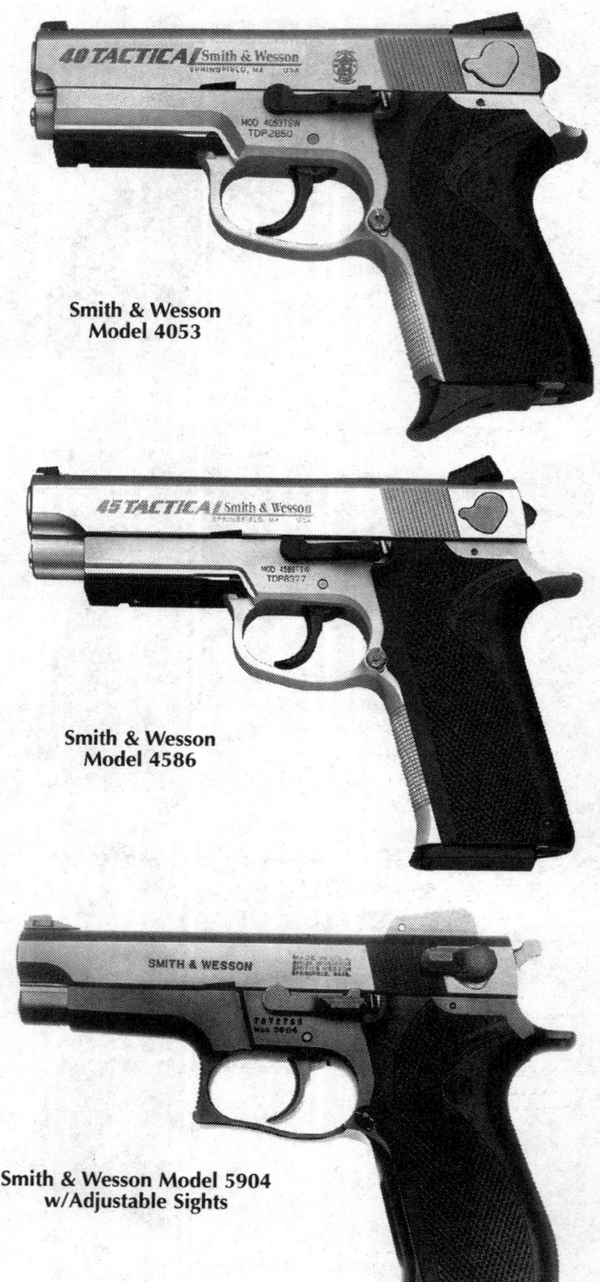

Smith & Wesson
Model 4053

Smith & Wesson
Model 4586

Smith & Wesson Model 5904
w/Adjustable Sights

MODEL 4013/4014 DA AUTOMATIC

Caliber: .40 S&W. Eight-round capacity, 3.5-inch bbl., 7 inches overall. Weight: 26 oz. Post front sight, fixed Novak LC rear w/3-dot system. One-piece Xenoy wraparound grips. Stainless or blued slide w/alloy frame. Made from 1991 to date.

Model 4013 w/stainless slide (disc. 1996) .... NiB $661 Ex $542 Gd $336
Model 4013 Tactical w/stainless slide .... NiB $805 Ex $650 Gd $486
Model 4014 w/blued slide (disc. 1993) ...... NiB $573 Ex $486 Gd $290

MODEL 4053/4054 DA AUTO PISTOL

Same general specifications as Model 4013/4014 except double action only. Alloy frame fitted w/blued steel slide. Made from 1991-97.

Model 4053 DA only w/stainless slide .... NiB $573 Ex $486 Gd $434
Model 4053 TSW w/ S&W Tactical options ... NiB $805 Ex $650 Gd $480
Model 4054 DA only w/blued slide
(disc. 1992)............................ NiB $573 Ex $486 Gd $434

MODEL 4500 SERIES DA AUTOMATIC

Caliber: .45 ACP. Six-, 7- or 8-round magazine, bbl. lengths: 3.75, 4.25 or 5 inches; 7.13 to 8.63 inches overall. Weight: 34.5 to 38.5 oz. Post front sight, fixed Novak LC rear w/3-dot system or adj. One-piece Xenoy wraparound grips. Satin stainless finish. Made from 1990 to date.

Model 4505 w/fixed sights, 5-inch bbl........ NiB $641 Ex $564 Gd $358
Model 4505 w/Novak LC sight, 5-inch bbl. ... NiB $669 Ex $592 Gd $386
Model 4506 w/fixed sights, 5-inch bbl........ NiB $749 Ex $615 Gd $471
Model 4506 w/Novak LC sight, 5-inch bbl. ... NiB $783 Ex $649 Gd $502
Model 4513T (TSW) w/3.75-inch bbl.
Tactical Combat........................ NiB $726 Ex $600 Gd $461
Model 4516 w/3.75-inch bbl.............. NiB $726 Ex $595 Gd $409
Model 4526 w/5-inch bbl., alloy frame,
decocking lever, fixed sights .... NiB $703 Ex $595 Gd $461
Model 4536, decocking lever .... NiB $708 Ex $605 Gd $471
Model 4546, w/3.75-inch bbl., DA only ..... NiB $708 Ex $605 Gd $471
Model 4553T (TSW) w/3.75-inch bbl.
Tactical Combat........................ NiB $669 Ex $592 Gd $381
Model 4556, w/3.75-inch bbl., DA only ..... NiB $641 Ex $564 Gd $359
Model 4563 TSW w/4.25-inch bbl.
Tactical Combat........................ NiB $724 Ex $600 Gd $461
Model 4566 w/4.25-inch bbl.,
ambidextrous safety, fixed sights............ NiB $693 Ex $580 Gd $409
Model 4566 TSW w/4.25-inch bbl.
Tactical Combat........................ NiB $724 Ex $600 Gd $461
Model 4576 w/4.25-inch bbl.,
decocking lever .... NiB $703 Ex $595 Gd $409
Model 4583T TSW w/4.25-inch bbl.
Tactical Combat........................ NiB $669 Ex $592 Gd $471
Model 4586 w/4.25-inch bbl., DA only ...... NiB $749 Ex $615 Gd $461
Model 4586 TSW w/4.25-inch bbl.
Tactical Combat........................ NiB $724 Ex $600 Gd $399

MODEL 5900 SERIES DA AUTOMATIC

Caliber: 9mm. 15-round magazine, 4-inch bbl., 7.5 inches overall. Weight: 26-38 oz. Fixed or adj. sights. One-piece Xenoy wraparound grips. Alloy frame w/stainless-steel slide (Model 5903) or blued slide (Model 5904) stainless-steel frame and slide (Model 5906). Made from 1989/90 to date.

Model 5903 w/adjustable sights .... NiB $765 Ex $626 Gd $332
Model 5903 w/Novak LC rear sight .... NiB $765 Ex $626 Gd $332
Model 5903 TSW w/4-inch bbl.,
Tactical Combat........................ NiB $765 Ex $640 Gd $346
Model 5904 w/adjustable sights .... NiB $603 Ex $506 Gd $364
Model 5904 w/Novak LC rear sight .... NiB $595 Ex $490 Gd $351
Model 5905 w/Adjustable Sights .... NiB $615 Ex $511 Gd $398
Model 5905 w/Novak LC rear sight .... NiB $703 Ex $609 Gd $423
Model 5906 w/adjustable sights .... NiB $698 Ex $614 Gd $398
Model 5906 w/Novak LC rear sight .... NiB $677 Ex $501 Gd $373
Model 5906 w/Tritium night sight........... NiB $801 Ex $696 Gd $552
Model 5906 TSW w/4-inch bbl.,
Tactical Combat........................ NiB $796 Ex $698 Gd $518
Model 5924 anodized frame, blued slide ..... NiB $636 Ex $487 Gd $291
Model 5926 Stain. frame, decocking lever .... NiB $724 Ex $595 Gd $461
Model 5943 alloy frame/
stainless slide, DA only .... NiB $698 Ex $600 Gd $379
Model 5943 TSW w/4-inch bbl., DA only .... NiB $667 Ex $541 Gd $385
Model 5944 alloy frame/
blued slide, DA only .... NiB $607 Ex $502 Gd $368
Model 5946 stainless frame/slide, DA only ... NiB $662 Ex $461 Gd $337
Model 5946 TSW w/4-inch bbl., DA only..... NiB $669 Ex $592 Gd $193

MODEL 6900 COMPACT SERIES
Double action. Caliber: 9mm. 12-round magazine, 3.5-inch bbl., 6.88 inches overall. Weight: 26.5 oz. Ambidextrous safety. Post front sight, fixed Novak LC rear w/3-dot system. Alloy frame w/blued carbon steel slide (Model 6904) or stainless steel slide (Model 6906). Made from 1989 to date.
Model 6904 .... NiB $640 Ex $475 Gd $344
Model 6906 w/fixed sights .... NiB $656 Ex $541 Gd $444
Model 6906 w/Tritium night sight .... NiB $779 Ex $579 Gd $506
Model 6926 same as model
6906 w/decocking lever .... NiB $666 Ex $547 Gd $344
Model 6944 same as model
6904 in DA only .... NiB $578 Ex $491 Gd $295
Model 6946 same as model
6906 in DA only ,fixed sights .... NiB $666 Ex $547 Gd $344
Model 6946 w/Tritium night sight .... NiB $728 Ex $604 Gd $403

SIGMA SW380 AUTOMATIC PISTOL..... NiB $338 Ex $296 Gd $219
Caliber: .380 ACP. Double-action only. Six-round magazine, 3-inch bbl., weight: 14 oz. Black integral polymer gripframe w/checkered back and front straps. Fixed channel sights. Polymer frame w/hammerless steel slide. Made from 1996 to date.

SIGMA SW9 SERIES AUTOMATIC PISTOL
Caliber: 9mm Parabellum. Double action only. 10-round magazine, 3.25-, 4- or 4.5-inch bbl., weight: 17.9 oz. to 24.7 oz. Polymer frame w/hammerless steel slide. Post front sight and drift adjustable rear w/3-dot system. Gray or black integral polymer gripframe w/checkered back and front straps. Made from 1994 to date.
Model SW9C (compact w/3.25-inch bbl.) .... NiB $511 Ex $414 Gd $321
Model SW9F (blue slide w/4.5-inch bbl.) ..... NiB $551 Ex $450 Gd $339
Model SW9M (compact w/3.25-inch bbl.) .... NiB $352 Ex $341 Gd $223
Model SW9V (stainless slide w/4-inch bbl.) ... NiB $414 Ex $352 Gd $300
Tritium night sight, add $210

SW40 SERIES AUTOMATIC PISTOL
Same general specifications as SW9 series except chambered for .40 S&W w/4- or 4.5-inch bbl., weight: 24.4 to 26 oz. Made 1994 to date.
Model SW40C (compact w/4inch bbl.) ...... NiB $510 Ex $413 Gd $320
Model SW40F (blue slide w/4.5inch bbl.)..... NiB $510 Ex $413 Gd $320
Model SW40V (stainless slide
w/4inch bbl.) .... NiB $418 Ex $356 Gd $304
Tritium night sight, add $210

MODEL 1891 SINGLE-SHOT TARGET PISTOL, FIRST MODEL
Hinged frame. Calibers: .22 LR, .32 S&W, .38 S&W. Bbl. lengths: 6-, 8- and 10-inches, approx. 13.5 inches overall (with 10-inch bbl.). Weight: About 25 oz. Target sights, barrel catch rear adj. for windage and elevation. Blued finish. Square butt, hard rubber grips. Made 1893-1905. Note: This model was available also as a combination arm w/accessory .38 revolver bbl. and cylinder enabling conversion to a pocket revolver. It has the frame of the .38 SA revolver Model 1891 w/side flanges, hand and cylinder stop slots.
Single-shot pistol, .22 LR .... NiB $876 Ex $721 Gd $387
Single-shot pistol, .32 S&W or .38 S&W..... NiB $1220 Ex $989 Gd $694
Combination set, revolver
and single-shot barrel................ NiB $1352 Ex $1096 Gd $768

MODEL 1891 SINGLE-SHOT TARGET PISTOL, SECOND MODEL .... NiB $1200 Ex $839 Gd $453
Similar to the First Model except side flanges, hand and stop slots eliminated, cannot be converted to revolver, redesigned rear sight. Caliber: .22 LR only, 10-inch bbl. only. Made from 1905-09.

PERFECTED SINGLE-SHOT TARGET PISTOL
Similar to Second Model except has double-action lockwork. Caliber: .22 LR only, 10-inch bbl. Checkered walnut grips, extended

Smith & Wesson Model 1

square-butt target type. Made 1909-23. Note: In 1920 and thereafter, this model was made w/barrels having bore diameter of .223 instead of .226 and tight, short chambering. The first group of these pistols was produced for the U.S. Olympic Team of 1920, thus the designation Olympic Model.
Pre-1920 type .... NiB $1818 Ex $839 Gd $376
Olympic model .... NiB $1509 Ex $1092 Gd $680

STRAIGHT LINE SINGLE-SHOT TARGET PISTOL .... NiB $1872 Ex $1306 Gd $636
Frame shaped like that of an automatic pistol, barrel swings to the left on pivot for extracting and loading, straight-line trigger and hammer movement. Caliber: .22 LR. 10-inch bbl., 11.25 inches overall. Weight: 34 oz. Target sights. Blued finish. Smooth walnut grips. Supplied in metal case w/screwdriver and cleaning rod. Made from 1925-36.

NOTE: *The following section contains only S&W Revolvers. For a complete listing of S&W handguns, please refer to the index.*

REVOLVERS

MODEL 1 HAND EJECTOR DA REVOLVER................. NiB $780 Ex $678 Gd $456
First Model. Forerunner of the .32 Hand Ejector and Regulation Police models, this was the first S&W revolver of the solid-frame, swing-out cylinder type. Top strap of this model is longer than those of later models, and it lacks the usual S&W cylinder latch. Caliber: .32 S&W Long. Bbl., lengths: 3.25-, 4.25-, and 6-inches. Fixed sights. Blued or nickel finish. Round butt, hard rubber stocks. Made from 1896-1903.

NO. 3 SA FRONTIER .... NiB $9428 Ex $6276 Gd $2053
Caliber: .44-40 WCF. Bbl., lengths: 4-, 5- and 6.5-inch. Fixed or target sights. Blued or nickel finish. Round, hard rubber or checkered walnut grips. Made from 1885-1908.

NO. 3 SA (NEW MODEL) ..... NiB $3951 Ex $3180 Gd $2193
Hinged frame. Six-round cylinder. Caliber: .44 S&W Russian. Bbl., lengths: 4-, 5-, 6-, 6.5-, 7.5- and 8-inches. Fixed or target sights. Blued or nickel finish. Round, hard rubber or checkered walnut grips. Made from 1878-1908. Note: Value shown is for standard model. Specialist collectors recognize numerous variations w/a range of higher values.

NO. 3 SA TARGET........... NiB $6805 Ex $3457 Gd $1336
Hinged frame. Six-round cylinder. Calibers: .32/.44 S&W, .38/.44 S&W Gallery & Target. 6.5-inch bbl. only. Fixed or target sights. Blued or nickel finish. Round, hard rubber or checkered walnut grips. Made from 1887-1910.

Smith & Wesson
Model 10 (Two-inch Barrel)

Smith & Wesson
Model 12 (Two-inch Barrel)

Smith & Wesson Model 13
(Heavy Barrel)

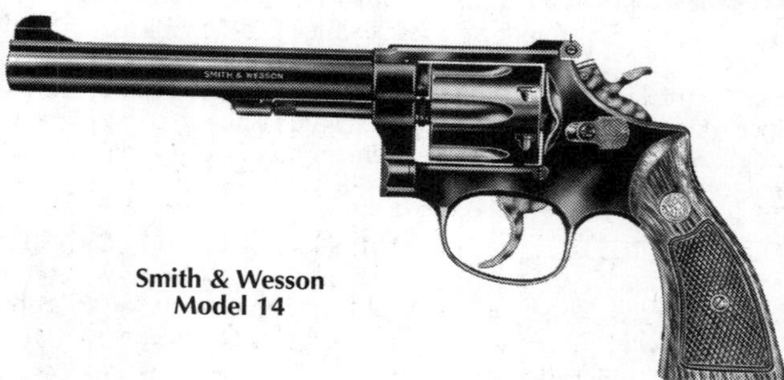

Smith & Wesson
Model 14

MODEL 10 .38 MILITARY & POLICE DA
Also called Hand Ejector Model of 1902, Hand Ejector Model of 1905, Model K. Manufactured substantially in its present form since 1902, this model has undergone numerous changes, most of them minor. Round- or square-butt models, the latter intro. in 1904. Caliber: .38 Special. Six-round cylinder, bbl. lengths: 2-(intro. 1933), 4-, 5-, 6- and 6.5-inch (latter disc. 1915) also 4-inch heavy bbl., (intro. 1957); 11.13 inches overall (square-butt model w/6-inch bbl.). Round-butt model is 1/4-inch shorter, weight: About 1/2 oz. less. Fixed sights. Blued or nickel finish. Checkered walnut grips, hard rubber available in round-butt style. Current Model 10 has short action. Made 1902 to date. Note: S&W Victory Model, wartime version of the M & P .38, was produced for the U.S. Government from 1940 to the end of the war. A similar revolver, designated .38/200 British Service Revolver, was produced for the British Government during the same period. These arms have either brush-polish or sandblast blued finish, and most of them have plain, smooth walnut grips, lanyard swivels.
Model of 1902 (1902-05) . . . . NiB $666 Ex $532 Gd $254
Model of 1905 (1905-40) . . . . NiB $563 Ex $445 Gd $254
.38/200 British Service (1940-45) . . . NiB $406 Ex $309 Gd $159
Victory Model (1942-45). . . . . NiB $413 Ex $340 Gd $246
Model of 1944 (1945-48) . . . . NiB $270 Ex $224 Gd $167
Model 10 (1948 - date) . . . . NiB $406 Ex $309 Gd $159

MODEL 10 .38 MILITARY
& POLICE HEAVY BARREL . . . . . . NiB $406 Ex $309 Gd $159
Same as standard Model 10 except has heavy 4-inch bbl., weight: 34 oz. Made from 1957 to date.

MODEL 12 .38 M
& PAIRWEIGHT. . . . . NiB $422 Ex $314 Gd $180
Same as standard Military & Police except has light alloy frame, f8rnished w/2- or 4-inch bbl. only, weight: 18 oz. (w/2-inch bbl.). Made from 1952-86.

MODEL 12/13 (AIR FORCE MODEL)
DA REVOLVER. . . . . NiB $886 Ex $809 Gd $551
Special "Air Force" Model designed with alloy cylinder and frame to be used as a "Survival Weapon" for air crews. Athough this weapon was actually a first-series Model 12, the Air Force stamped "M13" on the top strap. Issued 1953 but recalled for function problems in 1954.

MODEL 13 .357
MILITARY/POLICE. . . . . NiB $355 Ex $273 Gd $165
Same as Model 10 .38 Military & Police Heavy Barrel except chambered for .357 Magnum and .38 Special w/3- or 4-inch bbl. Round or square butt configuration. Made from1974-98.

MODELS 14 (K38) AND 16 (K32) MASTERPIECE REVOLVERS
Calibers: .22 LR, .22 Magnum Rimfire, .32 S&W Long, .38 Special. Six-round cylinder. DA/SA. Bbl. lengths: 4- (.22 WMR only), 6-, 8.38-inch (latter not available in K32), 11.13 inches overall (with 6-inch bbl.). Weight: 38.5 oz. (with 6-inch bbl.). Click adj. rear sight, Partridge front. Blued finish. Checkered walnut grips. Made from 1947 to date. (Model 16 disc. 1974, w/only 3,630 produced; reissued 1990-93.)
Model 14 (K-38 double-
action) . . . . NiB $345 Ex $293 Gd $190
Model 14 (K-38 single action,
6-inch bbl.) . . . . NiB $371 Ex $304 Gd $201
Model 14 (K-38 single action,
8.38-inch bbl.). . . . . NiB $403 Ex $330 Gd $231
Model 16 (K-32 double-
action) 1st Issue. . . . . NiB $1455 Ex $1250 Gd $837
Model 16 (K-32 double-
action) . . . . NiB $476 Ex $321 Gd $234

MODELS 15 (.38) AND 18 (.22) COMBAT MASTERPIECE DA REVOLVERS
Same as K-.22 and K-.38 Masterpiece but w/2- (.38) or 4-inch bbl., and Baughman quick-draw front sight. 9.13 inches overall w/4-inch bbl., Weight: 34 oz. (.38 cal.). Made from 1950 to date.
Model 15 . . . . NiB $388 Ex $244 Gd $223
Model 18 (disc. 1985) . . . . NiB $398 Ex $321 Gd $234
W/target options TH & TT, add $35

MODEL 17 K-.22 MASTERPIECE DA REVOLVER
Caliber: 22LR. Six-round cylinder, Bbl lengths: 4, 6 or 8.38 inches. 11.13 inches overall (with 6-inch bbl.). Weight: 38 oz. (with 6-inch bbl.). Partridge-type front sight, S&W micrometer click rear. Checkered walnut Service grips with S&W momogram. S&W blued finish. Made from 1947-93 and from 1996-98.
Model 17 (4-inch bbl.) . . . . .NiB $640 Ex $563 Gd $357
Model 17 (6-inch bbl.) . . . . NiB $640 Ex $563 Gd $357
Model 17 (8.38-inch bbl.) . . . . NiB $666 Ex $614 Gd $439
W/target options TH & TT, add $35

MODEL 19 .357 COMBAT MAGNUM DA REVOLVER
Caliber: .357 Magnum. Six-round cylinder, bbl. lengths: 2.5 (round butt), 4, or 6 inches, 9.5 inches overall (with 4-inch bbl.). Weight: 35 oz. (with 4-inch bbl.). Click adj. rear sight, ramp front. Blued or nickel finish. Target grips of checkered Goncalo Alves. Made from 1956 to date (2.5- and 6-inch bbls. were disc. in 1991).
Model 19 (2.5-inch bbl.) . . . . NiB $395 Ex $313 Gd $215
Model 19 (4-inch bbl.) . . . . NiB $405 Ex $323 Gd $224
Model 19 (6-inch bbl.) . . . . NiB $411 Ex $328 Gd $230
Model 19 (8.38-inch bbl.) . . . . NiB $394 Ex $323 Gd $233
W/target options TH & TT, add $60

MODEL 20 .38/.44 HEAVY DUTY DA
Caliber: .38 Special. Six-round cylinder, bbl. lengths: 4, 5 and 6.5 inches;10.38 inches overall (with 5-inch bbl.). Weight: 40 oz. (with 5-inch bbl.). Fixed sights. Blued or nickel finish. Checkered walnut grips. Short action after 1948. Made from 1930-56 and from 1957-67.
Pre-World War II. . . . . NiB $649 Ex $541 Gd $386
Postwar . . . . NiB $396 Ex $330 Gd $190

MODEL 21 1950 .44 MILITARY DA REVOLVER
Postwar version of the 1926 Model 44 Military. Caliber: .44 Special, 6-round cylinder. Bbl. lengths: 4-, 5- and 6.5-inches. 11.75 inches overall (w/6.5-inch bbl.) Weight: 39.5 oz. (w/6.5-inch bbl.). Fixed front sight w/square-notch rear sight; target model has micrometer click rear sight adj. for windage and elevation. Checkered walnut grips w/S&W monogram. Blued or nickel finish. Made from 1950-67.
Model 21 (4- or 5-inch bbl.) . . . . NiB $1886 Ex $1706 Gd $753
Model 21 (6.5-inch bbl.) . . . . NiB $2797 Ex $2526 Gd $1097

MODEL .22 1950 ARMY DA . . . . . . NiB $1886 Ex $1706 Gd $753
Postwar version of the 1917 Army w/same general specifications except redesigned hammer. Made from 1950-67.

.22/.32 TARGET DA REVOLVER
Also known as the "Bekeart Model." Design based upon ".32 Hand Ejector." Caliber: .22 LR (recessed head cylinder for high-speed cartridges intro. 1935). Six-round cylinder, 6-inch bbl., 10.5 inches overall. Weight: 23 oz. Adj. target sights. Blued finish. Checkered walnut grips. Made from 1911-53. Note: In 1911, San Francisco gun dealer Phil Bekeart, who suggested this model, received 292 pieces. These are the true "Bekeart Model" revolvers and are marked with separate identification numbers on the base of the wooden grip.
.22/.32 Target model . . . . NiB $349 Ex $297 Gd $174
.22/.32 Target model (early prod. 1-3000) . . . . NiB $486 Ex $357 Gd $233
.22/.32 Target model (Bekeart model). . . . . . . NiB $1178 Ex $972 Gd $277

.22/.32 KIT GUN. . . . . NiB $331 Ex $264 Gd $202
Same as .22/.32 Target except has 2- or 4-inch bbl., round grips, 6 or 8 inches overall, weight: 19-21oz. Made from 1935-53.

Smith & Wesson
Model 15

Smith & Wesson
Model 17 K-22

Smith & Wesson
Model 18 (See Model 15 for description)

Smith & Wesson
Model 19 (Round Butt)

**Smith & Wesson
Model 19 (Square Butt)**

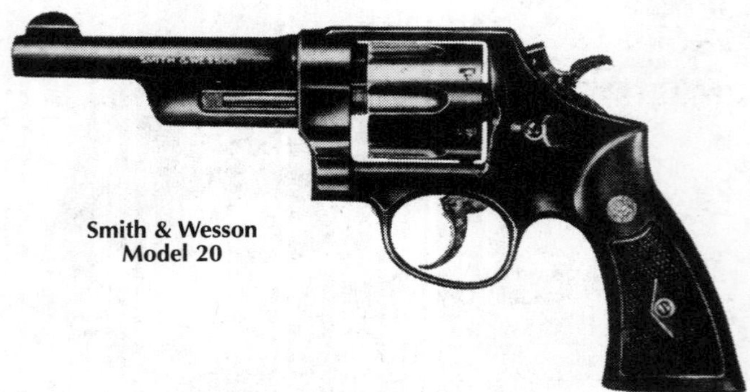

**Smith & Wesson
Model 20**

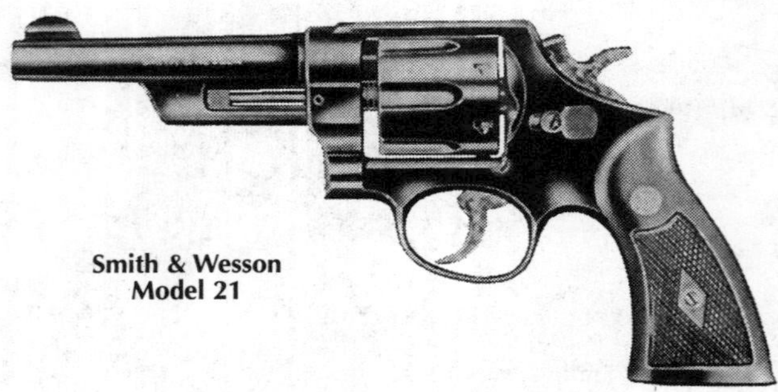

**Smith & Wesson
Model 21**

**Smith & Wesson
Model 22**

MODEL 23 .38/.44 OUTDOORSMAN DA REVOLVER

Target version of the .38/44 Heavy Duty. 6.5- or 8.75-inch bbl., weight: 41.75 oz. Target sights, micrometer-click rear on postwar models. Blued or nickel finish. 1950 transition model has ribbed barrel, redesigned hammer. Made from 1930-67.

Prewar model (plain bbl.) . . . . NiB $734 Ex $631 Gd $353
Postwar (ribbed bbl.). . . . . NiB $868 Ex $745 Gd $411

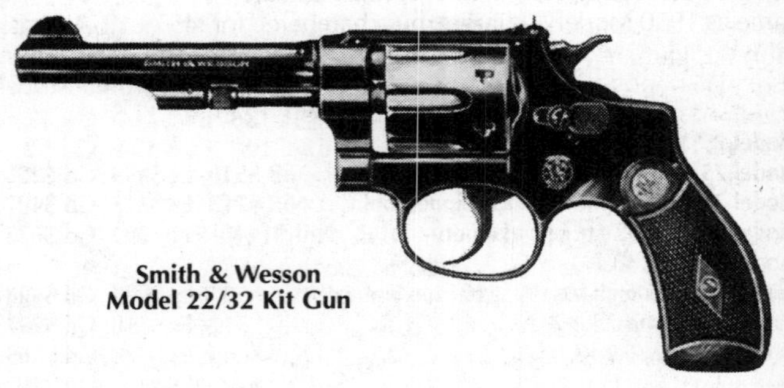

**Smith & Wesson
Model 22/32 Kit Gun**

**Smith & Wesson
Model 22/32 Target Revolver**

**Smith & Wesson
Model 23**

MODEL 24 1950 .44 TARGET DA REVOLVER

Postwar version of the 1921 Model .44 with 4-, 5- or 6.5-inch ribbed bbl., redesigned hammer, micrometer click rear sight. Matte or polished blue finish. Made from 1950-67. Model 24 reintroduced in 1983 only.

**Model 24 (1950)
w/4-inch bbl. . . . . NiB $1068 Ex $893 Gd $604**
**Model 24 (1950)
w/5-inch bbl. . . . . NiB $1081 Ex $908 Gd $620**
**Model 24 (1950)
w/6.5-inch bbl. . . . . NiB $775 Ex $651 Gd $445**
**Model 24 (1950) w/polished
blue finish, add 20%**
**Model 24 (1950)
w/nickel finish, add. 50%**
**Model 24
.44 Target reintroduced
(7,500 produced in 1983-84)**
Model 24 (w/4-inch bbl.) . . . . NiB $511 Ex $486 Gd $383
Model 24 (w/6.5-inch bbl.). . . . . NiB $460 Ex $434 Gd $341
**Model 24-3 .44
Lew Horton Special (produced in 1983)**
Model 24-3 (w/3-inch bbl.). . . . . NiB $439 Ex $383 Gd $305

MODEL .25 1955 .45 TARGET DA REVOLVER
Same as 1950 Model .44 Target, but chambered for .45 ACP, .45 Auto Rim or .45 LC w/4-, 6- or 6.5-inch bbl. Made from 1955 to 1991 in several variations. Note: In 1961, the .45 ACP was designated Model .25-2, and in 1978 the .45 LC was designated Model .25-5.
Model 25 1955 .45 Target
Model 25 (.45 ACP w/4- or 6-inch bbl.) . . . . . . NiB $510 Ex $459 Gd $253
Model 25 (.45 ACP w/6.5-inch pinned bbl.) . . . NiB $713 Ex $613 Gd $407
Model 25 (.45 LC early production) . . . . NiB $1445 Ex $1291 Gd $673
Model 25-2 .45 ACP
Model 25 (w/3-inch bbl., Lew Horton Special) NiB $557 Ex $505 Gd $428
Model 25 (w/4-inch bbl.). . . . . NiB $512 Ex $358 Gd $297
Model 24-3 (w/6.5-inch bbl.) . . . . NiB $525 Ex $428 Gd $305
Model 25-5 .45 LC
Model 25 (w/4-inch bbl.). . . . . NiB $512 Ex $418 Gd $297
Model 24-3 (w/6.5-inch bbl.) . . . . NiB $551 Ex $449 Gd $319

MODEL 26 1950 .45 LIGHT TARGET DA REVOLVER
Similar to 1950 Model Target except w/lighter bbl. Note: Lighter profile was not well received. (Only 2768 produced)
Model 26 (.45 ACP or .45 Auto Rim
w/6.5-inch bbl.). . . . . NiB $839 Ex $726 Gd $329
Model 26 (.45 LC, < 200 produced) . . . . NiB $2452 Ex $2112 Gd $923
W/4- or 5-inch bbl., add. 25%

MODEL 27 .357 MAGNUM DA
Caliber: .357 Magnum. Six-round cylinder, bbl. lengths: 3.5-, 4-, 5-, 6-, 6.5-and 8.38-inches, 11.38 inches overall (with 6-inch bbl.). Weight: 44 oz. (with 6-inch bbl.). Adj. target sights, Baughman quick-draw ramp front sight on 3.5-inch bbl., Blued or nickel finish. Checkered walnut grips. Made from 1935-94. Note: Until 1938, the .357 Magnum was custom made in any barrel length from 3.5-inch to 8.75-inch. Each of these revolvers was accompanied by a registration certificate and has its registration number stamped on the inside of the yoke. Postwar magnums have a redesigned hammer w/shortened fall and the new S&W micrometer click rear sight.
Prewar registered model
(Reg number on yoke) . . . . NiB $1351 Ex $1095 Gd $767
Prewar model without registration number . . . NiB $434 Ex $352 Gd $254
Early model w/pinned bbl., recessed cyl.. . . . . . NiB $474 Ex $383 Gd $275
Late model w/8.38-inch bbl. . . . . NiB $443 Ex $360 Gd $262
Late model, w/3.5-5-inch bbl. . . . . NiB $481 Ex $419 Gd $290
Late model, other bbl. lengths. . . . . NiB $481 Ex $419 Gd $290

MODEL 28 HIGHWAY PATROLMAN
Caliber: .357 Magnum. Six-round cylinder, bbl. lengths: 4- or 6-inches, 11.25 inches overall (with 6-inch bbl.). Weight: 44 oz. (with 6-inch bbl.). Adj.rear sight, ramp front. Blued finish. Checkered walnut grips, Magna or target type. Made from 1954-86.
Prewar registered model
(reg number on yoke) . . . . NiB $1349 Ex $1093 Gd $763
Prewar model without registration number . . . NiB $973 Ex $784 Gd $555
Early model w/pinned bbl.,
recessed cylinder, 5-screws . . . . NiB $413 Ex $365 Gd $305
Late model, all bbl. lengths . . . . NiB $329 Ex $293 Gd $247

MODEL 29 .44 MAGNUM DA REVOLVER
Caliber: .44 Magnum. Six-round cylinder. bbl., lengths: 4-, 5-, 6.5-, 8.38-inches. 11.88 inches overall (with 6.5-inch bbl.). Weight: 47 oz. (with 6.5-inch bbl.). Click adj. rear sight, ramp front. Blued or nickel finish. Checkered Goncalo Alves target grips. Made from 1956-98.
Early Production Standard Series (disc. 1983)
3-Screw model (1962-83) . . . . NiB $717 Ex $614 Gd $357
4-Screw model (1957-61) . . . . NiB $764 Ex $717 Gd $486
5-Screw model (1956-57) . . . . NiB $981 Ex $795 Gd $556
W/5-inch bbl., 3- or 4-screw models, add 95%

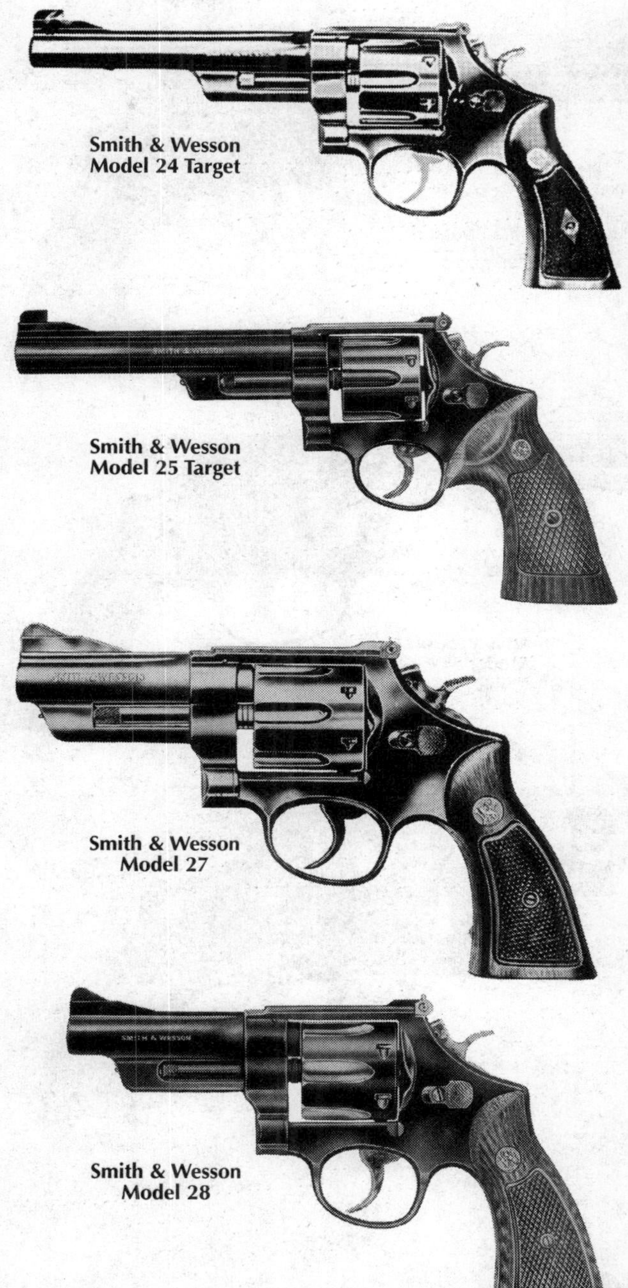
Smith & Wesson Model 24 Target

Smith & Wesson Model 25 Target

Smith & Wesson Model 27

Smith & Wesson Model 28

Late Production standard series (disc. 1998)
Model 29 (w/4- or 6.5-inch bbl.) . . . . NiB $489 Ex $400 Gd $287
Model 29 (w/3-inch bbl., Lew Horton Special) . . NiB $483 Ex $405 Gd $349
Model 29 (w/8.38-inch bbl.) . . . . NiB $542 Ex $439 Gd $352
Model 29 Classic (w/5- or 6.5-inch bbl.) . . . . . NiB $534 Ex $431 Gd $323
Model 29 Classic (w/8.38-inch bbl.) . . . . NiB $542 Ex $445 Gd $352
Model 29 Classic DX (w/6.5-inch bbl.). . . . . . . NiB $694 Ex $591 Gd $359
Model 29 Classic DX (w/8.38-inch bbl.) . . . . . NiB $697 Ex $584 Gd $362
Model 29 Magna Classic
(w/7.5-inch ported bbl.) . . . . NiB $937 Ex $809 Gd $469
Model 29 Silhouette (w/10.63-inch bbl.) . . . . . NiB $620 Ex $543 Gd $361

Smith & Wesson
Model 29

Smith & Wesson
Model 31

Smith & Wesson
Model 32

Smith & Wesson
Model 34

MODEL 30 .32 HAND EJECTOR DA REVOLVER . . . . NiB $335 Ex $294 Gd $206
Caliber: .32 S&W Long. Six-round cylinder, bbl. lengths: 2- (intro. 1949), 3-, 4- and 6-inches, 8 inches overall (with 4-inch bbl.). Weight: 18 oz. (with 4-inch bbl.). Fixed sights. Blued or nickel finish. Round, checkered walnut or hard rubber grips. Made from 1903-76.

MODELS 31 & 33 REGULATION POLICE DA REVOLVER
Same basic type as .32 Hand Ejector except has square buttgrips. Calibers: .32 S&W Long (Model 31) .38 S&W (Model 33). Six-round cylinder in .32 cal., 5-round in .38 caliber. Bbl., lengths: 2- (intro. 1949), 3-, 4- and 6-inches in .32 cal., 4-inch only in .38 cal., 8.5 inches overall (with 4-inch bbl.). Weight: 18 oz. (.38 cal. w/4-inch bbl.), 18.75 oz. (.32 cal. w/4-inch bbl.). Fixed sights. Blued or nickel finish. Checkered walnut grips. Made from 1917. Model 33 disc. in 1974; Model 31 disc. in 1992.
Model 31 . . . . NiB $325 Ex $268 Gd $206
Model 33 . . . . NiB $361 Ex $309 Gd $206

.32 DOUBLE-ACTION REVOLVER . . . . NiB $474 Ex $427 Gd $185
Hinged frame. Caliber: .32 S&W. Five-round cylinder, bbl. lengths: 3-, 3.5- and 6-inches. Fixed sights. Blued or nickel finish. Hard rubber grips. Made from 1880-1919. Note: Value shown applies generally to the several varieties. Exception is the rare first issue of 1880 (identified by squared sideplate and serial no. 1 to 30) valued up to $2,500.

MODEL .32 TERRIER DA . . . . NiB $376 Ex $263 Gd $165
Caliber: .38 S&W. Five-round cylinder, 2-inch bbl., 6.25 inches overall. Weight: 17 oz. Fixed sights. Blued or nickel finish. Checkered walnut or hard rubber grips. Built on .32 Hand Ejector frame. Made from 1936-74.

.32-20 MILITARY & POLICE DA . . .NiB $438 Ex $309 Gd $242
Same as M & P 38 except chambered for .32-20 Winchester cartridge. First intro. in the 1899 model, M & P revolvers were produced in this caliber until about 1940. Values same as M & P .38 models.

MODEL 34 1953 .22/.32 KIT GUN. . . . . NiB $337 Ex $270 Gd $208
Same general specifications as previous .22/.32 Kit Gun except w/2-inch or 4-inch bbl. and round or square grips, blued or nickel finish. Made from 1936-91.

MODEL 35 1953 .22/.32 TARGET. . . . . NiB $476 Ex $347 Gd $244
Same general specifications as previous model .22/.32 Target except has micrometer-click rear sight. Magna type target grips. Weight: 25 oz. Made from 1953-74.

MODEL 36 CHIEFS SPECIAL DA
Based on .32 Hand Ejector w/frame lengthened to permit longer cylinder for .38 Special cartridge. Caliber: .38 Special. Five-round cylinder, bbl. lengths: 2- or 3-inches, 6.5 inches overall (with 2-inch bbl.). Weight: 19 oz. Fixed sights. Blued or nickel finish. Checkered walnut grips, round or square butt. Made from 1952 to date.
Blued model . . . . NiB $337 Ex $270 Gd $193
Nickel model. . . . . NiB $345 Ex $282 Gd $205
Early model (5-screw, small trigger guard, SN 1-2500) . . . . NiB $417 Ex $341 Gd $237

MODEL 37 AIRWEIGHT
CHIEFS SPECIAL . . . . NiB $460 Ex $332 Gd $229
Same general specifications as standard Chiefs Special except has light alloy frame, weight: 12.5 oz. w/2-inch bbl., blued finish only. Made from 1954 to date.

MODEL 38 BODYGUARD AIRWEIGHT DA REVOLVER
Shrouded hammer. Light alloy frame. Caliber: .38 Special. Five-round cylinder, 2- or 3-inch bbl., 6.38 inches overall (w/2-inch bbl). Weight: 14.5 oz. Fixed sights. Blued or nickel finish. Checkered walnut grips. Made from 1955-98.
Blued model . . . . NiB $395 Ex $303 Gd $210
Nickel model. . . . . NiB $411 Ex $318 Gd $226
Early model (pinned & recessed, pre-1981) . . . . NiB $357 Ex $292 Gd $210

.38 DA REVOLVER. . . . . NiB $555 Ex $400 Gd $241
Hinged frame. Caliber: .38 S&W. Five-round cylinder, bbl. lengths: 4-, 4.25-, 5-, 6-, 8- and 10-inch. Fixed sights. Blued or nickel finish. Hard rubber grips. Made from 1880-1911. Note: Value shown applies generally to the several varieties. Exceptions are the first issue of 1880 (identified by squared sideplate and serial no. 1 to 4,000) and the 8- and 10-inch bbl. models of the third issue (1884-95).

MODEL .38 HAND EJECTOR DA
Military & Police — First Model. Resembles Colt New Navy in general appearance, lacks bbl., lug and locking bolt common to all later S&W hand ejector models. Caliber: .38 Long Colt. Six-round cylinder, bbl. lengths: 4-, 5-, 6- and 6.5-inch, 11.5 inches overall (with 6.5-inch bbl.). Fixed sights. Blued or nickel finish. Round, checkered walnut or hard rubber grips. Made from 1899-1902.
Standard model (civilian issue) . . . . NiB $721 Ex $618 Gd $263
Army Model (marked U.S. Army Model, 1000 issued) . . . . . NiB $2025 Ex $1716 Gd $712
Navy Model (marked USN, 1000 issued) . . . . NiB $1505 Ex $1711 Gd $707

.38 MILITARY & POLICE TARGET DA . . . . NiB $659 Ex $504 Gd $257
Target version of the Military & Police w/standard features of that model. Caliber: .38 Special, six-inch bbl. Weight: 32.25 oz. Adj. target sights. Blued finish. Checkered walnut grips. Made from 1899-1940. For values, add $175 for corresponding M&P 38 models.

MODEL .38 PERFECTED DA . . . . . . NiB $865 Ex $556 Gd $247
Hinged frame. Similar to earlier .38 DA Model but heavier frame, side latch as in solid-frame models, improved lockwork. Caliber: .38 S&W. Five-round cylinder, bbl. lengths: 3.25, 4, 5 and 6 inches. Fixed sights. Blued or nickel finish. Hard rubber grips. Made from 1909-20.

MODEL .40 CENTENNIAL DA HAMMERLESS REVOLVER. . . . . NiB $523 Ex $472 Gd $302
Similar to Chiefs Special but has Safety Hammerless-type mechanism w/grip safety. Two-inch bbl. Weight: 19 oz. Made from 1953-74.

MODEL 42 CENTENNIAL AIRWEIGHT
Same as standard Centennial model except has light alloy frame, weight: 13 oz. Made from 1954-74.
Blued model . . . . NiB $527 Ex $476 Gd $306
Nickel model. . . . . NiB $1084 Ex $1032 Gd $620

MODEL 43 1955 .22/.32 KIT GUN AIRWEIGHT . . . . NiB $476 Ex $398 Gd $229
Same as Model 34 Kit Gun except has light alloy frame, square grip. Furnished w/3.5-inch bbl., weight: 14.25 oz. Made from 1954-74.

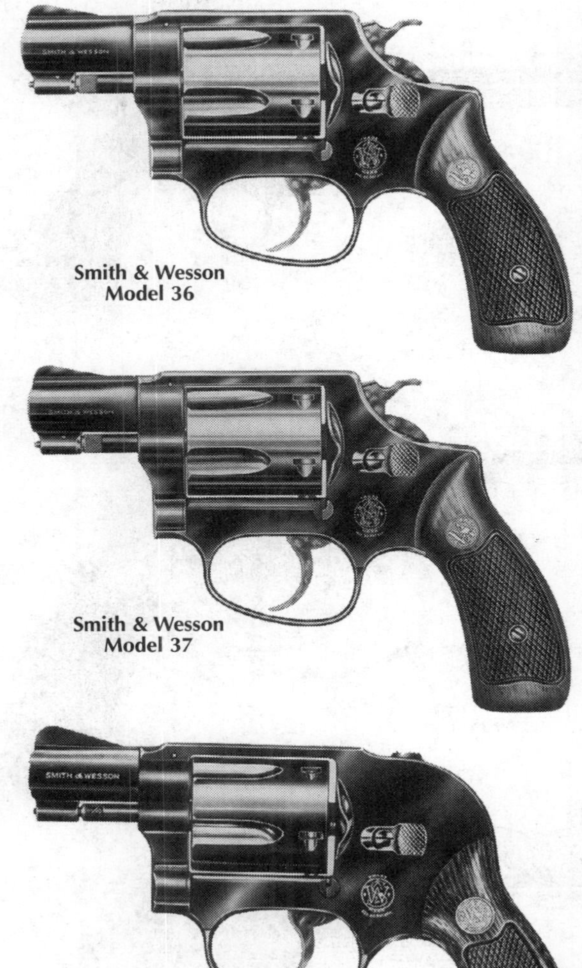
Smith & Wesson Model 36

Smith & Wesson Model 37

Smith & Wesson Model 38 Bodyguard Airweight

MODEL 44 1926 MILITARY DA REVOLVER
Same as the early New Century model with extractor rod casing but lacking the "Triple Lock" feature. Caliber: .44 S&W Special. Six-round cylinder, bbl. lengths: 4, 5 and 6.5 inches, 11.75 inches overall (with 6.5-inch bbl.). Weight: 39.5 oz. (with 6.5-inch bbl.). Fixed sights. Blued or nickel finish. Checkered walnut grips. Made from 1926-41.
Standard model . . . . NiB $947 Ex $768 Gd $539
Target model w/6.5-inch bbl., target sights, blued . . . . NiB $3906 Ex $3146 Gd $2174

.44 AND .38 DA REVOLVERS
Also called Wesson Favorite (lightweight model), Frontier (caliber .44-40). Hinged frame. Six-round cylinder. Calibers: .44 S&W Russian, .38-40, .44-40. Bbl. lengths: 4-, 5-, 6- and 6.5-inch. Weight: 37.5 oz. (with 6.5-inch bbl.). Fixed sights. Blued or nickel finish. Hard rubber grips. Made from 1881-1913, Frontier disc. 1910.
Standard model, .44 Russian . . . NiB $4797 Ex $2119 Gd $862
Standard model, .38-40. . . . . NiB $4797 Ex $2119 Gd $862
Frontier model. . . . . NiB $4797 Ex $2119 Gd $862
Favorite model . . . . NiB $10,300 Ex $8240 Gd $2884

Smith & Wesson
Model 48

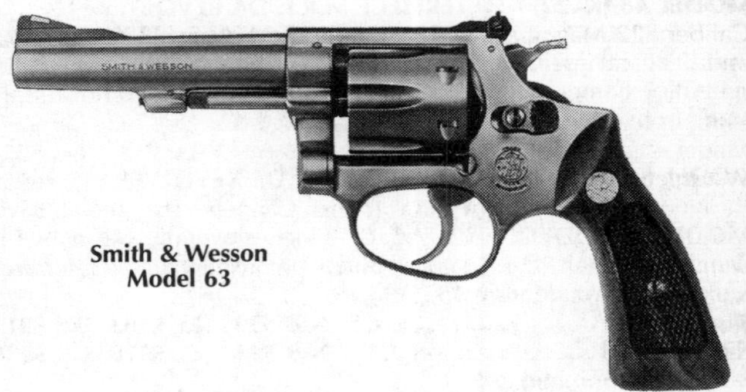

Smith & Wesson
Model 63

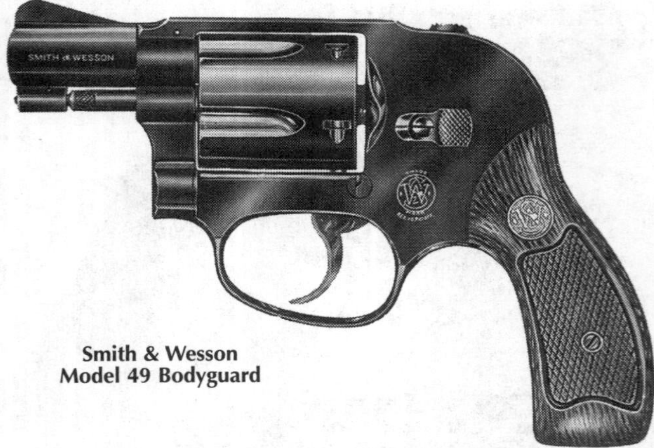

Smith & Wesson
Model 49 Bodyguard

Smith & Wesson
Model 64

Smith & Wesson
Model 57

Smith & Wesson
Model 60

.44 HAND EJECTOR MODEL DA REVOLVER
First Model, New Century, also called "Triple Lock" because of its third cylinder lock at the crane. Six-round cylinder. Calibers: .44 S&W Special, .450 Eley, .455 Mark II. Bbl. lengths: 4-, 5-, 6.5- and 7.5-inch. Weight: 39 oz. (with 6.5-inch bbl.). Fixed sights. Blued or nickel finish. Checkered walnut grips. Made 1907-66.
Second Model is basically the same as New Century except crane lock ("Triple Lock" feature) and extractor rod casing eliminated. Calibers: .44 S&W Special .44-40 Win. .45 Colt. Bbl. lengths: 4-, 5-, 6.5- and 7.5-inch; 11.75 inches overall (with 6.5-inch bbl.). Weight: 38 oz. (with 6.5-inch bbl.). Fixed sights. Blued or nickel finish. Checkered walnut grips. Made from 1915-37.
First Model series w/triple lock (1907-15)
Standard model,
.44 S&W Special . . . . NiB $2440 Ex $2028 Gd $962
Standard model w/
special calibers . . . . NiB $2440 Ex $2028 Gd $972
British 455
Target model . . . . NiB $3401 Ex $3143 Gd $964
Second Model series w/o triple lock (1915-37)
Standard model,
.44 S&W Special . . . . NiB $1818 Ex $1638 Gd $803
Standard model
w/special calibers . . . . NiB $2420 Ex $2008 Gd $942
Third Model series (see S&W Model .44/1926)
Fourth Model series (see S&W Model .44/1950)

.44 HAND EJECTOR,
SECOND MODEL
DA REVOLVER. . . . . NiB $741 Ex $659 Gd $345
Basically the same as New Century except crane lock ("Triple Lock" feature) and extractor rod casing eliminated. Calibers: .44 S&W Special .44-40 Win. .45 Colt. Bbl. lengths: 4-, 5-, 6.5- and 7.5-inches, 11.75 inches overall (with 6.5-inch bbl.). Weight: .38 oz. (with 6.5-inch bbl.). Fixed sights. Blued or nickel finish. Checkered walnut grips. Made from 1915-37.

MODEL 48 (K-.22) MASTERPIECE M.R.F. DA REVOLVER
Caliber: .22 Mag. and .22 RF. Six-round cylinder, bbl. lengths: 4, 6 and 8.38 inches, 11.13 inches overall (w/ 6-inch bbl.). Weight: 39 oz. Adj. rear sight, ramp front. Made from 1959-86.
Model 48 (4- or 6-inch bbl.) . . . . . . NiB $311 Ex $283 Gd $208
Model 48 (8.38-inch bbl.) . . . . NiB $347 Ex $327 Gd $224
W/target options TH & TT, add $50

MODEL 49 BODYGUARD
Same as Model 38 Bodyguard Airweight except has steel frame, weight: 20.5 oz. Made from 1959-96.
Blued model . . . . NiB $337 Ex $296 Gd $203
Nickel model. . . . . NiB $363 Ex $322 Gd $219

MODEL 51 1960 .22/.32 KIT GUN . . . . . . NiB $450 Ex $398 Gd $270
Same as Model 34 Kit Gun except chambered for .22 WMR 3.5-inch bbl., weight: 24 oz. Made from 1960-74.

MODEL 53 .22 MAGNUM DA
Caliber: .22 Rem. Jet C.F. Magnum. Six-round cylinder (inserts permit use of .22 Short, Long, or LR cartridges). Bbl. lengths: 4, 6, 8.38 inches, 11.25 inches overall (with 6-inch bbl.). Weight: 40 oz. (with 6-inch bbl.). Micrometer-click rear sight ramp front. Checkered walnut grips. Made from 1960-74.
Model 53 (4- or 6-inch bbl.) . . . . . . NiB $806 Ex $718 Gd $456
Model 53 (8.38-inch bbl.) . . . . NiB $827 Ex $749 Gd $466
W/target options TH & TT, add $35

MODEL 57 41 MAGNUM DA REVOLVER
Caliber: 41 Magnum. Six-round cylinder, bbl. lengths: 4-, 6-, 8.38-inch. Weight: 40 oz. (with 6-inch bbl.). Micrometer click rear sight, ramp front. Target grips of checkered Goncalo Alves. Made from 1964-93.
Model 57 (w/4- or 6-inch bbl.) . . . . NiB $394 Ex $297 Gd $214
Model 57 (w/8.63-inch bbl.). . . . . NiB $415 Ex $317 Gd $235
Model 57 (w/pinned bbl., recessed cylinder), add 10%

MODEL 58 41 MILITARY & POLICE DA REVOLVER . . . . NiB $546 Ex $496 Gd $340
Caliber: 41 Magnum. Six-round cylinder, 4-inch bbl. 9.25 inches overall. Weight: 41 oz. Fixed sights. Checkered walnut grips. Made from 1964-82.

MODEL 60 STAINLESS DA
Caliber: .38 Special or .357 Magnum. Five-round cylinder, bbl. lengths: 2, 2.1 or 3 inches, 6.5 or 7.5 inches overall. Weight: 19 to 23 oz. Square-notch rear sight, ramp front. Satin finish stainless steel. Made from 1965-96 (.38 Special) and from 1996 to date .357/.38).
.38 Special (disc. 1996). . . . . NiB $400 Ex $297 Gd $236
.357 Mag. . . . . NiB $452 Ex $344 Gd $256
Lady Smith (W/smaller grip) . . . . . . NiB $483 Ex $334 Gd $261

MODEL 63 (1977) KIT GUN DA . . . . NiB $416 Ex $292 Gd $241
Caliber: .22 LR. Six-round cylinder, 2- or 4-inch bbl., 6.5 or 8.5 inches overall. Weight: 19 to 24.5 oz. Adj. rear sight, ramp front. Stainless steel. Checkered walnut or synthetic grips.

MODEL 64 .38 M&P STAINLESS. . . . . NiB $442 Ex $313 Gd $246
Same as standard Model 10 except satin-finished stainless steel, square butt w/4-inch heavy bbl., or round butt w/2-inch bbl. Made from 1970 to date.

MODEL 65 .357 MILITARY/POLICE STAINLESS
Same as Model 13 except satin-finished stainless steel. Made from 1974 to date.
Model 65 M&P. . . . . NiB $447 Ex $297 Gd $251
Model 65 Lady Smith (W/smaller grip) . . . . . . NiB $483 Ex $349 Gd $272

Smith & Wesson
Model 66 Combat Magnum

Smith & Wesson
Model 67 Combat Masterpiece

MODEL 66 .357 COMBAT MAGNUM STAINLESS
Same as Model 19 except satin-finished stainless steel. Made from 1971 to date.
Model 66 (2.5-inch bbl.) . . . . NiB $517 Ex $373 Gd $265
Model 66 (3-inch bbl.) . . . . NiB $505 Ex $361 Gd $274
Model 66 (4-inch bbl.) . . . . NiB $505 Ex $361 Gd $274
Model 66 (6-inch bbl.) . . . . NiB $526 Ex $453 Gd $304
W/target options TH & TT, add $48

MODEL 67 .38 COMBAT MASTERPIECE STAINLESS. . . . . NiB $511 Ex $361 Gd $274
Same as Model 15 except satin-finished stainless steel available only w/4-inch bbl. Made from 1972-88 and from 1991 to date.

MODEL 68 .38 COMBAT MASTERPIECE STAINLESS. . . . . NiB $833 Ex $705 Gd $571
Same as Model 66 except w/4- or 6-inch bbl., chambered for .38 Special. Made to accommodate CA Highway Patrol because they were not authorized to carry .357 magnums. Made from 1976-83. (7500 produced)

125th Anniversary Commemorative
Issued to celebrate the 125th anniversary of the 1852 partnership of Horace Smith and Daniel Baird Wesson. Standard Edition is Model 25 revolver in .45 Colt w/6.5-inch bbl., bright blued finish, gold-filled bbl., roll mark "Smith & Wesson 125th Anniversary," sideplate marked w/gold-filled Anniversary seal, smooth Goncalo Alves grips, in presentation case w/nickel silver Anniversary medallion and book, "125 Years w/Smith & Wesson," by Roy Jinks. Deluxe Edition is same except revolver is Class A engraved w/gold-filled seal on sideplate, ivory grips, Anniversary medallion is sterling silver and book is leather bound. Limited to 50 units. Total issue is 10,000 units, of which 50 are Deluxe Edition and two are a Custom Deluxe Edition and not for sale. Made in 1977.
Standard edition . . . . NiB $831 Ex $678 Gd $482
Deluxe edition. . . . . NiB $2273 Ex $1836 Gd $1258

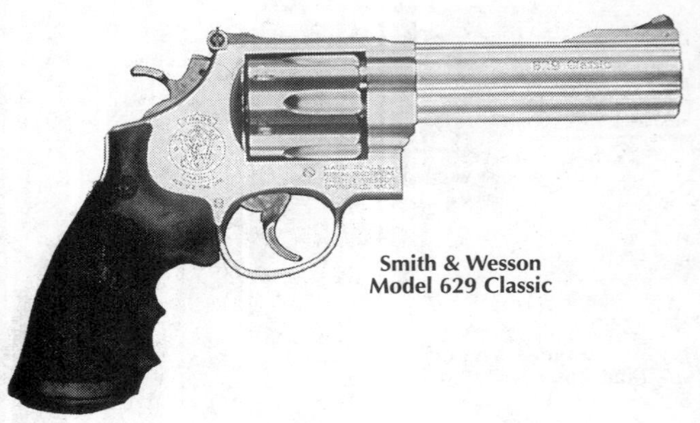
Smith & Wesson
Model 629 Classic

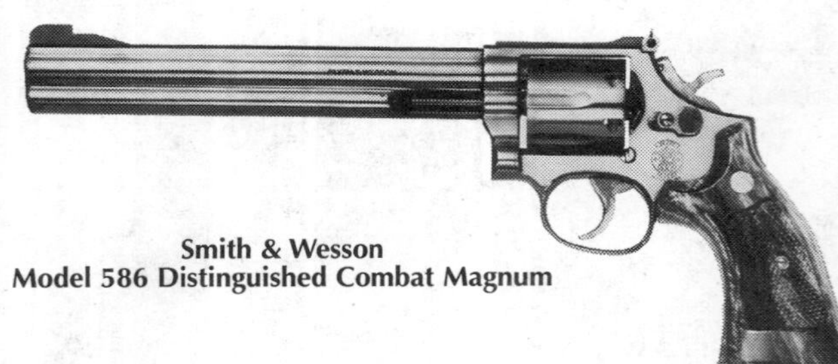
Smith & Wesson
Model 586 Distinguished Combat Magnum

Smith & Wesson
Model 625

Smith & Wesson
Model 629

317 AIRLITE DA REVOLVER
Caliber: .22 LR. Eight-round cylinder, 1.88- or 3-inch bbl., 6.3 or 7.2 inches overall. Weight: 9.9 oz. or 11 oz. Ramp front sight, notched frame rear. Aluminum, carbon fiber, stainless and titanium construction. Brushed aluminum finish. Synthetic or Dymondwood grips. Made from 1997 to date.
Model 317 (w/1.88-inch bbl.) . . . . NiB $482 Ex $353 Gd $271
Model 317 (w/3-inch bbl.) . . . . NiB $482 Ex $353 Gd $271
Model 317 (w/Dymondwood grips), add. $68

MODEL 520 DA REVOLVER. . . . . NiB $373 Ex $321 Gd $167
Caliber: .357 Mag. Six-round cylinder. N-Frame w/4-inch bbl. Weight: 40 oz. Fixed sights. In 1980, 3000 were made for the N.Y. State Police, but that agency did not purchase those firearms. (Sold commercially).

MODEL 547 DA REVOLVER. . . . . NiB $342 Ex $311 Gd $229
Caliber: 9mm. Six-round cylinder, bbl. length: 3 or 4 inches, 7.31 inches overall. Weight: 32 oz. Square-notch rear sight, ramp front. Disc. 1986.

MODEL 581 REVOLVER
Caliber: .357 Magnum. Bbl. lengths: 4 inches, weight: 34 oz. Serrated ramp front sight, square notch rear. Checkered walnut grips. Made from 1985-92.
Blued finish . . . . NiB $315 Ex $264 Gd $197
Nickel finish . . . . NiB $336 Ex $287 Gd $217

MODEL 586 DISTINGUISHED COMBAT MAGNUM
Caliber: .357 Magnum. Six-round cylinder, bbl. lengths: 4, 6 and 8.38 inches, overall length: 9.75 inches (with 4-inch bbl.). Weight: 42, 46, 53 oz., respectively. Red ramp front sight, micrometer-click adj. rear. Checkered grip. Blued or nickel finish. Made from 1980-99.
Model 586 (w/4- or 6-inch bbl.) . . . . NiB $418 Ex $331 Gd $228
Model 586 (w/8.63-inch bbl.) . . . . NiB $441 Ex $353 Gd $250
Model 586 (w/adjustable front sight), add. $35
Model 586 (w/nickel finish), add. $45

MODEL 610 DA REVOLVER . . . . . NiB $711 Ex $566 Gd $459
Similar to Model 625 except in caliber 10mm. Magna classic grips. Made from 1990-91 and from 1998 to date.

MODEL 617 DA REVOLVER
Similar to Model 17 except in stainless. Made from 1990 to date.
Semi-target model w/4- or 6-inch bbl. . . . . . . NiB $524 Ex $370 Gd $272
Target model w/6-inch bbl. . . . . NiB $524 Ex $370 Gd $272
Target model w/8.38-inch bbl. . . . . NiB $524 Ex $370 Gd $272
W/10-round cylinder, add. $94

MODEL 624 DOUBLE-ACTION REVOLVER
Same general specifications as Model 24 except satin finished stainless steel. Limited production of 10,000. Made from 1985-86.
Model 624 w/4-inch bbl. . . . . NiB $388 Ex $295 Gd $270
Model 624 w/6.5-inch bbl. . . . . NiB $413 Ex $310 Gd $284
Model 624 w/3-inch bbl., round butt (Lew Horton spec.) . . . . NiB $445 Ex $398 Gd $445

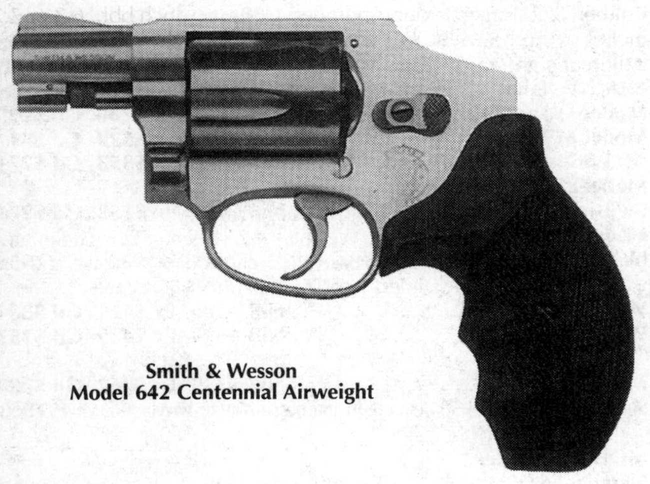
Smith & Wesson
Model 642 Centennial Airweight

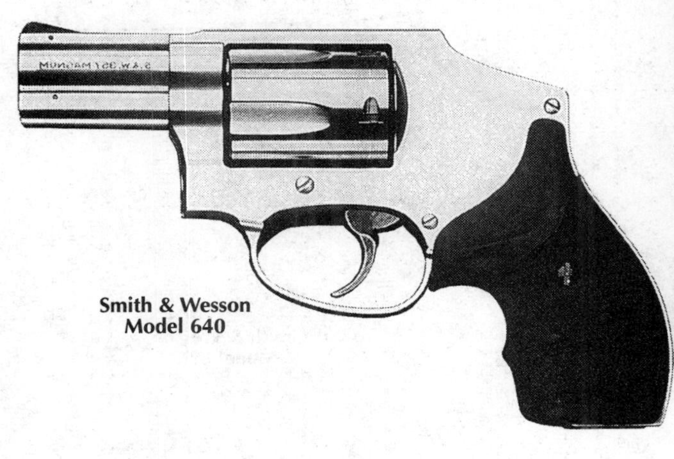
Smith & Wesson
Model 640

MODEL 625 DA REVOLVER . . . . . . NiB $534 Ex $390 Gd $282
Same general specifications as Model 25 except 3-, 4- or 5-inch bbl., round-butt Pachmayr grips and satin stainless steel finish. Made from 1989 to date.

MODEL 627 DA REVOLVER . . . . . . NiB $534 Ex $390 Gd $282
Same general specifications as Model 27 except satin stainless steel finish. Made from 1989-91.

MODEL 629 DA REVOLVER
Same as Model 29 in .44 Magnum except in stainless steel. Classic made from 1990 to date.
Model 629 (3-inch bbl., Backpacker) . . . . NiB $638 Ex $505 Gd $382
Model 629 (4- and 6-inch bbl.) . . . . NiB $662 Ex $528 Gd $402
Model 629 (8.38-inch bbl.) . . . . NiB $678 Ex $524 Gd $421
Model 629 Classic (5- and 6.5-inch bbl.) . . . . . NiB $665 Ex $516 Gd $402
Model 629 Classic (8.38-inch bbl.) . . . . NiB $691 Ex $541 Gd $428
Model 629 Classic DX (6.5-inch bbl.) . . . . NiB $866 Ex $701 Gd $572
Model 629 Classic DX (8.38-inch bbl.) . . . . . . NiB $904 Ex $739 Gd $610
Model 629 Magna Classic (w/7.5-inch ported bbl.) . . . . NiB $1062 Ex $862 Gd $607

MODEL 631 DA REVOLVER
Similar to Model 31 except chambered for .32 H&R Mag. Goncalo Alves combat grips. Made in 1991-92.
Fixed sights, 2-inch bbl. NiB $385 Ex $318 Gd $241
Adjustable sights, 4-inch bbl. . . . . NiB $389 Ex $318 Gd $228
Lady Smith, 2-inch bbl. NiB $411 Ex $339 Gd $267
Lady Smith, 2-inch bbl. (black stainless). . . . . . NiB $415 Ex $339 Gd $242

MODEL 632 CENTENNIAL DA
Same general specifications as Model 640 except chambered for .32 H&R Mag. 2- or 3-inch bbl., weight: 15.5 oz. Stainless slide w/alloy frame. Fixed sights. Santoprene combat grips. Made in 1991-92.
Model 632 w/2-inch bbl.. . . . . NiB $359 Ex $282 Gd $236
Model 632 w/3-inch bbl.. . . . . NiB $359 Ex $282 Gd $236

MODEL 637 CHIEFS SPECIAL AIRWEIGHT DA . . . . NiB $452 Ex $318 Gd $251
Same general specifications as Model 37 except w/clear anodized fuse alloy frame and stainless cylinder. 560 made in 1991 and reintroduced in 1996.

MODEL 638 BODYGUARD AIRWEIGHT DA . . . . NiB $468 Ex $344 Gd $272
Same general specifications as Model .38 except w/clear anodized fuse alloy frame and stainless cylinder. 1200 made in 1989 and reintroduced in 1998.

MODEL 640 CENTENNIAL DA . . . . NiB $468 Ex $324 Gd $272
Caliber: .38 Special. Five-round cylinder, 2, 2.1 or 3-inch bbl., 6.31 inches overall. Weight: 20-22 oz. Fixed sights. Stainless finish. Smooth hardwood service grips. Made from 1990 to date.

MODEL 642 CENTENNIAL AIRWEIGHT DA REVOLVER
Same general specifications as Model 640 except w/stainless steel/aluminum alloy frame and finish. Weight 15.8 oz. Santoprene combat grips. Made from 1990-93 and reintroduced 1996.
Model 642 Centennial . . . . NiB $468 Ex $344 Gd $262
Model 642 Lady Smith (W/smaller grip). . . . . NiB $468 Ex $344 Gd $262

MODEL 648 DA REVOLVER. . . . . NiB $392 Ex $289 Gd $233
Same general specifications as Models 17/617 except in stainless and chambered for .22 Mag. Made from 1990-93.

MODEL 649 BODYGUARD DA. . . . . NiB $493 Ex $344 Gd $262
Caliber: .38 Special. Five-round cylinder, bbl. length: 2 inches, 6.25 inches overall. Weight: 20 oz. Square-notch rear sight ramp front. Stainless frame and finish. Made from 1986 to date.

MODEL 650 REVOLVER. NiB $281 Ex $230 Gd $220
Caliber: .22 Mag. Six-round cylinder, 3-inch bbl., 7 inches overall. Weight: 23.5 oz. Serrated ramp front sight, fixed square-notch rear. Round butt, checkered walnut monogrammed grips. Stainless steel finish. Made from 1983-86.

Smith & Wesson Model 696

Smith & Wesson Model K-22 Outdoorsman

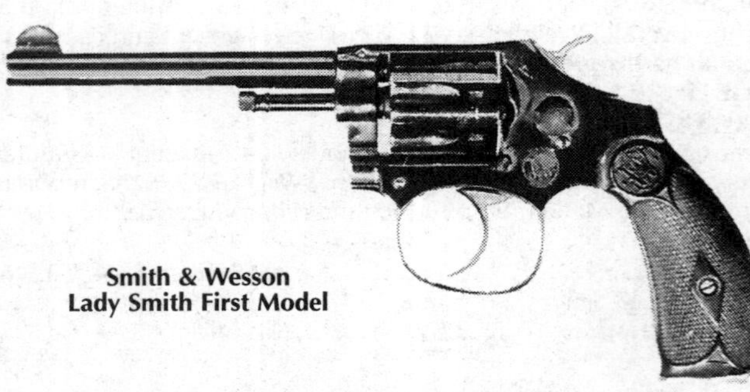
Smith & Wesson Lady Smith First Model

Smith & Wesson Lady Smith Second Model

MODEL 651 STAINLESS DA

Caliber: .22 Mag. Rimfire. Six-round cylinder, bbl. length: 3 and 4 inches, 7 and 8.63 inches, respectively, overall. Weight: 24.5 oz. Adj. rear sight, ramp front. Made from 1983-87 and from 1990-98. Note: Optional .22 LR cylinder available during early production.

Model 651 w/3- or 4-inch bbl. . . . . NiB $395 Ex $286 Gd $225
Model 651 w/extra cylinder . . . . . . NiB $603 Ex $520 Gd $417

MODEL 657 REVOLVER

Caliber: 41 Mag. Six-round cylinder. Bbl. lengths: 4, 6 or 8.4 inches; 9.6, 11.4, and 13.9 inches overall. Weight: 44.2, 48 and 52.5 oz. Serrated black ramp front sight on ramp base click rear, adj. for windage and elevation. Satin finished stainless steel. Made from 1986 to date.

W/4- or 6-inch bbl. . . . . NiB $586 Ex $421 Gd $334
W/8.4-inch bbl. . . . . NiB $603 Ex $439 Gd $351

MODEL 681 . . . . NiB $359 Ex $267 Gd $230

Same as S&W Model 581 except in stainless finish only. Made from 1991-93.

MODEL 686

Same as S&W Model 586 Distinguished Combat Magnum except in stainless finish w/additional 2.5-inch bbl. Made from 1991 to date.

Model 686 (w/2.5-inch bbl.). . . . . NiB $524 Ex $395 Gd $365
Model 686 (w/4- or 6-inch bbl.). . . . . NiB $550 Ex $421 Gd $390
Model 686 (w/8.63-inch bbl.). . . . . NiB $581 Ex $452 Gd $442
Model 686 (w/adjustable front sight), add. $35

MODEL 686 PLUS

Same as standard Model 686 Magnum except w/7-round cylinder and 2.5-, 4- or 6-inch bbl. Made from 1996 to date.

Model 686 Plus (w/2.5-inch bbl.) . . . . NiB $540 Ex $375 Gd $292
Model 686 Plus (w/4-inch bbl.) . . . . NiB $562 Ex $398 Gd $313
Model 686 Plus (w/6-inch bbl.) . . . . NiB $453 Ex $370 Gd $263

MODEL 696 . . . . NiB $535 Ex $359 Gd $292

Caliber: .44 S&W Special. L-Frame w/five-round cylinder, 3-inch shrouded bbl., 8.38 inches overall. Weight: 48 oz. Red ramp front sight, micrometer-click adj. rear. Checkered synthetic grip. Satin stainless steel. Made from 1997 to date.

MODEL 940 CENTENNIAL DA . . . . NiB $435 Ex $306 Gd $260

Same general specifications as Model 640 except chambered for 9mm. Two- or 3-inch bbl., Weight: 23-25 oz. Santoprene combat grips. Made from 1991 to date.

MODEL 1891 SA REVOLVER

Hinged frame. Caliber: .38 S&W. Five-round cylinder, bbl. lengths: 3.25, 4, 5 and 6-inches. Fixed sights. Blued or nickel finish. Hard rubber grips. Made 1891-1911. Note: Until 1906, an accessory single-shot target bbl. (see Model 1891 Single-Shot Target Pistol) was available for this revolver.

Revolver only. . . . . NiB $2449 Ex $1780 Gd $883
Set w/.22 single-shot bbl. . . . . . NiB $3170 Ex $2140 Gd $1625

1917 ARMY DA REVOLVER

Caliber: .45 Automatic, using 3-cartridge half-moon clip or .45 Auto Rim, without clip. Six-round cylinder, 5.5-inch bbl., 10.75 inches overall. Weight: 36.25 oz. Fixed sights. Blued finish (blue-black finish on commercial model, brush polish on military). Checkered walnut grips (commercial model, smooth on military). Made under U.S. Government contract 1917-19 and produced commercially 1919-1941. Note: About 175,000 of these revolvers were produced during WW I. The DCM sold these to NRA members during the 1930s at $16.15 each.

Commercial model . . . . NiB $708 Ex $554 Gd $333
Military model. . . . . NiB $863 Ex $657 Gd $266

K-22 MASTERPIECE DA. . . . . NiB $1292 Ex $1137 Gd $674
Improved version of K-22 Outdoorsman w/same specifications but w/micrometer-click rear sight, short action and antibacklash trigger. Fewer than 1100 manufactured in 1940.

K-22 OUTDOORSMAN DA. . . . . . . NiB $627 Ex $550 Gd $329
Design based on the .38 Military & Police Target. Caliber: .22 LR. Six-round cylinder, 11.13 inches overall. Weight: 35 oz. Adj. target sights. Blued finish. Checkered walnut grip. Made from 1931-40.

K32 AND K38 HEAVY MASTERPIECES
Same as K32 and K38 Masterpiece but w/heavy bbl. Weight: 38.5 oz. Made 1950-53. Note: All K32 and K38 revolvers made after September 1953 have heavy bbls. and the "Heavy Masterpiece" designation was disc. Values for Heavy Masterpiece models are the same as shown for Models 14 and 16. (See separate listing).

K-32 TARGET DA REVOLVER . . . . NiB $1445 Ex $1178 Gd $827
Same as .38 Military & Police Target except chambered for .32 S&W Long cartridge, slightly heavier bbl., weight: 34 oz. Only 98 produced. Made from 1938-40.

LADY SMITH (MODEL M HAND EJECTOR) DA REVOLVER
Caliber: .22 LR. Seven-round cylinder, bbl. length: 2.25-, 3-, 3.5- and 6-inch (Third Model only), approximately 7 inches overall w/3.5-inch bbl., weight: About 9.5 oz. Fixed sights, adj. target sights available on Third Model. Blued or nickel finish. Round butt, hard rubber grips on First and Second models; checkered walnut or hard rubber square buttgrips on Third Model. First Model —1902-06: Cylinder locking bolt operated by button on left side of frame, no bbl., lug and front locking bolt. Second Model —1906-11: Rear cylinder latch eliminated, has bbl. lug, forward cylinder lock w/draw-bolt fastening. Third Model —1911-21: Same as Second Model except has square grips, target sights and 6-inch bbl. available. Note: Legend has it that a straight-laced D.B. Wesson ordered discontinuance of the Lady Smith when he learned of the little revolver's reputed popularity w/ladies of the evening. The story, which undoubtedly has enhanced the appeal of this model to collectors, is not true: The Lady Smith was disc. because of difficulty of manufacture and high frequency of repairs.
First model . . . . NiB $3004 Ex $1974 Gd $568
Second model . . . . NiB $2180 Ex $1665 Gd $548
Third model, w/fixed sights,
2.25- or 3.5-inch bbl. . . . . NiB $2180 Ex $1665 Gd $568
Third model, w/fixed sights,
6-inch bbl. . . . . NiB $2180 Ex $1639 Gd $548
Third model, w/adj. sights,
6-inch bbl. . . . . NiB $4150 Ex $1771 Gd $849

REGULATION POLICE
DA (I FRAME) . . . . NiB $670 Ex $547 Gd $391
Calibers: .32 S&W (6-round) or .38 S&W (5-round) built on .32 Hand Ejector frames. Two-, 3-, 3.25-, 4-, 4.25- or 6-inch bbl., weight: 20-24 oz. Fixed sights. Blue or nickel finish. Checkered walnut grips. Made 1917-57. Note: After 1957 "J" Frames replaced the older "I" Frames and designations changed to Model 31 and 33 respectively.
Regulation Police, .32 S&W. . . . . . . NiB $386 Ex $334 Gd $170
Regulation Police, .38 S&W. . . . . . . NiB $386 Ex $334 Gd $170

REGULATION POLICE TARGET DA
Target version of the Regulation Police w/standard features of that model. Calibers: .32 S&W Long or .38 S&W. 6-inch bbl., 10.25 inches overall. Weight: 20 oz. Adjustable target sights. Blue or nickel finish. Checkered walnut grips. Made from about 1917-57.
Regulation Police Target, .32 S&W . . . . NiB $730 Ex $628 Gd $319
Regulation Police Target, .38 S&W . . . . NiB $730 Ex $628 Gd $319

Smith & Wesson
Regulation Police Target

Smith & Wesson
Safety Hammerless

SAFETY HAMMERLESS
REVOLVER . . . . NiB $1308 Ex $896 Gd $407
Also called New Departure Double Action. Hinged frame. Calibers: .32 S&W, .38 S&W. Five-round cylinder, bbl. lengths: 2, 3- and 3.5-inch (.32 cal.) or 2-, 3.25-, 4-, 5- and 6-inch (.38 cal.); 6.75 inches overall (.32 cal. w/3-inch bbl.) or 7.5 inches (.38 cal. w/3.25-inch bbl.). Weight: 14.25 oz. (.32 cal. w/3-inch bbl.) or 18.25 oz. (.38 cal. 2.5-inch bbl.). Fixed sights. Blued or nickel finish. Hard rubber grips. Made from 1888-1937 (.32 cal.); 1887-1941 (.38 cal. w/various minor changes.)

TEXAS RANGER
COMMEMORATIVE. . . . . NiB $1308 Ex $1014 Gd $738
Issued to honor the 150th anniversary of the Texas Rangers. Model 19 .357 Combat Magnum w/4-inch bbl., sideplate stamped w/Texas Ranger Commemorative Seal, smooth Goncalo Alves grips. Special Bowie knife in presentation case. 8,000 sets made in 1973. Top value is for set in new condition.

SPHINX ENGINEERING SA. — Porrentruy, Switzerland

MODEL AT-380 DA PISTOL
Caliber: .380 ACP. 10-round magazine, 3.27- inch bbl., 6.03 inches overall. Weight: 25 oz. Stainless steel frame w/blued slide or Palladium finish. Slide latch w/ambidextrous magazine release. Imported from 1993-96.
Model AT-380 two-tone
(w/blued slide) . . . . NiB $491 Ex $429 Gd $327
Model AT-380 N/pall
(w/Palladium finish) . . . . NiB $563 Ex $502 Gd $400

NOTE: *The AT-88 pistol series was previously manufactured by ITM in Switzerland and imported by Action Arms before Sphinx-Muller resumed production of these firearms, now designated as the AT-2000 series.*

Springfield Armory
1911-A1 Post '90 Series Trophy Model

Springfield Armory
1911-A1 PDP Series Defender

Springfield Armory
1911-A1 Champion

Springfield Armory
1911-A1 Compact

Sphinx
Model AT2000S Scope Optional

MODEL AT2000S DA AUTOMATIC PISTOL

Calibers: 9mm Parabellum, .40 S&W. 15- or 11-round magazine respectively, 4.53-inch bbl., (S-standard), 3.66-inch bbl., (P-compact), 3.34-inch bbl., (H-subcompact), 8.25 inches overall. Weight: 36.5 oz. Fixed sights w/3-dot system. Stainless frame w/blued slide or Palladium finish. Ambidextrous safety. Checkered walnut or neoprene grips. Imported 1993-96.

Model AT2000S (standard) . . . . NiB $1051 Ex $832 Gd $526
Model AT2000P (compact) . . . . NiB $931 Ex $701 Gd $482
Model AT2000H (subcompact) . . . . NiB $931 Ex $701 Gd $482
.40 S&W, add $90
For Palladium finish (disc. 1994). . . . . . NiB $258 Ex $235 Gd $205

MODEL AT2000C/2000CS COMPETITOR

Similar to the Model AT2000S except also chambered for 9x21mm. 10-round magazine, 5.31-inch compensated bbl., 9.84 inches overall. Weight: 40.56 oz. Fully adjustable BoMar or ProPoint sights. Made from 1993-96.

Model 2000C (w/BoMar sight) . . . . NiB $1830 Ex $1361 Gd $928
Model 2000CS (w/ProPoint sight). . . . . . NiB $1830 Ex $1361 Gd $928

MODEL AT2000GM/GMS GRAND MASTER

Similar to the AT2000C except single action only w/square trigger guard and extended beavertail grip. Imported 1993-96.

Model 2000GM (w/BoMar sight) . . . . NiB $2368 Ex $1910 Gd $1324
Model 2000GMS (w/ProPoint sight). . . . . . NiB $2495 Ex $2012 Gd $1394

SPRINGFIELD, INC. — Geneseo, Illinois (Formerly Springfield Armory)

MODEL M1911 SERIES AUTO PISTOL

Springfield builds the "PDP" (Personal Defense Pistol) Series based on the self-loading M 1911-A1 pistol (military specifications model) as adopted for a standard service weapon by the U.S. Army. With enhancements and modifications they produce a full line of firearms including Ultra-Compacts, Lightweights, Match Grade and Competition Models. For values see specific models.

MODEL 1911-A1 GOVERNMENT

Calibers: 9mm Para., .38 Super, .40 S&W, 10mm or .45 ACP., 7-, 8-, 9- or 10-round magazine, 4- or 5-inch bbl., 8.5 inches overall. Weight: 36 oz. Fixed combat sights. Blued, Parkerized or Duo-Tone finish. Checkered walnut grips. Note: This is an exact duplicate of the Colt M1911-A1 that was used by the U.S. Armed Forces as a service weapon.

Blued finish . . . . NiB $452 Ex $421 Gd $330
Parkerized finish . . . . NiB $452 Ex $421 Gd $330

MODEL 1911-A1 (PRE '90 SERIES)

Calibers: 9mm Parabellum, .38 Super, 10mm, .45 ACP. Seven-, 8-, 9- or 10-round magazine, bbl. length: 3.63, 4, 4.25 or 5 inches, 8.5 inches overall. Weight: 36 oz. Fixed combat sights. Blued, Duo-Tone or Parkerized finish. Checkered walnut stocks. Made from 1985-90.

Government model (blued) . . . . NiB $450 Ex $409 Gd $328
Government model (Parkerized) . . . NiB $450 Ex $409 Gd $328
Bullseye model (wadcutter) . . . . . NiB $1514 Ex $1295 Gd $836
Combat Commander model (blued) . . . NiB $486 Ex $435 Gd $322
Combat Commander model (Parkerized) . . . . NiB $486 Ex $435 Gd $322
Commander model (blued) . . . . NiB $501 Ex $465 Gd $333
Commander model (Duo-Tone) . . . . NiB $501 Ex $496 Gd $363
Commander model (Parkerized) . . . NiB $501 Ex $465 Gd $333
Compact model (blued) . . . . NiB $532 Ex $496 Gd $328
Compact model (Duo-Tone) . . . . . . NiB $583 Ex $547 Gd $379
Compact model (Parkerized) . . . . . . NiB $501 Ex $465 Gd $297
Defender model (blued) . . . . NiB $567 Ex $521 Gd $363
Defender model (Parkerized) . . . . . NiB $537 Ex $487 Gd $328
Defender model (Custom Carry) . . . NiB $872 Ex $795 Gd $525
National Match model (Hardball) . NiB $852 Ex $7019 Gd $525
Trophy Master (Competition) . . . NiB $1394 Ex $1190 Gd $833
Trophy Master (Distinguished) . . NiB $2110 Ex $1778 Gd $1115
Trophy Master (Competition) . . . NiB $1765 Ex $1547 Gd $976

MODEL 1911-A1 (POST '90 SERIES)

SA linkless operating system w/steel or alloy frame. Calibers: 9mm Parabellum, .38 Super, .40 S&W, 10mm, .45 ACP. Seven-, 8-, 9- or 10-round magazine, bbl. length: 3.63, 4, 4.25 or 5 inches; 8.5 inches overall. Weight: 28 oz. to 36 oz. Fixed combat sights. Blued, Duo-Tone, Parkerized or stainless finish. Checkered composition or walnut stocks. Made from 1990 to date.

Mil-Spec model (blued) . . . . NiB $516 Ex $424 Gd $328
Mil-Spec model (Parkerized) . . . . . . NiB $516 Ex $424 Gd $328
Standard model (blued) . . . . NiB $507 Ex $414 Gd $295
Standard model (Parkerized) . . . . . . NiB $705 Ex $552 Gd $399
Standard model (stainless) . . . . NiB $730 Ex $577 Gd $450
Trophy model (blued) . . . . NiB $1044 Ex $845 Gd $488
Trophy model (Duo-Tone) . . . . NiB $1024 Ex $856 Gd $499
Trophy model (stainless) . . . . NiB $1086 Ex $918 Gd $561

MODEL 1911-A1 PDP SERIES

PDP Series (Personal Defense Pistol). Calibers: .38 Super, .40 S&W, .45 ACP. Seven-, 8-, 9-, 10-, 13- or 17-round magazine, bbl. length: 4, 5, 5.5 or 5.63 inches, 9 to 11 inches overall w/compensated bbl. Weight: 34.5 oz. to 42.8 oz. Post front sight, adjustable rear w/3-dot system. Blued, Duo-Tone, Parkerized or stainless finish. Checkered composition or walnut stocks. Made from 1991 to date.

Defender model (blued) . . . . NiB $917 Ex $800 Gd $509
Defender model (Duo-Tone) . . . . . . NiB $917 Ex $800 Gd $509
Defender model (Parkerized) . . . . . NiB $917 Ex $800 Gd $509
.45 ACP Champion Comp model (blued) . . . . NiB $789 Ex $590 Gd $381
.45 ACP Compact Comp HC model (blued) . . . . NiB $875 Ex $784 Gd $540
.38 Sup Factory Comp model (blued) . . . . NiB $845 Ex $754 Gd $509
.45 ACP Factory Comp model (blued) . . . . NiB $845 Ex $754 Gd $509
.38 Sup Factory Comp HC model (blued) . . . . NiB $845 Ex $754 Gd $509
.45 ACP Factory Comp HC model (blued) . . . . NiB $845 Ex $754 Gd $509

MODEL M1911-A1 CHAMPION

Calibers: .38 ACP, .45 ACP. Six- or 7-round magazine, 4-inch bbl.

Springfield Armory
M1911-A1 Ultra
Compact Parkerized

Weight: 26.5 to 33.4 oz. Low profile post front sight and drift adjustable rear w/3-dot sighting system. Commander-style hammer and slide. Checkered walnut grips. Blue, Bi-Tone, Parkerized or stainless finish. Made from 1992 to date.

.380 ACP standard (disc. 1995) . . . . NiB $424 Ex $348 Gd $246
.45 ACP Parkerized . . . . NiB $501 Ex $399 Gd $246
.45 ACP blued . . . . NiB $501 Ex $409 Gd $271
.45 ACP Bi-Tone (B/H Model) . . . . NiB $763 Ex $564 Gd $355
.45 ACP stainless . . . . NiB $768 Ex $559 Gd $457
.45 super tuned . . . . NiB $946 Ex $615 Gd $513

MODEL M1911-A1 COMPACT

Similar to the standard M1911 w/champion length slide on a steel or alloy frame w/a shortened grip. Caliber: .45 ACP. Six- or 7-round magazine (10+ law enforcement only), 4-inch bbl. weight: 26.5 to 32 oz. Low profile sights w/3-dot system. Checkered walnut grips. Matte blue, Duo-Tone or Parkerized finish. Made from 1991-96.

Compact Parkerized . . . . NiB $473 Ex $412 Gd $279
Compact blued . . . . NiB $541 Ex $479 Gd $347
Compact Duo-Tone . . . . NiB $473 Ex $412 Gd $279
Compact stainless . . . . NiB $796 Ex $618 Gd $541
Compact comp (ported) . . . . NiB $904 Ex $796 Gd $516
High capacity blue . . . . NiB $604 Ex $466 Gd $390
High capacity stainless . . . . NiB $644 Ex $567 Gd $429

MODEL M1911-A1 ULTRA COMPACT

Similar to M1911 Compact except chambered for .380 ACP or .45 ACP. 6- or 7-round magazine, 3.5-inch bbl., weight: 22 oz. to 30 oz. Matte Blue, Bi-Tone, Parkerized (military specifiactions) or stainless finish. Made from 1995 to date.

.380 ACP Ultra (disc. 1996) . . . . NiB $745 Ex $551 Gd $337
.45 ACP Ultra Parkerized . . . . NiB $745 Ex $551 Gd $337
.45 ACP Ultra blued . . . . NiB $745 Ex $551 Gd $337
.45 ACP Ultra Bi-Tone . . . . NiB $857 Ex $664 Gd $449
.45 ACP Ultra stainless . . . . NiB $827 Ex $602 Gd $500
.45 ACP ultra high capacity Parkerized . . . . NiB $817 Ex $602 Gd $373
.45 ACP ultra high capacity blue . . . . NiB $817 Ex $602 Gd $373
.45 ACP ultra high capacity stainless . . . . NiB $827 Ex $602 Gd $500
.45 ACP V10 ultra comp Parkerized . . . . NiB $771 Ex $562 Gd $347
.45 ACP V10 ultra comp blue . . . . . NiB $771 Ex $562 Gd $347
.45 ACP V10 ultra comp stainless . . NiB $827 Ex $602 Gd $500
.45 ACP V10 ultra super tuned . . . NiB $1015 Ex $862 Gd $505

Springfield Armory
M1911-A1 Ultra Compact Bi-Tone

Springfield Armory
M1911-A1 Ultra Compact Stainless

Springfield Armory
M1911-A1 Ultra Compact
Super Tuned

FIRECAT
AUTOMATIC PISTOL
Calibers: 9mm, .40 S&W. Eight-round magazine (9mm) or 7-round magazine (.40 S&W), 3.5-inch bbl., 6.5 inches overall. Weight: 25.75 oz. Fixed sights w/3-dot system. Checkered walnut grip. Matte blued finish. Made from 1991-93.
9mm . . . . NiB $549 Ex $477 Gd $324
.40 S&W . . . . NiB $549 Ex $477 Gd $324

Springfield Armory
P9 Combat

Springfield Armory Panther

PANTHER
AUTO PISTOL . . . . NiB $590 Ex $503 Gd $324
Calibers: 9mm, .40 S&W. 15-round magazine (9mm) or 11-round magazine (.40 S&W), 3.8-inch bbl., 7.5 inches overall. Weight: 28.95 oz. Blade front sight, rear adj. for windage w/3-dot system. Checkered walnut grip. Matte blued finish. Made from 1991-93.

MODEL P9 DA COMBAT SERIES
Calibers: 9mm, .40 S&W, .45 ACP. Magazine capacity: 15-round (9mm), 11-round (.40 S&W) or 10-round (.45 ACP), 3.66-inch bbl., (Compact and Sub-Compact), or 4.75-inch bbl., (Standard), 7.25 or 8.1 inches overall. Weight: 32 to 35 oz. Fixed sights w/3-dot system. Checkered walnut grip. Matte blued, Parkerized, stainless or Duo-Tone finish. Made from 1990-94.
Compact model (9mm,
Parkerized) . . . . NiB $483 Ex $426 Gd $289
Sub-Compact model (9mm,
Parkerized) . . . . NiB $523 Ex $467 Gd $330
Standard model (9mm,
Parkerized) . . . . NiB $503 Ex $426 Gd $289
W/blued finish, add $25
W/Duo-Tone finish, add $235
W/stainless finish, add $20
.40 S&W, add $35
.45 ACP add $95

MODEL P9 COMPETITION SERIES
Same general specifications as Model P9 except in target configuration w/5-inch bbl., (LSP Ultra) or 5.25-inch bbl. Factory Comp model w/dual port compensator system, extended safety and magazine release.
Factory Comp model
(9mm Bi-Tone)................ NiB $658 Ex $536 Gd $381
Factory Comp model
(9mm stainless)............... NiB $772 Ex $628 Gd $444
LSP Ultra model
(9mm Bi-Tone)................ NiB $607 Ex $496 Gd $354
LSP Ultra model
(9mm stainless)............... NiB $645 Ex $526 Gd $374
.40 S&W, .45 ACP: add $90

STALLARD ARMS — Mansfield, Ohio

See listings under Hi-Point.

STAR PISTOLS — Eibar, Spain Star, Bonifacio Echeverria, S.A.

MODEL 30M DA AUTO PISTOL ... NiB $399 Ex $343 Gd $261
Caliber: 9mm Para. 15-round magazine, 4.38-inch bbl., 8 inches overall. Weight: 40 oz. Steel frame w/combat features. Adj. sights. Checkered composition grips. Blued finish. Made from 1984-91.

MODEL 30PK DA AUTO PISTOL .... NiB $399 Ex $343 Gd $261
Same gen. specifications as Star Model 30M except 3.8-inch bbl., weight: 30 oz. Alloy frame. Made from 1984-89.

MODEL 31P DA AUTO PISTOL
Same general specifications as Model 30M except removable backstrap houses complete firing mechanism. Weight: 39.4 oz. Made from 1990-94.
Blued finish .... NiB $399 Ex $343 Gd $251
Starvel finish .... NiB $430 Ex $373 Gd $287

MODEL 31 PK DA AUTO PISTOL....... NiB $399 Ex $343 Gd $256
Same general specifications as Model 31P except w/alloy frame. Weight: 30 oz. Made from 1990-97.

MODEL A AUTOMATIC PISTOL ... NiB $373 Ex $322 Gd $196
Modification of the Colt Government Model .45 Auto, which it closely resembles, but lacks grip safety. Caliber: .38 Super. Eight-round magazine, 5-inch bbl., 8 inches overall. Weight: 35 oz. Fixed sights. Blued finish. Checkered grips. Made from 1934-97. (No longer imported.)

MODELS AS, BS, PS............ NiB $379 Ex $348 Gd $256
Same as Models A, B and P except have magazine safety. Made in 1975.

MODEL B .... NiB $373 Ex $297 Gd $185
Same as Model A except in 9mm Para. Made from 1934-75.

MODEL BKM................ NiB $358 Ex $317 Gd $215
Similar to Model BM except has aluminum frame weight: 25.6 oz. Made from 1976-92.

MODEL BKS STARLIGHT
AUTOMATIC PISTOL .... NiB $306 Ex $169 Gd $184
Light alloy frame. Caliber: 9mm Para. Eight-round magazine, 4.25-inch bbl., 7 inches overall. Weight: 25 oz. Fixed sights. Blued or chrome finish. Plastic grips. Made from 1970-81.

Star Model 30M

Star Model 30PK

Star Model AS

Star Model BKS

Star Model F

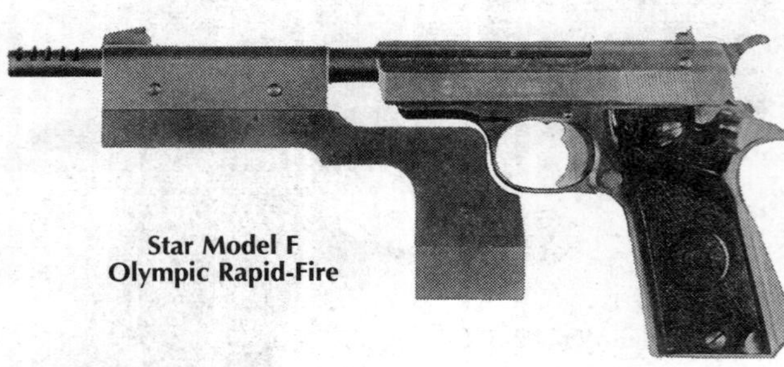
Star Model F
Olympic Rapid-Fire

Star Model FS

MODEL BM AUTOMATIC PISTOL
Caliber: 9mm. Eight-round magazine, 3.9-inch bbl., 6.95 inches overall. Weight: 34.5 oz. Fixed sights. Checkered walnut grips. Blued or Starvel finish. Made from 1976-92.
Blued finish . . . . NiB $320 Ex $279 Gd $187
Starvel finish . . . . NiB $354 Ex $313 Gd $222

MODEL CO POCKET AUTOMATIC PISTOL . . . . NiB $284 Ex $233 Gd $141
Caliber: .25 Automatic (6.35mm), 2.75-inch bbl., 4.5 inches overall. Weight: 13 oz. Fixed sights. Blued finish. Plastic grips. Made from 1941-57.

MODEL CU STARLET POCKET PISTOL . . . . NiB $269 Ex $233 Gd $141
Light alloy frame. Caliber: .25 Auto (6.35mm). Eight-round magazine, 2.38-inch bbl., 4.75 inches overall. Weight: 10.5 oz. Fixed sights. Blued or chrome-plated slide w/frame anodized in black, blue, green, gray or gold. Plastic grips. Made from 1957-97. (U.S. importation disc. 1968.)

MODEL F AUTOMATIC PISTOL . . . . NiB $364 Ex $262 Gd $135
Caliber: .22 LR. 10-round magazine, 4.5-inch bbl., 7.5 inches overall. Weight: 25 oz. Fixed sights. Blued finish. Plastic grips. Made from 1942-67.

MODEL F OLYMPIC RAPID-FIRE . . . . NiB $502 Ex $374 Gd $165
Caliber: .22 Short. Nine-round magazine, 7-inch bbl., 11.06 inches overall. Weight: 52 oz. w/weights. Adj. target sight. Adj. 3-piece bbl. weight. Aluminum alloy slide. Muzzle brake. Plastic grips. Made from 1942-67.

MODEL FM . . . . NiB $349 Ex $272 Gd $135
Similar to Model FR except has heavier frame w/web in front of trigger guard, 4.25-inch heavy bbl., Weight: 32 oz. Made from 1972-91.

MODEL FR . . . . NiB $374 Ex $272 Gd $135
Similar to Model F w/same general specifications but restyled, has slide stop and adj. rear sight. Made from 1967-72.

MODEL FRS. . . . . NiB $400 Ex $298 Gd $135
Same as Model FR except has 6-inch bbl., weight: 28 oz. Also avail. in chrome finish. Made from 1967-91.

MODEL FS. NiB $374 Ex $272 Gd $135
Same as regular Model F but w/6-inch bbl. and adj. sights. Weight: 27 oz. Made from 1942-67.

MODEL H . . . . NiB $410 Ex $298 Gd $135
Same as Model HN except .32 Auto (7.65mm), 7-round magazine, weight: 20 oz. Made from 1934-41.

MODEL HK LANCER AUTOMATIC PISTOL . . . . NiB $285 Ex $254 Gd $157
Similar to Starfire w/same general specifications except .22 LR. Made from 1955-68.

MODEL HN AUTOMATIC PISTOL . . . . NiB $423 Ex $311 Gd $143
Caliber: .380 Auto (9mm Short). Six-round magazine, 2.75-inch bbl., 5.56 inches overall. Weight: 20 oz. Fixed sights. Blued finish. Plastic grips. Made from 1934-41.

MODEL I AUTOMATIC PISTOL . . . . NiB $400 Ex $298 Gd $140
Caliber: .32 Auto (7.65mm). Nine-round magazine, 4.81-inch bbl., 7.5 inches overall. Weight: 24 oz. Fixed sights. Blued finish. Plastic grips. Made from 1934-36.

MODEL IN. . . . . .NiB $448 Ex $315 Gd $142
Same as Model I except caliber .380 Auto (9mm Short), 8-round magazine, weight: 24.5 oz. Made from 1934-36.

MODEL M MILITARY AUTOMATIC PISTOL . . . . NiB $372 Ex $321 Gd $204
Modification of the Colt Government Model .45 Auto, which it closely resembles, but without grip safety. Calibers: 9mm Bergmann (Largo), .45 ACP, 9mm Para. Eight-round magazine except 7-shot in .45 caliber, 5-inch bbl., 8.5 inches overall. Weight: 36 oz. Fixed sights. Blued finish. Checkered grips. Made from 1934-39.

MODELS M40, M43, M45 FIRESTAR AUTO PISTOLS
Calibers: 9mm, .40 S&W, .45 ACP. Seven-round magazine (9mm) or 6-round (other calibers). 3.4-inch bbl., 6.5 inches overall. Weight: 30.35 oz. Blade front sight, adj. rear w/3-dot system. Checkered rubber grips. Blued or Starvel finish. Made from 1990-97.
M40 blued (.40 S&W) . . . . NiB $338 Ex $292 Gd $190
M40 Starvel (.40 S&W) . . . . NiB $358 Ex $314 Gd $210
M43 blued (9mm) . . . . NiB $338 Ex $297 Gd $210
M43 Starvel (9mm) . . . . NiB $358 Ex $314 Gd $210
M45 blued (.45 ACP) . . . . NiB $368 Ex $338 Gd $210
M45 Starvel (.45 ACP) . . . . NiB $389 Ex $358 Gd $231

MEGASTAR AUTOMATIC PISTOL
Calibers: 10mm, .45 ACP. 12-round magazine, 4.6-inch bbl., 8.44 inches overall. Weight: 47.6 oz. Blade front sight, adj. rear. Checkered composition grip. finishes: Blued or Starvel. Made from 1992-97.
Blued finish, 10mm or .45 ACP . . . . NiB $501 Ex $424 Gd $422
Starvel finish, 10mm or .45 ACP . . . . NiB $531 Ex $454 Gd $352

MODEL P . . . . NiB $392 Ex $326 Gd $198
Same as Model A except caliber .45 Auto, has 7-round magazine. Made from 1934-75.

MODEL PD AUTOMATIC PISTOL
Caliber: .45 Auto. Six-round magazine, 3.75-inch bbl., 7 inches overall. Weight: 25 oz. Adj. rear sight, ramp front. Blued or Starvel finish. Checkered walnut grips. Made from 1975-92.
Blued finish . . . . NiB $389 Ex $333 Gd $210
Starvel finish . . . . NiB $409 Ex $353 Gd $231

MODEL S. . . . . NiB $270 Ex $235 Gd $133
Same as Model SI except caliber .380 Auto (9mm), 7-round magazine, weight: 19 oz. Made from 1941-65.

MODEL SL AUTOMATIC PISTOL . . . . NiB $311 Ex $272 Gd $184
Reduced-size modification of the Colt Government Model .45 Auto, lacks grip safety. Caliber: .32 Auto (7.65mm). Eight-round magazine, 4-inch bbl., 6.5 inches overall. Weight: 20 oz. Fixed sights. Blued finish. Plastic grips. Made from 1941-65.

STARFIRE DK AUTOMATIC PISTOL . . . . . . NiB $511 Ex $399 Gd $226
Light alloy frame. Caliber: .380 Automatic (9mm Short). Seven-round magazine, 3.13-inch bbl.. 5.5 inches overall. Weight: 14.5 oz. Fixed sights. Blued or chrome-plated slide w/frame anodized in black, blue, green, gray or gold. Plastic grips. Made 1957-97. U.S. importation disc. 1968.

MODEL SUPER A AUTOMATIC PISTOL . . . NiB $445 Ex $373 Gd $195
Caliber: .38 Super. Improved version of Model A but has disarming bolt permitting easier takedown, cartridge indicator, magazine safety, take-down magazine, improved sights w/luminous spots for aiming in darkness. This is the standard service pistol of the Spanish Armed Forces, adopted 1946.

MODEL SUPER B AUTOMATIC PISTOL
Caliber: 9mm Para. Similar to Model B except w/improvements described under Model Super A. Made circa 1946-89/90.
Super blued finish . . . . NiB $368 Ex $292 Gd $180
Starvel finish . . . . NiB $399 Ex $323 Gd $210

MODELS SUPER M, SUPER P . . . . . NiB $861 Ex $719 Gd $351
Calibers: .45 ACP, 9mm Parabellum or 9mm Largo, (Super M) and 9mm Parabellum (Super P). Improved versions of the Models M & P w/same general specifications, but has disarming bolt permitting easier takedown, cartridge indicator, magazine safety, take-down magazine, improved sights w/luminous spots for aiming in darkness.

MODELS SUPER SL, SUPER S . . . . . NiB $309 Ex $555 Gd $182
Same general specifications as the regular Model SI and S except w/improvements described under Super Star. Made circa 1946-72.

Star
Model M Military

Star
Model PD

MODEL SUPER SM . . . . NiB $309 Ex $269 Gd $207
Similar to Model Super S except has adj. rear sight, wood grips. Made from 1973-81.

SUPER TARGET MODEL . . . . NiB $1339 Ex $1033 Gd $574
Same as Super Star model except w/adj. target rear sight. (Disc.)

ULTRASTAR DA AUTOMATIC PISTOL . . . . NiB $336 Ex $290 Gd $203
Calibers: 9mm Parabellum or .40 S&W. Nine-round magazine, 3.57-inch bbl., 7 inches overall. Weight: 26 oz. Blade front, adjustable rear w/3-dot system. Polymer frame. Blue metal finish. Checkered black polymer grips. Imported from 1994-97.

STENDA-WERKE PISTOL — Suhl, Germany

POCKET AUTOMATIC PISTOL . . . . NiB $259 Ex $203 Gd $132
Essentially the same as the Beholla (see listing of that pistol for specifications). Made circa 1920-.25. Note: This pistol may be marked "Beholla" along w/the Stenda name and address.

STERLING ARMS CORPORATION — Gasport, New York

MODEL 283 TARGET 300
AUTO PISTOL . . . . NiB $179 Ex $123 Gd $108
Caliber: .22 LR. 10-round magazine, bbl. lengths: 4.5-, 6- 8-inch. 9 inches overall w/4.5-inch bbl., Weight: 36 oz. w/4.52-inch bbl. Adj. sights. Blued finish. Plastic grips. Made from 1970-71.

Sterling
Model 283Target 300

Sterling
Model 284 Target 300L

Sterling
Model 285 Husky

Sterling
Model 286 Trapper

Sterling
Model 300

Sterling
Model 400

MODEL 284 TARGET 300L . . . . NiB $192 Ex $141 Gd $106
Same as Model 283 except has 4.5- or 6-inch Luger-type bbl. Made from 1970-71.

MODEL 285 HUSKY . . . . NiB $192 Ex $141 Gd $106
Same as Model 283 except has fixed sights, 4.5-inch bbl only. Made from 1970-71.

MODEL 286 TRAPPER . . . . NiB $192 Ex $141 Gd $106
Same as Model 284 except w/fixed sights. Made from 1970-71.

MODEL 287 PPL-.380
AUTOMATIC PISTOL . . . . NiB $146 Ex $121 Gd $88
Caliber: .380 Auto. Six-round magazine, 1-inch bbl., 5.38 inches overall. Weight: 22.5 oz. Fixed sights. Blued finish. Plastic grips. Made from 1971-72.

MODEL 300
AUTOMATIC PISTOL . . . . NiB $146 Ex $116 Gd $70
Caliber: .25 Auto. Six-round magazine, 2.33-inch bbl., 4.5 inches overall. Weight: 13 oz. Fixed sights. Blued or nickel finish. Plastic grips. Made from 1972-83.

MODEL 300S. . . . . NiB $154 Ex $121 Gd $80
Same as Model 300 except in stainless steel. Made from 1976-83.

MODEL 302 . . . . NiB $146 Ex $116 Gd $70
Same as Model 300 except in .22 LR. Made from 1973-83.

MODEL 302S. . . . . NiB $146 Ex $116 Gd $70
Same as Model 302 except in stainless steel. Made from 1976-83.

MODEL 400 DA
AUTOMATIC PISTOL . . . . NiB $192 Ex $162 Gd $131
Caliber: .380 Auto. Seven-round magazine, 3.5-inch bbl., 6.5 inches overall. Weight: 24 oz. Adj. rear sight. Blued or nickel finish. Checkered walnut grips. Made from 1975-83.

MODEL 400S. . . . . NiB $218 Ex $172 Gd $131
Same as Model 400 except stainless steel. Made from 1977-83.

MODEL 450 DA
AUTO PISTOL . . . . NiB $248 Ex $218 Gd $172
Caliber: .45 Auto. Eight-round magazine, 4-inch bbl., 7.5 inches overall. Weight: 36 oz. Adj. rear sight. Blued finish. Smooth walnut grips. Made from 1977-83.

MODEL PPL-22
AUTOMATIC PISTOL . . . . NiB $197 Ex $146 Gd $111
Caliber: .22 LR. 10-round magazine, 1-inch bbl., 5.5 inches overall. Weight: About 24 oz. Fixed sights. Blued finish. Wood grips. Only 382 made in 1970-71.

J. STEVENS ARMS & TOOL CO. — Chicopee Falls, Mass.

This firm was established in Civil War era by Joshua Stevens, for whom the company was named. In 1936 it became a subsidiary of Savage Arms.

NO. 10
SINGLE-SHOT
TARGET PISTOL . . . . NiB $251 Ex $231 Gd $149
Caliber: .22 LR. 8-inch bbl., 11.5 inches overall. Weight: 37 oz. Target sights. Blued finish. Hard rubber grips. In external appearance this arm resembles an automatic pistol but it has a tip-up action. Made from 1919-39.

NO. 35
OFFHAND MODEL SINGLE-SHOT
TARGET PISTOL . . . . NiB $389 Ex $338 Gd $221
Tip-up action. Caliber: .22 LR. Bbl. lengths: 6, 8, 10, 12.25 inches. Weight: 24 oz. w/6-inch bbl. Target sights. Blued finish. Walnut grips. Note: This pistol is similar to the earlier "Gould" model. Made from 1907-39.

OFFHAND
NO. 35 SINGLE-SHOT
PISTOL/SHOTGUN . . . . NiB $389 Ex $338 Gd $185
Same general specifications as the standard No. 35 pistol except chambered for the .410 shotshell. Six-, 8-, 10-, or 12-inch half-ocatagonal bbl., iron frame either blued, nickel plated, or case-hardened. BATF Class 3 license required to purchase. Made from 1923-42.

NO. 36
SINGLE-SHOT PISTOL . . . . NiB $787 Ex $614 Gd $410
Tip-up action. Calibers: .22 Short and LR, .22 WRF, .25 Stevens, .32 Short Colt, .38 Long Colt, .44 Russian. 10- or 12-inch half-octagonal bbl., iron or brass frame w/nickel plated finish. Blued bbl. Checkered walnut grips. Made from 1880-1911.

NO. 37
SINGLE-SHOT PISTOL . . . . NiB $966 Ex $797 Gd $517
Similar specifications to the No. 38 except the finger spur on the trigger guard has been omitted. Made from 1889-1903.

NO. 38
SINGLE-SHOT PISTOL . . . . NiB $473 Ex $438 Gd $320
Tip-up action. Calibers: .22 Short and LR, .22 WRF, .25 Stevens, .32 Stevens, .32 Short Colt. Iron or brass frame. Checkered grips. Made from 1884-1903.

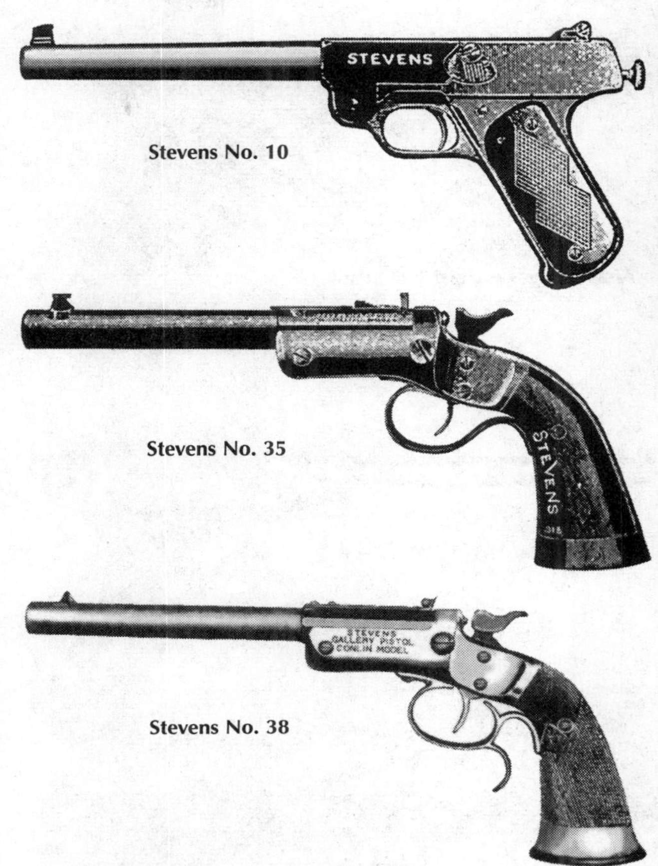

Stevens No. 10

Stevens No. 35

Stevens No. 38

NO. 41 TIP-UP
SINGLE-SHOT PISTOL . . . . NiB $310 Ex $259 Gd $178
Tip-up action. Caliber: .22 Short, 3.5-inch half-octagonal bbl. Blued metal parts w/optional nickel frame. Made from 1896-1915.

STEYR PISTOLS — Steyr, Austria

GB SEMIAUTOMATIC PISTOL
Caliber: 9mm Para. 18-round magazine, 5.4-inch bbl., 8.9 inches overall. Weight: 2.9 lbs. Post front sight, fixed, notched rear. Double, gas-delayed, blow-back action. Made from 1981-88.
Commercial model . . . . NiB $669 Ex $592 Gd $396
Military model
(Less than 1000 imported). . . . . NiB $617 Ex $514 Gd $442

M12 AUTOMATIC PISTOL
Caliber: 9mm Steyr. Eight-round fixed magazine, charger loaded; 5.1-inch bbl., 8.5 inches overall. Weight: 35 oz. Fixed sights. Blued finish. Checkered wood grips. Made from 1911-19. Adopted by the Austro-Hungarian Army in 1912. Note: Confiscated by the Germans in 1938, an estimated 250,000 of these pistols were converted to 9mm Para. and stamped w/an identifying "08" on the left side of the slide. Mfd. by Osterreichische Waffenfabrik-Gesellschaft.
Commercial model (9mm Steyr) . . . NiB $514 Ex $437 Gd $355
Military model (9mm Steyr-
Austro-Hungarian Army) . . . . NiB $520 Ex $442 Gd $200
Military model (9mm Parabellum
Conversion marked "08") . . . . NiB $992 Ex $837 Gd $467

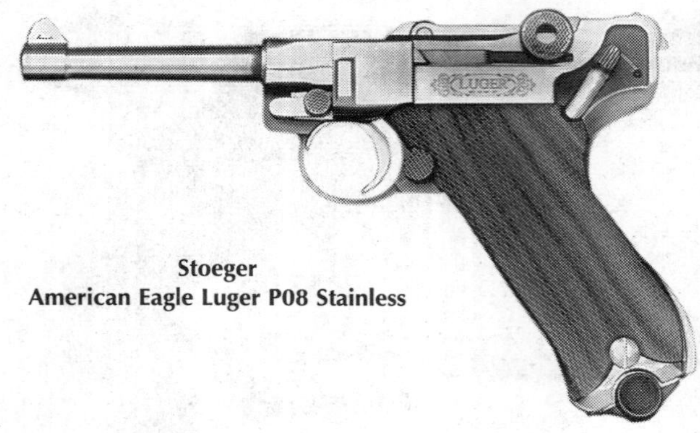

Stoeger
American Eagle Luger P08 Stainless

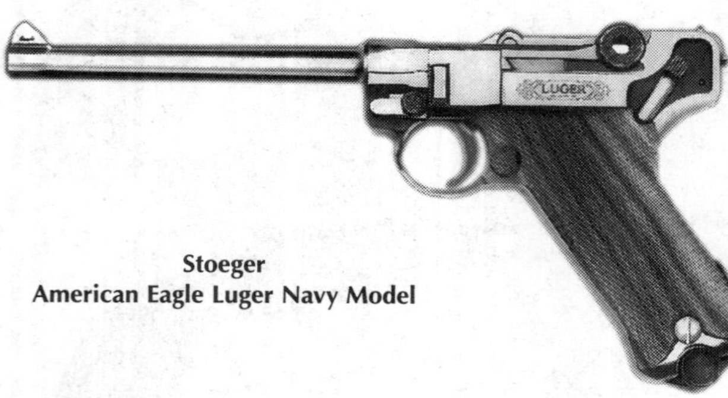

Stoeger
American Eagle Luger Navy Model

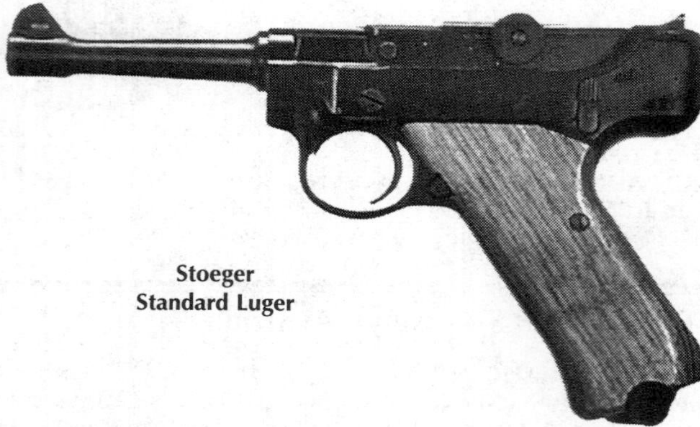

Stoeger
Standard Luger

Targa
Model GT380XE

STOEGER LUGERS
Formerly mfd. by Stoeger Industries, So. Hackensack, N.J.; later by Classic Arms, Union City, N.J.

AMERICAN EAGLE LUGER
Caliber: 9mm Para. Seven-round magazine, 4- or 6-inch bbl., 8.25 inches overall (with 4-inch bbl.). or 10.25 inches (with 6-inch bbl.). Weight: 30 or 32 oz. Checkered walnut grips. Stainless steel w/brushed or matte black finish. Made from 1994 to date.
Model P-08 stainless (4-inch bbl.)...... NiB $711 Ex $415 Gd $344
Navy model (6-inch bbl.)...... NiB $711 Ex $415 Gd $344
W/matte black finish, add $50

STANDARD LUGER .22 AUTOMATIC PISTOL ...... NiB $167 Ex $141 Gd $90
Caliber: .22 LR. 10-round magazine, 4.5- or 5.5-inch bbl., 8.88 inches overall (with 4.5-inch bbl.). Weight: 29.5 oz. (with 4.5-inch bbl.). Fixed sights. Black finish. Smooth wood grips. Made from 1969-86.

STEEL FRAME LUGER .22 AUTO PISTOL ...... NiB $172 Ex $146 Gd $106
Caliber: .22 LR. 10-round magazine, 4.5-inch bbl., 8.88 inches overall. Blued finish. Checkered wood grips. Features one piece forged and machined steel frame. Made from 1980-86.

TARGET LUGER .22 AUTO PISTOL ...... NiB $203 Ex $197 Gd $155
Same as Standard Luger .22 except has target sights 9.38 inches overall w/4.5-inch bbl., Checkered wood grips. Made from 1975-86.

TARGA PISTOLS — Italy
Manufactured by Armi Tanfoglio Guiseppe

MODEL GT26S AUTO PISTOL ...... NiB $115 Ex $96 Gd $71
Caliber: .25 ACP. Six-round magazine, 2.5-inch bbl., 4.63 inches overall. Weight: 15 oz. fixed sights. Checkered composition grips. Blued or chrome finish. Disc. 1990.

MODEL GT32 AUTO PISTOL
Caliber: .32 ACP. Six-round magazine, 4.88-inch bbl., 7.38 inches overall. Weight: 26 oz. fixed sights. Checkered composition or walnut grips. Blued or chrome finish.
Blued finished ...... NiB $146 Ex $121 Gd $90
Chrome finish ...... NiB $162 Ex $126 Gd $101

MODEL GT380 AUTOMATIC PISTOL
Same as the Targa GT32 except chambered for .380 ACP.
Blued finish ...... NiB $166 Ex $136 Gd $99
Chrome finish ...... NiB $178 Ex $146 Gd $106

MODEL GT380XE AUTOMATIC PISTOL ...... NiB $197 Ex $157 Gd $116
Caliber: .380 ACP. 11-round magazine, 3.75-inch bbl., 7.38 inches overall. Weight: 28 oz. Fixed sights. Blued or satin nickel finish. Smooth wooden grips. Made from 1980-90.

Taurus Model .44

Taurus Model 66

FORJAS TAURUS S.A. — Porto Alegre, Brazil

MODEL 44 DA REVOLVER
Caliber: .44 Mag. Six-round cylinder, 4-, 6.5-, or 8.38-inch bbl. Weight: 44.75 oz., 52.5 or 57.25 oz. Brazilian hardwood grips. Blued or stainless steel finish. Made from 1994 to date.
Blued finish . . . . NiB $447 Ex $370 Gd $202
Stainless. . . . . NiB $503 Ex $411 Gd $340

MODEL 65 DA REVOLVER
Caliber: .357 Magnum. 6-round cylinder, 3- or 4-inch bbl., weight: 32 oz. Front ramp sight, square notch rear. Checkered walnut target grip. Royal blued or satin nickel finish. Imported from 1992-97 and from 1999 to date.
Blue . . . . NiB $391 Ex $304 Gd $141
Stainless. . . . . NiB $396 Ex $309 Gd $151

MODEL 66 DA REVOLVER
Calibers: .357 Magnum, .38 Special. Six-round cylinder, 3-, 4- and 6-inch bbl., weight: 35 oz. Serrated ramp front sight, rear click adj. Checkered walnut grips. Royal blued or nickel finish. Imported from 1992-97 and from 1999 to date.
Blue . . . . NiB $350 Ex $279 Gd $182
Stainless. . . . . NiB $411 Ex $289 Gd $238

MODEL 73 DA REVOLVER . . . . NiB $202 Ex $177 Gd $126
Caliber: .32 Long. Six-round cylinder, 3-inch heavy bbl., weight: 20 oz. Checkered grips. Blued or satin nickel finish. Disc. 1993.

MODEL 74 TARGET
GRADE DA REVOLVER . . . . NiB $208 Ex $197 Gd $131
Caliber: .32 S&W Long. Six-round cylinder, 3-inch bbl., 8.25 inches overall. Weight: 20 oz. Adj. rear sight, ramp front. Blued or nickel finish. Checkered walnut grips. Made from 1971-90.

MODEL 80 DA REVOLVER
Caliber: .38 Special. Six-round cylinder, bbl. lengths: 3, 4 inches, 9.25 inches overall (with 4-inch bbl.). Weight: 30 oz. (with 4-inch bbl.) Fixed sights. Blued or nickel finish. Checkered walnut grips. Made from 1996-97.
Blued . . . . NiB $217 Ex $167 Gd $106
Stainless. . . . . NiB $269 Ex $203 Gd $152

MODEL 82 HEAVY BARREL
Same as Model 80 except has heavy bbl., weight: 33 oz. w/4-inch bbl., Made from 1971 to date.
Blued . . . . NiB $218 Ex $172 Gd $111
Stainless. . . . . NiB $223 Ex $182 Gd $121

MODEL 83 HEAVY BARREL TARGET GRADE
Same as Model 84 except has heavy bbl., weight: 34.5 oz. Made from 1977 to date.
Blued . . . . NiB $240 Ex $179 Gd $118
Stainless. . . . . NiB $276 Ex $210 Gd $159

Taurus
Model 74 Target Grade

Taurus Model 80

Taurus Model 82

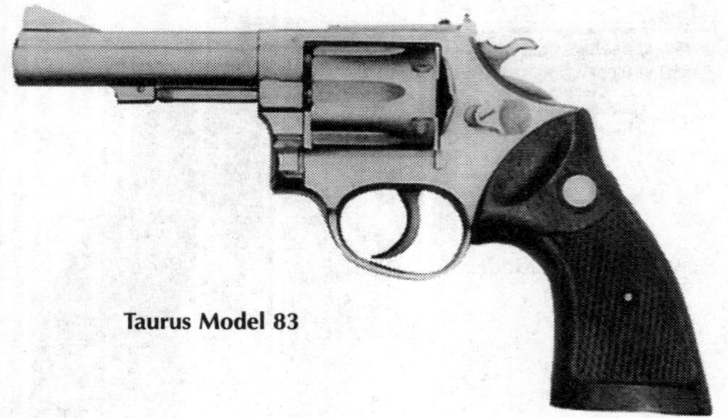
Taurus Model 83

Taurus
Model 85 w/Spur Hammer

Taurus Model 84

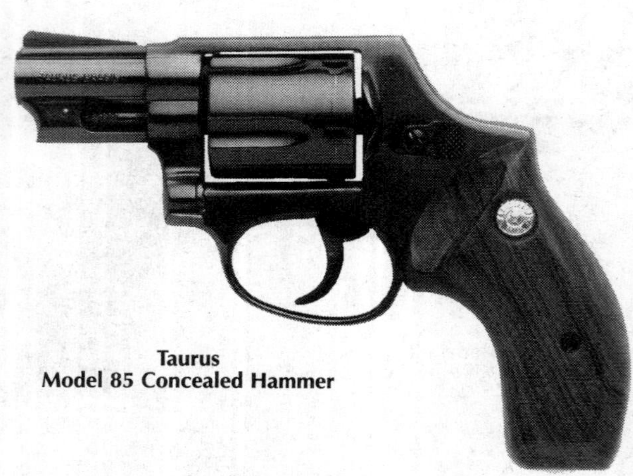
Taurus
Model 85 Concealed Hammer

Taurus Model 86

MODEL 84 TARGET GRADE REVOLVER . . . . NiB $278 Ex $222 Gd $156
Caliber: .38 Special. Six-round cylinder, 4-inch bbl., 9.25 inches overall. Weight: 31 oz. Adj. rear sight, ramp front. Blued or nickel finish. Checkered walnut grips. Made from 1971-89.

MODEL 85 DA REVOLVER
Caliber: .38 Special. Five-round cylinder, 2- or 3-inch. bbl., weight: 21 oz. Fixed sights. Checkered walnut grips. Blued, satin nickel or stainless-steel finish. Currently in production. Model 85CH is the same as the standard version except for concealed hammer.
Blued or satin nickel . . . . NiB $293 Ex $227 Gd $108
Stainless steel . . . . NiB $358 Ex $267 Gd $193

MODEL 86 TARGET MASTER DA REVOLVER . . . . NiB $298 Ex $227 Gd $156
Caliber: .38 Special. Six-round cylinder, 6-inch bbl., 11.25 inches overall. Weight: 34 oz. Adj. rear sight, Partridge-type front. Blued finish. Checkered walnut grips. Made from 1971-94.

MODEL 94 TARGET GRADE
Same as Model 74 except .22 LR. w/9-round cylinder, 3- or 4-inch bbl., weight: 25 oz. Blued or stainless finish. Made from 1971 to date.
Blued finish . . . . NiB $273 Ex $207 Gd $120
Stainless finish. . . . . NiB $323 Ex $241 Gd $180

MODEL 96 TARGET MASTER . . . . . NiB $303 Ex $227 Gd $156
Same as Model 86 except in .22 LR. Made from 1971 to date.

MODEL 431 DA REVOLVER
Caliber: .44 Spec. Five-round cylinder, 3- or 4-inch solid-rib bbl. w/ejector shroud. Weight: 35 oz. w/4-inch bbl., Serrated ramp front sight, notched topstrap rear. Blued or stainless finish. Made from 1992-97.
Blued finish . . . . NiB $247 Ex $196 Gd $125
Stainless finish. . . . . NiB $318 Ex $246 Gd $200

MODEL 441 DA REVOLVER
Similar to the Model 431 except w/6-inch bbl. and fully adj. target sights. Weight: 40 oz. Made from 1991-97.
Blued finish . . . . NiB $268 Ex $207 Gd $125
Stainless finish. . . . . NiB $389 Ex $282 Gd $231

MODEL 445 DA REVOLVER
Caliber: .44 Special. Five-round cylinder, 2-inch bbl., 6.75 inches overall. Weight: 28.25 oz. Serrated ramp front sight, notched frame rear. Standard or concealed hammer. Santoprene I grips. Blue or stainless finish. Imported from 1997 to date.
Blue model . . . . NiB $298 Ex $232 Gd $125
Stainless model . . . . NiB $394 Ex $256 Gd $185

MODEL .454 DA RAGING BULL REVOLVER
Caliber: .454 Casull. Five-round cylinder, ported 6.5- or 8.4-inch vent rib bbl., 12 inches overall (w/6.5-inch bbl.). Weight: 53 or 63 oz. Partridge front sight, micrometer adj. rear. Santoprene I or walnut grips. Blue or stainless finish. Imported from 1997 to date.
Blue model . . . . NiB $861 Ex $708 Gd $534
Stainless model . . . . NiB $846 Ex $774 Gd $698

MODEL 669/669VR DA REVOLVER
Caliber: .357 Mag. Six-round cylinder, 4- or 6-inch solid-rib bbl. w/ejector shroud Model 669VR has vent rib bbl., weight: 37 oz. w/4-inch bbl., Serrated ramp front sight, micro-adj. rear. Royal blued or stainless finish. Checkered Brazilian hardwood grips. Made from 1989 to date.
Model 669 blued. . . . . NiB $290 Ex $219 Gd $142
Model 669 stainless. . . . . NiB $356 Ex $275 Gd $219
Model 669VR blued. . . . . NiB $300 Ex $229 Gd $152
Model 669VR stainless . . . . NiB $367 Ex $285 Gd $229

MODEL 741/761 DA REVOLVER
Caliber: .32 H&R Mag. Six-round cylinder, 3- or 4-inch solid-rib bbl. w/ejector shroud. Weight: 20 oz. w/3-inch bbl., Serrated ramp front sight, micro-adj. rear. Blued or stainless finish. Checkered Brazilian hardwood grips. Made from 1991-97.
Model 741
blued. . . . . NiB $234 Ex $183 Gd $132
Model 741
stainless . . . . NiB $305 Ex $244 Gd $178
Model 761
(6-inch bbl.,
blued, 34 oz.) . . . . NiB $280 Ex $214 Gd $127

MODEL 941 TARGET REVOLVER
Caliber: .22 Magnum. Eight-round cylinder. Solid-rib bbl. w/ejector shroud. Micro-adj. rear sight. Brazilian hardwood grips. Blued or stainless finish.
Blued finish . . . . NiB $293 Ex $222 Gd $125
Stainless finish. . . . . NiB $329 Ex $263 Gd $181

MODEL PT .22 DA
AUTOMATIC PISTOL . . . . NiB $196 Ex $156 Gd $89
Caliber: .22 LR. Nine-round magazine, 2.75-inch bbl., weight: 12.3 oz. Fixed open sights. Brazilian hardwood grips. Blued finish. Made from 1991 to date.

MODEL PT .25 DA
AUTOMATIC PISTOL . . . . NiB $196 Ex $156 Gd $90
Same general specifications as Model PT 22 except in .25 ACP w/eight-round magazine, Made from 1992 to date.

MODEL PT58 SEMI-
AUTOMATIC PISTOL . . . . NiB $361 Ex $310 Gd $224
Caliber: .380 ACP. Twelve-round magazine, 4-inch bbl., 7.2 inches overall. Weight: 30 oz. Blade front sight, rear adj. for windage w/3-dot sighting system. Blued, satin nickel or stainless finish. Made from 1988-96.

MODEL PT 92AF
SEMIAUTOMATIC PISTOL
Double action. Caliber: 9mm Para. Fifteen-round magazine, 5-inch bbl., 8.5 inches overall. Weight: 24 oz. Blade front sight, notched bar rear. Smooth Brazilian walnut grips. Blued, satin nickel or stainless finish. Made from 1991 to date.
Blued finish . . . . NiB $476 Ex $384 Gd $236
Satin nickel finish . . . . NiB $516 Ex $425 Gd $277
Stainless finish. . . . . NiB $486 Ex $394 Gd $325

Taurus Model 669

Taurus Model PT .22

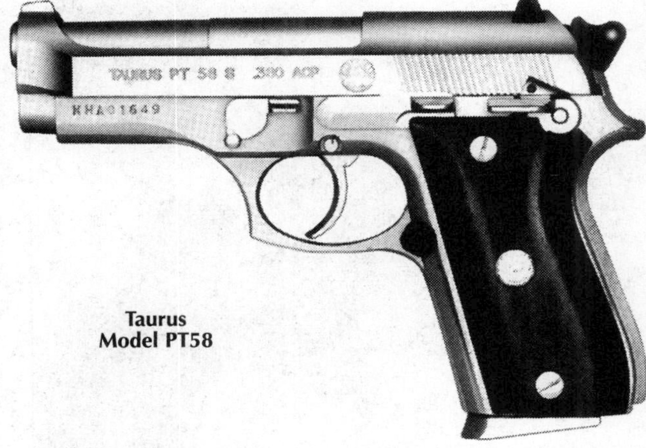

Taurus Model PT58

Taurus Model PT92

Taurus
Model PT-99AF

Taurus
Model PT-908

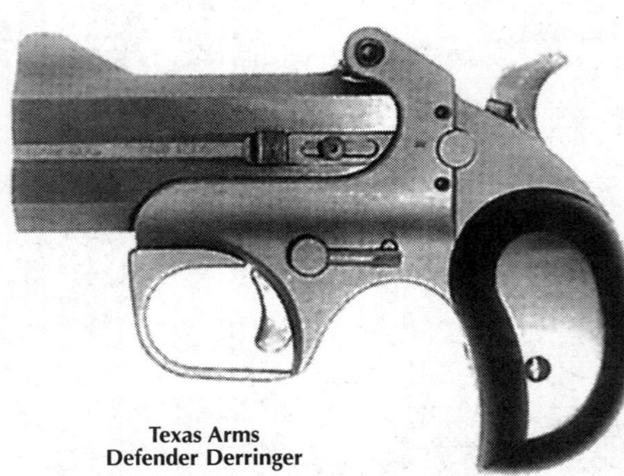
Texas Arms
Defender Derringer

MODEL PT-92AFC COMPACT PISTOL
Same general specifications as Model PT-92AF except w/13-round magazine, 4.25-inch bbl., 7.5 inches overall. Weight: 31 oz. Made 1991-96
Blued finish . . . . NiB $378 Ex $227 Gd $230
Satin nickel finish . . . . NiB $415 Ex $365 Gd $269
Stainless finish . . . . NiB $445 Ex $352 Gd $291

MODEL PT 99AF SEMI-AUTOMATIC PISTOL . . . . NiB $510 Ex $398 Gd $240
Same general specifications as Model PT-92AF except rear sight is adj. for elevation and windage, and finish is blued or satin nickel.

MODEL PT 100 DA AUTOMATIC PISTOL
Caliber: .40 S&W. Eleven-round magazine, 5-inch bbl., weight: 34 oz. Fixed front sight, adj. rear w/3-dot system. Smooth hardwood grip. Blued, satin nickel or stainless finish. Made from 1991-97.
Blued finish . . . . NiB $502 Ex $395 Gd $247
Satin finish. . . . . NiB $492 Ex $436 Gd $288
Stainless finish . . . . NiB $456 Ex $405 Gd $272

MODEL PT 101 DA AUTOMATIC PISTOL
Same general specifications as Model 100 except w/micrometer click adj. sights. Made from 1992-96.
Blued finish . . . . NiB $517 Ex $405 Gd $247
Satin nickel finish . . . . NiB $563 Ex $451 Gd $293
Stainless finish . . . . NiB $522 Ex $446 Gd $323

MODEL PT 111 MILLENNIUM DAO PISTOL
Caliber: 9mm Parabellum. 10-round magazine, 3.12-inch bbl., 6 inches overall. Weight: 19.1 oz. Fixed low-profile sights w/3-dot system. Black polymer grip/frame. Blue or stainless slide. Imported from 1998 to date.
Blue model . . . . NiB $400 Ex $232 Gd $176
Stainless model . . . . NiB $400 Ex $232 Gd $176

MODEL PT 908 SEMIAUTOMATIC PISTOL
Caliber: 9mm Para. Eight-round magazine, 3.8-inch bbl., 7 inches overall. Weight: 30 oz. Post front sight, drift-adj. combat rear w/3-dot system. Blued, satin nickel or stainless finish. Made from 1993-97.
Blued finish . . . . NiB $375 Ex $329 Gd $232
Satin nickel finish . . . . NiB $375 Ex $339 Gd $232
Stainless finish . . . . NiB $584 Ex $466 Gd $318

MODEL PT 911 COMPACT SEMIAUTOMATIC PISTOL
Caliber: 9mm Parabellum. 10-round magazine, 3.75-inch bbl., 7.05 inches overall. Weight: 28.2 oz. Fixed low-profile sights w/3-dot system. Santoprene II grips. Blue or stainless finish. Imported from 1997 to date.
Blue model . . . . NiB $463 Ex $382 Gd $229
Stainless model . . . . NiB $586 Ex $468 Gd $320

MODEL PT 938 COMPACT SEMIAUTOMATIC PISTOL
Caliber: 380 ACP. 10-round magazine, 3.72-inch bbl., 6.75 inches overall. Weight: 27 oz. Fixed low-profile sights w/3-dot system. Santoprene II grips. Blue or stainless finish. Imported from 1997 to date.
Blue model . . . . NiB $448 Ex $382 Gd $224
Stainless model . . . . NiB $403 Ex $331 Gd $238

MODEL PT 940 COMPACT SEMIAUTOMATIC PISTOL
Caliber: .40 S&W. 10-round magazine, 3.75-inch bbl., 7.05 inches overall. Weight: 28.2 oz. Fixed low-profile sights w/3-dot system. Santoprene II grips. Blue or stainless finish. Imported from 1997 to date.
Blue model . . . . NiB $473 Ex $402 Gd $234
Stainless model . . . . NiB $484 Ex $407 Gd $336

MODEL PT 945 COMPACT SEMIAUTOMATIC PISTOL
Caliber: .45 ACP. Eight-round magazine, 4.25-inch bbl., 7.48 inches overall. Weight: 29.5 oz. Fixed low-profile sights w/3-dot system. Santoprene II grips. Blue or stainless finish. Imported from 1995 to date.
Blue model . . . . NiB $499 Ex $412 Gd $254
Stainless model . . . . NiB $524 Ex $433 Gd $356

TEXAS ARMS — Waco, Texas

DEFENDER DERRINGER . . . . NiB $320 Ex $280 Gd $183
Calibers: 9mm, .357 Mag., .44 Mag., .45 ACP, .45 Colt/.410. Three-inch bbl., 5 inches overall. Weight: 21 oz. Blade front sight, fixed rear. Matte gun-metal gray finish. Smooth grips. Made from 1993 to date.

TEXAS LONGHORN ARMS — Richmond, Texas

"THE JEZEBEL" PISTOL . . . . NiB $290 Ex $236 Gd $168
Top-break, single-shot. Caliber: .22 Short, Long or LR. Six-inch half-round bbl., 8 inches overall. Weight: 15 oz. Bead front sight, adj. rear. One-piece walnut grip. Stainless finish. Intro. in 1987.

SA REVOLVER CASED SET
Set contains one each of the Texas Longhorn Single Actions. Each chambered in the same caliber and w/the same serial number. Intro. in 1984.
Standard set. . . . . NiB $5722 Ex $4600 Gd $3164
Engraved set . . . . NiB $7444 Ex $5977 Gd $4100

SOUTH TEXAS ARMY LIMITED EDITION SA REVOLVER . . . . . . NiB $1783 Ex $1329 Gd $1048
Calibers: All popular centerfire pistol calibers. Six-round cylinder, 4.75-inch bbl.,10.25 inches overall. Weight: 40 oz. Fixed sights. Color casehardened frame. One-piece deluxe walnut grips. Blued bbl., Intro. in 1984.

SESQUICENTENNIAL SA REVOLVER. . . . . NiB $2470 Ex $1987 Gd $1369
Same as South Texas Army Limited Edition except engraved and nickel-plated w/one-piece ivory grip. Intro. in 1986.

TEXAS BORDER SPECIAL SA REVOLVER . . . . NiB $1575 Ex $1270 Gd $880
Same as South Texas Army Limited Edition except w/3.5-inch bbl. and bird's-head grips. Intro. in 1984.

WEST TEXAS FLAT TOP TARGET SA REVOLVER . . . . NiB $1576 Ex $1326 Gd $1033
Same as South Texas Army Limited Edition except w/choice of bbl. lengths from 7 .5 to 15 inches. Same special features w/flat-top style frame and adj. rear sight. Intro. in 1984.

THOMPSON PISTOL — West Hurley, New York Mfd. by Auto-Ordnance Corporation

MODEL 27A-5 SEMIAUTOMATIC PISTOL
Similar to Thompson Model 1928A submachine gun except has no provision for automatic firing, does not have detachable buttstock. Caliber: .45 Auto, 20-round detachable box magazine (5-, 15- and 30-round box magazines, 39-round drum also available), 13-inch finned bbl., overall length: 26 inches. Weight: About 6.75 lbs. Adj. rear sight, blade front. Blued finish. Walnut grips. Intro. in 1977. See Auto-Ordnance in Handgun Section.

THOMPSON/CENTER ARMS — Rochester, NH Acquired by Smith & Wesson in 2006.

CONTENDER SINGLE-SHOT PISTOL
Break frame, underlever action. Calibers: (rimfire) .22 LR. .22 WMR, 5mm RRM; (standard centerfire), .218 Bee, .22 Hornet, .22 Rem. Jet, .221 Fireball, .222 Rem., .25-35, .256 Win. Mag., .30 M1 Carbine, .30-30, .38 Auto, .38 Special .357 Mag./Hot Shot, 9mm Para., .45 Auto, .45 Colt, .44 Magnum/Hot Shot; (wildcat centerfire) .17 Ackley Bee, .17 Bumblebee, .17 Hornet, .17 K Hornet, .17 Mach IV, .17-.222, .17-.223, .22 K Hornet, .30 Herrett, .357 Herrett, .357-4 B&D. Interchangeable bbls.: 8.75- or 10-inch standard octagon (.357 Mag., .44 Mag. and .45 Colt available w/detachable choke for use w/Hot Shot cartridges); 10-inch w/vent rib and detachable internal choke tube for Hot Shots, .357 and .44 Magnum only; 10-inch

Thompson Contender Single-Shot Pistol

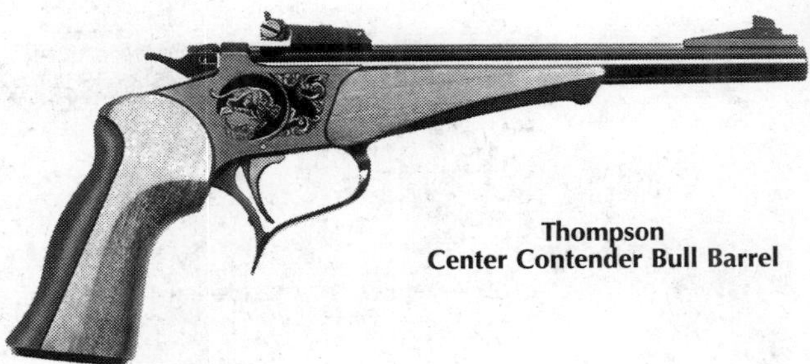
Thompson Center Contender Bull Barrel

bull bbl., .30 or .357 Herrett only. 13.5 inches overall w/10-inch bbl., Weight: 43 oz. (w/standard 10-inch bbl.). Adj. rear sight, ramp front; vent rib model has folding rear sight, adj. front; bull bbl., available w/or w/o sights. Lobo 1.5/ scope and mount (add $40 to value). Blued finish. Receiver photoengraved. Checkered walnut thumbrest grip and forearm (pre-1972 model has different grip w/silver grip cap). Made from 1967 to date, w/the following revisions and variations.
Standard model. . . . . NiB $346 Ex $295 Gd $183
Vent rib model . . . . NiB $448 Ex $346 Gd $208
Bull bbl. model, w/sights . . . . NiB $428 Ex $341 Gd $203
Bull bbl. model, without sights . . . . . . NiB $417 Ex $326 Gd $188
Extra standard bbl. . . . . NiB $269 Ex $218 Gd $116
Extra vent rib or bull bbl. . . . . NiB $315 Ex $229 Gd $132

CONTENDER BULL BARREL . . . . . . NiB $428 Ex $341 Gd $203
Caliber offerings of the bull bbl. version expanded in 1973 and 1978, making it the Contender model w/the widest range of caliber options: .22 LR, .22 Win. Mag., .22 Hornet, .223 Rem., 7mm T.C.U., 7x30 Waters, .30 M1 Carbine, .30-30 Win., .32 H&R Mag., .32-20 Win., .357 Rem. Max., .357 Mag., 10mm Auto, .44 Magnum, .445 Super Magnum. 10-inch heavy bbl., Partridge-style iron sights. Contoured Competitor grip. Blued finish.

CONTENDER INTERNAL CHOKE MODEL
Originally made in 1968-69 w/octagonal bbl., this Internal Choke version in .45 Colt/.410 caliber only was reintroduced in 1986 w/10-inch bull bbl. Vent rib also available. Fixed iron rear sight, bead front. Detachable choke screws into muzzle. Blued finish. Contoured American black walnut Competitor grip, also since 1986, has nonslip rubber insert permanently bonded to back of grip.
W/bull bbl . . . . NiB $448 Ex $361 Gd $224
W/vent rib . . . . NiB $473 Ex $387 Gd $276

CONTENDER OCTAGON BARREL . . . . NiB $395 Ex $300 Gd $213
The original Contender design, this octagonal bbl., version began to see the discontinuance of caliber offerings in 1980. Now it is available in .22 LR only, 10-inch octagonal bbl., Partridge-style iron sights. Contoured Competitor grip. Blued finish.

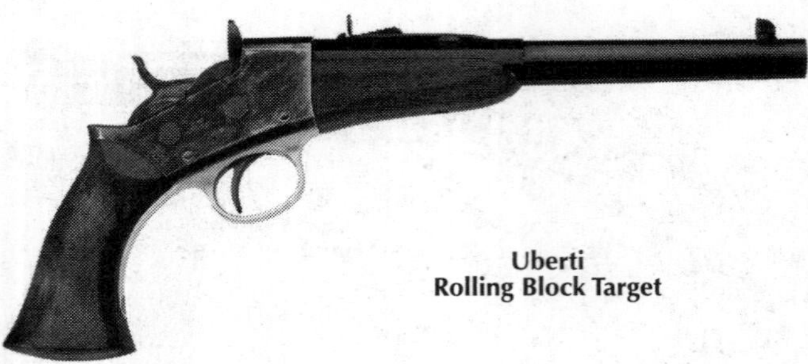
Uberti
Rolling Block Target

Uberti
Model 1873 Cattleman

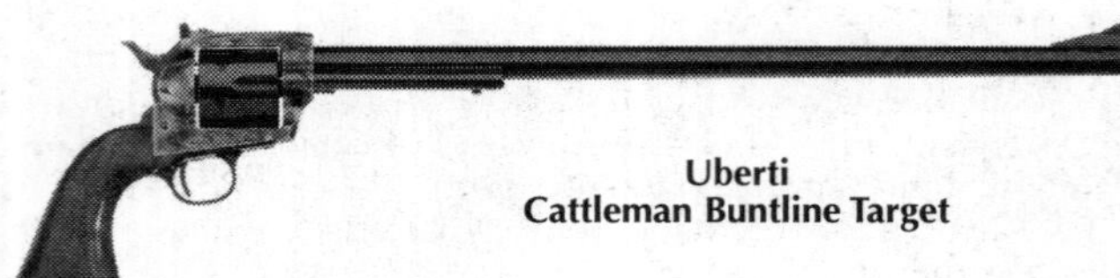
Uberti
Cattleman Buntline Target

CONTENDER STAINLESS
Similar to the standard Contender models except stainless steel w/blued sights. Black Rynite forearm and ambidextrous finger-groove grip. Made from 1993 to date.
Standard SS model (10-inch bbl.) . . . . NiB $487 Ex $364 Gd $267
SS Super 14. . . . . NiB $477 Ex $374 Gd $278
SS Super 16. . . . . NiB $502 Ex $380 Gd $283

CONTENDER SUPER 14/16
Calibers: .22 LR, .222 Rem., .223 Rem., 6mm T.C.U., 6.5mm T.C.U., 7mm T.C.U., 7x30 Waters, .30 Herrett, .30-30 Win., .357 Herrett, .357 Rem. Max., .35 Rem., 10mm Auto, .44 Mag., .445 Super Mag. 14- or 16.25-inch bull bbl., 18 or 20.25 inches overall. Weight: 43-65 oz. Partridge-style ramp front sight, adj. target rear. Blued finish. Made from 1978 to date.
Super 14 . . . . NiB $400 Ex $303 Gd $216
Super 16 . . . . NiB $415 Ex $308 Gd $221

CONTENDER TC ALLOY II
Calibers: .22 LR, .223 Rem., .357 Magnum, .357 Rem. Max., .44 Magnum, 7mm T.C.U., .30-30 Win., .45 Colt/.410 (w/internal choke), .35 Rem. and 7-30 Waters (14-inch bbl.). 10- or 14-inch bull bbl. or 10-inch vent rib bbl. (w/internal choke). All metal parts permanently electroplated w/T/C Alloy II, which is harder than stainless steel, ensuring smoother action, 30 percent longer bbl. life. Other design specifications the same as late model Contenders. Made from 1986-89.
T/C Alloy II 10-inch bull bbl. . . . . NiB $405 Ex $344 Gd $288
T/C Alloy II vent rib bbl. w/choke . . . . NiB $457 Ex $374 Gd $268
T/C Alloy II Super 14 . . . . NiB $490 Ex $400 Gd $286

ENCORE SINGLE-SHOT PISTOL
Similar to the standard Contender models except w/10-, 12- or 15-inch bbl., Calibers: .22-250 Rem., .223 Rem., .243 Win., .260 Rem., .270 Win., 7mm BR Rem., 7mm-08 Rem., 7.62x39mm, .308 Win., .30-06 Spfd., .44 Rem. Mag., .444 Marlin, .45-70 Govt., .45 LC/410. Blue or stainless finish. Walnut or composition, ambidextrous finger-groove grip. Hunter Model w/2.5-7x pistol scope. Note: Encore bbls. are not interchangeable with Contenter models. Made from 1998 to date.
Encore model w/10-inch
bbl. (blue, disc.) . . . . NiB $482 Ex $415 Gd $242
Encore model w/12-inch bbl. (blue) . . . . . . NiB $482 Ex $415 Gd $242
Encore model w/15-inch bbl. (blue) . . . . . . NiB $490 Ex $425 Gd $250
Hunter model w/2.5-7x scope . . . . NiB $762 Ex $658 Gd $415
Encore model (stainless), add $55

UBERTI HANDGUNS — Mfd. by Aldo Uberti, Ponte Zanano, Italy *(Imported by Uberti USA, Inc.)*

MODEL 1871 ROLLING BLOCK
TARGET PISTOL . . . . NiB $382 Ex $320 Gd $208
Single shot. Calibers: .22 LR, .22 Magnum, .22 Hornet and .357 Magnum; 9.5-inch bbl., 14 inches overall. Weight: 44 oz. Ramp front sight, fully adjustable rear. Smooth walnut grip and forearm. Color casehardened frame w/brass trigger guard. Blued half-octagon or full round barrel.

MODEL 1873 CATTLEMAN SA REVOLVER
Calibers: .357 Magnum, .38-40, .44-40, .44 Special, .45 Long Colt, .45 ACP. Six-round cylinder, Bbl length: 3.5, 4.5, 4.75, 5.5, 7.5 or 18 inches; 10.75 inches overall (5.5-inch bbl.). Weight: 38 oz. (5.5-inch bbl.). Color casehardened steel frame w/steel or brass back strap and trigger guard. Nickel-plated or blued barrel and cylinder. Imported from 1997 to date.
First issue . . . . .NiB $417 Ex $361 Gd $223
Bisley . . . . NiB $417 Ex $361 Gd $223
Bisley (flattop) . . . . NiB $417 Ex $361 Gd $223
Buntline (reintroduced 1992) . . . . NiB $417 Ex $361 Gd $223
Quick Draw . . . . NiB $417 Ex $361 Gd $223
Sabre (bird head) . . . . NiB $417 Ex $361 Gd $223
Sheriff's model . . . . NiB $417 Ex $361 Gd $223
Convertible cylinder, add $51
Stainless steel, add $125
Steel backstrap and trigger guard, add $55
Target sights, add $60

MODEL 1875 REMINGTON OUTLAW
Replica of Model 1875 Remington. Calibers: .357 Mag., .44-40, .45 ACP, .45 Long Colt. Six-round cylinder, 5.5- to 7.5-inch bbl., 11.75 to 13.75 inches overall. Weight: 44 oz. (with 7.5 inch bbl). Color casehardened steel frame w/steel or brass back strap and trigger guard. Blue or nickel finish.
Blue model . . . . NiB $443 Ex $341 Gd $193
Nickel model (disc. 1995). . . . . NiB $555 Ex $468 Gd $310
Convertible cylinder
(.45 LC/.45 ACP), add $92

MODEL 1890 REMINGTON POLICE
Similar to Model 1875 Remington except without the web under the ejector housing.
Blue Model . . . . NiB $443 Ex $341 Gd $193
Nickel Model (disc. 1995) . . . . NiB $550 Ex $463 Gd $305
Convertible Cylinder (.45 LC/.45 ACP), add. $92

ULTRA LIGHT ARMS, INC — Granville, WV.

MODEL 20 SERIES PISTOLS
Calibers: .22-250 thru .308 Win. Five-round magazine, 14-inch bbl., weight: 4 lbs. Composite Kevlar, graphite reinforced stock. Benchrest grade action available in right- or left-hand models. Timney adjustable trigger w/three function safety. Bright or matte finish. Made from 1987-99.
Model 20 Hunter's Pistol (disc. 1989). . . NiB $1393 Ex $1245 Gd $735
Model 20 Reb Pistol (disc. 1999) . . . . . . NiB $1576 Ex $1296 Gd $760

UNIQUE PISTOLS — Hendaye, France
Mfd. by Manufacture d'Armes des Pyrénées
Currently imported by Nygord Precision Products(Previously by Beeman Precision Arms)

MODEL B/CF AUTOMATIC PISTOL . . . . . . NiB $237 Ex $226 Gd $159
Calibers: .32 ACP, .380 ACP. Nine-round (.32) or 8-round (.38) magazine, 4-inch bbl., 6.6 inches overall. Weight: 24.3 oz. Blued finish. Plain or thumbrest plastic grips. Intro. in 1954. Disc.

MODEL D2 . . . . NiB $345 Ex $293 Gd $237
Same as Model D6 except has 4.5-inch bbl., 7.5 inches overall, weight: 24.5 oz. Made from 1954 to date.

MODEL D6 AUTOMATIC PISTOL. . . . . NiB $345 Ex $293 Gd $180
Caliber: .22 LR. 10-round magazine, 6-inch bbl., 9.25 inches overall. Weight: About 26 oz. Adj. sights. Blued finish. Plain or thumbrest plastic grips. Intro. in 1954. Disc.

MODEL DES/32U RAPID FIRE PISTOL
Caliber: .32 S&W Long (wadcutter). Five- or 6-round magazine, 5.9-inch bbl., weight: .40.2 oz. Blade front sight, micro-adj. rear. Trigger adj. for weight and position. Blued finish. Stippled handrest grips. Imported from 1990 to date.
Right-hand model . . . . NiB $1459 Ex $1324 Gd $706
Left-hand model . . . . NiB $1506 Ex $1388 Gd $770

MODEL DES/69-U TARGET PISTOL
Caliber: .22 LR. Five-round magazine, 5.9-inch bbl., w/250 gm counterweight. 10.6 inches overall. Trigger adjusts for position and pull. Weight: 35.3 oz. Blade front sight, micro-adj. rear. Checkered walnut thumbrest grips w/adj. handrest. Blued finish. Imported from 1969 to date.
Right-hand model . . . . NiB $1242 Ex $1082 Gd $567
Left-hand model . . . . NiB $1267 Ex $1113 Gd $603

MODEL DES/VO RAPID FIRE MATCH AUTOMATIC PISTOL . . . . NiB $1087 Ex $850 Gd $598
Caliber: .22 Short. Five-round magazine, 5.9-inch bbl., 10.4 inches overall. Weight: 43 oz. Click adj. rear sight blade front. Checkered walnut thumbrest grips w/adj. handrest. Trigger adj. for length of pull. Made from 1974 to date.

KRIEGS MODELL L AUTOMATIC PISTOL . . . . NiB $364 Ex $286 Gd $194
Caliber: .32 Auto (7.65mm). Nine-round magazine, 3.2-inch bbl., 5.8 inches overall. Weight: 26.5 oz. Fixed sights. Blued finish. Plastic grips. Mfd. during German occupation of France 1940-45. Note: Bears the German military acceptance marks and may have grips marked "7.65m/m 9 SCHUSS."

MODEL L AUTOMATIC PISTOL . . . . NiB $286 Ex $235 Gd $132
Calibers: .22 LR, .32 Auto (7.65mm), .380 Auto (9mm Short). 10-round magazine in .22, 7 in .32, 6 in .380; 3.3-inch bbl.; 5.8 inches overall. Weight: 16.5 oz. (.380 Auto w/light alloy frame), 23 oz. (w/steel frame). Fixed sights. Blued finish. Plastic grips. Intro. in 1955. Disc.

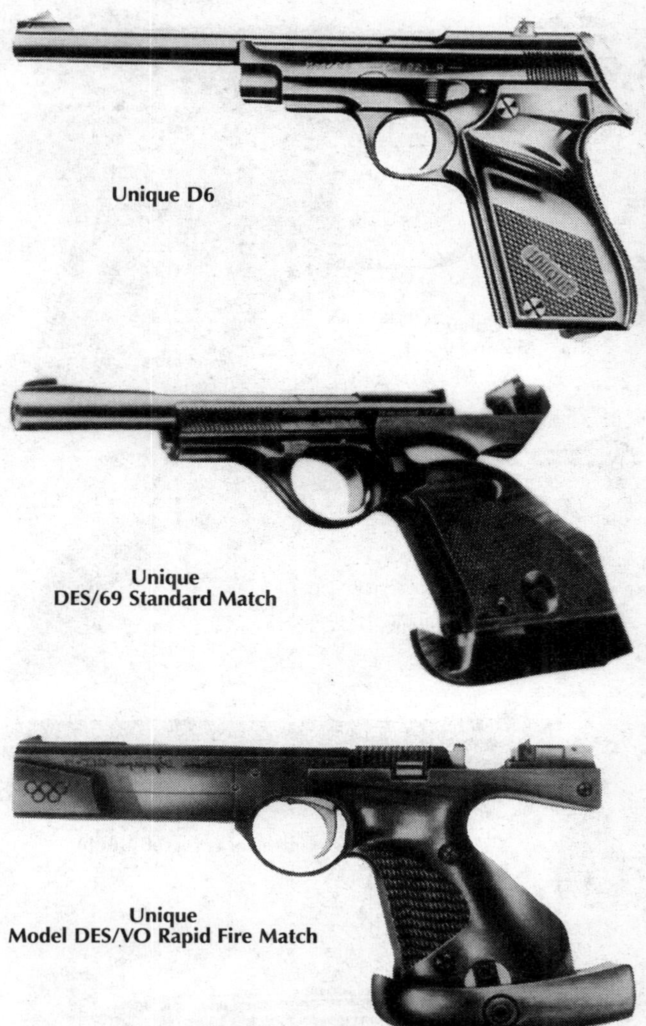

Unique D6

Unique DES/69 Standard Match

Unique Model DES/VO Rapid Fire Match

MODEL MIKROS POCKET AUTOMATIC PISTOL . . . . NiB $228 Ex $182 Gd $125
Calibers: .22 Short, .25 Auto (6.35mm). Six-round magazine, 2.25-inch bbl., 4.44 inches overall. Weight: 9.5 oz. (light alloy frame), 12.5 oz. (steel frame.). Fixed sights. Blued finish. Plastic grips. Intro. in 1957. Disc.

MODEL RR AUTOMATIC PISTOL . . . . NiB $204 Ex $194 Gd $132
Postwar commercial version of WWII Kriegsmodell w/same general specifications. Intro. in 1951. Disc.

MODEL 2000-U MATCH PISTOL
Caliber: .22 Short. Designed for U.I.T. rapid fire competitution. Five-round top-inserted magazine, 5.5-inch bbl., w/five vents for recoil reduction. 11.4 inches overall. Weight: 43.4 oz. Special light alloy frame, solid steel slide and shock absorber. Stippled French walnut w/adj. handrest. Imported from 1990-96.
Right-hand model . . . . NiB $1408 Ex $1150 Gd $644
Left-hand model . . . . NiB $1448 Ex $1190 Gd $624

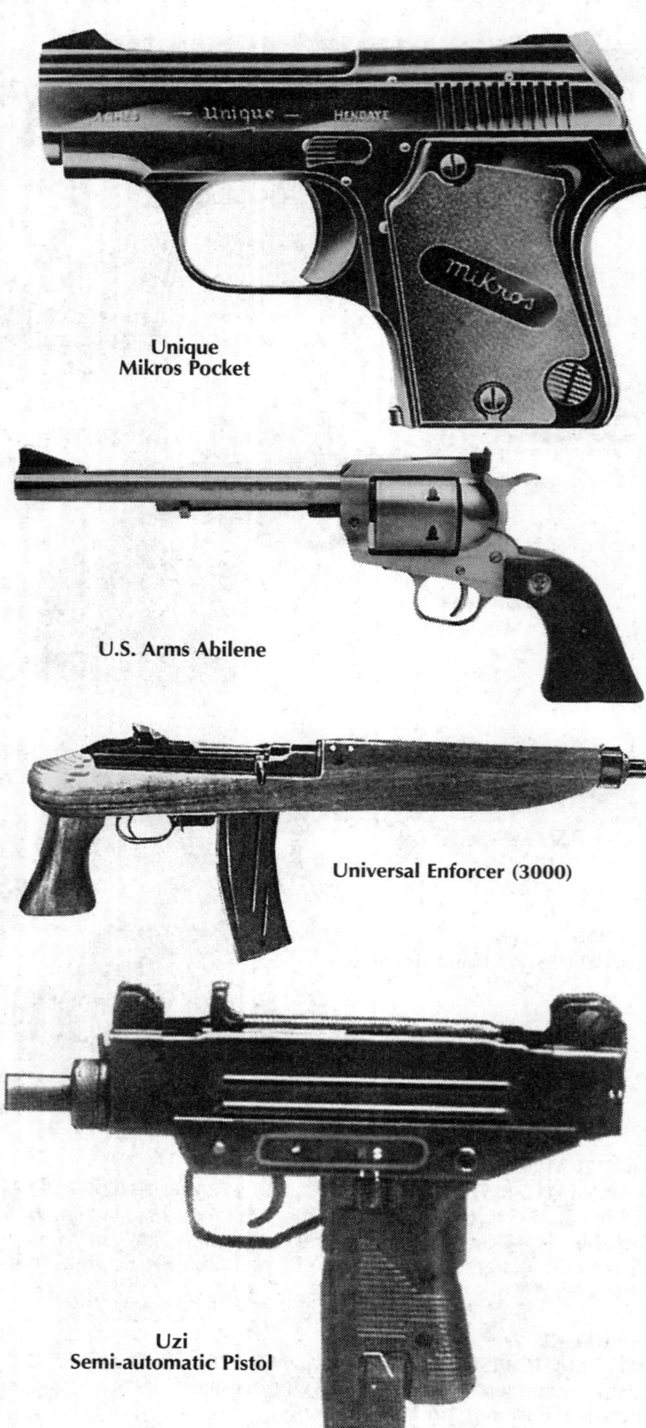

Unique
Mikros Pocket

U.S. Arms Abilene

Universal Enforcer (3000)

Uzi
Semi-automatic Pistol

UNITED STATES ARMS CORPORATION — Riverhead, New York

ABILENE SA REVOLVER

Safety Bar action. Calibers: .357 Mag., .41 Mag., .44 Mag., .45 Colt and .357/9mm convertible model w/two cylinders. Six-round cylinder, bbl. lengths: 4.63-, 5.5-, 6.5-inch, 7.5- and 8.5-inches in .44 Mag. only. Weight: About 48 oz. Adj. rear sight, ramp front. Blued finish or stainless steel. Smooth walnut grips. Made from 1976-83.

.44 Magnum, blued finish . . . . NiB $341 Ex $290 Gd $203
Magnum, stainless steel. . . . . NiB $392 Ex $331 Gd $239
Other calibers, blued finish. . . . . . . NiB $322 Ex $264 Gd $191
.357 Magnum, stainless steel. . . . . . NiB $386 Ex $315 Gd $226
Convertible, .357 Mag./9mm
Para., blued finish . . . . NiB $341 Ex $290 Gd $203

UNIVERSAL FIREARMS CORPORATION — Hialeah, Florida

This company was purchased by Iver Johnson Arms in the mid-1980s, when the Enforcer listed below was disc.. An improved version was issued under the Iver Johnson name (see separate listing).

ENFORCER (3000)
SEMIAUTOMATIC PISTOL . . . . NiB $302 Ex $251 Gd $185

M-1 Carbine-type action. Caliber: 30 Carbine. Five-, 15- or 30-round clip magazine, 10.25-inch bbl., 17.75 inches overall. Weight: 4.5 lbs. (with 30-round magazine). Adj. rear sight, blade front. Blued finish. Walnut stock w/pistol grip and handguard. Made from 1964-83.

UZI PISTOLS — Mfd. by Israel Military Industries, Israel

(Currently imported by UZI America)

SEMIAUTOMATIC PISTOL . . . . . . NiB $1033 Ex $916 Gd $712

Caliber: 9mm Para. 20-round magazine, 4.5-inch bbl., about 9.5 inches overall. Weight: 3.8 lbs. Front post-type sight, rear open-type, both adj. Disc. in 1993.

"EAGLE" SERIES
SEMIAUTOMATIC DA PISTOL

Caliber: 9mm Parabellum, .40 S&W, .45 ACP (Short Slide). 10-round magazine, 3.5-, 3.7- and 4.4-inch bbl., weight: 32 oz. to 35 oz. Blade front sight, drift adjustable tritium rear. Matte blue finish. Black synthetic grips. Imported from 1997 to date.

Compact model
(DA or DAO). . . . . NiB $529 Ex $483 Gd $371
Polymer compact model . . . . NiB $529 Ex $483 Gd $371
Full-size model . . . . NiB $529 Ex $483 Gd $371
Short slide model. . . . . NiB $529 Ex $483 Gd $371

WALTHER PISTOLS — Manufactured by German, French and Swiss firms

The following Walther pistols were made before and during World War II by Waffenfabrik Walther, Zella-Mehlis (Thür.), Germany.

MODEL 1
AUTOMATIC PISTOL . . . . NiB $712 Ex $584 Gd $275

Caliber: .25 Auto (6.35mm). Six-round. 2.1-inch bbl., 4.4 inches overall. Weight: 12.8 oz. Fixed sights. Blued finish. Checkered hard rubber grips. Intro. in 1908.

MODEL 2
AUTOMATIC PISTOL

Caliber: .25 Auto (6.35mm). Six-round magazine, 2.1-inch bbl., 4.2 inches overall. Weight: 9.8 oz. Fixed sights. Blued finish. Checkered hard rubber grips. Intro. in 1909.

Standard model. . . . . NiB $511 Ex $486 Gd $187
Pop-up sight model . . . . NiB $1503 Ex $1091 Gd $632

MODEL 3 AUTOMATIC PISTOL . . . . NiB $1605 Ex $1347 Gd $626
Caliber: .32 Auto (7.65mm). Six-round magazine, 2.6-inch bbl., 5 inches overall. Weight: 16.6 oz. Fixed sights. Blued finish. Checkered hard rubber grips. Intro. in 1910.

MODEL 4 AUTOMATIC PISTOL . . . . NiB $449 Ex $372 Gd $190
Caliber: .32 Auto (7.65mm). Eight-round magazine, 3.5-inch bbl., 5.9 inches overall. Weight: 18.6 oz. Fixed sights. Blued finish. Checkered hard rubber grips. Made from 1910-18.

MODEL 5 AUTOMATIC PISTOL . . . . NiB $537 Ex $475 Gd $176
Improved version of Model 2 w/same general specifications, distinguished chiefly by better workmanship and appearance. Intro. in 1913.

MODEL 6 AUTOMATIC PISTOL . . . . . . NiB $6307 Ex $4763 Gd $1208
Caliber: 9mm Para. Eight-round magazine, 4.75-inch bbl., 8.25 inches overall. Weight: 34 oz. Fixed sights. Blued finish. Checkered hard rubber grips. Made from 1915-17. Note: The powerful 9mm Para. cartridge is too much for the simple blow-back system of this pistol, so firing is not recommended.

MODEL 7 AUTOMATIC PISTOL . . . . NiB $720 Ex $566 Gd $257
Caliber: .25 Auto. (6.35mm). Eight-round magazine, 3-inch bbl., 5.3 inches overall. Weight: 11.8 oz. Fixed sights. Blued finish. Checkered hard rubber grips. Made from 1917-18.

MODEL 8 AUTOMATIC PISTOL . . . . NiB $592 Ex $510 Gd $200
Caliber: .25 Auto. (6.35mm). Eight-round magazine, 2.88-inch bbl., 5.13 inches overall. Weight: 12.38 oz. Fixed sights. Blued finish. Checkered plastic grips. Made from 1920-45.

MODEL 8 LIGHTWEIGHT
AUTOMATIC PISTOL . . . . NiB $555 Ex $453 Gd $323
Same as standard Model Eight except about 25 percent lighter due to use of aluminum alloys.

MODEL 9 VEST POCKET
AUTOMATIC PISTOL . . . . NiB $668 Ex $591 Gd $215
Caliber: .25 Auto (6.35mm). Six-round magazine, 2-inch bbl., 3.94 inches overall. Weight: 9 oz. Fixed sights. Blued finish. Checkered plastic grips. Made from 1921-45.

MODEL HP DOUBLE-ACTION AUTOMATIC
Prewar commercial version of the P38 marked with an "N" proof over an "Eagle" or "Crown." The "HP" is an abbreviation of "Heeres Pistole" (Army Pistol). Caliber: 9mm Para. 8-round magazine, 5-inch bbl., 8.38 inches overall. Weight: About 34.5 oz. Fixed sights. Blued finish. Checkered wood or plastic grips. The Model HP is distinguished by its notably fine material and workmanship. Made from 1937-44. (SN range 1000-25900)
First production (Swedish Trials
model H1000-H2000). . . . . NiB $3171 Ex $2565 Gd $1791
Standard commercial production
(2000-24,000) . . . . NiB $1609 Ex $1403 Gd $883
War production - marked "P38"
(24,000-26,000) . . . . NiB $1300 Ex $1089 Gd $733
W/Nazi proof "Eagle/359," add $240

OLYMPIA FUNFKAMPF
MODEL AUTOMATIC . . . . NiB $1840 Ex $1505 Gd $629
Caliber: .22 LR. 10-round magazine, 9.6-inch bbl., 13 inches overall. Weight: 33 oz., less weight. Set of 4 detachable weights. Adj. target sights. Blued finish. Checkered grips. Intro. in 1936.

OLYMPIA HUNTING
MODEL AUTOMATIC . . . . NiB $1711 Ex $1299 Gd $516
Same general specifications as Olympia Sport Model but w/4-inch bbl., Weight: 28.5 oz.

Walther Model 5

Walther Model 8

Walther Model 9

OLYMPIA RAPID FIRE
MODEL AUTOMATIC . . . . NiB $1711 Ex $1299 Gd $619
Caliber: .22 Short. Six-round magazine, 7.4-inch bbl., 10.7 inches overall. Weight: (without 12.38 oz. detachable muzzle weight,) 27.5 oz. Adj. target sights. Blued finish. Checkered grips. Made about 1936-40.

OLYMPIA SPORT
MODEL AUTOMATIC . . . . NiB $1067 Ex $913 Gd $496
Caliber: .22 LR. 10-round magazine, 7.4-inch bbl., 10.7 inches overall. Weight: 30.5 oz., less weight. Adj. target sights. Blued finish. Checkered grips. Set of four detachable weights was supplied at extra cost. Made about 1936-40.

Walther PP (Prewar)

P38 MILITARY DA AUTOMATIC

Modification of the Model HP adopted as an official German Service arm in 1938 and produced throughout WW II by Walther (code "ac"), Mauser (code "byf") and a few other manufacturers. General specifications and appearance same as Model HP, but w/a vast difference in quality, the P38 being a mass-produced military pistol. Some of the late wartime models were very roughly finished and tolerances were quite loose.

War Production w/Walther banner (1940)

Zero Ser. 1st Iss. (SN 01-01,000) .... NiB $7925 Ex $6071 Gd $2260
Zero Ser. 2nd Iss. (SN 01,000-03,500) .... NiB $6380 Ex $4989 Gd $2157
Zero Ser. 3rd Iss. (SN 03,500-013,000) ...... NiB $2952 Ex $2180 Gd $944

WALTHER CONTRACT PISTOLS (LATE 1940-44)

"480" code Series (SN 1-7,600) .... NiB $5607 Ex $3805 Gd $1436
"ac" code Ser. w/no date (SN 7,350-9,700)... NiB $5865 Ex $4526 Gd $2054
"ac" code Ser. w/.40 below
code (SN 9,700-9,900A) .... NiB $4320 Ex $3805 Gd $1745
"ac40" code inline Ser. (SN 1-9,900B)....... NiB $2225 Ex $1813 Gd $763
"ac" code Ser. w/41 below code (SN 1-4,5001) .. NiB $1685 Ex $1530 Gd $861
"ac" code Ser. w/42 below code
(SN 4,500I-9,300K) .... NiB $1427 Ex $1273 Gd $655
"ac" code Ser. w/43 date (inline or below)..... NiB $708 Ex $553 Gd $399
"ac" code Ser. w/45 (inline or below)......... NiB $656 Ex $553 Gd $373

MAUSER CONTRACT PISTOLS (LATE 1942-44)

"byf" code Ser. w/42 date (19,000 prod.) ..... NiB $1243 Ex $1140 Gd $728
"bcf" code Ser. w/43, 44 or 45 date
(inline or below) .... NiB $789 Ex $686 Gd $531
"svw" code Ser. (French prod. w/Nazi proofs).. NiB $1207 Ex $1027 Gd $537
"svw" code Ser. (French prod. w/star proof) .... NiB $508 Ex $421 Gd $302

SPREEWERKE CONTRACT PISTOLS (LATE 1942-45)

"cyq" code 1st Ser. w/Eagle over
359 (500 prod.) .... NiB $1752 Ex $1428 Gd $1001
"cyq" code Standard Ser. (300,000 prod.) ..... NiB $884 Ex $498 Gd $395
"cyq" code "0" Ser. (5,000 prod.)............. NiB $1121 Ex $715 Gd $529

MODEL PP DA AUTOMATIC PISTOL

Polizeipistole (Police Pistol). Calibers: .22 LR (5.6mm), .25 Auto (6.35mm), .32 Auto (7.65mm), .380 Auto (9mm). Eight-round magazine, (7-round in .380), 3.88-inch bbl., 6.94 inches overall. Weight: 23 oz. Fixed sights. Blued finish. Checkered plastic grips. 1929-45. Post-War production and importation 1952 to present.

NOTE: Wartime models are inferior in quality to prewar commercial pistols.

COMMERCIAL MODEL W/CROWN "N" PROOF

.22 cal. (w/comm. Crown "N" proof)....... NiB $1120 Ex $970 Gd $652
.25 cal. (w/comm. Crown "N" proof)....... NiB $3662 Ex $3298 Gd $1650
.32 cal. (w/comm. Crown "N" proof)......... NiB $569 Ex $507 Gd $316
.32 cal. (w/Dural (alloy) frame)............. NiB $545 Ex $563 Gd $355
.32 cal. (w/Verchromt Fin., pre-war)......... NiB $1163 Ex $1575 Gd $633
.32 cal. (A.F.Stoeger Contract, pre-war) ...... NiB $1832 Ex $1369 Gd $571
.32 cal. (Allemagne French contract,
pre-war) .... NiB $1369 Ex $1163 Gd $571
.380 cal. (w/Comm. Crown "N" proof) ...... NiB $1420 Ex $1158 Gd $674
.380 cal. (w/Verchromt Fin., pre-war)........ NiB $2622 Ex $2313 Gd $889

WARTIME MODEL WITH EAGLE "N" PROOF

.32 cal. (w/Waffenampt proofs)............... NiB $636 Ex $549 Gd $618
.32 cal. (w/Eagle "C" Nazi Police markings)...... NiB $925 Ex $791 Gd $46
.32 cal. (w/Eagle "F" Nazi Police markings) ..... NiB $928 Ex $791 Gd $466
.32 cal. (w/NSKK markings) .... NiB $3131 Ex $2281 Gd $891
.32 cal. (w/NSDAP Gruppe markings)....... NiB $2513 Ex $2153 Gd $839
.380 cal. (w/Waffenampt proofs)........ NiB $1372 Ex $1110 Gd $750

COMMERCIAL MODEL (POST-WAR)

.22 cal. (German manufacture).............. NiB $1028 Ex $899 Gd $487
.32 cal. (German manufacture).............. NiB $925 Ex $564 Gd $432
.380 cal. (German manufacture)............ NiB $1053 Ex $899 Gd $358
.22 cal. (French manufacture) .... NiB $521 Ex $465 Gd $228
.32 cal. (French manufacture) .... NiB $521 Ex $465 Gd $228
.380 cal. (French manufacture)............. NiB $568 Ex $505 Gd $244
.22, .32 or .380 Cal. (other foreign manuf.) ..... NiB $362 Ex $295 Gd $207

MODEL PP SPORT DA AUTOMATIC PISTOL

Target version of the Model PP. Caliber: .22 LR. Eight-round magazine, 5.75- to 7.75 inch bbl. w/adjustable sights. Blue or nickel finish. Checkered plastic grips w/thumbrest. Made from 1953-70.

PP Sport (Walther manufacture)............ NiB $976 Ex $873 Gd $516
PP Sport (Manurhin manufacture)........... NiB $796 Ex $744 Gd $518
PP Sport C model (comp./single act.)........ NiB $997 Ex $914 Gd $616
W/nickel finish, add $170
W/matched bbl., weights, add $75

MODEL PP DELUXE ENGRAVED

These elaborately engraved models are available in blued finish, silver- or gold-plated.

Blued finish .... NiB $1536 Ex $1351 Gd $1145
Silver-plated............... NiB $1866 Ex $1444 Gd $1248
Gold-plated................ NiB $2077 Ex $1753 Gd $1351
W/ivory grips, add.................................. $250
W/presentation case, add $700
.22 caliber, add $50
.380 caliber, add 95%

MODEL PP LIGHTWEIGHT

Same as standard Model PP except about 25 percent lighter due to use of aluminum alloys (Dural). Values 40 percent higher. (See individual listings).

WALTHER MODEL PP
SUPER DA PISTOL.............. NiB $922 Ex $754 Gd $540

Caliber: 9x18mm. Seven-round magazine, 3.6-inch bbl., 6.9 inches overall. Weight: 30 oz. Fixed sights. Blued finish. Checkered plastic grips. Made from 1974-81.

MODEL PP 7.65MM
PRESENTATION............. NiB $1972 Ex $1598 Gd $1121

Made of soft aluminum alloy in green-gold color, these pistols were not intended to be fired.

MODEL PPK DOUBLE-ACTION AUTOMATIC PISTOL

Polizeipistole Kriminal (Detective Pistol). Calibers: .22 LR (5.6mm), .25 Auto (6.35mm), .32 Auto (7.65mm), .380 Auto (9mm). Seven-round magazine, (6-round in .380), 3.25-inch bbl., 5.88 inches overall. Weight: 19 oz. Fixed sights. Blued finish. Checkered plastic grips. ***Note: Wartime models are inferior in workmanship to pre-war commercial pistols. Made 1931-45.***

NOTE: *After both World Wars, the Walther manufacturing facility was required to cease the production of "restricted" firearms as part of the armistice agreements. Following WW II, Walther moved its manufacturing facility from the original location in Zella/Mehilis, Germany to Ulm/Donau. In 1950, the firm Manufacture de Machines du Haut Rhine at Mulhouse, France was licensed by Walther and started production of PP and PPK models at the Manurhin facility in 1952. The MK II Walthers as produced at Manurhin were imported into the U.S. until 1968 when CGA importation requirements restricted the PPK firearm configuration from further importation. As a result, Walther developed the PPK/S to conform to the new regulations and licensed Interarms to produce the firearm in the U.S. from 1986-99. From 1984-86, Manurhin imported PP and PPK/S type firearms under the Manurhin logo. Additional manufacturing facilities (both licensed & unlicensed) that produced PP and PPK type firearms were established after WW II in various locations and other countries including: China, France, Hungary, Korea, Romania and Turkey. In 1996, Walther was sold to Umarex Sportwaffen GmbH and manufacturing facilities were relocated in Arnsberg, Germany. In 1999, Walther formed a partnership with Smith and Wesson and selected Walther firearms are licensed for production in the U.S.*

COMMERCIAL MODEL W/EAGLE "N" PROOF (PREWAR)

.22 cal. (w/Comm. Eagle "N" proof) ..... NiB $1412 Ex $1258 Gd $609
.25 cal. (w/Comm. Eagle "N" proof) ..... NiB $5290 Ex $3230 Gd $2818
.32 cal. (w/Comm. Eagle "N" proof) ..... NiB $734 Ex $528 Gd $425
.380 cal. (w/Comm. Eagle "N" proof)..... NiB $2707 Ex $2192 Gd $956

WARTIME MODEL W/EAGLE "N" PROOF

.22 cal. (w/Comm. Eagle "N" proof)...... NiB $1406 Ex $1150 Gd $822
.22 cal. (w/Dural frame) .... NiB $1670 Ex $1361 Gd $1258
.32 cal. (w/Comm. Eagle "N" proof)........ NiB $621 Ex $518 Gd $312
.32 cal. (w/Dural frame) .... NiB $859 Ex $699 Gd $493
.32 cal. (w/Verchromt Fin., Pre-War) ..... NiB $2313 Ex $1798 Gd $819
.380 cal. (w/Comm. Eagle "N" proof)..... NiB $2828 Ex $2210 Gd $871
.380 cal. (w/Dural frame) .... NiB $3034 Ex $2313 Gd $922
.380 cal. (w/Verchromt Fin., Pre-War) .... NiB $3494 Ex $2622 Gd $1927
.22 cal. (w/Comm. Eagle "N" proof) .... NiB $791 Ex $781 Gd $559
.32 cal. (w/Waffenampt proofs) .... NiB $1028 Ex $744 Gd $384
.32 cal. (w/Eagle "C" Nazi Police markings) . NiB $1028 Ex $744 Gd $343
.32 cal. (w/Eagle "F" Nazi Police markings) .... NiB $1382 Ex $1022 Gd $481
.32 cal. (w/NSKK markings)............ NiB $2201 Ex $1790 Gd $1265
.32 cal. (w/NSDAP Gruppe markings) .... NiB $2102 Ex $1587 Gd $1149
.380 cal. (w/Waffenampt proofs) .... NiB $1366 Ex $1057 Gd $799

COMMERCIAL MODEL (POST-WAR)

.22 cal. (German manufacture)........... NiB $1043 Ex $914 Gd $399
.32 cal. (German manufacture)........... NiB $940 Ex $579 Gd $373
.380 cal. (German manufacture).......... NiB $1058 Ex $579 Gd $476
.22 cal. (French manufacture) .... NiB $2190 Ex $902 Gd $516
.32 cal. (French manufacture) .... NiB $847 Ex $641 Gd $410
.380 cal. (French manufacture)........... NiB $1161 Ex $827 Gd $440
.22, .32 or .380 cal. (other foreign manuf.) .. NiB $327 Ex $270 Gd $196

COMMERCIAL MODEL (U.S. PRODUCTION)

.380 cal. (w/blue finish).................. NiB $539 Ex $426 Gd $380
.380 cal. (w/nickel finish) .... NiB $539 Ex $426 Gd $380
.32 or .380 Cal. (stainless steel)............ NiB $539 Ex $426 Gd $380

MODEL PPK DELUXE ENGRAVED

These elaborately engraved models are available in blued finish, chrome-, silver- or gold-plated.

Blued finish .... NiB $1836 Ex $1476 Gd $1141
Chrome-plated .... NiB $2918 Ex $1527 Gd $1162
Silver-plated .... NiB $2120 Ex $1579 Gd $1215

Walther PPK (WW II)

Walther PPK Silver-Plated

Gold-plated ....NiB $2464 Ex $1872 Gd $1386
W/ivory grips, add $250
W/Presentation case, add $700
.22 cal, add $50
.25 cal, add $100
.380 cal, add $95

MODEL PPK LIGHTWEIGHT

Same as standard Model PPK except about 25 percent lighter due to aluminum alloys. Values 50 percent higher.

MODEL PPK 7.65MM PRESENTATION

PRESENTATION.............. NiB $1752 Ex $1294 Gd $799

Made of soft aluminum alloy in green-gold color, these pistols were not intended to be fired.

MODEL PPK/S DA AUTOMATIC PISTOL

Designed to meet the requirements of the U.S. Gun Control Act of 1968, this model has the frame of the PP and the shorter slide and bbl., of the PPK. Overall length: 6.1 inches. Weight: 23 oz. Other specifications are the same as those of standard PPK except steel frame only. German, French and U.S. production 1971 to date. U.S. version made by Interarms 1978-99.

.22 cal. (German manufacture) ... NiB $1211 Ex $902 Gd $516
.32 cal. (German manufacture) ... NiB $897 Ex $691 Gd $429
.380 cal. (German manufacture) .. NiB $1211 Ex $877 Gd $439
.22 cal. (French manufacture) ..... NiB $832 Ex $600 Gd $445
.32 cal. (French manufacture) ..... NiB $837 Ex $523 Gd $383
.380 cal. (French manufacture) .... NiB $883 Ex $574 Gd $430
.22, .32 or .380 cal., blue
(U.S. manufacture) .... NiB $567 Ex $454 Gd $335
.22, .32 or .380 cal., stainless
(U.S. manuf.) .... NiB $567 Ex $454 Gd $413

NOTE: *Interarms (Interarmco) acquired a license from Walther in 1978 to manufacturer PP and PPK models at the Ranger Manufacturing Co., Inc. in Gadsden, Alabama. In 1988 the Ranger facility was licensed as EMCO and continued to produce Walther firearms for Interarms until 1996. From 1996-99, Black Creek in Gadsden, Alabama produced Walther pistols for Interarms. In 1999, Smith & Wesson acquired manufacturing rights for Walther firearms at the Black Creek facility.*

MODELS PPK/S DELUXE ENGRAVED
These elaborately engraved models are available in blued finish, chrome-, silver- or gold-plated.
Blued finish . . . . NiB $1544 Ex $1132 Gd $1080
Chrome-plated . . . . NiB $1429 Ex $1130 Gd $821
Silver-plated. . . . . NiB $1595 Ex $1183 Gd $1877
Gold-plated . . . . NiB $1771 Ex $1437 Gd $1011

NOTE: *The following Walther pistols are now manufactured by Carl Walther, Waffenfabrik, Ulm/Donau, Germany.*

SELF-LOADING
SPORT PISTOL . . . . NiB $783 Ex $731 Gd $500
Caliber: .22 LR. 10-round magazine, bbl. lengths: 6- and 9-inch, 9.88 inches overall w/6-inch bbl. Target sights. Blued finish. One-piece, wood or plastic grips, checkered. Intro. in 1932.

MODEL FREE PISTOL . . . . NiB $1898 Ex $1461 Gd $807
Single-Shot. Caliber: .22 LR. 11.7-inch heavy bbl., Weight: 48 oz. Adj. grips and target sights w/electronic trigger. Importation disc. 1991.

MODEL GSP TARGET AUTOMATIC PISTOL
Calibers: .22 LR, .32 S&W Long Wadcutter. Five-round magazine, 4.5-inch bbl., 11.8 inches overall. Weights: 44.8 oz. (.22 cal.) or 49.4 oz. (.32 cal.). Adj. target sights. Black finish. Walnut thumbrest grips w/adj. handrest. Made from 1969-94.
.22 LR . . . . NiB $1532 Ex $1331 Gd $581
.32 S&W Long
Wadcutter . . . . NiB $1738 Ex $1228 Gd $605
Conversion unit.
.22 Short
or .22 LR add. . . . . NiB $992 Ex $873 Gd $894

MODEL OSP RAPID
FIRE TARGET PISTOL. . . . . NiB $1609 Ex $1146 Gd $561
Caliber: .22 Short. Five-round magazine, 4.5-inch bbl., 11.8 inches overall. Weight: 42.3 oz. Adj. target sights. Black finish. Walnut thumbrest grips w/adj. handrest. .22 LR conversion unit available (add $275). Made from 1968-94.

MODEL P4 (P38-LV)
DA PISTOL . . . . NiB $746 Ex $643 Gd $329
Similar to P38 except has an uncocking device instead of a manual safety. Caliber: 9mm Para. 4.3-inch bbl., 7.9 inches overall. Other general specifications same as for current model P38. Made from 1974-82.

MODEL P5 DA PISTOL . . . . NiB $828 Ex $699 Gd $468
Alloy frame w/frame-mounted decocking levers. Caliber: 9mm Para. Eight-round magazine, 3.5-inch bbl., 7 inches overall. Weight: 28 oz. blued finish. Checkered walnut or synthetic grips. Made from 1988 to date.

MODEL P5
COMPACT PISTOL . . . . NiB $1008 Ex $880 Gd $442
Similar to model P5 except w/3.1-inch bbl. and weight: 26 oz. Made from 1988-96.

Walther Free Pistol

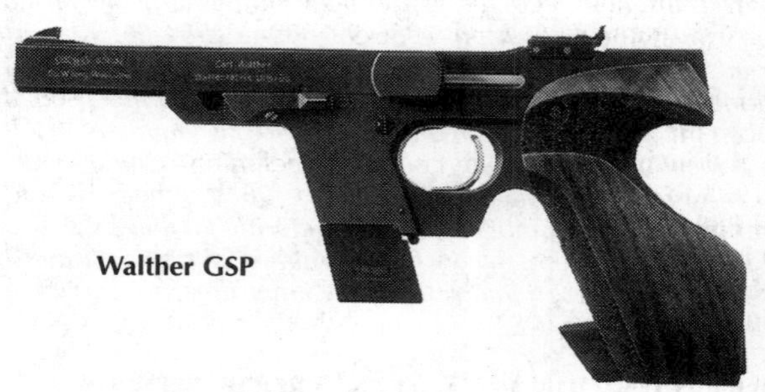
Walther GSP

Walther P5

MODEL P38 (P1) DA AUTOMATIC
Postwar commercial version of the P38, has light alloy frame. Calibers: .22 LR, 7.65mm Luger, 9mm Para. Eight-round magazine, bbl., lengths: 5.1-inch in .22 caliber, 4.9- inch in 7.65mm and 9mm, 8.5 inches overall. Weight: 28.2 oz. Fixed sights. Nonreflective black finish. Checkered plastic grips. Made from 1957-89. Note: The "P1" is W. German Armed Forces official pistol.
.22 LR . . . . NiB $751 Ex $638 Gd $390
Other calibers . . . . NiB $699 Ex $596 Gd $334

MODEL P38 DELUXE ENGRAVED PISTOL
Elaborately engraved, available in blued or chrome-, silver- or gold-plated finish.
Blued finish . . . . NiB $1949 Ex $1460 Gd $889
Chrome-plated . . . . NiB $1632 Ex $1297 Gd $860
Silver-plated . . . . NiB $1606 Ex $1297 Gd $905
Gold-plated . . . . NiB $1971 Ex $1587 Gd $1147

MODEL P38K . . . . NiB $778 Ex $680 Gd $345
Short-barreled version of current P38, the "K" standing for "kurz" (meaning short). Same general specifications as standard model except 2.8-inch bbl., 6.3 inches overall, weight: 27.2 oz. Front sight is slide mounted. Caliber: 9mm Para. Made from 1974-80.

MODEL P 88 DA AUTOMATIC PISTOL . . . . NiB $1455 Ex $1300 Gd $564
Caliber: 9mm Para. 15-round magazine, 4-inch bbl., 7.38 inches overall. Weight: 31.5 oz. Blade front sight, adj. rear. Checkered black synthetic grips. External hammer w/ambidextrous decocking levers. Alloy frame w/matte blued steel slide. Made from 1987-93.

MODEL P 88 DA COMPACT
Similar to the standard P 88 Model except w/10- or 13-round magazine, 3.8-inch bbl., 7.1 inches overall. Weight: 29 oz. Imported from 1993 to date.
Model P88 (early importation) . . . . NiB $940 Ex $812 Gd $554
Model P88 (post 94 importation) . . . . NiB $837 Ex $709 Gd $477

MODEL P99 DA AUTOMATIC PISTOL . . . . NiB $636 Ex $559 Gd $405
Calibers: 9mm Para., .40 S&W or 9x21mm. 10-round magazine, 4-inch bbl., 7.2 inches overall. Weight: 22-25 oz. Ambidextrous magazine release, decocking lever and 3-function safety. Interchangeable front post sight, micro-adj. rear. Polymer gripframe w/blued slide. Imported from 1997 to date.

MODEL TPH DA POCKET PISTOL
Light alloy frame. Calibers: .22 LR, .25 ACP (6.35mm). Six-round magazine, 2.25-inch bbl., 5.38 inches overall. Weight: 14 oz. Fixed sights. Blued finish. Checkered plastic grips. Made 1968 to date. Note: Few Walther-made models reached the U.S. because of import restrictions. A U.S.-made version was mfd. by Interarms from 1986-99.
German model . . . . NiB $878 Ex $724 Gd $358
U.S. model . . . . NiB $431 Ex $395 Gd $261

NOTE: The Walther Olympia Model pistols were manufactured 1952-1963 by Hämmerli AG Jagd-und Sportwaffenfabrik, Lenzburg, Switzerland, and marketed as "Hämmerli-Walther." See Hämmerli listings for specific data.

OLYMPIA MODEL 200 AUTO PISTOL, 1952 TYPE . . . . NiB $745 Ex $683 Gd $462
Similar to 1936 Walther Olympia Funfkampf Model.

For the following Hammerli-Walther Models (200, 201, 202, 203, 204, and 205) See listings under Hammerli Section.

WARNER PISTOL — Norwich, Connecticut Warner Arms Corp. (or Davis-Warner Arms Co.)

INFALLIBLE POCKET AUTOMATIC PISTOL . . . . NiB $518 Ex $415 Gd $158
Caliber: .32 Auto. Seven-round magazine, 3-inch bbl., 6.5 inches overall. Weight: About 24 oz. Fixed sights. Blued finish. Hard rubber grips. Made from 1917-19.

Walther P38

Walther P38K

Walther P88

Walther TPH (Current)

Webley 9MM Military Police Revolver

Webley Mark III 38 Military & Police Revolver

WEBLEY & SCOTT LTD. — London and Birmingham, England

MODEL 9MM MILITARY & POLICE AUTOMATIC . . . . NiB $1061 Ex $958 Gd $572
Caliber: 9mm Browning Long. Eight-round magazine, 8 inches overall. Weight: 32 oz. Fixed sights. Blued finish. Checkered Vulcanite grips. Made from 1909-30.

MODEL 25 HAMMER AUTOMATIC . . . . NiB $374 Ex $296 Gd $168
Caliber: .25 Automatic. Six-round magazine, overall length: 4.75 inches. Weight: 11.75 oz. No sights. Blued finish. Checkered Vulcanite grips. Made from 1906-40.

MODEL 25 HAMMERLESS AUTOMATIC . . . . NiB $425 Ex $271 Gd $168
Caliber: .25 Automatic. Six-round magazine, overall length: 4.25 inches, weight: 9.75 oz. Fixed sights. Blued finish. Checkered Vulcanite grips. Made from 1909-40.

MARK I 455 AUTOMATIC PISTOL . . . . NiB $1896 Ex $1433 Gd $660
Caliber: .455 Webley Auto. Seven-round magazine, 5-inch bbl., 8.5 inches overall. Weight: About 39 oz. Fixed sights. Blued finish. Checkered Vulcanite grips. Made 1913-31. Reissued during WWII. Total production about 9,300. Note: Mark I No. 2 is same pistol w/adj. rear sight and modified manual safety.

MARK III 38 MILITARY & POLICE REVOLVER . . . . NiB $396 Ex $340 Gd $180
Hinged frame. DA. Caliber: .38 S&W. Six-round cylinder, bbl. lengths: 3- and 4-inches. 9.5 inches overall (with 4-inch bbl.). Weight: 21 oz. (with 4-inch bbl.). Fixed sights. Blued finish. Checkered walnut or Vulcanite grips. Made from 1897-45.

MARK IV 22 CALIBER TARGET REVOLVER. . . . . NiB $753 Ex $624 Gd $264
Same frame and general appearance as Mark IV .38. Caliber: .22 LR. Six-round cylinder, 6-inch bbl., 10.13 inches overall. Weight: 34 oz. Target sights. Blued finish. Checkered grips. Disc. in 1945.

MARK IV 38 MILITARY & POLICE REVOLVER . . . . NiB $510 Ex $433 Gd $240
Identical in appearance to the double-action Mark IV .22 w/hinged frame except chambered for .38 S&W. Six-round cylinder, bbl. length: 3-, 4- and 5-inches; 9.13 inches overall (with 5-inch bbl.). Weight: 27 oz. (with 5-inch bbl.). Fixed sights. Blued finish. Checkered grips. Made from 1929-c. 1957.

MARK VI NO. 1 BRITISH SERVICE REVOLVER . . . . NiB $349 Ex $297 Gd $205
DA. Hinged frame. Caliber: 455 Webley. Six-round cylinder, bbl. lengths: 4-, 6- and 7.5-inches; 11.25 inches overall (with 6-inch bbl.). Weight: 38 oz. (with 6-inch bbl.). Fixed sights. Blued finish. Checkered walnut or Vulcanite grips. Made from 1915-1947.

MARK VI 22 TARGET REVOLVER. . . . . NiB $503 Ex $426 Gd $225
Same frame and general appearance as the Mark VI 455. Caliber: .22 LR. Six-round cylinder, 6-inch bbl., 11.25 inches overall. Weight: 40 oz. Target sights. Blued finish. Checkered walnut or Vulcanite grips. Disc. in 1945.

METROPOLITAN POLICE AUTOMATIC PISTOL . . . . NiB $503 Ex $349 Gd $210
Calibers: .32 Auto, .380 Auto. Eight-round (.32) or 7-round (.380) magazine, 3.5-inch bbl., 6.25 inches overall. weight: 20 oz. Fixed sights. Blued finish. Checkered Vulcanite grips. Made from 1906-40 (.32) and 1908-20 (.380).

RIC MODEL DA REVOLVER . . . . . . NiB $340 Ex $293 Gd $149
Royal Irish Constabulary or Bulldog Model. Solid frame. Caliber: .455 Webley. Five-round cylinder, 2.25-inch bbl., weight: 21 oz. Fixed sights. Blued finish. Checkered walnut or vulcanite grips. Disc.

SEMIAUTOMATIC SINGLE-SHOT PISTOL . . . . NiB $1055 Ex $849 Gd $566
Similar in appearance to the Webley Metropolitan Police Automatic, this pistol is "semiautomatic" in the sense that the fired case is extracted and ejected and the hammer cocked as in a blow-back automatic pistol; it is loaded singly and the slide manually operated in loading. Caliber: .22 Long, 4.5- or 9-inch bbl., 10.75 inches overall (with 9-inch bbl.). Weight: 24 oz. (with 9-inch bbl.). Adj. sights. Blued finish. Checkered Vulcanite grips. Made from 1911-27.

SINGLE-SHOT TARGET PISTOL . . . . . . NiB $425 Ex $296 Gd $142
Hinge frame. Caliber: .22 LR. 10-inch bbl., 15 inches overall. Weight: 37 oz. Fixed sights on earlier models, current production has adj. rear sight. Blued finish. Checkered walnut or Vulcanite grips. Made from 1909 to date.

FOSBERY AUTOMATIC REVOLVER
Hinged frame. Recoil action revolves cylinder and cocks hammer. Caliber: 455 Webley. Six-round cylinder, 6-inch bbl., 12 inches overall. Weight: 42 oz. Fixed or adjustable sights. Blued finish. Checkered walnut grips. Made 1901-1939. Note: A few were produced in caliber .38 Colt Auto w/an 8-shot cylinder (very rare).

1901 model . . . . NiB $6340 Ex $5845 Gd $3250
1902 model . . . . NiB $5825 Ex $4280 Gd $2705
1904 model . . . . NiB $5725 Ex $4280 Gd $2705
.38 Colt (8-round), add 100%
Target model w/adjustable sights, add 20%

WESSON FIREARMS CO., INC. — Palmer, Massachusetts Formerly Dan Wesson Firearms, Inc. Acquired by CZ-USA in 2005.

MODEL 8 SERVICE
Same general specifications as Model 14 except caliber .38 Special. Made from 1971-75. Values same as for Model 14.

MODEL 8-2 SERVICE
Same general specifications as Model 14-2 except caliber .38 Special. Made from 1975 to date. Values same as for Model 14-2.

MODEL 9 TARGET
Same as Model 15 except caliber .38 Special. Made from 1971-75. Values same as for Model 15.

MODEL 9-2 TARGET
Same as Model 15-2 except caliber .38 Special. Made from 1975 to date. Values same as for Model 15-2.

MODEL 9-2H HEAVY BARREL
Same general specifications as Model 15-2H except caliber .38 Special. Made from 1975 to date. Values same as for Model 15-2H. Disc. 1983.

MODEL 9-2HV VENT RIB HEAVY BARREL
Same as Model 15-2HV except caliber .38 Special. Made from 1975 to date. Values same as for Model 15-2HV.

MODEL 9-2V VENT RIB
Same as Model 15-2V except caliber .38 Special. Made from 1975 to date. Values same as for Model 15-2H.

MODEL 11 SERVICE DA REVOLVER
Caliber: .357 Magnum. Six-round cylinder. bbl. lengths: 2.5-, 4-, 6-inches interchangeable bbl. assemblies, 9 inches overall (with 4-inch bbl.). Weight: 38 oz. (with 4-inch bbl.). Fixed sights. Blued finish. Interchangeable grips. Made from 1970-71. Note: The Model 11 has an external bbl. nut.
W/one bbl. assembly and grip. . . . . NiB $224 Ex $196 Gd $151
Extra bbl. assembly, add $60
Extra grip, add $45

MODEL 12 TARGET
Same general specifications as Model 11 except has adj. sights. Made from 1970-71.
W/one-bbl. assembly and grip. . . . . NiB $271 Ex $227 Gd $164
Extra bbl. assembly, add $60
Extra grip, add $25

MODEL 14 SERVICE DA REVOLVER
Caliber: .357 Magnum. Six-round cylinder, bbl. length: 2.25-, 3.75, 5.75-inches; interchangeable bbl. assemblies, 9 inches overall (with 3.75-inch bbl.). Weight: 36 oz. (with 3.75-inch bbl.). Fixed sights. Blued or nickel finish. Interchangeable grips. Made from 1971-75. Note: Model 14 has recessed bbl. nut.
W/one-bbl. assembly and grip. . . . . NiB $250 Ex $212 Gd $164
Extra bbl. assembly, add $60
Extra grip, add $25

MODEL 14-2 SERVICE DA REVOLVER
Caliber: .357 Magnum. Six-round cylinder, bbl. lengths: 2.5-, 4-, 6-, 8-inch; interchangeable bbl. assemblies, 9.25 inches overall (with 4-inch bbl.) Weight: 34 oz. (with 4-inch bbl.). Fixed sights. Blued finish. Interchangeable grips. Made from 1975 to date. Note: Model 14-2 has recessed bbl. nut.

Dan Wesson
Model 14-2 Service

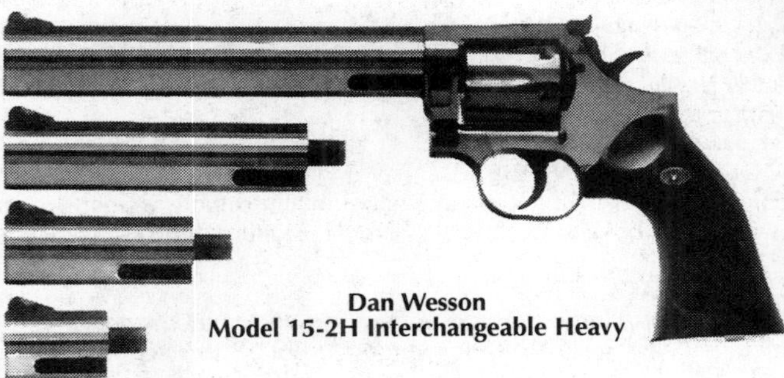
Dan Wesson
Model 15-2H Interchangeable Heavy

W/one bbl. assembly (8 inch) and grip . . . . NiB $240 Ex $194 Gd $143
W/one bbl. assembly (other lengths) and grip. . . . . NiB $240 Ex $194 Gd $143
Extra bbl. assembly, 8 inch, add $65
Extra bbl. assembly, other lengths, add $50
Extra grip, add $25

MODEL 15 TARGET
Same general specifications as Model 14 except has adj. sights. Made from 1971-75.
W/one bbl. assembly and grip. . . . . NiB $296 Ex $245 Gd $148
Extra bbl. assembly, add $60
Extra grip, add $25

MODEL 15-2 TARGET
Same general specifications as Model 14-2 except has adj. rear sight and interchangeable blade front; also avail. w/10-, 12- or 15-inch bbl., Made from 1975 to date.
W/one bbl. assembly (8 inch) and grip . NiB $310 Ex $259 Gd $151
W/one bbl. assembly (10 inch) and grip . . . NiB $310 Ex $259 Gd $151
W/one bbl. assembly (12 inch)/grip. Disc. . . . . NiB $310 Ex $259 Gd $151
W/one bbl. assembly (15 inch)/grip. Disc. . . . . NiB $310 Ex $259 Gd $151
W/one-bbl. assembly (other lengths)/grip. . . . . NiB $199 Ex $164 Gd $118
Extra bbl. assembly, add $65
Extra grip, add. $25

MODEL 15-2H HEAVY BARREL
Same as Model 15-2 except has heavy bbl., assembly weight: with 4-inch bbl., 38 oz. Made from 1975-83.
W/one bbl. assembly . . . . NiB $225 Ex $189 Gd $133
Extra bbl. assembly, add $65
Extra grip, add $25

MODEL 15-2HV VENT RIB HEAVY BARREL
Same as Model 15-2 except has vent rib heavy bbl. assembly; weight: (w/4-inch bbl.) 37 oz. Made from 1975 to date.
W/one bbl. assembly (8 inch) and grip ...... NiB $261 Ex $225 Gd $148
W/one bbl. assembly (10 inch) and grip ..... NiB $261 Ex $225 Gd $148
W/one bbl. assembly (12 inch) and grip ..... NiB $261 Ex $225 Gd $148
W/one bbl. assembly
(15 inch) and grip .... NiB $276 Ex $261 Gd $184
W/one bbl. assembly (other
lengths) and grip .... NiB $240 Ex $194 Gd $139
Extra bbl. assembly (8 inch), add $65
Extra bbl. assembly (10 inch), add $65
Extra bbl. assembly (12 inch), add $65
Extra bbl. assembly (15 inch), add $65
Extra bbl. assembly
(other lengths), add $65
Extra grip, add $25

MODEL 15-2V VENT RIB
Same as Model 15-2 except has vent rib bbl. assembly, weight: 35 oz. (with 4-inch bbl.). Made from 1975 to date. Values same as for 15-2H.

HUNTER PACS
Dan Wesson Hunter Pacs are offered in all Magnum calibers and include heavy vent rib 8-inch shrouded bbl., Burris scope mounts, bbl. changing tool in a case.
HP22M-V...................... NiB $835 Ex $656 Gd $437
HP22M-2 .... NiB $688 Ex $565 Gd $407
HP722M-V..................... NiB $790 Ex $646 Gd $462
HP722M-2 .... NiB $765 Ex $625 Gd $448
HP32-V .... NiB $739 Ex $592 Gd $434
HP32-2 .... NiB $650 Ex $534 Gd $385
HP732-V .... NiB $772 Ex $631 Gd $451
HP732-2 .... NiB $727 Ex $595 Gd $427
HP15-V .... NiB $727 Ex $595 Gd $427
HP15-2 .... NiB $676 Ex $554 Gd $399
HP715-V .... NiB $778 Ex $636 Gd $455
HP715-2 .... NiB $727 Ex $595 Gd $427
HP41-V .... NiB $644 Ex $529 Gd $382
HP741-V .... NiB $829 Ex $677 Gd $483
HP741-2 .... NiB $727 Ex $595 Gd $427
HP44-V .... NiB $816 Ex $677 Gd $476
HP44-2 .... NiB $727 Ex $595 Gd $427
HP744-V .... NiB $889 Ex $728 Gd $518
HP744-2 .... NiB $867 Ex $707 Gd $503
HP40-V .... NiB $574 Ex $473 Gd $344
HP40-2 .... NiB $790 Ex $646 Gd $462
HP740-V .... NiB $931 Ex $758 Gd $538
HP740-2 .... NiB $867 Ex $707 Gd $503
HP375-V .... NiB $561 Ex $463 Gd $337
HP375-2 .... NiB $906 Ex $739 Gd $525
HP45-V .... NiB $701 Ex $575 Gd $414

WHITNEY FIREARMS COMPANY — Hartford, Connecticut

WOLVERINE AUTOMATIC PISTOL
Dural frame/shell contains all operating components. Caliber: .22 LR. 10-round magazine, 4.63-inch bbl., 9 inches overall. Weight: 23 oz. Partridge-type sights. Blued or nickel finish. Plastic grips. Made from 1955-62.
Wolverine model, blue .... NiB $483 Ex $405 Gd $251
Wolverine model, nickel .... NiB $663 Ex $534 Gd $282

WICHITA ARMS — Wichita, Kansas

CLASSIC PISTOL
Caliber: Chambered to order. Bolt-action, single-shot. 11.25-inch octagonal bbl., 18 inches overall. Weight: 78 oz. Open micro sights. Custom-grade checkered walnut stock. Blued finish. Made from 1980-97.
Standard .... NiB $3515 Ex $2454 Gd $2197
Presentation grade
(engraved) .... NiB $5544 Ex $3793 Gd $2969

HUNTER PISTOL.............. NiB $1372 Ex $986 Gd $806
Bolt-action, single-shot. Calibers: .22 LR, .22 WRF, 7mm Super Mag., 7-30 Waters, .30-30 Win., .32 H&R Mag., .357 Mag., .357 Super Mag. 10.5-inch bbl., 16.5 inches overall, weight: 60 oz. No sights (scope mount only). Stainless steel finish. Walnut stock. Made from 1983-94.

INTERNATIONAL PISTOL .... NiB $753 Ex $531 Gd $413
Top-break, single-shot. SA. Calibers: 7-30 Waters, 7mm Super Mag., 7R (.30-30 Win. necked to 7mm), .30-30 Win. .357 Mag., .357 Super Mag., .32 H&R Mag., .22 Mag., .22 LR. 10- and 14-inch bbl. (10.5 inch for centerfire calibers). Weight: 50-71 oz. Partridge front sight, adj. rear. Walnut forend and grips.

MK-40 SILHOUETTE PISTOL.... NiB $1619 Ex $1144 Gd $938
Calibers: .22-250, 7mm IHMSA, .308 Win. Bolt-action, single-shot. 13-inch bbl., 19.5 inches overall. Weight: 72 oz. Wichita Multi-Range sight system. Aluminum receiver w/blued bbl., gray Fiberthane glass stock. Made from 1981 to date.

**SILHOUETTE
PISTOL (WSP) .... NiB $1999 Ex $1618 Gd $1324**
Calibers: .22-250, 7mm IHMSA 308 Win. Bolt-action, single-shot. 14.94-inch bbl., 21.38 inches overall. Weight: 72 oz. Wichita Multi-Range sight system. Blued finish. Walnut or gray Fiberthane glass stock. Walnut center or rear grip. Made from 1979 to date.

WILKINSON ARMS — Parma, Idaho

**"LINDA" SEMI-
AUTOMATIC PISTOL .... NiB $744 Ex $693 Gd $409**
Caliber: 9mm Para. Luger. 31-round magazine, 8.25-inch bbl., 12.25 inches overall. Weight: 77 oz. Rear peep sight w/blade front. Blued finish. Checkered composition grips.

**"SHERRY" SEMI-
AUTOMATIC PISTOL .... NiB $291 Ex $242 Gd $149**
Caliber: .22 LR. Eight-round magazine, 2.13-inch bbl., 4.38 inches overall. Weight: 9.25 oz. Crossbolt safety. Fixed sights. Blued or blue-gold finish. Checkered composition grips.

30th Edition
GUN TRADER'S GUIDE

Rifles

Action Arms Timber Wolfe

Alpha Arms Custom

Alpha Arms Alaskan

Alpha Arms Jaguar

AA ARMS — Monroe, North Carolina

AR-9 SEMIAUTOMATIC CARBINE . . . . NiB $807 Ex $679 Gd $399
Semiautomatic recoil-operated rifle w/side-folding metal stock design. Fires from a closed bolt. Caliber: 9mm Parabellum. 20-round magazine. 16.25-inch bbl., 33 inches overall. Weight: 6.5 lbs. Fixed blade, protected postfront sight adjustable for elevation, winged square notched rear. Matte phosphate/blue or nickel finish. Checkered polymer grip/frame. Made from 1991-94.

ACTION ARMS — Philadelphia, Pennsylvania

MODEL B SPORTER
SEMI-AUTOMATIC CARBINE . . . . . NiB $594 Ex $522 Gd $344
Similar to Uzi Carbine (see separate listing) except w/thumbhole stock. Caliber: 9mm Parabellum, 10-round magazine. 16-inch bbl. Weight: 8.75 lbs. Post front sight; adj. rear. Imported from 1993-94.

TIMBER WOLFE REPEATING RIFLE
Calibers: .357 Mag./.38 Special and .44 Mag. slide-action. Tubular magazine holds 10 and 8 rounds, respectively. 18.5-inch bbl. 36.5 inches overall. Weight: 5.5 lbs. Fixed blade front sight; adj. rear. Receiver w/integral scope mounts. Checkered walnut stock. Imported from 1989-94.

Blued model . . . . NiB $311 Ex $254 Gd $178
Chrome model, add. $50
.44 Mag., add $100

ALPHA ARMS, INC. — Dallas, Texas

CUSTOM BOLT-ACTION RIFLE . . . . NiB $1606 Ex $1275 Gd $816
Calibers: .17 Rem. thru .338 Win. Mag. Right or left-hand action in three action lengths w/three-lug locking system and 60-degree bolt rotation. 20- to 24-inch round or octagonal bbl. Weight: 6 to 7 lbs. No sights. Presentation-grade California Claro walnut stock w/hand-rubbed oil finish, custom inletted sling swivels and ebony forend tip. Made from 1984-89.

ALASKAN BOLT-ACTION RIFLE . . . . NiB $1611 Ex $1280 Gd $821
Similar to Custom model except w/stainless-steel bbl. and receiver w/all other parts coated w/Nitex. Weight: 6.75 to 7.25 lbs. Open sights w/bbl-band sling swivel. Classic-style Alpha wood stock w/Niedner-style steel grip cap and solid recoil pad. Made from 1984-89.

GRAND SLAM
BOLT-ACTION RIFLE. . . . . NiB $1270 Ex $1015 Gd $709
Same as Custom model except w/Alphawood (fiberglass and wood) classic-style stock featuring Niedner-style grip cap. Weight: 6.5 lbs.

JAGUAR BOLT-ACTION RIFLE
Same as Custom Rifle except designed on Mauser-style action w/claw extractor drilled and tapped for scope. Originally designated Alpha Model 1. Calibers: .243, 7mm-08, .308 original chambering (1984-85) up to .338 Win. Mag. in standard model; .338 thru .458 Win. Mag. in Big Five model (1984-85). Teflon-coated trigger guard/floorplate assembly. Made from1984-88.
Jaguar Grade I . . . . NiB $999 Ex $795 Gd $581
Jaguar Grade II . . . . NiB $1221 Ex $609 Gd $558
Jaguar Grade III. . . . . NiB $1272 Ex $1017 Gd $711
Jaguar Grade IV. . . . . NiB $1374 Ex $1017 Gd $711
Big Five model. . . . . NiB $1633 Ex $1174 Gd $919

AMERICAN ARMS — N. Kansas City, Missouri

1860 HENRY . . . . NiB $883 Ex $668 Gd $388
Replica of 1860 Henry rifle. Calibers: .44-40 or .45 LC. 24.25-inch half-octagonal bbl. 43.75 inches overall. Weight: 9.25 lbs. Brass frame and appointments. Straight-grip walnut buttstock.

1866 WINCHESTER
Replica of 1866 Winchester. Calibers: .44-40 or .45 LC. 19-inch round tapered bbl. (carbine) or 24.25-inch tapered octagonal bbl. (rifle). 38 to 43.25 inches overall. Weight: 7.75 or 8.15 lbs. Brass frame, elevator and buttplate. Walnut buttstock and forend.
Carbine . . . . NiB $693 Ex $591 Gd $372
Rifle. . . . . NiB $693 Ex $591 Gd $372

1873 WINCHESTER
Replica of 1873 Winchester rifle. Calibers: .44-40 or .45 LC. 24.25-inch tapered octagonal bbl. w/tubular magazine. Color casehardened steel frame w/brass elevator and ejection port cover. Walnut buttstock w/steel buttplate.
Standard model . . . . NiB $831 Ex $678 Gd $398
Deluxe model . . . . NiB $1073 Ex $867 Gd $602

AMERICAN SPIRIT ARMS CORP.— Scottsdale, Arizona

ASA BULL BARREL FLATTOP RIFLE . . . NiB $987 Ex $662 Gd $487
Semi-automatic. Caliber: ..223 Rem. Patterned after AR-15. Forged steel lower receiver, aluminum flattop upper receiver, 24-inch stainless bull barrel, free-floating aluminum hand guard, includes Harris bipod.

ASA BULL BARREL A2 RIFLE . . . . NiB $912 Ex $687 Gd $487
Similar to Flattop Rifle except has A2 upper receiver with carrying handle and sights. Introduced 1999.

OPEN MATCH RIFLE . . . . NiB $1395 Ex $995 Gd $695
Caliber: .223 Rem. Bbl.: 16-inch fluted and ported stainless steel match with round shroud. Flattop without sights, forged upper and lower receiver, match trigger. Introduced 2001.

LIMITED MATCH RIFLE . . . . NiB $1345 Ex $870 Gd $570
Caliber: .223 Rem. Bbl.: 16-inch fluted stainless steel match with round shroud. National Match front and rear sights; match trigger.

DCM SERVICE RIFLE. . . . . NiB $1345 Ex $914 Gd $570
Caliber: .223 Rem. Bbl.: 20-inch stainless steel match type with free-floating shroud. National Match front and rear sights; match trigger; pistol grip.

ASA M4 RIFLE. NiB $890 Ex $635 Gd $440
Caliber: .223 Rem. Non-collapsible stock, M4 hand guard, 16-inch bbl. w/muzzle brake; aluminum flattop upper receiver.

ASA A2 RIFLE . . . . NiB $860 Ex $590 Gd $465
Caliber: .223 Rem. A2 receiver; 20-inch National Match barrel. Intro. 1999.

ASA CARBINE. . . . . NiB $1010 Ex $665 Gd $565
Caliber: .223 Rem. or Short. Side-charging, flattop receiver; M4 hand guard; 16-inch National Match bbl. w/slotted muzzle brake.

POST-BAN CARBINE. . . . . NiB $870 Ex $608 Gd $453
Caliber: .223 Rem. Wilson 16-inch National Match bbl.; non-collapsible stock. Introduced 1999.

BULL BARREL A2 INVADER . . . . NiB $997 Ex $687 Gd $507
Caliber: .223 Rem. Similar to ASA 24-inch bull bbl. rifle except has 16-inch stainless steel bbl.. Introduced 1999.

A2 CAR CARBINE. . . . . NiB $992 Ex $687 Gd $517
Caliber: 9mm Parabellum. Forged receiver, non-collapsible stock. Bbl.: 16-inch Wilson w/o muzzle brake, bird cage flash hider (pre-ban) or muzzle brake (post-ban).

FLATTOP CAR RIFLE. . . . . NiB $992 Ex $767 Gd $567
Caliber: 9mm Parabellum. Similar to A2 CAR Rifle except flattop design w/o sights. Introduced 2002.

ASA TACTICAL RIFLE . . . . NiB $1728 Ex $1048 Gd $728
Caliber: .308 Win. Bbl.: 16-inch stainless steel regular or match; side-charging handle; pistol grip.
Match model (w/fluted bbl. match trigger, chrome finish) . Add $525

ASA 24-INCH MATCH RIFLE . . . . . . NiB $1728 Ex $1048 Gd $728
Caliber: .308 Win. Bbl.: 24-inch stainless steel match with or w/o fluting/porting. Side-charging handle; pistol grip. Introduced 2002.

AMT (ARCADIA MACHINE & TOOL) — Irwindale, California

BOLT-ACTION REPEATING RIFLE
Winchester-type push-feed or Mauser-type controlled-feed short-, medium- or long-action. Calibers: .223 Remington, .22-250 Remington, .243 A, .243 Winchester, 6mm PPC, .25-06 Remington, 6.5x08, .270 Winchester, 7x57 Mauser, 7mm-08 Remington, 7mm Remington Mag., 7.62x39mm, .308 Winchester, .30-06, .300 Winchester Mag., .338 Winchester Mag., .375 H&H, .416 Remington, .416 Rigby, .458 Winchester Mag. 22- to 28-inch number 3 contour bbl. Weight: 7.75 to 8.5 lbs. Sights: None furnished; drilled and tapped for scope mounts. Classic composite or Kevlar stock. Made from 1996-97.
Standard model. . . . . NiB $853 Ex $674 Gd $496
Deluxe model . . . . NiB $1073 Ex $8169 Gd $563

BOLT-ACTION SINGLE-SHOT RIFLE
Winchester-type cone breech push-feed or Mauser-type controlled-feed action. Calibers: .22 Hornet, .22 PPC, .222 Remington, .223 Remington, .22-250 Remington, .243 A, .243 Winchester, 6mm PPC, 6.5x08, .270 Win., 7mm-08 Remington, .308 Winchester 22- to 28-inch #3 contour bbl. Weight: 7.75 to 8.5 lbs. Sights: None furnished; drilled and tapped for scope mounts. Classic composite or Kevlar stock. Made from1996-97.
Standard model. . . . . NiB $884 Ex $706 Gd $553
Deluxe model . . . . NiB $1068 Ex $869 Gd $665

RIFLES

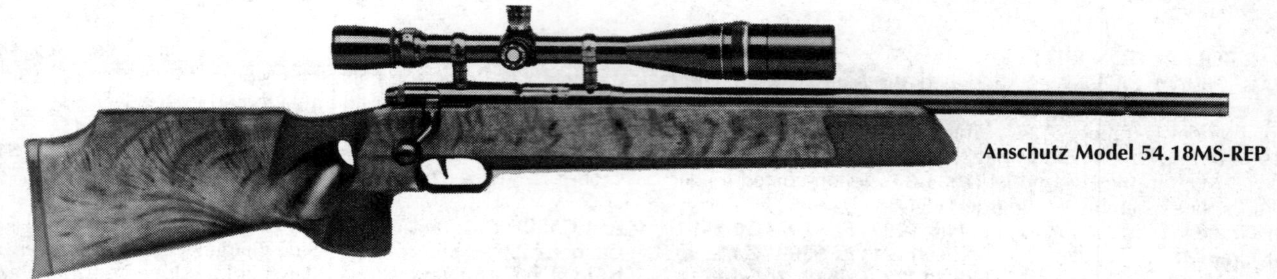
Anschutz Model 54.18MS-REP

CHALLENGER AUTOLOADING TARGET RIFLE SERIES I, II & III
Similar to Small Game Hunter except w/McMillan target fiberglass stock. Caliber: .22 LR. 10-round magazine. 16.5-, 18-, 20- or 22-inch bull bbl. Drilled and tapped for scope mount; no sights. Stainless steel finish. Made from 1994-98.
Challenger I Standard .... NiB $748 Ex $544 Gd $365
Challenger II w/muzzle brake..... NiB $882 Ex $722 Gd $518
Challenger III w/bbl extension .... NiB $787 Ex $646 Gd $466
W/jewelled trigger, add........................... $200

LIGHTNING 25/22
AUTOLOADING RIFLE .... NiB $258 Ex $212 Gd $146
Caliber: .22 LR. 25-round magazine. 18-inch tapered or bull bbl. Weight: 6 lbs. 37 inches overall. Sights: Adj. rear; ramp front. Folding stainless-steel stock w/matte finish. Made from 1984-94.

LIGHTNING SMALL GAME HUNTER SERIES
Similar to AMT 25/22 except w/conventional matte black fiberglass/nylon stock. 10-round rotary magazine. 22-inch bbl. 40.5 inches overall. Weight: 6 lbs. Grooved for scope; no sights. Made from 1987-94 (Series I), and from 1992-93 (Series II).
Hunter I..................... NiB $229 Ex $190 Gd $129
Hunter II (w/22-inch
heavy target bbl.) .... NiB $246 Ex $201 Gd $139

MAGNUM HUNTER AUTO RIFLE .... NiB $393 Ex $318 Gd $222
Similar to Lightning Small Game Hunter II model except chambered in .22 WRF w/22-inch match-grade bbl. Made from 1993 to date.

ANSCHUTZ RIFLES — Ulm, Germany Mfd. by J.G. Anschutz GmbH Jagd und Sportwaffenfabrik

Currently imported by AcuSport Corp.; Accuracy International; Champion's Choice; Champion Shooter's Supply, Go Sportsmen's Supply, Inc.; Gunsmithing Inc. (Previously by Precision Sales Int'l., Inc.)

Anschutz models 1407 ISU, 1408-ED, 1411, 1413, 1418, 1432, 1433, 1518 and 1533 were marketed in the U.S by Savage Arms. Further, Anschutz models 1403, 1416, 1422D, 1441, 1516 and 1522D were sold as Savage/Anschutz with Savage model designations (see also listings under Savage Arms

MODEL 54 18MS .... NiB $1289 Ex $1031 Gd $722
Bolt-action, single-shot, Caliber: .22 LR. 22-inch bbl. European hardwood stock w/cheekpiece. Stipple-checkered forend and Wundhammer swell pistol-grip. Receiver grooved, drilled and tapped for scope blocks. Weight: 8.4 lbs. Imported from 1982-97.

MODEL 54.18MS-REP REPEATING RIFLE
Same as model 54.18MS except w/repeating action and 5-round magazine. 22- to 30-inch bbl. 41-49 inches overall. Avg. weight: 7 lbs., 12 oz. Hardwood or synthetic gray thumbhole stock. Imported from 1989-97.
Standard MS-REP model .... NiB $1441 Ex $1184 Gd $772
Left-hand model .... NiB $1313 Ex $1081 Gd $720

MODEL 64S BOLT-ACTION SINGLE-SHOT RIFLE
Bolt-action, single-shot. Caliber: .22 LR. 26-inch bbl. Checkered European hardwood stock w/Wundhammer swell pistol-grip and adj. buttplate. Single-stage trigger. Aperture sights. Weight: 8.25 lbs. Imported from 1963-82.
Standard .... NiB $545 Ex $391 Gd $287
Left-hand model .... NiB $545 Ex $391 Gd $313

MODEL 64MS BOLT-ACTION
SINGLE-SHOT RIFLE
Bolt-action, single-shot. Caliber: .22 LR. 21.25-inch bbl. European hardwood silhouette-style stock w/cheekpiece. Forend base and Wundhammer swell pistol-grip, stipple-checkered. Adj. two-stage trigger. Receiver grooved, drilled and tapped for scope blocks. Weight: 8 lbs. Imported from 1982-96.
Standard or Featherweight
(disc. 1988) .... NiB $829 Ex $726 Gd $365
Left-hand model .... NiB $855 Ex $731 Gd $484

MODEL 64MSR BOLT-ACTION REPEATER
Similar to Anschutz Model 64MS except repeater w/5-round magazine. Imported from 1996 to date.
Standard model .... NiB $829 Ex $726 Gd $443
Left-hand model .... NiB $855 Ex $726 Gd $443

MODEL 520/61 SEMIAUTOMATIC....... NiB $434 Ex $285 Gd $131
Caliber: .22 LR. 10-round magazine. 24-inch bbl. Sights: Folding leaf rear, hooded ramp front. Receiver grooved for scope mounting. Rotary-style safety. Monte Carlo stock and beavertail forend, checkered. Weight: 6.5 lbs. Imported from 1982-83.

MODEL 525 AUTOLOADER
Caliber: .22 LR. 10-round magazine. 20- or 24-inch bbl. 39 to 43 inches overall. Weight: 6.1 to 6.5 lbs. Adj. folding rear sight; hooded ramp front. Checkered European hardwood Monte Carlo style buttstock and beavertail forend. Sling swivel studs. Imported since 1982.
Carbine model
(disc. 1986) .... NiB $419 Ex $285 Gd $182
Rifle model (24-inch bbl.) .... NiB $511 Ex $414 Gd $291

MODEL 1403B .... NiB $912 Ex $706 Gd $397
A lighter-weight model designed for Biathlon competition. Caliber: .22 LR. 21.5-inch bbl. Adj. two-stage trigger. Adj. grooved wood buttplate, stipple-checkered deep thumb-rest flute and straight pistol-grip. Weight: 9 lbs. w/sights. Imported from 1982-1992.

MODEL 1403D MATCH SINGLE-SHOT TARGET RIFLE
Caliber: .22 LR. 25-inch bbl. 43 inches overall. Weight: 8.6 lbs. No sights, receiver grooved for Anschutz target sights. Walnut-finished hardwood target stock w/adj. buttplate. Importation disc. 1992.
Standard model................ NiB $673 Ex $545 Gd $382
W/match sights .... NiB $932 Ex $753 Gd $524

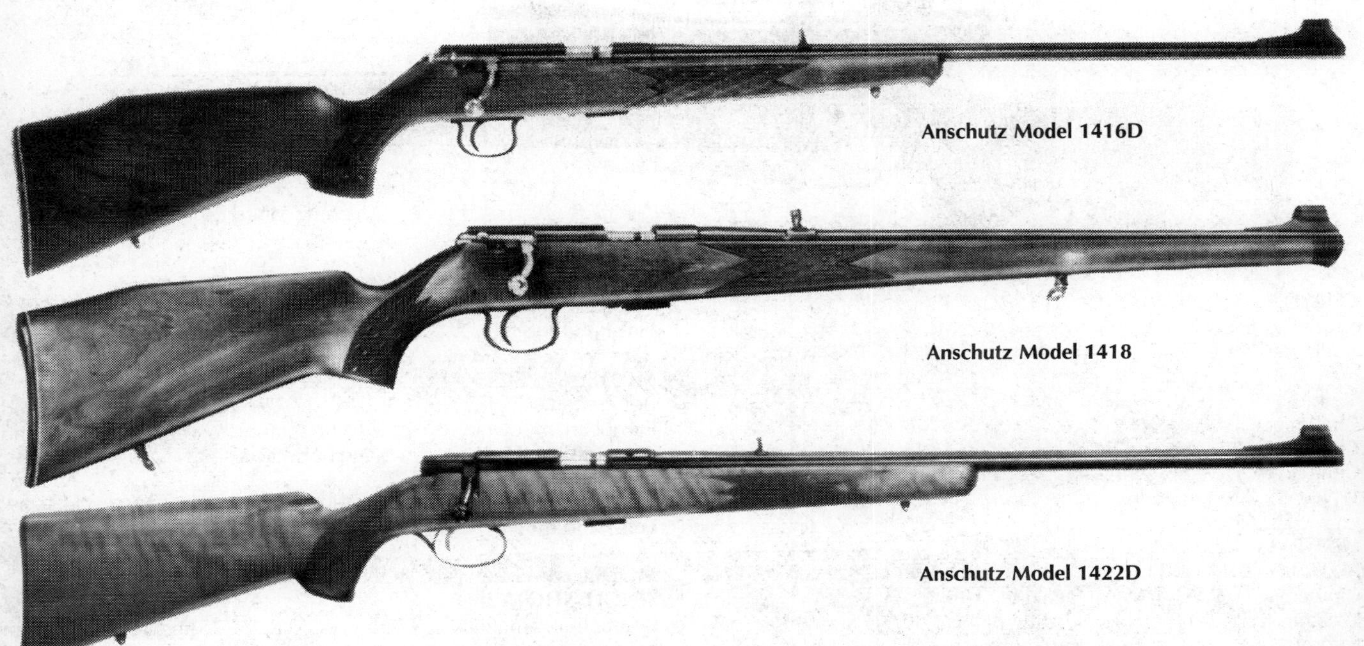

Anschutz Model 1416D

Anschutz Model 1418

Anschutz Model 1422D

MODEL 1407 ISU MATCH 54 RIFLE
Bolt-action, single-shot, caliber: .22 LR. 26.88-inch bbl. Scope bases. Receiver grooved for Anschutz sights. Single-stage adj. trigger. Select walnut target stock w/deep forearm for position shooting, adj. buttplate, hand stop and swivel. Weight: 10 lbs. Imported 1970-81.
Standard model . . . . NiB $596 Ex $519 Gd $262
Left-hand model . . . . NiB $596 Ex $519 Gd $262
W/international sights, add $65

MODEL 1408-ED
SUPER RUNNING BOAR . . . . NiB $442 Ex $390 Gd $339
Bolt-action, single-shot, caliber: .22 LR. 23.5-inch bbl. w/sliding weights. No metallic sights. Receiver drilled and tapped for scope-sight bases. Single-stage adj. trigger. Oversize bolt knob. Select walnut stock w/thumbhole, adj. comb and buttplate. Weight: 9.5 lbs. Intro. 1976. Disc.

MODEL 1411 MATCH 54 RIFLE
Bolt-action, single-shot. Caliber: .22 LR. 27.5-inch extra heavy bbl. w/mounted scope bases. Receiver grooved for Anschutz sights. Single-stage adj. trigger. Select walnut target stock w/cheekpiece (adj. in 1973 and later production), full pistol-grip, beavertail forearm, adj. buttplate, hand stop and swivel. Model 1411-L has left-hand stock. Weight: 11 lbs. Disc.
W/Non-adj. cheekpiece. . . . . NiB $442 Ex $390 Gd $236
W/adj. cheekpiece. . . . . NiB $610 Ex $493 Gd $345
with Anschutz
International Sight set $275

MODEL 1413 SUPER MATCH 54 RIFLE
Freestyle international target rifle w/specifications similar to those of Model 1411, except w/special stock w/thumbhole, adj. pistol grip, adj. cheekpiece in 1973 and later production, adj. hook buttplate, adj. palmrest. Model 1413-L has left-hand stock. Weight: 15.5 lbs. Disc.
W/Non-adj. cheekpiece. . . . . NiB $779 Ex $701 Gd $372
W/Adj. cheekpiece . . . . NiB $656 Ex $532 Gd $341
With Anschutz
International Sight set $275

MODEL 1416D . . . . NiB $564 Ex $545 Gd $339
Bolt-action sporter. Caliber: .22 LR. 22.5-inch bbl. Sights: Folding leaf rear; hooded ramp front. Receiver grooved for scope mounting. Select European stock w/cheekpiece, skip-checkered pistol grip and forearm. Weight: 6 lbs. Imported 1982 to date.

MODEL 1416D CLASSIC/CUSTOM SPORTERS
Same as Model 1416D except w/American classic-style stock (Classic) or modified European-style stock w/Monte Carlo roll-over cheekpiece and Schnabel forend (Custom). Weight: 5.5 lbs. (Classic); 6 lbs. (Custom). Imported 1986 to date.
Model 1416D Classic . . . . NiB $624 Ex $506 Gd $354
Model 1416D Classic,
"True" left-hand . . . . NiB $670 Ex $542 Gd $379
Model 1416D Custom. . . . . NiB $605 Ex $490 Gd $335
Model 1416D fiberglass (1991-92). . . . NiB $733 Ex $593 Gd $414

MODEL 1418 BOLT-ACTION
SPORTER. NiB $386 Ex $309 Gd $180
Caliber: .22 LR. 5- or 10-round magazine. 19.75-inch bbl. Sights: Folding leaf rear; hooded ramp front. Receiver grooved for scope mounting. Select walnut stock, Mannlicher type w/cheekpiece, pistol-grip and forearm skip checkered. Weight: 5.5 lbs. Intro. 1976. Disc.

MODEL 1418D BOLT-ACTION
SPORTER. NiB $963 Ex $850 Gd $504
Caliber: .22 LR. 5- or 10-round magazine. 19.75-inch bbl. European walnut Monte Carlo stock, Mannlicher type w/cheekpiece, pistol-grip and forend skip-line checkered, buffalo horn Schnabel tip. Weight: 5.5 lbs. Imported from 1982-95 and 1998 to date.

MODEL 1422D CLASSIC/CUSTOM RIFLE
Bolt-action sporter. Caliber: .22 LR. Five-round removable straight-feed clip magazine. 24-inch bbl. Sights: Folding leaf rear; hooded ramp front. Select European walnut stock, classic type (Classic); Monte Carlo w/hand-carved rollover cheekpiece (Custom). Weight: 7.25 lbs. (Classic) 6.5 lbs. (Custom). Imported 1982-89.
Model 1422D Classic . . . . NiB $782 Ex $627 Gd $395
Model 1422D Custom. . . . . NiB $859 Ex $782 Gd $447

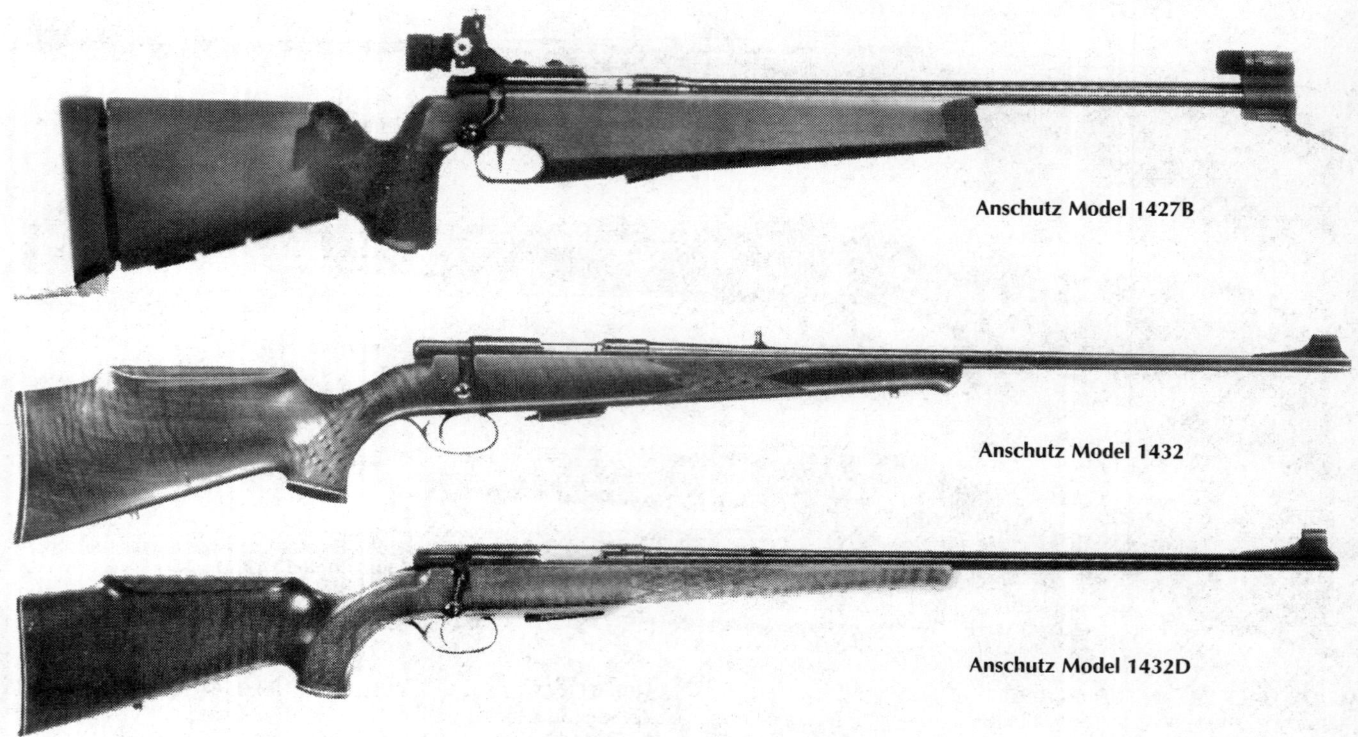
Anschutz Model 1427B

Anschutz Model 1432

Anschutz Model 1432D

MODEL 1427B BIATHLON RIFLE
Bolt-action clip repeater. Caliber: .22 LR. 21.5-inch bbl. Two-stage trigger w/wing-type safety. Hardwood stock w/deep fluting, pistol grip and deep forestock with adj. hand stop rail. Target sights w/adjustable weights. Advertised in 1981 but imported from 1982 to date as Model 1827B. (See that model designation for current values)

MODEL 1430D MATCH . . . . NiB $727 Ex $598 Gd $372
Improved version of Model 64S. Bolt-action, single-shot. Caliber: .22 LR. 26-inch medium-heavy bbl. Walnut Monte Carlo stock w/cheekpiece, adj. buttplate, deep midstock tapered to forend. Pistol-grip and contoured thumb groove w/stipple checkering. Single-stage adj. trigger. Target sights. Weight: 8.38 lbs. Imported from 1982-83.

MODEL 1432 BOLT-ACTION SPORTER
Caliber: .22 Hornet. 5-round box magazine. 24-inch bbl. Sights: Folding leaf rear, hooded ramp front. Receiver grooved for scope mounting. Select walnut stock w/Monte Carlo comb and cheekpiece, pistol-grip and forearm skip-checkered. Weight: 6.75 lbs. Imported from 1974-87. (Reintroduced as 1700/1730 series)
Early model
(1974-85). NiB $1284 Ex $933 Gd $676
Late model
(1985-87). NiB $1100 Ex $878 Gd $595

MODEL 1432D CLASSIC/CUSTOM RIFLE
Bolt-action sporter similar to Model 1422D except chambered for Caliber: .22 Hornet. 4-round magazine. 23.5-inch bbl. Weight: 7.75 lbs. (Classic); 6.5 lbs. (Custom). Classic stock on Classic model; fancy-grade Monte Carlo w/hand-carved rollover cheekpiece (Custom). Imported from 1982-87. (Reintroduced as 1700/1730 series)
Model 1432D Classic . . . . NiB $1285 Ex $934 Gd $677
Model 1432D Custom. . . . . NiB $1114 Ex $883 Gd $600

MODEL 1433 BOLT-ACTION SPORTER . . . . . NiB $1093 Ex $882 Gd $624
Caliber: .22 Hornet. 5-round box magazine. 19.75-inch bbl. Sights: Folding leaf rear, hooded ramp front. Receiver grooved for scope mounting. Single-stage or double-set trigger. Select walnut Mannlicher stock; cheekpiece, pistol-grip and forearm skip-checkered. Weight: 6.5 lbs. Imported from 1976-86.

MODEL 1448D CLAY BIRD. . . . . . NiB $329 Ex $298 Gd $210
Similar to Model 1449 except chambered for Caliber: .22 LR. w/22.5-inch smooth bore bbl. and no sights. Walnut-finished hardwood stock. Imported from 1999 to date.

MODEL 1449 YOUTH SPORTER . . . . NiB $262 Ex $216 Gd $154
Bolt-action sporter version of Model 2000. Caliber: .22 LR. 5-round box magazine. 16.25-inch bbl. Weight: 3.5 lbs. Hooded ramp front sight, addition. Walnut-finished hardwood stock. Imported from 1989-92.

MODEL 1450B TARGET RIFLE . . . . NiB $678 Ex $497 Gd $343
Biathlon rifle developed on 2000 Series action. 19.5-inch bbl. Weight: 5.5 lbs. Adj. buttplate. Target sights. Imported from 1993-94.

MODEL 1451 E/R SPORTER/TARGET
Bolt-action, single-shot (1451E) or repeater (1451R). Caliber: .22 LR. 22- or 22.75-inch bbl. w/o sights. Select hardwood stock w/stippled pistolgrip and vented forearm. beavertail forend, adj. cheekpiece, and deep thumb flute. Weight: 6.5 lbs. Imported from 1996 to date.
Model 1451E (disc. 1997) . . . . NiB $442 Ex $339 Gd $236
Model 1451R . . . . NiB $458 Ex $425 Gd $270

MODEL 1451D CLASSIC/CUSTOM RIFLE
Same as Model 1451R except w/walnut-finished hardwood stock (Classic) or modified European-style walnut stock w/Monte Carlo rollover cheekpiece and Schnabel forend (Custom). Weight: 5 lbs. Imported from 1996 to date.
Model 1451D Classic (Super) . . . . . NiB $335 Ex $258 Gd $180
Model 1451D Custom. . . . . NiB $474 Ex $433 Gd $294

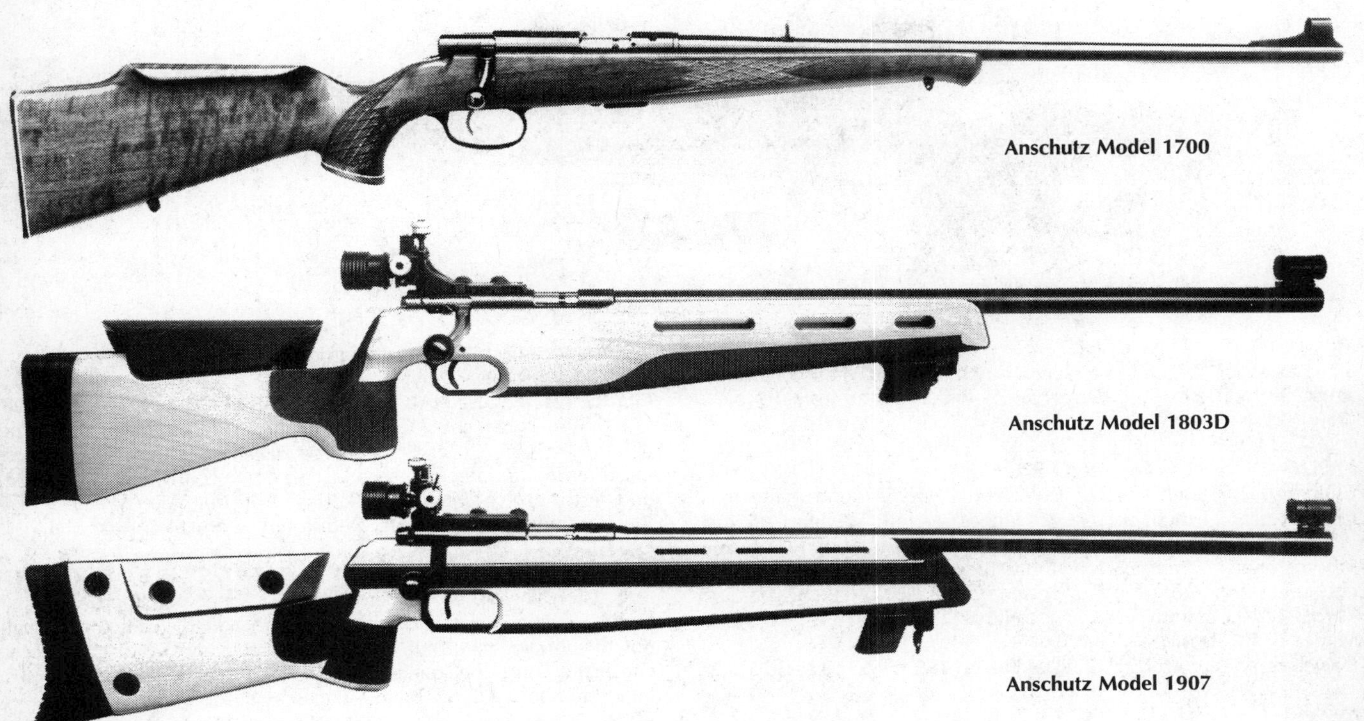

Anschutz Model 1700

Anschutz Model 1803D

Anschutz Model 1907

MODEL 1451 ST- R RIFLE . . . . NiB $459 Ex $419 Gd $304
Same as Model 1451R except w/two-stage trigger and walnut-finished hardwood uncheckered stock. Imported 1999 to date.

MODEL 1516D CLASSIC/CUSTOM RIFLE
Same as Model 1416D except chambered for Caliber: .22 Magnum RF, with American classic-style stock (Classic) or modified European-style stock w/Monte Carlo rollover cheekpiece and Schnabel forend (Custom). Weight: 5.5 lbs. (Classic), 6 lbs. (Custom). Imported from 1986 to date.
Model 1516D Classic . . . . NiB $680 Ex $530 Gd $355
Model 1516D Custom . . . . NiB $705 Ex $580 Gd $380

MODELS 1516D/1518D LUXUS RIFLES
The alpha designation for these models was changed from Custom to Luxus in 1996-98. (See current Custom listings for Luxus values.)

MODELS 1518/1518D SPORTING RIFLES
Same as Model 1418 except chambered for .22 Magnum RF, 4-round box magazine. Model 1518 intro. 1976. Disc. Model 1518D has full Mannlicher-type stock. Imported from 1982 to date.
Model 1518 . . . . NiB $733 Ex $613 Gd $383
Model 1518D . . . . NiB $928 Ex $738 Gd $508
W/set trigger, add $125

MODEL 1522D CLASSIC/CUSTOM RIFLE
Same as Model 1422D except chambered for .22 Magnum RF, 4-round magazine. Weight: 6.5 lbs. (Custom). Fancy-grade Classic or Monte Carlo stock w/hand-carved rollover cheekpiece. Imported 1982-89. (Reintroduced as 1700D/1730D series)
Model 1522D Classic . . . . NiB $1046 Ex $856 Gd $606
Model 1522D Custom . . . . NiB $1046 Ex $856 Gd $606

MODEL 1532D CLASSIC/CUSTOM RIFLE
Same as Model 1432D except chambered for .222 Rem. Three-round mag. Weight: 6.5 lbs. (Custom). Classic stock on Classic Model; fancy-grade Monte Carlo stock w/handcarved rollover cheekpiece (Custom). Imported from 1982-89. (Reintroduced as 1700D/174 D0 series)
Model 1532D Classic . . . . NiB $945 Ex $751 Gd $401
Model 1532D Custom . . . . NiB $1241 Ex $951 Gd $651

MODEL 1533 . . . . NiB $1055 Ex $805 Gd $555
Same as Model 1433 except chambered for .222 Rem. Three-shot box magazine. Imported from 1976-94.

MODEL 1700 SERIES BOLT-ACTION REPEATER
Match 54 Sporter. Calibers: .22 LR., .22 Magnum, .22 Hornet, .222 Rem. Five-shot removable magazine 24-inch bbl. 43 inches overall. Weight: 7.5 lbs. Folding leaf rear sight, hooded ramp front. Select European walnut stock w/cheekpiece and Schnabel forend tip. Imported from 1989 to date.
Standard Model 1700
Bavarian — rimfire cal. NiB $961 Ex $901 Gd $541
Standard Model 1700
Bavarian — centerfire cal. . . . . NiB $1281 Ex $1006 Gd $656
Model 1700D Classic (Classic
stock, 6.75 lbs.) rimfire cal. . . . . NiB $1131 Ex $951 Gd $656
Model 1700D Classic — centerfire cal. . . . . NiB $1244 Ex $1006 Gd $702
Model 1700D Custom — rimfire cal. . . . . NiB $1050 Ex $851 Gd $597
Model 1700D Custom — centerfire cal.. . . . NiB $1279 Ex $1035 Gd $723
Model 1700D Graphite Cust. (McMillan graphite
reinforced stock, 22 inch bbl., intro. 1991) . . NiB $1106 Ex $931 Gd $606
Select walnut and gold trigger . . . . add $181
Model 1700 FWT Feather-
weight (6.5 lbs.) rimfire calibers . . . . NiB $1087 Ex $881 Gd $617
Model 1700 FWT — centerfire cal. . . . . . . NiB $1256 Ex $1106 Gd $706

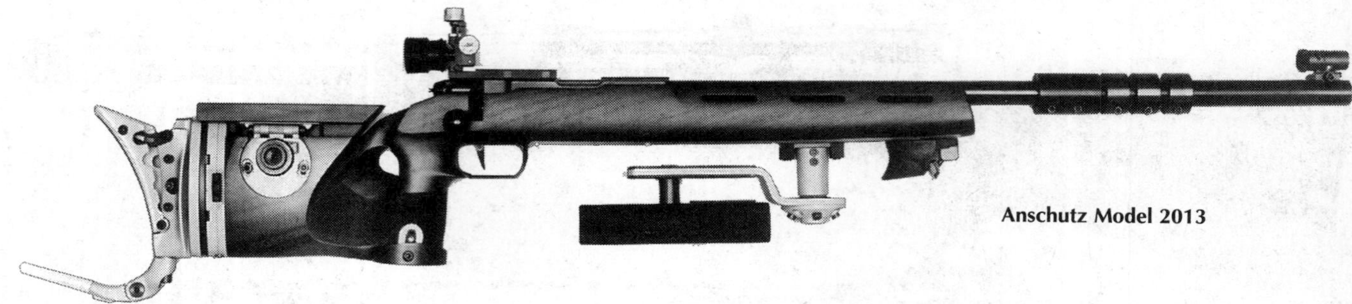

Anschutz Model 2013

MODEL 1733D MANNLICHER. . . . . . . NiB $1347 Ex $1135 Gd $826
Same as Model 1700D except w/19-inch bbl. and Mannlicher-style stock. 39 inches overall. Weight: 6.25 lbs. Imported from 1993-96 (Reintroduced in 1998).

MODEL 1740 MONTE CARLO SPORTER
Caliber: .22 Hornet or .222 Rem. Three and 5-round magazines respectively. 24-inch bbl. 43.25 inches overall. Weight: 6.5 lbs. Hooded ramp front, folding leaf rear. Drilled and tapped for scope mounts. Select European walnut stock w/roll-over cheekpiece, checkered grip and forend. Imported from 1997 to date.
Model 1740 Custom . . . . NiB $1298 Ex $1032 Gd $672
Model 1740 Classic
(Meistergrade) . . . . NiB $1466 Ex $1184 Gd $823

MODEL 1743 MONTE CARLO
SPORTER. . . . . NiB $1316 Ex $1084 Gd $723
Similar to Model 1740 except w/Mannlicher full stock. Imported from 1997 to date.

MODEL 1803D MATCH SINGLE-SHOT TARGET RIFLE
Caliber: .22 LR. 25.5-inch bbl. 43.75 inches overall. Weight: 8.5 lbs. No sights; receiver grooved, drilled and tapped for scope mounts. Blonde or walnut-finished hardwood stock w/adj. cheekpiece, stippled grip and forend. Left-hand version. Imported from 1987-92.
Right-hand model
(Reintroduced as 1903D) . . . . NiB $969 Ex $804 Gd $495
Left-hand model . . . . NiB $1030 Ex $830 Gd $575

MODEL 1807 ISU
STANDARD MATCH . . . . NiB $1312 Ex $1038 Gd $668
Bolt-action single-shot. Caliber: 22 LR. 26-inch bbl. Improved Super Match 54 action. Two-stage match trigger. Removable cheekpiece, adj. buttplate, thumbpiece and forestock w/stipple-checkered. Weight: 10 lbs. Imported from 1982-88. (Reintroduced as 1907 ISU)

MODEL 1808ED SUPER RUNNING TARGET
Bolt-action single-shot. Caliber: .22 LR. 23.5-inch bbl. w/sliding weights. Improved Super Match 54 action. Heavy beavertail forend w/adj.cheekpiece and buttplate. Adj. single-stage trigger. Weight: 9.5 lbs. Imported from 1982-96.
Right-hand model . . . . NiB $1593 Ex $1294 Gd $830
Left-hand model . . . . NiB $1635 Ex $1320 Gd $916

MODEL 1808MS-R
METALLIC SILHOUETTE . . . . NiB $1965 Ex $1502 Gd $884
Bolt-action repeater. Caliber: .22 LR. 19.2-inch bbl. w/o sights. Thumbhole Monte Carlo stock w/grooved forearm enhanced w/ "Anschutz" logo. Weight: 8.2 lbs. Imported from 1998 to date.

MODEL 1810 SUPER MATCH II . . . . . . NiB $1940 Ex $1399 Gd $884
A less detailed version of the Super Match 1813 model. Tapered forend w/deep receiver area. Select European hardwood stock. Weight: 13.5 lbs. Imported from 1982-88 (reintroduced as 1910 series).

MODEL 1811 PRONE MATCH . . . . NiB $1788 Ex $1577 Gd $820
Bolt-action single-shot. Caliber: .22 LR. 27.5-inch bbl. Improved Super Match 54 action. Select European hardwood stock w/beavertail forend, adj. cheekpiece, and deep thumb flute. Thumb groove and pistol grip w/stipple checkering. Adj. buttplate. Weight: 11.5 lbs. Imported from 1982-88. (Reintroduced as 1911Prone Match)

MODEL 1813 SUPER MATCH. . . . . NiB $2257 Ex $1927 Gd $845
Bolt-action single-shot. Caliber: .22 LR. 27.5-inch bbl. Improved Super Match 54 action w/light firing pin, one-point adj. trigger. European walnut thumbhole stock, adj. palm rest, forend and pistol grip stipple checkered. Adj. cheekpiece and hook buttplate. Weight: 15.5 lbs. Imported from 1982-88. (Reintroduced as 1913 Super Match)

MODEL 1827 BIATHLON RIFLE
Bolt-action clip repeater. Caliber: .22 LR. 21.5-inch bbl. 42.5 inches overall. Weight: 8.5 to 9 lbs. Slide safety. Adj. target sight set w/snow caps. European walnut stock w/cheekpiece, stippled pistol grip and forearm w/adj. weights. Fortner straight pull bolt option offered in 1986. Imported from 1982 to date.
Mdl. 1827B w/Sup. Mat. 54 action . . . . NiB $2335 Ex $2129 Gd $996
Model 1827B, left-hand . . . . NiB $2081 Ex $1696 Gd $1204
Model 1827BT w/Fortner
Option, right-hand . . . . NiB $2441 Ex $2235 Gd $996
Model 1827BT, left-hand . . . . NiB $2578 Ex $2101 Gd $1487
Model 1827BT w/laminated stock, add $175
W/stainless steel bbl., add $205

MODEL 1907 ISU INTERNATIONAL MATCH RIFLE
Updated version of Model 1807 w/same general specifications as Model 1913 except w/26-inch bbl. 44.5 inches overall. Weight: 11 lbs. Designed for ISU 3-position competition. Fitted w/vented beechwood or walnut, blonde or color-laminated stock. Imported from 1989 to date.
Right-hand model . . . . NiB $1532 Ex $1341 Gd $826
Left-hand model . . . . NiB $1718 Ex $1403 Gd $1000
W/laminated stock, add $135
W/walnut stock, add $100
W/stainless steel bbl., add $130

MODEL 1910 INTERNATIONAL SUPER MATCH RIFLE
Updated version of Model 1810 w/same general specifications Model 1913 except w/less-detailed hardwood stock w/tapered forend. Weight: 13.5 lbs. Imported from 1989 to date.
Right-hand model . . . . NiB $2546 Ex $2057 Gd $1083
Left-hand model . . . . NiB $2540 Ex $2077 Gd $1486

MODEL 1911 PRONE MATCH RIFLE
Updated version of Model 1811 w/same general specifications Model 1913 except w/specialized prone match hardwood stock w/beavertail forend. Weight: 11.5 lbs. Imported from 1989 to date.
Right-hand model . . . . NiB $1836 Ex $1746 Gd $831

Anschutz Achiever

MODEL 1912
LADIES' SPORT RIFLE . . . . NiB $1792 Ex $1576 Gd $824
Similar to the Model 1907 designed for ISU 3-position competition w/same general U.I.T. specifications except w/shorter dimensions to accomodate smaller competitors. Weight: 11.4 lbs. Imported from 1999 to date.

MODEL 1913 STANDARD RIFLE . . . . . . NiB $1554 Ex $1185 Gd $824
Similar to 1913 Super Match w/economized appointments. Imported from 1997 to date.

MODEL 1913 SUPER MATCH RIFLE
Bolt-action single-shot Super Match (updated version of Model 1813). Caliber: .22 LR. 27.5-inch bbl. Weight: 14.2 lbs. Adj. two-stage trigger. Vented International thumbhole stock w/adj. cheekpiece, hand and palm rest, fitted w/10-way butthook. Imported from 1989 to date.
Right-hand model . . . . NiB $2244 Ex $1915 Gd $833
Left-hand model . . . . NiB $2315 Ex $1863 Gd $1287
W/laminated stock, add $130
W/stainless steel bbl., add $140

MODEL 2007 ISU STANDARD RIFLE
Bolt-action single-shot. Caliber: .22 LR. 19.75-inch bbl. 43.5 to 44.5 inches overall. Weight: 10.8 lbs. Two-stage trigger. Standard ISU stock w/adj. cheekpiece. Imported from 1992 to date.
Right-hand model . . . . NiB $1940 Ex $1476 Gd $863
Left-hand model . . . . NiB $2047 Ex $1667 Gd $1181
W/stainless steel bbl., add $140

MODEL 2013
LADIES' SPORT RIFLE . . . . NiB $2146 Ex $1965 Gd $874
Similar to the Model 2007 designed for ISU 3-position competition w/same general U.I.T. specifications except w/shorter dimensions to accomodate smaller competitors. Weight: 11.4 lbs. Imported from 1999 to date.

MODEL 2013
BENCHREST RIFLE (BR-50) . . . . . NiB $1741 Ex $1576 Gd $829
Bolt-action single-shot. Caliber: .22 LR. 19.6-inch bbl. 43 inches overall. Weight: 10.3 lbs. Adjustable trigger for single or two-stage function. Benchrest-configuration stock. Imported from 1999 to date.

MODEL 2013 SILHOUETTE RIFLE . . . . NiB $2130 Ex $1605 Gd $884
Bolt-action single-shot. Caliber: .22 LR. 20-inch bbl. 45.5 inches overall. Weight: 11.5 lbs. Two-stage trigger. Thumbhole black synthetic or laminated stock w/adj. cheekpiece, hand and palm rest. Imported from 1994 to date.

MODEL 2013 SUPER MATCH RIFLE
Bolt-action single-shot. Caliber: .22 LR. 19.75- or 27.1-inch bbl. 43 to 50.1 inches overall. Weight: 15.5 lbs. Two-stage trigger. International thumbhole, black synthetic or laminated stock w/adj. cheekpiece, hand and palm rest; fitted w/10-way butthook. Imported from 1992 to date.
Right-hand model . . . . NiB $2489 Ex $2253 Gd $1099
Left-hand model . . . . NiB $2468 Ex $1205 Gd $1414
W/laminated stock, add $180

ACHIEVER BOLT-ACTION RIFLE. . . . . NiB $386 Ex $309 Gd $180
Caliber: .22 LR. 5-round magazine. Mark 2000-type repeating action. 19.5-inch bbl. 36.5 inches overall. Weight: 5 lbs. Adj. open rear sight; hooded ramp front. Plain European hardwood target-style stock w/vented forend and adj. buttplate. Imported since 1987.

ACHIEVER ST-SUPER TARGET . . . . . NiB $515 Ex $386 Gd $232
Same as Achiever except single-shot w/22-inch bbl. and adj. stock. 38.75 inches overall. Weight: 6.5 lbs. Target sights. Imported since 1994.

BR-50 BENCH REST RIFLE. . . . . . NiB $2058 Ex $1621 Gd $977
Single-shot. Caliber: .22 LR. 19.75-inch bbl. (23 inches w/muzzle weight). 37.75-42.5 inches overall. Weight: 11 lbs. Grooved receiver, no sights. Walnut-finished hardwood or synthetic benchrest stock w/adj. cheekpiece. Imported from 1994-97. (Reintroduced as Model 2013 BR-50)

KADETT BOLT-ACTION
REPEATING RIFLE . . . . NiB $328 Ex $225 Gd $148
Caliber: .22 LR. 5-round detachable box magazine. 22-inch bbl. 40 inches overall. Weight: 5.5 lbs. Adj. folding leaf rear sight; hooded ramp front. Checkered European hardwood stock w/walnut-finish. Imported from 1987-88.

MARK 2000 MATCH . . . . NiB $426 Ex $318 Gd $199
Takedown, bolt-action single-shot. Caliber: .22 LR. 26-inch heavy bbl. Walnut stock w/deep-fluted thumb-groove, Wundhammer swell pistol grip, beavertail forend. Adj. buttplate, single-stage adj. trigger. Weight: 8 lbs. Imported from 1982-89.

ARMALITE, INC. — Geneseo, Illinois (Formerly Costa Mesa, California)

Armalite was in Costa Mesa, California from 1959-73. Following the acquisition by Eagle Arms in 1995, production resumed under the Armalite, Inc. Logo in Geneseo, Illinois.
Production by ARMALITE

AR-7 EXPLORER SURVIVAL RIFLE. . . NiB $154 Ex $128 Gd $77
Takedown. Semiautomatic. Caliber: .22 LR. Eight-round box magazine. 16-inch cast aluminum bbl. w/steel liner. Sights: Peep rear; blade front. Brown plastic stock, recessed to stow barrel, action, and magazine. Weight: 2.75 lbs. Will float stowed or assembled. Made from 1959-1973 by Armalite; from 1974-90 by Charter Arms; from 1990-97 by Survival Arms, Cocoa, FL.; from 1997 to date by Henry Repeating Arms Co., Brooklyn, NY.

AR-7 EXPLORER CUSTOM RIFLE . . . NiB $206 Ex $170 Gd $92
Same as AR-7 Survival Rifle except w/deluxe walnut stock w/cheekpiece and pistol grip. Weight: 3.5 lbs. Made from 1964-70.

Armalite AR-10

Armalite AR-10 (T) Target Carbine

Armalite M-15A2 National Match

Armalite M-15A2 HBAR

AR-180 SEMIAUTOMATIC RIFLE

Commercial version of full automatic AR-18 Combat Rifle. Gas-operated semiautomatic. Caliber: .223 Rem. (5.56mm). 5-, 20-, 30-round magazines. 18.25-inch bbl. w/flash hider/muzzle brake. Sights: Flip-up "L" type rear, adj. for windage; post front, adj. for elevation. Accessory: 3x scope and mount (add $60 to value). Folding buttstock of black nylon, rubber buttplate and pistol grip, heat dissipating fiberglass forend (hand guard), swivels, sling. 38 inches overall, 28.75 inches folded. Weight: 6.5 lbs. Note: Made by Armalite Inc. 1969-72, manufactured for Armalite by Howa Machinery Ltd., Nagoya, Japan, from 1972-73; by Sterling Armament Co. Ltd., Dagenham, Essex, England, from 1976 to 94. Importation disc.

Armalite AR-180 (Mfg. by Armalite-Costa Mesa) . . . . NiB $1289 Ex $1083 Gd $774
Armalite AR-180 (Mfg. by Howa) . . . . . . NiB $1463 Ex $1180 Gd $820
Armalite AR-180 (Mfg. by Sterling). . . . . . NiB $1079 Ex $864 Gd $602
W/3x scope and mount, add. $225

Production by ARMALITE, Inc.

AR-10 (A) SEMIAUTOMATIC SERIES

Gas-operated semiautomatic action. Calibers: .243 Win. or .308 Win. (7.62 x 51mm). 10-round magazine. 16- or 20-inch bbl. 35.5 or 39.5 inches overall. Weight: 9 to 9.75 lbs. Post front sight, adj. aperature rear. Black or green composition stock. Made from 1995 to date.

AR-10 A2 (Std. carbine). . . . . NiB $1940 Ex $1631 Gd $678
AR-10 A2 (Std. rifle) . . . . NiB $1270 Ex $1085 Gd $652
AR-10 A4 (S.P. carbine) . . . . NiB $1322 Ex $1085 Gd $652
AR-10 A4 (S.P. rifle). . . . . NiB $1322 Ex $1085 Gd $652
W/stainless steel bbl., add. $120

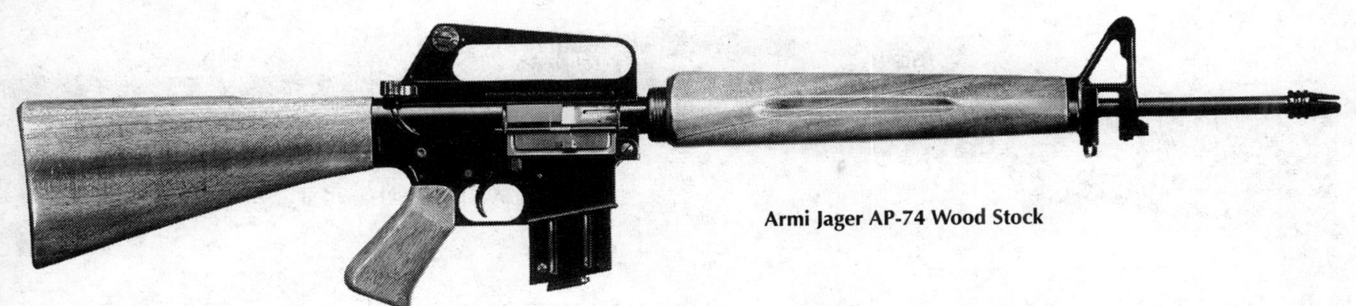
Armi Jager AP-74 Wood Stock

AR-10 (T) TARGET
Similar to Armalite Model AR-10A except in National Match configuration w/three-slot short Picatinny rail system and case deflector. 16- or 24-inch bbl. Weight: 8.25 to 10.4 lbs. Composite stock and handguard. No sights. Optional National Match carry handle and detachable front sight. Made from 1995 to date.
AR-10 T (Rifle)............... NiB $1936 Ex $1627 Gd $983
AR-10 T (Carbine)............ NiB $1936 Ex $1627 Gd $983

MODEL AR-50 SS BOLT-ACTION RIFLE.................... NiB $2451 Ex $2080 Gd $1308
Caliber: .50 BMG. 31-inch bbl. w/muzzle brake. 59 inches overall. Weight: 41 lbs. Modified octagonal-form receiver, drilled and slotted for scope rail. Single-stage trigger. Triple front-locking bolt lug w/spring-loaded plunger for automatic ejection. Magnesium phosphate steel, hard-anodized aluminum finish. Made from 1999 to date.

M15 SERIES
Gas-operated semiautomatic w/A2-style forward-assist mechanism and push-type pivot pin for easy takedown. Caliber: .223. 7-round magazine. 16-, 20- or 24-inch bbl. Weight: 7-9.2 lbs. Composite or retractable stock. Fully adj. sights. Black anodized finish. Made from 1995 to date.
M-15A2 (Carbine) .... NiB $891 Ex $763 Gd $607
M-15A2 (Service Rifle)............... NiB $942 Ex $813 Gd $618
M-15A2 (National Match)........... NiB $1313 Ex $1076 Gd $720
M-15A2 (Golden Eagle heavy bbl.)............ NiB $1287 Ex $1040 Gd $680
M-15A2 M4C (retractable stock, disc. 1997).......... NiB $1235 Ex $968 Gd $647
M-15A4 (Action Master, disc. 1997)..... NiB $1107 Ex $895 Gd $623
M-15A4 (Predator) .... NiB $942 Ex $813 Gd 618
M-15A4 (S.P. Rifle) .... NiB $916 Ex $762 Gd $504
M-15A4 (S.P. Carbine).................. NiB $865 Ex $710 Gd $453
M-15A4T (Eagle Eye Carbine)........ NiB $1287 Ex $1029 Gd $720
M-15A4T (Eagle Eye Rifle)........... NiB $1338 Ex $1004 Gd $720

ARMI JAGER — Turin, Italy

AP-74 COMMANDO............ NiB $276 Ex $215 Gd $143
Similar to standard AP-74 but styled to resemble original version of Uzi 9mm submachine gun w/wood buttstock. Lacks carrying handle and flash suppressor. Has different type front sight mount and guards, wood stock, pistol grip and forearm. Intro. 1976. Disc.

AP-74 SEMIAUTOMATIC RIFLE
Styled after U.S. M16 military rifle. Caliber: .22 LR, .32 Auto (pistol cartridge). Detachable clip magazine; capacity: 14 rounds caliber .22 LR, 9 rounds .32 ACP. 20-inch bbl. w/flash suppressor. Weight: 6.5 lbs. M16 type sights. Stock, pistol-grip and forearm of black plastic, swivels and sling. Intro. 1974. Disc.
.22 LR.......................... NiB $328 Ex $276 Gd $173
.32 Auto......................... NiB $354 Ex $302 Gd $184

AP-74 WOOD STOCK MODEL
Same as standard AP-74 except w/wood stock, pistol-grip and forearm weight: 7 lbs. Disc.
.22 LR .... NiB $407 Ex $330 Gd $217
.32 Auto....................... NiB $433 Ex $330 Gd $217

ARMSCOR (Arms Corp.) — Manila, Philippines *(Imported until 1991 by Armscor Precision, San Mateo, CA; 1991-95 by Ruko Products, Inc., Buffalo NY: Currently imported by K.B.I., Harrisburg, PA)*

MODEL 20 AUTO RIFLE
Caliber: .22 LR. 15-round magazine. 21-inch bbl. 39.75 inches overall. Weight: 6.5 lbs. Sights: Hooded front; adj. rear. Checkered or plain walnut finished mahogany stock. Blued finish. Imported 1990-91. (Reinstated by Ruko in the M series.)
Model 20 (checkered stock) .... NiB $137 Ex $113 Gd $82
Model 20C (carbine-style stock) .... NiB $124 Ex $103 Gd $75
Model 20P (plain stock) .... NiB $112 Ex $92 Gd $68

MODEL 1600 AUTO RIFLE
Caliber: .22 LR. 15-round magazine. 19.5-inch bbl. 38 inches overall. Weight: 6 lbs. Sights: Post front; aperture rear. Plain mahogany stock. Matte black finish. Imported 1987-91. (Reinstated by Ruko in the M series.)
Standard model................. NiB $159 Ex $118 Gd $87
Retractable stock model .... NiB $169 Ex $133 Gd $92

MODEL AK22 AUTO RIFLE
Caliber: .22 LR. 15- or 30-round magazine. 18.5-inch bbl. 36 inches overall. Weight: 7 lbs. Sights: Post front; adj. rear. Plain mahogany stock. Matte black finish. Imported 1987-91.
Standard model................. NiB $205 Ex $184 Gd $118
Folding stock model .... NiB $220 Ex $189 Gd $143

MODEL M14 SERIES BOLT-ACTION RIFLE
Caliber: .22 LR. 10-round magazine. 23-inch bbl. Weight: 6.25 lbs. Open sights. Walnut or walnut finished mahogany stock. Imported 1991-97.
M14P Standard model............. NiB $113 Ex $87 Gd $63
M14D Deluxe model (checkered stock, disc. 1995) .... NiB $99 Ex $82 Gd $71

MODEL M20 SERIES SEMIAUTOMATIC RIFLE
Caliber: .22 LR. 10- or 15-round magazine. 18.25- or 20.75-inch bbl. Weight:5.5 to 6.5 lbs. 38 to 40.5 inches overall. Hooded front sight w/windage adj. rear. Walnut finished mahogany stock. Imported 1990-97.
M20C carbine model .... NiB $118 Ex $98 Gd $67
M20P standard model.................. NiB $110 Ex $87 Gd $67
M20S Sporter Deluxe (checkered mahogany stock)...................... NiB $143 Ex $128 Gd $77
M20SC Super Classic (checkered walnut stock) .... NiB $276 Ex $220 Gd $103

A-Square — Hannibal

MODEL M1400 BOLT-ACTION RIFLE
Similar to Model 14P except w/checkered stock w/Schnabel forend. Weight: 6 lbs. Imported from 1990-97.
M1400LW (Lightweight, disc. 1992). . . . . . NiB $214 Ex $183 Gd $122
M1400S (Sporter) . . . . NiB $147 Ex $122 Gd $91
M1400SC (Super Classic) . . . . NiB $269 Ex $219 Gd $157

MODEL M1500 BOLT-ACTION RIFLE
Caliber: .22 Mag. 5-round magazine. 21.5-inch bbl. Weight: 6.5 lbs. Open sights. Checkered mahogany stock. Imported from 1991-97.
M1500 (standard) . . . . NiB $147 Ex $122 Gd $91
M1500LW (Euro-style walnut
stock, disc. 1992) . . . . NiB $198 Ex $173 Gd $122
M1500SC (Monte Carlo stock) . . . . NiB $204 Ex $173 Gd $132

MODEL M1600 AUTO RIFLE
Rimfire replica of Armalite Model AR 180 (M16) except chambered for Caliber .22 LR. 15-round magazine. 18-inch bbl. Weight: 5.25 lbs. Composite or retractable buttstock w/composite handguard and pistol grip. Carrying handle w/adj. aperture rear sight and protected post front. Black anodized finish. Imported from 1991-97.
M-1600 (standard w/fixed stock) . . . . . . NiB $166 Ex $136 Gd $99
M-1600R (retractable stock) . . . . NiB $178 Ex $146 Gd $106

MODEL M1800 BOLT-ACTION RIFLE
Caliber: .22 Hornet. 5-round magazine. 22-inch bbl. Weight: 6.6 lbs. Checkered hardwood or walnut stock. Sights: Post front; adj. rear. Imported from 1995 to date.
M-1800 (standard) . . . . NiB $277 Ex $206 Gd $149
M-1800SC (checkered walnut stock) . . . . . NiB $379 Ex $308 Gd $226

MODEL M2000 AUTO RIFLE
Similar to Model 20P except w/checkered mahogany stock and adj. sights. Imported from 1991 to date.
M2000S (standard) . . . . NiB $146 Ex $121 Gd $87
M2000SC (checkered walnut stock) . . . . . . NiB $255 Ex $208 Gd $148

ARNOLD ARMS — Arlington, Washington

AFRICAN SAFARI
Calibers: .243 to .458 Win. Magnum. 22- to 26-inch bbl. Weight: 7-9 lbs. Scope mount standard or w/optional M70 Express sights. Chrome-moly in four finishes. "A" and "AA" Fancy Grade English walnut stock with number 5 standard wraparound checkering pattern. Ebony forend tip. Made from 1996 to date.
With "A" Grade English
walnut: matte blue . . . . NiB $4651 Ex $3760 Gd $2620
Std. polish . . . . NiB $4906 Ex $3934 Gd $2758
Hi-Luster . . . . NiB $5104 Ex $4112 Gd $2865
Stainless steel matte . . . . NiB $4651 Ex $3760 Gd $2619
With "AA" Grade English
Walnut: C-M matte blue . . . . NiB $4626 Ex $3739 Gd $2605
Std. polish . . . . NiB $4906 Ex $3964 Gd $2758
Hi-Luster . . . . NiB $5104 Ex $4122 Gd $2865
Stainless steel matte . . . . NiB $4651 Ex $3759 Gd $2620

ALASKAN TROPHY
Calibers: .300 Magnum to .458 Win. Magnum. 24- to 26-inch bbl. Weight: 7-9 lbs. Scope mount w/Express sights standard. Stainless steel or chrome-moly Apollo action w/fibergrain or black synthetic stock. Barrel band on 357 H&H and larger magnums. Made from 1996 to 2000.
Matte finish . . . . NiB $3208 Ex $2598 Gd $1817
Std. polish . . . . NiB $3464 Ex $2801 Gd $1955
Stainless steel . . . . NiB $3279 Ex $2654 Gd $1854

A-SQUARE COMPANY INC. — Louisville, Kentucky (Formerly Bedford, KY)

CAESAR BOLT-ACTION RIFLE
Custom rifle built on Remington's 700 receiver. Calibers: Same as Hannibal, Groups I, II and III. 20- to 26-inch bbl. Weight: 8.5 to 11 lbs. Express 3-leaf rear sight, ramp front. Synthetic or classic Claro oil-finished walnut stock w/flush detachable swivels and Coil-Chek recoil system. Three-way adj. target trigger; 3-position safety. Right- or left-hand. Made from 1984 to date.
Synthetic stock model . . . . NiB $3314 Ex $2695 Gd $1872
Walnut stock model. . . . . NiB $2953 Ex $2284 Gd $1666

GENGHIS KHAN BOLT-ACTION RIFLE
Custom varmint rifle developed on Winchester's M70 receiver; fitted w/heavy tapered bbl. and Coil-Chek stock. Calibers: .22-250 Rem., .243 Win., .25-06 Rem., 6mm Rem. Weight: 8-8.5 lbs. Made from 1994 to date.
Synthetic stock model . . . . NiB $4055 Ex $3221 Gd $2252
Walnut stock model. . . . . NiB $3385 Ex $2767 Gd $1943

HAMILCAR BOLT-ACTION RIFLE
Similar to Hannibal Model except lighter. Calibers: .25-06, .257 Wby., 6.5x55 Swedish, .270 Wby., 7x57, 7mm Rem., 7mm STW, 7mm Wby., .280 Rem., .30-06, .300 Win., .300 Wby., .338-06, 9.3x62. Weight: 8-8.5 lbs. Made from 1994 to date.
Synthetic stock model . . . . NiB $3870 Ex $3123 Gd $2149
Walnut stock model. . . . . NiB $3425 Ex $2767 Gd $1927

HANNIBAL BOLT-ACTION RIFLE
Custom rifle built on reinforced P-17 Enfield receiver. Calibers: Group I: 30-06; Group II: 7mm Rem. Mag., .300 Win. Mag., .416 Taylor, .425 Express, .458 Win. Mag.; Group III: .300 H&H, .300 Wby. Mag., 8mm Rem. Mag., .340 Wby. Mag., .375 H&H, .375 Wby. Mag., .404 Jeffery, .416 Hoffman, .416 Rem Mag., .450 Ackley, .458 Lott; Group IV: .338 A-Square Mag., .375 A-Square Mag., .378 Wby. Mag., .416 Rigby, .416 Wby. Mag., .460 Short Square Mag., .500 A-Square Mag. 20- to 26-inch bbl. Weight: 9 to 11.75 lbs. Express 3-leaf rear sight, ramp front. Classic Claro oil-finished walnut stock or synthetic stock w/flush detachable swivels and Coil-Chek recoil system. Adj. trigger w/2-position safety. Made from 1983 to date.
Synthetic stock model . . . . NiB $3814 Ex $3080 Gd $2241
Walnut stock model. . . . . NiB $3615 Ex $2921 Gd $2043

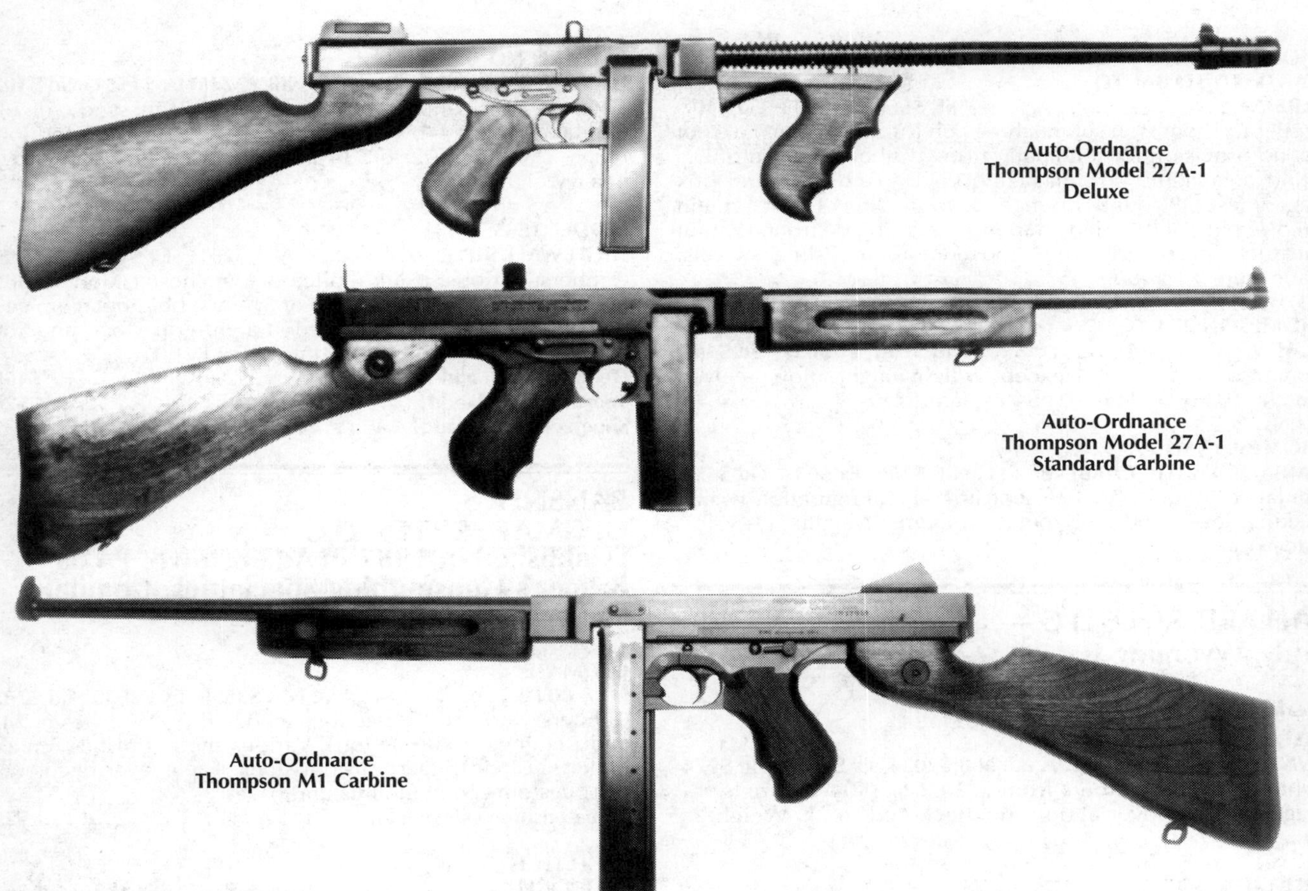

Auto-Ordnance
Thompson Model 27A-1
Deluxe

Auto-Ordnance
Thompson Model 27A-1
Standard Carbine

Auto-Ordnance
Thompson M1 Carbine

AUSTRIAN MILITARY RIFLES — Steyr, Austria Manufactured at Steyr Armory

MODEL 90
STEYR-MANNLICHER RIFLE . . . . . . NiB $297 Ex $174 Gd $121
Straight-pull bolt action. Caliber: 8mm. 5-round magazine. Open sights. 10-inch bayonet. Cartridge clip forms part of the magazine mechanism. Some of these rifles were provided with a laced canvas hand guard, others were of wood.

MODEL 90
STEYR-MANNLICHER CARBINE . . . NiB $299 Ex $203 Gd $121
Same general specifications as Model 90 rifle except w/19.5-inch bbl., weight 7 lbs. No bayonet stud or supplemental forend grip.

MODEL 95
STEYR-MANNLICHER CARBINE . . . NiB $299 Ex $204 Gd $121
Same general specifications as Model 95 rifle except w/19.5-inch bbl., weight 7 lbs. Post front sight; adj. rear carbine sight.

MODEL 95
STEYR-MANNLICHER
SERVICE RIFLE. . . . . NiB $274 Ex $152 Gd $116
Straight-pull bolt action. Caliber: 8x50R Mannlicher (many of these rifles were altered during World War II to use the 7.9mm German service ammunition). 5-round Mannlicher-type box magazine. 30-inch bbl. Weight: 8.5 lbs. Sights: Blade front; rear adj. for elevation. Military-type full stock.

AUTO-ORDNANCE CORPORATION — West Hurley, New York (Manufacturing rights acquired by Kahr Arms 1999)

THOMPSON
MODEL 22-27A-3 . . . . NiB $752 Ex $628 Gd $448
Same-bore version of Deluxe Model 27A-1. Same general specifications except 22 LR w/lightweight alloy receiver, weight 6.5 lbs. Magazines include 5-, 20-, 30- and 50-round box types, 80-round drum. Made from 1977-94.

THOMPSON
MODEL 27A-1 DELUXE
Same as Standard Model 27A-1 except w/finned bbl. w/compensator, adj. rear sight, pistol-grip forestock. Caliber: .22 LR, l0mm (1991-93) or 45 ACP. Weight: 11.5 lbs. Made from 1976-99.
.22 LR (Limited production) . . . . NiB $1328 Ex $1072 Gd $744
10mm or 45 ACP. . . . . NiB $757 Ex $634 Gd $505
50-round drum magazine, add $250
100-round drum magazine, add $450
Violin carrying case, add. $100

THOMPSON MODEL 27A-1 STANDARD SEMIAUTO CARBINE . . . . NiB $660 Ex $608 Gd $402
Similar to Thompson submachine gun ("Tommy Gun") except has no provision for automatic firing. Caliber: .45 Auto. 20-round detachable box magazine (5-,15- and 30-round box magazines, 39-round drum also available). 16-inch plain bbl. Weight: 14 lbs. Sights: Aperture rear; blade front. Walnut buttstock, pistol grip and grooved forearm, sling swivels. Made from 1976-86.

THOMPSON 27A-1C LIGHTWEIGHT CARBINE . . . . NiB $796 Ex $637 Gd $448
Similar to Model 27A-1 except w/lightweight alloy receiver. Weight: 9.25 lbs. Made 1984 to date.

THOMPSON M1 SEMI-AUTOMATIC CARBINE . . . . . NiB $760 Ex $637 Gd $457
Similar to Model 27A-1 except in M-1 configuration w/side cocking lever and horizontal forearm. Weight: 11.5 lbs. Made from 1986 to date.

BALLARD RIFLE LLC — Cody, Wyoming

Firearms manufactured since 1996.

BALLARD 1-1/2 HUNTER'S RIFLE . . . . NiB $2024 Ex $1374 Gd $974
Calibers: Seven calibers from .22 LR to .50-70. Single trigger, S-style lever action; unchecкered stock. Weight: 10.5 lbs.

BALLARD 1-3/4 FAR WEST RIFLE . . . . NiB $2124 Ex $1474 Gd $999
Calibers: Eight calibers from .32-40 WCF to .50-90 SS. Patterned after original Ballard Far West model. 30 or 32-inch bbl., standard or heavyweight octagon; double set triggers; ring-style lever. Weight: 9.75 to 10.5 lbs.

BALLARD NO. 5 PACIFIC . . . . NiB $2426 Ex $1701 Gd $1126
Calibers: Nine calibers between .32-40 WCF and .50-90 SS. Similar to No. 1-3/4 Far West model but with under-barrel wiping rod.

BALLARD NO. 4-1/2 MID-RANGE RIFLE . . . . NiB $2226 Ex $1526 Gd $1201
Calibers: .Five calibers between .32-40 WCF and .45-110. Designed for black powder silhouette shooting. 30 or 32-inch bbl., half-octagonal heavyweight; single or double set triggers; pistol grip stock; full loop lever; hard rubber Ballard buttplate; Vernier tang sight. Weight: 10.75 to 11.5 lbs.

BALLARD NO. 7 LONG-RANGE RIFLE. . . . . NiB $2226 Ex $1551 Gd $1026
Caliber: Five calibers between .40-65 Win. and .45-110. Similar to No. 4-1/2 Mid-Range Rifle; designed for long-range shooting. 32 or 34-inch half-octagon standard or heavyweight bbl.

MODEL 1885 HIGH WALL RIFLE . . . . NiB $2015 Ex $1370 Gd $995
Calibers: Various. Exact replica of Winchester Model 1885 (parts are interchangeable). 30 or 32-inch bbl., octagon; case-colored receiver, uncheckered straight-grip stock and forearm. Weight: Approx. 9 lbs. Introduced 2001.
Deluxe model, add $1500
Sporting model, add $200
Shuetzen model, add $325

BANSNER'S ULTIMATE RIFLES, LLC — Established in 1981 in Adamstown, PA as Basner's Gunsmithing Specialties. Company name changed in 2000.

ULTIMATE ONE RIFLE. . . . . NiB $3990 Ex $2650 Gd $2025
Calibers: Various. Bolt-action, modeled on Winchester M70 and Remington 700 actions. Various metal finishes; muzzle brake; custom trigger; custom stock; Pachmayer decelerator pad; custom scope mounts and bases.
Three-position safety, add. $250

HIGH TECH SERIES RIFLE . . . . NiB $1071 Ex $896 Gd $646
Calibers: Various. Steel or stainless steel action with factory bbl. Bansner's synthetic stock and Pachmayer decelerator pad.
Stainless steel model, add. $150

SAFARI HUNTER RIFLE . . . . NiB $4343 Ex $3268 Gd $2293
Calibers: Various dangerous game calibers. Based on Model 70 Classic action; muzzle brake; Lilja Precision stainless steel barrel; synthetic stock; matte black Teflon metal finish. Introduced 2003.

WORLD SLAM LIMITED EDITION RIFLE . . . . NiB $4243 Ex $2693 Gd $2018
Calibers: Various. Customized Model 700 action; fluted bold body. jeweled trigger. three-position safety; synthetic stock. Only 25 each of limited edition models were made beginning in 2003.

BARRETT FIREARMS MFG., INC. — Murfreesboro, Tennessee

MODEL 82 A-1
SEMI-AUTOMATIC RIFLE . . . . . NiB $7139 Ex $5543 Gd $3483
Caliber: .50 BMG. 10-round detachable box magazine. 29-inch recoiling bbl. w/muzzle brake. 57 inches overall. Weight: 28.5 lbs. Open iron sights and 10x scope. Composit stock w/Sorbothance recoil pad and self-leveling bipod. Blued finish. Made in various configurations from 1985 to date.

MODEL 90
BOLT-ACTION RIFLE . . . . NiB $3684 Ex $3169 Gd $1985
Caliber: .50 BMG. Five round magazine. 29-inch match bbl. 45 inches overall. Weight: 22 lbs. Composite stock w/retractable bipod. Made from 1990-95.

MODEL 95 BOLT-ACTION . . . . NiB $4755 Ex $3699 Gd $2762
Similar to Model 90 bullpup design chambered for .50 BMG except w/improved muzzle brake and extendable bipod. Made from 1995 to date.

BEEMAN PRECISION ARMS INC. — Santa Rosa, California

Since 1993 all European firearms imported by Beeman have been distributed by Beeman Outdoor Sports, Div., Roberts Precision Arms, Inc., Santa Rosa, CA.

WEIHRAUCH HW MODELS 60J AND 60J-ST
BOLT-ACTION RIFLES
Calibers: .22 LR (60J-ST), .222 Rem. (60J). 22.8-inch bbl. 41.7 inches overall. Weight: 6.5 lbs. Sights: Hooded blade front; open adj. rear. Blued finish. Checkered walnut stock w/cheekpiece. Made from 1988-94.
Model 60J . . . . NiB $501 Ex $738 Gd $604
Model 60J-ST. . . . . NiB $618 Ex $501 Gd $353

WEIHRAUCH HW MODEL 60M
SMALL BORE RIFLE. . . . . NiB $656 Ex $553 Gd $368
Caliber: .22 LR. Single-shot. 26.8-inch bbl. 45.7 inches overall. Weight: 10.8 lbs. Adj. trigger w/push-button safety. Sights: Hooded blade front on ramp, precision aperture rear. Target-style stock w/stippled forearm and pistol grip. Blued finish. Made from 1988-94.

WEIHRAUCH HW
MODEL 660 MATCH RIFLE. . . . . . . NiB $923 Ex $795 Gd $408
Caliber: .22 LR. 26-inch bbl. 45.3 inches overall. Weight: 10.7 lbs. Adj. match trigger. Sights: globe front, precision aperture rear. Match-style walnut stock w/adj. cheekpiece and buttplate. Made from 1988-94.

FEINWERKBAU MODEL 2600 SERIES TARGET RIFLE
Caliber: .22 LR. Single-shot. 26.3-inch bbl. 43.7 inches overall. Weight: 10.6 lbs. Match trigger w/fingertip weight adjustment dial. Sights: Globe front; micrometer match aperture rear. Laminated hardwood stock w/adj. cheekpiece. Made from 1988-94.
Standard Model 2600 (left-hand) . . . . NiB $1676 Ex $1295 Gd $883
Standard Model 2600
(right-hand) . . . . NiB $1501 Ex $1192 Gd $780
Free Rifle Model 2602
(left-hand) . . . . NiB $2119 Ex $1707 Gd $986
Free Rifle Model 2602
(right-hand) . . . . NiB $2110 Ex $1707 Gd $986

BELGIAN MILITARY RIFLES Mfd. by Fabrique Nationale D'Armes de Guerre, Herstal, Belgium; Fabrique D'Armes de L'Etat, Lunich, Belgium

Hopkins & Allen Arms Co. of Norwich, Conn., as well as contractors in Birmingham, England, also produced these guns during World War I.

MODEL 1889 MAUSER
MILITARY RIFLE . . . . NiB $221 Ex $150 Gd $99
Caliber: 7.65mm Belgian Service (7.65mm Mauser). 5-round projecting box magazine. 30.75-inch bbl. w/jacket. Weight: 8.5 lbs. Adj. rear sight, blade front. Straight-grip military stock. This, and the carbine version, was the principal weapon of the Belgian Army at the start of WWII. Made from 1889 to c.1935.

MODEL 1916
MAUSER CARBINE . . . . NiB $246 Ex $195 Gd $109
Same as Model 1889 Rifle except w/20.75-inch bbl. Weighs 8 lbs. and has minor differences in the rear sight graduations, lower band closer to the muzzle and swivel plate on side of buttstock.

MODEL 1935 MAUSER
MILITARY RIFLE . . . . NiB $323 Ex $246 Gd $144
Same general specifications as F.N. Model 1924; minor differences. Caliber: 7.65mm Belgian Service. Mfd. by Fabrique Nationale D'Armes de Guerre.

MODEL 1936 MAUSER
MILITARY RIFLE . . . . NiB $246 Ex $201 Gd $141
An adaptation of Model 1889 w/German M/98-type bolt, Belgian M/89 protruding box magazine. Caliber: 7.65mm Belgian Service. Mfd. by Fabrique Nationale D'Armes de Guerre.

BENTON & BROWN FIREARMS, INC. — Fort Worth, Texas

MODEL 93
BOLT-ACTION RIFLE
Similar to Blaser Model R84 (the B&B rifle is built on the Blaser action, see separate listing) with an interchangeable bbl. system. Calibers: .243 Win., 6mm Rem., .25-06, .257 Wby., .264 Win., .270 Win., .280 Rem., 7mm Rem Mag., .30-06, .308, .300 Wby., .300 Win. Mag., .338 Win., .375 H&H. 22- or 24-inch bbl. 41 or 43 inches overall. Bbl.-mounted scope rings and one-piece base; no sights. Two-piece walnut or fiberglass stock. Made from 1993 to date.
Walnut stock model. . . . . NiB $1849 Ex $1695 Gd $964
Fiberglass stock model. . . . . NiB $1643 Ex $1283 Gd $922
Extra bbl. assembly, add $475
Extra bolt assembly, add $425

Beretta 501
Bolt-Action Sporter

Beretta AR-70

BERETTA U.S.A. CORP. — Accokeek, Maryland, Manufactured by Fabbrica D'Armi Pietro Beretta, S.p.A., Gardone Val Trompia (Brescia), Italy

455 SxS EXPRESS DOUBLE RIFLE
Sidelock action w/removable sideplates. Calibers: .375 H&H, .458 Win. Mag., .470 NE, .500 NE (3 inches), .416 Rigby. Bbls.: 23.5 or 25.5-inch. Weight: 11 lbs. Double triggers. Sights: Blade front; V-notch folding leaf rear. Checkered European walnut forearm and buttstock w/recoil pad. Color casehardened receiver w/blued bbls. Made from 1990 to date.
Model 455 . . . . NiB $40,938 Ex $32,750 Gd $22,270
Model 455EELL. . . . . NiB $51,875 Ex $41,500 Gd $28,220

500 BOLT-ACTION SPORTER
Centerfire bolt-action rifle w/Sako A I short action. Calibers: .222 Rem., .223 Rem. Five round magazine. 23.63-inch bbl. Weight: 6.5 lbs. Available w/ or w/o iron sights. Tapered dovetailed receiver. European walnut stock. Disc. 1986.
Standard . . . . NiB $649 Ex $551 Gd $396
DL Model . . . . NiB $1532 Ex $1235 Gd $856
500 EELL
Engraved . . . . NiB $1596 Ex $1390 Gd $927
W/iron sights, add 10%

501 BOLT-ACTION SPORTER
Same as Model 500 except w/Sako A II medium action. Calibers: .243 Win., .308 Win. Weight: 7.5 lbs. Disc. 1986.
Standard . . . . NiB $674 Ex $546 Gd $383
Standard
w/iron sights . . . . NiB $649 Ex $602 Gd $396
DL model. . . . . NiB $1534 Ex $1245 Gd $885
501 EELL (engraved) . . . . NiB $1657 Ex $1400 Gd $936
W/iron sights, add 10%

502 BOLT-ACTION SPORTER
Same as Model 500 except w/Sako A III long action. Calibers: .270 Win., 7mm Rem. Mag., .30/06, 375 H&H. Weight: 8.5 lbs. Disc. 1986.
Standard model . . . . NiB $747 Ex $607 Gd $428
DL model. . . . . NiB $1710 Ex $1349 Gd $937
502 EELL (engraved) . . . . NiB $1858 Ex $1499 Gd $1034
W/iron sights, add 10%

AR-70 SEMIAUTOMATIC RIFLE . . . . . . NiB $1967 Ex $1736 Gd $1040
Caliber: .223 Rem. (5.56mm). 30-round magazine. 17.75-inch bbl. Weight: 8.25 lbs. Sights: Rear peep adj. for windage and elevation; blade front. High-impact synthetic buttstock. Imported from 1984-89.

EXPRESS S686/S689 SABLE O/U RIFLE
Calibers: .30-06 Spfld., 9.3x74R, and .444 Marlin. 24-inch bbl. Weight: 7.7 lbs. Drilled and tapped for scope mount. European-style cheek rest and ventilated rubber recoil pad. Imported from 1995 to date.
Model S686/S689 Silver Sable II. . . . . NiB $4637 Ex $3680 Gd $2135
Model S689 Gold Sable . . . . NiB $6255 Ex $5225 Gd $3062
Model S686/S689 EELL
Diamond Sable. . . . . NiB $12,875 Ex $9270 Gd $6180
W/extra bbl. set, add $325
W/detachable claw mounts, add $595

EXPRESS SSO O/U EXPRESS DOUBLE RIFLE
Sidelock. Calibers: .375 H&H Mag., .458 Win. Mag., 9.3 x 74R. 23-24- or 25.5-inch blued bbls. Weight: 11 lbs. Double triggers. Express sights w/blade front and V-notch folding leaf rear. Optional Zeiss scope w/claw mounts. Color casehardened receiver w/scroll engraving, game scenes and gold inlays on higher grades. Checkered European walnut forearm and buttstock w/cheekpiece and recoil pad. Imported from 1985 to date.
Model SS0 (disc. 1989) . . . . NiB $9380 Ex $8247 Gd $5260
Model SS05 (disc. 1990) . . . . NiB $10,410 Ex $8865 Gd $6290
Model SS06 Custom . . . . NiB $26,265 Ex $20,085 Gd $12,360
Model SS06 EELL Gold Custom . . . . NiB $29,767 Ex $26,265 Gd $14,935
Extra bbl. assembly, add $6250
Claw mounts, add $550

Blaser Model R84

MATO
Calibers: .270 Win., .280 Rem., 7mm Rem. Mag, .300 Win. Mag., .338 Win. Mag., .375 H&H. 23.6-inch bbl. Weight: 8 lbs. Adjustable trigger. Drop-out box magazine. Drilled and tapped for scope w/ or w/o adj. sights. Walnut or synthetic stock. Manufactured based on Mauser 98 action. Made from 1997 to date.
Standard model . . . . NiB $1296 Ex $987 Gd $678
Deluxe model . . . . NiB $1965 Ex $1605 Gd $884
.375 H&H w/iron sights, add. $300

SMALL BORE SPORTING CARBINE/TARGET RIFLE
Semiautomatic w/bolt handle in raised or conventional single-shot bolt-action w/handle in lowered position. Caliber: .22 LR. Four, 5-, 8-, 10- or 20-round magazines. 20.5-inch standard or heavy bbl. Sights: 3-leaf folding rear, partridge front. Target or sporting stock w/checkered pistol grip and forend and sling swivels. Weight: 5.5 to 6 lbs.
Sporter model (Super Sport X) . . . . NiB $415 Ex $338 Gd $230
Target model (Olympia X) . . . . NiB $289 Ex $467 Gd $312

BERNARDELLI, VINCENZO — Brescia, Italy

Currently headquartered in Brescia, Italy, Bernardelli arms were manufactured from 1721 to 1997 in Gardone, Italy. Imported and distributed by Armsport, Inc., Miami, Florida. Also handled by Magnum Research, Inc., Quality Arms, Inc., Armes De Chasse, Stoeger and Action Arms.

EXPRESS VB . . . . NiB $5640 Ex $4640 Gd $3590
Double barrel. Calibers: Various. Side-by-side sidelock action. Ejectors, double triggers. Imported from 1990 to1997.
Deluxe model (w/double triggers), add $1000

EXPRESS 2000 . . . . NiB $3085 Ex $2035 Gd $1475
Calibers: .30-06, 7x65R, 8x57JRS, 9.3x74R. Over/under boxlock design. Single or double triggers, extractors. Checkered walnut stock and forearm. Imported from 1994 to 1997.
Single trigger, add. $150

MINERVA EXPRESS . . . . NiB $5365 Ex $4290 Gd $3885
Caliber: Various. Exposed hammers. Extractors, double triggers. Moderate engraving. Imported from 1995 to 1997.

CARBINA .22. . . . . NiB $629 Ex $469 Gd $294
Semi-auto. Caliber: .22 rimfire. Blow-back action. Imported from 1990 to 1997.

MODEL 120 . . . . NiB $2151 Ex $1686 Gd $1136
Combination gun; over-under boxlock; 12 gauge over .22 Hornet, .222 Rem., 5.6x50R Mag., .243 Win., 6.5x57R, .270 Win., 7x57R, .308 Win., .30-06, 6.5x55, 7x65R, 8x57JRS, 9.3x74R. Iron sights. Checkered walnut stock and forearm. Double triggers, automatic ejectors or extractors. Ventilated recoil pad. Engraved action. Made in Italy. Discontinued.

MODEL 190 . . . . NiB $1401 Ex $1076 Gd $1021
Combination gun; over-under boxlock. Calibers: 12, 16 or 20 ga. Over .222 Rem., .243 Win., .30-06, .308 Win., 5.6x50R Mag., .5.6x57R, 6.5x55, 6.5x57R, 7x57R, 7x65R, 8x57JRS, 9.3x74R. Iron sights. Checkered walnut stock. Double triggers; extractors. Made in Italy. Introduced in 1969, discontinued 1989.

MODEL 2000 . . . . NiB $2222 Ex $1794 Gd $1319
Combination gun; over-under boxlock action. Calibers: 12, 16 or 20 ga. Over .222 Rem., .22 Hornet, 5.6x50R Mag., .243 Win., 6.5x55, 6.5x57R, .270 Win., 7x57R, .308 Win., .30-06, 8x57JRS, 9.3x74R. Bbl: 23 inches. Sights: Blade front, open rear. Hand checkered, oil-finished select European walnut stock, double-set triggers, auto ejectors. Silvered, engraved action. Made in Italy. Introduced in 1990, discontinued 1991.
Extra bbl. assembly, add $500

RIFLES

BLASER USA, INC. — Fort Worth, Texas Mfd. by Blaser Jagdwaffen GmbH, Germany *(Imported by Sigarms, Exeter, NH; Autumn Sales, Inc., Fort Worth, TX)*

MODEL R84 BOLT-ACTION RIFLE
Calibers: .22-250, .243, 6mm Rem., .25-06, .270, .280 Rem., .30-06- .257 Wby. Mag., .264 Win. Mag., 7mm Rem Mag., .300 Win. Mag., .300 Wby. Mag., .338 Win. Mag., .375 H&H. Interchangeable bbls. w/standard or Magnum bolt assemblies. Bbl. length: 23 inches (standard); 24 inches (Magnum). 41 to 42 inches overall. Weight: 7 to 7.25 lbs. No sights. Bbl.-mounted scope system. Two-piece Turkish walnut stock w/solid black recoil pad. Imported from 1989-94.
Model R84 Standard . . . . NiB $2231 Ex $1716 Gd $1093
Model R84 Deluxe
(game scene). . . . . NiB $3068 Ex $2048 Gd $1307
Model R84 Super Deluxe
(Gold and silver inlays). . . . . NiB $3694 Ex $2066 Gd $1438
Left-hand model, add $125
Extra bbl. assembly, add $650

MODEL R93 SAFARI SERIES BOLT-ACTION REPEATER
Similar to Model R84 except restyled action w/straight-pull bolt, unique safety and searless trigger mechanism. Additional chamberings: 6.5x55, 7x57, .308, .416 Rem. Optional open sights. Imported from 1994-98.
Model R93 Safari . . . . NiB $3777 Ex $3185 Gd $2052
Model R93 Safari Deluxe . . . . NiB $4226 Ex $4020 Gd $3196
Model R84 Safari
Super Deluxe . . . . NiB $4741 Ex $4226 Gd $3350
Extra bbl. assembly, add $525

MODEL R93 CLASSIC SERIES BOLT-ACTION REPEATER
Similar to Model R93 Safari except w/expanded model variations. Imported from 1998 to date.
Model R93 Attache
(Premium wood, fluted bbl.). . . . . NiB $4430 Ex $3762 Gd $2990
Model R93 Classic
(.22-250 to .375 H&H) . . . . NiB $3433 Ex $2765 Gd $1910
Model R93 Classic Safari (.416 Rem.). . . . . NiB $3820 Ex $3074 Gd $2120
Model R93 LX (.22-250 to .416 Rem.) . . . . . NiB $1735 Ex $1401 Gd $974
Model R93 Synthetic (.22-250
to .375 H&H) . . . . NiB $1347 Ex $1091 Gd $763
Extra bbl. assembly, add $550

Brno Model II

Brno Model 21H
Bolt-Action Sporting Rifle

Brno Model 22F

Brno Hornet
Bolt-Action Sporting Rifle

BRITISH MILITARY RIFLES
Mfd. at Royal Small Arms Factory, Enfield Lock, Middlesex, England, as well as private contractors

RIFLE NO. 1 MARK III. . . . . NiB $281 Ex $179 Gd $128
Short magazine Lee-Enfield (S.M.L.E.). Bolt action. Caliber: .303 British. 10-round box magazine. 25.25-inch bbl. Weight: 8.75 lbs. Sights: Adj. rear; blade front w/guards. Two-piece, full-length military stock. Note: The earlier Mark III (approved 1907) is virtually the same as Mark III (adopted 1918) except for sights and different magazine cut-off that was eliminated on the latter.

RIFLE NO. 3 MARK I (PATTERN 14) . . . . . . NiB $306 Ex $230 Gd $128
Modified Mauser-type bolt action. Except for caliber .303 British and long-range sight, this rifle is the same as U.S. Model 1917 Enfield. See listing of the latter for general specifications.

RIFLE NO. 4 MARK I. . . . . NiB $255 Ex $204 Gd $128
Post-World War I modification of the S.M.L.E. intended to simplify mass production. General specifications same as Rifle No. 1 Mark III except w/aperture rear sight and minor differences in construction and weighs 9.25 lbs.

LIGHT RIFLE NO. 4 MARK I . . . . . . NiB $204 Ex $153 Gd $118
Modification of the S.M.L.E. Caliber: .303 British. 10-round box magazine. 23-inch bbl. Weight: 6.75 lbs. Sights: Micrometer click rear peep; blade front. One-piece military-type stock w/recoil pad. Made during WWII.

RIFLE NO. 5 MARK I. . . . . NiB $332 Ex $230 Gd $153
Jungle Carbine. Modification of the S.M.L.E. similar to Light Rifle No. 4 Mark I except w/20.5-inch bbl. w/flash hider, carbine-type stock. Made during WWII, originally designed for use in the Pacific Theater.

BRNO SPORTING RIFLES — Brno, Czech Republic, Manufactured by Ceska Zbrojovka
Imported by Euro-Imports, El Cajon, CA (Previously by Bohemia Arms & Magnum Research)

See also CZ rifles.

MODEL I BOLT-ACTION
SPORTING RIFLE. . . . . NiB $654 Ex $587 Gd $396
Caliber: .22 LR. Five round detachable magazine. 22.75-inch bbl. Weight: 6 lbs. Sights: three-leaf open rear; hooded ramp front. Sporting stock w/checkered pistol grip, swivels. Made from 1946-73.

MODEL II BOLT-ACTION
SPORTING RIFLE. . . . . NiB $705 Ex $602 Gd $396
Same as Model I except w/deluxe grade stock. Made from 1949-57.

MODEL III BOLT-ACTION
TARGET RIFLE . . . . NiB $760 Ex $708 Gd $451
Same as Model I except w/heavy bbl. and target stock. Made from 1948-56.

MODEL IV BOLT-ACTION
TARGET RIFLE . . . . NiB $811 Ex $646 Gd $451
Same as Model III except w/improved target trigger mechanism. Made from 1956-62.

MODEL V BOLT-ACTION
SPORTING RIFLE. . . . . NiB $760 Ex $585 Gd $396
Same as Model I except w/improved trigger mechanism. Made from 1956-73.

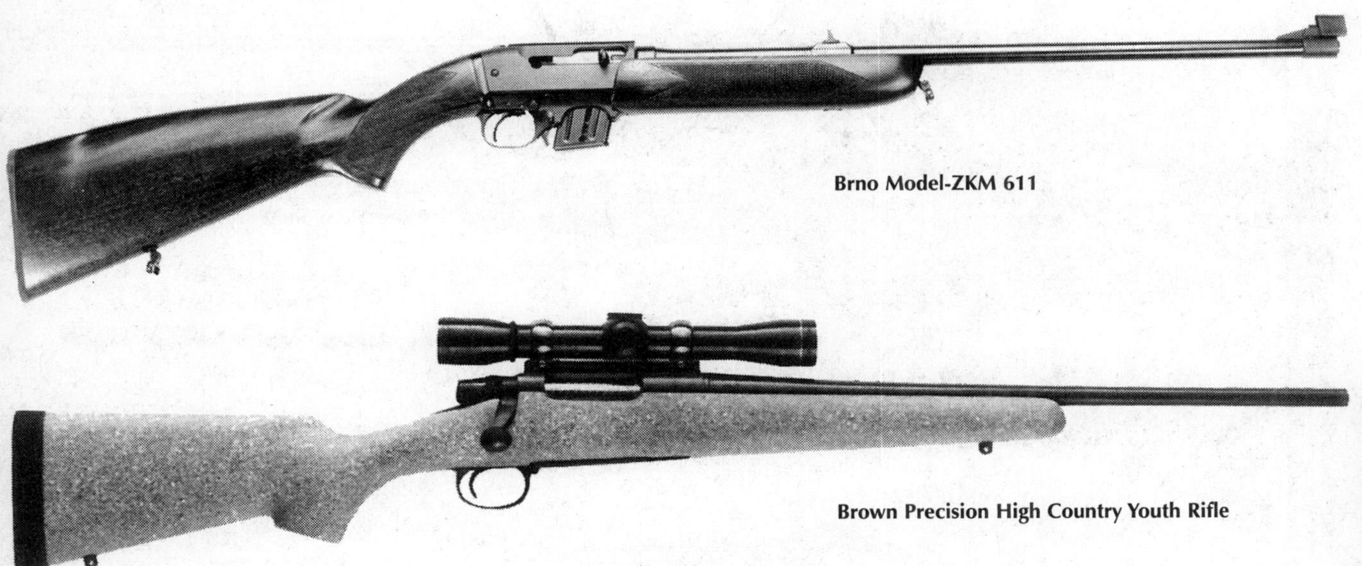

Brno Model-ZKM 611

Brown Precision High Country Youth Rifle

MODEL 21H BOLT-ACTION SPORTING RIFLE. . . . . NiB $810 Ex $656 Gd $450
Mauser-type action. Calibers: 6.5x57mm, 7x57mm 8x57mm. Five round box magazine. 20.5-inch bbl. Double set trigger. Weight: 6.75 lbs. Sights: Two-leaf open rear-hooded ramp front. Half-length sporting stock w/cheekpiece, checkered pistol-grip and forearm, swivels. Made from 1946-55.

MODEL 22F. . . . . NiB 1070 Ex $865 Gd $603
Same as Model 21H except w/full-length Mannlicher-type stock, weight: 6 lbs., 14 oz. Disc.

MODEL 98 STANDARD
Calibers: .243 Win., .270 Win., .30-06, .308 Win., .300 Win. Mag., 7x57mm, 7x64mm, or 9.3x62mm. 23.8-inch bbl. Overall 34.5 inches. Weight: 7.25 lbs. Checkered walnut stock w/Bavarian cheekpiece. Imported from 1998 to date.
Standard calibers . . . . NiB $476 Ex $387 Gd $274
Calibers .300 Win., Mag., 9.3x62mm . . . . . NiB $527 Ex $429 Gd $302
W/single set trigger, add. $100

MODEL 98 MANNLICHER
Similar to Model 98 Standard except full length stock and set triggers. Imported from 1998 to date.
Standard calibers . . . . NiB $645 Ex $510 Gd $354
Calibers .300 Win. Mag., 9.3x62mm. . . . . . NiB $709 Ex $574 Gd $401

ZBK-110 SINGLE-SHOT
Calibers: .22 Hornet, .222 Rem., 5.6x52R, 5.6x50 Mag., 6.5x57R, 7x57R, and 8x57JRS. 23.8-inch bbl. Weight: 6.1 lbs. Walnut checkered buttstock and forearm w/Bavarian cheekpiece. Imported from 1998 to date.
Standard model. . . . . NiB $249 Ex $192 Gd $141
Lux model. . . . . NiB $403 Ex $274 Gd $197
Calibers 7x57R and 8x57 JRS, add $25
W/interchangeable 12 ga. shotgun bbl., add $132

HORNET BOLT-ACTION SPORTING RIFLE. . . . . NiB $1015 Ex $887 Gd $500
Miniature Mauser action. Caliber: .22 Hornet. Five-round detachable box magazine. 23-inch bbl. Double set trigger. Weight: 6.25 lbs. Sights: Three-leaf open rear hooded ramp front. Sporting stock w/checkered pistol grip and forearm, swivels. Made 1949-74. Note: This rifle was also marketed in U.S. as "Z-B Mauser Varmint Rifle." (Reintroduced as Model ZKB 680)

MODEL ZKB 680 BOLT-ACTION RIFLE. . . . . NiB $509 Ex $412 Gd $289
Calibers: .22 Hornet, .222 Rem. Five-round detachable box magazine. 23.5-inch bbl. Weight: 5.75 lbs. Double-set triggers. Adj. open rear sight, hooded ramp front. Walnut stock. Imported from 1985-92.

MODEL ZKM 611 SEMIAUTOMATIC RIFLE
Caliber: .22 WMR. Six-round magazine. 20-inch bbl. 37 inches overall. Weight: 6.2 lbs. Hooded front sight; mid-mounted rear sight. Checkered walnut or beechwood stock. Single thumbscrew takedown. Grooved receiver for scope mounting. Imported from 1992 to date.
Standard beechwood model . . . . . . NiB $444 Ex $361 Gd $254
Deluxe walnut model . . . . NiB $546 Ex $438 Gd $283

BROWN PRECISION COMPANY — Los Molinos, California

MODEL 7 SUPER LIGHT SPORTER . . . . NiB $1063 Ex $1005 Gd $707
Lightweight sporter built on a Remington Model 7 barreled action w/18-inch factory bbl. Weight: 5.25 lbs. Kevlar stock. Made from 1984-92.

HIGH COUNTRY BOLT-ACTION SPORTER
Custom sporting rifles built on Blaser, Remington 700, Ruger 77 and Winchester 70 actions. Calibers: .243 Win., .25-06, .270 Win., 7mm Rem. Mag., .308 Win., .30-06. Five-round magazine (4-round in 7mm Mag.). 22- or 24-inch bbl. Weight: 6.5 lbs. Fiberglass stock w/recoil pad, sling swivels. No sights. Made from 1975 to date.
Standard High Country . . . . NiB $1192 Ex $1037 Gd $780
Custom High Country . . . . NiB $2119 Ex $1697 Gd $986
Left-hand action, add. $200
Stainless bbl., add $200
70, 77 or Blaser actions, add. $125
70 SG action, add $350

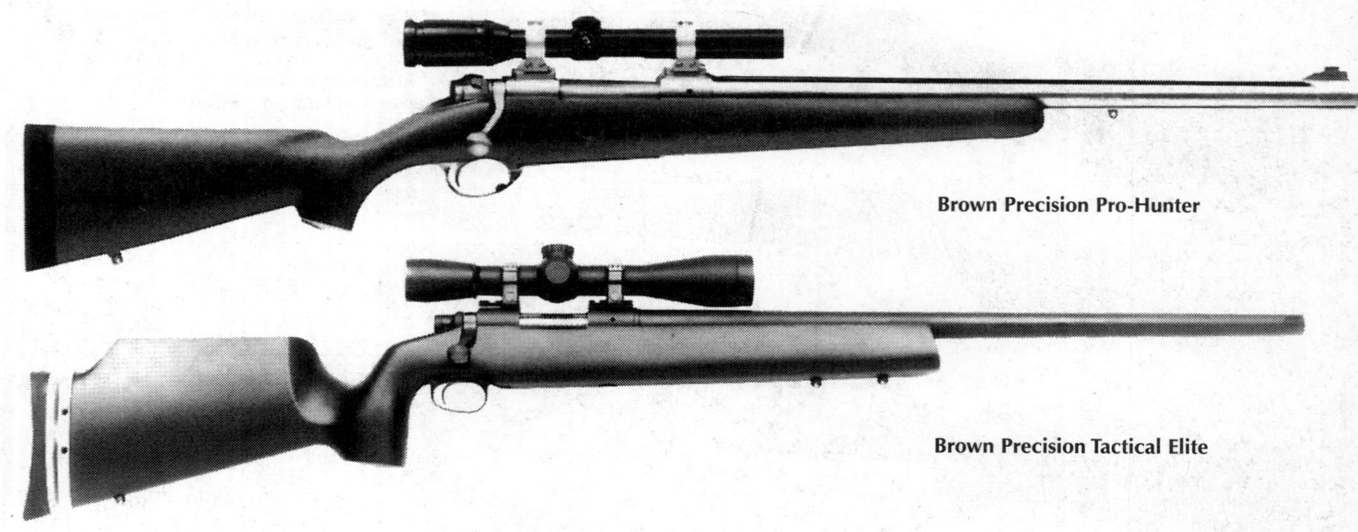

Brown Precision Pro-Hunter

Brown Precision Tactical Elite

HIGH COUNTRY YOUTH RIFLE .... **NiB $1279 Ex $970 Gd $661**
Similar to standard Model 7 Super Light except w/Kevlar or graphite stock, scaled-down to youth dimensions. Calibers: .223, .243, 6mm, 7mm-08, .308. Made from 1992 to date.

PRO-HUNTER BOLT-ACTION RIFLE
Custom sporting rifle built on Remington 700 or Winchester 70 SG action fitted w/match-grade Shilen bbl. chambered in customer's choice of caliber. Matte blued, nickel or Teflon finish. Express-style rear sight hooded ramp front. Synthetic stock. Made from 1989 to date
Standard Pro-Hunter............... **NiB $2507 Ex $2095 Gd $1220**
Pro-Hunter Elite (1993 to date) ...... **NiB $3537 Ex $2765 Gd $1889**

PRO-VARMINTER BOLT-ACTION RIFLE
Custom varminter built on a Remington 700 or 40X action fitted w/Shilen stainless steel benchrest bbl. Varmint or benchrest-style stock. Made from 1993 to date.
Standard Pro-Varminter .... **NiB $1906 Ex $1452 Gd $989**
Pro-Hunter w/Rem 40X action ...... **NiB $2482 Ex $1906 Gd $1288**

SELECTIVE TARGET MODEL ..... **NiB $1264 Ex $965 Gd $630**
Tactical law-enforcement rifle built on a Remington 700V action. Caliber: .308 Win. 20-, 22- or 24-inch bbl. Synthetic stock. Made from 1989-92.

TACTICAL ELITE RIFLE .... **NiB $2644 Ex $2345 Gd $1305**
Similar to Selective Target Model except fitted w/select match-grade Shilen benchrest heavy stainless bbl. Calibers: .223, .308, .300 Win. Mag. Black or camo Kevlar/graphite composite fiberglass stock w/adj. buttplate. Non-reflective black Teflon metal finish. Made from 1993 to date.

BROWNING RIFLES — Morgan, Utah Mfd. for Browning by Fabrique Nationale d'Armes de Guerre (now Fabrique Nationale Herstal), Herstal, Belgium; Miroku Firearms Mfg. Co., Tokyo, Japan; A.T.I., Salt Lake City, Ut; Oy Sako Ab, Riihimaki, Finland.

.22 AUTOMATIC RIFLE, GRADE I
Similar to discontinued Remington Model 241A. Autoloading. Take-down. Calibers: .22 LR. .22 Short (not interchangeably). Tubular magazine in buttstock holds 11 LR. 16 Short. Bbl. lengths: 19.25 inches (.22 LR), 22.25 inches (.22 Short). Weight: 4.75 lbs. (.22 LR); 5 lbs. (.22 Short). Receiver scroll engraved. Open rear sight, bead front. Checkered pistol-grip buttstock, semibeavertail forearm. Made from 1965-72 by FN; from 1972 to date by Miroku. Note: Illustrations are of rifles manufactured by FN.
FN manufacture................. **NiB $622 Ex $442 Gd $236**
Miroku manufacture .... **NiB $334 Ex $231 Gd $179**

.22 AUTOMATIC RIFLE, GRADE II
Same as Grade I except satin chrome-plated receiver engraved w/small game animal scenes, gold-plated trigger select walnut stock and forearm. .22 LR only. Made from 1972-84.
FN manufacture............... **NiB $1048 Ex $708 Gd $507**
Miroku manufacture .... **NiB $451 Ex $375 Gd $245**

.22 AUTOMATIC RIFLE, GRADE III
Same as Grade I except satin chrome-plated receiver elaborately hand-carved and engraved w/dog and game-bird scenes, scrolls and leaf clusters: gold-plated trigger, extra-fancy walnut stock and forearm, skip-checkered. .22 LR only. Made from 1972-84.
FN manufacture............ **NiB $2116 Ex $1704 Gd $1080**
Miroku manufacture .... **NiB $862 Ex $543 Gd $445**

.22 AUTOMATIC, GRADE VI ...... **NiB $755 Ex $549 Gd $369**
Same general specifications as standard .22 Automatic except for engraving, high-grade stock w/checkering and glossy finish. Made by Miroku from 1986 to date.

MODEL 52 BOLT-ACTION RIFLE .... **NiB $755 Ex $600 Gd $394**
Limited edition of Winchester Model 52C Sporter. Caliber: .22 LR. Five-round magazine. 24-inch bbl. Weight: 7 lbs. Micro-Motion trigger. No sights. Checkered select walnut stock w/rosewood forend and metal grip cap. Blued finish. Only 5000 made in 1991-92.

MODEL 53 LEVER-ACTION RIFLE .... **NiB $780 Ex $652 Gd $436**
Limited edition of Winchester Model 53. Caliber: .32-20. Seven-round tubular half-magazine. 22-inch bbl. Weight: 6.5 lbs. Adj. rear sight, bead front. Select walnut checkered pistol-grip stock w/high-gloss finish. Classic-style forearm. Blued finish. Only 5000 made in 1990.

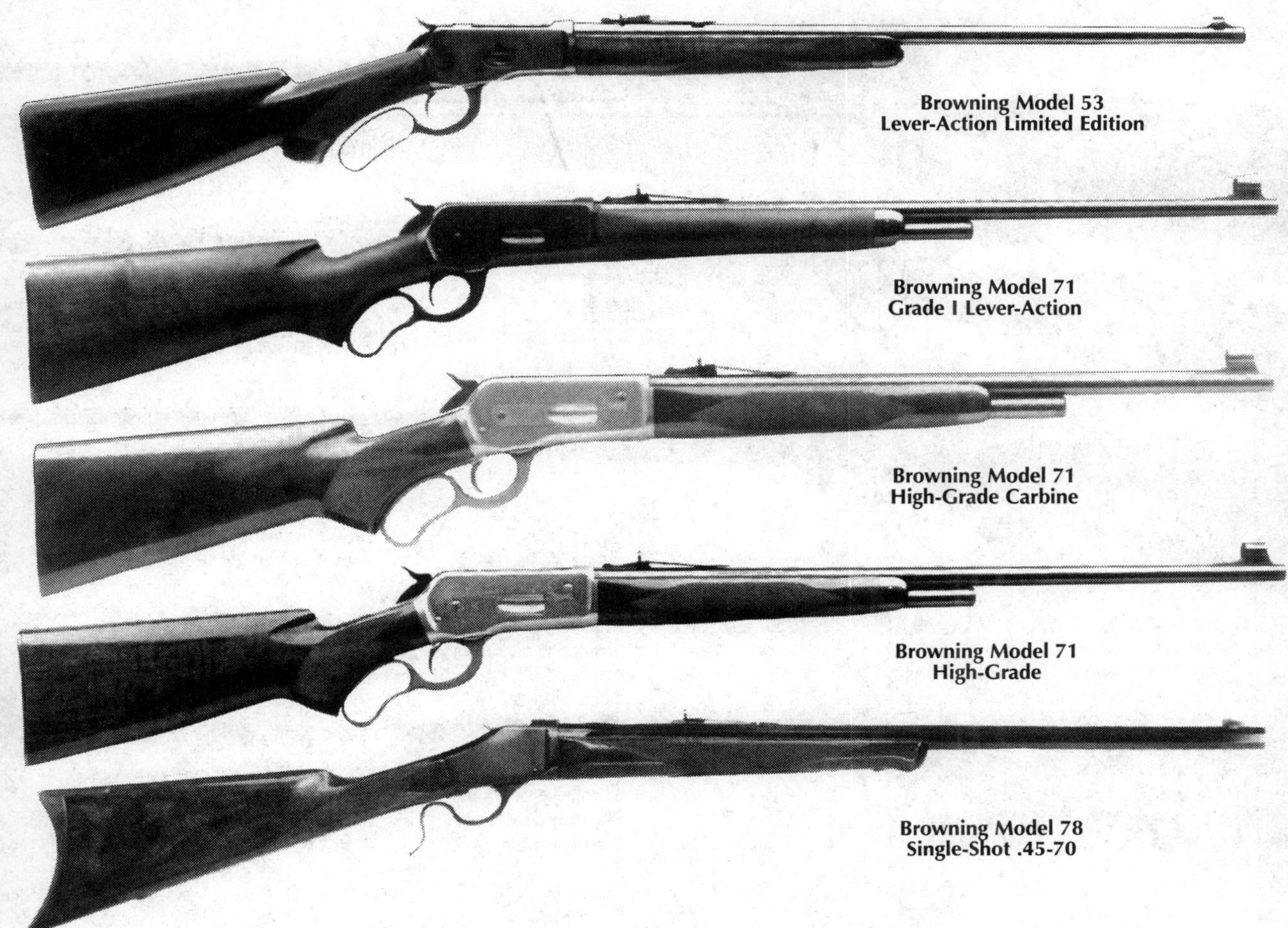
Browning Model 53
Lever-Action Limited Edition

Browning Model 71
Grade I Lever-Action

Browning Model 71
High-Grade Carbine

Browning Model 71
High-Grade

Browning Model 78
Single-Shot .45-70

MODEL 65 GRADE I
LEVER-ACTION RIFLE .... NiB $765 Ex $507 Gd $404
Caliber: .218 Bee. 7-round tubular half-magazine. 24-inch bbl. Weight: 6.75 lbs. Sights: Adj. buckhorn-style rear, hooded bead front. Select walnut pistol-grip stock w/high-gloss finish. Semibeavertail forearm. Limited edition of 3500 made in 1989.

MODEL 65 HIGH GRADE RIFLE .... NiB $1862 Ex $987 Gd $678
Same general specifications as Model 65 Grade I except w/engraving and gold-plated animals on grayed receiver. Cut checkering on pistol grip and forearm. Limited edition of 1500 made in 1989.

MODEL 71 GRADE I CARBINE .... NiB $763 Ex $583 Gd $402
Same general specifications as Model 71 Grade I Rifle except carbine w/20-inch round bbl. and weighs 8 lbs. Limited edition of 4000 made in 1986-87.

MODEL 71 GRADE I
LEVER-ACTION RIFLE........... NiB $862 Ex $666 Gd $460
Caliber: .348 Win. 4-round magazine. 24-inch round bbl. Weight: 8 lbs., 2 oz. Open buckhorn sights. Select walnut straight grip stock w/satin finish. Classic-style forearm, flat metal buttplate. Limited edition of 3000 made in 1986-87.

MODEL 71 HIGH-GRADE CARBINE ..... NiB $1244 Ex $1068 Gd $626
Same general specifications as Model 71 High Grade Rifle, except carbine w/20-inch round bbl. Limited edition of 3000 made in 1986-88.

MODEL 71 HIGH-GRADE RIFLE ...... NiB $1322 Ex $1038 Gd $755
Caliber: .348 Win. Four round magazine. 24-inch round bbl. Weight: 8 lbs., 2 oz. Engraved receiver. Open buckhorn sights. Select walnut checkered pistol-grip stock w/high-gloss finish. Classic-style forearm, flat metal buttplate. Limited edition of 3000 made in 1987.

78 BICENTENNIAL SET....... NiB $3702 Ex $3058 Gd $2054
Special Model 78 .45-70 w/same specifications as standard type, except sides of receiver engraved w/bison and eagle, scroll engraving on top of receiver, lever, both ends of bbl. and buttplate; high-grade walnut stock and forearm. Accompanied by an engraved hunting knife and stainless steel commemorative medallion, all in an alder wood presentation case. Each item in set has matching serial number beginning with "1776" and ending with numbers 1 to 1,000. Edition limited to 1,000 sets. Made in 1976.

78 SINGLE-SHOT RIFLE
Falling-block lever-action similar to Winchester 1885 High Wall single-shot rifle. Calibers: .22-250, 6mm Rem., .243 Win., .25-06, 7mm Rem. Mag., .30-06, .45-70 Govt. 26-inch octagon or heavy round bbl.; 24-inch octagon bull bbl. on .45-70 model. Weight: 7.75 lbs. w/octagon bbl.; w/round bbl., 8.5 lbs.; .45-70, 8.75 lbs. Furnished w/o sights except .45-70 model w/open rear sight, blade front. Checkered fancy walnut stock and forearm. .45-70 model w/straight-grip stock and curved buttplate; others have Monte Carlo comb and cheekpiece, pistol-grip w/cap, recoil pad. Made from 1973-83 by Miroku. Reintroduced in 1985 as Model 1885.
All calibers except .45-70 .... NiB $820 Ex $692 Gd $450
.45-70 .... NiB $898 Ex $717 Gd $460

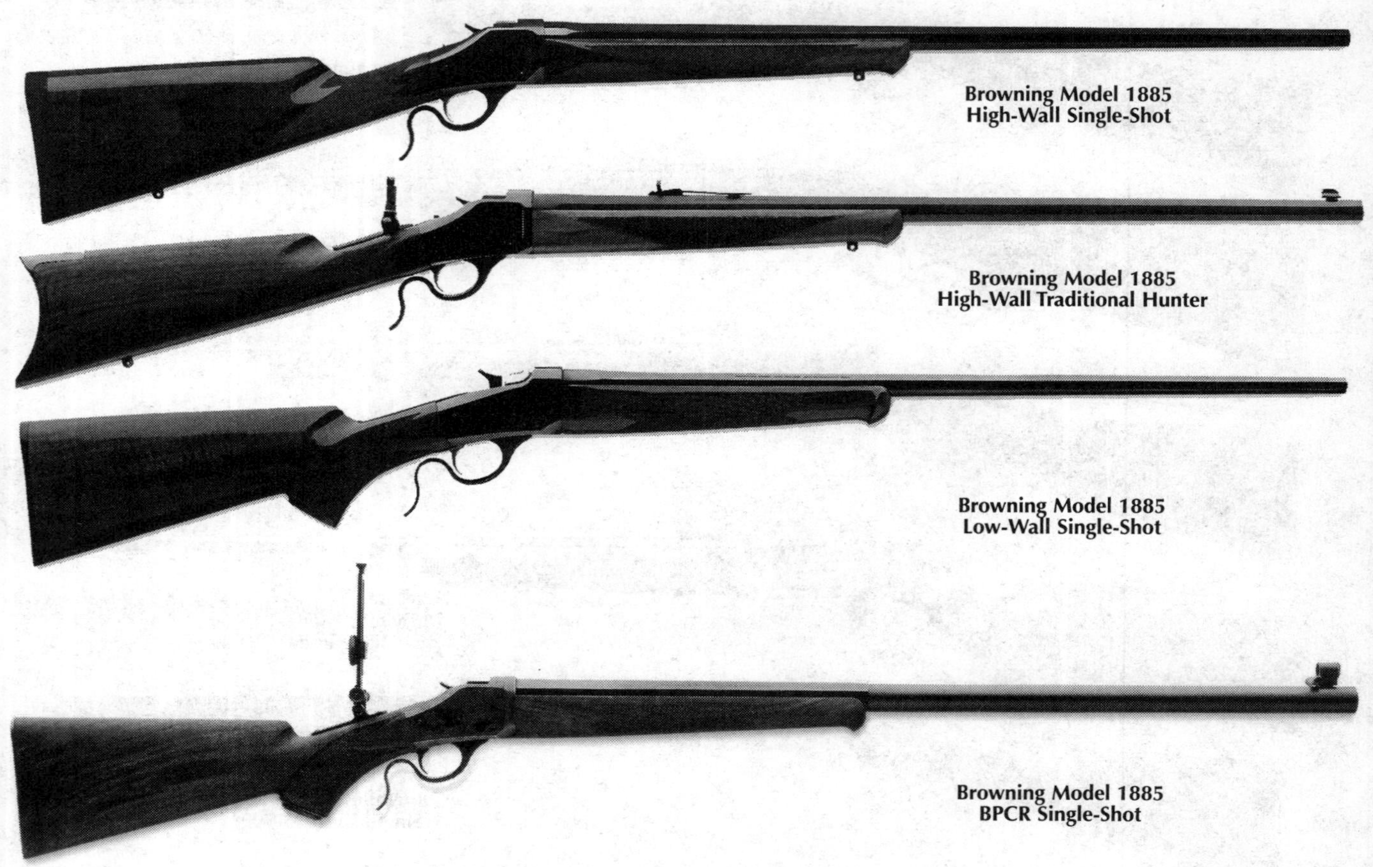

Browning Model 1885
High-Wall Single-Shot

Browning Model 1885
High-Wall Traditional Hunter

Browning Model 1885
Low-Wall Single-Shot

Browning Model 1885
BPCR Single-Shot

MODEL 1885 SINGLE-SHOT RIFLE
Calibers: .22 Hornet, .223, .243, (Low Wall); .357 Mag., .44 Mag., .45 LC (L/W Traditional Hunter); .22-250, .223 Rem., .270 Win., 7mm Rem. Mag., .30-06, .454 Casull Mag., .45.70 (High Wall); .30.30 Win., .38-55 WCF, .45 Govt. (H/W Traditional Hunter); .40-65, .45 Govt. and .45.90 (BPCR). 24-, 28-, 30 or 34-inch round, octagonal or octagonal and round bbl. 39.5, 43.5, 44.25 or 46.125 inches overall. Weight: 6.25, 8.75, 9, 11, or 11.75 lbs. respectively. Blued or color casehardened receiver. Gold-colored adj. trigger. Drilled and tapped for scope mounts w/no sights or vernier tang rear sight w/globe front and open sights on .45-70 Govt. Walnut straight-grip stock and Schnabel forearm w/cut checkering and high-gloss or oil finish. Made from 1985 to date.
Low Wall model w/o sights (Intro. 1995) . . NiB $812 Ex $709 Gd $478
Traditional Hunter model (Intro. 1998) . . . NiB $967 Ex $915 Gd $529
High Wall model w/o sights (Intro. 1985) . . . . NiB $761 Ex $606 Gd $452
Traditional Hunter model (Intro. 1997) . . NiB $1073 Ex $867 Gd $532
BPCR model w/no
ejector (Intro. 1996) . . . . NiB $1665 Ex $1356 Gd $981
BPCR Creedmoor Model .45-90
(Intro. 1998) . . . . NiB $1665 Ex $1292 Gd $944

MODEL 1886 MONTANA
CENTENNIAL RIFLE . . . . NiB $1979 Ex $1609 Gd $1027
Same general specifications as Model 1886 High Grade lever-action except w/specially engraved receiver designating Montana Centennial; also different stock design. Made in 1986 in limited issue by Miroku.

MODEL 1886 GRADE I
LEVER-ACTION RIFLE . . . . NiB $1288 Ex $963 Gd $731
Caliber: .45-70 Govt., 8-round magazine. 26-inch octagonal bbl. 45 inches overall. Weight: 9 lbs., 5 oz. Deep blued finish on receiver. Open buckhorn sights. Straight-grip walnut stock. Classic-style fore-arm. Metal buttplate. Satin finish. Made in 1986 in limited issue 7,000 by Miroku.

MODEL 1886 HIGH-
GRADE LA RIFLE . . . . NiB $1555 Ex $1195 Gd $881
Same general specifications as the Model 1886 Grade I except receiver is grayed, steel embellished w/scroll; elk and American bison engraving. High-gloss stock. Made in 1986 in limited issue of 3,000 by Miroku.

MODEL 1895 GRADE I LA RIFLE . . . . NiB $808 Ex $757 Gd $705
Caliber: .30-06, .30-40 Krag. Four round magazine. 24-inch round bbl. 42 inches overall. Weight: 8 lbs. French walnut stock and Schnabel forend. Sights: Rear buckhorn; gold bead on elevated ramp front. Made in 1984 in limited issue of 8,000 (2,000 chambered for .30-40 Krag and 6,000 chambered for .30-06). Mfd. by Miroku.

MODEL 1895 HIGH-
GRADE LA RIFLE. . . . . NiB $1446 Ex $1294 Gd $933
Same general specifications as Model 1895 Grade I except engraved receiver and Grade III French walnut stock and forend w/fine checkering. Made in 1985 in limited issue of 1000 in each caliber by Miroku.

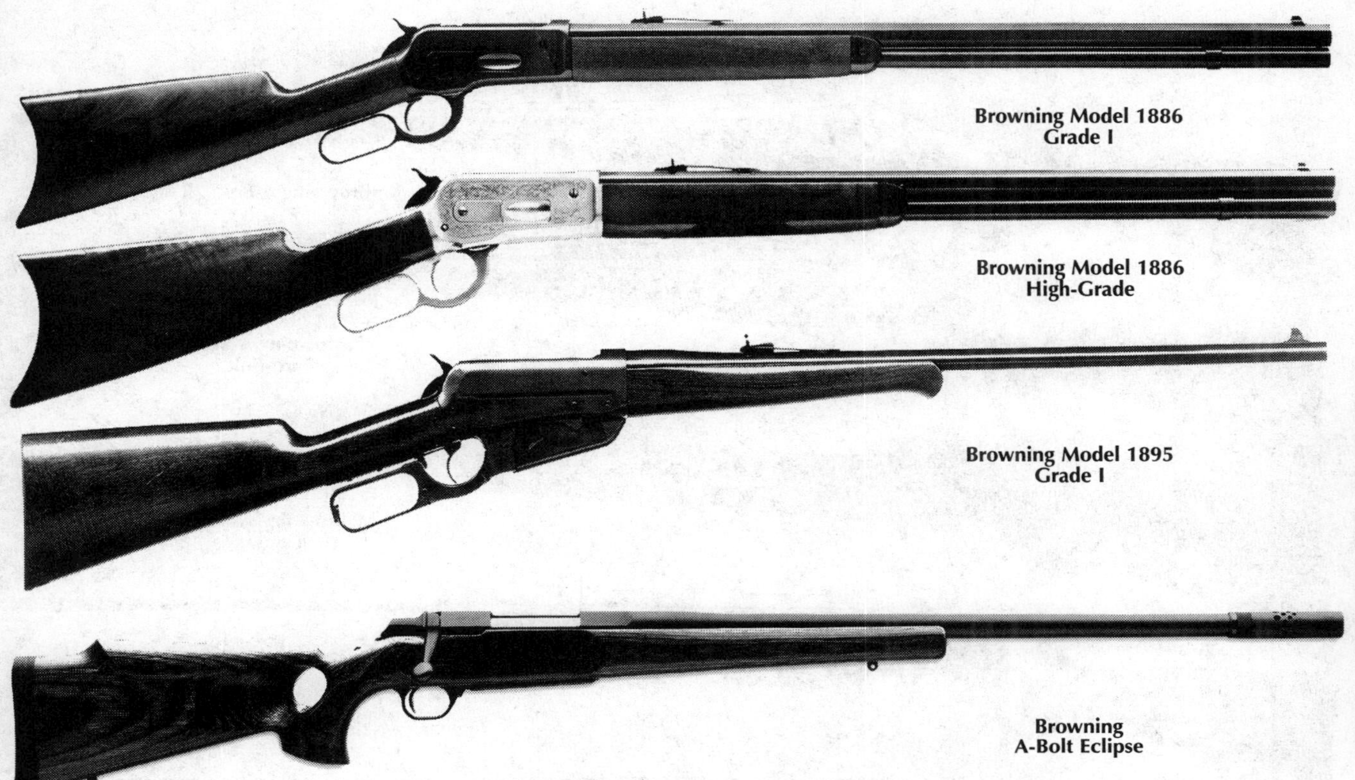

Browning Model 1886 Grade I

Browning Model 1886 High-Grade

Browning Model 1895 Grade I

Browning A-Bolt Eclipse

MODEL A-BOLT .22 RIFLE

Calibers: .22 LR. .22 Magnum. Five- and 15-round magazines. 22-inch round bbl. 40.25 inches overall. Weight: 5 lbs., 9 oz. Gold-colored adj. trigger. Laminated walnut stock w/checkering. Rosewood forend grip cap; pistol grip. With or w/o sights. Ramp front and adj. folding leaf rear on open sight model. 22 LR made 1985-96; 22 Magnum, 1990-96.

Grade I .22 LR. . . . . NiB $390 Ex $305 Gd $221
Grade I .22 Magnum . . . . NiB $468 Ex $385 Gd $236
Deluxe Grade
Gold Medallion . . . . NiB $571 Ex $442 Gd $329

MODEL A-BOLT ECLIPSE BOLT RIFLE

Same general specifications as Hunter Grade except fitted w/gray and black laminated thumbhole stock. Available in both short and long action w/two bbl. configurations w/BOSS. Mfd. by Miroku 1996 to date.

Eclipse w/standard bbl. . . . . NiB $907 Ex $779 Gd $640
Eclipse Varmint w/heavy bbl.. . . . . NiB $1067 Ex $917 Gd $789
Eclipse M-1000
(Target .300 Win. Mag.) . . . . NiB $1224 Ex $959 Gd $711

MODEL A-BOLT EURO-BOLT RIFLE

Same general specifications as Hunter Grade except w/checkered satin-finished walnut stock. W/continental-style cheekpiece, palm-swell grip and Schnabel forend. Mannlicher-style spoon bolt handle and contoured bolt shroud. 22- or 26-inch bbl. w/satin blued finish. Weight: 6.8 to 7.4 lbs. Calibers: .22-250 Rem., .243 Win., .270 Win., .30.06, .308 Win., 7mm Rem. Mag. Mfd. by Miroku 1993-94; 1994-96 (Euro-Bolt II).

Euro-Bolt . . . . NiB $638 Ex $493 Gd $334
Euro-Bolt II . . . . NiB $674 Ex $596 Gd $437
BOSS option, add $90

MODEL A-BOLT HUNTER GRADE RIFLE

Calibers: .22 Hornet, .223 Rem., .22-250 Rem., .243 Win., .257 Roberts, 7mm-08 Rem., .308 Win., (short action) .25-06 Rem., .270 Win., .280 Rem., .284 Win., .30-06, 7mm Rem. Mag., .300 Win. Mag., .338 Win. Mag. Four-round magazine (standard), 3-round (magnum). 22-inch bbl. (standard), 24-inch (magnum). Weight: 7.5 lbs. (standard), 8.5 lbs. (magnum). With or w/o sights. Classic-style walnut stock. Produced in two action lengths w/nine locking lugs, fluted bolt w/60 degree rotation. Mfd. by Miroku from 1985-93; from 1994 to date (Hunter II).

Hunter. . . . . NiB $648 Ex $596 Gd $432
Hunter II . . . . NiB $746 Ex $545 Gd $468
Hunter Micro. . . . . NiB $751 Ex $596 Gd $493
BOSS option, add $90
Open sights, add $50

MODEL A-BOLT MEDALLION GRADE RIFLE

Same as Hunter Grade except w/high-gloss deluxe stock rosewood grip cap and forend; high-luster blued finish. Also in .375 H&H w/open sights. Left-hand models available in long action only. Mfd. by Miroku from 1988-93; from 1994 to date (Medallion II). Bighorn Sheep Ltd. Ed.

(600 made 1986, .270 Win.). . . . . NiB $1345 Ex $1036 Gd $727
Gold Medallion Deluxe Grade . . . . NiB $736 Ex $571 Gd $398
Gold Medallion II Deluxe Grade . . . . NiB $731 Ex $591 Gd $412
Medallion, Standard Grade . . . . NiB $571 Ex $493 Gd $313
Medallion II, Standard Grade . . . . NiB $577 Ex $468 Gd $328
Medallion, .375 H&H . . . . NiB $947 Ex $725 Gd $442
Medallion II, .375 H&H . . . . NiB $957 Ex $699 Gd $493
Micro Medallion . . . . NiB $622 Ex $493 Gd $339
Micro Medallion II . . . . NiB $648 Ex $519 Gd $365
Pronghorn Antelope Ltd. Ed.
(500 made 1987, .243 Win.) . . . . NiB $1198 Ex $1050 Gd $870
BOSS option, add $90

Browning A-Bolt .22

Browning A-Bolt Euro-Bolt

Browning A-Bolt Hunter

Browning A-Bolt Hunter with BOSS

Browning A-Bolt Medallion Custom Trophy

Browning A-Bolt Medallion White Gold

Browning A-Bolt Medallion

Browning A-Bolt Medallion (Left-Handed)

Browning A-Bolt Composite Stalker

Browning A-Bolt Stainless Stalker

Browning BAR, Grade IV

Browning BAR, Grade V

MODEL A-BOLT STALKER RIFLE
Same general specifications as Model A-Bolt Hunter Rifle except w/checkered graphite-fiberglass composite stock and matte blued or stainless metal. Non-glare matte finish of all exposed metal surfaces. 3 models: Camo Stalker orig. w/multi-colored laminated wood stock, matte blued metal; Composite Stalker w/graphite-fiberglass stock, matte blued metal; w/composite stock, stainless metal. Made by Miroku from 1987-93; 1994 to date. (Stalker II).
Camo Stalker (orig. laminated stock) . . . . . NiB $608 Ex $449 Gd $274
Composite Stalker . . . . NiB $650 Ex $505 Gd $377
Composite Stalker II . . . . NiB $650 Ex $505 Gd $377
Stainless Stalker . . . . NiB $686 Ex $583 Gd $480
Stainless Stalker II . . . . NiB $711 Ex $608 Gd $505
Stainless Stalker, .375 H&H . . . . NiB $860 Ex $737 Gd $608
BOSS option, add $90
Left-hand model, add $90

MODEL A-BOLT
VARMINT II RIFLE . . . . NiB $763 Ex $711 Gd $552
Same general specifications as Stalker model except w/22-inch heavy bbl. w/BOSS system and varmint-style black laminated wood stock. Calibers: .22-250, .223 or .308. No sights. Bright blue or satin finish. Made by Miroku from 1994 to date.

MODEL B-92 LEVER-ACTION RIFLE . . . . . NiB $496 Ex $435 Gd $239
Calibers: .357 Mag. and .44 Rem. Mag. 11-round magazine. 20-inch round bbl. 37.5 inches overall. Weight: 5.5 to 6.4 lbs. Seasoned French walnut stock w/high gloss finish. Cloverleaf rear sight; steel post front. Made from1979-89 by Miroku.

BAR AUTOMATIC RIFLE,
GRADE I, STANDARD CALIBERS . . . . . NiB $753 Ex $583 Gd $428
Gas-operated semiautomatic. Calibers: .243 Win., .270 Win., .280 Rem., .308 Win., .30-06. Four-round box magazine. 22-inch bbl. Weight: 7.5 lbs. Folding leaf rear sight, hooded ramp front. French walnut stock and forearm checkered, QD swivels. Made from 1967-92 by FN.

BAR, GRADE I, MAGNUM CALIBERS . . . . NiB $763 Ex $711 Gd $547
Same as BAR in standard calibers, except w/24-inch bbl.chambered 7mm Rem. Mag. or .300 Win. Mag. .338 Win. Mag. w/3-round box magazine and recoil pad. Weight: 8.5 lbs. Made 1969-92 by FN.

BAR, GRADE II
Same as Grade I except receiver engraved w/big-game heads (deer and antelope on standard-caliber rifles, ram and grizzly on Magnum-caliber) and scrollwork, higher grade wood. Made from 1967-74 by FN.
Standard calibers . . . . NiB $975 Ex $830 Gd $624
Magnum calibers . . . . NiB $1083 Ex $805 Gd $568

BAR, GRADE III
Same as Grade I except receiver of grayed steel engraved w/big-game heads (deer and antelope on standard-caliber rifles, moose and elk on Magnum-caliber) framed in fine-line scrollwork, gold-plated trigger, stock and forearm of highly figured French walnut, hand-checkered and carved. Made from 1971-74 by FN.
Standard calibers . . . . NiB $1042 Ex $981 Gd $579
Magnum calibers . . . . NiB $1302 Ex $1215 Gd $710

BAR, GRADE IV
Same as Grade I except receiver of grayed steel engraved w/full detailed rendition of running deer and antelope on standard-caliber rifles, moose and elk on Magnum-caliber gold-plated trigger, stock and forearm of highly figured French walnut, hand checkered and carved. Made from 1971-86 by FN.
Standard calibers . . . . NiB $1681 Ex $1332 Gd $946
Magnum calibers . . . . NiB $1938 Ex $1564 Gd $1087

BAR, GRADE V
Same as Grade I except receiver w/complete big-game scenes executed by a master engraver and inlaid w/18K gold (deer and antelope on standard-caliber rifles, moose and elk on Magnum caliber), gold-plated trigger, stock and forearm of finest French walnut, intricately hand-checkered and carved. Made from 1971-74 by FN.
Standard calibers . . . . NiB $3238 Ex $2606 Gd $1799
Magnum calibers . . . . NiB $3688 Ex $3018 Gd $2091

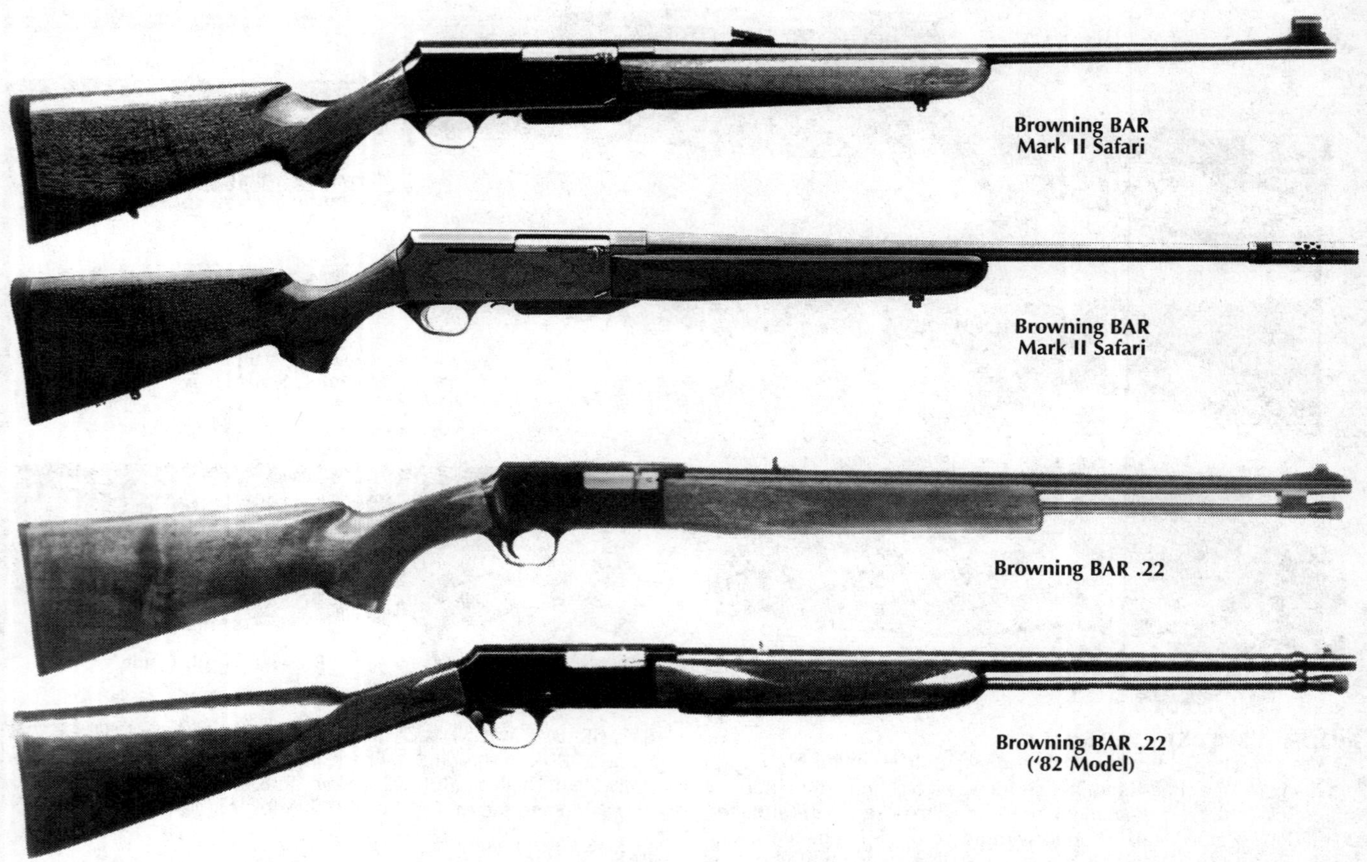
Browning BAR Mark II Safari

Browning BAR Mark II Safari

Browning BAR .22

Browning BAR .22 ('82 Model)

MODEL BAR MARK II SAFARI AUTOMATIC RIFLE
Same general specifications as standard BAR semiautomatic rifle, except w/redesigned gas and buffer systems, new bolt release lever, and engraved receiver. Made from 1993 to date.
Standard calibers . . . . NiB $699 Ex $638 Gd $442
Magnum calibers. NiB $777 Ex $674 Gd $468
Lightweight (Alloy receiver
w/20-inch bbl.) . . . . NiB $622 Ex $535 Gd $339
BAR Mk II Grade III (intro. 1996). . . . . NiB $2245 Ex $2065 Gd $1215
BAR Mk II Grade IV (intro. 1996). . . . . NiB $2446 Ex $1807 Gd $1369
W/BOSS option, add $60
W/open sights, add $15

BAR .22 AUTOMATIC RIFLE
Semiautomatic. Caliber: .22 LR. Tubular magazine holds 15 rounds. 20.25-inch bbl. Weight: 6.25 lbs. Sights: Folding-leaf rear, gold bead front on ramp. Receiver grooved for scope mounting. French walnut pistol-grip stock and forearm checkered. Made from 1977-85.
Grade I . . . . NiB $389 Ex $328 Gd $194
Grade II. . . . . NiB $467 Ex $431 Gd $235

BBR LIGHTNING BOLT-ACTION RIFLE . . . NiB $570 Ex $467 Gd $353
Bolt-action rifle w/short bolt throw of 60 degrees. Calibers: .25-06 Rem., .270 Win., .30-06, 7mm Rem. Mag., .300 Win. Mag. 24-inch bbl. Weight: 8 lbs. Made from 1979-84.

BL-.22 LEVER-ACTION REPEATING RIFLE
Short-throw lever-action. Caliber: .22 LR, Long, Short. Tubular magazine holds 15 LR, 17 Long 22 Short rounds. 20-inch bbl. Weight: 5 lbs. Sights: Folding leaf rear; bead front. Receiver grooved for scope mounting. Walnut straight-grip stock and forearm, bbl. band. Made from 1970 to date by Miroku.
Grade I . . . . NiB $359 Ex $225 Gd $158
Grade I7
w/scroll engraving. . . . . NiB $374 Ex $256 Gd $189

BLR LEVER-ACTION REPEATING RIFLE
Calibers: (short action only) .243 Win., .308 Win., .358 Win. Four round detachable box magazine. 20-inch bbl. Weight: 7 lbs. Sights: Windage and elevation adj. open rear; hooded ramp front. Walnut straight-grip stock and forearm, checkered, bbl. band, recoil pad. Made in 1966 by BAC/USA; from 1969-73 by FN; from 1974-80 by Miroku. Note: USA manufacture of this model was limited to prototypes and pre-production guns only and may be identified by the "MADE IN USA" roll stamp on the bbl.
FN model. . . . . NiB $750 Ex $523 Gd $369
Miroku model . . . . NiB $472 Ex $343 Gd $240
USA model . . . . NiB $1187 Ex $1032 Gd $620

BLR LIGHTNING MODEL
Lightweight version of the Browning BLR '81 w/forged alloy receiver and redesigned trigger group. Calibers: Short Action— .22-250 Rem., .223 Rem., .243 Win., 7mm-08 Rem., .308 Win.; Long Action— .270 Win., 7mm Rem. Mag., .30-06, .300 Win. Mag. Three or 4-round detachable box magazine. 20-, 22- or 24-inch bbl. Weight: 6.5 to 7.75 lbs. Pistol-grip style walnut stock and forearm, cut checkering and recoil pad. Made by Miroku from 1995 to date.
BLR Lightning model short action. . . . . . . NiB $492 Ex $431 Gd $235
BLR Lightning model long action . . . . NiB $518 Ex $467 Gd $312

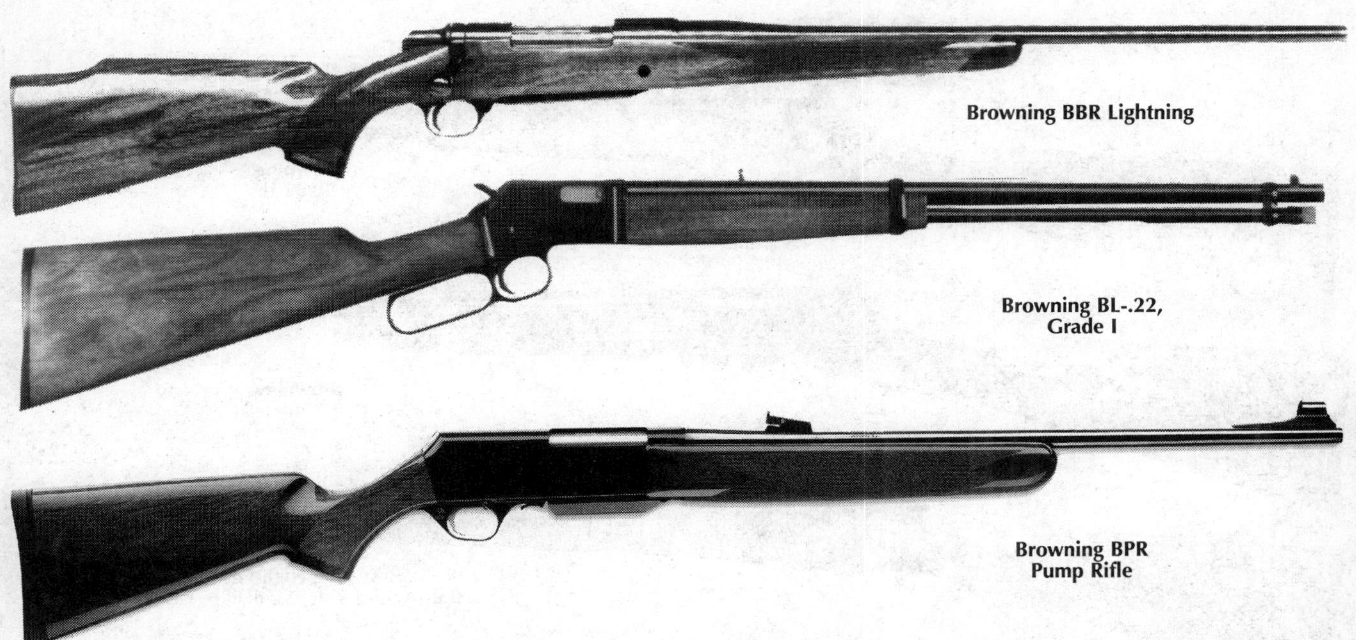

Browning BBR Lightning

Browning BL-.22, Grade I

Browning BPR Pump Rifle

BLR MODEL '81
Redesigned version of the Browning BLR. Calibers: .222-50 Rem., .243 Win., .308 Win., .358 Win; Long Action— .270 Win., 7mm Rem. Mag., .30-06. Fourround detachable box magazine. 20-inch bbl. Weight: 7 lbs. Walnut straight-grip stock and forearm, cut checkering, recoil pad. Made by Miroku from 1981-95; Long Action intro. 1991.
BLR Model '81 short action....... NiB $596 Ex $437 Gd $287
BLR Model '81 long action .... NiB $638 Ex $442 Gd $329

BPR-22 PUMP RIFLE
Hammerless slide-action repeater. Specifications same as for BAR-.22, except also available chambered for .22 Magnum RF; magazine capacity, 11 rounds. Made from 1977-82 by Miroku.
Model I .... NiB $280 Ex $229 Gd $167
Model II...................... NiB $488 Ex $432 Gd $257

BPR PUMP RIFLE
Slide-action repeater based on proven BAR designs w/forged alloy receiver and slide that cams down to clear bbl. and receiver. Calibers: .243 Win., .308 Win., .270 Win., .30-06, 7mm Rem. Mag. .300 Win. Mag. Three or 4-round detachable box magazine. 22- or 24-inch bbl. w/ramped front sight and open adj. rear. Weight: 7.2 to 7.4 lbs. Made from 1997 to date by Miroku.
BPR Model standard calibers...... NiB $862 Ex $688 Gd $461
BPR Model magnum calibers...... NiB $945 Ex $713 Gd $482

HIGH-POWER BOLT-ACTION RIFLE, MEDALLION GRADE .... NiB $1755 Ex $1596 Gd $978
Same as Safari Grade except receiver and bbl. scroll engraved, ram's head engraved on floorplate; select walnut stock w/rosewood forearm tip, grip cap. Made from 1961-74.

HIGH-POWER BOLT-ACTION RIFLE, OLYMPIAN GRADE .... NiB $3803 Ex $3417 Gd $1897
Same as Safari Grade except bbl. engraved; receiver, trigger guard and floorplate satin chrome-plated and engraved w/game scenes appropriate to caliber; finest figured walnut stock w/rosewood forearm tip and grip cap, latter w/18K-gold medallion. Made from 1961-74.

HIGH-POWER BOLT-ACTION RIFLE, SAFARI GRADE, MEDIUM ACTION..... NiB $1072 Ex $819 Gd $588
Same as Standard except medium action. Calibers: .22-250, .243 Win., .264 Win. Mag., .284 Win. Mag., .308 Win. Bbl.: 22-inch lightweight bbl.; .22-250 and .243 also available w/24-inch heavy bbl. Weight: 6 lbs., 12 oz. w/lightweight bbl.; 7 lbs. 13 oz. w/heavy bbl. Made from 1963-74 by Sako.

HIGH-POWER BOLT-ACTION RIFLE, SAFARI GRADE, SHORT ACTION....... NiB $1072 Ex $819 Gd $588
Same as Standard except short action. Calibers: .222 Rem., .222 Rem. Mag. 22-inch lightweight or 24-inch heavy bbl. No sights. Weight: 6 lbs., 2 oz. w/lightweight bbl.; 7.5 lbs. w/heavy bbl. Made from 1963-74 by Sako.

HIGH-POWER BOLT-ACTION RIFLE, SAFARI GRADE, STANDARD ACTION .. NiB $1362 Ex $1074 Gd $868
Mauser-type action. Calibers: .270 Win., .30-06, 7mm Rem. Mag., .300 H&H Mag., .300 Win. Mag., .308 Norma Mag. .338 Win. Mag., .375 H&H Mag., .458 Win. Mag. Cartridge capacity: 6 rounds in .270, .30-06; 4 in Magnum calibers. Bbl. length: 22 in., in .270, .30-06; 24 in., in Magnum calibers. Weight: 7 lbs., 2 oz., in .270, .30-06; 8.25 lbs. in Mag. calibers. Folding leaf rear sight, hooded ramp front. Checkered stock w/pistol grip, Monte Carlo cheekpiece, QD swivels; recoil pad on Magnum models. Made from 1959-74 by FN.

"T-BOLT" T-1 .22 REPEATING RIFLE
Straight-pull bolt action. Caliber: .22 LR. Five round clip magazine. 24-inch bbl. Peep rear sight w/ramped blade front. Plain walnut stock w/pistol grip and laquered finish. Weight: 6 lbs. Also left-hand model. Made from 1965-74 by FN.
Right-hand model .... NiB $494 Ex $433 Gd $263
Left-hand model .... NiB $520 Ex $438 Gd $263

"T-BOLT" T-2
Same as T-1 Model except w/checkered fancy figured walnut stock. Made from 1966-74 by FN. (Reintroduced briefly during the late 1980's with oil-finished stock)
Original model .... NiB $520 Ex $438 Gd $263
Reintroduced model .... NiB $469 Ex $391 Gd $237

Browning
BL-22 II

Browning
BLR Model '81

Browning High-Power
Bolt-Action Rifle, Medallion Grade

Browning High-Power
Safari Grade Medium Action, Heavy Barrel

Browning High-Power
Safari Grade Short Action, Heavy Barrel

Browning High-Power
Safari Grade Standard Action

F.N. BROWNING FAL SEMIAUTOMATIC RIFLE

Same as F.N. FAL Semiautomatic Rifle. See F.N. listing for specifications. Sold by Browning for a brief period c. 1960.

F.N. FAL standard model (G-series)...................... **NiB $4012 Ex $2879 Gd $2081**
F.N. FAL lightweight model (G-series)...................... **NiB $4811 Ex $4265 Gd $2725**
F.N. FAL heavy bbl.. model (G-series)...................... **NiB $7426 Ex $6073 Gd $4776**
BAC FAL model...................... **NiB $3106 Ex $2771 Gd $1783**

BSA GUNS LTD. — Birmingham, England (Previously Imported by Samco Global Arms, BSA Guns Ltd and Precision Sports)

NO. 12 MARTINI SINGLE-SHOT TARGET RIFLE.................. **NiB $624 Ex $495 Gd $367**

Caliber .22 LR. 29-inch bbl. Weight: 8.75 lbs. Parker-Hale Model 7 rear sight and Model 2 front sight. Straight-grip stock, checkered forearm. Note: This model was also available w/open sights or w/BSA No. 20 and 30 sights. Made before WWII.

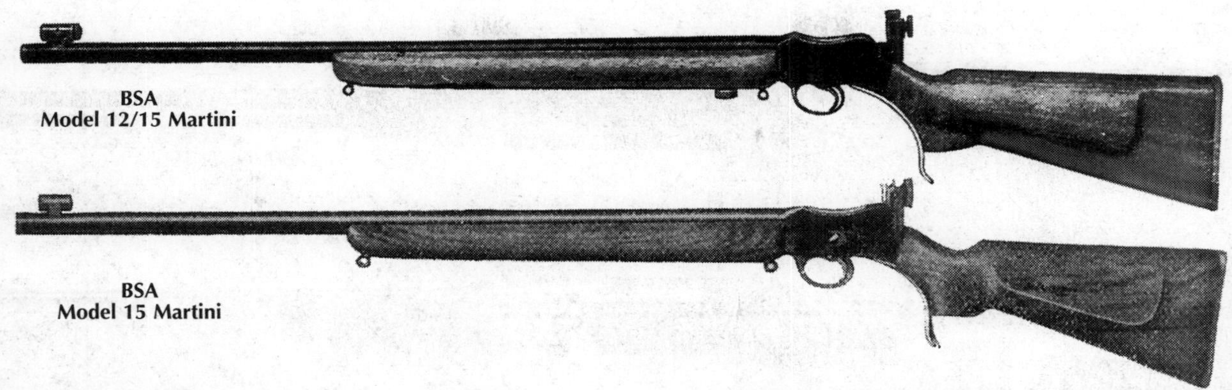

BSA
Model 12/15 Martini

BSA
Model 15 Martini

MODEL 12/15 MARTINI HEAVY . . . . NiB $651 Ex $501 Gd $337
Same as Standard Model 12/15 except w/extra heavy bbl., weighs 11 lbs.

MODEL 12/15 MARTINI SINGLE-SHOT TARGET RIFLE . . . . . NiB $579 Ex $445 Gd $323
Caliber: .22 LR. 29-inch bbl. Weight: 9 lbs. Parker-Hale No. PH-7A rear sight and No. FS-22 front sight. Target stock w/high comb and cheekpiece, beavertail forearm. Note: This is a post-WWII model; however, a similar rifle, the BSA-Parker Model 12/15, was produced c. 1938.

NO. 13 MARTINI SINGLE-SHOT TARGET RIFLE . . . . NiB $553 Ex $445 Gd $295
Caliber: .22 LR. Lighter version of the No.12 w/same general specifications except w/25-inch bbl., weighs 6.5lbs. Made before WWII.

NO. 13 SPORTING RIFLE
Same as No. 13 Target except fitted w/Parker-Hale "Sportarget" rear sight and bead front sight. Also available in .22 Hornet. Made before WWII.
.22 Long Rifle . . . . NiB $612 Ex $453 Gd $314
.22 Hornet. . . . . NiB $818 Ex $659 Gd $454

MODEL 15 MARTINI SINGLE-SHOT TARGET RIFLE. . . . . NiB $579 Ex $445 Gd $295
Caliber: .22 LR. 29-inch bbl. Weight: 9.5 lbs. BSA No. 30 rear sight and No. 20 front sight. Target stock w/cheekpiece and pistol-grip, long, semi-beavertail forearm. Made before WWII.

CENTURION MODEL MATCH RIFLE . . . . NiB $548 Ex $398 Gd $295
Same general specifications as Model 15 except w/"Centurion" match bbl. Made before WWII.

CF-2 BOLT-ACTION HUNTING RIFLE . . . . NiB $446 Ex $369 Gd $235
Mauser-type action. Calibers: 7mm Rem. Mag., .300 Win. Mag. Three-round magazine. 23.6-inch bbl. Weight: 8 lbs. Sights: Adj. rear; hooded ramp front. Checkered walnut stock w/Monte Carlo comb, rollover cheekpiece, rosewood forend tip, recoil pad, sling swivels. Made 1975-87. See Ithaca-BSA CF-2.

CF-2 STUTZEN RIFLE . . . . NiB $548 Ex $398 Gd $295
Calibers: .222 Rem., .22-250, .243 Win., .270 Win., .308 Win. .30-06. Four round capacity (5 in 222 Rem.). 20.6-inch bbl. 41.5 inches (approx.) overall length. Weight: 7.5 to 8 lbs. Williams front and rear sights. Hand-finished European walnut stock. Monte Carlo cheekpiece and Wundhammer palm swell. Double-set triggers. Importation disc. 1987.

CFT TARGET RIFLE . . . . NiB $872 Ex $667 Gd $492
Single-shot bolt action. Caliber: 7.62mm. 26.5-inch bbl. About 47.5 inches overall. Weight: 11 lbs., incl. accessories. Bbl. and action weight: 6 lbs., 12 oz. Importation disc. 1987.

MAJESTIC DELUXE FEATHERWEIGHT BOLT-ACTION HUNTING RIFLE
Mauser-type action. Calibers: .243 Win., .270 Win., .308 Win., .30-06, .458 Win. Mag. Four round magazine. 22-inch bbl. w/BESA recoil reducer. Weight: 6.25 lbs.; 8.75 lbs. in 458. Folding leaf rear sight, hooded ramp front. Checkered European-style walnut stock w/cheekpiece, pistol-grip, Schnabel forend, swivels, recoil pad. Made from 1959-65.
.458 Win. Mag. caliber . . . . NiB $596 Ex $468 Gd $313
Other calibers . . . . NiB $493 Ex $437 Gd $262

BSA MAJESTIC DELUXE STANDARD WEIGHT . . . . NiB $468 Ex $287 Gd $215
Same as Featherweight model except heavier bbl. w/o recoil reducer. Calibers: .22 Hornet, .222 Rem., .243 Win., 7x57mm, .308 Win., .30-06. Weight: 7.25 to 7.75 lbs. Disc.

MARTINI-INTERNATIONAL ISU MATCH RIFLE. . . . . NiB $1001 Ex $769 Gd $527
Similar to MK III, but modified to meet International Shooting Union "Standard Rifle" specifications. 28-inch standard weight bbl. Weight: 10.75 lbs. Redesigned stock and forearm, latter attached to bbl. w/"V" section alloy strut. Intro. 1968. Disc.

MARTINI-INTERNATIONAL MARK V MATCH RIFLE . . . . NiB $1028 Ex $797 Gd $560
Same as ISU model except w/heavier bbl. Weight: 12.25 lbs. Intro. 1976. Disc.

MARTINI-INTERNATIONAL MATCH RIFLE SINGLE-SHOT HEAVY PATTERN. . . . NiB $731 Ex $581 Gd $475
Caliber: .22 LR. 29-inch heavy bbl. Weight: 14 lbs. Parker-Hale "International" front and rear sights. Target stock w/full cheekpiece and pistol-grip, broad beavertail forearm, handstop, swivels. Right- or left-hand models. Made from 1950-53.

MARTINI-INTERNATIONAL MATCH RIFLE — LIGHT PATTERN. . . . . NiB $706 Ex $578 Gd $449
Same general specifications as Heavy Pattern except w/26-inch lighter weight bbl. Weight: 11 lbs. Disc.

MARTINI-INTERNATIONAL MK II MATCH RIFLE . . . . NiB $922 Ex $603 Gd $485
Same general specifications as original model. Heavy and Light Pattern. Improved trigger mechanism and ejection system. Redesigned stock and forearm. Made from 1953-59.

MARTINI-INTERNATIONAL MK III MATCH RIFLE . . . . NiB $1025 Ex $794 Gd $556
Same general specifications as MK II Heavy Pattern. Longer action frame w/I-section alloy strut to which forearm is attached; bbl. is fully floating. Redesigned stock and forearm. Made from 1959-67.

MONARCH DELUXE BOLT-ACTION HUNTING RIFLE................ NiB $359 Ex $323 Gd $225
Same as Majestic Deluxe Standard Weight model except w/redesigned stock of U.S. style w/contrasting hardwood forend tip and grip cap. Calibers: .222 Rem., .243 Win., .270 Win., 7mm Rem. Mag., .308 Win., .30-06. 22-inch bbl. Weight: 7 to 7.25 lbs. Made from 1965-74.

MONARCH DELUXE VARMINT RIFLE .... NiB $463 Ex $385 Gd $257
Same as Monarch Deluxe except w/24-inch heavy bbl. and weighs 9 lbs. Calibers: .222 Rem., .243 Win.

BUSHMASTER FIREARMS — (Quality Parts Company), Windham, Maine

M17S BULLPUP................ NiB $893 Ex $759 Gd $532
Caliber: .223. 21.5-inch bbl. Weight: 8.2 lbs. Polymer stocks. Handle w/fixed open sights w/Weaver-type rail for any optics. Semi-auto, self-compensating short stroke gas piston. Forward trigger/grip w/rear chamber. Bullpup style. Alloy receiver. Synthetic lower receiver is hinged to upper w/hinged takedown system. Accepts M-16 type magazines. Made from 1992 to date.

MODEL XM15 E2S SERIES
Caliber: .223. 16-, 20-, 24- or 26-inch bbl. Weight: 7 to 8.6 lbs. Polymer stocks. Adjustable sights w/dual flip-up aperture; optional flattop rail accepts scope. Direct gas-operated w/rotating bolt. Forged alloy receiver. All steel-coated w/manganese phosphate. Accepts M-16 type magazines. Made from 1989 to date.
XM15 E2S Carbine............. NiB $1132 Ex $952 Gd $707
XM15 E2S Target Rifle.......... NiB $1184 Ex $901 Gd $645

CABELA'S, INC. — Sidney, Nebraska

Cabela's is a sporting goods dealer and catalog company headquartered in Sidney, Nebraska. Cabela's imports black powder cartridge Sharps replicas, revolvers and other reproductions and replicas manufactured in Italy by A. Uberti, Pedersoli, Pietta and others.

1858 HENRY REPLICA .... NiB $643 Ex $568 Gd $493
Lever-action. Modeled after the original Henry rifle. Caliber: .44-40. Thirteen-round magazine; Bbl: 24 inches. Overall length: 43 inches. Weight: 9 pounds. European walnut stock. Sights: Bead front, open adjustable rear. Brass receiver and buttplate. Introduced 1994.

1866 WINCHESTER REPLICA ..... NiB $543 Ex $493 Gd $418
Lever-action modeled after the original Model 1866 rifle. Caliber: .44-40. Thirteen-round magazine. Bbl: 24 inches, octagonal; overall length: 43 inches. Weight: 9 pounds. European walnut stock, brass receiver, butt plate and forend cap. Sights: Bead front, open adjustable rear.

1873 WINCHESTER REPLICA ..... NiB $493 Ex $428 Gd $368
Lever-action modeled after the original Model 1873 rifle. Caliber: .44-40, .45 Colt. Thirteen-round magazine. Bbl: 30 inches. Overall length: 43 inches. Weight: 8 pounds. European walnut stock. Sights: Bead front, open adjustable rear or globe front and tang rear. Color case-hardened steel receiver. Introduced 1994.
W/tang rear sight, globe front: .... .add $150

1873 SPORTING
MODEL REPLICA............... NiB $622 Ex $537 Gd $477
Same as 1873 Winchester except with 30-inch bbl.
W/half-round, half-octagonal bbl., half magazine ...... add $100

CATTLEMAN CARBINE .... NiB $317 Ex $277 Gd $217
Revolver with shoulder stock. Caliber: .44-40; six-round cylinder. Bbl: 18 inches. Overall length: 34 inches. Weight: 4 pounds. European walnut stock. Sights: Blade front, notch rear. Color case-hardened frame, remainder blued. Introduced 1994.

SHARPS SPORTING RIFLE .... NiB $826 Ex $751 Gd $526
Single-shot. Caliber: .45-70. Bbl: Tapered octagon, 32 inches. Overall length: 47 inches. Weight: 9 pounds. Checkered walnut stock. Sights: Blade front, open adjustable rear. Color case-hardened receiver and hammer; remainder blued. Introduced 1995.

CALICO LIGHT WEAPONS SYSTEMS — Bakersville, California

LIBERTY 50/100 SEMIAUTOMATIC RIFLE
Retarded blowback action. Caliber: 9mm. 50- or 100-round helical-feed magazine. 16.1-inch bbl. 34.5 inches overall. Weight: 7 lbs. Adjustable post front sight and aperture rear. Ambidextrous rotating safety. Glass-filled polymer or thumbhole-style wood stock. Made 1995 to date.
Model Liberty 50............... NiB $775 Ex $622 Gd $367
Model Liberty 100.............. NiB $852 Ex $826 Gd $444

MODEL M-100 SEMIAUTOMATIC SERIES
Similar to the Liberty 100 Model except chambered for .22 LR. Weight: 5 lbs. 34.5 inches overall. Folding or glass-filled polymer stock and forearm. Made from 1986 to date.
Model M-100 w/folding
stock (disc. 1994)..................... NiB $460 Ex $323 Gd $180
Model M-100 FS w/fixed
stock (1996) .... NiB $634 Ex $435 Gd $307

MODEL M-105
SEMI-AUTOMATIC
SPORTER..................... NiB $328 Ex $256 Gd $180
Similar to the Liberty 100 Model except fitted w/walnut buttstock and forearm. Made from 1986 to date.

MODEL M-900
SEMIAUTOMATIC CARBINE
Caliber: 9mm Parabellum. 50- or 100-round magazine. 16.1-inch bbl. 28.5 inches overall. Weight: 3.7 lbs. Post front sight adj. for windage and elevation, fixed notch rear. Collapsible steel buttstock and glass-filled polymer grip. Matte black finish. Made from 1989-94.
Model M-100 w/folding
stock (disc. 1994) .... NiB $567 Ex $440 Gd $287
Model M-100 FS w/fixed
stock (Intro. 1996) .... NiB $537 Ex $389 Gd $261

MODEL M-951
TACTICAL CARBINE
Similar to Model 900 except w/long compensator and adj. forward grip. Made from 1990-94.
Model 951.................... NiB $537 Ex $389 Gd $292
Model 951-S .... NiB $567 Ex $333 Gd $312

CANADIAN MILITARY RIFLES — Quebec, Canada, Manufactured by Ross Rifle Co.

MODEL 1907 MARK II
ROSS MILITARY RIFLE .... NiB $352 Ex $250 Gd $220
Straight-pull bolt action. Caliber: .303 British. Five-round box magazine. 28-inch bbl. Weight: 8.5 lbs. Sights: adj. rear; blade front. Military-type full stock. Note: The Ross was originally issued as a Canadian service rifle in 1907. There were several variations; it was the official weapon at the start of WWI, but has been obsolete for many years. For Ross sporting rifle, see listing under Ross Rifle company.

CENTURY INTERNATIONAL ARMS, INC. — Boca Raton, Florida; (Formerly St. Albans, Vermont)

CENTURION M38/M96
BOLT-ACTION SPORTER
Sporterized Swedish M38/96 Mauser action. Caliber: 6.5x55mm. Five-round magazine. 24-inch bbl. 44 inches overall. Adj. rear sight. Blade front. Black synthetic or checkered European hardwood Monte Carlo stock. Holden Ironsighter see-through scope mount. Imported from 1987 to date.
W/hardwood stock .... NiB $194 Ex $143 Gd $98
W/synthetic stock .... NiB $210 Ex $169 Gd $118

CENTURION M98
BOLT-ACTION SPORTER
Sporterized VZ24 or 98 Mauser action. Calibers: .270 Win., 7.62x39mm, .308 Win., .30-06. Five round magazine. 22-inch bbl. 44 inches overall. Weight: 7.5 lbs. W/Millet or Weaver scope base(s), rings and no iron sights. Classic or Monte Carlo laminated hardwood, black synthetic or checkered European hardwood stock. Imported from 1992 to date.
M98 Action W/black
synthetic stock (w/o rings)................ NiB $245 Ex $194 Gd $137
M98 Action W/hardwood Stock
(w/o rings) .... NiB $215 Ex $169 Gd $108

RIFLES

VZ24 Action W/laminated Hardwood Stock (Elite) . . . . NiB $321 Ex $249 Gd $173
VZ24 Action W/black synthetic stock. . . . . NiB $307 Ex $249 Gd $176
W/Millet base and rings, add $25

CENTURION P-14 SPORTER
Sporterized P-14 action. Caliber: 7mm Rem. Mag., .300 Win. Mag. Five-round magazine. 24-inch bbl. 43.4 inches overall. Weight: 8.25 lbs. Weaver-type scope base. Walnut stained hardwood or fiberglass stock. Imported from 1987 to date.
W/hardwood stock . . . . NiB $239 Ex $198 Gd $137
W/fiberglass stock. . . . . NiB $275 Ex $198 Gd $137

ENFIELD SPORTER 4 BOLT-ACTION RIFLE
Sporterized Lee-Enfield action. Caliber: .303 British. 10-round magazine. 25.25-inch bbl. 44.5 inches overall. Blade front sight, adj. aperture rear. Sporterized beechwood military stock or checkered walnut Monte Carlo stock. Blued finish. Imported from 1987 to date.
W/sporterized military stock . . . . NiB $143 Ex $113 Gd $72
W/checkered walnut stock . . . . NiB $194 Ex $169 Gd $113

L1A1 FAL SPORTER . . . . NiB $866 Ex $688 Gd $530
Sporterized L1A1 FAL semiautomatic. Caliber: .308 Win. 20.75-inch bbl. 41 inches overall. Weight: 9.75 lbs. Protected front post sight, adj. aperture rear. Matte blued finish. Black or camo Bell & Carlson thumbhole sporter stock w/rubber buttpad. Imported from 1988-98.

M-14 SPORTER . . . . NiB $428 Ex $306 Gd $203
Sporterized M-14 gas operated semiautomatic action. Caliber: .308 Win. 10-round magazine. 22-inch bbl. 41 inches overall. Weight: 8.25 lbs. Blade front sight, adj. aperture rear sight. Parkerized finish. Walnut stock w/rubber recoil pad. Forged receiver. Imported from 1991 to date.

TIGER DRAGUNOV . . . . NiB $3680 Ex $2736 Gd $1359
Russian SVD semiautomatic sniper rifle. Caliber: 7.62x54R. Five-round magazine. 21-inch bbl. 43 inches overall. Weight: 8.5 lbs. Blade front sight, open rear adj. for elevation. Blued finish. European laminated hardwood thumbhole stock. 4x range-finding scope w/lighted reticle and sunshade. Quick detachable scope mount. Imported from 1994-95.

CHARTER ARMS CORPORATION — Stratford, Connecticut

AR-7 EXPLORER SURVIVAL RIFLE . . . . NiB $142 Ex $107 Gd $76
Same as Armalite AR-7, except w/black, instead of brown, "wood grain" plastic stock. See listing of that rifle for specifications. Made from 1973-90.

CHIPMUNK RIFLES — Prospect, Oregon MFD. by Rogue Rifle Company (Formerly Oregon Arms Company and Chipmunk Manufacturing, Inc.)

BOLT-ACTION SINGLE-SHOT RIFLE
Calibers: .22 LR. or .22 WMR. 16.13-inch standard or 18.13-inch bull bbl. Weight: 2.5 lbs. (standard) or 4 lbs. (Bull bbl.) Peep sight rear; ramp front. Plain or checkered American walnut, laminated or black hardwood stock. Made from 1982 to date.
Standard model w/plain walnut stock. . . . . NiB $186 Ex $130 Gd $84
Standard model w/black hardwood stock . . . . NiB $166 Ex $120 Gd $84
Standard model w/camouflage stock. . . . . NiB $196 Ex $150 Gd $99
Standard model w/laminated stock . . . . NiB $182 Ex $150 Gd $110
Deluxe grade w/checkered walnut stock. . . . . NiB $252 Ex $196 Gd $127
.22 WMR, add $20

CHURCHILL RIFLES — Mfd. in England. *Imported by Ellett Brothers, Inc., Chapin, SC (Previously by Kassnar Imports, Inc.)*

HIGHLANDER BOLT-ACTION RIFLE. . . . . NiB $476 Ex $385 Gd $270
Calibers: .243 Win., .25-06 Rem., .270 Win., .308 Win., .30-06, 7mm Rem. Mag., .300 Win. Mag. Four round magazine (standard); 3-round (magnum). Bbl. length: 22-inch (standard); 24-inch (magnum). 42.5 to 44.5 inches overall. Weight: 7.5 lbs. Adj. rear sight, blade front. Checkered European walnut pistol-grip stock. Imported from 1986-91.

"ONE OF ONE THOUSAND" RIFLE
. . . . . NiB $2648 Ex $2128 Gd $990
Made for Interarms to commemorate that firm's 20th anniversary. Mauser-type action. Calibers: .270, 7mm Rem. Mag., .308, .30-06, .300 Win. Mag., .375 H&H Mag., .458 Win. Mag. Five round magazine (3-round in Magnum calibers). 24-inch bbl. Weight: 8 lbs. Classic-style French walnut stock w/cheekpiece, black forend tip, checkered pistol grip and forearm, swivel-mounted recoil pad w/cartridge trap, pistol-grip cap w/trap for extra front sight, barrel-mounted sling swivel. Limited issue of 1,000 rifles made in 1973. See illustration next page.

REGENT BOLT-ACTION RIFLE . . . . NiB $603 Ex $547 Gd $423
Calibers: .243 Win., .25-06 Rem., .270 Win., .308 Win., .30-06, 7mm Rem. Mag., .300 Win. Mag. Four round magazine. 22-inch round bbl. 42.5 inches overall. Weight: 7.5 lbs. Ramp front sight w/gold bead; adj. rear. Hand-checkered Monte Carlo-style stock of select European walnut; recoil pad. Made from 1986-90. See illustration next page.

CIMARRON ARMS — Fredericksburg, Texas

1860 HENRY LEVER-ACTION REPLICA
Replica of 1860 Henry w/original Henry loading system.Calibers: .44-40, .44 Special, .45 Colt. 13-round magazine. 22-inch bbl. (carbine) or 24.25-inch bbl. (rifle). 43 inches overall (rifle). Weight: 9.5 lbs. (rifle). Bead front sight, open adj. rear. Brass receiver and buttplate. Smooth European walnut buttstock. Imported from 1991 to date.
Carbine model. . . . . NiB $916 Ex $757 Gd $479
Rifle model . . . . NiB $942 Ex $685 Gd $504
Civil War model (U.S. issue martially marked). . . . . . NiB $942 Ex $777 Gd $530
W/A-engraving, add. $395
W/B-engraving, add. $495
W/C-engraving, add. $695

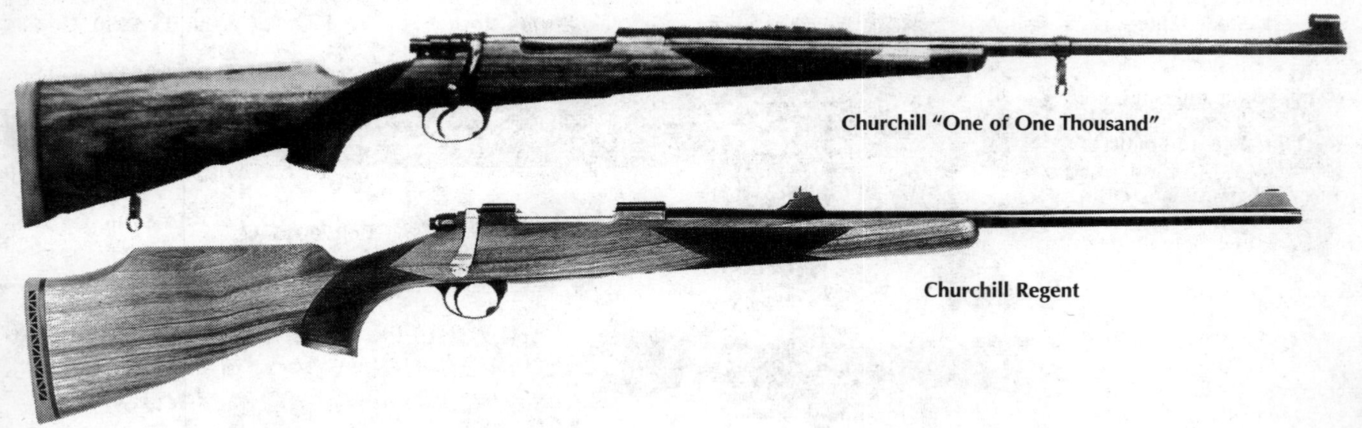
Churchill "One of One Thousand"

Churchill Regent

RIFLES

1866 YELLOWBOY LEVER-ACTION
Replica of 1866 Winchester. Calibers: .22 LR, 22WMR, .38 Special, .44-40, .45 Colt. 16-inch round bbl. (Trapper), 19-inch round bbl. (Carbine) or 24.25-inch ocatagonal bbl. (rifle). 43 inches overall (rifle). Weight: 9 lbs. (rifle). Bead front sight, open adj. rear. Brass receiver, buttplate and forend cap. Smooth European walnut stock. Imported 1991 to date.
Carbine .... NiB $731 Ex $577 Gd $371
Rifle .... NiB $854 Ex $602 Gd $396
Indian model (disc.) .... NiB $705 Ex $577 Gd $371
Trapper Model (.44-40 WCF only, disc.) ...... NiB $577 Ex $448 Gd $294
W/A-engraving, add $425
W/B-engraving, add $595
W/C-engraving, add $995

1873 LEVER-ACTION
Replica of 1873 Winchester. Calibers: .22 LR. .22WMR, .357 Magnum, .44-40 or .45 Colt. 16-inch round bbl. (Trapper), 19-inch round bbl. (SRC), 20-inch octagonal bbl. (short rifle), 24.25-inch octagonal bbl. (sporting rifle) and 30-inch octagonal bbl. (express rifle). 43 inches overall (sporting rifle). Weight: 8 lbs. Fixed blade front sight, adj. semi-buckhorn rear or tang peep sight. Walnut stock and forend. Color case-hardened receiver. Imported from 1989 to date.
Express Rifle .... NiB $926 Ex $695 Gd $494
Short Rifle (disc.) .... NiB $901 Ex $643 Gd $453
Sporting Rifle .... NiB $768 Ex $613 Gd $428
SRC Carbine .... NiB $794 Ex $613 Gd $433
Trapper (disc.) .... NiB $660 Ex $536 Gd $246
One of 1000 engraved model .... NiB $2319 Ex $1907 Gd $1238

1874 FALLING BLOCK SPORTING RIFLE
Replica of 1874 Sharps Sporting Rifle. Calibers: .45-65, .45-70, .45-90 or .45-120. 32- or 34-inch round or octagonal bbl. Weight: 9.5 to 10 lbs. Blade or globe front sight w/adj. open rear or sporting tang peep sight. Single or double set triggers. Checkered walnut stock and forend w/nose cap. Color case-hardened receiver. Imported from 1997 to date.
1874 Sporting Rifle - Billy Dixon Model .. NiB $1138 Ex $1035 Gd $799
1874 Sporting Rifle - Quigley Model ... NiB $1550 Ex $1370 Gd $829
Sharps Sporting No. 1 Rifle .... NiB $1082 Ex $855 Gd $598

CLERKE RECREATION PRODUCTS — Santa Monica, California

DELUXE HI-WALL .... NiB $389 Ex $318 Gd $221
Same as standard model, except w/adj. trigger, half-octagon bbl., select wood, stock w/cheekpiece and recoil pad. Made from 1972-74.

HI-WALL
SINGLE-SHOT RIFLE .... NiB $385 Ex $329 Gd $206
Falling-block lever-action similar to Winchester 1885 High Wall S.S. Color casehardened investment-cast receiver. Calibers: .222 Rem., .22-250, .243 Rem., 6mm Rem., .25-06, .270 Win., 7mm Rem. Mag., .30-06, .45-70 Govt. 26-inch medium-weight bbl. Weight: 8 lbs. Furnished w/o sights. Checkered walnut pistol-grip stock and Schnabel forearm. Made from 1972-74.

CLIFTON ARMS — Medina, Texas

SCOUT BOLT-ACTION RIFLE
Custom rifle built on the Dakota .76, Ruger .77 or Winchester .70 action. Shilen match-grade barrel cut and chambered to customer's specification. Clifton composite stock fitted and finished to customer's preference. Made from 1992-97.
African
Scout .... NiB $3735 Ex $3065 Gd $2391
Pseudo
Scout .... NiB $3606 Ex $2185 Gd $1392
Standard
Scout .... NiB $3580 Ex $2138 Gd $1366
Super
Scout .... NiB $3709 Ex $2988 Gd $1443

COLT INDUSTRIES, FIREARMS DIVISION — Hartford, Connecticut

NOTE: *On Colt AR-15 Sporter models currently produced (i.e., Competition H-BAR, Sporter Match Target Lightweight, and Sporter Target Rifle), add $200 to pre-ban models made prior to 10-13-94.*

AR-15 A2 DELTA
MATCH H-BAR RIFLE .... NiB $1705 Ex $1628 Gd $1396
Similar to AR-15A2 Government Model except w/standard stock and heavy refined bbl. Furnished w/3-9x rubber armored scope and removeable cheekpiece. Made from 1986-91.

AR-15 A2 GOVERNMENT
MODEL CARBINE .... NiB $2262 Ex $1927 Gd $1098
Caliber: .223 Rem., Five-round magazine. 16-inch bbl. w/flash suppressor. 35 inches overall. Weight: 5.8 lbs. Telescoping aluminum buttstock; sling swivels. Made from 1985-91.

Colt AR-15 A2

Colt AR-15 A2 Delta Match H-BAR

Colt AR-15 A2 Government Model

Colt AR-15 Sporter Competition H-BAR

AR-15 A2 SPORTER II . . . . NiB $1339 Ex $1184 Gd $1076
Same general specifications as standard AR-15 Sporter except heavier bbl., improved pistol-grip. Weight 7.5 lbs.; optional 3x or 4x scope. Made from 1985-89.

AR-15 COMPACT 9MM CARBINE . . . . NiB $1754 Ex $1497 Gd $1085
Semiautomatic. Caliber: 9mm NATO. 20-round detachable magazine. Bbl.: 16-inch round. Weight: 6.3 lbs. Adj. rear and front sights. Adj. buttstock. Ribbed round handguard. Made from 1985-86.

AR-15 SEMIAUTOMATIC SPORTER
Commercial version of U.S. M16 rifle. Gas-operated. Takedown. Caliber: .223 Rem. (5.56mm). 20-round magazine w/spacer to reduce capacity to 5 rounds. 20-inch bbl. w/flash suppressor. Sights: Rear peep w/windage adjustment in carrying handle; front adj. for windage. 3x scope and mount optional. Black molded buttstock of high-impact synthetic material, rubber buttplate. Barrel surrounded by handguard of black fiberglass w/heat-reflecting inner shield. Swivels, black web sling strap. Weight: w/o accessories, 6.3 lbs. Made from 1964-94.
Standard Sporter .... NiB $1328 Ex $1072 Gd $744
W/adj. stock, redesigned forearm (disc. 1988), add $200
W/3x scope and mount, add... $100

AR-15 SPORTER COMPETITION H-BAR RIFLE .... NiB $1334 Ex $1072 Gd $691
Similar to AR-15 Sporter Target model except w/integral Weaver-type mounting system on a flat-top receiver. 20-inch bbl. w/counter-bored muzzle and 1:9 rifling twist. Made from 1991 to date.

AR-15 SPORTER COMPETITION H-BAR (RS) .... NiB $1726 Ex $1391 Gd $871
Similar to AR-15 Sporter Competition H-BAR Model except "Range Selected" for accuracy w/3x9 rubber-clad scope w/mount. Carrying handle w/iron sights. Made from 1992-94.

AR-15 SPORTER MATCH TARGET LIGHTWEIGHT
Calibers: .223 Rem., 7.62x39mm, 9mm. Five-round magazine. 16-inch bbl. (non-threaded after 1994). 34.5-35.5 inches overall. Weight: 7.1 lbs. Redesigned stock and shorter handguard. Made from 1991 to date.
Standard LW Sporter (except 9mm) ..... NiB $1067 Ex $814 Gd $567
Standard LW Sporter, 9mm .... NiB $995 Ex $713 Gd $505
.22 LR conversion (disc. 1994), add $175

AR-15 SPORTER TARGET RIFLE
Caliber: .223 Rem. Five-round magazine. 20-inch bbl. w/flash suppressor (non-threaded after 1994). 39 inches overall. Weight: 7.5 lbs. Black composition stock, grip and handguard. Sights: post front; adj. aperture rear. Matte black finish. Made from 1993 to date.
Sporter Target Rifle .... NiB $1175 Ex $995 Gd $660
.22 LR conversion (disc. 1994), add $200

LIGHTNING MAGAZINE RIFLE - LARGE FRAME
Similar to Medium Frame model except w/large frame to accommodate larger calibers: .38-56, .44-60, .45-60, .45-65, .45-85, or .50-95 Express. Standard 22-inch (carbine & baby carbine) or 28-inch round or octagonal bbl. (rifle). Note: Additional bbl. lengths optional. Weight: 8 to 10.5 lbs. Sights: Open rear; bead or blade front. Walnut stock and checkered forearm. Made from 1887-94. (6,496 produced)
Rifle .... NiB $4290 Ex $3234 Gd $2333
Carbine .... NiB $8307 Ex $6350 Gd $4290
Baby Carbine .... NiB $10,393 Ex $8334 Gd $5700
.50-95 Express, add 35%

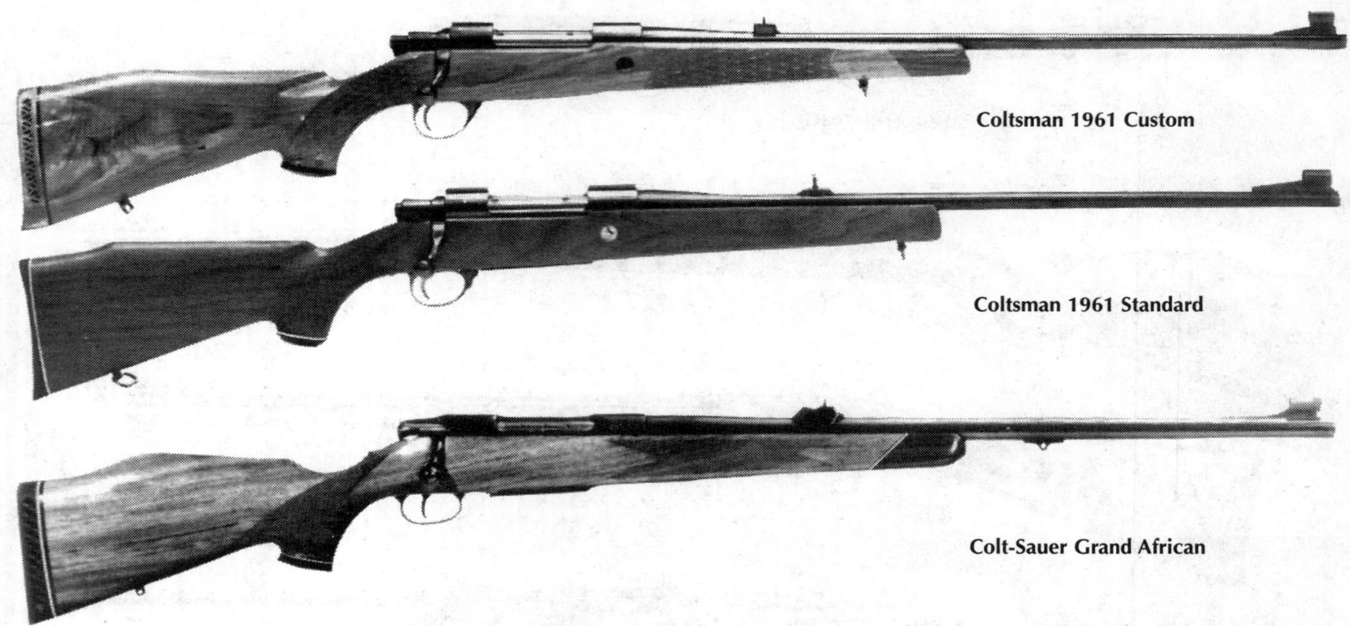

Coltsman 1961 Custom

Coltsman 1961 Standard

Colt-Sauer Grand African

LIGHTNING MAGAZINE RIFLE - MEDIUM FRAME
Slide-action w/12-round tubular magazine Carbine & Baby Carbine) or 15-round tubular magazine (rifle). Calibers: .32-20, .38-40, .44-40. Standard 20-inch (Carbine & Baby Carbine) or 26-inch round or octagonal bbl.(rifle). Note: Additional bbl. lengths optional. Weight: 5.5 lbs. (Baby Carbine), 6.25 lbs. (carbine) or 7 to 9 lbs. (rifle). Sights: Open rear; bead or blade front. Walnut stock and checkered forearm. Blue finish w/color casehardened hammer. Made from 1884-1902. (89,777 produced)
Rifle . . . . NiB $2341 Ex $1774 Gd $1208
Carbine . . . . NiB $3685 Ex $2845 Gd $1970
Baby Carbine . . . . NiB $5255 Ex $4132 Gd $2896
Military model
w/bayonet
lug & sling swivels . . . . NiB $5102 Ex $3698 Gd $2561

LIGHTNING MAGAZINE RIFLE - SMALL FRAME
Similar to Medium Frame model except w/smaller frame and chambered for .22 caliber only. Standard 24-inch round or octagonal bbl. w/half magazine. Note: Additional bbl. lengths optional. Weight: 6 lbs. Sights: Open rear; bead or blade front. Walnut stock and checkered forearm. Made from 1884-1902. (89,912 produced)
Standard Rifle model. . . . . NiB $1403 Ex $1074 Gd $744
W/Deluxe or optional features, add 20%

STAGECOACH .22 AUTOLOADER . . . . NiB $390 Ex $313 Gd $184
Same as Colteer .22 Autoloader except w/engraved receiver, saddle ring, 16.5-inch bbl. Weight: 4 lbs., 10 oz. Made from 1965-75.

1-.22 SINGLE-SHOT
BOLT-ACTION RIFLE. . . . . NiB $339 Ex $262 Gd $184
Caliber: .22 LR. Long, Short. 20- or 22-inch bbl. Sights: Open rear; ramp front. Pistol-grip stock w/Monte Carlo comb. Weight: 5 lbs. Made from 1957-67.

.22 AUTOLOADER . . . . NiB $339 Ex $262 Gd $184
Caliber: .22 LR. 15-round tubular magazine. 19.38-inch bbl. Sights: Open rear; hooded ramp front. Straight-grip stock, Western carbine-style forearm w/bbl. band. Weight: 4.75 lbs. Made from 1964-75.

CUSTOM BOLT-ACTION
SPORTING RIFLE. . . . . NiB $551 Ex $443 Gd $293
FN Mauser action, side safety, engraved floorplate. Calibers: .30-06, .300 H&H Mag. Five round box magazine. 24-inch bbl., rampfront sight. Fancy walnut stock. Monte Carlo comb, cheekpiece, pistol-grip, checkered, QD swivels. Weight: 7.25 lbs. Made from 1957-61.

DELUXE RIFLE . . . . NiB $916 Ex $710 Gd $504
FN Mauser action. Same as Custom model, except plain floorplate, plainer wood and checkering. Made from 1957-61. Value shown is for rifle as furnished by manufacturer w/o rear sight.

MODELS OF 1957 RIFLES
Sako medium action. Calibers: .243, .308. Weight: 6.75 lbs. Other specifications similar to those of models w/FN actions. Made from 1957-61.
Custom . . . . NiB $865 Ex $659 Gd $453
Deluxe. . . . . NiB $865 Ex $685 Gd $453
Standard . . . . NiB $709 Ex $452 Gd $375

MODEL OF 1961,
CUSTOM RIFLE. . . . . NiB $674 Ex $529 Gd $349
Sako action. Calibers: .222, .222 Mag., .223, .243, .264, .270, .308, .30-06, .300 H&H. 23-, 24-inch bbl. Sights: Folding leaf rear; hooded ramp front. Fancy French walnut stock w/Monte Carlo comb, rosewood forend tip and grip cap skip checkering, recoil pad, sling swivels. Weight: 6.5 - 7.5 lbs. Made from 1963-65.

MODEL OF 1961,
STANDARD RIFLE . . . . NiB $684 Ex $555 Gd $375
Same as Custom model except plainer, American walnut stock. Made from 1963-65.

STANDARD RIFLE . . . . NiB $658 Ex $503 Gd $349
FN Mauser action. Same as Deluxe model except in .243, .30-06, .308, .300 Mag. and stock w/o cheekpiece, bbl. length 22 inches. Made from 1957-61. Value shown is for rifle as furnished by manufacturer w/o rear sight.

COLT-SAUER DRILLINGS See Colt shotgun listings.

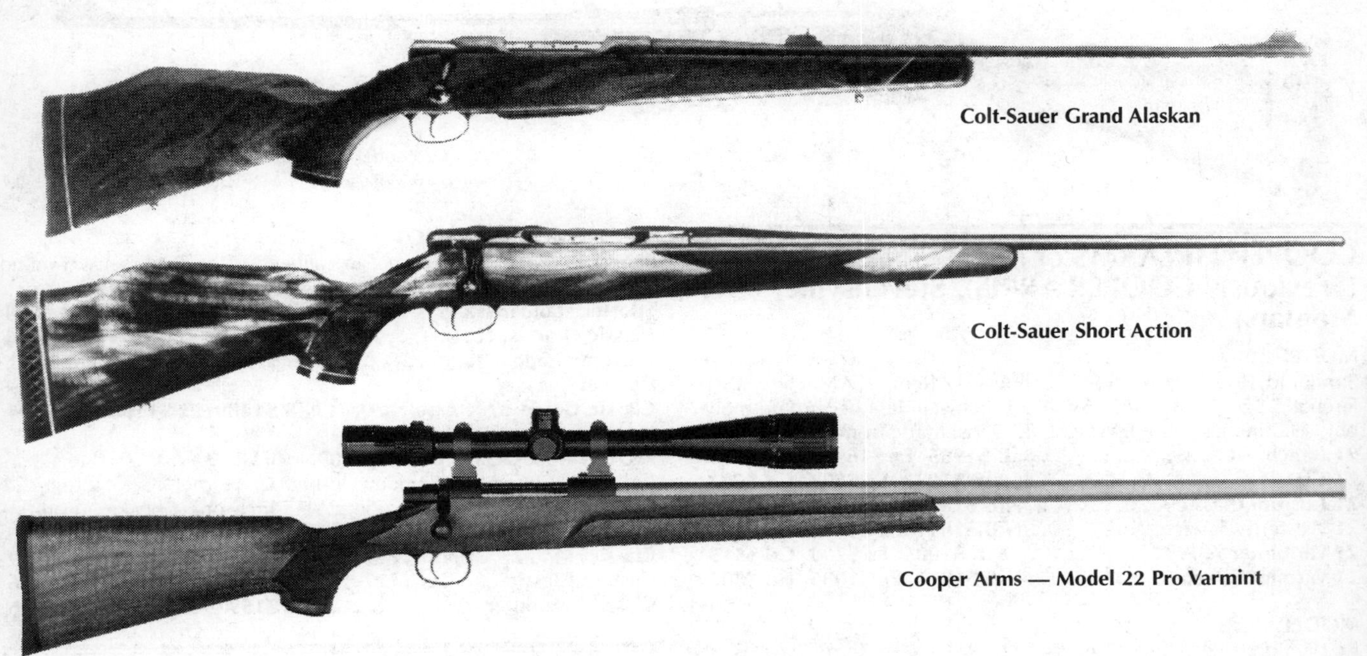

Colt-Sauer Grand Alaskan

Colt-Sauer Short Action

Cooper Arms — Model 22 Pro Varmint

GRAND AFRICAN . . . . NiB $1914 Ex $1502 Gd $1013
Same specifications as standard model except .458 Win. Mag., weight: 9.5 lbs. Sights: Adj. leaf rear; hooded ramp front. Magnum-style stock of Bubinga. Made from 1973-85.

GRAND ALASKAN . . . . NiB $1914 Ex $1322 Gd $884
Same specifications as standard model except .375 H&H, weight: 8.5 lbs. Sights: Adj. leaf rear; hooded ramp front. Magnum-style stock of walnut.

MAGNUM. . . . . NiB $1447 Ex $1037 Gd $729
Same specifications as standard model except calibers 7mm Rem. Mag., .300 Win. Mag., .300 Weatherby. Weight: 8.5 lbs. Made from 1973-85.

SHORT ACTION . . . . NiB $1292 Ex $1009 Gd $700
Same specifications as standard model except shorter action chambered for the following calibers: .22-250, .243 Win., .308 Win. and similar length cartridges. Weight: 7.5 1bs.; 8.25 lbs. (.22-250). Drilled and tapped for scope mount. No front or rear open sights. Made from 1973-88.

SPORTING RIFLE,
STANDARD MODEL . . . . NiB $1318 Ex $1034 Gd $725
Sauer 80 non-rotating bolt action. Calibers: .25-06, .270 Win., .30-06. Three-round detachable box magazine. 24-inch bbl. Weight: 7.75 lbs., 8.5 lbs. (.25-06). Furnished w/o sights. American walnut stock w/Monte Carlo cheekpiece, checkered pistol grip and forearm, rosewood forend tip and pistol-grip cap, recoil pad. Made from 1973-88.

COMANDO CARBINES — Knoxville, Tennessee, (Formerly Volunteer Enterprises, Inc.)

MARK III
SEMIAUTOMATIC CARBINE
Blow-back action, fires from closed bolt. Caliber: .45 ACP. 15- or 30-round magazine. 16.5-inch bbl. w/cooling sleeve and muzzle brake. Weight: 8 lbs. Sights: peep rear; blade front. "Tommy Gun" style stock and forearm or grip. Made from I969-76.
W/horizontal forearm . . . . NiB $469 Ex $366 Gd $263

MARK 9
Same specifications as Mark III and Mark 45 except caliber 9mm Luger. Made from 1976-81.
W/horizontal forearm . . . . NiB $494 Ex $402 Gd $283
W/vertical foregrip . . . . NiB $514 Ex $417 Gd $294

MARK 45
Same specifications as Mark III. Has redesigned trigger housing and magazines. Made from 1976-88.
W/horizontal forearm . . . . NiB $494 Ex $433 Gd $288
W/vertical foregrip . . . . NiB $591 Ex $479 Gd $336

CONTINENTAL RIFLES — Manufactured in Belgium for Continental Arms, Corp., New York, N.Y.

DOUBLE RIFLE
Calibers: .270, .303 Sav., .30-40, .348 Win., .30-06, .375 H&H, .400 Jeffrey, .465, .470, .475 No. 2, .500, .600. Side-by-side. Anson-Deeley reinforced boxlock action w/triple bolting lever work. Two triggers. Non-automatic safety. 24- or 26-inch bbls. Sights: Express rear; bead front. Checkered cheekpiece stock and forend. Weight: From 7 lbs., depending on caliber. Imported from 1956-75.
Calibers: .270 to .348 Win. . . . . NiB $5328 Ex $4304 Gd $2994
Calibers: .375 H&H & larger . . . . NiB $6584 Ex $5308 Gd $3677

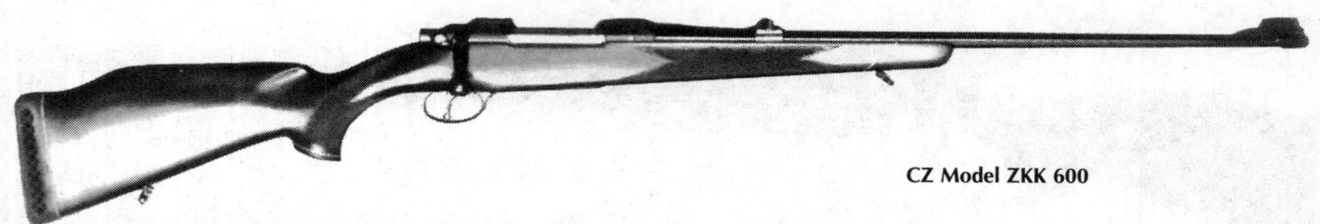

CZ Model ZKK 600

COOPER FIREARMS of MONTANA, INC. — (Previously COOPER ARMS), Stevensville, Montana

MODEL 21
Similar to Model 36C except in calibers .17 Rem., .17 Mach IV, .221 Fireball, .222, .223, 6x45, 6x47. 24-inch stainless or chrome-moly bbl. 43.5 inches overall. Weight: 8.75 lbs. Made from 1994 to date.

21 Benchrest . . . . NiB $1965 Ex $1656 Gd $1085
21 Classic . . . . NiB $1038 Ex $878 Gd $523
21 Custom Classic . . . . NiB $1811 Ex $1193 Gd $575
21 Western Classic . . . . NiB $1811 Ex $1193 Gd $575
21 Varminter . . . . NiB $1005 Ex $799 Gd $515
21 Varmint Extreme . . . . NiB $1811 Ex $1085 Gd $807

MODEL 22
Bolt-action, single-shot. Calibers: .22 BR. .22-250 Rem., .220 Swift, .243 Win., 6mm PPC, 6.5x55mm, 25-06 Rem., 7.62x39mm 26-inch bbl, 45.63 inches overall. Weight: 8 lbs., 12 oz. Single-stage trigger. AAA Claro walnut stock. Made from 1996 to date.

22 Benchrest . . . . NiB $1862 Ex $1528 Gd $1034
22 Classic . . . . NiB $1811 Ex $1255 Gd $677
22 Custom Classic . . . . NiB $1296 Ex $1193 Gd $832
22 Western Classic . . . . NiB $1909 Ex $1290 Gd $884
22 Varminter . . . . NiB $1090 Ex $879 Gd $575
22 Pro-Varmint Extreme . . . . NiB $1801 Ex $1085 Gd $781
22 Black Jack . . . . NiB $1801 Ex $1085 Gd $781

MODEL 36 RF/BR 50 . . . . NiB $1837 Ex $1193 Gd $808
Caliber: .22 LR. Bolt-action. Single-shot. 22-inch bbl. 40.5 inches overall. Weight: 6.8 lbs. No sights. Fully-adj. match-grade trigger. Stainless barrel. McMillan benchrest stock. Three mid-bolt locking lugs. Made from 1994 to date.

MODEL 36 CF BOLT-ACTION RIFLE
Calibers: .17 CCM, .22 CCM, .22 Hornet. Four-round mag. 23.75 inch bbl. 42.5 inch overall. Weight: 7 lbs. Walnut or synthetic stock. Made from 1992-94.

Marksman . . . . NiB $1008 Ex $776 Gd $565
Sportsman . . . . NiB $905 Ex $699 Gd $493
Classic Grade . . . . NiB $1804 Ex $1088 Gd $810
Custom Grade . . . . NiB $1088 Ex $882 Gd $624
Custom Classic Grade . . . . NiB $1814 Ex $1196 Gd $835

MODEL 36 RF BOLT-ACTION RIFLE
Similar to Model 36CF except in caliber .22 LR. Five round magazine. Weight: 6.5-7 lbs. Made from 1992 to date.

BR-50 (22-inch stainless bbl.) . . . NiB $1394 Ex $1083 Gd $724
Custom Grade . . . . NiB $1085 Ex $859 Gd $596
Custom Classic Grade . . . . NiB $1188 Ex $879 Gd $621
Featherweight . . . . NiB $1150 Ex $931 Gd $650

MODEL 36 TRP-1 SERIES
Similar to Model 36RF except in target configuration w/ ISU or silhouette-style stock. Made from 1991-93.

TRP-1 (ISU single-shot) . . . . NiB $975 Ex $795 Gd $483
TRP-1S (Silhouette) . . . . NiB $975 Ex $795 Gd $483

MODEL 38 SINGLE SHOT
Similar to Model 36CF except in calibers .17 or .22 CCM w/3-round magazine. Weight: 8 lbs. Walnut or synthetic stock. Made from 1992-93.

Sporter Standard . . . . NiB $979 Ex $773 Gd $618
Classic Grade. . . . . NiB $1077 Ex $871 Gd $618
Custom Grade . . . . NiB $1211 Ex $1030 Gd $618
Custom
Classic Grade . . . . NiB $1489 Ex $1190 Gd $804

MODEL 40 CLASSIC BOLT-ACTION RIFLE
Calibers: .17 CCM, .17 Ackley Hornet, .22 Hornet, .22K Hornet, .22 CCM, 4- or 5-round magazine. 23.75-inch bbl. Checkered oil-finished AAA Claro walnut stock. Made from 1995-97.

Classic. . . . . NiB $1484 Ex $1185 Gd $799
Custom Classic . . . . NiB $1487 Ex $1283 Gd $876
Classic Varminter . . . . NiB $1597 Ex $1283 Gd $876

CUMBERLAND MOUNTAIN ARMS — Winchester, Tennessee

PLATEAU RIFLE
Falling block action w/underlever. Calibers: .40-65, and .45-70. 32-inch round bbl. 48 inches overall. Weight: 10.5 lbs. American walnut stock. Bead front sight, adj. buckhorn rear. Blued finish. Lacquer finish walnut stock w/crescent buttplate. Made from 1995 to date.

Standard model . . . . NiB $967 Ex $787 Gd $555
Deluxe model . . . . NiB $1379 Ex $1096 Gd $751

CZ RIFLES — Strankonice, Czechoslovakia (Currently Uhersky Brod and Brno, Czecho.) Mfd. by Ceska Zbrojovka-Nardoni Podnik (Formerly Bohmische Waffenfabrik A.G.)

See also listings under Brno Sporting Rifles and Springfield, Inc.

ZKK 600 BOLT-ACTION RIFLE
Calibers: .270 Win., 7x57, 7x64, .30-06. Five round magazine. 23.5- inch bbl. Weight: 7.5 lbs. Adj. folding-leaf rear sight, hooded ramp front. Pistol-grip walnut stock. Imported from 1990 to date.

Standard model . . . . NiB $567 Ex $459 Gd $320
Deluxe model . . . . NiB $656 Ex $530 Gd $369

ZKK 601 BOLT-ACTION RIFLE
Similar to Model ZKK 600 except w/short action in calibers .223 Rem., .243 Win., .308 Win. 43 inches overall. Weight: 6 lbs., 13 oz. Checkered walnut pistol-grip stock w/Monte Carlo cheekpiece. Imported from 1990 to date.

Standard model . . . . NiB $535 Ex $458 Gd $382
Deluxe model . . . . NiB $586 Ex $525 Gd $382

ZKK 602 BOLT-ACTION RIFLE
Similar to Model ZKK 600 except w/Magnum action in calibers .300 Win. Mag., 8x68S, .375 H&H, .458 Win. Mag. 25-inch bbl. 45.5 inches overall. Weight: 9.25 lbs. Imported from 1990 to date.

Standard model . . . . NiB $718 Ex $616 Gd $428
Deluxe model . . . . NiB $846 Ex $693 Gd $463

CA Model ZKM 452 LUX Model

CZ 511

CZ Model ZKM 527

CZ 550 LUX Model

ZKM 452 BOLT-ACTION REPEATING RIFLE
Calibers: .22 LR. or .22 WMR. Five, 6- or 10-round magazine. 25-inch bbl. 43.5 inches overall. Weight: 6 lbs. Adj. rear sight, hooded bead front. Oil-finished beechwood or checkered walnut stock w/Schnabel forend. Imported 1995 to date.
Standard model (22 LR). . . . . NiB $381 Ex $310 Gd $160
Deluxe model (22 LR) . . . . NiB $422 Ex $279 Gd $192
Varmint model (22 LR) . . . . NiB $355 Ex $279 Gd $202
.22 WMR, add $35

ZKM 527 BOLT-ACTION RIFLE
Calibers: .22 Hornet, .222 Rem., .223 Rem., 7.62x39mm. Five round magazine. 23.5-inch bbl. 42.5 inches overall. Weight: 6.75 lbs. Adj. rear sight, hooded ramp front. Grooved receiver. Adj. double-set triggers. Oil-finished beechwood or checkered walnut stock . Imported 1995 to date.
Standard model. NiB $533 Ex $426 Gd $308
Classic model . . . . NiB $538 Ex $426 Gd $308
Carbine model (shorter configuration) . . . . NiB $563 Ex $431 Gd $308
Deluxe model . . . . NiB $620 Ex $528 Gd $334

ZKM 537 SPORTER BOLT-ACTION RIFLE
Calibers: .243 Win., .270 Win., 7x57mm, .308 Win., .30-06. Four or 5-round magazine. 19- or 23.5-inch bbl. 40.25 or 44.75 inches overall. Weight: 7 to 7.5 lbs. Adj. folding leaf rear sight, hooded ramp front. Shrouded bolt. Standard or Mannlicher-style checkered walnut stock. Imported 1992-94.
Standard model . . . . NiB $563 Ex $431 Gd $308
Mannlicher model . . . . NiB $793 Ex $538 Gd $385
Mountain Carbine model. . . . . NiB $563 Ex $426 Gd $283

511 SEMI-AUTO RIFLE . . . . NiB $220 Ex $199 Gd $123
Caliber: .22 LR. 8-round magazine. 22- inch bbl., 38.6 inches overall. Weight: 5.39 lbs. Receiver top fitted for telescopic sight mounts. Walnut wood-lacquered checkering stock. Imported 1998 to date.

550 BOLT-ACTION SERIES
Calibers: .243 Win., 6.5x55mm, .270 Win., 7mm Mag., 7x57, 7x64, .30-06, .300 Win Mag., .375 H&H, .416 Rem., .416 Rigby, .458 Win. Mag., 9.3x62. Four or 5-round detachable magazine. 20.5- or 23.6-inch bbl. Weight: 7.25 to 8 lbs. No sights or Express sights on magnum models. Receiver drilled and tapped for scope mount. Standard or Mannlicher-style checkered walnut stock w/buttpad. Imported 1995 to date.
Standard . . . . NiB $498 Ex $412 Gd $285
Magnum . . . . NiB $616 Ex $494 Gd $336
Delux . . . . NiB $535 Ex $428 Gd $310
Mannlicher . . . . NiB $601 Ex $463 Gd $336
Calibers .416 Rem., .416 Rigby, .458 Win. Mag., add. $70

CZECHOSLOVAKIAN MILITARY RIFLES — Brno, Czechoslovakia, Manufactured by Ceska Zbrojovka

MODEL 1924 (VZ24)
MAUSER MILITARY RIFLE . . . . NiB $274 Ex $213 Gd $146
Basically same as German Kar., 98k and F.N. (Belgian Model 1924.) Caliber: 7.9mm Mauser. Five round box magazine. 23.25-inch bbl. Weight: 8.5 lbs. Sights: Adj. rear; blade front w/guards. of Belgian-type military stock, full handguard. Made from 1924 thru WWII. Many of these rifles were made for export. As produced during the German occupation, this model was known as Gewehr 24t.

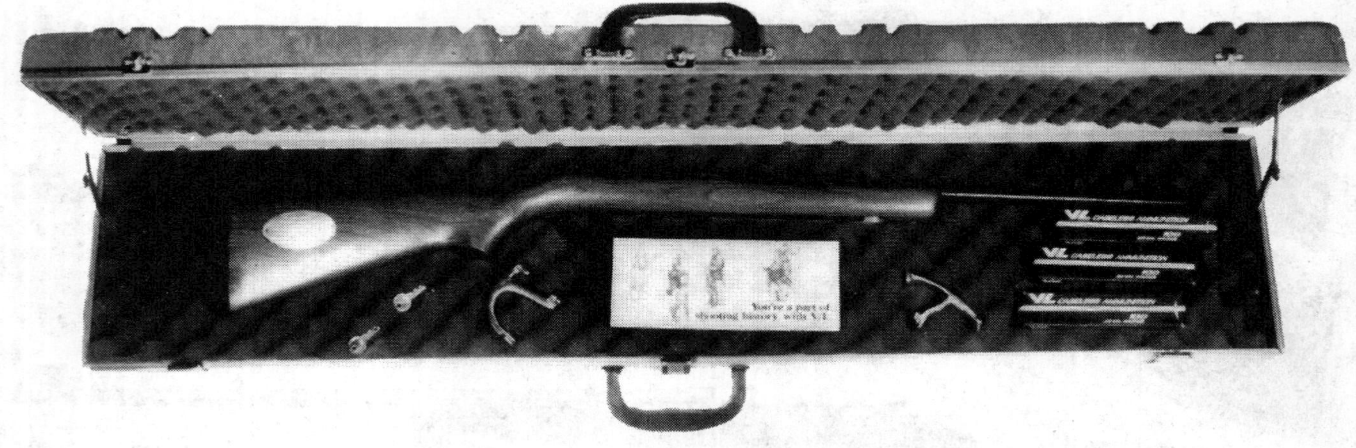

Daisy V/L Collector's Kit

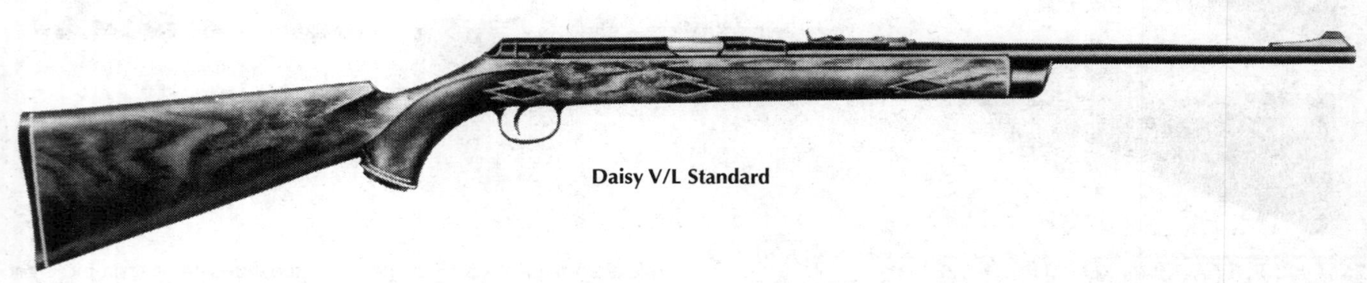

Daisy V/L Standard

MODEL 1933 (VZ33) MAUSER
MILITARY CARBINE . . . . NiB $358 Ex $280 Gd $203
Modification of German M/98 action w/smaller receiver ring. Caliber: 7.9mm Mauser. 19.25-inch bbl. Weight: 7.5 lbs. Sights: Adj. rear; blade front w/guards. Military-type full stock. Mfd. 1933 thru WWII. A similar model, produced during the German occupation, was designated Gew. 33/40.

DAEWOO PRECISION INDUSTRIES — Manufactured in Korea (Previously Imported by Kimber of America; Daewoo Precision Industries; Nationwide Sports and KBI, Inc.)

DR200 SA SEMIAUTOMATIC SPORTER
Caliber: .223 Rem. (5.56mm). Six or 10-round magazine. 18.4-inch bbl. 39.25 inches overall. Weight: 9 lbs. Protected post front sight, fully-adj. aperture rear. Forged aluminum receiver w/rotating locking bolt assembly. Synthetic sporterized thumbhole stock. Imported from 1994-96.
Sporter model . . . . NiB $705 Ex $551 Gd $421
Varmint model. . . . . NiB $602 Ex $551 Gd $319

DR300 SA SEMIAUTO-
MATIC SPORTER. . . . . NiB $628 Ex $541 Gd $371
Similar to Model Daewoo DR200 except chambered for 7.62x39mm. Imported from 1994-96.

DAISY RIFLES — Rogers, Arkansas

Daisy V/L rifles carry the first and only commercial caseless cartridge system. These rifles are expected to appreciate considerably in future years. The cartridge, no longer made, is also a collector's item. Production was discontinued following BATF ruling the V/L model to be a firearm.

COLLECTOR'S KIT. . . . . NiB $453 Ex $370 Gd $263
Presentation-grade rifle w/gold plate inscribed w/owner's name and gun serial number mounted on the stock. Also includes a special gun case, pair of brass gun cradles for wall-hanging, 300 rounds of 22 V/L ammunition and a certificate signed by Daisy president Cass S. Hough. Approx. 1,000 manufactured from 1968-69.

PRESENTATION
GRADE . . . . NiB $332 Ex $265 Gd $231
Same specifications as standard model except w/walnut stock. Approx. 4,000 manufactured from 1968-69.

STANDARD RIFLE . . . . NiB $265 Ex $213 Gd $157
Single-shot under-lever action. Caliber: .22 V/L (caseless cartridge, propellant ignited by jet of hot air). 18-inch bbl. Weight: 5 lbs. Sights: Adj. open rear, ramp w/blade front. Wood-grained Lustran stock (foam-filled). Approx. 19,000 manufactured from 1968-69.

Dakota Model 10 Single-Shot Rifle

Dakota Arms Model 76 African Grade

Dakota Arms Model 76 Classic Grade

Dakota Arms Model 97 Hunter

DAKOTA ARMS, INC. — Sturgis, South Dakota

MODEL 10 SINGLE-SHOT RIFLE

Chambered for most commercially-loaded calibers. 23-inch bbl. 39.5 inches overall. Weight: 5.5 lbs. Top tang safety. No sights. Checkered pistol-grip buttstock and semi-beavertail forearm, QD swivels, rubber recoil pad. Made from 1992 to date.

Standard calibers. . . . . NiB $3361 Ex $2944 Gd $1863
Magnum calibers. . . . . NiB $3845 Ex $3099 Gd $2120

MODEL 22 BOLT-ACTION SPORTER RIFLE . . . . NiB $1396 Ex $1138 Gd $767

Calibers: .22 LR. .22 Hornet. Five round magazine. 22-inch bbl. Weight: 6.5 lbs. Adj. trigger. Checkered classic-style Claro or English walnut stock w/black recoil pad. Made from 1992 to date.

MODEL 76 AFRICAN BOLT-ACTION RIFLE. . . . . NiB $4355 Ex $3912 Gd $2470

Same general specifications as Model 76 Safari. Calibers: .404 Jeffery, .416 Rigby, .416 Dakota, .450 Dakota. 24-inch bbl. Weight: 8 lbs. Checkered select walnut stock w/two crossbolts. Made from 1989 to date.

MODEL 76 ALPINE BOLT-ACTION RIFLE. . . . . NiB $2331 Ex $1666 Gd $1136

Same general specifications as Model 76 Classic except short action w/blind magazine. Calibers: .22-250, .243, 6mm Rem., .250-3000, 7mm-08, .308. 21-inch bbl. Weight: 7.5 lbs. Made from 1989-93.

MODEL 76 CLASSIC BOLT-ACTION RIFLE. . . . . NiB $2982 Ex $2333 Gd $1617

Calibers: .257 Roberts, .270 Win., .280 Rem., .30-06, 7mm Rem. Mag., .300 Win. Mag., .338 Win. Mag., .375 H&H Mag., .458 Win. Mag. 21- or 23-inch bbl. Weight: 7.5 lbs. Receiver drilled and tapped for sights. Adj. trigger. Classic-style checkered walnut stock w/steel grip cap and solid recoil pad. Right- and left-hand models. Made from 1988 to date.

MODEL 76 LONGBOW TACTICAL BOLT-ACTION RIFLE. . . . . NiB $4287 Ex $3304 Gd $2274

Calibers: .300 Dakota Mag., .330 Dakota Mag., .338 Lapua Mag. Blind magazine. Ported 28-inch bbl. 50 to 51 inches overall. Weight: 13.7 lbs. Black or oliver green fiberglass stock w/adj. cheekpiece and buttplate. Receiver drilled and tapped w/one-piece rail mount and no sights. Made from 1997 to date.

MODEL 76 SAFARI BOLT-ACTION RIFLE. . . . . NiB $4316 Ex $3286 Gd $2205

Calibers: .300 Win. Mag., .338 Win. Mag., .375 H&H Mag. .458 Win. Mag. 23-inch bbl. w/bbl. band swivel. Weight: 8.5 lbs. Ramp front sight, standing leaf rear. Checkered fancy walnut stock w/ebony forend tip and solid recoil pad. Made from 1988 to date.

MODEL 76 TRAVELER SERIES RIFLES

Threadless take-down action w/interchangeable bbl. capability based on the Dakota 76 design. Calibers: .257 through .458 Win (Standard-Classic & Safari) and .416 Dakota, .404 Jeffery, .416 Rigby, .338 Lapua and .450 Dakota Mag. (E/F Family-African Grade). 23- to 24- inch bbl. Weight: 7.5 to 9.5 lbs. Right or left-hand action. X grade (Classic) or XXX grade (Safari or African) oil finish English Bastogne or Claro walnut stock. Made from 1999 to date.

Classic Grade. . . . . NiB $4393 Ex $3338 Gd $2277
Safari Grade . . . . NiB $4368 Ex $3363 Gd $2745
African Grade . . . . NiB $5531 Ex $4390 Gd $3069
Interchangeable bbl. assemblies
Classic Grade, add. $1150
Safari Grade, add. $1450
African Grade, add $1595

MODEL 76 VARMINT
BOLT-ACTION RIFLE . . . . NiB $2409 Ex $1894 Gd $1091
Similar to Model 76 Classic except single-shot action w/ heavy bbl. chambered for .17 Rem. to 6mm PPC. Weight: 13.7 lbs. Checkered walnut or synthetic stock. Receiver drilled and tapped for scope mounts and no sights. Made from 1994-98.

MODEL 97 HUNTER BOLT-ACTION SERIES
Calibers: .22-250 Rem. to .330 Dakota Mag.(Lightweight), .25-06 to .375 Dakota Mag. (Long Range). 22-, 24- or 26-inch bbl. 43 to 46 inches overall. Weight: 6.16 lbs. to 7.7 lbs. Black composite fiberglass stock w/recoil pad. Fully adj. match trigger. Made from 1997 to date.
Lightweight . . . . NiB $1907 Ex $1551 Gd $872
Long Range . . . . NiB $1668 Ex $1345 Gd $933

MODEL 97 VARMINT HUNTER
BOLT-ACTION RIFLE . . . . NiB $1706 Ex $1474 Gd $830
Similar to Model 97 Hunter except single-shot action w/ heavy bbl. chambered .22-250 Rem. to .308 Win. Checkered walnut stock. Receiver drilled and tapped for scope mounts and no sights. Made from 1998 to date.

CHARLES DALY RIFLE — Harrisburg, Pennsylvania, *Imported by K.B.I., Inc., Harrisburg, PA, (Previously by Outdoor Sports Headquarters, Inc.)*

EMPIRE GRADE BOLT-ACTION RIFLE (RF)
Similar to Superior Grade except w/checkered California walnut stock w/rosewood grip cap and forearm cap. High polished blued finish and damascened bolt. Made from 1998. Disc.
Empire Grade (.22 LR). . . . . NiB $337 Ex $275 Gd $195
Empire Grade (.22WMR). . . . . NiB $363 Ex $295 Gd $209
Empire Grade (.22 Hornet) . . . . NiB $503 Ex $407 Gd $285

FIELD GRADE BOLT-ACTION RIFLE (RF)
Caliber: .22 LR. 16.25-, 17.5- or 22.63-inch bbl. 32 to 41 inches overall. Single-shot (True Youth) and 6- or 10-round magazine. Plain walnut-finished hardwood or checkered polymer stock. Blue or stainless finish. Imported from 1998. Disc.
Field Grade (Standard w/22.63-inch bbl.). . . NiB $129 Ex $108 Gd $80
Field Grade (Youth w/17.5-inch bbl.) . . . . . . NiB $136 Ex $113 Gd $83
Field Grade (True Youth
w/16.25-inch bbl.) . . . . NiB $173 Ex $142 Gd $104
Field Grade (Polymer w/stainless action) . . . NiB $142 Ex $118 Gd $87

FIELD GRADE HUNTER BOLT-ACTION RIFLE
Calibers: .22 Hornet, .223 Rem., .243 Win., .270 Win., 7mm Rem. Mag. .308 Win., .30-06, .300 Win. Mag., .300 Rem. Ultra Mag., .338 Win. Mag. Three, 4-, or 5-round magazine. 22- or 24-inch bbl. w/o sights. Weight: 7.2 to 7.4 lbs. Checkered walnut or black polymer stock. Receiver drilled and tapped. Blue or stainless finish. Imported from 1998. Disc.
Field Grade Hunter (walnut stock) . . . . NiB $524 Ex $428 Gd $303
Field Grade Hunter (polymer stock) . . . . . . NiB $544 Ex $443 Gd $314
w/Left-hand model, add $35

HAMMERLESS DRILLING
See listing under Charles Daly shotguns.

HORNET RIFLE . . . . NiB $1263 Ex $1010 Gd $710
Same as Herold Rifle. See listing of that rifle for specifications. imported during the 1930s. Disc.

MAUSER 98
Calibers: .243 Win., .270 Win., 7mm Rem. Mag. .308 Win., .30-06, .300 Win. Mag., .375 H&H, or .458 Win. Mag. Three, 4-, or 5-round magazine. 23-inch bbl. 44.5 inches overall. Weight: 7.5 lbs. Checkered European walnut (Superior) or fiberglass/graphic (Field) stock w/recoil pad. Ramped front sight, adj. rear. Receiver drilled and tapped w/side saftey. Imported from 1998. Disc.
Field Grade (standard calibers) Disc. . . . . . NiB $428 Ex $377 Gd $127
Field Grade (375 H&H
and 458 Win. Mag.) . . . . NiB $632 Ex $530 Gd $326
Superior Grade (standard calibers) Disc. . . NiB $632 Ex $484 Gd $326
Superior Grade (magnum calibers) Disc. . . NiB $860 Ex $734 Gd $573

MINI-MAUSER 98
Similar to Mauser 98 except w/19.25-inch bbl. chambered for .22 Hornet, .22-250 Rem., .223 Rem., or 7.62x39mm. Five round magazine. Imported from 1998. Disc.
Field Grade . . . . NiB $382 Ex $331 Gd $214
Superior Grade . . . . NiB $494 Ex $407 Gd $229

SUPERIOR GRADE BOLT-ACTION RIFLE
Calibers: .22 LR. .22 WMR, .22 Hornet. 20.25- to 22.63-inch bbl. 40.5 to 41.25 inches overall. Five, 6-, or 10-round magazine. Ramped front sight, adj. rear w/grooved receiver. Checkered walnut stock. Made from 1998. Disc.
Superior Grade (.22 LR) . . . . NiB $161 Ex $141 Gd $90
Superior Grade (.22WMR) . . . . NiB $197 Ex $157 Gd $111
Superior Grade (.22 Hornet) . . . . . . NiB $363 Ex $312 Gd $199

SEMIAUTOMATIC RIFLE
Caliber: .22 LR. 20.75-inch bbl. 40.5 inches overall. 10-round magazine. Ramped front sight, adj. rear w/grooved receiver. Plain walnut-finished hardwood stock (Field), checkered walnut (Superior), checkered polymer stock or checkered California walnut stock w/rosewood grip cap and forearm cap (Empire). Blue or stainless finish. Imported from 1998. Disc.
Field Grade . . . . NiB $131 Ex $111 Gd $75
Field Grade (Polymer
w/stainless action). . . . . NiB $143 Ex $121 Gd $80
Superior Grade . . . . NiB $197 Ex $172 Gd $111
Empire Grade . . . . NiB $315 Ex $248 Gd $172

BOLT ACTION RIFLE. . . . . NiB $875 Ex $625 Gd $515
Calibers: .22 Hornet. Bbl.: 24 inches. Five round box magazine, hinged floorplate. Sights: Ramp front, leaf rear. Walnut stock, checkered grip and forearm. Early version rifle, introduced 1931 by Franz Jaeger Co. Discontinued 1939. Imported by Charles Daly but same model was imported by A. F. Stoeger as Herold Rifle.

SUPERIOR
COMBINATION GUN. . . . . NiB $1300 Ex $1095 Gd $950
Calibers: 12-guage shotgun over .22 Hornet, .223 Remington, .22-250, .243 Win., .270 Win., or .30-06. Barrels: 23 1/2 inches. Shotgun choked Imp. Cyl. Weight: About 7.5 pounds. Checkered walnut, pistol grip, semi-beavertail forend. Silvered, engraved receiver. Chrome-moly steel barrels, double triggers, extractors. Gold bead front sight. Introduced 1997, imported by K.B.I.

EMPIRE COMBINATION GUN . NiB $1700 Ex $1490 Gd $1150
Similar to Superior Combination Gun but with fancy grade wood, European style comb and cheekpiece, slimmer forend. Introduced 1997, imported by K.B.I.

FIELD GRADE AUTO RIFLE. . . . . NiB $135 Ex $95 Gd $80
Calibers: .22 LR. Semiautomatic, 10-round magazine, shell deflector. Bbl.: 20 3/4 inches. Weight: 6.5 pounds. Overall length: 40.5

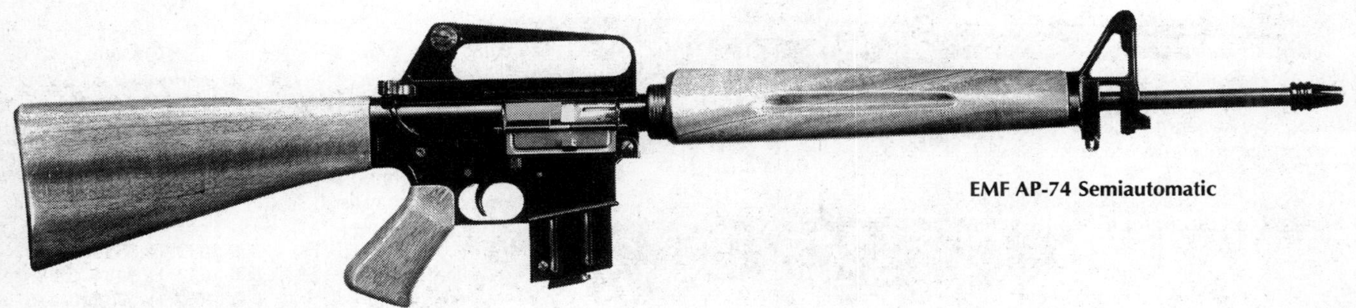

EMF AP-74 Semiautomatic

inches. Stock: Hardwood, walnut-finished, Monte Carlo style. Sights: Hooded front, adjustable open rear. Grooved for scope mounting. Blued finish. Introduced 1998. Imported by K. B. I.

EMPIRE GRADE AUTO RIFLE . . . . . NiB $175 Ex $140 Gd $110
Similar to Field Grade Auto Rifle but with select California walnut stock, hand checkering. Contrasting forend and grip caps. Damascened bolt, high-polish blued finish. Introduced 1998; discontinued.

TRUE YOUTH
BOLT-ACTION RIFLE . . . . NiB $120 Ex $90 Gd $60
Caliber: .22 LR. Single-shot., bolt-action. Bbl.: 16.25 inches. Weight: 3 pounds. Overall length: 32 inches. Walnut-finished hardwood stock. Sights: Blade front, adjustable rear. Blued finish. Introduced 1998. Imported by K. B. I.

EAGLE ARMS INC. — Geneseo, Illinois (Previously Coal Valley, Illinois)

In 1995, Eagle Arms Inc., became a division of ArmaLite and reintroduced that logo. For current ArmaLite production see models under that listing.

MODEL EA-15 CARBINE
Caliber: .223 Rem. (5.56mm). 30-round magazine. 16-inch bbl. and collapsible buttstock. Weight: 5.75 lbs. (E1); 6.25 lbs. (E2 w/heavy bbl. & National Match sights). Made from 1989 to 94.
E1 Carbine. . . . . NiB $846 Ex $686 Gd $480
E2 Carbine. . . . . NiB $911 Ex $737 Gd $515

MODEL EA-15 GOLDEN
EAGLE MATCH RIFLE . . . . NiB $1182 Ex $929 Gd $620
Same general specifications as EA-15 Standard, except w/E2-style National Match sights. 20-inch Douglas Heavy Match bbl. NM trigger and bolt-carrier group. Weight: 12.75 lbs. Made from 1991 to 94.

MODEL EA-15 SEMIAUTOMATIC RIFLE . . . . . NiB $864 Ex $689 Gd $462
Same as EA-15 Carbine except 20-inch bbl., 39 inches overall and weighs 7 lbs. Made from 1989 to date.

EMF COMPANY, INC. — Santa Ana, California

MODEL AP-74
SEMI-AUTOMATIC CARBINE . . . . . NiB $328 Ex $281 Gd $184
Calibers: .22 LR or .32 ACP, 15-round magazine. 20-inch bbl. w/flash reducer. 38 inches overall. Weight: 6.75 lbs. Protected pin front sight; protected rear peep sight. Lightweight plastic buttstock; ventilated snap-out forend. Importation. disc. 1989.

MODEL AP74-W
SPORTER CARBINE . . . . NiB $359 Ex $292 Gd $178
Sporterized version of AP-74 w/wood buttstock and forend. Importation disc. 1988.

MODEL AP74 PARATROOPER . . . . NiB $312 Ex $225 Gd $204
Same general specifications as Model AP74-W except w/folding tubular buttstock. Made in .22 LR. only. Importation disc. 1987.

MODEL 1860 HENRY RIFLE
Calibers: .44-40 and .45 LC. 24.25-inch bbl.; upper-half octagonal w/magazine tube in one-piece steel. 43.75-inches overall. Weight: 9.25 lbs. Varnished American walnut wood stock. Polished brass frame and brass buttplate. Original rifle was patented by B. Tyler Henry and produced by the New Haven Arms Company, when Oliver Winchester was president. Imported 1987 to date.
Deluxe model . . . . NiB $830 Ex $650 Gd $310
Engraved model. . . . . NiB $1057 Ex $779 Gd $521

MODEL 1866
YELLOW BOY RIFLE . . . . NiB $620 Ex $538 Gd $327
Calibers: .44-40, .45 LC and .38 Special. Lever-action. Bbl: 24 inches, 43 inches overall. Bead front sight. Exact reproduction. Offered w/blued finish, walnut stock and brass frame.

MODEL 1866 YELLOW BOY CARBINE
Same features as 1866 Yellow Boy Rifle except carbine.
Standard carbine . . . . NiB $641 Ex $430 Gd $285
Engraved carbine . . . . NiB $646 Ex $517 Gd $311

MODEL 1873 SPORTING RIFLE
Calibers: .22 LR. .22 WMR, .357 Mag., .44-40 and .45 LC. 24.25-inch octagonal bbl. 43.25 inches overall. Weight: 8.16 lbs. Color casehardened frame w/blued steel magazine tube. Walnut stock and forend.
Standard Rifle . . . . NiB $802 Ex $648 Gd $416
Engraved Rifle . . . . NiB $933 Ex $624 Gd $434
Boy's Rifle
(Youth Model, .22 LR). . . . . NiB $638 Ex $519 Gd $339

MODEL 1873
SPORTING RIFLE CARBINE
Same features as 1873 sporting rifle except w/19-inch bbl. Overall length: 38.25 inches. Weight: 7.38 lbs. Color casehardened or blued frame.
Standard carbine. NiB $802 Ex $648 Gd $416
Boy's carbine (Youth Model, .22 LR). . . . . . NiB $638 Ex $519 Gd $339

Erma — EG712

Erma — EGM1

Erma — EM1 22

ERMA-WERKE — Dachau, Germany (Previously imported by Precision Sales International; Nygord Precision Products; Mandall's Shooting Supplies)

MODEL EG72 PUMP-ACTION REPEATER . . . . NiB $146 Ex $116 Gd $90
Visible hammer. Caliber: .22 LR. 15-round magazine. 18.5-inch bbl. Weight: 5.25 lbs. Sights: open rear; hooded ramp front. Receiver grooved for scope mounting. Straight-grip stock, grooved slide handle. Imported from 1970-76.

MODEL EG73 . . . . NiB $289 Ex $254 Gd $146
Same as Model EG712 except chambered for .22 WMR w/12-round tubular magazine, 19.3-inch bbl. Imported from 1973-97.

MODEL EG712 LEVER-ACTION REPEATING CARBINE. . . . . NiB $284 Ex $254 Gd $140
Styled after Winchester Model 94. Caliber: .22 LR. Long, Short. Tubul33 magazine holds 15 LR, 17 Long, 21 Short. 18.5-inch bbl. Weight: 5.5 lbs. Sights: Open rear; hooded ramp front. Receiver grooved for scope mounting. Western carbine-style stock and forearm w/bbl. band. Imported 1976-97. Note: A similar carbine of Erma manufacture is marketed in U.S. as Ithaca Model 72 Saddle Gun.

MODEL EGM1. . . . . NiB $289 Ex $248 Gd $146
Same as Model EM1 except w/unslotted buttstock, ramp front sight, 5-round magazine standard. Imported from 1970-95.

MODEL EM1 .22 SEMIAUTOMATIC CARBINE. . . . . . NiB $378 Ex $301 Gd $199
Styled after U.S. Carbine cal. 30 M1. Caliber: .22 LR. 10- or 15-round magazine. 18-inch bbl. Weight: 5.5 lbs. Carbine-type sights. Receiver grooved for scope mounting. Military stock/handguard. Imported from 1966-97.

EUROPEAN AMERICAN ARMORY — Sharpes, Florida

MODEL HW 660 BOLT-ACTION SINGLE-SHOT RIFLE. . . . . NiB $855 Ex $705 Gd $448
Caliber: .22 LR. 26.8-inch bbl., 45.7 inches overall. Weight: 10.8 lbs. Match-type aperture rear sight; Hooded ramp front. Stippled walnut stock. Imported from 1992-96.

MODEL HW BOLT-ACTION SINGLE-SHOT TARGET RIFLE . . . . . NiB $850 Ex $705 Gd $499
Same general specification as Model HW 660 except equipped w/ target stock. Imported from 1995-96.

MODEL SABITTI SP1822
Caliber: .22 LR. 10-round detachable magazine. 18.5 inch bbl. 37.5 inches overall. Weight: 5.25 to 7.15 lbs. No sights. Hammer-forged heavy non-tapered bbl. Scope-mounted rail. Flush-mounted magazine release. Alloy receiver w/non-glare finish. Manual bolt lock. Wide claw extractor. Blowback action. Cross-trigger safety. Imported from 1994-96.
Traditional Sporter model. . . . . NiB $227 Ex $187 Gd $135
Thumbhole Sporter model (synthetic stock). . . . . NiB $349 Ex $284 Gd $202

FABRIQUE NATIONALE HERSTAL — Herstal & Liege, Belgium, (Formerly Fabrique Nationale d'Armes de Guerre)

MODELS 1924, 1934/30 AND 1930 MAUSER MILITARY RIFLES . . . . NiB $405 Ex $303 Gd $201
Similar to German Kar. 98k w/straight bolt handle. Calibers: 7mm, 7.65mm and 7.9mm Mauser. Five round box magazine. 23.5-inch bbl. Weight: 8.5 lbs. Sights: Adj. rear; blade front. Military stock of M/98 pattern w/slight modification. Model differences are minor. Also produced in a short carbine model w/17.25-inch bbl. Note: These rifles were manufactured under contract for Abyssinia, Argentina, Belgium, Bolivia, Brazil, Chile, China, Colombia, Ecuador, Iran, Luxembourg, Mexico, Peru, Turkey, Uruguay and Yugoslavia. Such arms usually bear the coat of arms of the country for which they were made together with the contractor's name and date of manufacture. Also sold commercially and exported to all parts of the world.

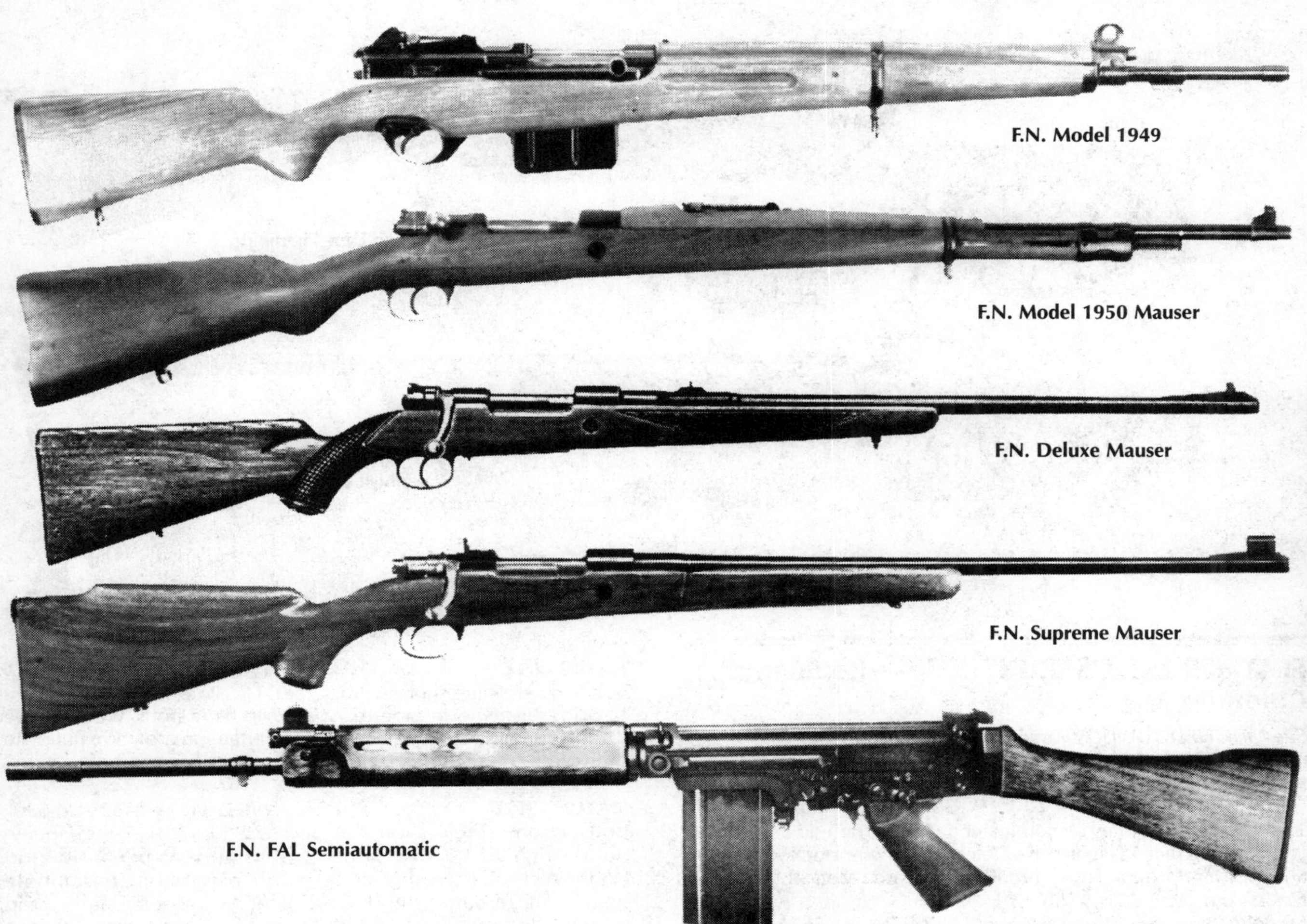

F.N. Model 1949

F.N. Model 1950 Mauser

F.N. Deluxe Mauser

F.N. Supreme Mauser

F.N. FAL Semiautomatic

MODEL 1949 SEMIAUTOMATIC MILITARY RIFLE .... NiB $744 Ex $616 Gd $285
Gas-operated. Calibers: 7mm, 7.65mm, 7.92mm, .30-06. 10-round box magazine, clip fed or loaded singly. 23.2-inch bbl. Weight: 9.5 lbs. Sights: Tangent rear-shielded post front. Pistol-grip stock, handguard. Note: Adopted by Belgium in 1949; also by Belgian Congo, Brazil, Colombia, Luxembourg, Netherlands, East Indies, and Venezuela. Approx. 160,000 were made.

MODEL 1950 MAUSER MILITARY RIFLE .... NiB $484 Ex $331 Gd $254
Same as previous F.N. models of Kar. 98k type except chambered for .30-06.

DELUXE MAUSER BOLT-ACTION SPORTING RIFLE.............. NiB $739 Ex $642 Gd $387
American calibers: .220 Swift, .243 Win., .244 Rem., .250/3000, .257 Roberts, .270 Win., 7mm, .300 Sav., .308 Win. .30-06. European calibers: 7x57, 8x57JS, 8x60S, 9.3x62, 9.5x57, 10.75x68mm. Five round box magazine. 24-inch bbl. Weight: 7.5-8.25 lbs. American model is standard w/hooded ramp front sight and Tri-Range rear; Continental model w/two-leaf rear. Checkered stock w/cheekpiece, pistol-grip, swivels. Made from 1947-63.

DELUXE MAUSER — PRESENTATION GRADE .... NiB $1262 Ex $707 Gd $701
Same as regular model except w/select grade stock; engraving on receiver, trigger guard, floorplate and bbl. breech. Disc. 1963.

FAL/FNC/LAR SEMIAUTOMATIC
Same as standard FAL military rifle except w/o provision for automatic firing. Gas-operated. Calibers: 7.62mm NATO (.308 Win.) or 5.56mm (.223 Rem.). 10- or 20-round box magazine. 25.5-inch bbl. (including flash hider). Weight: 9 lbs. Sights: Post front; aperture rear. Fixed wood or folding buttstock, pistol-grip, forearm/handguard w/carrying handle and sling swivels. Disc. 1988.
F.N. FAL/LAR model (Light Automatic Rifle) .... NiB $2490 Ex $2159 Gd $1343
F.N. FAL/HB model (heavy bbl.) ...... NiB $2810 Ex $2261 Gd $1559
F.N. FAL/PARA (Paratrooper) .... NiB $3439 Ex $2776 Gd $1756
F.N. FNC Carbine model (.223 cal.)................. NiB $2628 Ex $1904 Gd $1241
F.N. FNC Carbine model w/flash suppresser (.223 cal.) .... NiB $2720 Ex $1955 Gd $1291

SUPREME MAUSER BOLT-ACTION SPORTING RIFLE............. NiB $760 Ex $913 Gd $403
Calibers: .243, .270, 7mm, .308, .30-06. Four round magazine in .243 and .308; 5-round in other calibers. 22-inch bbl. in .308; 24-inch in other calibers. Sights: Hooded ramp front, Tri-Range peep rear. Checkered stock w/ Monte Carlo cheekpiece, pistol-grip, swivels. Weight: 7.75 lbs. Made from 1957-75.

SUPREME MAGNUM MAUSER .... NiB $811 Ex $658 Gd $428
Calibers: .264 Mag., 7mm Mag., .300 Win. Mag. Specifications same as for standard caliber model except 3-round magazine capacity.

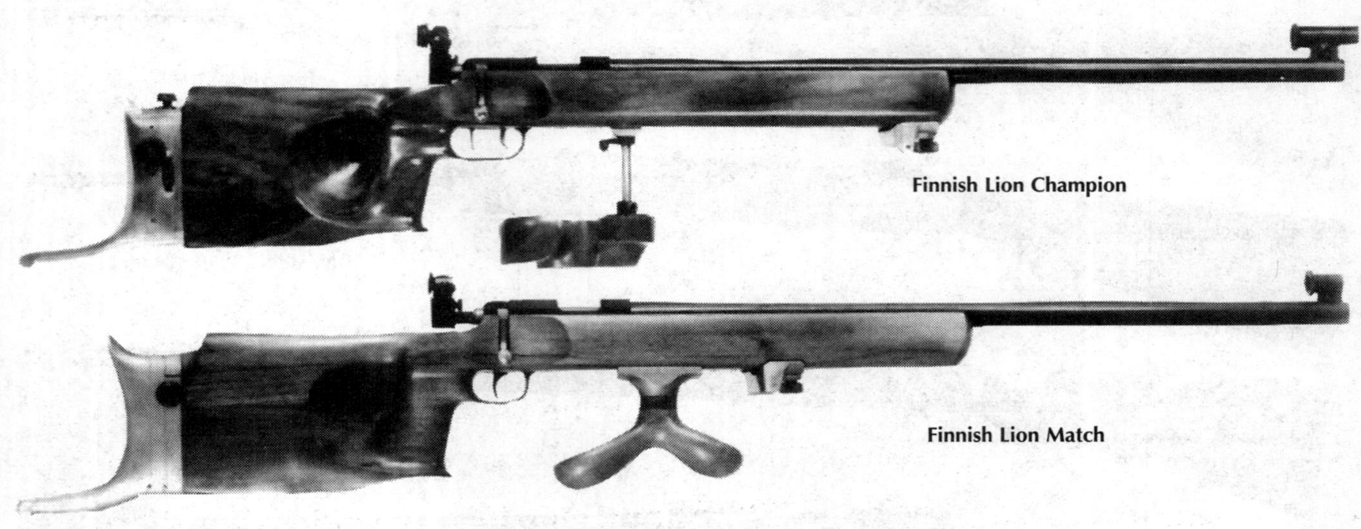
Finnish Lion Champion

Finnish Lion Match

FEATHER INDUSTRIES, INC. — Boulder, Colorado

See MITCHELL ARMS. For current production.

MODEL AT-9 SEMIAUTOMATIC RIFLE
Caliber: 9mm Parabellum. 10-, 25-, 32-, or 100-round magazine. 17-inch bbl. 35 inches overall (extended). Hooded post front sight, adj. aperture rear. Weight: 5 lbs. Telescoping wire stock w/composition pistol-grip and barrel-shroud handguard. Matte black finish. Made from 1988-95.
Model AT-9 .... NiB $751 Ex $674 Gd $442
W/32-round magazine, add. $75
W/100-round drum magazine, add $250

MODEL AT-22 .... NiB $250 Ex $199 Gd $143
Caliber: .22 LR. 20-round magazine. 17-inch bbl. 35 inches overall (extended). Hooded post front sight; adj. aperture rear. Weight: 3.25 lbs. Telescoping wire stock w/composition pistol-grip and barrel shroud handguard. Matte black finish.

MODEL F2 SA CARBINE .... NiB $277 Ex $215 Gd $132
Similar to AT-22, except w/fixed Polymer stock and pistol-grip. Made from 1992-95.

MODEL F9 SA CARBINE .... NiB $617 Ex $566 Gd $360
Similar to AT-9, except w/fixed Polymer stock and pistol-grip. Made from 1992-95.

FINNISH LION RIFLES — Jyväkylylä, Finland Manufactured by Valmet Oy, Tourula Works

CHAMPION FREE RIFLE .... NiB $637 Ex $514 Gd $358
Bolt-action single-shot target rifle. Double-set trigger. Caliber: .22 LR. 28.75-inch heavy bbl. Weight: 16 lbs. Sights: Extension rear peep; aperture front. Walnut free-rifle stock w/full pistol-grip, thumbhole, beavertail forend, hook buttplate, palm rest, hand stop, swivel. Made from 1965-72.

STANDARD ISU
TARGET RIFLE .... NiB $383 Ex $306 Gd $177
Bolt-action, single-shot. Caliber: .22 LR. 27.5-inch bbl. Weight: 10.5 lbs. Sights: extension rear peep; aperture front. Walnut target stock w/full pistol-grip, checkered beavertail forearm, adj. buttplate, sling swivel. Made from 1966-77.

MATCH RIFLE .... NiB $534 Ex $432 Gd $302
Bolt-action, single-shot. Caliber: .22 LR. 28.75-inch heavy bbl. Weight: 14.5 lbs. Sights: Extension rear peep; aperture front. Walnut free-rifle stock w/full pistol-grip, thumbhole, beavertail forearm, hook buttplate, palm rest, hand stop, swivel. Made from 1937-72.

STANDARD
TARGET RIFLE
Bolt-action, single-shot. Caliber: .22 LR. 27.5-inch bbl. 44.5 inches overall. Weight: 10.5 lbs. No sights; micrometer rear and globe front International-style sights available. Select walnut stock in target configuration. Currently in production.
Standard
model .... NiB $777 Ex $643 Gd $416
Thumbhole
stock model................. NiB $834 Ex $674 Gd $468
Standard
model .... NiB $383 Ex $280 Gd $177
Deluxe model .... NiB $409 Ex $332 Gd $229

LUIGI FRANCHI, S.P.A. — Brescia, Italy

CENTENNIAL AUTOMATIC RIFLE
Commemorates Franchi's 100th anniversary (1868-1968). Centennial seal engraved on receiver. Semiautomatic. Take-down. Caliber: .22 LR. 11-round magazine in buttstock. 21-inch bbl. Weight: 5.13 lbs. Sights: Open rear; gold bead front on ramp. Checkered walnut stock and forend. Deluxe model w/fully engraved receiver, premium grade wood. Made in 1968.
Standard model .... NiB $380 Ex $288 Gd $201
Engraved model............... NiB $446 Ex $354 Gd $246

Franchi Deluxe Centennial

Francotte Sidelock Double Rifle

Galil .223 AR Semiautomatic Rifle

Francotte Boxlock Mountain Rifle w/claw mounts and scope

FRANCOTTE RIFLES — Leige, Belgium
Imported by Armes de Chasse, Hertford, NC (Previously by Abercrombie & Fitch)

BOLT-ACTION RIFLE

Custom rifle built on Mauser style bolt action. Available in three action lengths. Calibers: .17 Bee to .505 Gibbs. Barrel length: 21- to 24.5-inches. Weight: 8 to 12 lbs. Stock dimensions, wood type and style to customer's specifications. Engraving, appointments and finish to customer's preference. Note: Deduct 25% for models w/o engraving.

Short action. . . . . NiB $9510 Ex $7460 Gd $4610
Standard action . . . . NiB $7935 Ex $6110 Gd $3710
Magnum Francotte action. . . . . NiB $13,750 Ex $10,800 Gd $7000

BOXLOCK MOUNTAIN RIFLE

Custom single-shot rifle built on Anson & Deeley style boxlock or Holland & Holland style sidelock action. 23- to 26-inch barrels chambered to customer's specification. Stock dimensions, wood type and style to customer's specifications. Engraving, appointments and finish to customer's preference. Note: Deduct 30% for models w/o engraving.

Boxlock . . . . NiB $13,900 Ex $11,700 Gd $7500
Sidelock . . . . NiB $22,438 Ex $17,950 Gd $12,206

DOUBLE RIFLE

Custom side-by-side rifle. Built on Francotte system boxlock or back-action sidelock. 23.5- to 26-inch barrels chambered to customer's specification. Stock dimensions, wood type and style to customer's specifications. Engraving, appointments and finish to customer's preference. Note: Deduct 30% for models w/o engraving.

Boxlock . . . . NiB $18,500 Ex $15,500 Gd $9500
Sidelock . . . . NiB $29,450 Ex $25,000 Gd $15,700

FRENCH MILITARY RIFLE — Saint Etienne, France

MODEL 1936

MAS MILITARY RIFLE . . . . NiB $170 Ex $129 Gd $78

Bolt-action. Caliber: 7.5mm MAS. Five-round box magazine. 22.5-inch bbl. Weight: 8.25 lbs. Sights: Adj. rear; blade front. Two-piece military-type stock. Bayonet carried in forend tube. Made from 1936-1940 by Manufacture Francaise d'Armes et de Cycles de St. Etienne (MAS).

GALIL RIFLES — Manufactured by Israel Military Industries, Israel, Imported by UZI America Inc., North Haven, CT (Previously by Action Arms, Springfield Armory and Magnum Research, Inc.)

AR SEMIAUTOMATIC RIFLE

Calibers: .308 Win. (7.62 NATO), .223 Rem. (5.56mm). 25-round (.308) or 35-round (.223) magazine. 16-inch (.223) or 18.5-inch (.308) bbl. w/flash suppressor. Weight: 9.5 lbs. Folding aperture rear sight, post front. Folding metal stock w/carrying handle. Imported 1982-94. Currently select fire models available to law enforcement only.

Model .223 AR. . . . . NiB $2338 Ex $1884 Gd $1112
Model .308 AR. . . . . NiB $2338 Ex $1884 Gd $1112
Model .223 ARM . . . . NiB $2786 Ex $2142 Gd $1540
Model .308 ARM . . . . NiB $2786 Ex $2142 Gd $1540

SPORTER SEMIAUTOMATIC RIFLE...... NiB $1072 Ex $971 Gd $636
Same general specifications as AR Model except w/hardwood thumbhole stock and 5-round magazine. Weight: 8.5 lbs. Imported from 1991-94.

GARCIA CORPORATION — Teaneck, New Jersey

BRONCO 22 SINGLE-SHOT RIFLE......... NiB $116 Ex $96 Gd $72
Swing-out action. Takedown. Caliber: .22 LR. Long, Short. 16.5-inch bbl. Weight: 3 lbs. Sights: Open rear-blade front. One-piece stock and receiver, crackle finish. Intro. 1967. Discontinued.

GERMAN MILITARY RIFLES — Mfd. by Ludwig Loewe & Co., Berlin, other contractors and by German arsenals and various plants under German government control

MODEL 24T (GEW. 24T) MAUSER RIFLE .... NiB $545 Ex $390 Gd $262
Same general specifications as Czech Model 24 (VZ24) Mauser Rifle w/minor modification and laminated wood stock. Weight: 9.25 lbs. Made in Czechoslovakia during German occupation; adopted 1940.

MODEL 29/40 (GEW. 29/40)
MAUSER RIFLE .... NiB $390 Ex $287 Gd $184
Same general specifications as Kar. 98K w/minor differences. Made in Poland during German occupation; adopted 1940.

MODEL 33/40 (GEW. 33/40)
MAUSER RIFLE .... NiB $1022 Ex $791 Gd $507
Same general specifications as Czech Model 33 (VZ33) Mauser Carbine w/minor modifications and laminated wood stock as found in war-time Model 98K carbines. Made in Czechoslovakia during German occupation; adopted 1940.

MODELS 41 AND 41-W (GEW. 41, GEW. 41-W)
SEMIAUTOMATIC MILITARY RIFLES
Gas-operated, muzzle cone system. Caliber: 7.9mm Mauser. Ten-round box magazine. 22.5-inch bbl. Weight: 10.25 lbs. Sights: Adj. leaf rear; blade front. Military-type stock w/semi-pistol grip, plastic handguard. Note: Model 41 lacks bolt release found on Model 41-W; otherwise, the models are the same. These early models were mfd. in Walther's Zella-Mehlis plant. Made c.1941-43.
Model 41.................. NiB $4293 Ex $3455 Gd $2384
Model 41-W .... NiB $3321 Ex $2678 Gd $1856

MODEL 43 (GEW. 43, KAR. 43)
SEMIAUTO MILITARY RIFLES......... NiB $1268 Ex $1022 Gd $709
Gas-operated, bbl. vented as in Russian Tokarev. Caliber: 7.9mm Mauser. 10-round detachable box magazine. 22- or 24-inch bbl. Weight: 9 lbs. Sights: Adj. rear; hooded front. Military-type stock w/semi-pistol-grip, wooden handguard. Note: These rifles are alike except for minor details, have characteristic late WWII mfg. short cuts: cast receiver and bolt cover, stamped steel parts, etc. Gew. 43 may have either 22- or 24-inch bbl. The former length was standardized in late 1944, when weapon designation was changed to "Kar. 43." Made from 1943-45.

MODEL 1888 (GEW. 88) MAUSER-
MANNLICHER SERVICE RIFLE .... NiB $385 Ex $231 Gd $179
Bolt-action w/straight bolt handle. Caliber: 7.9mm Mauser (8x57mm). Five round Mannlicher box magazine. 29-inch bbl. w/jacket. Weight: 8.5 lbs. Fixed front sight, adj. rear. Military-type full stock. Mfd. by Ludwig Loewe & Co., Haenel, Schilling and other contractors.

MODEL 1888 (KAR. 88) MAUSER-
MANNLICHER CARBINE......... NiB $278 Ex $227 Gd $205
Same general specifications as Gew. 88 except w/18-inch bbl., w/o jacket, flat turned-down bolt handle, weight: 6.75 lbs. Mfd. by Ludwig Loewe & Co., Haenel, Schilling and other contractors.

MODEL 1898 (GEW. 98)
MAUSER MILITARY RIFLE........ NiB $521 Ex $392 Gd $238
Bolt action with straight bolt handle. Caliber: 7.9mm Mauser (8x57mm). Five round box magazine. 29-inch stepped bbl. Weight: 9 lbs. Sights: Blade front; adj. rear. Military-type full stock w/rounded bottom pistol grip. Adopted 1898.

MODEL 1898A (KAR. 98A)
MAUSER CARBINE .... NiB $439 Ex $392 Gd $186
Same general specifications as Model 1898 (Gew.98) Rifle except has turned-down bolt handle, smaller receiver ring, light 23.5-inch-straight taper bbl., front sight guards, sling is attached to left side of stock, weight: 8 lbs. Note: Some of these carbines are marked "Kar. 98;" the true Kar. 98 is the earlier original M/98 carbine w/17-inch bbl. and is rarely encountered.

MODEL 1898B (KAR. 98B)
MAUSER CARBINE .... NiB $470 Ex $392 Gd $289
Same general specifications as Model 1898 (Gew.98) Rifle except has turned-down bolt handle and sling attached to left side of stock. This is post-WWI model.

MODEL 1898K (KAR. 98K)
MAUSER CARBINE .... NiB $470 Ex $392 Gd $289
Same general specifications as Model 1898 (Gew.98) Rifle except has turned-down bolt handle, 23.5-inch bbl., may have hooded front sight, sling attached to left side of stock, weighs about 8.5 lbs. Adopted in 1935, this was the standard German service rifle of WWII. Note: Late-war models had stamped sheet steel trigger guards and many of the Model 98K carbines made during WWII had laminated wood stocks These weigh .5 to .75 pound more than the previous Model 98K. Value shown is for earlier type.

MODEL VK 98
PEOPLE'S RIFLE ("VOLKSAEWEHR").. NiB $243 Ex $197 Gd $140
Kar. 98K-type action. Caliber: 7.9mm. Single-shot or repeater (latter w/rough hole-in-the-stock 5-round "magazine" or fitted w/10-round clip of German Model 43 semiauto rifle). 20.9-inch bbl. Weight: 7 lbs. Fixed V-notch rear sight dovetailed into front receiver ring; front blade welded to bbl. Crude, unfinished, half-length stock w/o buttplate. Last ditch weapon made in 1945 for issue to German civilians. Note: Of value only as a military arms collector's item, this hastily-made rifle should be regarded as unsafe to shoot.

GÉVARM RIFLE — Saint Etienne, France Manufactured by Gevelot

E-1 AUTOLOADING RIFLE .... NiB $194 Ex $169 Gd $118
Caliber: .22 LR. Eight-round clip magazine. 19.5-inch bbl. Sights: Open rear; post front. Pistol-grip stock and forearm of French walnut.

GOLDEN EAGLE RIFLES — Houston, Texas Mfd. by Nikko Firearms Ltd., Tochigi, Japan

MODEL 7000 GRADE I AFRICAN .... NiB $699 Ex $545 Gd $437
Same as Grade I Big Game except: Caliber: .375 H&H Mag. and .458 Win. Mag. Two-round magazine in .458, weight: 8.75 lbs. in .375 and 10.5 lbs. in .458, furnished w/sights. Imported from 1976-81.

Golden Eagle Model 7000

Carl Gustaf Model 2000

Carl Gustaf Deluxe

Carl Gustaf Grand Prix

Carl Gustaf Sporter

MODEL 7000 BIG GAME SERIES
Bolt action. Calibers: .22-250, .243 Win., .25-06, .270 Win., Weatherby Mag., 7mm Rem. Mag., .30-06, .300 Weatherby Mag., .300 Win. Mag., .338 Win. Mag. Magazine capacity: 4 rounds in .22-250, 3 rounds in other calibers. 24- or 26-inch bbl. (26-inch only in 338). Weight: 7 lbs., .22-250; 8.75, lbs., other calibers. Furnished w/o sights. Fancy American walnut stock, skip checkered, contrasting wood forend tip and grip cap w/gold eagle head, recoil pad. Imported 1976-81.
Model 7000 Grade I . . . . NiB $731 Ex $591 Gd $412
Model 7000 Grade II. . . . . NiB $796 Ex $643 Gd $447

GREIFELT & CO. — Suhl, Germany

SPORT MODEL 22 HORNET
BOLT-ACTION RIFLE . . . . NiB $2248 Ex $1811 Gd $1253
Caliber: .22 Hornet. Five round box magazine. 22-inch Krupp steel bbl. Weight: 6 lbs. Sights: Two-leaf rear; ramp front. Walnut stock, checkered pistol-grip and forearm. Made before WWII.

CARL GUSTAF RIFLES — Eskilstuna, Sweden Mfd. by Carl Gustaf Stads Gevärsfaktori

MODEL 2000 BOLT-ACTION RIFLE
Calibers: .243, 6.5x55, 7x64, .270, .308 Win., .30-06, 7mm Rem. Mag., .300 Win. Mag. Three round magazine. 24-inch bbl. 44 inches overall. Weight: 7.5 lbs. Receiver drilled and tapped. Hooded ramp front sight, open rear. Adj. trigger. Checkered European walnut stock w/Monte Carlo cheekpiece and Wundhammer palmswell grip. Imported 1991-95
Model 2000
w/o sights . . . . NiB $1460 Ex $1178 Gd $817
Model 2000 w/sights. . . . . NiB $1660 Ex $1337 Gd $925
Model 2000 LUXE . . . . NiB $1796 Ex $1595 Gd $977

DELUXE. . . . . NiB $777 Ex $628 Gd $439
Same specifications as Monte Carlo Standard. Calibers: 6.5x55, 308 Win., .30-06, 9.3x62. Four round magazine in 9.3x62. Jeweled bolt. Engraved floorplate and trigger guard. Deluxe French walnut stock w/rosewood forend tip. Imported 1970-77.

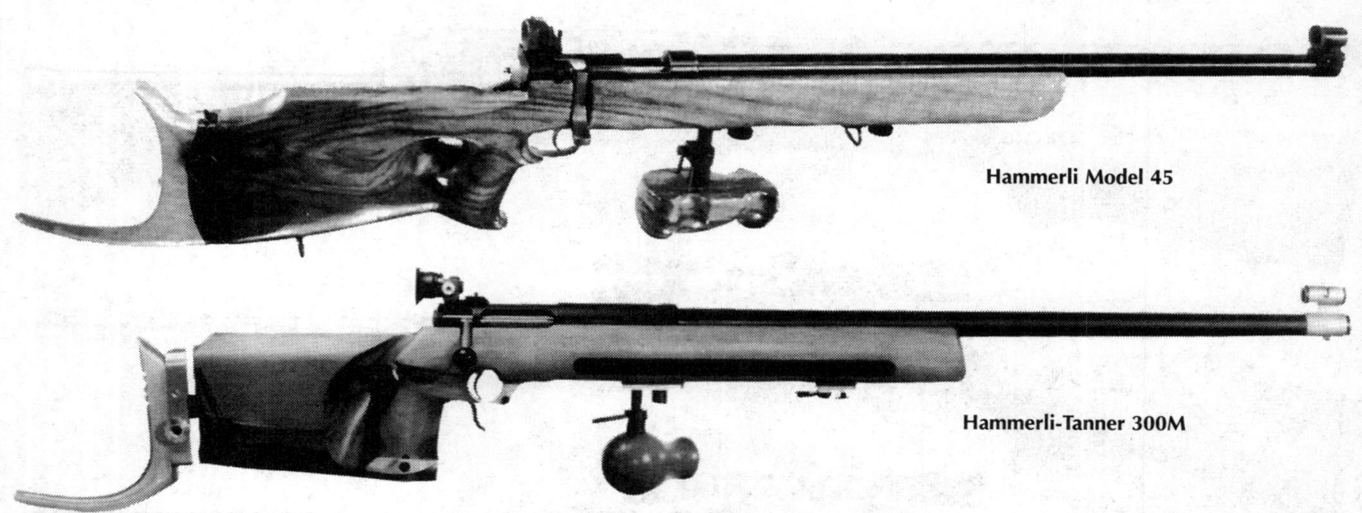

Hammerli Model 45

Hammerli-Tanner 300M

GRAND PRIX SINGLE-SHOT TARGET RIFLE . . . . NiB $643 Ex $540 Gd $370
Special bolt action with "world's shortest lock time." Single-stage trigger adjusts down to 18 oz. Caliber: .22 LR. 26.75-inch heavy bbl. w/adj. trim weight. Weight: 9.75 lbs. Furnished w/o sights. Target-type Monte Carlo stock of French walnut, adj. cork buttplate. Imported from 1970-77.

MONTE CARLO STANDARD BOLT-ACTION SPORTING RIFLE . . . . NiB $493 Ex $437 Gd $390
Carl Gustaf 1900 action. Calibers: 6.5x55, 7x64, .270 Win., 7mm Rem. Mag., .308 Win., .30-06, 9.3x62. Five round magazine, except 4-round in 9.3x62 and 3-round in 7mm Rem. Mag. 23.5-inch bbl. Weight: 7 lbs. Sights: Folding leaf rear; hooded ramp front. French walnut Monte Carlo stock w/cheekpiece, checkered forearm and pistol grip, sling swivels. Also available in left-hand model. Imported from 1970-77.

SPECIAL . . . . NiB $545 Ex $468 Gd $334
Also designated "Grade II" in U.S. and "Model 9000" in Canada. Same specifications as Monte Carlo Standard. Calibers: .22-250, .243 Win., .25-06, .270 Win., 7mm Rem. Mag., .308 Win., .30-06, .300 Win. Mag. Three round magazine in magnum calibers. Select wood stock w/rosewood forend tip. Left-hand model avail. Imported from 1970-77.

SPORTER . . . . NiB $642 Ex $519 Gd $363
Also designated "Varmint-Target" in U.S. Fast bolt action w/large Bakelite bolt knob. Trigger pull adjusts down to 18 oz. Calibers: .222 Rem., .22-250, .243 Win., 6.5x55. Five round magazine except 6-round in .222 Rem. 26.75-inch heavy bbl. Weight: 9.5 lbs. Furnished w/o sights. Target-type Monte Carlo stock of French walnut. Imported from 1970 to date.

STANDARD . . . . NiB $596 Ex $493 Gd $339
Same specifications as Monte Carlo Standard. Calibers: 6.5x55, 7x64, .270 Win., .308 Win., .30-06, 9.3x62. Classic-style stock w/o Monte Carlo. Imported from 1970-77.

TROFÉ . . . . NiB $856 Ex $656 Gd $460
Also designated "Grade III" in U.S. and "Model 8000" in Canada. Same specifications as Monte Carlo Standard. Calibers: .22-250, .25-06, 6.5x55, .270 Win., 7mm Rem. Mag., .308 Win., .30-06, .300 Win. Mag. Three round magazine in magnum calibers. Furnished w/o sights. Fancy wood stock w/rosewood forend tip, high-gloss lacquer finish. Imported from 1970-77.

C.G. HAENEL — Suhl, Germany

'88 MAUSER SPORTER . . . . NiB $571 Ex $447 Gd $339
Same general specifications as Haenel Mauser-Mannlicher except w/Mauser 5-round box magazine.

MAUSER-MANNLICHER BOLT-ACTION SPORTING RIFLE . . NiB $519 Ex $416 Gd $261
Mauser M/88-type action. Calibers: 7x57, 8x57, 9x57mm. Mannlicher clip-loading box magazine, 5-round. 22- or 24-inch half or full octagon bbl. w/raised matted rib. Double-set trigger. Weight: 7.5 lbs. Sights: Leaf-type open rear; ramp front. Sporting stock w/cheekpiece, checkered pistol-grip, raised side-panels, Schnabel tip, swivels.

HÄMMERLI AG JAGD-UND-SPORTWAFFEN-FABRIK —

Lenzburg, Switzerland, *Imported by Sigarms, Exetre, NH, (Previously by Hammerli USA; Mandall Shooting Supplies, Inc. & Beeman Precision Arms)*

MODEL 45 SMALLBORE BOLT-ACTION SINGLE-SHOT MATCH RIFLE . . . . NiB $715 Ex $601 Gd $395
Calibers: .22 LR. 22 Extra Long. 27.5-inch heavy bbl. Weight: 15.5 lbs. Sights: Micrometer peep rear; globe front. Free-rifle stock w/cheekpiece, full pistol-grip, thumbhole, beavertail forearm, palm-rest, Swiss-type buttplate, swivels. Made from 1945-57.

MODEL 54 SMALLBORE MATCH RIFLE . . . . NiB $725 Ex 601 Gd $370
Bolt-action, single-shot. Caliber: .22 LR. 27.5-inch heavy bbl. Weight: 15 lbs. Sights: Micrometer peep rear; globe front. Free-rifle stock w/cheekpiece, thumbhole, adj. hook buttplate, palm rest, swivel. Made from 1954-57.

MODEL 503 FREE RIFLE . . . . NiB $730 Ex $601 Gd $370
Bolt-action, single-shot. Caliber: .22 LR. 27.5-inch heavy bbl. Weight: 15 lbs. Sights: Micrometer peep rear; globe front. Free-rifle stock w/cheekpiece, thumbhole, adj. hook buttplate, palm rest, swivel. Made from 1957-62.

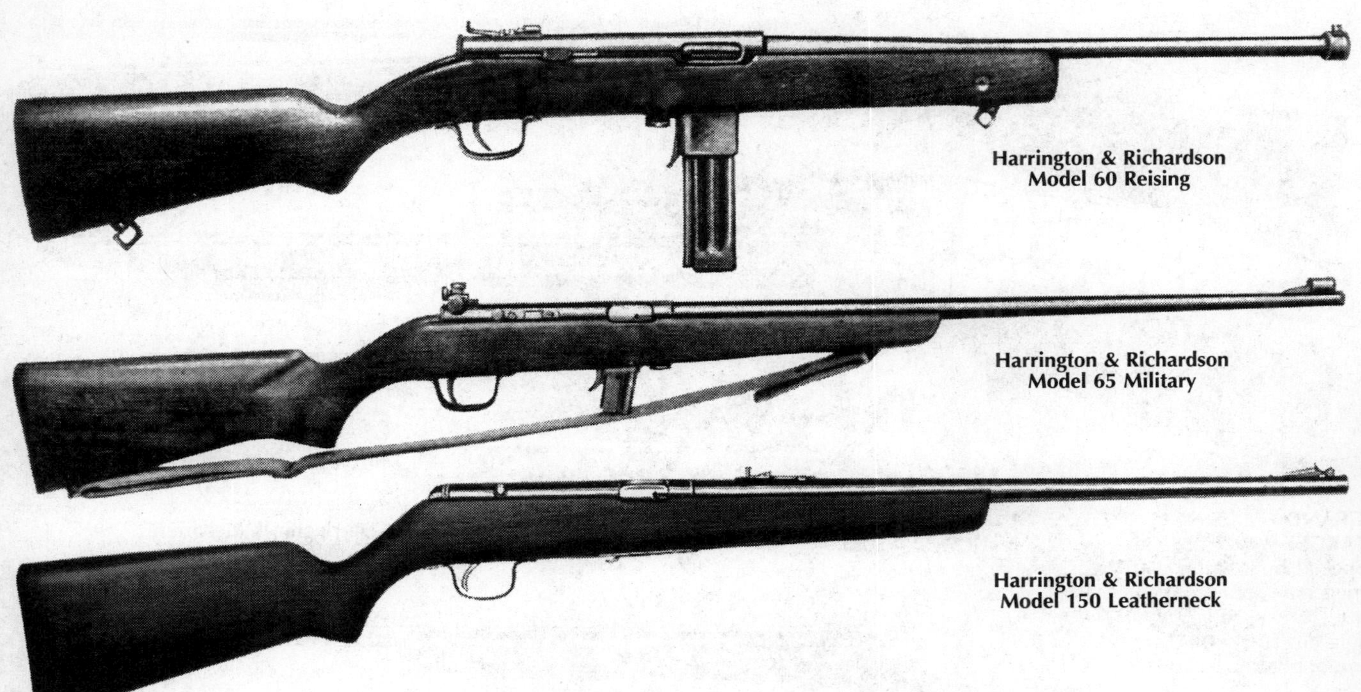

Harrington & Richardson Model 60 Reising

Harrington & Richardson Model 65 Military

Harrington & Richardson Model 150 Leatherneck

MODEL 506 SMALLBORE MATCH RIFLE .... NiB $730 Ex $601 Gd $395
Bolt-action, single-shot. Caliber: .22 LR. 26.75-inch heavy bbl. Weight: 16.5 lbs. Sights: Micrometer peep rear; globe front. Free-rifle stock w/cheekpiece, thumbhole adj. hook buttplate, palmrest, swivel. Made from 1963-66.

MODEL OLYMPIA 300 METER BOLT-ACTION SINGLE-SHOT FREE RIFLE................ NiB $943 Ex $814 Gd $505
Calibers: .30-06, .300 H&H Magnum for U.S.A.; ordinarily produced in 7.5mm, other calibers available on special order. 29.5-inch heavy bbl. Double-pull or double-set trigger. Sights: Micrometer peep rear, globe front. Free-rifle stock w/cheekpiece, full pistol grip, thumbhole, beavertail forend, palmrest, Swiss-type buttplate, swivels. Made from 1945-59.

TANNER 300 METER FREE RIFLE .... NiB $969 Ex $892 Gd $505
Bolt-action, single-shot. Caliber: 7.5mm standard, available in most popular centerfire calibers. 29.5-inch heavy bbl. Weight: 16.75 lbs. Sights: Micrometer peep rear; globe front. Free-rifle stock w/cheekpiece, thumbhole, adj. hook buttplate, palmrest, swivel. Intro. 1962. Disc. See Illustration previous page.

HARRINGTON & RICHARDSON, INC. — Gardner, Massachusetts (Now H&R 1871, INC., Gardner, Mass.)

Formerly Harrington & Richardson Arms Co. of Worcester, Mass. One of the oldest and most distinguished manufacturers of handguns, rifles and shotguns, H&R suspended operations on January 24, 1986. In 1987, New England Firearms was established as an independent company producing selected H&R models under the NEF logo. In 1991, H&R 1871, Inc. was formed from the residual of the parent company and that took over the New England Firearms facility. H&R 1871 produced firearms under both its logo and the NEF brand name until 1999, when the Marlin Firearms Company acquired the assets of H&R 1871.

MODEL 60 REISING SEMI-AUTOMATIC RIFLE............. NiB $539 Ex $513 Gd $256
Caliber: .45 Automatic. 12- and 20-round detachable box magazines. 18.25-inch bbl. Weight: 7.5 lbs. Sights: Open rear; blade front. Plain pistol-grip stock. Made from 1944-46.

MODEL 65 MILITARY AUTOLOADING RIFLE.......... NiB $333 Ex $271 Gd $163
Also called "General." Caliber: .22 LR. 10-round detachable box magazine. 23-inch heavy bbl. Weight: 9 lbs. Sights: Redfield 70 rear peep, blade front w/protecting "ears." Plain pistol-grip stock, "Garand" dimensions. Made from 1944-46. Note: This model was used as a training rifle by the U.S. Marine Corps.

MODEL 150 LEATHERNECK AUTOLOADER............. NiB $121 Ex $100 Gd $80
Caliber: .22 LR. only. Five round detachable box magazine. 22-inch bbl. Weight: 7.25 lbs. Sights: Open rear; blade front, on ramp. Plain pistol-grip stock. Made from 1949-53.

MODEL 151 .... NiB $175 Ex $109 Gd $93
Same as Model 150 except w/Redfield 70 rear peep sight.

MODEL 155 SINGLE-SHOT RIFLE................. NiB $206 Ex $155 Gd $103
Model 158 action. Calibers: .44 Rem. Mag., .45-70 Govt. 24- or 28-inch bbl. (latter in .44 only). Weight: 7 or 7.5 lbs. Sights: Folding leaf rear; blade front. Straight-grip stock, forearm w/bbl. band, brass cleaning rod. Made from 1972-82.

MODEL 157 SINGLE-SHOT RIFLE.................. NiB $206 Ex $124 Gd $93
Model 158 action. Calibers: .22 WMR, .22 Hornet, .30-30. 22-inch bbl. Weight: 6.25 lbs. Sights: Folding leaf rear; blade front. Pistol-grip stock, full-length forearm, swivels. Made from 1976-86.

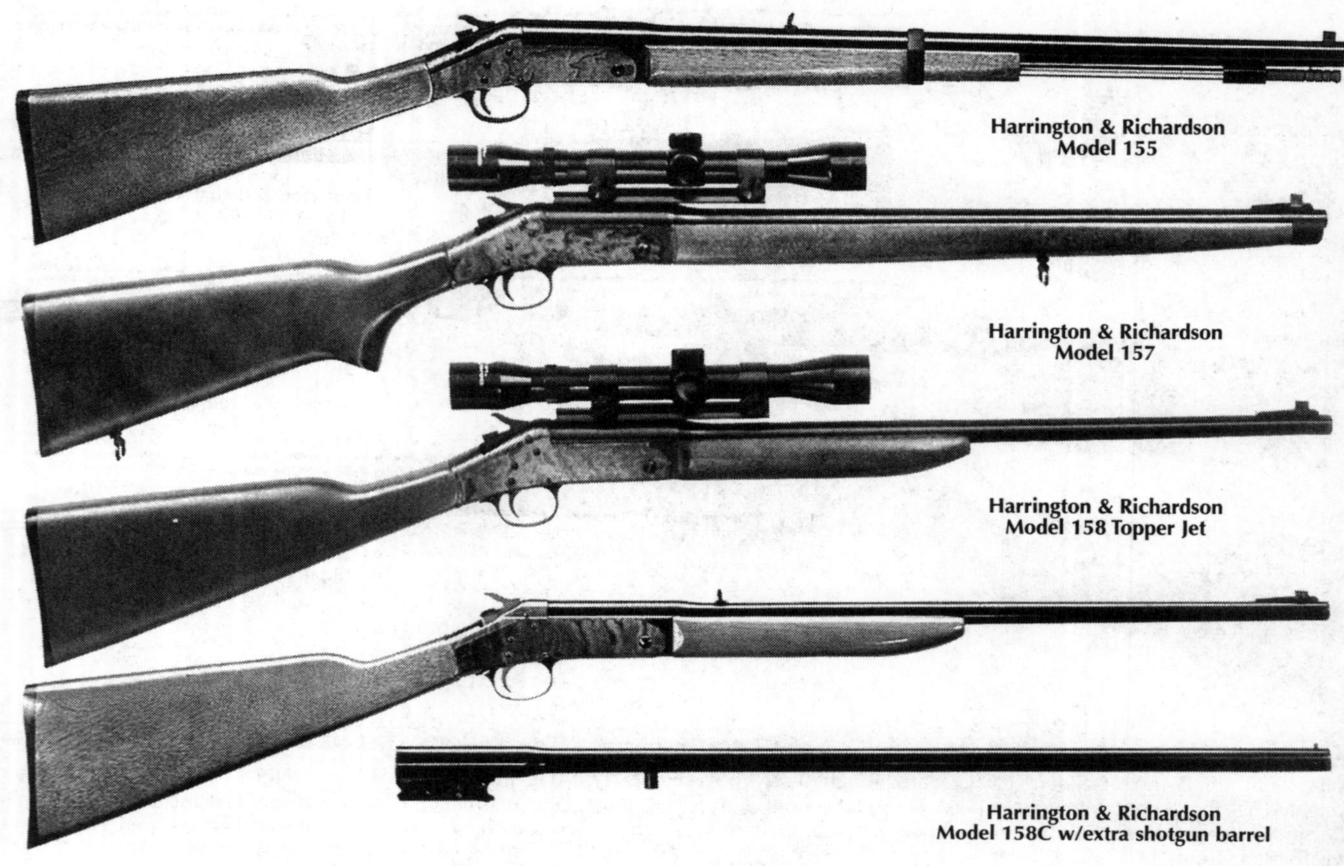

Harrington & Richardson
Model 155

Harrington & Richardson
Model 157

Harrington & Richardson
Model 158 Topper Jet

Harrington & Richardson
Model 158C w/extra shotgun barrel

MODEL 158 TOPPER JET SINGLE-SHOT COMBINATION RIFLE
Shotgun-type action w/visible hammer, side lever, auto ejector. Caliber: .22 Rem. Jet. 22-inch bbl. (interchanges with .30-30, .410 ga., 20 ga. bbls.). Weight: 5 lbs. Sights: Lyman folding adj. open rear; ramp front. Plain pistol-grip stock and forearm, recoil pad. Made from 1963-67.
Rifle only . . . . NiB $174 Ex $149 Gd $102
Interchangeable bbl.
.30-30, shotgun . . . . Add $50

MODEL 158C . . . . NiB $175 Ex $159 Gd $102
Same as Model 158 Topper Jet except calibers .22 Hornet, .30-30, .357 Mag., .357 Mag., .44 Mag. Straight-grip stock. Made from 1963-86.

MODEL 163 MUSTANG
SINGLE-SHOT RIFLE . . . . NiB $175 Ex $154 Gd $97
Same as Model 158 Topper except w/gold-plated hammer and trigger, straight-grip stock and contoured forearm. Made from 1964-67.

MODEL 165 LEATHERNECK AUTOLOADER . . . NiB $149 Ex $133 Gd $97
Caliber: .22 LR. 10-round detachable box magazine. 23-inch bbl. Weight: 7.5 lbs. Sights: Redfield 70 rear peep; blade front, on ramp. Plain pistol-grip stock, swivels, web sling. Made from 1945-61.

MODEL 171 . . . . NiB $385 Ex $334 Gd $221
Model 1873 Springfield Cavalry Carbine replica. Caliber: .45-70. 22-inch bbl. Weight: 7 lbs. Sights: Leaf rear; blade front. Plain walnut stock. Made from 1972-81.

MODEL 171 DELUXE . . . . NiB $439 Ex $387 Gd $282
Same as Model 171 except engraved action and different sights. Made from 1972-86. See illustration next page.

MODEL 172 . . . . NiB $730 Ex $680 Gd $525
Same as Model 171 Deluxe except silver-plated, w/fancy walnut stock, checkered, w/grip adapter; tang-mounted aperture sight. Made from 1972-86.

MODEL 173 . . . . NiB $755 Ex $655 Gd $430
Model 1873 Springfield Officer's Model replica, same as 100th Anniversary Commemorative except w/o plaque on stock. Made from 1972-86.

MODEL 174 . . . . NiB $439 Ex $387 Gd $284
Little Big Horn Commemorative Carbine. Same as Model 171 Deluxe except w/tang-mounted aperture sight, grip adapter. Made from 1972-84.

MODEL 178 . . . . NiB $439 Ex $387 Gd $284
Model 1873 Springfield Infantry Rifle replica. Caliber: .45-70. 32-inch bbl. Weight: 8 lbs. 10 oz. Sights: Leaf rear; blade front. Full-length stock w/bbl. bands, swivels, ramrod. Made from 1973-86.

MODEL 250 SPORTSTER BOLT-ACTION
REPEATING RIFLE . . . . NiB $119 Ex $98 Gd $72
Caliber: .22 LR. Five-round detachable box magazine. 23-inch bbl. Weight: 6.5 lbs. Sights: Open rear; blade front, on ramp. Plain pistol-grip stock. Made from 1948-61.

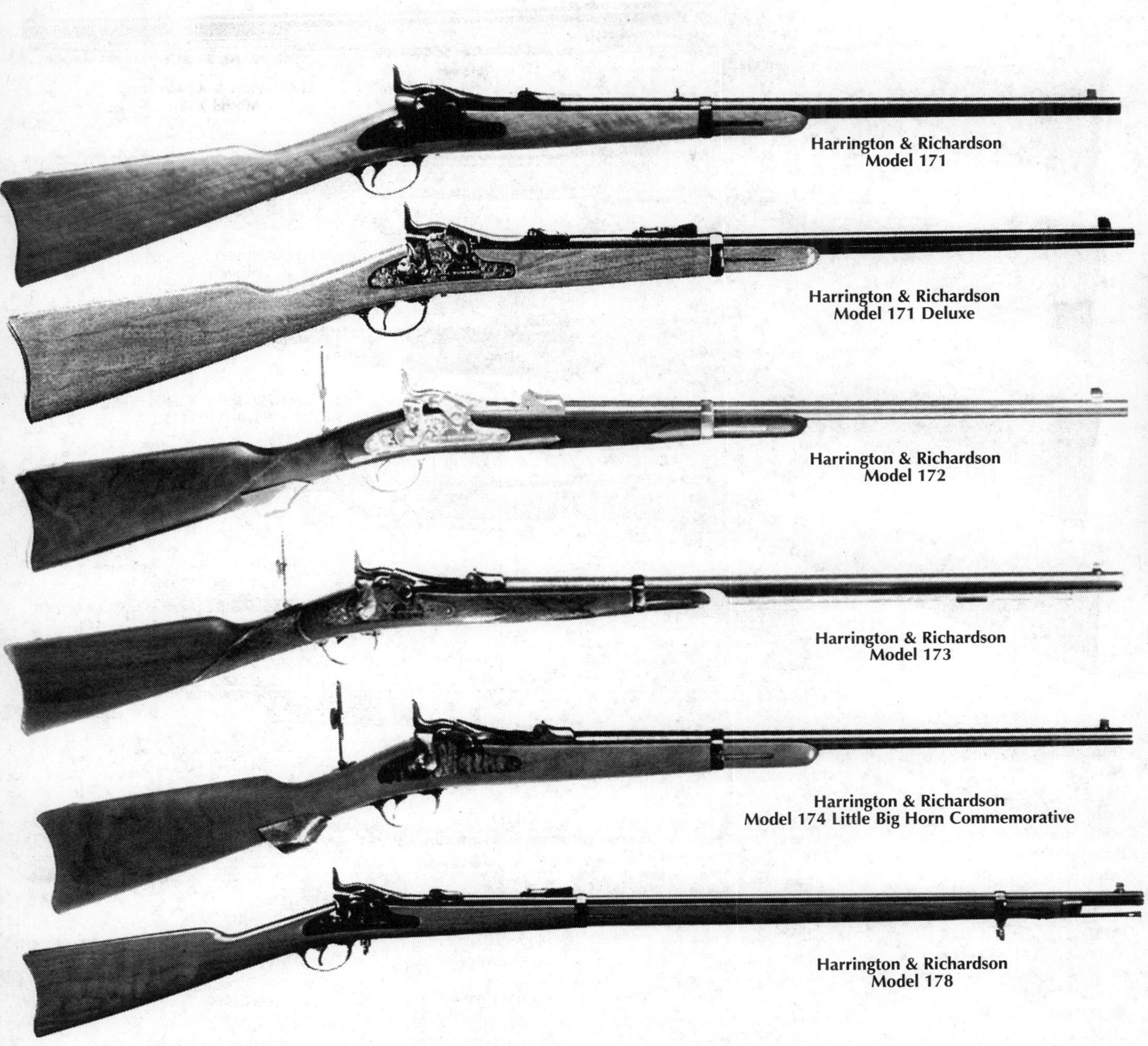

Harrington & Richardson
Model 171

Harrington & Richardson
Model 171 Deluxe

Harrington & Richardson
Model 172

Harrington & Richardson
Model 173

Harrington & Richardson
Model 174 Little Big Horn Commemorative

Harrington & Richardson
Model 178

MODEL 251 .... NiB $132 Ex $111 Gd $83
Same as Model 250 except w/Lyman No. 55H rear sight.

MODEL 265 "REG'LAR" BOLT-ACTION REPEATING RIFLE........ NiB $126 Ex $105 Gd $79
Caliber: .22 LR. 10-round detachable box magazine. 22-inch bbl. Weight: 6.5 lbs. Sights: Lyman No. 55 rear peep; blade front, on ramp. Plain pistol-grip stock. Made from 1946-49.

MODEL 300 ULTRA BOLT-ACTION RIFLE............ NiB $556 Ex $479 Gd $273
Mauser-type action. Calibers: .22-250, .243 Win., .270 Win., .30-06, .308 Win., 7mm Rem. Mag., .300 Win. Mag. Three round magazine in 7mm and .300 Mag. calibers, 5-round in others. 22- or 24-inch bbl. Sights: Open rear; ramp front. Checkered stock w/rollover cheekpiece and full pistol grip, contrasting wood forearm tip and pistol grip, rubber buttplate, sling swivels. Weight: 7.25 lbs. Made from 1965-82.

Harrington & Richardson Model 300

Harrington & Richardson Model 301 Carbine

Harrington & Richardson Model 317P

Harrington & Richardson Model 330

Harrington & Richardson Model 360 Ultra

Harrington & Richardson Model 370 Ultra Medalist

MODEL 301 CARBINE . . . . NiB $463 Ex $385 Gd $257
Same as Model 300 except w/18-inch bbl., Mannlicher-style stock, weighs 7.25 lbs.; not available in caliber .22-250. Made from 1967-82.

MODEL 308 AUTOMATIC RIFLE. . . NiB $443 Ex $360 Gd $253
Original designation of the Model 360 Ultra. Made from 1965-67.

MODEL 317 ULTRA WILDCAT BOLT-ACTION RIFLE. . . . . NiB $638 Ex $591 Gd $360
Sako short action. Calibers: .17 Rem. 17/.223 (handload), .222 Rem., .223 Rem. Six round magazine. 20-inch bbl. No sights, receiver dovetailed for scope mounts. Checkered stock w/cheekpiece and full pistol grip, contrasting wood forearm tip and pistol-grip cap, rubber buttplate. Weight: 5.25 lbs. Made from 1968-76.

MODEL 317P PRESENTATION GRADE . . . . NiB $757 Ex $628 Gd $448
Same as Model 317 except w/select grade fancy walnut stock w/basket weave carving on forearm and pistol-grip. Made from 1968-76.

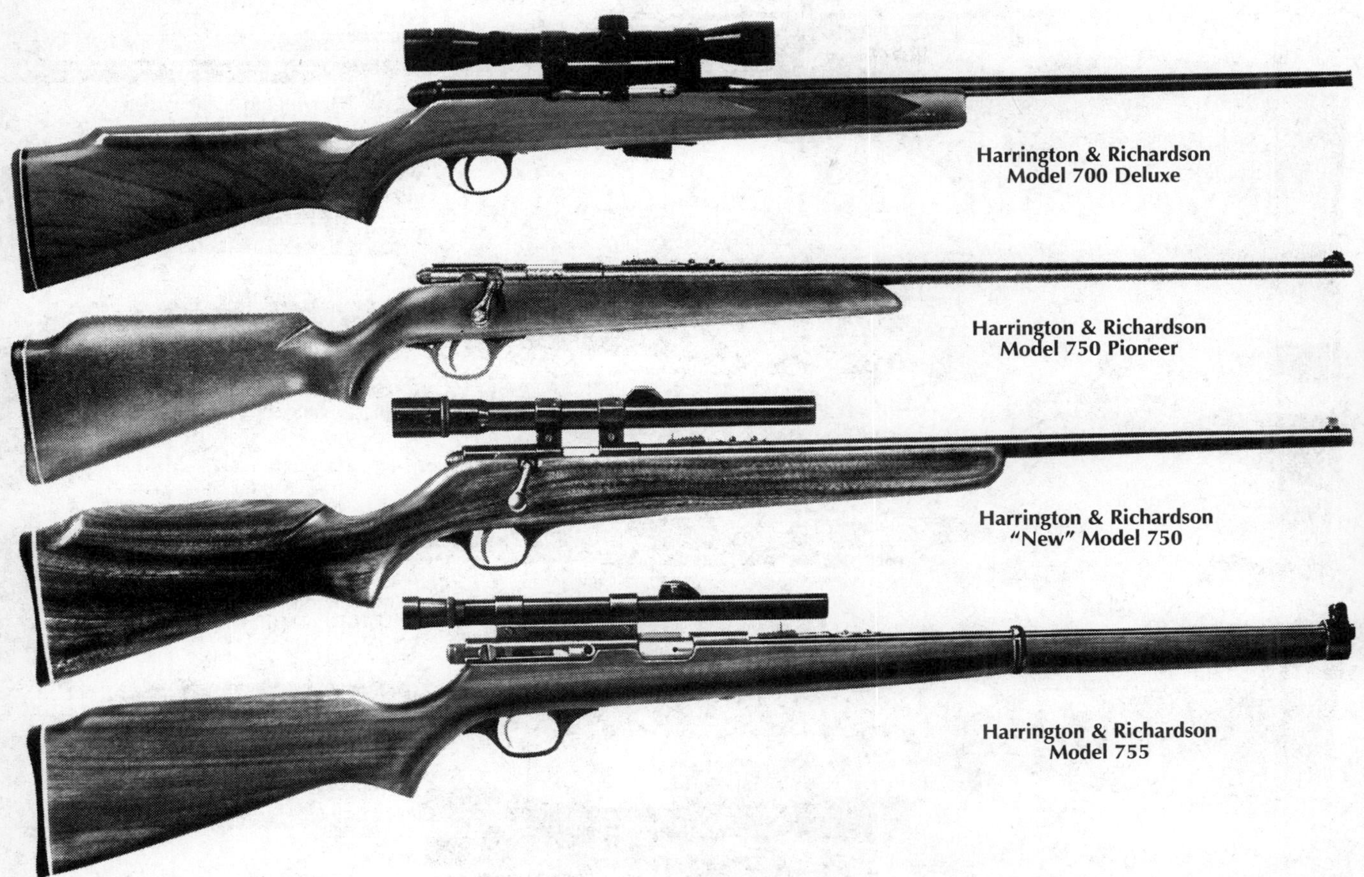

Harrington & Richardson Model 700 Deluxe

Harrington & Richardson Model 750 Pioneer

Harrington & Richardson "New" Model 750

Harrington & Richardson Model 755

MODEL 330 HUNTER'S RIFLE .... NiB $333 Ex $281 Gd $204
Similar to Model 300, but w/plainer stock. Calibers: .243 Win., .270 Win., .30-06, .308 Win., 7mm Rem. Mag., .300 Win. Mag. Weight: 7.13 lbs. Made from 1967-72.

MODEL 333 .... NiB $281 Ex $256 Gd $153
Plainer version of Model 300 w/uncheckered walnut-finished hardwood stock. Calibers: 7mm Rem. Mag. and .30-06. 22-inch bbl. Weight: 7.25 lbs. No sights. Made in 1974.

MODEL 340 .... NiB $410 Ex $333 Gd $225
Mauser-type action. Calibers: .243 Win., .308 Win., .270 Win., .30-06, 7x57. 22-inch bbl. Weight: 7.25 lbs. Hand-checkered American walnut stock. Made from 1982-84.

MODEL 360
ULTRA AUTOMATIC RIFLE .... NiB $442 Ex $360 Gd $257
Gas-operated semiautomatic. Calibers: .243 Win., .308 Win. Three round detachable box magazine. 22-inch bbl. Sights: Open rear; ramp front. Checkered stock w/rollover cheekpiece, full pistol grip, contrasting wood forearm tip and pistol-grip cap, rubber buttplate, sling swivels. Weight: 7.25 lbs. Made from 1967-78.

MODEL 361 .... NiB $498 Ex $421 Gd $292
Same as Model 360 except w/full rollover cheekpiece for right- or left-hand shooters. Made from 1970-73.

MODEL 365 ACE BOLT-ACTION
SINGLE-SHOT RIFLE .... NiB $134 Ex $129 Gd $82
Caliber: .22 LR. 22-inch bbl. Weight: 6.5 lbs. Sights: Lyman No. 55 rear peep, blade front, on ramp. Plain pistol-grip stock. Made from 1946-47.

MODEL 370 ULTRA MEDALIST ... NiB $524 Ex $498 Gd $301
Varmint and target rifle based on Model 300. Calibers: .22-250, .243 Win., 6mm Rem. Three round magazine. 24-inch varmint weight bbl. No sights. Target-style stock w/semibeavertail forearm. Weight: 9.5 lbs. Made from 1968-73.

MODEL 422 SLIDE-ACTION
REPEATER .... NiB $150 Ex $119 Gd $98
Caliber: .22 LR. Long, Short. Tubular magazine holds 21 Short, 17 Long, 15 LR. 24-inch bbl. Weight: 6 lbs. Sights: Open rear; ramp front. Plain pistol-grip stock grooved slide handle. Made from 1956-58.

MODEL 450 .... NiB $134 Ex $119 Gd $72
Same as Model 451 except w/o front and rear sights.

MODEL 451 MEDALIST
BOLT-ACTION TARGET RIFLE ..... NiB $203 Ex $177 Gd $103
Caliber: .22 LR. Five round detachable box magazine. 26-inch bbl. Weight: 10.5 lbs. Sights: Lyman No. 524F extension rear; Lyman No. 77 front, scope bases. Target stock w/full pistol-grip and forearm, swivels and sling. Made from 1948-61.

Harrington & Richardson Model 760

Harrington & Richardson Model 866

Harrington & Richardson Model 1873 — 100th Anniversary

Harrington & Richardson Model 5200 Sporter

Harrington & Richardson Ultra Varmint

MODEL 465 TARGETEER SPECIAL BOLT-ACTION REPEATER . . . . NiB $186 Ex $150 Gd $103
Caliber: .22 LR. 10-round detachable box magazine. 25-inch bbl. Weight: 9 lbs. Sights: Lyman No. 57 rear peep; blade front, on ramp. Plain pistol-grip stock, swivels, web sling strap. Made from 1946-47.

MODEL 700 AUTOLOADER . . . . NiB $318 Ex $282 Gd $154
Caliber: .22 WMR. Five-round magazine. 22-inch bbl. Weight: 6.5 lbs. Sights: Folding leaf rear; blade front, on ramp. Monte Carlo-style stock of American walnut. Made from 1977-86.

MODEL 700 DELUXE . . . . NiB $450 Ex $373 Gd $295
Same as Model 700 Standard except w/select custom polished and blued finish, select walnut stock, hand checkering, and no iron sights. Fitted w/H&R Model 432 4x scope. Made from 1980-86.

MODEL 750 PIONEER BOLT-ACTION SINGLE-SHOT RIFLE . . . . NiB $114 Ex $93 Gd $72
Caliber: .22 LR. Long, Short. 22- or 24-inch bbl. Weight: 5 lbs. Sights: Open rear; bead front. Plain pistol-grip stock. Made from 1954-81; redesigned 1982; disc. 1985.

MODEL 751 SINGLE-SHOT RIFLE . . . . NiB $95 Ex $75 Gd $54
Same as Model 750 except w/Mannlicher-style stock. Made in 1971.

MODEL 755 SAHARA SINGLE-SHOT RIFLE . . . . NiB $95 Ex $75 Gd $54
Blow-back action, automatic ejection. Caliber: .22 LR. Long, Short. 18-inch bbl. Weight: 4 lbs. Sights: Open rear; military-type front. Mannlicher-style stock. Made from 1963-71.

MODEL 760 SINGLE-SHOT . . . . NiB $114 Ex $93 Gd $72
Same as Model 755 except w/conventional sporter stock. Made from 1965-70.

MODEL 765 PIONEER BOLT-ACTION SINGLE-SHOT RIFLE .... NiB $90 Ex $75 Gd $54
Caliber: .22 LR. Long, Short. 24-inch bbl. Weight: 5 lbs. Sights: Open rear; hooded bead front. Plain pistol-grip stock. Made from 1948-54.

MODEL 800 LYNX AUTOLOADING RIFLE .... NiB $159 Ex $123 Gd $87
Caliber: .22 LR. Five or 10-round clip magazine. 22-inch bbl. Open sights. Weight: 6 lbs. Plain pistol-grip stock. Made from 1958-60.

MODEL 852 FIELDSMAN BOLT-ACTION REPEATER .... NiB $133 Ex $77 Gd $82
Caliber: .22 LR. Long, Short. Tubular magazine holds 21 Short, 17 Long, 15 LR. 24-inch bbl. Weight: 5.5 lbs. Sights: Open rear; bead front. Plain pistol-grip stock. Made from 1952-53.

MODEL 865 PLAINSMAN BOLT-ACTION REPEATER .... NiB $123 Ex $102 Gd $71
Caliber .22 LR. Long, Short. Five round detachable box magazine. 22- or 24-inch bbl. Weight: 5.25 lbs. Sights: Open rear, bead front. Plain pistol-grip stock. Made from 1949-86.

MODEL 866 BOLT-ACTION REPEATER .... NiB $123 Ex $102 Gd $71
Same as Model 865, except w/Mannlicher-style stock. Made 1971.

MODEL 1873 100TH ANNIVERSARY (1871-1971) COMMEMORATIVE OFFICER'S SPRINGFIELD REPLICA ... NiB $807 Ex $601 Gd $421
Model 1873 "trap door" single-shot action. Engraved breech block, receiver, hammer, lock, band and buttplate. Caliber: .45-70. 26-inch bbl. Sights: Peep rear; blade front. Checkered walnut stock w/anniversary plaque. Ramrod. Weight: 8 lbs. 10,000 made in 1971.

MODEL 5200 SPORTER .... NiB $648 Ex $550 Gd $352
Turn-bolt repeater. Caliber: .22 LR. 24-inch bbl. Classic-style American walnut stock. Adj. trigger. Sights: Peep receiver; hooded ramp front. Weight: 6.5 lbs. Disc. 1983.

MODEL 5200 MATCH RIFLE...... NiB $447 Ex $442 Gd $344
Same action as 5200 Sporter. Caliber: .22 LR. 28-inch target weight bbl. Target stock of American walnut. Weight: 11 lbs. Made from 1982-86.

CUSTER MEMORIAL ISSUE
Limited Edition Model 1873 Springfield Carbine replica, richly engraved and inlaid w/gold, fancy walnut stock, in mahogany display case. Made in 1973.
Officers' Model
Limited to 25 pieces .... NiB $5974 Ex $4815 Gd $3332
Enlisted Men's model, limited to 243 pieces............. NiB $3399 Ex $2755 Gd $1931

TARGETEER JR. BOLT-ACTION RIFLE .... NiB $177 Ex $151 Gd $115
Caliber: .22 LR. Five-round detachable box magazine. 20-inch bbl. Weight: 7 lbs. Sights: Redfield 70 rear peep; Lyman No. 17A front. Target stock, junior-size w/pistol grip, swivels and sling. Made from 1948-51.

ULTRA SINGLE-SHOT RIFLE
Side-lever single-shot. Calibers: .22-250 Rem., .223 Rem., .25-06 Rem., .308 Win. 22- to 26-inch bbl. Weight: 7-8 lbs. Curly maple or laminated stock. Barrel-mounted scope mount, no sights. Made from 1993 to date.
Ultra Hunter (.25-06, .308)....... NiB $219 Ex $152 Gd $126
Ultra Varmint................. NiB $255 Ex $203 Gd $152

HARRIS GUNWORKS — Phoenix, Arizona (Formerly McMillan Gun Works)

Sportintg line of firearms discontinued, now specializes in sniper and tactical arms.

SIGNATURE ALASKAN BOLT-ACTION RIFLE......... NiB $3622 Ex $2901 Gd $1974
Same general specifications as Classic Sporter except w/match-grade bbl. Rings and mounts. Sights: Single-leaf rear, bbl. band front. Checkered Monte Carlo stock w/palmswell and solid recoil pad. Nickel finish. Calibers: LA (long): .270 Win., .280 Rem., .30-06, MA (Magnum): 7mm Rem. Mag., .300 Win. Mag., .300 Wby. Mag., .340 Wby. Mag., .358 Win., .375 H&H Mag. Made from 1990. Disc.

SIGNATURE CLASSIC SPORTER
The prototype for Harris' Signature Series, this bolt-action rifle is available in three lengths: SA (standard/ short) — from .22-250 to .350 Rem Mag.; LA (long) — .25-06 to .30-06; MA (Magnum) — 7mm STW to .416 Rem. Mag. Four-round or 3-round (Magnum) magazine. Bbl. lengths: 22, 24 or 26 inches. Weight: 7 lbs. (short action). No sights; rings and bases provided. Harris fiberglass stock, Fibergrain or wood stock optional. Stainless, matte black or black chrome sulfide finish. Available in right- and left-hand models. Made from 1987. Disc. Has pre-64 Model 70-style action for dangerous game.
Classic Sporter Standard ...... NiB $2572 Ex $2263 Gd $1336
Classic Sporter Stainless ...... NiB $2768 Ex $2285 Gd $1342
Talon Sporter............... NiB $2778 Ex $2057 Gd $1439

RIFLES

SIGNATURE MOUNTAIN RIFLE...... NiB $3158 Ex $2798 Gd $1515
Same general specifications as Harris (McMillan) Classic Sporter except w/titanium action and graphite-reinforced fiberglass stock. Weight: 5.5 lbs. Calibers: .270 Win., .280 Rem., .30-06, 7mm Mag., .300 Win. Mag. Other calibers on special order. Made from 1995. Disc.

SIGNATURE SUPER VARMINTER ..... NiB $2584 Ex $2172 Gd $1348
Same general specifications as Harris (McMillan) Classic Sporter except w/heavy, contoured bbl., adj. trigger, fiberglass stock and field bipod. Calibers: .223, .22-250, .220 Swift, .244 Win., 6mm Rem., .25-06, 7mm-08, .308 Win., .350 Win. Mag. Made from 1995. Disc.

TALON SAFARI RIFLE
Same general specifications as Harris (McMillan) Classic Sporter except w/Harris Safari-grade action, match-grade bbl. and "Safari" fiberglass stock. Calibers: Magnum — .300 H&H Mag., .300 Win Mag., .300 Wby. Mag., .338 Win. Mag., .340 Wby. Mag., .375 H&H Mag., .404 Jeffrey, .416 Rem. Mag., .458 Win., Super Mag. — .300 Phoenix, .338 Lapua, .378 Wby. Mag., .416 Rigby, .416 Wby. Mag., .460 Wby. Mag. Matte black finish. Other calibers available on special order, and at a premium, but the "used gun" value remains the same. Imported 1989. Disc.
Safari Magnum .... NiB $3879 Ex $3045 Gd $2025
Safari Super Magnum .... NiB $4275 Ex $3514 Gd $2527

HECKLER & KOCH, GMBH — Oberndorf/Neckar, Germany Imported by Heckler & Koch, Inc., Sterling, VA

MODEL 911 SEMIAUTO RIFLE........ NiB $1859 Ex $1653 Gd $932
Caliber: .308 (7.62mm). Five-round magazine. 19.7-inch bull bbl. 42.4 inches overall. Sights: Hooded post front; adj. aperture rear. Weight: 11 lbs. Kevlar-reinforced fiberglass thumbhole-stock. Imported 1989-93.

MODEL HK91 A-2 SEMIAUTO .... NiB $2328 Ex $2019 Gd $1288

Heckler & Koch Model HK91 A-2

Heckler & Koch Model HK91 A-3

Heckler & Koch Model HK93 A-2

Heckler & Koch Model HK940 Carbine

MODEL HK91 A-3. . . . . NiB $2640 Ex $2382 Gd $1507
Same as Model HK91 A-2 except w/retractable metal buttstock, weighs 10.56 lbs. Disc. 1991.

MODEL HK93 SEMIAUTOMATIC
Delayed roller-locked blow-back action. Caliber: 5.56mm x 45 (.223 Rem.). 5- or 20-round magazine. 16.13-inch bbl. Weight: W/o magazine, 7.6 lbs. Sights: "V" and aperture rear; post front. Plastic buttstock and forearm. Disc. 1991.
HK93 A-2 . . . . NiB $2439 Ex $2276 Gd $1087
HK93 A-3 w/retractable stock. . . . . . . NiB $2482 Ex $2225 Gd $1967

MODEL HK94 SEMIAUTOMATIC CARBINE
Caliber: 9mm Para. 15-round magazine. 16-inch bbl. Weight: 6.75 lbs. Aperture rear sight, front post. Plastic buttstock and forend or retractable metal stock. Imported from 1983-91.
HK94-A2 w/standard stock. . . . . NiB $3175 Ex $3113 Gd $2660
HK94-A3 w/retractable stock . . . . NiB $4751 Ex $3819 Gd $2624

MODEL HK300 SEMIAUTOMATIC . . . . NiB $746 Ex $689 Gd $447
Caliber: .22 WMR. Five- or 15-round box magazine. 19.7-inch bbl. w/polygonal rifling. Weight: 5.75 lbs. Sights: V-notch rear; ramp front. High-luster polishing and bluing. European walnut stock w/cheekpiece, checkered forearm and pistol-grip. Disc. 1989.

MODEL HK630 SEMIAUTOMATIC. . . . . NiB $1260 Ex $1028 Gd $642
Caliber: .223 Rem. Four- or 10-round magazine. 24-inch bbl. Overall length: 42 inches. Weight: 7 lbs. Sights: Open rear; ramp front. European walnut stock w/Monte Carlo cheekpiece. Imported from 1983-90.

Heckler & Koch Model HK PSG-1

Heckler & Koch Model SL-8

Heckler & Koch Model USC Carbine

MODEL HK770 SEMIAUTOMATIC .... NiB $1945 Ex $1610 Gd $889
Caliber: .308 Win. Three- or 10-round magazine. Overall length: 44.5 inches. Weight: 8 lbs. Sights: Open rear; ramp front. European walnut stock w/Monte Carlo cheekpiece. Imported from 1983-90.

MODEL HK940 SEMIAUTOMATIC ...... NiB $2073 Ex $1867 Gd $1018
Caliber: .30-06 Springfield. Three- or 10-round magazine. Overall length: 47 inches. Weight: 8.8 lbs. Sights: Open rear; ramp front. European walnut stock w/Monte Carlo cheekpiece. Imported from 1983-90.

MODEL HK PSG-1
MARKSMAN'S RIFLE .... NiB $10,672 Ex $8547 Gd $5828
Caliber: .308 (7.62mm). Five- and 20-round magazine. 25.6-inch bbl. 47.5 inches overall. Hensoldt 6x42 telescopic sight. Weight: 17.8 lbs. Matte black composite stock w/pistol-grip. Imported from 1988 to date.

MODEL SL8-1 RIFLE .... NiB $1702 Ex $1341 Gd $929
Caliber: .223 Win. Ten-round magazine. 20.80- inch bbl. 38.58 inches overall. Weight: 8.6 lbs. Gas-operated, short-stroke piston w/rotary locking bolt. Rear adjustable sight w/ambidextrous safety selector lever. Polymer receiver w/adjustable buttstock. Introduced in 1999.

MODEL SR-9
SEMIAUTO RIFLE .... NiB $1858 Ex $1704 Gd $983
Caliber: .308 (7.62mm). Five round magazine. 19.7-inch bull bbl. 42.4 inches overall. Hooded post front sight; adj. aperture rear. Weight: 11 lbs. Kevlar-reinforced fiberglass thumbhole-stock w/wood grain finish. Imported from 1989-93.

MODEL SR-9
TARGET RIFLE.................... NiB $2644 Ex $2077 Gd $1408
Same general specifications as standard SR-9 except w/ PSG-1 trigger group and adj. buttstock. Imported from 1992-94.

MODEL USC
CARBINE RIFLE.................... NiB $1183 Ex $1075 Gd $719
Caliber: 45 ACP. 10-round magazine. 16- inch bbl., 35.43 inches overall. Weight: 6 lbs. Blow-back operating system. Polymer receiver w/integral grips. Rear adjustable sight w/ambidextrous safety selector lever. Introduced in 1999.

HERCULES RIFLES

See listings under "W" for Montgomery Ward.

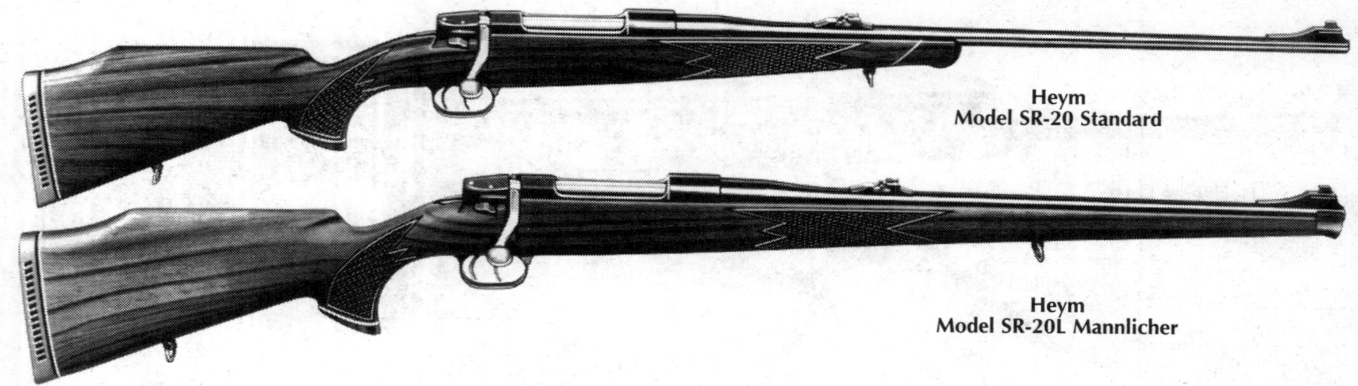

Heym
Model SR-20 Standard

Heym
Model SR-20L Mannlicher

HEROLD RIFLE — Suhl,Germany Made by Franz Jaeger & Company

BOLT-ACTION REPEATING
SPORTING RIFLE. . . . . NiB $1333 Ex $1071 Gd $690
"Herold-Repetierbüchse." Miniature Mauser-type action w/unique 5-round box magazine on hinged floorplate. Double-set triggers. Caliber: .22 Hornet. 24-inch bbl. Sights: Leaf rear; ramp front. Weight: 7.75 lbs. Fancy checkered stock. Made before WWII. Note: These rifles were imported by Charles Daly and A.F. Stoeger Inc. of New York City and sold under their names.

HEYM RIFLES AMERICA, INC. — Mfd. By Heym, GmbH & Co JAGWAFFEN KD., Gleichamberg, Germany, *(Previously imported by Heym America, Inc.; Heckler & Koch; JagerSport, Ltd.)*

MODEL 55B O/U DOUBLE RIFLE
Kersten boxlock action w/double cross bolt and cocking indicators. Calibers: .308 Win., .30-06, .375 H&H, .458 Win. Mag., .470 N.E. 25-inch bbl. 42 inches overall. Weight: 8.25 lbs. Sights: fixed V-type rear; front ramp w/silver bead. Engraved receiver w/optional sidelocks, interchangeable bbls. and claw mounts. Checkered European walnut stock. Imported from Germany.
Model 55 (boxlock) . . . . NiB $7660 Ex $6260 Gd $5660
Model 55 (sidelock. . . . . NiB $12,038 Ex $9650 Gd $6594
W\Extra rifle bbls., add $5500
W/Extra shotgun bbls., add $2800

MODEL 88B DOUBLE RIFLE
Modified Anson & Deeley boxlock action w/standing gears, double underlocking lugs and Greener extension w/crossbolt. Calibers: 8x57 JRS, 9.3x74R, .30-06, .375 H&H, .458 Win. Mag., .470 Nitro Express, .500 Nitro Express. Other calibers available on special order. Weight: 8 to 10 lbs. Top tang safety and cocking indicators. Double triggers w/front set. Fixed or 3-leaf express rear sight, front ramp w/silver bead. Engraved receiver w/optional sidelocks. Checkered French walnut stock. Imported from Germany.
Model 88B Boxlock . . . . NiB $11,069 Ex $8875 Gd $6067
Model 88B/SS Sidelock. . . . . NiB $13,538 Ex $10,850 Gd $7410
Model 88B Safari (Magnum). . . . . . NiB $15,038 Ex $12,050 Gd $8226

EXPRESS BOLT-ACTION RIFLE
Same general specifications as Model SR-20 Safari except w/modified magnum Mauser action. Checkered AAA-grade European walnut stock w/cheekpiece, solid rubber recoil pad, rosewood forend tip and grip cap. Calibers: .338 Lapua Magnum, .375 H&H, .378 Wby. Mag., .416 Rigby .450 Ackley, .460 Wby. Mag., .500 A-Square, .500 Nitro Express, .600 Nitro Express. Other calibers available on special order, but no change in used gun value. Imported from Germany 1989-95.
Standard Express Magnum . . . . NiB $5414 Ex $4376 Gd $3048
600 Nitro Express. . . . . NiB $5726 Ex $5026 Gd $3026
Left-hand models, add $600

SR-20 BOLT-ACTION RIFLE
Calibers: .243 Win., .270 Win., .308 Win., .30-06, 7mm Rem. Mag., .300 Win. Mag., .375 H&H. Five round (standard) or 3-round (Magnum) magazine. Bbl. length: 20.5-inch (SR-20L); 24-inch (SR-20N); 26-inch (SR-20G). Weight: 7.75 lbs. Adj. rear sight, blade front. Checkered French walnut stock in Monte Carlo style (N&G Series) or full Mannlicher (L Series). Imported from Germany. Disc. 1992.
SR-20L . . . . NiB $2038 Ex $1626 Gd $982
SR-20N . . . . NiB $2208 Ex $1801 Gd $1146
SR-20G . . . . NiB $2746 Ex $2179 Gd $1484

SR-20 CLASSIC BOLT-ACTION RIFLES
Same as SR-20 except w/.22-250 and .338 Win. Mag. plus metric calibers on request. 24-inch (standard) or 25-inch (Magnum) bbl. Checkered French walnut stock. Left-hand models. Imported from Germany since 1985; Sporter version 1989-93.
Classic (Standard) . . . . NiB $2378 Ex $1897 Gd $1345
Classic (Magnum) . . . . NiB $2568 Ex $2089 Gd $1375
Left-hand models, add $300
Classic Sporter (Std.
w/22-inch bbl.) . . . . NiB $2482 Ex $2121 Gd $1430
Classic Sporter (Mag.
w/24-inch bbl.) . . . . NiB $2722 Ex $2212 Gd $1559

SR-20 ALPINE, SAFARI AND TROPHY SERIES
Same general specifications as Model SR-20 Classic Sporter except Alpine Series w/20-inch bbl., Mannlicher stock, chambered in standard calibers only; Safari Series w/24-inch bbl., 3-leaf express sights and magnum action in calibers .375 H & H, .404 Jeffrey, .425 Express, .458 Win. Mag.; Trophy Series w/Krupp-Special tapered octagon bbl. w/quarter rib and open sights, standard and Magnum calibers. Imported from Germany from 1989-93.
Alpine Series . . . . NiB $2482 Ex $2021 Gd $1430
Safari Series. . . . . NiB $2529 Ex $2058 Gd $1455
Trophy Series (Stand. calibers) . . . . . . NiB $3193 Ex $2590 Gd $1819
Trophy Series
(Magnum calibers). . . . . NiB $3463 Ex $2806 Gd $1966

J.C. HIGGINS RIFLES

See Sears, Roebuck & Company.

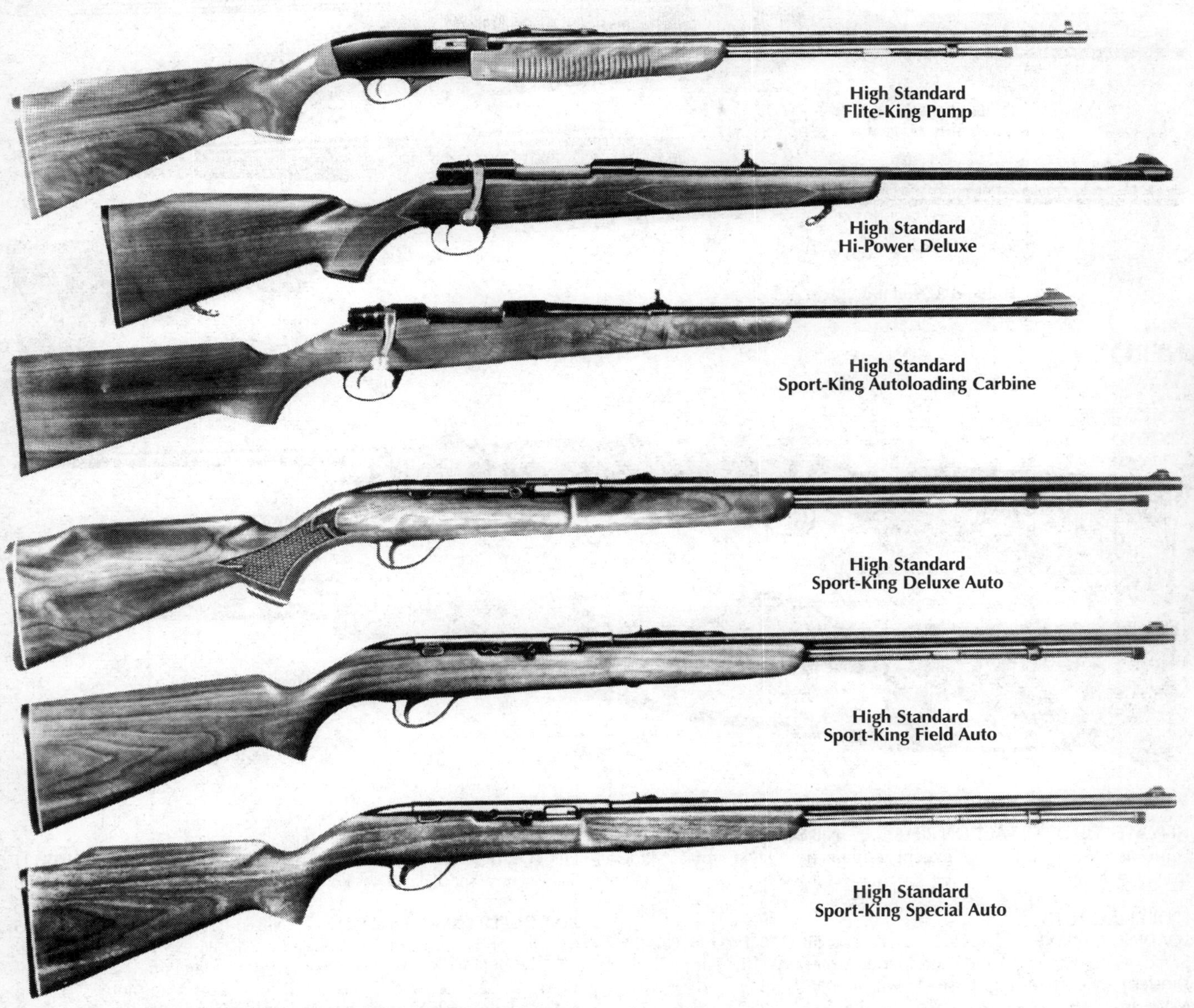

High Standard
Flite-King Pump

High Standard
Hi-Power Deluxe

High Standard
Sport-King Autoloading Carbine

High Standard
Sport-King Deluxe Auto

High Standard
Sport-King Field Auto

High Standard
Sport-King Special Auto

HI-POINT FIREARMS — Dayton, Ohio

MODEL 995 CARBINE
Semiautomatic recoil-operated carbine. Calibers: 9mm Parabellum or 40 S&W. 10-round magazine. 16.5-inch bbl. 31.5 inches overall. Protected post front sight, aperture rear w/integral scope mount. Matte blue, chrome or Parkerized finish. Checkered polymer grip/frame. Made from 1996 to date.
Model 995, 9mm (blue or Parkerized) .... NiB $182 Ex $150 Gd $109
Model 995, .40 S&W (blue or Parkerized) ... NiB $215 Ex $175 Gd $126
W/laser sights, add $35
W/chrome finish, add $15

HIGH STANDARD SPORTING FIREARMS — East Hartford, Connecticut, (Formerly High Standard Mfg. Co., Hamden, CT)

A long-standing producer of sporting arms, High Standard discontinued its operations in 1984.

FLITE-KING PUMP RIFLE .... NiB $175 Ex $124 Gd $83
Hammerless slide-action. Caliber: .22 LR. .22 Long, .22 Short. Tubular mag. holds 17 LR, 19 Long, or 24 Short. 24-inch bbl. Weight: 5.5 lbs. Sights: Partridge rear; bead front. Monte Carlo stock w/pistol grip, serrated semibeavertail forearm. Made from 1962-75.

HI-POWER DELUXE RIFLE .... NiB $564 Ex $383 Gd $228
Mauser-type bolt action, sliding safety. Calibers: .270, .30-06. Four round magazine. 22-inch bbl. Weight: 7 lbs. Sights: Folding open rear; ramp front. Walnut stock w/checkered pistol-grip and forearm, Monte Carlo comb, QD swivels. Made from 1962-66.

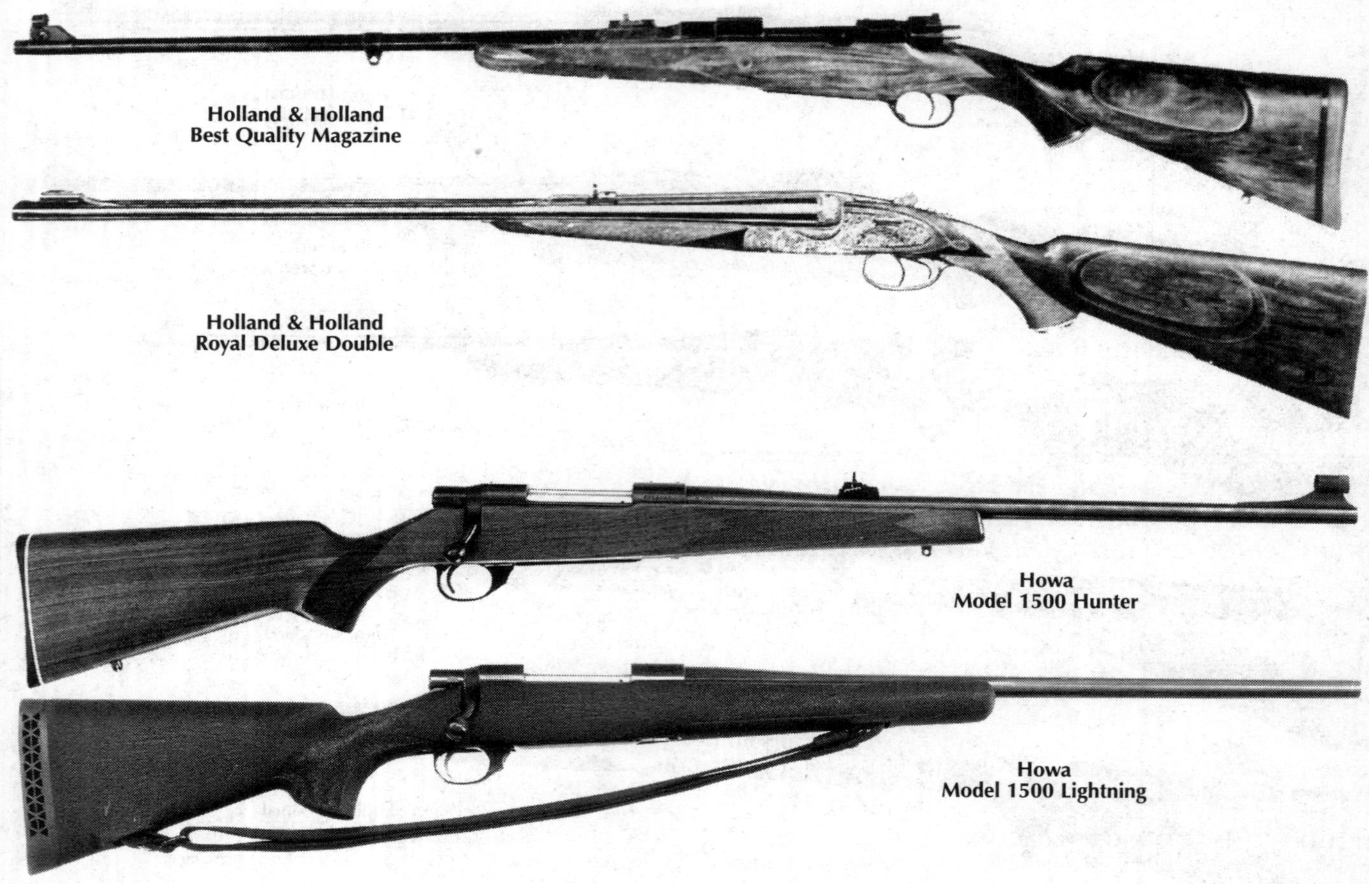
Holland & Holland
Best Quality Magazine

Holland & Holland
Royal Deluxe Double

Howa
Model 1500 Hunter

Howa
Model 1500 Lightning

HI-POWER FIELD BOLT-ACTION RIFLE...... NiB $490 Ex $336 Gd $207
Same as Hi-Power Deluxe except w/plain field style stock. Made from 1962-66.

SPORT-KING AUTO-LOADING CARBINE...................... NiB $170 Ex $109 Gd $88
Same as Sport-King Field Autoloader except w/18.25-inch bbl., Western-style straight-grip stock w/bbl. band, sling and swivels. Made from 1964-73.

SPORT-KING DELUXE AUTOLOADER........ NiB $248 Ex $196 Gd $93
Same as Sport-King Special Autoloader except w/checkered stock. Made from 1966-75.

SPORT-KING FIELD AUTOLOADER.......... NiB $129 Ex $109 Gd $73
Calibers: .22 LR. .22 Long, .22 Short (high speed). Tubular magazine holds 15 LR, 17 Long, or 21 Short. 22.25-inch bbl. Weight: 5.5 lbs. Sights: Open rear; beaded post front. Plain pistol-grip stock. Made from 1960-66.

SPORT-KING SPECIAL AUTOLOADER........ NiB $196 Ex $150 Gd $93
Same as Sport-King Field except stock w/Monte Carlo comb and semibeavertail forearm. Made from 1960-66.

HOLLAND & HOLLAND, LTD. — London, England, *Imported by Holland & Holland, NY, NY*

NO. 2 MODEL HAMMERLESS EJECTOR DOUBLE RIFLE........ NiB $14,943 Ex $11,955 Gd $8131
Same general specifications as Royal Model except plainer finish. Disc. 1960.

BEST QUALITY MAGAZINE RIFLE.... NiB $14,380 Ex $11,505 Gd $7825
Mauser or Enfield action. Calibers: .240 Apex, .300 H&H Mag., .375 H&H Magnum. Four round box magazine. 24-inch bbl. Weight: 7.25 lbs., 240 Apex; 8.25 lbs., .300 Mag. and .375 Mag. Sights: Folding leaf rear; hooded ramp front. Detachable French walnut stock w/cheekpiece, checkered pistol-grip and forearm, swivels. Currently mfd. Specifications given apply to most models.

DELUXE MAGAZINE RIFLE....... NiB $15,943 Ex $12,755 Gd $8675
Same specifications as Best Quality except w/exhibition-grade stock and special engraving. Currently mfd.

ROYAL HAMMERLESS EJECTOR RIFLE......... NiB $40,630 Ex $32,505 Gd $22,105
Sidelock. Calibers: .240 Apex, 7mm H&H Mag., .300 H&H Mag., .300 Win. Mag., .30-06, .375 H&H Mag., .458 Win. Mag., .465 H&H Mag. 24- to 28-inch bbls. Weight: From 7.5 lbs. Sights: Folding leaf rear, ramp front. Cheekpiece stock of select French walnut, checkered pistol-grip and forearm. Currently mfd. Same general specifications apply to prewar model.

ROYAL DELUXE DOUBLE RIFLE.... NiB $56,880 Ex $45,505 Gd $30,945
Formerly designated "Modele Deluxe." Same specifications as Royal Model except w/exhibition-grade stock and special engraving. Currently mfd.

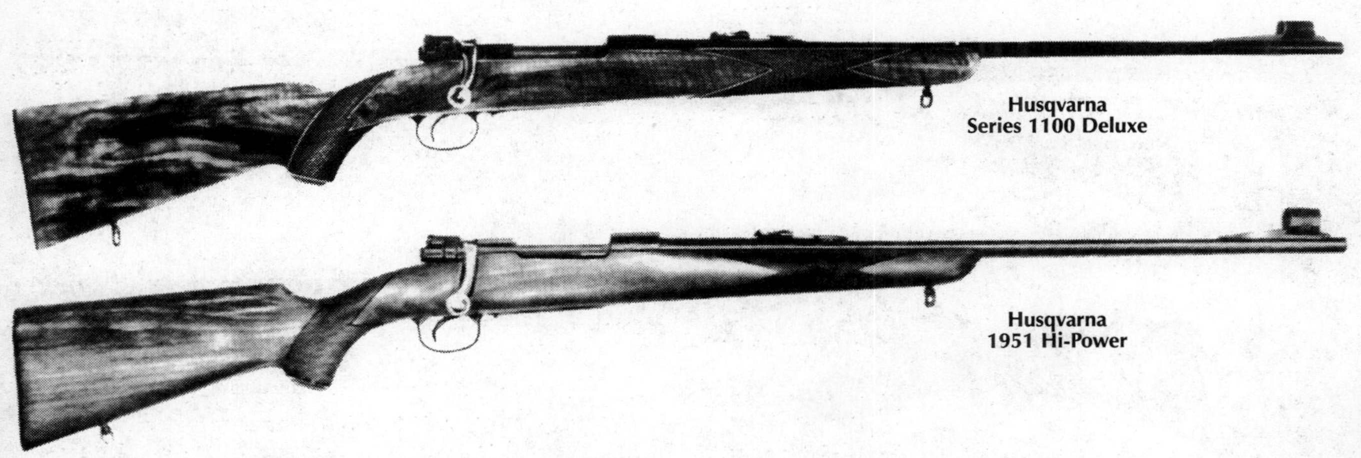

Husqvarna
Series 1100 Deluxe

Husqvarna
1951 Hi-Power

HOWA RIFLES — Mfg. By Howa Machinery Ltd., Shinkawa-Chonear, Nagoya 452, Japan, *Imported by Interarms, Alexandria, VA, and Legacy Sports Int., Reno, NV*

See also Mossberg (1500) Smith & Wesson (1500 & 1700) and Weatherby (Vanguard).

MODEL 1500 HUNTER
Similar to Trophy Model except w/standard walnut stock. No Monte Carlo cheekpiece or grip cap. Imported from 1988-89.
Standard calibers .... NiB $487 Ex $436 Gd $307
Magnum calibers .... NiB $468 Ex $384 Gd $277
Stainless steel, add............................. $85

MODEL 1500 LIGHTNING BOLT-ACTION RIFLE
Similar to Hunter Model except fitted w/black Bell & Carlson Carbelite stock w/checkered grip and forend. Weight: 7.5 lbs. Imported 1988.
Standard calibers .... NiB $451 Ex $364 Gd $225
Magnum calibers .... NiB $468 Ex $384 Gd $277

MODEL 1500 PCS BOLT-ACTION RIFLE
Similar to Hunter Model except in Police Counter Sniper configuration and chambered for .308 Win. only. Walnut or synthetic stock w/checkered grip and forend. Receiver drilled and tapped but w/o sights. Weight: 8.5 to 9.3 lbs. Imported from 1999 to date.
PCS Model w/walnut stock ...... NiB $451 Ex $364 Gd $225
PCS Model w/synthetic stock ..... NiB $430 Ex $359 Gd $268
Stainless steel, add $85

MODEL 1500 REALTREE
CAMO RIFLE .... NiB $513 Ex $436 Gd $307
Similar to Trophy Model except fitted w/Camo Bell & Carlson Carbelite stock w/checkered grip and forend. Weight: 8 lbs. Stock, action and barrel finished in Realtree camo. Available in standard calibers only. Imported from 1993 to date.

MODEL 1500 TROPHY/VARMINT BOLT-ACTION RIFLE
Calibers: .22-250, .223, .243 Win., .270 Win., .308 Win., .30-06, 7mm Mag., .300 Win. Mag.,. .338 Win. Mag. 22-inch bbl. (standard); 24-inch bbl. (Magnum). 42.5 inches overall (standard). Weight: 7.5 lbs. Adj. rear sight hooded ramp front. Checkered walnut stock w/Monte Carlo cheekpiece. Varmint Model w/24-inch heavy bbl., weight of 9.5 lbs. in calibers .22-250, .223 and .308 only. Imported from 1979-93.
Trophy Standard .... NiB $568 Ex $446 Gd $271
Trophy Magnum .... NiB $528 Ex $431 Gd $307
Varmint (Parkerized finish) .... NiB $436 Ex $354 Gd $249
Stainless steel, add $85

MODEL 1500 WOODGRAIN LIGHTNING RIFLE
Calibers: .243, .270, 7mm Rem. Mag., .30-06. Mag. Five round magazine 22-inch. 42 inches overall. Weight: 7.5 lbs. Receiver drilled and tapped for scope mount, no sights. Checkered woodgrain synthetic polymer stock. Imported from 1993-94.
Standard calibers .... NiB $487 Ex $426 Gd $256
Magnum calibers .... NiB $553 Ex $451 Gd $322

H-S PRECISION — Rapid City, South Dakota

PRO-SERIES
Custom rifle built on Remington 700 bolt action. Calibers: .22 to .416, 24- or 26-inch bbl. w/fluted option. Aluminum bedding block system w/take-down option. Kevlar/carbon fiber stock to customer's specifications. Appointments and options to customer's preference. Made from 1990 to date.
Sporter model.................... NiB $2097 Ex $1762 Gd $1041
Pro-Hunter model (PHR)............ NiB $1766 Ex $1425 Gd $988
Long-Range Model .... NiB $1991 Ex $1682 Gd $961
Long-Range
takedown model.................. NiB $2321 Ex $1869 Gd $1293
Marksman model .... NiB $2101 Ex $1766 Gd $1045
Marksman takedown model .... NiB $2426 Ex $1947 Gd $1303
Varmint takedown model (VTD)...... NiB $2075 Ex $1741 Gd $1020
Left-hand models, add................................ $200

HUNGARIAN MILITARY RIFLES — Budapest, Hungary, Manufactured at Government Arsenal

MODEL 1935M MANN-
LICHER MILITARY RIFLE .... NiB $318 Ex $255 Gd $152
Caliber: 8x52mm Hungarian. Bolt action, straight handle. Five round projecting box magazine. 24-inch bbl. Weight: 9 lbs. Adj. leaf rear sight, hooded front blade. Two-piece military-type stock. Made from 1935-40.

MODEL 1943M (GERMAN GEW 98/40) MANNLICHER
MILITARY RIFLE .... NiB $358 Ex $278 Gd $177
Modification, during German occupation, of Model 1935M. Caliber: 7.9mm Mauser. Turned-down bolt handle and Mauser M/98-type box magazine; other differences are minor. Made from 1940 to end of war in Europe.

HUSQVARNA VAPENFABRIK A.B. — Husqvarna, Sweden

MODEL 456 LIGHTWEIGHT FULL-STOCK SPORTER . . . . NiB $540 Ex $437 Gd $308
Same as Series 4000/4100 except w/sporting style full stock w/slope-away cheekrest. Weight: 6.5 lbs. Made from 1959-70.

SERIES 1000 SUPER GRADE . . . . . . NiB $534 Ex $432 Gd $302
Same as 1951 Hi-Power except w/European walnut sporter stock w/Monte Carlo comb and cheekpiece. Made from 1952-56.

SERIES 1100 DELUXE MODEL HI-POWER BOLT-ACTION SPORTING RIFLE . . . . NiB $540 Ex $437 Gd $305
Same as 1951 Hi-Power, except w/jeweled bolt, European walnut stock. Made from 1952-56.

1950 HI-POWER SPORTING RIFLE . . . . . . NiB $476 Ex $385 Gd $270
Mauser-type bolt action. Calibers: .220 Swift, .270 Win. .30-06 (see note below), 5-round box magazine. 23.75-inch bbl. Weight: 7.75 lbs. Sights: Open rear; hooded ramp front. Sporting stock of Arctic beech, checkered pistol grip and forearm, swivels. Note: Husqvarna sporters were first intro. in U.S. about 1948; earlier models were also available in calibers 6.5x55, 8x57 and 9.3x57. Made from 1946-1951.

1951 HI-POWER RIFLE . . . . NiB $508 Ex $411 Gd $288
Same as 1950 Hi-Power except w/high-comb stock, low safety.

SERIES 3000 CROWN GRADE . . . . NiB $514 Ex $385 Gd $257
Same as Series 3100, except w/Monte Carlo comb stock.

SERIES 3100 CROWN GRADE . . . . NiB $514 Ex $385 Gd $257
HVA improved Mauser action. Calibers: .243, .270, 7mm, .30-06, .308 Win. Five round box magazine. 23.75-inch bbl. Weight: 7.75 lbs. Sights: Open rear; hooded ramp front. European walnut stock, checkered, cheekpiece, pistol-grip cap, black forend tip, swivels. Made from 1954-72.

SERIES 4000 LIGHTWEIGHT RIFLE . . . . . . NiB $514 Ex $385 Gd $257
Same as Series 4100 except w/Monte Carlo comb stock and no rear sight.

SERIES 4100 LIGHTWEIGHT RIFLE . . . . . . NiB $509 Ex $385 Gd $231
HVA improved Mauser action. Calibers: .243, .270, 7mm, .30-06, .308 Win. Five round box magazine. 20.5-inch bbl. Weight: 6.25 lbs. Sights: Open rear; hooded ramp front. Lightweight walnut stock w/cheekpiece, pistol grip, Schnabel forend tip, checkered, swivels. Made from 1954-72.

SERIES 6000 IMPERIAL CUSTOM GRADE . NiB $672 Ex $543 Gd $363
Same as Series 3100 except fancy-grade stock, 3-leaf folding rear sight, adj. trigger. Calibers: .243, .270, 7mm Rem. Mag. .308, .30-06. Made from 1968-70.

SERIES 7000 IMPERIAL MONTE CARLO LIGHTWEIGHT. . . NiB $697 Ex $543 Gd $363
Same as Series 4000 Lightweight except fancy-grade stock, 3-leaf folding rear sight, adj. trigger. Calibers: .243, .270, .308, .30-06. Made from 1968-70.

MODEL 8000 IMPERIAL GRADE RIFLE . . . . NiB $697 Ex $543 Gd $363
Same as Model 9000 except w/jeweled bolt, engraved floorplate, deluxe French walnut checkered stock, no sights. Made from 1971-72.

MODEL 9000 CROWN GRADE RIFLE . . . . NiB $540 Ex $437 Gd $334
New design Husqvarna bolt action. Adj. trigger. Calibers: .270, 7mm Rem. Mag., .30-06, .300 Win. Mag. Five round box magazine, hinged floorplate. 23.75-inch bbl. Sights: Folding leaf rear; hooded ramp front. Checkered walnut stock w/Monte Carlo cheekpiece, rosewood forend tip and pistol-grip cap. Weight: 7 lbs. 3 oz. Made from 1971-72.

SERIES P-3000 PRESENTATION RIFLE . . . . NiB $851 Ex $696 Gd $465
Same as Crown Grade Series 3000 except w/selected stock, engraved action, adj. trigger. Calibers: .243, .270, 7mm Rem. Mag., .30-06. Made from 1968-70.

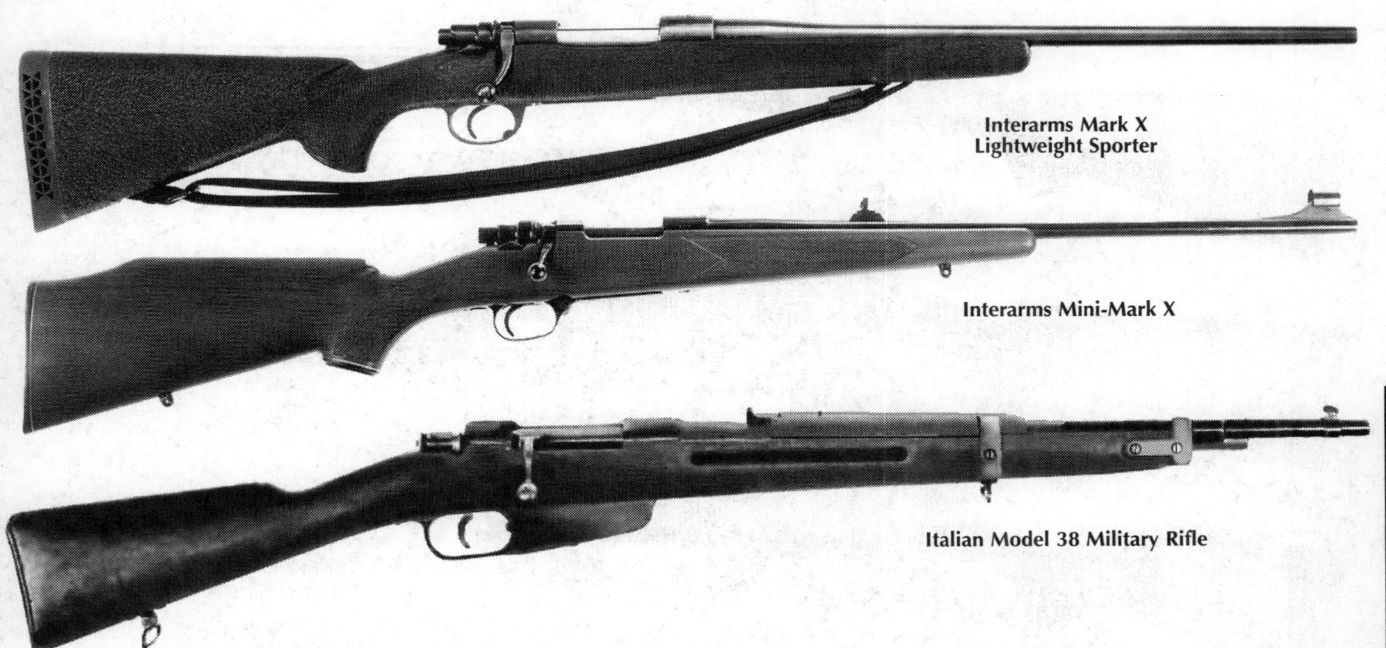

Interarms Mark X Lightweight Sporter

Interarms Mini-Mark X

Italian Model 38 Military Rifle

INTERARMS RIFLES — Alexandria, Virginia

The following Mark X rifles are manufactured by Zavodi Crvena Zastava, Belgrade, Yugoslavia.

MARK X ALASKAN . . . . NiB $509 Ex $382 Gd $280
Same specs as Mark X Sporter, except chambered for .375 H&H Mag. and .458 Win. Mag. w/3-round magazine. Stock w/recoil-absorbing cross bolt and heavy duty recoil pad. Weighs 8.25 lbs. Made from 1976-84.

MARK X BOLT-ACTION SPORTER SERIES
Mauser-type action. Calibers: .22-250, .243, .25-06, .270, 7x57, 7mm Rem. Mag., .308, .30-06, .300 Win. Mag. Five round magazine (3-round in magnum calibers). 24-inch bbl. Weight: 7.5 lbs. Sights: Adj. leaf rear; ramp front, w/hood. Classic-style stock of European walnut w/Monte Carlo comb and cheekpiece, checkered pistol grip and forearm, black forend tip, QD swivels. Made from 1972-97.
Mark X Standard . . . . NiB $401 Ex $326 Gd $230
Mark X Camo (Realtree) . . . . NiB $503 Ex $407 Gd $285
American Field, std.
(rubber recoil pad) . . . . NiB $618 Ex $499 Gd $347
American Field, Magnum
(rubber recoil pad) . . . . NiB $661 Ex $535 Gd $374

MARK X CAVALIER . . . . NiB $407 Ex $331 Gd $229
Same specifications as Mark X Sporter except w/contemporary-style stock w/rollover cheekpiece, rosewood forend tip/grip cap, recoil pad. Intro. 1974; Disc.

MARK X CONTINENTAL
MANNLICHER STYLE CARBINE . . . . NiB $433 Ex $382 Gd $254
Same specifications as Mark X Sporter except straight European-style comb stock w/sculptured cheekpiece. Precise double-set triggers and classic "butterknife" bolt handle. French checkering. Weight: 7.25 lbs. Disc.

MARK X LIGHTWEIGHT SPORTER . . . . . . NiB $382 Ex $321 Gd $229
Calibers: .22-250 Rem., .270 Win., 7mm Rem. Mag., .30-06 or 7mm Mag. Four- or 5-round magazine. 20-inch bbl. Synthenic Carbolite stock Weight: 7 lbs. Imported from 1988-90. (Reintroduced 1994-97.)

MARK X MARQUIS
MANNLICHER STYLE CARBINE . . . . NiB $465 Ex $377 Gd $265
Same specifications as Mark X Sporter except w/20-inch bbl., full-length Mannlicher-type stock w/metal forend/muzzle cap. Calibers: .270, 7x57, .308, .30-06. Imported 1976-84.

MINI-MARK X BOLT-ACTION RIFLE. . . . . NiB $407 Ex $326 Gd $229
Miniature M98 Mauser action. Caliber: .223 Rem. Five round magazine. 20-inch bbl. 39.75 inches overall. Weight: 6.25 lbs. Adj. rear sight, hooded ramp front. Checkered hardwood stock. Imported from 1987-94.

MARK X VISCOUNT . . . . NiB $407 Ex $331 Gd $229
Same specifications as Mark X Sporter except w/plainer field grade stock. Imported from 1974-87.

AFRICAN SERIES . . . . NiB $662 Ex $576 Gd $382
Mauser-type bolt-action. Calibers: .375 H&H Mag., .458 Win. Mag. Three round magazine. 24-inch bbl. Weight: 8 lbs. Sights: 3-leaf express open rear, ramp front w/hood. English-style stock of European walnut, w/cheekpiece, black forend tip, checkered pistol grip and forearm, recoil pad, QD swivels. Imported from 1974-96 by Whitworth Rifle Co., England.

ITALIAN MILITARY RIFLES
Manufactured by government plants at Brescia, Gardone, Terni and Turin, Italy

MODEL 38 MILITARY RIFLE . . . . NiB $118 Ex $108 Gd $67
Modification of Italian Model 1891 Mannlicher-Carcano Military Rifle w/turned-down bolt handle, detachable folding bayonet. Caliber: 7.35mm Italian Service (many arms of this model were later converted to the old 6.5mm caliber). Six round box magazine. 21.25-inch bbl. Weight: 7.5 lbs. Sights: Adj. rear-blade front. Military straight-grip stock. Adopted 1938.

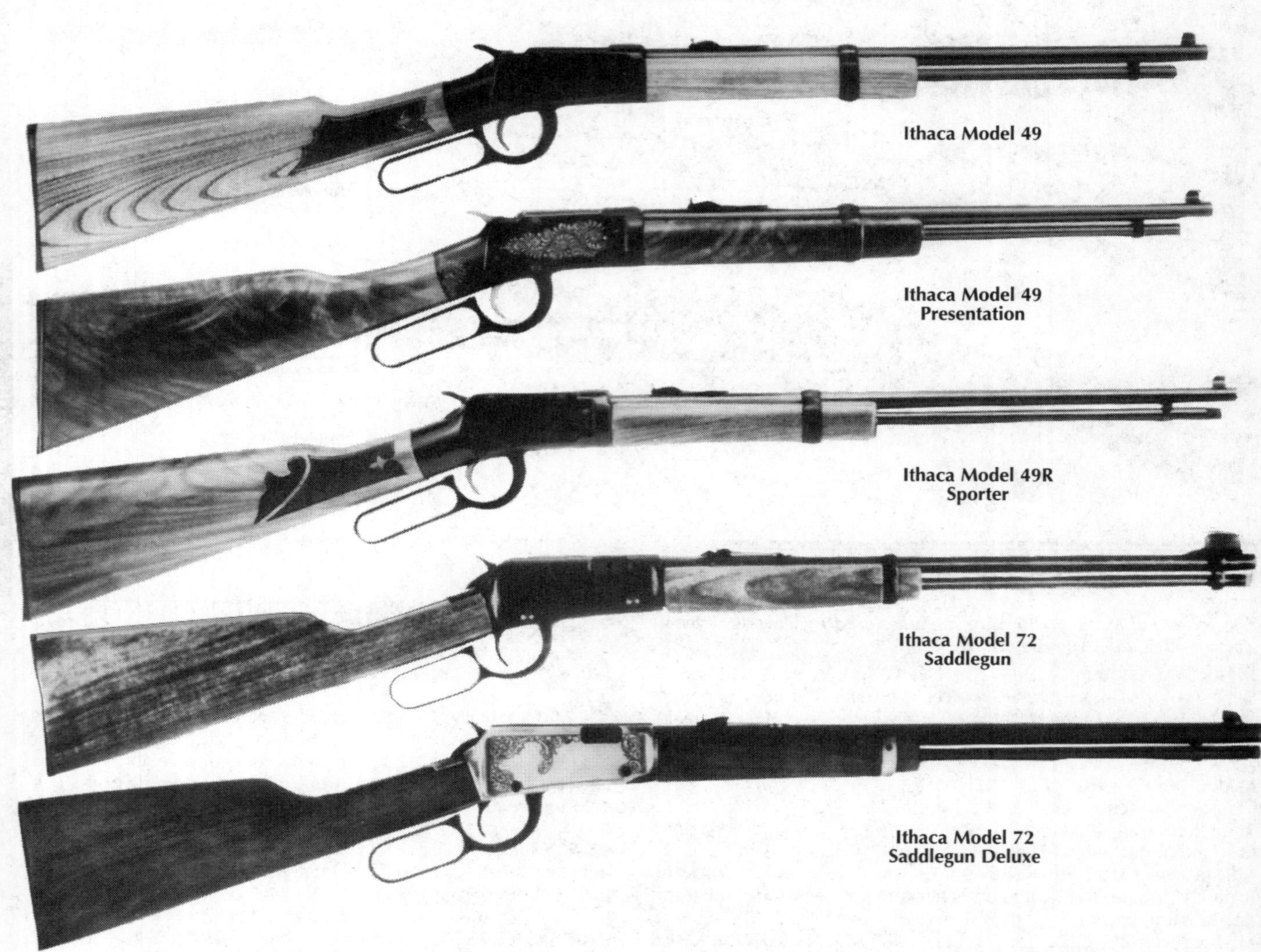

Ithaca Model 49

Ithaca Model 49 Presentation

Ithaca Model 49R Sporter

Ithaca Model 72 Saddlegun

Ithaca Model 72 Saddlegun Deluxe

ITHACA GUN COMPANY, INC. — King Ferry, New York, (Formerly Ithaca, NY)

MODEL 49 SADDLEGUN LEVER ACTION SINGLE-SHOT RIFLE . . . . **NiB $169 Ex $154 Gd $82**
Martini-type action. Hand-operated rebounding hammer. Caliber: .22 LR. Long, Short. 18-inch bbl. Open sights. Western carbine-style stock. Weight: 5.5 lbs. Made from 1961-78.

MODEL 49 SADDLEGUN — DELUXE . . . . . **NiB $199 Ex $148 Gd $97**
Same as standard Model 49 except w/gold-plated hammer and trigger, figured walnut stock, sling swivels. Made from 1962-75.

MODEL 49 SADDLEGUN — MAGNUM . . **NiB $194 Ex $174 Gd $113**
Same as standard Model 49 except chambered for .22 WMR cartridge. Made from 1962-78.

MODEL 49 SADDLEGUN —PRESENTATION. **NiB $319 Ex $303 Gd $145**
Same as standard Model 49 Saddlegun except w/gold-plated hammer and trigger, engraved receiver, full fancy-figured walnut stock w/gold nameplate. Available in .22 LR or .22 WMR. Made from 1962-74.

MODEL 49 SADDLEGUN — ST. LOUIS BICENTENNIAL. . . . . **NiB $319 Ex $303 Gd $145**
Same as Model 49 Deluxe except w/commemorative inscription. 200 made in 1964. Top value is for rifle in new, unfired condition.

MODEL 49R SADDLEGUN REPEATING RIFLE . . . . **NiB $293 Ex $273 Gd $125**
Similar in appearance to Model 49 Single-Shot. Caliber: .22 LR. Long, Short. Tubular magazine holds 15 LR, 17 Long, 21 Short. 20-inch bbl. Weight: 5.5 lbs. Sights: Open rear-bead front. Western-style stock, checkered grip. Made from 1968-71.

Ithaca
Model LSA-65 Standard

Ithaca
Model X5-T

Ithaca
Model X-15

Ithaca
BSA CF-2

MODEL 49 YOUTH SADDLEGUN . . . . NiB $159 Ex $123 Gd $92
Same as standard Model 49 except shorter stock for young shooters. Made from 1961-78.

REPEATING CARBINE . . . . NiB $354 Ex $278 Gd $176
Caliber: .22 LR. Long, Short. Tubular magazine holds 15 LR, 17 Long, 21 Short. 18.5-inch bbl. Weight: 5.5 lbs. Sights: Open rear; hooded ramp front. Receiver grooved for scope mounting. Western carbine stock and forearm of American walnut. Made from 1973-78.

MODEL 72 SADDLEGUN — DELUXE . . . . NiB $408 Ex $332 Gd $220
Same as standard Model 72 except w/silver-finished and engraved receiver, octagon bbl., higher grade walnut stock and forearm. Made from 1974-76.

MODEL LSA-65 BOLT ACTION STANDARD GRADE . . . . . NiB $459 Ex $408 Gd $278
Same as Model LSA-55 Standard Grade except calibers .25-06, .270, .30-06; 4-round magazine, 23-inch bbl., weight: 7 lbs. Made from 1969-77.

MODEL LSA-65 DELUXE . . . . NiB $538 Ex $487 Gd $308
Same as Model LSA-65 Standard Grade except w/special features of Model LSA-55 Deluxe. Made from 1969-77.

MODEL X5-C LIGHTNING AUTOLOADER . . . . NiB $199 Ex $148 Gd $97
Takedown. Caliber: .22 LR. Seven round clip magazine. 22-inch bbl. Weight: 6 lbs. Sights: Open rear; Ray-bar front. Pistol-grip stock, grooved forearm. Made from 1958-64.

MODEL X5-T LIGHTNING AUTOLOADER TUBULAR REPEATING RIFLE . . . . NiB $199 Ex $148 Gd $97
Same as Model X5-C except w/16-round tubular magazine, stock w/plain forearm.

MODEL X-15 LIGHTNING AUTOLOADER . . . . NiB $185 Ex $164 Gd $97
Same general specifications as Model X5-C except forend is not grooved. Made from 1964-67.

BSA CF-2 BOLT-ACTION REPEATING RIFLE . . . . NiB $331 Ex $305 Gd $198
Mauser-type action. Calibers: 7mm Rem. Mag., .300 Win. Mag. Three round magazine. 23.6-inch bbl. Weight: 8 lbs. Sights: Adj. rear; hooded ramp front. Checkered walnut stock w/Monte Carlo comb, rollover cheekpiece, rosewood forend tip, recoil pad, sling swivels. Imported from 1976-77. Mfd. by BSA Guns Ltd., Birmingham, England.

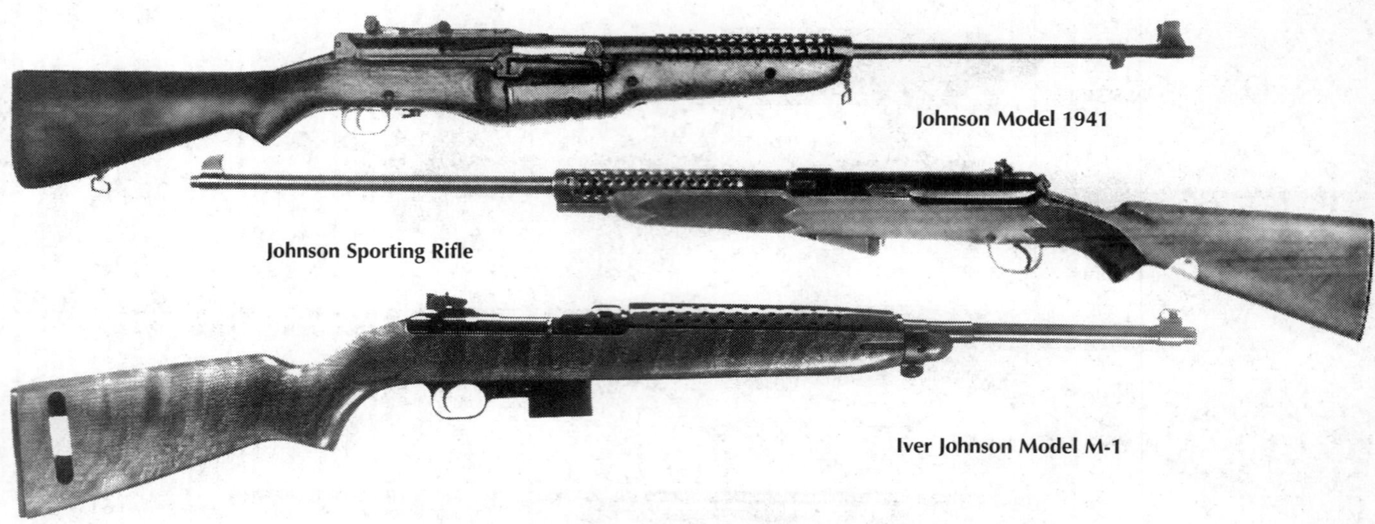

Johnson Model 1941

Johnson Sporting Rifle

Iver Johnson Model M-1

JAPANESE MILITARY RIFLES — Tokyo, Japan Manufactured by Government Plant

MODEL 38 ARISAKA SERVICE RIFLE . . . . . . NiB $50 Ex $356 Gd $203
Mauser-type bolt action. Caliber: 6.5mm Japanese. Five round box magazine. Bbl. lengths: 25.38 and 31.25 inches. Weight: 9.25 lbs. w/long bbl. Sights: fixed front, adj. rear. Military-type full stock. Adopted in 1905, the 38th year of the Meiji reign hence, the designation "Model 38."

MODEL 38 ARISAKA CARBINE. . . . NiB $509 Ex $356 Gd $203
Same general specifications as Model 38 Rifle except w/19-inch bbl., heavy folding bayonet, weight 7.25 lbs.

MODEL 44 CAVALRY CARBINE . . . NiB $688 Ex $611 Gd $331
Same general specifications as Model 38 Rifle except w/19-inch bbl., heavy folding bayonet, weight 8.5 lbs. Adopted in 1911, the 44th year of the Meiji reign, hence the designation, "Model 44."

MODEL 99 SERVICE RIFLE . . . . NiB $413 Ex $229 Gd $178
Modified Model 38. Caliber: 7.7mm Japanese. Five round box magazine. 25.75-inch bbl. Weight: 8.75 lbs. Sights: Fixed front; adj. aperture rear; anti-aircraft sighting bars on some early models; fixed rear sight on some late WWII rifles. Military-type full stock, may have bipod. Takedown paratroop model was also made during WWII. Adopted in 1939, (Japanese year 2599) from which the designation "Model 99" is taken. Note: The last Model 99 rifles made were of poor quality; some with cast steel receivers. Value shown is for earlier type.

JARRETT CUSTOM RIFLES — Jackson, South Carolina

MODEL NO. 2 WALKABOUT BOLT-ACTION RIFLE. . . . . NiB $3049 Ex $2698 Gd $1668
Custom lightweight rifle built on Remington M700 action. Jarrett match- grade barrel cut and chambered to customer's specification in short action calibers only. McMillan fiberglass stock pillar-bedded to action and finished to customer's preference.

MODEL NO. 3 CUSTOM BOLT-ACTION RIFLE. . . . . NiB $3033 Ex $2544 Gd $1591
Custom rifle built on Remington M700 action. Jarrett match grade barrel cut and chambered to customer's specification. McMillan classic fiberglass stock pillar-bedded to action and finished to customer's preference. Made from 1989 to date.

MODEL NO. 4 PROFESSIONAL HUNTER BOLT-ACTION RIFLE . . . . . . NiB $6763 Ex $5682 Gd $4343
Custom magnum rifle built on Winchester M70 "controlled feed" action. Jarrett match grade barrel cut and chambered to customer's specification in magnum calibers only. Quarter rib w/iron sights and two Leupold scopes w/Q-D rings and mounts. McMillan classic fiberglass stock fitted and finished to customer's preference.

JOHNSON AUTOMATICS, INC. — Providence, Rhode Island

MODEL 1941 SEMIAUTO MILITARY RIFLE . . . . NiB $2549 Ex $1624 Gd $1249
Short-recoil operated. Removable, air-cooled, 22-inch bbl. Caliber: .30-06, 7mm Mauser. 10-round rotary magazine. Two-piece wood stock, pistol grip, perforated metal radiator sleeve over rear half of bbl. Sights: Receiver peep; protected post front. Weight: 9.5 lbs. Note: The Johnson M/1941 was adopted by the Netherlands government in 1940-41 and the major portion of the production of this rifle, 1941-43, was on Dutch orders. A quantity was also bought by the U.S. government for use by Marine Corps parachute troops (1943) and for Lend Lease. All these rifles were caliber .30-06; the 7mm Johnson rifles were made for the South American government.

SPORTING RIFLE PROTOTYPE. . . . NiB $13,750 Ex $11,000 Gd $7480
Same general specifications as military rifle except fitted w/sporting stock, checkered grip and forend. Blade front sight; receiver peep sight. Less than a dozen made prior to World War II.

IVER JOHNSON ARMS, INC. — Jacksonville, Arkansas, (Formerly of Fitchburg, Massachusetts, and Middlesex, New Jersey)

LI'L CHAMP BOLT-ACTION RIFLE . . . NiB $108 Ex $82 Gd $66
Caliber: .22 S. L. LR. Single-shot. 16.25-inch bbl. 32.5 inches overall. Weight: 3.25 lbs. Adj. rear sight, blade front. Synthetic composition stock. Made from 1986-88.

Iver Johnson Model SC30FS

Iver Johnson Survival Semiautomatic Carbine

Iver Johnson Trailblazer

Iver Johnson Model XX (2X) Bolt-Action Rifle

MODEL M-1 SEMIAUTOMATIC CARBINE
Similar to U.S. M-1 Carbine. Calibers: 9mm Parabellum 30 U.S. Carbine. 15- or 30-round magazine. 18-inch bbl. 35.5 inches overall. Weight: 6.5 lbs. Sights: blade front, w/guards; adj. peep rear. Walnut, hardwood or collapsible wire stock. Parkerized finish.
Model M-1 (30 cal. w/hardwood). . . . . . . NiB $360 Ex $282 Gd $179
Model M-1 (30 cal. w/walnut) . . . . NiB $387 Ex $295 Gd $192
Model M-1 (30 cal. w/wire) . . . . NiB $439 Ex $362 Gd $197
Model M-1 (9mm w/hardwood) . . . . NiB $267 Ex $252 Gd $216
Model M-1 (9mm w/walnut). . . . . NiB $331 Ex $284 Gd $223
Model M-1 (9mm w/wire) . . . . NiB $387 Ex $326 Gd $212

MODEL PM.30
SEMIAUTOMATIC CARBINE . . . . . . NiB $367 Ex $284 Gd $181
Similar to U.S. Carbine, Cal. 30 M1. 18-inch bbl. Weight: 5.5 lbs. 15- or 30-round detachable magazine. Both hardwood and walnut stock.

MODEL SC30FS
SEMIAUTOMATIC CARBINE . . . . . . NiB $439 Ex $362 Gd $197
Similar to Survival Carbine except w/folding stock. Made from 1983 to date.

SURVIVAL SEMIAUTOMATIC CARBINE . . NiB $413 Ex $387 Gd $207
Similar to Model PM.30 except in stainless steel. Made from 1983 to date. W/folding high-impact plastic stock add $35.

TRAILBLAZER SEMIAUTO RIFLE . . . NiB $145 Ex $129 Gd $109
Caliber: .22 LR. 18-inch bbl. Weight: 5.5 lbs. Sights: Open rear, blade front. Hardwood stock. Made from 1983-85

MODEL X BOLT-ACTION RIFLE . . . . NiB $134 Ex $114 Gd $83
Takedown, Single-shot. Caliber: .22 Short, Long and LR. 22-inch bbl. Weight: 4 lbs. Sights: Open rear; blade front. Pistol-grip stock w/knob forend tip. Made from 1928-32.

MODEL XX (2X)
BOLT-ACTION RIFLE . . . . NiB $145 Ex $109 Gd $88
Improved version of Model X w/heavier 24-inch bbl. larger stock (w/o knob tip), weight: 4.5 lbs. Made from 1932-55.

K.B.I., INC. — Harrisburg, Pennsylvania

See listing under Armscor; Charles Daly; FEG; Liberty and I.M.I.

SUPER CLASSIC
Calibers: .22 LR, .22 Mag., RF, .22 Hornet. Five- or 10-round capacity. Bolt and semiauto action. 22.6- or 20.75-inch bbl. 41.25 or 40.5 inches overall. Weight: 6.4 to 6.7 lbs. Blue finish. Oil-finished American walnut stock w/hardwood grip cap and forend tip. Checkered Monte Carlo comb and cheekpiece. High polish blued barreled action w/damascened bolt. Dovetailed receiver and iron sights. Recoil pad. QD swivel posts.
.22 Long Rifle (M-1500 SC). . . . . NiB $245 Ex $203 Gd $148
.22 Magnum Rimfire (M-1500 SC) . . . . NiB $271 Ex $224 Gd $163
.22 Hornet (M-1800-S) . . . . NiB $413 Ex $337 Gd $240
.22 Long Rifle Semiauto (M-2000 SC). . . . . NiB $271 Ex $224 Gd $163

K.D.F. INC. — Sequin, Texas

MODEL K15
BOLT-ACTION RIFLE
Calibers: (Standard) .22-250, .243 Win., 6mm Rem., .25-06, .270 Win., .280 Rem., 7mm Mag., .30-60; (Magnum) .300 Wby., .300 Win., .338 Win., .340 Wby., .375 H&H, .411 KDF, .416 Rem., .458 Win. Four round magazine (standard), 3-shot (magnum). 22-inch (standard) or 24-inch (magnum) bbl. 44.5 to 46.5 inches overall. Weight: 8 lbs. Sights optional. Kevlar composite or checkered walnut stock in Classic, European or thumbhole-style. Note: U.S. Manufacture limited to 25 prototypes and pre-production variations.
Standard model . . . . NiB $1836 Ex $1655 Gd $935
Magnum model . . . . NiB $1887 Ex $1501 Gd $986

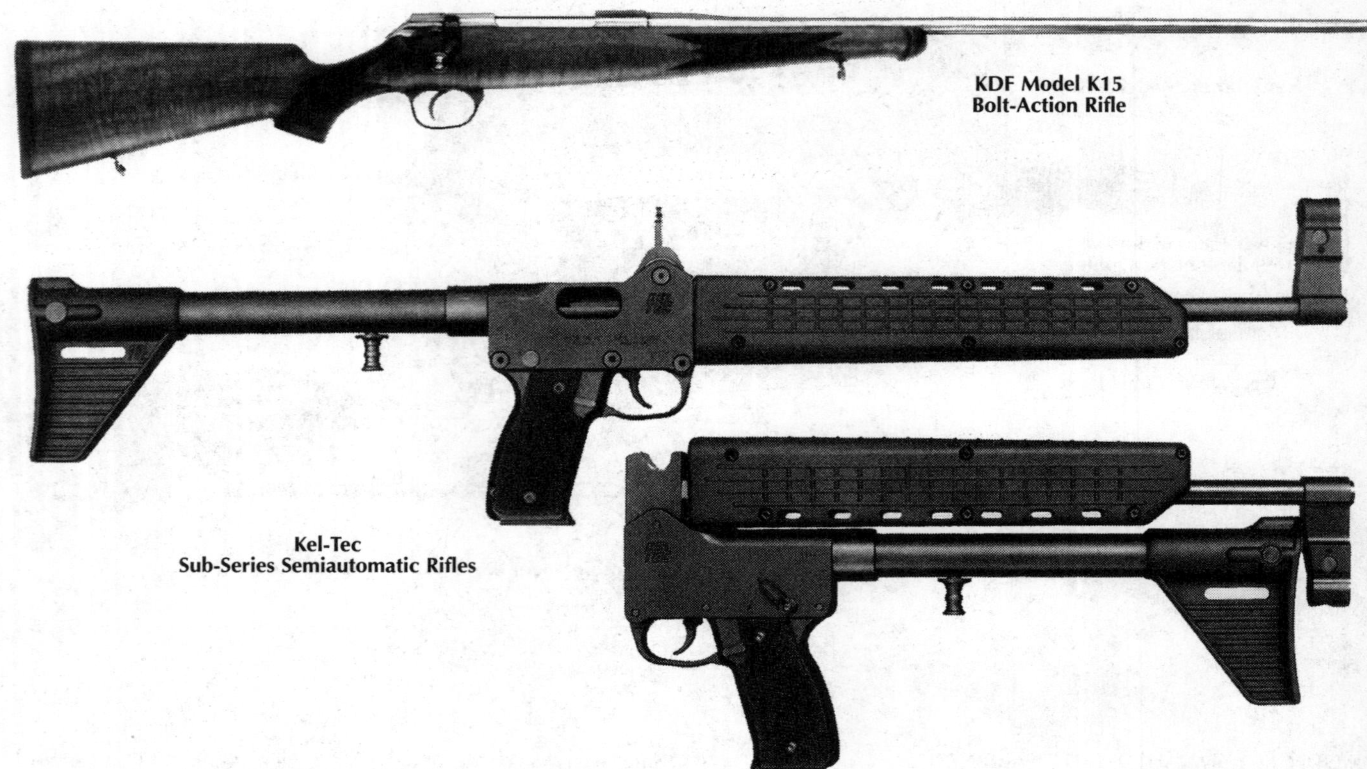

KDF Model K15
Bolt-Action Rifle

Kel-Tec
Sub-Series Semiautomatic Rifles

KEL-TEC CNC INDUSTRIES, INC. — Cocoa, Florida

SUB-SERIES SEMIAUTOMATIC RIFLES

Semiautomatic blow-back action w/pivoting bbl., takedown. 9mm Parabellum or 40 S&W. Interchangeable grip assembly accepts most double column, high capacity handgun magazines. 16.1-inch bbl. 31.5 inches overall. Weight: 4.6 lbs. Hooded post front sight, flip-up rear. Matte black finish. Tubular buttstock w/grooved polymer buttplate and vented handguard. Made from 1997 to date.

Sub-9 Model (9mm). . . . . NiB $427 Ex $308 Gd $231
Sub-40 Model (40 S&W) . . . . NiB $514 Ex $427 Gd $282

KIMBER RIFLES — Mfd. By Kimber Manufacturing, Inc., Yonkers, NY (Formerly Kimber of America, Inc.; Kimber of Oregon, Inc.)

Note: From 1980-91, Kimber of Oregon produced Kimber firearms. A redesigned action designated by serialization with a "B" suffix was introduced 1986. Pre-1986 production is recognized as the "A" series but is not so marked. These early models in rare configurations and limited-run calibers command premium prices from collectors. Kimber of America, in Clackamas, Oregon, acquired the Kimber trademark and resumed manufactured of Kimber rifles. During this transition, Nationwide Sports Distributors, Inc. in Pennsylvania and Nevada became exclusive distributors of Kimber products. In 1997, Kimber Manufacturing acquired the trademark with manufacturing rights and expanded production to include a 1911-A1-style semiautomatic pistol, the Kimber Classic 45.
Rifle production resumed in late 1998 with the announcement of an all-new Kimber .22 rifle and a refined Model 84 in both single-shot and repeater configurations.

MODEL 82 BOLT-ACTION RIFLE

Small action based on Kimber's "A" Model 82 rimfire receiver w/twin rear locking lugs. Calibers: .22 LR. .22 WRF, .22 Hornet, .218 Bee, .25-20. 5- or 10-round magazine (.22 LR); 5-round magazine (22WRF); 3-round magazine (.22 Hornet). .218 Bee and .25-20 are single-shot. 18- to 25-inch bbl. 37.63 to 42.5 inches overall. Weight: 6 lbs. (Light Sporter), 6.5 lbs. (Sporter), 7.5 lbs. (Varmint); 10.75 lbs. (Target). Right- and left-hand actions are available in distinctive stock styles.

Cascade (disc. 1987) . . . . NiB $913 Ex $836 Gd $553
Classic (disc. 1988) . . . . NiB $913 Ex $836 Gd $553
Continental . . . . NiB $1398 Ex $1127 Gd $781
Custom Classic
(disc. 1988) . . . . NiB $971 Ex $785 Gd $546
Mini Classic. . . . . NiB $624 Ex $517 Gd $356
Super America. . . . . NiB $1646 Ex $1054 Gd $796
Super Continental . . . . NiB $1585 Ex $1337 Gd $822
1990 Classifications
All-American Match . . . . NiB $937 Ex $808 Gd $577
Deluxe Grade
(disc. 1990) . . . . NiB $1333 Ex $1050 Gd $844
Hunter
(Laminated stock) . . . . NiB $862 Ex $707 Gd $476
Super America. . . . . NiB $1333 Ex $1071 Gd $717
Target
(Government Match). . . . . NiB $913 Ex $856 Gd $682

MODEL 82C CLASSIC BOLT-ACTION RIFLE

Caliber: .22 LR. Four- or 10-round magazine. 21-inch air-gauged bbl. 40.5 inches overall. Weight: 6.5 lbs. Receiver drilled and tapped for Warne scope mounts; no sights. Single-set trigger. Checkered Claro walnut stock w/red buttpad and polished steel grip cap. Reintroduced 1993.

Classic model . . . . NiB $888 Ex $749 Gd $450
Left-hand model, add. $75

Kimber Model 82 Rimfire Classic

Kimber Model 82C Rimfire Classic

Kimber Model 84 Classic

Kimber Model 89 Big Game 375 Caliber

Kimber Model 89 Big Game 375 H&H Caliber

Model 84 Bolt-Action Rifle

Classic (disc. 1988) Compact-medium action based on a scaled-down Mauser-type receiver, designed to accept small base centerfire cartridges. Calibers: .17 Rem., .221 Fireball, .222 Rem., .223 Rem. Five round magazine. Same general barrel and stock specifications as Model 82.

Classic (discontinued 1988) . . . . NiB $968 Ex $763 Gd $530
Continental . . . . NiB $1279 Ex $1033 Gd $720
Custom Classic (disc. 1988) . . . . NiB $1161 Ex $941 Gd $658
Super America (disc. 1988). . . . . NiB $1316 Ex $1064 Gd $743
Super Continental (disc. 1988) . . . . NiB $1379 Ex $1111 Gd $778
1990 Classifications
Deluxe Grade (disc. 1990) . . . . NiB $1213 Ex $982 Gd $687
Hunter/Sporter (laminated stock) . . . . . . NiB $1084 Ex $879 Gd $612
Super America (disc. 1991). . . . . NiB $1349 Ex $1093 Gd $765
Super Varmint (disc. 1991) . . . . NiB $1387 Ex $1124 Gd $785
Ultra Varmint (disc. 1991) . . . . NiB $1290 Ex $1044 Gd $728

MODEL 89 BIG-GAME RIFLE

Large action combining the best features of the pre-64 Model 70 Winchester and the Mauser 98. Three action lengths are offered in three stock styles. Calibers: .257 Roberts, .25-06, 7x57, .270 Win., .280 Win., .30-06, 7mm Rem. Mag., .300 Win. Mag., .300 H&H, .338 Win., 35 Whelen, .375 H&H, .404 Jeffrey, .416 Rigby, .460 Wby., .505 Gibbs (.308 cartridge family to follow). Five round magazine (standard calibers); 3-round magazine (Magnum calibers). 22- to 24-inch bbl. 42 to 44 inches overall. Weight: 7.5 to 10.5 lbs. Model 89 African features express sights on contoured quarter rib, banded front sight. Barrel-mounted recoil lug w/integral receiver lug and twin recoil crosspins in stock.

BGR Long Action
Classic (disc. 1988). . . . . NiB $941 Ex $762 Gd $533
Custom Classic (disc. 1988) . . . . NiB $1211 Ex $980 Gd $685
Super America. NiB $1470 Ex $1188 Gd $827
1990 Classifications
Deluxe Grade: Featherweight . . . . NiB $1939 Ex $1402 Gd $978
Medium. . . . . NiB $1777 Ex $1436 Gd $999
.375 H&H . . . . NiB $1867 Ex $1508 Gd $1048
Hunter Grade (laminated stock)
.270 and .30-06 . . . . NiB $1293 Ex $1047 Gd $734
.375 H&H . . . . NiB $1608 Ex $1300 Gd $907
Super America: Featherweight . . . . NiB $2011 Ex $1616 Gd $1123
Medium. . . . . NiB $2101 Ex $1697 Gd $1180
.375 H&H . . . . NiB $2669 Ex $2154 Gd $1494
African — All calibers. . . . . NiB $4723 Ex $3796 Gd $2612

Krico Model 400

KNIGHT'S MANUFACTURING COMPANY — Vero Beach, Florida

SR-15 SEMIAUTOMATIC MATCH RIFLE . . . . NiB $1709 Ex $1451 Gd $988
AR-15 configuration. Caliber: .223 Rem. (5.56mm). Five- or 10-round magazine. 20-inch w/free-floating, match-grade bbl., 38 inches overall. Weight: 7.9 lbs. Integral Weaver-style rail. Two-stage target trigger. Matte black oxide finish. Black synthetic AR-15A2-style stock and forearm. Made from 1997 to date.

SR-15 M-4 SEMIAUTOMATIC CARBINE
Similar to SR-15 rifle except w/16-inch bbl. Sights and mounts optional. Fixed synthetic or collapsible buttstock. Made from 1997 to date.
Model SR-15 Carbine (w/collapsible stock) . . . . NiB $1424 Ex $1291 Gd $930

SR-15 M-5 SEMIAUTOMATIC RIFLE . . . . . . NiB $1558 Ex $1368 Gd $1033
Caliber: .223 Rem. (5.56mm). Five- or 10-round magazine. 20-inch bbl. 38 inches overall. Weight: 7.6 lbs. Integral Weaver-style rail. Two-stage target trigger. Matte black oxide finish. Black synthetic AR-15A2-style stock and forearm. Made from 1997 to date.

SR-25 MATCH RIFLE
Similar to SR-25 Sporter except w/free floating 20- or 24-inch match bbl. 39.5-43.5 inches overall. Weight: 9.25 and 10.75 lbs., respectively. Integral Weaver-style rail. Sights and mounts optional. 1 MOA guaranteed. Made from 1993 to date.
Model SR-25 LW Match (w/20-inch bbl.). . . . . NiB $2814 Ex $2402 Gd $1553
W/RAS (Rail Adapter System), add $300

SR-25 SEMIAUTOMATIC CARBINE
Similar to SR-25 Sporter except w/free floating 16-inch bbl. 35.75 inches overall. Weight: 7.75 lbs. Integral Weaver-style rail. Sights and mounts optional. Made from 1995 to date.
Model SR-25 Carbine (w/o sights) . . . . NiB $2763 Ex $2505 Gd $1527
W/RAS (Rail Adapter System), add $300

SR-25 SEMIAUTOMATIC SPORTER RIFLE . . . . NiB $2866 Ex $2351 Gd $1630
AR-15 configuration. Caliber: .308 Win. (7.62 NATO). Five, 10- or 20-round magazine. 20-inch bbl. 39.5 inches overall. Weight: 8.75 lbs. Integral Weaver-style rail. Protected post front sight adjustable for elevation, detachable rear adjustable for windage. Two-stage target trigger. Matte black oxide finish. Black synthetic AR-15A2-style stock and forearm. Made from 1993-97.

SR-50 SEMIAUTOMATIC LONG RANGE PRECISION RIFLE. . . . . NiB $6696 Ex $5872 Gd $3503
Gas-operated semiautomatic action. Caliber: .50 BMG. 10-round magazine. 35.5-inch bbl. 58.5 inches overall. Weight: 31.75 lbs. Integral Weaver-style rail. Two-stage target trigger. Matte black oxide finish. Tubular-style stock. Made from 1996 to date.

KONGSBERG RIFLES — Kongsberg, Norway

(Imported by Kongsberg America L.L.C., Fairfield, CT)

MODEL 393 CLASSIC SPORTER
Calibers: .22-250 Rem., .243 Win., 6.5x55, .270 Win., 7mm Rem. Mag., .30-06, .308 Win. .300 Win. Mag., .338 Win. Mag. Three- or 4-round rotary magazine. 23-inch bbl. (Standard) or 26-inch bbl. (magnum). Weight: 7.5 to 8 lbs. 44 to 47 inches overall. No sights w/ dovetailed receiver or optional hooded blade front sight, adjustable rear. Blue finish. Checkered European walnut stock w/rubber buttplate. Imported from 1994-98.
Standard calibers . . . . NiB $948 Ex $825 Gd $540
Magnum calibers . . . . NiB $1227 Ex $1015 Gd $743
Left-hand model, add $135
W/optional sights, add $50

MODEL 393 DELUXE SPORTER
Similar to Classic Model except w/deluxe European walnut stock. Imported from 1994-98.
Standard calibers . . . . NiB $1025 Ex $866 Gd $536
Magnum calibers. . . . . NiB $1260 Ex $1041 Gd $761
Left-hand model, add. $135
W/optional sights, add $50

MODEL 393 THUMBHOLE SPORTER
Calibers: 22-250 Rem. or 308 Win. Four round rotary magazine. 23-inch heavy bbl. Weight: 8.5 lbs. 44 inches overall. No sights, dovetailed receiver. Blue finish. Stippled American walnut thumbhole stock w/adjustable cheekpiece. Imported from 1993-98.
Right-hand model . . . . NiB $1439 Ex $1259 Gd $564
Left-hand model . . . . NiB $1727 Ex $1419 Gd $1025

KRICO RIFLES — Stuttgart-Hedelfingen, Germany, Mfd. by Sportwaffenfabrik, Kriegeskorte GmbH

Imported by Northeast Arms, LLC, Ft. Fairfield, Maine. (Previously by Beeman Precision Arms, Inc and Mandell Shooting Supplies)

MODEL 260 SEMIAUTOMATIC RIFLE . . . . NiB $666 Ex $604 Gd $398
Caliber: .22 LR. 10-round magazine. 20-inch bbl. 38.9 inches overall. Weight: 6.6 lbs. Hooded blade front sight; adj. rear. Grooved receiver. Beech stock. Blued finish. Introduced 1989. Disc.

MODEL 300 BOLT-ACTION RIFLE
Calibers: .22 LR. .22 WMR, .22 Hornet. 19.6-inch bbl. (22 LR), 23.6-inch (22 Hornet). 38.5 inches overall. Weight: 6.3 lbs. Double-set triggers. Sights: Ramped blade front, adj. open rear. Checkered walnut-finished hardwood stock. Blued finish. Introduced 1989. Disc.
Model 300 Standard . . . . NiB $682 Ex $527 Gd $373
Model 300 Deluxe. . . . . NiB $708 Ex $553 Gd $398
Model 300 SA (Monte Carlo walnut stock) . . . . NiB $821 Ex $675 Gd $489
Model 300 Stutzen (full-length walnut stock) . . . . . NiB $943 Ex $814 Gd $557

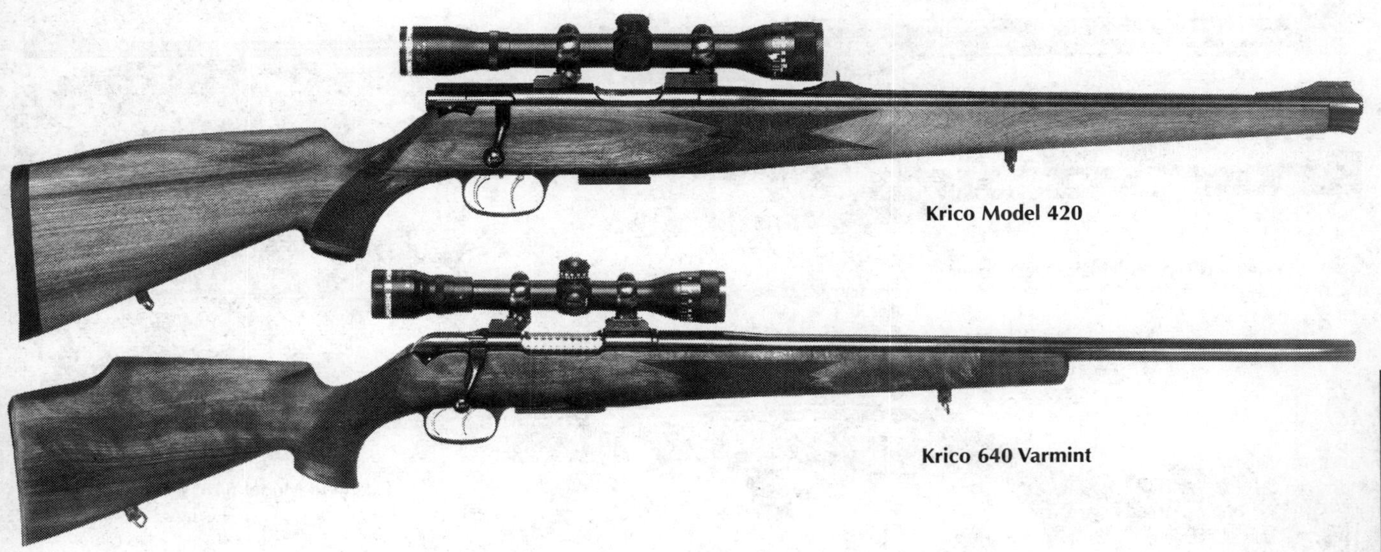

Krico Model 420

Krico 640 Varmint

MODEL 311 SMALL-BORE RIFLE
Bolt action. Caliber: .22 LR. Five or 10-round clip magazine. 22-inch bbl. Weight: 6 lbs. Single- or double-set trigger. Sights: Open rear; hooded ramp front; available w/factory-fitted Kaps 2.5x scope. Checkered stock w/cheekpiece, pistol-grip and swivels. Disc. 1962.
W/scope sight . . . . NiB $466 Ex $414 Gd $260
W/iron sights only . . . . NiB $388 Ex $285 Gd $234

MODEL 320 BOLT-ACTION SPORTER . . . . NiB $725 Ex $571 Gd $390
Caliber: .22 LR. Five round detachable box magazine. 19.5-inch bbl. 38.5 inches overall. Weight: 6 lbs. Adj. rear sight, blade ramp front. Checkered European walnut Mannlicher-style stock w/low comb and cheekpiece. Single or double-set triggers. Imported from 1986-88. Disc.

MODEL 340 METALLIC SILHOUETTE BOLT-ACTION RIFLE . . . . NiB $741 Ex $622 Gd $432
Caliber: .22 LR. Five round magazine. 21-inch heavy, bull bbl. 39.5 inches overall. Weight: 7.5 lbs. No sights. Grooved receiver for scope mounts. European walnut stock in off-hand, match-style configuration. Match or double-set triggers. Imported from 1983-88. Disc.

MODEL 360S BIATHLON RIFLE . . . . . . NiB $1384 Ex $1126 Gd $637
Caliber: .22 LR. Five 5-round magazines. 21.25-inch bbl. w/snow cap. 40.5 inches overall. Weight: 9.25 lbs. Straight-pull action. Match trigger w/17-oz. pull. Sights: Globe front, adj. match peep rear. Biathlon-style walnut stock w/high comb and adj. butt-plate. Imported from 1991. Disc.

MODEL 360 S2 BIATHLON RIFLE . . . . . NiB $1358 Ex $1075 Gd $611
Similar to Model 360S except w/pistol-grip activated action. Biathlon-style walnut stock w/black epoxy finish. Imported from 1991. Disc.

MODEL 400 BOLT-ACTION RIFLE . . . . NiB $901 Ex $727 Gd $505
Caliber: .22 Hornet. Five round detachable box magazine. 23.5-inch bbl. Weight: 6.75 lbs. Adj. open rear sight, ramp front. European walnut stock. Disc. 1990.

MODEL 420 BOLT-ACTION RIFLE . . . . NiB $933 Ex $753 Gd $521
Same as Model 400 except w/full-length Mannlicher-style stock and double-set triggers. Scope optional, extra. Disc. 1989.

MODEL 440 S BOLT-ACTION RIFLE. . . . . . NiB $876 Ex $707 Gd $490
Caliber: .22 Hornet. Detachable box magazine. 20-inch bbl. 36.5 inches overall. Weight: 7.5 lbs. No sights. French walnut stock w/ventilated forend. Disc. 1988.

MODEL 500 MATCH RIFLE . . . . NiB $3527 Ex $2844 Gd $971
Caliber: .22 LR. Single-shot. 23.6-inch bbl. 42 inches overall. Weight: 9.4 lbs. Kricotronic electronic ignition system. Sights: Globe front; match micrometer aperture rear. Match-style European walnut stock w/adj. butt.

MODEL 600 BOLT-ACTION RIFLE . . . . . . NiB $1223 Ex $977 Gd $682
Same general specifications as Model 700 except w/short action. Calibers: .17 Rem., .222, .223, .22-250, .243, 5.6x50 Mag. and 308. Introduced 1983. Disc.

MODEL 620 BOLT-ACTION RIFLE . . . . . NiB $1275 Ex $1069 Gd $688
Same as Model 600 except w/short-action-chambered for .308 Win. only and full-length Mannlicher-style stock w/Schnabel forend tip. 20.75-inch bbl. Weight: 6.5 lbs. No longer imported.

MODEL 640 SUPER SNIPER BOLT-ACTION REPEATING RIFLE . . NiB $1480 Ex $1198 Gd $838
Calibers: .223 Rem., .308 Win. Three round magazine. 26-inch bbl. 44.25 inches overall. Weight: 9.5 lbs. No sights drilled and tapped for scope mounts. Single or double-set triggers. Select walnut stock w/adj. cheekpiece and recoil pad. Disc. 1989.

MODEL 640 VARMINT RIFLE . . . . NiB $931 Ex $802 Gd $493
Caliber: .222 Rem. Four round magazine. 23.75-inch bbl. Weight: 9.5 lbs. No sights. European walnut stock. No longer imported.

MODEL 700 BOLT-ACTION RIFLE
Calibers: .17 Rem., .222, .222 Rem. Mag., .223, .22-250, 5.6x50 Mag., .243, 5.6x57 RSW, 6x62, 6.5x55, 6.5x57, 6.5x68 .270 Win., 7x64, 7.5 Swiss, 7mm Mag., .30-06, .300 Win., 8x68S, 9.3x64. 24-inch (standard) or 26-inch (magnum) bbl. 44 inches overall (standard). Weight: 7.5 lbs. Adj. rear sight; hooded ramp front. Checkered European-style walnut stock w/Bavarian cheekpiece and rosewood Schnabel forend tip. Imported from 1983 to date.
Model 700 . . . . NiB $1142 Ex $922 Gd $642
Model 700 Deluxe. . . . . NiB $1196 Ex $969 Gd $674
Model 700 Deluxe S . . . . NiB $1457 Ex $1174 Gd $814
Model 700 Stutzen . . . . NiB $1271 Ex $1025 Gd $712

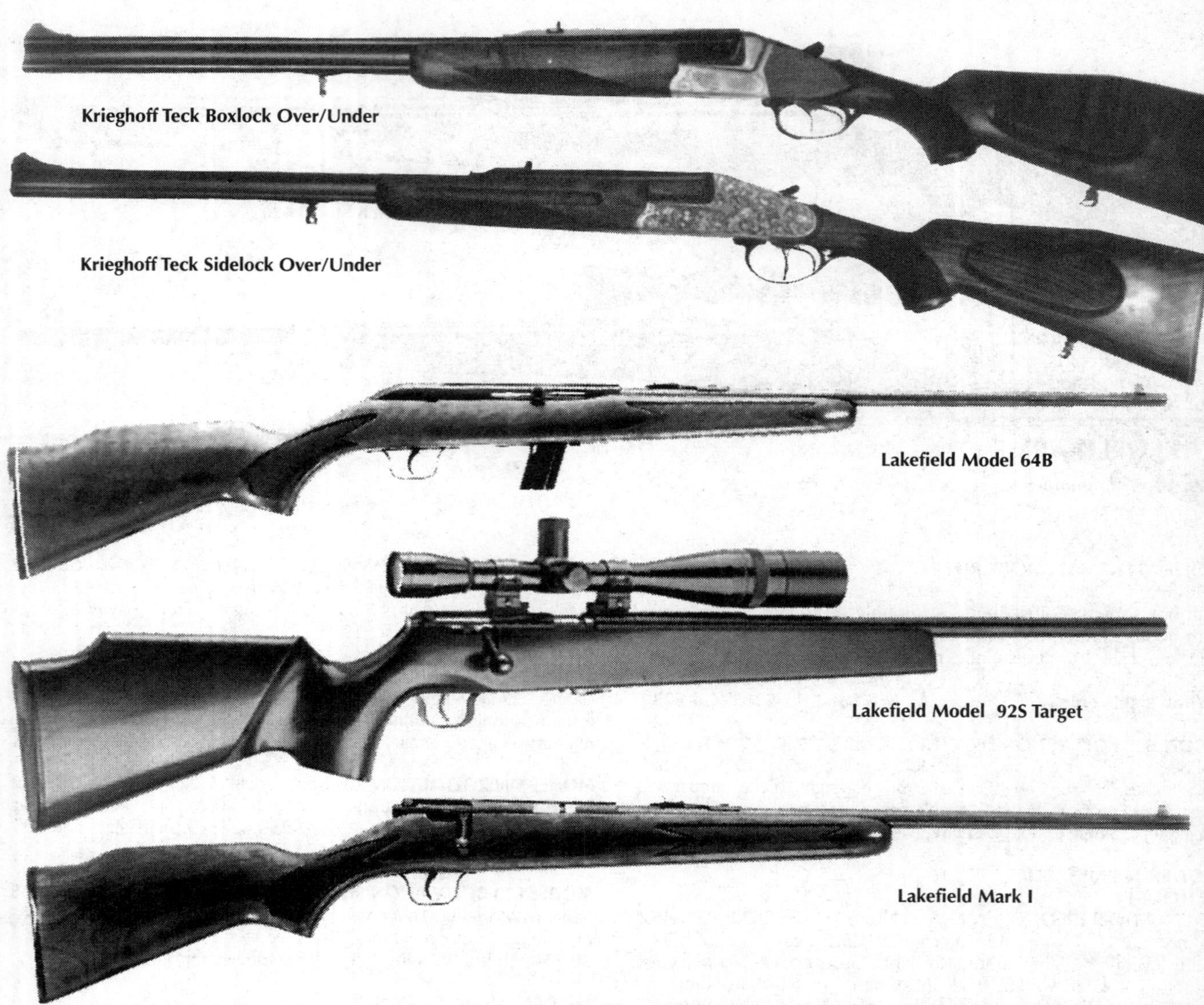
Krieghoff Teck Boxlock Over/Under
Krieghoff Teck Sidelock Over/Under
Lakefield Model 64B
Lakefield Model 92S Target
Lakefield Mark I

MODEL 720 BOLT-ACTION RIFLE
Same general specifications as Model 700 except in calibers .270 Win. and .30-06 w/full-length Mannlicher-style stock and Schnabel forend tip. 20.75-inch bbl. Weight: 6.75 lbs. Disc. importing 1990.
Sporter Model .... NiB $1198 Ex $967 Gd $672
Ltd. Edition .... NiB $2433 Ex $2114 Gd $1094

BOLT-ACTION SPORTING RIFLE .... NiB $648 Ex $596 Gd $416
Miniature Mauser action. Single- or double-set trigger. Calibers: .22 Hornet, .222 Rem. Four round clip magazine. 22-24- or 26-inch bbl. Weight: 6.25 lbs. Sights: Open rear; hooded ramp front. Checkered stock w/cheekpiece, pistol-grip, black forend tip, sling swivels. Imported from 1956-62. Disc.

CARBINE .... NiB $699 Ex $571 Gd $390
Same as Krico Sporting Rifle except w/20- or 22-inch bbl., full-length Mannlicher-type stock. Disc. 1962.

SPECIAL VARMINT RIFLE .... NiB $699 Ex $571 Gd $390
Same as Krico Rifle except w/heavy bbl., no sights, weight: 7.25 lbs. Caliber: .222 Rem. only. Disc. 1962.

KRIEGHOFF RIFLES — Ulm (Donau), Germany, Mfd. by H. Krieghoff Jagd und Sportwaffenfabrik

See also Combination Guns under Krieghoff shotgun listings.

TECK OVER/UNDER RIFLE
Kersten action, double crossbolt, double underlugs. Boxlock. Calibers: 7x57r5, 7x64, 7x65r5, .30-30, .308 Win. .30-06, .300 Win. Mag., 9.3x74r5, .375 H&H Mag. .458 Win. Mag. 25-inch bbls. Weight: 8 to 9.5 lbs. Sights: Express rear; ramp front. Checkered walnut stock and forearm. Made from 1967. Disc.
Standard calibers .... NiB $9116 Ex $6747 Gd $5305
.375 H&H Mag.
(Disc. 1988)
.458 Win. Mag .... NiB $9425 Ex $7056 Gd $6335

ULM OVER/
UNDER RIFLE .... NiB $14,729 Ex $10,609 Gd $6180
Same general specifications as Teck model except w/sidelocks w/leaf Arabesque engraving. Made from 1963. Disc.

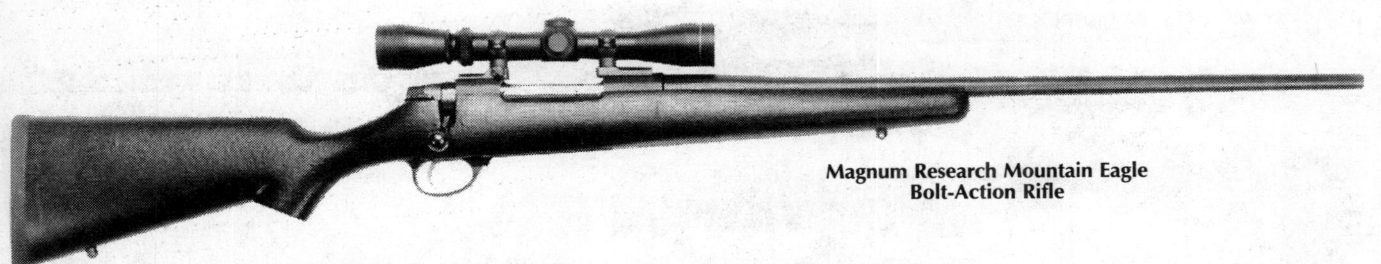
Magnum Research Mountain Eagle Bolt-Action Rifle

ULM-PRIMUS OVER/UNDER RIFLE... NiB $14,485 Ex $11,587 Gd $7879
Delux version of Ulm model, w/detachable sidelocks, higher grade engraving and stock wood. Made from 1963. Disc.

LAKEFIELD ARMS LTD. — Ontario, Canada

See also listing under Savage for production since 1994.

MODEL 64B SEMIAUTOMATIC RIFLE ...... NiB $160 Ex $99 Gd $78
Caliber: .22 LR. 10-round magazine. 20-inch bbl. Weight: 5.5 lbs. 40 inches overall. Bead front sight, adj. rear. Grooved receiver for scope mounts. Stamped checkering on walnut-finished hardwood stock w/Monte Carlo cheekpiece. Imported from 1990-94.

MODEL 90B
BOLT-ACTION TARGET RIFLE ..... NiB $456 Ex $329 Gd $202
Caliber: .22 LR. Five round magazine. 21-inch bbl. w/snow cap. 39.63 inches overall. Weight: 8.25 lbs. Adj. receiver peep sight; globe front w/colored inserts. Receiver drilled and tapped for scope mounts. Biathlon-style natural finished hardwood stock w/shooting rails, hand stop and butthook. Made from 1991-94.

MODEL 91T/91TR BOLT-ACTION TARGET RIFLE
Calibers: .22 Short, Long, LR. 25-inch bbl. 43.63 inches overall. Weight: 8 lbs. Adj. rear peep sight; globe front w/inserts. Receiver drilled and tapped for scope mounts. Walnut-finished hardwood stock w/shooting rails and hand stop. Model 91TR is a 5-round clip-fed repeater. Made from 1991-94.
Model 91T single-shot................. NiB $370 Ex $283 Gd $125
Model 91TR repeater (.22 LR only)....... NiB $380 Ex $227 Gd $135

MODEL 92S TARGET RIFLE....... NiB $310 Ex $252 Gd $179
Same general specifications as Model 90B except w/conventional target-style stock. 8 lbs. No sights, but drilled and tapped for scope mounts. Made from 1993-95.

MODEL 93M BOLT ACTION....... NiB $160 Ex $131 Gd $95
Caliber: .22 WMR. Five round magazine. 20.75-inch bbl. 39.5 inches overall. Weight: 5.75 lbs. Bead front sight, adj. open rear. Receiver grooved for scope mount. Thumb-operated rotary safety. Checkered walnut-finished hardwood stock. Blued finish. Made in 1995.

MARK I BOLT-ACTION RIFLE .... NiB $107 Ex $88 Gd $66
Calibers: .22 Short, Long, LR. Single-shot. 20.5-inch bbl. (19-inch Youth Model); available in smoothbore. Weight: 5.5 lbs. 39.5 inches overall. Bead front sight; adj. rear. Grooved receiver for scope mounts. Checkered walnut-finished hardwood stock w/Monte Carlo and pistol-grip. Blued finish. Made from 1990-94.

MARK II BOLT-ACTION RIFLE
Same general specifications as Mark I except has repeating action w/10-round detachable box magazine. .22 LR. only. Made from 1992-94.
Mark II Standard .... NiB $115 Ex $96 Gd $71
Mark II Youth (19-inch barrel)...... NiB $127 Ex $106 Gd $78
Mark II left-hand .... NiB $153 Ex $126 Gd $91

LAURONA RIFLES — Mfg. in Eibar, Spain Imported by Galaxy Imports, Victoria, TX

MODEL 2000X O/U EXPRESS RIFLE
Calibers: .30-06, 8x57 JRS, 8x75 JR, .375 H&H, 9.3x74R Five round magazine. 24-inch separated bbls. Weight: 8.5 lbs. Quarter rib drilled and tapped for scope mount. Open sights. Matte black chrome finish. Monte Carlo-style checkered walnut buttstock; tulip forearm. Imported from 1993 to date.
Standard calibers............ NiB $2982 Ex $2402 Gd $1661
Magnum calibers............ NiB $3685 Ex $2963 Gd $2043

L.A.R. MANUFACTURING, INC. — West Jordan, Utah

BIG BOAR COMPETITOR
BOLT-ACTION RIFLE......... NiB $2453 Ex $1976 Gd $1366
Single-shot, bull-pup action. Caliber: .50 BMG. 36-inch bbl. 45.5 inches overall. Weight: 28.4 lbs. Made from 1994 to date.

LUNA RIFLE — Mehlis, Germany Mfg. by Ernst Friedr. Büchel

SINGLE-SHOT TARGET RIFLE .... NiB $1066 Ex $921 Gd $612
Falling block action. Calibers: .22 LR. .22 Hornet. 29-inch bbl. Weight: 8.25 lbs. Sights: Micrometer peep rear tang; open rear; ramp front. Cheekpiece stock w/full pistol-grip, semibeavertail forearm, checkered, swivels. Made before WWII.

MAGNUM RESEARCH, INC. — Minneapolis, Minnesota

MOUNTAIN EAGLE BOLT-ACTION RIFLE SERIES
Calibers: .222 Rem., .223 Rem., .270 Win., .280 Rem., 7mm Rem. Mag., 7mm STW, .30-06, .300 Win. Mag., .338 Win. Mag., .340 Wby. Mag., .375 H&H, .416 Rem. Mag. Five round (std.) or 4-round (Mag.). 24- or 26-inch bbl. 44 to 46 inches overall. Weight: 7.75 to 9.75 lbs. Receiver drilled and tapped for scope mount; no sights. Blued finish. Fiberglass composite stock. Made from 1994. Disc. 2000.
Standard model.................. NiB $1421 Ex $1160 Gd $671
Magnum model................... NiB $1421 Ex $1160 Gd $671
Varmint model (Intro. 1996).......... NiB $1421 Ex $1160 Gd $671
Calibers .375 H&H, .416 Rem. Mag., add..................... $300

Mannlicher Model L Rifle

Mannlicher Model M Carbine

Mannlicher Model M Professional

Mannlicher Model M Rifle

MAGTECH — Las Vegas, Nevada Mfg. by CBC, Brazil

MODEL MT 122.2/S BOLT-ACTION RIFLE . . NiB $133 Ex $113 Gd $72
Calibers: .22 Short, Long, Long Rifle. Six- or 10-round clip. Bolt action. 25-inch free-floating bbl. 43 inches overall. Weight: 6.5 lbs. Double locking bolt. Red cocking indicator. Safety lever. Brazilian hardwood finish. Double extractors. Beavertail forearm. Sling swivels. Imported from 1994. Disc.

MODEL MT 122.2/R BOLT-ACTION RIFLE. . NiB $129 Ex $108 Gd $80
Same as Model MT 122.2/S except adj. rear sight and post front sight. Introduced 1994. Disc.

MODEL MT 122.2T BOLT-ACTION RIFLE . . NiB $136 Ex $113 Gd $83
Same as Model MT 122.2/S except w/adj. micrometer-type rear sight and ramp front sight. Introduced 1994. Disc.

MANNLICHER SPORTING RIFLES — Steyr, Austria, Mfg. by Steyr-Daimler-Puch, A.-G.

NOTE: *Certain Mannlicher-Schoenauer models were produced before WWII. Manufacture of sporting rifles and carbines was resumed at the Steyr-Daimler-Puch plant in Austria in 1950 during which time the Model 1950 rifles and carbines were introduced.*

In 1967, Steyr-Daimler-Puch introduced a series of sporting rifles with a bolt action that is a departure from the Mannlicher-Schoenauer system of earlier models. In the latter, the action is locked by lugs symmetrically arranged behind the bolt head as well as by placing the bolt handle ahead of the right flank of the receiver, the rear section of which is open on top for backward movement of the bolt handle. The current action, made in four lengths to accommodate different ranges of cartridges, has a closed-top receiver; the bolt locking lugs are located toward the rear of the bolt (behind the magazine). The Mannlicher-Schoenauer rotary magazine has been redesigned as a detachable box type made of Makrolon. Imported by Gun South, Inc. Trussville, AL

MODEL L CARBINE. . . . . NiB $1397 Ex $1126 Gd $780
Same general specifications as Model SL Carbine except w/type "L" action, weight: 6.2 lbs. Calibers same as for Model L Rifle. Imported from 1968-96.

Mannlicher Model SL
Rifle w/Single-Set Trigger

MODEL L RIFLE. . . . . NiB $1980 Ex $1439 Gd $873
Same general specifications as Model SL Rifle except w/type "L" action, weighs 6.3 lbs. Calibers: .22-250, 5.6x57 (disc. 1991), ..243 Win., 6mm Rem. .308 Win. Imported 1968-96.

MODEL L VARMINT RIFLE . . . . . NiB $2006 Ex $1481 Gd $863
Same general specifications as Model SL Varmint Rifle except w/type "L" action. Calibers: .22-250, .243 Win., .308 Win. Imported 1969-96.

MODEL LUXUS BOLT-ACTION RIFLE
Same general specifications as Models L and M except w/3-round detachable box magazine and single-set trigger. Full or half-stock w/low-luster oil or high-gloss lacquer finish. Disc. 1996.
Full stock. . . . . NiB $2058 Ex $1699 Gd $1239
Half stock . . . . NiB $2626 Ex $1878 Gd $859

MODEL M CARBINE
Same general specifications as Model SL Carbine except w/type "M" action, stock w/recoil pad, weighs 6.8 lbs. Left-hand version w/additional 6.5x55 and 9.3x62 calibers intro. 1977. Imported 1969-96.
Right-hand carbine . . . . NiB $2110 Ex $1498 Gd $828
Left-hand carbine . . . . NiB $2264 Ex $1904 Gd $1445

MODEL M PROFESSIONAL RIFLE . . . . . NiB $2007 Ex $1440 Gd $771
Same as standard Model M Rifle except w/synthetic (Cycolac) stock, weighs 7.5 lbs. Calibers: 6.5x55, 6.5x57, .270 Win., 7x57, 7x64, 7.5 Swiss, .30-06, 8x57JS, 9.3x62. Imported 1977-93.

MODEL M RIFLE
Same general specifications as Model SL Rifle except w/type "M" action, stock w/forend tip and recoil pad; weighs 6.9 lbs. Calibers: 6.5x57, .270 Win., 7x57, 7x64, .30-06, 8x57JS, 9.3x62. Made 1969 to date. Left-hand version also in calibers 6.5x55 and 7.5 Swiss. Imported 1977-96.
Right-hand rifle . . . . NiB $1595 Ex $1131 Gd $771
Left-hand rifle . . . . NiB $2260 Ex $1900 Gd $1441

MODEL S RIFLE. . . . . NiB $1595 Ex $1131 Gd $771
Same general specifications as Model SL Rifle except w/type "S" action, 4-round magazine, 25.63-inch bbl., stock w/forend tip and recoil pad, weighs 8.4 lbs. Calibers: 6.5x68, .257 Weatherby Mag., .264 Win. Mag., 7mm Rem. Mag., .300 Win. Mag., .300 H&H Mag., .308 Norma Mag., 8x68S, .338 Win. Mag., 9.3x64, .375 H&H Mag. Imported 1970-96.

MODEL SL CARBINE. . . . . NiB $1595 Ex $1131 Gd $771
Same general specifications as Model SL Rifle except w/20-inch bbl. and full-length stock, weight: 6 lbs. Imported 1968-96.

MODEL SL RIFLE. . . . . NiB $1595 Ex $1131 Gd $771
Steyr-Mannlicher SL bolt action. Calibers: .222 Rem., .222 Rem., .222 Rem. Mag., .223 Rem. Five round rotary magazine, detachable. 23.63-inch bbl. Weight: 6 lbs. Single- or double-set trigger (mechanisms interchangeable). Sights: Open rear; hooded ramp front. Half stock of European walnut w/Monte Carlo comb and cheekpiece, skip-checkered forearm and pistol grip, rubber buttpad, QD swivels. Imported 1967-96.

MODEL SL
VARMINT RIFLE . . . . NiB $1180 Ex $1154 Gd $794
Same general specifications as Model SL Rifle except caliber .222 Rem. only, w/25.63-inch heavy bbl., no sights, weighs 7.92 lbs. Imported 1969-96.

MODEL SSG MATCH TARGET RIFLE
Type "L" action. Caliber: .308 Win. (7.62x51 NATO). Five- or 10-round magazine, single-shot plug. 25.5-inch heavy bbl. Weight: 10.25 lbs. Single trigger. Sights: Micrometer peep rear; globe front. Target stock, European walnut or synthetic, w/full pistol-grip, wide forearm w/swivel rail, adj. rubber buttplate. Imported 1969 to date.
W/walnut stock. . . . . NiB $2331 Ex $1867 Gd $1200
W/synthetic stock . . . . NiB $1407 Ex $1073 Gd $646

MODEL S/T RIFLE. . . . . NiB $2113 Ex $1510 Gd $679
Same as Model S Rifle except w/heavy 25.63-inch bbl., weight: 9 lbs. Calibers: 9.3x64, .375 H&H Mag., .458 Win. Mag. Option of 23.63-inch bbl. in latter caliber. Imported 1975-96.

MODEL 1903
BOLT-ACTION
SPORTING CARBINE . . . . NiB $4101 Ex $4008 Gd $609
Caliber: 6.5x53mm (referred to in some European gun catalogs as 6.7x53mm, following the Austrian practice of designating calibers by bullet diameter). Five round rotary magazine. 450mm (17.7-inch) bbl. Weight: 6.5 lbs. Double-set trigger. Sights: Two-leaf rear; ramp front. Full-length sporting stock w/cheekpiece, pistol-grip, trap buttplate, swivels. Pre-WWII.

MODEL 1905 CARBINE . . . . NiB $1289 Ex $851 Gd $568
Same as Model 1903 except w/19.7-inch bbl.chambered 9x56mm and weight: 6.75 lbs. Pre-WWII.

MODEL 1908 CARBINE . . . . NiB $1388 Ex $1186 Gd $877
Same as Model 1905 except calibers 7x57mm and 8x56mm Pre-WWII.

MODEL 1910 CARBINE . . . . NiB $1601 Ex $1291 Gd $622
Same as Model 1905 except in 9.5x57mm. Pre-WWII.

MODEL 1924 CARBINE . . . . NiB $1704 Ex $1498 Gd $983
Same as Model 1905 except caliber .30-06 (7.62x63mm). Pre-WWII.

MODEL 1950
BOLT-ACTION
SPORTING RIFLE. . . . . NiB $1549 Ex $1395 Gd $519
Calibers: .257 Roberts, .270 Win., .30-06. Five round rotary magazine. 24-inch bbl. Weight: 7.25 lbs. Single trigger or double-set trigger. Redesigned low bolt handle, shotgun-type safety. Sights: Folding leaf open rear; hooded ramp front. Improved half-length stock w/cheekpiece, pistol grip, checkered, ebony forend tip, swivels. Made from 1950-52.

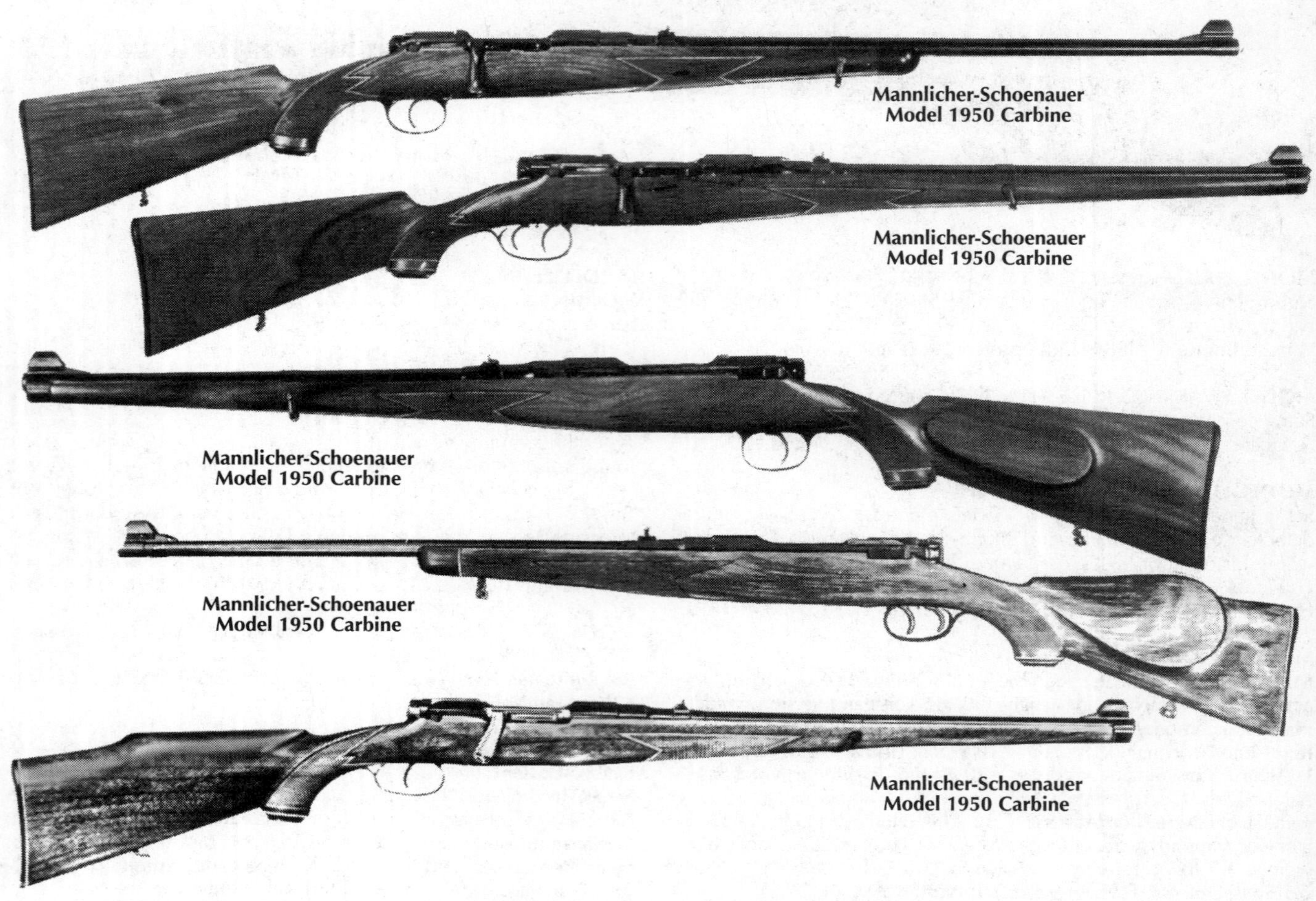

Mannlicher-Schoenauer Model 1950 Carbine

Mannlicher-Schoenauer Model 1950 Carbine

Mannlicher-Schoenauer Model 1950 Carbine

Mannlicher-Schoenauer Model 1950 Carbine

Mannlicher-Schoenauer Model 1950 Carbine

MODEL 1950 CARBINE . . . . NiB $1808 Ex $1499 Gd $932
Same general specifications as Model 1950 Rifle except w/20-inch bbl., full-length stock, weighs 7 lbs. Made from 1950-52.

MODEL 1950
6.5 CARBINE . . . . NiB $1911 Ex $1705 Gd $974
Same as other Model 1950 Carbines except caliber 6.5x53mm, w/18.25-inch bbl., weighs 6.75 lbs. Made from 1950-52.

MODEL 1952
IMPROVED CARBINE . . . . NiB $2017 Ex $1394 Gd $863
Same as Model 1950 Carbine except w/swept-back bolt handle, redesigned stock. Calibers: .257, .270, 7mm, .30-06. Made from 1952-56.

MODEL 1952 IMPROVED
6.5 CARBINE . . . . NiB $1133 Ex $1030 Gd $567
Same as Model 1952 Carbine except caliber 6.5x53mm, w/18.25-inch bbl. Made from 1952-56.

MODEL 1952 IMPROVED
SPORTING RIFLE . . . . NiB $1496 Ex $1290 Gd $826
Same as Model 1950 except w/swept-back bolt handle, redesigned stock. Calibers: .257, .270, .30-06, 9.3x62mm. Made from 1952-56 and imported exclusively by Stoeger Arms Corp.

MODEL 1956 CUSTOM CARBINE . . . . NiB $935 Ex $755 Gd $523
Same general specifications as Models 1950 and 1952 Carbines except w/redesigned stock w/high comb. Drilled and tapped for scope mounts. Calibers: .243, 6.5mm, .257, .270, 7mm, .30-06, .308. Made from 1956-60.

CARBINE, MODEL 1961-MCA . . NiB $2123 Ex $1968 Gd $578
Same as Model 1956 Carbine except w/universal Monte Carlo design stock. Calibers: .243 Win., 6.5mm, .270, .308, .30-06. Made from 1961-71.

RIFLE, MODEL 1961-MCA . . . . . NiB $1760 Ex $1296 Gd $626
Same as Model 1956 Rifle except w/universal Monte Carlo design stock. Calibers: .243, .270, .30-06. Made from 1961-71.

HIGH VELOCITY
BOLT-ACTION SPORTING RIFLE . . . NiB $2225 Ex $2019 Gd $963
Calibers: 7x64 Brenneke, .30-06 (7.62x63), 8x60 Magnum, 9.3x62, 10.75x68mm. 23.6-inch bbl. Weight: 7.5 lbs. Sights: British-style 3-leaf open rear; ramp front. Half-length sporting stock w/cheekpiece, pistol grip, checkered, trap buttplate, swivels. Also produced in a takedown model. Pre-WWII. See illustration next page.

M72 MODEL L/M CARBINE . . . . . . NiB $961 Ex $693 Gd $446
Same general specifications as M72 Model L/M Rifle except w/20-inch bbl. and full-length stock, weight: 7.2 lbs. Imported from 1972 to date.

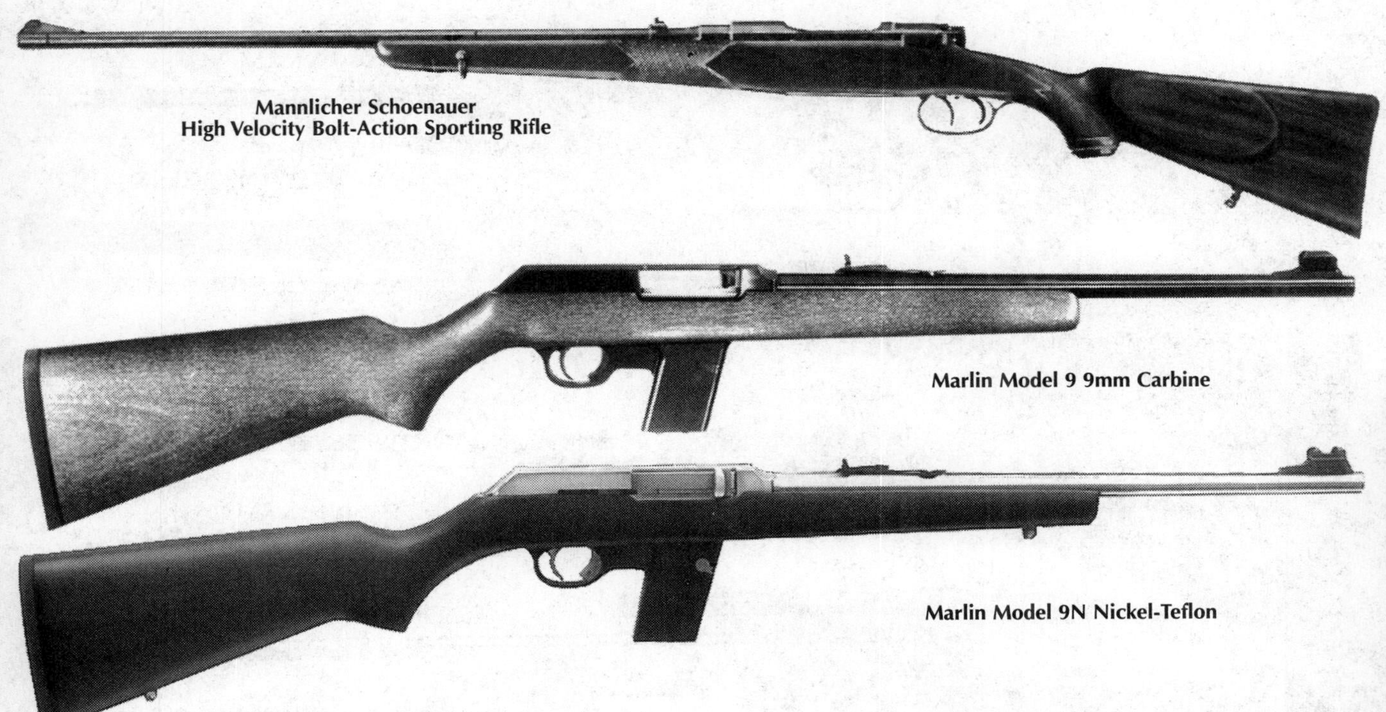
Mannlicher Schoenauer
High Velocity Bolt-Action Sporting Rifle

Marlin Model 9 9mm Carbine

Marlin Model 9N Nickel-Teflon

M72 MODEL L/M RIFLE .... NiB $854 Ex $777 Gd $545
M72 bolt-action, type L/M receiver front-locking bolt internal rotary magazine (5-round). Calibers: .22-250, 5.6x57, 6mm Rem., .243 Win., 6.5x57, .270 Win., 7x57, 7x64, .308 Win., .30-06. 23.63-inch bbl. Weight: 7.3 lbs. Single- or double-set trigger (mechanisms interchangeable). Sights: Open rear; hooded ramp front. Half stock of European walnut, checkered forearm and pistol-grip, Monte Carlo cheekpiece, rosewood forend tip, recoil pad QD swivels. Imported from 1972-81.

M72 MODEL S RIFLE .... NiB $828 Ex $725 Gd $493
Same general specifications as M72 Model L/M Rifle except w/magnum action, 4-round magazine, 25.63-inch bbl., weighs 8.6 lbs. Calibers: 6.5x68, 7mm Rem. Mag., 8x68S, 9.3x64, .375 H&H Mag. Imported from 1972-81.

M72 MODEL S/T RIFLE........ NiB $1407 Ex $1098 Gd $742
Same as M72 Model S Rifle except w/heavy 25.63-inch bbl., weighs 9.3 lbs. Calibers: .300 Win. Mag. 9.3x64, .375 H&H Mag., .458 Win. Mag. Option of 23.63-inch bbl. in latter caliber. Imported from 1975-81.

MODEL SBS FORESTER RIFLE
Calibers: .243 Win., .25-06 Rem., .270 Win., .6.5x55mm, 6.5x57mm, 7x64mm, 7mm-08 Rem., .30-06, .308 Win. 9.3x64mm. Four round detachable magazine. 23.6-inch bbl. 44.5 inches overall. Weight: 7.5 lbs. No sights w/drilled and tapped for Browning A-Bolt configuration. Checkered American walnut stock w/Monte Carlo cheekpiece and Pachmayr swivels. Polished or matte blue finish. Imported from 1997 to date.
SBS Forester Rifle (standard calibers) ..... NiB $844 Ex $674 Gd $437
SBS Forester Mountain Rifle (20-inch bbl.) .... NiB $809 Ex $648 Gd $432
For magnum calibers, add.. $25
For metric calibers, add $100

MODEL SBS PRO-HUNTER RIFLE
Similar to the Forester Model, except w/ASB black synthetic stock. Matte blue finish. Imported from 1997 to date.
SBS Pro-Hunter Rifle (standard calibers)...... NiB $792 Ex $648 Gd $432
SBS Pro-Hunter Rifle
Mountain Rifle (20-inch bbl.) .... NiB $844 Ex $638 Gd $437
SBS Pro-Hunter Rifle (.376 Steyr) .... NiB $834 Ex $674 Gd $468
SBS Pro-Hunter Youth/Ladies Rifle .... NiB $844 Ex $674 Gd $437
For magnum calibers, add.. $25
For metric calibers, add.. $100
W/walnut stock .... NiB $2284 Ex $1873 Gd $1348
W/synthetic stock .... NiB $1823 Ex $1489 Gd $1062

MARLIN FIREARMS CO. — North Haven, Connecticut

MODEL 9
SEMIAUTOMATIC CARBINE
Calibers: 9mm Parabellum. 12-round magazine. 16.5-inch bbl. 35.5 inches overall. Weight: 6.75 lbs. Manual bolt hold-open. Sights: Hooded post front; adj. open rear. Walnut-finished hardwood stock w/rubber buttpad. Blued or nickel-Teflon finish. Made from 1985-99.
Model 9 .... NiB $378 Ex $260 Gd $136
Model 9N, Nickel-Teflon (disc. 1994)........ NiB $414 Ex $285 Gd $141

MODEL 15Y/15YN
Bolt-action, single-shot "Little Buckaroo" rifle. Caliber: .22 Short, Long or LR. 16.25-inch bbl. Weight: 4.25 lbs. Thumb safety. Ramp front sight; adj. open rear. One-piece walnut Monte Carlo stock w/full pistol-grip. Made from 1984-88. Reintroduced in 1989 as Model 15YN.
Model 15Y..................... NiB $143 Ex $112 Gd $76
Model 15YN.....................NiB $148 Ex $117 Gd $81

MODEL 18 BABY SLIDE-ACTION
REPEATER .... NiB $324 Ex $308 Gd $179
Exposed hammer. Solid frame. Caliber: .22 LR, Long Short. Tubular magazine holds 14 Short cartridges. 20-inch bbl., round or octagon. Weight: 3.75 lbs. Sights: Open rear; bead front. Plain straight-grip stock and slide handle. Made from 1906-09.

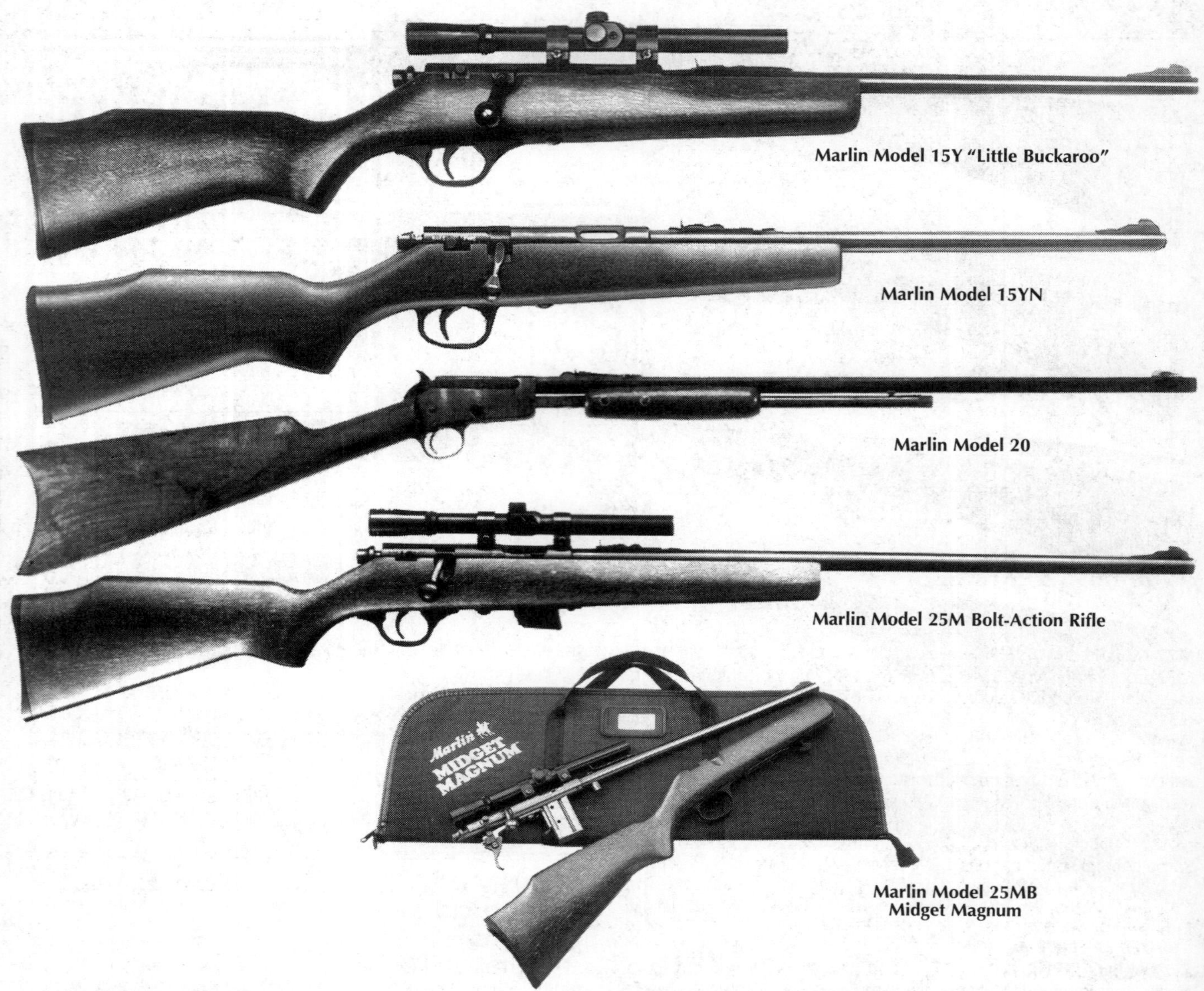

Marlin Model 15Y "Little Buckaroo"

Marlin Model 15YN

Marlin Model 20

Marlin Model 25M Bolt-Action Rifle

Marlin Model 25MB
Midget Magnum

MODEL 20 SLIDE-ACTION REPEATING RIFLE . . . . NiB $328 Ex $312 Gd $178
Exposed hammer. Takedown. Caliber: .22 LR. Long, Short. Tubular magazine: Half-length holds 15 Short, 12 Long, 10 LR; full-length holds 25 Short, 20 Long, 18 LR. 24-inch octagon bbl. Weight: 5 lbs. Sights: Open rear; bead front. Plain straight-grip stock, grooved slide handle. Made from 1907-22. Note: After 1920 was designated "Model 20-S."

MODEL 25 BOLT-ACTION RIFLE . . . . NiB $175 Ex $150 Gd $98
Caliber: .22 Short, Long or LR; 7-round clip. 22-inch bbl. Weight: 5.5 lbs. Ramp front sight, adj. open rear. One-piece walnut Monte Carlo stock w/full pistol-grip Mar-Shield finish. Made from 1984-88.

MODEL 25 SLIDE-ACTION REPEATER . . . . NiB $460 Ex $316 Gd $187
Exposed hammer. Takedown. Caliber: .22 Short (also handles 22 CB caps). Tubular magazine holds 15 Short. 23-inch bbl. Weight: 4 lbs. Sights: Open rear; beaded front. Plain straight-grip stock and slide handle. Made from 1909-10.

MODEL 25M BOLT ACTION W/SCOPE . . . NiB $169 Ex $139 Gd $101
Caliber: .22 WMR. 7-round clip. 22-inch bbl. Weight: 6 lbs. Ramp front sight w/brass bead, adj. open rear. Walnut-finished stock w/Monte Carlo styling and full pistol-grip. Sling swivels. Made from 1986-88.

MODEL 25MB MIDGET MAGNUM . . . . NiB $175 Ex $139 Gd $98
Bolt action. Caliber: .22 WMR. Seven round capacity.16.25-inch bbl. Weight: 4.75 lbs. Walnut-finished Monte Carlo-style stock w/full pistol grip and abbreviated forend. Sights: Ramp front w/brass bead, adj. open rear. Thumb safety. Made from 1986-88.

MODEL 25MG/25MN/25N/25NC BOLT-ACTION RIFLE
Caliber: .22 WMR (Model 25MN) or .22 LR. (Model 25N). Seven round clip magazine. 22-inch bbl. 41 inches overall. Weight: 5.5 to 6 lbs. Adj. open rear sight, ramp front; receiver grooved for scope mounts. One piece walnut-finished hardwood Monte Carlo stock w/pistol grip. Made from 1989 to date.
Marlin Model 25MG (Garden Gun) . . . . . . NiB $199 Ex $155 Gd $112
Marlin Model 25MN. . . . . NiB $169 Ex $139 Gd $100
Marlin Model 25N . . . . NiB $156 Ex $129 Gd $94
Marlin Model 25NC (camouflage stock). . . NiB $189 Ex $155 Gd $112

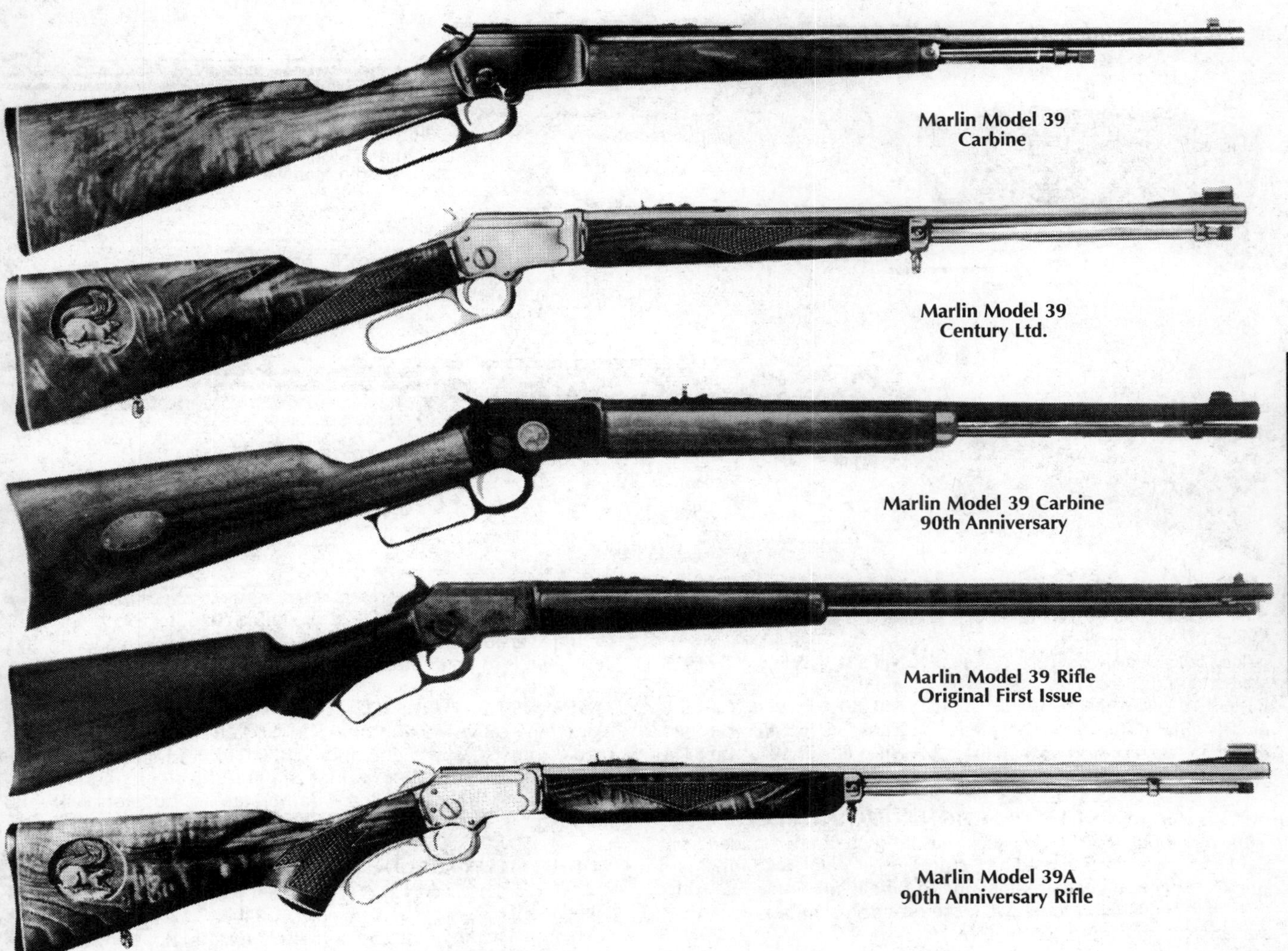
Marlin Model 39 Carbine

Marlin Model 39 Century Ltd.

Marlin Model 39 Carbine 90th Anniversary

Marlin Model 39 Rifle Original First Issue

Marlin Model 39A 90th Anniversary Rifle

MODEL 27 SLIDE-ACTION REPEATING RIFLE . . . . NiB $434 Ex $264 Gd $186
Exposed hammer. Takedown. Calibers: .25-20, .32-20. Magazine (tubular) holds 7 rounds. 24-inch octagon bbl. Weight: 5.75 lbs. Sights: Open rear; bead front. Plain, straight-grip stock, grooved slide handle. Made from 1910-16.

MODEL 27S. . . . . NiB $341 Ex $246 Gd $161
Same as Model 27 except w/round bbl., also chambered for .25 Stevens rimfire Made from 1920-32.

MODEL 29 SLIDE-ACTION REPEATER . . . . NiB $341 Ex $264 Gd $161
Similar to Model 20 w/23-inch round bbl., half magazine only, weight 5.75 lbs. Made from 1913-16.

MODEL 30/30A AND 30AS LEVER-ACTION
Caliber: .30/30 Win. Six-round tubular magazine. 20-inch bbl. w/Micro-Groove rifling. 38.25 inches overall. Weight: 7 lbs. Brass bead front sight, adj. rear. Solid top receiver, offset hammer spur for scope use. Walnut-finished hardwood stock w/pistol-grip. Mar-Shield finish. Made from 1964-2000.
Model 30/30A . . . . NiB $254 Ex $181 Gd $130
Model 30AS. . . . . NiB $254 Ex $181 Gd $130
Model 30AS w/4x scope, add $10

MODEL 32 SLIDE-ACTION REPEATER . . . . NiB $608 Ex $454 Gd $274
Hammerless. Takedown. Caliber: .22 LR. Long, Short. Tubular magazine holds 15 Short, 12 Long, 10 LR; full magazine, 25 Short, 20 Long, 18 LR. 24-inch octagon bbl. Weight: 5.5 lbs. Sights: Open rear; bead front. Plain pistol-grip stock, grooved slide handle. Made from 1914-15.

MODEL 36 LEVER-ACTION REPEATING CARBINE
Calibers: .30-30, .32 Special. Seven-round tubular magazine. 20-inch bbl. Weight: 6.5 lbs. Sights: Open rear; bead front. Pistol-grip stock, semibeavertail forearm w/carbine bbl. band. Early production w/receiver, lever and hammer color casehardened and the remaining metal blued. Late production w/blued receiver. Made 1936-48. Note: In 1936, this was designated "Model 1936" and was so marked on the upper tang. In 1937, the model designation was shortened to "36". An "RC" serial number suffix identifies a "Regular/Carbine".
Model 1936 (CC receiver, w/long tang, w/o SN prefix) . . . . NiB $818 Ex $690 Gd $458
Model 1936 (CC receiver, w/short tang, w/o SN prefix) . . . . NiB $589 Ex $479 Gd $340
Model 1936 (CC receiver, w/SN prefix) . . . NiB $483 Ex $402 Gd $287
Model 36 (CC receiver, w/SN prefix) . . . . . NiB $460 Ex $377 Gd $270
Model 36 (blued receiver, w/SN prefix) . . . NiB $416 Ex $340 Gd $243

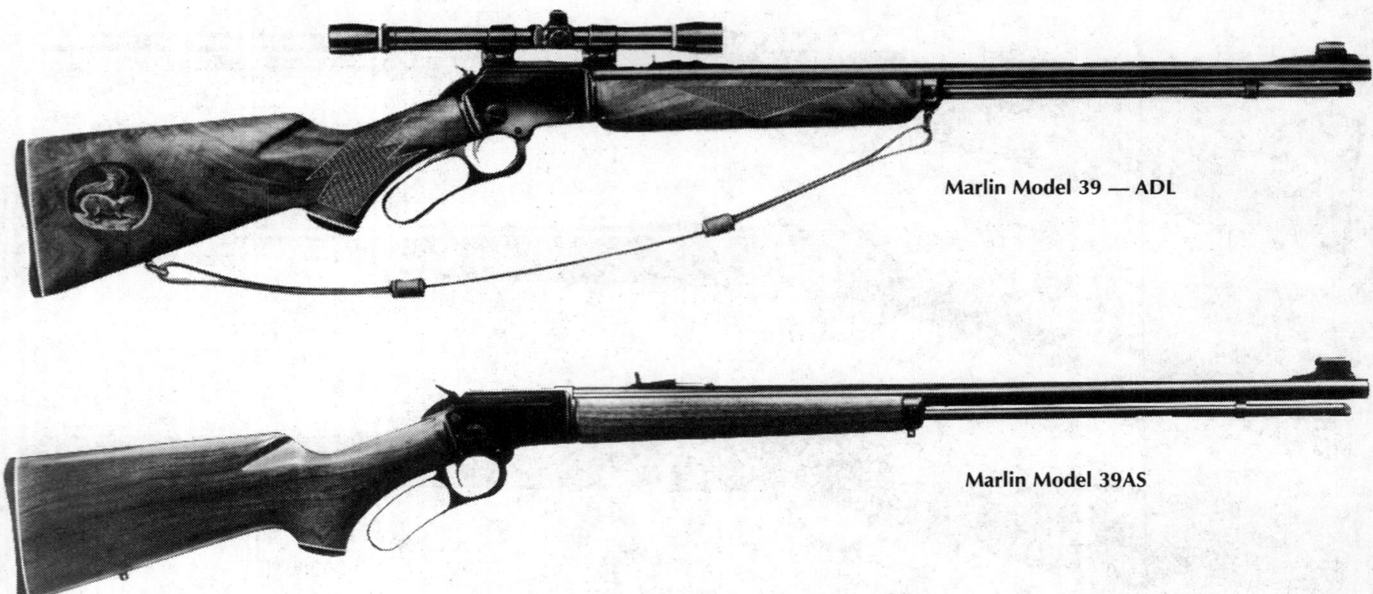

Marlin Model 39 — ADL

Marlin Model 39AS

MODEL 36 SPORTING CARBINE
Same as M36 carbine except w/6-round, (2/3 magazine) and weighs 6.25 lbs.
Model 1936 (CC receiver,
w/long tang, w/o SN prefix) . . . . NiB $819 Ex $665 Gd $459
Model 1936 (CC receiver,
w/short tang, w/o SN prefix) . . . . NiB $613 Ex $536 Gd $356
Model 1936 (CC receiver, w/SN prefix) . . . NiB $556 Ex $455 Gd $324
Model 36 (CC receiver, w/SN prefix) . . . . . NiB $505 Ex $413 Gd $294
Model 36 (blued receiver, w/SN prefix) . . . NiB $460 Ex $377 Gd $270

MODEL 36A/36A-DL LEVER-ACTION REPEATING RIFLE
Same as Model 36 Carbine except has 24-inch bbl. w/hooded front sight and 2/3 magazine holding 6 cartridges. Weight: 6.75 lbs. Note: An "A" serial number suffix identifies a Rifle while an "A-DL" suffix designates a Deluxe Model w/checkered stock, semibeavertail forearm, swivels and sling. Made from 1936-48.
Model 1936 (CC receiver,
w/long tang, w/o SN prefix) . . . . NiB $1241 Ex $1087 Gd $366
Model 1936 (CC receiver,
w/short tang, w/o SN prefix) . . . . NiB $598 Ex $521 Gd $341
Model 1936 (CC receiver, w/SN prefix) . . . NiB $579 Ex $470 Gd $330
Model 36 (CC receiver, w/SN prefix) . . . . . NiB $515 Ex $418 Gd $295
Model 36 (blued receiver, w/SN prefix) . . . NiB $483 Ex $392 Gd $277
For ADL model, add 25%

MODEL 37 SLIDE-ACTION
REPEATING RIFLE . . . . NiB $444 Ex $392 Gd $186
Similar to Model 29 except w/24-inch bbl. and full magazine. Weight: 5.25 lbs. Made from 1913-16.

MODEL 38 SLIDE-ACTION
REPEATING RIFLE . . . . NiB $387 Ex $284 Gd $191
Hammerless. Takedown. Caliber: .22 LR. Long, Short. 2/3 magazine (tubular) holds 15 Short, 12 Long, 10 LR. 24-inch octagon or round bbls. Weight: 5.5 lbs. Sights: Open rear; bead front. Plain shotgun-type pistol-grip buttstock w/hard rubber buttplate, grooved slide handle. Ivory bead front sight; adj. rear. About 20,000 Model 38 rifles were made between 1920-30.

MODEL 39 CARBINE . . . . NiB $280 Ex $203 Gd $152
Same as 39M except w/lightweight bbl., 3/4 magazine (capacity: 18 Short, 14 Long, 12 LR), slimmer forearm. Weight: 5.25 lbs. Made from 1963-67.

MODEL 39 90TH
ANNIVERSARY CARBINE . . . . NiB $1076 Ex $999 Gd $757
Carbine version of 90th Anniversary Model 39A. 500 made in 1960. Top value is for carbine in new, unfired condition.

MODEL 39 CENTURY LTD. . . . . NiB $488 Ex $334 Gd $221
Commemorative version of Model 39A. Receiver inlaid w/brass medallion, "Marlin Centennial 1870-1970." Square lever. 20-inch octagon bbl. Fancy walnut straight-grip stock and forearm; brass forend cap, buttplate, nameplate in buttstock. 35,388 made in 1970.

MODEL 39 LEVER-ACTION
REPEATER . . . . NiB $2138 Ex $1983 Gd $1098
Takedown. Casehardened receiver. Caliber: .22 LR. Long, Short. Tubular magazine holds 25 Short, 20 Long, 18 LR. 24-inch octagon bbl. Weight: 5.75 lbs. Sights: Open rear; bead front. Plain pistol-grip stock and forearm. Made from 1922-38.

MODEL 39A
General specifications same as Model 39 except w/blued receiver, round bbl., heavier stock w/semibeavertail forearm, weight 6.5 lbs. Made from 1938-60.
Early model (no prefix) . . . . NiB $1245 Ex $1007 Gd $702
Late model ("B" prefix) . . . . NiB $1015 Ex $821 Gd $574

MODEL 39A 90TH
ANNIVERSARY RIFLE . . . . NiB $1088 Ex $1032 Gd $765
Commemorates Marlin's 90th anniversary. Same general specifications as Golden 39A except w/chrome-plated bbl. and action, stock and forearm of select walnut-finely checkered, carved figure of a squirrel on right side of buttstock. 500 made in 1960. Top value is for rifle in new, unfired condition.

MODEL 39A
ARTICLE II RIFLE . . . . NiB $515 Ex $386 Gd $284
Commemorates National Rifle Association Centennial 1871-1971. "The Right to Bear Arms" medallion inlaid in receiver. Similar to Model 39A. Magazine capacity: 26 Short, 21 Long, 19 LR. 24-inch octagon bbl. Fancy walnut pistol-grip stock and forearm; brass forend cap, buttplate. 6,244. Made in 1971.

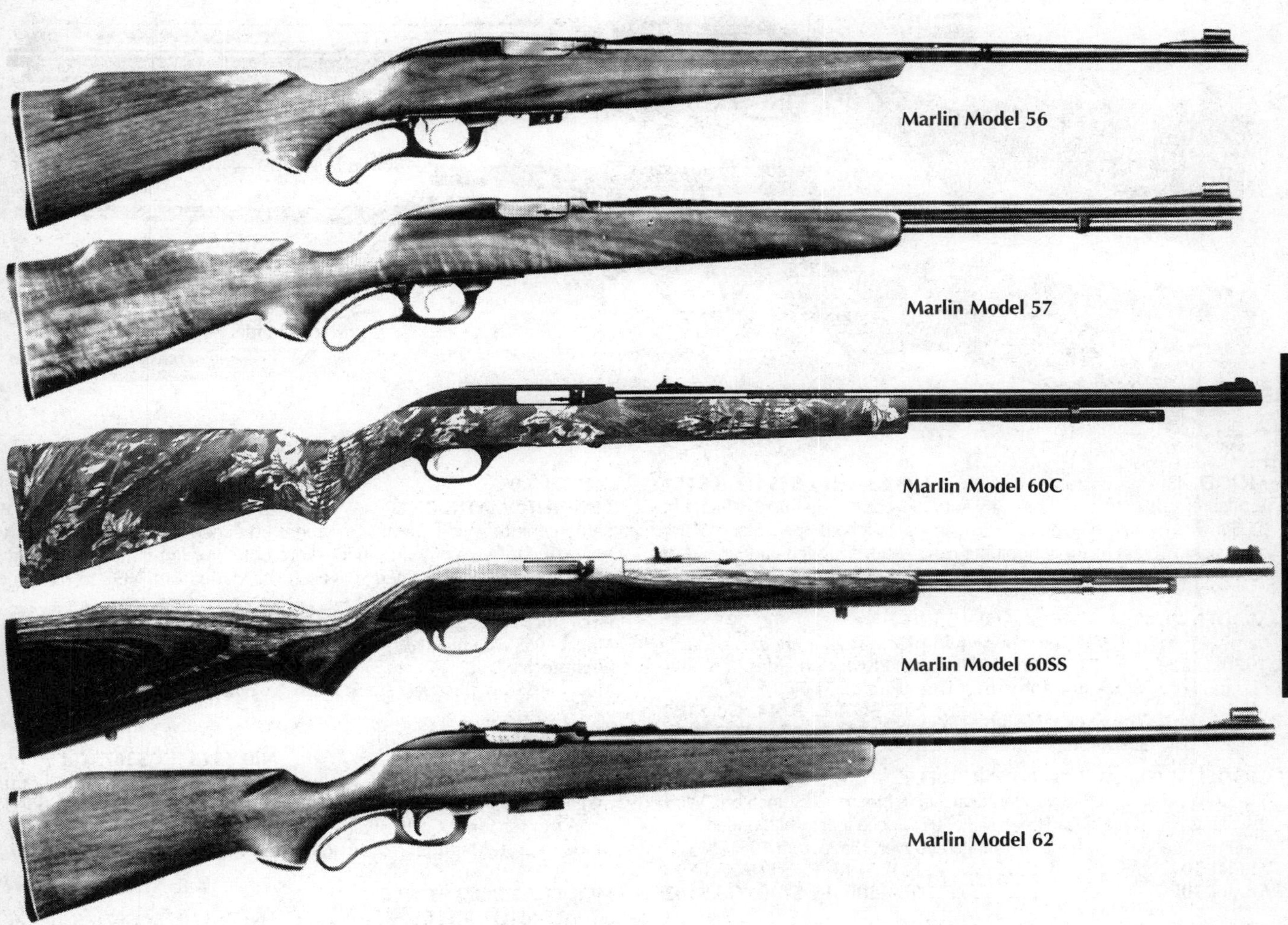
Marlin Model 56

Marlin Model 57

Marlin Model 60C

Marlin Model 60SS

Marlin Model 62

GOLDEN 39A/39AS RIFLE
Same as Model 39A except w/gold-plated trigger, hooded ramp front sight, sling swivels. Made from 1960-87 (39A); Model 39AS from 1988 to date.
Golden 39A........................ NiB $380 Ex $281 Gd $153
Golden 39AS (W/hammer block safety) .. NiB $261 Ex $164 Gd $137

MODEL 39A "MOUNTIE" LEVER-ACTION REPEATING RIFLE....... NiB $384 Ex $333 Gd $204
Same as Model 39A except w/lighter, straight-grip stock, slimmer forearm. Weight: 6.25 lbs. Made from 1953-60.

MODEL 39A OCTAGON......... NiB $695 Ex $541 Gd $335
Same as Golden 39A except w/oct. bbl., plain bead front sight, slimmer stock and forearm, no pistol-grip cap or swivels. Made in1973. (2551 produced)

MODEL 39D .... NiB $256 Ex $209 Gd $153
Same as Model 39M except w/pistol-grip stock, forearm w/bbl. band. Made from 1970-74.

39M ARTICLE II CARBINE....... NiB $487 Ex $431 Gd $256
Same as 39A Article II Rifle except w/straight-grip buttstock, square lever, 20-inch octagon bbl., reduced magazine capacity. 3,824 units, made in 1971.

GOLDEN 39M
Calibers: .22 Short, Long and LR. Tubular magazine holds 21 Short, 16 Long or 15 LR cartridges. 20-inch bbl. 36 inches overall. Weight: 6 lbs. Gold-plated trigger. Hooded ramp front sight, adj. folding semi-buckhorn rear. Two-piece, straight-grip American black walnut stock. Sling swivels. Mar-Shield finish. Made from 1960-87.
Model Golden 39M............. NiB $393 Ex $283 Gd $231
Model 39M Octagon (octagonal bbl. made 1973 only)............... NiB $463 Ex $432 Gd $334

MODEL 39M "MOUNTIE" CARBINE
Same as Model 39A "Mountie" Rifle except w/20-inch bbl. Weight: 6 lbs. 500 made in 1960. (For values See Marlin 39 90th Anniversary Carbine)

MODEL 39TDS CARBINE..................... NiB $329 Ex $226 Gd $149
Same general specifications as Model 39M except takedown style w/16.5-inch bbl. and reduced magazine capacity. 32.63 inches overall. Weight: 5.25 lbs. Made from 1988-95.

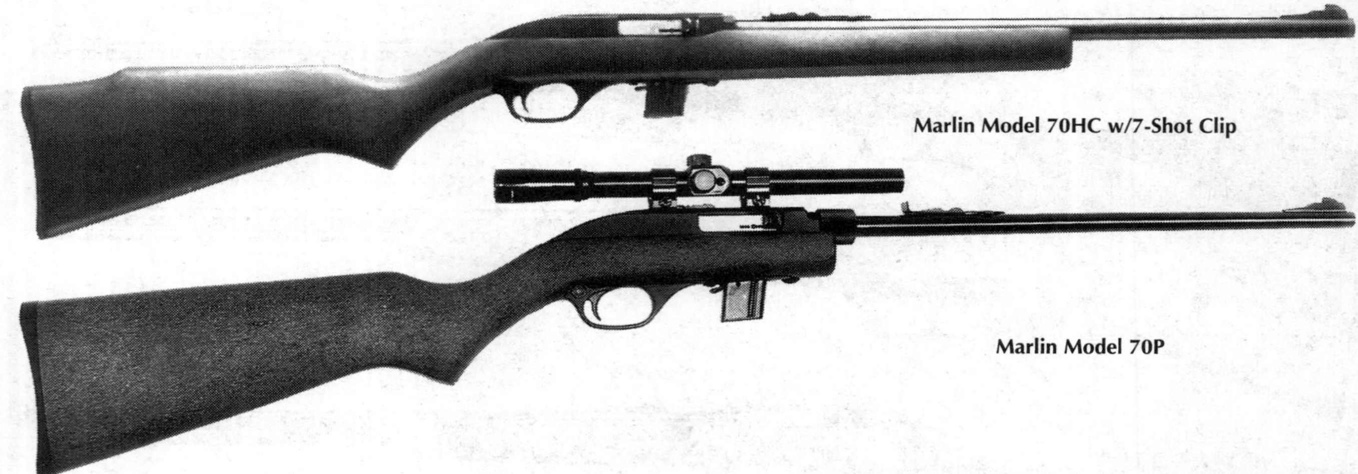

Marlin Model 70HC w/7-Shot Clip

Marlin Model 70P

MODEL 45 . . . . NiB $310 Ex $254 Gd $151
Semiautomatic action. Caliber: .45 Auto. Seven round clip.16.5-inch bbl. 35.5 inches overall. Weight: 6.75 lbs. Manual bolt hold-open. Sights: Ramp front sight w/brass bead, adj. folding rear. Receiver drilled and tapped for scope mount. Walnut-finished hardwood stock. Made from 1986 to date.

MODEL 49/49DL AUTOLOADING RIFLE
Same as Model 99C except w/two-piece stock, checkered after 1970. Made 1968-71. Model 49DL w/scrollwork on sides of receiver, checkered stock and forearm; made from 1971-78.
Model 49 . . . . NiB $174 Ex $144 Gd $104
Model 49DL . . . . NiB $181 Ex $149 Gd $108

MODEL 50/50E AUTOLOADING RIFLE
Takedown. Cal: .22 LR. Six round detachable box mag. 22 inch bbl. Wt: 6 lbs. Sights: Open rear; bead front; Mdl. 50E w/peep rear sight, hooded front. Plain pistol-grip stock, forearm w/finger grooves. Made from 1931-34.
Model 50. . . . . NiB $190 Ex $149 Gd $97
Model 50E. NiB $200 Ex $149 Gd $102

MODEL 56 LEVERMATIC RIFLE . . . NiB $281 Ex $220 Gd $127
Same as Model 57 except clip-loading. Magazine holds eight rounds. Weight: 5.75 lbs. Made from 1955-64.

MODEL 57 LEVERMATIC RIFLE . . . NiB $281 Ex $220 Gd $127
Lever-action. Cal: .22 LR. 22 Long, 22 Short. Tubular mag. holds 19 LR, 21 Long, 27 Short. 22 inch bbl. Wt: 6.25 lbs. Sights: Open rear, adj. for windage and elevation; hooded ramp front. Monte Carlo-style stock w/pistol-grip. Made from 1959-65.

MODEL 57M LEVERMATIC. . . . . . . NiB $272 Ex $211 Gd $128
Same as Model 57 except chambered for 22 WMR cartridge, w/24-inch bbl., 15-round magazine. Made from 1960-69.

MODEL 60 SEMIAUTOMATIC RIFLE . . . . NiB $121 Ex $95 Gd $69
Caliber: .22 LR. 14-round tubular magazine. 22-inch bbl. 40.5 inches overall. Weight: 5.5 lbs. Grooved receiver. Ramp front sight w/removable hood; adj. open rear. Anodized receiver w/blued bbl. Monte Carlo-style walnut-finished hardwood stock w/Mar-Shield finish. Made 1981 to date. Note: Marketed 1960-1980 under Glenfield promotion logo and w/slightly different stock configuration.

MODEL 60C SELF-LOADING RIFLE . . . . NiB $126 Ex $116 Gd $90
Caliber: .22 LR. 14- round tubular mag. 22 inch Micro-Groove bbl., 40.5 inch overall. Wt: 5.5 lbs. Screw-adjustable open rear and ramp front sights. Aluminum receiver, grooved for scope mount. Hardwood Monte Carlo stock w/Mossy Oak "Break-Up" camouflage pattern. Made from 1998 to date.

MODEL 60SS
SEMIAUTOMATIC RIFLE
Same general specifications as Model 60 except w/stainless bbl. and magazine tube. Synthetic, uncheckered birch or laminated black/gray birch stock w/nickel-plated swivel studs. Made from 1993 to date.
Model 60SB w/uncheckered
birch stock . . . . NiB $228 Ex $176 Gd $115
Model 60SS w/laminated
birch stock . . . . NiB $238 Ex $176 Gd $115
Model 60SSK w/fiberglass stock. . . . . NiB $228 Ex $176 Gd $115

MODEL 62
LEVERMATIC RIFLE . . . . NiB $513 Ex $387 Gd $259
Lever-action. Calibers: .256 Magnum, .30 Carbine. Four round clip magazine. 23-inch bbl. Weight: 7 lbs. Sights: Open rear; hooded ramp front. Monte Carlo-style stock w/pistol-grip, swivels and sling. Made in .256 Magnum from 1963-66; in .30 Carbine from 1966-69.

MODEL 65 BOLT-ACTION
SINGLE-SHOT RIFLE . . . . NiB $110 Ex $678 Gd $56
Takedown. Caliber: .22 LR. Long, Short. 24-inch bbl. Weight: 5 lbs. Sights: Open rear; bead front. Plain pistol-grip stock w/grooved forearm. Made 1932-38. Model 65E is same as Model 65 except w/rear peep sight and hooded front sight.

MODEL 70HC SEMIAUTOMATIC
Caliber: .22 LR. Seven and 15-round magazine. 18-inch bbl. Weight: 5.5 lbs. 36.75 inches overall. Ramp front sight; adj. open rear. Grooved receiver for scope mounts. Walnut-finished hardwood stock w/Monte Carlo and pistol-grip. Made from 1988-96.
Marlin model. . . . . NiB $166 Ex $141 Gd $114
Glenfield model. . . . . NiB $120 Ex $99 Gd $68

MODEL 70P
SEMIAUTOMATIC. . . . . NiB $171 Ex $146 Gd $89
"Papoose" takedown. Caliber: .22 LR. Seven round clip. 16.25-inch bbl. 35.25 inches overall. Weight: 3.75 lbs. Sights: Ramp front, adj. open rear. Side ejection, manual bolt hold-open. Cross-bolt safety. Walnut-finished hard-wood stock w/abbreviated forend, pistol-grip. Made from 1984-94.

MODEL 70PSS
SELF-LOADING CARBINE . . . . NiB $182 Ex $146 Gd $94
"Papoose" takedown carbine. Caliber: .22 LR. Seven round clip. 16.25- inch bbl., 35.25 inches overall. Weight: 3.25 lbs. Ramp front and adjustable open rear sights. Automatic last-shot hold open (1996). Black fiberglass synthetic stock. Made from 1995 to date.

Marlin Model 75C

Marlin Model 80C

Marlin Model 80DL

Marlin Model 81DL

MODEL 75C
SEMIAUTOMATIC . . . . NiB $171 Ex $120 Gd $94
Caliber: .22 LR. 13-round tubular magazine.18-inch bbl. 36.5 inches overall. Weight: 5 lbs. Side ejection. Cross-bolt safety. Sights: Ramp-mounted blade front; adj. open rear. Monte Carlo-style walnut-finished hardwood stock w/pistol-grip. Made from 1975-92.

MODEL 80 BOLT-ACTION REPEATING RIFLE
Takedown. Caliber: .22 LR. Long, Short. Eight round detachable box magazine. 24-inch bbl. Weight: 6 lbs. Sights: Open rear; bead front. Plain pistol-grip stock. Made from 1934-39. Model 80E, w/peep rear sight; hooded front, made from 1934-40.
Model 80 Standard . . . . NiB $141 Ex $110 Gd $79
Model 80E . . . . NiB $130 Ex $94 Gd $74

MODEL 80C/80DL
BOLT-ACTION REPEATER
Improved version of Model 80. Model 80C w/bead from sight, semibeavertail forearm; made 1940-70. Model 80DL w/peep rear sight; hooded blade front sight on ramp, swivels; made from 1940-65.
Model 80C. NiB $141 Ex $110 Gd $79
Model 80DL . . . . NiB $115 Ex $94 Gd $79

MODEL 81/81E BOLT-ACTION REPEATER
Takedown. .22 LR. Long, Short. Tubular magazine holds 24 Short, 20 Long, 18 LR. 24-inch bbl. Weight: 6.25 lbs. Sights: Open rear, bead front. Plain pistol-grip stock. Made from 1937-40. Model 81E w/peep rear sight; hooded front w/ramp.
Model 81 . . . . NiB $151 Ex $148 Gd $79
Model 81E. . . . . NiB $171 Ex $120 Gd $110

MODEL 81C/81DL BOLT-ACTION REPEATER
Improved version of Model 81 w/same general specifications. Model 81C w/bead front sight, semibeavertail forearm; made from 1940-70. Model 81 DL w/peep rear sight, hooded front, swivels; disc. 1965.
Model 81C. NiB $171 Ex $146 Gd $79
Model 81DL . . . . NiB $187 Ex $151 Gd $94

MODEL 88-C/88-DL AUTOLOADING
Takedown. Caliber: .22 LR. Tubular magazine in buttstock holds 14 cartridges. 24-inch bbl. Weight: 6.75 lbs. Sights: Open rear; hooded front. Plain pistol-grip stock. Made from 1947-56. Model 88-DL w/received peep sight, checkered stock and sling swivels, made from 1953-56.
Model 88-C . . . . NiB $197 Ex $171 Gd $110
Model 88-DL. . . . . NiB $202 Ex $182 Gd $115

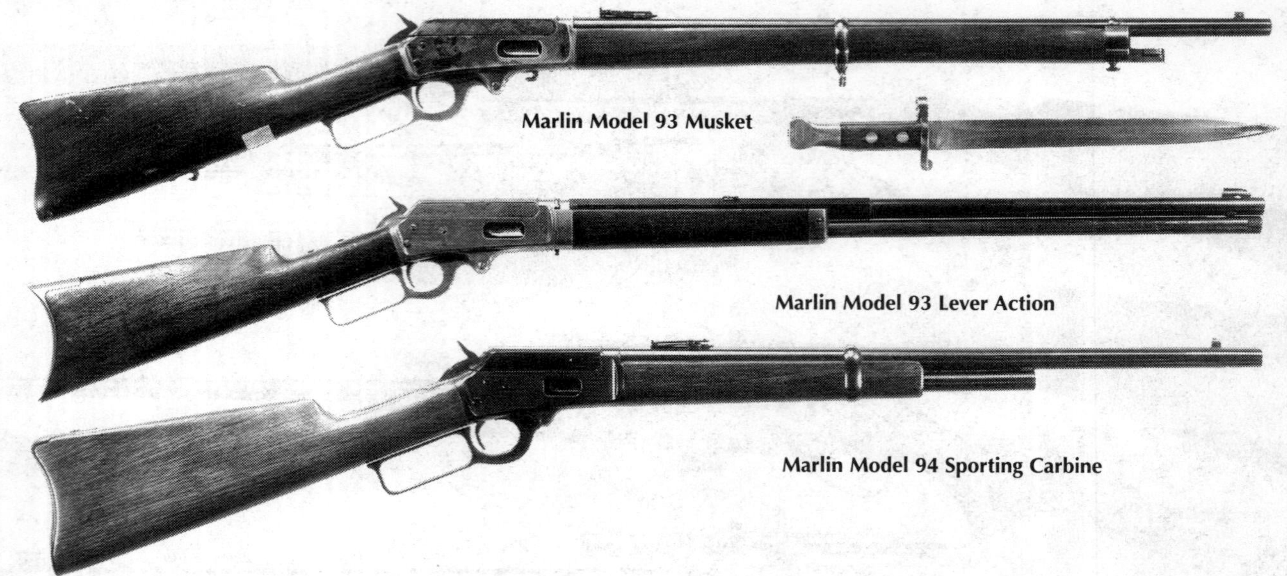

Marlin Model 93 Musket

Marlin Model 93 Lever Action

Marlin Model 94 Sporting Carbine

MODEL 89-C/89-DL AUTOLOADING RIFLE
Clip magazine version of Model 88-C. Seven round clip (12-round in later models); other specifications same. Made from 1950-61. Model 89-DL w/receiver peep sight, sling swivels.
Model 89-C . . . . NiB $189 Ex $153 Gd $112
Model 89-DL . . . . NiB $194 Ex $173 Gd $117

MODEL 92 LEVER-ACTION REPEATING RIFLE
Calibers: .22 Short, Long, LR. .32 Short, Long (rimfire or centerfire by changing firing pin). Tubular magazines holding 25 Short, 20 Long, 18 LR (.22); or 17 Short, 14 Long (.32); 16-inch bbl. model w/shorter magazine holding 15 Short, 12 Long, 10 LR. Bbl. lengths: 16 (.22 cal. only) 24, 26, 28 inches. Weight: 5.5 lbs. w/24-inch bbl. Sights: open rear; blade front. Plain straight-grip stock and forearm. Made from 1892-1916. Note: Originally designated "Model 1892."
Model 92 (.22 caliber). . . . . NiB $1911 Ex $1344 Gd $726
Model 92 (.32 caliber). . . . . NiB $1489 Ex $1190 Gd $860

MODEL 93/93SC CARBINE
Same as Standard Model 93 Rifle except in calibers .30-30 and .32 Special only. Model 93 w/7-round magazine. 20-inch round bbl., carbine sights, weight: 6.75 lbs. Model 93SC magazine capacity 5 rounds, weight 6.5 lbs.
Model 93 Carbine
(w/saddle ring) . . . . NiB $1600 Ex $1342 Gd $1059
Model 93 Carbine ("Bullseye"
w/o saddle ring) . . . . NiB $1085 Ex $972 Gd $621
Model 93SC Sporting Carbine. . . . . NiB $1703 Ex $1394 Gd $982

MODEL 93
LEVER-ACTION
REPEATING RIFLE . . . . NiB $2344 Ex $1932 Gd $1309
Solid frame or takedown. Calibers: .25-36 Marlin, .30-30, .32 Special, .32-40, .38-55. Tubular magazine holds 10 cartridges. 26-inch round or octagon bbl. standard; also made w/28-, 30- and 32-inch bbls. Weight: 7.25 lbs. Sights: Open rear; bead front. Plain straight-grip stock and forearm. Made from 1893-1936. Note: Before 1915 designated "Model 1893."

MODEL 93 MUSKET . . . . NiB $4128 Ex $3088 Gd $1749
Same as Standard Model 93 except w/30-inch bbl., angular bayonet, ramrod under bbl., musket stock, full-length military-style forearm. Weight: 8 lbs. Made from 1893-1915.

MODEL 94 LEVER-ACTION
REPEATING RIFLE . . . . NiB $2683 Ex $2138 Gd $2009
Solid frame or takedown. Calibers: .25-20, .32-20, .38-40, .44-40. 10-round tubular magazine. 24-inch round or octagon bbl. Weight: 7 lbs. Sights open rear; bead front. Plain straight-grip stock and forearm (also available w/pistol-grip stock). Made from 1894-1934. Note: Before 1906 designated "Model 1894."

MODEL 94 LEVER-ACTION COWBOY SERIES
Calibers: .357 Mag., .44-40, .44 Mag., .45 LC. 10-round magazine. 24-inch tapered octagon bbl. Weight: 7.5 lbs. 41.5 inches overall. Marble carbine front sight, adjustable semi-buckhorn rear. Blue finish. Checkered, straight-grip American black walnut stock w/hard rubber buttplate. Made from 1996 to date. Cowboy II introduced in 1997.
Cowboy model (.45 LC) . . . . NiB $545 Ex $416 Gd $287
Cowboy II model (.357 Mag.,
.44-40, .44 Mag) . . . . NiB $545 Ex $416 Gd $287

MODEL 97 LEVER-ACTION
REPEATING RIFLE . . . . NiB $2592 Ex $2108 Gd $1222
Takedown. Caliber: .22 LR. Long, Short. Tubular magazine; full length holds 25 Short, 20 Long, 18 LR; half length holds 16 Short, 12 Long and 10 LR. Bbl. lengths: 16, 24, 26, 28 inches. Weight: 6 lbs. Sights: Open rear; bead front. Plain, straight-grip stock and forearm (also avail. w/pistol-grip stock). Made from 1897-1922. Note: Before 1905 designated "Model 1897."

MODEL 98 AUTOLOADING RIFLE. . . . . NiB $169 Ex $113 Gd $92
Solid frame. Caliber: .22 LR. Tubular magazine holds 15 cartridges. 22-inch bbl. Weight: 6.75 lbs. Sights: Open rear; hooded ramp front. Monte Carlo stock w/cheekpiece. Made from 1950-61.

MODEL 99 AUTOLOADING RIFLE. . . . . NiB $169 Ex $113 Gd $92
Caliber: .22 LR. Tubular magazine holds 18 cartridges. 22-inch bbl. Weight: 5.5 lbs. Sights: Open rear; hooded ramp front. Plain pistol-grip stock. Made from 1959-61.

MODEL 99C . . . . NiB $182 Ex $146 Gd $99
Same as Model 99 except w/gold-plated trigger, receiver grooved for tip-off scope mounts, Monte Carlo stock (checkered in later production). Made from 1962-78.

MODEL 99DL . . . . NiB $225 Ex $200 Gd $118
Same as Model 99 except w/gold-plated trigger, jeweled breech bolt, Monte Carlo stock w/pistol-grip, swivels and sling. Made from 1960-65.

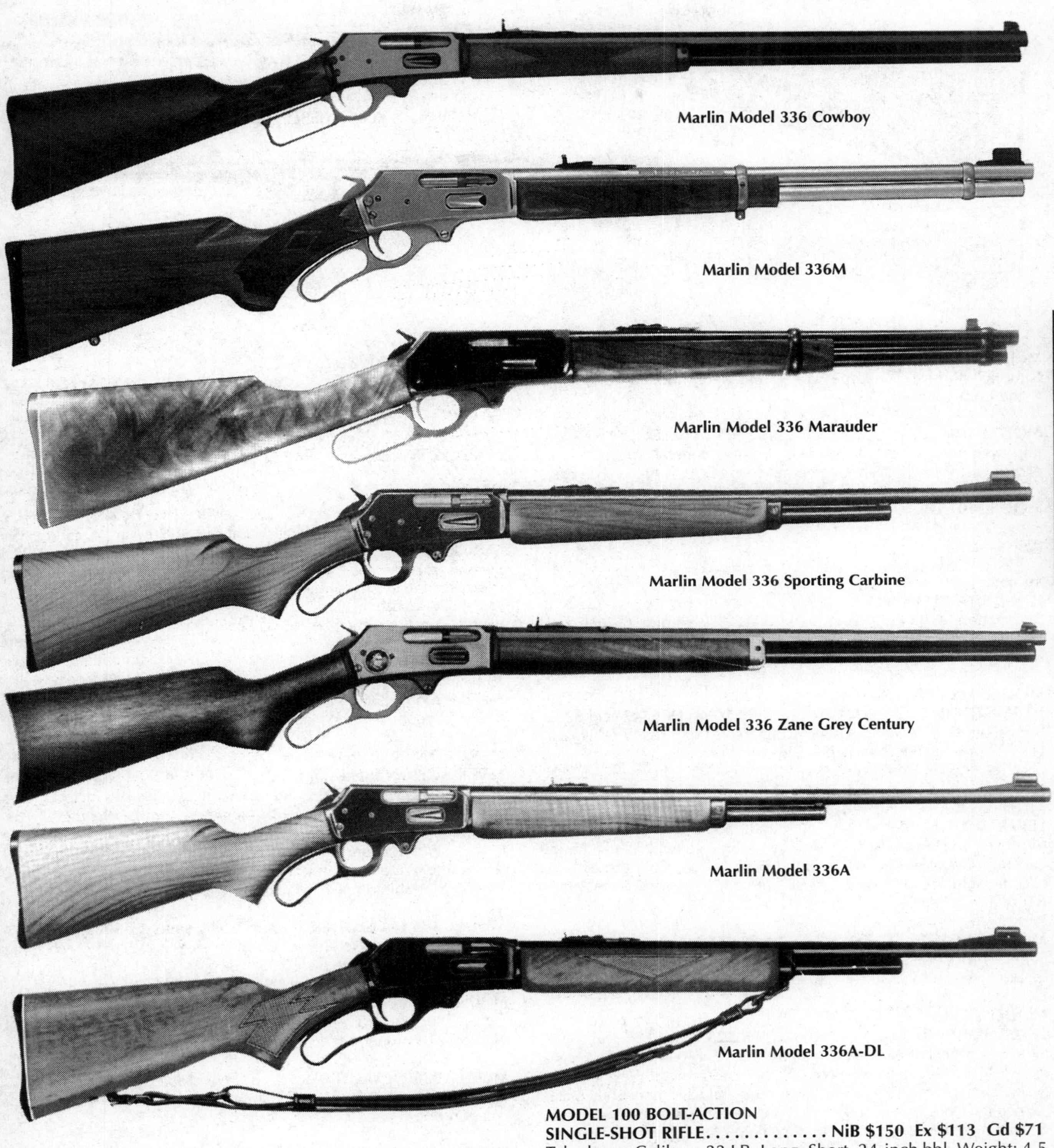

Marlin Model 336 Cowboy

Marlin Model 336M

Marlin Model 336 Marauder

Marlin Model 336 Sporting Carbine

Marlin Model 336 Zane Grey Century

Marlin Model 336A

Marlin Model 336A-DL

MODEL 99M1 CARBINE. . . . . NiB $239 Ex $177 Gd $126
Same as Model 99C except styled after U.S. .30 M1 Carbine; 9-round tubular magazine, 18-inch bbl. Sights: Open rear; military-style ramp front; carbine stock w/handguard and bbl. band, sling swivels. Weight: 4.5 lbs. Made from 1966-79.

MODEL 100 BOLT-ACTION SINGLE-SHOT RIFLE. . . . . NiB $150 Ex $113 Gd $71
Takedown. Caliber: .22 LR, Long, Short. 24-inch bbl. Weight: 4.5 lbs. Sights: Open rear; bead front. Plain pistol-grip stock. Made from 1936-60.

MODEL 100SB . . . . NiB $144 Ex $118 Gd $80
Same as Model 100 except smoothbore for use w/22 shot cartridges, shotgun sight. Made from 1936-41.

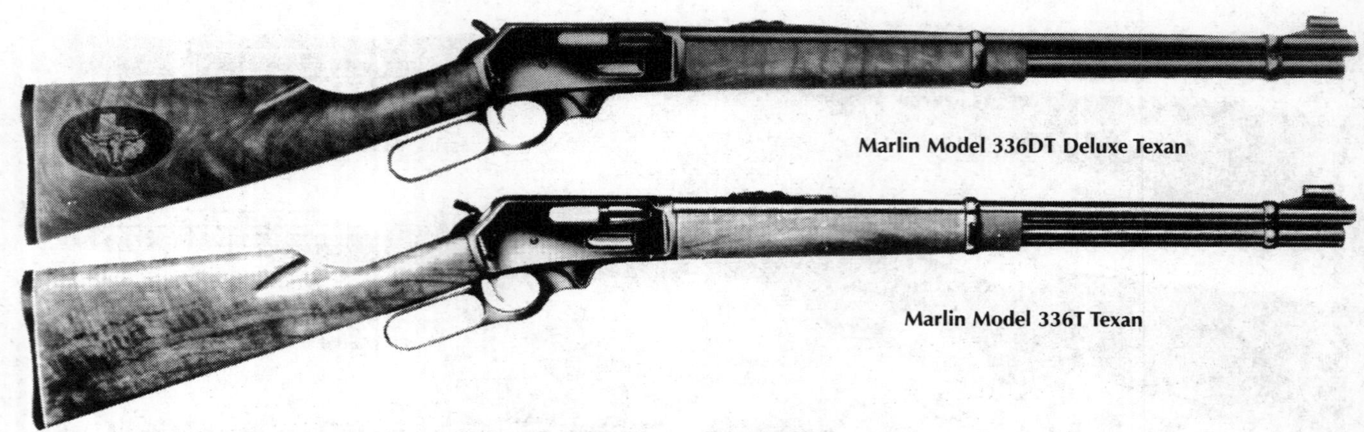

Marlin Model 336DT Deluxe Texan

Marlin Model 336T Texan

MODEL 100 TOM MIX SPECIAL........ NiB $416 Ex $329 Gd $231
Same as Model 100 except w/peep rear sight; hooded front; sling. Made from 1936-46.

MODEL 101 .... NiB $112 Ex $91 Gd $55
Improved version of Model 100 w/same general specifications, except w/stock w/beavertail forearm, weighs 5 lbs. Intro. 1951. Disc.

MODEL 101 DL................. NiB $117 Ex $86 Gd $55
Same as Model 101 except has peep rear sight; hooded front, swivels. Disc.

MODEL 122 SINGLE-SHOT JUNIOR TARGET RIFLE............ NiB $91 Ex $65 Gd $50
Bolt action. Caliber: .22 LR, .22 Long, .22 Short. 22-inch bbl. Weight: 5 lbs. Sights: Open rear; hooded ramp front. Monte Carlo stock w/pistol-grip, swivels, sling. Made from 1961-65.

MODEL 322 BOLT-ACTION VARMINT RIFLE .... NiB $594 Ex $543 Gd $332
Sako short Mauser action. Caliber: .222 Rem. Three round clip magazine. 24-inch medium weight bbl. Checkered stock. Sights: Two-position peep rear; hooded ramp front. Weight: 7.5 lbs. Made from 1954-57.

MODEL 336A LEVER-ACTION RIFLE........... NiB $334 Ex $205 Gd $188
Improved version of Model 36A Rifle w/same general specifications except w/improved action w/round breech bolt. Calibers: .30-30, .32 Special (disc. 1963), .35 Rem. (intro. 1952). Made from 1948-63; reintroduced 1973, disc. 1980.

MODEL 336A-DL .... NiB $569 Ex $490 Gd $311
Same as Model 336A Rifle except w/deluxe checkered stock and forearm, swivels and sling. Made from 1948-63.

MODEL 336AS LEVER-ACTION RIFLE........... NiB $253 Ex $186 Gd $134
Similar to Model 30AS. Caliber: .30-30 Win., Six round tubular magazine. 20- inch Micro-Groove bbl. 38.25 inches overall. Weight: 7 lbs. Maine birch pistol grip stock w/swivel studs and hard rubber butt plate. Tapped for scope mount and receiver sight. Screw-adjustable open rear and ramp front sight. Checkered walnut finish. Made from 1999 to date.

MODEL 336C LEVER-ACTION CARBINE........ NiB $304 Ex $248 Gd $173
Improved version of Model 36 Carbine w/same general specifications except w/improved action w/round breech bolt. Original calibers: .30-30 and .32 Win. Spec. Made from 1948-83. Note: Caliber .35 Rem. intro. 1953. Caliber .32 Winchester Special disc. 1963.

MODEL 336 COWBOY LEVER-ACTION RIFLE........... NiB $595 Ex $441 Gd $312
Calibers: .30-30 Win., or .38-55 Win., 6- round tubular magazine. 24- inch tapered octagon bbl. 42.5 inches overall. Weight: 7.5 lbs. American black walnut checkering stock. Marble carbine front sight w/solid top receiver drilled and tapped for scope mount. Mar-Shield finish. Made from 1998 to date.

MODEL 336CS W/SCOPE .... NiB $385 Ex $277 Gd $179
Lever-action w/hammer block safety. Caliber: .30/30 Win. or .35 Rem. Six round tubular magazine. 20-inch round bbl. w/Micro-Groove rifling. 38.5 inches overall. Weight: 7 lbs. Ramp front sight w/hood, adj. semi-buckhorn folding rear. Solid top receiver drilled and tapped for scope mount or receiver sight; offset hammer spur for scope use. American black walnut stock w/pistol-grip, fluted comb. Mar-Shield finish. Made from 1984 to date.

MODEL 336DT DELUXE TEXAN................ NiB $437 Ex $432 Gd $334
Same as Model 336T except w/select walnut stock and forearm, hand-carved longhorn steer and map of Texas on buttstock. Made from 1962-64.

MODEL 336M LEVER-ACTION RIFLE........... NiB $542 Ex $439 Gd $310
Calibers: .30-30 Win., 6- round tubular magazine. 20- inch stainless steel Micro Groove bbl., 38.5 inches overall. Weight: 7 lbs. American black walnut w/checkered pistol-grip stock. Adjustable folding semi-buckhorn rear and ramp front sight w/brass bead and removable Wide-Scan hood. Tapped for receiver sight and scope mount. Mar-Shield finish. Made from 1999 to date.

MODEL 336 MARAUDER .... NiB $490 Ex $439 Gd $253
Same as Model 336 Texan Carbine except w/16.25-inch bbl., weight: 6.25 lbs. Made from 1963-64.

MODEL 336-MICRO GROOVE ZIPPER ... NiB $568 Ex $490 Gd $331
General specifications same as Model 336 Sporting Carbine except caliber .219 Zipper. Made from 1955-61.

MODEL 336 OCTAGON .... NiB $542 Ex $475 Gd $212
Same as Model 336T except chambered for .30-30 only w/22-inch octagon bbl. Made in 1973.

MODEL 336 SPORTING CARBINE....... NiB $439 Ex $336 Gd $181
Same as Model 336A rifle except w/20-inch bbl., weight: 6.25 lbs. Made from 1948-63.

MODEL 336T TEXAN CARBINE .... NiB $279 Ex $228 Gd $202
Same as Model 336 Carbine except w/straight-grip stock and is not available in caliber .32 Special. Made 1953-83. Caliber .44 Magnum made from 1963-67.

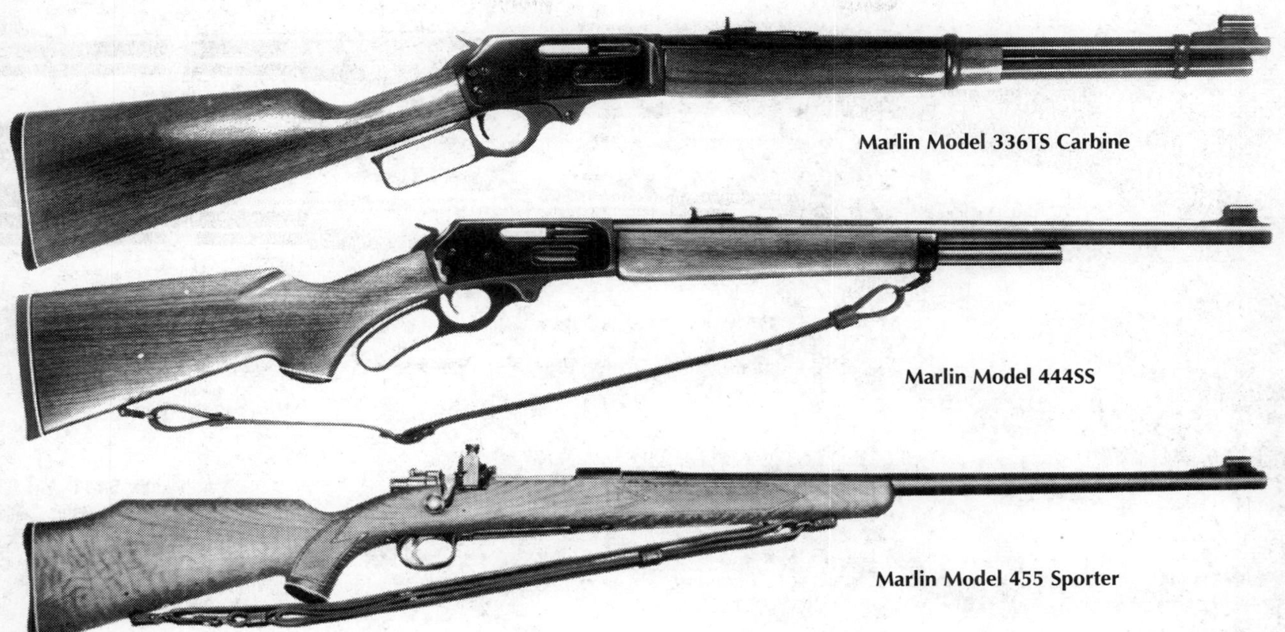
Marlin Model 336TS Carbine

Marlin Model 444SS

Marlin Model 455 Sporter

MODEL 336TS. . . . . NiB $358 Ex $306 Gd $152
Lever-action w/hammer-block safety. Caliber: .30-30 Win. Six round tubular magazine. 18.5-inch Micro-Groove bbl. 37 inches overall. Weight: 6.5 lbs. Ramp front sight, adj. semi-buckhorn folding rear. Straight-grip American black walnut stock. Made from 1983-87.

MODEL 336 ZANE GREY CENTURY . . . . NiB $488 Ex $385 Gd $257
Similar to Model 336A except w/22-inch octagonal bbl., caliber .30-30, Zane Grey Centennial 1872-1972 medallion inlaid in receiver; select walnut stock w/classic pistol-grip and forearm; brass buttplate, forend cap. Weight: 7 lbs. 10,000 produced (numbered ZG1 through ZG10,000). Made in 1972.

MODEL 444 LEVER-ACTION REPEATING RIFLE . . . . NiB $411 Ex $360 Gd $179
Action similar to Model 336. Caliber: .444 Marlin. Four round tubular magazine. 24-inch bbl. Weigh: 7.5 lbs. Sights: Open rear; hooded ramp front. Monte Carlo stock w/straight grip, recoil pad. Carbine-style forearm w/bbl. band. Swivels, sling. Made from 1965-71.

MARLIN MODEL 444 SPORTER. . . . . NiB $416 Ex $385 Gd $190
Same as Model 444 Rifle except w/22-inch bbl., pistol-grip stock and forearm as on Model 336A, recoil pad, QD swivels and sling. Made from 1972-83.

MODEL 444P (OUTFITTER) LEVER-ACTION RIFLE . . . . NiB $500 Ex $385 Gd $205
Caliber: .444 Marlin. Five round tubular magazine. 18.5-inch ported bbl., 37 inches overall. Weight: 6.75 lbs. Ramp front and adjustable folding rear sights. Black walnut straight grip stock w/cut checkering and Mar-Shield finish. Made from 1999-2002.

MODEL 444SS. . . . . NiB $514 Ex $385 Gd $205
Same general specifications as Model 444 except w/hammer safety. Made from 1984-2002. (Changed to M444 in 2001.)

MODEL 455 BOLT-ACTION SPORTER
FN Mauser action w/Sako trigger. Calibers: .30-06 or .308. Five round box magazine. 24-inch medium weight stainless-steel bbl. Monte Carlo stock w/cheekpiece, checkered pistol grip and forearm. Lyman No. 48 receiver sight; hooded ramp front. Weight: 8.5 lbs. Made from 1957-59.
Model 455 (chambered for .30-06, 1079 produced) . . . . NiB $599 Ex $471 Gd $265
Model 455 (chambered for .308, 59 produced). . . . NiB $599 Ex $471 Gd $265

MODEL 780 BOLT-ACTION REPEATER SERIES
Caliber: .22 LR. Long, Short. Seven round clip magazine. 22-inch bbl. Weight: 5.5 to 6 lbs. Sights: Open rear; hooded ramp front. Receiver grooved for scope mounting. Monte Carlo stock w/checkered pistol-grip and forearm. Made from 1971-88.
Model 780 Standard . . . . NiB $131 Ex $100 Gd $75
Model 781 (w/17-round tubular magazine) . NiB $131 Ex $100 Gd $75
Model 782 (.22 WMR, w/swivels, sling) . . . . NiB $131 Ex $100 Gd $75
Model 783 (w/12-round tubular magazine) . NiB $131 Ex $100 Gd $75

MODEL 795 SELF-LOADING RIFLE . . . . . . NiB $147 Ex $121 Gd $100
Caliber: .22 LR. 10- round clip. 18- inch Micro-Groove bbl., 37 inches overall. Weight: 5 lbs. Screw-adjustable open rear and ramp front sight. Monte Carlo synthetic stock with checkering swivel studs. Made from 1999 to date.

MODEL 880 BOLT-ACTION REPEATER SERIES
Caliber: .22 rimfire. Seven round magazine. 22-inch bbl. 41 inches overall. Weight: 5.5 to 6 lbs. Hooded ramp front sight; adj. folding rear. Grooved receiver for scope mounts. Checkered Monte Carlo-style walnut stock w/QD studs and rubber recoil pad. Made from 1989-97.
Model 880 (.22 LR). . . . . NiB $208 Ex $157 Gd $100
Model 880SS (Stainless .22 LR). . . . . NiB $229 Ex $188 Gd $135
Model 880SQ (Squirrel .22 LR). . . . . NiB $242 Ex $198 Gd $142
Model 881 (w/7-round tubular magazine. . NiB $213 Ex $162 Gd $100
Model 882 (.22 WMR) . . . . NiB $203 Ex $167 Gd $121
Model 882L (w/laminated hardwood stock) . . . . . NiB $213 Ex $162 Gd $100
Model 882SS (Stainless w/fire sights) . . . . . NiB $249 Ex $203 Gd $146
Model 882SSV (Stainless .22 LR) . . . . NiB $249 Ex $203 Gd $146
Model 883 (.22 WMR w/12-round tubular magazine). . . . . NiB $208 Ex $157 Gd $100
Model 883N (w/nickel-Teflon finish) . . . . . NiB $245 Ex $201 Gd $149
Model 883SS (stainless w/laminated stock) . . . . NiB $264 Ex $183 Gd $161

Marlin Model 780

Marlin Model 781

Marlin Model 783

Marlin Model 882L

Marlin Model 883N

MODEL 922 MAGNUM
SELF-LOADING RIFLE . . . . NiB $385 Ex $308 Gd $128
Similar to Model 9 except chambered for .22 WMR. Seven round magazine. 20.5-inch bbl. 39.5 inches overall. Weight: 6.5 lbs. American black walnut stock w/Monte Carlo. Blued finish. Made from 1993 -2001.

MODEL 980 .22 MAGNUM . . . . NiB $184 Ex $132 Gd $96
Bolt action. Caliber: .22 WMR. Eight round clip magazine. 24-inch bbl. Weight: 6 lbs. Sights: Open rear; hooded ramp front. Monte Carlo stock, swivels, sling. Made from 1962-70.

MODEL 989 AUTOLOADING RIFLE. . . . . . . NiB $163 Ex $117 Gd $91
Caliber: .22 LR. Seven round clip magazine. 22-inch bbl. Weight: 5.5 lbs. Sights: Open rear; hooded ramp front. Monte Carlo walnut stock w/pistol grip. Made from 1962-66.

MODEL 989M2
CARBINE . . . . NiB $163 Ex $112 Gd $88
Same as Model 99M1 except clip-loading, 7-round magazine. Made from 1966-79.

MODEL 990
SEMIAUTOMATIC
Caliber: .22 LR. 17-round tubular magazine. 22-inch bbl. 40.75 inches overall. Weight: 5.5 lbs. Side ejection. Cross-bolt safety. Ramp front sight w/brass bead; adj. semi-buckhorn folding rear. Receiver grooved for scope mount. Monte Carlo-style American black walnut stock w/checkered pistol grip and forend. Made from 1979-87.
Model 990 Semiautomatic . . . . NiB $163 Ex $132 Gd $91
Model 990L (w/14 rounds,
laminated hardwood stock, QD studs,
black recoil pad; 1992 to date). . . . . NiB $148 Ex $117 Gd $91

Marlin Model 980

Marlin Model 989

Marlin Model 989M2

Marlin Model 990

Marlin Model 990L

Marlin Model 995

RIFLES

MODEL 995 SEMIAUTOMATIC . . . . NiB $184 Ex $143 Gd $96
Caliber: .22 LR. Seven round clip magazine.18-inch bbl. 36.75 inches overall. Weight: 5 lbs. Cross-bolt safety. Sights: Ramp front w/brass bead; adj. folding semi-buckhorn rear. Monte Carlo-style American black walnut stock w/checkered pistol grip and forend. Made from 1979-94.

MODEL 1870-1970 CENTENNIAL MATCHED PAIR, MODELS 336 AND 39 . . . . NiB $1995 Ex $1660 Gd $1094
Presentation-grade rifles in luggage-style case. Matching serial numbers. Fancy walnut straight-grip buttstock and forearm brass buttplate and forend cap. Engraved receiver w/inlaid medallion; square lever. 20-inch octagon bbl. Model 336: .30-30, 7-round capacity; weight: 7 lbs. Model 39: .22 Short, Long, LR, tubular magazine holds 21 Short, 16 Long, 15 LR. 1,000 sets produced. Made in 1970. Top value is for rifles in new, unfired condition. See illustration on page 284.

MODEL 1892 LEVER-ACTION RIFLE
See Marlin Model 92 listed previously under this section.

MODEL 1893 LEVER-ACTION RIFLE
See Marlin Model 93 listed previously under this section.

MODEL 1894 LEVER-ACTION RIFLE
See Marlin Model 94 Lever-Action Rifle listed previously under this section.

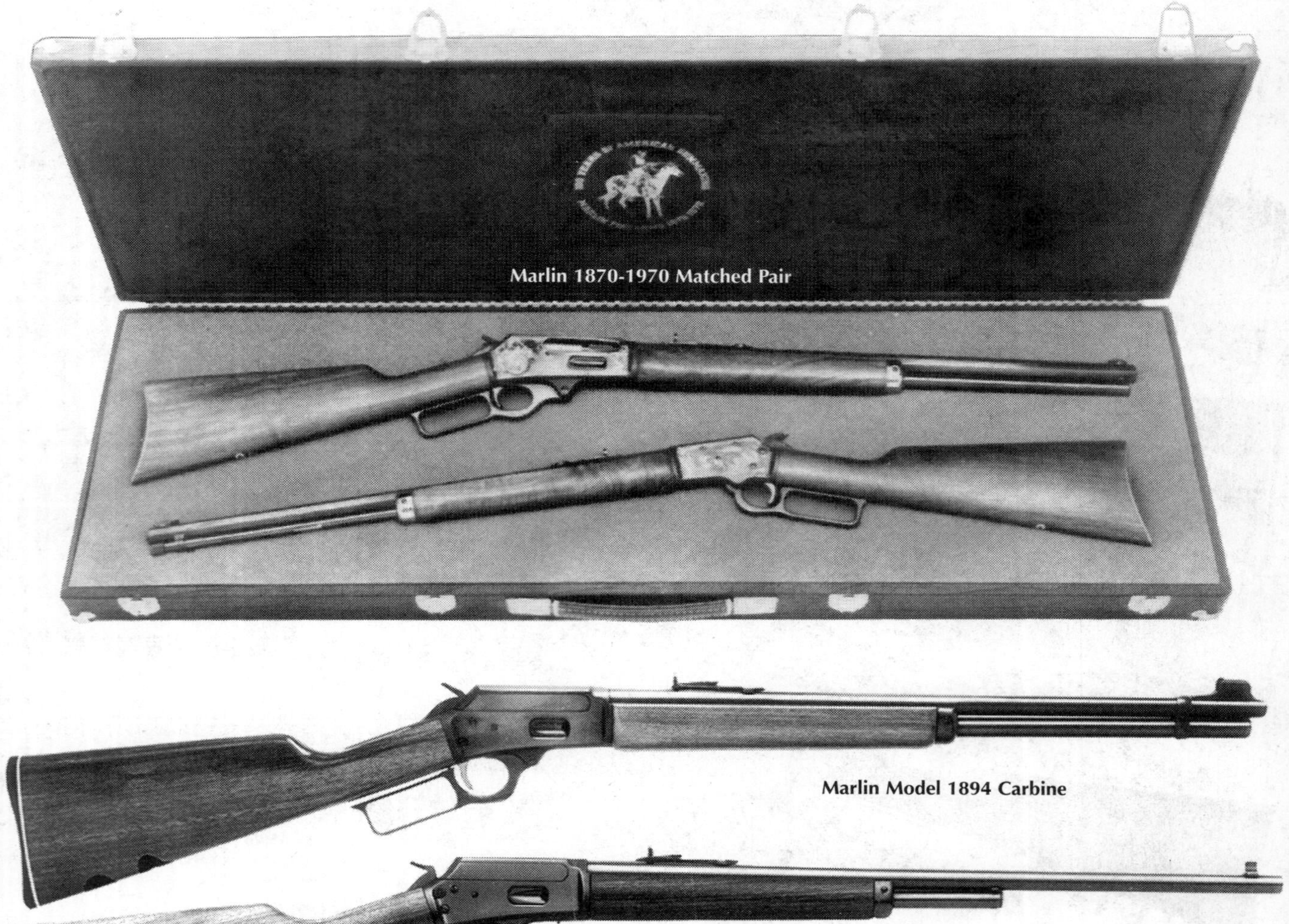

Marlin 1870-1970 Matched Pair

Marlin Model 1894 Carbine

Marlin Model 1894CL

MODEL 1894 CARBINE
Replica of original Model 94. Caliber: .44 Rem. 10-round magazine. 20-inch round bbl. Weight: 6 lbs. Sight: Open rear; ramp front. Straight-grip stock. Made from 1969-84.
Standard Model
1894 Carbine . . . . NiB $414 Ex $285 Gd $208
Model 1894 Octagon
(made 1973) . . . . NiB $440 Ex $363 Gd $213
Model 1894 Sporter (w/22-inch bbl.,
made 1973) . . . . NiB $414 Ex $285 Gd $260

MODEL 1894CL
CLASSIC . . . . NiB $493 Ex $365 Gd $210
Calibers: .218 Bee, .25-20 Win., .32-20 Win. Six round tubular magazine. 22-inch bbl. 38.75 inches overall. Weight: 6.25 lbs. Adj. semibuckhorn folding rear sight, brass bead front. Receiver tapped for scope mounts. Straight-grip American black walnut stock w/Mar-Shield finish. Made from 1988-94.

MODEL 1894CS LEVER-ACTION . . . . NiB $442 Ex $390 Gd $184
Caliber: .357 Magnum, .38 Special. Nine round tubular magazine. 18.5-inch bbl. 36 inches overall. Weight: 6 lbs. Side ejection. Hammer block safety. Square finger lever. Bead front sight, adj. semi-buckhorn folding rear. Offset hammer spur for scope use. Two-piece straight grip American black walnut stock w/white buttplate spacer. Mar-Shield finish. Made from 1984-2002.

MODEL 1894M LEVER-ACTION. . . . . NiB $338 Ex $286 Gd $183
Caliber: .22 WMR.11-round tubular magazine. 20-inch bbl. Weight: 6.25 lbs. Sights: Ramp front w/brass bead and Wide-Scan hood; adj. semi-buckhorn folding rear. Offset hammer spur for scope use. Straight-grip American black walnut stock w/white buttplate spacer. Squared finger lever. Made from 1986-88.

MODEL 1894S LEVER-ACTION . . . . NiB $389 Ex $312 Gd $209
Calibers: .41 Mag., .44 Rem. Mag., .44 S&W Special, .45 Colt.10-shot tubular magazine. 20-inch bbl.37.5 inches overall. Weight: 6 lbs. Sights and stock same as Model 1894M. Made from 1984-2002.

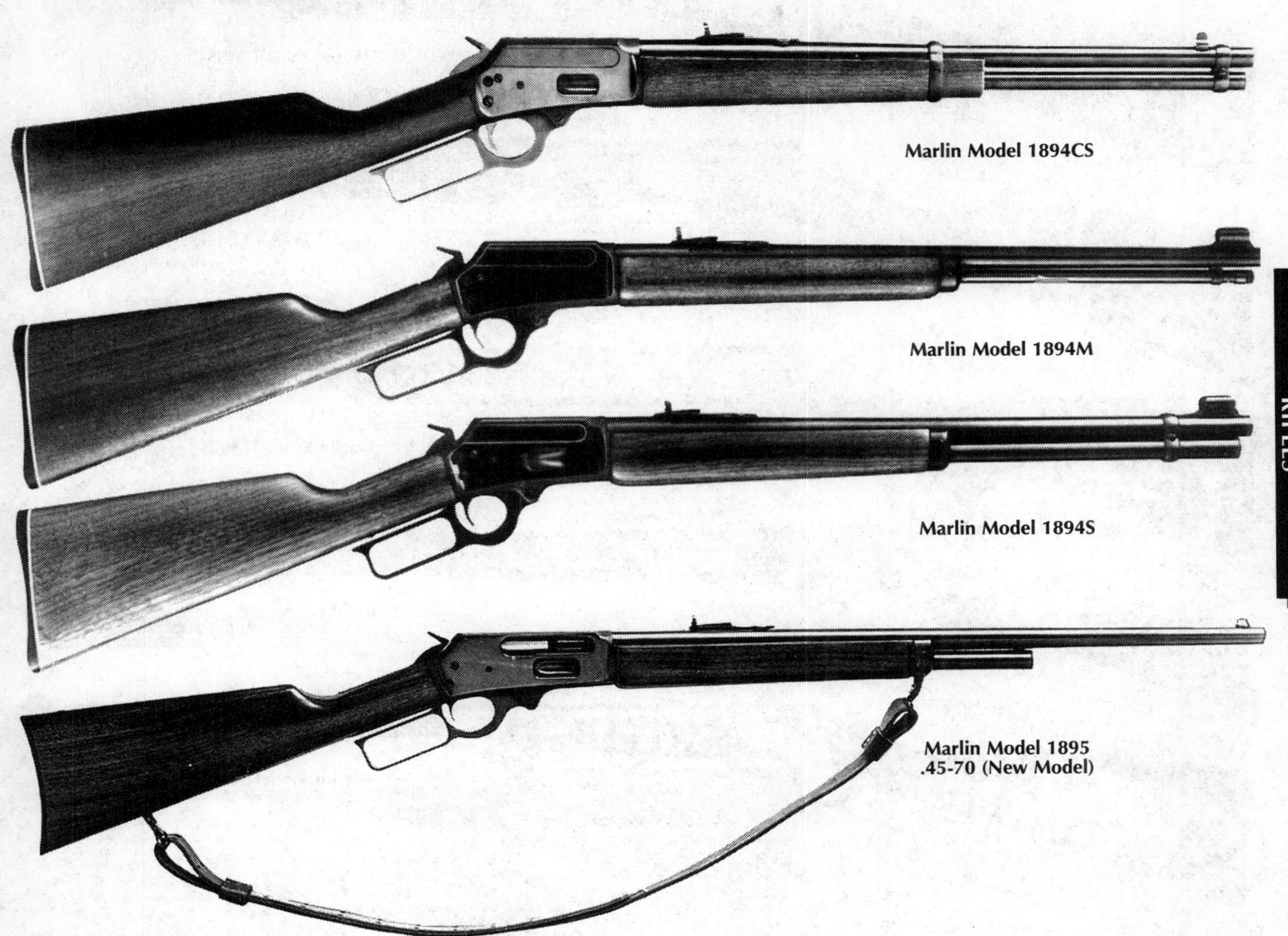
Marlin Model 1894CS

Marlin Model 1894M

Marlin Model 1894S

Marlin Model 1895 .45-70 (New Model)

MODEL 1895 .45-70 REPEATER . . . NiB $453 Ex $344 Gd $189
Model 336-type action. Caliber: .45-70 Government. Four round magazine. 22-inch bbl. Weight: 7 lbs. Sights: Open rear; bead front. Straight-grip stock, forearm w/metal end cap, QD swivels, leather sling. Made 1972-79.

MODEL 1895
LEVER-ACTION REPEATER . . . . NiB $344 Ex $313 Gd $241
Solid frame or takedown. Calibers: .33 WCF, .38-56, .40-65, .40-70, .40-82, .45-70. Nine round tubular magazine. 24-inch round or octagongon bbl. standard (other lengths available). Weight: 8 lbs. Sights: Open rear; bead front. Plain stock and forearm (also available w/pistol-grip stock). Made 1895-1915.

MODEL 1895G (GUIDE GUN)
LEVER-ACTION RIFLE . . . . NiB $721 Ex $545 Gd $448
Caliber: .45-70 Govt., 4- round magazine. 18.5-inch ported bbl., 37 inches overall. Weight: 6.75 lbs. Ramp front and adjustable folding rear sights. Black walnut straight grip stock w/cut checkering and Mar-Shield finish. Made 1998 to date.

MODEL 1895M
LEVER-ACTION RIFLE . . . . NiB $639 Ex $554 Gd $514
Caliber: .450 Marlin. Four round tubular magazine., 18.5- inch ported bbl. w/Ballard-type rifling. 37 inches overall. Weight: 6.75 lbs. Genuine American black walnut straight-grip stock w/checkering. Ventilated recoil pad. Adjustable folding semi-buckhorn rear and ramp front sights. Mar-Shield finish. Made 1999 to date.

MODEL 1895SS
LEVER-ACTION. . . . . NiB $370 Ex $292 Gd $215
Caliber: .45-70 Govt. Four round tubular magazine. 22-inch bbl. w/Micro-Groove rifling. 40.5 inches overall. Weight: 7.5 lbs. Ramp front sight w/brass bead and Wide-Scan hood; adj. semi-buckhorn folding rear. Solid top receiver tapped for scope mount or receiver sight. Off-set hammer spur for scope use. Two-piece American black walnut stock w/fluted comb, pistol-grip, sling swivels. Made 1984 to date. (Changed to M1895 in 2001.)

MODEL 1897 LEVER-ACTION RIFLE
See Marlin Model 97 listed previously under this section.

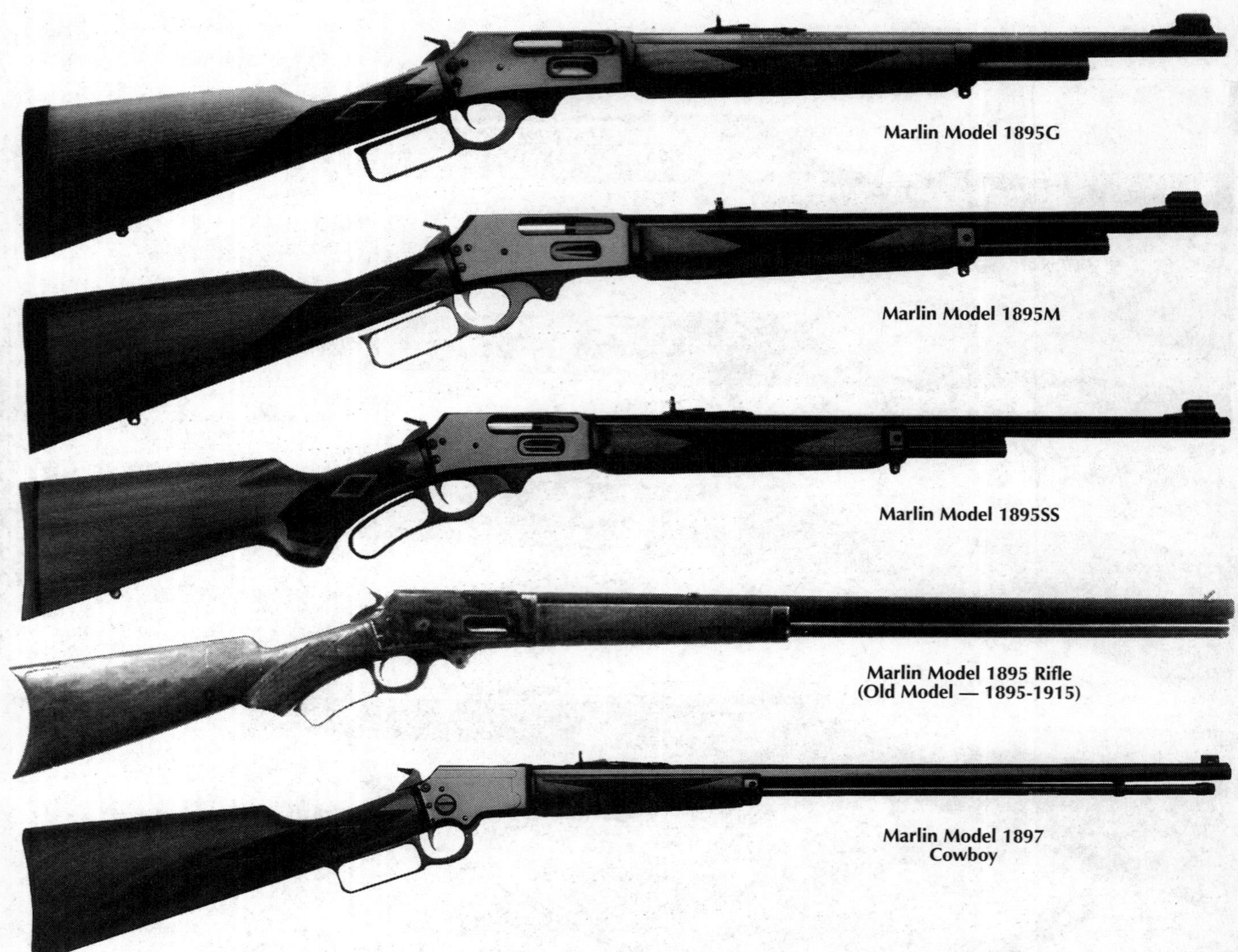

Marlin Model 1895G

Marlin Model 1895M

Marlin Model 1895SS

Marlin Model 1895 Rifle (Old Model — 1895-1915)

Marlin Model 1897 Cowboy

MODEL 1897 COWBOY LEVER-ACTION RIFLE . . . . **NiB $650 Ex $547 Gd $315**
Caliber: .22 LR., capacity: 19 LR, 21 L, or 26 S, tubular magazine. 24-inch tapered octagon bbl., 40 inches overall. Weight: 6.5 lbs. Marble front and adjustable rear sight, tapped for scope mount. Black walnut straight grip stock w/cut checkering and Mar-Shield finish. Made from 1999-2001.

MODEL 1936 LEVER-ACTION CARBINE
See Marlin Model 36 listed previously under this section.

MODEL 2000 TARGET RIFLE
Bolt-action single-shot. Caliber: .22 LR. Optional 5-round adapter kit available. 22-inch bbl. 41 inches overall. Weight: 8 lbs. Globe front sight, adj. peep or aperture rear. two-stage target trigger. Textured composite Kevlar or black/gray laminated stock. Made from 1991-95.
Model 2000 (disc. 1995) . . . . **NiB $519 Ex $447 Gd $287**
Model 2000A w/Adj. comb (Made 1994 only) . . . . **NiB $571 Ex $468 Gd $287**
Model 2000L w/laminated stock (intro. 1996) . . . . **NiB $601 Ex $493 Gd $357**

MODEL 7000 . . . . **NiB $239 Ex $197 Gd $142**
Caliber: .22 LR. 10-round magazine. 18-inch bbl. Weight: 5.5 lbs. Synthetic stocks. No sights; receiver grooved for scope. Semi-auto. Side ejection. Manual bolt hold-open. Cross-bolt safety. Matte finish. Made from 1997-2001.
Model 7000 . . . . **NiB $260 Ex $208 Gd $157**
Model 7000T . . . . **NiB $414 Ex $337 Gd $285**

MODEL A-1 AUTOLOADING RIFLE . . . . **NiB $202 Ex $125 Gd $99**
Takedown. Caliber: .22 LR. Six round detachable box magazine. 24-inch bbl. Weight: 6 lbs. Open rear sight. Plain pistol-grip stock. Made from 1935-46.

MODEL A-1C AUTOLOADING RIFLE . . . . **NiB $176 Ex $115 Gd $84**
Improved version of Model A-1 w/same general specifications, stock w/semibeavertail forend. Made from 1940-46.

MODEL A-1DL . . . . **NiB $176 Ex $115 Gd $84**
Same as Model A-1C above, except w/peep rear sight; hooded front, swivels.

Marlin Model 2000

Marlin Model 2000L

Marlin Model 7000

Marlin Model 7000T

MODEL A-1E . . . . NiB $173 Ex $112 Gd $81
Same as Model A-1 except w/peep rear sight; hooded front.

MODEL MR-7 BOLT-ACTION RIFLE
Calibers: .25-06 Rem., .270 Win., .280 Rem., .308 Win. or .30-06. Four round magazine. 22-inch bbl. w/ or w/o sights. 43.31 inches overall. Weight: 7.5 lbs. Checkered American walnut or birch stock w/recoil pad and sling-swivel studs. Jeweled bolt w/cocking indicator and 3-position safety. Made from 1996-99.
Model MR-7 . . . . NiB $489 Ex $361 Gd $258
Model MR7B w/birch stock (Intro. 1998) . . . . NiB $155 Ex $150 Gd $119
Open sights, add $35

MODEL 10 . . . . NiB $122 Ex $101 Gd $75
Same as Marlin Model 101 except w/walnut-finished hardwood stock. Made 1966-79. Note: Later production featuring hot-ironstamped wood pistol grip to simulate checkering/carving; plain forend.

MODEL 20 . . . . NiB $122 Ex $101 Gd $75
Same as Marlin Model 80/780 except w/bead front sight, walnut-finished hardwood stock. Made 1966-82. Note: Recent production has stamped pistol-grip to simulate checkering; plain forend.

MODEL 30 . . . . NiB $173 Ex $112 Gd $81
Same as Marlin Model 336C except chambered for .30-30 only, w/4-round magazine, plainer stock and forearm of walnut-finished hardwood. Made 1966-68.

MODEL 30A . . . . NiB $255 Ex $177 Gd $126
Same as Marlin Model 336C except chambered for .30-30 only, w/checkered stock of walnut-finished hardwood. Made 1969-83.

MODEL 36G . . . . NiB $280 Ex $177 Gd $120
Same as Marlin Model 336C except chambered for .30-30 only, w/5-round magazine, plainer stock. Made 1960-65.

MODEL 60 . . . . NiB $95 Ex $69 Gd $54
Same as Marlin Model 99C except w/walnut-finished hardwood stock. Made 1960-80.

MODEL 70 . . . . NiB $100 Ex $80 Gd $59
Same as Marlin Model 989M2 except w/walnut-finished hardwood stock; no handguard. Made 1966-69.

MODEL 80G . . . . NiB $100 Ex $80 Gd $59
Same as Marlin Model 80C except w/plain stock, bead front sight. Made 1960-65.

Marlin Model A-1 Autoloader

Marlin-Glenfield Model 10

Marlin-Glenfield Model 30A

Marlin-Glenfield Model 60

Marlin-Glenfield Model 70

Marlin-Glenfield Model 80G

MODEL 81G . . . . NiB $93 Ex $67 Gd $57
Same as Marlin Model 81C except w/plain stock, bead front sight. Made from 1960-65.

MODEL 99G . . . . NiB $98 Ex $83 Gd $67
Same as Marlin Model 99C except w/plain stock, bead front sight. Made from 1960-65.

MODEL 101G . . . . NiB $92 Ex $66 Gd $56
Same as Marlin Model 101 except w/plain stock. Made from 1960-65.

MODEL 989G
AUTOLOADING RIFLE. . . . . NiB $92 Ex $66 Gd $56
Same as Marlin Model 989 except w/plain stock, bead front sight. Made from 1962-64.

MAUSER SPORTING RIFLES — Oberndorf am Neckar, Germany, Mfg. by Mauser-Werke GmbH, *Imported by Brolin Arms, Pomona, CA, (Previously by Gun South, Inc.; Gibbs Rifle Co.; Precision Imports, Inc. and KDF, Inc.)*

Before the end of WWI the name of the Mauser firm was "Waffenfabrik Mauser A.-G." Shortly after WWI it was changed to "Mauser-Werke A.-G." This information may be used to determine the age of genuine original Mauser sporting rifles made before WWII because all bear either of these firm names as well as the Mauser banner trademark.

The first four rifles listed were manufactured before WWI. Those that follow were produced between World Wars I and II. The early Mauser models can generally be identified by the pistol grip, which is rounded instead of capped, and the M/98 military-type magazine floorplate and catch. The later models have hinged magazine floorplates with lever or button release.

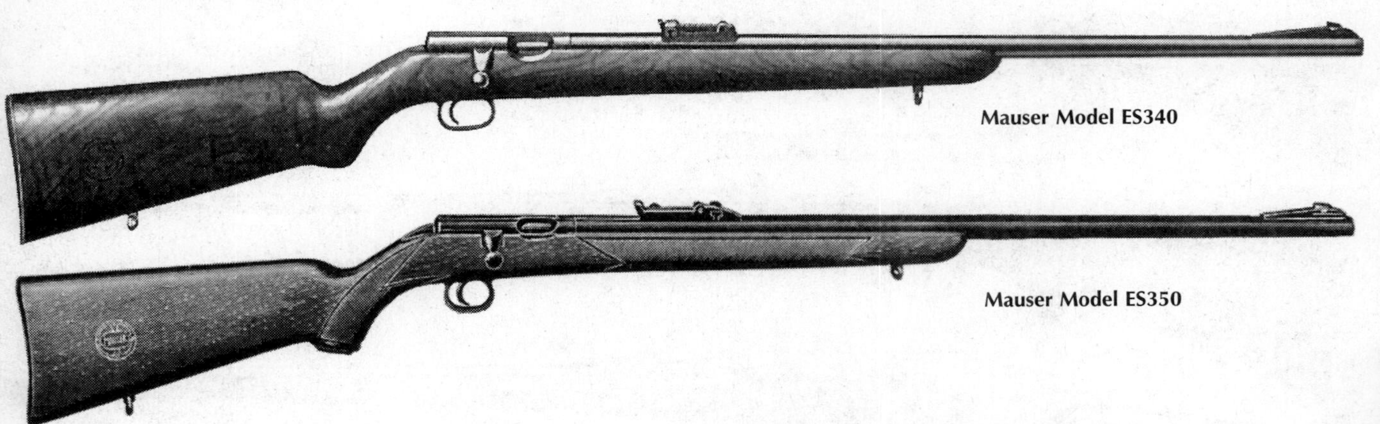

NOTE: *The "B" series of Mauser .22 rifles (Model ES340B, MS350B, etc.) were improved versions of their corresponding models and were introduced about 1935.*

PRE-WORLD WAR I MODELS

BOLT-ACTION SPORTING CARBINE
Calibers: 6.5x54, 6.5x58, 7x57, 8x57, 957mm. 19.75-inch bbl. Weight: 7 lbs. Full-stocked to muzzle. Other specifications same as for standard rifle.
Sporting Carbine w/20-inch bbl. (Type M). NiB $2400 Ex $1938 Gd $1347
Sporting Carbine w/20 or 24-inch bbl. (Type S). . . . . NiB $2471 Ex $1994 Gd $1385

BOLT-ACTION SPORTING RIFLE
Calibers: 6.5x55, 6.5x58, 7x57, 8x57, 9x57, 9.3x62 10.75x68.Five-round box magazine, 23.5-inch bbl. Weight: 7 to 7.5 lbs. Pear-shaped bolt handle. Double-set or single trigger. Sights: Tangent curve rear; ramp front. Pistol-grip stock, forearm w/Schnabel tip and swivels.
Sporting Rifle (Type A, English export) . NiB $2545 Ex $2144 Gd $1487
Sporting Rifle (Type B) . . . . NiB $1746 Ex $1412 Gd $985

BOLT-ACTION SPORTING RIFLE, MILITARY MODEL TYPE C . . . . NiB $740 Ex $598 Gd $417
So called because of stepped M/98-type bbl., military front sight and double-pull trigger. Calibers: 7x57, 8x57, 9x57mm. Other specifications same as for standard rifle.

BOLT-ACTION SPORTING RIFLE SHORT MODEL TYPE K . . . . NiB $3759 Ex $3014 Gd $2085
Calibers: 6.5x54, 8x51mm. 19.75-inch bbl. Weight: 6.25 lbs. Other specifications same as for standard rifle.

PRE-WORLD WAR II MODELS

MODEL DSM34 BOLT-ACTION SINGLE-SHOT SPORTING RIFLE . . . . NiB $508 Ex $411 Gd $288
Also called "Sport-model." Caliber: .22 LR. 26-inch bbl. Weight: 7.75 lbs. Sights: Tangent curve open rear; Barleycorn front. M/98 military-type stock, swivels. Intro. c. 1935.

MODEL EL320 BOLT-ACTION SINGLE-SHOT SPORTING RIFLE . . . . NiB $488 Ex $396 Gd $277
Caliber: .22 LR. 23.5-inch bbl. Weight: 4.25 lbs. Sights: Adj. open rear; bead front. Sporting stock w/checkered pistol grip, swivels.

MODEL EN310 BOLT-ACTION SINGLE-SHOT SPORTING RIFLE . . . . NiB $443 Ex $360 Gd $253
Caliber: .22 LR. ("22 Lang fur Buchsen.") 19.75-inch bbl. Weight: 4 lbs. Sights: Fixed open rear, blade front. Plain pistol-grip stock.

MODEL ES340 BOLT-ACTION SINGLE-SHOT TARGET RIFLE . . . . NiB $508 Ex $411 Gd $288
Caliber: .22 LR. 25.5-inch bbl. Weight: 6.5 lbs. Sights: Tangent curve rear; ramp front. Sporting stock w/checkered pistol-grip and grooved forearm, swivels.

MODEL ES340B BOLT-ACTION SINGLE-SHOT TARGET RIFLE . . . . NiB $508 Ex $411 Gd $288
Caliber: .22 LR. 26.75-inch bbl. Weight: 8 lbs. Sights: Tangent curve open rear; ramp front. Plain pistol-grip stock, swivels.

MODEL ES350 BOLT-ACTION SINGLE-SHOT TARGET RIFLE . . . . NiB $704 Ex $569 Gd $396
"Meistershaftsbuchse" (Championship Rifle). Caliber: .22 LR. 27.5-inch bbl. Weight: 7.75 lbs. Sights: Open micrometer rear; ramp front. Target stock w/checkered pistol-grip and forearm, grip cap, swivels.

MODEL ES350B BOLT-ACTION SINGLE-SHOT TARGET RIFLE . . . . NiB $640 Ex $517 Gd $361
Same general specifications as Model MS350B except single-shot, weight: 8.25 lbs.

MODEL KKW BOLT-ACTION SINGLE-SHOT TARGET RIFLE. . . . . NiB $509 Ex $414 Gd $291
Caliber: .22 LR. 26-inch bbl. Weight: 8.75 lbs. Sights: Tangent curve open rear; Barleycorn front. M/98 military-type stock, swivels. Note: This rifle has an improved design Mauser 22 action w/separate nonrotating bolt head. In addition to being produced for commercial sale, this model was used as a training rifle by the German armed forces; it was also made by Walther and Gustoff. Intro. just before WWII.

MODEL M410 BOLT-ACTION REPEATING SPORTING RIFLE . . . . NiB $904 Ex $730 Gd $508
Caliber: .22 LR. Five round detachable box magazine. 23.5-inch bbl. Weight: 5 lbs. Sights: Tangent curve open rear; ramp front. Sporting stock w/checkered pistol-grip, swivels.

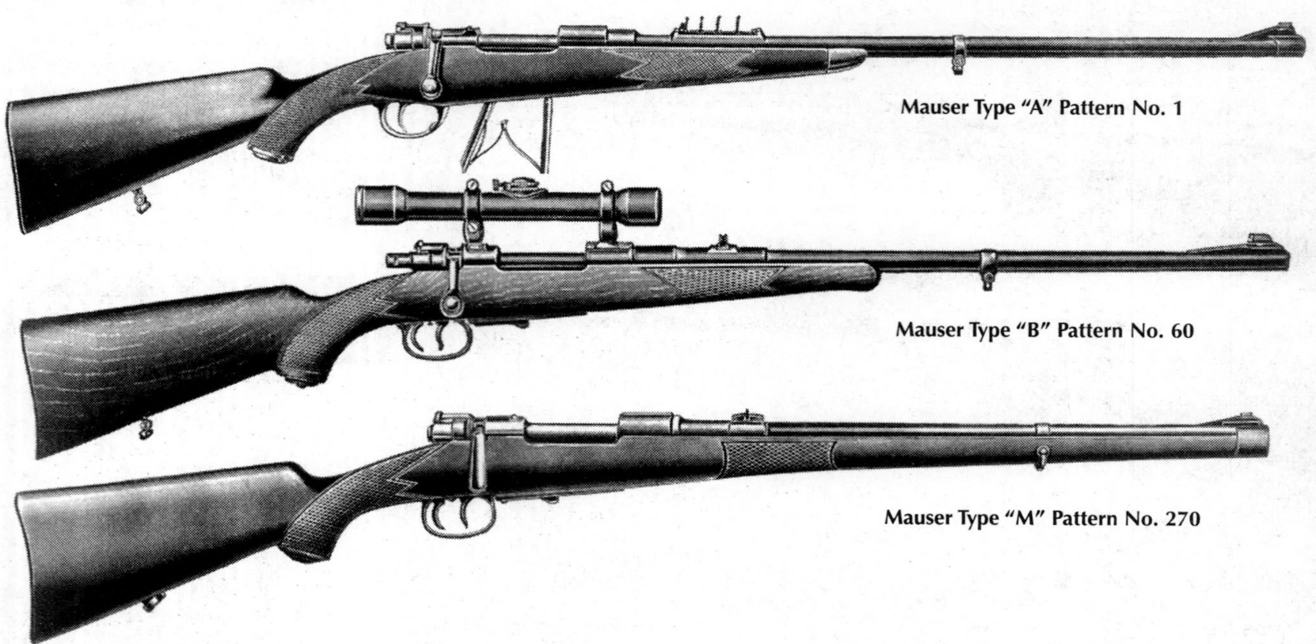

Mauser Type "A" Pattern No. 1

Mauser Type "B" Pattern No. 60

Mauser Type "M" Pattern No. 270

MODEL MM410B BOLT-ACTION REPEATING SPORTING RIFLE .... NiB $927 Ex $748 Gd $519
Caliber: .22 LR. Five round detachable box magazine. 23.5-inch bbl. Weight: 6.25 lbs. Sights: Tangent curve open rear; ramp front. Lightweight sporting stock w/checkered pistol-grip, swivels.

MODEL MS350B BOLT-ACTION REPEATING TARGET RIFLE............. NiB $927 Ex $748 Gd $519
Caliber: .22 LR. Five round detachable box magazine. Receiver and bbl. grooved for detachable rear sight or scope. 26.75-inch bbl. Weight: 8.5 lbs. Sights: Micrometer open rear; ramp front. Target stock w/checkered pistol grip and forearm, grip cap, sling swivels.

MODEL MS420 BOLT-ACTION REPEATING SPORTING RIFLE .... NiB $998 Ex $804 Gd $557
Caliber: .22 LR. Five round detachable box magazine. 25.5-inch bbl. Weight: 6.5 lbs. Sights: Tangent curve open rear; ramp front. Sporting stock w/checkered pistol grip, grooved forearm swivels.

MODEL MS420B BOLT-ACTION REPEATING TARGET RIFLE............. NiB $836 Ex $676 Gd $470
Caliber: .22 LR. Five round detachable box magazine. 26.75-inch bbl. Weight: 8 lbs. Sights: Tangent curve open rear; ramp front. Target stock w/checkered pistol grip, grooved forearm, swivels.

STANDARD MODEL RIFLE .... NiB $706 Ex $571 Gd $398
Refined version of German Service Kar. 98k. Straight bolt handle. Calibers: 7mm Mauser (7x57mm), 7.9mm Mauser (8x57mm). Five round box magazine. 23.5-inch bbl. Weight: 8.5 lbs. Sights: Blade front; adj. rear. Walnut stock of M/98 military-type. Note: These rifles were made for commercial sale and are of the high quality found in the Oberndorf Mauser sporters. They bear the Mauser trademark on the receiver ring.

TYPE "A" BOLT-ACTION SPORTING RIFLE............ NiB $2637 Ex $2123 Gd $1466
Special British Model. 7x57, 30-06 (7.62x63), 8x60, 9x57, 9.3x62mm. Five round box mag. 23.5-inch round bbl. Weight: 7.25 lbs. Mil.-type single trigger. Sights: Express rear; hooded ramp front. Circassian walnut sporting stock w/checkered pistol-grip and forearm, w/ or w/o cheekpiece, buffalo horn forend tip and grip cap, detachable swivels. Variations: Octagon bbl., double-set trigger, shotgun-type safety, folding peep rear sight, tangent curve rear sight, three-leaf rear sight.

TYPE "A" BOLT-ACTION SPORTING RIFLE, MAGNUM MODEL.......... NiB $2899 Ex $2334 Gd $1641
Same general specifications as standard Type "A" except w/Magnum action, weighs 7.5 to 8.5 lbs. Calibers: .280 Ross, .318 Westley Richards Express, 10.75x68mm, .404 Nitro Express.

TYPE "A" BOLT-ACTION SPORTING RIFLE, SHORT MODEL............. NiB $2384 Ex $1921 Gd $1331
Same as standard Type "A" except w/short action, 21.5-inch round bbl., weight 6 lbs. Calibers: .250-3000, 6.5x54, 8x51mm.

TYPE "B" BOLT-ACTION SPORTING RIFLE..................... NiB $1794 Ex $1445 Gd $1001
Normal Model. Calibers: 7x57, .30-06 (7.62x63), 8x57, 8x60, 9x57, 9.3x62, 10.7568mm. Five round box magazine. 23.5-inch round bbl. Weight: 7.25 lbs. Double-set trigger. Sights: Three-leaf rear, ramp front. Fine walnut stock w/checkered pistol-grip, Schnabel forend tip, cheekpiece, grip cap, swivels. Variations: Octagon or half-octagon bbl., military-type single trigger, shotgun-type safety, folding peep rear sight, tangent curve rear sight, telescopic sight.

TYPE "K" BOLT-ACTION SPORTING RIFLE............ NiB $3766 Ex $3021 Gd $2092
Light Short Model. Same specifications as Normal Type "B" model except w/short action, 21.5-inch round bbl., weight: 6 lbs. Calibers: .250-3000, 6.5x54, 8x51mm.

TYPE "M" BOLT-ACTION SPORTING CARBINE .... NiB $2378 Ex $1916 Gd $1325
Calibers: 6.5x54, 7x57, .30-06 (7.62x63), 8x51, 8x60, 9x57mm. Five round box magazine. 19.75-inch round bbl. Weight: 6 to 6.75 lbs. Double-set trigger, flat bolt handle. Sights: Three-leaf rear; ramp front. Stocked to muzzle, cheekpiece, checkered pistol-grip and forearm, grip cap, steel forend cap, swivels. Variations: Military-type single trigger, shotgun-type trigger, shotgun-type safety, tangent curve rear sight, telescopic sight.

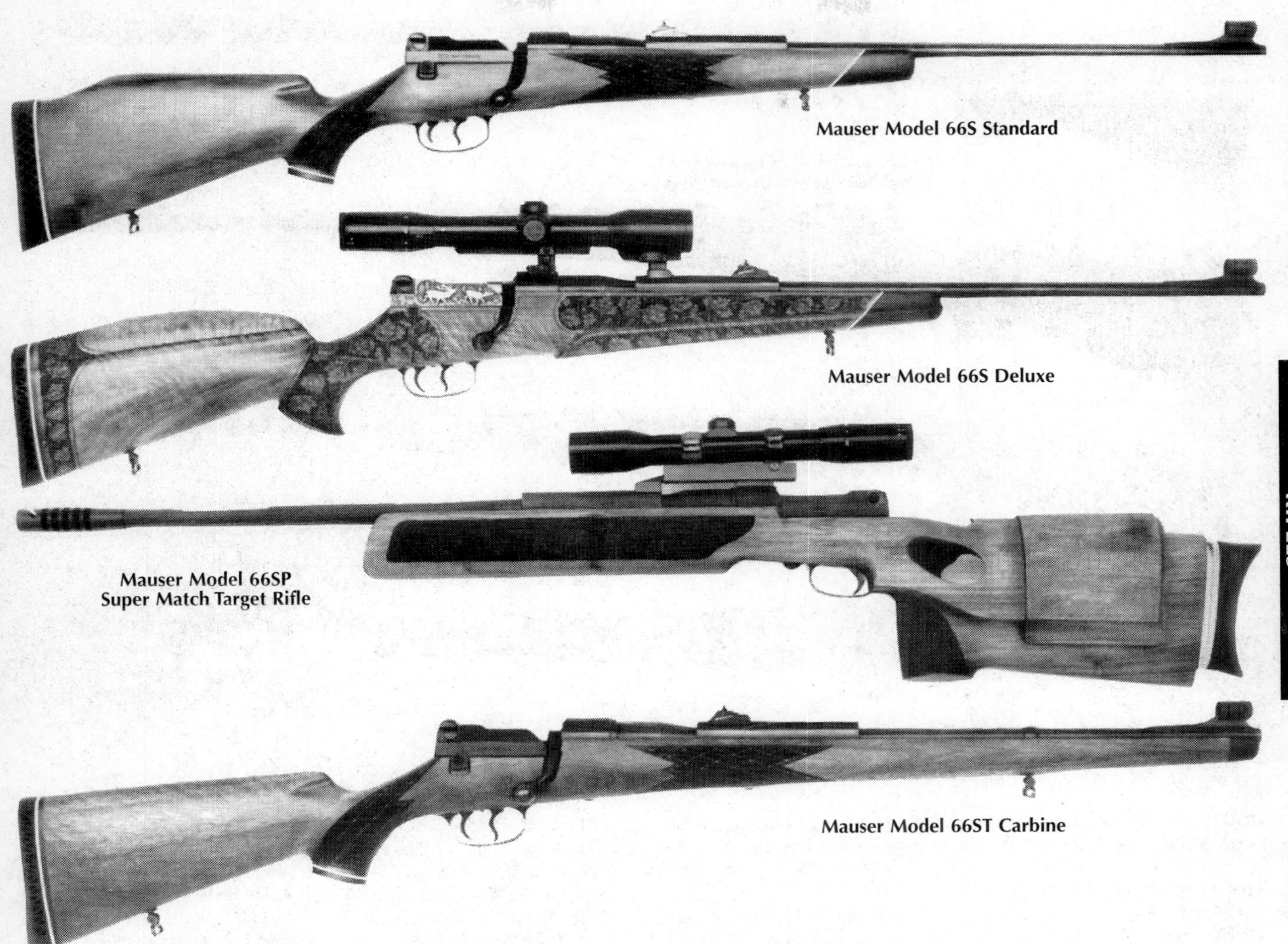
Mauser Model 66S Standard

Mauser Model 66S Deluxe

Mauser Model 66SP Super Match Target Rifle

Mauser Model 66ST Carbine

TYPE "S" BOLT-ACTION SPORTING CARBINE .... NiB $2463 Ex $2076 Gd $1330
Calibers: 6.5x54 7x57, 8x51, 8x60, 9x57mm. Five-round box magazine. 19.75-inch round bbl. Weight: 6 to 6.75 lbs. Double-set trigger. Sights: Three-leaf rear; ramp front. Stocked to muzzle, Schnabel forend tip, cheekpiece, checkered pistol-grip w/cap, swivels. Variations: Same as listed for Normal Model Type "B."

POST-WORLD WAR II MODELS

NOTE: *Production of original Mauser sporting rifles (66 series) resumed at the Oberndorf plant in 1965 by Mauser-Jagdwaffen GmbH, now Mauser-Werke Oberndorf GmbH. The Series 2000-3000-4000 rifles, however, were made for Mauser by Friedrich Wilhelm Heym Gewehrfabrik, Muennerstadt, West Germany.*

MODEL 66S BOLT-ACTION STANDARD SPORTING RIFLE
Telescopic short action. Bbls. interchangeable within cal. group. Single- or double-set trigger (interchangeable). Cal: .243 Win., 6.5x57, .270 Win., 7x64, .308 Win., .30-06. Three round mag. 23.6 inch bbl. (25.6inch in 7x64). Wt: 7.3 lbs. (7.5 lbs. in 7x64). Sights: Adj. open rear, hooded ramp front. Select Eur. walnut stock, Monte Carlo w/cheekpiece, rosewood forend tip and pistol-grip cap, skip checkering, recoil pad, sling swivels. Made from 1965 to date, export to U.S. disc. 1974. Note: U.S. designation, 1971-73, was "Model 660."
Model 66S .... NiB $2429 Ex $2120 Gd $1090
W/extra bbl. assembly, add $550

MODEL 66S DELUXE SPORTER
Limited production special order. Model 66S rifles and carbines are available with /elaborate engraving, gold and silver inlays and carved select walnut stocks. Added value is upward of $4500.

MODEL 66S ULTRA
Same general specifications as Model 66S Standard except with 20.9-inch bbl., weight: 6.8 lbs.
Model 66S Ultra .... NiB $1665 Ex $1578 Gd $1021
W/extra bbl. assembly, add $550

MODEL 66SG BIG GAME
Same general specifications as Model 66S Standard except w/25.6-inch bbl., weight 9.3 lbs. Calibers: .375 H&H Mag., .458 Win. Mag. Note: U.S. designation, 1971-73, was "Model 660 Safari."
Model 66SG .... NiB $3062 Ex $2006 Gd $1249
W/ extra bbl. assembly, add $550

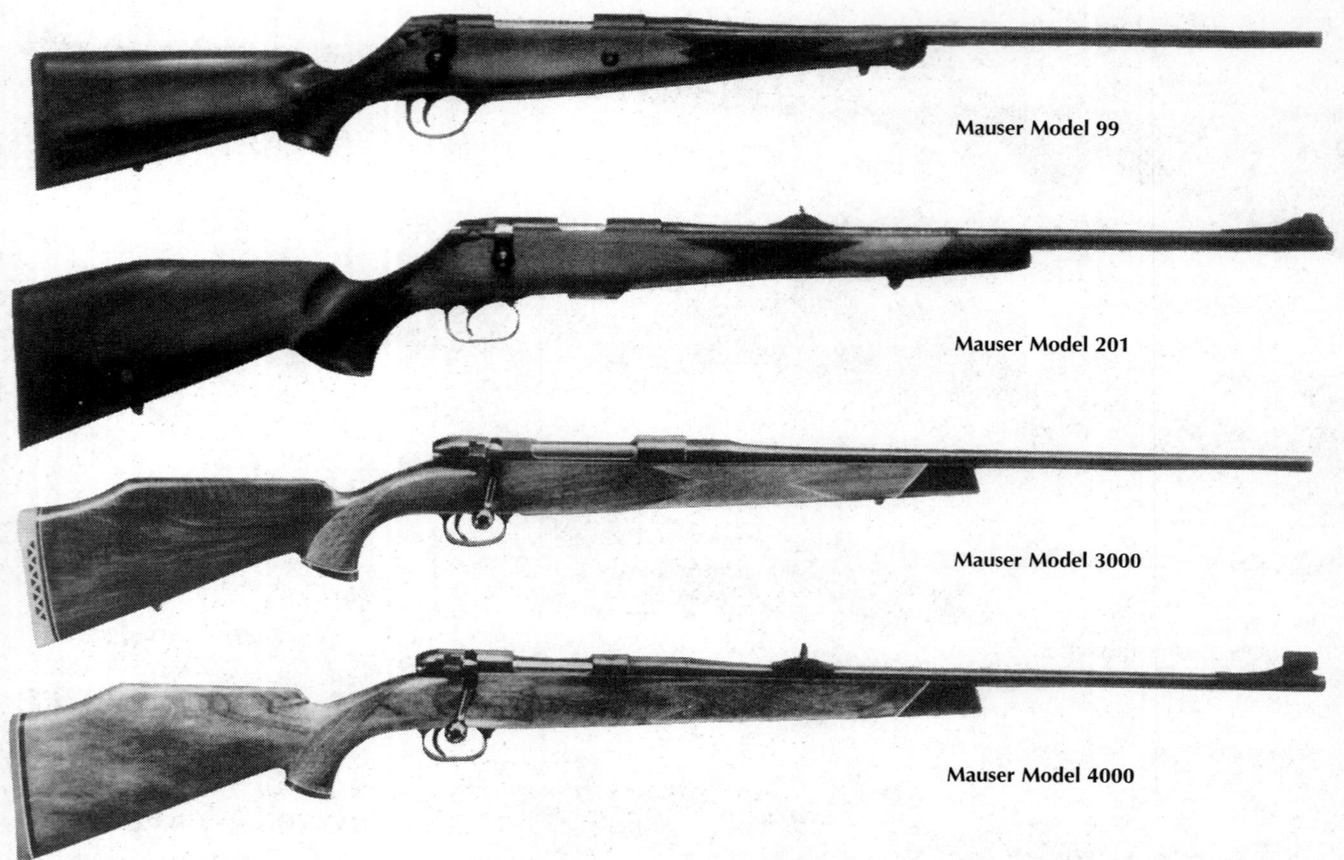

Mauser Model 99

Mauser Model 201

Mauser Model 3000

Mauser Model 4000

MODEL 66SH HIGH PERFORMANCE . NiB $1623 Ex $1448 Gd $1023
Same general specifications as Model 66S Standard except w/25.6-inch bbl., weighs 7.5 lbs. (9.3 lbs. in 9.3x64). Calibers: 6.5x68, 7mm Rem. Mag., 7mm S.E.v. Hoffe, .300 Win. Mag., 8x68S, 9.3x64.

MODEL 66SP SUPER MATCH
BOLT-ACTION TARGET RIFLE. . . . . NiB $4215 Ex $3597 Gd $1897
Telescopic short action. Adj. single-stage trigger. Caliber: .308 Win. (chambering for other cartridges available on special order). Three round magazine. 27.6-inch heavy bbl. w/muzzle brake, dovetail rib for special scope mount. Weight: 12 lbs. Target stock w/wide and deep forearm, full pistol-grip, thumbhole adj. cheekpiece, adj. rubber buttplate.

MODEL 66ST CARBINE
Same general specifications as Model 66S Standard except w/20.9-inch bbl., full-length stock, weight: 7 lbs.
Model 66ST . . . . NiB $6364 Ex $1581 Gd $1143
W/extra bbl. assembly, add $550

MODEL 83 BOLT-ACTION RIFLE . . . . . NiB $2467 Ex $2080 Gd $1308
Centerfire single-shot, bolt-action rifle for 300-meter competition. Caliber: .308 Win. 25.5-inch fluted bbl. Weight: 10.5 lbs. Adj. micrometer rear sight globe front. Fully adj. competition stock. Disc. 1988.

MODEL 96 . . . . NiB $708 Ex $573 Gd $400
Calibers: .25-06, .270 Win., 7x64, .308 Win., .30-06, 7mm Rem. Mag., .300 Win. Mag. 22-inch bbl.; magnums 24-inch. Weight: 6.25 lbs. No sights; drilled and tapped for scope. Walnut stock. Five-round top-loading magazine. 3-position safety.

MODEL 99 CLASSIC BOLT-ACTION RIFLE
Calibers: .243 Win., .25-06, .270 Win., .30-06, .308 Win., .257 Wby., .270 Wby., 7mm Rem. Mag., .300 Win., .300 Wby. .375 H&H. Four round magazine (standard), 3-round (Magnum). Bbl.: 24-inch (standard) or 26-inch (Magnum). 44 inches overall (standard). Weight: 8 lbs. No sights. Checkered European walnut stock w/rosewood grip cap available in Classic and Monte Carlo styles w/High-Luster or oil finish. Disc. importing 1994.
Standard Classic or
Monte Carlo (oil finish). . . . . NiB $1208 Ex $1008 Gd $672
Magnum Classic or
Monte Carlo (oil finish). . . . . NiB $1298 Ex $1053 Gd $740
Standard Classic or
Monte Carlo (H-L finish). . . . . NiB $1238 Ex $1032 Gd $689
Magnum Classic or
Monte Carlo (H-L finish). . . . . NiB $1268 Ex $1073 Gd $756

MODEL 107 BOLT-ACTION RIFLE . . . . NiB $400 Ex $297 Gd $194
Caliber: .22 LR. Mag. Five round magazine. 21.5-inch bbl. 40 inches overall. Weight: 5 lbs. Receiver drilled and tapped for rail scope mounts. Hooded front sight, adj. rear. Disc. importing 1994.

MODEL 201/201 LUXUS BOLT-ACTION RIFLE
Calibers: .22 LR. .22 Win. Mag. Five round magazine. 21-inch bbl. 40 inches overall. Weight: 6.5 lbs. Receiver drilled and tapped for scope mounts. Sights optional. Checkered walnut-stained beech stock w/Monte Carlo. Model 201 Luxus w/checkered European walnut stock QD swivels, rosewood forend and rubber recoil pad. Made from 1989 to date. Disc. importing 1994.
Model 201 Standard . . . . NiB $763 Ex $711 Gd $355
Model 201 Magnum . . . . NiB $705 Ex $579 Gd $355
Model 201 Luxus Standard . . . . NiB $789 Ex $711 Gd $428
Model 201 Luxus Magnum . . . . NiB $898 Ex $736 Gd $531

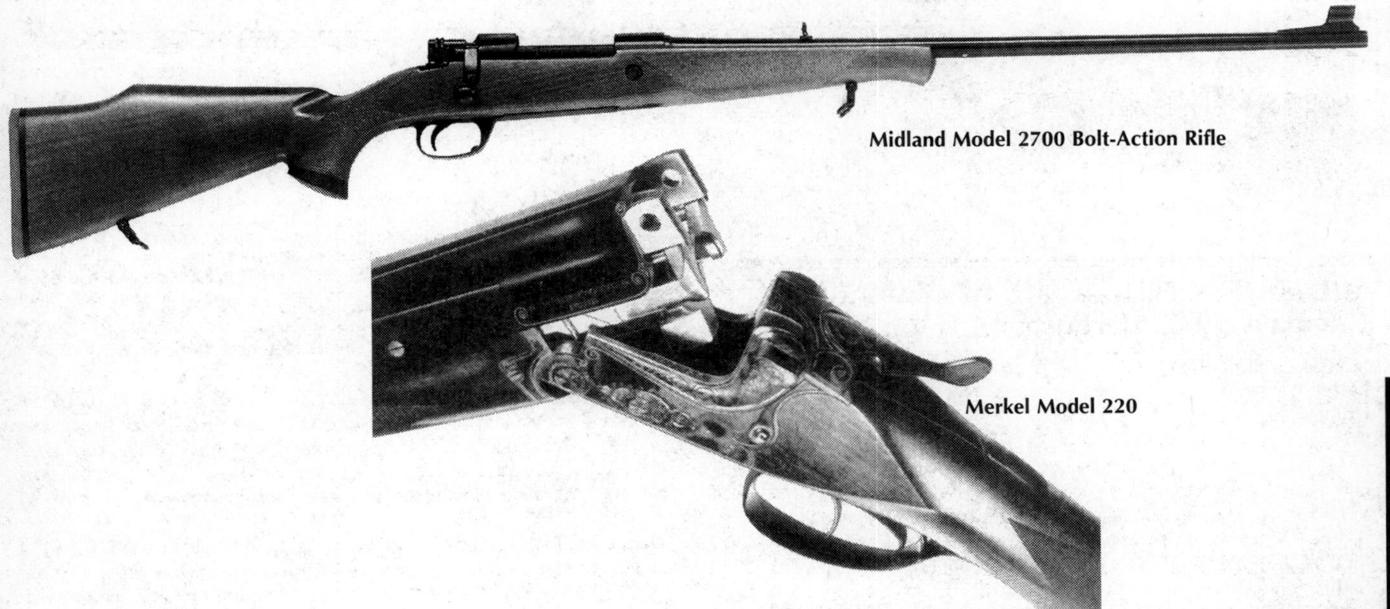

Midland Model 2700 Bolt-Action Rifle

Merkel Model 220

MODEL 2000 BOLT-ACTION SPORTING RIFLE. . . . . NiB $611 Ex $513 Gd $333
Modified Mauser-type action. Calibers: .270 Win., .308 Win., .30-06. Five-round magazine. 24-inch bbl. Weight: 7.5 lbs. Sights: Folding leaf rear; hooded ramp front. Checkered walnut stock w/Monte Carlo comb and cheekpiece, forend tip, sling swivels. Made from 1969-71. Note: Model 2000 is similar in appearance to Model 3000.

MODEL 2000 CLASSIC BOLT-ACTION SPORTING RIFLE
Calibers: .22-250 Rem., .234 Win., .270 Win., 7mm Mag., .308 Win., .30-06, .300 Win. Mag. Three or 5-round magazine. 24-inch bbl. Weight: 7.5 lbs. Sights: Folding leaf rear; hooded ramp front. Checkered walnut stock w/Monte Carlo comb and cheekpiece, forend tip, sling swivels. Imported 1998. Note: The Model 2000 Classic is designed to interchange bbl. assemblies within a given caliber group.
Model 2000 Classic. . . . . NiB $1631 Ex $1316 Gd $912
Model 2000 Professional w/Recoil Compensator . . . . NiB $3282 Ex $2649 Gd $1927
Model 2000 Sniper . . . . NiB $1852 Ex $1494 Gd $1023
Model 2000 Varmint. . . . . NiB $1695 Ex $1446 Gd $1002
Extra bbl. assembly, add $895

MODEL 3000 BOLT-ACTION SPORTING RIFLE. . . . . NiB $622 Ex $493 Gd $360
Modified Mauser-type action. Calibers: .243 Win., .270 Win., .308 Win., .30-06. Five round magazine. 22-inch bbl. Weight: 7 lbs. No sights. Select European walnut stock, Monte Carlo style w/cheekpiece, rosewood forend tip and pistol-grip cap, skip checkering, recoil pad, sling swivels. Made from 1971-74.

MODEL 3000 MAGNUM . . . . NiB $622 Ex $545 Gd $442
Same general specifications as standard Model 3000, except w/3-round magazine, 26-inch bbl., weight: 8 lbs. Calibers: 7mm Rem. Mag., .300 Win. Mag., .375 H&H Mag.

MODEL 4000 VARMINT RIFLE . . . . NiB $545 Ex $442 Gd $329
Same general specifications as standard Model 3000, except w/smaller action, folding leaf rear sight; hooded ramp front, rubber buttplate instead of recoil pad, weight 6.75 lbs. Calibers: .222 Rem., .223 Rem. 22-inch bbl. Select European walnut stock w/rosewood forend tip and pistol-grip cap. French checkering and sling swivels.

McMILLAN GUN WORKS — Phoenix, Arizona Harris Gunworks

See Harris Gunworks.

GEBRÜDER MERKEL — Suhl, Germany

For Merkel combination guns and drillings, see listings under Merkel shotguns.

OVER/UNDER RIFLES ("BOCK-DOPPELBÜCHSEN")
Calibers: 5.6x35 Vierling, 6.5x58r5, 7x57r5, 8x57JR, 8x60R Magnum, 9.3x53r5, 9.3x72r5, 9.3x74r5, 10.3x60R as well as most of the British calibers for African and Indian big game. Various bbl. lengths, weights. In general, specifications correspond to those of Merkel over/under shotguns. Values of these over/under rifles (in calibers for which ammunition is obtainable) are about the same as those of comparable shotgun models currently manufactured. For more specific data, see Merkel shotgun models indicated below.
Model 220. . . . . NiB $9000 Ex $8000 Gd $4000
Model 220E. . . . . NiB $9575 Ex $8400 Gd $7400
Model 221. . . . . NiB $7438 Ex $5950 Gd $4046
Model 221E. . . . . NiB $9813 Ex $7850 Gd $5338
Model 320. . . . . NiB $8125 Ex $6500 Gd $4420
Model 320E. . . . . NiB $15,000 Ex $12,000 Gd $8160
Model 321. . . . . NiB $16,563 Ex $13,250 Gd $9010
Model 321E. . . . . NiB $17,500 Ex $14,000 Gd $9520
Model 322. . . . . NiB $18,125 Ex $14,500 Gd $9860
Model 323E . . . . NiB $23,125 Ex $18,500 Gd $12,580
Model 324 . . . . NiB $26,875 Ex $21,500 Gd $14,620

MEXICAN MILITARY RIFLE Mfd. by Government Arsenal, Mexico, D.F.

MODEL 1936 MAUSER MILITARY RIFLE . . . NiB $216 Ex $164 Gd $90
Same as German Kar.98k w/minor variations and U.S. M/1903 Springfield-type knurled cocking piece.

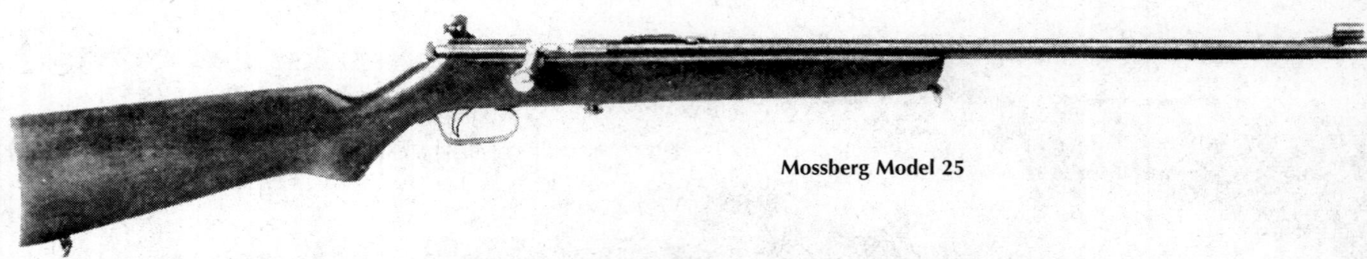

Mossberg Model 25

MIDLAND RIFLES — Mfg. by Gibbs Rifle Company, Inc., Martinsburg, WV

MODEL 2100 BOLT-ACTION RIFLE............................ NiB $369 Ex $301 Gd $213
Calibers: .22-250, .243 Win., 6mm Rem., .270 Win., 6.5x55, 7x57, 7x64, .308 Win., and .30-06. Springfield 1903 action. Four-round magazine. 22-inch bbl. 43 inches overall. Weight: 7 lbs. Flip-up rear sight; hooded ramp front. Finely finished and checkered walnut stock w/pistol-grip cap and sling swivels. Steel recoil bar. Action drilled and tapped for scope mounts. Production disc.1997.

MODEL 2600 BOLT-ACTION RIFLE ...... NiB $388 Ex $316 Gd $193
Same general specifications as Model 2100 except no pistol-grip cap, and stock is walnut-finished hardwood. Made from 1992-97.

MODEL 2700 BOLT-ACTION RIFLE ...... NiB $388 Ex $211 Gd $208
Same general specifications as Model 2100 except the weight of this rifle as been reduced by utilizing a tapered bbl., anodized aluminum trigger housing and lightened stock. Weight: 6.5 lbs. Disc.

MODEL 2800 LIGHTWEIGHT RIFLE ..... NiB $395 Ex $322 Gd $228
Same general specifications as Model 2100 except w/laminated birch stock. Made from 1992-94 and from 1996-97.

MITCHELL ARMS. INC. — Fountain Valley, California, (Formerly Santa Ana, CA)

MODEL 15/22 SEMIAUTOMATIC
High Standard-style action. Caliber: .22 LR. 15-round magazine (10-round after 10/13/94). 20.5-inch bbl. 37.5 inches overall. Weight: 6.25 lbs. Ramp front sight; adj. open rear. Blued finish. Mahogany stock; Monte Carlo-style American walnut stock on Deluxe model. Made from 1994-96.
Model 15/22 SP (Special) w/plastic buttplate .... NiB $111 Ex $91 Gd $67
Model 15/22 Carbine .... NiB $149 Ex $122 Gd $87
Model 15/22D Deluxe .... NiB $175 Ex $143 Gd $102

MODEL 9300 SERIES BOLT-ACTION RIFLE
Calibers: .22 LR. .22 Mag. Five or 10-round magazine. 22.5-inch bbl. 40.75 inches overall. Weight: 6.5 lbs. Beaded ramp front sight; adj. open rear. Blued finish. American walnut stock. Made from 1994-95.
Model 9302 (.22 LR, checkered, rosewood caps)............ NiB $262 Ex $215 Gd $154
Model 9302 (.22 Mag., checkered, rosewood caps) .... NiB $2705 Ex $225 Gd $161
Model 9303 (.22 LR, plain stock) .... NiB $210 Ex $173 Gd $126
Model 9304 (.22 Mag., checkered, No rosewood caps).......... NiB $224 Ex $184 Gd $132
Model 9305 (.22 LR, special stock)....... NiB $183 Ex $151 Gd $210

AK-22 SEMIAUTOMATIC RIFLE .... NiB $260 Ex $215 Gd $154
Replica of AK-47 rifle. .22 LR. .22 WMR., 20-round magazine (.22 LR), 10-round (.22 WMR). 18-inch bbl. 36 inches overall. Weight: 6.5 lbs. Sights: Post front; open adj. rear. European walnut stock and forend. Matte black finish. Made from 1985-94.

CAR-15 22 SEMIAUTOMATIC RIFLE...... NiB $262 Ex $215 Gd $154
Replica of AR-15 CAR rifle. Caliber: .22 LR. 15-round magazine.16.25-inch bbl. 32 inches overall. Sights: Adj. post front; adj. aperture rear. Telescoping buttstock and ventilated forend. Matte black finish. Made from 1990-94.

GALIL 22 SEMIAUTOMATIC RIFLE....... NiB $307 Ex $256 Gd $168
Replica of Israeli Galil rifle. Calibers: .22 LR. .22 WMR., 20-round magazine (.22 LR), 10-round (.22 WMR). 18-inch bbl. 36 inches overall. Weight: 6.5 lbs. Sights: Adj. post front; rear adj. for windage. Folding metal stock w/European walnut grip and forend. Matte black finish. Made from 1987-93.

M-16A 22 SEMIAUTOMATIC RIFLE ...... NiB $262 Ex $215 Gd $154
Replica of AR-15 rifle. Caliber: .22 LR. 15-round magazine. 20.5-inch bbl. 38.5 inches overall. Weight: 7 lbs. Sights: Adj. post front, adj. aperture rear. Black composite stock and forend. Matte black finish. Made from 1990-94.

MAS 22 SEMIAUTOMATIC RIFLE........ NiB $307 Ex $251 Gd $178
Replica of French MAS bullpup rifle. Caliber: .22 LR. 20-round magazine. 18-inch bbl. 28 inches overall. Weight: 7.5 lbs. Sights: Adj. post front, folding aperture rear. European walnut buttstock and forend. Matte black finish. Made from 1987-93.

PPS SEMIAUTOMATIC RIFLE
Caliber: .22 LR. 20-round magazine, 50-round drum. 16.5-inch bbl. 33.5 inches overall. Weight: 5.5 lbs. Sights: Blade front; adj. rear. European walnut stock w/ventilated bbl. shroud. Matte black finish. Made from 1989-94.
Model PPS (20-round).......... NiB $281 Ex $230 Gd $164
Model PPS/50 (50-round drum) ... NiB $548 Ex $465 Gd $358

O.F. MOSSBERG & SONS, INC. — North Haven, Connecticut, (Formerly New Haven, CT)

MODEL 10 BOLT-ACTION SINGLE-SHOT RIFLE........... NiB $177 Ex $126 Gd $100
Takedown. Caliber: .22 LR, Long, Short. 22-inch bbl. Weight: 4 lbs. Sights: Open rear; bead front. Plain pistol-grip stock w/swivels, sling. Made from 1933-35.

MODEL 14 BOLT-ACTION SINGLE-SHOT RIFLE........... NiB $188 Ex $126 Gd $101
Takedown. Caliber: .22 LR. Long, Short. 24-inch bbl. Weight: 5.25 lbs. Sights: Peep rear; hooded ramp front. Plain pistol-grip stock w/semi-beavertail forearm, 1.25-inch swivels. Made from 1934-35.

MODEL 20 BOLT-ACTION SINGLE-SHOT RIFLE........... NiB $188 Ex $126 Gd $100
Takedown. Caliber: .22 LR. Long, Short. 24-inch bbl. Weight: 4.5 lbs. Sights: Open rear; bead front. Plain pistol-grip stock and forearm w/finger grooves, sling and swivels. Made from 1933-35.

MODEL 25/25A BOLT-ACTION SINGLE-SHOT RIFLE
Takedown. Caliber: .22 LR. Long, Short. 24-inch bbl. Weight: 5 lbs. Sights: Peep rear; hooded ramp front. Plain pistol-grip stock w/semi-beavertail forearm. 1.25-inch swivels. Made from 1935-36.
Model 25........................... NiB $188 Ex $126 Gd $95
Model 25A (Improved Model 25, 1936-38).... NiB $198 Ex $126 Gd $100

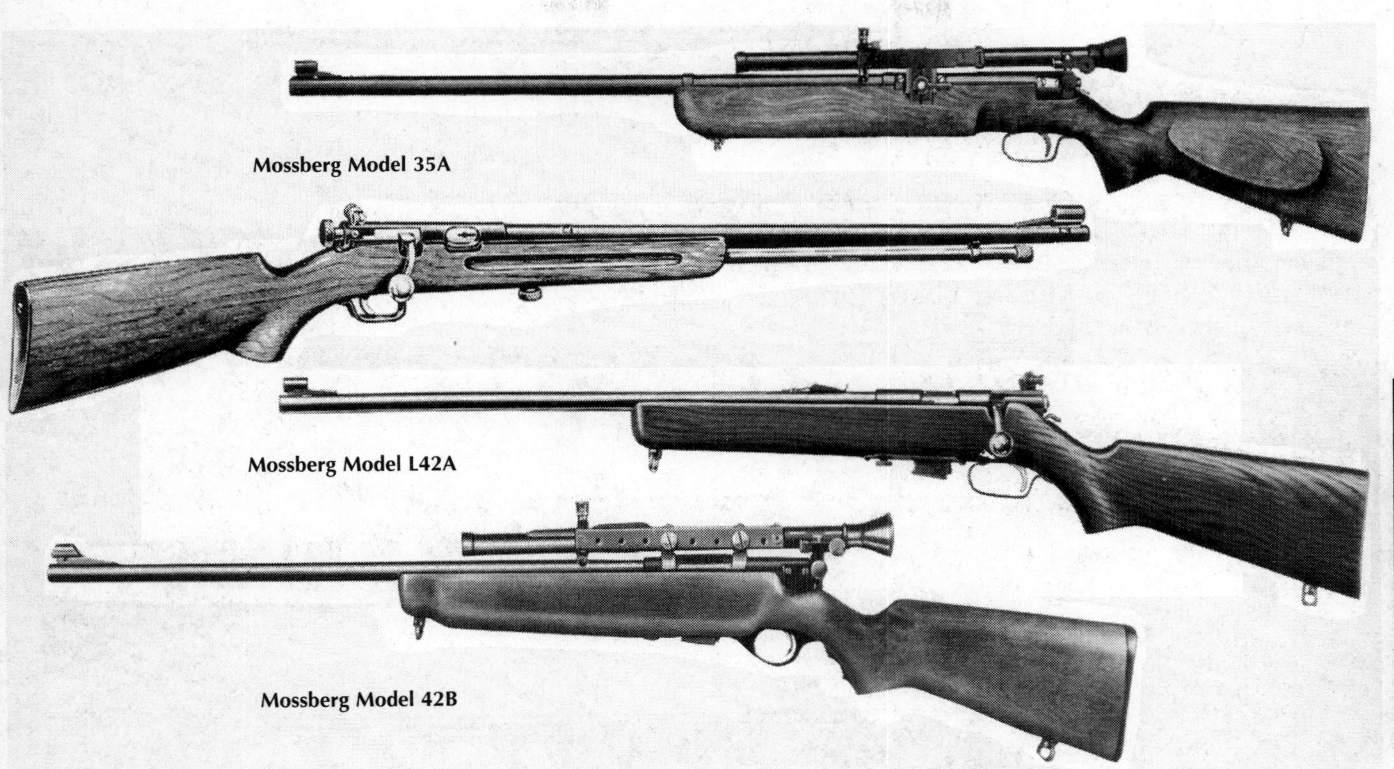

Mossberg Model 35A

Mossberg Model L42A

Mossberg Model 42B

MODEL 26B/26C BOLT-ACTION SINGLE-SHOT
Takedown. Caliber: .22 LR. Long, Short. 26-inch bbl. Weight: 5.5 lbs. Sights; Rear, micrometer click peep or open; hooded ramp front. Plain pistol-grip stock swivels. Made fiom 1938-41.
Model 26B .... NiB $199 Ex $158 Gd $101
Model 26C
(No rear sight/swivels) .... NiB $178 Ex $127 Gd $86

MODEL 30 BOLT-ACTION
SINGLE-SHOT RIFLE .... NiB $158 Ex $127 Gd $96
Takedown. Caliber: .22 LR. Long, Short. 24-inch bbl. Weight: 4.5 lbs. Sights: Peep rear; bead front, on hooded ramp. Plain pistol-grip stock, forearm w/finger grooves. Made from 1933-35.

MODEL 34 BOLT-ACTION
SINGLE-SHOT RIFLE .... NiB $180 Ex $127 Gd $96
Takedown. Caliber: .22 LR. Long, Short. 24-inch bbl. Weight: 5.5 lbs. Sights: Peep rear; hooded ramp front. Plain pistol-grip stock w/semibeavertail forearm, 1.25-inch swivels. Made from 1934-35.

MODEL 35 TARGET GRADE
BOLT-ACTION SINGLE-SHOT RIFLE...... NiB $362 Ex $254 Gd $111
Caliber: .22 LR. 26-inch heavy bbl. Weight: 8.25 lbs. Sights: Micrometer click rear peep; hooded ramp front. Large target stock w/full pistol grip, cheekpiece, full beavertail forearm, 1.25-inch swivels. Made from 1935-37.

MODEL 35A BOLT-ACTION
SINGLE-SHOT RIFLE .... NiB $362 Ex $253 Gd $109
Caliber: .22 LR. 26-inch heavy bbl. Weight: 8.25 lbs. Sights: Micrometer click peep rear; hooded front. Target stock w/cheekpiece full pistol grip and forearm, 1.25-inch sling swivels. Made from 1937-38.

MODEL 35A-LS .... NiB $421 Ex $287 Gd $200
Caliber .22 LR. Same as Model 35A but w/Lyman No. 57 rear sight, 17A front. Target stock w/checkpiece, full pistol-grip and forearm.

MODEL 35B .... NiB $411 Ex $277 Gd $195
Same specifications as Model 44B except single-shot. Made from 1938-40.

MODEL 40 BOLT-ACTION REPEATER...... NiB $175 Ex $124 Gd $93
Takedown. Caliber: .22 LR. Long, Short, 16-round tubular magazine. 24-inch bbl. Weight: 5 lbs. Sights: Peep rear; bead front, on hooded ramp. Plain pistol-grip stock, forearm w/finger grooves. Madefrom 1933-35.

MODEL 42 BOLT-ACTION REPEATER...... NiB $175 Ex $124 Gd $93
Takedown. Caliber: .22 LR. Long, Short. Seven-round detachable box magazine. 24-inch bbl. Weight: 5 lbs. Sights: Receiver peep, open rear; hooded ramp front. Pistol-grip stock. 1.25-inch swivels. Made from 1935-37.

MODEL 42A/L42A BOLT-ACTION REPEATERS
Takedown. Caliber: .22 LR. Long, Short. Seven-round detachable box magazine. 24-inch bbl. Weight: 5 lbs. Sights: Receiver peep, open rear; ramp front. Plain pistol-grip stock. Made from 1937-38. Model L42A (left-hand action) made from 1937-1941.
Model 42A.................... NiB $175 Ex $145 Gd $105
Model L42A.................. NiB $263 Ex $216 Gd $155

MODEL 42B/42C BOLT-ACTION REPEATERS
Takedown. Caliber: .22 LR. Long, Short. Five-round detachable box magazine. 24-inch bbl. Weight: 6 lbs. Sights: Micrometer click receiver peep, open rear hooded ramp front. Plain pistol-grip stock, swivels. Made from 1938-41.
Model 42B..................... NiB $175 Ex $150 Gd $83
Model 42C (No rear peep sight) .... NiB $144 Ex $119 Gd $88

Mossberg Model 42C

Mossberg Model L-43

Mossberg Model 43B

Mossberg Model 44US

Mossberg Model L45A Left-Hand Model

Mossberg Model 45B

Mossberg Model L46A-LS

Mossberg Model 46B

MODEL 42M BOLT-ACTION REPEATER .... **NiB $203 Ex $177 Gd $105**
Caliber: .22 LR. Long, Short. Seven-round detachable box magazine. 23-inch bbl. Weight: 6.75 lbs. Sights: Microclick receiver peep, open rear; hooded ramp front. Two-piece Mannlicher-type stock w/cheekpiece and pistol-grip, swivels. Made from 1940-50.

MODEL 43/L43 BOLT-ACTION REPEATERS .... **NiB $446 Ex $363 Gd $256**
Speedlock, adj. trigger pull. Caliber: .22 LR. Seven-round detachable box magazine. 26-inch heavy bbl. Weight: 8.25 lbs. Sights: Lyman No. 57 rear; selective aperture front. Target stock w/cheekpiece, full pistol-grip, beavertail forearm, adj. front swivel. Made from 1937-38. Model L43 is same as Model 43 except w/left-hand action.

MODEL 43B .... **NiB $384 Ex $281 Gd $122**
Same as Model 44B except w/Lyman No. 57 receiver sight and No. 17A front sight. Made from 1938-39.

Mossberg Model 46M

Mossberg Model 50

Mossberg Model 51

Mossberg Model 51M

MODEL 44 BOLT-ACTION REPEATER..... NiB $677 Ex $236 Gd $123
Takedown. Caliber: .22 LR. Long, Short. Tubular magazine holds 16 LR. 24-inch bbl. Weight: 6 lbs. Sights: Peep rear; hooded ramp front. Plain pistol-grip stock w/semi-beavertail forearm, 1.25-inch swivels. Made from 1934-35. Note: Do not confuse this rifle w/later Models 44B and 44US, which are clip repeaters.

MODEL 44B BOLT-ACTION TARGET RIFLE................. NiB $301 Ex $229 Gd $126
Caliber: .22 LR. Seven-round detachable box magazine. Made from 1938-41.

MODEL 44US BOLT-ACTION REPEATER
Caliber: .22 LR. Seven round detachable box magazine. 26-inch heavy bbl. Weight: 8.5 lbs. Sights: Micrometer click receiver peep, hooded front. Target stock, swivels. Made from 1943-48. Note: This model was used as a training rifle by the U.S. Armed Forces during WWII.
Model 44US .... NiB $280 Ex $255 Gd $116
Model 44US (marked U.S. Property) ..... NiB $358 Ex $306 Gd $229

MODEL 45 BOLT-ACTION REPEATER..... NiB $199 Ex $173 Gd $112
Takedown. Caliber: .22 LR. Long, Short. Tubular magazine holds 15 LR. 18 Long, 22 Short. 24-inch bbl. Weight: 6.75 lbs. Sights: Rear peep; hooded ramp front. Plain pistol-grip stock, 1.25-inch swivels. Made from 1935-37.

MODEL 45A, L45A, 45AC BOLT-ACTION REPEATERS
Takedown. Caliber: .22 LR. Long, Short. Tubular magazine holds 15 LR, 18 Long, 22 Short. 24-inch bbl. Weight: 6.75 lbs. Sights: Receiver peep, open rear; hooded blade front sight mounted on ramp. Plain pistol-grip stock, 1.25-inch sling swivels. Made 1937-38. See illustration on previous page.
Model 45A .... NiB $199 Ex $163 Gd $117
Model L45A (Left-hand action).......... NiB $251 Ex $204 Gd $145
Model 45AC (No receiver peep sight)..... NiB $184 Ex $143 Gd $101

MODEL 45B/45C BOLT-ACTION REPEATERS
Takedown. Caliber: .22 LR. Long, Short. Tubular magazine holds 15 LR, 18 Long, 22 Short. 24-inch bbl. Weight: 6.25 lbs. Open rear sight; hooded blade front sight mounted on ramp. Plain pistol-grip stock w/sling swivels. Made from 1938-40.
Model 45B .... NiB $180 Ex $148 Gd $107
Model 45C (No sights, made 1935-37)..... NiB $161 Ex $132 Gd $86

MODEL 46 BOLT-ACTION REPEATER..... NiB $199 Ex $204 Gd $112
Takedown. Caliber: .22 LR. Long, Short. Tubular magazine holds 15 LR, 18 Long, 22 Short. 26-inch bbl. Weight: 7.5 lbs. Sights: Micrometer click rear peep; hooded ramp front. Pistol-grip stock w/cheekpiece, full beavertail forearm, 1.25-inch swivels. Made from 1935-37.

MODEL 46A, 46A-LS, L46A-LS BOLT-ACTION REPEATERS
Takedown. Caliber: .22 LR. Long, Short. Tubular magazine holds 15 LR, 18 Long, 22 Short. 26-inch bbl. Weight: 7.25 lbs. Sights: Micrometer click receiver peep, open rear; hooded ramp front. Pistol-grip stock w/cheekpiece and beavertail forearm, quick-detachable swivels. Made from 1937-38.
Model 46A .... NiB $207 Ex $170 Gd $123
Mdl. 46A-LS (w/Lyman No. 57 receiver sight).... NiB $276 Ex $226 Gd $162
Model L46A-LS (Left-hand action) .... NiB $391 Ex $319 Gd $225

Mossberg Model 140B

Mossberg Model 140K

Mossberg Model 144LS

Mossberg Model 146B

MODEL 46B BOLT-ACTION REPEATER . . . . **NiB $168 Ex $138 Gd $100**
Takedown. Caliber: .22 LR. Long, Short. Tubular magazine holds 15 LR, 18 Long, 22 Short. 26-inch bbl. Weight: 7 lbs. Sights: Micrometer click receiver peep, open rear, hooded front. Plain pistol-grip stock w/cheekpiece, swivels. Note: Postwar version of this model has full magazine holding 20 LR, 23 Long, 30 Short. Made from 1938-50.

MODEL 46BT . . . . **NiB $234 Ex $192 Gd $137**
Same as Model 46B except w/heavier bbl. and stock. Weight: 7.75 lbs. Made from 1938-39.

MODEL 46C . . . . **NiB $228 Ex $176 Gd $115**
Same as Model 46 except w/a heavier bbl. and stock than that model. Weight: 8.5 lbs. Made from 1936-37.

MODEL 46M BOLT-ACTION REPEATER . . . . **NiB $228 Ex $176 Gd $115**
Caliber: .22 LR. Long, Short. Tubular magazine holds 22 Short, 18 Long, 15 LR. 23-inch bbl. Weight: 7 lbs. Sights: Microclick receiver peep, open rear; hooded ramp front. Two-piece Mannlicher-type stock w/cheekpiece and pistol-grip, swivels. Made from 1940-52.

MODEL 50 AUTOLOADING RIFLE . . . . **NiB $202 Ex $166 Gd $120**
Same as Model 51 except w/plain stock w/o beavertail cheekpiece, swivels or receiver peep sight. Made from 1939-42.

MODEL 51 AUTOLOADING RIFLE . . . . **NiB $195 Ex $149 Gd $118**
Takedown. Caliber: .22 LR. Fifteen-round tubular magazine in buttstock. 24-inch bbl. Weight: 7.25 lbs. Sights: Micrometer click receiver peep, open rear; hooded ramp front. Cheekpiece stock w/full pistol grip and beavertail forearm, swivels. Made in 1939 only.

MODEL 51M AUTOLOADING RIFLE . . . . . **NiB $195 Ex $149 Gd $118**
Caliber: .22 LR. Fifteen-round tubular magazine. 20-inch bbl. Weight: 7 lbs. Sights: Microclick receiver peep, open rear; hooded ramp front. Two-piece Mannlicher-type stock w/pistol-grip and cheekpiece, hard-rubber buttplate and sling swivels. Made from 1939-46.

MODEL 140B SPORTER-TARGET RIFLE . . . **NiB $195 Ex $149 Gd $118**
Same as Model 140K except w/peep rear sight, hooded ramp front sight. Made from 1957-58.

MODEL 140K BOLT-ACTION REPEATER . . **NiB $174 Ex $144 Gd $104**
Caliber: .22 LR. .22 Long, .22 Short. Seven-round clip magazine. 24.5-inch bbl. Weight: 5.75 lbs. Sights: Open rear; bead front. Monte Carlo stock w/cheekpiece and pistol-grip, sling swivels. Made from 1955-58.

MODEL 142-A BOLT-ACTION REPEATING CARBINE . . . . **NiB $214 Ex $174 Gd $125**
Caliber: .22 Short Long, LR. Seven-round detachable box magazine. 18-inch bbl. Weight: 6 lbs. Sights: Peep rear, military-type front. Monte Carlo stock w/pistol-grip, hinged forearm pulls down to form hand grip; sling swivels mounted on left side of stock. Made from 1949-57.

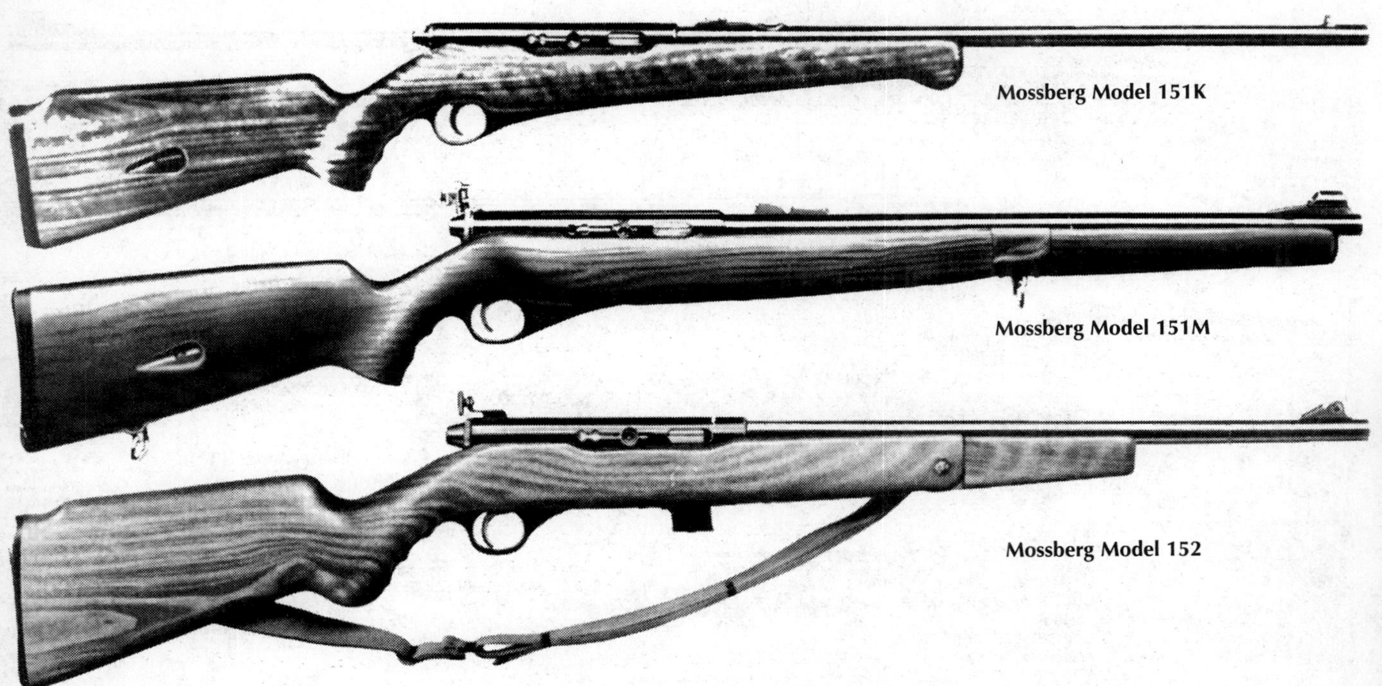

MODEL 142K . . . . NiB $151 Ex $124 Gd $89
Same as Model 142 except w/open rear sight. Made from 1953-57.

MODEL 144 BOLT-ACTION TARGET RIFLE . . . . NiB $437 Ex $360 Gd $205
Caliber: .22 LR. Seven-round detachable box magazine. 26-inch heavy bbl. Weight: 8 lbs. Sights: Microclick receiver peep; hooded front. Pistol-grip target stock w/beavertail forearm, adj. hand stop, swivels. Made from 1949-54. Note: This model designation was resumed c.1973 to replace Model 144LS, and then disc. again in 1985.

MODEL 144LS. . . . . NiB $483 Ex $427 Gd $195
Same as Model 144 except w/Lyman No. 57MS or Mossberg S331 receiver sight and Lyman 17A front sight. Made from 1954 to date. Note: Since 1973, this model has been marketed as Model 144.

MODEL 146B BOLT-ACTION REPEATER . . NiB $225 Ex $173 Gd $122
Takedown. Caliber: .22 LR. Long, Short. Tubular magazine holds 30 Short, 23 Long, 20 LR. 26-inch bbl. Weight: 7 lbs. Sights: Micrometer click rear peep, open rear; hooded front. Plain stock w/pistol-grip, Monte Carlo comb and cheekpiece, knob forend tip, swivels. Made from 1949-54.

MODEL 151K . . . . NiB $204 Ex $163 Gd $112
Same as Model 151M except w/24-inch bbl., weight: 6 lbs., w/o peep sight, plain stock w/Monte Carlo comb and cheekpiece, pistol-grip knob, forend tip, w/o swivels. Made from 1950-51.

MODEL 151M AUTOLOADING RIFLE . . . . NiB $204 Ex $164 Gd $112
Improved version of Model 51M w/same general specifications, complete action is instantly removable w/o use of tools. Made from 1946-58.

MODEL 152 AUTOLOADING CARBINE . . NiB $204 Ex $163 Gd $112
Caliber: .22 LR. Seven-round detachable box magazine. 18-inch bbl. Weight: 5 lbs. Sights: Peep rear; military-type front. Monte Carlo stock w/pistol-grip, hinged forearm pulls down to form hand grip, sling mounted on swivels on left side of stock. Made from 1948-57.

MODEL 152K . . . . NiB $183 Ex $147 Gd $100
Same as Model 152 except w/open instead of peep rear sight. Made from 1950-57.

MODEL 320B BOY SCOUT TARGET RIFLE . . . . NiB $184 Ex $152 Gd $109
Same as Model 340K except single-shot w/auto. safety. Made from 1960-71.

MODEL 320K HAMMERLESS BOLT-ACTION SINGLE-SHOT . . . . . . NiB $144 Ex $118 Gd $85
Same as Model 346K except single-shot, w/drop-in loading platform, automatic safety. Weight: 5.75 lbs. Made from 1958-60.

MODEL 321B . . . . NiB $163 Ex $133 Gd $95
Same as Model 321K except w/receiver peep sight. Made from 1972-75.

MODEL 321K BOLT-ACTION SINGLE-SHOT . . . . NiB $169 Ex $139 Gd $99
Same as Model 341 except single-shot. Made from 1972-80.

MODEL 333 AUTOLOADING CARBINE . . NiB $169 Ex $144 Gd $118
Caliber: .22 LR. 15-round tubular magazine. 20-inch bbl. Weight: 6.25 lbs. Sights: Open rear; ramp front. Monte Carlo stock w/checkered pistol grip and forearm, bbl. band, swivels. Made from 1972-73.

MODEL 340B TARGET SPORTER . . . . NiB $203 Ex $172 Gd $121
Same as Model 340K except w/peep rear sight, hooded ramp front sight. Made from 1958-81.

MODEL 340K HAMMERLESS BOLT-ACTION REPEATER . . . . NiB $172 Ex $147 Gd $121
Same as Model 346K except clip type, 7-round magazine. Made from 1958-71.

MODEL 340M . . . . NiB $320 Ex $260 Gd $184
Same as Model 340K except w/18.5-inch bbl., Mannlicher-style stock w/swivels and sling. Weight: 5.25 lbs. Made from 1970-71.

Mossberg Model 320B

Mossberg Model 320K

Mossberg Model 333

Mossberg Model 340B

Mossberg Model 340K

Mossberg Model 341

Mossberg Model 342K

Mossberg Model 346B

Mossberg Model 346K

Mossberg Model 350K Autoloading — Clip Type

Mossberg Model 351K Automatic Sporter

Mossberg Model 352K Carbine

Mossberg Model 353 Carbine

Mossberg Model 377 Plinkster

MODEL 341 BOLT-ACTION REPEATER. . . . . NiB $147 Ex $116 Gd $90
Caliber: .22 Short. Long, LR. Seven-round clip magazine. 24-inch bbl. Weight: 6.5 lbs. Sights: Open rear, ramp front. Monte Carlo stock w/checkered pistol-grip and forearm, sling swivels. Made from 1972-85.

MODEL 342K HAMMERLESS BOLT-ACTION CARBINE. . . . . NiB $172 Ex $147 Gd $111
Same as Model 340K except w/18-inch bbl., stock w/no cheekpiece, extension forend is hinged, pulls down to form hand grip; sling swivels and web strap on left side of stock. Weight: 5 lbs. Made from 1958-74.

MODEL 346B . . . . NiB $172 Ex $147 Gd $111
Same as Model 346K except w/peep rear sight, hooded ramp front sight. Made from 1958-67.

MODEL 346K HAMMERLESS BOLT-ACTION REPEATER . . . . NiB $156 Ex $136 Gd $98
Caliber: .22 Short. Long, LR. Tubular magazine holds 25 Short, 20 Long, 18 LR. 24-inch bbl. Weight: 6.5 lbs. Sights: Open rear; bead front. Walnut stock w/Monte Carlo comb, cheekpiece, pistol-grip, sling swivels. Made from 1958-71.

MODEL 350K AUTOLOADING RIFLE — CLIP TYPE . . . . NiB $162 Ex $116 Gd $90
Caliber: .22 Short (High Speed), Long, LR. Seven-round clip magazine. 23.5-inch bbl. Weight: 6 lbs. Sights: Open rear; bead front. Monte Carlo stock w/pistol-grip. Made from 1958-71.

MODEL 351C AUTOLOADING CARBINE . NiB $184 Ex $153 Gd $112
Same as Model 351K except w/18.5-inch bbl., Western carbine-style stock w/barrel band and sling swivels. Weight: 5.5 lbs. Made from 1965-71.

MODEL 351K AUTOLOADING SPORTER. . . . . NiB $184 Ex $153 Gd $112
Caliber: .22 LR. Fifteen-round tubular magazine in buttstock. 24-inch bbl. Weight: 6 lbs. Sights: Open rear; bead front. Monte Carlo stock w/pistol-grip. Made from 1960-71.

MODEL 352K AUTOLOADING CARBINE. . . . . NiB $184 Ex $153 Gd $112
Caliber: .22 Short, Long, LR. Seven-round clip magazine. 18-inch bbl. Weight: 5 lbs. Sights: Open rear; bead front. Monte Carlo stock w/pistol grip; extension forend of Tenite is hinged, pulls down to form hand grip; sling swivels, web strap. Made from 1958-71.

MODEL 353 AUTOLOADING CARBINE . . NiB $184 Ex $153 Gd $112
Caliber: .22 LR. Seven round clip magazine. 18-inch bbl. Weight: 5 lbs. Sights: Open rear; ramp front. Monte Carlo stock w/checkered pistol-grip and forearm; black Tenite extension forend pulls down to form hand grip. Made from 1972-85.

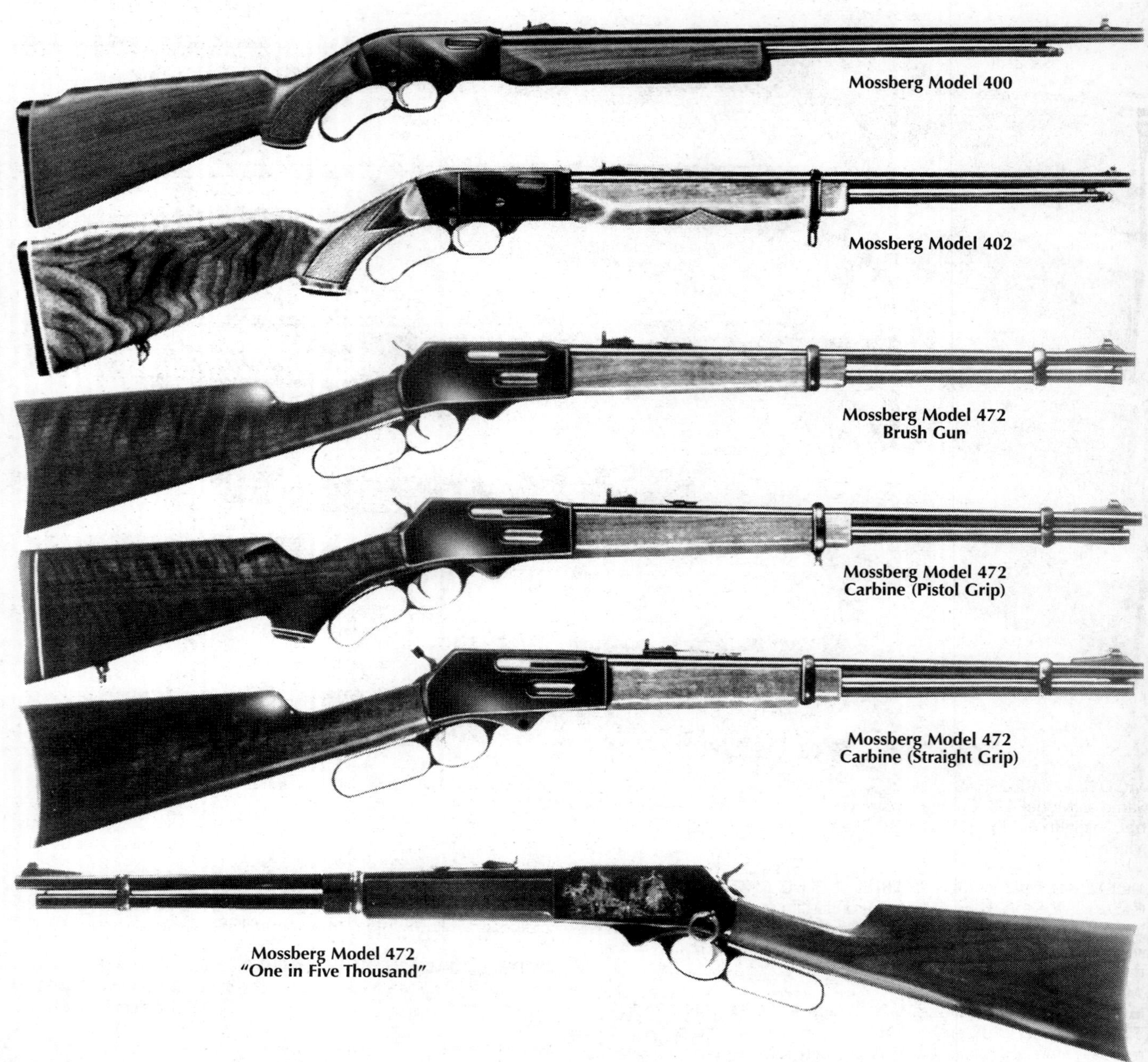

Mossberg Model 400

Mossberg Model 402

Mossberg Model 472 Brush Gun

Mossberg Model 472 Carbine (Pistol Grip)

Mossberg Model 472 Carbine (Straight Grip)

Mossberg Model 472 "One in Five Thousand"

MODEL 377 PLINKSTER AUTOLOADER . . NiB $208 Ex $165 Gd $119
Caliber: .22 LR. Fifteen-round tubular magazine. 20-inch bbl. Weight: 6.25 lbs. 4x scope sight. Thumbhole stock w/rollover cheekpiece, Monte Carlo comb, checkered forearm; molded of modified polystyrene foam in walnut-finish; sling swivel studs. Made from 1977-79.

MODEL 380 SEMIAUTOMATIC RIFLE . . . . NiB $175 Ex $145 Gd $105
Caliber: .22 LR. Fifteen-round buttstock magazine. 20-inch bbl. Weight: 5.5 lbs. Sights: Open rear; bead front. Made from 1980-85.

MODEL 400 PALOMINO LEVER-ACTION. . . . . NiB $280 Ex $219 Gd $126
Hammerless. Caliber: .22 Short, Long, LR. Tubular magazine holds 20 Short, 17 Long, 15 LR. 24-inch bbl. Weight: 5.5 lbs. Sights: Open rear; bead front. Monte Carlo stock w/checkered pistol-grip; beavertail forearm. Made from 1959-64.

MODEL 402 PALOMINO CARBINE . . . . . . NiB $280 Ex $229 Gd $203
Same as Model 400 except w/18.5-inch (1961-64) or 20-inch bbl. (1964-71), forearm w/bbl. band, swivels; magazine holds two fewer rounds. Weight: 4.75 lbs. Made from 1961-71.

MODEL 430 AUTOLOADING RIFLE. . . . . . . NiB $165 Ex $135 Gd $97
Caliber: .22 LR. Eighteen-round tubular magazine. 24-inch bbl. Weight: 6.25 lbs. Sights: Open rear; bead front. Monte Carlo stock w/checkered pistol grip; checkered forearm. Made from 1970-71.

MODEL 432 WESTERN-STYLE AUTO . . . . . . NiB $159 Ex $130 Gd $94
Same as Model 430 except w/plain straight-grip carbine-type stock and forearm, bbl. band, sling swivels. Magazine capacity: 15 cartridges. Weight: 6 lbs. Made from 1970-71.

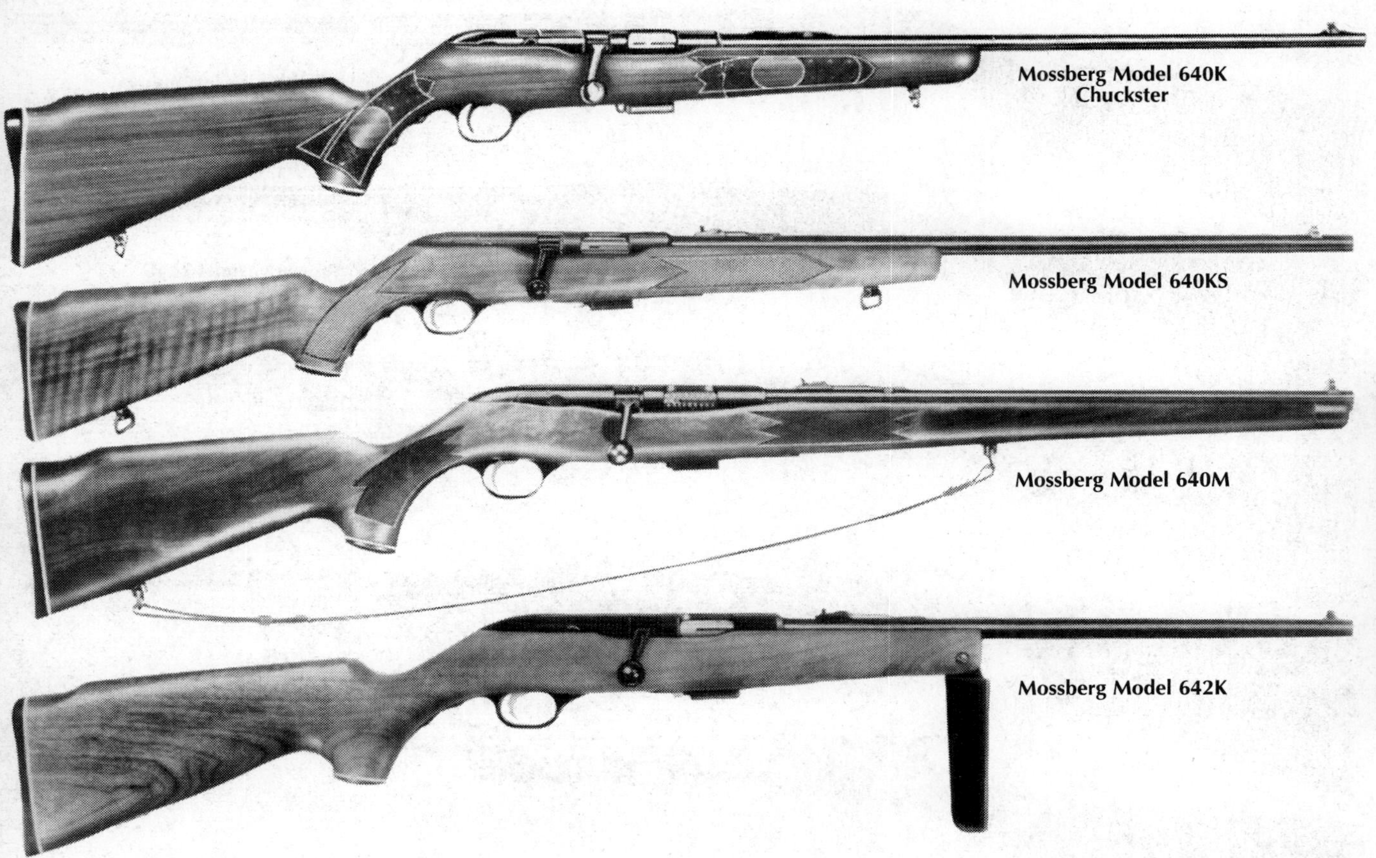

Mossberg Model 640K Chuckster

Mossberg Model 640KS

Mossberg Model 640M

Mossberg Model 642K

MODEL 472 BRUSH GUN .... NiB $227 Ex $201 Gd $124
Same as Model 472 Carbine w/straight-grip stock except w/18-inch bbl., weight: 6.5 lbs. Caliber: .30-30. Magazine capacity: 5 rounds. Made from 1974-76.

MODEL 472 LEVER-ACTION CARBINE ... NiB $206 Ex $175 Gd $124
Calibers: .30-30, .35 Rem. Six round tubular magazine. 20-inch bbl. Weight: 6.75 to 7 lbs. Sights: Open rear; ramp front. Pistol-grip or straight-grip stock, forearm w/bbl. band; sling swivels on pistol-grip model saddle ring on straight-grip model. Made from 1972-79.

MODEL 472 ONE IN FIVE THOUSAND... NiB $475 Ex $346 Gd $181
Same as Model 472 Brush Gun except w/Indian scenes etched on receiver; brass buttplate, saddle ring and bbl. bands, gold-plated trigger, bright blued finish, select walnut stock and forearm. Limited edition of 5,000; serial numbered 1 to 5,000. Made in 1974.

MODEL 472 RIFLE.............. NiB $228 Ex $202 Gd $125
Same as Model 472 Carbine w/pistol-grip stock except w/24-inch bbl., 5-round magazine, weight: 7 lbs. Made from 1974-76.

MODEL 479
Caliber: .30-30. Six-round tubular magazine. 20-inch bbl. Weight: 6.75 to 7 lbs. Sights: Open rear; ramp front. Made from 1983-85.
Model 479 Rifle .... NiB $218 Ex $202 Gd $146
Model 479PCA
(Carbine w/20-inch bbl.).............. NiB $218 Ex $202 Gd $146
Model 479RR
(Roy Rogers, 5000 Ltd. Edition)......... NiB $359 Ex $307 Gd $148

MODEL 620K HAMMERLESS SINGLE-SHOT BOLT-ACTION RIFLE........... NiB $183 Ex $162 Gd $116
Single shot. Caliber: .22 WMR. 24-inch bbl. Weight: 6 lbs. Sights: Open rear; bead front. Monte Carlo stock w/cheekpiece, pistol-grip, sling swivels. Made from 1959-60.

MODEL 620K-A............... NiB $179 Ex $147 Gd $106
Same as Model 640K except w/sight modification. Made from 1960-68.

MODEL 640K CHUCKSTER HAMMERLESS BOLT-ACTION RIFLE........... NiB $183 Ex $162 Gd $116
Caliber: .22 WMR. Five-round detachable clip magazine. 24-inch bbl. Weight: 6 lbs. Sights: Open rear; bead front. Monte Carlo stock w/cheekpiece, pistol grip, sling swivels. Made from 1959-84.

MODEL 640KS .... NiB $224 Ex $172 Gd $121
Deluxe version of Model 640K w/select walnut stock hand checkering; gold-plated front sight, rear sight elevator, and trigger. Made from 1960-64.

MODEL 640M................. NiB $331 Ex $305 Gd $202
Similar to Model 640K except w/heavy receiver and jeweled bolt. 20-inch bbl., full length Mannlicher-style stock w/Monte Carlo comb and cheekpiece, swivels and leather sling. 40.75 inches overall. Weight: 6 lbs. Made from 1971-73.

MODEL 642K CARBINE .... NiB $254 Ex $202 Gd $151
Caliber: .22 WMR. Five-round detachable clip magazine. 18-inch bbl. Weight: 5 lbs. 38.25 inches overall. Sights: Open rear; bead front. Monte Carlo walnut stock w/black Tenite forearm extension that pulls down to form hand grip. Made from 1961-68.

Mossberg Model 800

Mossberg Model 800D

Mossberg Model 800M

Mossberg Model 810

Mossberg Model L

Mossberg Model R

MODEL 800 BOLT-ACTION CENTERFIRE RIFLE . . . . NiB $248 Ex $202 Gd $145
.222 Rem., .22-250, .243 Win., .308 Win. Four-round mag., 3-round in .222. 22-inch bbl. Weight: 7.5 lbs. Sights: Folding leaf rear; ramp front. Monte Carlo stock w/cheekpiece, checkered pistol-grip and forearm, sling swivels. Made from 1967-79.

MODEL 800D SUPER GRADE. . . . . NiB $389 Ex $316 Gd $222
Deluxe version of Model 800 except w/stock w/rollover comb and cheekpiece, rosewood forend tip and pistol-grip cap. Weight: 6.75 lbs. Chambered for all calibers listed for the Model 800 except for .222 Rem. Sling swivels. Made from 1970-73.

MODEL 800M . . . . NiB $305 Ex $279 Gd $176
Same as Model 800 except w/flat bolt handle, 20-inch bbl., Mannlicher-style stock. Weight: 6.5 lbs. Calibers: .22-250, .243 Win., .308 Win. Made from 1969-72.

MODEL 800VT VARMINT/TARGET . . . . . . NiB $254 Ex $202 Gd $152
Similar to Model 800 except w/24-inch heavy bbl., no sights. Weight: 9.5 lbs. Calibers: .222 Rem., .22-250, .243 Win. Made from 1968-79.

MODEL 810 BOLT-ACTION CENTERFIRE RIFLE
Calibers: .270 Win., .30-06, 7mm Rem. Mag., .338 Win. Mag. Detachable box magazine (1970-75) or internal magazine w/hinged floorplate (1972 to date). Capacity: Four-round in .270 and .30-06, 3-round in Magnums. 22-inch bbl. in .270 and .30-06, 24-inch in Magnums. Weight: 7.5 to 8 lbs. Sights: Leaf rear; ramp front. Stock w/Monte Carlo comb and cheekpiece, checkered pistol-grip and forearm, grip cap, sling swivels. Made from 1970-79.
Standard calibers. . . . . NiB $360 Ex $293 Gd $207
Magnum calibers. . . . . NiB $385 Ex $308 Gd $221

MODEL 1500 MOUNTAINEER GRADE I CENTERFIRE RIFLE. . . . . . NiB $411 Ex $334 Gd $257
Calibers: .223, .243, .270, .30-06, 7mm Mag. 22-inch or 24-inch (7mm Mag.) bbl. Weight: 7 lbs. 10 oz. Hardwood walnut-finished checkered stock. Sights: Hooded ramp front w/gold bead; fully adj. rear. Drilled and tapped for scope mounts. Sling swivel studs. Imported from 1986-87.

Musgrave Premier NR5

Musgrave RSA NR1

Musgrave Valiant NR6

Musketeer Mauser Sporter

MODEL 1500 VARMINT BOLT-ACTION RIFLE
Same as Model 1500 Grade I except w/22-inch heavy bbl. Chambered in .222, .22-250, .223 only. High-luster blued finish or Parkerized satin finished stock. Imported from Japan 1986-87.
High-luster blue . . . . NiB $411 Ex $334 Gd $257
Parkerized satin finish . . . . NiB $431 Ex $349 Gd $245

MODEL 1700LS CLASSIC HUNTER BOLT-ACTION RIFLE . . . . NiB $463 Ex $385 Gd $257
Same as Model 1500 Grade I except w/checkered classic-style stock and Schnabel forend. Chambered in 243, 270, 30-06 only. Imported from Japan 1986-87.

MODEL B BOLT-ACTION RIFLE . . . . NiB $196 Ex $170 Gd $88
Takedown. Caliber: .22 LR. Long, Short. Single-shot. 22-inch bbl. Sights: Open rear; bead front. Plain pistol-grip stock. Made from 1930-32.

MODEL K SLIDE-ACTION REPEATER . . . . . . NiB $201 Ex $145 Gd $98
Hammerless. Takedown. Caliber: .22 LR. Long, Short. Tubular magazine holds 20 Short, 16 Long, 14 LR. 22-inch bbl. Weight: 5 lbs. Sights: Open rear; bead front. Plain, straight-grip stock. Grooved slide handle. Made from 1922-31.

MODELS L42A, L43, L45A, L46A-LS
See Models 42A, 43, 45A and 46A-LS respectively; "L" refers to a left-hand version of those rifles.

MODEL L SINGLE-SHOT RIFLE . . . . NiB $469 Ex $380 Gd $267
Martini-type falling-block lever-action. Takedown. Caliber: .22 LR, Long, Short. 24-inch bbl. Weight: 5 lbs. Sights: Open rear; bead front. Plain pistol-grip stock and forearm. Made from 1929-32.

MODEL M SLIDE-ACTION REPEATER . . . . NiB $310 Ex $253 Gd $179
Specifications same as for Model K except w/24-inch octagon bbl., pistol-grip stock, weighs 5.5 lbs. Made from 1928-31.

MODEL R BOLT-ACTION REPEATER . . . . . NiB $298 Ex $242 Gd $171
Takedown. Caliber: .22 LR, Long, Short. Tubular magazine. 24-inch bbl. Sights: Open rear; bead front. Plain pistol-grip stock. Made from 1930-32.

MUSGRAVE RIFLES, MUSGRAVE MFRS. & DIST. (PTY) LTD. — Bloemfontein, South Africa

PREMIER NR5 BOLT-ACTION HUNTING RIFLE . . . . NiB $473 Ex $390 Gd $262
Calibers: .243 Win., .270 Win., .30-06, .308 Win., 7mm Rem. Mag. Five-round magazine. 25.5-inch bbl. Weight: 8.25 lbs. Furnished w/o sights, but drilled and tapped for scope mount. Select walnut Monte Carlo stock w/cheekpiece, checkered pistol-grip and forearm, contrasting pistol-grip cap and forend tip, recoil pad, swivel studs. Made from 1971-76.

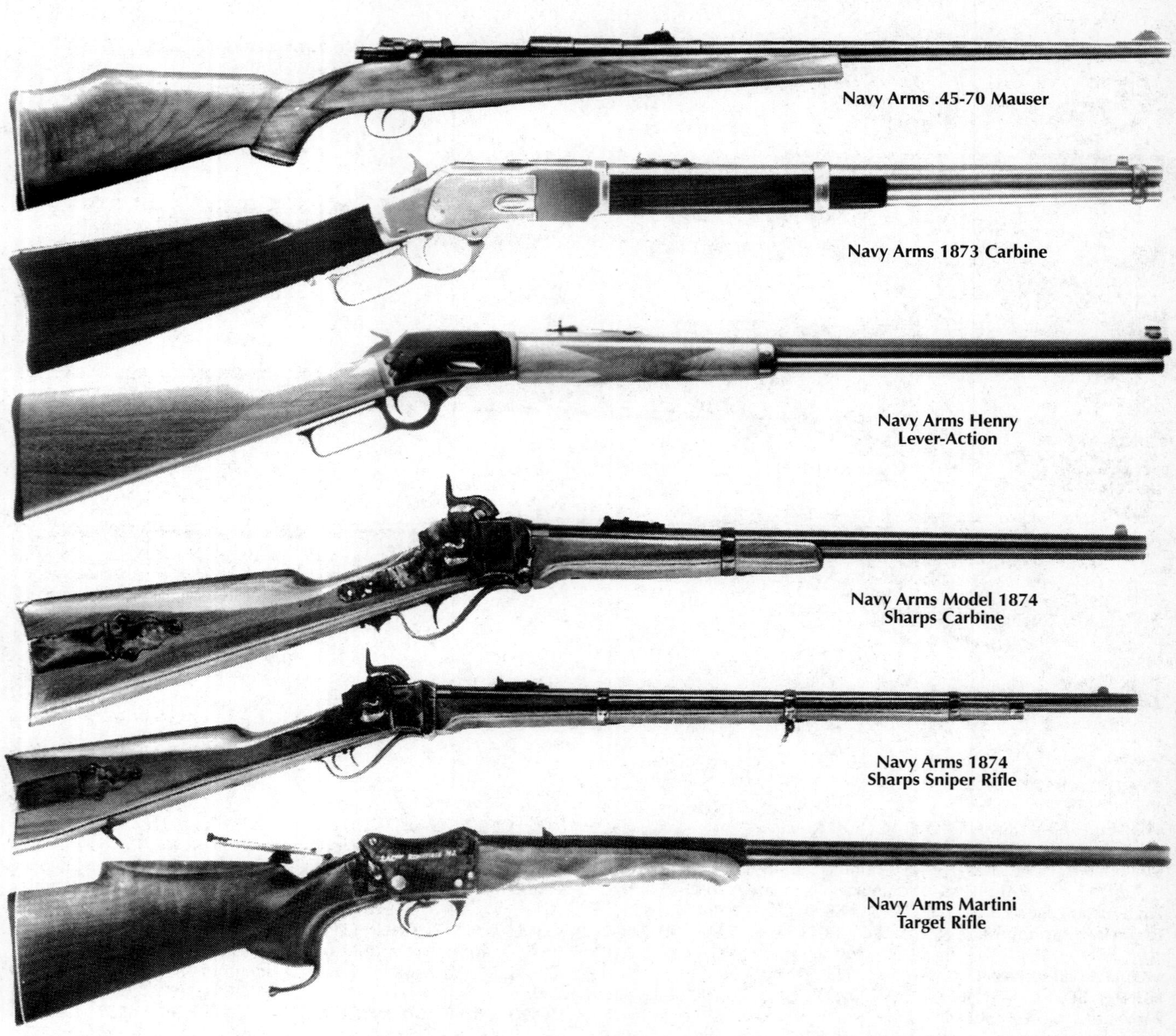

Navy Arms .45-70 Mauser

Navy Arms 1873 Carbine

Navy Arms Henry Lever-Action

Navy Arms Model 1874 Sharps Carbine

Navy Arms 1874 Sharps Sniper Rifle

Navy Arms Martini Target Rifle

RSA NR1 BOLT-ACTION SINGLE-SHOT TARGET RIFLE . . . . . NiB $474 Ex $385 Gd $272
Caliber: .308 Win. (7.62mm NATO). 26.4-inch heavy bbl. Weight: 10 lbs. Sights: Aperture receiver; tunnel front. Walnut target stock w/beavertail forearm, handguard, bbl. band, rubber buttplate, sling swivels. Made from 1971-76.

VALIANT NR6 HUNTING RIFLE . . . NiB $437 Ex $339 Gd $231
Similar to Premier except w/24-inch bbl.; stock w/straight comb, skip French-style checkering, no grip cap or forend tip. Sights: Leaf rear; hooded ramp front bead sight. Weight: 7.7 lbs. Made from 1971-76.

MUSKETEER RIFLES — Washington, D.C. Mfd. by Firearms International Corp.

MAUSER SPORTER
FN Mauser bolt action. .243, .25-06, .270, .264 Mag., .308, .30-06, 7mm Mag., .300 Win. Mag. Magazine holds 5 standard, 3 Magnum cartridges. 24-inch bbl. Weight: 7.25 lbs. No sights. Monte Carlo stock w/checkered pistol-grip and forearm, swivels. Made from 1963-72.
Standard Sporter . . . . NiB $416 Ex $365 Gd $231
Deluxe Sporter . . . . NiB $468 Ex $390 Gd $236
Standard Carbine. . . . . NiB $401 Ex $3339 Gd $231

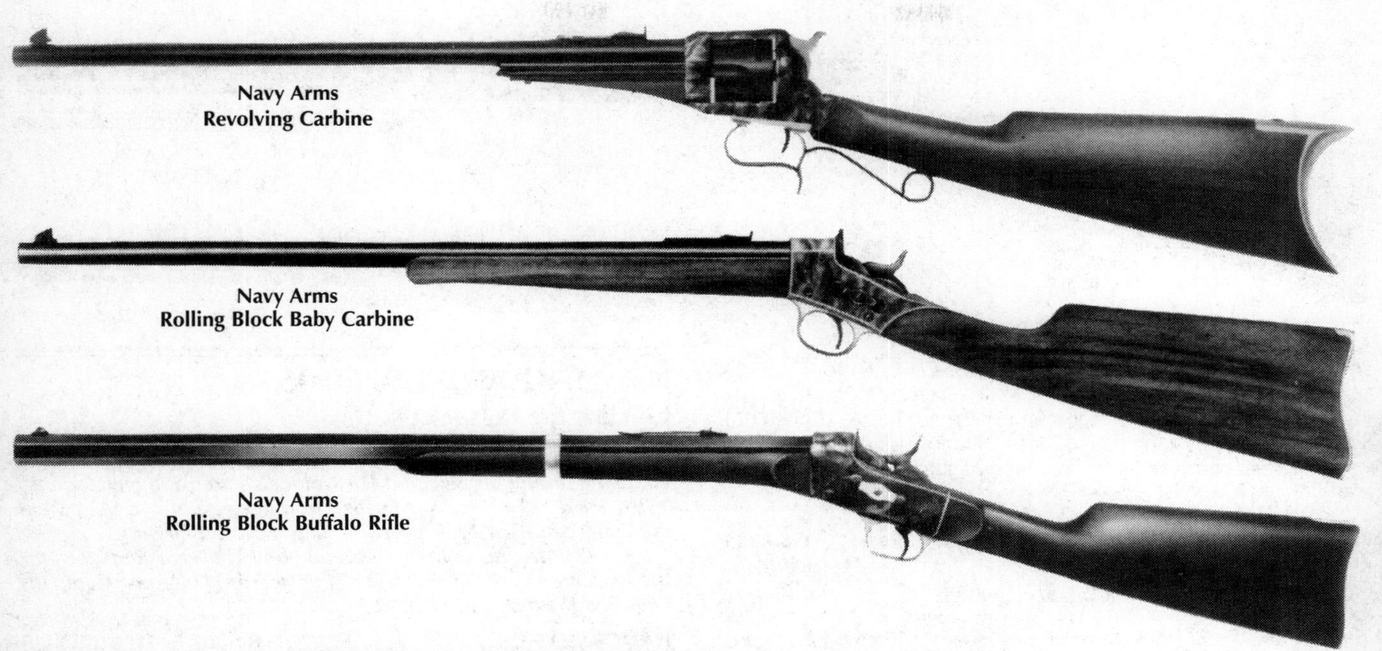

NAVY ARMS — Ridgefield, New Jersey

.45-70 MAUSER CARBINE . . . . NiB $252 Ex $201 Gd $145
Same as .45-70 Mauser Rifle except w/18-inch bbl., straight-grip stock w/low comb, weight: 7.5 lbs. Disc.

.45-70 MAUSER RIFLE . . . . NiB $227 Ex $186 Gd $134
Siamese Mauser bolt action. Caliber: .45-70 Govt. Three-round magazine. 24- or 26-inch bbl. Weight: 8.5 lbs. w/26-inch bbl. Sights: Open rear; ramp front: Checkered stock w/Monte Carlo comb. Intoduced 1973. Disc.

MODEL 1873 WINCHESTER BORDER RIFLE . . . . NiB $822 Ex $695 Gd $333
Replica of Winchester Model 1873 Short Rifle. Calibers: .357 Mag., .44-40, and .45 Colt. 20- inch bbl., 39.25 inches overall. Weight: 7.6 lbs. Blued full octagonal barrel, color casehardened receiver w/walnut stocks. Made from 1999 to date.

MODEL 1873 CARBINE . . . . NiB $797 Ex $695 Gd $363
Similar to Model 1873 Rifle except w/blued receiver, 10-round magazine, 19-inch round bbl. carbine-style forearm w/bbl. band, weighs 6.75 lbs. Disc. Reissued in 1991 in .44-40 or .45 Colt.

MODEL 1873 LEVER-ACTION RIFLE . . . . . NiB $797 Ex $720 Gd $389
Replica of Winchester Model 1873. Casehardened receiver. Calibers: .22 LR. .357 Magnum, .44-40. 15-round magazine. 24-inch octagon bbl. Weight: 8 lbs. Sights: Open rear; blade front. Straight-grip stock, forearm w/end cap. Disc. Reissued in 1991 in .44-40 or .45 Colt w/12-round magazine. Disc. 1994.

MODEL 1873 TRAPPER'S . . . . NiB $622 Ex $514 Gd $377
Same as Model 1873 Carbine, except w/16.5-inch bbl., 8-round magazine, weighs 6.25 lbs. Disc.

MODEL 1873 SPORTING CARBINE/RIFLE
Replica of Winchester Model 1873 Sporting Rifle. Calibers: .357 Mag. (24.25-inch bbl. only), .44-40 and .45 Colt. 24.25-inch bbl. (Carbine) or 30-inch bbl. (Rifle). 48.75 to 53 inches overall. Weight: 8.14 to 9.3 lbs. Octagonal barrel, casehardened receiver and checkered walnut pistol-grip. Made from 1992 to date.
Carbine model. . . . . NiB $905 Ex $776 Gd $419
Rifle model . . . . NiB $955 Ex $878 Gd $470

MODEL 1874 SHARPS CAVALRY CARBINE. . . . . NiB $774 Ex $596 Gd $443
Replica of Sharps 1874 Cavalry Carbine. Similar to Sniper Model, except w/22-inch bbl. and carbine stock. Caliber: .45-70. Imported from 1994 to date.

MODEL 1874 SHARPS SNIPER RIFLE
Replica of Sharps 1874 Sharpshooter's Rifle. Caliber: .45-70. Falling breech, single-shot. 30-inch bbl. 46.75 inches overall. Weight: 8.5 lbs. Double-set triggers. Color casehardened receiver. Blade front sight; rear sight w/elevation leaf. Polished blued bbl. Military three-band stock w/patch box. Imported from 1994 to date.
Infantry model (single trigger) . . . . NiB $1174 Ex $1046 Gd $638
Sniper model (double set trigger) . . . . . NiB $1684 Ex $1480 Gd $740

ENGRAVED MODELS
Yellowboy and Model 1873 rifles are available in deluxe models w/select walnut stocks and forearms and engraving in three grades. Grade "A" has delicate scrollwork in limited areas. Grade "B" is more elaborate with 40 percent coverage. Grade "C" has highest grade engraving. Add to value:
Grade "A" . . . . NiB $257 Ex $212 Gd $155
Grade "B" . . . . NiB $283 Ex $233 Gd $170
Grade "C" . . . . NiB $665 Ex $539 Gd $378

HENRY LEVER-ACTION RIFLE
Replica of the Winchester Model 1860 Henry Rifle. Caliber: .44-40. Twelve round magazine. 16.5-, 22- or 24.25-inch octagon bbl. Weight: 7.5 to 9 lbs. 35.4 to 43.25 inches overall. Sights: Blade front, adjustable ladder rear. European walnut straight grip buttstock w/bbl. and side stock swivels. Imported from 1985 to date. Brass or steel receiver. Blued or color casehardened metal.
Carbine model w/22-inch bbl., introduced 1992) . . . . NiB $828 Ex $650 Gd $420
Military rifle model (w/brass frame) . . . . . . NiB $828 Ex $650 Gd $420
Trapper model (w/brass frame) . . . . NiB $828 Ex $650 Gd $420
Trapper model (w/iron frame). . . . . NiB $879 Ex $777 Gd $441
W/"A" engraving, add $300
W/"B" engraving, add. $500
W/"C" engraving, add. $900

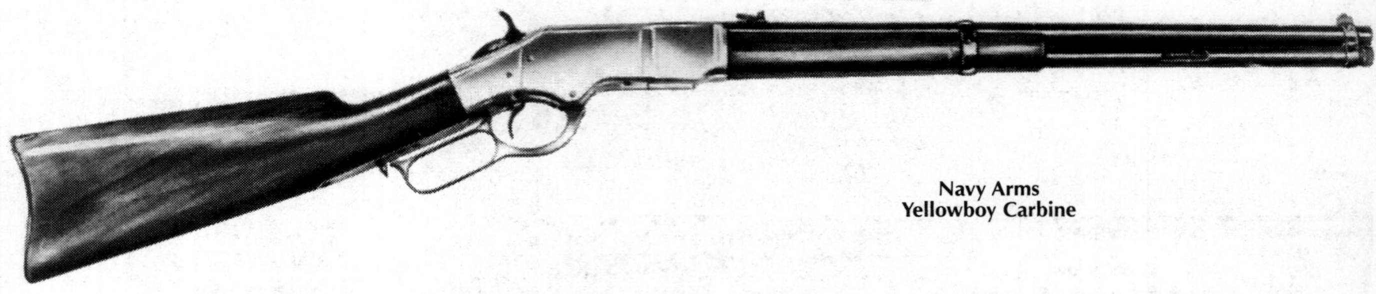

Navy Arms
Yellowboy Carbine

MARTINI TARGET RIFLE . . . . **NiB $512 Ex $436 Gd $293**
Martini single-shot action. Calibers: .444 Marlin, .45-70. 26- or 30-inch half-octagon or full-octagon bbl. Weight: 9 lbs. w/26-inch bbl. Sights: Creedmoor tang peep, open middle, blade front. Stock w/cheekpiece and pistol-grip, forearm w/Schnabel tip, both checkered. Intro. 1972. Disc.

REVOLVING CARBINE . . . . **NiB $574 Ex $512 Gd $359**
Action resembles that of Remington Model 1875 Revolver. Casehardened frame. Calibers: .357 Magnum, .44-40, .45 Colt. Six round cylinder. 20-inch bbl. Weight: 5 lbs. Sights: Open rear; blade front. Straight-grip stock brass trigger guard and buttplate. Intro. 1968. Disc.

ROLLING BLOCK BABY CARBINE . . . . **NiB $244 Ex $199 Gd $142**
Replica of small Remington Rolling Block single-shot action. Casehardened frame, brass trigger guard. Calibers: .22 LR. .22 Hornet, .357 Magnum, .44-40. 20-inch octagon or 22-inch round bbl. Weight: 5 lbs. Sights: Open rear; blade front. Straight-grip stock, plain forearm, brass buttplate. Imported from 1968-81.

ROLLING BLOCK BUFFALO CARBINE. . . . NiB $420 Ex $385 Gd $334
Same as Buffalo Rifle except w/18-inch bbl., weight: 10 lbs

ROLLING BLOCK BUFFALO RIFLE. . . . . . . NiB $630 Ex $528 Gd $273
Replica Remington Rolling Block single-shot action. Casehardened frame, brass trigger guard. Calibers: .444 Marlin, .45-70, .50-70. 26- or 30-inch heavy half-octagon or full-octagon bbl. Weight: 11 to 12 lbs. Sights: Open rear; blade front. Straight-grip stock w/brass buttplate, forearm w/brass bbl. band. Made from 1971 to date.

ROLLING BLOCK CREEDMOOR RIFLE
Same as Buffalo Rifle except calibers .45-70 and .50-70 only, 28- or 30-inch heavy half-octagon or full-octagon bbl., Creedmoor tang peep sight.
Target model . . . . **NiB $833 Ex $608 Gd $338**
Deluxe target model (disc. 1998) . . . . . **NiB $1548 Ex $1268 Gd $1038**

YELLOWBOY CARBINE. . . . . **NiB $570 Ex $461 Gd $323**
Similar to Yellowboy Rifle except w/19-inch bbl., 10-round magazine (14-round in 22 Long Rifle), carbine-style forearm. Weight: 6.75 lbs. Disc. Reissued 1991 in .44-40 only.

YELLOWBOY LEVER-ACTION REPEATER . . . . . **NiB $665 Ex $538 Gd $334**
Replica of Winchester Model 1866. Calibers: .38 Special, .44-40. 15-round magazine. 24-inch octagon bbl. Weight: 8 lbs. Sights: Folding leaf rear; blade front. Straight-grip stock, forearm w/end cap. Intro. 1966. Disc. Reissued 1991 in .44-40 only w/12-round magazine and adj. ladder-style rear sight.

YELLOWBOY TRAPPER'S MODEL. . . . . **NiB $595 Ex $482 Gd $337**
Same as Yellowboy Carbine except w/16.5-inch bbl., 8-round magazine, weighs 6.25 lbs. Disc.

NEW ENGLAND FIREARMS — Gardner, Massachusetts

In 1987, New England Firearms was established as an independent company producing selected H&R models under the NEF logo. In 1991, H&R 1871, Inc. was formed from the residual of the parent company and that took over the New England Firearms facility. H&R 1871 produced firearms under both its logo and the NEF brand name until 1999, when the Marlin Firearms Company acquired the assets of H&R 1871.

HANDI-RIFLE. **NiB $226 Ex $165 Gd $119**
Single-shot, break-open action w/side-lever release. Calibers: .22 Hornet, .22-250, .223, .243, .270, .30-30, .30-06, .45-70. 22-inch bbl. Weight: 7 lbs. Sights: Ramp front; folding rear. Drilled and tapped for scope mounts. Walnut-finished hardwood or synthetic stock. Blued finish. Made from 1989 to date.

NEWTON SPORTING RIFLES — Buffalo, New York

Mfd. by Newton Arms Co., Charles Newton Rifles Corp. and Buffalo Newton Rifle Co.

BUFFALO
SPORTING RIFLE. . . . . **NiB $1336 Ex $1130 Gd $821**
Same general specifications as Standard Model — Second Type. Made c. 1922-32 by Buffalo Newton Rifle Co.

MAUSER
SPORTING RIFLE. . . . . **NiB $1285 Ex $1172 Gd $770**
Mauser (Oberndorf) action. Caliber: .256 Newton. Five round box magazine, hinged floorplate. Double-set triggers. 24-inch bbl. Open rear sight, ramp front sight. Sporting stock w/checkered pistol-grip. Weight: 7 lbs. Made c. 1914 by Newton Arms Co.

STANDARD MODEL
SPORTING RIFLE — FIRST TYPE . . . . . . **NiB $1233 Ex $1053 Gd $657**
Newton bolt action, interrupted screw-type breech-locking mechanism, double-set triggers. Calibers: .22, .256, .280, .30, .33, .35 Newton; ,30-06. 24-inch bbl. Sights: Open rear or cocking-piece peep; ramp front. Checkered pistol-grip stock. Weight: 7 to 8 lbs., depending on caliber. Made c. 1916-18 by Newton Arms Co.

STANDARD MODEL
SPORTING RIFLE
SECOND TYPE. . . . . **NiB $987 Ex $797 Gd $555**
Newton bolt action, improved design; distinguished by reversed-set trigger and 1917-Enfield-type bolt handle. Calibers: .256, .30, .35 Newton and .30-06. Five round box magazine. 24-inch bbl. Sights: Open rear; ramp front. Checkered pistol-grip stock. Weight: 7.75 to 8.25 lbs. Made c. 1921 by Charles Newton Rifle Corp.

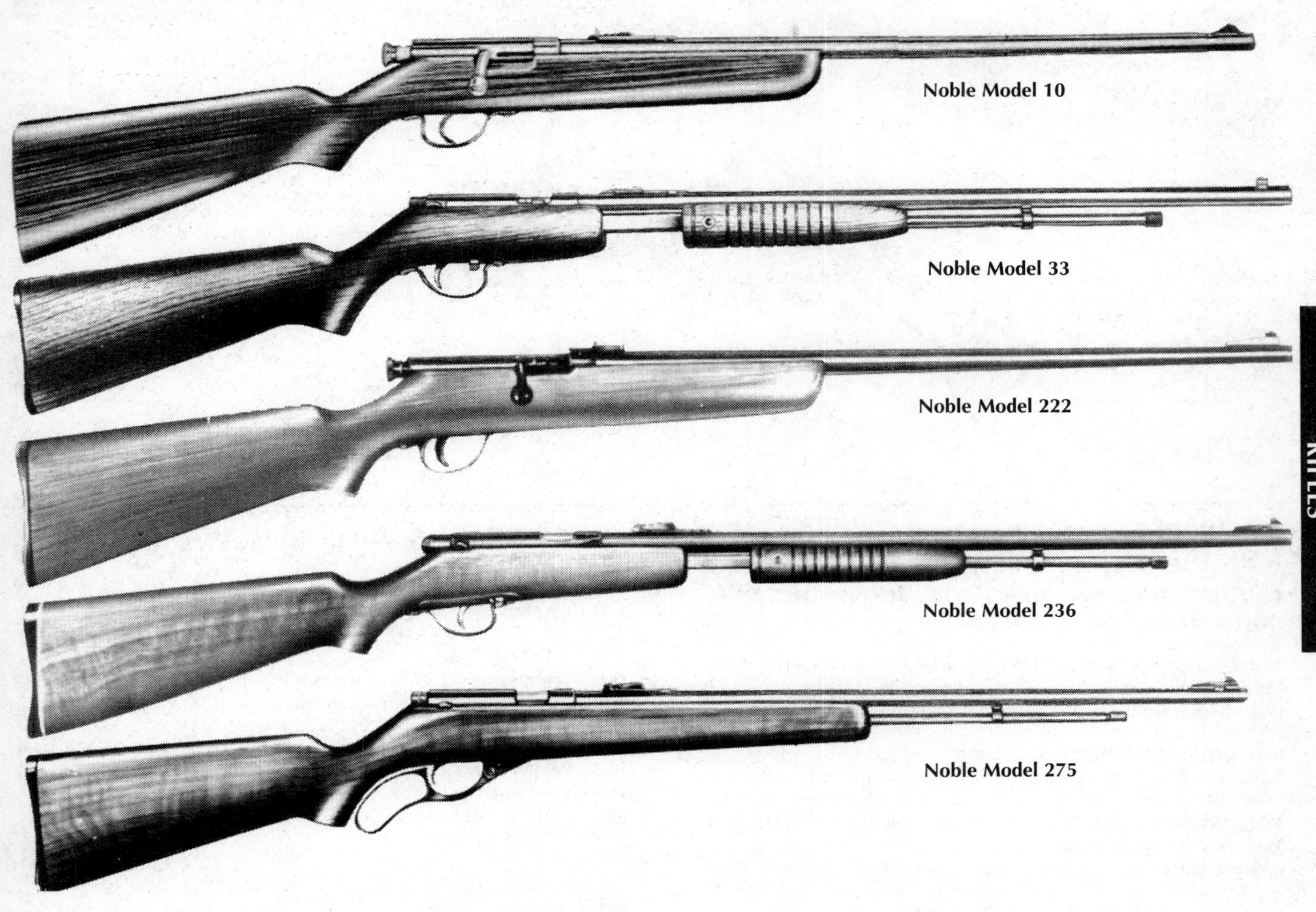

Noble Model 10

Noble Model 33

Noble Model 222

Noble Model 236

Noble Model 275

NIKKO FIREARMS, LTD. — Tochiga, Japan

See listings under Golden Eagle Rifles.

NOBLE MFG. CO. — Haydenville, Massachusetts

MODEL 10 BOLT-ACTION SINGLE-SHOT RIFLE . . . . NiB $89 Ex $82 Gd $61
Caliber: .22 LR. Long, Short. 24-inch bbl. Plain pistol-grip stock. Sights: Open rear, bead front. Weight: 4 lbs. Made from 1955-58.

MODEL 20 BOLT-ACTION SINGLE-SHOT RIFLE . . . . NiB $92 Ex $77 Gd $58
Manually cocked. Caliber: .22 LR. Long, Short. 22-inch bbl. Weight: 5 lbs. Sights: Open rear; bead front. Walnut stock w/pistol grip. Made from 1958-63.

MODEL 33 SLIDE-ACTION REPEATER . . . . . . NiB $112 Ex $92 Gd $68
Hammerless. Caliber: .22 LR. Long, Short. Tubular magazine holds 21 Short, 17 Long, 15 LR. 24-inch bbl. Weight: 6 lbs. Sights: Open rear; bead front. Tenite stock and slide handle. Made from 1949-53.

MODEL 33A . . . . NiB $99 Ex $82 Gd $61
Same general specifications as Model 33 except w/wood stock and slide handle. Made from 1953-55.

MODEL 222 BOLT-ACTION SINGLE-SHOT RIFLE . . . . NiB $112 Ex $92 Gd $68
Manually cocked. Caliber: .22 LR. Long, Short. Barrel integral w/receiver. Overall length: 38 inches. Weight: 5 lbs. Sights: Interchangeable V-notch and peep rear; ramp front. Scope mounting base. Pistol-grip stock. Made from 1958-71.

MODEL 236 SLIDE-ACTION REPEATING RIFLE . . . . NiB $124 Ex $105 Gd $88
Hammerless. Caliber: .22 Short, Long, LR. Tubular magazine holds 21 Short, 17 Long, 15 LR. 24-inch bbl. Weight: 5.5 lbs. Sights: Open rear; ramp front. Pistol-grip stock, grooved slide handle. Made from 1951 to date.

MODEL 275 LEVER-ACTION RIFLE . . . . NiB $169 Ex $113 Gd $87
Hammerless. Caliber: .22 Short, Long, LR. Tubular magazine holds 21 Short, 17 Long, 15 LR. 24-inch bbl. Weight: 5.5 lbs. Sights: Open rear; ramp front. Stock w/semipistol-grip. Made from 1958-71.

Parker-Hale Model 81 Classic

Parker-Hale Model 87

NORINCO — Mfd. by Northern China Industries Corp., Beijing, China, *Imported by Century International Arms; Interarms; KBI and China Sports, Inc.*

MODEL 81S/AK SEMIAUTOMATIC RIFLE

Semiautomatic Kalashnikov style AK-47 action. Caliber: 7.62x39mm. Five, 30- or 40-round magazine. 17.5-inch bbl. 36.75 inches overall. Weight: 8.5 lbs. Hooded post front sight, 500 meters leaf rear sight. Oil-finished hardwood (military style) buttstock, pistol grip, forearn and handguard or folding metal stock. Black oxide finish. Imported from 1988-89.

Model 81S (w/wood stock)........... NiB $1057 Ex $800 Gd $568
Model 81S-1 (w/under-folding metal stock) .. NiB $1206 Ex $975 Gd $680
Model 81S-5/56S-2 (w/side-folding metal stock) .... NiB $1077 Ex $872 Gd $610

MODEL 84S/AK SEMIAUTOMATIC RIFLE

Semiautomatic Kalashnikov style AK-47 action. Caliber: .223 (5.56mm). 30-round magazine. 16.25-inch bbl. 35.5 inches overall. Weight: 8.75 lbs. Hooded post front sight, 800 meters leaf rear sight. Oil-finished hardwood (military style) buttstock, pistol grip, forearn and handguard; sporterized composite fiberglass stock or folding metal stock. Black oxide finish. Imported from 1988-89.

Model 84S (w/wood stock)............. NiB $595 Ex $483 Gd $350
Model 84S-1 (w/under-folding metal stock) ... NiB $747 Ex $604 Gd $423
Model 84S-3 (w/fiberglass stock) .... NiB $714 Ex $579 Gd $406
Model 84S-5 (w/side-folding metal stock).... NiB $1201 Ex $969 Gd $675

MODEL AK-47 THUMBHOLE SPORTER

Semiautomatic AK-47 sporterized variant. Calibers: .223 (5.56mm) or 7.62x39mm. Five round magazine. 16.25-inch bbl. or 23.25-inch bbl. 35.5 or 42.5 inches overall. Weight: 8.5 to 10.3 lbs. Adj. post front sight, open adj. rear. Forged receiver w/black oxide finish. Walnut-finished thumbhole stock w/recoil pad. Imported from 1991-93.

Model AK-47 Sporter (5.56mm) .... NiB $537 Ex $435 Gd $305
Model AK-47 Sporter (7.62x39mm) ...... NiB $511 Ex $414 Gd $291

MODEL MAK 90/01 SPORT ...... NiB $517 Ex $440 Gd $311

Similar to Model AK-47 Thumbhole Sporter except w/minor modifications implemented to meet importation requirements. Imported from 1994-95.

OLYMPIC ARMS — Olympia, Washington

PCR SERIES

Gas-operated semi-auto action. Calibers: .17 Rem., .223, 7.62x39, 6x45, 6PPC or 9mm, .40 S&W, 4.5ACP (in carbine version only). Ten-round magazine. 16-, 20- or 24-inch bbl. Weight: 7 to 10.2 lbs. Black composite stocks. Post front, rear adj. sights; scope ready flattop. Barrel fluting. William set trigger. Made from 1994 to date.

PCR-1/Ultra Match.................. NiB $1038 Ex $924 Gd $564
PCR-2/MultiMatch ML-1.............. NiB $1073 Ex $868 Gd $606
PCR-3/MultiMatch ML-2.............. NiB $1130 Ex $924 Gd $615
PCR-4/AR-15 Match .... NiB $1284 Ex $1037 Gd $721
PCR-5/CAR-15 (.223 Rem.)............ NiB $1038 Ex $770 Gd $487
PCR-5/CAR-15 (9mm, 40S&W, 45ACP) .... NiB $862 Ex $764 Gd $501
PCR-5/CAR-15 (.223 Rem.)............. NiB $804 Ex $651 Gd $455
PCR-6/A-2 (7.62x39mm)............... NiB $842 Ex $682 Gd $476

PARKER-HALE LIMITED — Birmingham, England

MODEL 81 AFRICAN .... NiB $939 Ex $759 Gd $501

Same general specifications as Model 81 Classic except in caliber .375 H&H only. Sights: African Express rear; hooded blade front. Barrel-band swivel. All-steel trigger guard. Checkered European walnut stock w/pistol grip and recoil pad. Engraved receiver. Imported from 1986-91.

MODEL 81 CLASSIC BOLT-ACTION RIFLE............ NiB $780 Ex $604 Gd $398

Calibers: .22-250, .243 Win., .270 Win., 6mm Rem., 6.5x55, 7x57, 7x64, .308 Win., .30-06, .300 Win. Mag., 7mm Rem. Mag. Four round magazine. 24-inch bbl. Weight: 7.75 lbs. Sights: Adj. open rear, hooded ramp front. Checkered pistol-grip stock of European walnut. Imported from 1984-91.

MODEL 85 SNIPER RIFLE ...... NiB $1847 Ex $1513 Gd $920

Caliber: .308 Win. Ten or 20-round M-14-type magazine. 24.25-inch bbl. 45 inches overall. Weight: 12.5 lbs. Blade front sight, folding aperture rear. McMillan fiberglass stock w/detachable bipod. Imported from 1989-91.

Parker-Hale Model 1100 Lightweight

Parker-Hale Model 1200 Super Clip

MODEL 87 BOLT-ACTION REPEATING TARGET RIFLE . . . . . NiB $1469 Ex $1186 Gd $722
Calibers: .243 Win., 6.5x55, .308 Win., .30-06 Springfield, .300 Win. Mag. Five-round detachable box magazine. 26-inch bbl. 45 inches overall. Weight: 10 lbs. No sights; grooved for target-style scope mounts. Stippled walnut stock w/adj. buttplate. Sling swivel studs. Parkerized finish. Folding bipod. Imported from 1988-91.

MODEL 1000 STANDARD RIFLE . . . . NiB $440 Ex $363 Gd $229
Calibers: .22-250, .243 Win., .270 Win., 6mm Rem., .308 Win., .30-06. Four-round magazine. Bolt action. 22-inch or 24-inch (22-250) bbl. 43 inches overall. 7.25 lbs. Checkered walnut Monte Carlo-style stock w/satin finish. Imported from 1984-88.

MODEL 1100 LIGHTWEIGHT BOLT-ACTION RIFLE . . . . NiB $517 Ex $440 Gd $306
Same general specifications as Model 1000 Standard except w/22-inch lightweight profile bbl., hollow bolt handle, alloy trigger guard and floorplate, 6.5 lbs., Schnabel forend. Imported from 1984-91.

MODEL 1100M AFRICAN MAGNUM RIFLE . . . . NiB $854 Ex $709 Gd $478
Same as Model 1000 Standard except w/24-inch bbl. in calibers .404 Jeffery, .458 Win. Mag. Weight: 9.5 lbs. Sights: Adj. rear; hooded post front. Imported from 1984-91.

MODEL 1200 SUPER CLIP BOLT-ACTION RIFLE . . . . NiB $584 Ex $491 Gd $311
Same as Model 1200 Super except w/detachable box magazine in calibers .243 Win., 6mm Rem., .270 Win. .30-06 and .308 Win., .300 Win. Mag., 7mm Rem. Mag. Imported from 1984-91.

MODEL 1200 SUPER BOLT-ACTION SPORTING RIFLE . . . . NiB $574 Ex $481 Gd $301
Mauser-type bolt action. Calibers: .22-250, .243 Win., 6mm Rem., .25-06, .270 Win., .30-06, .308 Win. Four round magazine. 24-inch bbl. Weight: 7.25 lbs. Sights: Folding open rear, hooded ramp front. European walnut stock w/rollover Monte Carlo cheekpiece, rosewood forend tip and pistol-grip cap, skip checkering, recoil pad, sling swivels. Imported from 1968-91.

MODEL 1200 SUPER MAGNUM . . . . NiB $626 Ex $507 Gd $327
Same general specifications as 1200 Super except calibers 7mm Rem. Mag. and .300 Win. Mag., 3-round magazine. Imported from 1988-91.

MODEL 1200P PRESENTATION . . . . NiB $537 Ex $435 Gd $305
Same general specifications as 1200 Super except w/scroll-engraved action, trigger guard and floorplate, no sights. QD swivels. Calibers: .243 Win. and .30-06. Imported from 1969-75.

MODEL 1200V VARMINT . . . . NiB $569 Ex $466 Gd $409
Same general specifications as 1200 Super, except w/24-inch heavy bbl., no sights, weight: 9.5 lbs. Calibers: .22-250, 6mm Rem., .25-06, .243 Win. Imported from 1969-89.

MODEL 1300C SCOUT . . . . NiB $755 Ex $652 Gd $523
Calibers: .243, .308 Win. 10-round magazine. 20-inch bbl. w/muzzle brake. 41 inches overall. Weight: 8.5 lbs. No sights, drilled and tapped for scope. Checkered laminated birch stock w/QD swivels. Imported in 1991.

MODEL 2100 MIDLAND BOLT-ACTION RIFLE . . . . NiB $360 Ex $303 Gd $205
Calibers: .22-250, .243 Win., 6mm Rem., .270 Win., 6.5x55, 7x57, 7x64, .308 Win, .30-06. Four-round box magazine. 22-inch or 24-inch (22-250) bbl. 43-inches overall. Weight: 7 lbs. Sights: Adj. folding rear; hooded ramp front. Checkered European walnut Monte Carlo stock w/pistol-grip. Imported from 1984-91.

MODEL 2700 LIGHTWEIGHT . . . . NiB $385 Ex $308 Gd $205
Same general specifications as Model 2100 Midland except w/tapered lightweight bbl. and aluminum trigger guard. Weight: 6.5 lbs. Imported in 1991.

MODEL 2800 MIDLAND . . . . NiB $334 Ex $282 Gd $229
Same general specifications as model 2100 except w/laminated birch stock. Imported in 1991.

PEDERSEN CUSTOM GUNS — North Haven, Connecticut, Division of O.F. Mossberg & Sons, Inc.

MODEL 3000 GRADE I BOLT-ACTION RIFLE . . . . NiB $1070 Ex $865 Gd $603
Richly engraved w/silver inlays, full-fancy American black walnut stock. Mossberg Model 810 action. Calibers: .270 Win., .30-06, 7mm Rem. Mag., .338 Win. Mag. Three-round magazine, hinged floorplate. 22-inch bbl. in .270 and .30-06, 24-inch in Magnums. Weight: 7 to 8 lbs. Sights: Open rear; hooded ramp front. Monte Carlo stock w/roll-over cheekpiece, wraparound hand checkering on pistol grip and forearm, rosewood pistol-grip cap and forend tip, recoil pad or steel buttplate w/trap, detachable swivels. Imported from 1973-75.

MODEL 3000 GRADE II . . . . NiB $796 Ex $643 Gd $447
Same as Model 3000 Grade I except less elaborate engraving, no inlays, fancy grade walnut stock w/recoil pad. Imported from 1973-75.

MODEL 3000 GRADE III. . . . . NiB $667 Ex $540 Gd $377
Same as Model 3000 Grade I except no engraving or inlays, select grade walnut stock w/recoil pad. Imported from 1973-74.

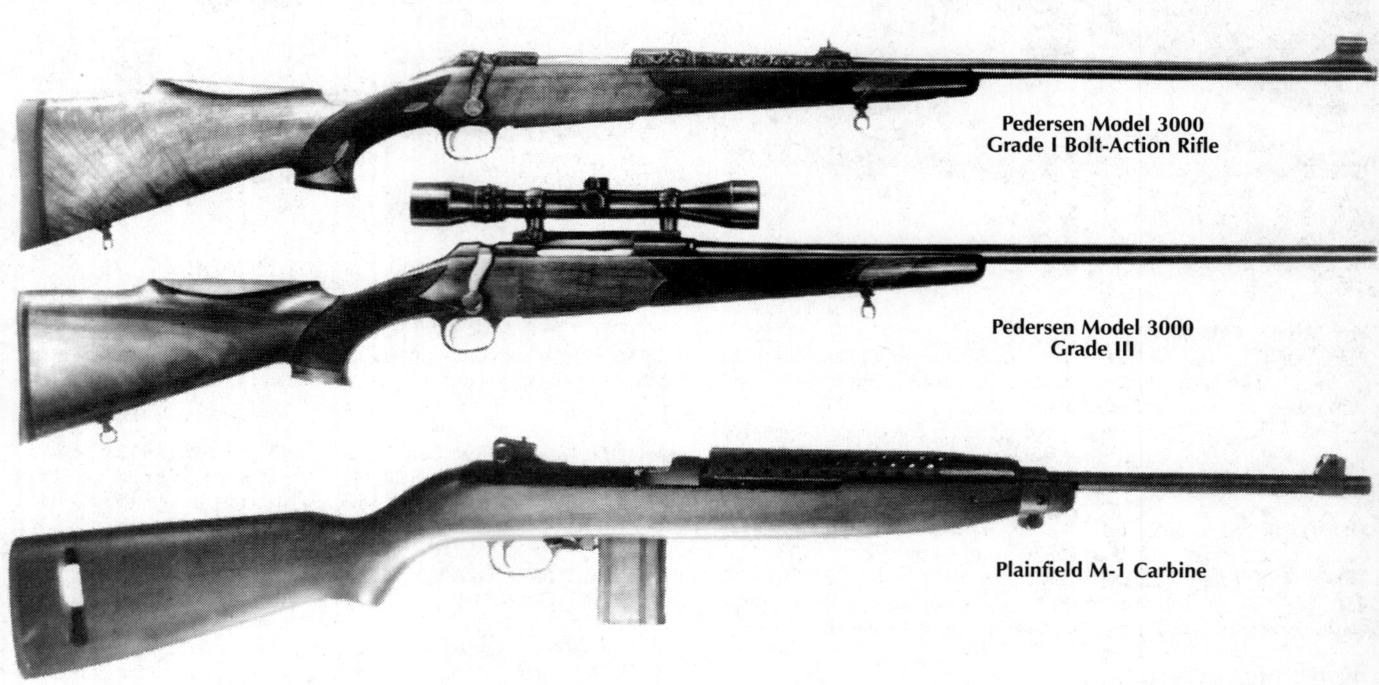

Pedersen Model 3000
Grade I Bolt-Action Rifle

Pedersen Model 3000
Grade III

Plainfield M-1 Carbine

MODEL 4700 CUSTOM
DELUXE LEVER-ACTION RIFLE. . . . . NiB $275 Ex $225 Gd $161
Mossberg Model .472 action. Calibers: .30-30, 35 Rem. Five-round tubular magazine. 24-inch bbl. Weight: 7.5 lbs. Sights: Open rear, hooded ramp front. Hand-finished black walnut stock and beavertail forearm, barrel band swivels. Imported in 1975.

J.C. PENNEY CO., INC. — Dallas, Texas

Firearms sold under the J.C. Penney label were mfd. by Marlin, High Standard, Stevens, Savage and Springfield.

MODEL 2025 BOLT-ACTION REPEATER. . . . . . NiB $87 Ex $57 Gd $52
Takedown. Caliber: .22 RF. Eight round detachable box magazine. 24-inch bbl. Weight: 6 lbs. Sights: Open rear; bead front. Plain pistol-grip stock. Manufactured by Marlin.

MODEL 2035 BOLT-ACTION REPEATER. . . . . . NiB $87 Ex $57 Gd $52
Takedown. Caliber: .22 RF. Eight round detachable box magazine. 24-inch bbl. Weight: 6 lbs. Sights: Open rear; bead front. Plain pistol-grip stock. Manufactured by Marlin.

MODEL 2935 LEVER-ACTION RIFLE . . . . . NiB $196 Ex $161 Gd $110
Same general specifications as Marlin Model 336.

MODEL 6400 BOLT-ACTION
CENTERFIRE RIFLE . . . . NiB $181 Ex $145 Gd $100
Same general specifications as Savage Model 340.

MODEL 6660
AUTOLOADING RIFLE. . . . . NiB $92 Ex $77 Gd $67
Caliber: .22 RF. Tubular magazine. 22-inch bbl. Weight: 5.5 lbs. Sights: Open rear; hooded ramp front. Plain pistol-grip stock. Manufactured by Marlin.

PLAINFIELD MACHINE COMPANY — Dunellen, New Jersey

M-1 CARBINE . . . . NiB $197 Ex $152 Gd $116
Same as U.S. Carbine, Cal. .30, M-1 except also available in caliber 5.7mm (.22 caliber w/necked-down .30 Carbine cartridge case). Current production w/ventilated metal handguard and barrel band w/o bayonet lug; earlier models have standard military-type fittings. Made from 1960-77.

M-1 CARBINE,
COMMANDO MODEL. . . . . NiB $203 Ex $172 Gd $126
Same as M-1 Carbine except w/paratrooper-type stock w/telescoping wire shoulderpiece. Made from 1960-77.

M-1 CARBINE, MILITARY SPORTER. . . . . . NiB $197 Ex $167 Gd $131
Same as M-1 Carbine except w/unslotted buttstock and wood handguard. Made from 1960-77.

M-1 DELUXE SPORTER. . . . . NiB $203 Ex $172 Gd $126
Same as M-1 Carbine except w/Monte Carlo sporting stock Made from 1960-73.

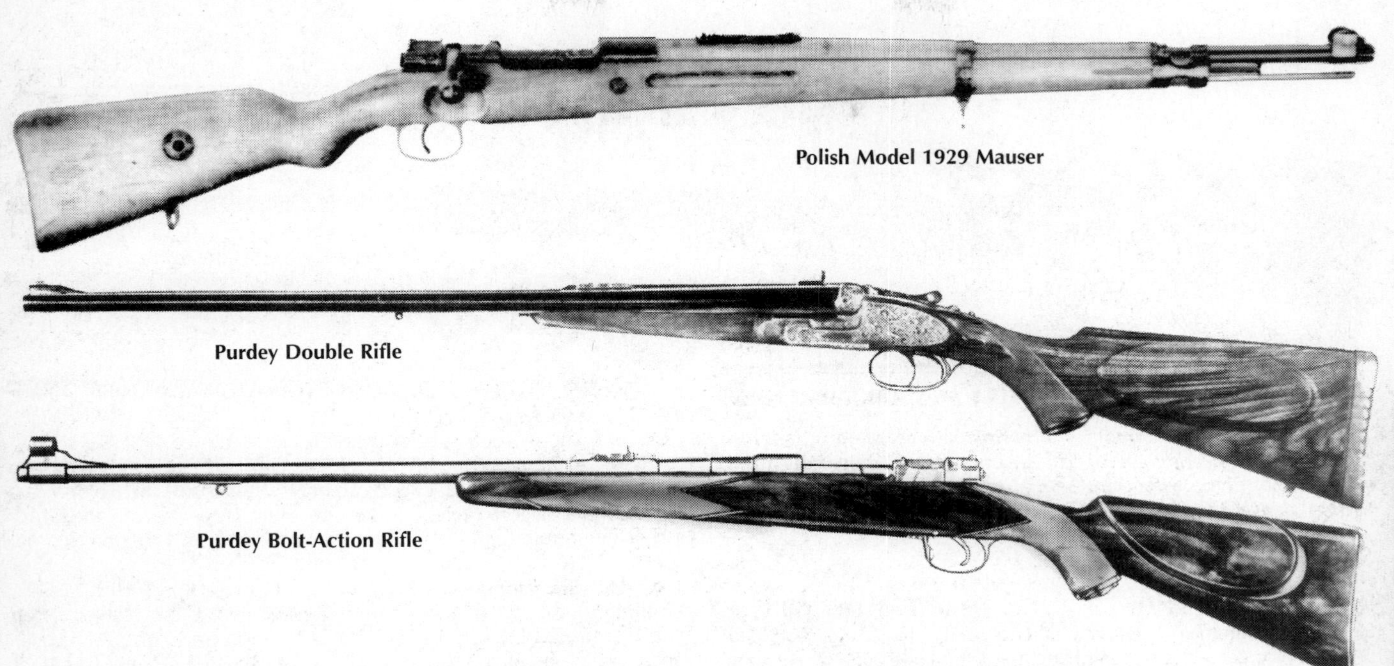
Polish Model 1929 Mauser

Purdey Double Rifle

Purdey Bolt-Action Rifle

POLISH MILITARY RIFLES — Manufactured by Government Arsenals at Radom and Warsaw, Poland

MODEL 1898 (KARABIN 98, K98)
MAUSER MILITARY CARBINE. . . . . Nib $299 Ex $192 Gd $151
Same as German Kar. 98A except for minor details. First manufactured during early 1920s.

MODEL 1898 (KARABIN 98, WZ98A)
MAUSER MILITARY RIFLE. . . . . NiB $261 Ex $172 Gd $136
Same as German Kar. 98 used in WWI except for minor details. Manufacture began c. 1921.

MODEL 1929 (KARABIN 29, WZ29)
MAUSER MILITARY RIFLE. . . . . NiB $299 Ex $202 Gd $151
Same as Czech Model 24, mfd. 1929 thru WWII except for minor details. A similar model produced during German occupation was designated Gew. 29/40.

WILLIAM POWELL & SON LTD. — Birmingham, England

DOUBLE-BARREL RIFLE. . . . . NiB $31,250 Ex $25,000 Gd $17,000
Boxlock. Made to order in any caliber during the time that rifle was manufactured. Bbls.: Made to order in any legal length, but 26 inches recommended. Highest grade French walnut buttstock and forearm w/fine checkering. Metal is elaborately engraved. Imported by Stoeger from 1938-51.

BOLT-ACTION RIFLE. . . . . NiB $2790 Ex $2265 Gd $1593
Mauser-type bolt action. Calibers: 6x54 through .375 H&H Magnum. Three and 4-shot magazine, depending upon chambering. 24-inch bbl. Weight: 7.5 to 8.75 lbs. Sights: Folding leaf rear; hooded ramp front. Cheekpiece stock, checkered forearm and pistol grip, swivels. Imported by Stoeger from 1938-51.

JAMES PURDEY & SONS LTD. — London, England

DOUBLE RIFLE
Sidelock action, hammerless, ejectors. Almost any caliber is available but the following are the most popular: .375 Flanged Magnum Nitro Express, .500/465 Nitro Express .470 Nitro Express, .577 Nitro Express. 25.5-inch bbls. (25-inch in .375). Weight: 9.5 to 12.75 lbs. Sights: Folding leaf rear; ramp front. Cheekpiece stock, checkered forearm and pistol-grip, recoil pad, swivels. Currently manufactured to individual measurements and specifications; same general specifications apply to pre-WWII model.
H&H calibers. . . . . NiB $69,375 Ex $55,500 Gd $37,740
NE calibers. . . . . NiB $85,000 Ex $55,500 Gd $37,774

BOLT-ACTION RIFLE . . . . NiB $22,000 Ex $19,000 Gd $12,000
Mauser-type bolt action. Calibers: 7x57, .300 H&H Magnum, .375 H&H Magnum, 10.75x73. Three round magazine. 24-inch bbl. Weight: 7.5 to 8.75 lbs. Sights: Folding leaf rear; hooded ramp front. Cheekpiece stock, checkered forearm and pistol-grip, swivels. Currently manufactured; same general specifications apply to pre-WWII model.

RAPTOR ARMS COMPANY, INC. — Newport, New Hampshire

BOLT-ACTION RIFLE
Calibers: .243 Win., .270 Win., .30-06 or .308 Win. Four round magazine. 22-inch sporter or heavy bbl. Weight: 7.3 to 8 lbs. 42.5 inches overall. No sights w/drilled and tapped receiver or optional blade front, adjustable rear. Blue, stainless or "Taloncote" rust-resistant finish. Checkered black synthetic stock w/Monte Carlo cheepiece and vented recoil pad. Imported from 1997-99.
Raptor Sporter model . . . . NiB $275 Ex $225 Gd $161
Raptor Deluxe Peregrine model (Disc. 1998). . . . NiB $327 Ex $449 Gd $189
Raptor heavy barrel model . . . . NiB $313 Ex $256 Gd $182
Raptor stainless barrel model . . . . NiB $339 Ex $261 Gd $196
W/optional oights, add $30

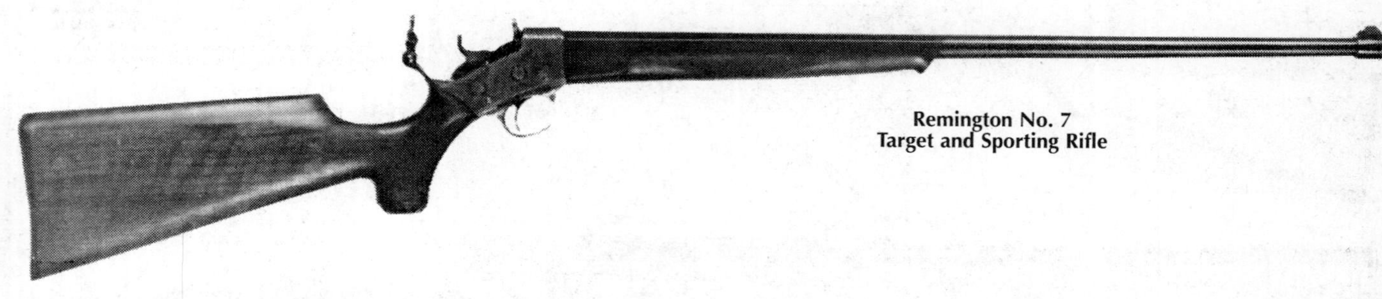

Remington No. 7
Target and Sporting Rifle

REMINGTON ARMS COMPANY — Ilion, New York

To facilitate locating Remington firearms, models are grouped into four categories: Single-shot rifles, bolt-action repeating rifles, slide-action (pump) rifles, and semiautomatic rifles. For a complete listing, please refer to the index.

SINGLE-SHOT RIFLES

NO. 1 SPORTING RIFLE . . . . NiB $1946 Ex $1689 Gd 1066
Single-Shot, rolling-block action. Calibers: .40-50, .40-70, .44-77, .50-45, .50-70 Gov't. centerfire and .44 Long, .44 Extra Long, .45-70, .46 Long, .46 Extra Long, .50-70 rimfire. Bbl. lengths: 28- or 30-inch part octagon. Weight: 5 to 7.5 lbs. Sights: Folding leaf rear sight; sporting front, dovetail bases. Plain walnut straight stock; flanged-top, semicarbine buttplate. Plain walnut forend with thin, rounded front end. Made from 1868 to 1902.

NO. 1 1/2 SPORTING RIFLE . . . . NiB $3675 Ex $3160 Gd $729
Single-Shot, rolling-block action. Calibers: .22 Short, Long, or Extra Long. 25 Stevens, .32, and .38 rimfire cartridges. .32-20, .38-40 and .44-40 centerfire. Bbl. lengths: 24-, 26-, 28- or 30-inch part octagon. Remaining features similar to Remington No. 1. Made from 1869 to 1902.

NO. 2 SPORTING RIFLE
Single-shot, rolling-block action. Calibers: .22, .25, .32, .38, .44 rimfire or centerfire. Bbl. lengths: 24, 26, 28 or 30 inches. Weight: 5 to 6 lbs. Sights: Open rear; bead front. Straight-grip sporting stock and knobtip forearm of walnut. Made from 1873-1910.
Calibers: .22, .25, .32 . . . . NiB $854 Ex $648 Gd $313
Calibers: .38, .44 . . . . NiB $905 Ex $674 Gd $339

NO. 3 CREEDMOOR AND SCHUETZEN RIFLES
. . . . NiB to $32,187 Ex to $25,750 Gd to $17,510
Produced in a variety of styles and calibers, these are collector's items and bring far higher prices than the sporting types. The Schuetzen Special, which has an under-lever action, is especially rare — perhaps fewer than 100 have been made.

NO. 3 HIGH POWER RIFLE
Single-shot, Hepburn falling-block action w/side lever. Calibers: .30-30, .30-40, .32 Special, .32-40, .38-55, .38-72 (high-power cartridges). Bbl. lengths: 26-, 28-, 30-inch. Weight: About 8 lbs. Open sporting sights. Checkered pistol-grip stock and forearm. Made from 1893-1907.
Calibers: .30-30, .30-40,
.32 Special, .32-40 . . . . NiB $2123 Ex $1612 Gd $1041
Calibers: .38-55, .38-72 . . . . NiB $2317 Ex $1865 Gd $1289

NO. 3 SPORTING RIFLE . . . . . . NiB $2638 Ex $2123 Gd 1088
Single-shot, Hepburn falling-block action w/side lever. Calibers: .22 WCF, .22 Extra Long, .25-20 Stevens, .25-21 Stevens, .25-25 Stevens, .32 WCF, .32-40 Ballard & Marlin, .32-40 Rem., .38 WCF, .38-40 Rem., 38-.38-50 Rem., .38-55 Ballard & Marlin, .40-60 Ballard & Marlin, .40-60 WCF, .40-65 Rem. Straight, .40-82 WCF, .45-70 Gov., .45-90 WCF, also was supplied on special order in bottle-necked .40-50, .40-70, .40-90, .44-77, .44-90, .44-105, .50-70 Gov., .50-90 Sharps Straight. Bbl. lengths: 26-inch (22, 25, 32 cal. only), 28-inch, 30-inch; half-octagon or full-octagon. Weight: 8 to 10 lbs. Sights: Open rear; blade front. Checkered pistol-grip stock and forearm. Made from 1880 to c. 1911.

NO. 4 SINGLE-SHOT RIFLE . . . . NiB $931 Ex $699 Gd $442
Rolling-block action. Solid frame or takedown. Calibers: .22 Short and Long, .22 LR. .25 Stevens R.F., .32 Short and Long R.F. 22.5-inch octagon bbl., 24-inch available in .32 caliber only. Weight: About 4.5 lbs. Sights: Open rear; blade front. Plain walnut stock and forearm. Made from 1890-1933.

NO. 4S MILITARY MODEL 22 SINGLE-SHOT RIFLE . . . . NiB $905 Ex $777 Gd $545
Rolling-block action. Calibers: .22 Short only, .22 LR. only. 28-inch bbl. Weight: About 5 lbs. Sights: Military-type rear; blade front. Military-type stock w/handguard, stacking swivel, sling. Has a bayonet stud on the barrel; bayonet and scabbard were regularly supplied. Note: At one time the Military Model was the official rifle of the Boy Scouts of America and was called the Boy Scout Rifle. Made from 1913-33.

NO. 5 SPECIAL SINGLE-SHOT RIFLE
Single-shot, rolling-block action. Calibers: 7mm Mauser, .30-30, .30-40 Krag, .303 British, .32-40, .32 Special, .38-55 (high-power cartridges). Bbl. lengths: 24, 26 and 28 inches. Weight: About 7 lbs. Open sporting sights. Plain straight-grip stock and forearm. Made 1902-18. Note: Models 1897 and 1902 Military Rifles, intended for the export market, are almost identical with the No. 5, except for 30-inch bbl. full military stock and weight (about 8.5 lbs.); a carbine was also supplied. The military rifles were produced in caliber 8mm Lebel for France, 7.62mm Russian for Russia and 7mm Mauser for the Central and South American government trade. At one time, Remington also offered these military models to retail buyers.
Sporting model . . . . NiB $867 Ex $699 Gd $485
Military model. . . . . NiB $642 Ex $519 Gd $363

NO. 6 TAKEDOWN RIFLE . . . . NiB $566 Ex $406 Gd $231
Single-shot, rolling-block action. Calibers: .22 Short, .22 Long, .22 LR, .32 Short/Long RF. 20-inch bbl. Weight: Avg. 4 lbs. Sights: Open front and rear; tang peep. Plain straight-grip stock, forearm. Made from 1901-33.

NO. 7 TARGET AND SPORTING RIFLE . . . .NiB $2571 Ex $2068 Gd $1426
Single-shot. Rolling-block Army Pistol frame. Calibers: .22 Short, .22 LR. 25-10 Stevens R.F. (other calibers as available in No. 2 Rifle were supplied on special order). Half-octagon bbls.: 24-, 26-, 28-inch. Weight: About 6 lbs. Sights: Lyman combination rear; Beach combination front. Fancy walnut stock and forearm, Swiss buttplate available as an extra. Made from 1903-11.

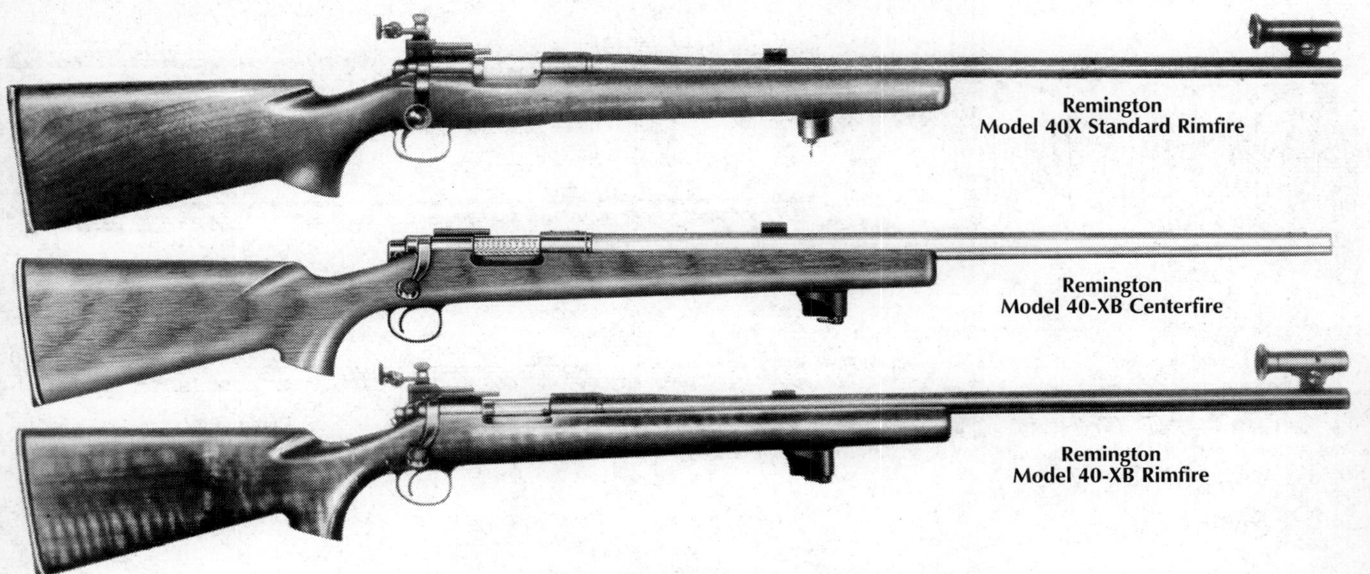

Remington
Model 40X Standard Rimfire

Remington
Model 40-XB Centerfire

Remington
Model 40-XB Rimfire

MODEL 33 BOLT-ACTION SINGLE-SHOT RIFLE . . . . NiB $225 Ex $163 Gd $117
Takedown. Caliber: .22 Short, Long, LR. 24-inch bbl. Weight: About 4.5 lbs. Sights: Open rear, bead front. Plain, pistol-grip stock, forearm with grasping grooves. Made from 1931-36.

MODEL 33 NRA JUNIOR TARGET RIFLE . . . . NiB $328 Ex $276 Gd $122
Same as Model 33 Standard except has Lyman peep rear sight, Partridge-type front sight, 0.88-inch sling and swivels, weighs about 5 lbs.

MODEL 40X CENTERFIRE RIFLE . . . . NiB $1284 Ex $820 Gd $383
Specifications same as for Model 40X Rimfire (heavy weight). Calibers: .222 Rem., .222 Rem. Mag., 7.62mm NATO, .30-06 (others were available on special order). Made from 1961-64. Value shown is for rifle w/o sights.

MODEL 40X HEAVYWEIGHT BOLT-ACTION TARGET RIFLE (RIMFIRE)
Caliber: .22 LR. Single shot. Action similar to Model 722. Click adj. trigger. 28-inch heavy bbl. Redfield Olympic sights. Scope bases. High-comb target stock bedding device, adj. swivel, rubber buttplate. Weight: 12.75 lbs. Made from 1955-1964.
With sights. . . . . NiB $1170 Ex $1073 Gd $537
Without sights . . . . NiB $1181 Ex $970 Gd $434

MODEL 40-X SPORTER . . . . NiB $1658 Ex $1335 Gd $923
Same general specifications as Model 700 C Custom (see that listing in this section) except in caliber .22 LR. Made from 1972-77.

MODEL 40X STANDARD BARREL
Same as Model 40X Heavyweight except has lighter barrel. Weight: 10.75 lbs.
With sights. NiB $751 Ex $586 Gd $236
Without sights . . . . NiB $844 Ex $699 Gd $329

MODEL 40-XB CENTERFIRE MATCH RIFLE . . NiB $1284 Ex $820 Gd $429
Bolt-action, single-shot. Calibers: .222 Rem., .222 Rem. Mag., .223 Rem., .22-250, 6x47mm, 6mm Rem., .243 Win., .25-06, 7mm Rem. Mag., .30-06, .308 Win. (7.62mm NATO), .30-338, (7.62mm NATO), .30-338, .300 Win. Mag. 27 25-inch standard or heavy bbl. Target stock w/adj. front swivel block on guide rail, rubber buttplate. Weight w/o sights: Standard bbl., 9.25 lbs.; heavy bbl., 11.25 lbs. Value shown is for rifle without sights. Made from 1964 to date.

MODEL 40-XB RANGEMASTER CENTERFIRE
Single-shot target rifle with same basic specifications as Model 40-XB Centerfire Match. Additional calibers in .220 Swift, 6mm BR Rem. and 7mm BR Rem., and stainless bbl. only. American walnut or Kevlar (weighs 1 lb. less) target stock with forend stop. Discontinued 1994.
Model 40-XB right-hand model. . . . . NiB $1067 Ex $861 Gd $600
Model 40-XB left-hand model. . . . . NiB $1138 Ex $918 Gd $638
For 2-oz. trigger, add $100
Model 40-XB KS (Kevlar stock, R.H.) . . . . NiB $1196 Ex $965 Gd $670
Model 40-XB KS (Kevlar stock, L.H.). . . . . NiB $1138 Ex $918 Gd $638
For 2-oz. trigger, add $100
For Repeater model, add. $100

MODEL 40-XB RANGEMASTER RIMFIRE MATCH RIFLE . . . . NiB $854 Ex $741 Gd $365
Bolt-action, single-shot. Caliber: .22 LR. 28-inch standard or heavy bbl. Target stock with adj. front swivel block on guide rail, rubber buttplate. Weight w/o sights: Standard bbl., 10 lbs.; heavy bbl., 11.25 lbs. Value shown is for rifle without sights. Made from 1964-74.

MODEL 40-XB VARMINT SPECIAL RIFLE . . . . NiB $1281 Ex $817 Gd $426
Same general specifications as Model 40-XB Repeater except has synthetic stock (Kevlar). Made from 1987-94.

MODEL 40-XBBR BENCH REST RIFLE
Bolt action, single shot. Calibers: .222 Rem., .222 Rem. Mag., .223 Rem., 6x47mm, .308 Win. (7.62mm NATO). 20- or 26-inch unblued stainless-steel bbl. Supplied w/o sights. Weight: With 20-inch bbl., 9.25 lbs., with 26-inch bbl.,12 lbs. (Heavy Varmint class; 7.25 lbs. w/Kevlar stock (Light Varmint class). Made from 1969 to date.
Model 40-XBBR (discontinued). . . . . NiB $932 Ex $753 Gd $519
Model 40-XBBR KS (Kevlar stock) . . . . . NiB $1192 Ex $961 Gd $667

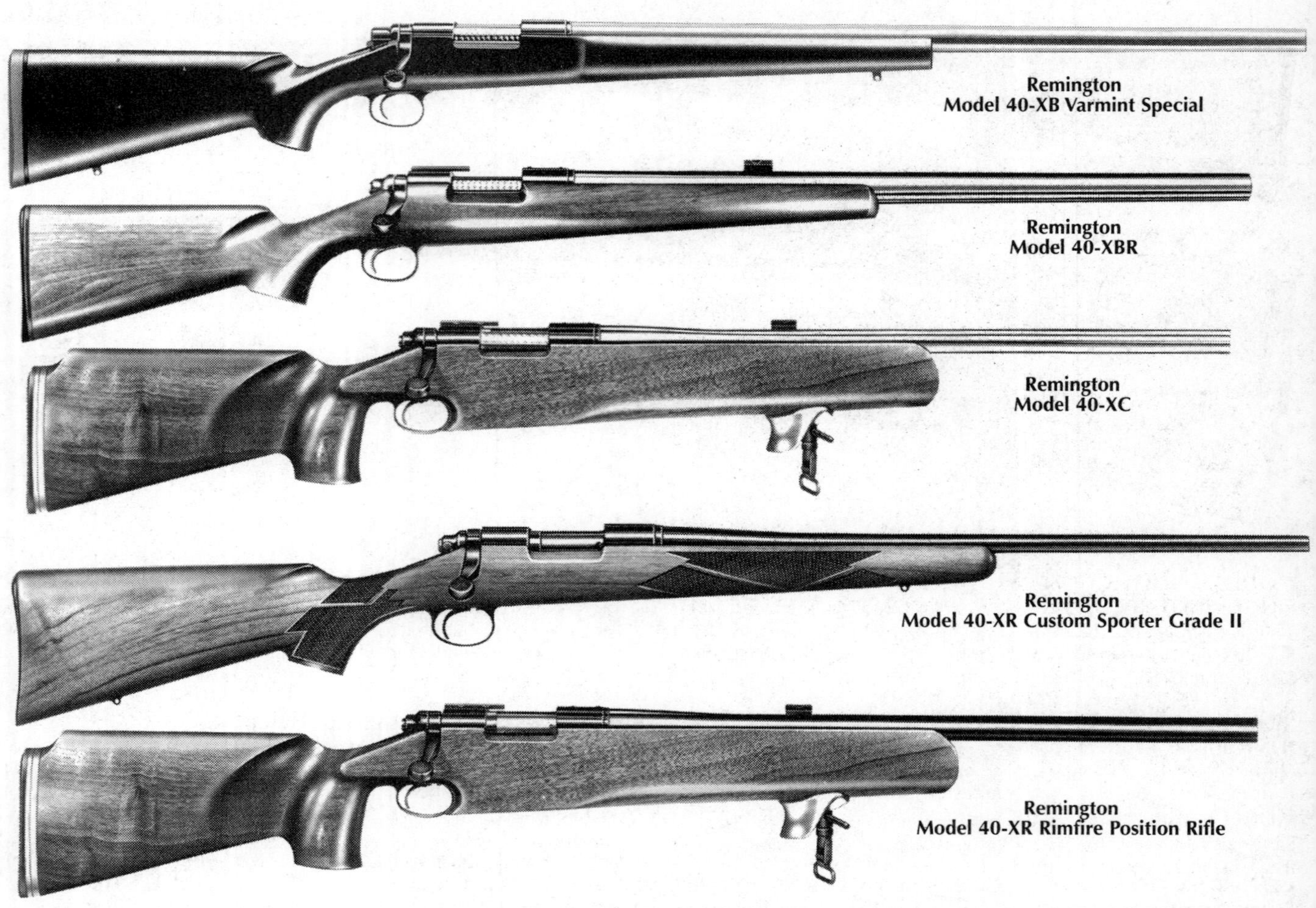

Remington
Model 40-XB Varmint Special

Remington
Model 40-XBR

Remington
Model 40-XC

Remington
Model 40-XR Custom Sporter Grade II

Remington
Model 40-XR Rimfire Position Rifle

MODEL 40-XC NATIONAL MATCH COURSE RIFLE
Bolt-action repeater. Caliber: .308 Win. (7.62mm NATO). Five round magazine, clip slot in receiver. 24-inch bbl. Supplied w/o sights. Weight: 11 lbs. Thumb groove stock w/adj. hand stop and sling swivel, adj. buttplate. Made from 1974 to date.
Mdl. 40-XC (wood stock) (disc.) . . . . NiB $932 Ex $705 Gd $474
Mdl. 40-XC KS (Kevlar stk. disc. 1994) . . . NiB $1370 Ex $967 Gd $632

MODEL 40-XR CUSTOM SPORTER RIFLE
Caliber: .22 RF. 24-inch contoured bbl. Supplied w/o sights. Made in four grades of checkering, engraving and other custom features. Made from 1987 to date. High grade model discontinued 1991.
Grade I . . . . NiB $1173 Ex $993 Gd $761
Grade II . . . . NiB $2123 Ex $1767 Gd $1098
Grade III . . . . NiB $3082 Ex $2299 Gd $1218
Grade IV . . . . NiB $5141 Ex $4951 Gd $2788

MODEL 40-XR RIMFIRE POSITION RIFLE
Bolt action, single shot. Caliber: .22 LR. 24-inch heavy bbl. Supplied w/o sights. Weight: 10 lbs. Position-style stock w/thumb groove, adj. hand stop and sling swivel on guide rail, adj. buttplate. Made from 1974. Discontinued 2004.
Model 40-XR . . . . NiB $1176 Ex $996 Gd $584
Model 40-XR KS (Kevlar stock) . . . . NiB $1279 Ex $1068 Gd $661

MODEL 41A TARGETMASTER BOLT-ACTION SINGLE-SHOT RIFLE . . . . NiB $221 Ex $169 Gd $113
Takedown. Caliber: .22 Short, Long, LR. 27-inch bbl. Weight: About 5.5 lbs. Sights: Open rear; bead front. Plain pistol-grip stock. Made from 1936-40.

MODEL 41AS . . . . NiB $221 Ex $169 Gd $113
Same as Model 41A except chambered for .22 Remington Special (.22 W.R.F.).

MODEL 41P . . . . NiB $221 Ex $169 Gd $113
Same as Model 41A except has peep rear sight, hooded front sight.

MODEL 41SB . . . . NiB $200 Ex $144 Gd $118
Same as Model 41A except smoothbore for use with shot cartridges.

MODEL 510A TARGETMASTER BOLT-ACTION SINGLE-SHOT RIFLE . . . . . NiB $176 Ex $144 Gd $103
Takedown. Caliber: 22 Short, Long, LR. 25-inch bbl. Weight: About 5.5 lbs. Sights: Open rear; bead front. Plain pistol-grip stock. Made from 1939-62.

MODEL 510P . . . . NiB $188 Ex $154 Gd $111
Same as Model 510A except has peep rear sight, Partridge front on ramp.

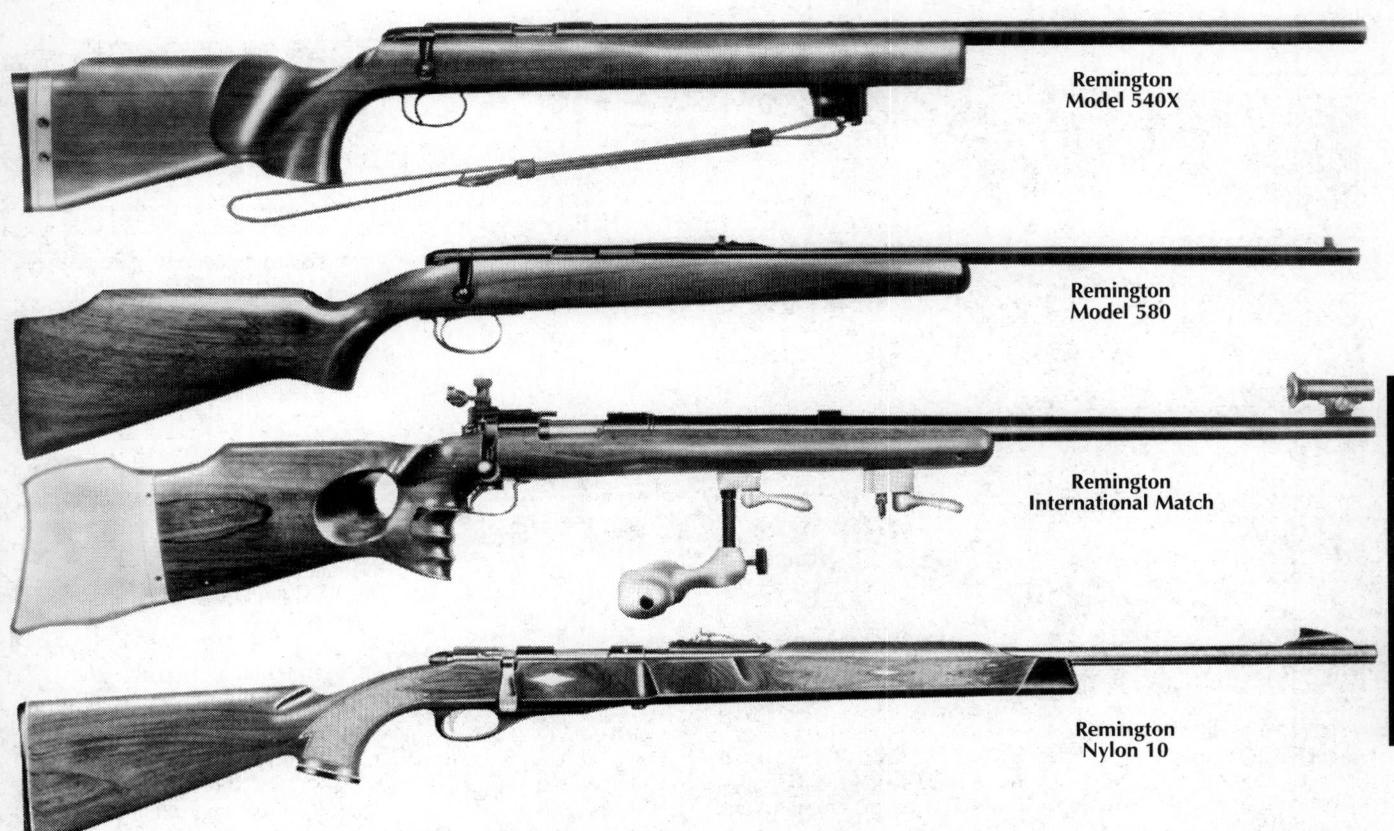

MODEL 510SB .... **NiB $327 Ex $224 Gd $172**
Same as Model 510A except smoothbore for use with shot cartridges, shotgun bead front sight, no rear sight.

MODEL 510X BOLT-ACTION SINGLE-SHOT RIFLE .... **NiB $221 Ex $169 Gd $108**
Same as Model 510A except improved sights. Made from1964-66.

MODEL 514 BOLT-ACTION SINGLE-SHOT .... **NiB $168 Ex $144 Gd $108**
Takedown. Caliber: .22 Short, Long, LR. 24-inch bbl. Weight: 4.75 lbs. Sights: Open rear; bead front. Plain pistol-grip stock. Made from1948-71.

MODEL 514BC BOY'S CARBINE .... **NiB $180 Ex $149 Gd $113**
Same as Model 514 except has 21-inch bbl., 1-inch shorter stock. Made from1961-71.

MODEL 514P .... **NiB $180 Ex $149 Gd $113**
Same as Model 514 except has receiver peep sight.

MODEL 540-X RIMFIRE TARGET RIFLE ... **NiB $361 Ex $283 Gd $129**
Bolt-action, single-shot. Caliber: .22 R. 26-inch heavy bbl. Supplied w/o sights. Weight: About 8 lbs. Target stock w/Monte Carlo cheekpiece and thumb groove, guide rail for hand stop and swivel, adj. buttplate. Made from 1969-74.

MODEL 540-XR POSITION RIFLE .... **NiB $386 Ex $309 Gd $179**
Bolt-action, single-shot. Caliber: .22 LR. 26-inch medium-weight bbl. Supplied w/o sights. Weight: 8 lbs., 13 oz. Position-style stock w/thumb groove, guide rail for hand stop and swivel, adj. buttplate. Made from 1974-84.

MODEL 540-XRJR .... **NiB $386 Ex $309 Gd $180**
Same as Model 540-XR except 1.75-inch shorter stock. Made from 1974-84.

MODEL 580 BOLT-ACTION SINGLE-SHOT .... **NiB $169 Ex $139 Gd $99**
Caliber: .22 Short, Long, LR. 24-inch bbl. Weight: 4.75 lbs. Sights: Bead front; U-notch rear. Monte Carlo stock. Made from 1967-78.

MODEL 580BR BOY'S RIFLE ...... **NiB $183 Ex $149 Gd $106**
Same as Model 580 except w/1-inch shorter stock. Made from 1971-78.

MODEL 580SB SMOOTH BORE ... **NiB $241 Ex $195 Gd $138**
Same as Model 580 except smooth bore for .22 Long Rifle shot cartridges. Made from 1967-78.

INTERNATIONAL FREE RIFLE .... **NiB $1008 Ex $751 Gd $442**
Same as Model 40-XB rimfire and centerfire except has free rifle-type stock with adj. buttplate and hook, adj. palm rest, movable front sling swivel, 2-oz. trigger. Weight: About 15 lbs. Made from 1964-74. Value shown is for rifle with professionally finished stock, no sights.

INTERNATIONAL MATCH FREE RIFLE ... **NiB $1070 Ex $941 Gd $529**
Calibers: .22 LR, .222 Rem., .222 Rem. Mag., 7.62mm NATO, .30-06 (others were available on special order). Model 40X-type bolt-action, single-shot. 2-oz. adj. trigger. 28-inch heavy bbl. Weight: About 15.5 lbs. Free rifle-style stock with thumbhole (furnished semifinished by mfr.); interchangeable and adj. rubber buttplate and hook buttplate, adj. palm rest, sling swivel. Made from 1961-64. Value shown is for rifle with professionally-finished stock, no sights.

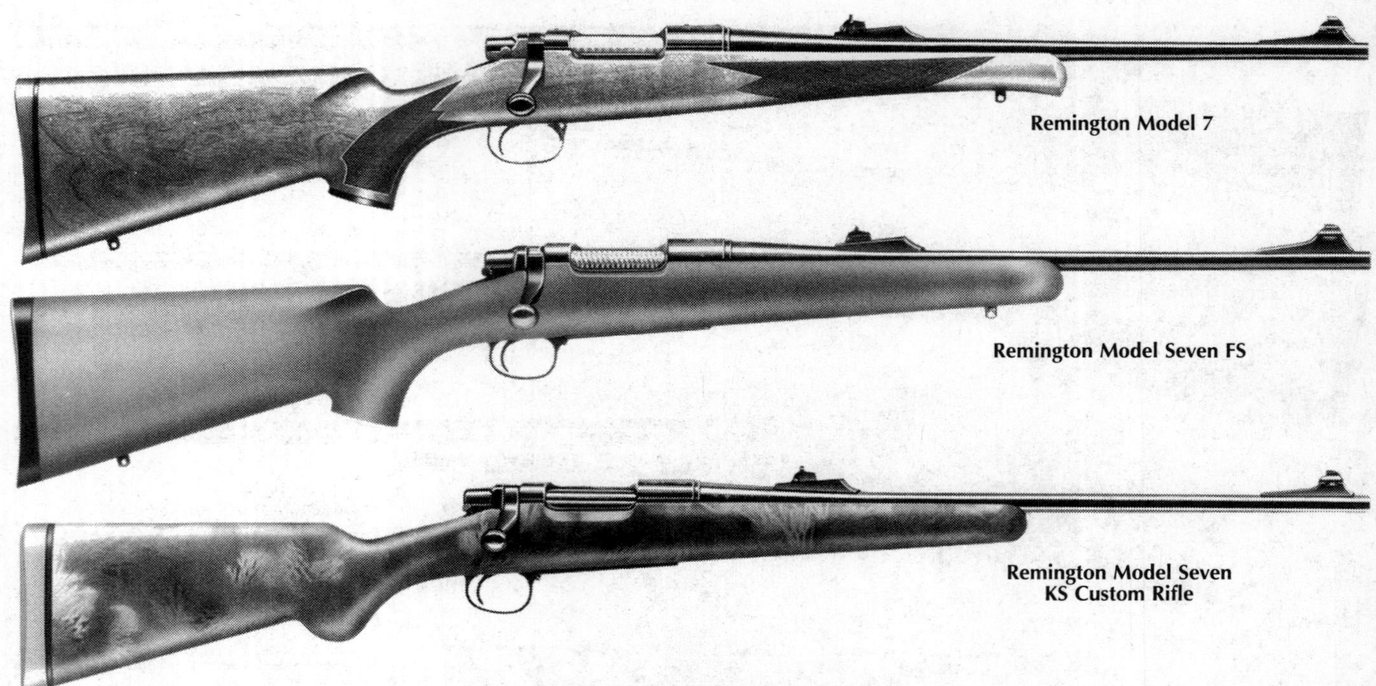

Remington Model 7

Remington Model Seven FS

Remington Model Seven KS Custom Rifle

NYLON 10 BOLT-ACTION SINGLE-SHOT RIFLE . . . . NiB $172 Ex $147 Gd $116
Caliber: .22 Short, Long, LR. 19.13-inch bbl. Weight: 4.25 lbs. Open rear sight; ramped blade front. Receiver grooved for scope mount. Brown nylon stock. Made from 1962-1966.

BOLT-ACTION REPEATING RIFLES

MODEL SEVEN (7) CF BOLT-ACTION RIFLE
Calibers: .17 Rem., .222 Rem., .223 Rem., .243 Win., 6mm Rem., 7mm-08 Rem., .308 Win. Magazine capacity: 5-round in .17 Rem., .222 Rem., .223 Rem., 4-round in other calibers. 18.5-inch bbl. Weight: 6.5 lbs. Walnut stock checkering, and recoil pad. Made from 1983 to date. .223 Rem. added in 1984.
Standard calibers except
.17 Rem. & .222 Rem. . . . . NiB $488 Ex $411 Gd $282
Caliber .17 Rem & .222 Rem.. . . . . NiB $514 Ex $432 Gd $293

MODEL SEVEN (7) FS RIFLE. . . . . NiB $572 Ex $463 Gd $323
Calibers: .243, 7mm-08 Rem., .308 Win. 18.5-inch bbl. 37.5 inches overall. Weight: 5.25 lbs. Hand layup fiberglass stock, reinforced with DuPont Kevlar at points of bedding and stress. Made from 1987-90.

MODEL SEVEN (7) KS RIFLE . . . . . . NiB $832 Ex $678 Gd $446
Calibers: .223 Rem., 7mm-08, .308, .35 Rem. and .350 Rem. Mag. 20-inch bbl. Custom-made in Remington's Custom Shop with Kevlar stock. Made from 1987 to date.

MODEL SEVEN (7) LS RIFLE . . . . . . NiB $540 Ex $463 Gd $283
Calibers: .223 Rem., .243 Win., .260 Rem., 7mm-08 and 308 Win. 20-inch matte bbl. Laminated hardwood stock w/matte brown finish. Weight: 6.5 lbs. Made from 2000 to date.

MODEL SEVEN (7) LSS RIFLE . . . . . NiB $591 Ex $463 Gd $308
Similar to Model 7 LS except stainless bbl. w/o sights. Calibers: .22-250 Rem., .243 Win. or 7mm-08. Made from 2000-2003.

MODEL SEVEN (7) MS CUSTOM RIFLE . . NiB $1028 Ex $900 Gd $539
Similar to the standard Model 7 except fitted with a laminated full Mannlicher-style stock. Weight: 6.75 lbs. Calibers: .222 Rem., .22-250, .243, 6mm Rem.,7mm-08, .308, .350 Rem. Additional calibers available on special order. Made from 1993 to date.

MODEL SEVEN (7) SS RIFLE . . . . . . NiB $566 Ex $437 Gd $308
Same as Model 7 except 20-inch stainless bbl., receiver and bolt; black synthetic stock. Calibers: .243, 7mm-08 or .308. Made from 1994 to date.

MODEL SEVEN (7) YOUTH RIFLE. . . . . NiB $383 Ex $332 Gd $255
Similar to the standard Model 7 except fitted with hardwood stock with a 12.19-inch pull. Calibers: .243, 6mm, 7mm-08 only. Made from 1993 to date.

MODEL 30A BOLT-ACTION EXPRESS RIFLE. . . . . NiB $601 Ex $486 Gd $340
Standard Grade. Modified M/1917 Enfield Action. Calibers: .25, .30, .32 and .35 Rem., 7mm Mauser, .30-06. Five round box magazine. 22-inch bbl. Weight: About 7.25 lbs. Sights: Open rear; bead front. Walnut stock w/checkered pistol grip and forearm. Made 1921-40. Note: Early Model 30s had a slender forend with Schnabel tip, military-type double-pull trigger.

MODEL 30R CARBINE . . . . NiB $614 Ex $517 Gd $394
Same as Model 30A except has 20-inch bbl., plain stock weighs about 7 lbs.

MODEL 30S SPORTING RIFLE . . . . NiB $740 Ex $600 Gd $421
Special Grade. Same action as Model 30A. Calibers: .257 Roberts, 7mm Mauser, .30-06. Five round box magazine. 24-inch bbl. Weight: About 8 lbs. Lyman No. 48 Receiver sight, bead front sight. Special high comb stock with long, full forearm, checkered. Made from 1930-40.

MODEL 34 BOLT-ACTION REPEATER. . . . . NiB $173 Ex $147 Gd $112
Takedown. Caliber: .22 Short, Long, LR. Tubular magazine holds 22 Short, 17 Long or 15 LR. 24-inch bbl. Weight: 5.25 lbs. Sights: Open rear; bead front. Plain, pistol-grip stock, forearm w/grasping grooves. Made from 1932-36.

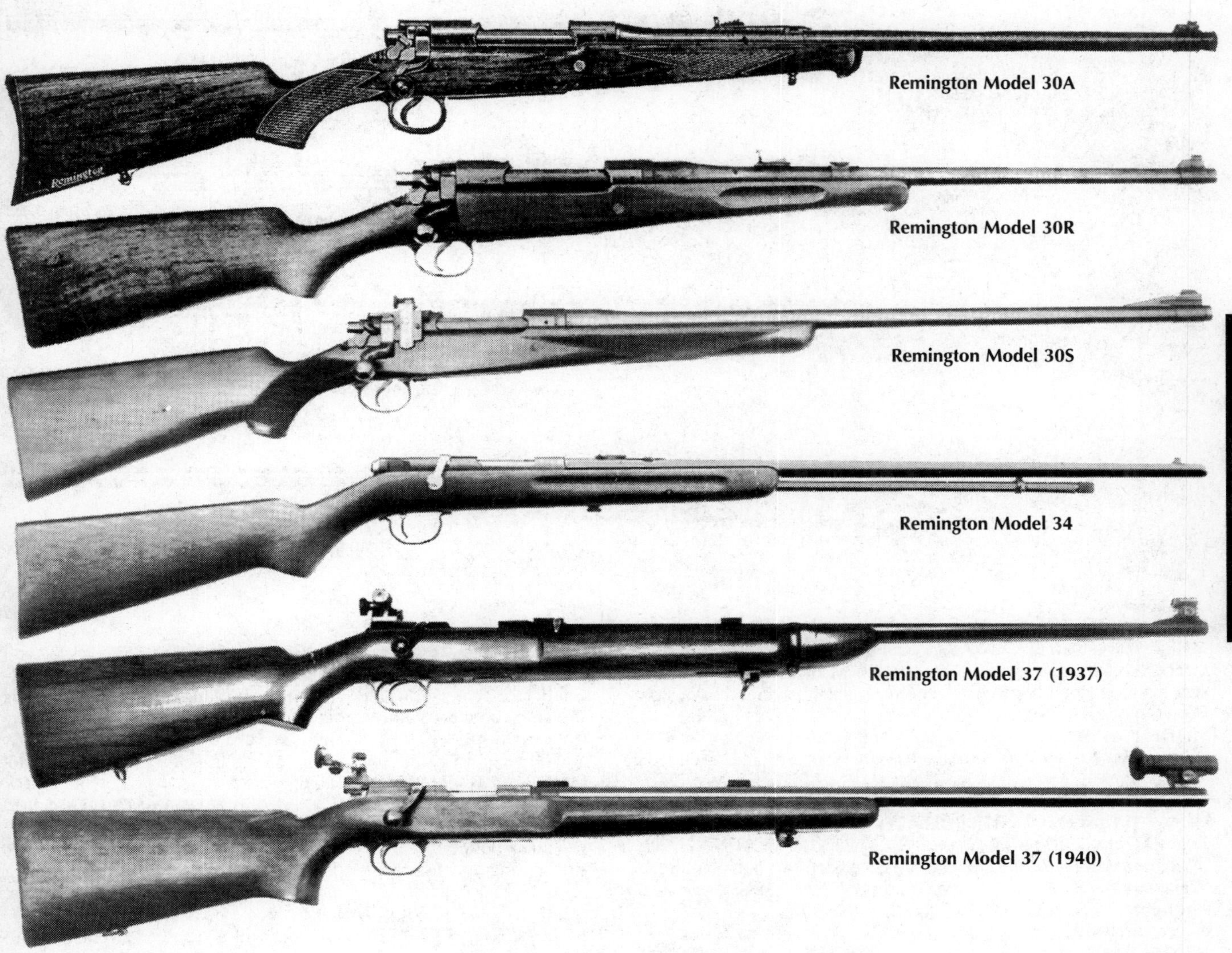
Remington Model 30A

Remington Model 30R

Remington Model 30S

Remington Model 34

Remington Model 37 (1937)

Remington Model 37 (1940)

MODEL 34 NRA TARGET RIFLE . . . . NiB $442 Ex $365 Gd $236
Same as Model 34 Standard except has Lyman peep rear sight, Partridge-type front sight, .88-inch sling and swivels, weight: About 5.75 lbs.

MODEL 37 RANGEMASTER BOLT-ACTION TARGET RIFLE (I)
Model of 1937. Caliber: .22 LR. Five round box magazine, single shot adapter also supplied as standard equipment. 28-inch heavy bbl. Weight: About 12 lbs. Remington front and rear sights, scope bases. Target stock, swivels, sling. Note: Original 1937 model had a stock with outside bbl. band similar in appearance to that of the old-style Winchester Model 52, forearm design was modified and bbl. band eliminated in 1938. Made from 1937-40.
With factory sights . . . . NiB $576 Ex $468 Gd $339
Without sights . . . . NiB $520 Ex $442 Gd $262

MODEL 37 RANGEMASTER BOLT-ACTION TARGET RIFLE (II)
Model of 1940. Same as Model of 1937 except has "Miracle" trigger mechanism and Randle-design stock with high comb, full pistol-grip and wide beavertail forend. Made from 1940-54.
With factory sights . . . . NiB $745 Ex $602 Gd $421
Without sights . . . . NiB $545 Ex $443 Gd $313

MODEL 40-XB
CENTERFIRE REPEATER. . . . . NiB $1128 Ex $913 Gd $638
Same as Model 40-XB Centerfire except 5-round repeater. Calibers: .222 Rem., .222 Rem. Mag., .223 Rem., .22-250, 6x47mm, 6mm Rem., .243 Win., .308 Win. (7.62mm NATO). Heavy bbl. only. Discontinued.

MODEL 78 SPORTSMAN
BOLT-ACTION RIFLE . . . . NiB $311 Ex $254 Gd $682
Similar to Model 700 ADL except with straight-comb walnut-finished hardwood stock in calibers .223 Rem., .243 Win, .270 Win., .30-06 Springfield and .308 Win. 22-inch bbl. Weight: 7 lbs. Adj. sights. Made from 1984-91.

MODEL 341A SPORTSMASTER
BOLT-ACTION REPEATER . . . . NiB $192 Ex $154 Gd $110
Takedown. Caliber: .22 Short, Long, LR. Tubular magazine holds 22 Short, 17 Long, 15 LR. 27-inch bbl. Weight: About 6 lbs. Sights: Open rear; bead front. Plain pistol-grip stock. Made from 1936-40.

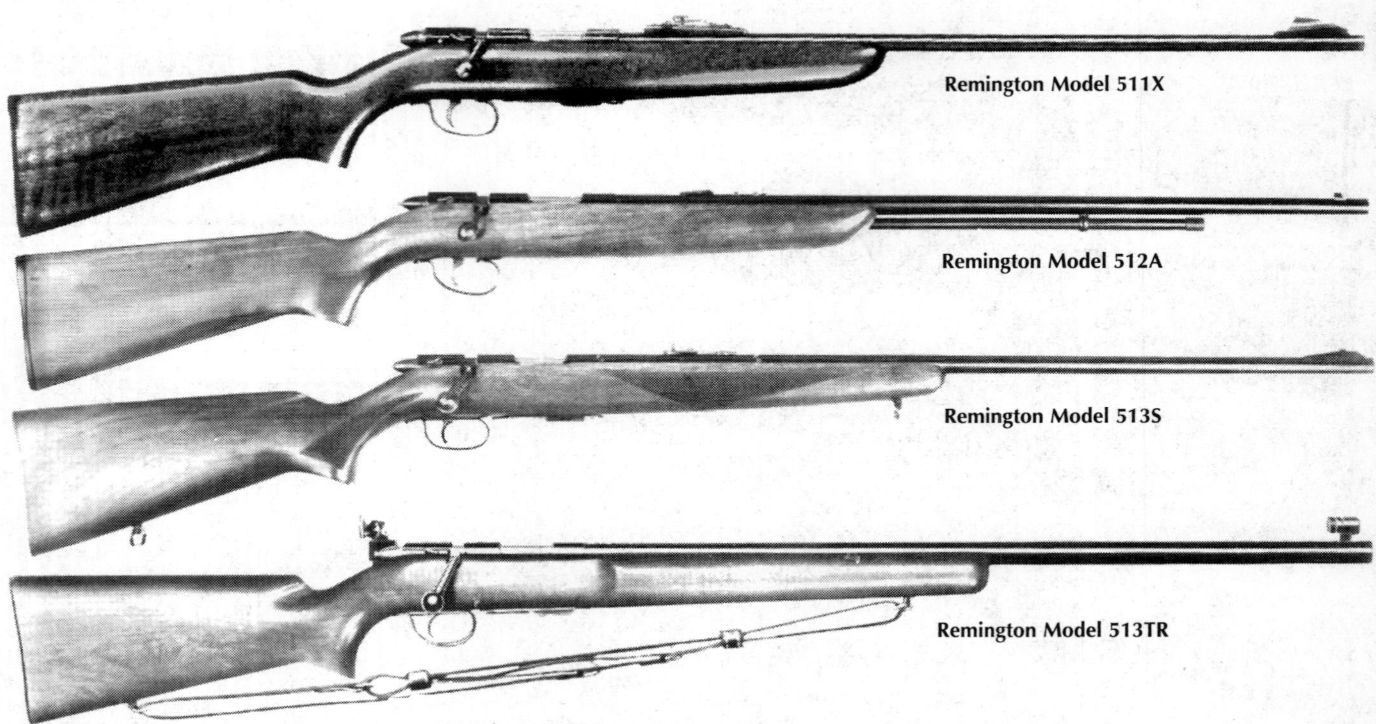

MODEL 341P . . . . NiB $220 Ex $180 Gd $128
Same as Model 341A except has peep rear sight, hooded front sight.

MODEL 341SB . . . . NiB $226 Ex $252 Gd $174
Same as Model 341A previously listed except smoothbore for use with shot cartridges.

MODEL 511A SCOREMASTER BOLT-ACTION BOX MAGAZINE REPEATER . . . . NiB $206 Ex $169 Gd $121
Takedown. Caliber: 22 Short, Long, LR. Six round detachable box magazine. 25-inch bbl. Weight: About 5.5 lbs. Sights: Open rear; bead front. Plain pistol-grip stock. Made 1939-62.

MODEL 511P . . . . NiB $214 Ex $174 Gd $125
Same as Model 511A except has peep rear sight, Partridge-type blade front on ramp.

MODEL 511X BOLT-ACTION REPEATER . . NiB $220 Ex $180 Gd $128
Clip type. Same as Model 511A except improved sights. Made from 1964-66.

MODEL 512A SPORTSMASTER BOLT-ACTION REPEATER . . . . NiB $194 Ex $160 Gd $125
Takedown. Caliber: .22 Short, Long, LR. Tubular magazine holds 22 Short, 17 Long, 15 LR. 25-inch bbl. Weight: About 5.75 lbs. Sights: Open rear; bead front. Plain pistol-grip stock w/semibeavertail forend. Made from 1940-62.

MODEL 512P . . . . NiB $246 Ex $200 Gd $143
Same as Model 512A except has peep rear sight, blade front, on ramp.

MODEL 512X BOLT-ACTION REPEATER . . NiB $2527 Ex $210 Gd $150
Tubular magazine type. Same as Model 512A except has improved sights. Made from 1964-66.

MODEL 513S BOLT-ACTION RIFLE . . . . . . NiB $539 Ex $487 Gd $307
Caliber: .22 LR. Six round detachable box magazine. 27-inch bbl. Weight: About 6.75 lbs. Marble open rear sight, Partridge-type front. Checkered sporter stock. Made from 1941-56.

MODEL 513TR MATCHMASTER BOLT-ACTION TARGET RIFLE . . . . . NiB $362 Ex $294 Gd $206
Caliber: .22 LR. Six round detachable box magazine. 27-inch bbl. Weight: About 9 lbs. Sights: Redfield No. 75 rear; globe front. Target stock. Sling and swivels. Made from 1941-69.

MODEL 521TL JUNIOR TARGET BOLT-ACTION REPEATER . . . . NiB $323 Ex $262 Gd $186
Takedown. Caliber: .22 LR. Six round detachable box magazine. 25-inch bbl. Weight: About 7 lbs. Sights: Lyman No. 57RS rear; dovetailed blade front. Target stock. Sling and swivels. Made from 1947-69.

MODEL 522 VIPER . . . . NiB $174 Ex $123 Gd $97
Calibers: .22 LR. 10-round magazine. 20-inch bbl. 40 inches overall. Weight: 4.63 lbs. Checkered black PET resin stock with beavertail forend. Dupont high-tech synthetic lightweight receiver. Matte black finish on all exposed metal. Made from 1993 to date.

MODEL 541-S CUSTOM SPORTER. . . . . . . NiB $737 Ex $594 Gd $413
Bolt-action repeater. Scroll engraving on receiver and trigger guard. Caliber: .22 Short, Long, LR. Five round clip magazine. 24-inch bbl. Weight: 5.5 lbs. Supplied w/o sights. Checkered walnut stock w/rosewood-finished forend tip, pistol-grip cap and buttplate. Made from 1972-84.

MODEL 541-T BOLT-ACTION RIFLE
Caliber: .22 RF. Clip-fed, Five round. 24-inch bbl. Weight: 5.88 lbs. Checkered walnut stock. Made from 1986 to date; heavy bbl. model intro. 1993.
Model 541-T Standard . . . . NiB $435 Ex $306 Gd $188
Model 541-T-HB heavy bbl.. . . . . NiB $461 Ex $332 Gd $244

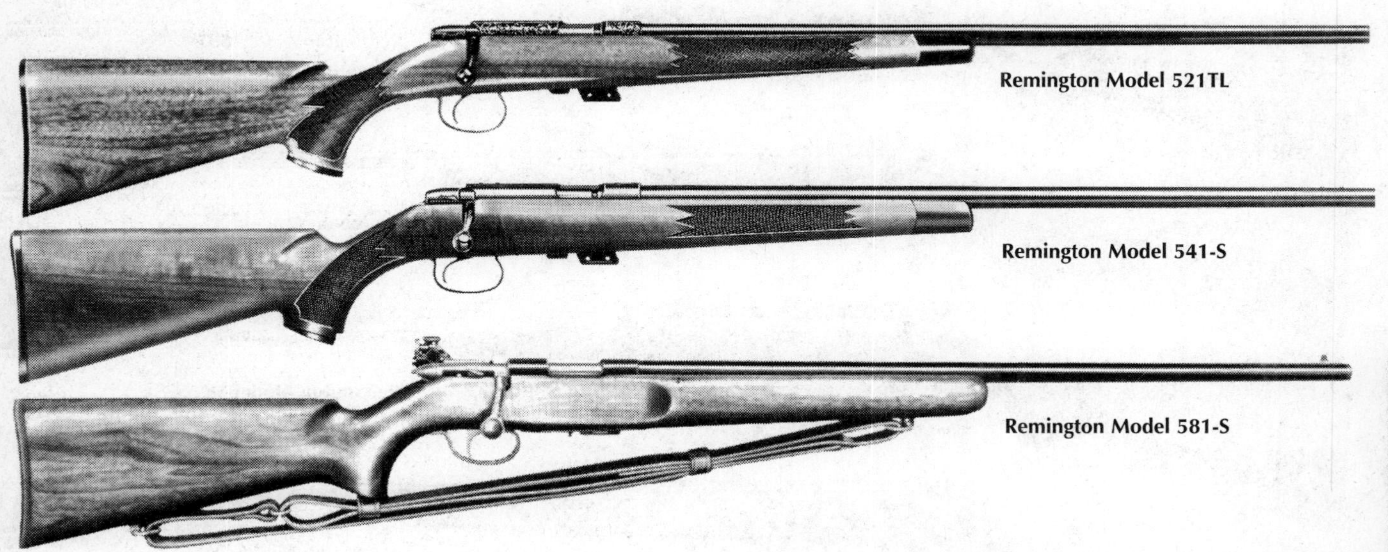

MODEL 581 CLIP REPEATER
Same general specifications as Model 580 except has 5-round clip magazine. Made from 1967-84.
Model 581. . . . . NiB $182 Ex $150 Gd $109
Model 581 left hand
(made 1969-1984) . . . . NiB $216 Ex $175 Gd $127

MODEL 581-S BOLT-ACTION RIFLE. . . . . . NiB $201 Ex $175 Gd $124
Caliber: .22 RF. Clip-fed, 5-round. 24-inch bbl. Weight: 4.75 lbs. Plain walnut-colored stock. Made from 1987-92.

MODEL 582 TUBULAR REPEATER . . . . NiB $189 Ex $155 Gd $112
Same general specifications as Model 580 except has tubular magazine holding 20 Short,15 Long,14 LR. Weight: About 5 lbs. Made from 1967-84.

MODEL 591 BOLT-ACTION
CLIP REPEATER. . . . . NiB $272 Ex $222 Gd $158
Caliber: 5mm Rimfire Magnum. Four round clip magazine. 24-inch bbl. Weight: 5 lbs. Sights: Bead front; U-notch rear. Monte Carlo stock. Made from 1970-73.

MODEL 592 TUBULAR REPEATER . . . . NiB $208 Ex $170 Gd $123
Same as Model 591 except has tubular magazine holding 10 rounds, weight: 5.5 lbs. Made from 1970-73.

MODEL 600 BOLT-ACTION CARBINE
Calibers: .222 Rem., .223 Rem., .243 Win., 6mm Rem., .308 Win., 35 Rem., 5-round magazine (6-round in .222 Rem.) 18.5-inch bbl. with ventilated rib. Weight: 6 lbs. Sights: Open rear; blade ramp front. Monte Carlo stock w/pistol-grip. Made from 1964-67.
.222 Rem. NiB $866 Ex $789 Gd $480
.223 Rem. . . . . NiB $1400 Ex $1173 Gd $783
.35 Rem. NiB $846 Ex $686 Gd $480
Standard calibers. . . . . NiB $675 Ex $547 Gd $384

MODEL 600 MAGNUM . . . . NiB $1070 Ex $905 Gd $603
Same as Model 600 except calibers 6.5mm Mag. and .350 Rem. Mag., 4-round magazine, special Magnum-type bbl. with bracket for scope back-up, laminated walnut and beech stock w/recoil pad. QD swivels and sling; weight: About 6.5 lbs. Made from 1965-67.

MODEL 600 MONTANA
TERRITORIAL CENTENNIAL $802
Same as Model 600 except has commemorative medallion embedded in buttstock. Made in 1964. Value is for rifle in new, unfired condition.

MODEL 660 STP
Calibers: .222 Rem., 6mm Rem., .243 Win., .308 Win., 5-round magazine. (6-round in .222 Rem.) 20-inch bbl. Weight: 6.5 lbs. Sights: Open rear; bead front on ramp. Monte Carlo stock, checkered, black pistol-grip cap and forend tip. Made from 1968-71.
.222 Rem. NiB $652 Ex $528 Gd $368
Other calibers . . . . NiB $608 Ex $491 Gd $383

MODEL 660 MAGNUM . . . . NiB $903 Ex $723 Gd $594
Same as Model 660 except calibers 6.5mm Rem. Mag. and .350 Rem. Mag., 4-round magazine, laminated walnut-and-beech stock with recoil pad. QD swivels and sling. Made from 1968-71.

MODEL 700 ADL CENTERFIRE RIFLE. . . . . NiB $407 Ex $325 Gd $221
Calibers: .22-250, .222 Rem., .25-06, 6mm Rem., .243 Win., .270 Win., .30-06, .308 Win., 7mm Rem. Mag. Magazine capacity: 6-round in .222 Rem.; 4-round in 7mm Rem. Mag. Five round in other calibers. Bbl. lengths: 24-inch in .22-250, .222 Rem., .25-06, 7mm Rem. Mag.; 22-inch in other calibers. Weight: 7 lbs. standard; 7.5 lbs. in 7mm Rem. Mag. Sights: Ramp front; sliding ramp open rear. Monte Carlo stock w/cheekpiece, skip checkering, recoil pad on Magnum. Laminated stock also avail. Made from 1962-93.

MODEL 700 APR BOLT-ACTION RIFLE . NiB $1274 Ex $1028 Gd $715
Acronym for African Plains Rifle. Calibers: 7mm Rem. Mag., 7mm STW, 300 Win. Mag., 300 Wby. Mag., 300 Rem. Ultra Mag., 338 Win. Mag., 375 H&H. Three round magazine. 26-inch bbl. on a magnum action. 46.5 inches overall. Weight: 7.75 lbs. Matte blue finish. Checkered classic-style laminated wood stock w/black magnum recoil pad. Made from 1994 to date.

MODEL 700 AS BOLT-ACTION RIFLE
Similar to the Model 700 BDL except with non-reflective matte black metal finish, including the bolt body. Weight: 6.5 lbs. Straight comb synthetic stock made of Arylon, a fiberglass-reinforced thermoplastic resin with non-reflective matte finish. Made from 1988-92.
Standard caliber . . . . NiB $493 Ex $399 Gd $278
Magnum caliber . . . . NiB $532 Ex $430 Gd $300

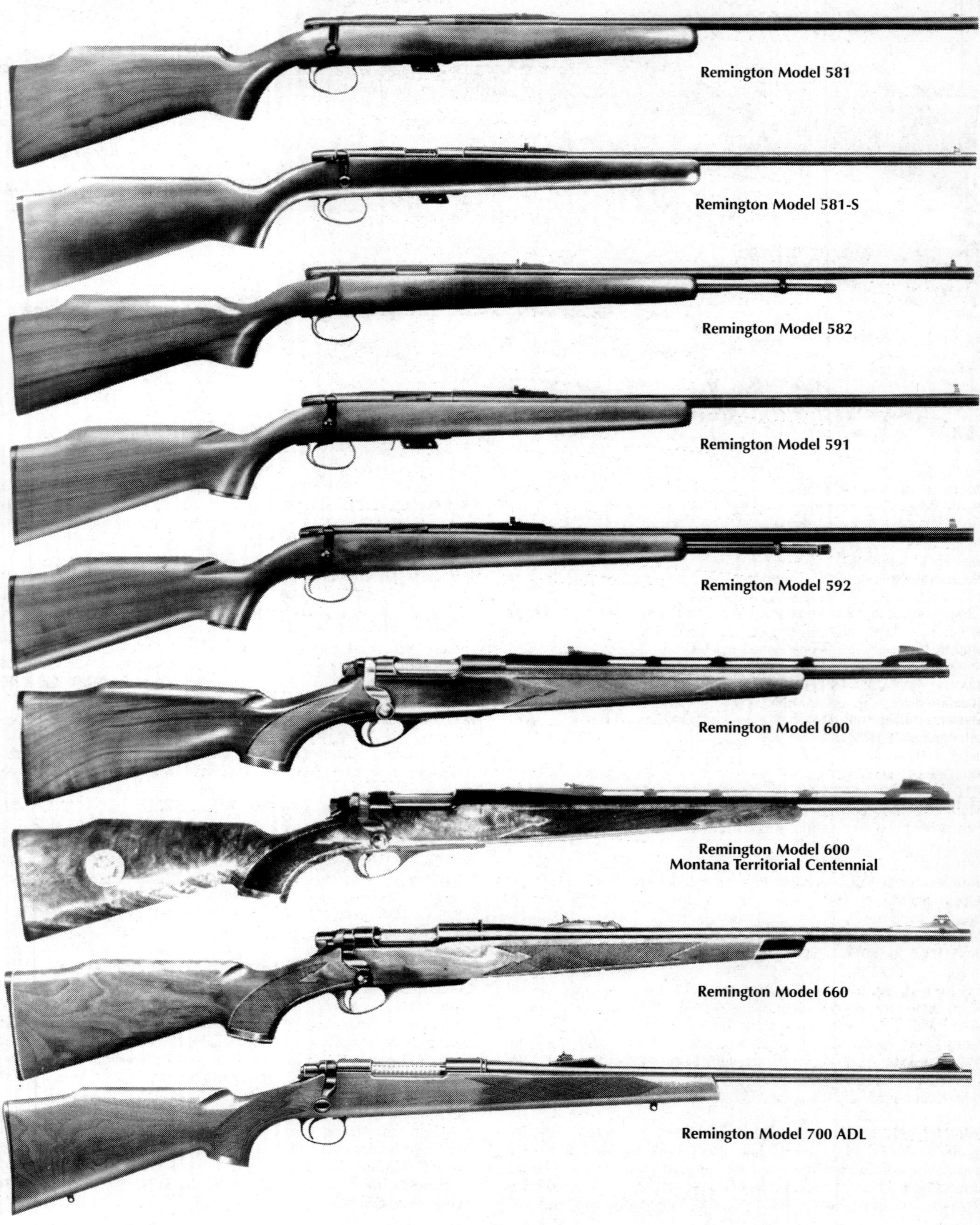

Remington Model 581

Remington Model 581-S

Remington Model 582

Remington Model 591

Remington Model 592

Remington Model 600

Remington Model 600
Montana Territorial Centennial

Remington Model 660

Remington Model 700 ADL

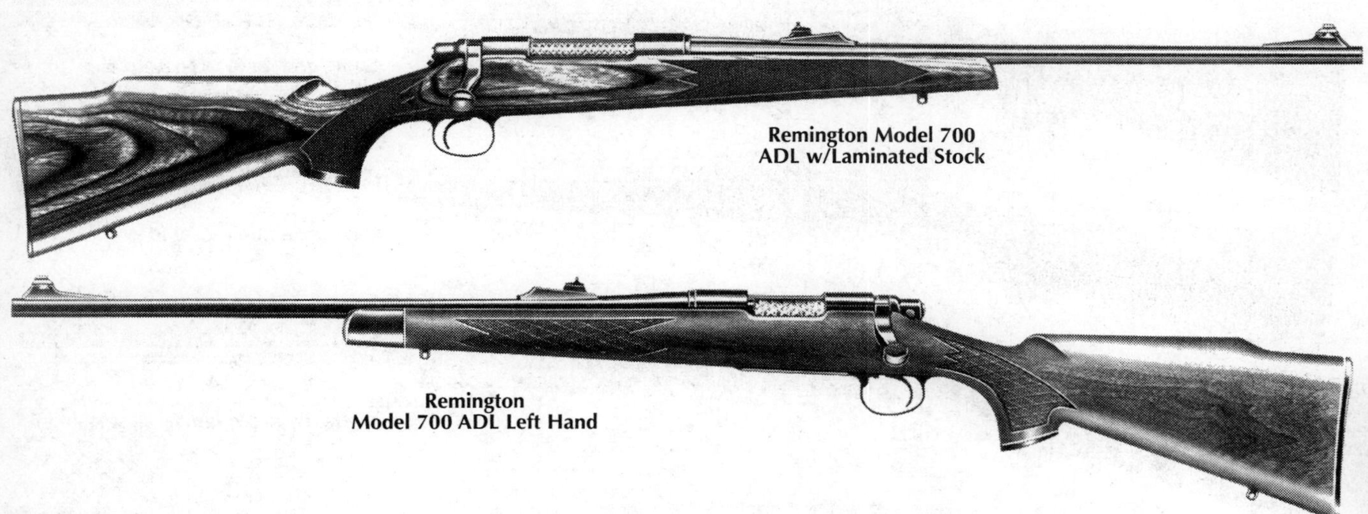

Remington Model 700
ADL w/Laminated Stock

Remington
Model 700 ADL Left Hand

MODEL 700 AWR
BOLT-ACTION RIFLE.......... NiB $1392 Ex $1186 Gd $1031
Acronym for Alaskan Wilderness Rifle, similar to Model 700 APR except w/24-inch stainless bbl. and black chromed action. Matte gray or black Kevlar stock w/straight comb and raised cheekpiece fitted w/black magnum recoil pad. Made from 1994 to date.

MODEL 700 BDL CENTERFIRE RIFLE
Same as Model 700 ADL except has hinged floorplate hooded ramp front sight, stock w/black forend tip and pistol-grip cap, cut checkering, QD swivels and sling. Additional calibers: .17 Rem., .223 Rem., .264 Win. Mag., 7mm-08, .280, .300 Sav., .300 Win. Mag., 8mm Rem. Mag., .338 Win. Mag., .35 Whelen. All have 24-inch bbls. Magnums have 4-round magazine, recoil pad, weighs 7.5 lbs; .17 Rem. has 6-round magazine, weighs 7 lbs. Made 1962 to date. Made from 1973 to date.
Standard calibers except .17 Rem........ NiB $522 Ex $424 Gd $297
Magnum calibers and .17 Rem. .... NiB $587 Ex $475 Gd $332
Left-hand, .270 Win. and .30-06......... NiB $536 Ex $434 Gd $304
Left-hand, 7mm
Rem. Mag and .222 Rem................ NiB $593 Ex $516 Gd $439

MODEL 700 BDL EUROPEAN RIFLE
Same general specifications as Model 700 BDL, except has oil-finished walnut stock. Calibers: .243, .270, 7mm-08, 7mm Mag., .280 Rem., .30-06. Made from 1993-95.
Standard calibers............... NiB $542 Ex $439 Gd $310
Magnum calibers............... NiB $542 Ex $500 Gd $387

MODEL 700 BDL SS BOLT-ACTION RIFLE
Same as Model 700 BDL except w/24-inch stainless bbl., receiver and bolt plus black synthetic stock. Calibers: .223 Rem., .243 Win., 6mm Rem., .25-06 Rem., .270 Win. .280 Rem., 7mm-08, 7mm Rem. Mag., 7mm Wby. Mag., .30-06, .300 Win., .308 Win., .338 Win. Mag. .375 H&H. Made from 1992 to date.
Standard calibers............... NiB $593 Ex $516 Gd $315
Magnum calibers, add $80
DM (detachable magazine), add $40
DM-B (muzzle brake), add $90

MODEL 700 BDL
VARMINT SPECIAL .... NiB $542 Ex $439 Gd $305
Same as Model 700 BDL except has 24-inch heavy bbl., no sights, weighs 9 lbs. (8.75 lbs. in 308 Win.). Calibers: .22-250, .222 Rem., .223 Rem., .25-06, 6mm Rem., .243 Win., .308 Win. Made from 1967-94.

REMINGTON MODEL 700 CS BOLT-ACTION RIFLE
Similar to Model 700 BDL except with nonreflective matte black metal finish, including the bolt body. Straight comb synthetic stock camouflaged in Mossy Oak Bottomland pattern. Made from 1992-94.
Standard calibers................ NiB $536 Ex $434 Gd $304
Magnum calibers................ NiB $574 Ex $465 Gd $325

MODEL 700 CLASSIC
Same general specifications as Model 700 BDL except has "Classic" stock of high-quality walnut with full-pattern cut-checkering, special satin wood finish; Schnabel forend. Brown rubber buttpad. Hinged floorplate. No sights. Weight: 7 lbs. Also chambered for "Classic" cartridges such as .257 Roberts and .250-3000. Introduced in 1981.
Standard calibers............... NiB $542 Ex $387 Gd $284
Magnum calibers............... NiB $593 Ex $439 Gd $305

MODEL 700 CUSTOM BOLT-ACTION RIFLE
Same general specifications as Model 700 BDL except custom-built; available in choice of grades, each with higher quality wood, different checkering patterns, engraving, high-gloss blued finish. Introduced in 1965.
Model 700 C Grade I .... NiB $1284 Ex $1028 Gd $715
Model 700 C Grade II......... NiB $2195 Ex $1759 Gd $1226
Model 700 C Grade III .... NiB $2839 Ex $2274 Gd $1576
Model 700 C Grade IV .... NiB $5176 Ex $4158 Gd $2857
Model 700 D Peerless .... NiB $2030 Ex $1507 Gd $1047
Model 700 F Premier......... NiB $3509 Ex $2825 Gd $1949

MODEL 700 FS BOLT-ACTION RIFLE
Similar to Model 700 ADL except with straight comb fiberglass stock reinforced with DuPont Kevlar, finished in gray or gray camo with Old English-style recoil pad. Made from 1987-89.
Standard calibers............... NiB $602 Ex $540 Gd $334
Magnum calibers............... NiB $643 Ex $540 Gd $385

MODEL 700 KS CUSTOM MOUNTAIN RIFLE
Similar to standard Model 700 MTN Rifle, except with custom Kevlar reinforced resin synthetic stock with standard or wood-grain finish. Calibers: .270 Win., .280 Rem., 7mm Rem Mag., .30-06, .300 Win. Mag., .300 Wby. Mag., 8mm Rem. Mag., .338 Win. Mag., .35 Whelen, .375 H&H. Four round magazine. 24-inch bbl. Weight: 6.75 lbs. Made from 1986 to date.
Standard KS stock (disc. 1993) .... NiB $1109 Ex $929 Gd $518
Wood-grain KS stock.................. NiB $1032 Ex $801 Gd $562
SS Model Stainless Synthetic (1995-97) . NiB $1245 Ex $1048 Gd $796
Left-hand model, add $75

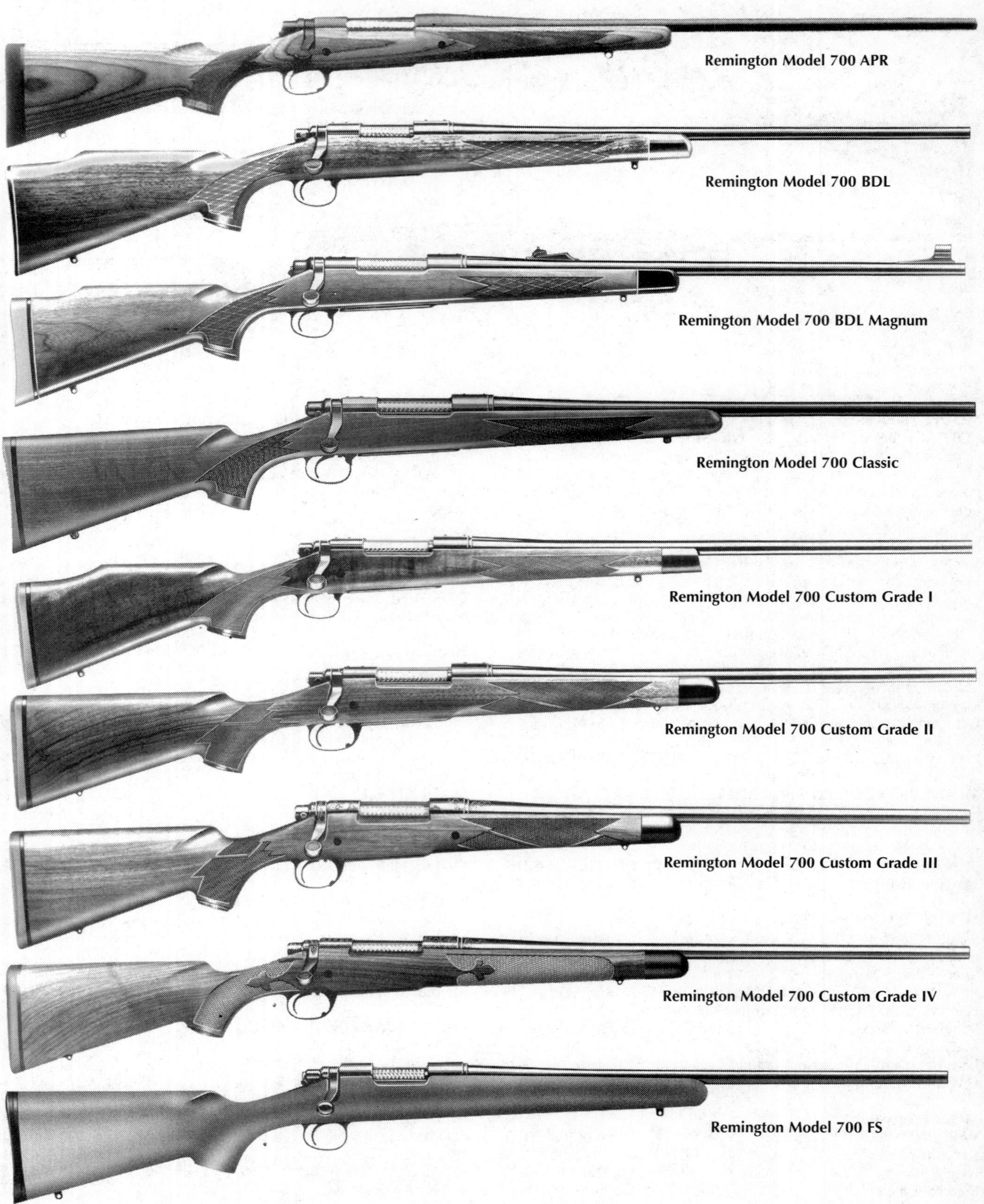

Remington Model 700 APR

Remington Model 700 BDL

Remington Model 700 BDL Magnum

Remington Model 700 Classic

Remington Model 700 Custom Grade I

Remington Model 700 Custom Grade II

Remington Model 700 Custom Grade III

Remington Model 700 Custom Grade IV

Remington Model 700 FS

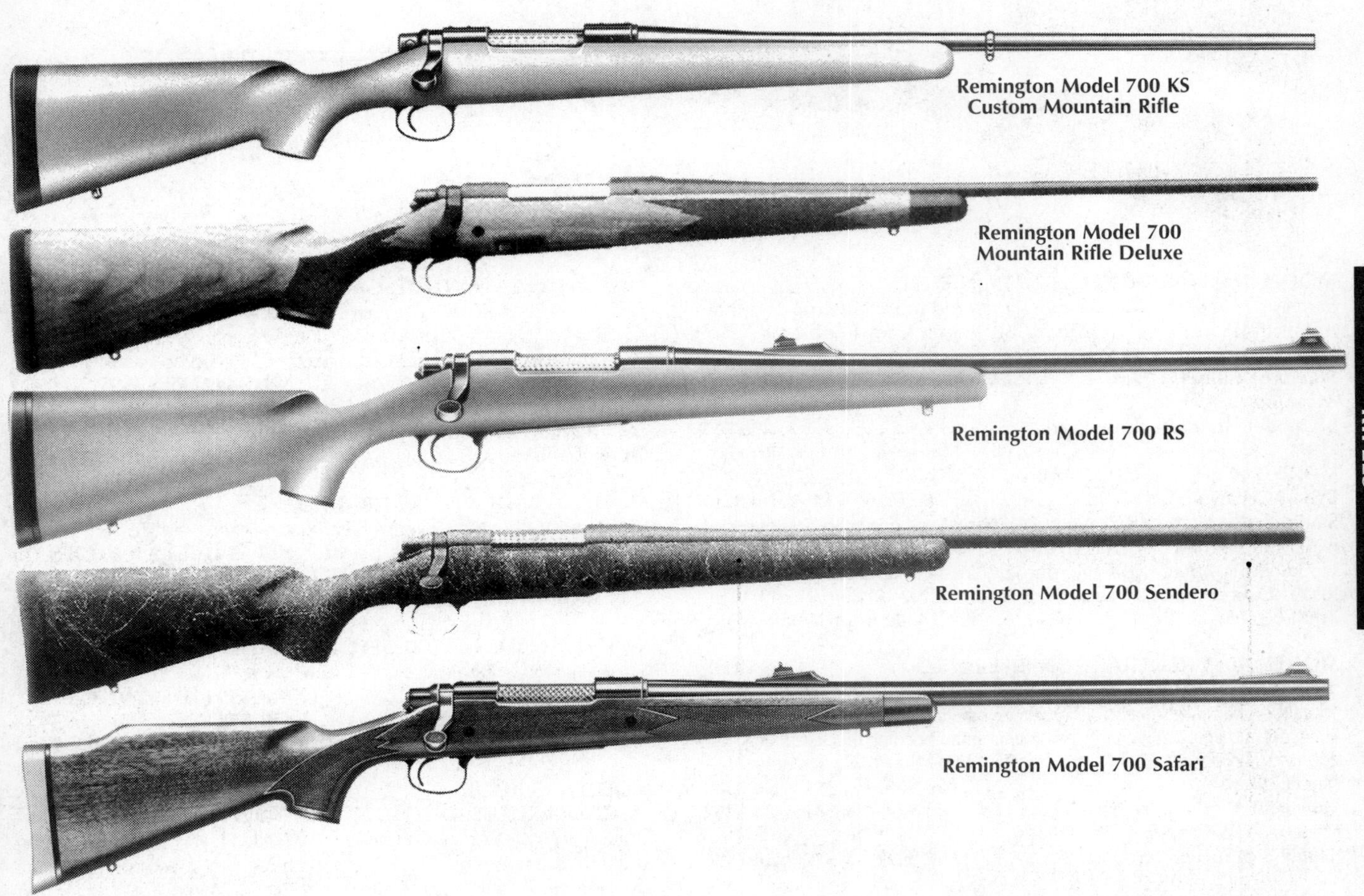

Remington Model 700 KS Custom Mountain Rifle

Remington Model 700 Mountain Rifle Deluxe

Remington Model 700 RS

Remington Model 700 Sendero

Remington Model 700 Safari

MODEL 700 LS BOLT-ACTION RIFLE

Similar to Model 700 ADL except with checkered Monte Carlo-style laminated wood stock with alternating grain and wood color, impregnated with phenolic resin and finished with a low satin luster. Made from 1988-93

Standard calibers . . . . NiB $591 Ex $488 Gd $316
Magnum calibers . . . . NiB $617 Ex $498 Gd $360

MODEL 700 LSS BOLT-ACTION RIFLE

Similar to Model 700 BDL except with stainless steel barrel and action. Checkered Monte Carlo-style laminated wood stock with alternating grain and gray tinted color impregnated with phenolic resin and finished with a low satin luster. Made from 1996 to date.

Standard calibers . . . . NiB $591 Ex $514 Gd $360
Magnum calibers . . . . NiB $643 Ex $566 Gd $385

MODEL 700 MOUNTAIN RIFLE

Lightweight version of Model 700. Calibers: .243 Win., .25-06, .257 Roberts, .270 Win., 7x57, 7mm-08 Rem., .280 Rem., .30-06 and .308 Win. Four round magazine. 22-inch bbl. Weight: 6.75 lbs. Satin blue or stainless finish. Checkered walnut stock and redesigned pistol grip, straight comb, contoured cheekpiece, Old English-style recoil pad and satin oil finish or black synthetic stock with pressed checkering and blind magazine. Made from 1986. Disc.

Standard w/blind magazine . . . . NiB $488 Ex $385 Gd $247
Standard w/hinged floorplate (disc. 1994) . NiB $548 Ex $458 Gd $342
DM Model (New 1995). . . . . NiB $602 Ex $488 Gd $334
SS Model stainless synthetic (disc. 1993) . . NiB $499 Ex $385 Gd $282

MODEL 700 RS BOLT-ACTION RIFLE

Similar to the Model 700 BDL except with straight comb DuPont Rynite stock finished in gray or gray camo with Old English style recoil pad. Made from 1987-90.

Standard calibers . . . . NiB $591 Ex $488 Gd $334
Magnum calibers. NiB $617 Ex $488 Gd $360
.280 Rem. calibers (Limited production). . . NiB $734 Ex $591 Gd $410

MODEL 700 SAFARI GRADE

Big game heavy magnum version of the Model 700 BDL. 8mm Rem. Mag., .375 H&H Mag., .416 Rem. Mag. and .458 Win. Mag. 24-inch heavy bbl. Weight: 9 lbs. Blued or stainless finish. Checkered walnut stock in synthetic/Kevlar stock with standard matte or wood-grain finish with old English style recoil pad. Made from 1962 to date.

Safari Classic/Monte Carlo . . . . NiB $1102 Ex $973 Gd $535
Safari KS (Kevlar stock) intro. 1989 . . . . NiB $1276 Ex $1071 Gd $809
Safari KS (Wood-grain) intro. 1992. . . . . . NiB $1197 Ex $978 Gd $698
Safari KS SS (Stainless) intro. 1993 . . . . . NiB $1481 Ex $1235 Gd $922
Safari left-hand, add $95

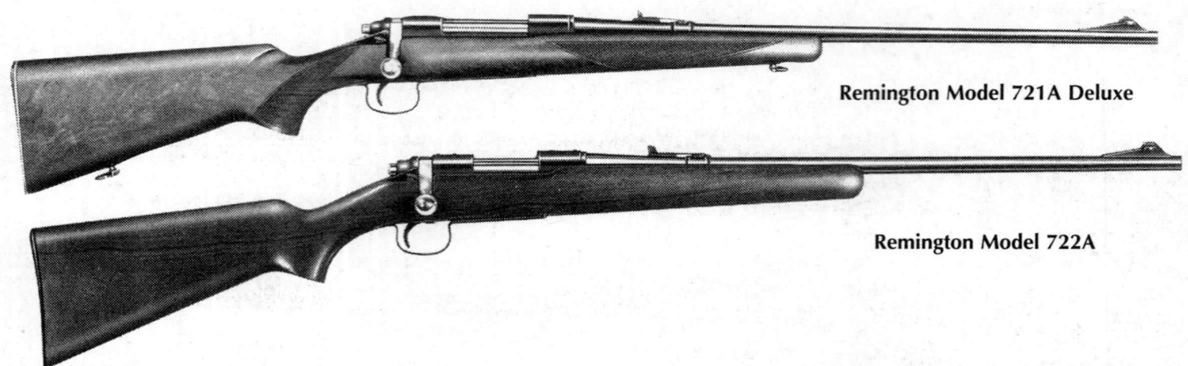

Remington Model 721A Deluxe

Remington Model 722A

MODEL 700 SENDERO BOLT-ACTION RIFLE
Same as Model 700 VS except chambered in long action and magnum .25-06 Rem., .270 Win., .280 Rem., 7mm Rem. Mag., .300 Win. Made from 1994 to date.
Standard calibers. . . . . NiB $697 Ex $594 Gd $363
Magnum calibers, add $30
SF Model (stainless fluted), add. $115

MODEL 700 VLS (VARMINT LAMINATED STOCK) BOLT-ACTION RIFLE. . . . . NiB $620 Ex $491 Gd $337
Same as Model 700 BDL Varmint Special except with 26-inch polished blue barrel. Laminated wood stock with alternating grain and wood color impregnated with phenolic resin and finished with a satin luster. Calibers: .222 Rem., .223 Rem., .22-250 Rem., .243 Win., 7mm-08 Rem., .308 Win. Weight: 9.4 lbs. Made from 1995 to date.

MODEL 700 VS BOLT-ACTION RIFLE
Same as Model 700 BDL Varmint Special except w/26-inch matte blue or fluted stainless barrel. Textured black or gray synthetic stock reinforced with Kevlar, fiberglass and graphite with full length aluminum bedding block. Calibers: .22-250 Rem., .220 Swift, .223 Rem., .308 Win. Made from 1992 to date.
Model 700 VS . . . . NiB $697 Ex $517 Gd $388
Model 700 VS SF (fluted barrel) . . . . NiB $743 Ex $615 Gd $452
Model 700 VS SF/SF-P (Fluted & ported barrel) . . . . NiB $912 Ex $777 Gd $604

MODEL 720A BOLT-ACTION HIGH POWER . . . . NiB $1356 Ex $1176 Gd $1021
Modified M/1917 Enfield action. .257 Roberts, .270 Win., .30-06. Five round box magazine. 22-inch bbl. Weight: About 8 lbs. Sights: Open rear; bead front, on ramp. Pistol-grip stock, checkered. Model 720R has 20-inch bbl.; Model 720S has 24-inch bbl. Made in 1941.

MODEL 721A STANDARD GRADE BOLT-ACTION HIGH-POWER RIFLE . . . . . NiB $435 Ex $383 Gd $322
Calibers: .270 Win., .30-06. Four round box magazine. 24-inch bbl. Weight: About 7.25 lbs. Sights: Open rear; bead front, on ramp. Plain sporting stock. Made from 1948-62.

MODEL 721A MAGNUM STANDARD GRADE . . . . NiB $589 Ex $461 Gd $383
Caliber: .264 Win. Mag. or .300 H&H Mag. Same as standard model except has 26-inch bbl. Three round magazine and recoil pad. Weight: 8.25 lbs.

MODEL 721ADL/BDL DELUXE
Same as Model 721A Standard or Magnum except has deluxe checkered stock and/or select wood.
Model 721ADL Deluxe Grade. . . . . NiB $672 Ex $594 Gd $466
Model 721ADL .300 Magnum Deluxe . . . . NiB $794 Ex $672 Gd $515
Model 721BDL Deluxe Special Grade . . . . NiB $679 Ex $569 Gd $428
Model 721BDL .300 Magnum Deluxe. . . . . NiB $752 Ex $636 Gd $487

MODEL 722A STANDARD GRADE SPORTER
Same as Model 721A bolt-action except shorter action. .222 Rem. mag., .243 Win., .257 Roberts, .308 Win., .300 Savage. Four or 5-round magazine. Weight: 7-8 lbs. .222 Rem. introduced 1950; .244 Rem. introduced 1955. Made from 1948-62.
.222 Rem. . . . . NiB $442 Ex $359 Gd $252
.244 Rem. . . . . NiB $404 Ex $328 Gd $232
.222 Rem. Mag. & .243 Win. . . . . . . NiB $407 Ex $410 Gd $287
Other Calibers. . . . . NiB $436 Ex $359 Gd $230

MODEL 722ADL DELUXE GRADE
Same as Model 722A except has deluxe checkered stock.
Standard calibers. . . . . NiB $591 Ex $488 Gd $334
.222 Rem. Deluxe Grade. . . . . NiB $643 Ex $540 Gd $411
.244 Rem. Deluxe Grade. . . . . NiB $759 Ex $672 Gd $414

MODEL 722BDL DELUXE SPECIAL GRADE
Same as Model 722ADL except select wood.
Standard calibers. . . . . NiB $591 Ex $540 Gd $437
.222 Rem. Deluxe Special Grade. . . NiB $591 Ex $540 Gd $437
.224 Rem. Deluxe Special Grade. . . NiB $606 Ex $538 Gd $414

MODEL 725 KODIAK MAGNUM RIFLE. . . . . NiB $4227 Ex $3506 Gd $2167
Similar to Model 725ADL. Calibers: .375 H&H Mag., .458 Win. Mag. Three round magazine. 26-inch bbl. with recoil reducer built into muzzle. Weight: About 9 lbs. Deluxe, reinforced Monte Carlo stock with recoil pad, black forend tip swivels, sling. Fewer than 100 made in 1961.

MODEL 725ADL BOLT-ACTION REPEATING RIFLE
Calibers: .222, .243, .244, .270, .280, .30-06. Four round box mag. (5-round in 222). 22-inch bbl. (24-inch in .222). Weight: About 7 lbs. Sights: Open rear, hooded ramp front. Monte Carlo comb stock w/pistol-grip, checkered, swivels. Made from 1958-61.
.222 Rem., .243 Win., .244 Rem . . . NiB $779 Ex $630 Gd $441
.270 Win.. NiB $789 Ex $604 Gd $398
.280 Win.. NiB $862 Ex $733 Gd $450
.30-06 . . . . NiB $630 Ex $501 Gd $398

MODEL 788 CENTERFIRE BOLT-ACTION
Calibers: .222 Rem., .22-250, .223 Rem., 6mm Rem., .243 Win., 7mm-08 Rem., .308 Win., .30-30, .44 Rem. Mag. Three round clip magazine (4-round in .222 and .223 Rem.). 24-inch bbl. in .22s, 22-inch in other calibers. Weight: 7.5 lbs. with 24-inch bbl.; 7.25 lbs. with 22-inch bbl. Sights: Blade front on ramp; U-notch rear. Plain Monte Carlo stock. Made from 1967-84.
.22-250, .223 Rem., 6mm Rem., .243 Win., .308 Win.. . . . . NiB $409 Ex $306 Gd $219
.30-30 Win.. . . . . NiB $472 Ex $389 Gd $282
7mm-08 Rem.. . . . . NiB $474 Ex $383 Gd $268
.44 Mag. . . . . NiB $518 Ex $420 Gd $293
Left-hand (6mm Rem. and .308 Win. 1972-79). . . . . NiB $419 Ex $348 Gd $254

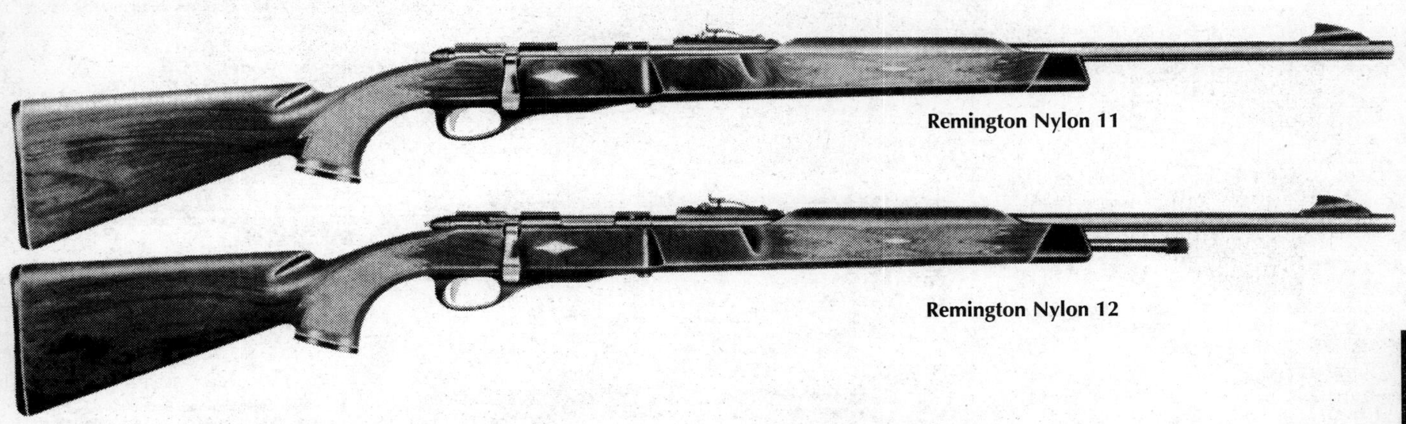

Remington Nylon 11

Remington Nylon 12

NYLON 11 BOLT-ACTION REPEATER .... NiB $282 Ex $179 Gd $118
Clip type. Caliber: .22 Short, Long, LR. Six- or 10-round clip mag. 19.63-inch bbl. Weight: 4.5 lbs. Sights: Open rear; blade front. Nylon stock. Made from 1962-66.

NYLON 12 BOLT-ACTION REPEATER .... NiB $282 Ex $179 Gd $118
Same as Nylon 11 except has tubular magazine holding 22 Short, 17 Long, 15 LR. Made from 1962-66.

SLIDE- AND LEVER-ACTION RIFLES

MODEL SIX (6) SLIDE-ACTION REPEATER .... NiB $443 Ex $360 Gd $253
Hammerless. Calibers: 6mm Rem., .243 Win., .270 Win. 7mm Express Rem., .30-06, .308 Win. 22-inch bbl. Weight: 7.5 lbs. Checkered Monte Carlo stock and forearm. Made from 1981-88.

MODEL SIX (6) SLIDE-ACTION REPEATER, PEERLESS GRADE .... NiB $1848 Ex $1591 Gd $973
Same as Model Six Standard except has engraved receiver. Made from 1981-88.

MODEL SIX (6) SLIDE-ACTION REPEATER, PREMIUM GRADES
Same as Model Six Standard except has engraved receiver with gold inlay. Made from 1981-88.

Peerless D Grade .... NiB $1863 Ex $1657 Gd $1014
Premier F Grade .... NiB $4290 Ex $3452 Gd $2381
Premier Gold F Grade .... NiB $6021 Ex $4818 Gd $3324

MODEL 12A, 12B, 12C, 12CS SLIDE-ACTION REPEATERS
Standard Grade. Hammerless. Takedown. Caliber: .22 Short, Long or LR. Tubular magazine holds 15 Short, 12 Long or 10 LR cartridges. 22- or 24-inch round or octagonal bbl. Open rear sight, bead front. Plain, half-pistol-grip stock and grooved slide handle of walnut. Made from 1909-36.

Model 12A .... NiB $540 Ex $334 Gd $231
Model 12B (22 Short only w/octagon bbl.) .... NiB $669 Ex $514 Gd $334
Model 12C (w/24-inch octagon bbl.) .... NiB $566 Ex $488 Gd $308
Model 12CS (22 WRF w/24-inch octagon bbl.) .... NiB $540 Ex $411 Gd $282

MODEL 14A HIGH POWER SLIDE-ACTION REPEATING RIFLE .... NiB $576 Ex $437 Gd $385
Standard grade. Hammerless. Takedown. Calibers: .25, .30, .32 and .35 Rem. Five round tubular magazine. 22-inch bbl. Weight: About 6.75 lbs. Sights: Open rear; bead front. Plain half-pistol-grip stock and grooved slide handle of walnut. Made from 1912-35.

MODEL 14R CARBINE .... NiB $910 Ex $730 Gd $447
Same as Model 14R except has 18.5-inch bbl., straight-grip stock, weight: About 6 lbs.

MODEL 14.5 CARBINE .... NiB $910 Ex $704 Gd $421
Same as Model 14A Rifle previously listed, except has 9-round magazine, 18.5-inch bbl.

MODEL 14.5 RIFLE .... NiB $1017 Ex $734 Gd $502
Similar to Model 14A except calibers: .38-40 and .44-40, 11-round full magazine, 22.5-inch bbl. Made from 1912 to early 1920's.

MODEL 25A SLIDE-ACTION REPEATER .... NiB $914 Ex $554 Gd $425
Standard Grade. Hammerless. Takedown. Calibers: .25-20, .32-20. 10-round tubular magazine. 24-inch bbl. Weight: About 5.5 lbs. Sights: Open rear; bead front. Plain, pistol-grip stock, grooved slide handle. Made from 1923-36.

MODEL 25R CARBINE .... NiB $968 Ex $580 Gd $451
Same as Model 25A except has 18-inch bbl. Six round magazine, straight-grip stock, weight: About 4.5 lbs.

MODEL 121A FIELDMASTER SLIDE-ACTION REPEATER........ NiB $591 Ex $437 Gd $282
Standard Grade. Hammerless. Takedown. Caliber: .22 Short, Long, LR. Tubular magazine holds 20 Short, 15 Long or 14 LR cartridges. 24-inch round bbl. Weight: 6 lbs. Plain, pistol-grip stock and grooved semi-beavertail slide handle. Made from 1936-54.

MODEL 121S.................. NiB $572 Ex $463 Gd $323
Same as Model 121A except chambered for .22 Remington Special (.22 W.R.F.). Magazine holds 12 rounds. Disc.

MODEL 121SB .... NiB $663 Ex $535 Gd $372
Same as Model 121A except smoothbore. Disc.

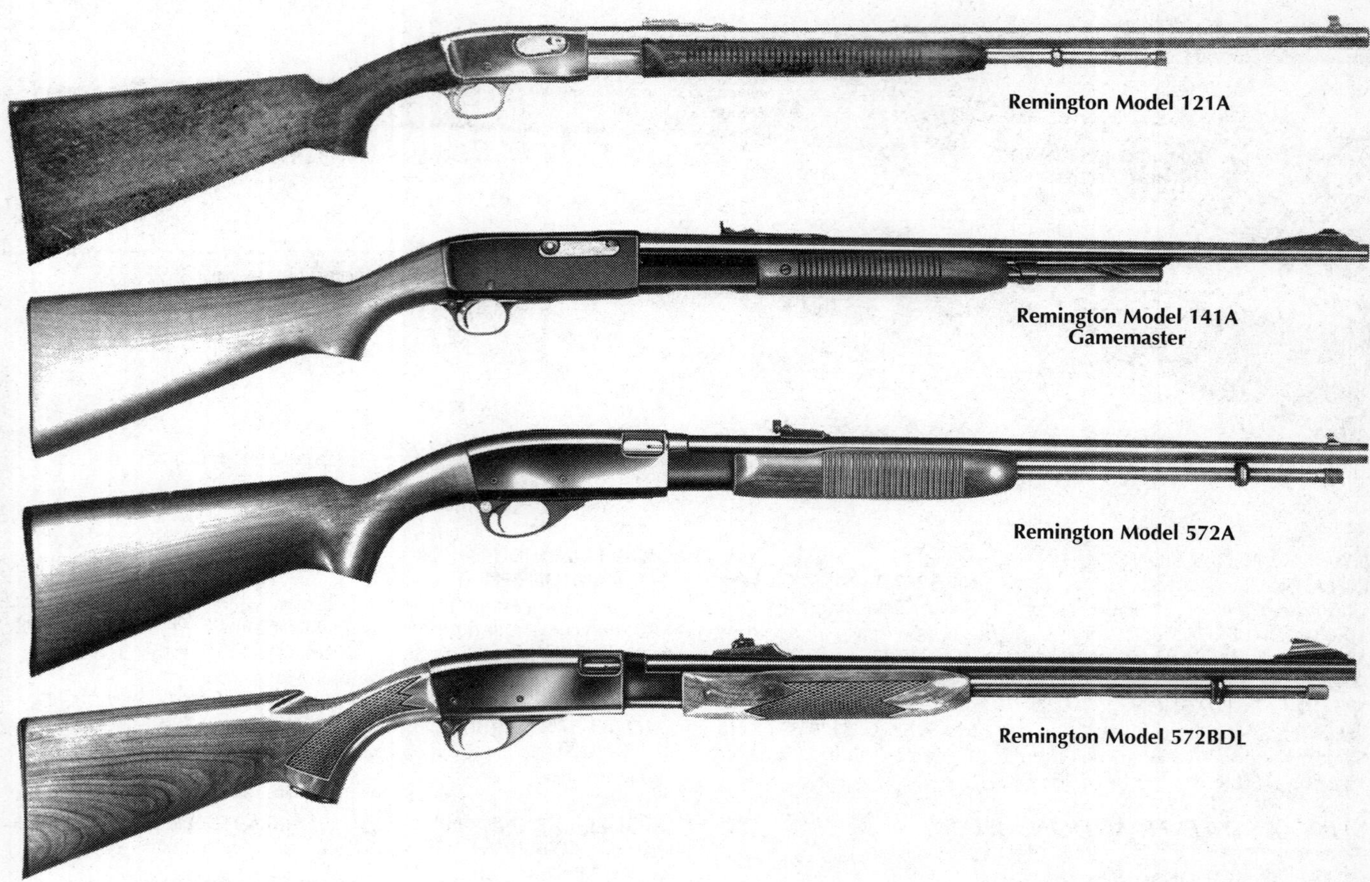

Remington Model 121A

Remington Model 141A Gamemaster

Remington Model 572A

Remington Model 572BDL

MODEL 141A GAMEMASTER SLIDE-ACTION REPEATER........ NiB $437 Ex $308 Gd $221
Standard Grade. Hammerless. Takedown. Calibers: .30, .32 and .35 Rem. Five round tubular magazine. 24-inch bbl. Weight: About 7.75 lbs. Sights: Open rear; bead front, on ramp. Plain, pistol-grip stock, semibeavertail forend (slide-handle). Made from 1936-50.

MODEL 572A FIELDMASTER SLIDE-ACTION REPEATER........ NiB $278 Ex $150 Gd $114
Hammerless. Caliber: .22 Short, Long, LR. Tubular magazine holds 20 Short, 17 Long, 15 LR. 23-inch bbl. Weight: About 5.5 lbs. Sights: Open rear; ramp front. Pistol-grip stock, grooved forearm. Made from 1955-88.

MODEL 572BDL DELUXE........ NiB $330 Ex $227 Gd $124
Same as Model 572A except has blade ramp front sight, sliding ramp rear; checkered stock and forearm. Made from 1966 to date.

MODEL 572SB SMOOTH BORE... NiB $343 Ex $278 Gd $196
Same as Model 572A except smoothbore for .22 LR shot cartridges. Made from 1961 to date.

MODEL 760 BICENTENNIAL COMMEMORATIVE............. NiB $750 Ex $544 Gd $415
Same as Model 760 except has commemorative inscription on receiver. Made in 1976.

MODEL 760 CARBINE .... NiB $591 Ex $473 Gd $231
Same as Model 760 Rifle except made in calibers .270 Win., .280 Rem., .30-06 and .308 Win. only, has 18.5-inch bbl., weight: 7.25 lbs. Made from 1961-80.

MODEL 760 GAMEMASTER STANDARD GRADE SLIDE-ACTION REPEATING RIFLE
Hammerless. Calibers: .223 Rem., 6mm Rem., .243 Win., .257 Roberts, .270 Win. .280 Rem., .30-06, .300 Sav., .308 Win., .35 Rem. 22-inch bbl. Weight: About 7.5 lbs. Sights: Open rear; bead front, on ramp. Plain pistol-grip stock, grooved slide handle on early models; current production has checkered stock and slide handle. Made from 1952-80.

.222 Rem. .... NiB $1260 Ex $977 Gd $616
.223 Rem. .... NiB $1440 Ex $1069 Gd $668
.257 Roberts .... NiB $957 Ex $735 Gd $452
Other calibers .... NiB $915 Ex $761 Gd $272

MODEL 760ADL DELUXE GRADE.................... NiB $5012 Ex $409 Gd $280
Same as Model 760 except has deluxe checkered stock, standard or high comb, grip cap, sling swivels. Made from 1953-63.

MODEL 760BDL CUSTOM DELUXE .... NiB $493 Ex $399 Gd $268
Same as Model 760 Rifle except made in calibers .270, .30-06 and .308 only, has Monte Carlo cheekpiece stock forearm with black tip, basket-weave checkering. Available also in left-hand model. Made from 1953-80.

MODEL 760D PEERLESS GRADE.................. NiB $1330 Ex $1073 Gd $815
Same as Model 760 except scroll engraved, fancy wood. Made from 1953-80.

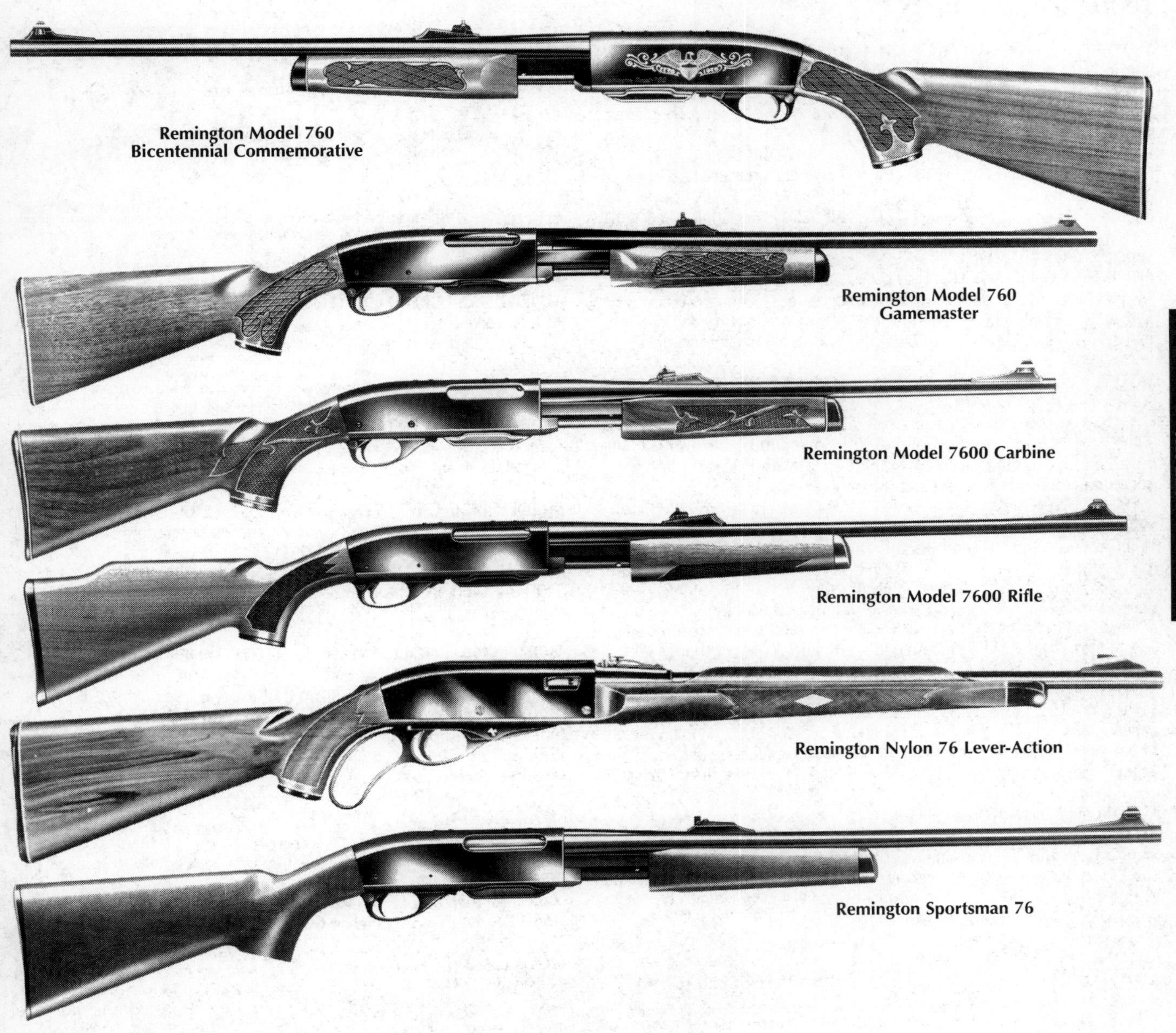

Remington Model 760
Bicentennial Commemorative

Remington Model 760
Gamemaster

Remington Model 7600 Carbine

Remington Model 7600 Rifle

Remington Nylon 76 Lever-Action

Remington Sportsman 76

MODEL 760F PREMIER GRADE
Same as Model 760 except extensively engraved with game scenes and scroll, finest grade wood. Also available with receiver inlaid with gold; adds 50 percent to value. Made from 1953-80.
Premier F Grade . . . . **NiB $2601 Ex $2098 Gd $1456**
Premier Gold F Grade . . . . **NiB $6034 Ex $4848 Gd $3334**

MODEL 7600 SLIDE-ACTION CARBINE . . . . **NiB $540 Ex $360 Gd $257**
Same general specifications as Model 7600 Rifle except has 18.5-inch bbl. and weighs 7.25 lbs. Made from 1987 to date.

MODEL 7600 SLIDE-ACTION RIFLE . . . . . . **NiB $514 Ex $416 Gd $252**
Similar to Model Six except has lower grade finishes. Made from 1981 to date.

MODEL 7600 SPECIAL PURPOSE . . . . **NiB $488 Ex $385 Gd $231**
Same general specification as the Model 7600, except chambered only in .270 or .30-06. Special Purpose matte black finish on all exposed metal. American walnut stock with SP non-glare finish.

NYLON 76 LEVER-ACTION REPEATER . . . . **NiB $332 Ex $280 Gd $177**
Short-throw lever action. Caliber: .22 LR. 14-round buttstock tubular magazine. Weight: 4 lbs. Black or brown nylon stock and forend. Made 1962-64. Remington's only lever-action rifle.

SPORTSMAN 76 SLIDE-ACTION RIFLE . . . **NiB $322 Ex $255 Gd $177**
Caliber: .30-06, 4-round magazine. 22-inch bbl. Weight: 7.5 lbs. Open rear sight; front blade mounted on ramp. Uncheckered hardwood stock and forend. Made from 1985-87.

SEMIAUTOMATIC RIFLES

MODEL FOUR (4) AUTOLOADING RIFLE
Hammerless. Calibers: 6mm Rem., .243 Win., .270 Win. 7mm Express Rem., .30-06, .308 Win. 22-inch bbl. Weight: 7.5 lbs. Sights: Open rear; bead front, on ramp. Monte Carlo checkered stock and forearm. Made from 1981-88.
Standard .... NiB $746 Ex $617 Gd $282
Peerless Grade (Engr. receiver) .... NiB $2123 Ex $1217 Gd $835
Premier Grade (Engr. receiver) .... NiB $3872 Ex $3101 Gd $2139
Prem. Gr. (Engr. rec., gold inlay)..... NiB $6349 Ex $5095 Gd $3497

MODEL FOUR DIAMOND ANNIVERSARY LTD. EDITION $1065
Same as Model Four Standard except has engraved receiver w/inscription, checkered high-grade walnut stock and forend. Only 1,500 produced. Made in 1981 only. (Value for new condition.)

MODEL 8A AUTOLOADING RIFLE ...... NiB $802 Ex $648 Gd $895
Standard Grade. Takedown. Calibers: .25, .30, .32 and .35 Rem. Five-round, clip-loaded magazine. 22-inch bbl. Weight: 7.75 lbs. Sights: Adj. and dovetailed open rear; dovetailed bead front. Half-moon metal buttplate on plain straight-grip walnut stock; plain walnut forearm with thin curved end. Made from 1906-1936.

MODEL 16 AUTOLOADING RIFLE....... NiB $437 Ex $334 Gd $205
Takedown. Closely resembles the Winchester Model 03 semiautomatic rifle. Calibers: .22 Short, .22 LR, 22 Rem. Auto. 15-round tubular magazine in buttstock. 22-inch bbl. Weight: 5.75 lbs. Sights: Open rear; dovetailed bead front. Plain straight-grip stock and forearm. Made from 1914-1928. Note: In 1918 this model was discontinued in all calibers except .22 Rem. Auto; specifications are for that model.

MODEL 24A AUTOLOADING RIFLE ..... NiB $437 Ex $308 Gd $205
Standard Grade. Takedown. Calibers: .22 Short only, .22 LR. only. Tubular magazine in buttstock, holds 15 Short or 10 LR. 21-inch bbl. Weight: About 5 lbs. Sights: Dovetailed adj. open rear; dovetailed bead front. Plain walnut straight-grip buttstock; plain walnut forearm. Made from 1922-35.

MODEL 81A WOODSMASTER AUTOLOADER .... NiB $566 Ex $437 Gd $257
Standard Grade. Takedown. Calibers: .30, .32 and .35 Rem., .300 Sav. Five round box magazine (not detachable). 22-inch bbl. Weight: 8.25 lbs. Sights: Open rear; bead front. Plain walnut pistol-grip stock, forearm. Made from 1936-50.

MODEL 241A SPEEDMASTER AUTOLOADER .... NiB $330 Ex $278 Gd $175
Standard Grade. Takedown. Calibers: .22 Short only, .22 LR. only. Tubular magazine in buttstock, holds 15 Short or 10 LR. 24-inch bbl. Weight: About 6 lbs. Sights: Open rear, bead front. Plain walnut stock and forearm. Made from 1935-51.

MODEL 550A AUTOLOADER..... NiB $253 Ex $175 Gd $100
Has "Power Piston" or floating chamber, which permits interchangeable use of 22 Short, Long or LR cartridges. Tubular magazine holds 22 Short, 17 Long, 15 LR. 24-inch bbl. Weight: About 6.25 lbs. Sights: Open rear; bead front. Plain, one-piece pistol-grip stock. Made from 1941-71.

MODEL 550P .... NiB $253 Ex $175 Gd $100
Same as Model 550A except has peep rear sight, blade front, on ramp.

MODEL 550-2G .... NiB $330 Ex $253 Gd $150
"Gallery Special." Same as Model 550A except has 22-inch bbl., screw eye for counter chain and fired shell deflector.

Remington Sportsman 742 Canadian Centennial

MODEL 552A SPEEDMASTER AUTOLOADER .... NiB $257 Ex $179 Gd $102
Caliber: .22 Short, Long, LR. Tubular magazine holds 20 Short, 17 Long, 15 LR. 25-inch bbl. Weight: About 5.5 lbs. Sights: Open rear; bead front. Pistol-grip stock, semi-beavertail forearm. Made from 1957-88.

MODEL 552BDL DELUXE........ NiB $324 Ex $221 Gd $154
Same as Model 552A except has checkered walnut stock and forearm. Made from 1966 to date.

MODEL 552C CARBINE .... NiB $282 Ex $179 Gd $128
Same as Model 552A except has 21-inch bbl. Made from 1961-77.

MODEL 552GS GALLERY SPECIAL...... NiB $324 Ex $221 Gd $154
Same as Model 552A except chambered for .22 Short only. Made from 1957-77.

MODEL 740A WOODSMASTER AUTOLOADER
Standard Grade. Gas-operated. Calibers: .30-06 or .308. Four round detachable box magazine. 22-inch bbl. Weight: About 7.5 lbs. Plain pistol-grip stock, semibeavertail forend with finger grooves. Sights: Open rear; ramp front. Made from 1955-60.
Rifle model .... NiB $414 Ex $337 Gd $224
Carbine model................. NiB $466 Ex $388 Gd $260

MODEL 740ADL/BDL DELUXE
Same as Model 740A except has deluxe checkered stock, standard or high comb, grip cap, sling swivels. Model 740 BDL also has select wood. Made from 1955-60.
Model 740 ADL Deluxe Grade .... NiB $624 Ex $495 Gd $264
Model 740 BDL Deluxe Special Grade ... NiB $701 Ex $547 Gd $392

MODEL 742 BICENTENNIAL COMMEMORATIVE.............................. $753
Same as Model 742 Woodsmaster rifle except has commemorative inscription on receiver. Made in 1976. (Value for new condition.)

MODEL 742 CANADIAN CENTENNIAL $753
Same as Model 742 rifle except has commemorative inscription on receiver. Made in 1967. Value is for rifle in new, unfired condition.

MODEL 742 CARBINE .... NiB $701 Ex $495 Gd $228
Same as Model 742 Woodsmaster Rifle except made in calibers .30-06 and .308 only, has 18.5-inch bbl., weight 6.75 lbs. Made from 1961-80.

MODEL 742 WOODSMASTER AUTOMATIC BIG GAME RIFLE .... NiB $640 Ex $444 Gd $233
Gas-operated semiautomatic. Calibers: 6mm Rem., .243 Win., .280 Rem., .30-06, .308 Win. Four round clip magazine. 22-inch bbl. Weight: 7.5 lbs. Sights: Open rear; bead front, on ramp. Checkered pistol-grip stock and forearm. Made from 1960-80.

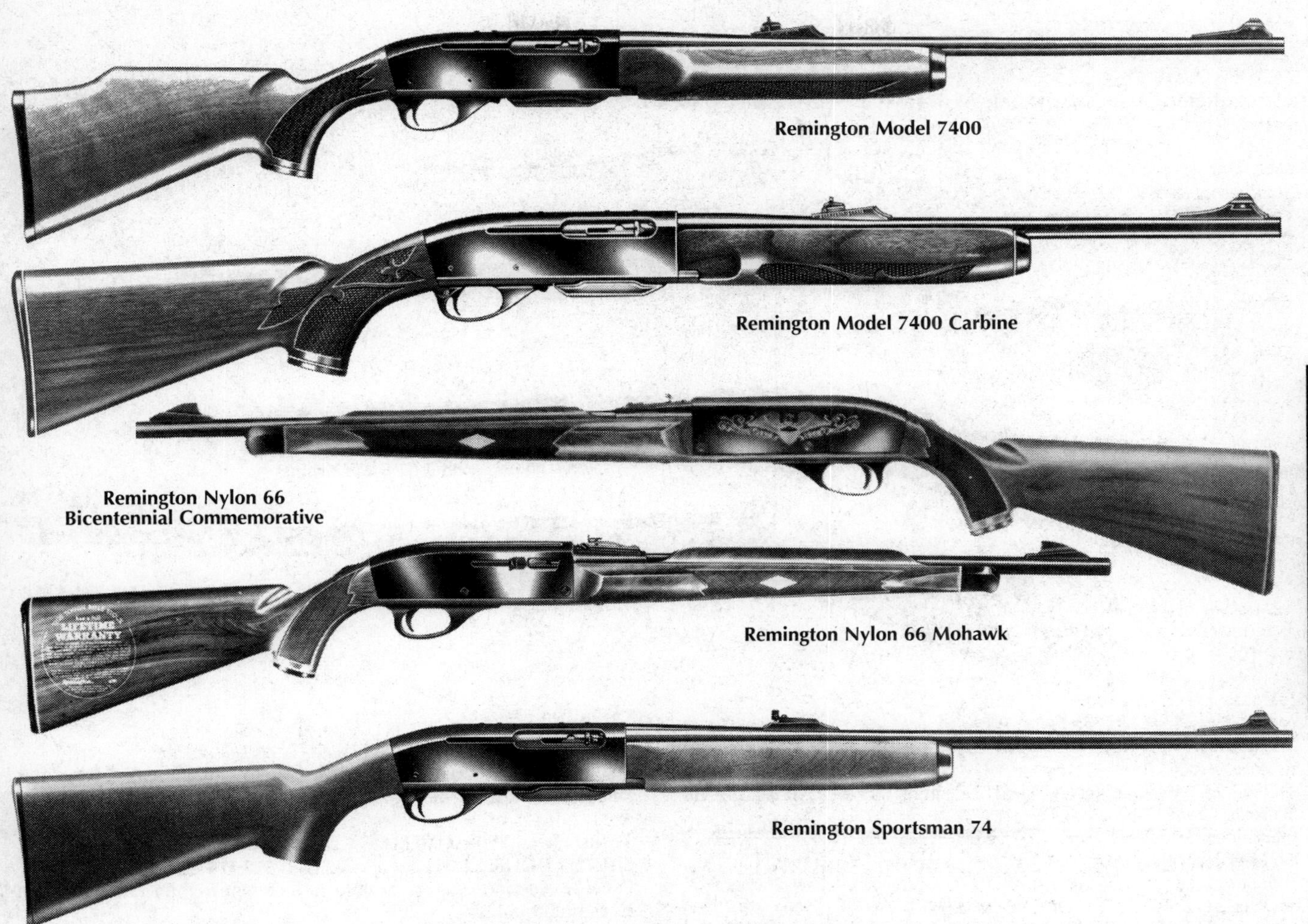

Remington Model 7400

Remington Model 7400 Carbine

Remington Nylon 66 Bicentennial Commemorative

Remington Nylon 66 Mohawk

Remington Sportsman 74

MODEL 742BDL CUSTOM DELUXE...... NiB $591 Ex $488 Gd $257
Same as Model 742 Rifle except made in calibers .30-06 and .308 only, Monte Carlo cheekpiece stock, forearm with black tip, basket-weave checkering. Available in left-hand model. Made from 1966-80.

MODEL 742D PEERLESS GRADE......... NiB $1830 Ex $1521 Gd $980
Same as Model 742 except scroll engraved, fancy wood. Made from 1961-80.

MODEL 742F PREMIER GRADE
Same as Model 742 except extensively engraved with game scenes and scroll, finest grade wood. Also available with receiver inlaid with gold; adds 50 percent to value. Made from 1961-1980.
Premier F Grade .... NiB $3881 Ex $3130 Gd $2158
Premier Gold F Grade........ NiB $6020 Ex $4837 Gd $3323

MODEL 7400 AUTOLOADER
Similar to Model Four w/lower grade finishes. Made from 1981 to date.
Model 7400 Standard .... NiB $463 Ex $385 Gd $226
Model 7400 HG
(High gloss finish).................... NiB $469 Ex $380 Gd $267

MODEL 7400 CARBINE .... NiB $463 Ex $334 Gd $257
Caliber: .30-06 only. Similar to the Model 7400 rifle except has 18.5-inch bbl. and weight: 7.25 lbs. Made from 1988 to date.

MODEL 7400 SPECIAL PURPOSE........ NiB $463 Ex $360 Gd $231
Same general specification as the Model 7400 except chambered only in .270 or .30-06. Special Purpose matte black finish on metal. American walnut stock with SP nonglare finish. Made from 1993-95.

NYLON 66 APACHE BLACK ...... NiB $225 Ex $148 Gd $112
Same as Nylon 66 Mohawk Brown listed below except bbl. and receiver cover chrome-plated, black stock. Made from 1962-84.

NYLON 66 BICENTENNIAL
COMMEMORATIVE .... NiB $245 Ex $173 Gd $122
Same as Nylon 66 Mohawk Brown listed below except has commemorative inscription on receiver. Made 1976 only.

NYLON 66MB AUTOLOADING RIFLE.... NiB $225 Ex $148 Gd $112
Similar to the early production Nylon 66 Black Apache except with blued bbl. and receiver cover. Made from 1978-87.

NYLON 66 MOHAWK
BROWN AUTOLOADER .... NiB $172 Ex $121 Gd $106
Caliber: .22 LR. Tubular magazine in buttstock holds 14 rounds. 19.5-inch bbl. Weight: About 4 lbs. Sights: Open rear; blade front. Brown nylon stock and forearm. Made from 1959-87.

NYLON 77 CLIP REPEATER....... NiB $201 Ex $147 Gd $111
Same as Nylon 66 except has 5-round clip magazine. Made from 1970-71.

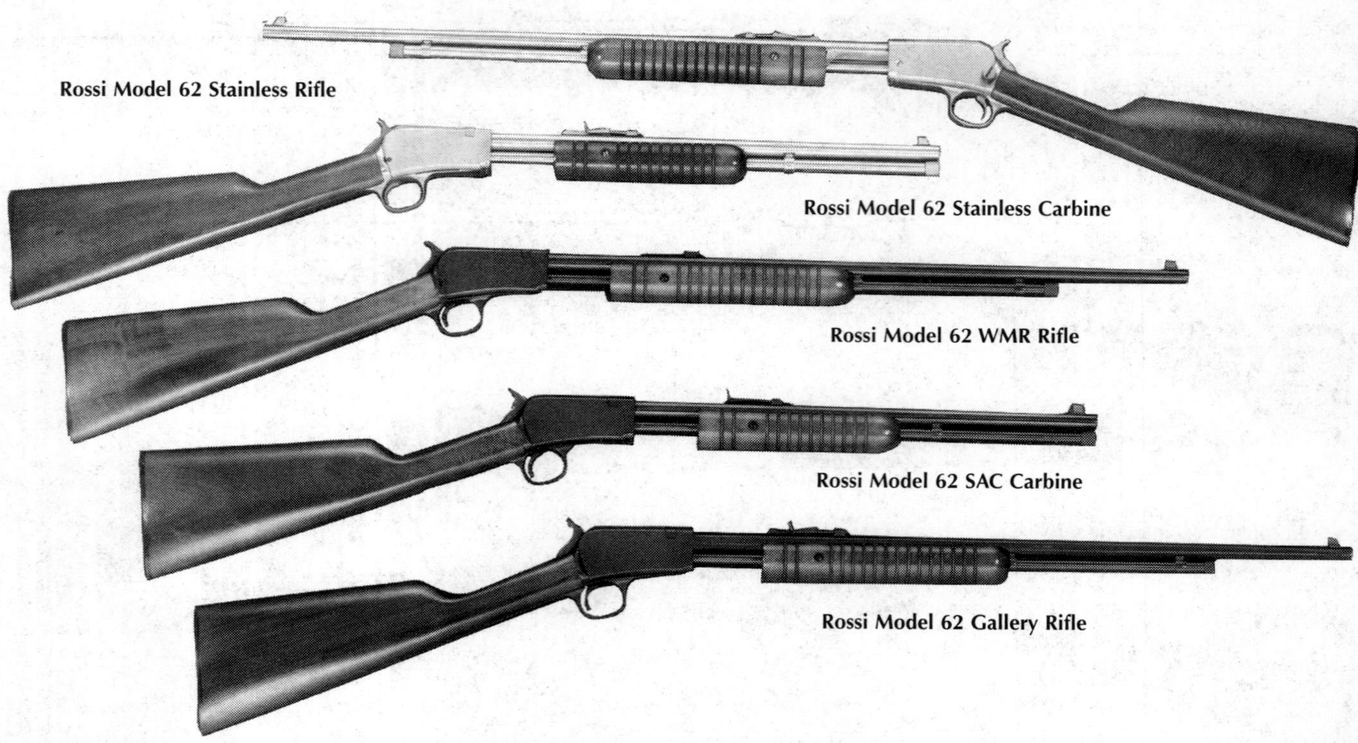
Rossi Model 62 Stainless Rifle

Rossi Model 62 Stainless Carbine

Rossi Model 62 WMR Rifle

Rossi Model 62 SAC Carbine

Rossi Model 62 Gallery Rifle

SPORTSMAN 74 AUTOLOADING RIFLE..... NiB $355 Ex $257 Gd $174
Caliber: .30-06, 4-round magazine. 22-inch bbl. Uncheckered buttstock and forend. Open rear sight; ramped blade front sight. Made from 1985-88.

JOHN RIGBY & CO. — London, England

MODEL 275 MAGAZINE SPORTING RIFLENiB $6250 Ex $5000+ Gd $3400
Mauser action. Caliber: .275 High Velocity or 7x57mm; 5-round box magazine. 25-inch bbl. Weight: about 7.5 lbs. Sights: Folding leaf rear; bead front. Sporting stock w/half-pistol-grip, checkered. Specifications given are those of current model; however, in general, they apply also to prewar model.

MODEL 275 LIGHTWEIGHT
MAGAZINE RIFLE................. NiB $5000 Ex $4000 Gd $2720
Same as standard .275 rifle except has 21-inch bbl. Weight: 6.75 lbs.

MODEL 350 MAGNUM
MAGAZINE SPORTING RIFLE .... NiB $4375 Ex $3500 Gd $2380
Mauser action. Caliber: .350 Magnum. Five round box magazine. 24-inch bbl. Weight: About 7.75 lbs. Sights: Folding leaf rear; bead front. Sporting stock with full pistol-grip, checkered. Currently mfd.

MODEL 416 BIG GAME
MAGAZINE SPORTING RIFLE .... NiB $7500 Ex $6000 Gd $4080
Mauser action. Caliber: .416 Big Game. Four round box magazine. 24-inch bbl. Weight: 9 to 9.25 lbs. Sights: Folding leaf rear; bead front. Sporting stock with full pistol-grip, checkered. Currently mfd.

BEST QUALITY HAMMERLESS
EJECTOR DOUBLE RIFLE....... NiB $48,750 Ex $39,000 Gd $26,520
Sidelocks. Calibers: .275 Magnum, .350 Magnum, .470 Nitro Express. 24- to 28-inch bbls. Weight: 7.5 to 10.5 lbs. Sights: Folding leaf rear; bead front. Checkered pistol-grip stock and forearm.

SECOND QUALITY HAMMERLESS
EJECTOR DOUBLE RIFLE....... NiB $21,875 Ex $17,500 Gd $11,900
Same general specifications as Best Quality double rifle except boxlock.

THIRD QUALITY HAMMERLESS
EJECTOR DOUBLE RIFLE.......... NiB $12,375 Ex $9900 Gd $6732
Same as Second Quality double rifle except plainer finish and not of as high quality.

ROSS RIFLE CO. — Quebec, Canada

MODEL 1910 BOLT-ACTION
SPORTING RIFLE............... NiB $652 Ex $235 Gd $214
Straight-pull bolt-action with interrupted screw-type lugs. Calibers: .280 Ross, .303 British. Four round or 5-round magazine. Bbl. lengths: 22, 24, 26 inches. Sights: Two-leaf open rear; bead front. Checkered sporting stock. Weight: About 7 lbs. Made c. 1910 to end of World War I. Note: Most firearm authorities agree that this and other Ross models with interrupted screw-type lugs are unsafe to fire.

ROSSI RIFLES — Sao Leopoldo, Brazil Manufactured by Amadeo Rossi, S.A.

62 GALLERY MODEL SAC CARBINE
Same as standard Gallery Model except in .22 LR only with 16.25-inch bbl.; weight 5.5 lbs. Imported 1975-98.
Blued finish .... NiB $212 Ex $175 Gd $114
Nickel finish .... NiB $227 Ex $186 Gd $139
Stainless....................... NiB $238 Ex $206 Gd $145

62 GALLERY MODEL MAGNUM .... NiB $217 Ex $186 Gd $124
Same as standard Gallery Model except chambered for .22 WMR, 10-shot magazine. Imported from 1975-98.

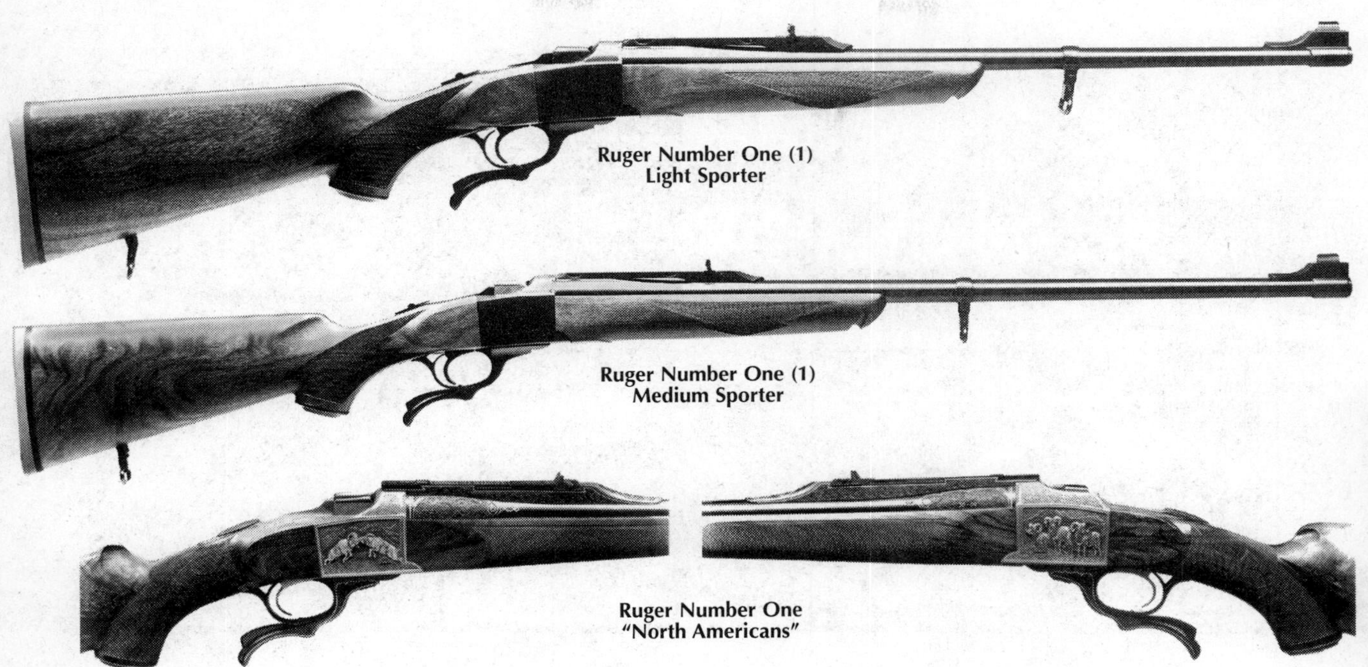

Ruger Number One (1)
Light Sporter

Ruger Number One (1)
Medium Sporter

Ruger Number One
"North Americans"

62 GALLERY MODEL SLIDE-ACTION REPEATER
Similar to Winchester Model 62. Calibers: .22 LR. Long, Short or .22 WMR. Tubular magazine holds 13 LR, 16 Long, 20 Short. 23-inch bbl. 39.25 inches overall. Weight: 5.75 lbs. Sights: Open rear; bead front. Straight-grip stock, grooved slide handle. Blued, nickel or stainless finish. Imported from 1970-98. Values same as SAC Model.

LEVER-ACTION 65/92 CARBINE
Similar to Winchester Model 92. Caliber: .38 Special/.357 Mag., .44 Mag., .44-40, .45 LC. 8- or 10-round magazine. 16-, 20- or 24-inch round or half-octagonal bbl. Weight: 5.5 to 6 lbs. 33.5- to 41.5-inches overall. Satin blue, chrome or stainless finish. Brazilian hardwood buttstock and forearm. Made from 1978-98.
Model M92 SRC .45LC . . . . NiB $383 Ex $306 Gd $219
Model M92 SRC .38/357, .44 Mag . . . . . . NiB $383 Ex $306 Gd $219
Model M92 w/octagon bbl . . . . NiB $409 Ex $229 Gd $224
Model M92 LL Lever . . . . NiB $383 Ex $255 Gd $203
Engraved, add $75
Chrome, add $25
Stainless, add $75

RUGER RIFLES — Southport, Connecticut Manufactured by Sturm, Ruger & Co.

NUMBER ONE (1) LIGHT SPORTER. . . . . . NiB $699 Ex $571 Gd $287
Same as No.1 Standard except has 22-inch bbl., folding leaf rear sight on quarter-rib and ramp front sight, Henry pattern forearm. Made from 1966 to date.

NUMBER ONE (1) MEDIUM SPORTER . . . NiB $648 Ex $519 Gd $313
Same as No. 1 Light Sporter except has 26-inch bbl. 22-inch in 45-70); weight: 8 lbs (7.25 lbs. in .45-70). Calibers: 7mm Rem. Mag., .300 Win. Mag., .45-70. Made from 1966 to date.

NUMBER ONE (1) "NORTH AMERICANS"
PRESENTATION RIFLE $52,570
Same general specifications as the Ruger No. 1 Standard except highly customized with elaborate engravings, carvings, fine-line checkering and gold inlays. This was a series of 21 rifles depicting a North American big-game animal, chambered in the caliber appropriate to the game. Stock is of Northern California English walnut. Comes in trunk-style Huey case with Leupold scope and other accessories.

NUMBER ONE (1) RSI INTERNATIONAL
SINGLE-SHOT RIFLE. . . . . NiB $648 Ex $493 Gd $329
Similar to the No. 1 Light Sporter except with lightweight 20-inch bbl. and full Mannlicher-style forend, in calibers .243 Win., .270 Win., 7x57mm, .30-06. Weight: 7.25 lbs.

NUMBER ONE (1)
SPECIAL VARMINTER . . . . NiB $648 Ex $493 Gd $329
Same as No. 1 Standard except has heavy 24-inch bbl. with target scope bases, no quarter-rib. Weight: 9 lbs. Calibers: .22-250, .25-06, 7mm Rem. Mag., .300 Win. Mag. Made from 1966 to date.

NUMBER ONE (1)
STANDARD RIFLE. . . . . NiB $638 Ex $468 Gd $313
Falling-block single-shot action with Farquharson-type lever. Calibers: .22-250, .243 Win., 6mm Rem., .25-06, .270 Win., .30-06, 7mm Rem. Mag., .300 Win. Mag. 26-inch bbl. Weight: 8 lbs. No sights, has quarter-rib for scope mounting. Checkered pistol-grip buttstock and semibeavertail forearm, QD swivels, rubber buttplate. Made from 1966 to date.

NUMBER ONE (1) TROPICAL RIFLE. . . . . NiB $699 Ex $566 Gd $339
Same as No. 1 Light Sporter except has heavy 24-inch bbl.; calibers are .375 H&H .404 Jeffery, .416 Rigby, and .458 Win. Mag. Weight: 8.25 to 9 lbs. Made from 1966 to date.

NUMBER THREE (3) SINGLE-SHOT
CARBINE . . . . NiB $493 Ex $442 Gd $262
Falling-block action with American-style lever. Calibers: .22 Hornet .223 Rem., .30-40 Krag, .357 Win., .44 Mag., .45-70. 22-inch bbl. Weight: 6 lbs. Sights: Folding leaf rear; gold bead front. Carbine-style stock w/curved buttplate, forearm with bbl. band. Made from 1972-87.

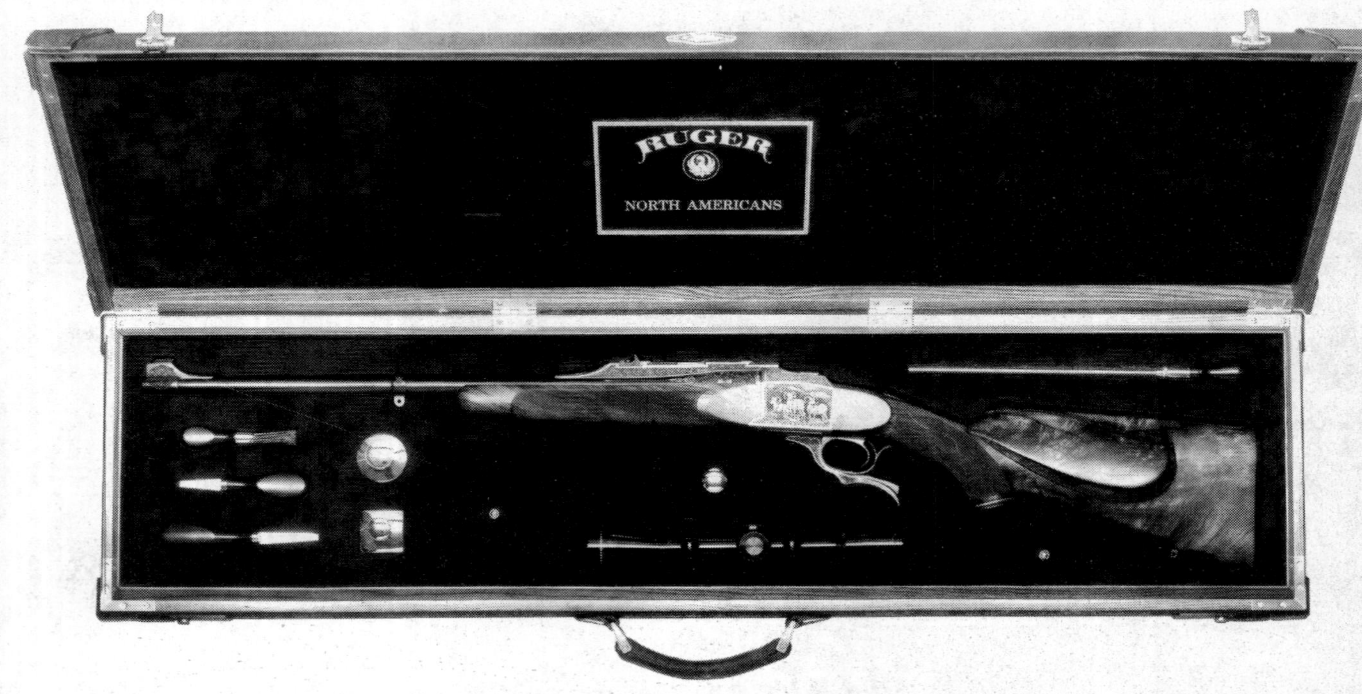

Ruger Number One "North Americans" Presentation Set

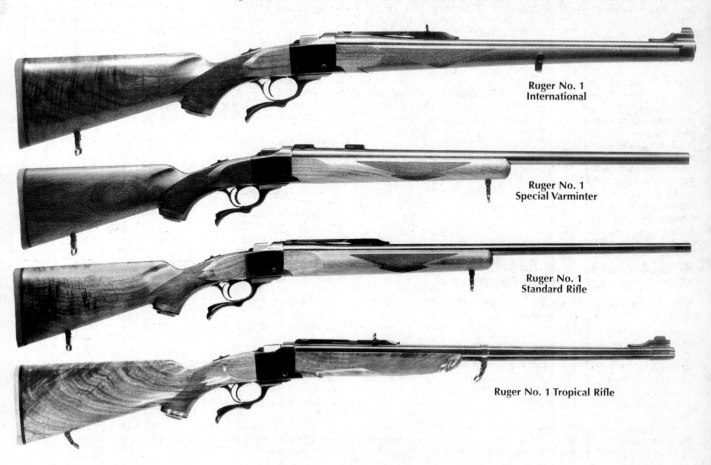

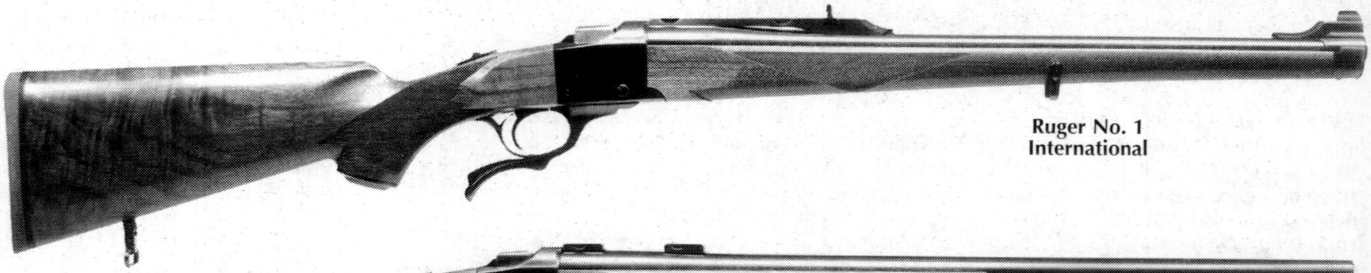

Ruger No. 1
International

Ruger No. 1
Special Varminter

Ruger No. 1
Standard Rifle

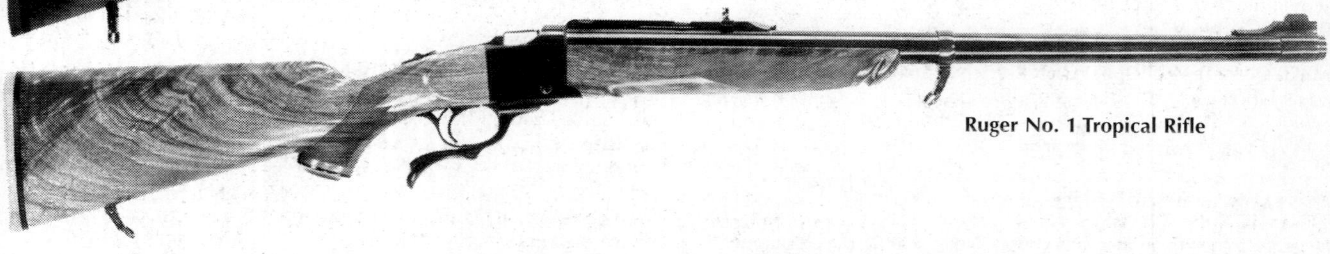

Ruger No. 1 Tropical Rifle

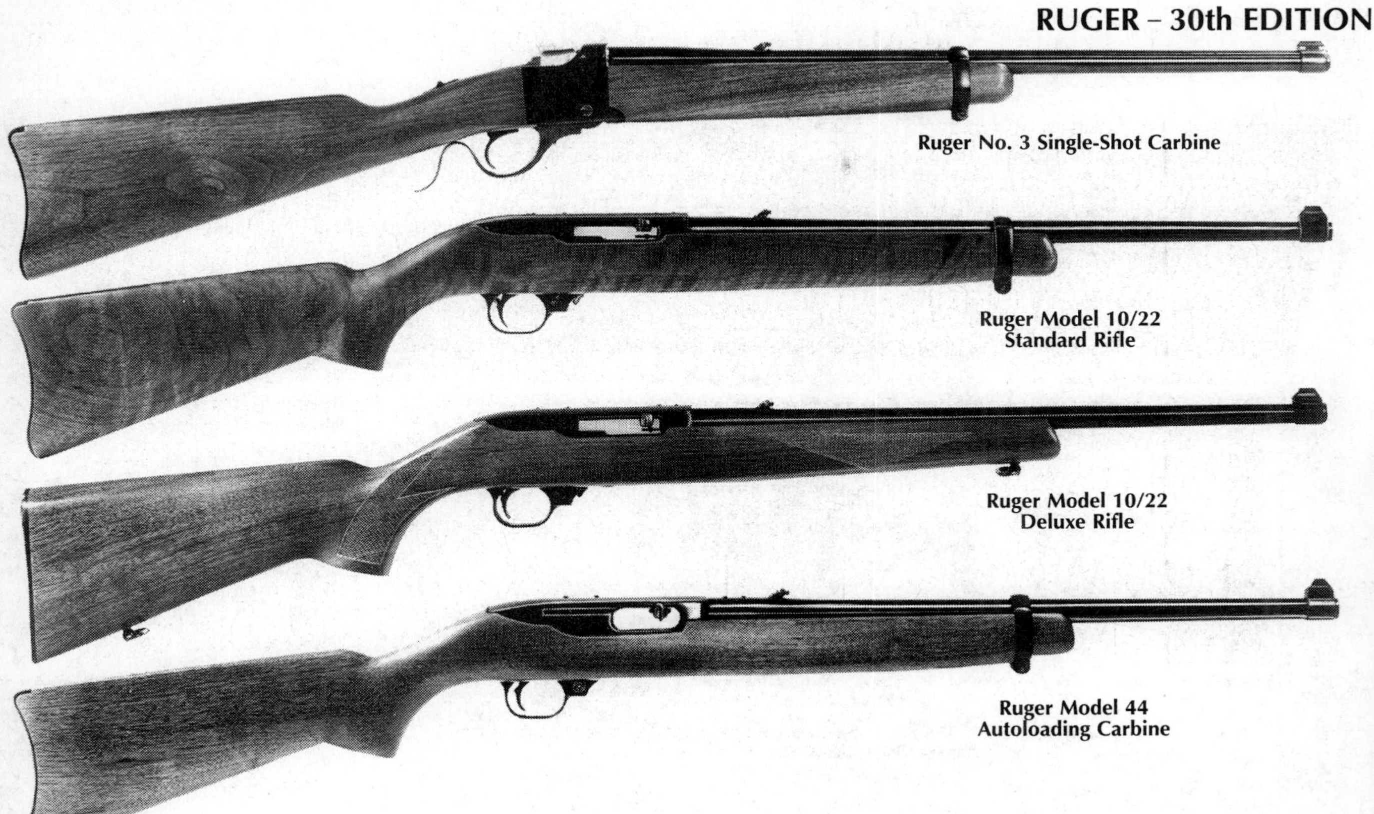

Ruger No. 3 Single-Shot Carbine

Ruger Model 10/22 Standard Rifle

Ruger Model 10/22 Deluxe Rifle

Ruger Model 44 Autoloading Carbine

RIFLES

MODEL 10/22 AUTOLOADING CARBINE

Caliber: .22 LR. Detachable 10-round rotary magazine. 18.5-inch bbl. Weight: 5 lbs. Sights: Folding leaf rear; bead front. Carbine-style stock with bbl. band and curved buttplate (walnut stock discontinued 1980). Made from 1964 to date. International and Sporter versions discontinued 1971.

10/22 Standard Carbine (Walnut stock) .... NiB $285 Ex $224 Gd $131
10/22 Int'l. (w/Mannlicher style stock, swivels) Disc.1971 .... NiB $596 Ex $442 Gd $339
10/22 RB (Birch stock, blued) .... NiB $208 Ex $157 Gd $121
K10/22 RB (Birch stock, stainless) .... NiB $213 Ex $182 Gd $131
10/22 Sporter (MC stock, flat buttplate, swivels) Disc.1971 .... NiB $213 Ex $182 Gd $131
10/22 SP Deluxe Sporter (made since 1966).... NiB $266 Ex $218 Gd $158
10/22 RBI Int'l. (blued); made since 1994... NiB $254 Ex $206 Gd $151
10/22 RBI Int'l. (stainless); made since 1995 .... NiB $279 Ex $229 Gd $165

MODEL 44 AUTOLOADING CARBINE

Gas-operated. Caliber: .44 Magnum. Four round tubular magazine (with magazine release button since 1967). 18.5-inch bbl. Weight: 5.75 lbs. Sights: Folding leaf rear; gold bead front. Carbine-style stock w/bbl. band and curved buttplate. Made from 1961-86. International and Sporter versions discontinued 1971.

Model 44 Standard autoloading carbine... NiB $498 Ex $395 Gd $282
Model 44 Int'l (w/Mannlicher-style stock, swivels).................. NiB $646 Ex $550 Gd $447
Mdl. 44 Sporter (MC stk. w/fingergroove)... NiB $653 Ex $704 Gd $498
Model 44RS Carbine (w/rear peep sight, disc. 1978).......... NiB $601 Ex $447 Gd $339

MODEL 77 BOLT-ACTION RIFLE

Receiver with integral scope mount base or with round top. Short stroke or magnum length action (depending on caliber) in the former type receiver, magnum only in the latter. .22-250, .220 Swift, 6mm Rem., .243 Win., .250-3000, .25-06, .257 Roberts, 6.5 Rem. Mag., .270 Win., 7x57mm, 7mm-08 7mm Rem. Mag., .280 Rem., .284 Win., .308 Win., .30-06, .300 Win. Mag. .338 Win. Mag., .350 Rem. Mag., .458 Win. Mag. Five round magazine standard, 4-round in .220 Swift, 3-round in magnum calibers. 22 24- or 26-inch bbl. (depending on caliber). Weight: About 7 lbs.; .458 Mag. model, 8.75 lbs. Round-top model furnished w/folding leaf rear sight and ramp front; integral base model furnished w/scope rings,with or w/o open sights. Stock w/checkered pistol grip and forearm, pistol-grip cap, rubber recoil pad, QD swivel studs. Made from 1968-92.

Model 77, integral base, no sights .... NiB $496 Ex $424 Gd $239
6.5 Rem. Mag., add $75
.284 Win., add $30
.338 Win. Mag., add $50
.350 Rem. Mag., 6.5 Rem. Mag., add $75
Model 77RL Ultra Light, no sights, ... NiB $496 Ex $393 Gd $265
Model 77RL Ultra Light, open sights, ... NiB $507 Ex $414 Gd $290
Model 77RS, integral base, open sights ... NiB $503 Ex $408 Gd $288
.338 Win. Mag., .458 Win. Mag., with standard stock, add $75
Model 77RSC, .458 Win. Mag. with fancy Circassian walnut stock, add $525
Model 77RSI International, Mannlicher stock, short action, 18.5-inch bbl., 7 lbs. ... NiB $496 Ex $393 Gd $265
Model 77ST, round top, open sights ...... NiB $507 Ex $404 Gd $321
.338 Win. Mag., add $50
Model 77V, Varmint, integral base, no sights .... NiB $496 Ex $424 Gd $239
Model 77NV, Varmint, integral base, no sights, stainless steel barrel, laminated wood stock .... NiB $522 Ex $435 Gd $290

MODEL 77 MARK II ALL-WEATHER RIFLE ... NiB $496 Ex $393 Gd $265

Revised Model 77 action. Same general specifications as Model M-77 Mark II except with stainless bbl. and action. Zytel injection-molded stock. Calibers: .223, .243, .270, .308, .30-06, 7mm Mag., .300 Win. Mag., .338 Win. Mag. Made from 1990 to date.

Ruger Model 77 Round Top Receiver

Ruger Model 77
Ultra-Light Carbine

Ruger Model 77
International Carbine

Ruger Model 77
Varmint Rifle

Ruger Model 77 Mark II
All-Weather Rifle

MODEL 77 MARK II BOLT-ACTION RIFLE

Revised Model 77 action. Same general specifications as Model M-77 except with new 3-position safety and fixed blade ejector system. Calibers .22 PPC, .223 Rem., 6mm PPC, 6.5x55 Swedish, .375 H&H, .404 Jeffery and .416 Rigby also available. Weight: 6 to 10.25 lbs. Made from 1989 to date.

Model 77 MKIIR, integral base, no sights . . NiB $486 Ex $383 Gd $255
Left-hand Model 77LR MKII, add $25
Model 77RL MKII, Ultra Light, no sights. . . NiB $486 Ex $414 Gd $229
Model 77RLS MKII, Ultra Light, open sights . . . . NiB $486 Ex $425 Gd $280
Model 77RS MKII, integral base, open sights . . . NiB $493 Ex $399 Gd $278
Model 77RS MKII, Express, with fancy French walnut stock, integral base, open sights . NiB $1286 Ex $1054 Gd $719
Model 77RSI MKII, International, Mannlicher. . . . . NiB $532 Ex $430 Gd $300
Model 77RSM MKII magnum, with fancy Circassian walnut stock, integral base, open sights. . . . . NiB $1369 Ex $1060 Gd $751
Model 77VT (VBZ or VTM) MKII Varmint/Target stainless steel action, laminated wood stock. . . . . NiB $512 Ex $425 Gd $280

MODEL 77/.22 HORNET BOLT-ACTION RIFLE

Mini-Sporter built on the 77/.22 action in caliber .22 Hornet. Six round rotary magazine. 20- inch bbl. 40 inches overall. Weight: 6 lbs. Receiver machined for Ruger rings (included). Beaded front sight and open adj. rear, or no sights. Blued or stainless finish. Checkered American walnut stock. Made from 1994 to date.

Model 77/.22RH (rings, no sights) . . . . NiB $361 Ex $335 Gd $232
Model 77/.22RSH (rings & sights). . . . . NiB $386 Ex $335 Gd $232
Model 77/.22VHZ (S/S w/ laminated wood stock) . . . . NiB $412 Ex $386 Gd $258

MODEL 77/.22 RIMFIRE BOLT-ACTION RIFLE

Calibers: .22 LR. or .22 WMR. 10-shot (.22 LR) or 9-shot (.22 WMR) rotary magazine. 20-inch bbl. 39.75 inches overall. Weight: 5.75 lbs. Integral scope bases; with or w/o sights. Checkered American walnut or Zytel injection-molded stock. Stainless or blued finish. Made 1983 to date. (Blued); stainless. Introduced 1989.

77/.22 R, rings, no sights, walnut stock . . . . . . NiB $380 Ex $309 Gd $219
77/.22 RS, rings, sights, walnut. . . . . NiB $386 Ex $309 Gd $232
77/.22 RP, rings, no sights, synthetic stock . . . . NiB $315 Ex $258 Gd $184
77/.22 RSP, rings, sights, synthetic stock . . . . . NiB $341 Ex $278 Gd $198
K77/.22 RP, S/S rings, no sights, synthetic . . . . NiB $393 Ex $320 Gd $226
K77/.22 RSP, S/S, rings, sights, synthetic . . . . . NiB $406 Ex $330 Gd $232
77/.22 RM, .22 WMR, rings, no sights, walnut . . . . NiB $386 Ex $309 Gd $222
77/.22 RSM, .22 WMR, rings, sights, walnut . . . NiB $412 Ex $325 Gd $232
K77/.22 RSMP, .22 WMR, S/S, rings, sights, synthetic. . . . . NiB $406 Ex $330 Gd $233
K77/.22 RMP, .22 WMR, S/S, no sights, synthetic . . . . NiB $380 Ex $309 Gd $219
K77/.22 VBZ, .22 WMR, no sights, laminated. (1993) . . . . NiB $406 Ex $330 Gd $233

Ruger Model 77 Mark II

Ruger Model 77/.22 Rimfire

Ruger Model 77/.22 All Weather

Ruger Model 77/.44 All Weather

MODEL 77/.44 BOLT-ACTION

Short-action, carbine-style M77 similar to the 77/.22RH. Chambered .44 Rem. Mag. Four round rotary magazine. 18.5-inch bbl. 38.25 inches overall. Weight: 6 lbs. Gold bead front sight, folding adjustable rear w/integral scope base and Ruger rings. Blue or stainless finish. Synthetic or checkered American walnut stock w/rubber buttpad and swivels. Made from 1997-2004. Disc.

Model 77/.44 blued. . . . . NiB $516 Ex $387 Gd $259
Model 77/.44 stainless. . . . . NiB $532 Ex $398 Gd $264

MODEL 96 LEVER ACTION CARBINE

Caliber: .22 LR. .22 Mag., .44 Mag. Detachable 10-, 9- or 4-round magazine. 18.5-inch bbl. Weight: 5.25 lbs. Front gold bead sights. Drilled and tapped for scope. American hardwood stock. Made from 1996 to date.

.22 Long Rifle . . . . NiB $278 Ex $227 Gd $155
.22 Magnum . . . . NiB $289 Ex $253 Gd $165
.44 Magnum . . . . NiB $465 Ex $376 Gd $263

MINI-14 SEMIAUTOMATIC RIFLE

Gas-operated. Caliber: .223 Rem. (5.56mm). 5-, 10- or 20-round box magazine. 18.5-inch bbl. Weight: About 6.5 lbs. Sights: Peep rear; blade front mounted on removable barrel band. Pistol-grip stock w/curved buttplate, handguard. Made from 1976 to date.

Mini-14/5 blued . . . . NiB $568 Ex $532 Gd $336
K-Mini-14/5 stainless steel . . . . NiB $593 Ex $542 Gd $387
Mini-14/5F blued, folding stock . . . . NiB $758 Ex $645 Gd $449
K-Mini-14/5F stainless, folding stock . . . . . NiB $784 Ex $655 Gd $475
Mini-14 Ranch Rifle,
scope model, 6.25 lbs. . . . . NiB $603 Ex $552 Gd $346
K-Mini-1H Ranch Rifle,
scope model, stainless. . . . . NiB $629 Ex $578 Gd $371

MINI-THIRTY (30) AUTOLOADER

Caliber: 7.62 x 39mm. 5-round detachable magazine. 18.5-inch bbl. 37.25 inches overall. Weight: 7 lbs. 3 oz. Designed for use with telescopic sights. Walnut stained stock. Sights: Peep rear; blade front mounted on bbl. band. Blued or stainless finish. Made from 1986 to date.

Blued . . . . NiB $594 Ex $543 Gd $327
Stainless. . . . . NiB $620 Ex $594 Gd $337

PC SERIES SEMIAUTOMATIC CARBINES

Calibers: 9mm Parabellum or .40 S&W. 10-round magazine. 15.25-inch bbl. Weight: 6.25 lbs. Integral Ruger scope mounts with or without sights. Optional blade front sight, adjustable open rear. Matte black oxide finish. Matte black Zytel stock w/checkered pistol-grip and forearm. Made from 1997 to date.

Model PC9 (w/o sights). . . . . NiB $462 Ex $411 Gd $257
Model PC4 (w/o sights). . . . . NiB $488 Ex $437 Gd $282
W/adjustable sights, add $40

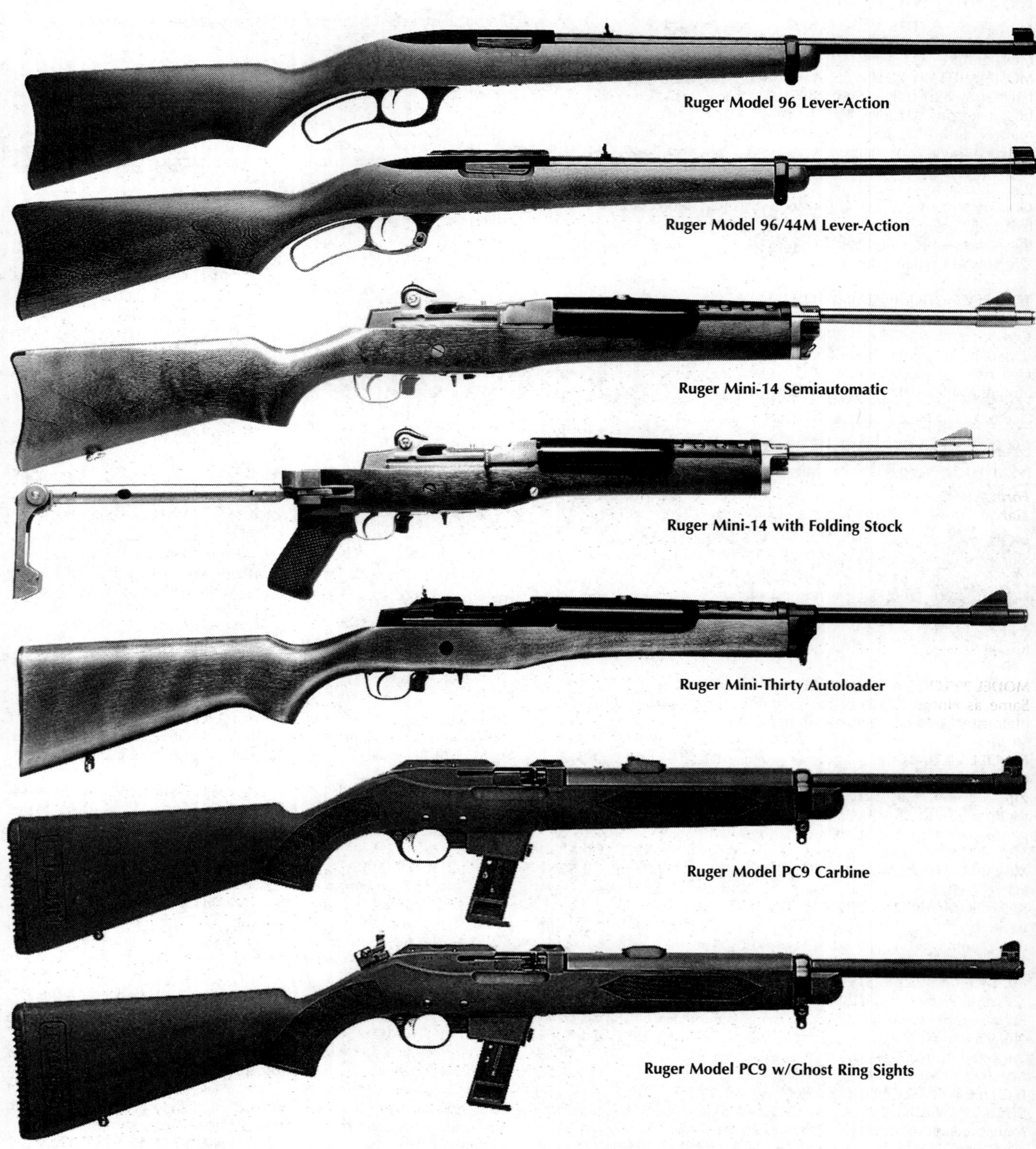
Ruger Model 96 Lever-Action
Ruger Model 96/44M Lever-Action
Ruger Mini-14 Semiautomatic
Ruger Mini-14 with Folding Stock
Ruger Mini-Thirty Autoloader
Ruger Model PC9 Carbine
Ruger Model PC9 w/Ghost Ring Sights

RUSSIAN MILITARY RIFLES — Principal U.S.S.R. Arms Plant, Tula

MODEL 1891
MOSIN MILITARY RIFLE. . . . . NiB $435 Ex $126 Gd $80
Nagant system bolt action. Caliber: 7.62mm Russian. Five round box magazine. 31.5-inch bbl. Weight: About 9 lbs. Sights: Open rear; blade front. Full stock w/straight grip. Specifications given are for WWII version; earlier types differ slightly. Note: In 1916, Remington Arms Co. and New England Westinghouse Co. produced 250,000 of these rifles on a contract from the Imperial Russian Government. Few were delivered to Russia and the balance bought by the U.S. Government for training in 1918. Eventually, many of these rifles were sold to N.R.A. members for about $3 each by the Director of Civilian Marksmanship.

TOKAREV MODEL 40 SEMIAUTOMATIC
MILITARY RIFLE . . . . NiB $805 Ex $395 Gd $241
Gas-operated. Caliber: 7.62mm Russian. 10-round detachable box magazine. 24.5-inch bbl. Muzzle brake. Weight: About 9 lbs. Sights: Leaf rear, hooded post front. Full stock w/pistol grip. Differences among Models 1938,1940 and 1941 are minor.

SAKO RIFLES — Riihimaki, Finland Manufactured by Sako L.T.D.

Formerly imported by Stoeger Industries, Wayne NJ (formerly by Garcia Corp.) until 2000. Imported by Beretta USA 2001 to date.

MODEL 72 . . . . NiB $1020 Ex $814 Gd $608
Single model designation replacing Vixen Sporter, Vixen Carbine, Vixen Heavy Barrel, Forester Sporter, Forester Carbine, Forester Heavy Barrel, Finnbear Sporter, and Finnbear Carbine, with same specifications, except all but heavy barrel models fitted with open rear sight. Values same as for corresponding earlier models. Imported from 1972-74.

MODEL 73 LEVER-ACTION RIFLE . . . . . NiB $1072 Ex $917 Gd $608
Same as Finnwolf except has 3-round clip magazine, flush floorplate; stock has no cheekpiece. Imported from 1973-75.

MODEL 74 CARBINE . . . . NiB $1020 Ex $686 Gd $547
Long Mauser-type bolt action. Caliber: .30-06. Five round magazine. 20-inch bbl. Weight: 7.5 lbs. No sights. Checkered Mannlicher-type full stock of European walnut, Monte Carlo cheekpiece. Imported from 1974-78.

MODEL 74 HEAVY BARREL RIFLE,
LONG ACTION. . . . . NiB $1020 Ex $686 Gd $454
Same specifications as short action except w/24-inch heavy bbl., weighs 8.75 lbs.; magnum w/4-round magazine. Calibers: .25-06, 7mm Rem. Mag. Imported from 1974-78.

MODEL 74 HEAVY BARREL RIFLE,
MEDIUM ACTION . . . . NiB $1020 Ex $686 Gd $454
Same specifications as short action except w/23-inch heavy bbl., weighs 8.5 lbs. Calibers: .220 Swift, .22-250, .243 Win., .308 Win. Imported from 1974-78.

MODEL 74 HEAVY BARREL RIFLE,
SHORT ACTION . . . . NiB $1072 Ex $866 Gd $505
Mauser-type bolt action. Calibers: .222 Rem., .223 Rem. Five round magazine. 23.5-inch heavy bbl. Weight: 8.25 lbs. No sights. Target-style checkered European walnut stock w/beavertail forearm. Imported from 1974-78.

MODEL 74 SUPER SPORTER,
LONG ACTION. NiB $1020 Ex $720 Gd $454
Same specifications as short action except w/24-inch bbl., weight: 8 lbs.; magnums have 4-round magazine, recoil pad. Calibers: .25-06, .270 Win. 7mm Rem. Mag., .30-06, .300 Win. Mag., .338 Win. Mag., .375 H&H Mag. Imported from 1974-78.

MODEL 74 SUPER SPORTER,
MEDIUM ACTION. . . . . NiB $1046 Ex $737 Gd $480
Same specifications as short action except weight: 7.25 lbs. Calibers: .220 Swift, .22-250, .243 Win. Imported from 1974-78.

MODEL 74 SUPER SPORTER,
SHORT ACTION . . . . NiB $1046 Ex $711 Gd $454
Mauser-type bolt action. Calibers: .222 Rem., .223 Rem. Five round magazine. 23.5-inch bbl. Weight: 6.5 lbs. No sights. Checkered European walnut stock w/Monte Carlo cheekpiece, QD swivel studs. Imported 1974. Disc.

MODEL 75 DELUXE . . . . NiB $1323 Ex 1067 Gd $739
Same specifications as Sako 75 Hunter Model except w/hinged floor plate, deluxe high gloss checkered walnut stock w/rosewood forend cap and grip cap w/silver inlay. Imported from 1998-2006. Disc.

RIFLES

MODEL 75 HUNTER. . . . . NiB $1056 Ex $779 Gd $557
New bolt action design available in four action lengths fitted with a new bolt featuring three front locking lugs with an external extractor positioned under the bolt. Calibers: .17 Rem., .222 Rem., .223 Rem., (I); .22-250 Rem., .243 Win., 7mm-08 Rem., .308 Win., (III); .25-06 Rem., .270 Win., .280 Rem., .30-06, (IV); 7mm Rem Mag., .300 Win. Mag., .300 Wby. Mag., .338 Win. Mag. 7mm STW, .300 Wby. Mag., .340 Wby. Mag., .375 H&H Mag. and .416 Rem. Mag.,(V). 4-, 5- or 6-round magazine w/detachable magazine. 22-, 24-, and 26-inch bbls. 41.75 to 45.6 inches over all. Weight: 6.3 to 9 lbs. Sako dovetail scope base integral with receiver with no sights. Checkered high-grade walnut stock w/recoil pad and sling swivels. Made from 1997-2006. Disc.

MODEL 75 STAINLESS SYNTHETIC . . . . . NiB $1104 Ex $892 Gd $620
Similar to Model 75 Hunter except chambered for .22-250 Rem., .243 Win., .25-06 Rem., .270 Win., 7mm-08 Rem., 7mm STW, .30-06, .308 Win., 7mm Rem Mag., .300 Win. Mag., .338 Win. Mag. or .375 H&H Mag. 22-, 24-, and 26-inch bbls. Black composite stock w/soft rubber grips inserts. Matte stainless steel finish. Made from 1997-2006. Disc.

MODEL 75 VARMINT RIFLE . . . . . . NiB $800 Ex $594 Gd $414
Similar to Model 75 Hunter except chambered .17 Rem., .222 Rem., .223 Rem. and .22-250 Rem. 24-inch bbl. Matte lacquered walnut stock w/beavertail forearm. Made from 1998-2006. Disc.

MODEL 78 SUPER HORNET SPORTER. . . . NiB $594 Ex $466 Gd $311
Same specifications as Model 78 Rimfire except chambered for .22 Hornet, 4-round magazine. Imported from 1977-87.

MODEL 78 SUPER RIMFIRE SPORTER . . . . NiB $543 Ex $440 Gd $260
Bolt action. Caliber: .22 LR. Five round magazine. 22.5-inch bbl. Weight, 6.75 lbs. No sights. Checkered European walnut stock, Monte Carlo cheekpiece. Imported from 1977-86.

CLASSIC BOLT-ACTION RIFLE
Medium Action (.243. Win.) or Long Action (.270 Win. .30-06, 7mm Rem. Mag.). American walnut stock. Made 1980-86. Reintroduced in 1993 w/matte lacquer finish stock, 22- or 24-inch bbl., overall length of 42 to 44 inches, weight 6.88 to 7.25lbs. Imported from 1992-97.
Standard calibers. . . . . NiB $901 Ex $727 Gd $505
Magnum caliber . . . . NiB $965 Ex $779 Gd $530
Left-hand models. . . . . NiB $978 Ex $789 Gd $547

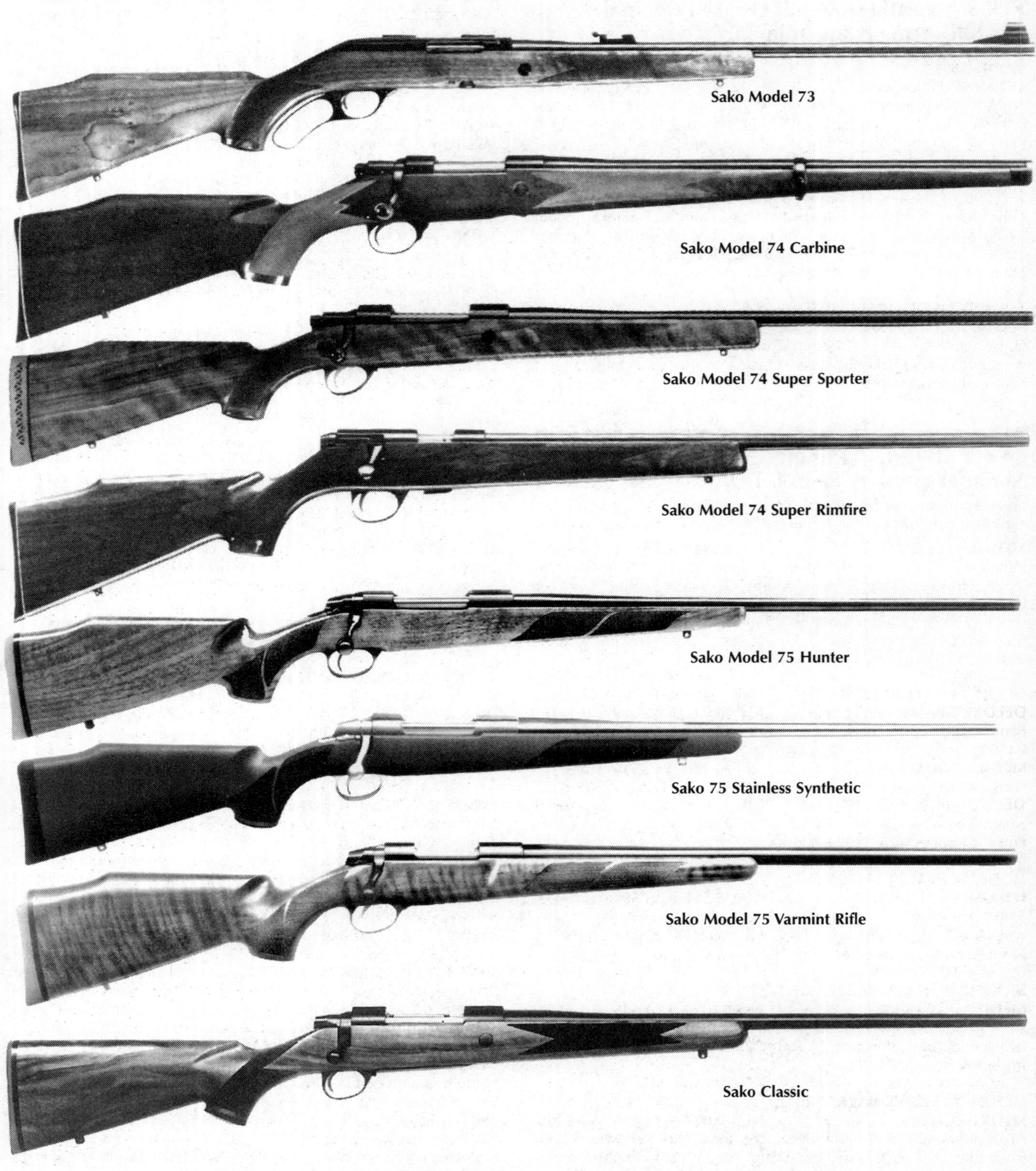

Sako Model 73

Sako Model 74 Carbine

Sako Model 74 Super Sporter

Sako Model 74 Super Rimfire

Sako Model 75 Hunter

Sako 75 Stainless Synthetic

Sako Model 75 Varmint Rifle

Sako Classic

Sako Deluxe Lightweight

Sako Fiberglass

Sako Finnfire

Sako Finnfire Heavy Barrel

Sako Finnwolf

DELUXE GRADE AI . . . . NiB $1027 Ex $718 Gd $487
Same specifications as Standard Grade except w/22 lines to the inch French checkering, rosewood grip cap and forend tip, semibeavertail forend. Disc.

DELUXE GRADE AII . . . . NiB $1053 Ex $744 Gd $512
Same specifications as Standard Grade except w/22 lines per inch French checkering, rosewood grip cap and forend tip, semi beavertail forend. Disc.

DELUXE GRADE AIII . . . . NiB $1362 Ex $1058 Gd $667
Same specifications as w/standard except w/French checkering, rosewood grip cap and forend tip, semibeavertail forend. Disc.

DELUXE LIGHTWEIGHT BOLT-ACTION RIFLE . . . . NiB $1137 Ex $919 Gd $641
Same general specifications as Hunter Lightweight except w/beautifully grained French walnut stock; superb high-gloss finish, fine hand-cut checkering, rosewood forend tip and grip cap. Imported from 1985-97.

FIBERCLASS BOLT-ACTION RIFLE . . . . NiB $1079 Ex $976 Gd $590
All-weather fiberglass stock version of Sako barreled long action. Calibers: .25-06, .270, .30-06, 7mm Rem. Mag., .300 Win. Mag., .338 Win. Mag., .375 H&H Mag. Bbl. length: 22.5 inches. Overall length: 44.25 inches. Weight: 7.25 lbs. Imported from 1984-96.

FINNBEAR CARBINE . . . . NiB $1182 Ex $873 Gd $538
Same as Finnbear Sporter except w/20-inch bbl., Mannlicher-type full stock. Imported 1971. Disc.

FINNBEAR SPORTER . . . . NiB $1130 Ex $893 Gd $538
Long Mauser-type bolt action. Calibers: .25-06, .264 Mag. .270, .30-06, .300 Win. Mag., .338 Mag., 7mm Mag., .375 H&H Mag. Magazine holds 5 standard or 4 magnum cartridges. 24-inch bbl. Weight: 7 lbs. Hooded ramp front sight. Sporter stock w/Monte Carlo cheekpiece, checkered pistol-grip and forearm, recoil pad, swivels. Imported from 1961-71.

FINNFIRE BOLT-ACTION RIFLE
Mini-Sporter built for rimfires on a scaled-down Sako design. Caliber: .22 LR. 5- or 10-round magazine. 22-inch bbl. 39.5 inches overall. Weight: 5.25 lbs. Receiver machined for 11mm dovetail scope rings. Beaded blade front sight, open adj. rear. Blued finish. Checkered European walnut stock. Imported from 1994 to date.
Hunter model . . . . NiB $754 Ex $641 Gd $471
Varmint model. . . . . NiB $852 Ex $651 Gd $496
Sporter model . . . . NiB $966 Ex $780 Gd $541

FINNWOLF LEVER-ACTION RIFLE . . . . . NiB $1038 Ex $838 Gd $573
Hammerless. Calibers: .243 Win., .308 Win. Four round clip magazine. 23-inch bbl. Weight: 6.75 lbs. Hooded ramp front sight. Sporter stock w/Monte Carlo cheekpiece, checkered pistol-grip and forearm, swivels (available w/right- or left-hand stock). Imported from 1963-72.

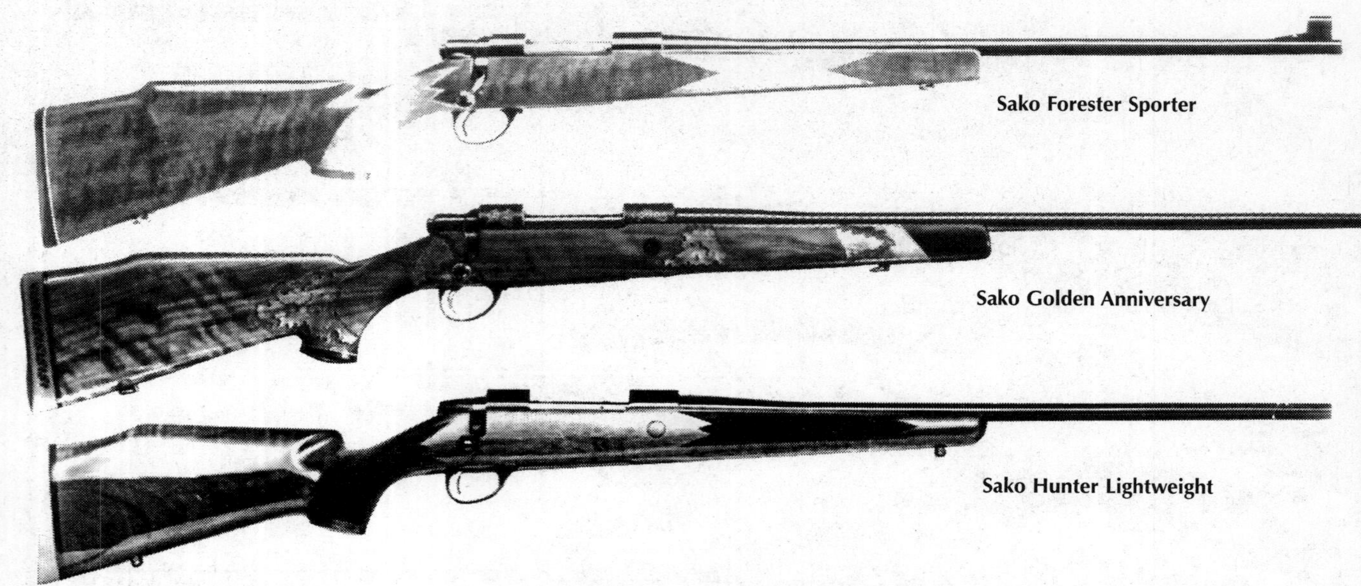

Sako Forester Sporter

Sako Golden Anniversary

Sako Hunter Lightweight

FINSPORT 2700 .... **NiB $910 Ex $756 Gd $498**
Bolt-action centerfire rifle. Calibers: .270, .30-06, 7mm Rem. Mag., .300 Win. Mag. Bbl. length: 24 inches. Weight: 8 lbs. Imported from 1984-86.

FORESTER CARBINE .... **NiB $1116 Ex $988 Gd $524**
Same as Forester Sporter except w/20-inch bbl., Mannlicher-type full stock. Imported from 1958-71.

FORESTER HEAVY BARREL ...... **NiB $1065 Ex $962 Gd $473**
Same as Forester Sporter except w/24-inch heavy bbl. Weight 7.5 lbs. Imported from 1958-71.

FORESTER SPORTER .... **NiB $1168 Ex $988 Gd $498**
Medium-length Mauser-type bolt action. Calibers: .22-250, .243 Win., .308 Win. Five round magazine. 23-inch bbl. Weight: 6.5 lbs. Hooded ramp front sight. Sporter stock w/Monte Carlo cheekpiece, checkered pistol grip and forearm, swivels. Imported from 1957-71.

GOLDEN ANNIVERSARY MODEL .... **NiB $2737 Ex $2103 Gd $1418**
Special presentation-grade rifle issued in 1973 to commemorate Sako's 50th anniversary. 1,000 (numbered 1 to 1,000) made. Same specifications as Deluxe Sporter: Long action, 7mm Rem. Mag. receiver, trigger guard and floorplate decorated w/gold oak leaf and acorn motif. Stock of select European walnut, checkering bordered w/hand-carved oak leaf pattern.

HIGH-POWER MAUSER SPORTING RIFLE...... **NiB $1080 Ex $977 Gd $771**
FN Mauser action. Calibers: .270, .30-06. Five round magazine. 24-inch bbl. Sights: Open rear leaf; Partridge front; hooded ramp. Checkered stock w/Monte Carlo comb and cheekpiece. Weight: 7.5 lbs. Imported from 1950-57.

HUNTER LIGHTWEIGHT BOLT-ACTION RIFLE
5- or 6-round magazine. Bbl. length: 21.5 inches, AI; 22 inches, AII; 22.5 inches, AIII. Overall length: 42.25-44.5 inches. Weight: 5.75 lbs., AI; 6.75 lbs. AII; 7.25 lbs., AIII. Monte Carlo-style European walnut stock, oil finished. Hand-checkered pistol-grip and forend. Imported from 1985-97. Left-hand version intro. 1987.
AI (Short Action) .17 Rem. .... **NiB $1039 Ex $757 Gd $550**
.222 Rem., .223 Rem. .... **NiB $1013 Ex $782 Gd $550**
AII (medium action)
.22-250 Rem., .243 Win., .308 Win. .... **NiB $910 Ex $756 Gd $498**
AIII (long action) .25-06 Rem.,
.270 Win., .30-06 .... **NiB $968 Ex $782 Gd $543**
.338 Win. Mag. .... **NiB $1105 Ex $905 Gd $650**
.375 H&H Mag. .... **NiB $1202 Ex $983 Gd $702**
Left-hand model (standard cal.) .... **NiB $1232 Ex $993 Gd $686**
Magnum calibers .... **NiB $1495 Ex $1219 Gd $867**

LAMINATED STOCK BOLT-ACTION RIFLES
Similar in style and specifications to Hunter Grade except w/stock of resin-bonded hardwood veneers. Available 18 calibers in AI (Short), AII (Medium) or AV action, left-hand version in 10 calibers, AV only. Imported from 1987-95.
Short or medium action .... **NiB $1013 Ex $833 Gd $550**
Long action/Magnum .... **NiB $1039 Ex $859 Gd $576**

MAGNUM MAUSER .... **NiB $1492 Ex $1183 Gd $848**
Similar specifications as Standard Model except w/recoil pad and redesigned longer AIII action to handle longer magnum cartridges. Calibers: .300 H&H Magnum, .375 H&H Magnum, standard at time of introduction. Disc.

MANNLICHER-STYLE CARBINE
Similar to Hunter Model except w/full Mannlicher-style stock and 18.5-inch bbl. Weighs 7.5 lbs. Chambered in .243, .25-06, .270, .308, .30-06, 7mm Rem. Mag., .300 Win. Mag., .338 Win. Mag., .375 H&H. Intro. in 1977. Disc.
Standard calibers .... **NiB $1232 Ex $949 Gd $614**
Magnum calibers (except .375)......... **NiB $1258 Ex $975 Gd $656**
.375 H&H .... **NiB $1274 Ex $1001 Gd $692**

SAFARI GRADE .... **NiB $2465 Ex $1903 Gd $1074**
Classic bolt-action. Calibers: .300 Win. Mag., .338 Win. Mag., .375 H&H. Oil-finished European walnut stock w/hand-checkering. Barrel band swivel, express-type sight rib; satin or matte blue finish. Imported from 1980-96.

SPORTER DELUXE............ **NiB $1228 Ex $945 Gd $610**
Same as Vixen, Forester, Finnbear and Model 74 except w/fancy French walnut stock w/skip checkering, rosewood forend tip and pistol-grip cap, recoil pad, inlaid trigger guard and floorplate. Disc.

Sako Mannlicher-Style Carbine

Sako Sporter Deluxe

Sako TRG-21 Target Rifle

STANDARD GRADE AI .... NiB $1016 Ex $733 Gd $398
Short bolt-action. Calibers: .17 Rem., .222 Rem., .223 Rem. Five round magazine. 23.5-inch bbl. Weight: 6.5 lbs. No sights. Checkered European walnut stock w/Monte Carlo cheekpiece, QD swivel studs. Imported from 1978-85.

STANDARD GRADE AII......... NiB $1027 Ex $749 Gd $424
Medium bolt-action. Calibers: .22-250 Rem., .243 Win., .308 Win. 23.5-inch bbl. in .22-250; 23-inch bbl. in other calibers. Five round magazine. Weight: 7.25 lbs. Checkered European walnut stock w/Monte Carlo cheekpiece, QD swivel studs. Imported from 1978-85.

STANDARD GRADE AIII .... NiB $1063 Ex $785 Gd $476
Long bolt action. Calibers: .25-06 Rem., .270 Win., .30-06, 7mm Rem. Mag., .300 Win. Mag., .338 Win. Mag., .375 H&H. 24-inch bbl. 4-round magazine. Weight: 8 lbs. Imported from 1978-84.

SUPER DELUXE RIFLE .... NiB $2377 Ex $2094 Gd $1244
Available in AI, AII, AIII calibers. Select European walnut stock, hand-checkered, deep oak leaf hand-engraved design. Disc.

TRG-BOLT-ACTION TARGET RIFLE
Caliber: .308 Win., .330 Win. or .338 Lapua Mag. Detachable 10-round magazine. 25.75- or 27.2-inch bbl. Weight: 10.5 to 11 lbs. Blued action w/stainless barrel. Adjustable two-stage trigger. modular reinforced polyurethane target stock w/adj. cheekpiece and buttplate. Options: Muzzle break; detachable bipod; QD sling swivels and scope mounts w/1-inch or 30mm rings. Imported from 1993 to date.

TRG-21 .308 Win .... NiB $2627 Ex $2122 Gd $1462
TRG-22 .308 Win.................. NiB $2702 Ex $2183 Gd $1508
TRG-41 .338 Lapua................ NiB $3169 Ex $2552 Gd $1763
TRG-42 .300 Win. or .338 Lapua ..... NiB $3240 Ex $2617 Gd $1801

TRG-S BOLT-ACTION RIFLE
Calibers: .243, 7mm-08, .270, .30-06, 7mm Rem. Mag., .300 Win. Mag., .338 Win. Mag. Five shot magazine (standard calibers), 4-shot (magnum), 22- or 24-inch bbl. 45.5 inches overall. Weight: 7.75 lbs. No sights. Reinforced polyurethane stock w/Monte Carlo. Introduced in 1993.
Standard calibers............... NiB $756 Ex $679 Gd $421
Magnum calibers............... NiB $801 Ex $648 Gd $452

VIXEN CARBINE .... NiB $1124 Ex $997 Gd $867
Same as Vixen Sporter except w/20-inch bbl., Mannlicher-type full stock. Imported from 1947-71.

VIXEN HEAVY BARREL .... NiB $1074 Ex $868 Gd $492
Same as Vixen Sporter except calibers .222 Rem., .222 Rem. Mag., .223 Rem., heavy bbl., target-style stock w/beavertail forearm. Weight: 7.5 lbs. Imported from 1947-71.

VIXEN SPORTER .... NiB $1125 Ex $1022 Gd $507
Short Mauser-type bolt-action. Cals.: .218 Bee, .22 Hornet, .222 Rem., .222 Rem. Mag., .223 Rem. Five round magazine. 23.5-inch bbl. Weight: 6.5 lbs. Hooded ramp front sight. Sporter stock w/Monte Carlo cheekpiece, checkered pistol-grip and forearm, swivels. Imported from 1946-71.

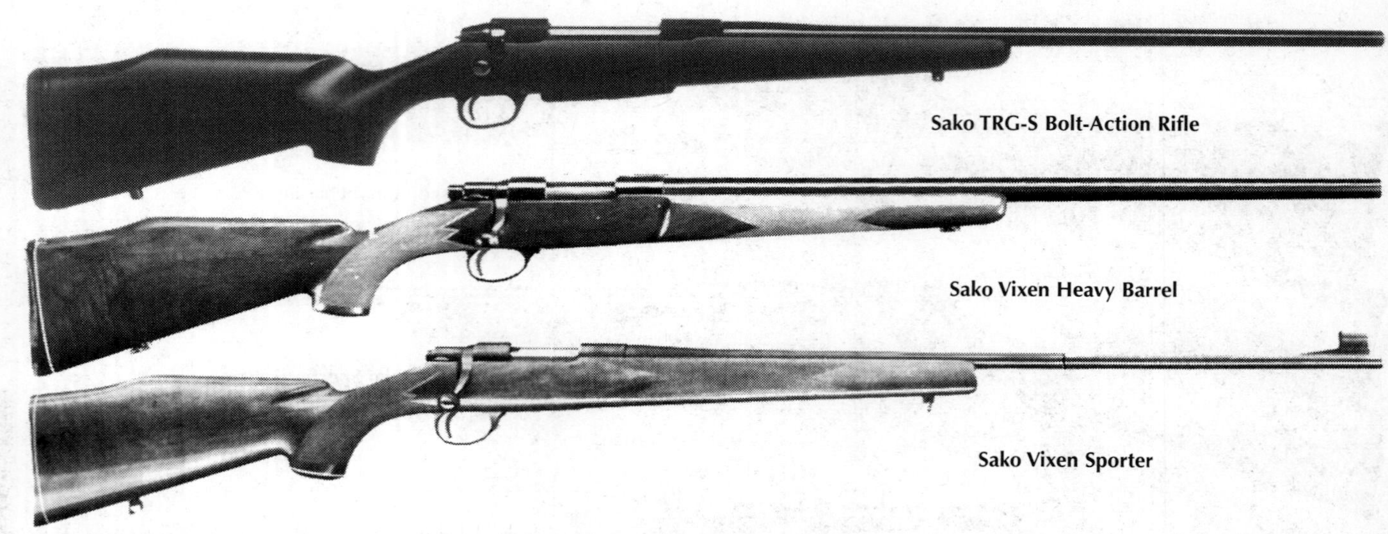
Sako TRG-S Bolt-Action Rifle

Sako Vixen Heavy Barrel

Sako Vixen Sporter

J. P. SAUER & SOHN — Eckernforde, Germany, (Formerly Suhl, Germany), Imported by Sigarms Exeter, NH , (Previously by Paul Company Inc. and G.U. Inc.)

MAUSER BOLT-ACTION SPORTING RIFLE . . . . NiB $1309 Ex $1042 Gd $717
Calibers: 7x57 and 8x57mm most common, but these rifles were produced in a variety of calibers including most of the popular Continental calibers as well as our .30-06. Five round box magazine. 22- or 24-inch Krupp steel bbl., half-octagon w/raised matted rib. Double-set trigger. Weight: 7.5 lbs. Sights: Three-leaf open rear; ramp front. Sporting stock w/cheekpiece, checkered pistol grip, raised side-panels, Schnabel tip, swivels. Also made w/20-inch bbl. and full-length stock. Mfd. before WWII.

MODEL S-90 BOLT-ACTION RIFLES
Calibers: .243 Win., .308 Win. (Short action); .25-06, .270 Win., .30-06 (Medium action); 7mm Rem. Mag., .300 Win. Mag., .300 Wby., .338 Win., .375 H&H (Magnum action). Four round (standard) or 3-round magazine (magnum). Bbl. length: 20-inch (Stutzen), 24-inch. Weight: 7.6 to 10.75 lbs. Adjustable (Supreme) checkered Monte Carlo style stock. contrasting forend and pistol grip cap w/high-gloss finish or European (Lux) checkered Classic-style European walnut stock w/satin oil finish. Imported from 1983-89.
S-90 Standard . . . . NiB $1077 Ex $948 Gd $536
S-90 Lux . . . . NiB $1293 Ex $1025 Gd $562
S-90 Safari. . . . . NiB $1267 Ex $1000 Gd $562
S-90 Stutzen . . . . NiB $1087 Ex $948 Gd $536
S-90 Supreme . . . . NiB $1396 Ex $1128 Gd $768
Grade I engraving, add $600
Grade II engraving, add $800
Grade III engraving add $1000
Grade IV engraving, add. $1500

MODEL 200 BOLT-ACTION RIFLES
Calibers: .243 Win., .25-06, .270 Win., 7mm Rem Mag., .30-06, .308 Win., .300 Win. Mag., Detachable box magazine. 24-inch (American) or 26-inch (European) interchangeable bbl. Standard (steel) or lightweight (alloy) action. Weight: 6.6 to 7.75 lbs. 44 inches overall. Stock options: American Model w/checkered Monte Carlo style 2-piece stock contrasting forend and pistol grip cap w/high gloss finish and no sights. European walnut stock w/Schnabel forend, satin oil finish and iron sights. Contemporary Model w/synthetic carbon fiber stock. Imported from 1986-93.
Standard model. NiB $1309 Ex $999 Gd $639
Lightweight model . . . . NiB $1083 Ex $953 Gd $541
Contemporary model . . . . NiB $1205 Ex $1005 Gd $593
American model . . . . NiB $1288 Ex $1030 Gd $593
European model . . . . NiB $1314 Ex $1056 Gd $518
Left-hand model, add $125
Magnum calibers, add. $115
Interchangeable barrel assembly, add. $295

MODEL 202 BOLT-ACTION RIFLES
Calibers: .243 Win., 6.5x55, 6.5x57, 6.6x68, .25-06, .270 Win., .280 7x64, .308, .30-06, Springfield, 7mm Rem. Mag., .300 Win. Mag., .300 Wby. Mag., 8x68S, .338 Win. Mag., .375 H&H Mag. Removable 3-round box magazine. 23.6- and 26-inch interchangable bbl. 44.3 and 46 inches overall. Modular receiver drilled and tapped for scope bases. Adjustable two-stage trigger w/dual release safety. Weight: 7.7 to 8.4 lbs. Stock options: Checkered Monte Carlo-style select American walnut two-piece stock; Euro-classic French walnut two-piece stock w/semi Schnabel forend and satin oil finish; Super Grade Claro walnut two-piece stock fitted w/rosewood forend and grip cap w/high-gloss epoxy finish. Imported from 1994 to date.
Standard model. NiB $1236 Ex $799 Gd $541
Euro-Classic model . . . . NiB $1278 Ex $824 Gd $541
Super Grade model. . . . . NiB $1288 Ex $850 Gd $567
Left-hand model, add $150
Magnum calibers, add. $125
Interchangeable barrel assembly, add. $295

SAVAGE INDUSTRIES — Westfield, Massachusetts, (Formerly Chicopee Falls, MA and Utica, NY)

MODEL 3 BOLT-ACTION SINGLE-SHOT RIFLE . . . . NiB $173 Ex $148 Gd $96
Takedown. Caliber: .22 Short, Long, LR. 26-inch bbl. on prewar rifles, postwar production w/24-inch bbl. Weight: 5 lbs. Sights: Open rear; bead front. Plain pistol-grip stock. Made from 1933-52.

MODEL 3S. NiB $209 Ex $173 Gd $112
Same as Model 3 except w/peep rear sight, hooded front. Made from 1933-42.

MODEL 3ST. . . . . NiB $215 Ex $199 Gd $117
Same as Model 3S except fitted w/swivels and sling. Made from 1933-42.

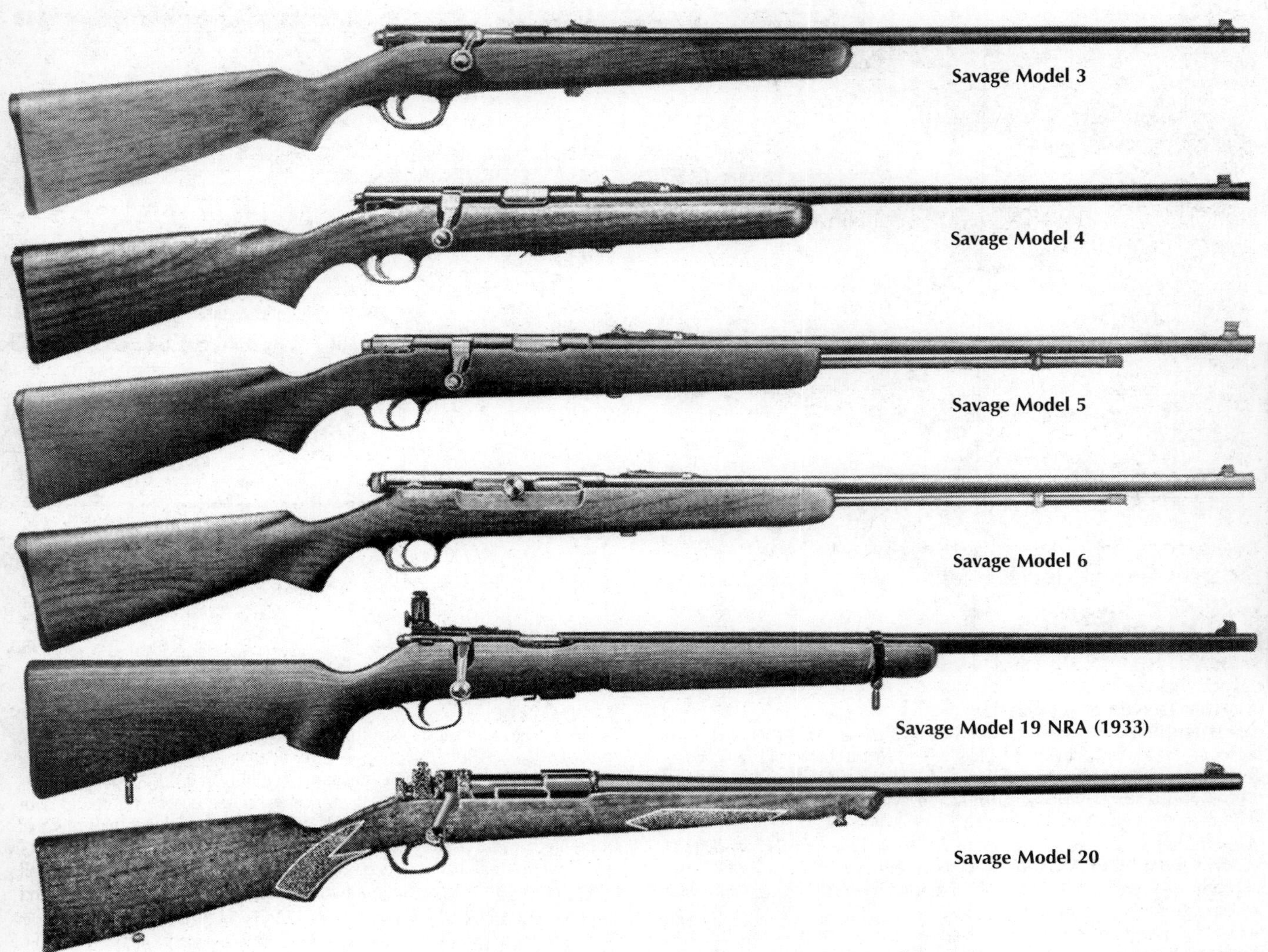

Savage Model 3

Savage Model 4

Savage Model 5

Savage Model 6

Savage Model 19 NRA (1933)

Savage Model 20

MODEL 4 BOLT-ACTION REPEATER...... NiB $199 Ex $158 Gd $117
Takedown. Caliber: .22 Short, Long, LR. Five round detachable box magazine. 24-inch bbl. Weight: 5.5 lbs. Sights: Open rear; bead front. Checkered pistol-grip stock on prewar models, early production had grooved forearm; postwar rifles have plain stocks. Made from 1933-65.

MODEL 4M..................... NiB $173 Ex $107 Gd $91
Same as Model 4 except chambered for .22 Rimfire Magnum. Made from 1961-65.

MODEL 4S...................... NiB $215 Ex $117 Gd $96
Same as Model 4 except w/peep rear sight, hooded front. Made from 1933-42.

MODEL 5 BOLT-ACTION REPEATER......................... NiB $199 Ex $117 Gd $96
Same as Model 4 except w/tubular magazine (holds 21 Short, 17 Long, 15 LR), weight: 6 lbs. Made from 1936-61.

MODEL 5S................... NiB $201 Ex $163 Gd $117
Same as Model 5 except w/peep rear sight, hooded front. Made from 1936-42.

MODEL 6 AUTOLOADING RIFLE........ NiB $199 Ex $173 Gd $122
Takedown. Caliber: .22 Short, Long, LR. Tubular magazine holds 21 Short, 17 Long, 15 LR. 24-inch bbl. Weight: 6 lbs. Sights: Open rear; bead front. Checkered pistol-grip stock on prewar models, postwar rifles have plain stocks. Made from 1938-68.

MODEL 6S................... NiB $215 Ex $184 Gd $127
Same as Model 6 except w/peep rear sight, bead front. Made from 1938-42.

MODEL 7 AUTOLOADING RIFLE........ NiB $225 Ex $199 Gd $132
Same general specifications as Model 6 except w/5-round detachable box magazine. Made from 1939-51.

MODEL 7S................... NiB $204 Ex $143 Gd $122
Same as Model 7 except w/peep rear sight, hooded front. Made from 1938-42.

MODEL 19 BOLT-ACTION TARGET RIFLE..... NiB $383 Ex $280 Gd $177
Model of 1933. Speed lock. Caliber: .22-LR. Five round detachable box magazine. 25-inch bbl. Weight: 8 lbs. Adj. rear peep sight, blade front on early models, later production equipped w/extension rear sight, hooded front. Target stock w/full pistol-grip and beavertail forearm. Made from 1933-46.

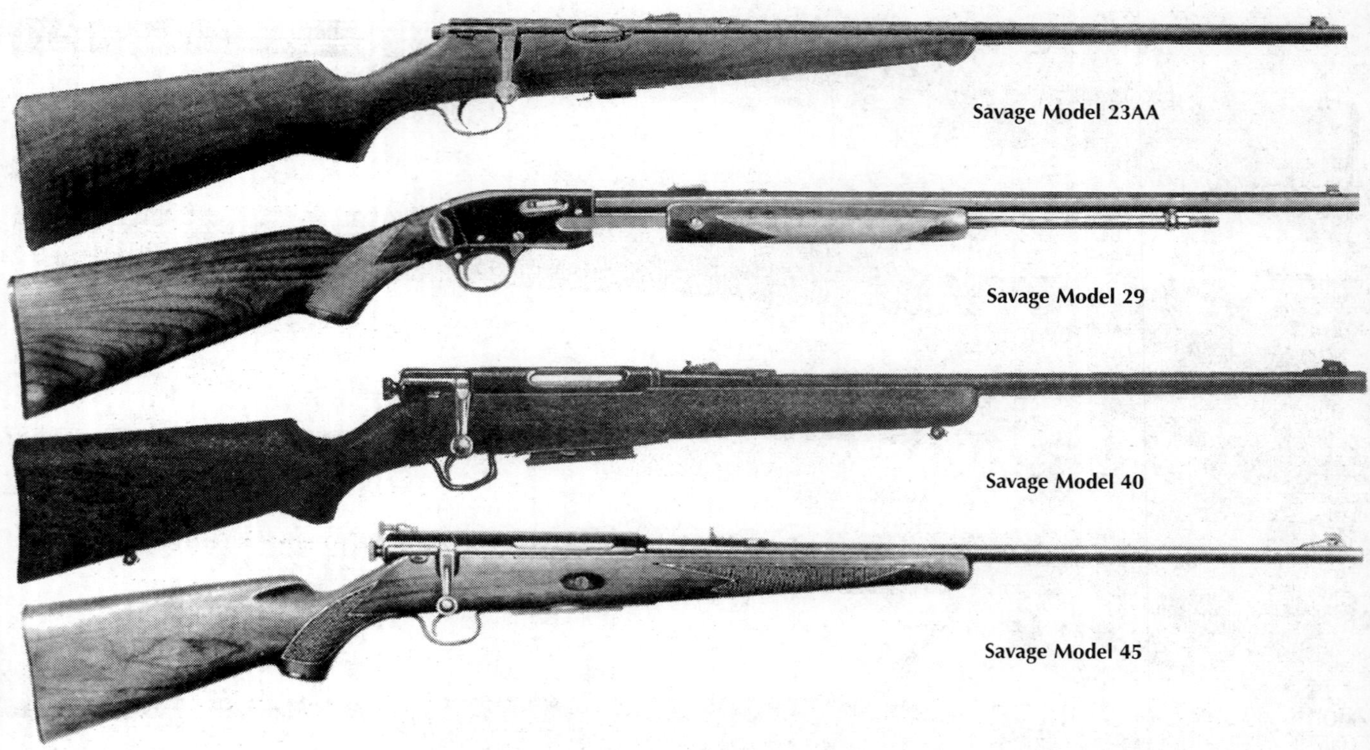

Savage Model 23AA

Savage Model 29

Savage Model 40

Savage Model 45

MODEL 19 NRA BOLT-ACTION MATCH RIFLE . . . . NiB $543 Ex $491 Gd $260
Model of 1919. Caliber: .22 LR. Five round detachable box magazine. 25-inch bbl. Weight: 7 lbs. Sights: Adj. rear peep; blade front. Full military stock w/pistol-grip. Made from 1919-33.

MODEL 19H . . . . NiB $620 Ex $517 Gd $337
Same as standard Model 19 (1933) except chambered for .22 Hornet, w/Model 23D-type bolt mechanism, loading port and magazine. Made from 1933-42.

MODEL 19L. . . . . NiB $383 Ex $280 Gd $177
Same as standard Model 19 (1933) except equipped w/Lyman No. 48Y receiver sight, 17A front sight. Made from 1933-42.

MODEL 19M . . . . NiB $491 Ex $440 Gd $208
Same as standard Model 19 (1933) except w/heavy 28-inch bbl. w/scope bases, weight: 9.25 lbs. Made from 1933-42.

MODEL 20-1926 HI-POWER . . . . NiB $491 Ex $388 Gd $285
Same as Model 1920, listed on page 354, except w/24-inch medium weight bbl., improved stock, Lyman 54 rear peep sight, weight: 7 lbs. Made from 1926-29.

MODEL 23A BOLT-ACTION SPORTING RIFLE. . . . . NiB $268 Ex $191 Gd $155
Caliber: 22 LR. Five round detachable box magazine. 23-inch bbl. Weight: 6 lbs. Sights: Open rear, blade or bead front. Plain pistol-grip stock w/slender forearm and Schnabel tip. Made from 1923-33.

MODEL 23AA . . . . NiB $325 Ex $278 Gd $186
Model of 1933. Improved version of Model 23A w/same general specifications except w/speed lock, improved stock, weighs 6.5 lbs. Made from 1933-42.

MODEL 23B . . . . NiB $304 Ex $201 Gd $150
Same as Model 23A except caliber .25-20, 25-inch bbl. Model of 1933 w/improved stock w/full forearm instead of slender forearm w/Schnabel found on earlier production. Weight: 6.5 lbs. Made from 1923-42.

MODEL 23C . . . . NiB $330 Ex $248 Gd $155
Same as Model 23B except caliber .32-20. Made from 1923-42.

MODEL 23D . . . . NiB $406 Ex $278 Gd $201
Same as Model 23B except caliber .22 Hornet. Made from 1933-47.

MODEL 25 SLIDE-ACTION REPEATER . . . . NiB $541 Ex $386 Gd $232
Takedown. Hammerless. Caliber: .22 Short, Long, LR. Tubular magazine holds 20 Short, 17 Long, 15 LR. 24-inch octagon bbl. Weight: 5.75 lbs. Sights: Open rear; blade front. Plain pistol-grip stock, grooved slide handle. Made from 1925-29.

MODEL 29 SLIDE-ACTION REPEATER . . . . NiB $468 Ex $339 Gd $236
Takedown. Hammerless. Caliber: .22 Short, Long, LR. Tubular magazine holds 20 Short, 17 Long, 15 LR. 24-inch bbl., octagon on prewar, round on postwar production. Weight: 5.5 lbs. Sights: Open rear; bead front. Stock w/checkered pistol grip and slide handle on prewar, plain stock and grooved forearm on postwar production. Made from 1929-67.

MODEL 40 BOLT-ACTION SPORTING RIFLE. . . . . NiB $409 Ex $255 Gd $208
Standard Grade. Calibers: .250-3000, .300 Sav., .30-30, .30-06. Four round detachable box magazine. 22-inch bbl. in calibers .250-3000 and .30-30; 24-inch in .300 Sav. and .30-06. Weight: 7.5 lbs. Sights: Open rear; bead front, on ramp. Plain pistol-grip stock w/tapered forearm and Schnabel tip. Made from 1928-40.

MODEL 45 SUPER SPORTER. . . . . . NiB $571 Ex $437 Gd $287
Special Grade. Same as Model 40 except w/checkered pistol-grip and forearm, Lyman No. 40 receiver sight. Made from 1928-40.

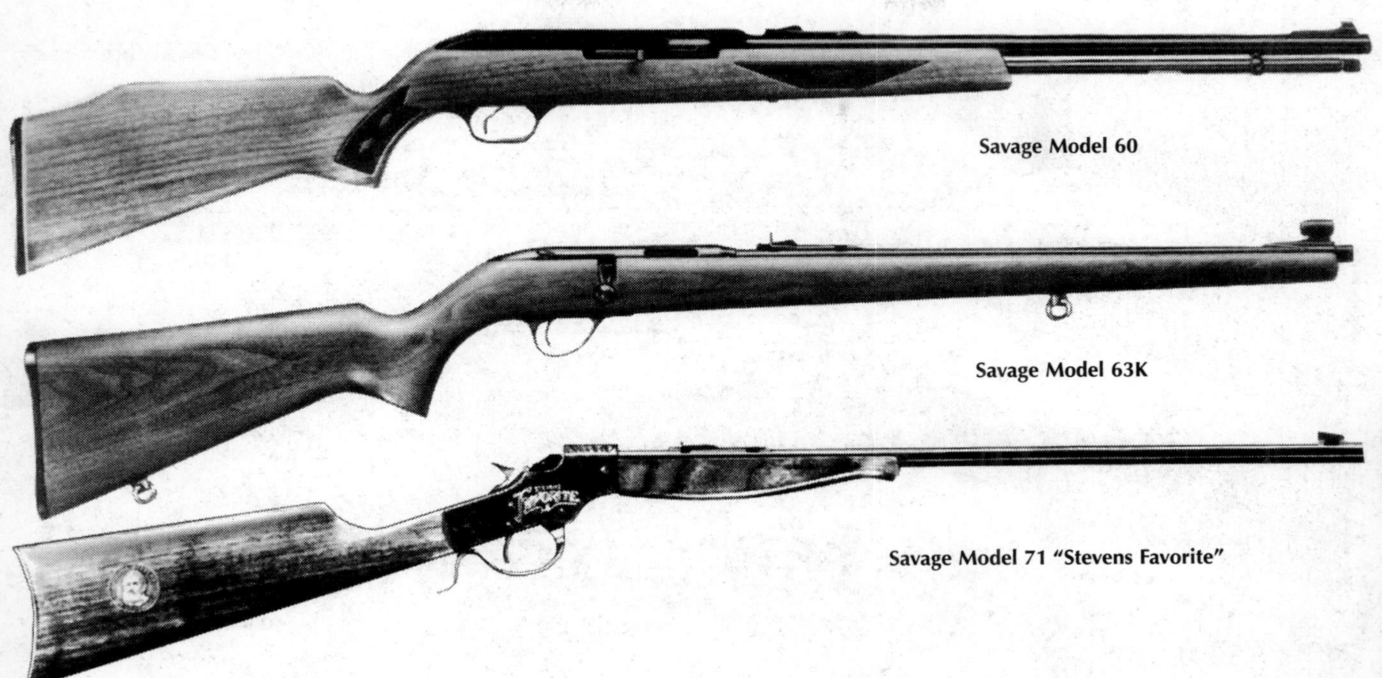

Savage Model 60

Savage Model 63K

Savage Model 71 "Stevens Favorite"

MODEL 60 AUTOLOADING RIFLE. . . . . . . NiB $173 Ex $121 Gd $98
Caliber: .22 LR. 15-round tubular magazine. 20-inch bbl. Weight: 6 lbs. Sights: Open rear, ramp front. Monte Carlo stock of walnut w/checkered pistol-grip and forearm. Made from 1969-72.

MODEL 63K KEY LOCK BOLT-ACTION SINGLE-SHOT RIFLE . . . . NiB $121 Ex $90 Gd $69
Trigger locked w/key. Caliber: .22 Short, Long, LR. 18-inch bbl. Weight: 4 lbs. Sights: Open rear; hooded ramp front. Full-length stock w/pistol grip, swivels. Made from 1970-72.

MODEL 63KM. . . . . NiB $136 Ex $95 Gd $80
Same as Model 63K except chambered for .22 WMR. Made from 1970-72.

MODEL 64F AUTOLOADING RIFLE. . . . . NiB $121 Ex $95 Gd $80
Same general specifications as Model 64G except w/black graphite/polymer stock. Weight: 5 lbs. Made from 1997 to date.

MODEL 64G AUTOLOADING RIFLE . . . . . . NiB $131 Ex $111 Gd $90
Caliber: 22 LR. 10-round magazine. 20-inch bbl. Weight: 5.5 lbs. 40 inches overall. Sights: Adj. open rear; bead front. Grooved receiver for scope mounts. Stamped checkering on walnut-finished hardwood stock w/Monte Carlo cheekpiece. Made from 1996 to date.

MODEL 71 "STEVENS FAVORITE" SINGLE-SHOT LEVER-ACTION RIFLE. . . . . NiB $275 Ex $198 Gd $147
Replica of original Stevens Favorite issued as a tribute to Joshua Stevens, "Father of .22 Hunting." Caliber: .22 LR. 22-inch full-octagon bbl. Brass-plated hammer and lever. Sights: Open rear; brass blade front. Weight: 4.5 lbs. Plain straight-grip buttstock and Schnabel forend; brass commemorative medallion inlaid in buttstock, brass crescent-shaped buttplate. 10,000 produced. Made in 1971 only. Top value is for new, unfired gun.

MODEL 90 AUTO-LOADING CARBINE. . . . . NiB $172 Ex $142 Gd $102
Similar to Model 60 except w/16.5-inch bbl. w/folding leaf rear sight, bead front. 10-round tubular magazine. Uncheckered, carbine-style walnut stock w/bbl. Band and sling swivels. Weight: 5.75 lbs. Made from 1969-72.

MODEL 93G BOLT-ACTION RIFLE. . . . . . . NiB $172 Ex $147 Gd $111
Caliber: .22 Win Mag. 5-round magazine. 20.75-inch bbl. 39.5 inches overall. Weight: 5.75 lbs. Sights: Adj. open rear; bead front. Grooved receiver for scope mounts. Stamped checkering on walnut-finished hardwood stock w/Monte Carlo cheekpiece. Made from 1996 to date.

MODEL 93F BOLT-ACTION RIFLE . . . . NiB $147 Ex $100 Gd $95
Same general specifications as Model 93G except w/black graphite/polymer stock. Weight: 5.2 lbs. Made from 1997 to date.

NOTE: MODEL 99 LEVER-ACTION REPEATER
Introduced in 1899, this model has been produced in a variety of styles and calibers. Original designation "Model 1899" was changed to "Model 99" c.1920. Earlier rifles and carbines — similar to Models 99A, 99B and 99H — were supplied in calibers .25-35, .30-30, .303 Sav., .32-40 and .38-55. Post-WWII Models 99A, 99C, 99CD, 99DE, 99DL, 99F and 99PE have top tang safety other 99s have slide safety on right side of trigger guard. Models 99C and 99CD have detachable box magazine instead of traditional Model 99 rotary magazine.

MODEL 99A (I) . . . . NiB $910 Ex $704 Gd $318
Hammerless. Solid frame. Calibers: .30-30, .300 Sav., .303 Sav. Five-round rotary magazine. 24-inch bbl. Weight: 7.25 lbs. Sights: Open rear; bead front, on ramp. Plain straight-grip stock, tapered forearm. Made from 1920-36.

MODEL 99A (II) . . . . NiB $859 Ex $807 Gd $498
Current model. Similar to original Model 99A except w/top tang safety, 22-inch bbl., folding leaf rear sight, no crescent buttplate. Calibers: .243 Win., .250 Sav., .300 Sav., .308 Win. Made from 1971-82.

MODEL 99B . . . . NiB $1060 Ex $854 Gd $524
Takedown. Otherwise same as Model 99A except weight: 7.5 lbs. Made from 1920-36.

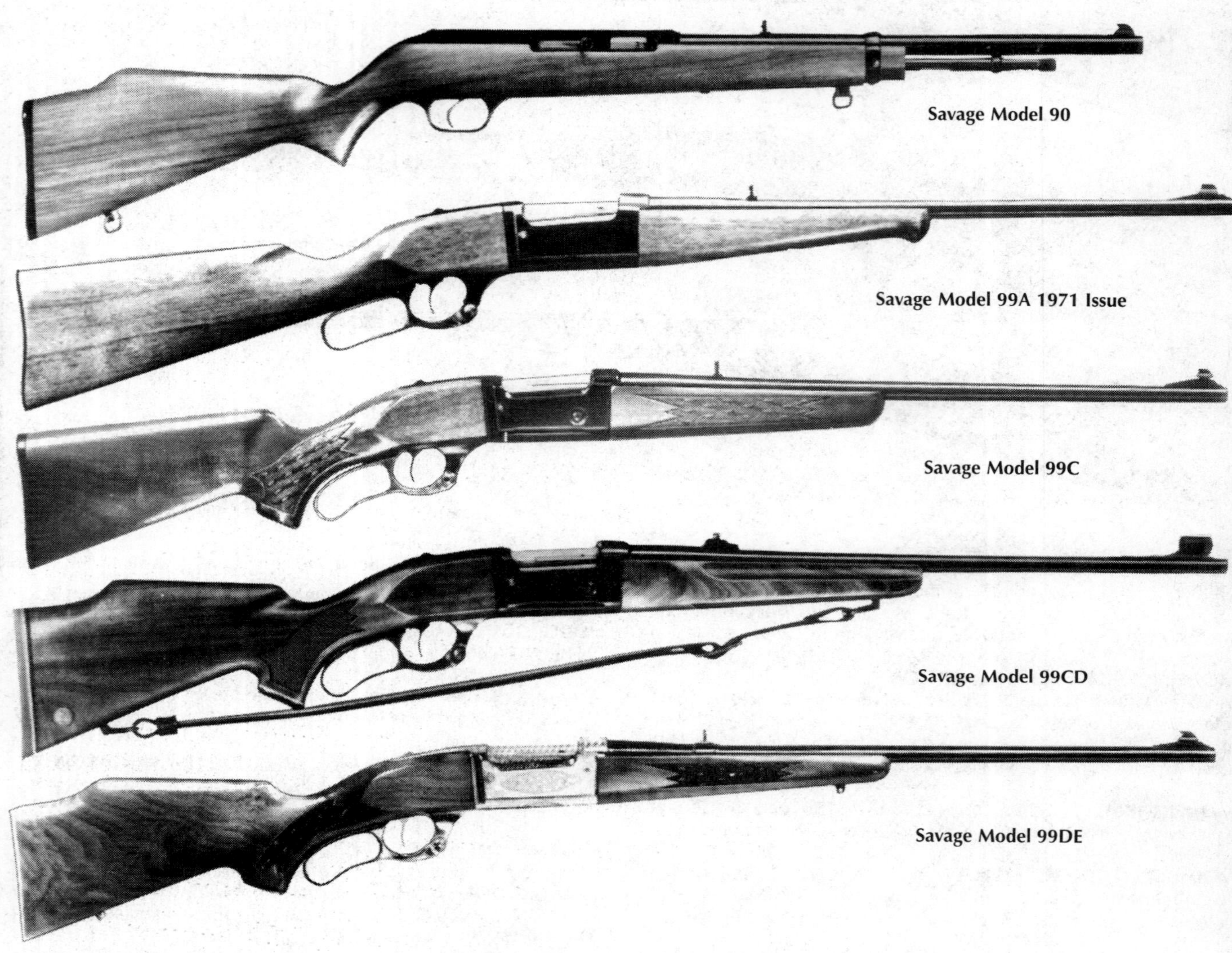

MODEL 99C . . . . NiB $525 Ex $435 Gd $375
Current model. Same as Model 99F except w/clip magazine instead of rotary. Calibers: .243 Win., .284 Win., .308 Win. Four round detachable magazine holds one round less in .284. Weight: 6.75 lbs. Made from 1965-98.

MODEL 99CD . . . . NiB $651 Ex $574 Gd $342
Deluxe version of Model 99C. Calibers: .243 Win., .250 Sav., .308 Win. Hooded ramp front sight. Weight: 8.25 lbs. Stock w/Monte Carlo comb and cheekpiece, checkered pistol-grip, grooved forearm, swivels and sling. Made from 1975 to 81.

MODEL 99DE CITATION GRADE. . . . . . . NiB $908 Ex $625 Gd $445
Same as Model 99PE, listed on page 348, except w/less elaborate engraving. Made from 1968-70.

MODEL 99DL DELUXE . . . . NiB $437 Ex $334 Gd $231
Postwar model. Calibers: .243 Win., .308 Win. Same as Model 99F, except w/high comb Monte Carlo stock, sling swivels. Weight: 6.75 lbs. Made from 1960-73.

MODEL 99E CARBINE (I) . . . . NiB $797 Ex $643 Gd $360
Pre-WWII type. Solid frame. Calibers: .22 Hi-Power, .250/3000, .30/30, .300 Sav., .303 Sav. w/22-inch bbl.; .300 Sav. 24-inch. Weight: 7 lbs. Other specifications same as Model 99A. Made from 1920-36.

MODEL 99E CARBINE (II). . . . . NiB $427 Ex $293 Gd $179
Current model. Solid frame. Calibers: .250 Sav., .243 Win., .300 Sav., .308 Win. 20- or 22-inch bbl. Checkered pistol-grip stock and forearm. Made from 1960-89.

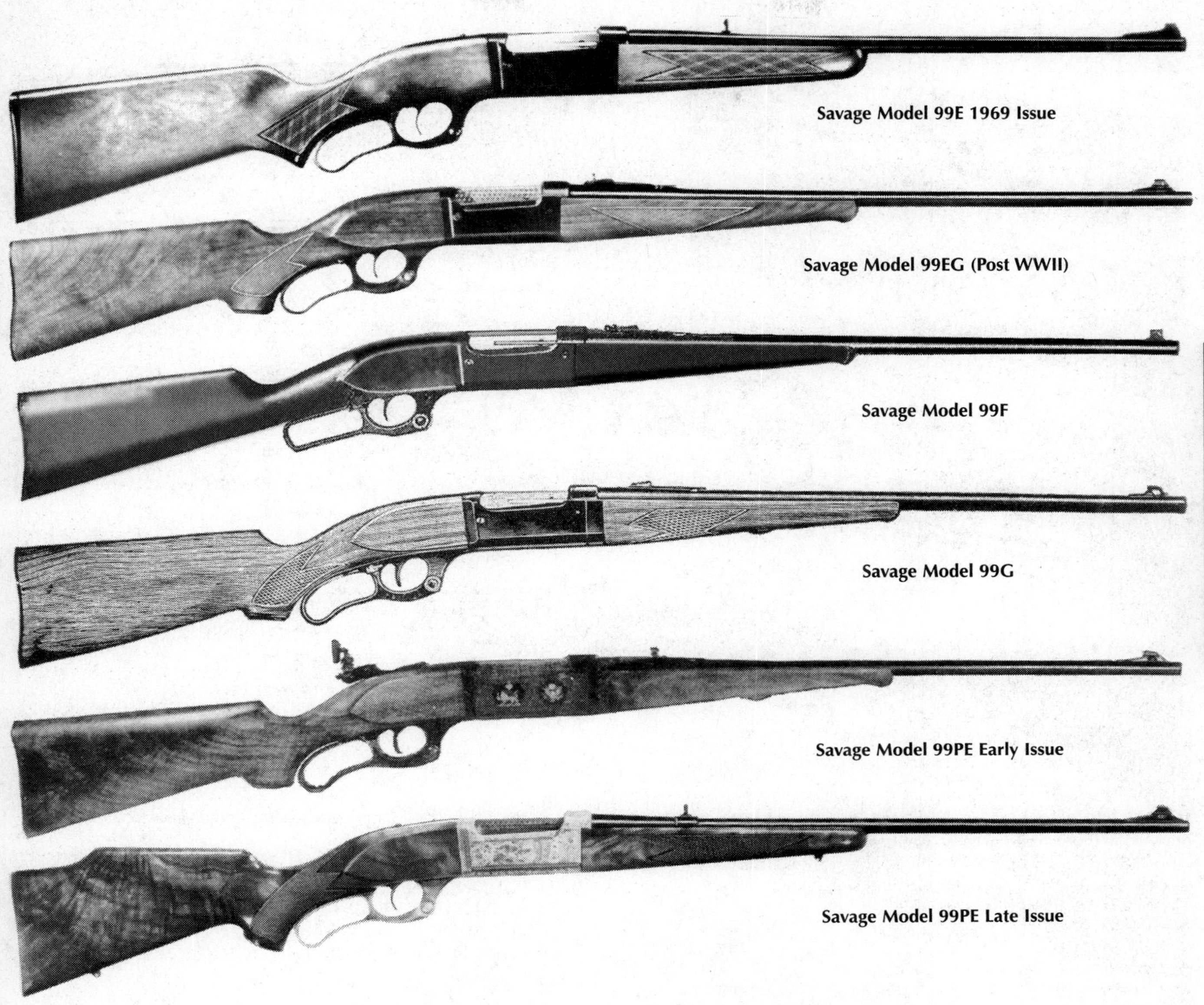
Savage Model 99E 1969 Issue

Savage Model 99EG (Post WWII)

Savage Model 99F

Savage Model 99G

Savage Model 99PE Early Issue

Savage Model 99PE Late Issue

MODEL 99EG (I) . . . . NiB $843 Ex $709 Gd $426
Pre-WWII type. Solid frame. Plain pistol-grip stock and forearm. Otherwise same as Model G. Made from 1936-41.

MODEL 99EG (II) . . . . NiB $658 Ex $452 Gd $349
Post-WWII type. Same as prewar model except w/checkered stock and forearm. Calibers: .250 Sav., .300 Sav., .308 Win. (intro. 1955), .243 Win., and .358 Win. Made from 1946-60.

MODEL 99F FEATHERWEIGHT (I) . . . . NiB $915 Ex $658 Gd $467
Pre-WWII type. Takedown. Specifications same as Model 99E, except weight: 6.5 lbs. Made from 1920-42.

MODEL 99F FEATHERWEIGHT (II) . . . . NiB $596 Ex $390 Gd $236
Postwar model. Solid frame. Calibers: .243 Win., .300 Sav., .308 Win. 22-inch bbl. Checkered pistol-grip stock and forearm. Weight: 6.5 lbs. Made from 1955-73.

MODEL 99G . . . . NiB $915 Ex $658 Gd $467
Takedown. Checkered pistol-grip stock and forearm. Weight: 7.25 lbs. Other specifications same as Model 99E. Made from 1920-42.

MODEL 99H CARBINE . . . . NiB $854 Ex $545 Gd $390
Solid frame. Calibers: .250/3000, .30/30, .303 Sav. 20-inch special weight bbl. Walnut carbine stock w/metal buttplate; walnut forearm w/bbl. band. Weight: 6.5 lbs. Open rear sights; ramped blade front sight. Other specifications same as Model 99A. Made from 1931-42.

MODEL 99K . . . . NiB $2341 Ex $2006 Gd $1095
Deluxe version of Model G w/similar specifications except w/fancy stock and engraving on receiver and bbl. Lyman peep rear sight and folding middle. Made from 1931-42.

MODEL 99PE PRESENTATION GRADE . . . NiB $1904 Ex $1646 Gd $771
Same as Model 99DL except w/engraved receiver (game scenes on sides), tang and lever, fancy walnut Monte Carlo stock and forearm w/hand checkering, QD swivels. Calibers: .243, .284, .308. Made from 1968-70.

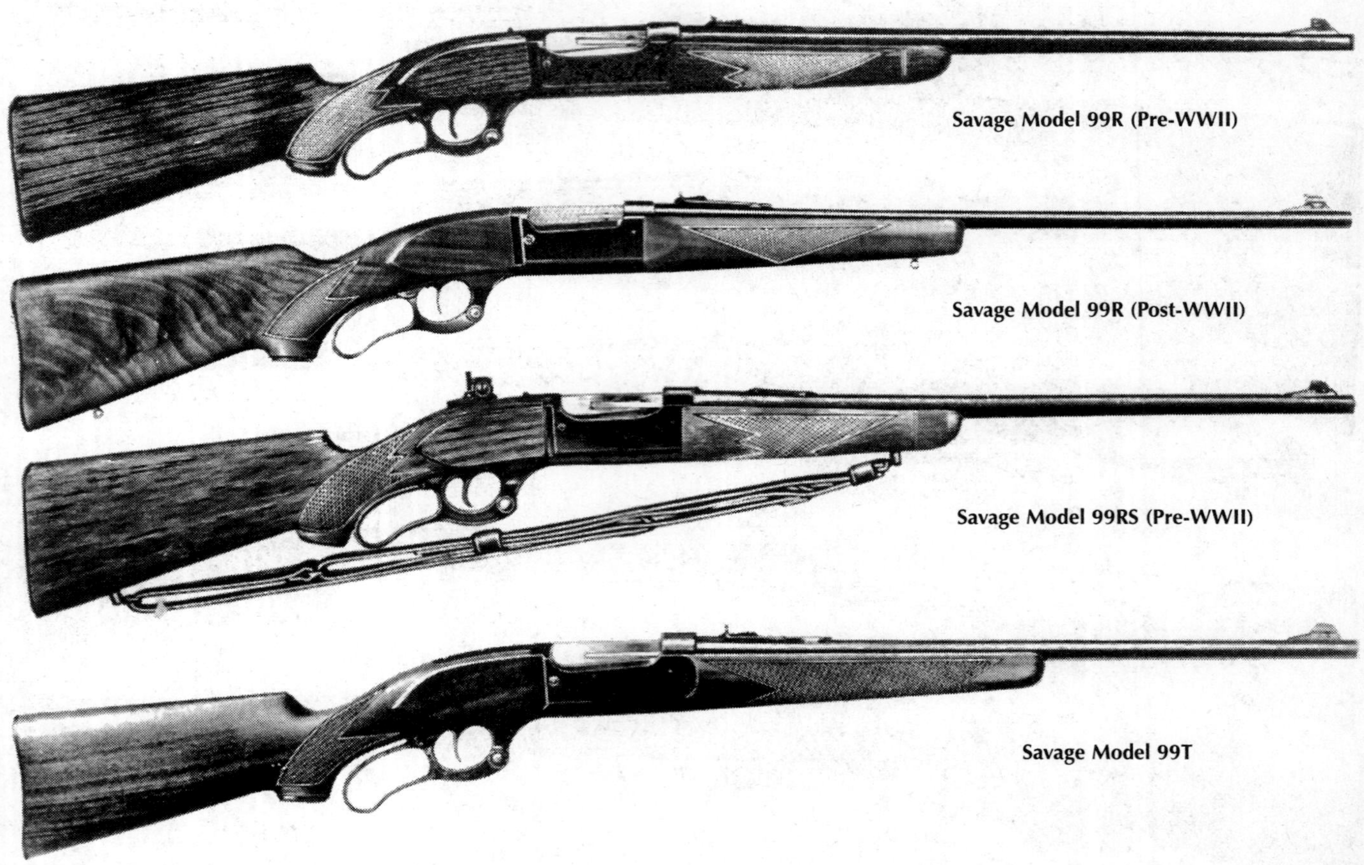

Savage Model 99R (Pre-WWII)

Savage Model 99R (Post-WWII)

Savage Model 99RS (Pre-WWII)

Savage Model 99T

MODEL 99R (I) . . . . NiB $910 Ex $653 Gd $473
Pre-WWII type. Solid frame. Calibers: .250-3000 (22-inch bbl.), .300 Sav. (24-inch bbl.). Weight: 7.5 lbs. Special large pistol-grip stock and forearm, checkered. General specifications same as other Model 99 rifles. Made from 1936-42.

MODEL 99R (II) . . . . NiB $838 Ex $447 Gd $318
Post-WWII type. Same as prewar mod except w/24-inch bbl. only, w/screw eyes for sling swivels. Calibers: .250 Sav., .300 Sav., .308 Win., .243 Win. and .358 Win. Made from 1946-60.

MODEL 99RS (I) . . . . NiB $833 Ex $576 Gd $447
Pre-WWII type. Same as prewar Model 99R except equipped w/Lyman rear peep sight and folding middle sight, quick detachable swivels and sling. Made from 1936-42.

MODEL 99RS (II). . . . . NiB $833 Ex $550 Gd $421
Post-WWII type. Same as postwar Model 99RS except equipped w/Redfield 70LH receiver sight, blank in middle sight slot. Made from 1946-58.

MODEL 99T . . . . NiB $838 Ex $473 Gd $359
Featherweight. Solid frame. Calibers: .22 Hi-Power, .30/30, .303 Sav. w/20-inch bbl.; .300 Sav. w/22-inch bbl. Checkered pistol-grip stock and beavertail forearm. Weight: 7 lbs. General specifications same as other Model 99 rifles. Made from 1936-42.

MODEL 99-358 . . . . NiB $589 Ex $435 Gd $332
Similar to current Model 99A except caliber .358 Win. has grooved forearm, recoil pad, swivel studs. Made from 1977-80.

MODEL 110 SPORTER
BOLT-ACTION RIFLE. . . . . NiB $237 Ex $175 Gd $124
Calibers: .243, .270, .308, .30-06. Four round box magazine. 22-inch bbl. Weight: About 6.75 lbs. Sights: Open rear; ramp front. Standard sporter stock with checkered pistol-grip. Made from 1958-63.

MODEL 110B BOLT-ACTION RIFLE
Same as Model 110E except with checkered select walnut Monte Carlo-style stock (early models) or brown laminated stock (late models). Calibers: .243 Win., .270 Win. .30-06, 7mm Rem. Mag., .338 Win. Mag. Made from 1976-91.
Early model . . . . NiB $343 Ex $278 Gd $196
Laminated stock model . . . . NiB $362 Ex $294 Gd $206

MODEL 110BL . . . . NiB $401 Ex $325 Gd $228
Same as Model 110B except has left-hand action.

MODEL 110C
Calibers: .22-250, .243, .25-06, .270, .308, .30-06, 7mm Rem. Mag., .300 Win. Mag. Four round detachable clip magazine (3-round in Magnum calibers). 22-inch bbl. (24-inch in .22-250 Magnum calibers). Weight: 6.75 lbs., Magnum, 7.75 to 8 lbs. Sights: Open rear; ramp front. Checkered Monte Carlo-style walnut stock (Magnum has recoil pad). Made from 1966-88.
Standard calibers. . . . . NiB $628 Ex $391 Gd $211
Magnum calibers. . . . . NiB $675 Ex $417 Gd $237

Savage Model 110

Savage Model 110B

Savage Model 110BL

Savage Model 110C

Savage Model 110E

Savage Model 110 MCL

MODEL 110CL

Same as Model 110C except has left-hand action. (Available only in .243 Win., .30-06, .270 Win. and 7mm Mag.) Made from 1963-66.

Standard calibers............... NiB $382 Ex $305 Gd $218
Magnum calibers............... NiB $408 Ex $310 Gd $228

MODEL 110CY
YOUTH/LADIES RIFLE .... NiB $382 Ex $331 Gd $202

Same as Model 110G except with walnut-finished hardwood stock with 12.5-inch pull. Calibers: .243 Win. and .300 Savage. Made from 1991 to date.

MODEL 110D

Similar to Model 110C except has internal magazine with hinged floorplate. Calibers: .243 Win., .270 Win., .30-06, 7mm Rem. Mag., .300 Win. Mag. Made from 1972-88.

Standard calibers.............. NiB $382 Ex $311 Gd $221
Magnum calibers.............. NiB $408 Ex $332 Gd $235

MODEL 110DL

Same as Model 110D except has left-hand action. Discontinued.

Standard calibers.............. NiB $446 Ex $363 Gd $256
Magnum calibers.............. NiB $479 Ex $388 Gd $273

Savage Model 110P

Savage Model 110PE

MODEL 110E. . . . . NiB $322 Ex $229 Gd $177
Calibers: .22-250, .223 Rem., .243 Win., .270 Win., .308, 7mm Rem. Mag., .30-06. Four round box magazine (3-round in Magnum). 20- or 22-inch bbl. (24-inch stainless steel in Magnum). Weight: 6.75 lbs.; Magnum, 7.75 lbs. Sights: Open rear; ramp front. Plain Monte Carlo stock on early production; current models have checkered stocks of walnut-finished hardwood (Magnum has recoil pad). Made from 1963-89.

MODEL 110EL. . . . . NiB $338 Ex $275 Gd $195
Same as Model 110E except has left-hand action made in .30-06 and 7mm Rem. Mag. only. Made from 1969-73.

MODEL 110F/110K BOLT-ACTION RIFLE
Same as Model 110E except Model 110F has black Rynite synthetic stock, swivel studs; made 1988-93. Model 110K has laminated camouflage stock; made from 1986-88.
Model 110F, adj. sights . . . . NiB $377 Ex $306 Gd $216
Model 110FNS, no sights . . . . NiB $393 Ex $317 Gd $223
Model 110K, standard calibers . . . . NiB $403 Ex $327 Gd $230
Model 110K, magnum calibers . . . . NiB $455 Ex $368 Gd $258

MODEL 110FM SIERRA ULTRA LIGHT. . . . NiB $383 Ex $306 Gd $208
Calibers: .243 Win., .270 Win., .30-06, .308 Win. Five round magazine. 20-inch bbl. 41.5 inches overall. Weight: 6.25 lbs. No sights w/drilled and tapped receiver. Black graphite/fiberglass composition stock. Non-glare matte blue finish. Made 1996 to date.

MODEL 110FP POLICE RIFLE . . . . . NiB $420 Ex $322 Gd $219
Calibers: .223, .308 Win. Four round magazine. 24-inch bbl. 45.5 inches overall. Weight: 9 lbs. Black Rynite composite stock. Matte blue finish. Made from 1990 to date.

MODEL 110G BOLT-ACTION RIFLE
Calibers: .223, .22-250, .243 Win., .270, 7mm Rem. Mag., .308 Win., .30-06, .300 Win. Mag. Five round (standard) or 4-round magazine (magnum). 22- or 24-inch bbl. 42.38 overall (standard). Weight: 6.75 to 7.5 lbs. Ramp front sight, adj. rear. Checkered walnut-finished hardwood stock with rubber recoil pad. Made from 1989-93.
Model 110G, standard calibers. . . . . NiB $383 Ex $280 Gd $177
Model 110G, magnum calibers. . . . . NiB $409 Ex $306 Gd $219
Model 110GLNS, left-hand, no sights . . . . . NiB $415 Ex $337 Gd $236

MODEL 110GV VARMINT RIFLE . . . . NiB $383 Ex $306 Gd $203
Similar to the Model 110G except fitted with medium-weight varmint bbl. with no sights. Receiver drilled and tapped for scope mounts. Calibers .22-250 and .223 only. Made from 1989-93.

MODEL 110M MAGNUM
Same as Model 110MC except calibers: 7mm Rem. Mag. .264, .300 and .338 Win. 24-inch bbl. Stock with recoil pad. Weight: 7.75 to 8 lbs. Made from 1963-69.
Model 110M Magnum . . . . NiB $435 Ex $419 Gd $239
Model 110ML Magnum. . . . . NiB $460 Ex $445 Gd $419

MODEL 110MC
Same as Model 110 except has Monte Carlo-style stock. Calibers: .22-250, .243 Win., .270, .308, .30-06. 24-inch bbl. in .22-250. Made from 1959-69.
Model 110MC. . . . . NiB $253 Ex $201 Gd $134
Model 110MCL . . . . NiB $259 Ex $212 Gd $151

MODEL 110P PREMIER GRADE
Calibers: .243 Win., 7mm Rem. Mag., .30-06. Four round magazine (3-round in Magnum). 22-inch bbl. (24-inch stainless steel in Magnum). Weight: 7 lbs.; Magnum, 7.75 lbs. Sights: Open rear folding leaf; ramp front. French walnut stock w/Monte Carlo comb and cheekpiece, rosewood forend tip and pistol-grip cap, skip checkering, sling swivels (Magnum has recoil pad). Made from 1964-70.
Calibers .243 Win. and .30-06. . . . . NiB $486 Ex $358 Gd $255
Caliber 7mm Rem. Mag. . . . . NiB $502 Ex $383 Gd $280

MODEL 110PE PRESENTATION GRADE
Same as Model 110P except has engraved receiver, floorplate and trigger guard, stock of choice grade French walnut. Made from 1968-70.
Calibers .243 Win. and .30-06. . . . . NiB $740 Ex $597 Gd $416
Caliber 7mm Rem. Mag. . . . . NiB $797 Ex $644 Gd $448

MODEL 110PEL PRESENTATION GRADE
Same as Model 110PE except has left-hand action.
Calibers .243 Win. and .30-06. . . . . NiB $797 Ex $644 Gd $448
Caliber 7mm Rem. Mag. . . . . NiB $869 Ex $700 Gd $486

MODEL 110PL PREMIER GRADE
Same as Model 110P except has left-hand action.
Calibers .243 Win. and .30-06. . . . . NiB $520 Ex $393 Gd $263
Caliber 7mm Rem. Mag. . . . . NiB $541 Ex $393 Gd $285

MODEL 110S/110V
Same as Model 110E except Model 110S in .308 Win. only; discontinued 1985. Model 110V in .22-250 and .223 Rem. w/heavy 2-inch barrel, 47 inches overall, weight: 9 lbs. Discontinued. 1989.
Model 110S . . . . NiB $382 Ex $311 Gd $221
Model 110V. NiB $408 Ex $329 Gd $235

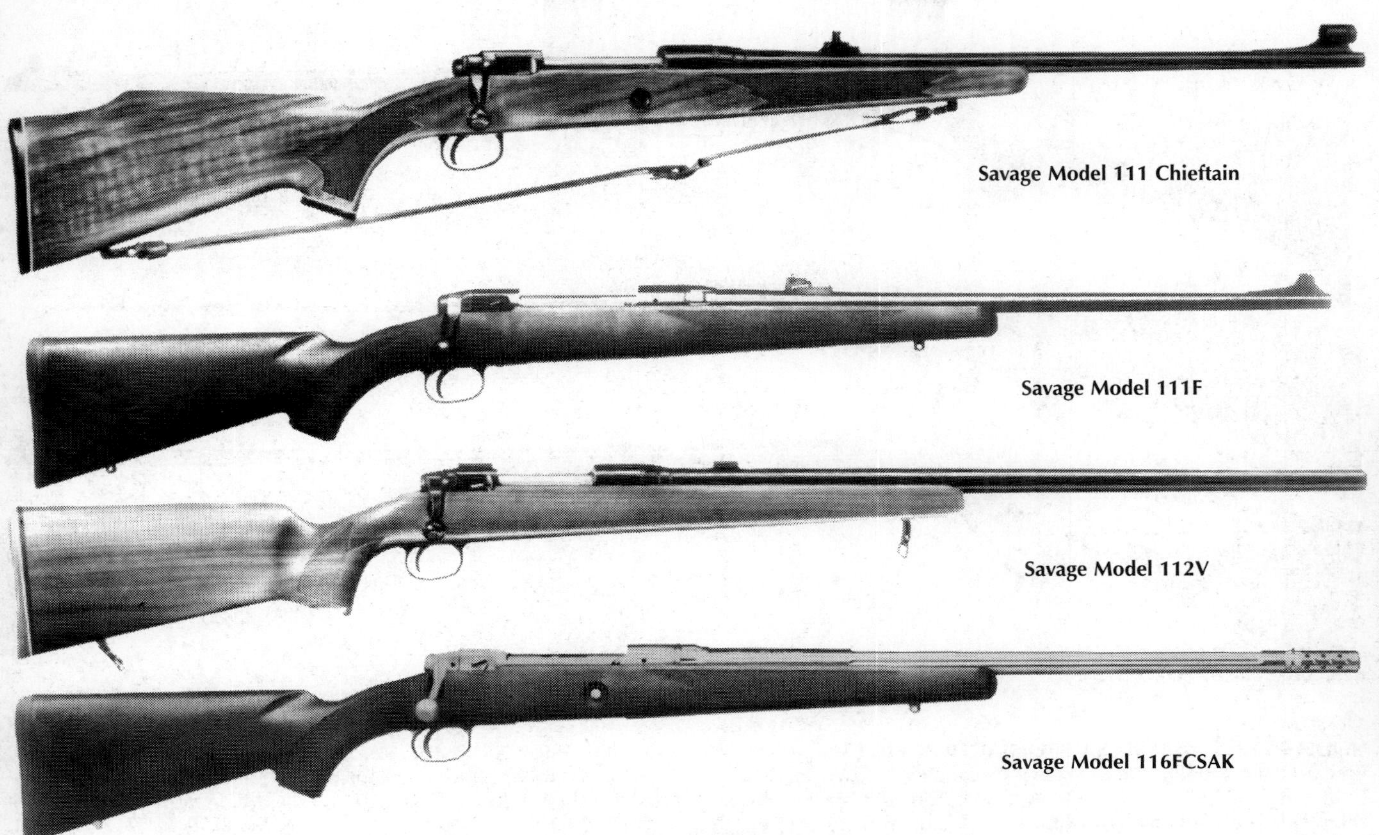
Savage Model 111 Chieftain

Savage Model 111F

Savage Model 112V

Savage Model 116FCSAK

MODEL 111 CHIEFTAIN BOLT-ACTION RIFLE
Calibers: .243 Win., .270 Win., 7x57mm, 7mm Rem. Mag. .30-06. 4-round clip magazine (3-round in Magnum). 22-inch bbl. (24-inch in Magnum). Weight: 7.5 lbs., 8.25 lbs. Magnum. Sights: Leaf rear; hooded ramp front. Select walnut stock w/Monte Carlo comb and cheekpiece, checkered, pistol-grip cap, QD swivels and sling. Made from 1974-79.
Standard calibers. . . . . NiB $440 Ex $363 Gd $234
Magnum calibers. . . . . NiB $493 Ex $404 Gd $291

MODELS 111F, 111FC, 111FNS CLASSIC HUNTERS
Similar to the Model 111G except with graphite/fiberglass composite stock. Weight: 6.25 lbs. Made from 1994 to date.
Model 111F (Box mag., right/left hand). . . NiB $388 Ex $260 Gd $208
Model 111FC (Detachable magazine). . . . . NiB $466 Ex $337 Gd $234
Model 111FNS (Box mag., no sights, R/L hand) . . . . NiB $363 Ex $296 Gd $211

MODELS 111G, 111GC, 111GNS CLASSIC HUNTERS
Calibers: .22-250 Rem., .223 Rem., .243 Win., .25-06 Rem. .250 Sav., .270 Win., 7mm-08 Rem., 7mm Rem. Mag., .30-06, .300 Sav., .300 Win. Mag., .308 Win., .338 Win. 22- or 24-inch bbl. Weight: 7 lbs. Ramp front sight, adj. open rear. Walnut-finished hardwood stock. Blued finish. Made from 1994 to date.
Model 111G (Box mag., right/left hand). . . NiB $388 Ex $311 Gd $182
Model 111GC (Detachable mag., R/L hand) . . . . NiB $409 Ex $316 Gd $193
Model 111GNS (Box mag., no sights). . . . . NiB $368 Ex $285 Gd $157

MODEL 112BV,112BVSS HEAVY VARMINT RIFLES
Similar to the Model 110G except fitted with 26-inch heavy bbl. Laminated wood stock with high comb. .22-250 and .223 only.
Model 112BV (Made 1993-94) . . . . NiB $601 Ex $447 Gd $334
Model 112BVSS (Fluted stainless bbl.; made since 1994) . . . . NiB $627 Ex $473 Gd $370

MODEL 112FV,112FVS,112FVSS VARMINT RIFLES
Similar to the Model 110G except fitted with 26-inch heavy bbl. and Dupont Rynite stock. Calibers: .22-250, .223 and .220 Swift (112FVS only). Blued or stainless finish. Made from 1991 to date.
Model 112FV (blued) . . . . NiB $387 Ex $316 Gd $226
Model 112FV-S (blued, single round), disc. 1993. . . . . NiB $421 Ex $395 Gd $251
Model 112FVSS (stainless) . . . . NiB $550 Ex $473 Gd $292
Model 112 FVSS-S (stainless, single round). NiB $576 Ex $498 Gd $318

MODEL 112V VARMINT RIFLE . . . . NiB $441 Ex $359 Gd $255
Bolt action, single shot. Caliber: .220 Swift, .222 Rem., .223 Rem., .22-250, .243 Win., .25-06. 26-inch heavy bbl. with scope bases. Supplied w/o sights. Weight: 9.25 lbs. Select walnut stock in varmint style w/checkered pistol-grip, high comb, QD sling swivels. Made from 1975-79.

MODEL 114C, 114CE, 114CU RIFLES
Calibers: .270 Win., 7mm Rem. Mag., .30-06, .300 Win. Mag. 22- or 24-inch bbl. Weight: 7 lbs. Detachable 3- or 4-round magazine. Ramp front sight; adjustable, open rear; (114CU has no sights). Checkered select walnut stock w/oil finish, red butt pad. Schnabel forend and skip-line checkering (114CE). High-luster blued finish. Made from 1991 to date.
Model 114C (Classic) . . . . NiB $524 Ex $447 Gd $272
Model 114CE (Classic European) . . . . NiB $529 Ex $447 Gd $277
Model 114CU (Classic Ultra) . . . . NiB $545 Ex $421 Gd $292

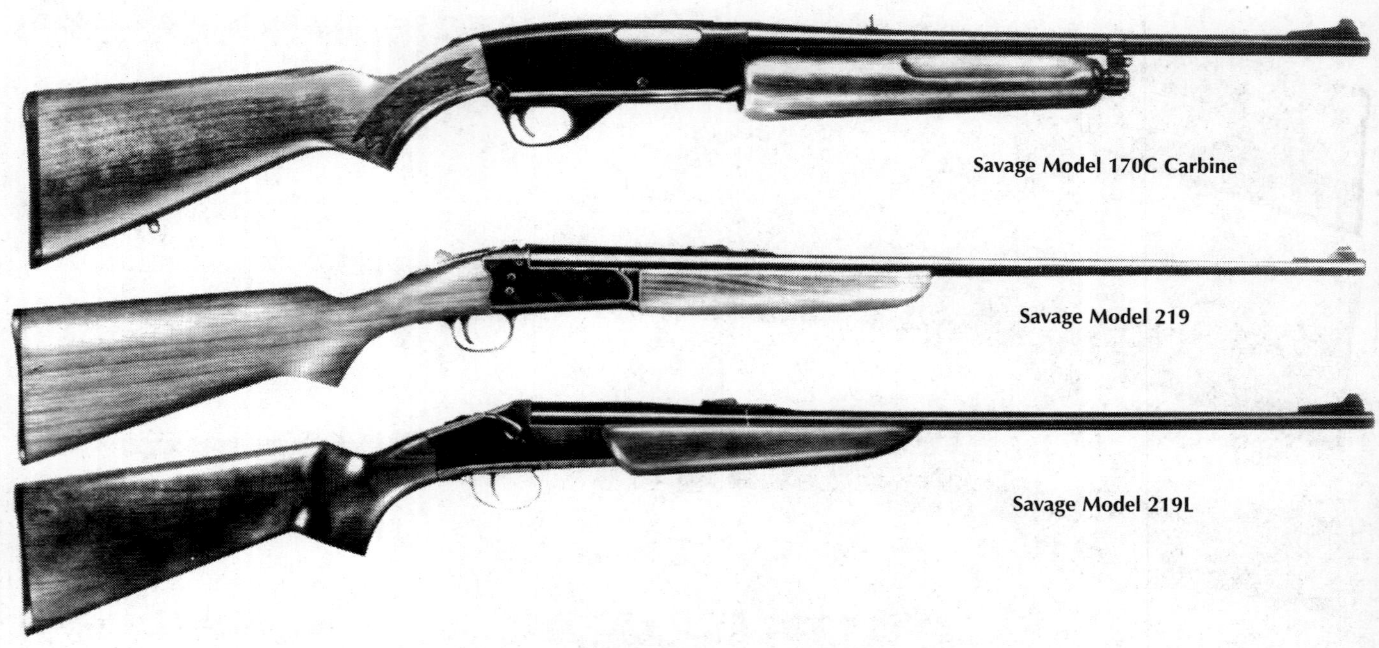
Savage Model 170C Carbine

Savage Model 219

Savage Model 219L

MODELS 116FSAK, 116FCSAK BOLT-ACTION RIFLES
Similar to the Model 116FSK except in calibers .270 Win., .30-06, 7mm Mag., .300 Win. Mag., .338 Win. Mag. Fluted 22-inch stainless bbl. w/adj. muzzle brake. Weight: 6.5 lbs. Made from 1994 to date.
Model 116FSAK .... NiB $545 Ex $493 Gd $313
Model 116FCSAK (detachable mag.)...... NiB $596 Ex $499 Gd $339

MODELS 116FSC, 116FSS BOLT-ACTION RIFLES
Improved Model 110 with satin stainless action and bbl. Calibers: .223, .243, .270, .30-06, 7mm Rem. Mag., .300 Win. Mag., .338 Win. Mag. 22- or 24-inch bbl. Four or 5-round capacity. Weight: About 7.5 lbs. Black Rynite stock w/recoil pad and swivel studs. Receiver drilled and tapped for scope mounts, no sights. Made from 1991 to date.
Model 116FSS...................... NiB $571 Ex $503 Gd $313
Model 116FSC, detachable magazine..... NiB $596 Ex $516 Gd $340

MODEL 116FSK KODIAK RIFLE......... NiB $622 Ex $442 Gd $339
Similar to the Model 116FSS except with 22-inch bbl. chambered for 338 Win. Mag. only. "Shock Suppressor" recoil reducer. Made from 1993 to date.

MODEL 116SE, 116US RIFLES
Calibers: .270 Win., 7mm Rem Mag., .30-06, .300 Win. Mag. (116US); .300 Win. Mag., .338 Win. mag., .425 Express, .458 Win. Mag. (116SE). 24-inch stainless barrel (with muzzle brake 116SE only). 45.5 inches overall. Weight: 7.2 to 8.5 lbs. Three round magazine. 3-leaf Express sights 116SE only. Checkered Classic style select walnut stock with ebony forend tip. Stainless finish. Made from 1994 to date.
Model 116SE (Safari Express) ..... NiB $938 Ex $732 Gd $500
Model 116US (Ultra Stainless) .... NiB $703 Ex $552 Gd $372

MODEL 170 PUMP-ACTION CENTERFIRE RIFLE .... NiB $268 Ex $217 Gd $150
Calibers: .30-30, .35 Rem. Three round tubular magazine. 22-inch bbl. Weight: 6.75 lbs. Sights: Folding leaf rear; ramp front. Select walnut stock w/checkered pistol-grip Monte Carlo comb, grooved slide handle. Made from 1970-81.

MODEL 170C CARBINE .... NiB $304 Ex $222 Gd $150
Same as Model 170 Rifle except has 18.5-inch bbl., straight comb stock, weight: 6 lbs.; caliber .30-30 only. Made from 1974-81.

MODEL 219 SINGLE-SHOT RIFLE
Hammerless. Takedown. Shotgun-type action with top lever. Calibers: .22 Hornet, .25-20, .32-20, .30-30. 26-inch bbl. Weight: about 6 lbs. Sights: Open rear; bead front. Plain pistol-grip stock and forearm. Made from 1938-65.
Model 219........................... NiB $278 Ex $201 Gd $145
Model 219L (w/side lever, made 1965-67) . NiB $201 Ex $150 Gd $114

MODEL 221-229 UTILITY GUNS
Same as Model 219 except in various calibers, supplied in combination with an interchangeable shotgun bbl. All versions discontinued.
Model 221 (.30-30,12-ga. 30-inch bbl.)... NiB $201 Ex $165 Gd $119
Model 222 (.30-30,16-ga. 28-inch bbl.) ... NiB $182 Ex $150 Gd $109
Model 223 (.30-30, 20-ga. 28-inch bbl.).... NiB $163 Ex $134 Gd $98
Model 227 (.22 Hornet, 12-ga. 30-inch bbl.)... NiB $215 Ex $175 Gd $126
Model 228 (.22 Hornet, 16-ga. 28-inch bbl.).. NiB $207 Ex $170 Gd $123
Model 229 (.22 Hornet, 20-ga. 28-inch bbl.) . NiB $201 Ex $165 Gd $119

MODEL 340 BOLT-ACTION REPEATER
Calibers: .22 Hornet, .222 Rem., .223 Rem., .225 Win., .30-30. Clip magazine; 4-round capacity (3-round in 30-30). Bbl. lengths: Originally 20-inch in .30-30, 22-inch in .22 Hornet; later 22-inch in .30-30, 24-inch in other calibers. Weight: 6.5 to 7.5 lbs. depending on caliber and vintage. Sights: Open rear (folding leaf on recent production); ramp front. Early models had plain pistol-grip stock, checkered since 1965. Made from 1950-85. (Note: Those rifles produced between 1947-1950 were .22 Hornet Stevens Model .322 and .30-30 Model .325. The Savage model, however, was designated Model .340 for all calibers.)
Pre-1965 with plain stock .... NiB $317 Ex $217 Gd $150
Current model.................. NiB $227 Ex $186 Gd $133
Savage Model 340C Carbine ...... NiB $330 Ex $217 Gd $150

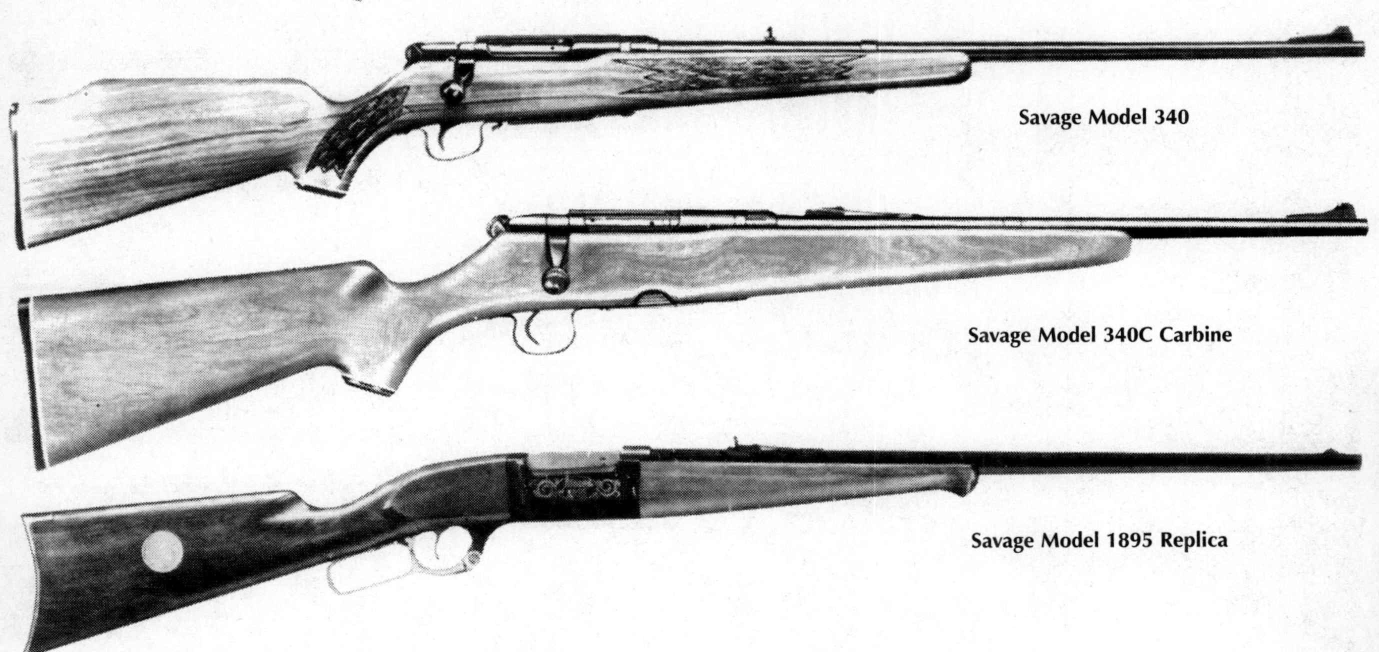
Savage Model 340

Savage Model 340C Carbine

Savage Model 1895 Replica

MODEL 340S DELUXE .... NiB $382 Ex $272 Gd $166
Same as Model 340 except has checkered stock, screw eyes for sling, peep rear sight, hooded front. Made from 1955-60.

MODEL 342 .... NiB $372 Ex $279 Gd $176
Designation, 1950 to 1955, of Model 340 .22 Hornet.

MODEL 342S DELUXE .... NiB $408 Ex $305 Gd $176
Designation, 1950 to 1955, of Model 340S .22 Hornet.

**ANNIVERSARY MODEL
1895 LEVER-ACTION .... NiB $1585 Ex $1379 Gd $1070**
Replica of Savage Model 1895 Hammerless Lever-Action Rifle issued to commemorate the 75th anniversary (1895-1970) of Savage Arms. Caliber: .308 Win. Five round rotary magazine. 24-inch full-octagon bbl. Engraved receiver. Brass-plated lever. Sights: Open rear; brass blade front. Plain straight-grip buttstock, Schnabel-type forend; brass medallion inlaid in buttstock, brass crescent-shaped buttplate. 9,999 produced. Made in 1970 only. Top value is for new, unfired specimen.

**MODEL 1903 SLIDE-ACTION
REPEATER .... NiB $408 Ex $279 Gd $218**
Hammerless. Takedown. Caliber: .22 Short, Long, LR. Detachable box magazine. 24-inch octagon bbl. Weight: About 5 lbs. Sights: Open rear; bead front. Pistol-grip stock, grooved slide handle. Made from 1903-21.

**MODEL 1904 BOLT-ACTION
SINGLE-SHOT RIFLE .... NiB $176 Ex $125 Gd $73**
Takedown. .22 Short, Long, LR. 18-inch bbl. Weight: About 3 lbs. Sights: Open rear; bead front. Plain, straight-grip, one-piece stock. Made from 1904-17.

**MODEL 1905 BOLT-ACTION
SINGLE-SHOT RIFLE .... NiB $176 Ex $125 Gd $73**
Takedown. .22 Short, Long, LR. 22-inch bbl. Weight: About 5 lbs. Sights: Open rear; bead front. Plain, straight-grip one-piece stock. Made from 1905-19.

**MODEL 1909 SLIDE-ACTION
REPEATER .... NiB $402 Ex $281 Gd $204**
Hammerless. Takedown. Similar to Model 1903 except has 20-inch round bbl., plain stock and forearm, weight: Approximately 4.75 lbs. Made from 1909-15.

**MODEL 1912
AUTOLOADING RIFLE................ NiB $519 Ex $329 Gd $194**
Takedown. Caliber: 22 LR. only. Seven round detachable box magazine. 20-inch bbl., plain stock and forearm. Made from 1912-16.

**MODEL 1914 SLIDE-ACTION
REPEATER .... NiB $405 Ex $281 Gd $204**
Hammerless. Takedown. Caliber: .22 Short, Long, LR, Tubular magazine holds 20 Short, 17 Long, 15 LR. 24-inch octagon bbl. Weight: About 5.75 lbs. Sights: Open rear; bead front. Plain pistol-grip stock, grooved slide handle. Made from 1914-24.

MODEL 1920 HI-POWER BOLT-ACTION RIFLE
Short Mauser-type action. Calibers: .250/3000, .300 Sav. Five round box magazine. 22-inch bbl. in .250 cal.; 24-inch in .300 cal. Weight: About 6 lbs. Sights: Open rear; bead front. Checkered pistol-grip stock w/slender forearm and Schnabel tip. Made from 1920-26.
**Model 1920
Hi-Power
(.250-3000 Sav.)..................... NiB $599 Ex $419 Gd $265**
**Model 1920
Hi-Power
(.300 Sav.)......................... NiB $548 Ex $368 Gd $239**

NOTE: *In 1965, Savage began the importation of rifles manufactured by J. G. Anschutz GmbH, Ulm, West Germany. Models designated "Savage/Anschutz" are listed in this section, those marketed in the U.S. under the "Anschutz" name are included in that firm's listings. Anschutz rifles are now distributed in the U.S. by Precision Sales Int'l., Westfield, Mass. See "Anschutz" for detailed specifications.*

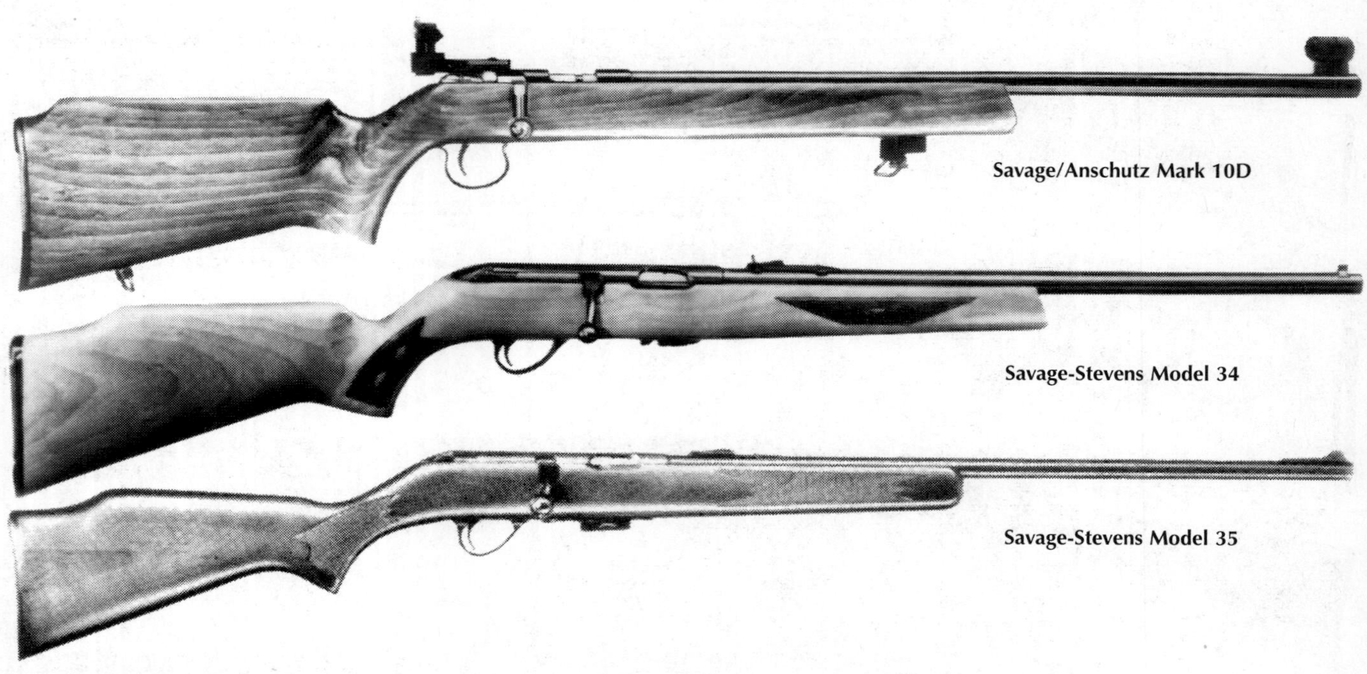

Savage/Anschutz Mark 10D

Savage-Stevens Model 34

Savage-Stevens Model 35

MARK 10 BOLT-ACTION TARGET RIFLE. . . . . NiB $488 Ex $329 Gd $231
Single shot. Caliber: .22 LR. 26-inch bbl. Weight: 8.5 lbs. Sights: Anschutz micrometer rear; globe front. Target stock w/full pistol-grip and cheekpiece, adj. hand stop and swivel. Made from 1967-72.

MARK 10D . . . . NiB $514 Ex $334 Gd $231
Same as Mark 10 except has redesigned stock with Monte Carlo comb, different rear sight. Weight: 7.75 lbs. Made in 1972.

MODEL 54 CUSTOM SPORTER. . . . . NiB $730 Ex $601 Gd $344
Same as Anschutz Model 1422D.

MODEL 54M . . . . NiB $892 Ex $634 Gd $402
Same as Anschutz Model 1522D.

MODEL 64 BOLT-ACTION TARGET RIFLE . . . . NiB $601 Ex $447 Gd $292
Same as Anschutz Model 1403.

MODEL 153 BOLT-ACTION SPORTER . . . . NiB $653 Ex $447 Gd $318
Caliber: .222 Rem. Three round clip magazine. 24-inch bbl. Sights: Folding leaf open rear; hooded ramp front. Weight: 6.75 lbs. French walnut stock w/cheekpiece, skip checkering, rosewood forend tip and grip cap, swivels. Made from 1964-67.

MODEL 153S. . . . . NiB $730 Ex $524 Gd $344
Same as Model 153 except has double-set trigger. Made from 1965-67.

MODEL 164 CUSTOM SPORTER. . . . . NiB $550 Ex $395 Gd $241
Same as Anschutz Model 1416.

MODEL 164M. . . . . NiB $627 Ex $421 Gd $267
Same as Anschutz Model 1516.

MODEL 184 SPORTER . . . . NiB $601 Ex $447 Gd $241
Same as Anschutz Model 1441.

NOTE: *Since J. Stevens Arms (see also separate listing) is a division of Savage Industries, certain Savage models carry the "Stevens" name.*

MODEL 34 BOLT-ACTION REPEATER . . . . NiB $165 Ex $109 Gd $72
Caliber: .22 Short, Long, LR. 20-inch bbl. Weight: 4.75 lbs. Sights: Open rear; bead front. Plain pistol-grip stock. Made from 1965-80.

MODEL 34M . . . . NiB $150 Ex $114 Gd $83
Same as Model 34 except chambered for 22 WMR. Made from 1969-73.

MODEL 35 . . . . NiB $150 Ex $114 Gd $83
Bolt-action repeater. Caliber: 22 LR. Six round clip magazine. 22-inch bbl. Weight: About 5 lbs. Sights: Open rear; ramp front. Monte Carlo stock w/checkered pistol grip and forearm. Made from 1982-85.

MODEL 35M . . . . NiB $175 Ex $124 Gd $88
Same as Model 35 except chambered for 22 WMR. Made from 1982-85.

MODEL 46 BOLT-ACTION RIFLE . . . . NiB $160 Ex $114 Gd $83
Caliber: .22 Short, Long, LR. Tubular magazine holds 22 Short, 17 Long, 15 LR. 20-inch bbl. Weight: 5 lbs. Plain pistol-grip stock on early production; later models have Monte Carlo stock w/checkering. Made from 1969-73.

MODEL 65 BOLT-ACTION RIFLE. . . . . NiB $175 Ex $124 Gd $83
Caliber: .22 Short, Long, LR. Five round clip magazine. 20-inch bbl. Weight: 5 lbs. Sights: Open rear; ramp front. Monte Carlo stock w/checkered pistol grip and forearm. Made from 1969-73.

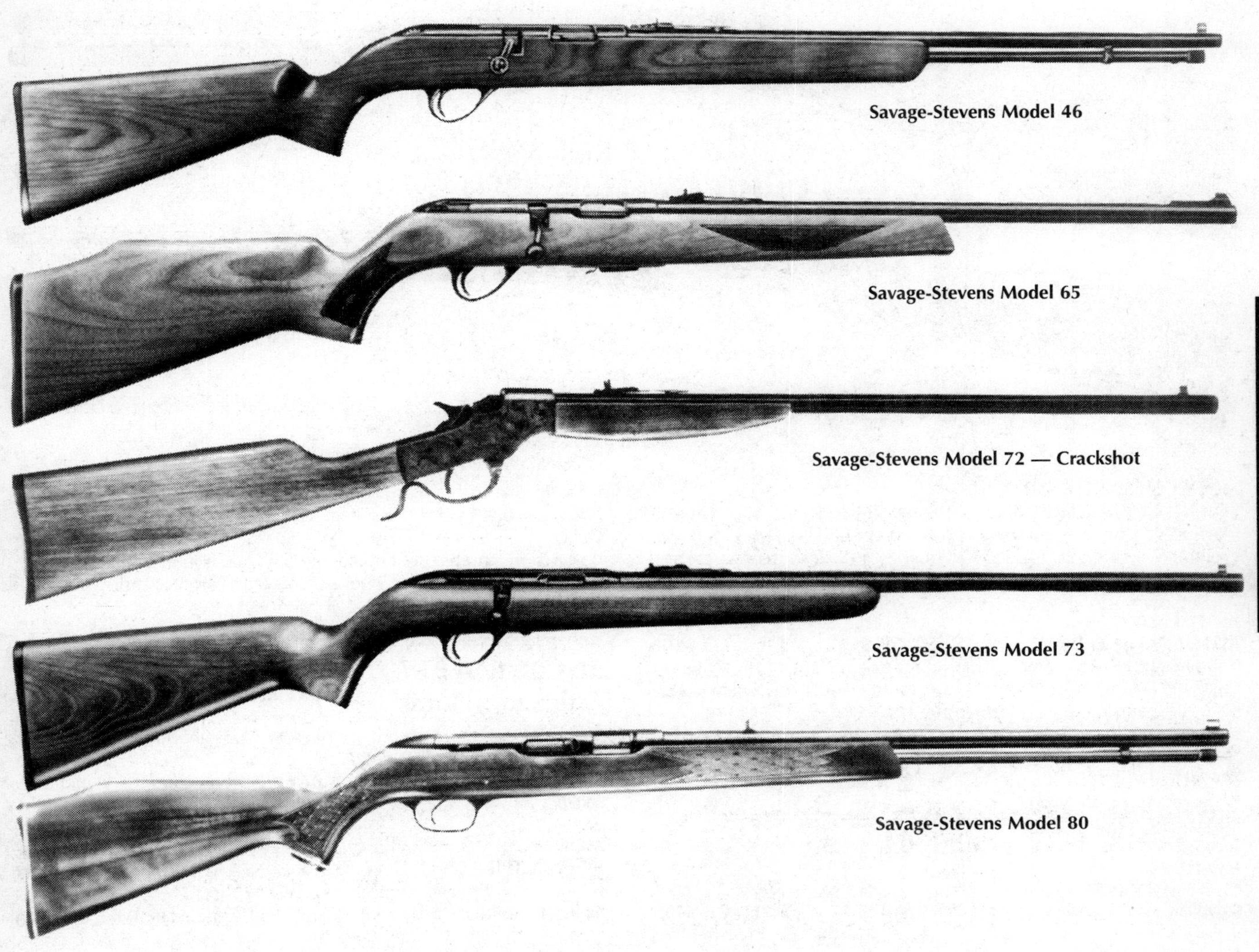

Savage-Stevens Model 46

Savage-Stevens Model 65

Savage-Stevens Model 72 — Crackshot

Savage-Stevens Model 73

Savage-Stevens Model 80

MODEL 65M . . . . NiB $175 Ex $134 Gd $93
Same as Model 65 except chambered for .22 WMR, has 22-inch bbl., weighs 5.25 lbs. Made from 1969-81.

NOTE: *The Model 72 is a "Favorite"-type single-shot unlike the smaller, original "Crackshot" made by Stevens from 1913-39.*

MODEL 72 CRACKSHOT SINGLE-SHOT LEVER-ACTION RIFLE . . . . NiB $278 Ex $227 Gd $150
Falling-block action. Casehardened frame. Caliber: .22 Short, Long, LR. 22-inch octagon bbl. Weight: 4.5lbs. Sights: Open rear; bead front. Plain straight-grip stock and forend of walnut. Made from 1972 to date.

MODEL 73 BOLT-ACTION SINGLE-SHOT . . NiB $124 Ex $103 Gd $83
Caliber: .22 Short, Long, LR. 20-inch bbl. Weight: 4.75 lbs. Sights: Open rear; bead front. Plain pistol-grip stock. Made from 1965-80.

MODEL 73Y YOUTH MODEL . . . . . . NiB $129 Ex $109 Gd $83
Same as Model 73 except has 18-inch bbl., 1.5-inch shorter butt-stock, weight: 4.5 lbs. Made from 1965-80.

MODEL 74 LITTLE FAVORITE . . . . NiB $196 Ex $184 Gd $114
Same as Model 72 Crackshot except has black-finished frame, 22-inch round bbl., walnut-finished hardwood stock. Weight: 4.75 lbs. Made from 1972-74.

MODEL 80 AUTOLOADING RIFLE . . . . NiB $175 Ex $145 Gd $105
Caliber: 22 LR. 15-round tubular magazine. 20-inch bbl. Weight: 6 lbs. Sights: Open rear, bead front. Monte Carlo stock of walnut w/checkered pistol-grip and forearm. Made from 1976 to date. (Note: This rifle is essentially the same as the Model 60 of 1969-72 except for a different style of checkering, side instead of top safety and plain bead instead of ramp front sight.)

MODEL 88 AUTOLOADING RIFLE . . . . NiB $180 Ex $169 Gd $108
Similar to Model 60 except has walnut-finished hardwood stock, plain bead front sight. Weight: 5.75 lbs. Made from 1969-72.

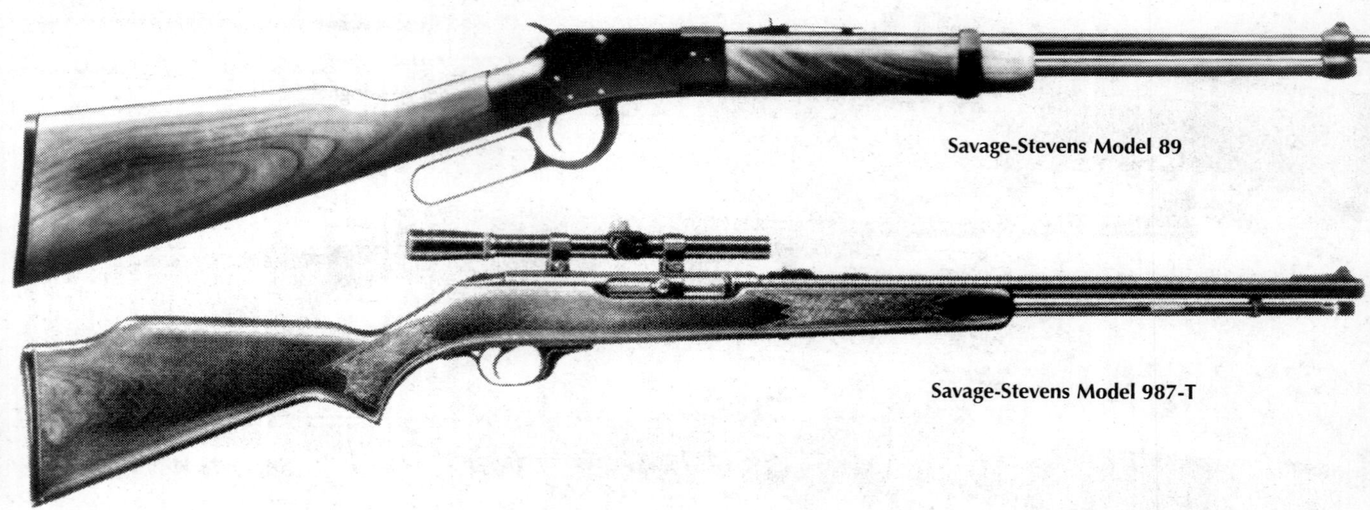

MODEL 89 SINGLE-SHOT LEVER-ACTION CARBINE . . . . NiB $113 Ex $98 Gd $72
Martini-type action. Caliber: .22 Short, Long, LR. 18.5-inch bbl. Weight: 5 lbs. Sights: Open rear; bead front. Western-style carbine stock w/straight grip, forearm with bbl. band. Made from 1976-89.

MODEL 987-T AUTOLOADING RIFLE . . . . NiB $175 Ex $145 Gd $105
Caliber: .22 LR. 15-round tubular magazine. 20-inch bbl. Weight: 6 lbs. Sights: Open rear; ramp front. Monte Carlo stock w/checkered pistol grip and forearm. Made from 1981-89.

"STEVENS FAVORITE"
See Savage Model 71.

V.C. SCHILLING — Suhl, Germany

MAUSER-MANNLICHER BOLT ACTION SPORTING RIFLE . . NiB $877 Ex $709 Gd $495
Same general specifications as given for the Haenel Mauser-Mannlicher Sporter. See separate listing.

'88 MAUSER SPORTER . . . . NiB $844 Ex $684 Gd $478
Same general specifications as Haenel '88 Mauser Sporter. See separate listing.

SCHULTZ & LARSEN GEVAERFABRIK — Otterup, Denmark

MATCH RIFLE NO. 47. . . . . NiB $761 Ex $709 Gd $529
Caliber: .22 LR. Bolt-action, single-shot, set trigger. 28.5-inch heavy bbl. Weight: 14 lbs. Sights: Micrometer receiver, globe front. Free-rifle stock w/cheekpiece, thumbhole, adj. Schuetzen-type buttplate, swivels, palmrest.

FREE RIFLE MODEL 54 . . . . NiB $1018 Ex $838 Gd $555
Calibers: 6.5x55mm or any standard American centerfire caliber. Schultz & Larsen M54 bolt-action, single-shot, set trigger. 27.5-inch heavy bbl. Weight: 15.5 lbs. Sights: Micrometer receiver; globe front. Free-rifle stock w/cheekpiece, thumbhole, adj. Schuetzen-type buttplate, swivels, palm rest.

MODEL 54J SPORTING RIFLE. . . . . NiB $725 Ex $596 Gd $390
Calibers: .270 Win., .30-06, 7x61 Sharpe & Hart. Schultz & Larsen bolt action. Three-round magazine. 24-inch bbl. in .270 and .30-06, 26-inch in 7x61 S&H. Checkered stock w/Monte Carlo comb and cheekpiece. Value shown is for rifle less sights.

SEARS, ROEBUCK & COMPANY — Chicago, Illinois

The most encountered brands or model designations used by Sears are J. C. Higgins and Ted Williams. Firearms sold under these designations have been mfd. by various firms including Winchester, Marlin, Savage, Mossberg, etc.

MODEL 2C BOLT-ACTION RIFLE. . . . . NiB $121 Ex $101 Gd $83
Caliber: .22RF. Seven round clip mag. 21-inch bbl. Weight: 5 lbs. Sights: Open rear; ramp front. Plain Monte Carlo stock. Mfd. by Win.

MODEL 42 BOLT-ACTION REPEATER. . . . . NiB $121 Ex $101 Gd $74
Takedown. Caliber: .22RF. Eight round detachable box magazine. 24-inch bbl. Weight: 6 lbs. Sights: Open rear; bead front. Plain pistol-grip stock. Mfd. by Marlin.

MODEL 42DL BOLT-ACTION REPEATER . . . . NiB $121 Ex $101 Gd $80
Same general specifications as Model 42 except fancier grade w/peep sight, hooded front sight and swivels.

MODEL 44DL LEVER-ACTION RIFLE . . . . NiB $197 Ex $157 Gd $111
Caliber: .22RF. Tubular magazine holds 19 LR cartridges. 22-inch bbl. Weight: 6.25 lbs. Sights: Open rear; hooded ramp front. Monte Carlo-style stock w/pistol grip. Mfd. by Marlin.

MODEL 53 BOLT-ACTION RIFLE. . . . . NiB $248 Ex $172 Gd $131
Calibers: .243, .270, .308, .30-06. Four-round magazine. 22-inch bbl. Weight: 6.75 lbs. Sights: Open rear; ramp front. Standard sporter stock w/pistol-grip, checkered. Mfd. by Savage.

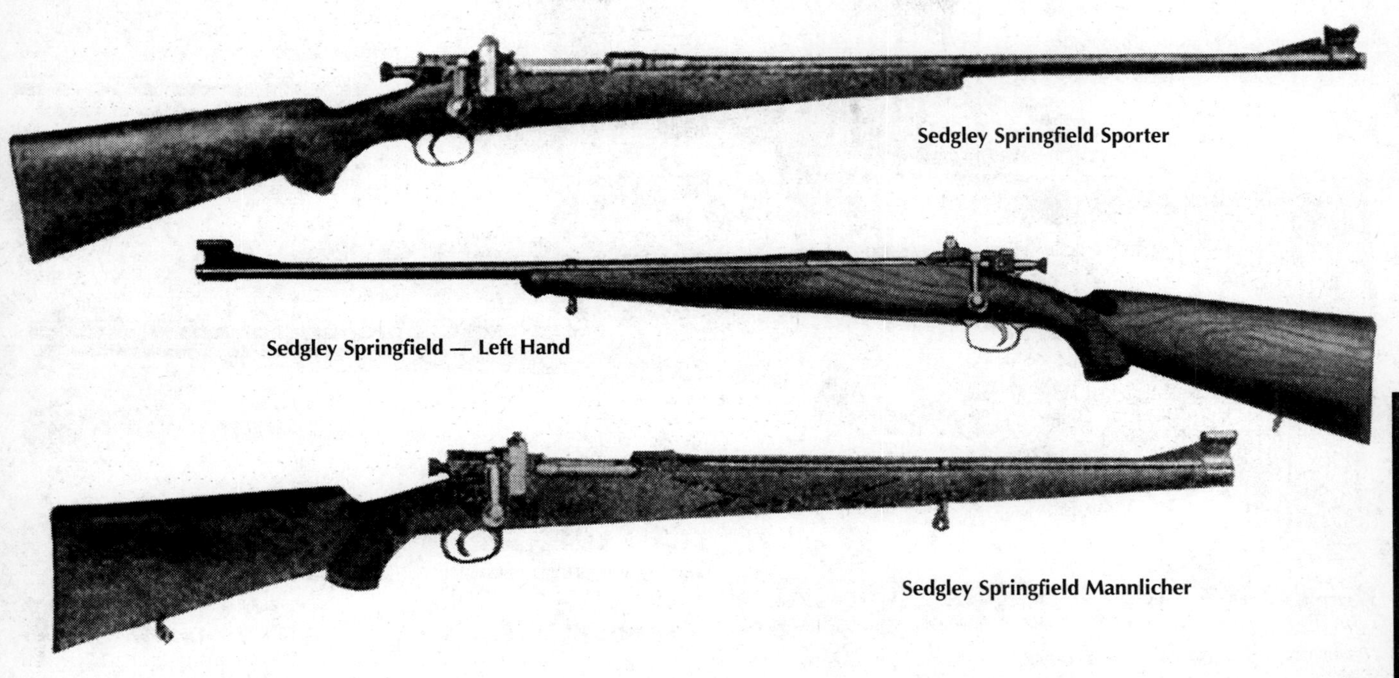

Sedgley Springfield Sporter

Sedgley Springfield — Left Hand

Sedgley Springfield Mannlicher

MODEL 54 LEVER-ACTION RIFLE . . . . NiB $199 Ex $174 Gd $123
Similar general specifications as Winchester Model 94 carbine. Made in .30-30 caliber only. Mfd. by Winchester.

MODEL 103 SERIES BOLT-ACTION REPEATER . . . . NiB $205 Ex $97 Gd $77
Same general specifications as Model 103.2 w/minor changes. Mfd. by Marlin.

MODEL 103.2 BOLT-ACTION REPEATER . . . . NiB $123 Ex $97 Gd $77
Takedown. Caliber: .22RF. Eight-round detachable box magazine. 24-inch bbl. Weight: 6 lbs. Sights: Open rear; bead front. Plain pistol-grip stock. Mfd. by Marlin.

R. F. SEDGLEY, INC. — Philadelphia, Pennsylvania

SPRINGFIELD SPORTER . . . . NiB $1376 Ex $1093 Gd $578
Springfield '03 bolt action. Calibers: .220 Swift, .218 Bee, .22-3000, R, .22-4000, .22 Hornet, .25-35, .250-3000, .257 Roberts, .270 Win., 7mm, .30-06. 24-inch bbl. Weight: 7.5 lbs. Sights: Lyman No. 48 receiver; bead front on matted ramp. Checkered walnut stock, grip cap, sling swivels. Disc. 1941.

SPRINGFIELD LEFT-HAND SPORTER . . . NiB $1556 Ex $1289 Gd $861
Bolt-action reversed for left-handed shooter; otherwise the same as standard Sedgley Springfield Sporter. Disc. 1941.

SEDGLEY SPRINGFIELD MANNLICHER-TYPE SPORTER . . . . NiB $1659 Ex $1376 Gd $990
Same as standard Sedgley Springfield Sporter except w/20-inch bbl., Mannlicher-type full stock w/cheekpiece, weight: 7.75 lbs. Disc. 1941.

SHILEN RIFLES, INC. — Ennis, Texas

DGA BENCHREST RIFLE . . . . NiB $1553 Ex $1170 Gd $887
DGA single-shot bolt-action. Calibers as listed for Sporter. 26-inch medium-heavy or heavy bbl. Weight: From 10.5 lbs. No sights. Fiberglass or walnut stock, classic or thumbhole pattern. Currently manufactured.

DGA SPORTER . . . . NiB $1608 Ex $1088 Gd $774
DGA bolt action. Calibers: .17 Rem., .222 Rem., .223 Rem. .22-250, .220 Swift, 6mm Rem., .243 Win., .250 Sav., .257 Roberts, .284 Win., .308 Win., .358 Win. Three round blind magazine. 24-inch bbl. Average weight: 7.5 lbs. No sights. Select Claro walnut stock w/cheekpiece, pistol grip, sling swivel studs. Currently manufactured.

DGA VARMINTER . . . . NiB $1500 Ex $1144 Gd $799
Same as Sporter except w/25-inch medium-heavy bbl. Weight: 9 lbs.

SHILOH RIFLE MFG. Co. — Big Timber, Montana (Formerly Shiloh Products)

SHARPS MODEL 1874 BUSINESS RIFLE . . . . NiB $1137 Ex $1060 Gd $674
Replica of 1874 Sharps similar to No. 3 Sporting Rifle. .32-40, .38-55, .40-50 BN, .40-70 BN, .40-90 BN, .45-70 ST, .45-90 ST, .50-70 ST, .50-100 ST. 28-inch round heavy bbl. Blade front sight, buckhorn rear. Double-set triggers. Straight-grip walnut stock w/steel crescent buttplate. Made from 1986 to date.

SHARPS MODEL 1874 LONG RANGE EXPRESS RIFLE . . . . NiB $1709 Ex $1657 Gd $1086
Replica of 1874 Sharps w/single-shot falling breech action. .32-40, .38-55, .40-50 BN, .40-70 BN, .40-90 BN, .45-70 ST, .45-90 ST, .45-110 ST, .50-70 ST, .50-90 ST, .50-110 ST. 34-inch tapered octagon bbl. 51 inches overall. Weight: 10.75 lbs. Globe front sight, sporting tang peep rear. Walnut buttstock w/pistol-grip and Schnabel-style forend. Color casehardened action w/double-set triggers Made from 1986 to date.

Shilen DGA Benchrest Rifle

Shilen DGA Sporter

Shilen DGA Varminter

SHARPS MODEL 1874 SADDLE RIFLE . . NiB $1186 Ex $1078 Gd $671
Similar to 1874 Express Rifle except w/30-inch bbl., blade front sight and buckhorn rear. Made from 1986 to date.

SHARPS MODEL 1874 SPORTING RIFLE NO. 1 . . . . NiB $1279 Ex $1078 Gd $679
Similar to 1874 Express Rifle except w/30-inch bbl., blade front sight and buckhorn rear. Made from 1986 to date.

SHARPS MODEL 1874 SPORTING RIFLE NO. 3 . . . . NiB $1083 Ex $954 Gd $645
Similar to 1874 Sporting Rifle No. 1 except w/straight-grip stock w/steel crescent buttplate. Made from 1986 to date.

SHARPS MODEL 1874 MONTANA ROUGHRIDER
Similar to 1874 Sporting Rifle No. 1 except w/24- to 34-inch half-octagon or full-octagon bbl. Standard or deluxe walnut stock w/pistol-grip or military-style buttstock. Made from 1989 to date.
Standard model . . . . NiB $1078 Ex $671 Gd $594
Deluxe model . . . . NiB $1212 Ex $928 Gd $568

SIG SWISS INDUSTRIAL COMPANY — Neuhausen-Rhine Falls, Switzerland

AMT SEMIAUTOMATIC RIFLE . . . . NiB $4255 Ex $3103 Gd $2890
.308 Win.(7.62 NATO). Five, 10, or 20-round magazine. 18.5-inch bbl. w/flash suppressor. Weight: 9.5 lbs. Sights: Adj. aperture rear, post front. Walnut buttstock and forend w/synthetic pistol grip. Imported from 1980-88.

AMT SPORTING RIFLE . . . . NiB $3971 Ex $2941 Gd $2164
Semiautomatic version of SG510-4 automatic assault rifle based on Swiss Army SIGW57. Roller-delayed blowback action. Caliber: 7.62x51mm NATO (.308 Win.). Five, 10- and 20-round magazines. 19-inch bbl. Weight: 10 lbs. Sights, aperture rear, post front. Wood buttstock and forearm, folding bipod. Imported from 1960-88.

PE57 SEMIAUTOMATIC RIFLE . . . . NiB $5263 Ex $4234 Gd $2918
Caliber: 7.5 Swiss. 24-round magazine. 23.75-inch bbl. Weight: 12.5 lbs. Sights: Adj. aperture rear; post front. High-impact synthetic stock. Imported from Switzerland during the 1980s.

Smith & Wesson Model 1500DL

Smith & Wesson Model 1700 LS Classic Hunter

Springfield Armory BM-59

SMITH & WESSON — Springfield, Massachusetts, Mfd. by Husqvarna, Vapenfabrik A.B., Huskvarna, Sweden & Howa Machinery LTD., Shinkawa-Chonear, Nagota 452, Japan

MODEL 1500 . . . . NiB $383 Ex $306 Gd $208
Bolt-action. .243 Win., .270 Win., .30-06, 7mm Rem. Mag. 22-inch bbl. (24-inch in 7mm Rem. Mag.). Weight: 7.5 lbs. American walnut stock w/Monte Carlo comb and cheekpiece, cut checkering. Sights: Open rear, hooded ramp, gold bead-front. This model was also imported by Mossberg (see separate listings); Imported from 1979-84.

MODEL 1500DL DELUXE . . . . NiB $383 Ex $306 Gd $208
Same as standard model, except w/o sights; w/engine-turned bolt, decorative scroll on floorplate, French checkering. Imported from 1983-84.

MODEL 1700 LS "CLASSIC HUNTER" . . . . NiB $435 Ex $383 Gd $229
Bolt action. Calibers: .243 Win., .270 Win., .30-06, 5-round magazine. 22-inch bbl. Weight: 7.5 lbs. Solid recoil pad, no sights, Schnabel forend, checkered walnut stock. Imported from 1983-84.

MODEL A BOLT-ACTION RIFLE . . . . NiB $5012 Ex $383 Gd $270
Similar to Husqvarna Model 9000 Crown Grade. Mauser-type bolt action. Calibers: .22-250, .243 Win., .270 Win., .308 Win., .30-06, 7mm Rem. Mag., .300 Win. Mag. Five round magazine except 3-round capacity in latter two calibers. 23.75-inch bbl. Weight: 7 lbs. Sights: Folding leaf rear; hooded ramp front. Checkered walnut stock w/Monte Carlo cheekpiece, rosewood forend tip and pistol-grip cap, swivels. Made from 1969-72.

MODEL B . . . . NiB $461 Ex $337 Gd $203
Same as Model A except w/20.25-inch extra-light bbl., Monte Carlo cheekpiece w/Schnabel-style forearm, weight: 6 lbs., 10 oz. Calibers: .243 Win., .30-06.

MODEL C . . . . NiB $461 Ex $342 Gd $203
Same as Model B except w/cheekpiece stock w/straight comb.

MODEL D . . . . NiB $589 Ex $435 Gd $306
Same as Model C except w/full-length Mannlicher-style forearm.

MODEL E. . . . . NiB $589 Ex $435 Gd $306
Same as Model B except w/full-length Mannlicher-style forearm.

SPRINGFIELD, INC. — Colona, Illinois (Formerly Springfield Armory of Geneseo, Ill.)

This is a private firm not to be confused with the former U.S. Government facility in Springfield, Mass.

BM-59 SEMIAUTOMATIC RIFLE
Gas-operated. Caliber: .308 Win. (7.62mm NATO). 20-round detachable box magazine. 19.3-inch bbl. w/flash suppressor. About 43 inches overall. Weight: 9.25 lbs. Adj. military aperture rear sight, square post front; direct and indirect grenade launcher sights. European walnut stock w/handguard or folding buttstock (Alpine Paratrooper). Made from 1981-90.
Standard model . . . . NiB $2123 Ex $1714 Gd $1189
Paratrooper model . . . . NiB $2131 Ex $1745 Gd $1384

Springfield Armory
SAR-8 Sporter Rifle

M-1 GARAND SEMIAUTOMATIC RIFLE
Gas-operated. Calibers: .308 Win. (7.62 NATO), .30-06. Eight round stripper clip. 24-inch bbl. 43.5 inches overall. Weight: 9.5 lbs. Adj. aperture rear sight, military square blade front. Standard "Issue-grade" walnut stock or folding buttstock. Made from 1979-90.
Standard model . . . . NiB $961 Ex $735 Gd $503
National match . . . . NiB $967 Ex $761 Gd $555
Ultra match . . . . NiB $1018 Ex $915 Gd $606
Sniper model . . . . NiB $1018 Ex $915 Gd $606
Tanker model. . . . . NiB $812 Ex $709 Gd $426
Paratrooper w/folding stock . . . . . NiB $1044 Ex $812 Gd $581

MATCH M1A
Same as Standard M1A except w/National Match-grade bbl. w/modified flash suppressor, National Match sights, turned trigger pull, gas system assembly in one unit, modified mainspring guide glass-bedded walnut stock. Super Match M1A w/premium-grade heavy bbl. (weighs 10 lbs).
Match M1A . . . . NiB $1596 Ex $1380 Gd $875
Super Match M1A . . . . NiB $1801 Ex $1390 Gd $1004

STANDARD M1A SEMIAUTOMATIC
Gas-operated. Similar to U.S. M14 service rifle except w/o provision for automatic firing. Caliber: 7.65mm NATO (.308 Win.). Five, 10- or 20-round detachable box magazine. 25.13-inch bbl w/flash suppressor. Weight: 9 lbs. Sights: Adj. aperture rear; blade front. Fiberglass, birch or walnut stock, fiberglass handguard, sling swivels. Made from 1974 to date.
W/fiberglass or birch stock . . . . . . NiB $1097 Ex $844 Gd $561
W/walnut stock . . . . NiB $1242 Ex $1029 Gd $758

M-6 SCOUT RIFLE/SHOTGUN COMBO
Similar to (14-inch) short-barrel Survival Gun provided as backup weapon to U.S. combat pilots. Calibers: .22 LR/.410 and .22 Hornet/.410. 18.5-inch bbl. 32 inches overall. Weight: 4 lbs. Parkerized or stainless steel finish. Folding detachable stock w/storage for fifteen .22 LR cartridges and four .410 shells. Drilled and tapped for scope mounts. Intro. 1982 and imported from Czech Republic 1995 to date.
First Issue (no trigger guard) . . . NiB $2016 Ex $1560 Gd $1086
Second Issue (w/trigger guard) . . NiB $1706 Ex $1346 Gd $986

SAR-8 SPORTER RIFLE
Similar to H&K 911 semiautomatic rifle. Calibers: .308 Win., (7.62x51) NATO. Detachable 5- 10- or 20-round magazine. 18- or 20-inch bbl. 38.25 or 45.3 inches overall. Weight: 8.7 to 9.5 lbs. Protected front post and rotary adj. rear sight. Delayed roller-locked blow-back action w/fluted chamber. Kevlar-reinforced fiberglass thumb-hole style wood stock. Imported from 1990-95.
SAR-8 w/wood stock (disc. 1994) . . . . . NiB $1388 Ex $1132 Gd $819
SAR-8 w/thumb-hole stock . . . . NiB $1107 Ex $926 Gd $643

SAR-48, SAR-4800
Similar to Browning FN FAL/LAR semiautomatic rifle. Calibers: .233 Rem. (5.56x45) and 3.08 Win. (7.62x51) NATO. Detachable 5- 10- or 20-round magazine. 18- or 21-inch chrome-lined bbl. 38.25 or 45.3 inches overall. Weight: 9.5 to 13.25 lbs. Protected post front and adj. rear sight. Forged receiver and bolt w/adj. gas system. Pistol-grip or thumb-hole style; synthetic or wood stock. Imported 1985; reintroduced 1995.
SAR-48 w/pistol-grip stock
(disc. 1989) . . . . NiB $1230 Ex $1050 Gd $638
SAR-48 w/wood stock (disc. 1989) . . . . NiB $2424 Ex $1956 Gd $1396
SAR-48 w/folding stock (disc. 1989) . . . NiB $2718 Ex $2185 Gd $1547
SAR-48 w/thumb-hole stock . . . . NiB $1257 Ex $1019 Gd $714

SQUIRES BINGHAM CO., INC. — Makati, Rizal, Philippines

MODEL 14D DELUXE BOLT-ACTION
REPEATING RIFLE . . . . NiB $123 Ex $98 Gd $72
Caliber: .22 LR. Five round box magazine. 24-inch bbl. Sights: V-notch rear; hooded ramp front. Receiver grooved for scope mounting. Pulong Dalaga stock w/contrasting forend tip and grip cap, checkered forearm and pistol-grip. Weight: 6 lbs. Disc.

MODEL 15 . . . . NiB $148 Ex $103 Gd $97
Same as Model 14D except chambered for .22 WMR. Importation. Disc.

MODEL M16 SEMIAUTOMATIC RIFLE. . . . NiB $143 Ex $148 Gd $113
Styled after U.S. M16 military rifle. Caliber: .22 LR. 15-round box magazine. 19.5-inch bbl. w/muzzle brake/flash hider. Rear sight in carrying handle, post front on high ramp. Black-painted mahogany buttstock and forearm. Weight: 6.5 lbs. Importation. Disc.

MODEL M20D DELUXE . . . . NiB $225 Ex $199 Gd $118
Caliber: .22 LR. 15-round box magazine. 19.5-inch bbl. w/muzzle brake/flash hider. Sights: V-notch rear; blade front. Receiver grooved for scope mounting. Pulong Dalaga stock w/contrasting forend tip and grip cap, checkered forearm/pistol-grip. Weight: 6 lbs. Importation. Disc.

STANDARD ARMS COMPANY — Wilmington, Delaware

MODEL G AUTOMATIC RIFLE . . . . NiB $650 Ex $341 Gd $233
Gas-operated. Autoloading. Hammerless. Takedown. .25-35, .30-30, .25 Rem., .30 Rem., .35 Rem. Magazine capacity: 4 rounds in .35 Rem., 5 rounds in other calibers. 22.38-inch bbl. Weight: 7.75 lbs. Sights: Open sporting rear; ivory bead front. Shotgun-type stock. Made c. 1910. Note: This was the first gas-operated rifle manufactured in the U.S. While essentially an autoloader, the gas port can be closed and the rifle may be operated as a slide-action repeater.

Star
Rolling Block Carbine

MODEL M HAND-OPERATED RIFLE . . . . . NiB $332 Ex $306 Gd $177
Slide-action repeater w/same general specifications as Model G except lacks autoloading feature. Weight: 7 lbs.

STAR — Eibar, Spain Mfd. by Bonifacio Echeverria, S.A.

ROLLING BLOCK CARBINE . . . . . . NiB $229 Ex $188 Gd $135
Single-shot action similar to Remington Rolling Block. .30-30, .357 Mag., .44 Mag. 20-inch bbl. Weight: 6 lbs. Sights: Folding leaf rear; ramp front. Walnut straight-grip stock w/crescent buttplate, forearm w/bbl. band. Imported 1973-75.

STERLING — Imported by Lanchester U.S.A., Inc., Dallas, Texas

MARK 6 SEMIAUTOMATIC CARBINE. . . . . NiB $807 Ex $627 Gd $442
Caliber: 9mm Para 34-round magazine. Bbl.: 16.1 inches. Weight: 7.5 lbs. Flip-type rear peep sight, ramp front. Folding metal skeleton stock. Made from 1983-94.

J. STEVENS ARMS CO. — Chicopee Falls, Massachusetts, Div. of Savage Industries, Westfield, Mass.

J. Stevens Arms eventually became a division of Savage Industries. Consequently, the "Stevens" brand name is used for some rifles by Savage; see separate Savage-Stevens listings under Savage.

NO. 12 MARKSMAN SINGLE-SHOT RIFLE. . NiB $227 Ex $176 Gd $99
Lever-action, tip-up. Takedown. Calibers: .22 LR, .25 R.F., .32 R.F. 22-inch bbl. Plain straight-grip stock, small tapered forearm.

**NO. 14 LITTLE SCOUT
SINGLE-SHOT RIFLE. . . . . NiB $227 Ex $120 Gd $74**
Caliber: .22 RF. 18-inch bbl. One-piece slab stock readily distinguishes it from the No. 14X that follows. Made from 1906-1910.

**NO. 14.5 LITTLE SCOUT
SINGLE-SHOT RIFLE . . . . NiB $227 Ex $125 Gd $99**
Rolling block. Takedown. Caliber: .22 LR. 18- or 20-inch bbl. Weight: 2.75 lbs. Sights: open rear; blade front. Plain straight-grip stock, small tapered forearm.

MODEL 15 . . . . NiB $201 Ex $125 Gd $115
Same as Stevens-Springfield Model 15 except w/24-inch bbl., weight: 5 lbs., w/redesigned stock. Made from 1948-65.

MODEL 15Y YOUTH'S RIFLE . . . . . NiB $176 Ex $120 Gd $105
Same as Model 15 except w/21-inch bbl., short buttstock, weight: 4.75 lbs. Made from 1958-65.

**NO. 44 IDEAL
SINGLE-SHOT RIFLE. . . . . NiB $786 Ex $634 Gd $440**
Rolling block. Lever-action. Takedown. Calibers: .22 LR. .25 R.F., .32 R.F., .25-20 S.S., .32-20, .32-40, .38-40, .38-55, .44-40. Bbl. lengths: 24-inch, 26-inch (round, half-octagon, full-octagon). Weight: 7 lbs w/26-inch round bbl. Sights: Open rear; Rocky Mountain front. Plain straight-grip stock and forearm. Made from 1894-32.

NO. 44.5 IDEAL SINGLE-SHOT RIFLE . . . . NiB $989 Ex $797 Gd $552
Falling-block. Lever-action rifle. Aside from the new design action intro. 1903, specifications of this model are the same as those of Model 44. Model 44X disc. 1916.

NOS. 45 TO 54 IDEAL SINGLE-SHOT RIFLES
These are higher-grade models, differing from the standard No. 44 and 44.5 chiefly in finish, engraving, set triggers, levers, bbls., stock, etc. The Schuetzen types (including the Stevens-Pope models) are in this series. Model Nos. 45 to 54 were intro. 1896 and originally had the No. 44-type rolling-block action, which was superseded in 1903 by the No. 44.5-type falling-block action. These models were all disc. about 1916. Generally speaking, the 45-54 series rifles, particularly the Stevens Pope and higher grade Schuetzen models are collector's items, bringing much higher prices than the ordinary No. 44 and 44.5.

**MODEL 66 BOLT-ACTION
REPEATING RIFLE . . . . NiB $204 Ex $123 Gd $105**
Takedown. Caliber: .22 Short, Long, LR. Tubular magazine holds 13 LR, 15 Long, 19 Short. 24-inch bbl. Weight: 5 lbs. Sights: Open rear, bead front. Plain pistol-grip stock w/grooved forearm. Made from 1931-35.

**NO. 70 VISIBLE LOADING
SLIDE-ACTION . . . . NiB $327 Ex $276 Gd $123**
Exposed hammer. Caliber: .22 LR., Long, Short. Tubular magazine holds 11 LR., 13 Long, 15 Short. 22-inch bbl. Weight: 4.5 lbs. Sights: Open rear; bead front. Plain straight-grip stock, grooved slide handle. Made 1907-34. Note: Nos. 702, 71, 712, 72, 722 essentially the same as No. 70, differing chiefly in bbl. length or sight tooling.

MODEL 87 AUTOLOADING RIFLE. . . . . . NiB $199 Ex $148 Gd $113
Takedown. Caliber: .22 LR. 15-round tubular magazine. 24-inch bbl. (20-inch on current model). Weight: 6 lbs. Sights: Open rear, bead front. Pistol-grip stock. Made 1938 to date. Note: This model originally bore the "Springfield" brand name, disc. in 1948.

**MODEL 322 HI-POWER
BOLT-ACTION CARBINE. . . . . NiB $327 Ex $276 Gd $148**
Caliber: .22 Hornet. 4-round detachable magazine. 21-inch bbl. Weight: 6.75 lbs. Sights: Open rear; ramp front. Pistol-grip stock. Made 1947-50 (See Savage models 340, 342.)

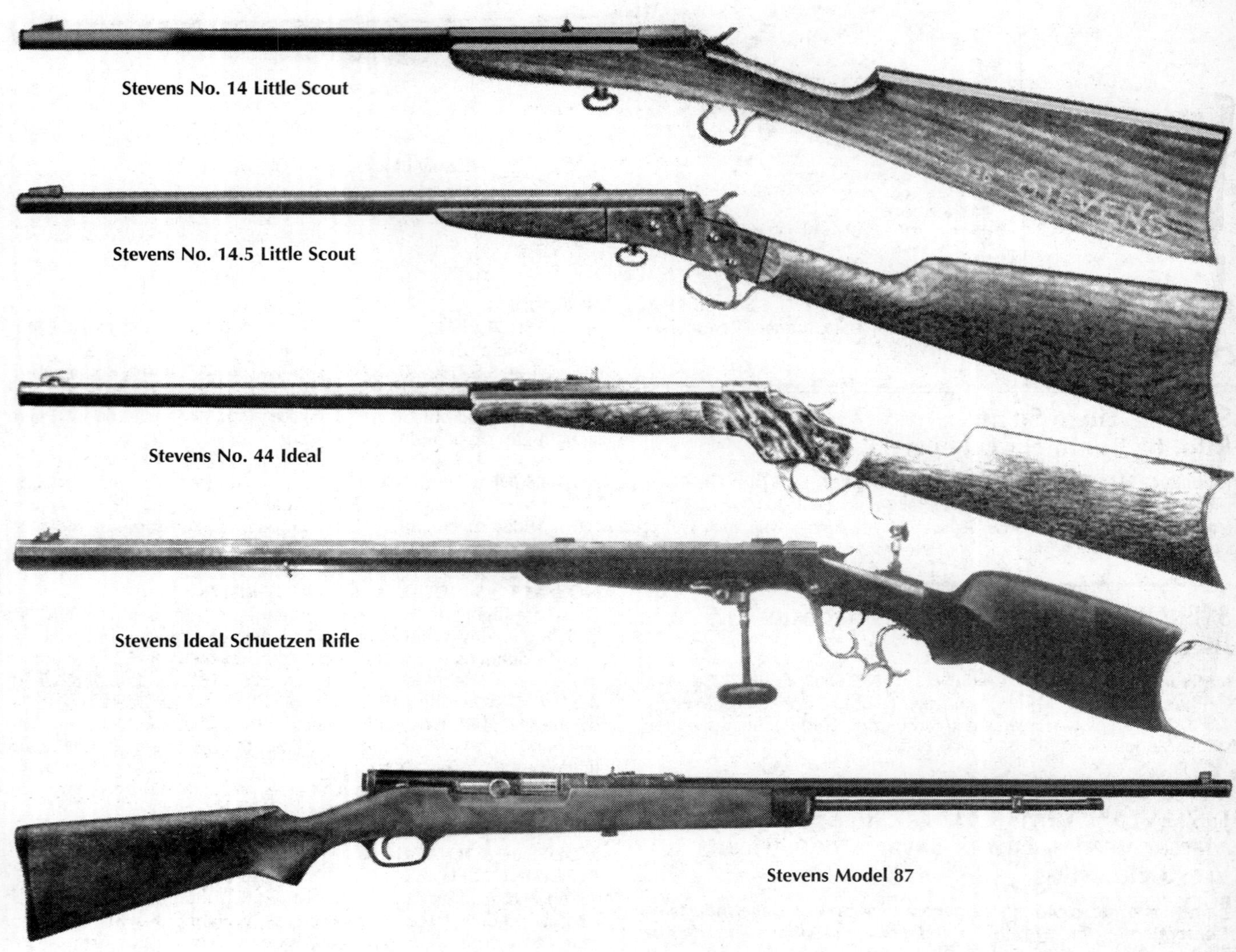

Stevens No. 14 Little Scout

Stevens No. 14.5 Little Scout

Stevens No. 44 Ideal

Stevens Ideal Schuetzen Rifle

Stevens Model 87

6MODEL 322-S . . . . NiB $384 Ex $307 Gd $180
Same as Model 325 except w/peep rear sight. (See Savage models 340S, 342S.)

MODEL 325 HI-POWER BOLT-ACTION CARBINE. . . . . NiB $333 Ex $282 Gd $154
Caliber: .30-30. Three round detachable box magazine. 21-inch bbl. Weight: 6.75 lbs. Sights: Open rear; bead front. Plain pistol-grip stock. Made from 1947-50. (See Savage Model 340.)

MODEL 325-S . . . . NiB $677 Ex $310 Gd $183
Same as Model 325 except w/peep rear sight. (See Savage Model 340S.)

NO. 414 ARMORY MODEL SINGLE-SHOT RIFLE . . . . NiB $540 Ex $463 Gd $310
No. 44-type lever-action. Calibers: .22 LR only, .22 Short only. 26-inch bbl. Weight: 8 lbs. Sights: Lyman receiver peep; blade front. Plain straight-grip stock, military-type forearm, swivels. Made from 1912-32.

MODEL 416 BOLT-ACTION TARGET RIFLE . . . . NiB $355 Ex $252 Gd $207
Caliber: .22 LR. Five round detachable box magazine. 26-inch heavy bbl. Weight: 9.5 lbs. Sights: Receiver peep; hooded front. Target stock, swivels, sling. Made from 1937-49.

NO. 419 JUNIOR TARGET MODEL BOLT-ACTION SINGLE-SHOT RIFLE. . . . . . NiB $380 Ex $278 Gd $201
Takedown. Caliber: .22 LR. 26-inch bbl. Weight: 5.5 lbs. Sights: Lyman No. 55 rear peep; blade front. Plain junior target stock w/pistol grip and grooved forearm, swivels, sling. Made from 1932-36.

BUCKHORN MODEL 053 BOLT-ACTION SINGLE-SHOT RIFLE . . . . NiB $160 Ex $131 Gd $95
Takedown. Calibers: .22 Short, Long, LR., .22 WRF. .25 Stevens R.F. 24-inch bbl. Weight: 5.5 lbs. Sights: Receiver peep; open middle; hooded front. Sporting stock w/pistol-grip and black forend tip. Made from 1935-48.

BUCKHORN MODEL 53. . . . . NiB $203 Ex $172 Gd $111
Same as Buckhorn Model 053 except w/open rear sight and plain bead front sight.

Stevens No. 414 Armory

Stevens Model 416

Stevens Buckhorn Model 53

Stevens Buckhorn Model 055

Stevens Buckhorn Model 56

BUCKHORN 055. . . . . NiB $205 Ex $174 Gd $113
Takedown. Same as Model 056 except in single-shot configuration. Weight: 5.5 lbs. Caliber: .22 LR., Long, Short. 24-inch bbl. Weight: 6 lbs. Sights: Receiver peep, open middle, hooded front. Made from 1935-48.

BUCKHORN MODEL 056
BOLT-ACTION . . . . NiB $210 Ex $174 Gd $118
Takedown. Caliber: .22 LR., Long, Short. Five round detachable box magazine. 24-inch bbl. Weight: 6 lbs. Sights: Receiver peep, open middle, hooded front. Sporting stock w/pistol grip and black forend tip. Made from 1935-48.

BUCKHORN
MODEL 56 . . . . NiB $199 Ex $148 Gd $113
Same as Buckhorn Model 056 except w/open rear sight and plain bead front sight.

BUCKHORN NO. 057. . . . . NiB $184 Ex $123 Gd $97
Same as Buckhorn Model 076 except w/5-round detachable box magazine. Made from 1939-48.

BUCKHORN NO. 57. . . . . NiB $184 Ex $123 Gd $97
Same as Buckhorn Model 76 except w/5-round detachable box magazine. Made from 1939-48.

BUCKHORN MODEL 066
BOLT-ACTION REPEATING RIFLE . . . . NiB $252 Ex $201 Gd $107
Takedown. Caliber: .22 LR, Long, Short. Tubular magazine holds 21 Short, 17 Long, 15 LR. 24-inch bbl. Weight: 6 lbs. Sights: Receiver peep; open middle; hooded front. Sporting stock w/pistol grip and black forend tip. Made from 1935-48.

BUCKHORN MODEL 66. . . . . NiB $184 Ex $123 Gd $97
Same as Buckhorn Model 066 except w/open rear sight, plain bead front sight.

BUCKHORN NO. 076
AUTOLOADING RIFLE . . . . NiB $199 Ex $174 Gd $118
Takedown. Caliber: .22 LR. 15-round tubular magazine. 24-inch bbl. Weight: 6 lbs. Sights: Receiver peep; open middle; hooded front. Sporting stock w/pistol grip, black forend tip. Made from 1938-48.

BUCKHORN NO. 76. . . . . NiB $199 Ex $174 Gd $113
Same as Buckhorn No. 076 except w/open rear sight, plain bead front sight.

CRACKSHOT NO. 26
SINGLE-SHOT RIFLE . . . . NiB $278 Ex $222 Gd $150
Lever-action. Takedown. Calibers: .22 LR, .32 R.F. 18-inch or 22-inch bbl. Weight: 3.25 lbs. Sights: Open rear; blade front. Plain straight-grip stock, small tapered forearm. Made from 1913-39.

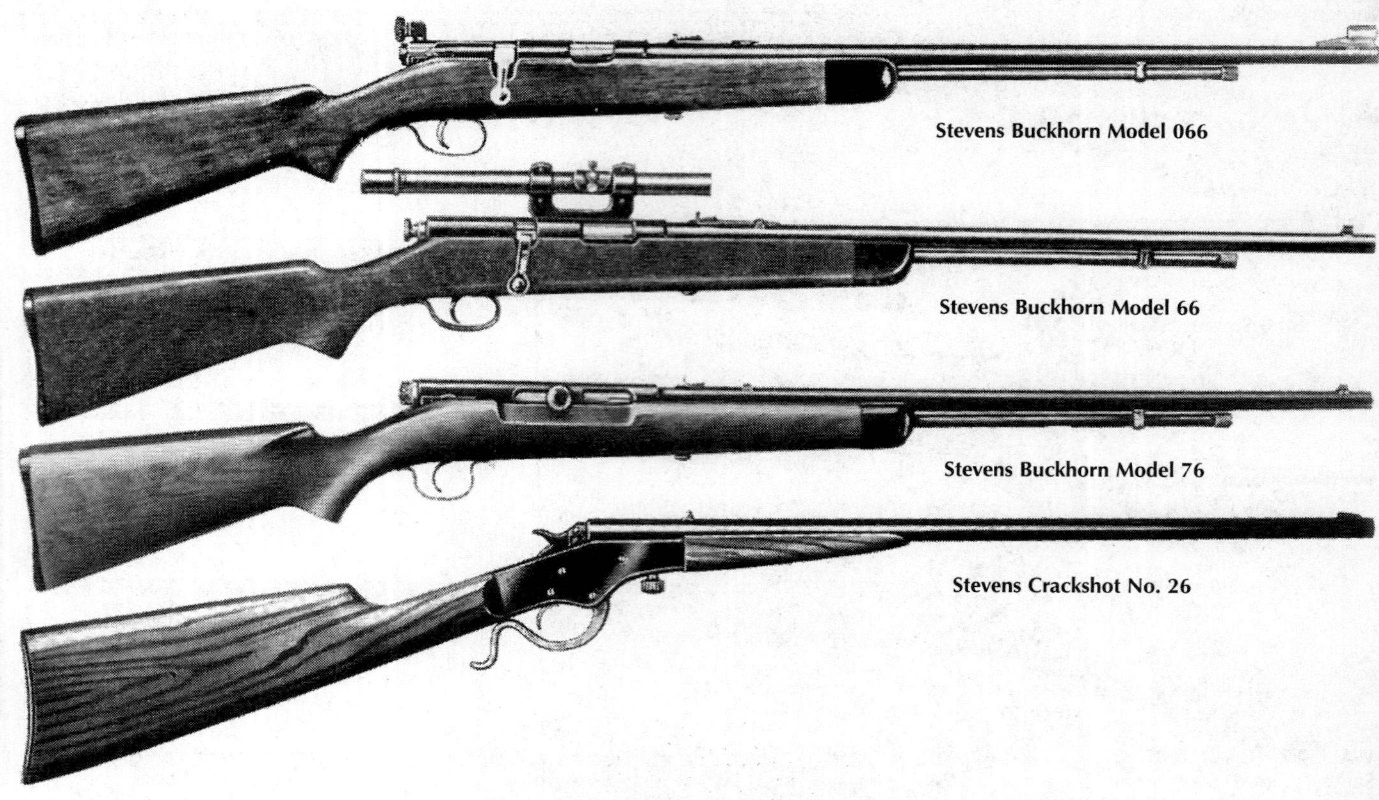
Stevens Buckhorn Model 066

Stevens Buckhorn Model 66

Stevens Buckhorn Model 76

Stevens Crackshot No. 26

CRACKSHOT NO. 26.5 . . . . NiB $319 Ex $201 Gd $176
Same as Crackshot No. 26 on previous page except w/smoothbore bbl. for shot cartridges.

FAVORITE NO. 17
SINGLE-SHOT RIFLE . . . . NiB $303 Ex $201 Gd $150
Lever-action. Takedown. Calibers: .22 LR, .25 R.F., .32 R.F. 24-inch round bbl; other lengths were available. Weight: 4.5 lbs. Sights: Open rear; Rocky Mountain front. Plain straight-grip stock, small tapered forearm. Made from 1894-1935.

FAVORITE NO. 18. . . . . NiB $380 Ex $278 Gd $150
Same as Favorite No. 17 except w/Vernier peep rear sight, leaf middle sight, Beach combination front sight.

FAVORITE NO. 19. . . . . NiB $405 Ex $303 Gd $176
Same as Favorite No. 17 except w/Lyman combination rear sight, leaf middle sight, Lyman front sight.

FAVORITE NO. 20. . . . . NiB $380 Ex $303 Gd $201
Same as Favorite No. 17 except w/smoothbore barrel.

FAVORITE NO. 27. . . . . NiB $405 Ex $303 Gd $217
Same as Favorite No. 17 except w/octagon bbl.

FAVORITE NO. 28. . . . . NiB $380 Ex $278 Gd $201
Same as Favorite No. 18 except w/octagon bbl.

FAVORITE NO. 29. . . . . NiB $405 Ex $278 Gd $201
Same as Favorite No. 19 except w/octagon bbl.

WALNUT HILL NO. 417-0
SINGLE-SHOT TARGET RIFLE . . . . NiB $932 Ex $728 Gd $473
Lever-action. Calibers: .22 LR only, .22 Short only, .22 Hornet. 28-inch heavy bbl. (extra heavy 29-inch bbl. also available). Weight: 10.5 lbs. Sights: Lyman No. 52L extension rear; 17A front, scope bases mounted on bbl. Target stock w/full pistol-grip, beavertail forearm, bbl. band, swivels, sling. Made from 1932-47.

WALNUT HILL NO. 417-1 . . . . NiB $958 Ex $932 Gd $550
Same as No. 417-0 except w/Lyman No. 48L receiver sight.

WALNUT HILL NO. 417-2 . . . . . . NiB $1009 Ex $932 Gd $575
Same as No. 417-0 except w/Lyman No. 144 tang sight.

WALNUT HILL NO. 417-3 . . . . NiB $948 Ex $805 Gd $448
Same as No. 417-0 except w/o sights.

WALNUT HILL NO. 417.5
SINGLE-SHOT RIFLE . . . . NiB $958 Ex $881 Gd $499
Lever-action. Calibers: .22 LR, .22 WMR, .25 R.F., .22 Hornet. 28-inch bbl. Weight: 8.5 lbs. Sights: Lyman No. 144 tang peep, folding middle; bead front. Sporting stock w/pistol-grip, semi-beavertail forearm, swivels, sling. Made from 1932-40.

WALNUT HILL NO. 418
SINGLE-SHOT RIFLE . . . . NiB $584 Ex $431 Gd $354
Lever-action. Takedown. Calibers: .22 LR only, .22 Short only. 26-inch bbl. Weight: 6.5 lbs. Sights: Lyman No. 144 tang peep; blade front. Pistol-grip stock, semi-beavertail forearm, swivels, sling. Made from 1932-40.

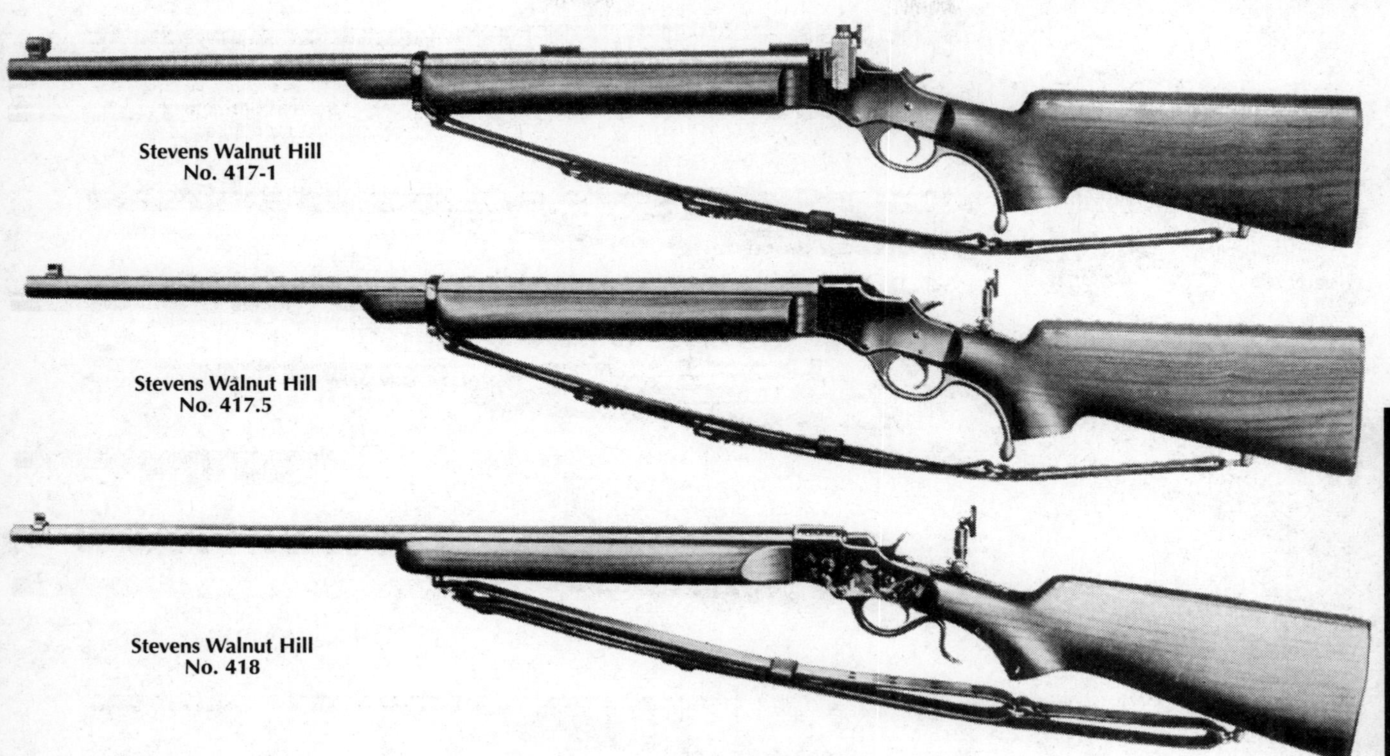

Stevens Walnut Hill No. 417-1

Stevens Walnut Hill No. 417.5

Stevens Walnut Hill No. 418

WALNUT HILL NO. 418.5 . . . . NiB $662 Ex $586 Gd $423
Same as No. 418 except also available in calibers .22 WRF and .25 Stevens R.F., w/Lyman No. 2A tang peep sight, bead front sight.

MODEL 15 SINGLE-SHOT BOLT-ACTION RIFLE . . . . NiB $172 Ex $121 Gd $95
Takedown. Caliber: .22 LR, Long, Short. 22-inch bbl. Weight: 4 lbs. Sights: Open rear, bead front. Plain pistol-grip stock. Made from 1937-48.

MODEL 82 BOLT-ACTION SINGLE-SHOT RIFLE . . . . NiB $143 Ex $126 Gd $95
Takedown. Caliber: .22 LR, Long, Short. 22-inch bbl. Weight: 4 lbs. Sights: Open rear; gold bead front. Plain pistol-grip stock w/grooved forearm. Made from 1935-39.

MODEL 83 BOLT-ACTION SINGLE-SHOT RIFLE . . . . NiB $172 Ex $111 Gd $90
Takedown. Calibers: .22 LR, Long, Short; .22 WRF, .25 Stevens R.F. 24-inch bbl. Weight: 4.5 lbs. Sights: Peep rear; open middle; hooded front. Plain pistol-grip stock w/grooved forearm. Made from 1935-39.

MODEL 84 . . . . NiB $195 Ex $172 Gd $113
Same as Model 86 except w/5-round detachable box magazine. Pre-1948 rifles of this model were designated Springfield Model 84, later known as Stevens Model 84. Made from 1940-65.

MODEL 84-S (084) . . . . NiB $195 Ex $172 Gd $116
Same as Model 84 except w/peep rear sight and hooded front sight. Pre-1948 rifles of this model were designated Springfield Model 084, later known as Stevens Model 84-S. Disc.

MODEL 85 . . . . NiB $213 Ex $131 Gd $101
Same as Stevens Model 87 except w/5-round detachable box magazine. Made 1939 to date. Pre-1948 rifles of this model were designated Springfield Model 85, currently known as Stevens Model 85. Earlier models command slight premiums.

MODEL 85-S (085) . . . . NiB $197 Ex $146 Gd $111
Same as Model 85 except w/peep rear sight and hooded front sight. Pre-1948 models were designated Springfield Model 085; also known as Stevens Model 85-S.

MODEL 86 BOLT-ACTION . . . . NiB $197 Ex $151 Gd $111
Takedown. Caliber: .22 LR, Long, Short. Tubular magazine holds 15 LR, 17 Long, 21 Short. 24-inch bbl. Weight: 6 lbs. Sights: Open rear, gold bead front. Pistol-grip stock, black forend tip on later production. Made 1935-65. Note: The Springfield brand name was disc. in 1948.

MODEL 86-S (086) . . . . NiB $205 Ex $172 Gd $121
Same as Model 86 except w/peep rear sight and hooded front sight. Pre-1948 rifles of this model were designated as Springfield Model 086, later known as Stevens Model 86-S. Disc.

MODEL 87-S (087) . . . . NiB $213 Ex $197 Gd $126
Same as Stevens Model 87 except w/peep rear sight and hooded front sight. Pre-1948 rifles of this model were designated as Springfield Model 087, later known as Stevens Model 87-S. Disc.

STEYR-DAIMLER-PUCH A.-G. — Steyr, Austria

See also listings under Mannlicher.

AUG-SA SEMIAUTOMATIC RIFLE . . . . NiB $3972 Ex $3191 Gd $2214
Gas-operated. Caliber: .223 Rem. (5.56mm). Thirty or 40-round magazine. 20-inch bbl. standard; optional 16-inch or 24-inch heavy bbl. w/folding bipod. 31 inches overall. Weight: 8.5 lbs. Sights: Integral 1.5x scope and mount. Green high-impact synthetic stock w/folding vertical grip.

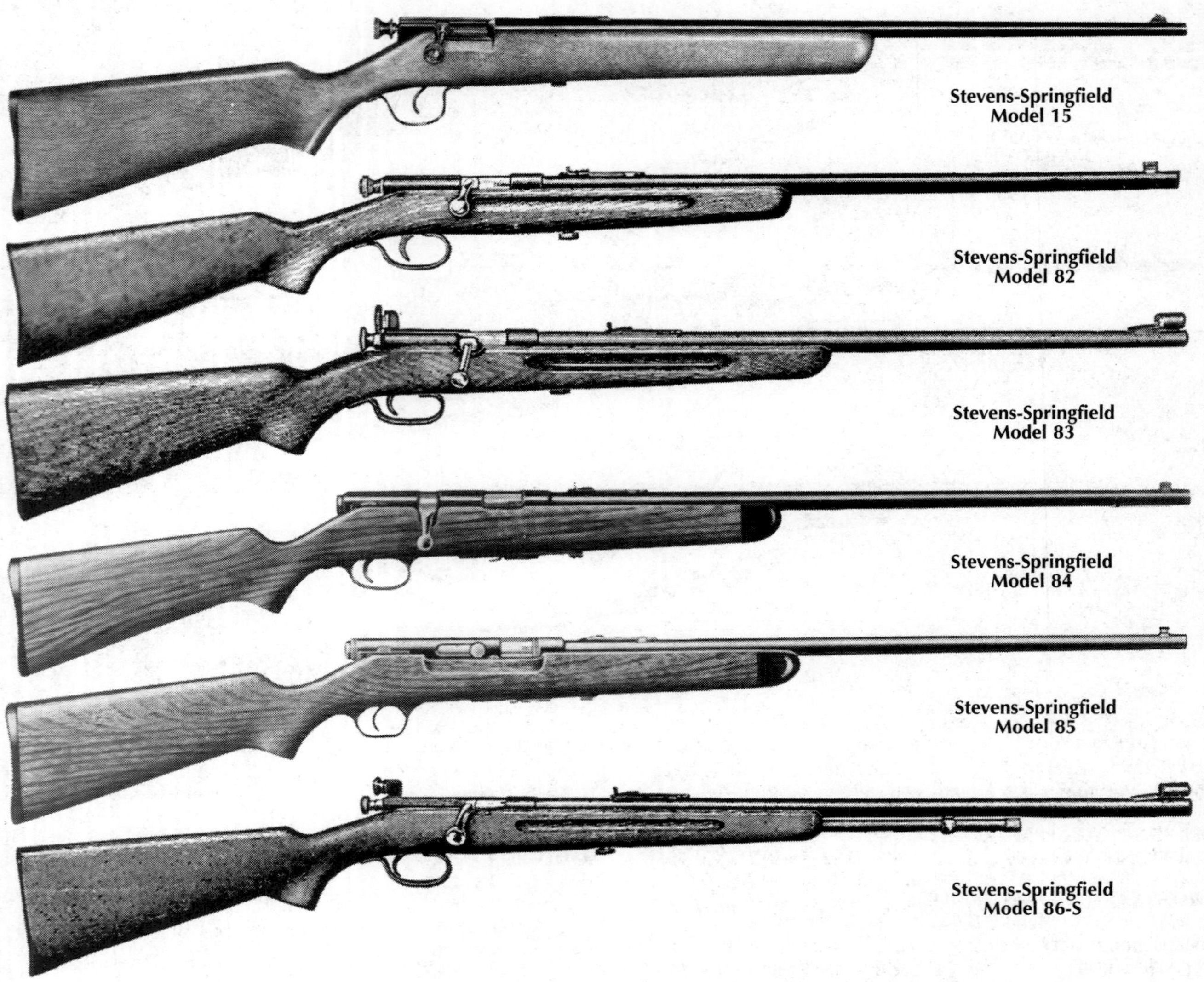
Stevens-Springfield Model 15

Stevens-Springfield Model 82

Stevens-Springfield Model 83

Stevens-Springfield Model 84

Stevens-Springfield Model 85

Stevens-Springfield Model 86-S

SMALL BORE CARBINE.......... NiB $572 Ex $463 Gd $323
Bolt-action repeater. Caliber: .22 LR. Five round detachable box magazine. 19.5-inch bbl. Sights: Leaf rear; hooded bead front. Mannlicher-type stock, checkered, swivels. Made from 1953-67.

STOEGER RIFLE — Mfd. by Franz Jaeger & Co., Suhl, Germany; dist. in the U.S. by A. F. Stoeger, Inc., New York, N.Y.

HORNET RIFLE .... NiB $1336 Ex $950 Gd $615
Same specifications as Herold Rifle, designed and built on a Miniature Mauser-type action. See listing under Herold Bolt-Action Repeating Sporting Rifle for additional specifications. Imported during the 1930s.

SURVIVAL ARMS — Orange, CT

AR-7 EXPLORER .... NiB $164 Ex $123 Gd $82
Caliber: .22 LR. Eight round magazine. Weight: 3 lbs. Polymer stocks. Drift adj. sights. Disassembles into five separate elements, allowing barrel, action and magazine to fit into buttstock; assembles quickly w/o tools. Choice of camo, silvertone or black matte finishes. Made from 1992-95.

THOMPSON/CENTER ARMS — Rochester, New Hampshire

CONTENDER CARBINE
Calibers: .22 LR, .22 Hornet, .222 Rem., .223 Rem., 7mm T.C.U., 7x30 Waters, .30-30 Win., .35 Rem., .44 Mag., .357 Rem. Max. and .410 bore. 21-inch interchangeable bbls. 35 inches overall. Adj. iron sights. Checkered American walnut or Rynite stock and forend. Made from 1985 to date.

Standard model (rifle calibers) .... NiB $446 Ex $343 Gd $266
Standard model (.410 bore)....... NiB $506 Ex $415 Gd $300
Rynite stock model (rifle calibers) .... NiB $569 Ex $497 Gd $407
Rynite stock model (.410 bore).... NiB $594 Ex $518 Gd $421
Extra bbls. (rifle calibers)......... NiB $290 Ex $245 Gd $187
Extra bbls. (.410 bore)........... NiB $306 Ex $255 Gd $192
Youth model (all calibers and .410 bore).................. NiB $385 Ex $317 Gd $214

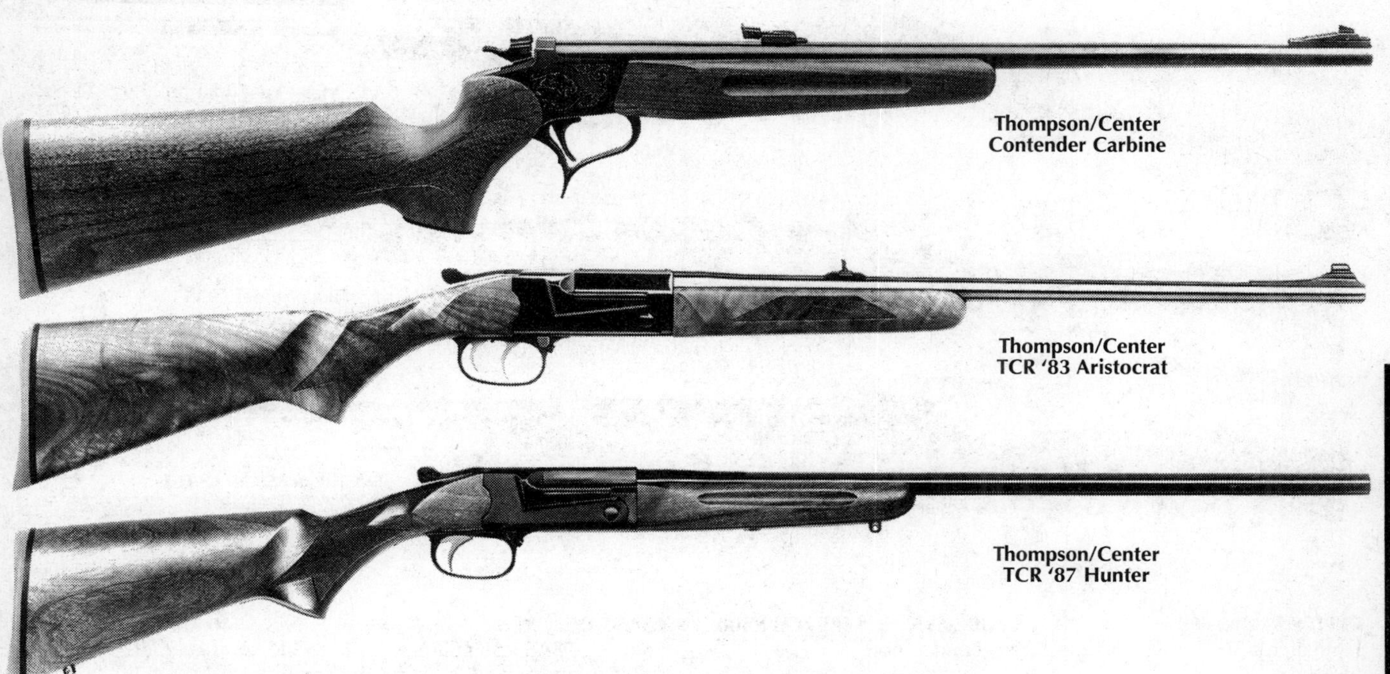

Thompson/Center
Contender Carbine

Thompson/Center
TCR '83 Aristocrat

Thompson/Center
TCR '87 Hunter

CONTENDER CARBINE
SURVIVAL SYSTEM . . . . NiB $617 Ex $437 Gd $334
Similar to standard Contender Carbine w/Rynite stock and forend. Comes w/two 16.25-inch bbls. chambered in .223 and .45/.410 bore. Camo Cordura case.

STAINLESS CONTENDER CARBINE
Same as standard Contender Carbine Model, except stainless steel w/blued sights. Calibers: .22 LR, .22 Hornet, .223 Rem., 7-30 Waters, .30-30 Win., .410. Walnut or Rynite stock and forend. Made from 1993 to date.
Walnut stock model. . . . . NiB $488 Ex $411 Gd $282
Rynite stock model . . . . NiB $463 Ex $385 Gd $272
Youth stock model. . . . . NiB $437 Ex $360 Gd $257
Extra bbls. (rifle calibers). . . . . NiB $249 Ex $203 Gd $146

TCR '83 ARISTOCRAT MODEL
Break frame, overlever action. Calibers: .223 Rem., .22/250 Rem., .243 Win., 7mm Rem. Mag., .30-06 Springfield. Interchangeable bbls.: 23 inches in length. Weight: 6 lbs., 14 oz. American walnut stock and forearm, checkered, black rubber recoil pad, cheekpiece. Made from 1983-87.
TCR '83 Standard model . . . . NiB $463 Ex $411 Gd $231
TCR '83 Aristocrat. . . . . NiB $535 Ex $385 Gd $257
Extra bbls. (rifle calibers). . . . . NiB $251 Ex $205 Gd $148

TCR '87 HUNTER RIFLE
Similar to TCR '83 except in calibers .22 Hornet, ..222 Rem., 223 Rem., .22-250 Rem., .243 Win., .270 Win., 7mm-08, .308 Win., .30-06, .32-40 Win. Also 12-ga. slug and 10- and 12-ga. field bbls. 23-inch standard or 25.88-inch heavy bbl. interchangeable. 39.5 to 43.38 inches overall. Weight: 6 lbs., 14 oz. to 7.5 lbs. Iron sights optional. Checkered American black walnut buttstock w/fluted end. Disc. 1993.

Standard model. NiB $540 Ex $437 Gd $257
Extra bbl. (rifle calibers and
10- or 12-ga. Field). . . . . NiB $270 Ex $221 Gd $158
Extra bbl. (12-ga. slug) . . . . NiB $314 Ex $257 Gd $183

TIKKA RIFLES — Mfg. by Sako, Ltd. of Riihimaki, Finland & Armi Marocchi in Italy

Imported by Beretta USA

Note: *Tikka New Generation, Battue and Continental series bolt action rifles are being manufactured by Sako, Ltd., in Finland. Tikka O/U rifles (previously Valmet) are being manufactured in Italy by Armi Marocchi. For earlier importation see additional listings under Ithaca LSA and Valmet 412S models.*

T3 HUNTER. . . . . NiB $600 Ex $480 Gd $355
Calibers:..223, .22-250, .243Win., .308 Win., .25-06, .270 Win., 6.5x55, 270 WSM, 7mm Rem. Mag., .30-06, 300 WSM, .300 Win. Mag., .338 Win. Mag., Bbl: 22 7/16 inches (24 3/8 in magnum calibers. Weight: 6 3/4 pounds. No sights. Walnut stock with rubber butt pad. Introduced 2003.

T3 LAMINATED
STAINLESS. NiB $820 Ex $725 Gd $595
Same as T3 Hunter but with stainless barrel and action; laminated stock.

T3 LITE . . . . NiB $560 Ex $465 Gd $400
Similar to T3 Hunter but with synthetic stock; weight: 6 pounds, 3 ounces. Introduced 2003.

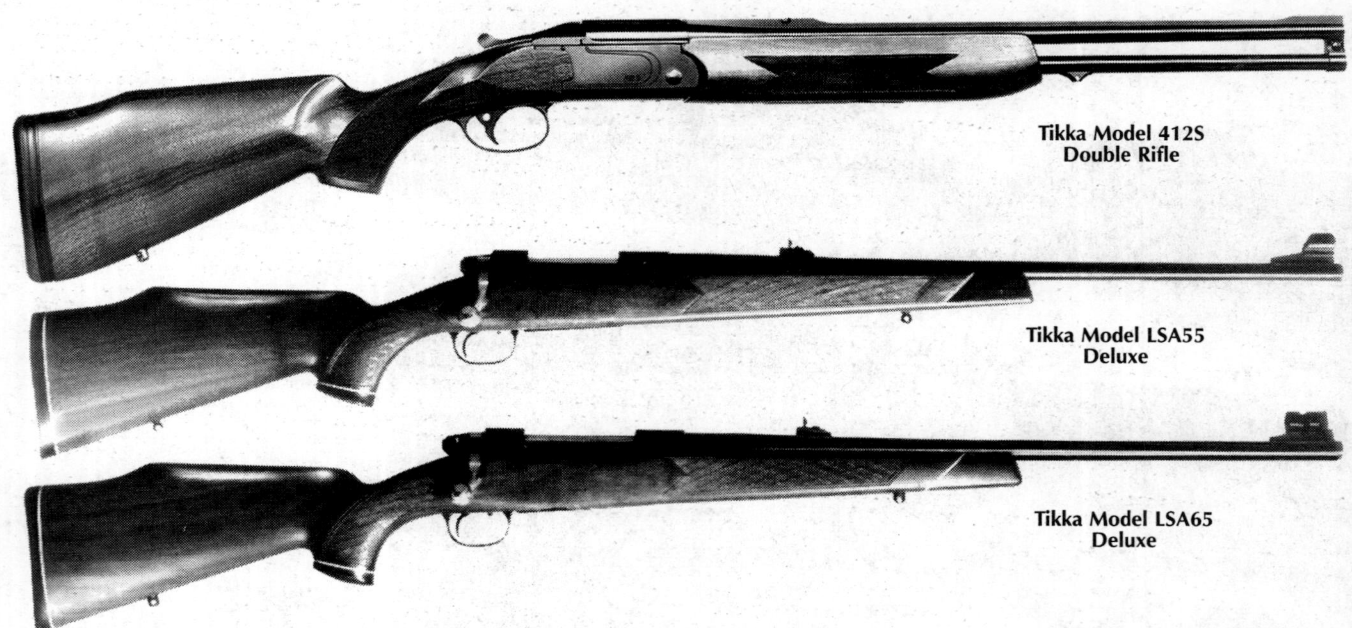

Tikka Model 412S Double Rifle

Tikka Model LSA55 Deluxe

Tikka Model LSA65 Deluxe

T3 LITE STAINLESS . . . . NiB $615 Ex $485 Gd $400
Same as T3 Lite but with stainless barrel and action.

T3 TACTICAL . . . . NiB $1325 Ex $1150 Gd $950
Calibers: .223, .308 Win. Similar to T3 Hunter but designed for law enforcement. Bbl.: 20 inches. Black phosphate finish, synthetic stock with adjustable comb. Five round detachable magazine. Picatinny rail on action, fitted for muzzle brake and bipod use.

T3 VARMINT . . . . NiB $775 Ex $700 Gd $525
Calibers: .223, .22-250, .308 Win. Similar to T3 Hunter but with heavy bull barrel, synthetic stock, adjustable trigger. Five round detachable magazine.

T3 VARMINT
STAINLESS. NiB $815 Ex $725 Gd $550
Similar to T3 Varmint but with stainless barrel and action.

MODEL 412S
DOUBLE RIFLE
Calibers: .308 Win., .30-06, 9.3x74R. 24-inch bbl. w/quarter rib machined for scope mounts; automatic ejectors (9.3x74R only). 40 inches overall. Weight: 8.5 lbs. Ramp front and folding adj. rear sight. Barrel selector on trigger and cocking indicators in tang. European walnut buttstock and forearm. Model 412S was replaced by the 512S version in 1994. Imported from 1989-93.
Model 412S
(disc. 1993) . . . . NiB $1485 Ex $1083 Gd $825
Extra barrel assembly
(O/U shotgun), add $650
Extra barrel assembly
(O/U Combo), add $775
Extra barrel assembly
(O/U rifle), add. $995

MODEL 512S DOUBLE RIFLE
Formerly Valmet 412S. In 1994, following the joint venture of 1989, the model designation was changed to 512S. Imported from 1994 to date.
Model 512S. . . . . NiB $1499 Ex $1370 Gd $1010
Extra barrel assembly
(O/U rifle), add. $755

LSA55 DELUXE . . . . NiB $540 Ex $488 Gd $411
Same as LSA55 Standard except w/rollover cheekpiece, rosewood grip cap and forend tip, skip checkering, high-luster blue. Imported from 1965-88.

LSA55 SPORTER . . . . NiB $533 Ex $432 Gd $302
Same as LSA55 except has 22.8-inch heavy bbl. w/o sights, special stock w/beavertail forearm, not available in 6mm Rem. Weighs 9 lbs. Imported from 1965-88.

LSA55 STANDARD
BOLT-ACTION REPEATER . . . . NiB $488 Ex $360 Gd $231
Mauser-type action. Calibers: .222 Rem., .22-250, 6mm Rem. Mag., .243 Win., .308 Win. Three round clip magazine. 22.8-inch bbl. Weight: 6.8 lbs. Sights: Folding leaf rear; hooded ramp front. Checkered walnut stock w/Monte Carlo cheekpiece, swivels. Made from 1965-88.

LSA65 DELUXE . . . . NiB $566 Ex $488 Gd $334
Same as LSA65 Standard except w/special features of LSA55 Deluxe. Imported from 1970-88.

LSA65 STANDARD . . . . NiB $453 Ex $360 Gd $231
Same as LSA55 Standard except calibers: .25-06, 6.5x55 .270 Win., .30-06. Five round magazine, 22-inch bbl., weight: 7.5 lbs. Imported from 1970-88.

MODEL M 55
Bolt action. Calibers: .222 Rem., .22-250 Rem., .223 Rem. .243 Win., .308 Win. (6mm Rem. and 17 Rem. available in Standard and Deluxe models only). 23.2-inch bbl. (24.8-inch in Sporter and Heavy Barrel models). 42.8 inches overall (44 inches in Sporter and Heavy Barrel models). Weight: 7.25 to 9 lbs. Monte Carlo-style stock w/pistol-grip. Sling swivels. Imported from 1965-88.
Continental . . . . NiB $699 Ex $519 Gd $370
Deluxe model . . . . NiB $741 Ex $524 Gd $390
Sporter. . . . . NiB $674 Ex $545 Gd $365
Sporter w/sights . . . . NiB $699 Ex $522 Gd $369
Standard . . . . NiB $622 Ex $493 Gd $339
Super Sporter . . . . NiB $779 Ex $640 Gd $392
Super Sporter w/sights . . . . NiB $846 Ex $418 Gd $444
Trapper . . . . NiB $712 Ex $505 Gd $367

Tikka
Model M65 Sporter

Tikka
Model M65 Wild Boar

MODEL M65
Bolt action. Calibers: .25-06, .270 Win., .308 Win., .30-06, 7mm Rem. Mag., .300 Win. Mag. (Sporter and Heavy Bbl. models in .270 Win., .308 Win. and .30-06 only). 22.4-inch bbl. (24.8-inch in Sporter and Heavy Bbl. models). 43.2 inches overall (44 inches in Sporter, 44.8 inches in Heavy Bbl.). Weight: 7.5 to 9.9 lbs. Monte Carlo-style stock w/pistol-grip. Disc. 1989.
Continental . . . . NiB $701 Ex $521 Gd $382
Deluxe Magnum . . . . NiB $779 Ex $640 Gd $439
Deluxe model . . . . NiB $727 Ex $521 Gd $367
Magnum . . . . NiB $676 Ex $470 Gd $392
Sporter. . . . . NiB $547 Ex $495 Gd $341
Sporter w/sights . . . . NiB $732 Ex $598 Gd $392
Standard . . . . NiB $624 Ex $495 Gd $341
Super Sporter . . . . NiB $851 Ex $650 Gd $444
Super Sporter w/sights . . . . NiB $856 Ex $646 Gd $495
Super Sporter Master. . . . . NiB $1083 Ex $883 Gd $568

MODEL M65 WILDBOAR . . . . NiB $725 Ex $596 Gd $432
Same general specifications as Model M 65 except 20.8-inch bbl., overall length of 41.6 inches, weight: of 7.5 lbs. Disc. 1989.

NEW GENERATION RIFLES
Short-throw bolt available in three action lengths. Calibers: .22-250 Rem., .223 Rem., .243 Win., .308 Win., (medium action) .25-06 Rem., .270 Win., .30.06, (Long Action) 7mm Rem. Mag., .300 Win. Mag., .338 Win. Mag., (Magnum Action). 22- to 26-inch bbl. 42.25 to 46 inches overall. Weight: 7.2 to 8.5 lbs. Available w/o sights or w/hooded front and open rear sight on quarter rib. Quick-release 3- or 5-round detachable magazine w/recessed side release. Barrel selector on trigger and cocking indicators in tang. European walnut buttstock and forearm matte lacquer finish. Imported from 1989-94.
Standard calibers. . . . . NiB $806 Ex $642 Gd $430
Magnum calibers. . . . . NiB $832 Ex $652 Gd $446

PREMIUM GRADE RIFLE
Similar to New Generation rifles except w/hand-checkered deluxe wood stock w/roll-over check-piece and rosewood grip cap and forend tip. High polished blued finish. Imported from 1989-94.
Standard calibers. . . . . NiB $853 Ex $701 Gd $446
Magnum calibers. . . . . NiB $935 Ex $701 Gd $523

WHITETAIL BOLT-ACTION RIFLE SERIES
New Generation design in multiple model configurations and three action lengths chambered .22-250 to .338 Win. Mag.

BATTUE MODEL
Similar to Hunter Model except designed for snapshooting w/hooded front and open rear sights on quarter rib. Blued finish. Checkered select walnut stock w/matt lacquered finish. Imported from 1991-97.
Battue model (standard w/sights) . . NiB $617 Ex $493 Gd $339
Magnum calibers, add $40

CONTINENTAL MODEL
Similar to Hunter Model except w/prone-style stock w/wider forearm and 26-inch heavy bbl. chambered for 17 Rem., .22-250 Rem., .223 Rem., .308 Win. (Varmint); .25-06 Rem., .270 Win., 7mm Rem. Mag., .300 Win. Mag. (Long Range). Weight: 8.6 lbs. Imported from 1991 to date.
Continental Long-Range model . . . . NiB $725 Ex $519 Gd $370
Continental Varmint model . . . . NiB $674 Ex $519 Gd $365
Magnum calibers, add $40

SPORTER MODEL . . . . NiB $905 Ex $725 Gd $571
Similar to Hunter Model except 23.5-inch bbl. Five round detachable mazigine. Chambered .22-250 Rem., .223 Rem., .308 Win. Weight: 8.6 lbs. Adjustable buttplate and cheekpiece w/stippled pistol grip and forend. Imported from 1998 to date.

WHITETAIL HUNTER MODEL
Calibers: .22-250 Rem., .223 Rem., .243 Win., .25-06 Rem., .270 Win., 7mm Rem. Mag., .308 Win .30.06, .300 Win. Mag., .338 Win. Mag. Three or 5-round detachable box magazine. 20.5- to 24.5-inch bbl. with no sights. 42 to 44.5 inches overall. Weight: 7 to 7.5 lbs. Adj. single-stage or single-set trigger. Blued or stainless finish. All-Weather synthetic or checkered select walnut stock w/matt lacquered finish. Imported from 1991-2002.
Standard model . . . . NiB $622 Ex $493 Gd $339
Deluxe model . . . . NiB $751 Ex $596 Gd $416
Synthetic model. . . . . NiB $725 Ex $493 Gd $365
Stainless model . . . . NiB $730 Ex $540 Gd $365
Magnum calibers, add $40
Left-hand model, add. $70

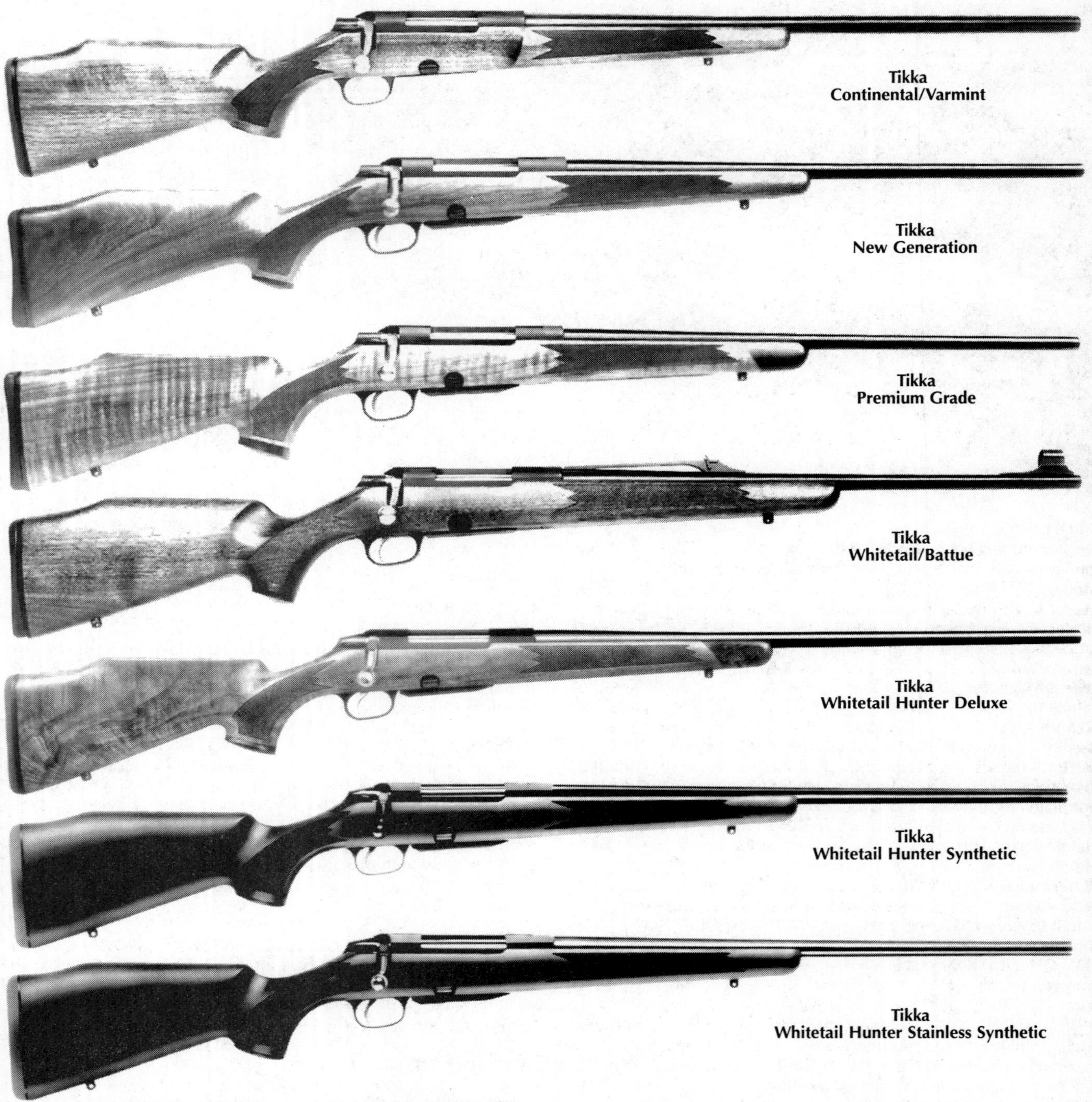

UBERTI RIFLES — Lakeville, Connecticut
Mfd. By Aldo Uberti, Ponte Zanano, Italy
Imported by Stoeger Industries, Accokeek, MD

MODEL 1866 SPORTING RIFLE

Replica of Winchester Model 1866 lever-action repeater. Calibers: .22 LR, .22 WMR, .38 Spec., .44-40, .45 LC. 24.25-inch octagonal bbl. 43.25 inches overall. Weight: 8.25 lbs. Blade front sight,rear elevation leaf. Brass frame and buttplate. Bbl., magazine tube, other metal parts blued. Walnut buttstock and forearm.

Model 1866 Rifle. . . . . NiB $811 Ex $631 Gd $348
Model 1866 Carbine
(19-inch round bbl.) . . . . NiB $701 Ex $580 Gd $374
Model 1866 Trapper
(16-inch bbl.)
Disc. 1989. NiB $631 Ex $502 Gd $369
Model 1866
Rimfire
(Indian Rifle) . . . . NiB $580 Ex $477 Gd $348
Model 1866 Rimfire
(Indian Carbine) . . . . NiB $554 Ex $456 Gd $343

Uberti Model
1873 Carbine

MODEL 1873 SPORTING RIFLE

Replica of Winchester Model 1873 lever-action repeater. Calibers: .22 LR, .22 WMR, .38 Spec., .357 Mag., .44-40, .45 LC. 24.25- or 30-inch octagonal bbl. 43.25 inches overall. Weight: 8 lbs. Blade front sight; adj. open rear. Color case-hardened frame. Bbl., magazine tube, hammer, lever and buttplate blued. Walnut buttstock and forearm.

Model 1873 Rifle.............. NiB $885 Ex $643 Gd $395
Model 1873 Carbine (19-inch round bbl.) .... NiB $782 Ex $612 Gd $385
Model 1873 Trapper (16-inch bbl.) Disc. 1990................... NiB $730 Ex $550 Gd $370

HENRY RIFLE

Replica of Henry lever-action repeating rifle. Calibers: .44-40, .45 LC. 24.5-inch half-octagon bbl. 43.75 inches overall. Weight: 9.25 lbs. Blade front sight; rear sight adj. for elevation. Brass frame, buttplate and magazine follower. Bbl., magazine tube and remaining parts blued. Walnut buttstock.

Henry Rifle .... NiB $833 Ex $601 Gd $421
Henry Carbine (22.5-inch bbl.) .... NiB $807 Ex $576 Gd $395
Henry Trapper (16- or 18-inch bbl.) .... NiB $756 Ex $612 Gd $427
Steel frame, add.................................. $85

MODEL 1875 ARMY TARGET .... NiB $415 Ex $340 Gd $265

Calibers: .357 Mag., .44-40 Colt. Six-round cylinder. Bbl.: 18 inches. Overall length: 37 inches. Weight: 4 1/2 pounds. Carbine version of Model 1875 single-action revolver. Sights: Adjustable rear, ramp front. Plain walnut stock, polished brass butt plate and trigger guard. Case-hardened frame. Blued or nickel-plated cylinder and barrel. Made in Italy. Introduced in 1987, discontinued 1989.

Nickel finish, add.................................. $25

ROLLING BLOCK BABY CARBINE................ NiB $395 Ex $325 Gd $285

Calibers: .22 LR, .22WMR, .22 Hornet, .357 Mag. Bbl.: 22 inches. Overall length: 35 1/2 inches. Weight: 4 3/4 pounds. Copy of Remington New Model No. 4 carbine featuring brass butt plate and trigger guard; blued barrel; color case-hardened frame. Introduced in 1986.

ULTRA-HI PRODUCTS COMPANY — Hawthorne, New Jersey

MODEL 2200 SINGLE-SHOT BOLT-ACTION RIFLE............ NiB $175 Ex $134 Gd $98

Caliber: .22 LR, Long, Short. .23-inch bbl. Weight: 5 lbs. Sights: Open rear; blade front. Monte Carlo stock w/pistol grip. Made in Japan. Intro. 1977; Disc.

ULTRA LIGHT ARMS COMPANY — Granville, West Virginia

MODEL 20 BOLT-ACTION RIFLE

Calibers: .22-250 Rem., .243 Win., 6mm Rem., .250-3000 Savage, .257 Roberts, .257 Ack., 7mm Mauser, 7mm Ack., 7mm-08 Rem., .284 Win., .300 Savage, .308 Win., .358 Win. Box magazine. 22-inch ultra light bbl. Weight: 4.75 lbs. No sights. Synthetic stock of Kevlar or graphite finished, seven different colors. Nonglare matte or bright metal finish. Medium-length action available L.H. models. Made from 1985 to date.

Standard model............ NiB $2363 Ex $1976 Gd $1096
Left-hand model .... NiB $2138 Ex $1745 Gd $1242

MODEL 20S BOLT-ACTION RIFLE

Same general specifications as Model 20 except w/short action in calibers 17 Rem., .222 Rem., .223 Rem., .22 Hornet only.

Standard model .... NiB $2378 Ex $2002 Gd $1101
Left-hand model .... NiB $2228 Ex $1817 Gd $1292

MODEL 24 BOLT-ACTION RIFLE

Same general specifications as Model 20 except w/long action in calibers .25-06, .270 Win., .30-06 and 7mm Express only.

Standard model............ NiB $2466 Ex $2018 Gd $1096
Left-hand model .... NiB $2170 Ex $1770 Gd $1260

MODEL 28 BOLT-ACTION RIFLE ..... NiB $2655 Ex $1924 Gd $1213

Same general specifications as Model 20 except w/long magnum action in calibers .264 Win. Mag., 7mm Rem. Mag., .300 Win. Mag., .338 Win. Mag. only. Offered w/recoil arrester. Left-hand model available.

MODEL 40 BOLT-ACTION RIFLE

Similar to Model 28 except in calibers .300 Wby. and .416 Rigby. Weight: 5.5 lbs. Made from 1994 to date.

Standard model............ NiB $2655 Ex $1924 Gd $1213
Left-hand, model............ NiB $2623 Ex $2033 Gd $1511

U.S. Model 1903-A1 Springfield

U.S. Model 1903-A3 Springfield

U.S. Model 1917 Enfield

UNIQUE RIFLE — Hendaye, France Mfd. by Manufacture d'Armes des Pyrénées Francaises

T66 MATCH RIFLE. . . . . NiB $512 Ex $435 Gd $306
Single-shot bolt-action rifle. Caliber: .22 LR. 25.5-inch bbl. Weight: 10.5 lbs. Sights: Micrometer aperture rear; globe front. French walnut target stock w/Monte Carlo comb, bull pistol-grip, wide and deep forearm, stippled grip surfaces, adj. swivel on accessory track, adj. rubber buttplate. Made in 1966. Disc.

U.S. MILITARY RIFLES — Mfd. by Springfield Armory, Remington Arms Co., Winchester Repeating Arms Co., Inland Mfg. Div. of G.M.C., and other contractors. See notes.

Unless otherwise indicated, the following U.S. military rifles were mfg. at Springfield Armory, Springfield, Mass.

MODEL 1898
KRAG-JORGENSEN CARBINE . . NiB $1999 Ex $1793 Gd $1046
Same general specifications as Model 1898 Rifle except w/22-inch bbl., weight: 8 lbs., carbine-type stock. Note: The foregoing specifications apply, in general, to Carbine models 1896 and 1899, which differed from Model 1898 only in minor details.

MODEL 1898
KRAG-JORGENSEN MILITARY RIFLE . . NiB $1999 Ex $1693 Gd $1046
Bolt action. Caliber: .30-40 Krag. Five round hinged box magazine. 30-inch bbl. Weight: 9 lbs. Sights: Adj. rear; blade front. Military-type stock, straight grip. Note: The foregoing specifications apply, in general, to Rifle models 1892 and 1896, which differed from Model 1898.

MODEL 1903 MARK I SPRINGFIELD . . . NiB $1973 Ex $1767 Gd $866
Same as Standard Model 1903 except altered to permit use of the Pedersen Device. This device, officially designated "U.S. Automatic Pistol Model 1918," converted the M/1903 to a semiautomatic weapon firing a .30 caliber cartridge similar to .32 automatic pistol ammunition. Mark I rifles have a slot milled in the left side of the receiver to serve as an ejection port when the Pedersen Device was in use; these rifles were also fitted w/a special sear and cut-off. Some 65,000 of these devices were manufactured and, presumably, a like number of M/1903 rifles were converted to handle them. During the early 1930s, all Pedersen Devices were ordered destroyed and the Mark I rifles were reconverted by replacement of the special sear and cut-off w/standard components. Some 20-odd specimens are known to have escaped destruction and are in government museums and private collections. Probably more are extant. Rarely is a Pedersen Device offered for sale, so a current value cannot be assigned. However, many of the altered rifles were bought by members of the National Rifle Association through the Director of Civilian Marksmanship. Value shown is for the Mark I rifle w/o the Pedersen Device.

MODEL 1903 NATIONAL
MATCH SPRINGFIELD . . . . NiB $1637 Ex $1484 Gd $886
Same general specifications as Standard Model 1903 except specially selected w/star-gauged bbl., Type C pistol-grip U.S. Model 1903 National Match Springfield (Con't) stock, polished bolt assembly; early types have headless firing pin assembly and reversed safety lock. Produced especially for target shooting.

MODEL 1903 SPRINGFIELD MILITARY RIFLE
Modified Mauser-type bolt action. Caliber: .30-06. Five round box magazine. 23.79-inch bbl. Weight: 8.75 lbs. Sights: Adj. rear; blade front. Military-type stock straight grip. Note: M/1903 rifles of Springfield manufacture w/serial numbers under 800,000 (1903-1918) have casehardened receivers; those between 800,000 and 1,275,767 (1918-1927) were double heat-treated; rifles numbered over 1,275,767 have nickle steel bolts and receivers. Rock Island production from No. 1 to 285,507 have case-hardened receivers. Improved heat treatment was adopted in May 1918 with No. 285,207; about three months later, with No. 319,921, the use of nickel steel was begun, but the production of some double-heat-treated carbon-steel receivers and bolts continued. Made 1903-30 at Springfield Armory during WWI, M/1903 rifles were also made at Rock Island Arsenal, Rock Island, Ill.
W/case-hardened receiver. . . . . NiB $5350 Ex $4577 Gd $2105
W/double heat-treated receiver . . . NiB $4268 Ex $3547 Gd $1549
W/nickel steel receiver . . . . NiB $1628 Ex $1422 Gd $907

MODEL 1903 SPRINGFIELD SPORTER. . NiB $1351 Ex $1875 Gd $768
Same general specifications as National Match except w/sporting design stock, Lyman No. 48 receiver sight.

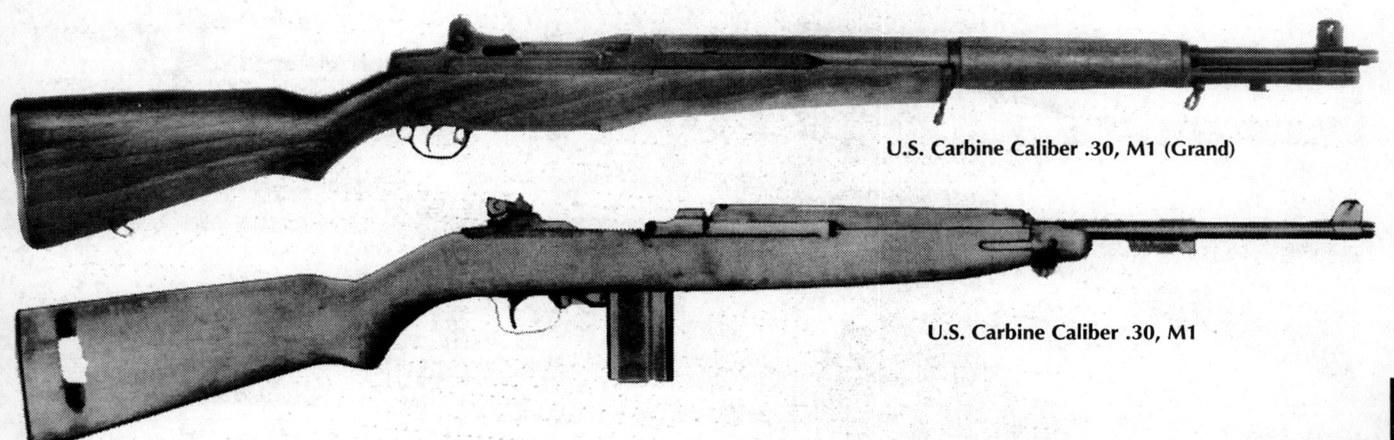

U.S. Carbine Caliber .30, M1 (Grand)

U.S. Carbine Caliber .30, M1

MODEL 1903 STYLE T SPRINGFIELD MATCH RIFLE . . . . NiB $1532 Ex $1235 Gd $856
Same specifications as Springfield Sporter except w/heavy bbl. (26-, 28- or 30-inch), scope bases, globe front sight, weight: 12.5 lbs. w/26-inch bbl.

MODEL 1903 TYPE A SPRINGFIELD FREE RIFLE . . . . . NiB $1822 Ex $1467 Gd $1014
Same as Style T except made w/28-inch bbl. only, w/Swiss buttplate, weight: 13.25 lbs.

MODEL 1903 TYPE B SPRINGFIELD FREE RIFLE . . . . . NiB $2416 Ex $1947 Gd $1345
Same as Type A, except w/cheekpiece stock, palm rest, Woodie double-set triggers, Garand fast firing pin, weight: 14.75 lbs.

MODEL 1903-A1 SPRINGFIELD
Same general specifications as Model 1903 except may have Type C pistol-grip stock adopted in 1930. The last Springfields produced at the Springfield Armory were of this type; final serial number was 1,532,878, made in 1939. Note: Late in 1941, Remington Arms Co., Ilion, N.Y., began production, under government contract, of Springfield rifles of this type w/a few minor modifications. These rifles are numbered 3,000,001-3,348,085 and were manufactured before the adoption of Model 1903-A3.
Springfield manufacture . . . . NiB $1329 Ex $1175 Gd $660
Remington manufacture . . . . NiB $879 Ex $741 Gd $497

MODEL 1903-A3 SPRINGFIELD. . . . . . . NiB $1582 Ex $1386 Gd $382
Same general specifications as Model 1903-A1, except modified to permit increased production and lower cost; may have either straight-grip or pistol-grip stock, bolt is not interchangeable w/earlier types, w/receiver peep sight, many parts are stamped sheet steel, including the trigger guard and magazine assembly. Quality of these rifles, lower than that of other 1903 Springfields, reflects the emergency conditions under which they were produced. Mfd. during WWII by Remington Arms Co. and L. C. Smith Corona Typewriters, Inc.

MODEL 1922-M1 22 SPRINGFIELD TARGET RIFLE . . . . NiB $1180 Ex $954 Gd $666
Modified Model 1903. Caliber: .22 LR. Five round detachable box magazine. 24.5-inch bbl. Weight: 9 lbs. Sights: Lyman No. 48C receiver, blade front. Sporting-type stock similar to that of Model 1903 Springfield Sporter. Issued 1927. Note: The earlier Model 1922, which is seldom encountered, differs from the foregoing chiefly in the bolt mechanism and magazine.

M2 22 SPRINGFIELD TARGET RIFLE . . . . NiB $1273 Ex $995 Gd $557
Same general specifications as Model 1922-M1 except w/speed-lock, improved bolt assembly adj. for headspace. Note: These improvements were later incorporated in many rifles of the preceding models (M1922, M1922MI) and arms so converted were marked "M1922M2" or "M1922MII."

NOTE: *The WWII-vintaqe .30-caliber U.S. Carbine was mfd. by Inland Mfg. Div. of G.M.C., Dayton, OH; Winchester Repeating Arms Co., New Haven, CT, and other contractors: International Business Machines Corp., Poughkeepsie, NY; National Postal Meter Co., Rochester, NY; Quality Hardware & Machine Co., and Rock-Ola Co., Chicago, IL; Saginaw Steering Gear Div. of G.M.C., Saginaw, M1; Standard Products Co., Port Clinton, OH; Underwood-Elliott-Fisher Co., Hartford, CT.*

CALIBER .30, M1 (GARAND) MIL. RIFLE . . . . NiB $1329 Ex $1123 Gd $1046
Clip-fed, gas-operated, air-cooled semiautomatic. Uses a clip containing 8 rounds. 24-inch bbl. Weight: W/o bayonet, 9.5 lbs. Sights: Adj. peep rear; blade front w/guards. Pistol-grip stock, handguards. Made 1937-57. Note: Garand rifles have also been produced by Winchester Repeating Arms Co., Harrington & Richardson Arms Co., and International Harvester Co. Deduct 25% for arsenal-assembled mismatches.

CALIBER .30, M1, NATIONAL MATCH . . . . NiB $2217 Ex $1650 Gd $672
Accurized target version of the Garand. Glass-bedded stock; match grade bbl., sights, gas cylinder. "NM" stamped on bbl. forward of handguard.

MODEL 1917 ENFIELD MILITARY RIFLE . . NiB $849 Ex $735 Gd $287
Modified Mauser-type bolt action. Caliber: .30-06. Five round box magazine. 26-inch bbl. Weight: 9.25 lbs. Sights: Adj. rear; blade front w/guards. Military-type stock w/semi-pistol-grip. This design originated in Great Britain as the, "Pattern 14" and was mfd. in caliber .303 for the British Government in three U.S. plants. In 1917, the U.S. Government contracted w/these firms to produce the same rifle in caliber .30-06; over two million of these Model 1917 Enfields were mfd. While no more were produced after WWI, the U.S. supplied over a million of them to Great Britain during WWII.

NOTE: *The U.S. Model 1917 Enfield was mfd. 1917-18 by Remington Arms Co. of Delaware (later Midvale Steel & Ordnance Co., Eddystone, PA); Remington Arms Co., Ilion, NY; Winchester Repeating Arms Co., New Haven, CT.*

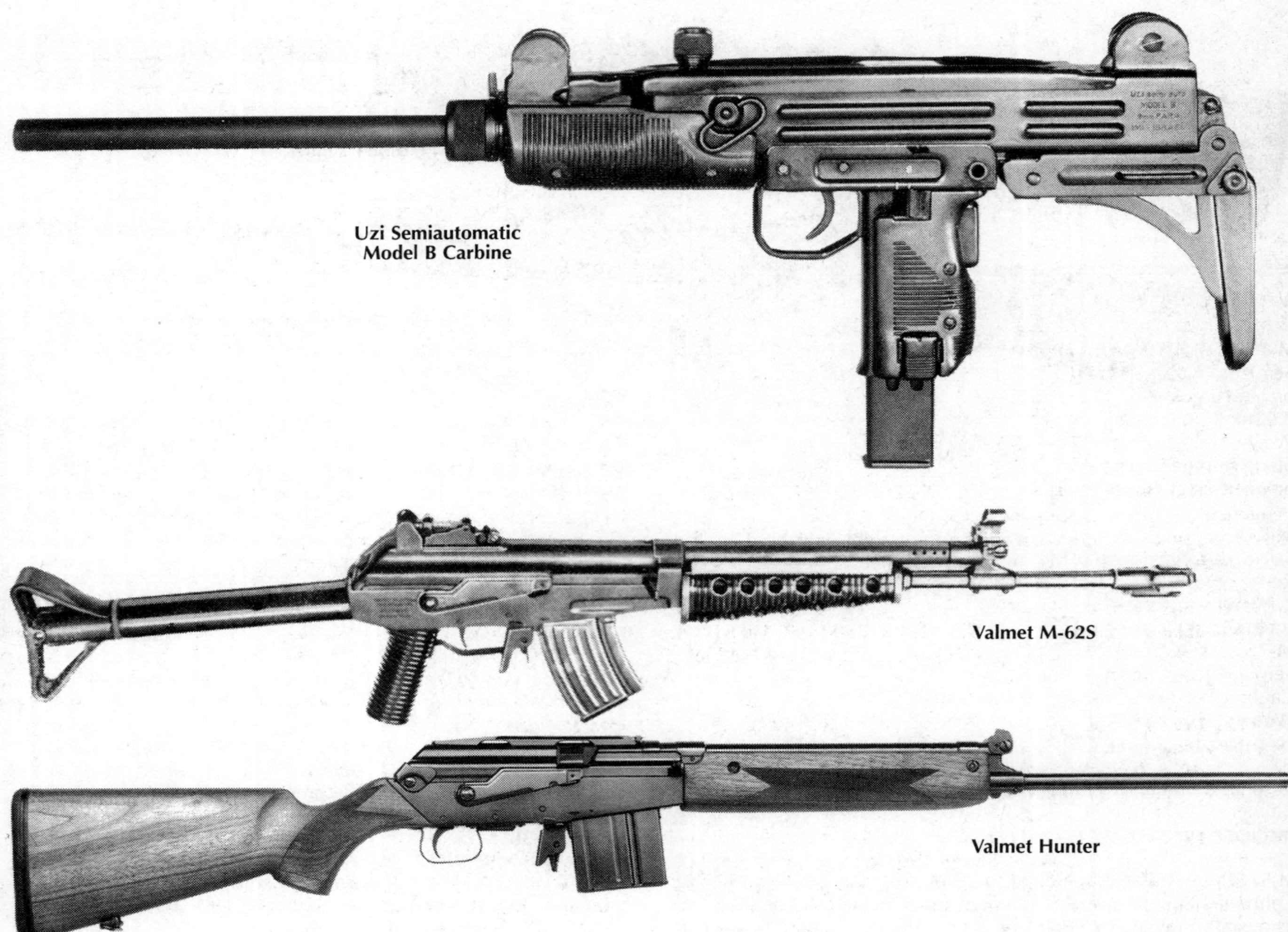

Uzi Semiautomatic Model B Carbine

Valmet M-62S

Valmet Hunter

CARBINE, CALIBER 30, M1 . . . . NiB $776 Ex $628 Gd $439
Gas-operated (short-stroke piston), semiautomatic. 15- or 30-round detachable box magazine. 18-inch bbl. Weight: 5.5 lbs. Sights: adj. rear; blade front sight w/guards. Pistol-grip stock w/handguard, side-mounted web sling. Made 1942-45. In 1963, 150,000 surplus M1 Carbines were sold at $20 each to members of the National Rifle Assn. by the Dept. of the Army. Note: For Winchester and Rock-Ola, add 30%; for Irwin Pedersen, add 80%. Quality Hardware did not complete its production run. Guns produced by other manufacturers were marked "Unquality" & command premium prices.

U.S. REPEATING ARMS CO.

See Winchester Rifle listings.

UNIVERSAL SPORTING GOODS, INC. — Miami, Florida

DELUXE CARBINE. . . . . NiB $354 Ex $303 Gd $176
Same as standard model except also available in caliber .256, w/deluxe walnut Monte Carlo stock and handguard. Made fro 1965 to date.

STANDARD M-1 CARBINE . . . . NiB $252 Ex $201 Gd $150
Same as U.S. Carbine, Cal. .30, M1 except may have either wood or metal handguard, bbl. band w/ or w/o bayonet lug; 5-round magazine standard. Made from 1964 to date.

UZI CARBINE — Mfd. by Israel Military Industries, Israel

SEMIAUTOMATIC MODEL B CARBINE
Calibers: 9mm Parabellum, .41 Action Express, .45 ACP. 20- to 50-round magazine. 16.1-inch bbl. Weight: 8.4 lbs. Metal folding stock. Front post-type sight, open rear, both adj. Imported by Action Arms 1983-89. NFA (Selective Fire) models imported by UZI America, INC., 1994 to date.

Model B Carbine (9mm or .45 ACP) . . . . NiB $1357 Ex $1135 Gd $749
Model B Carbine (.41 AE) . . . . NiB $1590 Ex $1285 Gd $941
Centerfire conversion unit, add $250
Rimfire conversion unit, add. $175

SEMIAUTOMATIC MINI CARBINE . . . . NiB $2596 Ex $2133 Gd $1515
Similar to Uzi Model B except with 19.75-inch bbl.and chambered 9mm Parabellum only. 20-round magazine. Weight: 7.2 lbs. Imported in 1989.

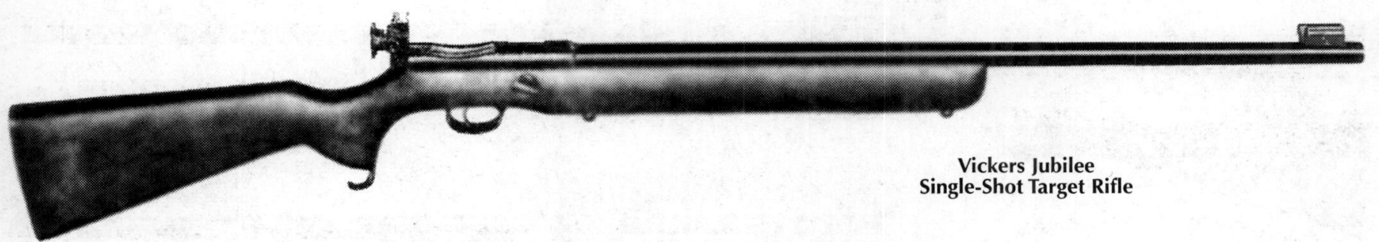

Vickers Jubilee
Single-Shot Target Rifle

VALMET OY — Jyväskylä, Finland

M-62S SEMIAUTOMATIC RIFLE . . . . . . NiB $1887 Ex $1521 Gd $1051
Semiautomatic version of Finnish M-62 automatic assault rifle based on Russian AK-47. Gas-operated rotating bolt action. Caliber: 7.62mmX39 Russian. 15- and 30-round magazines. 16.63-inch bbl. Weight: 8 lbs. w/metal stock. Sights: Tangent aperture rear; hooded blade front w/luminous flip-up post for low-light use. Tubular steel or wood stock. Intro. 1962. Disc.

M-71S . . . . NiB $1894 Ex $1675 Gd $954
Same specifications as M-62S except caliber 5.56mmx45 (.223 Rem.), w/open rear sight, reinforced resin or wood stock, weight: 7.75 lbs. w/former. Made from 1971-89.

M-76 SEMIAUTOMATIC RIFLE
Semiautomatic assault rifle. Gas-operated, rotating bolt action. Caliber: 223 Rem. 15- and 30-round magazines. Made 1984-89.
Wood stock . . . . NiB $1592 Ex $1284 Gd $936
Folding stock . . . . NiB $1978 Ex $1593 Gd $1101

M-78 SEMIAUTOMATIC RIFLE . . . . NiB $1792 Ex $1443 Gd $204
Caliber: 7.62x51 (NATO). 24.13-inch bbl. Overall length: 43.25 inches. Weight: 10.5 lbs.

M-82 SEMIAUTOMATIC CARBINE . . . . NiB $2649 Ex $2082 Gd $1078
Caliber: .223 Rem. 15- or 30-round magazine. 17-inch bbl. 27 inches overall. Weight: 7.75 lbs.

MODEL 412 S DOUBLE RIFLE . . . . NiB $1408 Ex $1147 Gd $791
Boxlock. Manual or automatic extraction. Calibers: .243, .308, .30-06, .375 Win., 9.3x74R. Bbls.: 24-inch over/under. Weight: 8.63 lbs. American walnut checkered stock and forend.

HUNTER SEMIAUTOMATIC RIFLE . . . . . . NiB $1021 Ex $815 Gd $558
Similar to M-78 except in calibers .223 Rem. (5.56mm), .243 Win., .308 Win. (7.62 NATO) and .30-06. Five , 9- or 15-round magazine. 20.5-inch plain bbl. 42 inches overall. Weight: 8 lbs. Sights: Adj. combination scope mount/rear; blade front, mounted on gas tube. Checkered European walnut buttstock and extended checkered forend and handguard. Imported from 1986-89.

VICKERS LTD. — Crayford, Kent, England

**JUBILEE MODEL SINGLE-SHOT-
TARGET RIFLE . . . . NiB $461 Ex $358 Gd $229**
Round-receiver Martini-type action. Caliber: .22 LR. 28-inch heavy bbl. Weight: 9.5 lbs. Sights: Parker-Hale No. 2 front; Perfection rear peep. One-piece target stock w/full forearm and pistol-grip. Made before WWII.

EMPIRE MODEL . . . . NiB $512 Ex $383 Gd $255
Similar to Jubilee Model except w/27- or 30-inch bbl., straight-grip stock, weight: 9.25 lbs. w/30-inch bbl. Made before WWII.

VOERE — Manufactured in Kufstein, Austria Imported by JagerSport, Cranston, Rhode Island

**VEC-91 LIGHTNING
BOLT-ACTION RIFLE . . . . NiB $2577 Ex $2074 Gd $1432**
Features unique electronic ignition system to activate or fire caseless ammunition. Calibers: .5.56 UCC (.222 Cal.), 6mm UCC caseless. Five round magazine. 20-inch bbl. 39 inches overall. Weight: 6 lbs. Open adj. rear sight. Drilled and tapped for scope mounts. European walnut stock w/cheekpiece. Twin forward locking lugs. Imported from 1992 to date.

VOERE, VOELTER & COMPANY — Vaehrenbach, Germany

Mauser-Werke acquired Voere in 1987 and all models are now marketed under new designations.

MODEL 1007 BIATHLON REPEATER . . . . . NiB $383 Ex $306 Gd $203
Caliber: 22 LR. Five round magazine. 19.5-inch bbl. 39 inches overall. Weight: 5.5 lb. Sights: Adj. rear, blade front. Plain beechwood stock. Imported from 1984-86.

MODEL 1013 BOLT-ACTION REPEATER . . . . . NiB $700 Ex $494 Gd $340
Same as Model 1007 except w/military-style stock in 22 WMR caliber. Double-set triggers optional. Imported 1984-86 by KDF, Inc.

MODEL 2107 BOLT-ACTION REPEATER
Caliber: 22 LR. Five or 8-round magazine. 19.5-inch bbl. 41 inches overall. Weight: 6 lbs. Sights: Adj. rear sight, hooded front. European hardwood Monte Carlo-style stock. Imported 1986 by KDF, Inc.
Standard model . . . . NiB $383 Ex $255 Gd $177
Deluxe model . . . . NiB $435 Ex $306 Gd $229

WALTHER RIFLES — Mfd. by the German firms of Waffenfabrik Walther and Carl Walther Sportwaffenfabrik

The following Walther rifles were mfd. before WWII by Waffenfabrik Walther, Zella-Mehlis (Thür.), Germany.

**MODEL 1 AUTOLOADING
RIFLE (LIGHT) . . . . NiB $754 Ex $656 Gd $398**
Similar to Standard Model 2 but w/20-inch bbl., lighter stock, weight: 4.5 lbs.

MODEL 2 AUTOLOADING RIFLE. . . . . NiB $733 Ex $604 Gd $373
Bolt-action, may be used as autoloader, manually operated repeater or single-shot. Caliber: .22 LR. Five or 9-round detachable box magazine. 24.5-inch bbl. Weight: 7 lbs. Sights: Tangent-curve rear; ramp front. Sporting stock w/checkered pistol grip, grooved forearm, swivels. Disc.

Walther Model 1

Walther Model 2

Walther Model GX-1

Walther Model KKM-S

Walther Model U.I.T. Super Match

OLYMPIC BOLT-ACTION MATCH RIFLE . . . . NiB $1244 Ex $1005 Gd $701
Single-shot. Caliber: .22 LR. 26-inch heavy bbl. Weight: 13 lbs. Sights: Micrometer extension rear; interchangeable front. Target stock w/checkered pistol-grip, thumbhole, full beavertail forearm covered w/corrugated rubber, palm rest, adj. Swiss-type buttplate, swivels. Disc.

MODEL V BOLT-ACTION SINGLE-SHOT RIFLE . . . . NiB $591 Ex $427 Gd $308
Caliber: .22 LR. 26-inch bbl. Weight: 7 lbs. Sights: Open rear; ramp front. Plain pistol-grip stock w/grooved forearm. Disc.

MODEL V MEISTERBÜCHSE (CHAMPION) . . . . NiB $669 Ex $488 Gd $329
Same as standard Model V except w/micrometer open rear sight and checkered pistol-grip. Disc.

POST WWII MODELS
The Walther rifles listed below have been manufactured since WWII by Carl Walther Sportwaffenfabrik, Ulm (Donau), Germany.

MODEL GX-1 FREE RIFLE . . . . . . NiB $1985 Ex $1470 Gd $852
Bolt-action, single-shot. Caliber: .22 LR. 25.5-inch heavy bbl. Weight: 15.9 lbs. Sights: Micrometer aperture rear; globe front. Thumbhole stock w/adj. cheekpiece and buttplate w/removable hook, accessory rail. Left-hand stock available. Accessories furnished include hand stop and sling swivel, palm rest, counterweight assembly.

MODEL KKJ SPORTER. . . . . NiB $1284 Ex $1052 Gd $558
Bolt action. Caliber: .22 LR. Five round box magazine. 22.5-inch bbl. Weight: 5.5 lbs. Sights: Open rear; hooded ramp front. Stock w/cheekpiece, checkered pistol-grip and forearm, sling swivels. Disc.

MODEL KKJ-HO . . . . NiB $1538 Ex $1332 Gd $998
Same as Model KKJ except chambered for .22 Hornet. Disc.

MODEL KKJ-MA . . . . NiB $1332 Ex $1178 Gd $550
Same as Model KKJ except chambered for .22 WMR. Disc.

MODEL KKM INTERNATIONAL MATCH RIFLE . . . . NiB $998 Ex $817 Gd $560
Bolt-action, single-shot. Caliber: .22 LR. 28-inch heavy bbl. Weight: 15.5 lbs. Sights: Micrometer aperture rear; globe front. Thumbhole stock w/high comb, adj. hook buttplate, accessory rail. Left-hand stock available. Disc.

MODEL KKM-S . . . . NiB $1049 Ex $869 Gd $586
Same specifications as Model KKM, except w/adj. cheekpiece. Disc.

MOVING TARGET MATCH RIFLE. . . . . NiB $995 Ex $737 Gd $485
Bolt-action, single-shot. Caliber: .22 LR. 23.6-inch bbl. w/weight. Weight: 8.6 lbs. Supplied w/o sights. Thumbhole stock w/adj. cheekpiece and buttplate. Left-hand stock available.

PRONE 400 TARGET RIFLE . . . . NiB $835 Ex $681 Gd $449
Bolt-action, single-shot. Caliber: .22 LR. 25.5-inch heavy bbl. Weight: 10.25 lbs. Supplied w/o sights. Prone stock w/adj. cheekpiece and buttplate, accessory rail. Left-hand stock available. Disc.

MODEL SSV VARMINT RIFLE . . . . . NiB $777 Ex $653 Gd $447
Bolt-action, single-shot. Calibers: .22 LR, .22 Hornet. 25.5-inch bbl. Weight: 6.75 lbs. Supplied w/o sights. Monte Carlo stock w/high cheekpiece, full pistol grip and forearm. Disc.

MODEL U.L.T. SPECIAL MATCH RIFLE . . . . . NiB $1331 Ex $997 Gd $713
Bolt-action, single-shot. Caliber: .22 LR. 25.5-inch bbl. Weight: 10.2 lbs. Sights: Micrometer aperture rear; globe front. Target stock w/high comb, adj. buttplate, accessory rail. Left-hand stock avail. Disc. 1993.

MODEL U.L.T. SUPER MATCH RIFLE. . . . . . NiB $1357 Ex $1022 Gd $739
Bolt-action, single-shot. Caliber: .22 LR. 25.5-inch heavy bbl. Weight: 10.2 lbs. Micrometer aperture rear; globe front. Target stock w/support for off-hand shooting, high comb, adj. buttplate and swivel. Left-hand stock available. Disc. 1993.

MONTGOMERY WARD — Chicago, Illinois Western Field and Hercules Models

Firearms under the "private label" names of Western Field and Hercules are manufactured by such firms as Mossberg, Stevens, Marlin, and Savage for distribution and sale by Montgomery Ward.

MODEL 14M-497B WESTERN FIELD BOLT-ACTION RIFLE. . . . . NiB $121 Ex $101 Gd $74
Caliber: .22 RF. Seven round detachable box magazine. 24-inch bbl. Weight: 5 lbs. Sights: Receiver peep; open rear; hooded ramp front. Pistol-grip stock. Mfg. by Mossberg.

MODEL M771 WESTERN FIELD LEVER-ACTION RIFLE . . . . NiB $172 Ex $146 Gd $116
Calibers: .30-30, .35 Rem. Six round tubular magazine. 20-inch bbl. Weight: 6.75 lbs. Sights: Open rear; ramp front. Pistol-grip or straight stock, forearm w/barrel band. Mfg. by Mossberg.

MODEL M772 WESTERN FIELD LEVER-ACTION RIFLE . . . . NiB $197 Ex $172 Gd $121
Calibers: .30-30, .35 Rem. Six round tubular magazine. 20-inch bbl. Weight: 6.75 lbs. Sights: Open rear; ramp front. Pistol-grip or straight stock, forearm w/bbl. band. Mfg. by Mossberg.

MODEL M775 BOLT-ACTION RIFLE. . . . . NiB $131 Ex $116 Gd $90
Calibers: .222 Rem., .22-250, .243 Win., .308 Win. Four round magazine. Weight: 7.5 lbs. Sights: Folding leaf rear; ramp front. Monte Carlo stock w/cheekpiece, pistol-grip. Mfg by Mossberg.

MODEL M776 BOLT-ACTION RIFLE. . . . . NiB $223 Ex $197 Gd $139
Calibers: .222 Rem., .22-250, .243 Win., .308 Win. Four round magazine. Weight: 7.5 lbs. Sights: Folding leaf rear; ramp front. Monte Carlo stock w/cheekpiece, pistol-grip. Mfg. by Mossberg.

MODEL M778 LEVER-ACTION . . . . NiB $218 Ex $172 Gd $121
Calibers: .30-30, .35 Rem. Six round tubular magazine. 20-inch bbl. Weight: 6.75 lbs. Sights: Open rear; ramp front. Pistol-grip or straight stock, forearm w/bbl. band. Mfg. by Mossberg.

MODEL M780 BOLT-ACTION RIFLE. . . . . NiB $223 Ex $197 Gd $146
Calibers: .222 Rem., .22-250, .243 Win., .308 Win. Four round magazine. Weight: 7.5 lbs. Sights: Folding leaf rear; ramp front. Monte Carlo stock w/cheekpiece, pistol grip. Mfg. by Mossberg.

MODEL M782 BOLT-ACTION RIFLE. . . . . NiB $223 Ex $197 Gd $146
Same general specifications as Model M780.

MODEL M808 . . . . NiB $123 Ex $106 Gd $79
Takedown. Caliber: .22RF. Fifteen round tubular magazine. Bbls.: 20- and 24-inch. Weight: 6 lbs. Sights: Open rear; bead front. Pistol-grip stock. Mfg. by Stevens.

MODEL M832 BOLT-ACTION RIFLE. . . . . . NiB $131 Ex $111 Gd $80
Caliber: .22 RF. Seven round clip magazine. 24-inch bbl. Weight: 6.5 lbs. Sights: Open rear; ramp front. Mfg. by Mossberg.

MODEL M836 . . . . NiB $136 Ex $111 Gd $90
Takedown. Caliber: .22RF. Fifteen round tubular magazine. Bbls.: 20- and 24-inch. Weight: 6 lbs. Sights: Open rear; bead front. Pistol-grip stock. Mfg. by Stevens.

MODEL M865 LEVER-ACTION CARBINE. . NiB $162 Ex $121 Gd $106
Hammerless. Caliber: .22RF. Tubular magazine. Made w/both 18.5-inch and 20-inch bbls., forearm w/bbl. band, swivels. Weight: 5 lbs. Mfg. by Mossberg.

MODEL M894 AUTO-LOADING CARBINE . . . . NiB $146 Ex $121 Gd $95
Caliber: .22 RF. Fifteen round tubular magazine. 20-inch bbl. Weight: 6 lbs. Sights: Open rear; ramp front. Monte Carlo stock w/pistol-grip. Mfg. by Mossberg.

MODEL M-SD57 . . . . NiB $131 Ex $111 Gd $80
Takedown. Caliber: .22RF. 15-round tubular magazine. Bbls.: 20- and 24-inch. Weight: 6 lbs. Sights: Open rear; bead front. Pistol-grip stock. Mfg. by Stevens.

WEATHERBY, INC. — Atascadero, CA (Formerly South Gate, CA)

CROWN CUSTOM RIFLE . . . . . NiB $6051 Ex $4171 Gd $2214
Calibers: .240, .30-06, .257, .270, 7mm, .300, and .340. Bbl.: Made to order. Super fancy walnut stock. Also available w/engraved barreled action including gold animal overlay.

RIFLES

Weatherby Mark V Classicmark I

Weatherby Crown Custom

Weatherby Fiberguard

Weatherby Fibermark

DELUXE .378 MAGNUM RIFLE . . . . . . NiB $2797 Ex $2050 Gd $1416
Same general specifications as Deluxe Magnum in other calibers except caliber .378 W. M. Schultz & Larsen action; 26-inch bbl. Disc. 1958.

DELUXE MAGNUM RIFLE. . . . . NiB $2010 Ex $1510 Gd $1092
Calibers: .220 Rocket, .257 Weatherby Mag., .270 W.M. 7mm W.M., .300 W.M., .375 W.M. Specially processed FN Mauser action. 24-inch bbl. (26-inch in .375 cal.). Monte Carlo-style stock w/cheekpiece, black forend tip, grip cap, checkered pistol-grip and forearm, quick-detachable sling swivels. Value shown is for rifle w/o sights. Disc. 1958.

DELUXE RIFLE. . . . . NiB $1453 Ex $1119 Gd $810
Same general specifications as Deluxe Magnum except chambered for standard calibers such as .270, .30-06, etc. Disc. 1958.

FIBERGUARD RIFLE . . . . NiB $747 Ex $618 Gd $438
Same general specifications as Vanguard except for fiberglass stock and matte metal finish. Disc, 1988.

FIBERMARK RIFLE. . . . . NiB $1289 Ex $959 Gd $650
Same general specifications as Mark V except w/molded fiberglass stock, finished in a nonglare black wrinkle finish. The metal is finished in a non-glare matte finish. Disc. 1993.

MARK V ACCUMARK BOLT-ACTION REPEATING
Weatherby Mark V magnum action. Calibers: .257 Wby., .270 Wby., 7mm Rem. Mag., 7mm Wby., 7mm STW, .300 Win. Mag., .300 Wby. Mag., .30-338 Wby., .30-378 Wby. and .340 Wby. 26- or 28-inch stainless bbl. w/black oxide flutes. 46.5 or 48.5 inches overall. Weight: 8 to 8.5 lbs. No sights, drilled and tapped for scope. Stainless finish w/blued receiver. H-S Precision black synthetic stock w/aluminum bedding plate, recoil pad and sling swivels. Imported from 1996 to date.

Mark V Accumark (.30-338
& .30-378 Wby. Mag.). . . . . NiB $1401 Ex $1130 Gd $784
Mark V Accumark (All other calibers). . . . NiB $1202 Ex $971 Gd $676
Mark V Left-Action, add $75

MARK V ACCUMARK
LIGHT WEIGHT RIFLE. . . . . NiB $1300 Ex $1105 Gd $667
Similar to the Mark V Accumark except w/LightWeight Mark V action designed for standard calibers w/sixlocking lugs rather than nine. 24-inch stainless bbl. Weight: 5.75 lbs. Gray or black Monte Carlo-style composite Kevlar/fiberglass stock w/Pachmayr "Decelerator" pad. No sights. Imported from 1997 to date.

MARK V
CLASSICMARK I RIFLE
Same general specifications as Mark V except w/checkered select American Claro walnut stock w/oil finish and presentation recoil pad. Satin metal finish. Imported from 1992-93.

Calibers .240 to .300 Wby. . . . . . . NiB $1159 Ex $824 Gd $515
Caliber .340 Wby. . . . . NiB $1180 Ex $850 Gd $515
Caliber .378 Wby. . . . . NiB $1365 Ex $850 Gd $515
Caliber .416 Wby. . . . . NiB $1236 Ex $902 Gd $515
Caliber .460 Wby. . . . . NiB $1339 Ex $979 Gd $541

Weatherby Mark V Deluxe

Weatherby Mark V Euromark

Weatherby Mark V Lazermark

Weatherby Mark V Safari Grade

MARK V CLASSICMARK LL RIFLE
Same general specifications as Classicmark I except w/checkered select American walnut stock w/oil finish steel grip cap and Old English recoil pad. Satin metal finish. Right-hand only. Imported from 1992-93.
Calibers .240 to .340 Wby.
(26-inch bbl.). . . . . NiB $1441 Ex $1132 Gd $772
Caliber .378 Wby. . . . . NiB $1493 Ex $1158 Gd $823
Caliber .416 Wby. . . . . NiB $1621 Ex $1385 Gd $971
Caliber .460 Wby. . . . . NiB $1673 Ex $1416 Gd $1004

MARK V DELUXE RIFLE. . . . . NiB $1061 Ex $783 Gd $545
Similar to Mark V Sporter except w/Lightweight Mark V action designed for standard calibers w/sixlocking lugs rather than nine, 4- or 5-round magazine. 24-inch bbl. 44 inches overall. Weight: 6.75 lbs. Checkered Monte Carlo American walnut stock w/rosewood forend and pistol grip and diamond inlay. Imported from 1997 to date.

WEATHERBY MARK V DELUXE BOLT-ACTION SPORTING RIFLE
Mark V action, right or left hand. Calibers: .22-250, .30-06- .224 Weatherby Varmintmaster; .240, .257, .270, 7mm, .300, .340, .375, .378, .416, .460 Weatherby Magnums. Box magazine holds 2 to 5 cartridges depending on caliber. 24- or 26-inch bbl. Weight: 6.5 to 10.5 lbs. Monte Carlo-style stock w/cheekpiece, skip checkering, forend tip, pistol-grip cap, recoil pad, QD swivels. Values shown are for rifles w/o sights. Made in Germany 1958-69; in Japan 1970-94. Values shown for Japanese production.
Calibers .22-250, .224 . . . . NiB $1107 Ex $859 Gd $607
Caliber .375 H&H Magnum . . . . NiB $1184 Ex $1004 Gd $695
Caliber .378 Weatherby Magnum . . . . . . NiB $1364 Ex $1081 Gd $849
Caliber .416 Weatherby Magnum . . . . . . NiB $1441 Ex $1132 Gd $772
Caliber .460 Weatherby Magnum . . . . . NiB $1853 Ex $1359 Gd $1029

MARK V EUROMARK BOLT-ACTION RIFLE
Same general specifications as other Mark V rifles except w/hand-rubbed, satin oil finish Claro walnut stock and nonglare special process blue matte barreled action. Left-hand models available. Imported from 1986-93. Reintroduced in 1995.
Caliber .378 Wby. Mag. . . . . NiB $1437 Ex $1128 Gd $768
Caliber .416 Wby. Mag. . . . . NiB $1540 Ex $1206 Gd $871
Caliber .460 Wby Mag. . . . . NiB $1826 Ex $1414 Gd $1027
Other calibers . . . . NiB $999 Ex $762 Gd $509

MARK V LAZERMARK RIFLE
Same general specifications as Mark V except w/laser-carved stock.
Caliber .378 Wby. Mag. . . . . NiB $1929 Ex $1517 Gd $868
Caliber .416 Wby. Mag. . . . . NiB $1929 Ex $1517 Gd $868
Caliber .460 Wby. Mag. . . . . NiB $2284 Ex $1615 Gd $1074
Other calibers . . . . NiB $1387 Ex $1078 Gd $697

MARK V SAFARI GRADE RIFLE. . . . . . . NiB $2248 Ex $1811 Gd $1253
Same general specifications as Mark V except extra capacity magazine, bbl. sling swivel, and express rear sight typical "Safari" style.

MARK V SPORTER RIFLE
Sporter version of Mark V Magnum w/low-luster metal finish. Checkered Carlo walnut stock w/o grip cap or forend tip. No sights. Imported from 1993 to date.
Calibers .257 to .300 Wby. . . . . . . NiB $1009 Ex $844 Gd $458
.340 Weatherby . . . . NiB $1071 Ex $700 Gd $484
.375 H&H . . . . NiB $1102 Ex $793 Gd $587

MARK V LIGHTWEIGHT SPORTER RIFLE. . NiB $967 Ex $787 Gd $452
Similar to Mark V Sporter except w/Lightweight Mark V action designed for standard calibers w/six locking lugs rather than nine. Imported from 1997 to date.

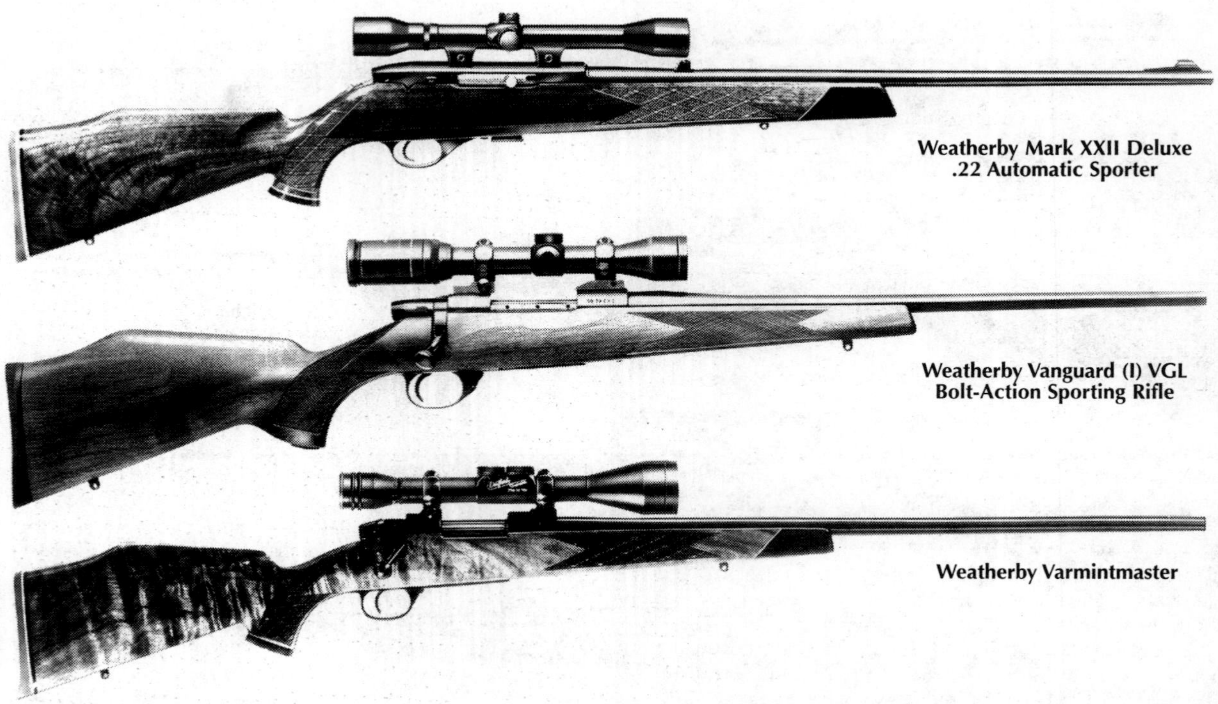

Weatherby Mark XXII Deluxe .22 Automatic Sporter

Weatherby Vanguard (I) VGL Bolt-Action Sporting Rifle

Weatherby Varmintmaster

MARK V STAINLESS RIFLE
Similar to the Mark V Magnum except in 400-series stainless steel w/bead-blasted matte finish. Weight: 8 lbs. Monte Carlo synthetic stock w/aluminum bedding block. Imported from 1995 to date.
Mark V Stainless (.30-.378 Wby.). . NiB $1204 Ex $987 Gd $534
Mark V Stainless (.375 H&H.) . . . . NiB $1204 Ex $987 Gd $534
All other calibers. . . . . NiB $1049 Ex $762 Gd $534
W/fluted bbl., add. $100

MARK V (LW) STAINLESS RIFLE . . . . NiB $828 Ex $643 Gd $437
Similar to the Mark V (standard calibers) except in 400-series stainless steel w/bead-blasted matte finish. Five round magazine. 24-inch bbl. 44 inches overall. Weight: 6.5 lbs. Monte Carlo synthetic stock w/aluminum bedding block. Imported from 1995 to date.

MARK V SLS RIFLE
Acronym for Stainless Laminated Sporter. Similar to the Mark V Magnum Sporter, except w/stainless 400-series action and 24- or 26-inch stainless bbl. Laminated wood stock. Weight: 8.5 lbs. Black oxide bead-blasted matte blue finish. Imported from 1997 to date.
Mark V SLS (.340 Wby.). . . . . NiB $1206 Ex $999 Gd $536
All other calibers. . . . . NiB $1051 Ex $763 Gd $536

MARK V SYNTHETIC RIFLE
Similar to the Mark V Magnum except w/Monte Carlo synthetic stock w/aluminum bedding block. 24- or 26-inch standard tapper or fluted bbl. Weight: 7.75 to 8 lbs. Matte blue finish. Imported from 1995 to date.
Mark V Synthetic (.340 Wby.) . . . . NiB $1051 Ex $763 Gd $506
Mark V Synthetic (.30-378 Wby.) . . . . NiB $1072 Ex $742 Gd $506
All other calibers . . . . NiB $777 Ex $596 Gd $416
W/fluted bbl., add. $100

MARK V ULTRA LIGHT WEIGHT RIFLE
Similar to the Mark V Magnum except w/skeletonized bolt handle. 24- or 26-inch fluted stainless bbl. chambered .257 Wby., .270 Wby., 7mm Rem. Mag., 7mm Wby., .300 Win. Mag., .300 Wby. Monte Carlo synthetic stock w/aluminum bedding block. Weight: 6.75 lbs. Imported from 1998 to date.
Mark V Ultra Lightweight (standard calibers). . . . . NiB $1935 Ex $1497 Gd $802
Mark V Ultra Lightweight (Weatherby calibers) . . . . NiB $1960 Ex $1548 Gd $827
Mark V Ultra Lightweight (Left-hand action), add $100

MARK XXII DELUXE .22 AUTOMATIC SPORTER, CLIP-FED MODEL . . . . NiB $535 Ex $488 Gd $360
Semiautomatic w/single-shot selector. Caliber: .22 LR. Five and 10-round clip magazines. 24-inch bbl. Weight: 6 lbs. Sights: Folding leaf open rear; ramp front. Monte Carlo-type stock w/cheekpiece, pistol-grip, forend tip, grip cap, skip checkering, QD swivels. Intro. 1964. Made in Italy from 1964-69; in Japan, from 1970-1981; in the U.S., from 1982-90.

MARK XXII, TUBULAR MAGAZINE MODEL . . . . NiB $432 Ex $355 Gd $225
Same as Mark XXII, clip-fed model except w/15-round tubular magazine. Made in Japan from 1973-81; in the U.S., from 1982-90.

VANGUARD (I) BOLT-ACTION SPORTING RIFLE
Mauser-type action. Calibers: .243 Win., .25-06, .270 Win., 7mm Rem. Mag., .30-06, .300 Win. Mag. Five round magazine; (3-round in Magnum calibers). 24-inch bbl. Weight: 7 lbs. 14 oz. No sights. Monte Carlo-type stock w/cheekpiece, rosewood forend tip and pistol-grip cap, checkering, rubber buttpad, QD swivels. Imported from 1970-84.
Vanguard Standard . . . . NiB $488 Ex $411 Gd $257
Vanguard VGL (w/shorter 20-inch bbl., plain checkered stock matte finish, 6.5 lbs . . . . NiB $463 Ex $385 Gd $262
Vanguard VGS (w/24-inch bbl., plain checkered stock, matte finish. . . . . NiB $514 Ex $396 Gd $282
Vanguard VGX (w/higher grade finish) . . . . NiB $566 Ex $463 Gd $308

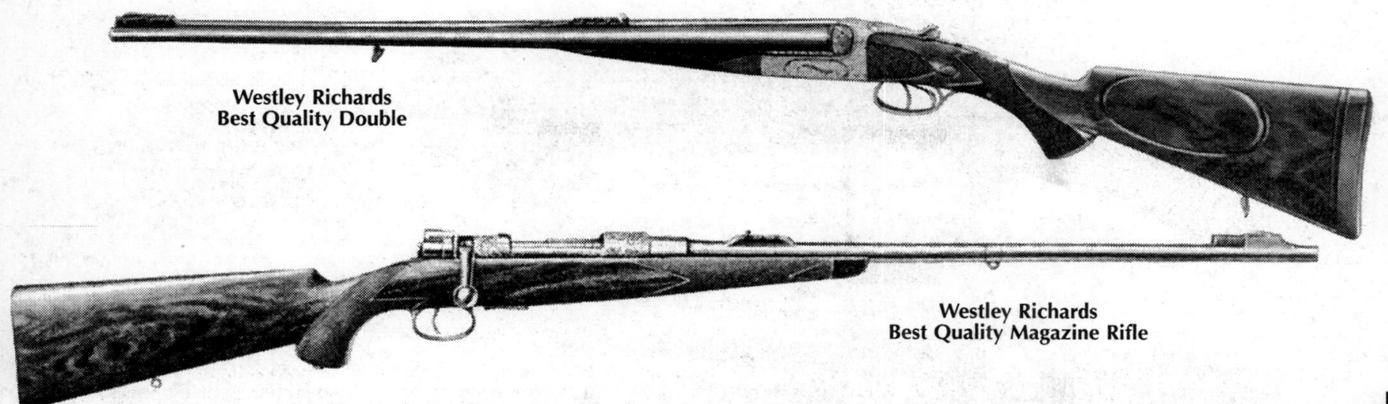

Westley Richards
Best Quality Double

Westley Richards
Best Quality Magazine Rifle

VANGUARD CLASSIC I RIFLE. . . . . NiB $519 Ex $406 Gd $288
Same general specifications as Vanguard VGX Deluxe except w/hand-checkered classic-style stock, black buttpad and satin finish. Calibers .223 Rem., .243 Win. .270 Win., 7mm-08, 7mm Rem. Mag., .30-06 and .308 Win. Imported 1989-94.

VANGUARD CLASSIC II RIFLE . . . . NiB $741 Ex $617 Gd $411
Same general specifications as Vanguard VGX Deluxe except custom checkered classic-style American walnut stock w/black forend tip, grip cap and solid black recoil pad, satin finish. Imported 1989-94.

VANGUARD VGX DELUXE . . . . NiB $669 Ex $535 Gd $385
Calibers: .22-250 Rem., .243 Rem., .270 Wby. Mag., .270 Win., 7mm Rem. Mag., .30-06, .300 Win. Mag., .300 Wby. Mag., .338 Win. Mag. Three or 5-round capacity. 24-inch bbl. About 44 inches overall. Weight: 7 to 8.5 lbs. Custom checkered American walnut stock w/Monte Carlo and recoil pad. Rosewood forend tip and pistol-grip cap. High-luster finish. Disc. 1994.

VARMINTMASTER BOLT-ACTION RIFLE. . NiB $1904 Ex $1487 Gd $822
Calibers: .224 Wby., .22-250, 4-round magazine. 26-inch bbl. 45 inches overall. Weight: 7.75 lbs. Checkered walnut stock. No sights. Disc.

WEATHERMARK RIFLE
Same gen. specs. as Classicmark except w/checkered blk. Weathermark composite stock. Mark V bolt act. Cal: .240, .257, .270, .300, .340, .378, .416 and .460 Weatherby Mag.; plus .270 Win., 7mm Rem. Mag., .30-06 and .375 H&H Mag. Wt: 8 to 10 lbs. Right-hand only. Imp. 1992-94.
Calibers .257 to .300 Wby. . . . . NiB $746 Ex $571 Gd $390
Caliber .340 Weatherby. . . . . NiB $777 Ex $596 Gd $401
Caliber .375 H&H . . . . NiB $1008 Ex $699 Gd $493
Other non-Wby. calibers . . . . NiB $745 Ex $540 Gd $390

WEATHERMARK ALASKAN RIFLE. . . . . NiB $828 Ex $674 Gd $468
Same general specifications as Weathermark except w/nonglare electroless nickel finish. Right-hand only. Imported from 1992-94.

WEIHRAUCH — Melrichstadt, West Germany *Imported by European American Armory, Sharpes, FL.*

MODEL HW 60 TARGET RIFLE . . . . NiB $671 Ex $593 Gd $384
Single-shot. Caliber: .22 LR. 26.75-inch bbl. Walnut stock. Adj. buttplate and trigger. Hooded ramp front sight. Push button safety. Imported from 1995-97.

MODEL HW 66 BOLT-ACTION RIFLE . . . . NiB $619 Ex $532 Gd $336
Caliber: .22 Hornet. 22.75-inch bbl. 41.75 inches overall. Weight: 6.5 lbs. Walnut stock w/cheekpiece. Hooded blade ramp front sight. Checkered pistol grip and forend. Imported from1989-90.

MODEL HW 660 MATCH
BOLT-ACTION RIFLE. . . . . NiB $903 Ex $775 Gd $440
Caliber: .22 LR. 26-inch bbl. 45.33 inches overall. Weight: 10.75 lbs. Walnut or laminated stock w/adj. cheekpiece and buttplate. Checkered pistol grip and forend. Adj. trigger. Imported 1991 to date.

WESTERN FIELD RIFLES

See listings under "W" for Montgomery Ward.

WESTLEY RICHARDS & CO., LTD. — London, England

BEST QUALITY
DOUBLE RIFLE. . . . . NiB $34,375 Ex $27,500 Gd $18,700
Boxlock, hammerless, ejector. Hand-detachable locks. Calibers: .30-06, .318 Accelerated Express, .375 Mag., .425 Mag. Express, .465 Nitro Express, .470 Nitro Express. 25-inch bbls. Weight: 8.5 to 11 lbs. Sights: leaf rear; hooded front. French walnut stock w/cheekpiece, checkered pistol grip and forend.

BEST QUALITY MAGAZINE RIFLE
Mauser or Magnum Mauser action. Calibers: 7mm High Velocity, .30-06, .318 Accelerated Express, .375 Mag., .404 Nitro Express, .425 Mag. Bbl. lengths: 24-inch; 7mm, 22-inch; .425 caliber, 25-inch. Weight 7.25 to 9.25 lbs. Sights: Leaf rear; hooded front.
Standard action . . . . NiB $8728 Ex $6990 Gd $4766
Magnum action . . . . NiB $12,813 Ex $10,250 Gd $6970

WICHITA ARMS — Wichita, Kansas

MODEL WCR CLASSIC BOLT-ACTION RIFLE
Single-shot. Calibers: .17 Rem through .308 Win. 21-inch octagon bbl. Hand-checkered walnut stock. Drilled and tapped for scope w/no sights. Right or left-hand action w/Canjar trigger. Non-glare blued finish. Made from 1978 to date.
Right-hand model . . . . NiB $3466 Ex $2694 Gd $1767
Left-hand model . . . . NiB $3383 Ex $2766 Gd $1977

MODEL WSR SILHOUETTE BOLT-ACTION RIFLE
Single-shot, bolt action, chambered in most standard calibers. Right or left-hand action w/fluted bolt. Drilled and tapped for scope mount with no sights. 24-inch bbl. Canjar trigger. Metallic gray Fiberthane stock w/vented rubber recoil pad. Made from 1983-95.
Right-hand model . . . . NiB $2631 Ex $1936 Gd $1344
Left-hand model . . . . NiB $2574 Ex $2116 Gd $1531

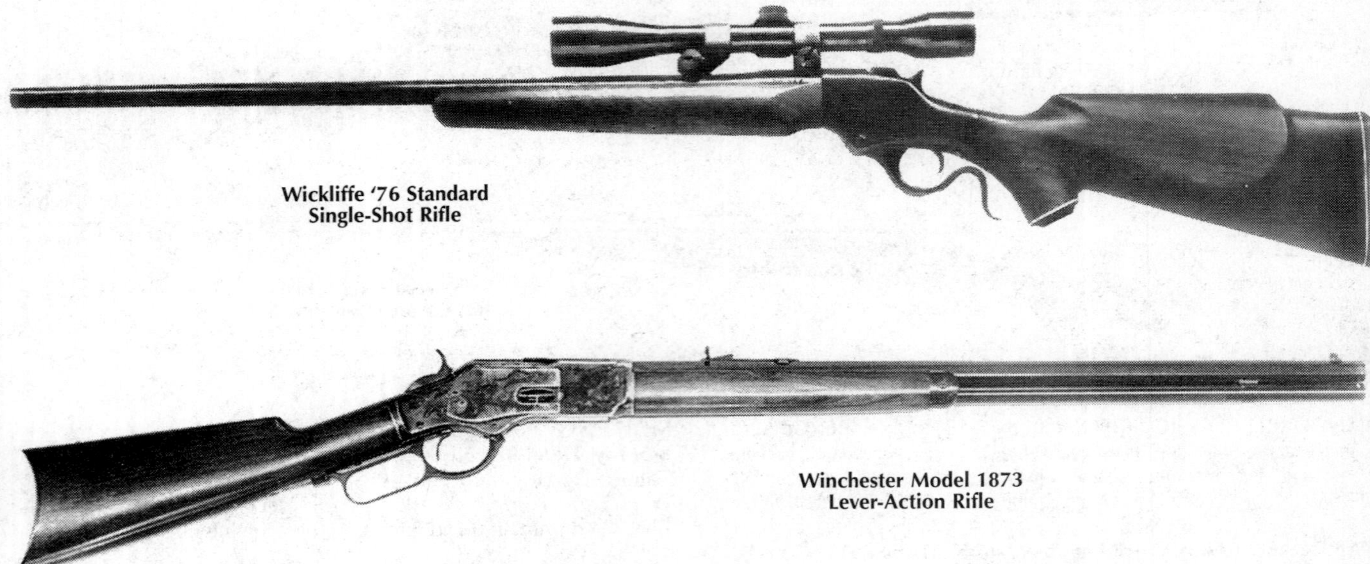

Wickliffe '76 Standard
Single-Shot Rifle

Winchester Model 1873
Lever-Action Rifle

MODEL WMR STAINLESS
MAGNUM BOLT-ACTION RIFLE . . . . NiB $2127 Ex $1813 Gd $1092
Single-shot or w/blind magazine action chambered .270 Win. through .458 Win. Mag. Drilled and tapped for scope with no sights. Fully adj. trigger. 22- or 24-inch bbl. Hand-checkered select walnut stock. Made from 1980-84.

MODEL WVR VARMINT RIFLE
Calibers: .17 Rem through .308 Win. Three round magazine. Right or left-hand action w/jeweled bolt. 21-inch bbl. w/o sights. Drilled and tapped for scope. Hand-checkered American walnut pistol-grip stock. Made from 1978 to date.
Right-hand model . . . . NiB $2656 Ex $1925 Gd $1214
Left-hand model . . . . NiB $2611 Ex $2131 Gd $1539

WICKLIFFE RIFLES — Wickliffe, Ohio Mfd. by Triple S Development Co., Inc.

'76 COMMEMORATIVE
MODEL . . . . NiB $1292 Ex $10134 Gd $854
Limited edition of 100. Same as Deluxe Model except w/filled etching on receiver sidewalls, U.S. silver dollar inlaid in stock, 26-inch bbl. only, comes in presentation case. Made in 1976 only.

'76 DELUXE MODEL . . . . NiB $536 Ex $434 Gd $304
Same as Standard Model except w/22-inch bbl. in .30-06 only; high-luster blued finish, fancy-grade figured American walnut stock w/nickel silver grip cap.

'76 STANDARD MODEL
SINGLE-SHOT RIFLE . . . . NiB $459 Ex $372 Gd $262
Falling-block action. Calibers: .22 Hornet, .223 Rem., .22-250, .243 Win., .25-06, .308 Win., .30-06, .45-70. 22-inch lightweight bbl. (.243 and .308 only) or 26-inch heavy sporter bbl. Weight: 6.75 or 8.5 lbs., depending on bbl. No sights. Select American walnut Monte Carlo stock w/right or left cheekpiece and pistol-grip, semi-beavertail forearm. Intro. 1976. Disc.

STINGER MODEL . . . . NiB $476 Ex $385 Gd $270
Falling block, single-shot. Calibers: .22 Hornet and .223 Rem. .22-inch bbl. w/no sights. American walnut Monte Carlo stock w/continental-type forend. Made from 1979-80.

TRADITIONALIST MODEL . . . . NiB $478 Ex $375 Gd $267
Falling block single-shot. Calibers: .30-06, .45-70. 24-inch bbl. w/open sights. Hand-checkered. American walnut classic-style buttstock and forearm. Made from 1979-80.

WILKINSON ARMS CO. — Covina, California

TERRY CARBINE . . . . NiB $514 Ex $401 Gd $282
Caliber: 9mm Para. Semiautomatic. Thirty round magazine. 16-inch bbl. 30 inches overall. Weight: 6 lbs. Dovetailed receiver for scope mounting. Bolt-type safety. Ejection port w/automatic trap door. Blowback action. Fires from closed bolt. Made from 1975 to date.

TED WILLIAMS RIFLES

See Sears, Roebuck and Company.

WINCHESTER RIFLES — Winchester Repeating Arms Company, New Haven, CT

Formerly Winchester Repeating Arms Co., and then mfd. by Winchester-Western Div., Olin Corp., later by U.S. Repeating Arms Company. In 1999, production rights were acquired by Browning Arms Company.

EARLY MODELS 1873 – 1918

NOTE: *Most Winchester rifles manufactured prior to 1918 used the date of approximate manufacture as the model number. For example, the Model 1894 repeating rifle was manufactured from 1894 to 1937. When Winchester started using two-digit model numbers after 1918, the "18" was dropped and the rifle was then called the Model 94. The Model 1892 was called the Model 92, etc. In light of the recent shut-down, Winchester is no longer made at New Haven.*

Winchester Model 1886 w/Case-colored Receiver

Winchester Model 1886 w/Blued Receiver

Winchester Model 1886 Saddle-Ring Carbine

At Right: Close-up barrel engraving on Winchester Model 1873 One of One Thousand.

MODEL 1873 LEVER-ACTION CARBINE . . . . NiB $9721 Ex $7802 Gd $5347
Same as Standard Model 1873 Rifle except w/20-inch bbl., 12-round magazine, weight: 7.25 lbs.

MODEL 1873 LEVER-ACTION RIFLE . . . . NiB $9072 Ex $7281 Gd $4981
Calibers: .32-20, .38-40, .44-40; a few were chambered for .22 rimfire. Fifteen round magazine, also made w/6-round half magazine. 24-inch bbl. (round, half-octagon, octagon). Weight: 8.5 lbs. Sights: Open rear; bead or blade front. Plain straight-grip stock and forearm. Made 1873-1924. 720,610 rifles of this model were mfd.

MODEL 1873 — ONE OF ONE THOUSAND . . . . NiB $195,700+ Ex $82,400+ Gd $51,500+
During the late 1870s, Winchester offered Model 1873 rifles of superior accuracy and extra finish, designated "One of One Thousand" grade, at $100. These rifles are marked "1 of 1000" or "One of One Thousand." Only 136 of this model are known to have been manufactured. This is one of the rarest of shoulder arms and, because so few have been sold in recent years, it is extremely difficult to assign a value; however, an "excellent" specimen would probably bring a price upward of $200,000.

MODEL 1873 SPECIAL SPORTING RIFLE . . . . NiB $10,475 Ex $8930 Gd $5325
Same as Standard Model 1873 Rifle except this type has receiver case-hardened in colors, pistol-grip stock of select walnut, octagon bbl. only.

MODEL 1885 SINGLE-SHOT RIFLE
Designed by John M. Browning, this falling-block, lever-action rifle was manufactured from 1885 to 1920 in a variety of models and chambered for most of the popular cartridges of the period — both rimfire and centerfire — from .22 to .50 caliber. There are two basic styles of frames, low-wall and high-wall. The low-wall was chambered only for the lower-powered cartridges, while the high-wall was supplied in all calibers and made in three basic types. The standard model for No. 3 and heavier barrels is the type commonly encountered; the thin-walled version was supplied with No. 1 and No. 2 light barrels and the thick-walled action in the heavier calibers. Made in both solid frame and takedown versions. Barrels were available in five weights ranging from the lightweight No. 1 to the extra-heavy No. 5 in round, half-octagon and full-octagon styles. Many other variations were also offered.

MODEL 1885 HIGH-WALL SPORTING RIFLE. . . . . NiB $3795 Ex $2147 Gd $1735
Solid frame or takedown. No. 3, 30-inch bbl., standard. Weight: 9.5 lbs. Standard trigger and lever. Open rear sights; blade front sight. Plain stock and forend.

MODEL 1885 LOW-WALL SPORTING RIFLE. . . . . NiB $1715 Ex $1391 Gd $964
Solid frame. No. 1, 28-inch round or octagon bbl. Weight: 7 lbs. Open rear sight; blade front sight. Plain stock and forend.

MODEL 1885 SCHUETZEN RIFLE . . . . NiB $5804 Ex $4708 Gd $3224
Solid frame or takedown. High-wall action. Schuetzen double-set trigger. Spur finger lever. No. 3, 30-inch octagon bbl. Weight: 12 lbs. Vernier rear peep sight; wind-gauge front sight. Fancy walnut Schuetzen stock with checkered pistol-grip and forend. Schuetzen buttplate; adj. palm rest.

MODEL 1885 SPECIAL SPORTING RIFLE . . . . . . NiB $2656 Ex $2141 Gd $1523
Same general specifications as the standard high-wall model except with checkered fancy walnut stock and forend.

Winchester Model 1890

Winchester Model 1892

MODEL 1885 SINGLE-SHOT MUSKET . . . . **NiB $1330 Ex $1074 Gd $746**
Solid frame. Low-wall. .22 Short and Long Rifle. 28-inch round bbl. Weight: 8.6 lbs. Lyman rear peep sight; blade front sight. Military-type stock and forend. Note: The U.S. Government purchased a large quantity of these muskets during World War I for training purposes.

MODEL 1885 SINGLE-SHOT "WINDER" MUSKET . . . . **NiB $1014 Ex $850 Gd $551**
Solid frame or takedown. High-wall. Plain trigger. 28-inch round bbl. Weight: 8.5 lbs. Musket rear sight; blade front sight. Military-type stock and forend w/bbl. band and sling stud/rings.

MODEL 1886 LEVER-ACTION RIFLE
Solid frame or takedown. .33 Win., .38-56, .38-70, .40-65, .40-70, .40-82, .45-70, .45-90, .50-100, .50-110. The .33 Win. and .45-70 were the last calibers in which this model was supplied. Eight round tubular magaine; also 4-round half-magazine. 26-inch bbl. (round, half-octagon, octagon). Weight: 7.5 lbs. Sights: Open rear; bead or blade front. Plain straight-grip stock and forend or standard models. Made from 1886-1935.
Standard model . . . . **NiB $5236 Ex $4218 Gd $2917**
Takedown model . . . . **NiB $6453 Ex $5192 Gd $3579**
Deluxe model (pistol-grip and high-quality walnut) . . . . **NiB $10,375 Ex $9850 Gd $6255**

MODEL 1886 SADDLE-RING CARBINE . . . . **NiB $12,425 Ex $9939 Gd $6759**
Same as standard rifle except with 22-inch bbl., carbine buttstock and forend. Carbine rear sight. Saddle ring on left side of receiver.

MODEL 1890 SLIDE-ACTION RIFLE
Visible hammer. Calibers: .22 Short, Long, LR; .22 WRF (not interchangeable). Tubular magazine holds 15 Short, 12 Long, 11 LR; 12 WRF. 24-inch octagon bbl. Weight: 5.75 lbs. Sights: Open rear; bead front. Plain straight-grip stock, grooved slide handle. Originally solid frame; after No. 15,499, all rifles of this model were takedown-type. Fancy checkered pistol-grip stock, nickel-steel bbl. supplied at extra cost, which can also increase the value by 100% or more. Made from 1890-1932.
Blue WRF . . . . **NiB $2010 Ex $1650 Gd $1083**
Blue (.22 LR) . . . . **NiB $2067 Ex $2015 Gd $1114**
Color casehardened receiver . . . . **NiB $6468 Ex $5207 Gd $3594**

MODEL 1892 LEVER-ACTION RIFLE . . . . **NiB $2590 Ex $2102 Gd $1478**
Solid frame or takedown. Calibers: .25-20, .32-20, .38-40, .44-40. Thirteen round tubular magazine; also 7-round half-magazine. 24-inch bbl. (round, octagon, half-octagon). Weight: from 6.75 lbs. up. Sights: Open rear; bead front. Plain straight-grip stock and forend. Pistol-grip fancy walnut stocks were available at extra cost and also doubles the value of the current value for standard models.

MODEL 1892 SADDLE-RING CARBINE . . . . **NiB $2714 Ex $2405 Gd $1787**
Same general specifications as the Model 1892 rifle except carbine buttstock, forend and sights. 20-inch bbl. Saddle ring on left side of receiver.

MODEL 1894 LEVER-ACTION RIFLE . . . . **NiB $1981 Ex $1596 Gd $1104**
Solid frame or takedown. .25-35, .30-30, .32-40, .32 Special, .38-55. Seven round tubular magazine or 4-round half-magazine. 26-inch bbl. (round, octagon, half-octagon). Weight: about 7.35 lbs. Sights: Open rear; bead front. Plain straight-grip stock and forearm on standard model; crescent-shaped or shotgun-style buttplate. Made from 1894-1937. See also Winchester Model 94 for later variations of this model.

MODEL 1894 LEVER-ACTION DELUXE. NiB $2482 Ex $1205 Gd $1326
Same general specifications as the standard rifle except checkered pistol-grip buttstock and forend using high-grade walnut. Engraved versions are considerably higher in value.

MODEL 1894 SADDLE-RING CARBINE . . . . **NiB $1602 Ex $1494 Gd $939**
Same general specifications as the Model 1894 standard rifle except 20-inch bbl., carbine buttstock, forend, and sights. Saddle ring on left side of receiver. Weight: about 6.5 lbs.

MODEL 1894 STANDARD CARBINE . . . NiB $1338 Ex $1082 Gd $754
Same general specifications as Saddle-Ringle Carbine except shotgun type buttstock and plate, no saddle ring, standard open rear sight. Sometimes called "Eastern Carbine." See also Winchester Model 94 carbine.

1895 LEVER-ACTION CARBINE . . . . **NiB $2872 Ex $2317 Gd $1609**
Same as Model 95 Standard Rifle except has 22-inch bbl., carbine-style buttstock and forend, weight: About 8 lbs., calibers .30-40 Krag, .30-03, .30-06 and .303, solid frame only.

1895 LEVER-ACTION RIFLE . . . . NiB $3190 Ex $2005 Gd $1130
Calibers: .30-40 Krag, .30-03, .30-60, .303 British, 7.62mm Russian, .35 Win., .38-72, .40-72, .405 Win. Four round box magazine except .30-40 and .303, which have 5-round magazines. Bbl. lengths: 24-, 26-, 28-inches (round, half-octagon, octagon). Weight: About 8.5 lbs. Sights: Open rear; bead or blade front. Plain straight-grip stock and forend (standard). Both solid frame and takedown models were made from1897-1931.

MODEL (1897) LEE BOLT-ACTION RIFLE
Straight-pull bolt-action. .236 U.S. Navy, 5-round box magazine, clip loaded. 24- and 28-inch bbl. Weight: 7.5 to 8.5 lbs. Sights: Folding leaf rear sight on musket; open sporting sight on sporting rifle.
Musket model . . . . **NiB $1864 Ex $1710 Gd $1066**
Sporting rifle . . . . **NiB $1967 Ex $1761 Gd $1066**

Winchester Model 1894

Winchester Model 1894
Fancy-Grade Takedown

Winchester Model 1894
Saddle-Ring Carbine

Winchester Model 1895
Carbine

Winchester Model 1895
Rifle

Winchester Model 1897
Lee Sporting Rifle

MODEL 1900 BOLT-ACTION
SINGLE-SHOT RIFLE . . . . NiB $575 Ex $466 Gd $326
Takedown. Caliber: .22 Short and Long. 18-inch bbl. Weight: 2.75 lbs. Open rear sight; blade front sight. One-piece, straight-grip stock. Made from 1899 to 1902.

MODEL 1902
BOLT-ACTION
SINGLE-SHOT RIFLE . . . . NiB $440 Ex $337 Gd $234
Takedown. Basically the same as Model 1900 with minor improvements. Calibers: .22 Short and Long, .22 Extra Long, .22 LR. Weight: 3 lbs. Made from 1902-1931.

MODEL 1903
SELF-LOADING RIFLE . . . . NiB $1054 Ex $812 Gd $529
Takedown. Caliber: .22 WRA. Ten round tubular magazine in buttstock. 20-inch bbl. Weight: 5.75 lbs. Sights: Open rear; bead front. Plain straight-grip stock and forearm (fancy grade illustrated). Made from 1903-36.

MODEL (1904) 99 THUMB-TRIGGER BOLT-ACTION
SINGLE-SHOT RIFLE . . . . NiB $794 Ex $641 Gd $445
Takedown. Same as Model 1902 except fired by pressing a button behind the cocking piece. Made from 1904-23.

MODEL 1904
BOLT-ACTION
SINGLE-SHOT RIFLE . . . . NiB $437 Ex $334 Gd $231
Similar to Model 1902. Takedown. Caliber: 22 Short, Long Extra Long, LR. 21-inch bbl. Weight: 4 lbs. Made from 1904-31.

MODEL 1905
SELF-LOADING RIFLE . . . . NiB $777 Ex $545 Gd $468
Takedown. Calibers: .32 Win. S. and L., .35 Win. S. and L. Five or 10-round detachable box magazine. 22-inch bbl. Weight: 7.5 lbs. Sights: Open rear; bead front. Plain pistol-grip stock and forearm. Made from 1905-20.

MODEL 1906
SLIDE-ACTION REPEATER . . . . . NiB $858 Ex $806 Gd $549
Takedown. Visible hammer. Caliber: .22 Short, Long, LR. Tubular magazine holds 20 Short, 16 Long or 14 LR. 20-inch bbl. Weight: 5 lbs. Sights: Open rear; bead front. Straight-grip stock and grooved forearm. Made from 1906-32.

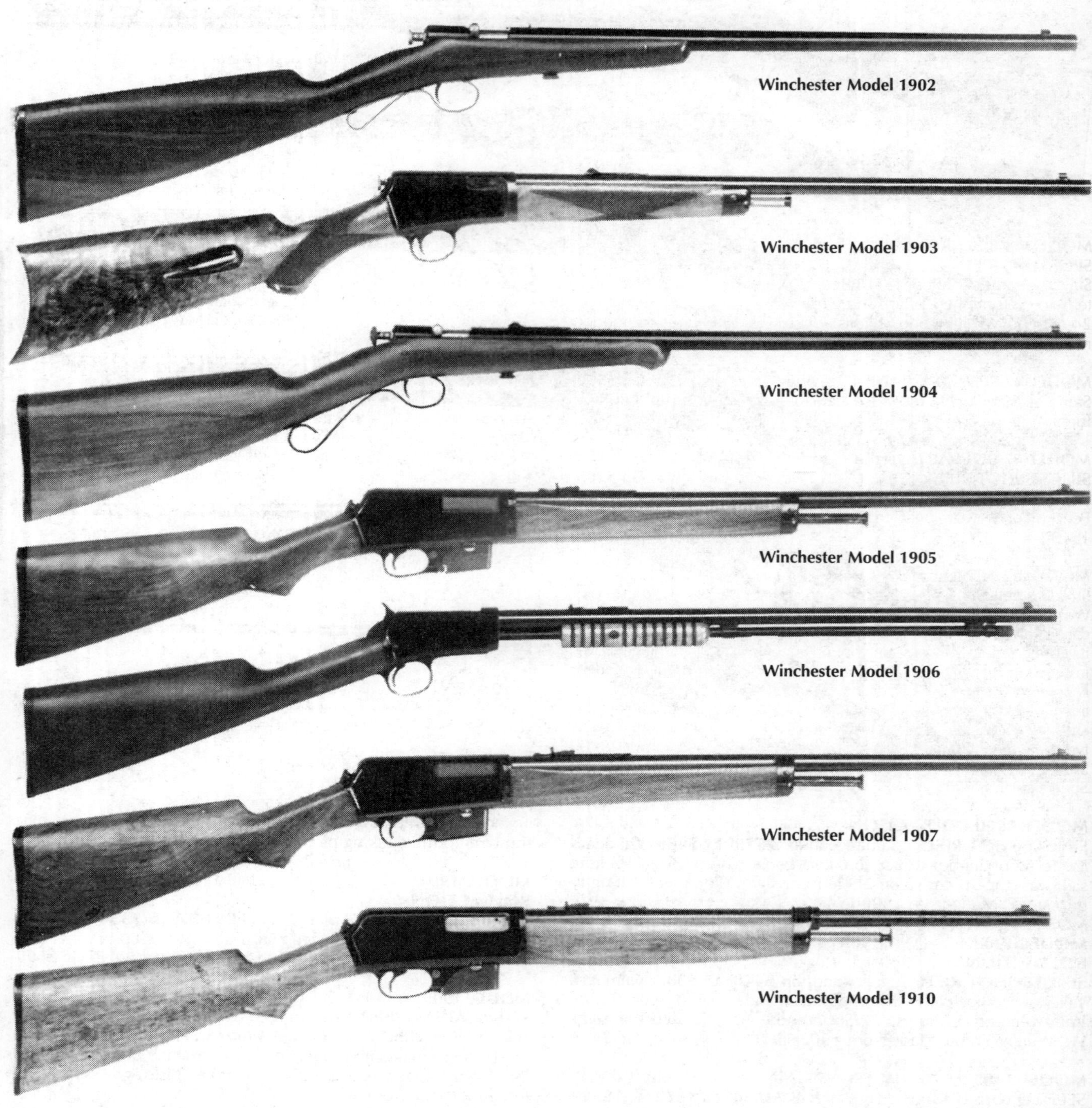

Winchester Model 1902

Winchester Model 1903

Winchester Model 1904

Winchester Model 1905

Winchester Model 1906

Winchester Model 1907

Winchester Model 1910

MODEL 1907 SELF-LOADING RIFLE . . . . . NiB $673 Ex $545 Gd $382
Takedown. Caliber: .351 Win. S. and L. Five or 10-round detachable box magazine. 20-inch bbl. Weight: 7.75 lbs. Sights: Open rear; bead front. Plain pistol-grip stock and forearm. Made from 1907-57.

MODEL 1910 SELF-LOADING RIFLE . . . . . NiB $805 Ex $652 Gd $456
Takedown. Caliber: .401 Win. S. and L. Four round detachable box magazine. 20-inch bbl. Weight: 8.5 lbs. Sights: Open rear; bead front. Plain pistol-grip stock and forearm. Made from 1910-36.

Winchester Model 43
Special Grade

MODEL 43 BOLT-ACTION SPORTING RIFLE. . . . . NiB $810 Ex $650 Gd $444
Standard Grade. Calibers: .218 Bee, .22 Hornet, .25-20, .32-20 (latter two discontinued 1950). Three round detachable box magazine. 24-inch bbl. Weight: 6 lbs. Sights: Open rear, bead front on hooded ramp. Plain pistol-grip stock with swivels. Made from 1949-57.

MODEL 43 SPECIAL GRADE. . . . . NiB $1049 Ex $812 Gd $550
Same as Standard Model 43 except has checkered pistol-grip and forearm, grip cap.

MODEL 47 BOLT-ACTION SINGLE-SHOT RIFLE . . . . NiB $383 Ex $306 Gd $203
Caliber: .22 Short, Long, LR. 25-inch bbl. Weight: 5.5 lbs. Sights: Peep or open rear; bead front. Plain pistol-grip stock. Made from 1949-54.

MODEL 52 BOLT-ACTION TARGET RIFLE
Standard bbl. First type. .22 LR. Five round box magazine. 28-inch bbl. Weight: 8.75 lbs. Sights: Folding leaf peep rear; blade front sight; standard sights various other combinations available. Scope bases. Semi-military-type target stock w/pistol grip; original model has grasping grooves in forearm; higher comb and semi-beavertail forearm on later models. Numerous changes were made in this model; the most important was the adoption of the speed lock in 1929. Model 52 rifles produced before this change are generally referred to as "slow lock" models. Last arms of this type bore serial numbers followed by the letter "A." Made from 1919-37.
Slow Lock model. . . . . NiB $577 Ex $468 Gd $328
Speed Lock model . . . . NiB $771 Ex $622 Gd $433

MODEL 52 HEAVY BARREL . . . . . . NiB $842 Ex $682 Gd $476
First type speed lock. Same general specifications as Standard Model 52 of this type except has heavier bbl., Lyman No. 17G front sight, weight: 10 lbs.

MODEL 52 INTERNATIONAL MATCH RIFLE
Similar to Model 52-D Heavy Barrel except has special lead-lapped bbl., laminated "free rifle"-style stock with high comb, thumbhole, hook buttplate, accessory rail, handstop/swivel assembly, palm rest. Weight: 13.5 lbs. Made from 1969-78.
With standard trigger . . . . NiB $1072 Ex $1020 Gd $840
With Kenyon or I.S.U. trigger . . . . . NiB $751 Ex $608 Gd $427

MODEL 52 INTERNATIONAL PRONE . . NiB $1098 Ex $1067 Gd $845
Similar to Model 52-D Heavy Barrel except has special lead-lapped bbl., prone stock with full pistol-grip, rollover cheekpiece removable for bore-cleaning. Weight 11.5 lbs. Made from 1975-80.

MODEL 52 SPORTING RIFLE
First type. Same as Standard Model 52 of this type except has lightweight 24-inch bbl., Lyman No. 48 receiver sight and gold bead front sight on hooded ramp, deluxe checkered sporting stock with cheekpiece, black forend tip, etc. Weight: 7.75 lbs. Made from 1934-58. Reintroduced 1993.
Model 52 Sporter . . . . NiB $2611 Ex $2108 Gd $1466
Model 52A Sporter . . . . NiB $3709 Ex $2979 Gd $2058
Model 52B Sporter . . . . NiB $2926 Ex $2361 Gd $1637
Model 52C Sporter . . . . NiB $3641 Ex $2922 Gd $2026
Model 52 C Sporter (1993 BAC re-issue) . . . . NiB $709 Ex $550 Gd $380

MODEL 52-B BOLT-ACTION RIFLE
Standard bbl. Extensively redesigned action. Supplied with choice of "Target" stock, an improved version of the previous Model 52 stock, or "Marksman" stock with high comb, full pistol grip and beavertail forearm. Weight: 9 lbs. Offered with a wide choice of target sight combinations (Lyman, Marble-Goss, Redfield, Vaver, Winchester), value shown is for rifle less sight equipment. Other specifications as shown for first type. Made from 1935-47. Reintroduced 1997.
Target model . . . . NiB $864 Ex $709 Gd $993
BAC model (1997 BAC re-issue). . . . . NiB $678 Ex $550 Gd $387
USRAC Sporting model . . . . NiB $709 Ex $551 Gd $400

MODEL 52-B BULL GUN HEAVY BARREL. . . . . NiB $919 Ex $735 Gd $513
Same specifications as Standard Model 52-B except Bull Gun has extra heavy bbl., Marksman stock only, weight: 12 lbs. Heavy Bbl. model weight: 11 lbs. Made 1940-47.

MODEL 52-C BOLT-ACTION RIFLE
Improved action with "Micro-Motion" trigger mechanism and new-type "Marksman" stock. General specifications same as shown for previous models. Made from 1947-61, Bull Gun from 1952. Value shown is for rifle less sights.
Bull Gun (extra heavy barrel, Wt. 12 lbs.) . . . . NiB $1077 Ex $871 Gd $603
Standard barrel (Wt. 9.75 lbs.). . . . . NiB $866 Ex $711 Gd $598
Target model (heavy barrel) . . . . NiB $1017 Ex $817 Gd $608

NOTE: *Following WWI, Winchester had financial difficulties and, like many other firearm firms of the day, failed. However, Winchester continued to operate in the hands of receivers. Then, in 1931, The Western Cartridge Co. — under the leadership of John Olin — purchased all assets of the firm. After that, Winchester leaped ahead of all other firms of the day in firearm and ammunition development.*
The first sporting firearm to come out of the Winchester plant after WWI was the Model 20 shotgun, but this was quickly followed by the famous Model 52 bolt-action rifle. This was also a time when Winchester dropped the four-digit model numbers and began using two-digit numbers instead. This model-numbering procedure, with one exception (Model 677), continued for the next several years.

Winchester Model 47

Winchester Model 52
Standard Barrel

Winchester Model 52
International Match

Winchester Model 52
International Prone Target

MODEL 52-D BOLT-ACTION TARGET RIFLE . . . . NiB $850 Ex $806 Gd $443
Redesigned Model 52 action, Single-Shot. Caliber: .22 LR. 28-inch standard or heavy bbl., free-floating, with blocks for standard target scopes. Weight: With standard bbl., 9.75 lbs., with heavy barrel, 11 lbs. Restyled Marksman stock with accessory channel and forend stop, rubber buttplate. Made from 1961-78. Value shown is for rifle without sights.

MODEL 53 LEVER-ACTION REPEATER . . . . NiB $2248 Ex $1811 Gd $1253
Modification of Model 92. Solid frame or takedown. Calibers: .25-20, .32-20, .44-40. Six round tubular half-magazine in solid frame model. Seven round in takedown. 22-inch nickel steel bbl. Weight: 5.5 to 6.5 lbs. Sights: Open rear; bead front. Redesigned straight-grip stock and forearm. Made from 1924-32.

MODEL 54 BOLT-ACTION HIGH POWER SPORTING RIFLE (I) . . . . . . NiB $962 Ex $859 Gd $601
First type. Calibers: .270 Win., 7x57mm, .30-30, .30-06, 7.65x53mm, 9x57mm. Five round box magazine. 24-inch bbl. Weight: 7.75 lbs. Sights: Open rear; bead front. Checkered stock w/pistol grip, tapered forearm w/Schnabel tip. This type has two-piece firing pin. Made from 1925-30.

MODEL 54 BOLT-ACTION HIGH POWER SPORTING RIFLE (II) . . . . NiB $1013 Ex $885 Gd $550
Standard Grade. Improved type with speed lock and one-piece firing pin. Calibers: .22 Hornet, .220 Swift, .250/3000, .257 Roberts, .270 Win., 7x57mm, .30-06. Five round box magazine. 24-inch bbl., 26-inch in cal. .220 Swift. Weight: About 8 lbs. Sights: Open rear, bead front on ramp. NRA-type stock w/checkered pistol-grip and forearm. Made 1930-36. Add $200 for .22 Hornet caliber.

MODEL 54 CARBINE (I) . . . . NiB $1080 Ex $874 Gd $591
First type. Same as Model 54 rifle except has 20-inch bbl., plain lightweight stock with grasping grooves in forearm. Weight: 7.25 lbs.

MODEL 54 CARBINE (II). . . . . NiB $1080 Ex $925 Gd $616
Improved type. Same as Model 54 Standard Grade Sporting Rifle of this type except has 20-inch bbl. Weight: About 7.5 lbs. This model may have either NRA-type stock or the lightweight stock found on the first-type Model 54 Carbine.

MODEL 54 NATIONAL MATCH RIFLE . . . . NiB $1112 Ex $900 Gd $628
Same as Standard Model 54 except has Lyman sights, scope bases, Marksman-type target stock, weighs 9.5 lbs. Same calibers as Standard Model.

MODEL 54 SNIPER'S MATCH RIFLE . . . . NiB $1599 Ex $1337 Gd $565
Similar to the earlier Model 54 Sniper's Rifle except has Marksman-type target stock, scope bases, weight: 12.5 lbs. Available in same calibers as Model 54 Standard Grade.

MODEL 54 SNIPER'S RIFLE . . . . . . NiB $1209 Ex $977 Gd $668
Same as Standard Model 54 except has heavy 26-inch bbl., Lyman No. 48 rear peep sight and blade front sight semi-military stock, weight: 11.75 pounds, cal. .30-06 only.

MODEL 54 SUPER GRADE . . . . . NiB $1595 Ex $1337 Gd $874
Same as Standard Model 54 Sporter except has deluxe stock with cheekpiece, black forend tip, pistol-grip cap, quick detachable swivels, 1-inch sling strap.

Winchester Model 52-B Standard Barrel

Winchester Model 52-B Sporter

Winchester Model 52-C Heavy Barrel

Winchester Model 53

Winchester Model 54 Super Grade

MODEL 54 TARGET RIFLE....... NiB $1114 Ex $902 Gd $630
Same as Standard Model 54 except has 24-inch medium-weight bbl. (26-inch in cal. .220 Swift), Lyman sights, scope bases, Marksman-type target stock, weight: 10.5 lbs., same calibers as Standard Model.

MODEL 55 "AUTOMATIC" SINGLE-SHOT................. NiB $344 Ex $267 Gd $189
Caliber: .22 Short, Long, LR. 22-inch bbl. Sights: Open rear, bead front. One-piece walnut stock. Weight: About 5.5 lbs. Made from 1958-60.

MODEL 55 LEVER-ACTION REPEATER
Modification of Model 94. Solid frame or takedown. Calibers: .25-35, .30-30, .32 Win. Special. Three round tubular half magazine. 24-inch nickel steel bbl. Weight: About 7 lbs. Sights: Open rear; bead front. Made from 1924-32.
Standard model (straight grip) .... NiB $1274 Ex $1030 Gd $717
Deluxe model (pistol grip) .... NiB $3283 Ex $2640 Gd $1818

MODEL 56 BOLT-ACTION SPORTING RIFLE............. NiB $1294 Ex $1080 Gd $647
Solid frame. Caliber: .22 LR., .22 Short. Five or 10-round detachable box magazine. 22-inch bbl. Weight: 4.75 lbs. Sights: Open rear; bead front. Plain pistol-grip with Schnabel forend. Made from 1926-29.

MODEL 57 BOLT-ACTION RIFLE
Solid frame. Same as Model 56 except available (until 1929) in .22 Short as well as LR with 5- or 10-round magazine. Has semi-military style target stock, bbl. band on forend, swivels and web sling, Lyman peep rear sight, weight: 5 lbs. Made from 1926-36.
Sporter model .... NiB $737 Ex $608 Gd $454
Target model .... NiB $686 Ex $634 Gd $480

MODEL 58 BOLT-ACTION SINGLE-SHOT...................... NiB $455 Ex $372 Gd $265
Similar to Model 52. Takedown. Caliber. .22 Short, Long LR. 18-inch bbl. Weight: 3 lbs. Sights, Open rear; blade front. Plain, flat, straight-grip hardwood stock. Not serial numbered. Made from 1928-31.

MODEL 59 BOLT-ACTION SINGLE-SHOT...................... NiB $578 Ex $449 Gd $320
Improved version of Model 58, has 23-inch bbl., redesigned stock w/pistol grip, weight: 4.5 lbs. Made in 1930.

MODEL 60, 60A BOLT-ACTION SINGLE-SHOT
Redesign of Model 59. Caliber: .22 Short, Long, LR. 23-inch bbl. (27-inch after 1933). Weight: 4.25 lbs. Sights: Open rear, blade front. Plain pistol-grip stock. Made from 1930-34 (60), 1932-39 (60A).
Model 60..................... NiB $346 Ex $243 Gd $181
Model 60A.................... NiB $423 Ex $253 Gd $191

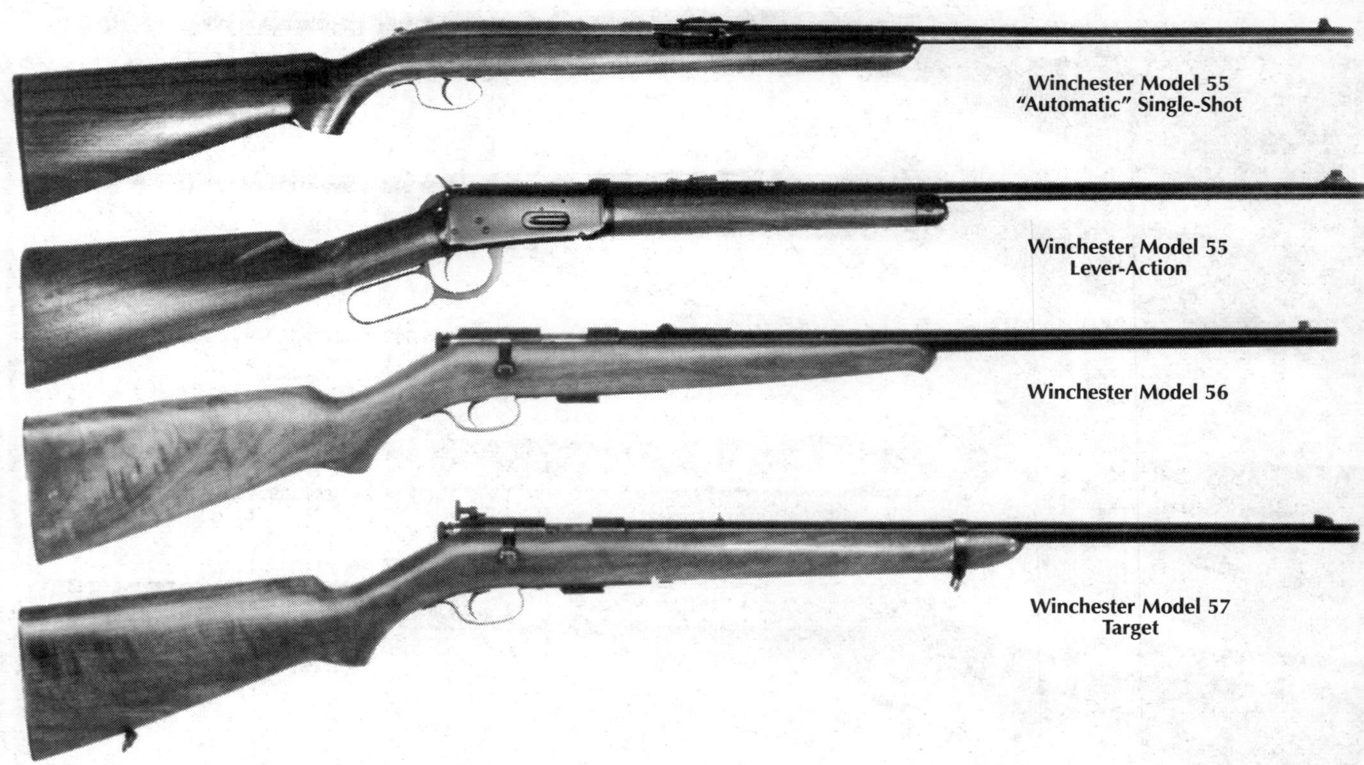

Winchester Model 55 "Automatic" Single-Shot

Winchester Model 55 Lever-Action

Winchester Model 56

Winchester Model 57 Target

MODEL 60A TARGET RIFLE . . . . . . NiB $486 Ex $409 Gd $280
Essentially the same as Model 60 except has Lyman peep rear sight and square top front sight, semi-military target stock and web sling, weight: 5.5 lbs. Made from 1932-39.

MODEL 61 HAMMERLESS SLIDE-ACTION REPEATER
Takedown. Caliber: .22 Short, Long, LR. Tubular magazine holds 20 Short, 16 Long, 14 LR. 24-inch round bbl. Weight: 5.5 lbs. Sights: Open rear; bead front. Plain pistol-grip stock, grooved semi-beavertail slide handle. Also available with 24-inch full-octagon bbl. and only calibers .22 Short, .22 LR or .22 WRF. Note: Octagon barrel model discontinued 1943-44; assembled 1948.
Model 61 (round barrel) . . . . NiB $796 Ex $643 Gd $447
Model 61 (grooved receiver) . . . . . NiB $1007 Ex $813 Gd $566
Model 61 (octagon barrel) . . . . . NiB $1715 Ex $1381 Gd $954

MODEL 61 MAGNUM . . . . NiB $988 Ex $807 Gd $524
Same as Standard Model 61 except chambered for .22 WMR; magazine holds 12 rounds. Made from 1960-63.

MODEL 62 VISIBLE HAMMER. . . . . NiB $674 Ex $545 Gd $390
Modernized version of Model 1890. Caliber: .22 Short, Long, LR. 23-inch bbl. Weight: 5.5 lbs. Plain straight-grip stock, grooved semi-beavertail slide handle. Also available in Gallery Model chambered for .22 Short only. Made from 1932-1959. Note: Pre-WWII model (small forearm) commands 25% higher price.

MODEL 63 SELF-LOADING RIFLE
Takedown. Caliber: .22 LR High Speed only. Ten round tubular magazine in buttstock. 23-inch bbl. Weight: 5.5 lbs. Sights: Open rear, bead front. Plain pistol-grip stock and forearm. Originally available with 20-inch bbl. as well as 23-inch. Made from 1933-59. Reintroduced in 1997.
Model 63 w/23-inch bbl. . . . . NiB $98 Ex $759 Gd $530
Model 63 w/20-inch bbl. . . . . NiB $1395 Ex $1124 Gd $778
Model 63 grooved receiver) . . . . NiB $1282 Ex $1041 Gd $723
Model 63 Grade I (1997 BAC reissue) . . . . NiB $774 Ex $630 Gd $443
Model 63 High Grade (1997 BAC reissue). . . NiB $1360 Ex $1072 Gd $716

MODEL 64 DELUXE
DEER RIFLE . . . . NiB $1328 Ex $1072 Gd $744
Same as Standard Model 64 calibers .30-30 and .32 Win. Special, except has checkered pistol-grip and semi-beavertail forearm, swivels and sling, weighs 7.75 lbs. Made from 1933-56.

MODEL 64 LEVER-ACTION REPEATER
Standard Grade. Improved version of Models 94 and 55. Solid frame. Calibers: .25-35, .30-30, .32 Win. Special. Five round tubular two-thirds magazine. 20- or 24-inch bbl. Weight: About 7 lbs. Sights: Open rear; bead front on ramp w/sight cover. Plain pistol-grip stock and forearm. Made from 1933-56. Production resumed in 1972 (caliber .30-30, 24-inch bbl.). Discontinued in 1974.
Original model . . . . NiB $884 Ex $755 Gd $575
1972-74 model . . . . NiB $703 Ex $524 Gd $394

MODEL 64 .219 ZIPPER . . . . . . NiB $2518 Ex $2030 Gd $1406
Same as Standard Grade Model 64 except has 26-inch bbl., peep rear sight. Made from 1937-47.

MODEL 65 LEVER-ACTION
REPEATER . . . . NiB $2647 Ex $2133 Gd $1476
Improved version of Model 53. Solid frame. Calibers: .25-20 and .32-20. Six round tubular half-magazine. 22-inch bbl. Weight: 6.5 lbs. Sights: Open rear, bead front on ramp base. Plain pistol-grip stock and forearm. Made from 1933-47.

MODEL 65 .218 BEE . . . . NiB $2852 Ex $2297 Gd $1589
Same as Standard Model 65 except has 24-inch bbl., peep rear sight. Made from 1938-47.

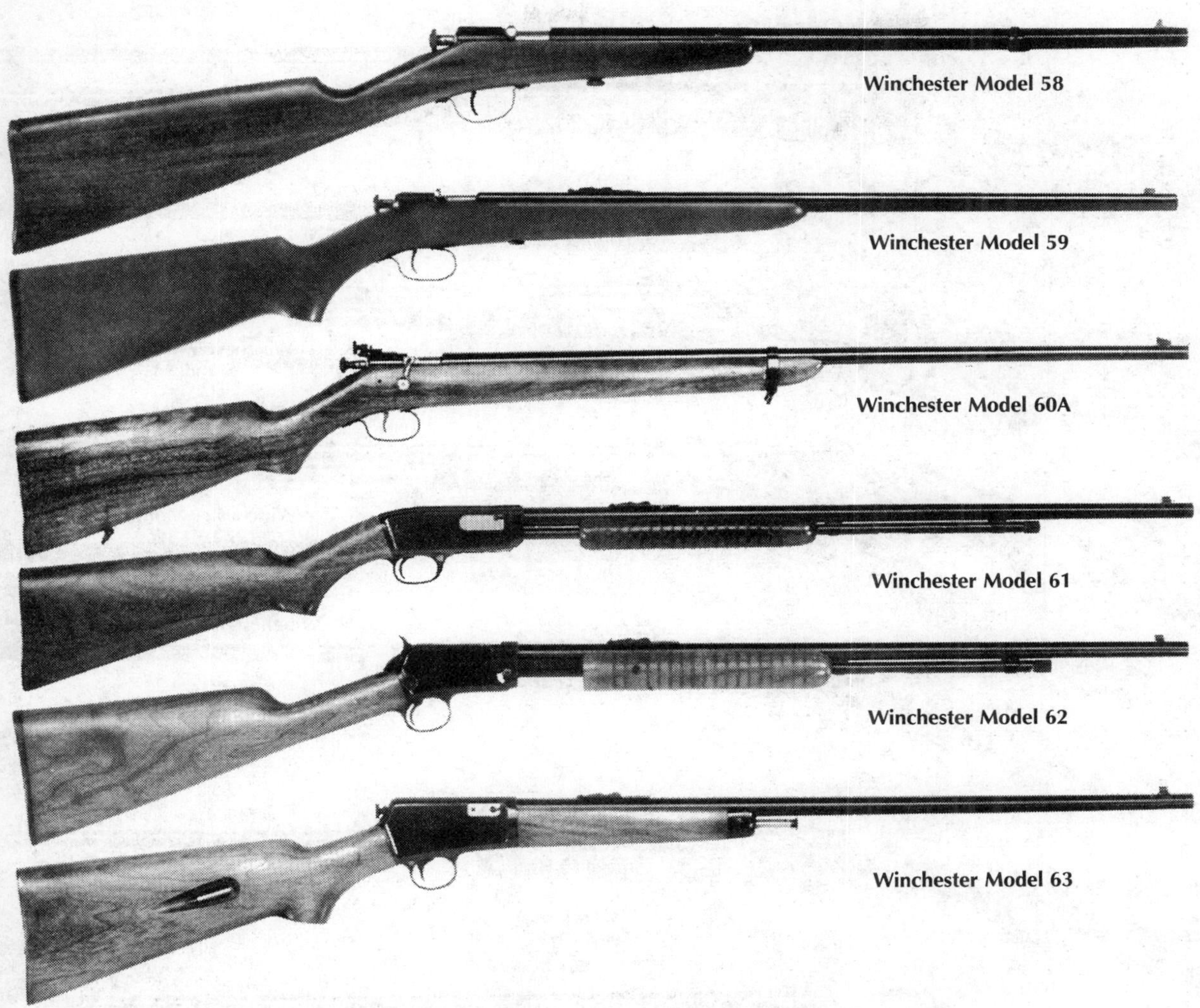
Winchester Model 58

Winchester Model 59

Winchester Model 60A

Winchester Model 61

Winchester Model 62

Winchester Model 63

MODEL 67 BOLT-ACTION SINGLE-SHOT RIFLE . . . . NiB $227 Ex $201 Gd $124
Takedown. Calibers: .22 Short, Long, LR, .22 LR round (smoothbore), .22 WRF. 27-inch bbl. Weight: 5 lbs. Sights: Open rear, bead front. Plain pistol-grip stock (original model had grasping grooves in forearm). Made from 1934-63.

MODEL 67 BOY'S RIFLE . . . . NiB $253 Ex $201 Gd $134
Same as Standard Model 67 except has shorter stock, 20-inch bbl., weighs 4.25 lbs.

MODEL 68 BOLT-ACTION SINGLE-SHOT . . . . NiB $278 Ex $201 Gd $160
Same as Model 67 except has rear peep sight. Made from 1934-1946.

MODEL 69 BOLT-ACTION RIFLE . . NiB $395 Ex $308 Gd $179
Takedown. Caliber: .22 S, L, LR. Five or 10-round box magazine. 25-inch bbl. Weight: 5.5 lbs. Peep or open rear sight. Plain pistol-grip stock. Rifle cocks on closing motion of the bolt. Made from 1935-37.

MODEL 69A BOLT-ACTION RIFLE
Same as the Model 69 except cocking mechanism was changed to cock the rifle by the opening motion of the bolt. Made from 1937-63. Note: Models with grooved receivers command 20% higher prices.

Model 69A standard. . . . . NiB $445 Ex $362 Gd $255
Match Mdl. w/Lyman No. 57E W receiver sight . . . . NiB $538 Ex $436 Gd $306
(Target Model w/Winchester peep rear sight, swivels, sling . . . . . NiB $645 Ex $522 Gd $366

MODEL 70
Introduced in 1937, the Model 70 Bolt-Action Repeating Rifle was offered in several styles and calibers. Only minor design changes were made over a period of 27 years and more than 500,000 of these rifles were sold. The original model was dubbed "The Rifleman's Rifle." In 1964, the original Model 70 was superseded by a revised version with redesigned action, improved bolt, swaged (free-floating) barrel, restyled stock. This model again underwent major changes in 1972. Most visible: New stock with contrasting forend tip and grip cap, cut checkering (instead of impressed as in predecessor) knurled bolt handle. The action was machined from a solid block of steel with barrels made from chrome molybdenum steel. Other changes in the design and style of the Model 70 continued. The XTR models were added in 1978 along with the Model 70A, the latter omitting the white liners, forend caps and floor plates. In 1981, an XTR Featherweight Model was added to the line, beginning with serial number G1,440,000. This version featured lighter barrels, fancy-checkered stocks with Schnabel forend. After U.S. Repeating Arms took over the Winchester plant, the Model 70 went through even more changes as described under that section of Winchester rifles.

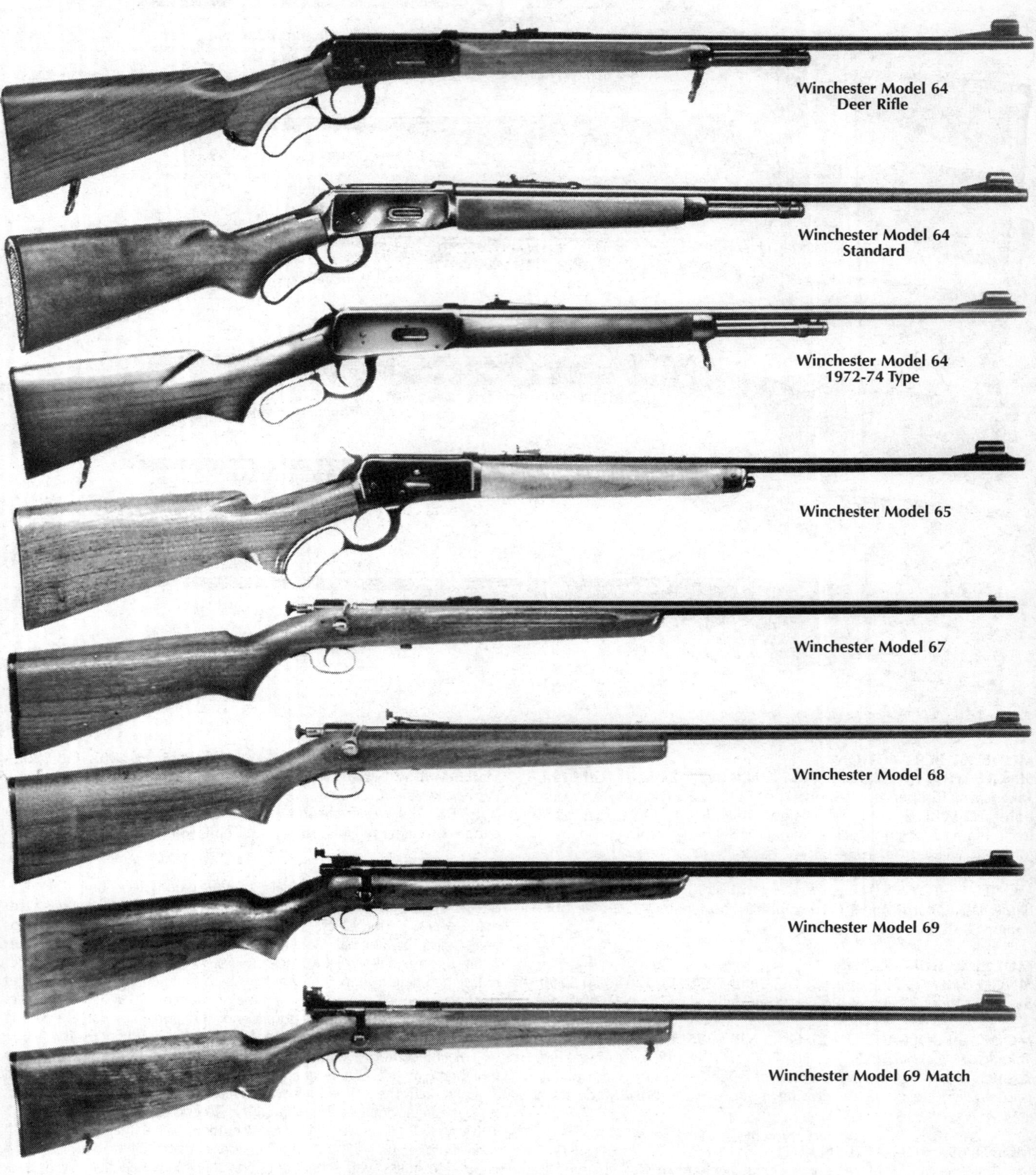

Winchester Model 64
Deer Rifle

Winchester Model 64
Standard

Winchester Model 64
1972-74 Type

Winchester Model 65

Winchester Model 67

Winchester Model 68

Winchester Model 69

Winchester Model 69 Match

Winchester Model 70 Basic Post-WWII Model

Winchester Model 70 Standard Model

Winchester Model 70 Super Grade

Winchester Model 70 African (1964)

Winchester Model 70 Deluxe (1964)

PRE-1964 MODEL 70

MODEL 70
AFRICAN RIFLE............. NiB $5303 Ex $4736 Gd $2728
Same general specifications as Super Grade Model 70 except w/25-inch bbl., 3-round magazine, Monte Carlo stock w/recoil pad. Weight: 9.5 lbs. Caliber: .458 Winchester Magnum. Made from 1956–63.

MODEL 70 ALASKAN
Same as Standard Model 70 except calibers .338 Win. Mag., .375 H&H Mag.; 3-round magazine in .338, 4-round in .375 caliber; 25-inch bbl.; stock w/recoil pad. Weight: 8 lbs. in .338; 8.75 lbs. in .375 caliber. Made from 1960–63.

.338 Win.
Magnum .... NiB $1854 Ex $1494 Gd $1034
.375 H&H .... NiB $2371 Ex $1909 Gd $1318

MODEL 70 BULL GUN....... NiB $4260 Ex $3745 Gd $2200
Same as Standard Model 70 except w/heavy 28-inch bbl., scope bases, Marksman stock, weighs 13.25 lbs., caliber .300 H&H Magnum and .30-06 only. Disc. in 1963.

MODEL 70
FEATHERWEIGHT SPORTER
Same as Standard Model 70 except w/redesigned stock and 22-inch bbl., aluminum trigger guard, floorplate and buttplate. Calibers: .243 Win., .264 Win. Mag., .270 Win., .308 Win., .30-06, .358 Win. Weight: 6.5 lbs. Made from 1952–63.

.243 Win.................... NiB $1104 Ex $898 Gd $637
.264 Win.................... NiB $1619 Ex $1311 Gd $917
.270 Win.................... NiB $1361 Ex $1105 Gd $777
.30-06 Springfield .... NiB $1036 Ex $842 Gd $595
.308 Win...................... NiB $965 Ex $786 Gd $557
.358 Win.................... NiB $2283 Ex $1846 Gd $1288

Winchester Model 70
Standard Weight Target Rifle

Winchester Model 70
Heavy Weight Target Rifle

Winchester Model 70
Bull Gun

Winchester Model 70
(Pre-1964) Standard Model

MODEL 70 NATIONAL MATCH RIFLE . . . . **NiB $2131 Ex $1796 Gd $1513**
Same as Standard Model 70 except w/scope bases, Marksman-type target stock, weight: 9.5 lbs. caliber .30-06 only. Disc. 1960.

MODEL 70 STANDARD GRADE
Calibers: .22 Hornet, .220 Swift, .243 Win., .250-3000, .257 Roberts, .270 Win., 7x57mm, .30-06, .308 Win., .300 H&H Mag., .375 H&H Mag. Five round box magazine (4-round in Magnum calibers). 24-inch bbl. standard; 26-inch in .220 Swift and .300 Mag.; 25-inch in .375 Mag.; at one time a 20-inch bbl. was available. Sights: Open rear; hooded ramp front. Checkered walnut stock; Monte Carlo comb standard on later production. Weight: From 7.75 lbs. depending on caliber and bbl. length. Made from 1937–63.

.22 Hornet (1937-58) . . . . **NiB $2063 Ex $1673 Gd $1163**
.220 Swift (1937-63) . . . . **NiB $1463 Ex $1181 Gd $820**
.243 Win. (1955-63) . . . . **NiB $1206 Ex $975 Gd $720**
.250-3000 Sav. (1937-49) . . . . **NiB $2648 Ex $2135 Gd $1478**
.257 Roberts (1937-59) . . . . **NiB $1849 Ex $1490 Gd $1030**
.264 Win. Mag. (1959-63) limited . . . . . . **NiB $1334 Ex $1078 Gd $750**
.270 Win. (1937-63) . . . . **NiB $1077 Ex $871 Gd $610**
7x57mm Mauser (1937-49) . . . . **NiB $2911 Ex $2346 Gd $1623**
7.65 Argentine (1937 only) limited . . . . **Very Rare**
.30-06 Springfield (1937-63) . . . . **NiB $882 Ex $714 Gd $500**
.308 Win. (1952-63) special order . . . . **Very Rare**
.300 H&H (1937-63) . . . . **NiB $1532 Ex $1235 Gd $856**
.300 Sav. (1944-50) limited . . . . **Rare**
.300 Win. Mag. (1962-63) . . . . **NiB $1981 Ex $1596 Gd $1104**
.338 Win. Mag. (1959-63)
special order only . . . . **NiB $1890 Ex $1524 Gd $1054**
.35 Rem. (1941-47) limited . . . . **Very Rare**
.358 Win. (1955-58) . . . . **Very Rare**
.375 H&H (1937-63) . . . . **NiB $2391 Ex $1929 Gd $1338**
.458 Win. Mag. (1956-63)
Super Grade only . . . . **NiB $4754 Ex $3828 Gd $2643**
9x57 Mauser (1937 only) limited . . . . **Very Rare**

MODEL 70 SUPER GRADE
Same as Standard Grade Model 70 except w/deluxe stock w/cheekpiece, black forend tip, pistol-grip cap, quick detachable swivels, sling. Disc. 1960. Prices for Super Grade models also reflect rarity in both production and caliber. Values are generally twice that of standard models of similar configuration.

MODEL 70 SUPER GRADE FEATHERWEIGHT
Same as Standard Grade Featherweight except w/deluxe stock w/cheekpiece, black forend tip, pistol-grip cap, quick detachable swivels, sling. Disc. 1960. Note: SG-FWs are very rare, but unless properly documented will not command premium prices. Prices for authenticated Super Grades Featherweight models are generally 4 to 5 times that of a standard production Featherweight model w/similar chambering.

MODEL 70 TARGET RIFLE
Same as Standard Model 70 except w/24-inch medium-weight bbl., scope bases, Marksman stock, weight 10.5 lbs. Originally offered in all of the Model 70 calibers, this rifle was available later in calibers .243 Win. and .30-06. Disc. 1963. Values are generally twice that of standard models of similar configuration.

MODEL 70 TARGET HEAVY WEIGHT . . . . **NiB $3807 Ex $1926 Gd $1309**
Same general specifications as Standard Model 70 except w/either 24- or 26-inch heavy weight bbl. weight: 10.5 lbs. No checkering. .243 and .30-06 calibers.

MODEL 70 TARGET BULL BARREL . . . . **NiB $4241 Ex $2387 Gd $1784**
Same general specifications as Standard Model 70 except 28-inch heavy weight bbl. and chambered for either .30-06 or .300 H&H Mag. Drilled and tapped for front sight base. Receiver slotted for clip loading. Weight: 13.25 lbs.

Winchester Model 70
International Army Match (1964)

Winchester Model 70
Mannlicher (1964)

Winchester Model 70
Standard (1964)

Winchester Model 70
Target (1964)

MODEL 70
VARMINT RIFLE . . . . NiB $1291 Ex $1214 Gd $1059
Same general specifications as Standard Model 70 except w/26-inch heavy bbl., scope bases, special varminter stock. Calibers: .220 Swift, .243 Win. Made from 1956–63.

MODEL 70
WESTERNER . . . . NiB $1239 Ex $1080 Gd $956
Same as Standard Model 70 except calibers .264 Win. Mag., .300 Win. Mag.; 3-round magazine; 26-inch bbl. in former caliber, 24-inch in latter. Weight: 8.25 lbs. Made from 1960–63.

1964-TYPE MODEL 70

MODEL 70 AFRICAN . . . . NiB $1188 Ex $750 Gd $565
Caliber: .458 Win. Mag. Three round magazine. 22-inch bbl. Weight: 8.5 lbs. Special "African" sights. Monte Carlo stock w/ebony forend tip, hand-checkering, twin stock-reinforcing bolts, recoil pad, QD swivels. Made from 1964–71.

MODEL 70 DELUXE . . . . NiB $1075 Ex $7697 Gd $488
Calibers: .243, .270 Win., .30-06, .300 Win. Mag. Five round box magazine (3-round in Magnum). 22-inch bbl. (24-inch in Magnum). Weight: 7.5 lbs. Sights: Open rear; hooded ramp front. Monte Carlo stock w/ebony forend tip, hand-checkering, QD swivels, recoil pad on Magnum. Made from 1964–71.

MODEL 70 INTERNATIONAL
ARMY MATCH RIFLE. . . . . NiB $1020 Ex $856 Gd $634
Caliber: .308 Win. (7.62 NATO). Five round box magazine. 24-inch heavy barrel. Externally adj. trigger. Weight: 11 lbs. ISU stock w/military oil finish, forearm rail for standard accessories, vertically adj. buttplate. Made in 1971. Value shown is for rifle w/o sights.

MODEL 70 MAGNUM
Calibers: 7mm Rem. Mag.; .264, .300, .338 Win. Mag.; .375 H&H Mag. Three round magazine. 24-inch bbl. Weight: 7.75 to 8.5 lbs. Sights: Open rear; hooded ramp front. Monte Carlo stock w/cheekpiece, checkering, twin stock-reinforcing bolts, recoil pad, swivels. Made from 1964–71.
Caliber .375 H&H Mag. . . . . NiB $750 Ex $608 Gd $427
Other calibers . . . . NiB $515 Ex $418 Gd $295

MODEL 70 MANNLICHER . . . . NiB $759 Ex $656 Gd $553
Calibers: .243, .270, .308 Win., .30-06. Five round box magazine. 19-inch bbl. Sights: open rear; hooded ramp front. Weight: 7.5 lbs. Mannlicher-style stock w/Monte Carlo comb and cheekpiece, checkering, steel forend cap, QD sling swivels. Made from 1969–71.

MODEL 70 STANDARD. . . . . NiB $463 Ex $385 Gd $262
Calibers: .22-250, .222 Rem., .225, .243, .270, .308 Win., .30-06. Five round box magazine. 22-inch bbl. Weight: 7.5 lbs. Sights: Open rear; hooded ramp front. Monte Carlo stock w/cheekpiece, checkering, swivels. Made from 1964–71.

Winchester Model 70
African (1972)

MODEL 70 TARGET. . . . . NiB $706 Ex $571 Gd $398
Calibers: .308 Win. (7.62 NATO) and .30-06. Five round box magazine. 24-inch heavy bbl. Blocks for target scope. No factory sights installed, but drilled and tapped for front and rear sights. Weight: 10.25 lbs. High-comb Marksman-style stock, aluminum hand stop, swivels. Straight-grain, one-piece stock w/sling swivels, but no checkering. Made from 1964-71.

MODEL 70 VARMINT . . . . NiB $507 Ex $409 Gd $311
Same as Model 70 Standard except w/24-inch target weight bbl., blocks for target scope. No factory sights installed, but drilled and tapped for front and rear sights. Available in calibers .22-250, .222 Rem., and .243 Win. only. Weight: 9.75 lbs. Made from 1964-71.

1972-TYPE MODEL 70

MODEL 70 AFRICAN . . . . NiB $801 Ex $648 Gd $452
Similar to Model 70 Magnum except w/22-inch bbl. caliber .458 Win. Mag. w/special African open rear sight, reinforced stock w/ebony forend tip, detachable swivels and sling; front sling swivel stud attached to bbl. Weight: 8.5 lbs. Made from 1972-92.

MODEL 70 CLASSIC SM
Similar to Model 70 Classic Sporter except w/checkered black composite stock and matte metal finish. Made from 1994-96.
Model 70 Classic SM. . . . . NiB $512 Ex $435 Gd $285
Caliber .375 H&H . . . . NiB $622 Ex $493 Gd $339
W/BOSS, add. $100
W/open sights, add $40

MODEL 70 CLASSIC SPORTER
Similar to Model 70 Sporter except w/pre-64-style action w/controlled round feeding, classic-style stock. Optional open sights. Made from 1994-2006.
Standard model . . . . NiB $471 Ex $397 Gd $141
W/BOSS, add. $100
W/open sights, add $40

MODEL 70 CLASSIC SPORTER STAINLESS
Similar to Model 70 Classic Sporter except w/matte stainless steel finish. Weight: 7.5 lbs. No sights. Made from 1994-2006.
Standard model . . . . NiB $663 Ex $571 Gd $283
Magnum model . . . . NiB $725 Ex $596 Gd $365
W/BOSS, add. $100

MODEL 70 CUSTOM SHARPSHOOTER
Calibers: .22-250, .223, .308 Win., .300 Win. Mag. 24- or 26-inch bbl. 44.5 inches overall (24-inch bbl.). Weight: 11 lbs. Custom-fitted, hand-honed action. McMillan A-2 target-style stock. Matte blue or stainless finish. Made from 1992-96.
Model 70 Custom
Sharpshooter (blued). . . . . NiB $1890 Ex $1452 Gd $963
Model 70 Custom
Sharpshooter (stainless) . . . . NiB $1966 Ex $1444 Gd $1015

MODEL 70 CUSTOM SPORTING SHARPSHOOTER
Similar to Custom Sharpshooter Model except w/sporter-style gray composite stock. Stainless 24- or 26-inch bbl. w/blued receiver. Calibers: .270, 7mm STW, .300 Win. Mag. Made from 1993-2006.
Model 70 Custom Sharpshooter
blued (disc. 1995). . . . . NiB $1893 Ex $1455 Gd $966
Model 70 Custom Sharpshooter, stainless NiB $1970 Ex $1507 Gd $1018

MODEL 70 GOLDEN 50TH ANNIVERSARY EDITION
BOLT-ACTION RIFLE $1069
Caliber: .300 Win. Three round magazine. 24-inch bbl. 44.5 inches overall. Weight: 7.75 lbs. Checkered American walnut stock. Hand-engraved American scroll pattern on bbl., receiver, magazine cover, trigger guard and pistol-grip cap. Sights: Adj. rear; hooded front ramp. Inscription on bbl. reads "The Rifleman's Rifle 1937–1987." Only 500 made 1986–87. (Value for guns in new condition.)

MODEL 70 FEATHERWEIGHT CLASSIC. . . . . NiB $577 Ex $468 Gd $328
Similar to Model 70 XTR Featherweight except w/controlled-round feeding system. Calibers: .270, .280 and .30-06. Made from 1992-2006.

MODEL 70 INTERNATIONAL
ARMY MATCH . . . . NiB $966 Ex $837 Gd $554
Caliber: .308 Win. (7.62mm NATO). Five round magazine, clip slot in receiver bridge. 24-inch heavy barrel. Weight: 11 lbs. No sights, but drilled and tapped for front and rear iron sights, and/or scope mounts. ISU target stock. Intro. 1973; disc.

MODEL 70 LIGHTWEIGHT. . . . . . NiB $622 Ex $390 Gd $174
Calibers: .22-250 and .223 Rem.; .243, .270 and .308 Win.; .30-06 Springfield. Five round mag. capacity (6-round .223 Rem.). 22-inch barrel. 42 to 42.5 inches overall. Weight: 6 to 6.25 lbs. Checkered classic straight stock. Sling swivel studs. Made from 1986-95.

MODEL 70 MAGNUM
Same as Model 70 except w/3-round magazine, 24-inch bbl., reinforced stock w/recoil pad. Weight: 7.75 lbs. (except 8.5 lbs. in .375 H&H Mag.). Calibers: .264 Win. Mag., 7mm Rem. Mag., .300 Win. Mag., .338 Win. Mag., .375 H&H Mag. Made from 1972-80.
.375 H&H Magnum. . . . . NiB $650 Ex $530 Gd $330
Other magnum calibers. . . . . NiB $596 Ex $405 Gd $325

MODEL 70 STANDARD. . . . . NiB $446 Ex $363 Gd $256
Same as Model 70A except w/5-round magazine, Monte Carlo stock w/cheekpiece, black forend tip and pistol-grip cap w/white spacers, checkered pistol grip and forearm, detachable sling swivels. Same calibers plus .225 Win. Made from 1972-80.

MODEL 70 STANDARD CARBINE . . . . NiB $453 Ex $368 Gd $258
Same general specifications as Standard Model 70 except 19-inch bbl. and weight: 7.25 lbs. Shallow recoil pad. Walnut stock and forend w/traditional Model 70 checkering. Swivel studs. No sights, but drilled and tapped for scope mount.

Winchester Model 70 Featherweight

Winchester Model 70 Golden 50th Anniversary

Winchester Model 70 Featherweight Classic

Winchester Model 70 Lightweight

Winchester Model 70 Magnum

Winchester Model 70 Carbine

MODEL 70 SPORTER DBM

Same general specifications as Model 70 Sporter SSM except w/detachable box magazine. Calibers: .22-250 (disc. 1994), .223 (disc. 1994), .243 (disc. 1994), .270, 7mm Rem. Mag., .308 (disc. 1994), .30-06, .300 Win. Mag. Made from 1992-94.

Model 70 DBM .... **NiB $512 Ex $430 Gd $280**
Model 70 DBM-S (w/iron sights) .... **NiB $532 Ex $430 Gd $300**

MODEL 70 STAINLESS SPORTER SSM .... **NiB $532 Ex $430 Gd $300**

Same general specifications as Model 70 XTR Sporter except w/checkered black composite stock and matte finished receiver, bbl. and other metal parts. Calibers: .270, 7mm Rem. Mag., .30-06, .300 Win. Mag., .338 Win. Mag. Weight: 7.75 lbs. Made from 1992-94.

MODEL 70 CLASSIC SUPER GRADE ..... **NiB $859 Ex $782 Gd $442**

Calibers: .270, 7mm Rem. Mag., .30-06, .300 Win. Mag., .338 Win. Mag. Five round magazine (standard), 3-round (magnum). 24-inch bbl. 44.5 inches overall. Weight: 7.75 lbs. Checkered walnut stock w/sculptured cheekpiece and tapered forend. Scope bases and rings, no sights. Controlled-round feeding system. Made from 1990-95. Improved in 1999. Disc. 2006.

MODEL 70 TARGET .... **NiB $883 Ex $806 Gd $445**

Calibers: .30-06 and .308 Win. (7.62mm NATO). Five round magazine. 26-inch heavy bbl. Weight: 10.5 lbs. No sights, but drilled and tapped for scope mount and open sights. High-comb Marksman-style target stock, aluminum hand stop and swivels. Intro. 1972. Disc.

MODEL 70 ULTRA MATCH .... **NiB $911 Ex $834 Gd $474**

Similar to Model 70 Target but custom grade w/26-inch heavy bbl. w/deep counterbore, glass bedding, externally adj. trigger. Intro. 1972. Disc.

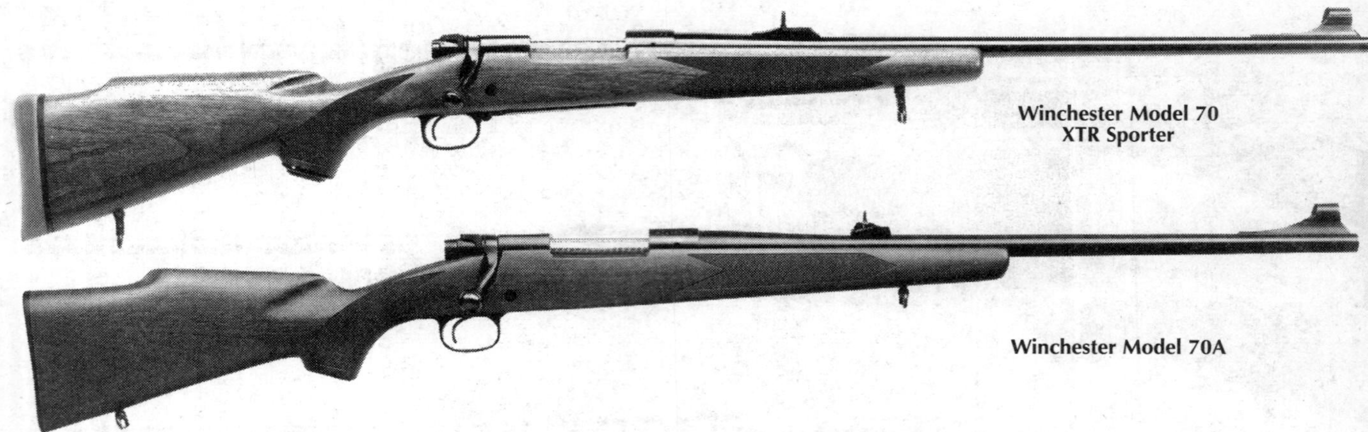
Winchester Model 70 XTR Sporter

Winchester Model 70A

MODEL 70 VARMINT (HEAVY BARREL)
Same as Model 70 Standard except w/medium-heavy, counter-bored 26-inch bbl., no sights, stock w/less drop. Weight: 9 lbs. Calibers: .22-250 Rem., .223 Rem., .243 Win., .308 Win. Made 1972-93. Model 70 SHB, in .308 Win. only w/black synthetic stock and matte blue receiver/bbl. Made from 1992-93.
Model 70 Varmint . . . . NiB $706 Ex $578 Gd $325
Model 70 SHB (synthetic heavy barrel) . . . NiB $504 Ex $416 Gd $287

MODEL 70 WIN-CAM RIFLE. . . . . . NiB $492 Ex $389 Gd $235
Caliber: .270 Win. and .30-06 Springfield. 24-inch barrel. Camouflage one-piece laminated stock. Recoil pad. Drilled and tapped for scope. Made from 1986 to date.

MODEL 70 WINLITE BOLT-ACTION RIFLE. . . . . NiB $681 Ex $500 Gd $377
Calibers: .270 Win., .280 Rem., .30-06 Springfield, 7mm Rem., .300 Win. Mag., and .338 Win. Mag. Five round magazine; 3-round for Magnum calibers. 22-inch bbl.; 24-inch for Magnum calibers. 42.5 inches overall; 44.5, Magnum calibers. Weight: 6.25 to 7 lbs. Fiberglass stock w/rubber recoil pad, sling swivel studs. Made from 1986-90.

MODEL 70 WIN-TUFF BOLT-ACTION RIFLE
Calibers: .22-250, .223, .243, .270, .308 and .30-06 Springfield. 22-inch bbl. Weight: 6.25–7 lbs. Laminated dye-shaded brown wood stock w/recoil pad. Barrel drilled and tapped for scope. Swivel studs. FWT Model made from 1986–94. LW Model intro. 1992.
Featherweight model . . . . NiB $5427 Ex $418 Gd $300
Lightweight model (Made 1992–93) . . . . . . NiB $492 Ex $379 Gd $266

MODEL 70 XTR FEATHERWEIGHT. . . . . . . NiB $512 Ex $415 Gd $292
Similar to Standard Win. Model 70 except lightweight American walnut stock w/classic Schnabel forend, checkered. 22-inch bbl., hooded blade front sight, folding leaf rear sight. Stainless-steel magazine follower. Weight: 6.75 lbs. Made from 1984-94.

MODEL 70 XTR SPORTER RIFLE. . . . . NiB $547 Ex $418 Gd $289
Calibers: .264 Win. Mag., 7mm Rem. Mag., .300 Win. Mag., .200 Weatherby Mag., and .338 Win. Mag. Three round magazine. 24-inch barrel. 44.5 inches overall. Weight: 7.75 lbs. Walnut Monte Carlo stock. Rubber buttpad. Receiver tapped and drilled for scope mounting. Made from 1986-94.

MODEL 70 XTR SPORTER MAGNUM . . . . NiB $547 Ex $418 Gd $289
Calibers: .264 Win. Mag., 7mm Rem. Mag., .300 Win. Mag., .338 Win. Mag. Three round magazine. 24-inch bbl. 44.5 inches overall. Weight: 7.75 lbs. No sights furnished, optional adj. folding leaf rear; hooded ramp. Receiver drilled and tapped for scope. Checkered American walnut Monte Carlo-style stock w/satin finish. Made from 1986-94.

MODEL 70 XTR
SPORTER VARMINT . . . . NiB $503 Ex $415 Gd $263
Same general specifications as Model 70 XTR Sporter, except in calibers .223, .22-250, .243 only. Checkered American walnut Monte Carlo-style stock w/cheekpiece. Made from 1986-94.

MODEL 70A . . . . NiB $396 Ex $308 Gd $226
Calibers: .222 Rem., .22-250, .243 Win., .25-06, .270 Win., .30-06, .308 Win. Four round magazine. 22-inch bbl. (except 24- or 26-inch in 25-06). Weight: 7.5 lbs. Sights: Open rear; hooded ramp front. Monte Carlo stock w/checkered pistol grip and forearm, sling swivels. Made from 1972-78.

MODEL 70A MAGNUM . . . . NiB $411 Ex $308 Gd $231
Same as Model 70A except w/3-round magazine, 24-inch bbl., recoil pad. Weight: 7.75 lbs. Calibers: .264 Win. Mag., 7mm Rem. Mag., .300 Win. Mag. Made from 1972-78

MODEL 70 ULTIMATE CLASSIC BOLT-ACTION RIFLE
Calibers: .25-06 Rem., .264 Win., .270 Win., .270 Wby. Mag., .280 Rem., 7mm Rem. Mag., 7mm STW, .30-06, Mag., .300 Win. Mag., .300 Wby. Mag., .300 H&H Mag., .338 Win. Mag., .340 Wby. Mag., .35 Whelen, .375 H&H Mag., .416 Rem. Mag. and .458 Win. Mag. Three, 4- or 5-round magazine. 22- 24- 26-inch stainless bbl. in various configurations including: full-fluted tapered round, half round and half octagonal or tapered full octagonal. Weight: 7.75 to 9.25 lbs. Checkered fancy walnut stock. Made in 1995.
Model 70
Ultimate Classic . . . . NiB $2441 Ex $1977 Gd $1076
For Mag. calibers (.375 H&H,
.416 and .458), add. $250

MODEL 70 LAMINATED STAINLESS
BOLT-ACTION RIFLE. . . . . NiB $910 Ex $782 Gd $442
Calibers: .270 Win., .30-06 Spfld., 7mm Rem. Mag., .300 Win. Mag., and .338 Win. Mag. Five round magazine. 24-inch bbl. 44.75 inches overall. Weight: 8 to 8.525 lbs. Gray/Black laminated stock. Made from 1998-99.

MODEL 70 CHARACTERISTICS

MODEL 70 FIRST MODEL (SERIAL NUMBERS 1 – 80,000)
First manufactured in 1936; first sold in 1937. Receiver drilled for Lyman No. 57W or No. 48WJS receiver peep sights. Also drilled and tapped for Lyman or Fecker scope sight block. Weight w/24-inch bbl. in all calibers except .375 H&H Mag.: 8.25 lbs. 9 lbs. in H&H Mag. Early type safety located on bolt top. Production of this model ended in 1942 near serial number 80,000 due to World War II.

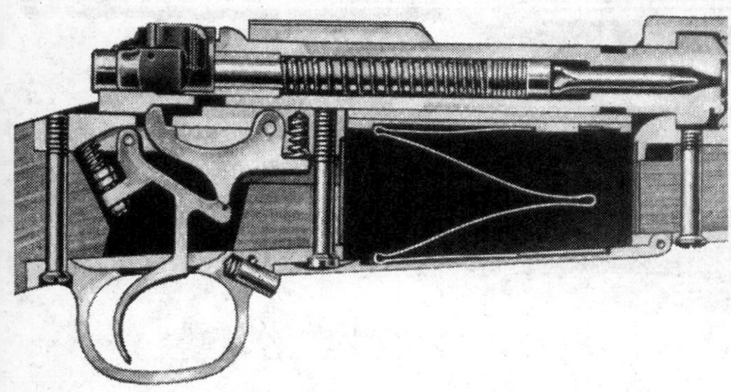

Cross-sectional view of the pre-1964 Winchester Model 70's speed lock action. This action cocks on the opening movement of the bolt with polished, smooth-functioning cams and guide lug, insuring fast and smooth operation.

MODEL 70 SECOND MODEL (SERIAL NUMBERS 80,000 – 350,000)
All civilian production of Winchester Model 70 rifles halted during World War II. Production resumed in 1947 w/improved safety and integral front-sight ramp. Serial numbers started at around 80,000. This model type was produced until 1954, ending around serial number 350,000.

MODEL 70 THIRD MODEL (SERIAL NUMBERS 350,000 – 400,000)
This variety was manufactured from 1954 to 1960 and retained many features of the Second Model except that a folding rear sight replaced the earlier type and front-sight ramps were brazed onto the bbl. rather than being an integral part of the bbl. The Model 70 Featherweight Rifle was intro. in 1954 in .308 WCF caliber. It was fitted w/light 22-inch bbl. and was also available w/either a Monte Carlo or Standard stock. The .243 Win. cartridge was added in 1955 in all grades of the Winchester Model 70 except the National Match and Bull Gun models. The .358 Win. cartridge was also intro. in 1955, along w/new Varmint Model chambered in .243 caliber only.

MODEL 70 FOURTH MODEL (SERIAL NUMBERS 400,000 – 500,000)
Different markings were inscribed on the barrels of these models and new magnum calibers were added; that is, .264 Win Mag., .338 Win. Mag, and .458 Win. Mag. All bbls. of this variation were about 0.13 inch shorter than previous ones. The .22 Hornet and .257 Roberts were disc. in 1962; the .358 Win. caliber in 1963.

MODEL 70 FIFTH MODEL (SERIAL NUMBERS 500,000 TO ABOUT 570,000)
These rifles may be recognized by slightly smaller checkering patterns and slightly smaller lightweight stocks. Featherweight bbls. were marked "Featherweight." Webbed recoil pads were furnished on magnum calibers.

POST-1964 MODEL 70 RIFLES

In 1964, the Winchester-Western Division of Olin Industries claimed that they were losing money on every Model 70 they produced. Both labor and material costs had increased to a level that could no longer be ignored. Other models followed suit. Consequently, sweeping changes were made to the entire Winchester line. Many of the older, less popular models were discontinued. Models that were to remain in production were modified for lower production costs.

1964 WINCHESTER MODEL 70 RIFLES
SERIAL NUMBERS 570,000 TO ABOUT 700,000)
The first version of the "New Model 70s" utilized a free-floating barrel, swaged rifle bore, new stock and sights, new type of bolt and receiver, and a different finish throughout on both the wood and metal parts. The featherweight grade was dropped, but six other grades were available in this new line:

Standard
Deluxe (Replaced Previous Super Grade)
Magnum
Varmint
Target
African

1966 MODEL 70 RIFLES
(SERIAL NUMBERS 700,000-G TO ABOUT 1,005,000)
In general, this group of Model 70s had fancier wood checkering, cross-bolt stock reinforcement, improved wood finish and improved action. One cross-bolt reinforcement was used on standard guns. Magnum calibers, however, used an additional forward cross-bolt and red recoil pad. The free-floating barrel clearance forward of the breech taper was reduced in thickness. Impressed checkering was used on the Deluxe models until 1968. Hand checkering was once again used on Deluxe and Carbine models in 1969; the big, red "W" was removed from all grip caps. A new, red safety-indicator and undercut cheekpiece was introduced in 1971.

1972 MODEL 70 RIFLES
(SERIAL NUMBERS G1,005,000 TO ABOUT G1,360,000)
Both the barrels and receivers for this variety of Model 70s were made from chrome molybdenum (C-M) steel. The barrels were tapered w/spiral rifling, ranging in length from 22 to 24 inches. Calibers .222 Rem., .225 Win. .22-250, .243 Win., .25-06, .270, .308 Win., .30-06 and .458 WM used the 22-inch length, while the following calibers used the 24-inch length: .222 Rem., .22-250, .243 Win., .264 Win. Mag., 7mm Mag., .300 and .375 H&H Mag. The .225 Win caliber was dropped in 1973; Mannlicher stocks were also disc. in 1973. The receiver for this variety of Model 70s was machined from a block of C-M steel. A new improved anti-bind bolt was introduced along with a new type of ejector. Other improvements included hand-cut checkering, pistol-grip stocks with pistol-grip and dark forend caps. An improved satin wood finish was also utilized.

1978 MODEL 70 RIFLES
(SERIAL NUMBERS BEGAN AROUND G1,360,000)
This variety of Model 70 was similar to the 1972 version except that a new XTR style was added which featured high-luster wood and metal finishes, fine-cut checkering, and similar embellishments. All Model 70 rifles made during this period used the XTR style; no standard models were available. In 1981, beginning with serial number G1,440,000 (approximately), a Featherweight version of the Model 70 XTR was introduced. The receiver was identical to the 1978 XTR, but lighter barrels were fitted. Stocks were changed to a lighter design with larger scroll checkering patterns and a Schnabel forend with no Monte Carlo comb. A satin sheen stock finish on the featherweight version replaced the high-luster finish used on the other XTR models. A new-style red buttplate with thick, black rubber liner was used on the Featherweight models. The grip cap was also redesigned for this model.

RIFLES

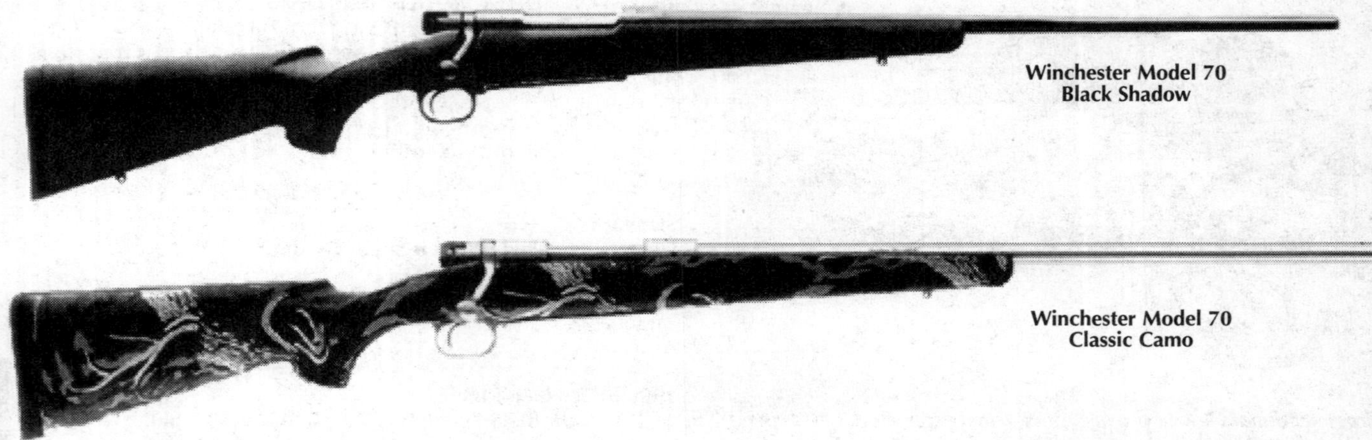

Winchester Model 70
Black Shadow

Winchester Model 70
Classic Camo

U.S. REPEATING ARMS MODEL 70 — 2006

In the early 1980s, negotiations began between Olin Industries and an employee-based corporation. The result of these negotiations ended with Olin selling all tools, machinery, supplies, etc. at the New Haven plant to the newly-formed corporation which was eventually named U.S. Repeating Arms Company. Furthermore, U.S. Repeating Arms Company purchased the right to use the Winchester name and logo. Winchester Model 70s went through very few changes the first two years after the transistion. However, in 1984, the Featherweight Model 70 XTR rifles were offered in a new short action for .22-250 Rem., .223 Rem., .243 Win. and .308 Win. calibers, in addition to their standard action which was used for the longer cartridges. A new Model 70 lightweight carbine was also introduced this same year. Two additional models were introduced in 1985 — the Model 70 Lightweight Mini-Carbine Short Action and the Model 70 XTR Sporter Varmint. The Model 70 Winlite appeared in the 1986 "Winchester" catalog, along with two economy versions of the Model 70 — the Winchester Ranger and the Ranger Youth Carbine. Five or six different versions of the Winchester Model 70 had been sufficient for 28 years (1937 - 1964). Now, changes in design and the addition of new models each year seemed to be necessary to keep the rifle alive. New models were added, old models dropped, changed in design, etc., on a regular basis. Still, the Winchester Model 70 Bolt-Action Repeating Rifle — in any of its variations — is the most popular bolt-action rifle ever built.

MODEL 70 BLACK SHADOW..... NiB $422 Ex $334 Gd $257
Calibers: .243 Win., .270 Win., .300 Win. Mag., .308 Win., .338 Win. Mag., .30-06 Spfld., 7mm STW., 7mm Rem. Mag. and 7mm-08 Rem. Three, 4- or 5-round magazine. 20- 24- 25- or 26-inch bbls. 39.5 to 46.75 inches overall.Weight: 6.5 to 8.25 lbs. Composite, Walnut or Gray/Black laminated stocks. Made from 1998-2006.

MODEL 70 CLASSIC
CAMO BOLT-ACTION RIFLE...... NiB $893 Ex $815 Gd $455
Calibers: .270 Win., 30-06 Spfld., 7mm Rem. Mag., .300 Win. Mag. Three or 5-round magazine. 24- or 26-inch bbl. 44.75 to 46.75 inches overall. Weight; 7.25 to 7.5 lbs. Mossy Oak finish and composite stock. Made from 1998-2006.

MODEL 70 CLASSIC
COMPACT BOLT-ACTION RIFLE... NiB $539 Ex $437 Gd $307
Calibers: .243 Win., .308 Win., and 7mm-08 Rem. Three round magazine. 20-inch bbl., 39.5 inches overall. Weight: 6.5 lbs. Walnut stock. Made from 1998-2006.

MODEL 70 CLASSIC LAREDO RANGE HUNTER
BOLT-ACTION RIFLE
Calibers: 7mm STW, 7mm Rem. mag., .300 Win. Mag. Three round magazine. 26-inch bbl. 46.75 inches overall. Weight: 9.5 lbs. Composite stock. Made from 1996-99.
Classic Laredo........................ NiB $711 Ex $583 Gd $449
Classic Laredo Fluted
(Made 1998 to date).................. NiB $737 Ex $608 Gd $428
Bossâ Classic Laredo.................. NiB $718 Ex $583 Gd $410

MODEL 70 COYOTE .... NiB $600 Ex $502 Gd $322
Calibers: .22-250 Rem., .223 Rem., and .243 Win. Five or 6-round magazine. 24- inch bbl., 44 inches overall. Weight: 9 lbs. Medium-heavy stainless steel barrel w/laminated stock. Reverse taper forend. Made from 1999. Disc.

MODEL 70 RANGER
COMPACT RIFLE..................... NiB $411 Ex $319 Gd $205
Calibers: .22-250 Rem., .223 Rem., .243 Win., 7mm-08 Rem., Mag., and .308 Win. Five or 6-round magazine. 20- or 22-inch bbl. 41 inches overall. Weight: 6.5 lbs. Adjustable TRUGLO front and rear fiber optic sights. Push-feed action. Made from 1999-2000.

MODEL 70
STEALTH RIFLE .... NiB $736 Ex $644 Gd $374
Varminter style bolt-action rifle. Calibers: .22-250 Rem., .223 Rem., and .308 Win. Five or 6-round magazine. 26- inch bbl. 46 inches overall. Weight: 10.75 lbs. Black synthetic stock w/Pillar Plus Accu Block and full-length aluminum bedding block. Matte blue finish. Made from 1999. Disc.

MODEL 71 LEVER-ACTION REPEATER
Solid frame. Caliber: .348 Win. Four round tubular magazine. 20- or 24-inch bbl. Weight: 8 lbs. Sights: Open or peep rear; bead front on ramp w/hood. Walnut stock. Made from 1935–57.
Special Grade (checkered pistol-grip
and forearm, grip cap, quick-detachable
swivels and sling.................. NiB $1988 Ex $1602 Gd $1061
Special Grade Carbine
(20-inch bbl.; disc. 1940) .... NiB $2517 Ex $2029 Gd $1405
Standard Grade
(lacks checkering,
grip cap, sling and swivels)........... NiB $1190 Ex $1035 Gd $598
Standard Grade
Carbine (20-inch
bbl.; disc. 1940) .... NiB $2132 Ex $1720 Gd $1097

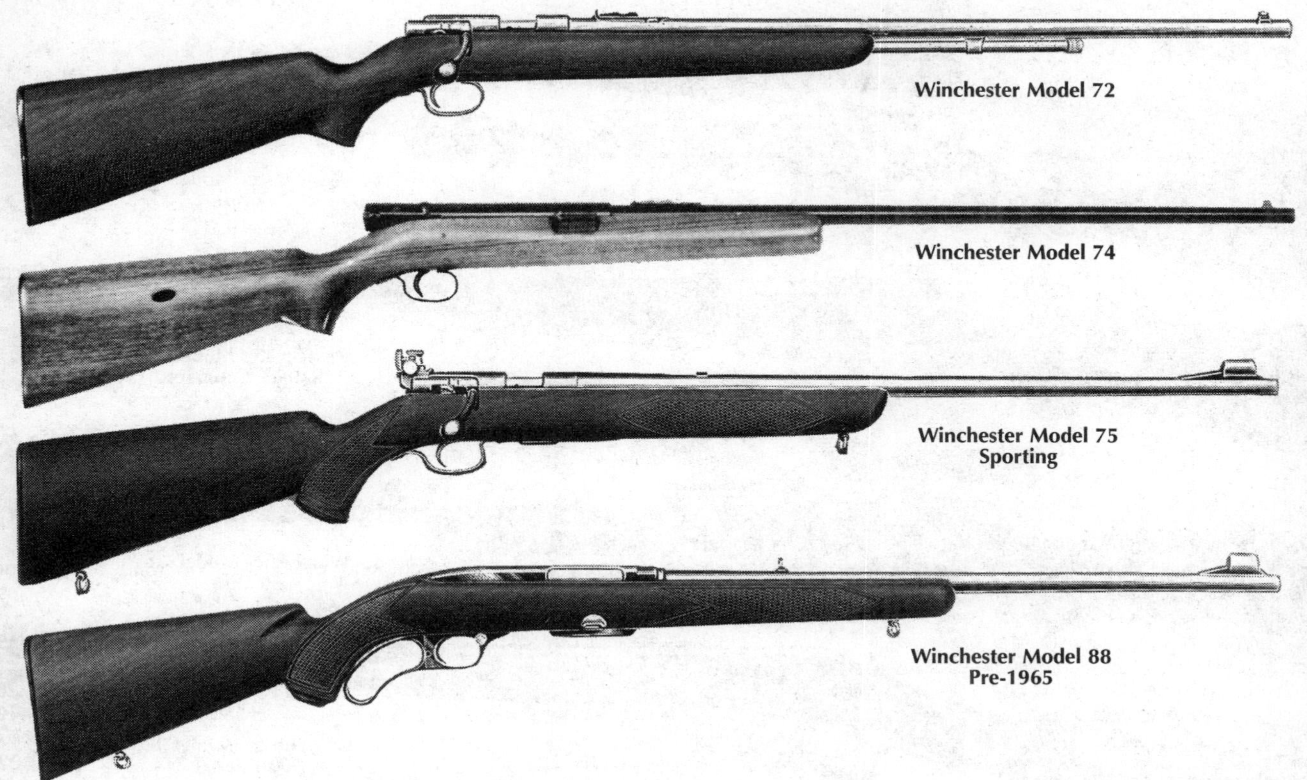

Winchester Model 72

Winchester Model 74

Winchester Model 75 Sporting

Winchester Model 88 Pre-1965

MODEL 72 BOLT-ACTION REPEATER. . . . . NiB $490 Ex $362 Gd $233
Tubular magazine. Takedown. Caliber: .22 Short, Long, LR. Magazine holds 20 Short, 16 Long or 15 LR. 25-inch bbl. Weight: 5.75 lbs. Sights: Peep or open rear; bead front. Plain pistol-grip stock. Made from 1938–59.

MODEL 73 LEVER-ACTION REPEATER
See Model 1873 rifles, carbines, "One of One Thousand" and other variations of this model at the beginning of Winchester Rifle Section. Note: The Winchester Model 1873 was the first lever-action repeating rifle bearing the Winchester name.

MODEL 74 SELF-LOADING RIFLE . . . . NiB $307 Ex $256 Gd $178
Takedown. Calibers: .22 Short only, .22 LR only. Tubular magazine in buttstock holds 20 Short, 14 LR. 24-inch bbl. Weight: 6.25 lbs. Sights: Open rear; bead front. Plain pistol-grip stock, one-piece. Made from 1939–55.

MODEL 75 SPORTING RIFLE . . . . . NiB $858 Ex $761 Gd $452
Same as Model 75 Target except has 24-inch bbl., checkered sporter stock, open rear sight; bead front on hooded ramp, weight: 5.5 lbs.

MODEL 75 TARGET RIFLE. . . . . NiB $596 Ex $442 Gd $287
Caliber: .22 LR. 5- or 10-round box magazine. 28-inch bbl. Weight: 8.75 lbs. Target sights (Lyman, Redfield or Winchester). Target stock w/pistol grip and semi-beavertail forearm, swivels and sling. Made from 1938–59.

MODEL 77 SEMIAUTOMATIC RIFLE,
CLIP TYPE . . . . NiB $307 Ex $256 Gd $168
Solid frame. Caliber: .22 LR. Eight round clip magazine. 22-inch bbl. Weight: About 5.5 lbs. Sights: Open rear; bead front. Plain, one-piece pistol-grip stock. Made from 1955–63.

MODEL 77,
TUBULAR MAGAZINE . . . . NiB $307 Ex $256 Gd $178
Same as Model 77. Clip type except has tubular magazine holding 15 rounds. Made from 1955–63.

MODEL 86 CARBINE AND RIFLE
See Model 1886 at beginning of Winchester Rifle section.

MODEL 88 CARBINE
Same as Model 88 Rifle except has 19-inch bbl., plain carbine-style stock and forearm with bbl. band. Weight: 7 lbs. Made from 1968-73.
88 Carbine. . . . . NiB $674 Ex $540 Gd $365
.284 Win.. . . . . NiB $1390 Ex $1287 Gd $978

MODEL 88 LEVER-ACTION RIFLE
Hammerless. Calibers: .243 Win., .284 Win., .308 Win., .358 Win. Four round box magazine. Three round in pre-1963 models and in .284. 22-inch bbl. Weight: About 7.25 lbs. One-piece walnut stock with pistol-grip, swivels (1965 and later models have basket-weave ornamentation instead of checkering). Made from 1955–1973. Note: .243 and .358 introduced 1956, later discontinued 1964; .284 introduced 1963.
Model 88 (checkered stock) . . . . NiB $704 Ex $550 Gd $380
Model 88 (basketweave stock) . . . . NiB $601 Ex $498 Gd $350
.284 Win. . . . . NiB $1152 Ex $932 Gd $652
.358 Win. . . . . NiB $1338 Ex $1082 Gd $754

MODEL 92 LEVER-ACTION RIFLE
Similar to the original Model 1892. Calibers: .357 Mag., .44-40, .44 Mag., .45 LC. Ten round magazine. 24-inch round bbl. Weight: 6.25 lbs. 41.25 inches overall. Bead front sight, adjustable buckhorn rear. Etched receiver and gold trigger. Blue finish. Smooth straight-grip walnut stock and forewarn w/ metal grip cap. Made from 1997. Disc.
Standard Rifle . . . . NiB $605 Ex $488 Gd $340
Short Rifle w/20-inch bbl. (.44 Mag. only) . . . . NiB $585 Ex $473 Gd $330

Winchester Model 70 Coyote

Winchester Model 70 Ranger Compact

Winchester Model 70 Stealth

Winchester Model 94 Traditional

MODEL 94
ANTIQUE CARBINE .... NiB $304 Ex $278 Gd $201
Same as standard Post-64 Model 94 Carbine except has decorative scrollwork and casehardened receiver, brass-plated loading gate, saddle ring; caliber .30-30 only. Made from 1964–84.

MODEL 94 CARBINE
Same as Model 1894 Rifle except 20-inch round bbl., 6-round full-length magazine. Weight: About 6.5 lbs. Originally made in calibers .25-35, .30-30, .32 Special and .38-55. Original version discontinued 1964. See 1894 Models at beginning of Winchester Rifle Section.
Pre-World War II
(under No. 1,300,000) .... NiB $1338 Ex $1082 Gd $754
Postwar, pre-1964
(under No. 2,700,000) .... NiB $738 Ex $596 Gd $415

MODEL 94
CLASSIC CARBINE .... NiB $419 Ex $311 Gd $260
Same as Canadian Centennial '67 Commemorative Carbine except without commemorative details; has scroll-engraved receiver, gold-plated loading gate. Made from 1968–70.

MODEL 94
CLASSIC RIFLE .... NiB $394 Ex $280 Gd $255
Same as Model 67 Rifle except without commemorative details; has scroll-engraved receiver, gold-plated loading gate. Made from 1968–70.

MODEL 94
DELUXE CARBINE.............. NiB $390 Ex $317 Gd $224
Caliber: .30-30 Win. Six round magazine. 20-inch bbl. 37.75 inches overall. Weight: 6.5 lbs. Semi-fancy American walnut stock with rubber buttpad, long forearm and specially cut checkering. Engraved with "Deluxe" script. Made from 1987-2006.

MODEL 94 LONG BARREL RIFLE........ NiB $358 Ex $306 Gd $177
Caliber: .30-30 Win. Seven round magazine. 24-inch bbl. 41.75 inches overall. Weight: 7 lbs. American walnut stock. Blade front sight. Made from 1987-2006.

MODEL 94 TRAPPER............ NiB $358 Ex $280 Gd $188
Same as Winchester Model 94 Carbine except 16-inch bbl. and weight: 6 lbs., 2 oz. Made from 1980-2006.

MODEL 94 WIN-TUFF RIFLE ..... NiB $332 Ex $255 Gd $188
Caliber: .30-30 Win. Six round magazine. 20-inch bbl. 37.75 inches overall. Weight: 6.5 lbs. Brown laminated wood stock. Made from 1987-2006.

MODEL 94 WRANGLER CARBINE
Same as standard Model 94 Carbine except has 16-inch bbl., engraved receiver and chambered for .32 Special & .38-55 Win.
Wrangler, Top
Eject (disc.1984)..................... NiB $358 Ex $280 Gd $203
Wrangler II,
Angle Eject (disc. 1985) .... NiB $306 Ex $219 Gd $177

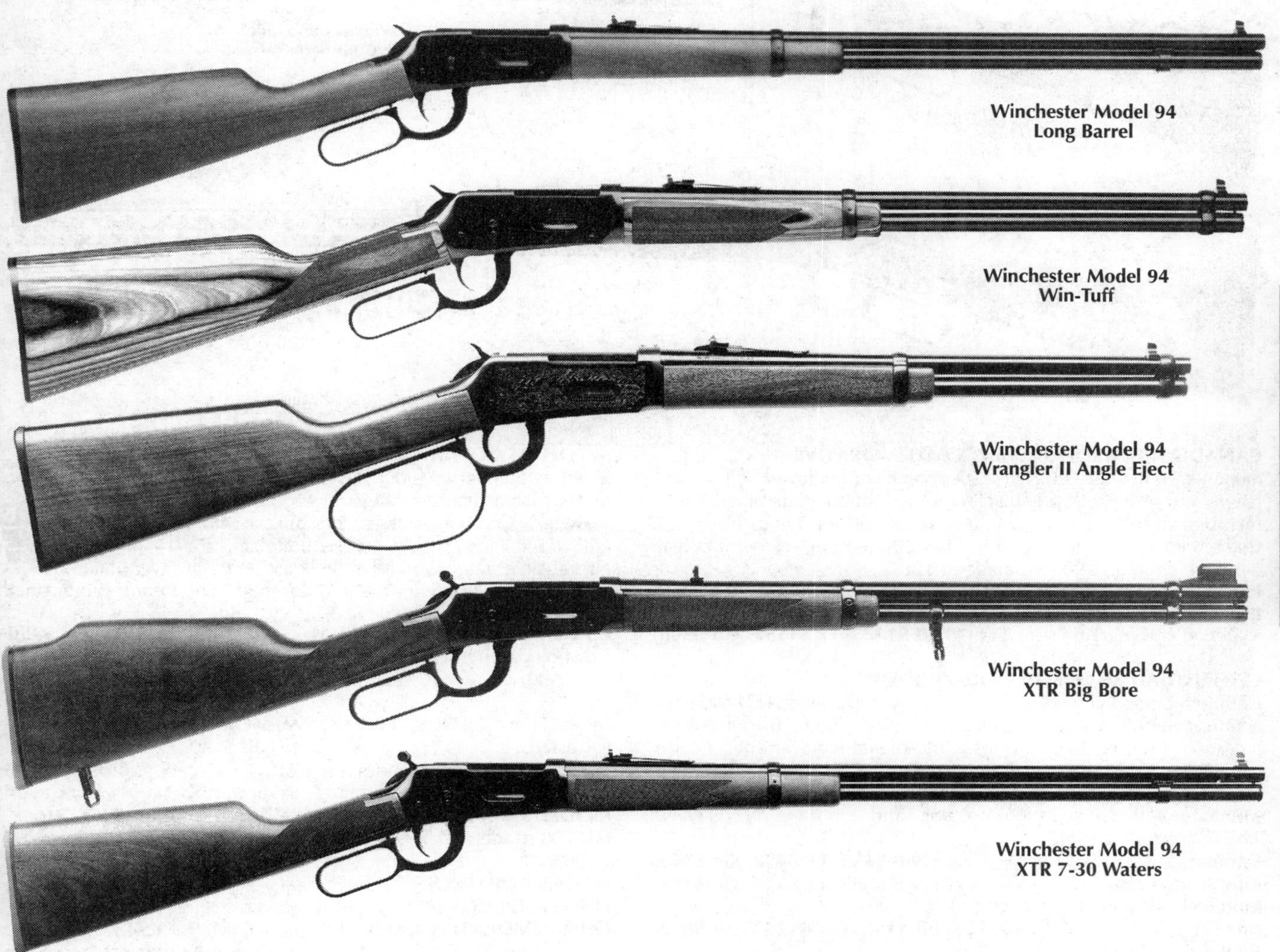

MODEL 94 XTR BIG BORE. . . . . . . NiB $389 Ex $286 Gd $188
Modified Model 94 action for added strength. Caliber: .375 Win. 20-inch bbl. Rubber buttpad. Checkered stock and forearm. Weight: 6.5 lbs. Made from 1978-2006.

MODEL 94 XTR
LEVER-ACTION RIFLE. . . . . NiB $332 Ex $229 Gd $167
Same general specifications as standard Angle Eject M94 except chambered .30-30 and 7-30 Waters and has 20- or 24-inch bbl. Weight: 7 lbs. Made 1985 to date by U.S. Repeating Arms.

MODEL 94 COMMEMORATIVES

MODEL 94 ANTLERED GAME. . . . . NiB $711 Ex $576 Gd $403
Standard Model 94 action. Gold-colored medallion inlaid in stock. Antique gold-plated receiver, lever tang and bbl. bands. Medallion and receiver engraved with elk, moose, deer and caribou. 20.5-inch bbl. Curved steel buttplate. In .30-30 caliber. 19,999 made in 1978.

MODEL 94 BICENTENNIAL
'76 CARBINE. . . . . NiB $864 Ex $735 Gd $545
Same as Standard Model 94 Carbine except caliber .30-30 Win. only; antique silver-finished, engraved receiver; stock and forearm of fancy walnut, checkered, Bicentennial medallion embedded in buttstock, curved buttplate. 20,000 made in 1976.

MODEL 94 BUFFALO BILL COMMEMORATIVE
Same as Centennial '66 Rifle except receiver is black-chromed, scroll-engraved and bears name "Buffalo Bill"; hammer, trigger, loading gate, saddle ring, forearm cap, and buttplate are nickel-plated; Buffalo Bill Memorial Assn. commemorative medallion embedded in buttstock; "Buffalo Bill Commemorative" inscribed on bbl., facsimile signature "W.F. Cody, Chief of Scouts" on tang. Carbine has 20-inch bbl., 6-round magazine, 7-lb. weight. 112,923 made in 1968.
Carbine . . . . NiB $615 Ex $498 Gd $350
Rifle. . . . . NiB $647 Ex $524 Gd $368
Matched carbine rifle set. . . . . . . NiB $1475 Ex $1198 Gd $837

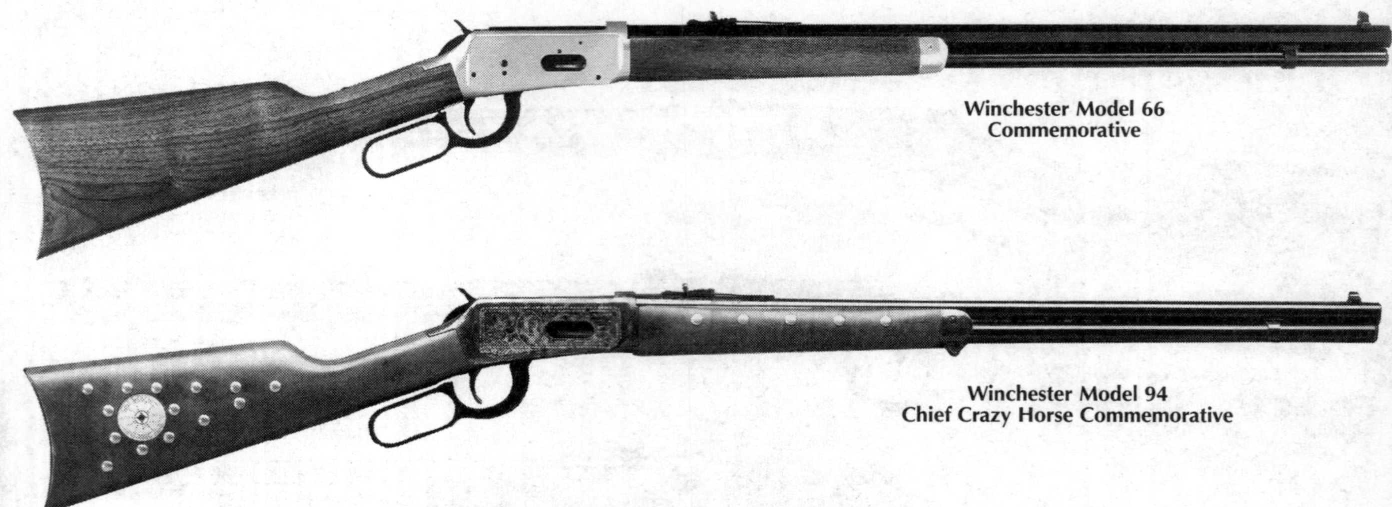

Winchester Model 66 Commemorative

Winchester Model 94 Chief Crazy Horse Commemorative

CANADIAN CENTENNIAL '67 COMMEMORATIVE
Same as Centennial '66 Rifle except receiver engraved with maple leaves and forearm cap is black-chromed, buttplate is blued, commemorative inscription in gold on barrel and top tang: "Canadian Centennial 1867–1967." Carbine has 20-inch bbl., 6-round magazine, weight: 7 lb., 90,398 made in 1967.
Carbine . . . . NiB $615 Ex $498 Gd $350
Rifle. . . . . NiB $647 Ex $524 Gd $368
Matched carbine/rifle set . . . . . . NiB $1423 Ex $1152 Gd $806

CENTENNIAL '66 COMMEMORATIVE
Commemorates Winchester's 100th anniversary. Standard Model 94 action. Caliber: .30-30. Full-length magazine holds 8 rounds. 26-inch octagon bbl. Weight: 8 lbs. Gold-plated receiver and forearm cap. Sights: Open rear; post front. Saddle ring. Walnut buttstock and forearm with high-gloss finish, solid brass buttplate. Commemorative inscription on bbl. and top tang of receiver. 100,478 made in 1966.
Carbine . . . . NiB $615 Ex $498 Gd $350
Rifle. . . . . NiB $647 Ex $524 Gd $368
Matched carbine/
rifle set . . . . NiB $1485 Ex $1203 Gd $842

MODEL 94 CHEYENNE
COMMEMORATIVE. . . . . NiB $1083 Ex $815 Gd $759
Available in Canada only. Same as Standard Model 94 Carbine except chambered for .44-40. 11,225 made in 1977.

MODEL 94
CHIEF CRAZY HORSE
COMMEMORATIVE. . . . . NiB $744 Ex $601 Gd $420
Cailber: .38-55, 7-round tubular magazine. 24-inch bbl., 41.75 inches overall. Walnut stock with medallion of the United Sioux Tribes; buttstock and forend also decorated with brass tacks. Engraved receiver. Open rear sights; bead front sight. 19,999 made in 1983.

MODEL 94 COLT COMMEMORATIVE
CARBINE SET. . . . . NiB $3985 Ex $3204 Gd $2227
Standard Model 94 action. Caliber: .44-40 Win. 20-inch bbl. Weight: 6.25 lbs. Features the horse-and-rider trademark and distinctive WC monogram in gold etching on left side of receiver. Sold in set with Colt Single Action Revolver chambered for same caliber.

MODEL 94 COWBOY COMMEMORATIVE CARBINE
Same as Standard Model 94 Carbine except caliber .30-30 only; nickel-plated receiver, tangs, lever, bbl. bands; engraved receiver, "Cowboy Commemorative" on bbl., commemorative medallion embedded in buttstock; curved buttplate. 20,915 made in 1970. Nickel-silver medallion inlaid in stock. Antique silver-plated receiver engraved with scenes of the old frontier. Checkered walnut stock and forearm. 19,999 made in 1970.
Cowboy carbine . . . . NiB $615 Ex $498 Gd $350
Cowboy carbine
(1 of 300) . . . . NiB $3841 Ex $3095 Gd $2141

MODEL 94 GOLDEN SPIKE COMMEMORATIVE
CARBINE. NiB $539 Ex $437 Gd $307
Same as Standard Model 94 Carbine except caliber .30-30 only; gold-plated receiver, tangs and bbl. bands; engraved receiver, commemorative medallion embedded in stock. 64,758 made in 1969.

MODEL 94 ILLINOIS
SESQUICENTENNIAL
COMMEMORATIVE CARBINE. . . . . NiB $539 Ex $437 Gd $307
Same as Standard Model 94 Carbine except caliber .30-30 only; gold-plated buttplate, trigger, loading gate, and saddle ring; receiver engraved with profile of Lincoln, commemorative inscription on receiver, bbl.; souvenir medallion embedded in stock. 31,124 made in 1968.

MODEL 94 LEGENDARY
FRONTIERSMEN
COMMEMORATIVE. . . . . NiB $711 Ex $576 Gd $403
Standard Model 94 action. Caliber: .39-55. 24-inch round bbl. Nickel-silver medallion inlaid in stock. Antique silver-plated receiver engraved with scenes of the old frontier. Checkered walnut stock and forearm. 19,999 made in 1979.

MODEL 94
LEGENDARY LAWMEN
COMMEMORATIVE. . . . . NiB $711 Ex $576 Gd $403
Same as Standard Model 94 Carbine except .30-30 Win. only; antique silver-plated receiver engraved with action law-enforcement scenes. 16-inch Trapper bbl., antique silver-plated bbl. bands. 19,999 made in 1978.

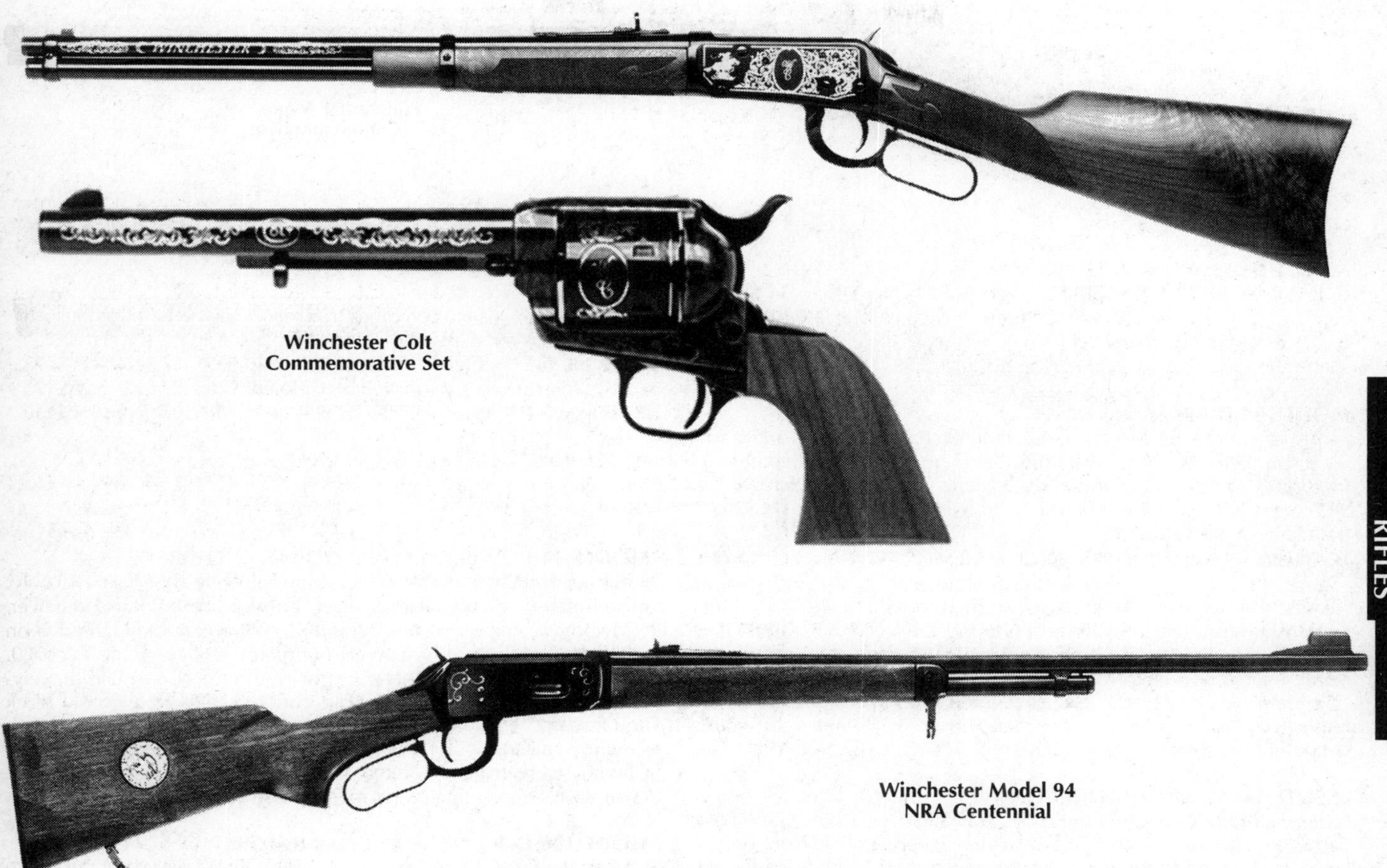

Winchester Colt Commemorative Set

Winchester Model 94 NRA Centennial

RIFLES

MODEL 94 LONE STAR COMMEMORATIVE
Same as Theodore Roosevelt Rifle except yellow-gold plating; "Lone Star" engraving on receiver and bbl., commemorative medallion embedded in buttstock. 30,669 made in 1970.
Rifle or carbine . . . . NiB $613 Ex $496 Gd $348
Matched carbine/rifle set . . . . . . NiB $1462 Ex $1180 Gd $820

MODEL 94 NRA CENTENNIAL MUSKET . . . . NiB $580 Ex $471 Gd $331
Commemorates 100th anniversary of National Rifle Association of America. Standard Model 94 action. Caliber: .30-30. Seven round magazine. 26-inch bbl. Sights: Military folding rear; blade front. Black chrome-finished receiver engraved "NRA 1871–1971" plus scrollwork. Barrel inscribed "NRA Centennial Musket." Musket-style buttstock and full-length forearm; commemorative medallion embedded in buttstock. Weight: 7.13 lbs. Made in 1971.

MODEL 94 NRA CENTENNIAL RIFLE . . . . NiB $613 Ex $493 Gd $345
Same as Model 94 Rifle except has commemorative details as in NRA Centennial Musket (barrel inscribed "NRA Centennial Rifle"); caliber .30-30, 24-inch bbl., QD sling swivels. Made in 1971.

MODEL 94 NRA CENTENNIAL MATCHED SET . . . NiB $1279 Ex $1033 Gd $720
Rifle and musket were offered in sets with consecutive serial numbers. Note: Production figures not available. These rifles offered in Winchester's 1972 catalog.

MODEL 94 NEBRASKA CENTENNIAL COMMEMORATIVE CARBINE . . . . NiB $1811 Ex $1427 Gd $1008
Same as Standard Model 94 Carbine except caliber .30-30 only; gold-plated hammer, loading gate, bbl. band, and buttplate; souvenir medallion embedded in stock, commemorative inscription on bbl. 2,500 made in 1966.

MODEL 94 THEODORE ROOSEVELT COMMEMORATIVE RIFLE/CARBINE
Standard Model 94 action. Caliber: .30-30. Rifle has 6-round half-magazine, 26-inch octagon bbl., weight: 7.5-lb. Carbine has 6-round full magazine, 20-inch bbl., weight: 7-lb. White gold-plated receiver, upper tang, and forend cap; receiver engraved with American Eagle, "26th President 1901–1909," and Roosevelt's signature. Commemorative medallion embedded in buttstock. Saddle ring. Half pistol-grip, contoured lever. 49,505 made in 1969.
Carbine . . . . NiB $580 Ex $471 Gd $331
Rifle. . . . . NiB $613 Ex $496 Gd $348
Matched set. . . . . NiB $1410 Ex $1148 Gd $792

MODEL 94 TEXAS RANGER ASSOCIATION CARBINE . . . . . NiB $3450 Ex $2772 Gd $1917
Same as Texas Ranger Commemorative Model 94 except special edition of 150 carbines, numbered 1 through 150, with hand-checkered full-fancy walnut stock and forearm. Sold only through Texas Ranger Association. Made in 1973.

Winchester Model 100

MODEL 94 TEXAS RANGER COMMEMORATIVE CARBINE. . . . . NiB $997 Ex $805 Gd $560
Same as Standard Model 94 Carbine except caliber .30-30 Win. only, stock and forearm of semi-fancy walnut, replica of Texas Ranger star embedded in buttstock, curved buttplate. 5,000 made in 1973.

MODEL 94 TRAPPER
Same as Winchester Model 94 Carbine except w/16-inch bbl. and weighs 6 lbs. 2 oz. Angle Eject introduced in 1985 also chambered for .357 Mag., .44 Mag. and .45 LC. Made from 1980 to date.
94 Trapper, Top Eject (disc. 1984) . . . . NiB $360 Ex $282 Gd $205
94 Trapper, Angle Eject (.30-30) . . . . NiB $334 Ex $226 Gd $154
.357 Mag., .44 Mag. or .45 LC., add $25

MODEL 94 JOHN WAYNE COMMEMORATIVE CARBINE. . . NiB $1275 Ex $1029 Gd $716
Standard Model 94 action. Caliber: .32-40. 18.5-inch bbl. Receiver is pewter-plated with engraving of Indian attack and cattle drive scenes. Oversized bow on lever. Nickel-silver medallion in buttstock bears a bas-relief portrait of Wayne. Selected American walnut stock with deep-cut checkering. Introduced by U.S. Repeating Arms in 1981.

MODEL 94 WELLS FARGO & CO. COMMEMORATIVE CARBINE. . . . . NiB $711 Ex $576 Gd $403
Same as Standard Model 94 Carbine except .30-30 Win. only; antique silver-finished, engraved receiver; stock and forearm of fancy walnut, checkered, curved buttplate. Nickel-silver stagecoach medallion (inscribed "Wells Fargo & Co. —1852–1977—125 Years") embedded in buttstock. 20,000 made in 1977.

MODEL 94 O. F. WINCHESTER COMMEMORATIVE RIFLE. . . . . NiB $973 Ex $787 Gd $547
Standard Model 94 action. Caliber: .38-55. 24-inch octagonal bbl. Receiver is satin gold-plated with distinctive engravings. Stock and forearm semi-fancy American walnut with high grade checkering.

MODEL 94 WRANGLER CARBINE
Same as standard Model 94 Carbine except w/16-inch bbl., engraved receiver and chambered for .32 Special and .38-55 Win. Angle Eject introduced in 1985 as Wrangler II, also chambered for .30-30 Win., .44 Mag. and .45 LC. Made from 1980-86. Re-introduced in 1992.
94 Wrangler, Top Eject (disc. 1984) . . . . . . NiB $311 Ex $255 Gd $177
94 Wrangler II, Angle Eject (.30-30) . . . . . . NiB $306 Ex $229 Gd $167
.44 Mag. or .45 LC., add $25

MODEL 94 WYOMING DIAMOND JUBILEE COMMEMORATIVE CARBINE . . . . NiB $1985 Ex $1600 Gd $1108
Same as Standard Model 94 Carbine except caliber .30-30 Win. only, receiver engraved and casehardened in colors, brass saddle ring and loading gate, souvenir medallion embedded in buttstock, commemorative inscription on bbl. 1,500 made in 1964.

MODEL 94 ALASKAN PURCHASE CENTENNIAL COMMEMORATIVE CARBINE . . . . NiB $2114 Ex $1703 Gd $1178
Same as Wyoming issue except different medallion and inscription. 1,501 made in 1967.

MODEL 94 XTR BIG BORE
Modified Model 94 action for added strength. Calibers: .307 Win., .356 Win., .375 Win. or .444 Marlin. 20-inch bbl. Six round magazine. Rubber buttpad. Checkered stock and forearm. Weight: 6.5 lbs. Made from 1978 to date.
94 XTR BB, Top Eject (disc. 1984). . . . . NiB $391 Ex $282 Gd $179
94 XTR BB, Angle Eject (intro. 1985) . . . . . NiB $308 Ex $226 Gd $179
.356 Win. or .375 Win., add $150

MODEL 94 XTR LEVER-ACTION RIFLE
Same general specifications as standard M94 and Angle Eject M94 except chambered for .30-30 Win. and 7-30 Waters and has 20- or 24-inch bbl. Weight: 6.5 to 7 lbs. Made from 1978-88 by U.S. Repeating Arms.
94 XTR Top Eject (disc. 1984) . . . . NiB $360 Ex $267 Gd $179
94 XTR Angle Eject (.30-30) . . . . NiB $329 Ex $257 Gd $164
94 XTR Deluxe Angle Eject (.30-30) . . . . . . NiB $411 Ex $329 Gd $221
7-30 Waters, add. $80

MODEL 100 AUTOLOADING RIFLE. . . . . . . NiB $596 Ex $468 Gd $13
Gas-operated semiautomatic. Calibers: .243, .284, .308 Win. Four round clip magazine (3-round in .284). 22-inch bbl. Weight: 7.25 lbs. Sights: Open rear; hooded ramp front. One-piece stock w/pistol grip, basket-weave checkering, grip cap, sling swivels. Made from 1961–73.

MODEL 100 CARBINE . . . . NiB $653 Ex $524 Gd $344
Same as Model 100 Rifle except has 19-inch bbl., plain carbine-style stock and forearm with bbl. band. Weight: 7 lbs. Made from 1967–73.

MODEL 121 DELUXE . . . . NiB $182 Ex $150 Gd $109
Same as Model 121 Standard except has ramp front sight, stock with fluted comb and sling swivels. Made from 1967-73.

MODEL 121 STANDARD BOLT-ACTION SINGLE SHOT. . . . . NiB $175 Ex $145 Gd $105
Caliber: .22 Short, Long, LR. 20.75-inch bbl. Weight: 5 lbs. Sights: Open rear; bead front. Monte Carlo-style stock. Made from 1967–73.

MODEL 121 YOUTH. . . . . NiB $175 Ex $145 Gd $114
Same as Model 121 Standard except has 1.25-inch shorter stock. Made from 1967–73.

MODEL 131 BOLT-ACTION REPEATER. . . . NiB $195 Ex $160 Gd $116
Caliber: .22 Short, Long or LR. Seven round clip magazine. 20.75-inch bbl. Weight: 5 lbs. Sights: Open rear; ramp front. Plain Monte Carlo stock. Made from 1967–73.

MODEL 135 . . . . NiB $182 Ex $150 Gd $109
Same as Model 131 except chambered for .22 WMR cartridge. Magazine holds 5 rounds. Made in 1967.

MODEL 141 BOLT-ACTION TUBULAR REPEATER. . . . . NiB $217 Ex $175 Gd $119
Same as Model 131 except has tubular magazine in buttstock; holds 19 Short, 15 Long, 13 LR. Made from 1967-73.

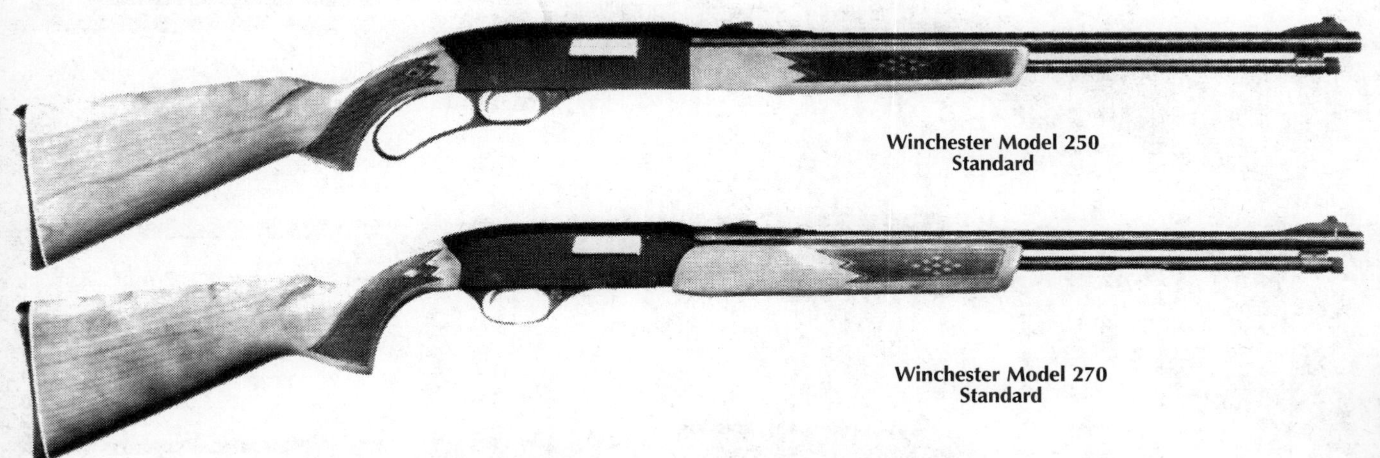

Winchester Model 250 Standard

Winchester Model 270 Standard

MODEL 145 . . . . NiB $206 Ex $175 Gd $119
Same as Model 141 except chambered for .22 WMR; magazine holds 9 rounds. Made in 1967.

MODEL 150 LEVER-ACTION CARBINE . . . . NiB $175 Ex $150 Gd $98
Same as Model 250 except has straight loop lever, plain carbine-style straight-grip stock and forearm with bbl. band. Made from 1967–73.

MODEL 190 CARBINE . . . . NiB $175 Ex $150 Gd $98
Same as Model 190 rifle except has carbine-style forearm with bbl. band. Made from 1967–73.

MODEL 190 SEMIAUTOMATIC RIFLE . . . . NiB $155 Ex $124 Gd $88
Same as current Model 290 except has plain stock and forearm. Made from 1966–78.

MODEL 250 DELUXE RIFLE . . . . . . NiB $253 Ex $201 Gd $124
Same as Model 250 Standard Rifle except has fancy walnut Monte Carlo stock and forearm, sling swivels. Made from 1965–71.

MODEL 250 STANDARD LEVER-ACTION RIFLE . . . . NiB $175 Ex $145 Gd $105
Hammerless. Caliber: .22 Short, Long or LR. Tubular magazine holds 21 Short, 17 Long, 15 LR. 20.5-inch bbl. Sights: Open rear; ramp front. Weight: About 5 lbs. Plain stock and forearm on early production; later model has checkering. Made from 1963–73.

MODEL 255 DELUXE RIFLE . . . . . . NiB $253 Ex $217 Gd $103
Same as Model 250 Deluxe Rifle except chambered for .22 WMR cartridge. Magazine holds 11 rounds. Made 1965–73.

MODEL 255 STANDARD RIFLE. . . . NiB $215 Ex $166 Gd $126
Same as Model 250 Standard Rifle except chambered for .22 WMR cartridge. Magazine holds 11 rounds. Made from 1964–70.

MODEL 270 DELUXE RIFLE . . . . . . NiB $221 Ex $175 Gd $114
Same as Model 270 Standard Rifle except has fancy walnut Monte Carlo stock and forearm. Made from 1965–73.

MODEL 270 STANDARD SLIDE-ACTION RIFLE . . . . NiB $154 Ex $124 Gd $93
Hammerless. Caliber: .22 Short, Long or LR. Tubular magazine holds 21 Short, 17 Long, 15 LR. 20.5-inch bbl. Sights: Open rear; ramp front. Weight: About 5 lbs. Early production had plain walnut stock and forearm (slide handle); latter also furnished in plastic (Cycolac); last model has checkering. Made from 1963–73.

MODEL 275 DELUXE RIFLE . . . . . . NiB $253 Ex $201 Gd $124
Same as Model 270 Deluxe Rifle except chambered for .22 WMR cartridge. Tubular magazine holds 11 rounds. Made 1965–70.

MODEL 275 STANDARD RIFLE . . . . NiB $186 Ex $150 Gd $114
Same as Model 270 Standard Rifle except chambered for .22 WMR cartridge. Magazine holds 11 rounds. Made from 1964–70.

MODEL 290 DELUXE RIFLE . . . . . . NiB $253 Ex $217 Gd $103
Same as Model 290 Standard Rifle except has fancy walnut Monte Carlo stock and forearm. Made from 1965–73.

MODEL 290 STANDARD SEMIAUTOMATIC RIFLE
Caliber: .22 Long or LR. Tubular magazine holds 17 Long, 15 LR. 20.5-inch bbl. Sights: Open rear; ramp front. Weight: About 5 lbs. Plain stock and forearm on early production; current model has checkering. Made from 1963–77.
W/plain stock/forearm . . . . NiB $253 Ex $217 Gd $103
W/checkered stock/forearm . . . . NiB $278 Ex $227 Gd $119

MODEL 310 BOLT-ACTION SINGLE SHOT . . . . NiB $278 Ex $222 Gd $160
Caliber: .22 Short, Long, LR. 22-inch bbl. Weight: 5.63 lbs. Sights: Open rear; ramp front. Monte Carlo stock w/checkered pistol-grip and forearm, sling swivels. Made from 1972–75.

MODEL 320 BOLT-ACTION REPEATER . . . . NiB $325 Ex $283 Gd $180
Same as Model 310 except has 5-round clip magazine. Made from 1972–74.

MODEL 490 SEMIAUTOMATIC RIFLE . . . . NiB $325 Ex $258 Gd $180
Caliber: .22 LR. Five round clip magazine. 22-inch bbl. Weight: 6 lbs. Sights: Folding leaf rear; hooded ramp front. One-piece walnut stock w/checkered pistol grip and forearm. Made from 1975–77.

MODEL 670 BOLT-ACTION SPORTING RIFLE. . . . . NiB $386 Ex $283 Gd $211
Calibers: .225 Win., .243 Win., .270 Win., .30-06, .308 Win. Four round magazine. 22-inch bbl. Weight: 7 lbs. Sights: Open rear; ramp front. Monte Carlo stock w/checkered pistol-grip and forearm. Made from 1967–73.

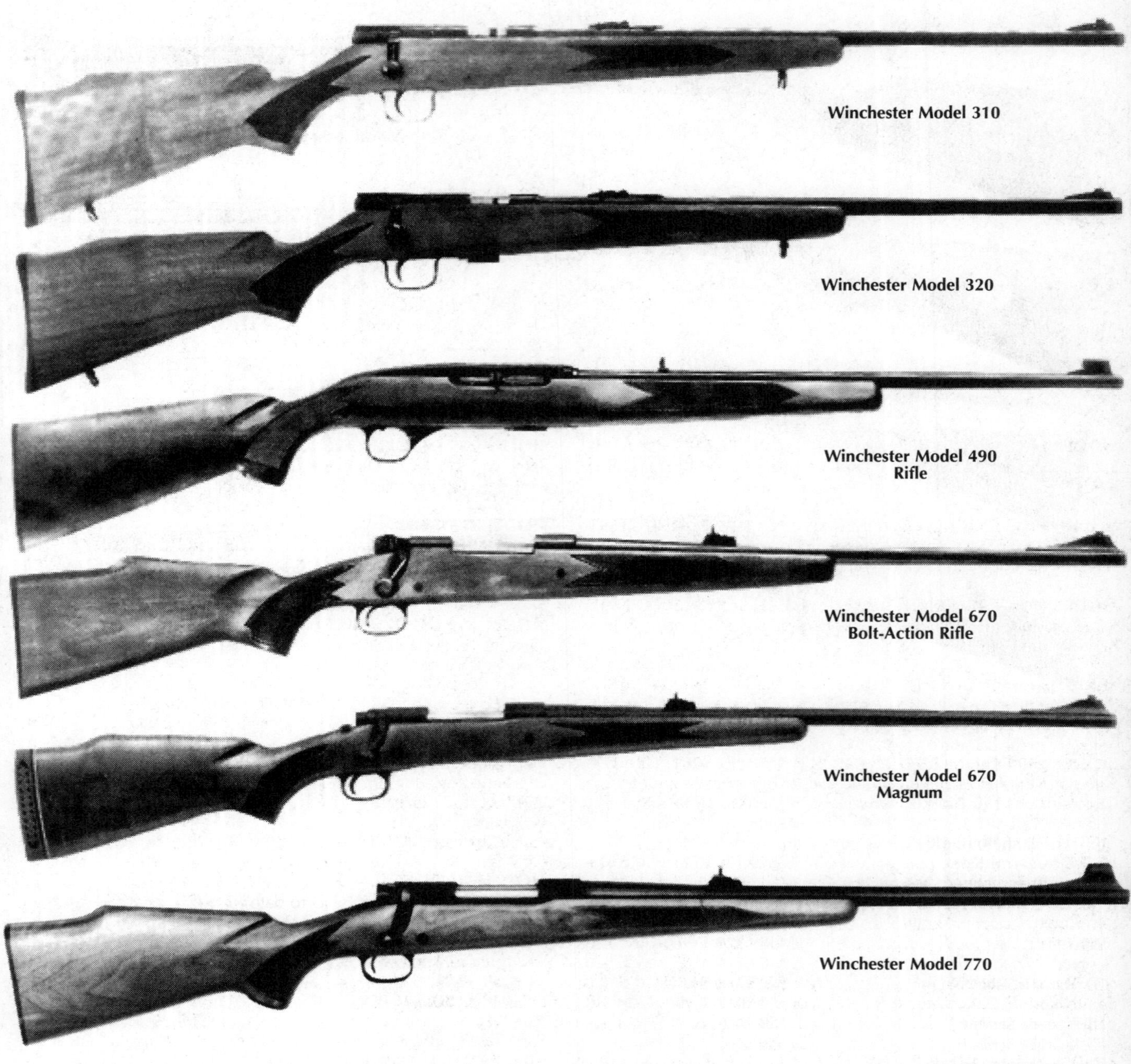

Winchester Model 310

Winchester Model 320

Winchester Model 490 Rifle

Winchester Model 670 Bolt-Action Rifle

Winchester Model 670 Magnum

Winchester Model 770

MODEL 670 CARBINE .... NiB $383 Ex $311 Gd $214
Same as Model 670 Rifle except has 19-inch bbl. Weight: 6.75 lbs. Calibers: .243 Win., .270 Win., .30-06. Made from 1967–70.

MODEL 670 MAGNUM .... NiB $430 Ex $306 Gd $244
Same as Model 670 Rifle except has 24-inch bbl., reinforced stock with recoil pad with slightly different checkering pattern. Weight: 7.25 lbs. Calibers: .264 Win. Mag., 7mm Rem. Mag., .300 Win. Mag. Open rear sight; ramp front sight with hood. Made from 1967–70.

MODEL 770 BOLT-ACTION SPORTING RIFLE.............. NiB $409 Ex $306 Gd $229
Model 70-type action. Calibers: .22-250, .222 Rem., .243, .270 Win., .30-06. Four round box magazine. 22-inch bbl. Sights: Open rear; hooded ramp front. Weight: 7.13 lbs. Monte Carlo stock, checkered pistol-grip and forend; sling swivels. Made from 1969–71.

MODEL 770 MAGNUM .... NiB $435 Ex $358 Gd $280
Same as Standard Model 770 except 24-inch bbl., weight: 7.25 lbs., recoil pad. Calibers: 7mm Rem. Mag., .264 and .300 Win. Mag. Made from 1969–71.

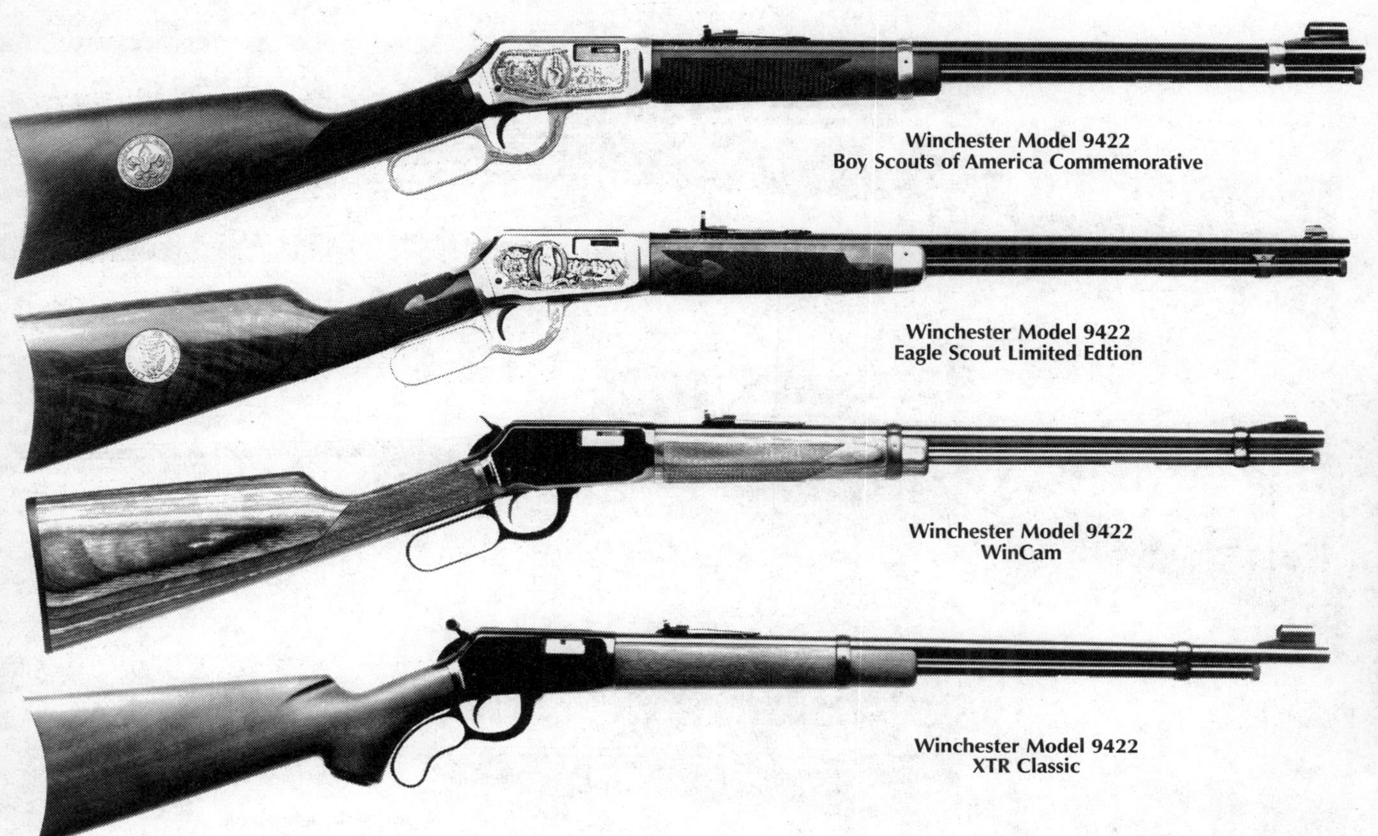

Winchester Model 9422
Boy Scouts of America Commemorative

Winchester Model 9422
Eagle Scout Limited Edtion

Winchester Model 9422
WinCam

Winchester Model 9422
XTR Classic

MODEL 9422 LEVER-ACTION RIMFIRE RIFLES
Similar to the standard Model 94 except chambered for .22 Rimfire. Calibers: .22 Short, Long, LR. (9422) or .22 WMR (9422M). Tubular magazine holds 21 or 15 Short.17 or 12 Long, 15 or 11 LR (9422 or Trapper) or 11 or 8 WRM (9422M or Trapper M). 16.5- or 20.5 inch bbl. 33.125- to 37.125 inches overall. Weight: 5.75 to 6.25 lbs. Open rear sight; hooded ramp front. Carbine-style stock and barrel-band forearm. Stock options: Walnut (Standard), laminated brown (WinTuff), laminated green (WinCam). Made from 1972. Disc.

Walnut (Standard) . . . . **NiB $378 Ex $306 Gd $203**
WinCam . . . . **NiB $383 Ex $311 Gd $208**
WinTuff . . . . **NiB $326 Ex $265 Gd $188**
Legacy . . . . **NiB $414 Ex $358 Gd $203**
Trapper (16.5-inch bbl.) . . . . **NiB $368 Ex $291 Gd $203**
XTR Classic . . . . **NiB $512 Ex $486 Gd $332**
High Grade Series I . . . . **NiB $450 Ex $383 Gd $250**
High Grade Series II . . . . **NiB $409 Ex $306 Gd $229**
25th Anniversary Edition
Grade I(1of 2500) . . . . **NiB $586 Ex $493 Gd $390**
25th Anniversary Edition
High Grade (1of 250) . . . . **NiB $1279 Ex $1052 Gd $743**
Boy Scout
Commemorative (1of 15,000) . . . . **NiB $702 Ex $589 Gd $393**
Eagle Scout
Commemorative (1of 1000) . . . . **NiB $3563 Ex $2868 Gd $1981**
22 WRM, add **10%**

DOUBLE XPRESS RIFLE . . . . **NiB $2905 Ex $2340 Gd $1617**
Over/under double rifle. Caliber: .30-06. 23.5-inch bbl. Weight: 8.5 lbs. Made for Olin Corp. by Olin-Kodensha in Japan. Introduced 1982.

RANGER YOUTH
BOLT-ACTION CARBINE . . . . **NiB $385 Ex $282 Gd $179**
Calibers: .223 (discontinued 1989), .243 Win., and .308 Win. Four and 5-round magazine. Bbl.: 20-inch. Weight: 5.75 lbs. American hardwood stock. Open rear sight. Made from 1985 to date by U.S. Repeating Arms.

RANGER LEVER-ACTION CARBINE . . . . . . **NiB $274 Ex $223 Gd $160**
Caliber: .30-30. Five round tubular magazine. Bbl.: 20-inch round. Weight: 6.5 lbs. American hardwood stock. Economy version of Model 94. Made from 1985 to date by U.S. Repeating Arms.

RANGER BOLT-ACTION CARBINE . . . . **NiB $360 Ex $293 Gd $207**
Calibers: .223 Rem., .243 Win., .270, .30-06, 7mm Rem. (discontinued 1985), Mag. Three and 4-round magazine. Bbl.: 24-inch in 7mm; 22-inch in .270 and .30-06. Open sights. American hardwood stock. Made from 1985 to date by U.S. Repeating Arms.

MODEL 1892 GRADE I LEVER-ACTION RIFLE
Similar to the original Model 1892. Calibers: .357 Mag., .44-40, .44 Mag., .45 LC. 10-round magazine. 24-inch round bbl. Weight: 6.25 lbs. 41.25 inches overall. Bead front sight, adjustable buckhorn rear. Etched receiver and gold trigger. Blue finish. Smooth straight-grip walnut stock and forearm w/ metal grip cap. Made from 1997. Disc.

Standard Rifle . . . . **NiB $724 Ex $636 Gd $374**
Short Rifle w/20-inch bbl.
(.44 Mag. only) . . . . **NiB $599 Ex $487 Gd $344**

MODEL 1892 GRADE
II LEVER-ACTION RIFLE . . . . **NiB $1216 Ex $1060 Gd $669**
Similar to the Grade I Model 1892 except w/gold appointments and receiver game scene. Chambered .45 LC only. Limited production of 1,000 in 1997.

Winslow Commander Grade

Winslow Crown Grade

Winslow Regent Grade
Bushmaster Stock

WINSLOW ARMS COMPANY — Camden, South Carolina

BOLT-ACTION SPORTING RIFLE
Action: FN Supreme Mauser, Mark X Mauser, Remington 700 and 788, Sako, Winchester 70. Standard calibers: .17-222, .17-223, .222 Rem., .22-250, .243 Win., 6mm Rem., .25-06, .257 Roberts, .270 Win., 7x57, .280 Rem., .284 Win., .308 Win., .30-06, .358 Win. Magnum calibers: .17-222 Mag., .257 Wby., .264 Win., .270 Wby., 7mm Rem., 7mm Wby., .300 H&H, .300 Wby., .300 Win., .308 Norma, 8mm Rem., .338 Win., .358 Norma, .375 H&H, .375 Wby., .458 Win. Three-round magazine in standard calibers, 2-round in magnum. 24-inch barrel in standard calibers, 26-inch in magnum. Weight: With 24-inch bbl., 7 to 7.5 lbs.; with 26-inch bbl., 8 to 9 lbs. No sights. Stocks: "Bushmaster" with slender pistol-grip and beavertail forearm, "Plainsmaster" with full curl pistol-grip and flat forearm; both styles have Monte Carlo cheekpiece. Values shown are for basic rifle in each grade; extras such as special fancy wood, more elaborate carving, inlays and engraving can increase these figures considerably. Made from 1962–89.

Commander Grade . . . . **NiB $550 Ex $524 Gd $380**
Regal Grade. . . . . **NiB $668 Ex $643 Gd $447**
Regent Grade. . . . . **NiB $807 Ex $704 Gd $519**
Regimental Grade . . . . **NiB $955 Ex $792 Gd $663**
Crown Grade. . . . . **NiB $1501 Ex $1295 Gd $837**
Royal Grade. . . . . **NiB $1707 Ex $1501 Gd $1140**
Imperial Grade. . . . . **NiB $3715 Ex $3200 Gd $2376**
Emperor Grade . . . . **NiB $6790 Ex $6066 Gd $4310**

ZEPHYR DOUBLE RIFLES Manufactured by Victor Sarasqueta Company — Eibar, Spain

DOUBLE RIFLE. . . . . **NiB $21,025 Ex $16,900 Gd $11,625**
Boxlock. Calibers: Available in practically every caliber from .22 Hornet to .505 Gibbs. Bbls.: 22 to 28 inches standard, but any lengths were available on special order. Weight: 7 lbs. for the smaller calibers up to 12 or more lbs. for the larger calibers. Imported by Stoeger from about 1938 to 1951.

30th Edition

GUN TRADER'S GUIDE

Shotguns

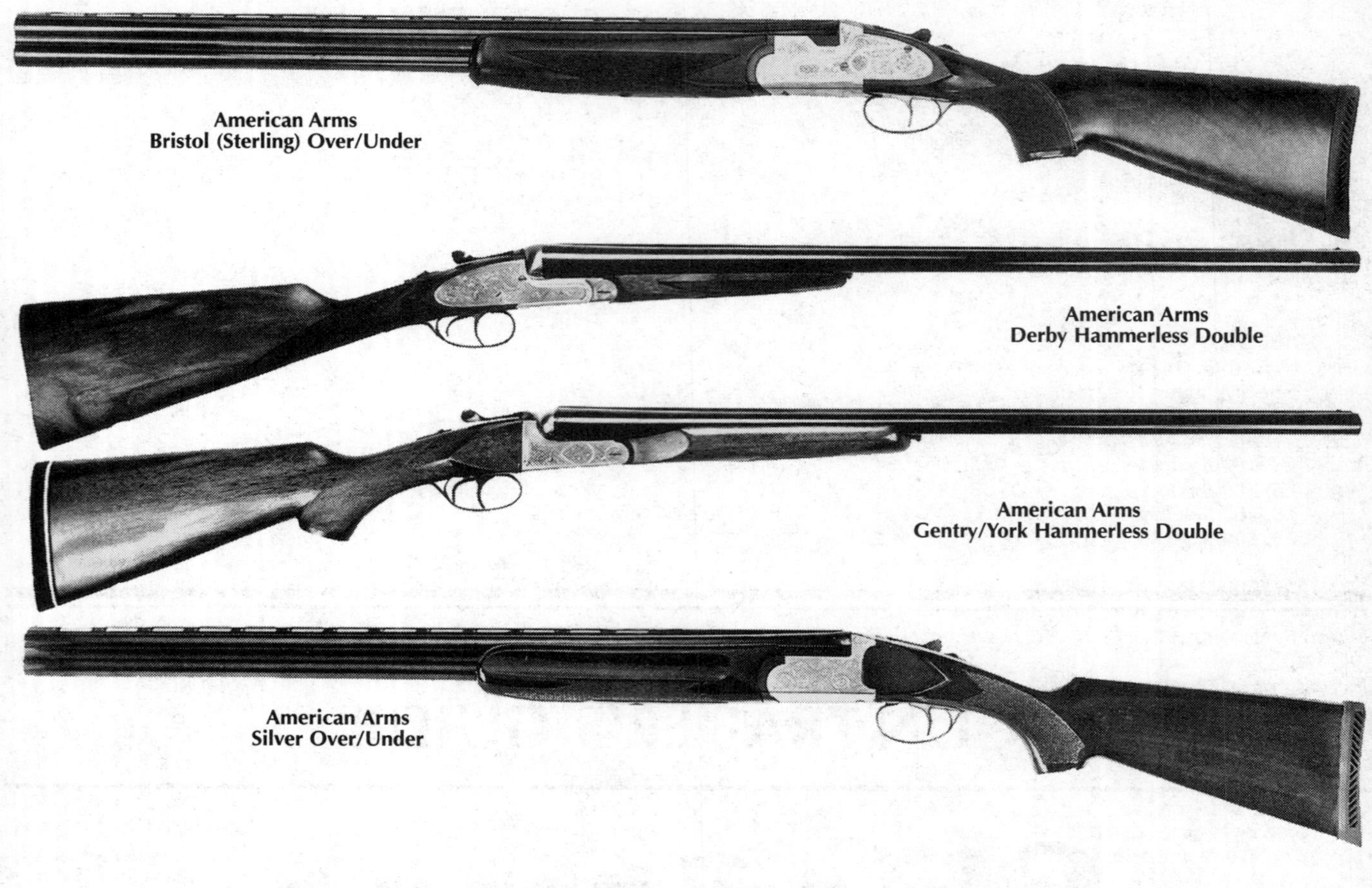

American Arms
Bristol (Sterling) Over/Under

American Arms
Derby Hammerless Double

American Arms
Gentry/York Hammerless Double

American Arms
Silver Over/Under

American Arms
Camper Special

ALDENS SHOTGUN — Chicago, Illinois

MODEL 670 CHIEFTAIN SLIDE ACTION . . NiB $238 Ex $204 Gd $139
Hammerless. Gauges: 12, 20 and others. Three round tubular magazine. Bbl.: 26- to 30-inch; various chokes. Weight: 6.25 to 7.5 lbs. depending on bbl. length and ga. Walnut-finished hardwood stock.

AMERICAN ARMS — N. Kansas City, Missouri

See also Franchi Shotguns.

BRISTOL (STERLING) O/U . . . . NiB $767 Ex $575 Gd $441
Boxlock w/Greener crossbolt and engraved sideplates. Single selective trigger. Selective automatic ejectors. Gauges: 12, 20; 3-inch chambers. 26-, 28-, 30-, or 32-inch vent-rib bbls. w/screw-in choke tubes (Improved Cylinder/Modified/Full). Weight: 7 lbs. Antique-silver receiver w/game scene or scroll engraving. Checkered full pistol-grip-style buttstock and forearm w/high-gloss finish. Imported 1986-88 with the model designation Bristol; redesignated Sterling 1989-90.

BRITTANY HAMMERLESS DOUBLE . . . . . . NiB $762 Ex $629 Gd $441
Boxlock w/engraved case-colored receiver. Single selective trigger. Selective automatic ejectors. Gauges: 12, 20. 3-inch chambers. Bbls.: 25- or 27-inch w/screw-in choke tubes (IC/M/F). Weight: 6.5 lbs. (20 ga.). Checkered English-style walnut stock w/semi-beavertail forearm or pistol-grip stock w/high-gloss finish. Imported 1989-2000.

CAMPER SPECIAL . . . . NiB $128 Ex $107 Gd $79
Similar to the Single Barrel except takedown model w/21-inch bbl., M choke and pistol-grip stock. Made in 1989 only.

COMBO . . . . NiB $218 Ex $178 Gd $127
Similar to the Single-Barrel model except available w/interchangeable rifle and shotgun bbls. .22 LR/20-ga. shotgun or .22 Hornet/12-ga. shotgun. Rifle bbl. has adj. rear sights; blade-type front sight. Made in 1989.

DERBY HAMMERLESS DOUBLE
Sidelock w/engraved sideplates. Single non-selective or double triggers. Selective automatic ejectors. Gauges: 12, 20, 28 and .410. 3 inch chambers. Bbls.: 26-inch (IC/M) or 28-inch (M/F). Weight: 6 lbs. (20 ga.). Checkered English-style walnut stock and splinter forearm w/hand-rubbed oil finish. Engraved frame/sideplates w/antique silver finish. Imported 1986-94.
12 or 20 ga. . . . . NiB $961 Ex $833 Gd $527
28 or .410 ga. (disc. 1991) . . . . . . NiB $1025 Ex $833 Gd $588

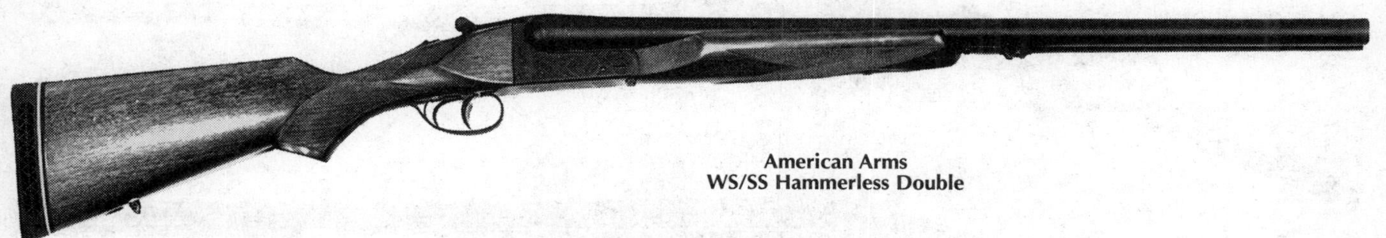

American Arms
WS/SS Hammerless Double

F.S. SERIES O/U
Greener crossbolt in Trap and Skeet configuration. Single selective trigger. Selective automatic ejectors. 12 gauge only. 26-, 28-, 30-, or 32-inch separated bbls. Weight: 6.5 to 7.25 lbs. Black or chrome receiver. Checkered walnut buttstock and forearm. Imported 1986-87.
Model F.S. 200 Boxlock . . . . NiB $761 Ex $618 Gd $440
Model F.S. 300 Boxlock . . . . NiB $899 Ex $746 Gd $542
Model F.S. 400 Sidelock . . . . NiB $1265 Ex $1061 Gd $755
Model F.S. 500 Sidelock . . . . NiB $1265 Ex $1061 Gd $755

GENTRY/YORK HAMMERLESS DOUBLE
Chrome, coin-silver or color casehardened boxlock receiver w/scroll engraving. Double triggers. Extractors. Gauges: 12, 16, 20, 28, .410. 3-inch chambers (16 and 28 have 2.75-inch). Bbls.: 26-inch (IC/M) or 28-inch (M/F, 12, 16 and 20). Weight: 6.75 lbs. (12 ga.). Checkered walnut buttstock w/pistol-grip and beavertail forearm; both w/semi-gloss oil finish. Imported as York from 1986-88, redesignated Gentry 1989-2000.
Gentry 12, or 16 or 20 ga. . . . . NiB $691 Ex $512 Gd $359
Gentry 28 or .410 ga. . . . . NiB $752 Ex $614 Gd $451
York 12, 16 or 20 ga. (disc. 1988) . . . . NiB $557 Ex $456 Gd $327
York 28 or .410 ga. (disc. 1988) . . . . NiB $659 Ex $538 Gd $382

GRULLA #2 HAMMERLESS DOUBLE
True sidelock w/engraved detachable sideplates. Double triggers. Extractors and cocking indicators. Gauges: 12, 20, .410 w/3-inch chambers; 28 w/2.75-inch. 26-inch bbl. Imported 1989-2000.
Standard model . . . . NiB $3341 Ex $2705 Gd $1891
Two-bbl. set (disc. 1995) . . . . . . NiB $4304 Ex $3475 Gd $2414

SILVER I O/U
Boxlock. Single selective trigger. Extractors. Gauges: 12, 20 and .410 w/3-inch chambers; 28 w/2.75 inch. Bbls.: 26-inch (IC/M), 28-inch (M/F, 12 and 20 ga. only). Weight: 6.75 lbs. (12 ga.). Checkered walnut stock and forearm. Antique-silver receiver w/scroll engraving. Imported 1987-2000.
12 or 20 ga. . . . . NiB $586 Ex $483 Gd $331
28 or .410 ga. . . . . NiB $624 Ex $509 Gd $362

SILVER II O/U
Similar to Model Silver I except w/selective automatic ejectors and 26-inch bbls. w/screw-in tubes (12 and 20 ga.). Fixed chokes (28 and .410). Made 1987-2000.
12 or 20 ga . . . . NiB $724 Ex $591 Gd $419
28 or .410 ga. . . . . NiB $788 Ex $642 Gd $454
Upland Lite II . . . . NiB $873 Ex $711 Gd $504
Two-bbl. set . . . . NiB $1117 Ex $907 Gd $637

SILVER LITE O/U
Similar to Model Silver II except w/blued, engraved alloy receiver. Available in 12 and 20 ga. only. Imported from 1990-92.
Standard Model . . . . NiB $734 Ex $616 Gd $463
Two-bbl. Set . . . . NiB $1147 Ex $929 Gd $652

SILVER SKEET/TRAP. . . . . NiB $886 Ex $720 Gd $509
Similar to the Silver II Model except has 28-inch (Skeet) or 30-inch (Trap) ported bbls. w/target-style rib and mid-bead sight. Imported 1992-94.

SILVER SPORTING O/U . . . . NiB $899 Ex $761 Gd $508
Boxlock. Single selective trigger. Selective automatic ejectors. Gauges: 12, 2.75-inch chambers. 28-inch bbls.w/Franchoke tubes (SK, IC, M and F). Weight: 7.5 lbs. Checkered walnut stock and forearm. Special broadway rib and vented side ribs. Engraved receiver w/chrome-nickel finish. Imported from 1990-2000.

SINGLE-SHOT SHOTGUN
Break-open action. Gauges: 10 (3.5), 12, 20, .410, 3-inch chamber. Weight: about 6.5 lbs. Bead front sight. Walnut-finished hardwood stock w/checkered grip and forend. Made from 1988 to 1990.
10 ga. (3.5-inch) . . . . NiB $154 Ex $128 Gd $95
12, 20 or .410 ga. . . . . NiB $134 Ex $113 Gd $85
Multi-choke bbl., add $30

SLUGGER SINGLE-SHOT SHOTGUN. . . . . . NiB $147 Ex $123 Gd $92
Similar to the Single-Shot model except in 12 and 20 ga. only w/24-inch slug bbl. Rifle-type sights and recoil pad. Made from 1989 to 1990.

TS/OU 12 SHOTGUN. . . . . NiB $766 Ex $639 Gd $450
Turkey Special. Boxlock. Single selective trigger. Selective automatic ejectors. Gauge: 12, 3.5-inch chambers. Bbls.: 24-inch O/U w/screw-in choke tubes (IC, M, F). Weight: 6 lbs. 15 oz. Checkered European walnut stock and beavertail forearm. Matte blue metal finish. Imported 1987-2000.

TS/SS 10 HAMMERLESS DOUBLE . . . . NiB $721 Ex $588 Gd $436
Turkey Special. Same general specifications as Model WS/ SS 10, except w/26-inch side-by-side bbls., screw-in choke tubes (F/F) and chambered for 10-ga. 3.5-inch shells. Weight: 10 lbs., 13 oz. Imported 1987 to 1993.

TS/SS 12 HAMMERLESS DOUBLE . . . . NiB $662 Ex $560 Gd $382
Same general specifications as Model WS/SS 10 except in 12 ga. w/26-inch side-by-side bbls. and 3 screw-in choke tubes (IC/M/F). Weight: 7 lbs., 6 oz. Imported 1987-2000.

WS/OU 12 SHOTGUN . . . . NiB $698 Ex $560 Gd $392
Waterfowl Special. Boxlock. Single selective trigger. Selective automatic ejectors. Gauge: 12; 3.5-inch chambers. Bbls.: 28-inch O/U w/screw-in tubes (IC/M/F). Weight: 7 lbs. Checkered European walnut stock and beavertail forearm. Matte blue metal finish. Imported 1987-2000.

WS/SS 10 HAMMERLESS DOUBLE. . . . . . NiB $766 Ex $639 Gd $440
Waterfowl Special. Boxlock. Double triggers. Extractors. Gauge: 10; 3.5-inch chambers. Bbls.: 32-inch side/side choked F/F. Weight: About 11 lbs. Checkered walnut stock and beavertail forearm w/satin finish. Parkerized metal finish. Imported from 1987-1995.

Armalite AR-17 Golden Gun

Armsport 1050

Armsport 1125

WT/OU 10 Shotgun .... **NiB $980 Ex $802 Gd $562**
Same general specifications as Model WS/OU 12 except chambered for 10-ga. 3.5-inch shells. Extractors. Satin wood finish and matte blue metal. Imported 1987-2000.

ARMALITE, INC. — Costa Mesa, California

AR-17 GOLDEN GUN............ **NiB $738 Ex $560 Gd $438**
Recoil-operated semiautomatic. High-test aluminum bbl. and receiver housing. 12 ga. only. Two round capacity. 24-inch bbl. w/interchangeable choke tubes: IC/M/F. Weight: 5.6 lbs. Polycarbonate stock and forearm recoil pad. Gold-anodized finish standard, also made w/black finish. Made 1964-65. Fewer than 2,000 produced.

ARMSCOR (Arms Corp.) — Manila, Philippines, *Imported until 1991 by Armscor Precision, San Mateo, CA; 1991-95 by Ruko Products, Inc., Buffalo NY: Currently imported by K.B.I., Harrisburg, PA*

MODEL M-30 FIELD PUMP SHOTGUN
Double slide-action bars w/damascened bolt. Gauge: 12 only w/3-inch chamber. Bbl.: 28-inch w/fixed chokes or choke tubes. Weight: 7.6 lbs. Walnut or walnut finished hardwood stock.
Model M30-F (w/hard-
wood stock and fixed chokes) ..... **NiB $255 Ex $205 Gd $118**
Model M-30F (w/hard-
wood stock and choke tubes) ..... **NiB $281 Ex $210 Gd $123**
Model M-30F/IC (w/walnut
stock and choke tubes) .... **NiB $291 Ex $215 Gd $128**

MODEL M-30 RIOT PUMP
Double-action slide bar w/damascened bolt. Gauge: 12 only w/3-inch chamber. Bbls: 18.5 and 20-inch w/IC bore. Five- or 7-round magazine. Weight: 7 lbs, 2 ozs. Walnut finished hardwood stock.
Model M-30R6 (5-round magazine) ...... **NiB $199 Ex $173 Gd $120**
Model M-30R8 (7-round magazine) ...... **NiB $209 Ex $183 Gd $122**

MODEL M-30 SPECIAL COMBO
Simlar to Special Purpose Model except has detachable synthetic stock that removes to convert to pistol-grip configuration.
Model M-30C (disc. 1995) .... **NiB $237 Ex $202 Gd $145**
Model M-30RP (disc. 1995) ..... **NiB $246 Ex $202 Gd $144**

MODEL M-30 SPECIAL PURPOSE
Double-action slide bar w/damascened bolt. Seven round magazine. Gauge: 12 only w/3-inch chamber. 20-inch bbl. w/cylinder choke. Iron sights (DG Model) or venter handguard (SAS Model). Weight: 7.5 lbs. Walnut finished hardwood stock.
Model M-30DG (Deer Gun) .... **NiB $233 Ex $193 Gd $139**
Model M-30SAS (Special Air Services) .... **NiB $261 Ex $214 Gd $184**

ARMSPORT, INC. — Miami, Florida

1000 SERIES HAMMERLESS DOUBLES
Side-by-side w/engraved receiver, double triggers and extractors. Gauges: 10 (3.5), 12, 20, .410- 3-inch chambers. Model 1033: 10 ga., 32-inch bbl. Model 1050/51: 12 ga., 28-inch bbl., M/F choke. Model 1052/53: 20 ga., 26-inch bbl., I/M choke. Model 1054/57: .410 ga., 26-inch bbl., I/M. Model 1055: 28 ga., Weight: 5.75 to 7.25 lbs. European walnut buttstock and forend. Made in Italy. Importation disc. 1993.
Model 1033 (10 ga. disc. 1989) ...... **NiB $781 Ex $635 Gd $445**
Model 1050 (12 ga. disc. 1993) ...... **NiB $697 Ex $648 Gd $427**
Model 1051 (12 ga. disc. 1985) ...... **NiB $457 Ex $374 Gd $269**
Model 1052 (20 ga. disc. 1985) ...... **NiB $429 Ex $352 Gd $253**
Model 1053 (20 ga. disc. 1993) ...... **NiB $740 Ex $602 Gd $423**
Model 1054 (.410 disc. 1992)........ **NiB $817 Ex $663 Gd $465**
Model 1055 (28 ga. disc. 1992) ...... **NiB $499 Ex $408 Gd $292**
Model 1057 (.410 disc. 1985)........ **NiB $535 Ex $437 Gd $310**

MODEL 1125 SINGLE-SHOT SHOTGUN ...... **NiB $110 Ex $95 Gd $69**
Bottom-opening lever. Gauges: 12, 20. 3-inch chambers. Bead front sight. Plain stock and forend. Imported 1987-89.

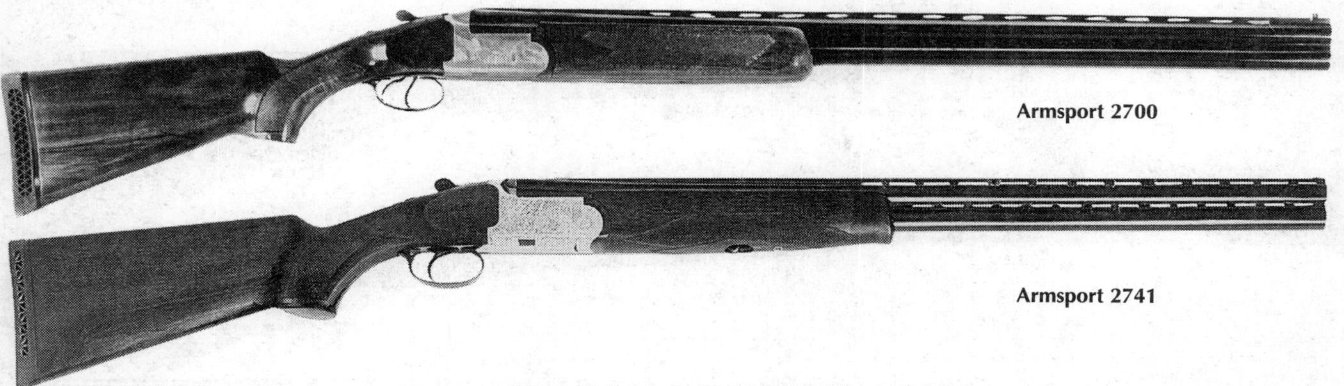

Armsport 2700

Armsport 2741

MODEL 2700 GOOSE GUN
Similar to the 2700 Standard Model except 10 ga. w/3.5-inch chambers. Double triggers w/28-inch bbl. choked IC/M or 32-inch bbl., F/F. 12mm wide vent rib. Weight: 9.5 lbs. Canada geese engraved on receiver. Antiqued silver-finished action. Checkered European walnut stock w/rubber recoil pad. Imported from Italy 1986 to 1993.
W/fixed chokes . . . . NiB $1047 Ex $843 Gd $578
W/choke tubes . . . . NiB $1329 Ex $919 Gd $639

MODEL 2700 OVER/UNDER SERIES
Hammerless, takedown shotgun w/engraved receiver. Selective single or double triggers. Gauges: 10, 12, 20, 28 and .410. Bbl.: 26-or 28-inch w/fixed chokes or choke tubes. Weight: 8 lbs. Checkered European walnut buttstock and forend. Made in Italy. Importation disc. 1993.
Model 2701 12 ga. (disc. 1985) . . . . NiB $546 Ex $445 Gd $316
Model 2702 12 ga. NiB $584 Ex $476 Gd $337
Model 2703 20 ga. (disc. 1985) . . . . NiB $571 Ex $465 Gd $330
Model 2704 20 ga. NiB $616 Ex $501 Gd $354
Model 2705 (.410, DT, fixed chokes) . . . . . NiB $716 Ex $583 Gd $411
Model 2730/31 (Boss-style action,
SST Choke tubes) . . . . NiB $806 Ex $657 Gd $460
Model 2733/35 (Boss-style
action, extractors) . . . . NiB $749 Ex $608 Gd $428
Model 2741 (Boss-style
action, ejectors) . . . . NiB $653 Ex $532 Gd $376
Model 2742 Sporting Clays
(12 ga./choke tubes) . . . . NiB $780 Ex $634 Gd $446
Model 2744 Sporting Clays
(20 ga./choke tubes) . . . . NiB $793 Ex $634 Gd $453
Model 2750 Sporting Clays
(12 ga./sideplates) . . . . NiB $848 Ex $689 Gd $485
Model 2751 Sporting Clays
(20 ga./sideplates) . . . . NiB $880 Ex $714 Gd $493

MODEL 2755 SLIDE-ACTION SHOTGUN
Gauge: 12 w/3-inch chamber. Tubular magazine. Bbls.: 28- or 30-inch w/fixed choke or choke tubes. Weight: 7 lbs. European walnut stock. Made in Italy 1986-87.
Standard model, fixed choke . . . . . . NiB $366 Ex $315 Gd $207
Standard model, choke tubes . . . . . NiB $544 Ex $432 Gd $309
Police model, 20-inch bbl.. . . . . NiB $335 Ex $289 Gd $197

MODEL 2900 TRI-BARREL (TRILLING) SHOTGUN
Boxlock. Double triggers w/top-tang bbl. selector. Extractors. Gauge: 12; 3-inch chambers. Bbls.: 28-inch (IC, M and F). Weight: 7.75 lbs. Checkered European walnut stock and forearm. Engraved silver receiver. Imported 1986-87 and 1990-93.
Model 2900 (fixed chokes) . . . . NiB $2188 Ex $1775 Gd $1244
Model 2900 (choke tubes). . . . . NiB $2916 Ex $2356 Gd $1640
Deluxe grades, add $500

ARRIETA, S.L. — Elgoibar, Spain
Imported by New England Arms Corp., Wingshooting Adventures Quality Arms, Griffin & Howe and Orvis.

Custom double-barreled shotguns with frames scaled to individual gauges. Standard guages are 12 and 16 gauge. Add: 5% for small gauges (20, 24, 28, 32 and .410 bore) on currently manufactured models; $900 for single trigger (most actions); 5% for matched pairs; 10% for rounded action on standard models; extra bbls., add $1375 to $2000 per set.

MODEL 557 STANDARD
Gauges: 12, 16 or 20. Demi-Bloc steel barrels, detachable engraved sidelocks, double triggers, ejectors **. NiB $3155 Ex $1655 Gd $1005**

MODEL 570 LIEJA
Gauges: 12, 16 or 20. Non-detachable sidelocks.
. . . . . NiB $3905 Ex $1980 Gd $1180

MODEL 578 VICTORIA
Gauges: 12, 16 or 20. Similar to Model 570 but with fine English scrollwork. . . . . **NiB $4200 Ex $2225 Gd $1240**

LIGERA MODEL
Available in all gauges. Lightweight 12 ga. has 2-inch chambers, lightweight or standard action. Includes unique frame engraving and Turkish wood upgrade. Wt. appox. 6 pounds
. . . . . NiB $5465 Ex $4090 Gd $2940

MODEL 590 REGINA
Gauges: 12, 16 or 20. Similar to Model 570 but has more elaborate engraving. . . . . **NiB $3395 Ex $3020 Gd $2095**

MODEL 595 PRINCIPE
Available in all gauges, sidelock, engraved hunting scenes, ejectors,double triggers. . . . . **NiB $5415 Ex $4175 Gd $3265**

MODEL 600 IMPERIAL
Gauges: 12, 16 or 20. Self-opening action, very ornate engraving throughout. . . . . **NiB $4615 Ex $3740 Gd $2415**

MODEL 601 IMPERIAL TYRO
Available in all gauges, sidelock, nickel plating, ejectors,single selective trigger, border engraving. . . . . **NiB $6655 Ex $3830 Gd $3055**

MODEL 801
Available in all gauges, detachable sidelocks, ejectors,coin-wash finish, Churchill-style engraving. **NiB $8265 Ex $6815 Gd $5540**

SHOTGUNS

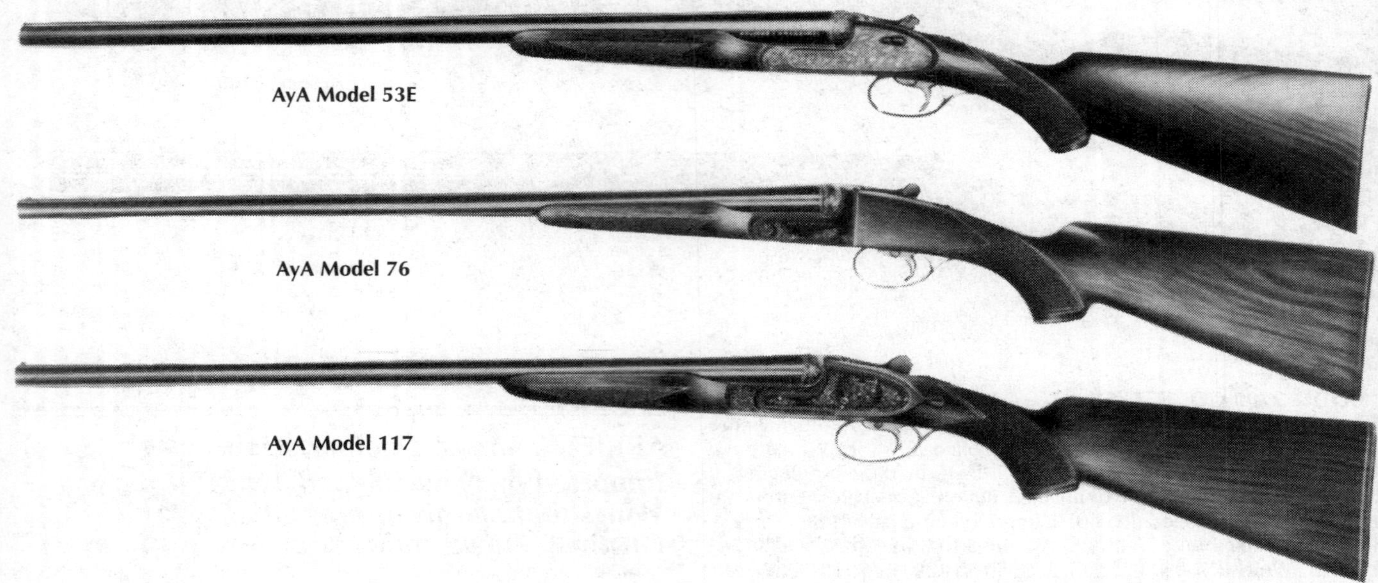
AyA Model 53E

AyA Model 76

AyA Model 117

MODEL 802
Gauges: 12, 16 or 20. Similar to Model 801 except with non-detachable sidelocks, finest Holland-style engraving.
. . . . **NiB $8505 Ex $7030 Gd $5480**

BOSS ROUND BODY
Available in all gauges, Boss pattern best quality engraving, wood upgrade.. . . . . **NiB $9795 Ex $7520 Gd $6265**

MODEL 803
Available in all gauges. Similar to Model 801 except finest Purdey-style engraving. . . . . **NiB $6495 Ex $5115 Gd $3815**

MODEL 871 . . . . **NiB $4777 Ex $4027 Gd $2477**
Available in all gauges. Rounded frame sidelock action with Demi-Bloc barrels, scroll engraving, ejectors,double triggers. . . . .

MODEL 871 EXTRA FINISH
Similar to Model 871 except with standard game scene engraving with woodcock and ruffed grouse. . . . . . **NiB $6020 Ex $4595 Gd $3795**

RENAISSANCE MODEL
Available in all gauges. Best quality sidelock, custom engraving, wood upgrade, manufactured in Spain in made in Italy. Prices range from $8,000 to $17,000 depending on engraving and wood options.

MODEL 872
Available in all gauges, rounded frame sidelock action, Demi-Bloc barrels, elaborate scroll engraving with third lever fastener.
. . . . **NiB $11,275 Ex $9225 Gd $6100**

MODEL 873
Available in all gauges. Sidelock, gold line engraved action, ejectors, single selective trigger. . . . . **NiB $7800 Ex $4920 Gd $3600**

MODEL 874
Available in all gauges. Sidelock, gold line engraved action, Demi-Bloc barrels.. . . . . **NiB $8375 Ex $6115 Gd $4900**

MODEL 875
Available in all gauges. Custom model built to individual specifications only, elaborate engraving, gold inlays
. . . . **NiB $14,000 Ex $11,975 Gd $9600**

MODEL 931
Available in all gauges. Self-opening action, elaborate engraving, H&H selective ejectors. . . . . **NiB $14,995 Ex $12,595 Gd $9650**

ASTRA SHOTGUNS — Guernica, Spain Manufactured by Unceta y Compania

MODEL 650 O/U SHOTGUN
Hammerless, takedown w/double triggers. 12 ga. w/.75-inch chambers. Bbls.: 28-inch (M/F or SK/SK); 30-inch (M/F). Weight: 6.75 lbs. Checkered European walnut buttstock and forend. Disc. 1987.
W/extractors . . . . NiB $622 Ex $495 Gd $367
W/ejectors . . . . NiB $750 Ex $612 Gd $418

MODEL 750 O/U SHOTGUN
Similar to the Model 650 except w/selective single trigger and ejectors. Made in field, skeet and trap configurations from1980. Disc. 1987.
Field model w/extractors. . . . . NiB $701 Ex $575 Gd $412
Field model w/ejectors . . . . NiB $824 Ex $672 Gd $478
Trap or Skeet . . . . NiB $951 Ex $774 Gd $547

AYA (Aguirre Y Aranzabal) — Eibar, Spain (Previously Mfd. by Diarm, *Imported by Armes De Chasse, Hertford, NC*

MODEL 1
HAMMERLESS DOUBLE
A Holland & Holland sidelock similar to the Model 2 except in 12 and 20 ga. only, w/special engraving and exhibition-grade wood. Weight: 5-8 lbs., depending on ga. Imported by Diarm until 1987, since 1992 by Armes de Chasse.
Model 1 Standard . . . . NiB $6688 Ex $3277 Gd $2034
Model 1 Deluxe. . . . . NiB $8170 Ex $3802 Gd $2242
Extra set of bbls., add $2550

AyA Matador II

AyA Model XXV Boxlock

MODEL 2
HAMMERLESS DOUBLE
Sidelock action w/selective single or double triggers automatic ejectors and safety. Gauges: 12, 20, 28, (2.75-inch chambers); .410 (3-inch chambers). Bbls.: 26- or 28-inch w/various fixed choke combinations. Weight: 7 lbs. (12 ga.). English-style straight walnut buttstock and splinter forend. Imported by Diarm until 1987, since 1992 by Armes de Chasse.
12 or 20 ga. w/double triggers . NiB $3167 Ex $1664 Gd $1300
12 or 20 ga. w/single trigger . . . NiB $3224 Ex $2496 Gd $1399
28 or .410 ga. w/double triggers NiB $3250 Ex $2501 Gd $1430
28 or .410 ga. w/single trigger . NiB $3276 Ex $2635 Gd $1430
Extra set of bbls., add $1325

MODEL 4
HAMMERLESS DOUBLE
Lightweight Anson & Deely boxlock, scalloped frame. Gauges: 12, 16, 20, 28, and .410. Bbls.: 25- to 28-inch w/concave rib. Importation disc. 1987 and resumed in 1992 by Armes de Chasse.
12 ga. . . . . NiB $1308 Ex $1255 Gd $631
16 ga. (early importation) . . . . NiB $719 Ex $595 Gd $437
20 ga. . . . . NiB $985 Ex $803 Gd $569
28 ga. . . . . NiB $1120 Ex $886 Gd $548
.410 ga. NiB $1125 Ex $886 Gd $574
Deluxe grades, add $500

MODEL 37 SUPER
O/U SHOTGUN . . . . NiB $3529 Ex $2854 Gd $1991
Sidelock. automatic ejectors. Selective single trigger. Made in all gauges, bbl. lengths and chokes. Vent rib bbls. Elaborately engraved. Checkered stock (w/straight or pistol grip) and forend. Disc. 1995.

MODEL 37 SUPER A
O/U SHOTGUN . . . . NiB $6143 Ex $4949 Gd $3420
Similar to the Standard Model 37 Super except has nickel steel frame and is fitted w/detachable sidelocks engraved w/game scenes. Importation disc. 1987 and resumed 1992 by Armes de Chasse. Disc.

MODEL 53E. . . . . NiB $2446 Ex $1979 Gd $1382
Same general specifications as Model 117 except more elaborate engraving and select figured wood. Importation disc. 1987 and resumed in 1992 by Armes de Chasse.

MODEL 56 HAMMERLESS DOUBLE
Pigeon weight Holland & Holland sidelock w/Purdey-style third lug and sideclips. Gauges: 12, 16, 20. Receiver has fine-line scroll and rosette engraving; gold-plated locks. Importation disc. 1987 and resumed 1992 by Armes de Chasse.
12 ga. . . . . NiB $7574 Ex $3674 Gd $3102
16 ga. (early importation) . . . . . NiB $6950 Ex $2530 Gd $1781
20 ga. (early importation). . . . . NiB $7730 Ex $3804 Gd $2374

MODEL 76 HAMMERLESS DOUBLE . . NiB $876 Ex $732 Gd $449
Anson & Deeley boxlock. Auto ejectors. Selective single trigger. Gauges: 12, 20 (3-inch). Bbls.: 26-, 28-, 30-inch (latter in 12 ga. only), any standard choke combination. Checkered pistol-grip stock/beavertail forend. Disc.

MODEL 76—.410 GA.. . . . . NiB $900 Ex $730 Gd $514
Same general specifications as 12 and 20 ga. Model 76 except chambered for 3-inch shells in .410, has extractors, double triggers, 26-inch bbls. only, English-style stock w/straight grip and small forend. Disc.

MODEL 117 HAMMERLESS DOUBLE. NiB $1005 Ex $817 Gd $576
Holland & Holland-type sidelocks, hand-detachable. Engraved action. Automatic ejectors. Selective single trigger. Gauges: 12, 20 (3-inch). Bbls.: 26-, 27-, 28-, 30-inch; 27- and 30-inch in 12 ga. only; any standard choke combination. Checkered pistol-grip stock and beavertail forend of select walnut. Manufactured in 1985.

BOLERO . . . . NiB $530 Ex $440 Gd $320
Same general specifications as Matador except non-selective single trigger and extractors. Gauges: 12 16, 20, 20 Magnum (3-inch), .410 (3-inch). Note: This model, prior to 1956, was designated F. I. Model 400 by the importer. Made from 1955-63.

CONTENTO OVER/UNDER SHOTGUN
Boxlock w/Woodward side lugs and double internal bolts. Gauge: 12 (2.75-inch chambers). Bbls.: 26-, 28-inch field; 30-, 32-inch trap; fixed chokes as required or screw-in choke tubes. Hand-checkered European walnut stock and forend. Single selective trigger and automatic ejectors.
M.K.2. . . . . NiB $1008 Ex $820 Gd $579
M.K.3. . . . . NiB $1736 Ex $1418 Gd $989
W/Interchangeable single bbl., add. $400

MATADOR
HAMMERLESS DOUBLE . . . . NiB $508 Ex $410 Gd $285
Anson & Deeley boxlock. Selective automatic ejectors. Selective single trigger. Gauges: 12, 16, 20, 20 Magnum (3-inch). Bbls: 26-, 28-, 30-inches; any standard choke combination. Weight: 6.5 to 7.5 lbs., depending on ga. and bbl. length. Checkered pistol-grip stock and beavertail forend. Note: This model, prior to 1956, was designated F. I. Model 400E by the U. S. importer, Firearms Int'l. Corp. of Washington, D.C. Made from 1955-63.

SHOTGUNS

MATADOR II . . . . NiB $602 Ex $492 Gd $351
Improved version of Matador w/same general specifications except has vent-rib bbls. Made 1964-69.

MATADOR III . . . . NiB $862 Ex $700 Gd $492
Same general specifications as AyA Matador II. Made 1970-85.

MODEL XXV BOXLOCK
Anson & Deeley boxlock w/double locking lugs. Gauges: 12 and 20. 25-inch chopper lump, satin blued bbls. w/Churchill rib. Weight: 5 to 7 lbs. Double triggers. Automatic safety and ejectors. Color-casehardened receiver w/Continental-style scroll and floral engraving. European walnut stock. Imported 1979-86 and 1991.
12 or 20 ga. . . . . NiB $2729 Ex $1580 Gd $961
Extra set of bbls., add $1050

MODEL XXV SIDELOCK
Holland & Holland-type sidelock. Gauges: 12, 20, 28 and .410; 25-, 26-, 27- 28-, 29-, and 32-inch bbls. Chopper lump, satin blued bbls. w/Churchill rib. Weight: 5 to 7 lbs. Double triggers standard or selective or non-selective single trigger optional. Automatic safety and ejectors. Cocking indicators. Color-casehardened or coin-silver-finished receiver w/Continental-style scroll and floral engraving. Select European walnut stock w/hand-cut checkering and oil finish. Imported 1979-86 and 1991.
12 or 20 ga. . . . . NiB $3902 Ex $1978 Gd $1193
28 ga. (disc. 1997). . . . . NiB $2439 Ex $1962 Gd $1399
.410 ga. (disc. 1997) . . . . NiB $2775 Ex $2250 Gd $1581
Single trigger, add $75
Single selective trigger, add. $120
Extra set of bbls., add $1700

BAIKAL SHOTGUNS — Izhevsk and Tula, Russia

MODEL IJ-18M SINGLE SHOT . . . . NiB $86 Ex $73 Gd $57
Hammerless w/cocking indicator. Automatic ejector. Manual safety. Gauges: 12 , 20, 16 w/2.75-inch chamber or .410 w/3-inch chamber. Bbls.: 26-, 28-inch w/fixed chokes (IC, M, F). Weight: 5.5 to 6 lbs. Made in Russia.

MODEL IJ-27 FIELD O/U . . . . NiB $392 Ex $316 Gd $229
Boxlock. Double triggers w/extractors. 12 ga.; 2.75-inch chambers. Bbls.: 26-inch, IC/M; 28-inch, M/F w/fixed chokes. Weight: 6.75 lbs. Made in Russia.

MODEL IJ-43 FIELD SIDE-BY-SIDE
Side-by-side; boxlock. Double triggers; extractors. 12 or 20 ga. w/2.75-inch chambers. Bbls: 20-inch cylinder bbl and 26-or 28-inch modified full bbl. Weight: 6.75 to 7 lbs. Checkered walnut stock, forend. Blued, engraved receiver. Imported 1994-96.
Model IJ-43 Field w/20-inch bbls . . . . NiB $264 Ex $217 Gd $157
Model IJ-43 Field
w/26- or 28-inch bbls . . . . NiB $238 Ex $196 Gd $142

IZH-43 SERIES SIDE-BY-SIDE
Boxlock. Gauges: 12, 16, 20 or .410 w/2.75- or 3-inch chambers. Bbls.: 20-, 24-, 26- or 28-inch w/fixed chokes or choke tubes. Single selective or double triggers. Weight: 6.75 lbs. Checkered hardwood (standard on Hunter II Model) or walnut stock and forend (standard on Hunter Model). Blued, engraved receiver. Imported 1994-1996.
Model IZH-43Hunter
(12 ga. w/walnut stock). . . . . NiB $370 Ex $324 Gd $166
Model IZH-43 Hunter
(20, 16 or .410 ga.) . . . . NiB $373 Ex $303 Gd $217
Model IZH-43 Hunter II
(12 ga. w/external hammers) . . . . . NiB $384 Ex $314 Gd $224
Model IZH-43 Hunter II
(12 ga. hammerless) . . . . NiB $256 Ex $212 Gd $154
Model IZH-43 Hunter II
(20, 16 or .410 ga.) . . . . NiB $268 Ex $222 Gd $162
Hunter II w/walnut stock, add $35
Hunter II w/single selective trigger, add $45

MODEL IJ-27 O/U
Boxlock. Single selective trigger w/automatic ejectors or double triggers w/extractors. Gauges: 12 or 20 w/2.75-inch chambers. Bbls.: 26-inch or 28-inch w/fixed chokes. Weight: 7 lbs. Checkered European hardwood stock and forearm. Made in Russia.
Model IJ-27 (w/double
triggers and extractors.) . . . . NiB $370 Ex $314 Gd $166
Model IJ-27
(single selective
trigger and ejectors) . . . . NiB $390 Ex $329 Gd $166

BAKER SHOTGUNS — Batavia, New York Made 1903-1933 by Baker Gun Company

BATAVIA LEADER HAMMERLESS DOUBLE
Sidelock. Plain extractors or automatic ejectors. Double triggers. Gauges: 12, 16, 20. Bbls.: 26- to 32-inch; any standard boring. Weight: About 7.75 lbs. (12 ga. w/30-inch bbls.). Checkered pistol-grip stock and forearm.
W/plain extractors . . . . NiB $879 Ex $421 Gd $328
W/automatic ejectors . . . . NiB $910 Ex $498 Gd $328

BATAVIA EJECTOR . . . . NiB $1159 Ex $896 Gd $633
Same general specifications as the Batavia Leader except higher quality and finer finish throughout; has Damascus or homotensile steel bbls., checkered pistol-grip stock and forearm of select walnut; automatic ejectors standard; 12 and 16 ga. only. Deduct 60% for Damascus bbls.

BATAVIA SPECIAL . . . . NiB $545 Ex $339 Gd $236
Same general specifications as the Batavia Leader except 12 and 16 ga. only; extractors, homotensile steel bbls.

BLACK BEAUTY
Same general specifications as the Batavia Leader except higher quality and finer finish throughout; has line engraving, special steel bbls., select walnut stock w/straight, full or half-pistol-grip.
Black Beauty w/plain extractors . . . NiB $597 Ex $365 Gd $288
Black Beauty Special
w/plain extractors . . . . NiB $1075 Ex $694 Gd $462
Black Beauty Special
w/automatic ejectors. . . . . NiB $1133 Ex $823 Gd $565

GRADE R. . . . . NiB $1450 Ex $1068 Gd $729
High-grade gun w/same general specifications as the Batavia Leader except has fine Damascus or Krupp fluid steel bbls., engraving in line, scroll and game scene designs, checkered stock and forearm of fancy European walnut; 12 and 16 ga. only. Deduct 60% for Damascus bbls.

GRADE S
Same general specifications as the Batavia Leader except higher quality and finer finish throughout; has Flui-tempered steel bbls., line and scroll engraving, checkered stock w/half-pistol-grip and forearm of semi-fancy imported walnut; 10, 12 and 16 ga.
Non-ejector . . . . NiB $1151 Ex $842 Gd $581
W/automatic ejectors . . . . NiB $1463 Ex $1071 Gd $742

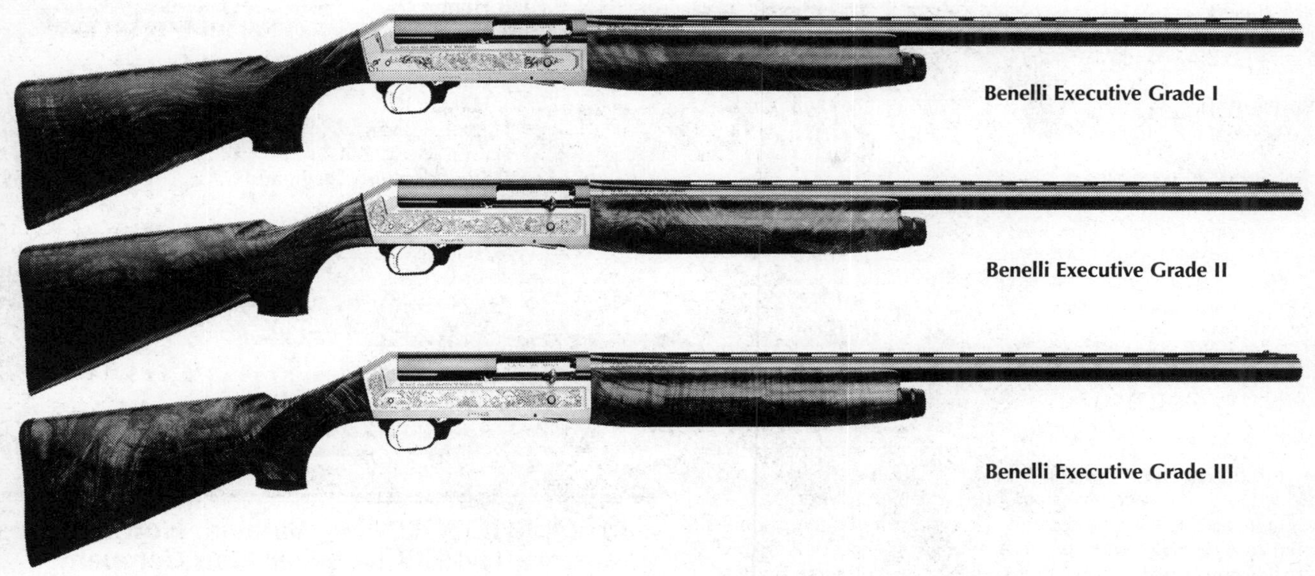

Benelli Executive Grade I

Benelli Executive Grade II

Benelli Executive Grade III

PARAGON, EXPERT AND DELUXE GRADES
Made to order only, these are the higher grades of Baker hammerless sidelock double-bbl. shotguns. After 1909, the Paragon Grade, as well as the Expert and Deluxe intro. that year, had a crossbolt in addition to the regular Baker system taper wedge fastening. There are early Paragon guns w/Damascus bbls. and some are non-ejector, but this grade was also produced w/automatic ejectors and w/the finest fluid steel bbls., in lengths to 34 inches, standard on Expert and Deluxe guns. Differences among the three models are in overall quality, finish, engraving and grade of fancy figured walnut in the stock and forearm; Expert and Deluxe wood may be carved as well as checkered. Choice of straight, full or half-pistol grip was offered. A single trigger was available in the two higher grades. The Paragon was available in 10 ga (Damascus bbls. only), and the other two models were regularly produced in 12, 16 and 20 ga.
Paragon grade, non-ejector . . . . NiB $1874 Ex $1515 Gd $1055
Paragon grade, Auto ejectors. . . NiB $2134 Ex $1723 Gd $1165
Expert grade . . . . NiB $3103 Ex $2462 Gd $1705
Deluxe grade. . . . . NiB $4293 Ex $3456 Gd $2384
For single trigger, add $250

BELKNAP SHOTGUNS — Louisville, Kentucky

MODEL B-68 SINGLE-SHOT SHOTGUN . NiB $144 Ex $119 Gd $88
Takedown. Visible hammer. Automatic ejector. Gauges: 12, 16, 20 and .410. Bbls.: 26-inch to 36-inch; F choke. Weight: 6 lbs. Plain pistol-grip stock and forearm.

MODEL B-63 SINGLE-SHOT SHOTGUN . . . NiB $130 Ex $109 Gd $81
Takedown. Visible hammer. Automatic ejector. Gauges: 12, 20 and .410. Bbls.: 26- to 36-inch, F choke. Weight: Average 6 lbs. Plain pistol-grip stock and forearm.

MODEL B-63E SINGLE-SHOT SHOTGUN . . . NiB $130 Ex $109 Gd $81
Same general specifications as Model B-68 except has side lever opening instead of top lever.

MODEL B-64
SLIDE-ACTION SHOTGUN. . . . . NiB $259 Ex $203 Gd $146
Hammerless. Gauges: 12, 16, 20 and .410. Three round tubular magazine. Various bbl. lengths and chokes from 26-inch to 30-inch. Weight: 6.25 to 7.5 lbs. Walnut-finished hardwood stock.

MODEL B-65C
AUTOLOADING SHOTGUN. . . . . . NiB $402 Ex $329 Gd $233
Browning-type lightweight alloy receiver. 12 ga. only. Four round tubular magazine. Bbl.: plain, 28-inch. Weight: About 8.25 lbs. Disc. 1949.

BENELLI SHOTGUNS — Urbino, Italy
Imported by Benelli USA, Accokeek, MD

MODEL 121 M1 MILITARY/POLICE
AUTOLOADING SHOTGUN . . . . NiB $518 Ex $450 Gd $310
Gauge: 12. Seven round magazine. 19.75-inch bbl. 39.75 inches overall. Cylinder choke, 2.75-inch chamber. Weight: 7.4 lbs. Matte black finish and European hardwood stock. Post front sight, fixed buckhorn rear sight. Imported in 1985. Disc.

BLACK EAGLE
AUTOLOADING SHOTGUN
Two-piece aluminum and steel receiver. Ga: 12; 3-inch chamber. Four round magazine. Screw-in choke tubes (SK, IC, M, IM, F). Bbls.: Ventilated rib; 21, 24, 26 or 28 inches w/bead front sight; 24-inch rifled slug. 42.5 to 49.5 inches overall. Weight: 7.25 lbs. (28-inch bbl.). Matte black lower receiver w/blued upper receiver and bbl. Checkered walnut stock w/high-gloss finish and drop adjustment. Imported from 1989-90 and 1997-98.
Limited edition. . . . . NiB $1878 Ex $1618 Gd $1098
Competition model . . . . NiB $1124 Ex $880 Gd $526
Slug model (disc. 1992) . . . . NiB $794 Ex $560 Gd $404
Standard model (disc. 1992) . . . . NiB $898 Ex $716 Gd $446

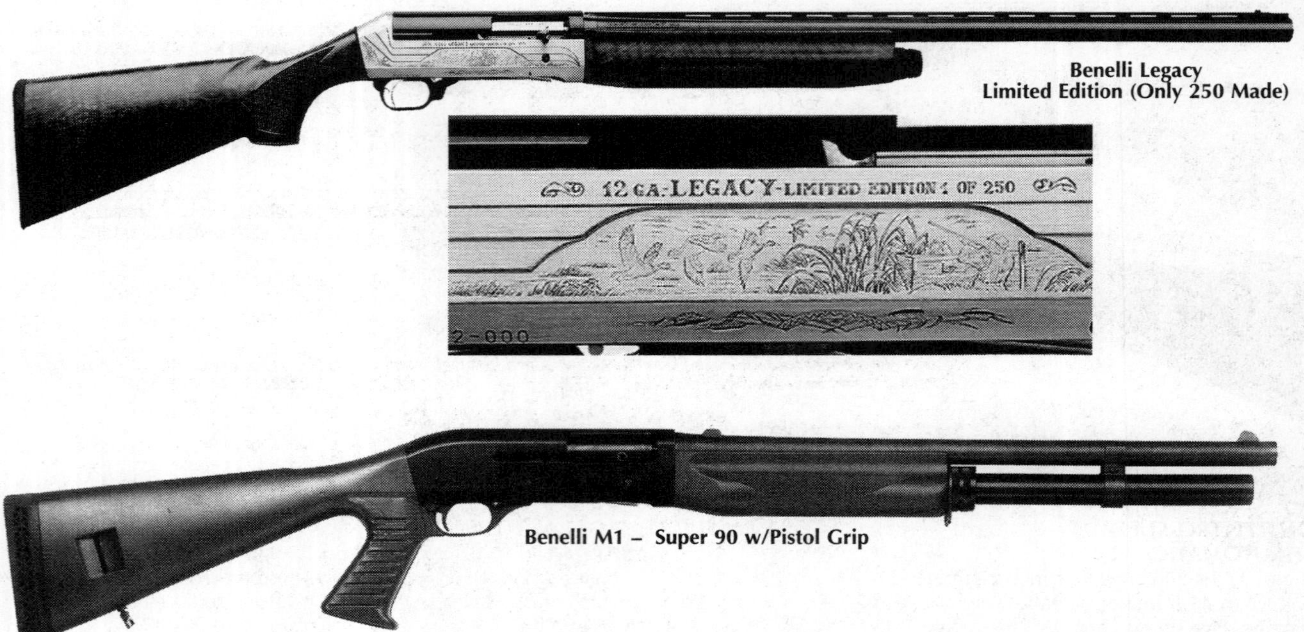

Benelli Legacy Limited Edition (Only 250 Made)

Benelli M1 – Super 90 w/Pistol Grip

BLACK EAGLE EXECUTIVE
Custom Black Eagle Series. Montefeltro-style rotating bolt w/three locking lugs. All-steel lower receiver engraved, gold inlay by Bottega Incisione di Cesare Giovanelli. 12 ga. only. 21-, 24-, 26-, or 28-inch vent-rib bbl. w/5 screw-in choke tubes (Type I) or fixed chokes. Custom deluxe walnut stock and forend. Built to customer specifications on special order.
Executive Grade I . . . . NiB $3959 Ex $3180 Gd $2183
Executive Grade II . . . . NiB $4291 Ex $3445 Gd $2363
Executive Grade III . . . . NiB $5038 Ex $4043 Gd $2770

LEGACY AUTOLOADING SHOTGUN
Gauges: 12 and 20 ga. w/3-inch chambers. 24- 26- or 28-inch bbl. 47.63 to 49.62 inches overall. Weight: 5.8 to 7.5 lbs. Four round magazine. Five screw-in choke tubes. Lower alloy receiver and upper steel reciever cover. Features Benelli's inertia recoil operating system. Imported 1998 to date.
Legacy model . . . . NiB $1232 Ex $971 Gd $816
Legacy model Limited edition . . . NiB $1820 Ex $1534 Gd $936

M1 FIELD AUTO SHOTGUN. . . . . NiB $800 Ex $685 Gd $570
Gauge: 20. Chambers: 2.75 or 3 inches. Bbl. 24 or 26 inches, stepped ventilated rib and red bar sights. Stock: Synthetic, black or camo. Weight: 5.7 to 5.8 lbs. Includes set of five choke tubes. Imported from Italy.

M1 SUPER 90
AUTO-LOADING SHOTGUN . . . . . NiB $868 Ex $738 Gd $452
Gauge: 12. Seven round magazine. Cylinder choke. 19.75-inch bbl. 39.75 inches overall. Weight: 7 lbs., 4 oz. to 7 lbs., 10 oz. Matte black finish. Stock and forend made of fiberglass-reinforced polymer. Sights: Post front, fixed buckhorn rear, drift adj. Introduced 1985; when the model line expanded in 1989, this configuration was discontinued.

M1 SUPER 90
DEFENSE AUTOLOADER. . . . . NiB $998 Ex $790 Gd $426
Same general specifications as Model Super 90 except w/pistol-grip stock. Available w/Ghost-Ring sight option. Imported 1986-98.

M1 SUPER 90 FIELD
Inertia-recoil semiautomatic shotgun. Gauge: 12; 3-inch chamber. Three round magazine. Bbl.: 21, 24, 26 or 28 inches. 42.5 to 49.5 inches overall. Choke: SK, IC, M, IM, F. Matte receiver. Standard polymer stock or satin walnut (26- or 28-inch bbl. only). Bead front sight. Imported from 1990 to date.
W/Realtree camo . . . . NiB $769 Ex $639 Gd $405
W/polymer stock . . . . NiB $655 Ex $481 Gd $353
W/walnut stock . . . . NiB $691 Ex $509 Gd $379

M1 SUPER 90 SLUG AUTOLOADER
Same general specifications as M1 Super 90 Field except w/5-round magazine. 18.5-inch bbl. Cylinder bore. 39.75 inches overall. Weight: 6.5 lbs. Polymer standard stock. Rifle or Ghost-Ring sights. Imported 1986-98.
W/rifle sights . . . . NiB $717 Ex $561 Gd $457
W/ghost-ring sights . . . . NiB $769 Ex $587 Gd $457
W/Realtree camo finish, add $100

M1 SUPER 90 SPORTING
SPECIAL AUTOLOADER . . . . NiB $824 Ex $720 Gd $434
Same general specifications as M1 Super 90 Field except w/18.5-inch bbl. 39.75 inches overall. Weight: 6.5 lbs. Ghost-ring sights. Polymer stock. Imported from 1994-98.

M3 SUPER 90 PUMP/AUTOLOADER
Inertia-recoil semiautomatic and/or pump action. Gauge: 12. Seven round magazine. Cylinder choke. 19.75-inch bbl. 41 inches overall (31 inches folded). Weight: 7 to 7.5 lbs. Matte black finish. Stock: standard synthetic, pistol-grip or folding tubular steel. Standard rifle or Ghost-Ring sights. Imported 1989 to date. Caution: Increasing the magazine capacity to more than 5 rounds in M3 shotguns w/pistol-grip stocks violates provisions of the 1994 Crime Bill. This model may be used legally only by the military and law-enforcement agencies.
Standard model . . . . NiB $895 Ex $749 Gd $453
Pistol-grip model . . . . NiB $1024 Ex $828 Gd $578
W/folding stock . . . . NiB $1090 Ex $883 Gd $619
W/laser sight . . . . NiB $1350 Ex $1091 Gd $760
For ghost ring sights, add $50

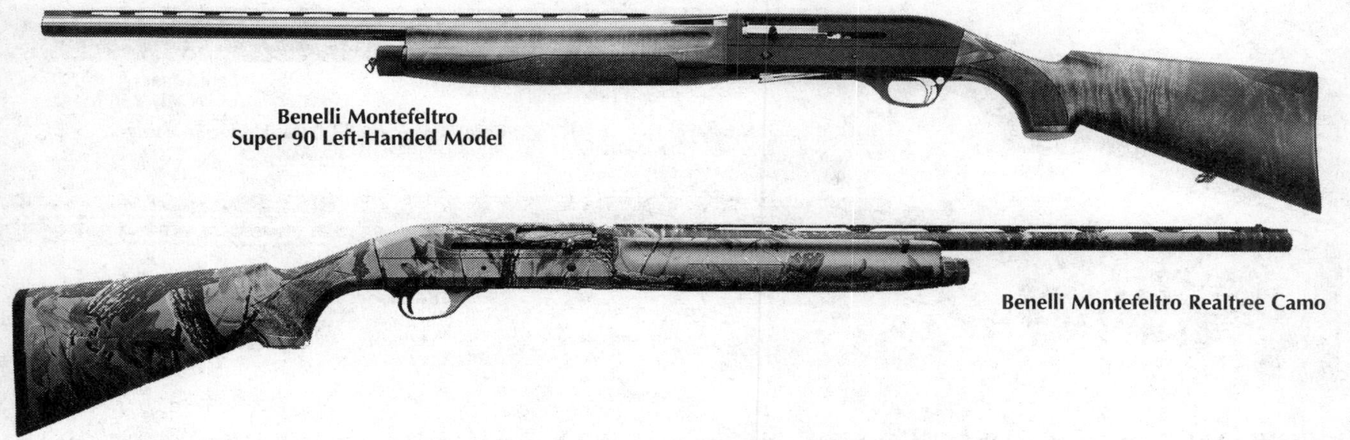

Benelli Montefeltro
Super 90 Left-Handed Model

Benelli Montefeltro Realtree Camo

MONTEFELTRO/SUPER 90 SEMIAUTOMATIC
Gauges: 12 or 20 gauge w/3-inch chamber. 21- 24- 26- or 28-inch bbl. 43.7 to 49.5 inches overall. Weight: 5.3 to 7.5 lbs. Four round magazine. Five screw-in choke tubes (C, IC, M, IM, F). High gloss or satin walnut or Realtree Camo stock. Blued metal finish. Imported 1987-92.
Standard Hunter model .... NiB $895 Ex $751 Gd $453
Slug model (disc. 1992).......... NiB $718 Ex $562 Gd $354
Turkey model .... NiB $718 Ex $562 Gd $354
Uplander model .... NiB $718 Ex $562 Gd $354
Limited Edition (1995-96) ..... NiB $1929 Ex $1559 Gd $1077
20 ga. w/Realtree camo .... NiB $736 Ex $614 Gd $431
20 ga. Youth Model w/short stock, add.................. $40
Left-hand model, add $25

NOVA PUMP SHOTGUN .... NiB $300 Ex $225 Gd $190
Gauge: 12 or 20. Chambers: 2.75 or 3 inches; 3.5 inch chambers in 12 gauge only Four-round magazine. Bbl. 24, 26 or 28 inches; red bar sights. Stock: Synthetic,(Xtra Brown in 12 gauge or Timber HD in 20 gauge). Montefeltro rotating bolt, magazine cutoff, synthetic trigger assembly. Introduced 1999. Imported from Italy.

SL 121V SEMIAUTO
(SL-80 SERIES)................... NiB $577 Ex $343 Gd $291
Recoil-operated semiautomaticw/split receiver design. Gauge: 12. Five round capacity. 26-, 28- or 30-inch ventilated rib bbl. (26-inch choked M, IM, IC, 28-inch, F, M, IM; 30-inch, F choke - Mag.). Straight walnut stock w/hand-checkered pistol grip and forend. Importation disc. in 1985.

SL 121V SLUG SHOTGUN
(SL-80 SERIES)................ NiB $587 Ex $369 Gd $301
Same general specifications as Benelli SL 121V except designed for rifled slugs and equipped w/rifle sights. Disc. in 1985.

SL 123V SEMIAUTO
(SL-80 SERIES)................... NiB $499 Ex $405 Gd $286
Gauge: 12. 26- and 28-inch bbls. 26-inch choked IM, M, IC; 28-inch choked F, IM, M. Disc. in 1985.

SL 201 SEMIAUTOMATIC
(SL-80 SERIES)................ NiB $447 Ex $364 Gd $258
Gauge: 20. 26-inch bbl. Mod. choke. Weight: 5 lbs., 10 oz. Ventilated rib. Disc. in 1985.

SPORT AUTOLOADING
SHOTGUN .... NiB $1028 Ex $831 Gd $581
Similar to the Black Eagle Competition model except has one-piece matte- finished alloy receiver w/inscribed red Benelli logo. 26 or 28 inches bbl. w/2 inchangable carbon fiber vent ribs. Oil-finished checkered walnut stock w/adjustable buttpad and buttstock. Imported 1997-2002.

SUPER BLACK EAGLE AUTOLOADING SHOTGUN
Same general specifications as Black Eagle except w/3.5-inch chamber that accepts 2.75-, 3- and 3.5-inch shells. Two round magazine (3.5-inch), 3-round magazine (2.75- or 3-inch). High-gloss, satin finish or camo stock. Realtree camo, matte black or blued metal finish. Imported 1991 to date.
Standard model .... NiB $1093 Ex $872 Gd $622
Realtree camo .... NiB $1223 Ex $990 Gd $692
Custom slug model .... NiB $1035 Ex $839 Gd $589
Limited edition .... NiB $1926 Ex $1546 Gd $1072
W/wood stock, add.................................. $25
Left-hand model, add................................ $30

BERETTA USA CORP. — Accokeek, Maryland Mfd. by Fabbrica D'Armi Pietro Beretta S.p.A. in Gardone Val Trompia (Brescia), Italy *Imported by Beretta USA (Previously by Garcia Corp.)*

MODEL 409PB
HAMMERLESS DOUBLE .... NiB $1052 Ex $730 Gd $465
Boxlock. Double triggers. Plain extractors. Gauges: 12, 16, 20, 28. Bbls.: 27.5-, 28.5- and 30-inch, IC/M choke or M/F choke. Weight: from 5.5 to 7.75 lbs., depending on ga. and bbl. length. Straight or pistol-grip stock and beavertail forearm, checkered. Imported 1934-64.

MODEL 410E
Same general specifications as Model 409PB except has automatic ejectors and is of higher quality throughout. Imported 1934-64.
Model 410E (12 ga.) .... NiB $1367 Ex $1213 Gd $795
Model 410E (20 ga.) .... NiB $1855 Ex $1497 Gd $1039
Model 410E (28 ga.) .... NiB $4635 Ex $3725 Gd $2560

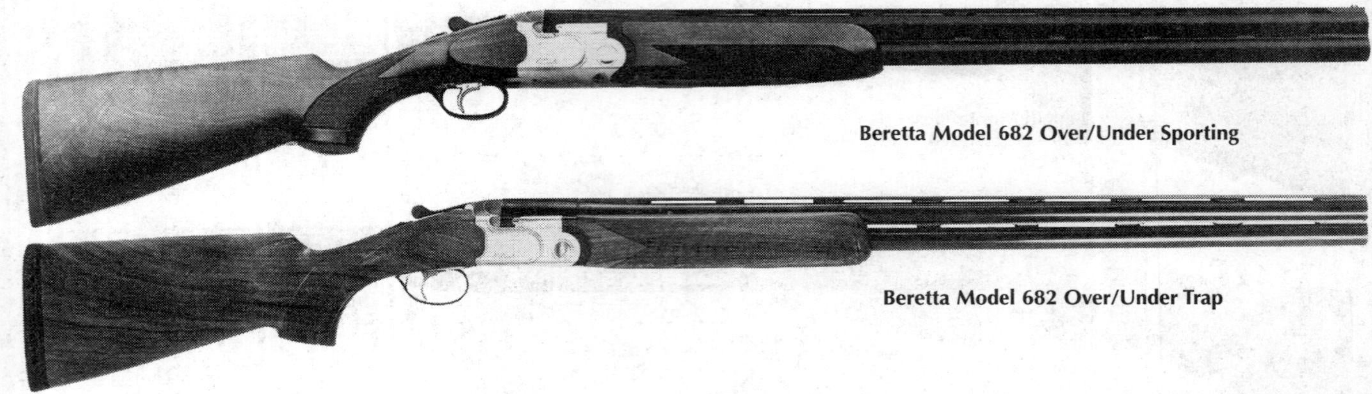

Beretta Model 682 Over/Under Sporting

Beretta Model 682 Over/Under Trap

MODEL 410 10-GA. MAGNUM . . NiB $1286 Ex $1042 Gd $726
Same as Model 410E except heavier construction. Plain extractors. Double triggers. 10-ga. Magnum, 3.5-inch chambers. 32-inch bbls., both F choke. Weight: about 10 lbs. Checkered pistol-grip stock and forearm, recoil pad. Imported 1934-84.

MODEL 411E
Same general specifications as Model 409PB except has sideplates, automatic ejectors and is of higher quality throughout. Imported 1934-64.
Model 411E (12 ga.) . . . . NiB $1998 Ex $1609 Gd $1112
Model 411E (20 ga.) . . . . NiB $2602 Ex $2095 Gd $1456
Model 411E (28 ga.) . . . . NiB $4770 Ex $3835 Gd $2639

MODEL 424 HAMMERLESS DOUBLE . . . . NiB $1468 Ex $1182 Gd $819
Boxlock. Light border engraving. Plain extractors. Gauges: 12, 20; chambers 2.75-inch in former, 3-inch in latter. Bbls.: 28-inch M/F choke, 26-inch IC/M choke. Weight: 5 lbs. 14 oz. to 6 lbs. 10 oz., depending on ga. and bbl. length. English-style straight-grip stock and forearm, checkered. Imported 1977-84.

MODEL 426E. . . . . NiB $1968 Ex $1500 Gd $1058
Same as Model 424 except action body is finely engraved, silver pigeon inlaid in top lever; has selective automatic ejectors and selective single trigger, stock and forearm of select European walnut. Imported 1977-84.

MODEL 450 SERIES HAMMERLESS DOUBLES
Custom English-style sidelock. Single, non-selective trigger or double triggers. Manual safety. Selective automatic ejectors. Gauge: 12; 2.75- or 3-inch chambers. Bbls.: 26, 28 or 30 inches choked to customers' specifications. Weight: 6.75 lbs. Checkered high-grade walnut stock. Receiver w/coin-silver finish. Imported 1948. Disc.
Model 450 EL (disc. 1982). . . . . NiB $7774 Ex $6241 Gd $4279
Model 450 EELL (disc. 1982). . . NiB $8236 Ex $6610 Gd $4520
Model 451 (disc. 1987) . . . . NiB $6734 Ex $5409 Gd $3714
Model 451 E (disc. 1989) . . . . . NiB $7383 Ex $5929 Gd $4067
Model 451 EL (disc. 1985) . . . . . NiB $12,936 Ex $10,348 Gd $7037
Model 451 EELL (disc. 1990) . . . NiB $14,202 Ex $11,362 Gd $7726
Model 452 (Intro. 1990) . . . . . NiB $20,750 Ex $18,200 Gd $12,376
Model 452 EELL (intro. 1992) . . NiB $30,226 Ex $24,180 Gd $16,442
Extra set of bbls., add 30%

MODEL 470 SERIES HAMMERLESS DOUBLE
Gauge: 12 and 20 ga. w/3-inch chambers. 26- or 28-inch bbl. Weight: 5.9 to 6.5 lbs. Low profile, improved box lock action w/single selective trigger. Selected walnut, checkered stock and forend. Metal front bead sight. Scroll-engraved receiver w/gold inlay and silver chrome finish. Imported 1999 to date.
Model 470 Silver Hawk 12 ga. . . . . . NiB $2462 Ex $1980 Gd $1365
Model 470 Silver Hawk 20 ga. . . . . . NiB $2650 Ex $2131 Gd $1467
Model 470 EL Silver Hawk 12 ga. . . . NiB $4085 Ex $3876 Gd $2240
Model 470 EL Silver Hawk 20 ga. . . . NiB $4253 Ex $4001 Gd $2342
Model 470 EELL (Jubilee II) 12 ga. . . . NiB $8064 Ex $6065 Gd $4451
Model 470 EELL (Jubilee II) 20 ga. . . . NiB $8526 Ex $6848 Gd $4701
Extra set of bbls., add. 30%

MODEL 625 S/S HAMMERLESS DOUBLE
Boxlock. Gauges: 12 or 20. Bbls.: 26-, 28- or 30-inch w/fixed choke combinations. Single selective or double triggers w/extractors. Checkered English-style buttstock and forend. Imported 1984-87.
W/double triggers . . . . NiB $1013 Ex $825 Gd $584
W/single selective trigger . . . . NiB $1180 Ex $958 Gd $675
20 ga., add. $150

MODEL 626 S/S HAMMERLESS DOUBLE
Field Grade side-by-side. Boxlock action w/single selective trigger, extractors and automatic safety. Gauges: 12 (2.75-inch chambers); 20 (3-inch chambers). Bbls.: 26- or 28-inch w/Mobilchoke or various fixed-choke combinations. Weight: 6.75 lbs. (12 ga.). Bright chrome finish. Checkered European walnut buttstock and forend in straight English style. Imported 1985-94.
Model 626 Field (disc. 1988). . . . NiB $1270 Ex $1062 Gd $568
Model 626 Onyx . . . . NiB $1400 Ex $1140 Gd $848
Model 626 Onyx (3.5-inch Magnum, disc. 1993). . . . . NiB $1498 Ex $1213 Gd $849
20 ga., add. $200

MODEL 627 S/S HAMMERLESS DOUBLE
Same as Model 626 S/S except w/engraved sideplates and pistol-grip or straight English-style stock. Imported 1985-94.
Model 627 EL Field . . . . NiB $2604 Ex $2090 Gd $1460
Model 627 EL Sport. . . . . NiB $2625 Ex $2147 Gd $1498
Model 627 EELL. . . . . NiB $4605 Ex $3687 Gd $2559

MODEL 682 O/U SHOTGUN
Hammerless takedown w/single selective trigger. Gauges: 12, 20, 28, .410. Bbls.: 26- to 34-inch w/fixed chokes or Mobilchoke tubes. Checkered European walnut buttstock/forend in various grades and configurations. Imported 1984-2000.
Model 682 Comp Skeet . . . . . . NiB $2015 Ex $1626 Gd $1129
Model 682 Comp Skeet Deluxe. . . . . NiB $2925 Ex $2354 Gd $1624
Mdl. 682 Comp Super Skeet . . . . NiB $2405 Ex $1938 Gd $1341
Mdl. 682 Comp Skeet 2-bbl. set (disc. 1989) . . . . NiB $4913 Ex $3952 Gd $2723
Mdl. 682 Comp Skeet 4 bbl. Set (disc. 1996) . . . . NiB $5635 Ex $4529 Gd $3115
Mdl. 682 Sporting Continental. . . . . . NiB $2011 Ex $1622 Gd $1125
Mdl. 682 Sporting Combo . . . . NiB $3141 Ex $2519 Gd $1737

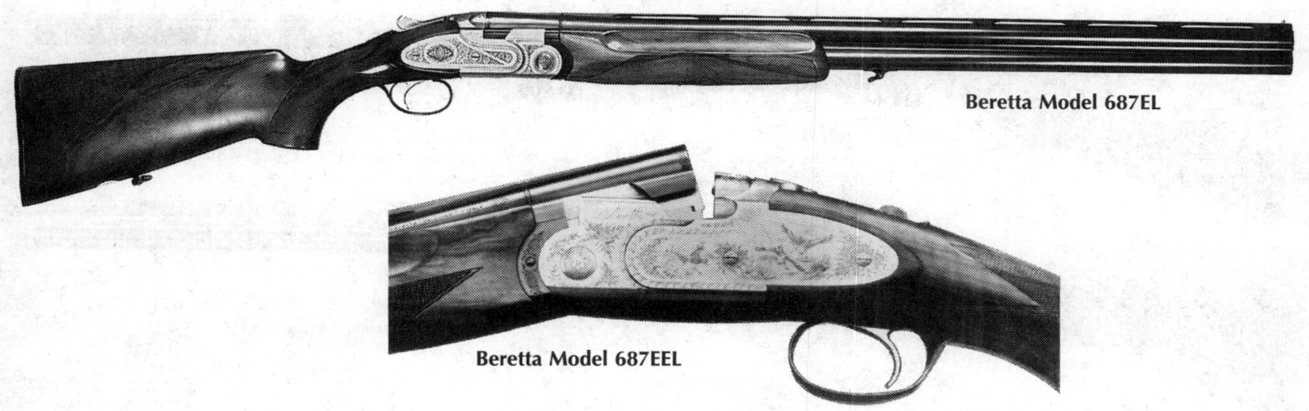

Beretta Model 687EL

Beretta Model 687EEL

Mdl. 682 Sporting Gold . . . . NiB $1885 Ex $1522 Gd $1158
Mdl. 682 Sporting Super Sport . . . . NiB $1253 Ex $1657 Gd $1149
Mdl. 682 Comp Trap Gold X . . . . NiB $2015 Ex $1626 Gd $1129
Mdl. 682 Comp Trap Top Sgle. (1986-95) . . NiB $1957 Ex $1579 Gd $1065
Mdl. 682 Comp Trap Live Pig. (1990-98) . . . NiB $2596 Ex $2096 Gd $1455
Mdl. 682 Comp Mono/ComboTrp. Gld. X . . NiB $2800 Ex $2330 Gd $1604
Mdl. 682 Comp Mono Trap (1985-88) . . . . . . NiB $1755 Ex $1418 Gd $987
Mdl. 682 Super Trap Gold X (1991-95) . . . . NiB $2094 Ex $1690 Gd $1164
Mdl. 682 Sup. Trap
Combo Gld. X (1991-97) . . . . NiB $2939 Ex $2368 Gd $1638
Mdl. 682 Super Trap
Top Sgle. Gld. X (1991-95) . . . . NiB $2154 Ex $1739 Gd $1208
Mdl. 682 Sup. Trap Unsingle (1992-94) . . . . NiB $2019 Ex $1630 Gd $1135

MODEL 686 O/U SHOTGUN

Low-profile improved boxlock action. Single selective trigger. Selective automatic ejectors. Gauges: 12, 20, 28 w/3.5- 3- or 2.75-inch chambers, depending upon ga. Bbls.: 26-, 28-, 30-inch w/fixed chokes or Mobilchoke tubes. Weight: 5.75 to 7.5 lbs. Checkered American walnut stock and forearm of various qualities, depending upon model. Receiver finishes also vary, but all have blued bbls. Sideplates to simulate sidelock action on EL models. Imported 1988-95.

Model 686 Field Onyx . . . . NiB $1378 Ex $1025 Gd $604
Mdl. 686 (3.5-inch Mag., disc.
1993 & reintro.1996) . . . . NiB $1436 Ex $1056 Gd $708
Model 686 EL Gold Perdiz (1992-97) . . . . NiB $1716 Ex $1389 Gd $948
Model 686 Essential (1994-96) . . . . NiB $950 Ex $764 Gd $525
Model 686 Silver Essential (1997-98) . . . . NiB $1056 Ex $859 Gd $584
Model 686 Sil. Pig. Onyx (intro. 1996) . . . . NiB $1395 Ex $1113 Gd $773
Mdl. 686 Sil. Perdiz Onyx (disc. 1996) . . . . . NiB $1358 Ex $1084 Gd $755
Model 686 Sil. Pig./Perdiz Onyx Combo . . . . NiB $1930 Ex $1541 Gd $859
Model 686 L Silver Perdiz (disc. 1994) . . . . . . NiB $1108 Ex $884 Gd $619
Model 686 Skeet Silver Pigeon (1996-98) . . . . NiB $1173 Ex $935 Gd $655
Model 686 Skeet Silver Perdiz (1994-96) . . . . NiB $1394 Ex $1113 Gd $774
Model 686 Skeet Sil. Pig./Perdiz Combo . . . . NiB $1394 Ex $1113 Gd $774
Model 686 Sporting Special (1987-93) . . . . . . NiB $1601 Ex $1278 Gd $888
Model 686 Sporting English (1991-92) . . . . NiB $1680 Ex $1352 Gd $930
Model 686 Sporting Onyx
w/fixed chokes (1991-92) . . . . NiB $1601 Ex $1288 Gd $888
Model 686 Sporting Onyx
w/tubes (intro. 1992) . . . . NiB $1215 Ex $979 Gd $680
Mdl. 686 Sporting Onyx Gld. (disc. 1993) . . . NiB $1747 Ex $1405 Gd $968
Mdl. 686 Sporting Sil. Pig. (intro. 1996) . . . . NiB $1429 Ex $1151 Gd $794
Model 686 Sporting Sil. Perdiz (1993-96) . . . . NiB $1394 Ex $1123 Gd $774
Mdl. 686 Sporting Coll. Sport (1996-97) . . . . NiB $1072 Ex $865 Gd $600
Model 686 Sporting Combo . . . . NiB $2484 Ex $2000 Gd $1380
Model 686 Trap International (1994-95) . . . . NiB $1044 Ex $846 Gd $592
Model 686 Trap Silver Pigeon (intro. 1997) . . . NiB $1133 Ex $909 Gd $634
Model 686 Trap Top Mono (intro. 1998) . . . . NiB $1159 Ex $947 Gd $653
Model 686 Ultralight Onyx (intro. 1992) . . . NiB $1474 Ex $1189 Gd $825
Mdl. 686 Ultralight Del. Onyx (intro. 1998) . . . NiB $1879 Ex $1481 Gd $1023

MODEL 687 O/U SHOTGUN

Same as Model 686 except w/decorative sideplates and varying grades of engraving and game-scene motifs.

Model 687 L Onyx (disc. 1991) . . . . NiB $1383 Ex $1119 Gd $780
Model 687 L Onyx Gold Field (1988-89) . . NiB $1583 Ex $1262 Gd $877
Model 687 L Onyx Silver Pigeon . . . . NiB $1991 Ex $1605 Gd $1110
Model 687 EL Onyx (disc. 1990) . . . . NiB $2721 Ex $2189 Gd $1522
Model 687 EL Gold Pigeon . . . . NiB $3100 Ex $2498 Gd $1735
Model 687 EL Gold Pigeon Sm. Fr. . . . . . NiB $2883 Ex $2335 Gd $1621
Mdl. 687 EL Gld. Pig. Sporting (Int. 1993) . . . . NiB $4252 Ex $3424 Gd $2365
Model 687 EELL Diamond Pigeon . . . . . . NiB $4252 Ex $3424 Gd $2365
Mdl. 687 EELL Diamond Pig. Skeet . . . . . . NiB $4110 Ex $3410 Gd $2278
Mdl. 687 EELL Diam. Pig. Sporting . . . . . . NiB $4331 Ex $3488 Gd $2407
Mdl. 687 EELL Diam. Pig. X Trap . . . . NiB $3795 Ex $3058 Gd $2116
Mdl. 687 EELL Diam. Pig. Mono Trap . . . . NiB $3873 Ex $3145 Gd $2174
Mdl. 687 EELL Diam. Pig. Trap Combo . . . NiB $5278 Ex $4249 Gd $2934
Model 687 EELL Field Combo . . . . NiB $4420 Ex $3563 Gd $2467
Model 687 EELL Skeet 4-bbl. set . . . . NiB $7231 Ex $5815 Gd $3403
Model 687 EELL Gallery Special . . . . NiB $6718 Ex $5403 Gd $3618
Model 687 EELL Gallery Special Combo . NiB $8098 Ex $6511 Gd $4469
Model 687 EELL Gallery Special pairs . NiB $15,730 Ex $12,584 Gd $8557
Model 687 Sporting English (1991-92) . . . NiB $2161 Ex $1746 Gd $1214
Mdl. 687 Sporting Sil. Pig. (intro. 1996) . NiB $1938 Ex $1568 Gd $1095
Mdl. 687 Sporting Sil. Perdiz (1993-96) . . NiB $2017 Ex $1631 Gd $1230

MODEL 1200 SERIES SEMIAUTOLOADING SHOTGUN

Short recoil action. Gauge: 12; 2.75- or 3-inch chamber. Six round magazine. 24-, 26- or 28-inch vent-rib bbl. w/fixed chokes or Mobilchoke tubes. Weight: 7.25 lbs. Matte black finish. Adj. technopolymer stock and forend. Imported 1988-90.

Model 1200 w/fixed choke (disc. 1989) . . . . . . NiB $582 Ex $473 Gd $332
Model 1200 Riot (disc. 1989) . . . . NiB $596 Ex $480 Gd $341
Model 1201 w/Mobilchoke (disc. 1994) . . . . . . NiB $611 Ex $496 Gd $349
Model 1201 Riot . . . . NiB $654 Ex $531 Gd $372
W/Pistol-grip stock, add $72
W/Tritium sights, add $56

MODEL A-301
AUTOLOADING SHOTGUN. . . . . . NiB $483 Ex $394 Gd $279

Field Gun. Gas-operated. Scroll-decorated receiver. Gauge: 12 or 20; 2.75-inch chamber in former, 3-inch in latter. Three round magazine. Bbl.: Ventilated rib; 28-inch F or M choke, 26-inch IC. Weight: 6 lbs., 5 oz. – 6 lbs., 14 oz., depending on gauge and bbl. length. Checkered pistol-grip stock/forearm. Imported 1977-82.

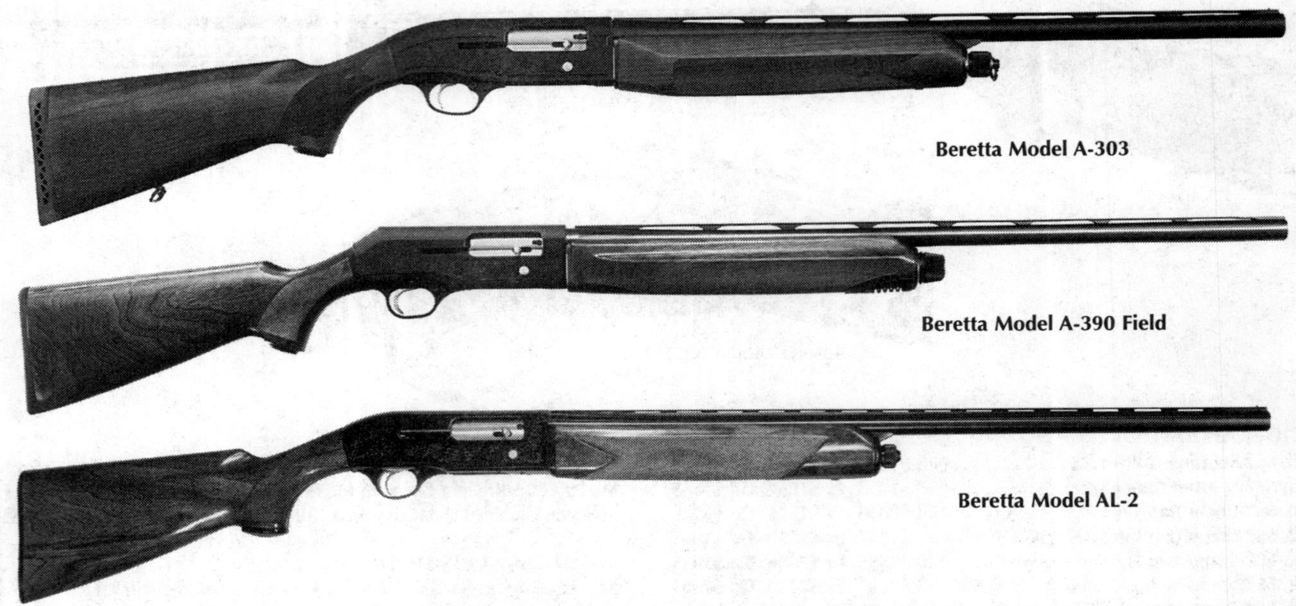
Beretta Model A-303

Beretta Model A-390 Field

Beretta Model AL-2

MODEL A-301 MAGNUM........ NiB $501 Ex $408 Gd $290
Same as Model A-301 Field Gun except chambered for 12 ga. Three inch Magnum shells, 30-inch F choke bbl. only, stock w/recoil pad. Weight: 7.25 lbs.

MODEL A-301 SKEET GUN....... NiB $527 Ex $429 Gd $304
Same as Model A-301 Field Gun except 26-inch bbl. SK choke only, skeet-style stock, gold-plated trigger.

MODEL A-301 SLUG GUN....... NiB $495 Ex $403 Gd $287
Same as Model A-301 Field Gun except has plain 22-inch bbl., slug choke, w/rifle sights. Weight: 6 lbs., 14 oz.

MODEL A-301 TRAP GUN .... NiB $527 Ex $429 Gd $304
Same as Model A-301 Field Gun except has 30-inch bbl. in F choke only, checkered Monte Carlo stock w/recoil pad, gold-plated trigger. Blued bbl. and receiver. Weight: 7 lbs., 10 oz. Imported 1978-82.

MODEL A-302 SEMIAUTOLOADING SHOTGUN
Similar to gas-operated Model 301. Hammerless, takedown shotgun w/tubular magazine and Mag-Action that handles both 2.75- and 3-inch Magnum shells. Gauge: 12 or 20; 2.75- or 3-inch Mag. chambers. Bbl.: Vent or plain; 22-inch/Slug (12 ga.); 26-inch/IC (12 or 20) 28-inch/M (20 ga.), 28-inch/Multi-choke (12 or 20 ga.) 30-inch/F (12 ga.). Weight: 6.5 lbs., 20 ga.; 7.25.lbs., 12 ga. Blued/ black finish. Checkered European walnut, pistol-grip stock and forend. Imported from 1983 to c. 1987.
Standard model w/fixed choke .... NiB $501 Ex $408 Gd $290
Standard model w/multi-choke.... NiB $553 Ex $450 Gd $319

MODEL A-302 SUPER LUSSO.. NiB $2398 Ex $2364 Gd $1462
A custom A-302 in presentation grade w/hand-engraved receiver and custom select walnut stock.

MODEL A-303 SEMIAUTOLOADER
Similar to Model 302, except w/target specifications in Trap, Skeet and Youth configurations, and weighs 6.5 to 8 lbs. Imported from 1983-96.
Field and Upland models......... NiB $582 Ex $551 Gd $512
Skeet and Trap (disc. 1994) .... NiB $712 Ex $577 Gd $404
Slug model (disc. 1992)........... NiB $777 Ex $629 Gd $439
Sporting Clays .... NiB $799 Ex $657 Gd $459
Super Skeet .... NiB $1177 Ex $951 Gd $663
Super Trap .... NiB $1120 Ex $906 Gd $641
Waterfowl/Turkey (disc. 1992) .... NiB $747 Ex $605 Gd $435
Mobil choke, add.......................... $50

MODEL A-303 YOUTH GUN ..... NiB $716 Ex $508 Gd $300
Locked-breech, gas-operated action. Ga: 12 and 20; 2-round magazine. Bbls.: 24, 26, 28, 30 or 32-inches, vent rib. Weight: 7 lbs. (12 ga.), 6 lbs. (20 ga.). Crossbolt safety. Length of pull shortened to 12.5 inches. Imported 1988-96.

MODEL A-390
SEMIAUTOMATIC SHOTGUN
Gas-operated, self-regulating action designed to handle any size load. Gauges: 12 or 20 w/ 3-inch chamber. Three round magazine. Bbl.: 24, 26, 28 or 30 inches w/vent rib and Mobilchoke tubes. Weight: 7.5 lbs. Select walnut stock w/adj. comb. Blued or matte black finish. Imported 1992-96. Superseded by AL-390 series.
Standard model/Slug model ...... NiB $606 Ex $492 Gd $348
Field model/Silver Mallard .... NiB $618 Ex $501 Gd $355
Deluxe model/Gold Mallard ...... NiB $670 Ex $544 Gd $383
Turkey/Waterfowl model
(matte finish).................. NiB $632 Ex $513 Gd $355
For 20 ga., add $35

MODEL A-390 TARGET
Similar to the Model 390 Field except w/2.75-inch chamber. Skeet: 28-inch ported bbl. w/wide vent rib and fixed choke (SK). Trap: 30- or 32-inch w/Mobilchoke tubes. Weight: 7.5 lbs. Fully adj. buttstock. Imported from 1993-96.
Sport Trap model............... NiB $618 Ex $503 Gd $355
Sport Skeet model.............. NiB $606 Ex $492 Gd $348
Sporting Clays model (unported)... NiB $632 Ex $514 Gd $364
Super Trap model (ported)........ NiB $818 Ex $663 Gd $465
Super Skeet model (ported)....... NiB $804 Ex $652 Gd $458
W/ported bbl., add $85
20 ga., add.................................. $35

MODEL AL-1 FIELD GUN .... NiB $488 Ex $399 Gd $284
Same as Model AL-2 gas-operated Field Gun except has bbl. w/o rib, no engraving on receiver. Imported from 1971-73.

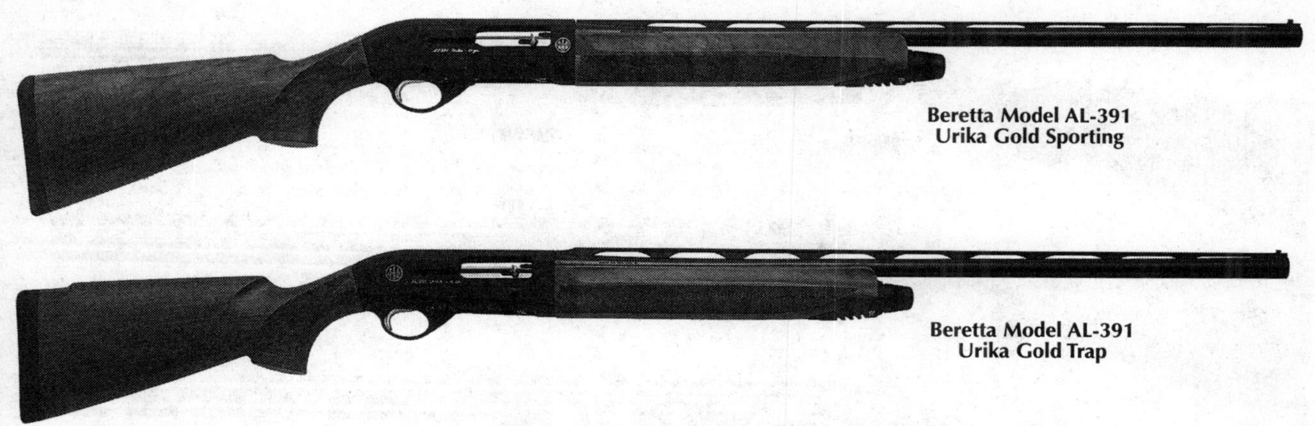

Beretta Model AL-391
Urika Gold Sporting

Beretta Model AL-391
Urika Gold Trap

MODEL AL-2 AUTOLOADING SHOTGUN
Field Gun. Gas-operated. Engraved receiver (1968 version, 12 ga. only, had no engraving). Gauge: 12 or 20. 2.75-inch chamber. Three round magazine. Bbls.: Vent rib; 30-inch F choke, 28-inch F or M choke, 26-inch IC. Weight: 6.5 to 7.25 lbs, depending on ga. and bbl. length. Checkered pistol-grip stock and forearm. Imported from 1968-75.
W/Plain receiver . . . . NiB $420 Ex $346 Gd $252
W/Engraved receiver . . . . NiB $564 Ex $461 Gd $330

MODEL AL-2 MAGNUM . . . . NiB $512 Ex $419 Gd $301
Same as Model AL-2 Field Gun except chambered for 12 ga. 3-inch Magnum shells; 30-inch F or 28-inch M choke bbl. only. Weight: About 8 lbs. Imported from 1973-75.

MODEL AL-2 SKEET GUN . . . . NiB $486 Ex $398 Gd $287
Same as Model AL-2 Field Gun except has wide rib, 26-inch bbl. in SK choke only, checkered pistol-grip stock and beavertail forearm. Imported 1973-75.

MODEL AL-2 TRAP GUN . . . . NiB $472 Ex $388 Gd $280
Same as Model AL-2 Field Gun except has wide rib, 30 inch bbl. in F choke only, beavertail forearm. Monte Carlo stock w/recoil pad. Weight: About 7.75 lbs. Imported from 1973-75.

MODEL AL-3
Similar to corresponding AL-2 models in design and general specifications. Imported from 1975-76.
Field model . . . . NiB $486 Ex $398 Gd $287
Magnum model . . . . NiB $498 Ex $409 Gd $294
Skeet model . . . . NiB $506 Ex $414 Gd $298
Trap model . . . . NiB $460 Ex $378 Gd $273

MODEL AL-3 DELUXE TRAP GUN . . . . NiB $952 Ex $774 Gd $542
Same as standard Model AL-3 Trap Gun except has fully-engraved receiver, gold-plated trigger and safety, stock and forearm of premium-grade European walnut, gold monogram escutcheon inlaid in buttstock. Imported 1975-76.

AL390 FIELD SHOTGUN
Lightweight version of A-390 series. Gauges: 12 or 20 ga. 22- 24-, 26-, 28-, or 30-inch bbl., 41.7 to 47.6 inches overall. Weight: 6.4 to 7.5 lbs. Imported 1992-1999.
Mdl. AL390 Field/Sil. Mallard (12 or 20 ga.) . . . NiB $734 Ex $599 Gd $425
Mdl. AL390 Field/Sil. Mallard Yth. (20 ga.) . . . . NiB $742 Ex $605 Gd $428
Model AL390 Field/Slug (12 ga. only) . . . . . . NiB $718 Ex $586 Gd $416
Model AL390 Silver Mallard camouflage . . NiB $796 Ex $649 Gd $456
Model AL390 Silver Mallard synthetic . . . . NiB $750 Ex $611 Gd $434
Model AL390 Gold Mallard (12 or 20 ga.) . NiB $824 Ex $684 Gd $486
Model AL390 NWTF Spec. camouflage . . . NiB $994 Ex $808 Gd $571
Model AL390 NWTF Spec. synthetic . . . . . NiB $807 Ex $659 Gd $468
Mdl. AL390 NWTF Spec. Yth. . . . . NiB $856 Ex $508 Gd $347

AL390 SPORT SPORTING SHOTGUN
Similar to Model AL-390 Sport Skeet. Gauges: 12 or 20 ga., 28- or 30-inch bbls. Weight: 6.8 to 8 lbs. Imported from 1995-1999.
Model AL390 Sport Sporting . . . . NiB $732 Ex $603 Gd $426
Model AL390 Sport Sporting Collection . . . . . . NiB $687 Ex $631 Gd $450
Mdl. AL390 Sport Sporting
Yth. (20 ga. only) . . . . NiB $710 Ex $578 Gd $408
Model AL390 Sport Gold Sporting . . . . NiB $980 Ex $795 Gd $557
Mdl. AL390 EELL Sport
Diamond Sporting. . . . . NiB $3558 Ex $2873 Gd $1997
W/Ported bbl., add $75

AL390 SPORT SKEET SHOTGUN
Gauges: 12 ga. only. 26- or 28-inch bbl. w/3-round mqagazine. Weight: 7.6 to 8 lbs. Matte finish wood and metal. Imported 1995 to date.
Model AL390 Sport Skeet . . . . NiB $751 Ex $609 Gd $429
Mdl. AL390 Sport Super Skeet (Semi-Auto) . . . NiB $1011 Ex $817 Gd $570
W/ported bbl., add $95

BERETTA AL390 SPORT TRAP SHOTGUN
Gauges: 12 ga. only. 30- or 32-inch bbl. w/3-round chamber. Weight: 7.8 to 8.25 lbs. Matte finish wood and metal. Black recoil rubber pad. Imported from 1995-1999.
Model AL390 Sport Trap . . . . NiB $751 Ex $609 Gd $429
Model AL390 Sport Super Trap . . . NiB $1053 Ex $850 Gd $590
Multi-choke bbl. (30" only), add $40
Ported bbl., add $95

AL391 URIKA AUTOLOADING SHOTGUN
Gauge: 12 and 20 ga. w/3-inch chambers. 28- 30- or 32-inch bbl. Weight: 6.6 to 7.7 lbs. Self-compensating gas valve. Adjustable synthetic and walnut stocks w/ five interchangeable chokes. Imported from 2000 to date.
Model AL391 Urika. . . . . NiB $862 Ex $709 Gd $490
Model AL391 Urika synthetic . . . . NiB $880 Ex $714 Gd $500
Model AL391 Urika camo
w/Realtree Hardwoods . . . . NiB $967 Ex $783 Gd $547
Model AL391 Urika
Gold w/black receiver . . . . NiB $1017 Ex $824 Gd $576
Model AL391 Urika Gold
w/silver receiver, lightweight . . . . NiB $1096 Ex $887 Gd $620
Model AL391 Urika Youth. . . . . NiB $870 Ex $706 Gd $486
Model AL391 Urika Sporting . . . . NiB $986 Ex $798 Gd $558
Model AL391 Urika Gold
Sporting w/black receiver. . . . . NiB $1071 Ex $859 Gd $600
Model AL391 Urika
Gold Sporting w/silver receiver . . . . NiB $1132 Ex $915 Gd $639
Model AL391 Urika Trap. . . . . NiB $994 Ex $805 Gd $562
Model AL391 Gold Trap . . . . NiB $1096 Ex $887 Gd $620
Model AL391 Parallel Target . . . . NiB $966 Ex $782 Gd $547

SHOTGUNS

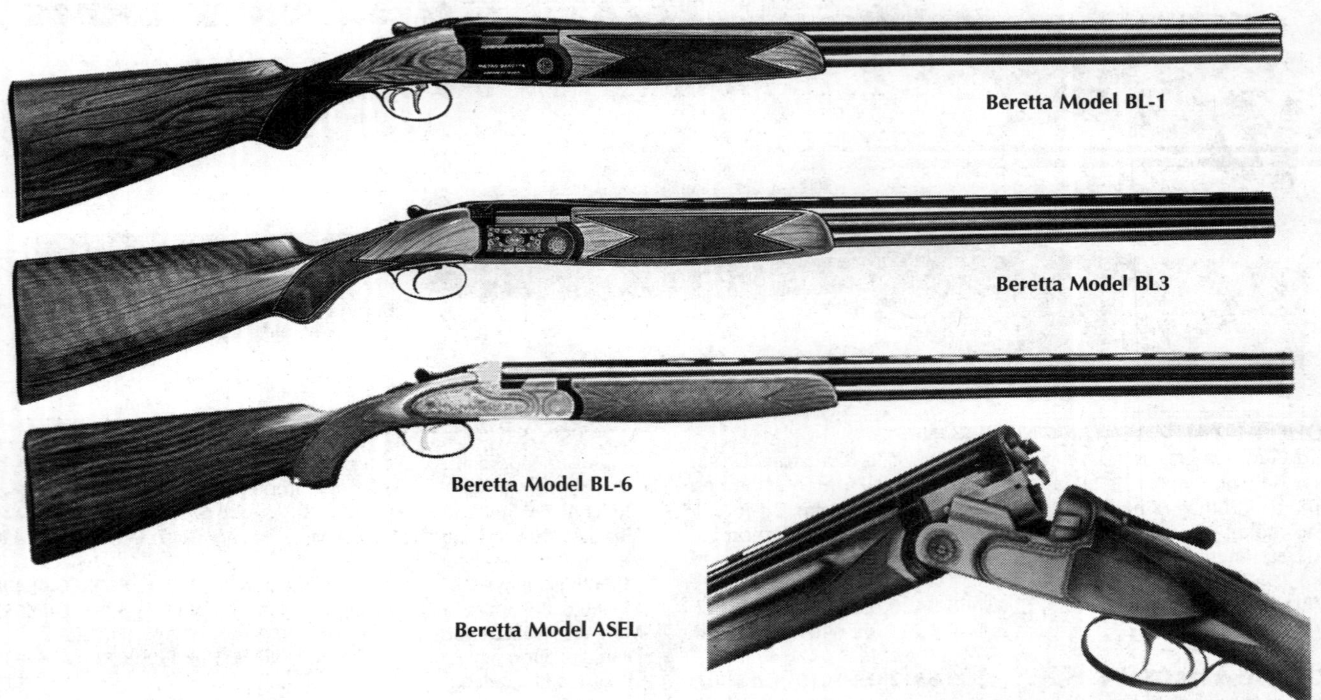
Beretta Model BL-1

Beretta Model BL3

Beretta Model BL-6

Beretta Model ASEL

MODEL ASE 90 O/U SHOTGUN
Competition-style receiver w/coin-silver finish and gold inlay featuring drop-out trigger group. Gauge: 12; 2.75-inch chamber. Bbls.: 28- or 30-inch w/fixed or Mobilchoke tubes; vent rib. Weight: 8.5 lbs. (30-inch bbl.). Checkered high-grade walnut stock. Imported 1992 to date.
Pigeon, Skeet, Trap models . . . . NiB $7760 Ex $6243 Gd $4291
Sporting Clays model. . . . . NiB $7948 Ex $6389 Gd $4394
Trap Combo model. . . . . NiB $12,140 Ex $9774 Gd $6656
Deluxe (introduced 1996) . . . . NiB $15,130 Ex $11,294 Gd $7756

MODEL ASE SERIES O/U SHOTGUN
Boxlock. Single non-selective trigger. Selective automatic ejectors. gauges: 12 and 20. Bbls. 26-, 28-, 30-inch; IC and M choke or M and F choke. Weight: about 5.75-7 lbs. Checkered pistol-grip stock and forearm. Receiver w/various grades of engraving. Imported 1947-64.
Model ASE (light scroll engraving). . . . . . . NiB $2228 Ex $1801 Gd $1254
Model ASEL (half coverage engraving) . . . . NiB $3165 Ex $2551 Gd $1759
Model ASEELL (full coverage engraving) . . . NiB $4829 Ex $3887 Gd $2682
For 20 ga. models, add 95%

MODEL BL-1/BL-2 O/U
Boxlock. Plain extractors. Double triggers.12 gauge, 2.75-inch chambers only. Bbls.: 30-and 28-inch M/F choke, 26-inch IC/M choke. Weight: 6.75-7 lbs., depending on bbl. length. Checkered pistol-grip stock and forearm. Imported 1968-73.
Model BL-1. . . . . NiB $436 Ex $348 Gd $248
Model BL-2 (single selective trigger) . . . . NiB $524 Ex $426 Gd $301

MODEL BL-2/S . . . . NiB $540 Ex $440 Gd $312
Similar to Model BL-1, except has selective "Speed-Trigger," vent-rib bbls., 2.75- or 3-inch chambers. Weight: 7-7.5 lbs. Imported 1974-76.

MODEL BL-3 . . . . NiB $762 Ex $617 Gd $432
Same as Model BL-1, except has deluxe engraved receiver, selective single trigger, vent-rib bbls., 12 or 20 ga., 2.75-inch or 3-inch chambers in former, 3-inch in latter. Weight: 6-7.5 lbs. depending on ga. and bbl. length. Imported 1968-76.

MODELS BL-4, BL-5 AND BL-6
Higher grade versions of Model BL-3 w/more elaborate engraving and fancier wood; Model BL-6 has sideplates. Selective automatic ejectors standard. Imported 1968-76.
Model BL-4 . . . . NiB $931 Ex $755 Gd $530
Model BL-5 . . . . NiB $1223 Ex $990 Gd $692
Model BL-6 (1973-76) . . . . NiB $1515 Ex $1223 Gd $849

SERIES BL SKEET GUNS
Models BL-3, BL-4, BL-5 and BL-6 w/standard features of their respective grades plus wider rib and skeet-style stock, 26-inch bbls. SK choked. Weight: 6-7.25 lbs. depending on ga.
Model BL-3 skeet gun . . . . NiB $833 Ex $677 Gd $466
Model BL-4 skeet gun . . . . NiB $957 Ex $776 Gd $545
Model BL-5 skeet gun . . . . NiB $1263 Ex $1023 Gd $735
Model BL-6 skeet gun . . . . NiB $1693 Ex $1366 Gd $948

SERIES BL TRAP GUNS
Models BL-3, BL-4, BL-5 and BL-6 w/standard features of their respective grades plus wider rib and Monte Carlo stock w/recoil pad; 30-inch bbls., improved M/F or both F choke. Weight: About 7.5 lbs.
Model BL-3 trap gun . . . . NiB $739 Ex $609 Gd $432
Model BL-4 trap gun . . . . NiB $827 Ex $672 Gd $474
Model BL-5 trap gun . . . . NiB $1263 Ex $1023 Gd $715
Model BL-6 trap gun . . . . NiB $1615 Ex $1304 Gd $907

MODEL FS-1
FOLDING SINGLE . . . . NiB $255 Ex $175 Gd $123
Formerly "Companion." Folds to length of bbl. Hammerless. Underlever. Gauge: 12, 16, 20, 28 or .410. Bbl.: 30-inch in 12 ga., 28-inch in 16 and 20 ga.; 26-inch in 28 and .410 ga.; all F choke. Checkered semipistol-grip stock/forearm. Weight: 4.5-5.5 lbs. depending on ga. Disc. 1971.

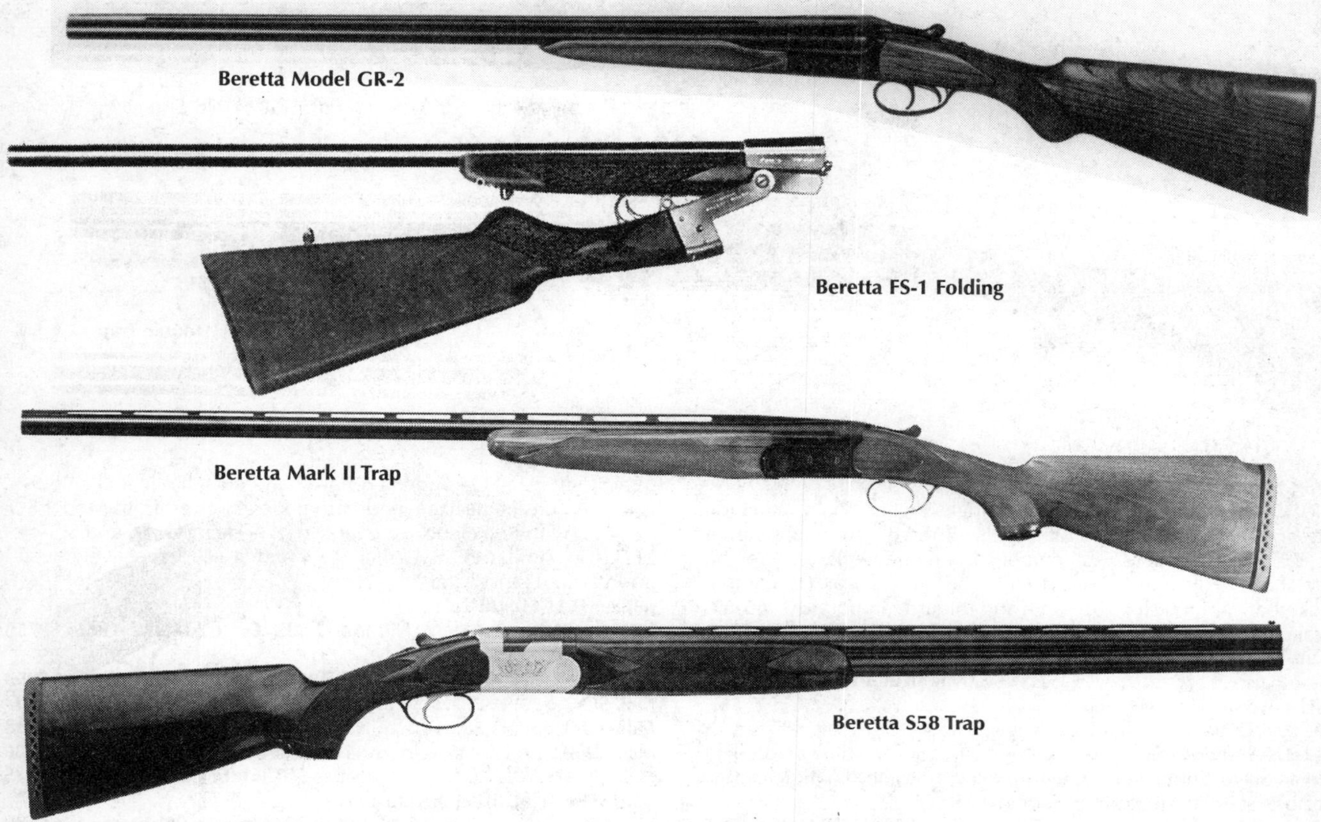
Beretta Model GR-2

Beretta FS-1 Folding

Beretta Mark II Trap

Beretta S58 Trap

MODEL GR-2 HAMMERLESS DOUBLE . . NiB $1017 Ex $823 Gd $556
Boxlock. Plain extractors. Double triggers. Gauges: 12, 20; 2.75-inch chambers in former, 3-inch in latter. Bbls.: Vent rib; 30-inch M/F choke (12 ga. only); 28-inch M/F choke, 26-inch IC/M choke. Weight: 6.5 to 7.5 lbs. depending on ga. and bbl. length. Checkered pistol-grip stock and forearm. Imported 1968-76.

MODEL GR-3 . . . . NiB $1151 Ex $931 Gd $650
Same as Model GR-2 except has selective single trigger chambered for 12-ga. Three inch or 2.75-inch shells. Magnum model has 30-inch M/F choke bbl., recoil pad. Weight: about 8 lbs. Imported 1968-76.

MODEL GR-4 . . . . NiB $1559 Ex $1258 Gd $873
Same as Model GR-2 except has automatic ejectors and selective single trigger, higher grade engraving and wood. 12 ga., 2.75-inch chambers only. Imported 1968-76.

GRADE 100 O/U
SHOTGUN . . . . NiB $2005 Ex $1616 Gd $1119
Sidelock. Double triggers. Automatic ejectors. 12 ga. only. Bbls.: 26-, 28-, 30-inch, any standard boring. Weight: About 7.5 lbs. Checkered stock and forend, straight or pistol grip. Disc.

GRADE 200 . . . . NiB $2632 Ex $2125 Gd $1476
Same general specifications as Grade 100 except higher quality; bores and action parts hard chrome plated. Disc.

MARK II SINGLE-BARREL TRAP GUN . . . . NiB $624 Ex $506 Gd $356
Boxlock action similar to that of Series "BL" over-and-unders. Engraved receiver. Automatic ejector. 12 ga. only. 32- or 34-inch bbl. w/wide vent rib. Weight: About 8.5 lbs. Monte Carlo stock w/pistol grip and recoil pad, beavertail forearm. Imported 1972-76.

MODEL S55B O/U
SHOTGUN . . . . NiB $662 Ex $610 Gd $480
Boxlock. Plain extractors. Selective single trigger. Gauges: 12, 20; 2.75- or 3-inch chambers in former, 3-inch in latter. Bbls. vent rib; 30-inch M/F choke or both F choke in 12-ga. Three inch Magnum only; 28-inch M/F choke; 26 inch IC/M choke. Weight: 6.5 to 7.5 lbs. depending on ga. and bbl. length. Checkered pistol-grip stock and forearm. Introduced in 1977. Disc.

MODEL S56E. . . . . NiB $926 Ex $666 Gd $458
Same as Model S55B except has scroll-engraved receiver selective automatic ejectors. Introduced in 1977. Disc.

MODEL S58 SKEET GUN . . . . NiB $874 Ex $624 Gd $458
Same as Model S56E except has 26-inch bbls. of Boehler Antinit Anticorro steel, SK choked, w/wide vent rib; skeet-style stock and forearm. Weight: 7.5 lbs. Introduced in 1977.

MODEL S58 TRAP GUN . . . . NiB $869 Ex $484 Gd $458
Same as Model S58 Skeet Gun except has 30-inch bbls. bored IM/F Trap, Monte Carlo stock w/recoil pad. Weight: 7 lbs. 10 oz. Introduced in 1977. Disc.

SILVER HAWK FEATHERWEIGHT
HAMMERLESS DOUBLE-BARREL SHOTGUN
Boxlock. Double triggers or non-selective single trigger. Plain extractor. Gauges: 12, 16, 20, 28, 12 Mag. Bbls.: 26- to 32-inch w/high matted rib, all standard choke combinations. Weight: 7 lbs. (12 ga. w/26-inch bbls.). Checkered walnut stock w/beavertail forearm. Disc. 1967.
W/double triggers . . . . NiB $712 Ex $532 Gd $350
For non-selective single trigger, add $65

SHOTGUNS

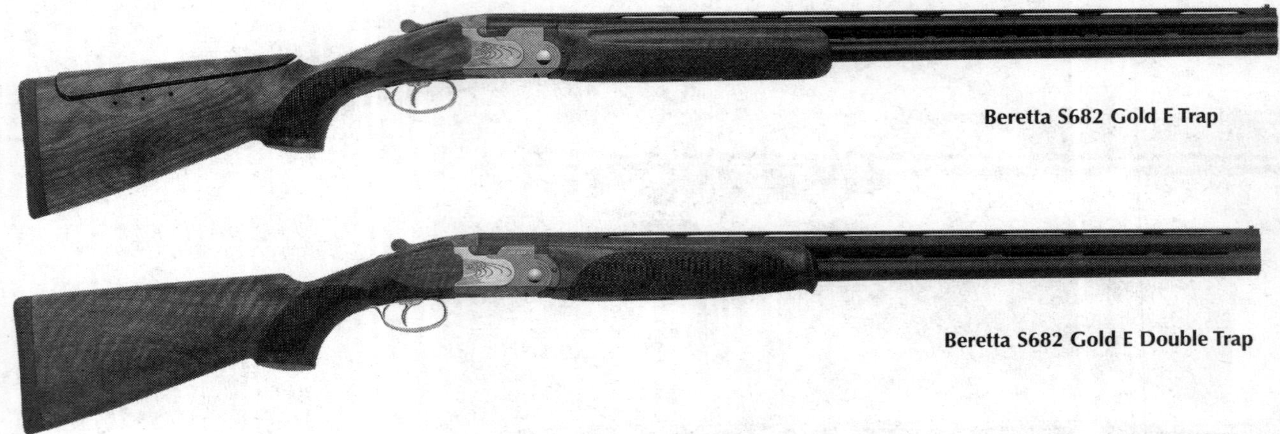

Beretta S682 Gold E Trap

Beretta S682 Gold E Double Trap

SILVER SNIPE O/U SHOTGUN

Boxlock. Non-selective or selective single trigger. Plain extractor. Gauges: 12, 20, 12 Mag., 20 Mag. Bbls.: 26-, 28-, 30-inch; plain or vent rib; chokes IC/M, M/F, SK number 1 and number 2, F/F. Weight: From about 6 lbs. in 20 ga. to 8.5 lbs. in 12 ga. (Trap gun). Checkered walnut pistol-grip stock and forearm. Imported 1955-67.

W/plain bbl., non-selective trigger .... NiB $812 Ex $734 Gd $376
W/vent rib bbl., non-selective single trigger .... NiB $838 Ex $760 Gd $422
For selective single trigger, add $65

GOLDEN SNIPE O/U

Same as Silver Snipe (see page 430) except has automatic ejectors, vent rib is standard feature. Imported 1959-67.

W/non-selective single trigger .... NiB $1089 Ex $924 Gd $512
W/selective single trigger, add $100

MODEL 57E O/U

Same general specifications as Golden Snipe, but higher quality throughout. Imported 1955-67.

W/non-selective single trigger ... NiB $1094 Ex $969 Gd $553
W/selective single trigger .... NiB $1131 Ex $917 Gd $642

MODEL SL-2 PIGEON SERIES PUMP GUN

Hammerless. Takedown.12 ga. only. Three round magazine. Bbls.: Vent rib; 30-inch F choke, 28-inch M, 26-inch IC. Weight: 7-7.25 lbs., depending on bbl. length. Receiver w/various grades of engraving. Checkered pistol-grip stock and forearm. Imported 1968-71.

Model SL-2 .... NiB $450 Ex $368 Gd $263
Silver Pigeon .... NiB $375 Ex $307 Gd $221
Gold Pigeon.................. NiB $562 Ex $457 Gd $323
Ruby Pigeon.................. NiB $712 Ex $577 Gd $404

"SO" SERIES SHOTGUNS

Jubilee Series introduced in 1998. The Beretta Boxlock is made with mechanical works from a single block of hot forged, high- resistance steel. The gun is richly engraved in scroll and game scenes. All engraving is signed by master engravers. High-quality finishing on the inside with high polishing of all internal points. Sidelock. Selective automatic ejectors. Selective single trigger or double triggers. 12 ga. only, 2.75- or 3-inch chambers. Bbls.: Vent rib (wide type on skeet and trap guns); 26-, 27-, 29-, 30-inch; any combination of standard chokes. Weight: 7 to 7.75 lbs., depending on bbl. length, style of stock and density of wood. Stock and forearm of select walnut, finely checkered; straight or pistol-grip, field, skeet and trap guns have appropriate styles of stock and forearm. Models differ chiefly in quality of wood and grade of engraving. Models SO-3EL, SO-3EELL, SO4 and SO-5 have hand-detachable locks. "SO-4" is used to designate skeet and trap models derived from Model SO-3EL, but with less elaborate engraving. Models SO3EL and SO-3EELL are similar to the earlier SO-4 and SO-5, respectively. Imported 1933 to date.

Jubilee O/U 410-28-20-12 .... NiB to $17,933 Ex to $14,347 Gd to $9756
Jubilee II Side-by-side .... NiB to $19,441 Ex to $14,637 Gd to $9953
Mdl. SO-2 .... NiB to $8573 Ex to $4570 Gd to $3107
Mdl. SO-3 .... NiB to $7143 Ex to $6629 Gd to $4508
Mdl. SO-3EL .... NiB to $9145 Ex to $7773 Gd to $5286
Mdl. SO-3EELL............... NiB to $10,861 Ex to $11,434 Gd to $7775
Mdl. SO-4 Field, Skeet or Trap gun .... NiB to $9147 Ex to $8313 Gd to $6220
Model SO-5 Sporting, Skt. or Trp. .... NiB to $11,830 Ex to $9880 Gd to $7768
W/extra bbl. set, add 25%

MODELS SO-6 AND SO-9 PREMIUM GRADE SHOTGUNS

High-grade over/unders in the SO series. Gauges: 12 ga. only (SO-6); 12, 20, 28 and .410 (SO-9). Fixed or Mobilchoke (12 ga. only). Sidelock action. Silver or casehardened receiver (SO-6); English custom hand-engraved scroll or game scenes (SO-9). Supplied w/leather case and accessories. Imported from about 1990 to date.

SO-6 O/U .... NiB $7996 Ex to $6812 Gd to $4632
SO-6 EELL O/U .... NiB to $5714 Ex to $8730 Gd to $5937
SO-9 O/U .... to $48,667
SO-9 EELL special engraving......................... to $93,600
W/extra bbl. set, add................................ 25%

MODEL SO6/SO-7 S/S DOUBLES

Side-by-side shotgun w/same general specifications as SO Series over/unders except higher grade w/more elaborate engraving, fancier wood.

SO-6 SxS (imported 1948-82).................... to $6,937
SO-7 SxS (imported 1948-90).................... to $8,856

MODEL TR-1 SINGLE-SHOT TRAP GUN .... NiB $392 Ex $253 Gd $233

Hammerless. Underlever action. Engraved frame.12 ga. only. 32-inch bbl. w/vent rib. Weight: About 8.25 lbs. Monte Carlo stock w/pistol grip and recoil pad, beavertail forearm. Imported 1968-71.

MODEL TR-2 .... NiB $436 Ex $357 Gd $256

Same as Model TR-1 except has extended ventilated rib. Imported 1969-73.

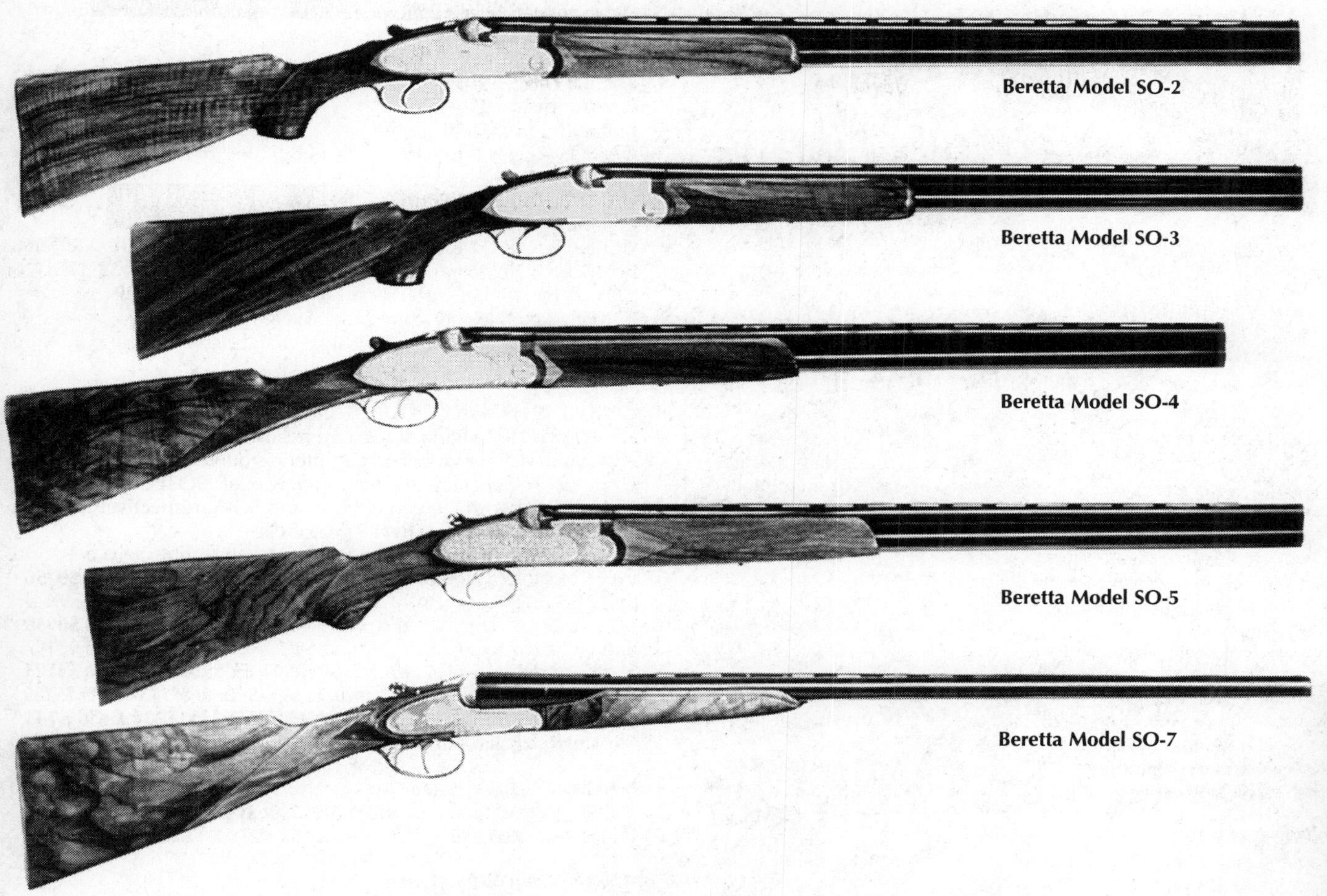

Beretta Model SO-2

Beretta Model SO-3

Beretta Model SO-4

Beretta Model SO-5

Beretta Model SO-7

VICTORIA PINTAIL (ES100) SEMIAUTOLOADER
Short Montefeltro-type recoil action. Gauge: 12 w/3-inch chamber. Bbl.: 24-inch slug, 24-, 26- or 28-inch vent rib w/Mobilchoke tubes. Weight: 7 lbs. to 7 lbs., 5 oz. Checkered synthetic or walnut buttstock and forend. Matte finish on both metal and stock. Imported 1993 and 2005.

Field model w/synthetic stock (intro. 1998) .... **NiB $659 Ex $548 Gd $382**
Field model w/walnut stock (disc. 1998)...... **NiB $617 Ex $503 Gd $359**
Rifled slug model w/synthetic stock (intro. 1998) .... **NiB $802 Ex $652 Gd $460**
Standard slug model w/walnut stock (disc. 1998) .... **NiB $588 Ex $481 Gd $343**
Wetland Camo model (intro. 2000) ...... **NiB $759 Ex $608 Gd $437**

VINCENZO BERNARDELLI — Gardone V.T. (Brescia), Italy

Previously imported by Armsport, Miami, FL (formerly by Magnum Research, Inc., Quality Arms, Stoeger Industries, Inc. & Action Arms, LTD).

115 SERIES O/U SHOTGUNS
Boxlock w/single trigger and ejectors. 12 ga. only. 25.5-, 26.75-, and 29.5-inch bbls. Concave top and vented middle rib. Anatomical grip stock. Blued or coin-silver finish w/various grades of engraving. Imported 1985-97.

Hunting Model 115 (disc. 1990)..... **NiB $1916 Ex $1546 Gd $1073**
Hunting Model 115E (disc. 1990)..... **NiB $5694 Ex $4579 Gd $3153**
Hunting Model 115L (disc. 1990)..... **NiB $3162 Ex $2548 Gd $1760**
Hunting Model 115S (disc. 1990) .... **NiB $2691 Ex $2171 Gd $1501**
Target Model 115 (disc. 1992) ...... **NiB $2156 Ex $1741 Gd $1209**
Target Model 115E (disc. 1992) ..... **NiB $6440 Ex $5180 Gd $3573**
Target Model 115L (disc. 1992) ..... **NiB $3992 Ex $3214 Gd $2216**
Target Model 115S (disc. 1992) ..... **NiB $2877 Ex $2320 Gd $1605**
Trap/Skeet Model 115S (imported 1996-97) .... **NiB $2942 Ex $2371 Gd $1641**
Sporting Clays Model 115S (imported 1995-97)................ **NiB $4335 Ex $3492 Gd $2411**

BRESCIA HAMMER DOUBLE............ **NiB $1036 Ex $840 Gd $590**
Back-action sidelock. Plain extractors. Double triggers. Gauges: 12, 20. Bbls.: 27.5 or 29.5-inch M/F choke in 12 ga. 25.5-inch IC/M choke in 20 ga.. Weight: From 5.75 to 7 lbs., depending on ga. and bbl. length. English-style stock and forearm, checkered. No longer imported.

ELIO .... **NiB $1224 Ex $991 Gd $693**
Lightweight game gun, 12 ga. only, w/same general specifications as Standard Gamecock (S. Uberto 1) except weight: About 6 to 6.25 lbs.; has automatic ejectors, fine English-pattern scroll engraving. No longer imported.

Bernardelli Gamecock

Bernardelli Standard Gamecock

Bernardelli Gardone

Bernardelli Italia

Bernardelli Roma 6

GAMECOCK, PREMIER (ROME 3)
Same general specifications as Standard Gamecock (S. Uberto 1) except has sideplates, auto ejectors, single trigger. No longer imported.
Roma 3 (disc. 1989,
Reintroduced 1993-97) . . . . NiB $1681 Ex $1355 Gd $939
Roma 3E (disc. 1950) Roma 3M
w/single trigger (disc. 1997) . . . NiB $1869 Ex $1506 Gd $1042

GAMECOCK, STANDARD
(S. UBERTO 1) HAMMERLESS
DOUBLE-BARREL SHOTGUN . . . . NiB $1180 Ex $956 Gd $668
Boxlock. Plain extractors. Double triggers. Gauges: 12, 16, 20; 2.75-inch chambers in 12 and 16, 3-inch in 20 ga. Bbls. 25.5-inch IC/M choke; 27.5-inch M/F choke. Weight: 5.75-6.5 lbs., depending on ga. and bbl. length. English-style straight-grip stock and forearm, checkered. No longer imported.

GARDONE HAMMER DOUBLE . . . NiB $2643 Ex $2138 Gd $1511
Same general specifications as Brescia except for higher grade engraving and wood, but not as high as the Italia. Half-cock safety. Disc. 1956.

HEMINGWAY HAMMERLESS DOUBLE
Boxlock. Single or double triggers w/hinged front. Selective automatic ejectors. Gauges: 12 and 20 w/2.75- or 3-inch chambers, 16 and 28 w/2.75-inch. Bbls.: 23.5- to 28-inch w/fixed chokes. Weight: 6.25 lbs. Checkered English-style European walnut stock. Silvered and engraved receiver.
Standard model . . . . NiB $2137 Ex $1732 Gd $1215
Deluxe model
w/sideplates (disc. 1993). . . . . . NiB $2486 Ex $2009 Gd $1405
For single trigger, add $100

ITALIA . . . . NiB $3482 Ex $2797 Gd $1920
Same general specifications as Brescia except higher grade engraving and wood. Disc. 1986.

ROMA 4 AND ROMA 6
Same as Premier Gamecock (Rome 3) except higher grade engraving and wood, double triggers. Disc. 1997.
Roma 4 (disc. 1989) . . . . NiB $1372 Ex $1113 Gd $782
Roma 4E (disc. 1997) . . . . NiB $1704 Ex $1378 Gd $962
Roma 6 (disc. 1989) . . . . NiB $1400 Ex $1144 Gd $803
Roma 6E (disc. 1997) . . . . NiB $2101 Ex $1701 Gd $1189

ROMA 7, 8, AND 9
Side-by-side. Anson & Deeley boxlock; hammerless. Ejectors; double triggers. 12 ga. Barrels: 27.5-or 29.5-inch. M/F chokes. Fancy hand-checkered European walnut straight or pistol-grip stock, forearm. Elaborately engraved, silver-finished sideplates. Imported 1994-97.
Roma 7 . . . . NiB $2508 Ex $2027 Gd $1411
Roma 8 . . . . NiB $3034 Ex $2448 Gd $1749
Roma 9 . . . . NiB $3742 Ex $3115 Gd $2085

S. UBERTO 2 . . . . NiB $1477 Ex $1192 Gd $828
Same as Standard Gamecock (S. Uberto 1) except higher grade engraving and wood. Currently imported.

S. UBERTO F.S.
Same as Standard Gamecock except w/higher grade engraving, wood and has auto-ejectors. Disc. 1989, reintroduced 1993-97.
Model FS . . . . NiB $1828 Ex $1470 Gd $1012
Model V.B. Incisio . . . . NiB $2085 Ex $1678 Gd $1156
W/single trigger, add $75

HOLLAND V.B. SERIES SHOTGUNS
Holland & Holland-type sidelock action. Auto-ejectors. Double triggers. 12 ga. only. Bbl. length or choke to custom specification. Silver-finish receiver (Liscio) or engraved coin finish receiver (Incisio). Extra-select wood and game scene engraving (Lusso). Checkered stock (straight or pistol-grip). Imported 1992-97.
Model V.B. Liscio. . . . . NiB $6274 Ex $5027 Gd $3431
Model V.B. Incisio . . . . NiB $7796 Ex $6248 Gd $4268
Model V.B. Lusso . . . . NiB $9298 Ex $7455 Gd $5093
Model V.B. Extra. . . . . NiB $10,726 Ex $8580 Gd $5834
Model V.B. Gold. . . . . NiB $37,636 Ex $30,108 Gd $20,473
Engraving Pattern No. 4, add. $950
Engraving Pattern No. 12, add. $4450
Engraving Pattern No. 20, add $8750
Single trigger, add $595

BOSS & COMPANY — London, England

HAMMERLESS DOUBLE-BARREL SHOTGUN. . . . . NiB $62,676 Ex $50,000 Gd $32,800
Sidelock. Automatic ejectors. Double triggers, non-selective or selective single trigger. Made in all gauges, bbl. lengths and chokes. Checkered stock and forend, straight or pistol-grip.

HAMMERLESS O/U SHOTGUN. . . . . NiB $109,683 Ex $80,500 Gd $40,000
Sidelock. Automatic ejectors. Selective single trigger. Made in all gauges, bbl. lengths and chokes. Checkered stock and forend, straight or pistol-grip. Disc.

BREDA MECCANICA BRESCIANA — Brescia, Italy, *formerly* ERNESTO BREDA, Milan, Italy

Previously imported by Tristar (Kansas City, MO), Gryphon International (Kansas City, MO) and Diana Imports Co., (San Francisco, CA).

VEGA SPECIAL O/U SHOTGUN . . . NiB $605 Ex $460 Gd $335
12 or 20 gauge. Box lock action. Bbl. 26 or 28 inches; single trigger; ejectors. Blue only.

VEGA SPECIAL TRAP. . . . . NiB $962 Ex $807 Gd $687
12 or 20 gauge. Box lock action. Competition triggers and lock. Bbl. 30 or 32 inches; single trigger; ejectors. Blue only.

VEGA LUSSO . . . . NiB $2013 Ex $1193 Gd $968
12 gauge only, 3-inch chambers. Scalloped box lock action, single selective trigger, ejectors. Bbl. 26 or 28 inches, ventilated rib. Coin finished receiver with light engraving. Deluxe checkered Circassian walnut stock and forearm. Imported 2001-02.

SIRIO STANDARD. . . . . NiB $2220 Ex $1670 Gd $1215
12 or 20 gauge. Engraved box lock action. Bbl. 26 or 28 inches; single trigger; ejectors. Blue only. Also available in skeet model.

ANDROMEDA SPECIAL . . . . NiB $735 Ex $560 Gd $405
Side-by-side.12 gauge, single trigger; ejectors, select checkered walnut stock; satin finish on receiver with elaborate engraving.

GOLD SERIES SEMIAUTOMATIC SHOTGUN
12 or (lightweight) 20 gauge, 2.75-inch chamber. Bbl. 25 or 27 inches; ventilated rib standard. Recoil operated
Antares Standard Model . . . . NiB $535 Ex $405 Gd $285

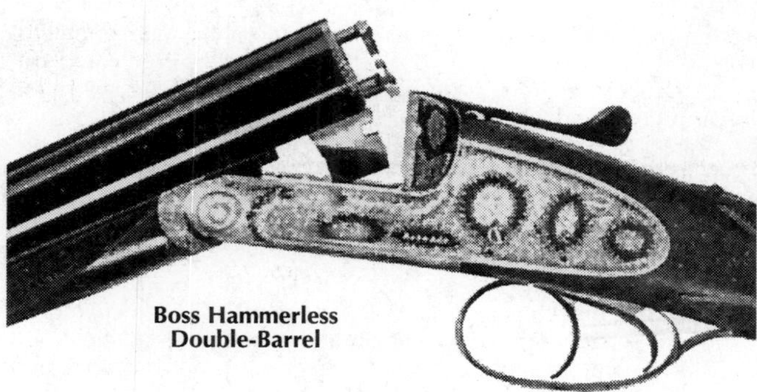
Boss Hammerless Double-Barrel

Argus Model . . . . NiB $545 Ex $415 Gd $305
Aries Model. . . . . NiB $565 Ex $435 Gd $325

STANDARD GRADE GOLD SERIES. NiB $360 Ex $235 Gd $200
12 gauge, 2-3/4-inch chamber. Recoil operated. Bbl. 25 or 27 inches. Light engraving. Disc.

GRADE 1. . . . . NiB $635 Ex $495 Gd $385
Similar to Standard model but with fancier wood and engraving.

GRADE 2. NiB $725 Ex $535 Gd $410
Similar to Grade 1 but with more engraving, etc.

GRADE 3 . . . . NiB $914 Ex $739 Gd $564
Same as Grade 1 but with custom-quality embellishments.

MAGNUM MODEL . . . . NiB $535 Ex $410 Gd $305
Similar to Standard Grade but with 3-inch chambers.

ALTAIR SPECIAL . . . . NiB $505 Ex $330 Gd $270
12 gauge, 2.75-inch chamber. Gas-operated. Bbl. 25 or 27 inches, ventilated rib standard. Alloy construction, blue or chrome receiver.

ASTRO. . . . . NiB $1115 Ex $765 Gd $540
12 gauge (disc. 2002) or 20 gauge, 3-inch chamber. Inertia action. Bbl. 22 (slug), 24, 26, 28 or 30 inches; ventilated rib. Black synthetic, Advantage camo, or Circassian walnut stock and forearm. Imported 2001.
Advantage camo model, add. $100

ASTROLUX . . . . NiB $1545 Ex $1270 Gd $945
Similar to Astro model except has two-tone receiver with engraving and deluxe checkered Circassian walnut stock and forearm. Imported 2001-02.

ERMES SERIES . . . . NiB $1135 Ex $905 Gd $760
12 gauge, 3-inch chamber. Semiautomatic. Inertia recoil operating system, aluminum alloy receiver, nickeel plated or blue finish on lower receiver. Bbl. 24, 26, or 28 inches. Deluxe checkered Circassian walnut stock and forearm. Imported 2001.
Ermes Silver. . . . . NiB $1849 Ex $1119 Gd $919
Ermes Gold. . . . . NiB $2019 Ex $1699 Gd $1419

MIRA . . . . NiB $965 Ex $740 Gd $610
12 gauge, 3-inch chamber. Semiautomatic, gas-operated. Aluminum alloy receiver; black or Advantage camo finish. Bbl. 22 (slug), 24, 26, 28 or 30 inches, ventilated rib. Circassian walnut or black synthetic stock and forearm. Imported 2001.
Black synthetic stock and forearm, deduct 10%
Sporting Clays model, add $25

SHOTGUNS

ARIES 2 .... NiB $935 Ex $760 Gd $605
12 gauge, 2-3/4-inch chamber. Semiautomatic, gas-operated. Engraved two-tone receiver. Bbl. 20 or 30 inches, ventilated rib. Deluxe checkered Circassian walnut or black synthetic stock and forearm. Imported 2001 only.

BRETTON SHOTGUNS — St. Etienne (Cedex1), France

BABY STANDARD SPRINT O/U .... NiB $1087 Ex $979 Gd $629
Inline sliding breech action. 12 or 20 gauge w/2.75-inch chambers. 27.5-inch separated bbls. w/vent rib and choke tubes. Weight: 4.8 to 5 lbs. Engraved alloy receiver. Checkered walnut buttstock and forearm w/satin oil finish. Imported 1992 to date.

SPRINT DELUXE O/U.................... NiB $980 Ex 856 Gd $568
Similar to the Standard Model except w/engraved coin-finished receiver and chambered 12, 16 and 20 ga. Discontinued 1994.

FAIR PLAY O/U................ NiB $1040 Ex $881 Gd $551
Lightweight action similar to the Sprint Model except w/hinged action that pivots open and is chambered 12 or 20 gauge only.

BRNO SHOTGUNS — Brno and Uherski Brod, Czech Republic, (formerly Czechoslovakia)

500 O/U SHOTGUN .... NiB $933 Ex $805 Gd $496
Hammerless boxlock w/double triggers and ejectors.12 ga. w/2.75-inch chambers. 27.5-inch bbls.. choked M/F. 44 inches overall. Weight: 7 lbs. Etched receiver. Checkered walnut stock w/classic style cheekplece. Imported from 1987-91.

500 SERIES O/U COMBINATION GUNS
Similar to the 500 Series over/under shotgun above, except w/lower bbl. chambered in rifle calibers and set trigger option. Imported from 1987-95.
Model 502 12/222, 12/243 (disc. 1991)..... NiB $1138 Ex $924 Gd $649
Model 502 12/308, 12/30.06 (disc. 1991) ... NiB $1185 Ex $961 Gd $674
Model 571 12/6x65R (disc. 1993) .... NiB $1030 Ex $838 Gd $590
Model 572 12/7x65R (imported since 1992)..... NiB $1107 Ex $899 Gd $631
Model 584 12/7x57R (imported since 1992) ..... NiB $1138 Ex $924 Gd $649
Sport Series 4-bbl. set (disc. 1991) .... NiB $2978 Ex $2406 Gd $1674

CZ 581 SOLO O/U SHOTGUN........... NiB $854 Ex $691 Gd $483
Hammerless boxlock w/double triggers, ejectors and automatic safety. 12 ga. w/2.75- or 3-inch chambers. 28-inch bbls. choked M/F. Weight: 7.5 lbs. Checkered walnut stock. Disc. 1996.

SUPER SERIES O/U SHOTGUN
Hammerless sidelock w/selective single or double triggers and ejectors. 12 ga. w/2.75- or 3-inch chambers. 27.5-inch bbls. choked M/F. 44.5 inches overall. Weight: 7.25 lbs. Etched or engraved side plates. Checkered European walnut stock w/classic-style cheekpiece. Imported from 1987-91.
Super Series Shotgun (disc. 1992)......... NiB $1072 Ex $867 Gd $604
Super Series Combo (disc. 1992) .... NiB $1254 Ex $1013 Gd $684
Super Ser. 3-bbl. set (disc. 1990)......... NiB $2474 Ex $1994 Gd $1380
Super Series engraving, add $1250

ZH 300 SERIES O/U SHOTGUNS
Hammerless boxlock w/double triggers. Gauge: 12 or 16 w/2.75- or 3-inch chambers. Bbls.: 26, 27.5 or 30 inches; choked M/F. Weight: 7 lbs. Skip-line checkered walnut stock w/classic-style cheekpiece. Imported from 1986-93.
Model 300 (disc. 1993) .... NiB $615 Ex $498 Gd $347
Model 301 Field (disc. 1991) .... NiB $630 Ex $509 Gd $355
Model 302 Skeet (disc. 1992) .... NiB $701 Ex $566 Gd $394
Model 303 Trap (disc. 1992) .... NiB $728 Ex $588 Gd $409

ZH 300 SERIES O/U COMBINATION GUNS
Similar to the 300 Series over/under shotgun except lower bbl. chambered in rifle calibers.
Model 300 Combo
8-bbl. Set (disc. 1991) .... NiB $3501 Ex $2743 Gd $1978
Model 304 12 ga./7x57R (disc. 1995) .... NiB $726 Ex $591 Gd $418
Model 305 12 ga./5.6x52R (disc. 1993) ...... NiB $816 Ex $663 Gd $467
Model 306 12 ga./5.6x50R (disc. 1993) ...... NiB $854 Ex $694 Gd $488
Model 307 12 ga./.22 Hornet
(Imported since 1995) .... NiB $759 Ex $617 Gd $435
Model 324 16 ga./7x57R (disc. 1987 .... NiB $791 Ex $642 Gd $453

ZP 149 HAMMERLESS DOUBLE
Sidelock action w/double triggers, automatic ejectors and automatic safety.12 ga. w/2.75- or 3-inch chambers. 28.5-inch bbls. choked M/F. Weight: 7.25 lbs. Checkered walnut buttstock with cheekpiece.
Standard model .... NiB $662 Ex $539 Gd $483
Engraved model .... NiB $720 Ex $586 Gd $515

BROLIN ARMS, INC. — Pomona, California

ARMS HAWK PUMP SHOTGUN, FIELD SERIES
Slide-action. Gauge: 12 ga. w/3-inch chamber. 24-, 26-, 28- or 30-inch bbl. 44 and 50 inches overall. Weight: 7.3 to 7.6 lbs. Cross-bolt safety. Vent rib bbl. w/screw-in choke tube and bead sights. Non-reflective metal finish. Synthetic or oil-finished wood stock w/swivel studs. Made from 1997-98.
Synthetic stock model .... NiB $252 Ex $212 Gd $150
Wood stock model.............. NiB $239 Ex $197 Gd $142

ARMS HAWK PUMP SHOTGUN COMBO MODEL
Similar to the Field Model except w/extra 18.5- or 22-inch bbl. w/bead or rifle sight. Made from 1997-98.
Synthetic stock model .... NiB $274 Ex $224 Gd $161
Wood stock model.............. NiB $261 Ex $213 Gd $149

ARMS HAWK PUMP SHOTGUN LAWMAN MODEL
Similar to the Field Model except has 18.5-inch bbl. w/cylinder bore fixed choke. Weight: 7 lbs. Dual operating bars. Bead, rifle or ghost ring sights. Black synthetic or wood stock. Matte chrome or satin nickel finish. Made from 1997-99.
Synthetic stock model .... NiB $235 Ex $193 Gd $139
Wood stock model .... NiB $223 Ex $183 Gd $132
Rifle sights, add.. $20
Ghost ring sights, add..................................... $35
Satin nickel finish (disc. 1997), add $25

ARMS HAWK SLUG MODEL
Similar to the Field Model except has 18.5- or 22-inch bbl. w/IC fixed choke or 4-inch extended rifled choke. Rifle or ghost ring sights or optional cantilevered scope mount. Black synthetic or wood stock. Matte blued finish. Made from 1998-99.
Synthetic stock model .... NiB $235 Ex $193 Gd $139
Wood stock model .... NiB $223 Ex $183 Gd $132
W/rifled bbl., add.. $20
W/cantilevered scope mount, add $35

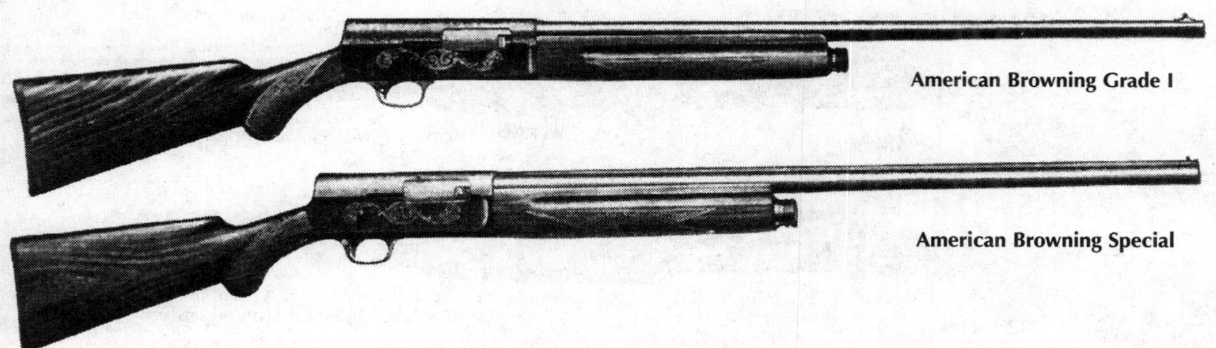

American Browning Grade I

American Browning Special

ARMS HAWK TURKEY SPECIAL
Similar to the Field Model except has 22-inch vent-rib bbl. w/extended extra-full choke. Rifle or ghost ring sights or optional cantilevered scope mount. Black synthetic or wood stock. Matte blued finish. Made from 1998-99.
Synthetic stock model .... NiB $227 Ex $186 Gd $134
Wood stock model .... NiB $215 Ex $176 Gd $127
W/cantilevered
scope mount, add $25

BROWNING SHOTGUNS — Morgan (formerly Ogden), Utah

AMERICAN BROWNING SHOTGUNS

Designated "American" Browning because they were produced in Ilion, New York, the following Remington-made Brownings are almost identical to the Remington Model 11A and Sportsman and the Browning Auto-5. They are the only Browning shotguns manufactured in the U.S. during the 20th century and were made for Browning Arms when production was suspended in Belgium because of WW II.

NOTE: *Fabrique Nationale Herstal (formerly Fabrique Nationale d'Armes de Guerre) of Herstal, Belgium, is the longtime manufacturer of Browning shotguns dating back to 1900. Miroku Firearms Mfg. Co. of Tokyo, Japan, bought into the Browning company and has, since the early 1970s, undertaken some of the production. The following shotguns were manufactured for Browning by these two firms.*

GRADE I AUTOLOADER (AUTO-5)
Recoil-operated autoloader. Similar to the Remington Model 11A except w/different style engraving and identified w/the Browning logo. Gauges: 12, 16 or 20. Plain 26- to 32-inch bbl. w/any standard boring. Two or four shell tubular magazine w/magazine cut-off. Weight: About 6.88 lbs. (20 ga.) to 8 lbs. (12 ga.). Checkered pistol-grip stock and forearm. Made from 1940-49.
American Browning Grade I
Auto-5, 12 or 16 ga.................. NiB $735 Ex $632 Gd $298
20 ga., add.. 20%

SPECIAL 441
Same general specifications as Grade I except supplied w/raised matted rib or vent rib. Disc. 1949.
W/raised matted rib .... NiB $813 Ex $710 Gd $375
W/vent rib .... NiB $838 Ex $735 Gd $385
20 ga., add.. 20%

SPECIAL SKEET MODEL .... NiB $716 Ex $581 Gd $408
Same general specifications as Grade I except has 26-inch bbl. w/vent rib and Cutts Compensator. Disc. 1949.

UTILITY FIELD GUN............ NiB $555 Ex $349 Gd $246
Same general specifications as Grade I except has 28-inch plain bbl. w/Poly Choke. Disc. 1949.

MODEL 12 PUMP SHOTGUN
Special limited edition Winchester Model 12. Gauge: 20 or 28. Five-round tubular magazine. 26-inch bbl., M choke. 45 inches overall. Weight: about 7 lbs. Grade I has blued receiver, checkered walnut stock w/matte finish. Grade V has engraved receiver, checkered deluxe walnut stock w/high-gloss finish. Made from 1988-92. See illustration next page.
Grade I,
20 ga. (8600)................... NiB $620 Ex $504 Gd $355
Grade I, 28 ga. .... NiB $652 Ex $529 Gd $373
Grade V, 20 ga (4000).......... NiB $1081 Ex $876 Gd $613
Grade V, 28 ga .... NiB $1046 Ex $846 Gd $591

MODEL 42 LIMITED EDITION SHOTGUN
Special limited edition Winchester Model 42 pump shotgun. Same general specifications as Model 12 except w/smaller frame in .410 ga. and 3-inch chamber. Made from 1991-93.
Grade I
(6000 produced) .... NiB $680 Ex $552 Gd $389
Grade V
(6000 produced) .... NiB $1081 Ex $866 Gd $614

2000 BUCK SPECIAL............ NiB $446 Ex $364 Gd $260
Same as Field Model except has 24-inch plain bbl. Bored for rifled slug and buckshot, fitted w/rifle sights (open rear, ramp front). 12 ga., 2.75-inch or 3-inch chamber; 20 ga., 2.75-inch chamber. Weight: 12 ga., 7 lbs., 8 oz.; 20 ga., 6 lbs., 10 oz. Made from 1974-81 by FN.

2000 GAS AUTOMATIC SHOTGUN, FIELD MODEL
Gas-operated. Gauge: 12 or 20. 2.75-inch chamber. Four-round magazine. Bbl.: 26-, 28-, 30-inch, any standard choke plain matted bbl. (12 ga. only) or vent rib. Weight: 6 lbs. 11 oz.-7 lbs. 12 oz. depending on ga. and bbl. length. Checkered pistol-grip stock/forearm. Made from 1974-81 by FN; assembled in Portugal.
W/plain matted bbl. .... NiB $610 Ex $378 Gd $275
W/vent rib bbl.................. NiB $620 Ex $404 Gd $280

2000 MAGNUM MODEL .... NiB $620 Ex $404 Gd $280
Same as Field Model except chambered for 3-inch shells, three-round magazine. Bbl.: 26- (20 ga. only), 28-, 30- or 32-inch (latter two 12 ga. only); any standard choke; vent rib. Weight: 6 lbs., 11 oz.-7 lbs., 13 oz. depending on ga. and bbl. Made from 1974-81 by FN.

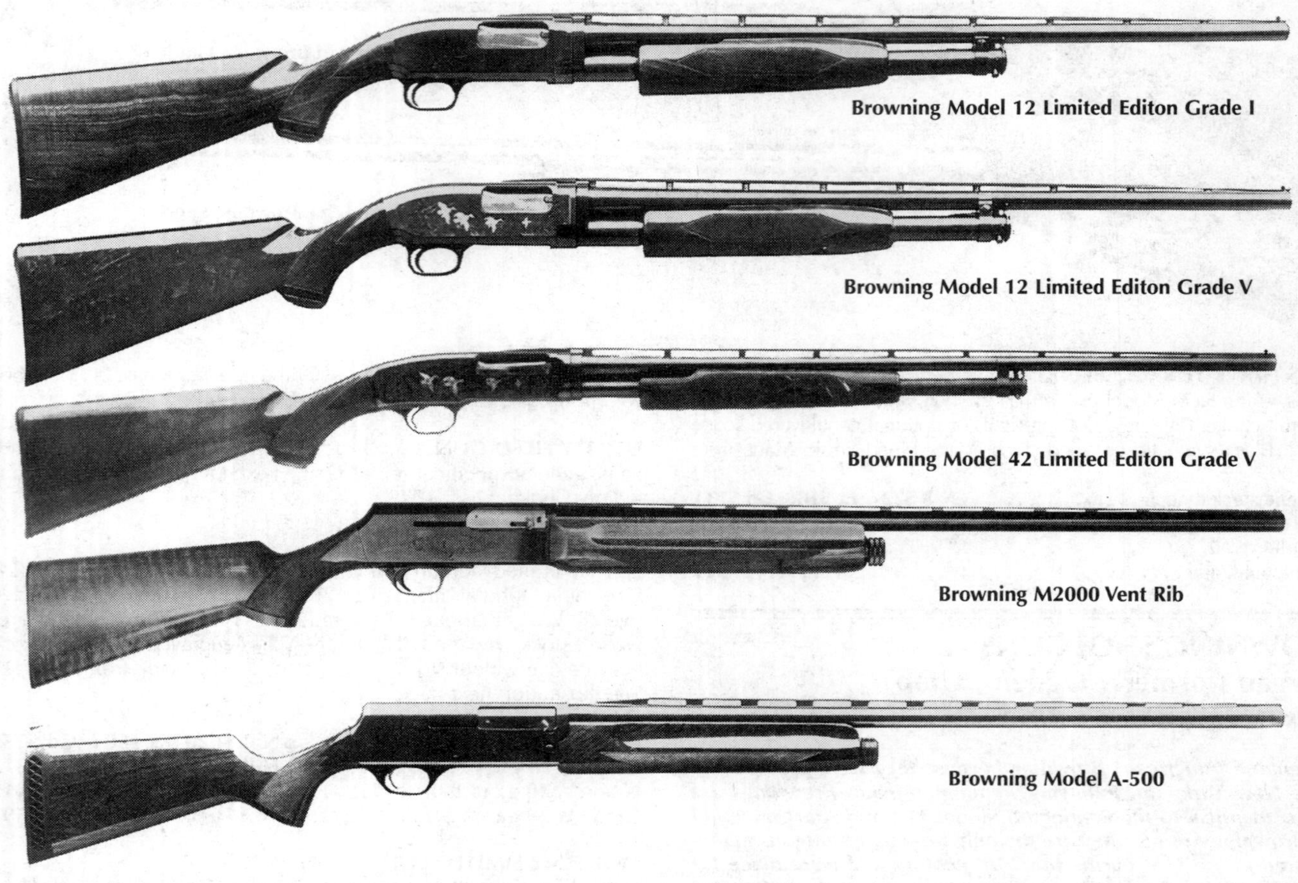

Browning Model 12 Limited Editon Grade I

Browning Model 12 Limited Editon Grade V

Browning Model 42 Limited Editon Grade V

Browning M2000 Vent Rib

Browning Model A-500

2000 SKEET MODEL . . . . NiB $479 Ex $390 Gd $277
Same as Field Model except has skeet-style stock w/recoil pad, 26-inch vent-rib bbl., SK choke. 12 or 20 ga., 2.75-inch chamber. Weight: 8 lbs., 1 oz. (12 ga.); 6 lbs., 12 oz. (20 ga.) Made 1974-81 by FN.

2000 TRAP MODEL. . . . . NiB $479 Ex $390 Gd $277
Same as Field Model except has Monte Carlo stock w/recoil pad, 30- or 32-inch bbl. w/high-post vent rib and receiver extension, M/I/F chokes. 12 ga., 2.75-inch chamber. Weight: About 8 lbs., 5 oz. Made 1974-81 by FN.

A-500G GAS-OPERATED SEMIAUTOMATIC
Same general specifications as Browning Model A-500R except gas-operated. Made 1990-93.
Buck Special . . . . NiB $603 Ex $493 Gd $353
Hunting model . . . . NiB $616 Ex $504 Gd $360

A-500G SPORTING CLAYS . . . . NiB $616 Ex $504 Gd $360
Same general specifications as Model A-500G except has matte blued receiver w/"Sporting Clays" logo. 28- or 30-inch bbl. w/Invector choke tubes. Made 1992-93.

A-500R SEMIAUTOMATIC
Recoil-operated. Gauge: 12. 26- to 30-inch vent-rib bbls. 24-inch Buck Special. Invector choke tube system. 2.75- or 3-inch Magnum cartridges. Weight: 7 lbs., 3 oz.-8 lbs., 2 oz. Cross-bolt safety. Gold-plated trigger. Scroll-engraved receiver. Gloss-finished walnut stock and forend. Made by FN from 1987-93.
Hunting model . . . . NiB $608 Ex $493 Gd $347
Buck Special . . . . NiB $647 Ex $524 Gd $368

A-BOLT SERIES SHOTGUN
Bolt-action repeating single-barrel shotgun. 12 ga. only w/3-inch chambers, 2-round magazine. 22- or 23-inch rifled bbl., w/or w/o a rifled invector tube. Receiver drilled and tapped for scope mounts. Bbl. w/ or w/o open sights. Checkered walnut or graphite/fiberglass composite stock. Matte black metal finish. Imported 1995-98.
Stalker model w/
composite stock . . . . NiB $441 Ex $359 Gd $255
Hunter model w/walnut stock . . . . NiB $421 Ex $344 Gd $245
W/rifled bbl., add $95
W/open sights, add $25

AUTOLOADING SHOTGUNS, GRADES II, III AND IV
These higher grade models differ from the Standard or Grade I in general quality, grade of wood, checkering, engraving, etc., otherwise specifications are the same. Grade IV guns, sometimes called Midas Grade, are inlaid w/yellow and green gold. Disc. in 1940.
Grade II, plan bbl. . . . . NiB $1470 Ex $1268 Gd $885
Grade III, plain bbl. . . . . NiB $2815 Ex $2455 Gd $1697
Grade IV, plain bbl.. . . . . NiB $4198 Ex $3915 Gd $3725
For raised matte rib bbl., add 15%
For vent rib bbl., add. 30%

Browning Model A-Bolt Hunter

Browning Model A-Bolt Stalker

Browning Automatic-5 Gold Classic

Browning Automatic-5 Buck Special

Browning Automatic-5 Classic

AUTOMATIC-5, LIGHT 20
Same general specifications as Standard Model except lightweight and 20 ga. Bbl.: 26- or 28-inch; plain or vent rib. Weight: About 6.25-6.5 lbs. depending on bbl. Made 1958-76 by FN, since then by Miroku.
FN manuf., plain bbl.. . . . . NiB $718 Ex $585 Gd $350
FN manuf., vent-rib bbl. . . . . NiB $931 Ex $853 Gd $518
Miroku manuf., vent rib,fixed choke . . NiB $853 Ex $668 Gd $364
Miroku manuf., vent rib, invectors . . . NiB $905 Ex $725 Gd $415

AUTOMATIC-5, BUCK SPECIAL MODELS
Same as Light 12, Magnum 12, Light 20, Magnum 20, in respective gauges, except 24-inch plain bbl. bored for rifled slug and buckshot, fitted w/rifle sights (open rear, ramp front). Weight: 6.13-8.25 lbs. depending on ga. Made 1964-76 by FN, since then by Miroku.
FN manuf., w/plain bbl. . . . . NiB $931 Ex $668 Gd $405
Miroku manuf., ... NiB $802 Ex $621 Gd $390
W/3-inch mag. rec., add 10%

AUTOMATIC-5 CLASSIC . . . . NiB $1199 Ex $947 Gd $844
Gauge: 12. 5-round capacity. 28-inch vent rib bbl./M choke. 2.75-inch chamber. Engraved silver-gray receiver. Gold-plated trigger. Crossbolt safety. High-grade, hand-checkered select American walnut stock w/rounded pistol grip. 5,000 issued; made in Japan in 1984, engraved in Belgium.

AUTOMATIC-5 GOLD CLASSIC . . . . . NiB $4094 Ex $3424 Gd $2549
Same general specifications as Automatic-5 Classic except engraved receiver inlaid w/gold. Pearl border on stock and forend plus fine-line hand-checkering. Each gun numbered "1 of Five Hundred," etc. 500 issued in 1984; made in Belgium.

AUTOMATIC-5, LIGHT 12
12 ga. only. Same general specifications as Standard Model except lightweight (about 7.25 lbs.), has gold-plated trigger. Guns w/rib have striped matting on top of bbl. Fixed chokes or Invector tubes. Made 1948-76 by FN, since then by Miroku.
FN manuf., plain bbl. . . . . NiB $649 Ex $532 Gd $384
FN manuf., raised matte rib . . . . . NiB $739 Ex $635 Gd $517
FN manuf., ventilated rib . . . . NiB $945 Ex $816 Gd $532
Miroku manuf., vent rib, fixed choke . . NiB $649 Ex $532 Gd $384
Miroku manuf., vent rib, invectors . . . NiB $867 Ex $682 Gd $429

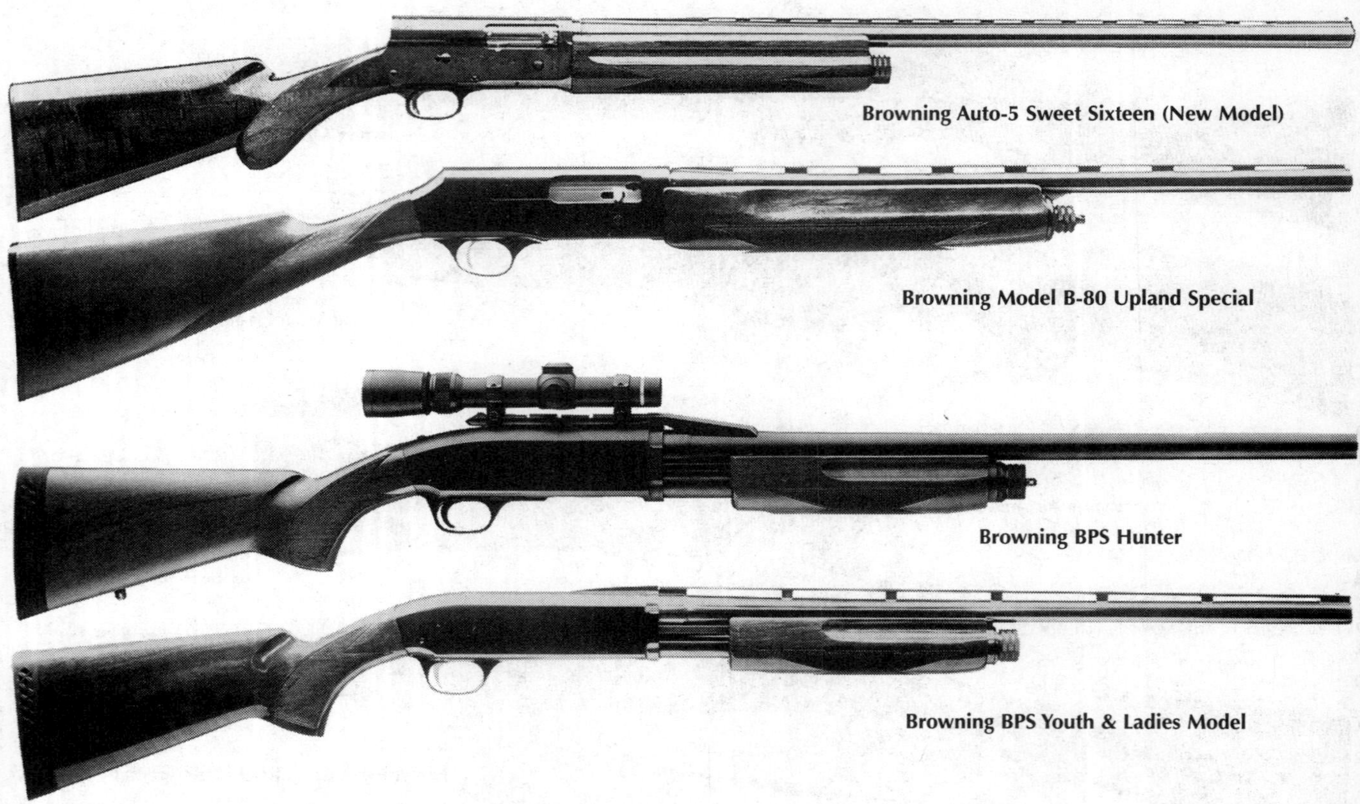

Browning Auto-5 Sweet Sixteen (New Model)

Browning Model B-80 Upland Special

Browning BPS Hunter

Browning BPS Youth & Ladies Model

AUTOMATIC-5, MAGNUM 12 GAUGE

Same general specifications as Standard Model. Chambered for 3-inch Magnum 12-ga. shells. Bbl.: 28-inch M/F, 30- or 32-inch F/F, plain or vent rib. Weight: 8.5-9 lbs. depending on bbl. Buttstock has recoil pad. Made 1958-76 by FN, since then by Miroku. Fixed chokes or Invector tubes.

FN manuf., plain bbl. . . . . NiB $846 Ex $687 Gd $485
FN manuf., vent rib bbl. . . . . NiB $918 Ex $747 Gd $527
Miroku manuf., vent rib, fixed chokes . . NiB $698 Ex $573 Gd $404
Miroku manuf., vent rib, invectors . . . . NiB $786 Ex $640 Gd $453

AUTOMATIC-5, MAGNUM 20 GAUGE

Same general specifications as Standard Model except chambered for 3-inch Magnum 20-ga. shell. Bbl.: 26- or 28-inch, plain or vent rib. Weight: 7 lbs., 5 oz.-7 lbs., 7 oz. depending on bbl. Made 1967-76 by FN, since then by Miroku.

FN manuf., plain bbl. . . . . NiB $845 Ex $688 Gd $487
FN manuf., vent rib bbl. . . . . NiB $889 Ex $709 Gd $510
Miroku manuf., vent rib, invectors . NiB $703 Ex $573 Gd $406

AUTOMATIC-5, SKEET MODEL

12 ga. only. Same general specifications as Light 12. Bbl.: 26-or 28-inch, plain or vent rib, SK choke. Weight: 7 lbs., 5 oz.-7 lbs., 10 oz. depending on bbl. Made by FN prior to 1976, since then by Miroku.

FN manuf., plain bbl. . . . . NiB $790 Ex $644 Gd $457
FN manuf., vent rib bbl. . . . . NiB $835 Ex $679 Gd $480
Miroku manuf., vent rib bbl. . . . . . NiB $639 Ex $522 Gd $372

AUTOMATIC-5 STALKER

Same general specifications as Automatic-5 Light and Magnum models except w/matte blue finish and black graphite fiberglass stock and forearm. Made from 1992 to date.

Light model . . . . NiB $854 Ex $735 Gd $502
Magnum model . . . . NiB $903 Ex $734 Gd $517

AUTOMATIC-5, STANDARD (GRADE I)

Recoil-operated. Gauge: 12 or 16 (16-gauge guns made prior to WW II were chambered for 2-inch shells; standard 16 disc. 1964). Four shell magazine in 5-round model, prewar guns were also available in 3-round model. Bbls.: 26- to 32-inch; plain, raised matted or vent rib; choice of standard chokes. Weight: About 8 lbs., in 12 ga., 7.5 lbs., in 16 ga. Checkered pistol-grip stock and forearm. (Note: Browning Special, disc. about 1940.) Made from 1900-73 by FN.

Grade I, plain bbl. . . . . NiB $688 Ex $560 Gd $398
Grade I or Browning Special,
Raised matted rib . . . . NiB $875 Ex $713 Gd $504
Grade I or Browning Special, vent rib . . . . NiB $899 Ex $733 Gd $518

AUTOMATIC-5, SWEET 16

16 ga. Same general specifications as Standard Model except lightweight (about 6.75 lbs.), has gold plated trigger. Guns w/rib have striped matting on top of bbl. Made 1937-76 by FN.

W/plain bbl. . . . . NiB $787 Ex $642 Gd $456
W/raised matted or ventilated rib . . . . NiB $859 Ex $700 Gd $507

AUTO-5,
SWEET SIXTEEN NEW MODEL . . . . NiB $960 Ex $782 Gd $553

Reissue of popular 16-gauge Hunting Model w/5-round capacity, 2.75-inch chamber, scroll-engraved blued receiver, high-gloss French walnut stock w/rounded pistol grip. 26- or 28-inch vent-rib bbl. F choke tube. Weight: 7 lbs., 5 oz. Reintro. 1987-93.

Browning BPS
Waterfowl – Mossy Oak Shadow Grass

Browning BPS Stalker

AUTOMATIC-5, TRAP MODEL . . . . NiB $934 Ex $727 Gd $470
12 ga. only. Same general specifications as Standard Model except has trap-style stock, 30-inch vent-rib bbl. F choke. Weight: 8.5 lbs. Disc. 1971.

MODEL B-80 GAS-OPERATED AUTOMATIC . . . . NiB $557 Ex $455 Gd $325
Gauge: 12 or 20; 2.75-inch chamber. Four round magazine. Bbl.: 26-, 28- or 30-inch, any standard choke, vent-rib bbl. w/fixed chokes or Invector tubes. Weight: 6 lbs., 12 oz.-8 lbs., 1 oz. depending on ga. and bbl. Checkered pistol-grip stock and forearm. Made 1981-88.

MODEL B-80 PLUS . . . . NiB $608 Ex $496 Gd $353
Same general specifications as Browning Model B-80 except chambered for 3-inch shotshells. Made in 1988 only.

MODEL B-80 SUPERLIGHT. . . . . . . NiB $557 Ex $455 Gd $325
Same as Standard Model except weighs 1 lb. less.

MODEL B-80 UPLAND SPECIAL . . NiB $569 Ex $465 Gd $331
Gauge: 12 or 20. 22-inch vent-rib bbl. Invector choke tube system. 2.75-inch chambers. 42 inches overall. Weight: 5 lbs., 7 oz. (20 ga.); 6 lbs., 10 oz. (12 ga.). German nickel silver sight bead. Crossbolt safety. Checkered walnut straight-grip stock and forend. Disc. 1988.

BPS DEER HUNTER SPECIAL . . . . . NiB $499 Ex $408 Gd $293
Same general specifications as Standard BPS model except has 20.5-inch bbl. w/adj. rifle-style sights. Solid scope mounting system. Checkered walnut stock w/sling swivel studs. Made from 1992 to date.

BPS GAME GUN TURKEY SPECIAL . . . . . . NiB $512 Ex $419 Gd $300
Same general specifications as Standard BPS model except w/matte blue metal finish and satin-finished stock. Chambered for 12 ga. 3-inch only. 20.5-inch bbl. w/extra full invector choke system. Receiver drilled and tapped for scope. Made from 1992-2001.

BPS PIGEON GRADE . . . . NiB $664 Ex $541 Gd $385
Same general specifications as Standard BPS model except w/select grade walnut stock and gold-trimmed receiver. Available in 12 ga. from only w/26- or 28-inch vent-rib bbl. Made 1992-1998.

BPS PUMP INVECTOR STALKER
Same general specifications as BPS Pump Shotgun except in 10 and 12 ga. w/Invector choke system, 22-, 26-, 28- or 30-inch bbls.; matte blue metal finish w/matte black stock. Made from 1987 to date.
12 ga. model (3-inch) . . . . NiB $482 Ex $395 Gd $285
10- & 12 ga. model (3.5-inch). . . . . NiB $648 Ex $529 Gd $375

BPS PUMP SHOTGUN
Takedown. Gauges: 10, 12 (3.5-inch chamber); 12, 20 and .410 (3-inch) and 28 ga. chambered 2.75-inch. Bbls.: 22-, 24-, 26-, 28-, 30-, or 32-inch; fixed choke or Invector tubes. Weight: 7.5 lbs. (w/28-inch bbl.). Checkered select walnut pistol-grip stock and semi-beavertail forearm, recoil pad. Introduced in 1977. Made by Miroku.
Model BPS Magnum Hunter . . . . NiB $656 Ex $531 Gd $390
Model BPS Magnum Stalker . . . . NiB $634 Ex $516 Gd $379
Model BPS Magnum Camo . . . . NiB $711 Ex $578 Gd $422
Model BPS Hunter . . . . NiB $551 Ex $449 Gd $334
Model BPS Upland. . . . . NiB $551 Ex $449 Gd $334
Model BPS Stalker (26- 28- or 30-inch bbl.) . . . NiB $531 Ex $433 Gd $323
Model BPS Stalker 24-inch bbl . . . . NiB $557 Ex $454 Gd $337
Model BPS Game Gun—Turkey Special . . . . . . NiB $589 Ex $480 Gd $355
Model BPS Game Gun—fully rifled bbl. . . . . . . NiB $660 Ex $536 Gd $393
Model BPS Hunter 20 ga. . . . . NiB $551 Ex $449 Gd $334
Model BPS Upland 20 ga. . . . . NiB $551 Ex $449 Gd $334
Model BPS Micro . . . . NiB $551 Ex $449 Gd $334
Model BPS Hunter 28 ga. . . . . NiB $583 Ex $475 Gd $352
Model BPS Bore Hunter .410 . . . . NiB $583 Ex $475 Gd $352
Model BPS Buck Spec. (10 or 12 ga., 3.5-inch) . NiB $637 Ex $521 Gd $372
Model BPS Buck Spec. (12 or 20 ga.) . . . . NiB $463 Ex $381 Gd $277
Model BPS Waterfowl (10 or 12 ga., 3.5-inch) . . . . NiB $695 Ex $567 Gd $404
W/fixed choke, deduct $50

BPS YOUTH AND LADIES' MODEL
Lightweight (6 lbs., 11 oz.) version of BPS Pump Shotgun in 20 ga. w/22-inch bbl. and floating vent rib, F choke (invector) tube. Made 1986-2002.
Standard Invector model (disc. 1994) . . . . NiB $425 Ex $349 Gd $252
Invector Plus model . . . . NiB $463 Ex $380 Gd $273

BSA 10 SEMIAUTOMATIC SHOTGUN
Gas-operated short-stroke action. 10 ga.; 3.5-inch chamber. Five round magazine. Bbls.: 26-, 28-or 30-inches w/Invector tubes and vent rib. Weight: 10.5 lbs. Checkered select walnut buttstock and forend. Blued finish. Made 1993 to date. Note: Although intro. as the BSA 10, this model is now marketed as the Gold Series. See separate listing for pricing.

B-SS SIDE-BY-SIDE
Boxlock. Automatic ejectors. Non-selective single trigger (early production) or selective-single trigger (late production). Gauges: 12 or 20 w/3-inch chambers. Bbls.: 26-, 28-, or 30-inches; IC/M, M/F, or F/F chokes; matte solid rib. Weight: 7 to 7.5 lbs. Checkered straight-grip stock and beavertail forearm. Made from 1972-88 by Miroku.
Standard model (early/NSST) . . . . NiB $592 Ex $483 Gd $343
Standard model (late/SST) . . . . NiB $683 Ex $555 Gd $392
Grade II (antique silver receiver). . . . . NiB $1154 Ex $935 Gd $654
20 ga. models, add $100

SHOTGUNS

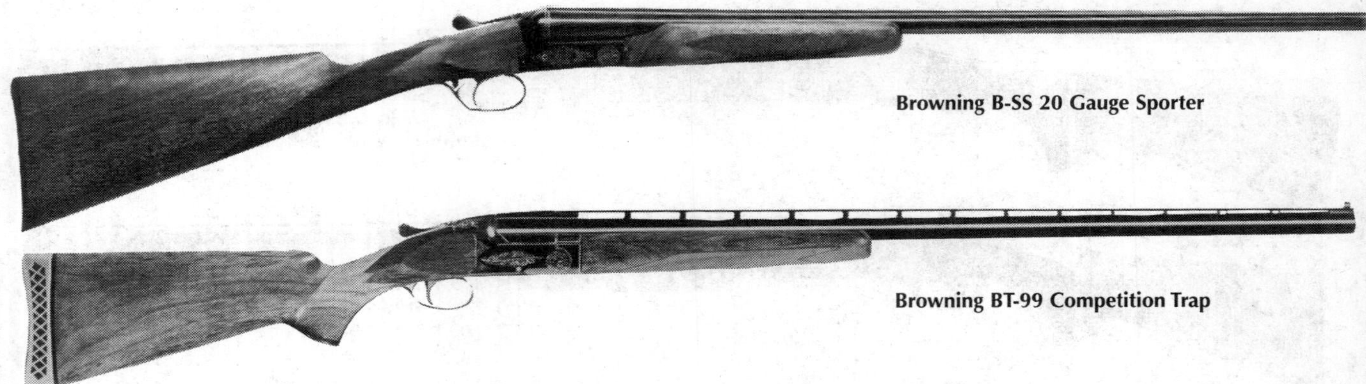
Browning B-SS 20 Gauge Sporter

Browning BT-99 Competition Trap

B-SS SIDE-BY-SIDE SIDELOCK
Same general specifications as B-SS boxlock models except sidelock version available in 26- or 28-inch bbl. lengths. 26-inch choked IC/M; 28-inch, M/F. Double triggers. Satin-grayed receiver engraved w/rosettes and scrolls. German nickel-silver sight bead. Weight: 6.25 lbs. to 6 lbs., 11 oz. 12 ga. made in 1983; 20 ga. Made in 1984. Disc. 1988.
12 ga. model . . . . NiB $980 Ex $753 Gd $1037
20 ga. model . . . . NiB $2558 Ex $2065 Gd $1435

B-SS S/S 20 GAUGE SPORTER . . . . NiB $793 Ex $644 Gd $454
Same as standard B-SS 20 ga. except has selective single trigger, straight-grip stock. Introduced 1977. Disc. 1987.

BT-99 GRADE I SINGLE BBL. TRAP . . . . . . NiB $849 Ex $690 Gd $485
Boxlock. Automatic ejector. 12 ga. only. 32- or 34-inch vent rib bbl., M, IM or F choke. Weight: About 8 lbs. Checkered pistol-grip stock and beavertail forearm, recoil pad. Made 1971-76 by Miroku.

BT-99 MAX
Boxlock. 12 ga. only w/ejector selector and no safety. 32- or 34-inch ported bbl. w/high post vent rib. Checkered select walnut buttstock and finger-grooved forend w/high luster finish. Engraved receiver w/blued or stainless metal finish. Made 1995-96.
Blued . . . . NiB $1238 Ex $1002 Gd $702
Stainless . . . . NiB $1840 Ex $1476 Gd $1023

BT-99 PLUS
Similar to the BT-99 Competition except w/Browning Recoil Reduction System. Made 1989-95.
Grade I . . . . NiB $1214 Ex $983 Gd $688
Pigeon grade . . . . NiB $1380 Ex $1117 Gd $769
Signature grade . . . . NiB $1342 Ex $1086 Gd $758
Stainless model . . . . NiB $1471 Ex $1187 Gd $828
Golden Clays . . . . NiB $2539 Ex $2360 Gd $2102

BT-99 PLUS MICRO. . . . . NiB $1250 Ex $1022 Gd $707
Same general specifications as BT-99 Plus except scaled down for smaller shooters. 30-inch bbl. w/adj. rib and Browning's recoil reducer system. Made 1991 to date.

BT-100 COMPETITION TRAP SPECIAL
Same as BT-99 except has super-high wide rib and standard Monte Carlo or fully adj. stock. Available w/adj. choke or Invector Plus tubes w/optional porting. Made 1976-94.
Grade I w/fixed
choke (disc. 1992). NiB $927 Ex $776 Gd $530
Grade I w/Invectors . . . . NiB $1149 Ex $930 Gd $649
Grade I stainless (disc. 1994) . . . . NiB $1217 Ex $976 Gd $681
Grade I Pigeon Grade (disc. 1994) . . . . . . NiB $1106 Ex $904 Gd $632

BT-100 SINGLE-SHOT TRAP
Similar to the BT-99 Max, except w/additional stock options and removable trigger group. Made 1995-2002.
Model BT-100 Grade I blued. . . . . NiB $1470 Ex $1187 Gd $824
Model BT-100 stainless . . . . NiB $1696 Ex $1367 Gd $947
Model BT-100 satin . . . . NiB $1373 Ex $1105 Gd $769
Model BT-100 w/adj. comb, add. $250
Thumbhole stock, add $295
Replacement trigger assembly, add $495
Fixed choke, deduct $65

CITORI HUNTING O/U MODELS
Boxlock. Gauges: 12, 16 (disc. 1989), 20, 28 (disc. 1992) and .410 bore (disc. 1989). Bbl. lengths: 24-, 26-, 28-, or 30-inch w/vent rib. Chambered 2.75-, 3- or 3.5-inch mag. Chokes: IC/M, M/F (Fixed Chokes); Standard Invector, or Invector plus choke systems. Overall length ranges from 41-47 inches. 2.75-, 3- or 3-inch Mag. loads, depending on ga. Weight: 5.75 lbs. to 7 lbs. 13 oz. Single selective, gold-plated trigger. Medium raised German nickel-silver sight bead. Checkered, rounded pistol-grip walnut stock w/beavertail forend. Invector Chokes and Invector Plus became standard in 1988 and 1995, respectively. Made from 1973 to date by Miroku.
Grade I (disc. 1994) . . . . NiB $844 Ex $684 Gd $478
Grade I - 3.5-inch Mag.(1989 to date) . . . NiB $1134 Ex $916 Gd $638
Grade II (disc. 1983). . . . . NiB $1034 Ex $844 Gd $589
Grade III (1985-95) . . . . NiB $1199 Ex $968 Gd $673
Grade V (disc. 1984). . . . . NiB $1664 Ex $1342 Gd $930
Grade VI (1985-95). . . . . NiB $1850 Ex $1491 Gd $1031
Model Sporting Hunter
(12 and 20 ga.; 1998 to date) . . . . NiB $1006 Ex $813 Gd $565
Model Satin Hunter
(12 ga. only; 1998 to date). . . . . NiB $909 Ex $735 Gd $513
Mdls. w/o Inv. choke syst., deduct $120
For 3.5-inch Mag., add $90
For disc. ga 16, 28 and .410, add 15%

CITORI LIGHTNING O/U MODELS
Same general specifications as the Citori Hunting models except w/classic Browning rounded pistol-grip stock. Made from 1988 to date by Miroku.
Grade I . . . . NiB $872 Ex $707 Gd $496
Grade III . . . . NiB $1300 Ex $1052 Gd $716
Grade VI . . . . NiB $1858 Ex $1499 Gd $1039
Gran Lightning model . . . . NiB $1373 Ex $1110 Gd $769
Feather Model (alloy receiver) . . . . NiB $1052 Ex $852 Gd $597
Feather Combo model (2-bbl. set) . . . . NiB $2471 Ex $1995 Gd $1385
Privilege Mdl. (engraved w/sideplates) . . . . NiB $4739 Ex $3813 Gd $2628
Micro model, add 10%
Models w/o Invector
choke system, deduct $120
28 and .410 ga., add 15%

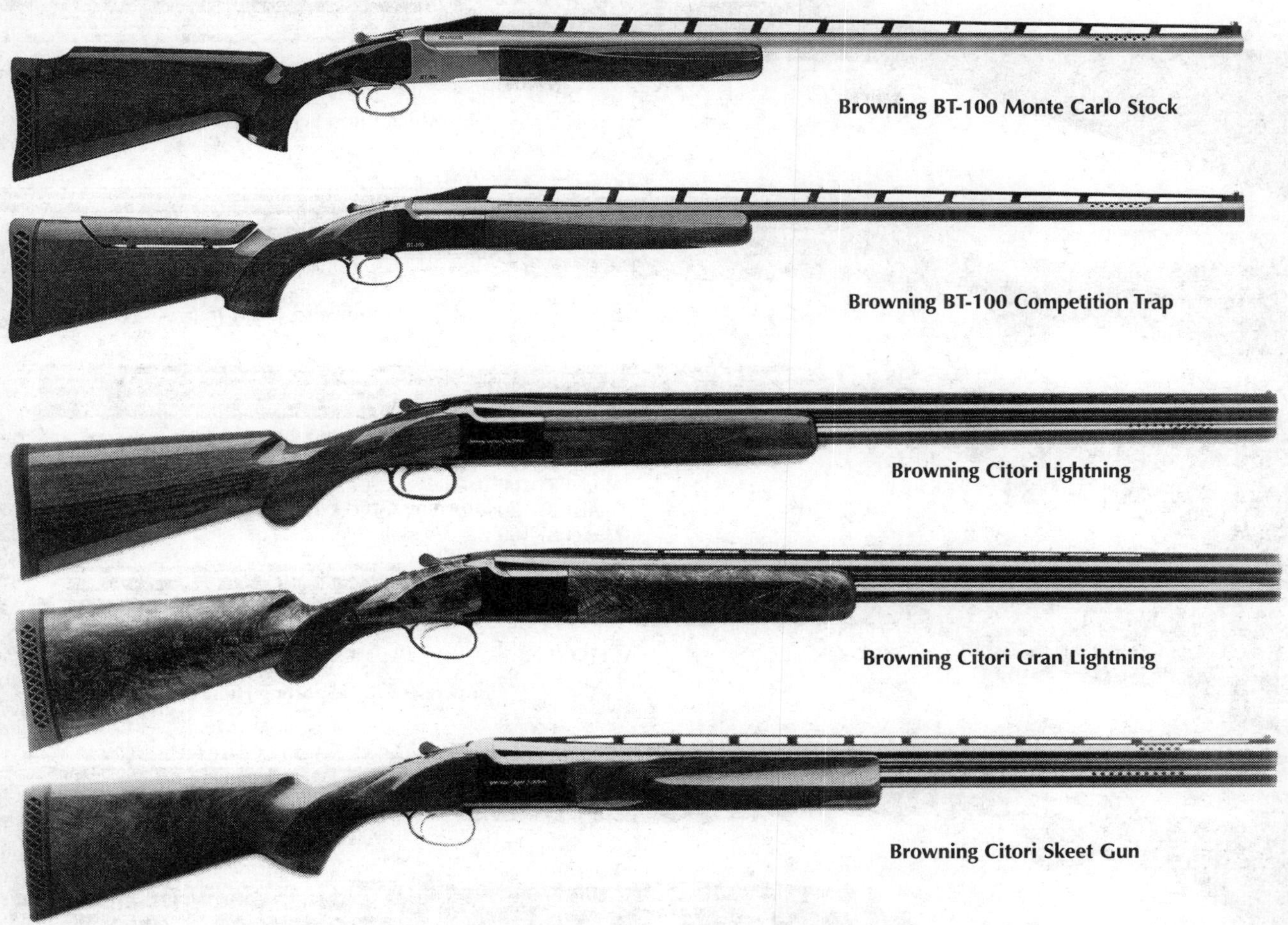

Browning BT-100 Monte Carlo Stock

Browning BT-100 Competition Trap

Browning Citori Lightning

Browning Citori Gran Lightning

Browning Citori Skeet Gun

CITORI SKEET GUN

Same as Hunting model except has skeet-style stock and forearm, 26- or 28-inch bbls., both bored SK choke. Available w/either standard vent rib or special target-type, high-post, wide vent rib. Weight (w/26-inch bbls.): 12 ga., 8 lbs., 20 ga., 7 lbs. Made 1974 to date by Miroku.

Grade I . . . . NiB $1498 Ex $1039 Gd $627
Grade II . . . . NiB $1156 Ex $937 Gd $656
Grade III . . . . NiB $1342 Ex $1086 Gd $758
Grade VI (disc. 1995) . . . . NiB $1993 Ex $1608 Gd $1116
Golden Clays. . . . . NiB $2202 Ex $1777 Gd $123
28 and .410 ga., add 15%
3-bbl. Set, Grade I (disc. 1996). . . . . . . NiB $2401 Ex $1950 Gd $1376
3-bbl. Set, Grade III (disc. 1996) . . . . . NiB $2587 Ex $2099 Gd $1465
3-bbl. Set, Grade VI (disc. 1994). . . . . . NiB $2924 Ex $2369 Gd $1661
3-bbl. Set, Golden Clays (disc. 1995) . . . . . NiB $3762 Ex $2942 Gd $2121
4-bbl. Set, Grade I . . . . NiB $3458 Ex $2799 Gd $1955
4-bbl. Set, Grade III . . . . NiB $3840 Ex $3105 Gd $2166
4-bbl. Set, Grade VI (disc. 1994). . . . . . NiB $3769 Ex $3255 Gd $2309
4-bbl. Set, Golden Clays (disc. 1995) . . NiB $4756 Ex $3842 Gd $2671

CITORI SPORTING CLAYS

Similar to the standard Citori Lightning model except Classic-style stock with rounded pistol-grip. 30-inch back-bored bbls. with Invector Plus tubes. Receiver with "Lightning Sporting Clays Edition" logo. Made from 1989 to date.

GTI model (disc. 1995). . . . . NiB $1364 Ex $978 Gd $643
GTI Golden Clays model (1993-94) . . . NiB $2033 Ex $1648 Gd $1156
Lightning model (intro. 1989). . . . . NiB $1209 Ex $987 Gd $702
Lightning Golden Clays (1993-98) . . . . NiB $2102 Ex $1702 Gd $1192
Lightning Pigeon Grade (1993-94) . . . . . NiB $1287 Ex $1049 Gd $744
Micro Citori Lightning model
(w/low rib) . . . . NiB $1429 Ex $978 Gd $658
Special Sporting model (intro. 1989) . . . NiB $1461 Ex $1003 Gd $682
Special Sporting
Golden Clays (1993-98) . . . . NiB $2430 Ex $1952 Gd $1367
Special Sporting Pigeon Gr. (1993-94) . . NiB $1319 Ex $1074 Gd $760
Ultra mdl.
(intro. 1995-previously GTI) . . . . NiB $1351 Ex $1099 Gd $778
Ultra Golden Clays (intro. 1995) . . . . . NiB $2432 Ex $1970 Gd $1379
Model 325 (1993-94) . . . . NiB $1296 Ex $1058 Gd $753
Model 325 Golden Clays (1993-94) . . . NiB $2081 Ex $1689 Gd $1196
Model 425 Grade I (intro. 1995) . . . . . . NiB $1386 Ex $1130 Gd $802
Model 425 Golden Clays (intro. 1995) . . . . NiB $2429 Ex $1967 Gd $1376
Model 425 WSSF (intro. 1995) . . . . NiB $1329 Ex $1084 Gd $770
Model 802 Sporter (ES)
Extended Swing (intro. 1996 . . . . NiB $1453 Ex $1183 Gd $836
For 2 bbl. set add $850
For adjustable stock, add $200
For high rib, add $85
For ported barrels, add $65

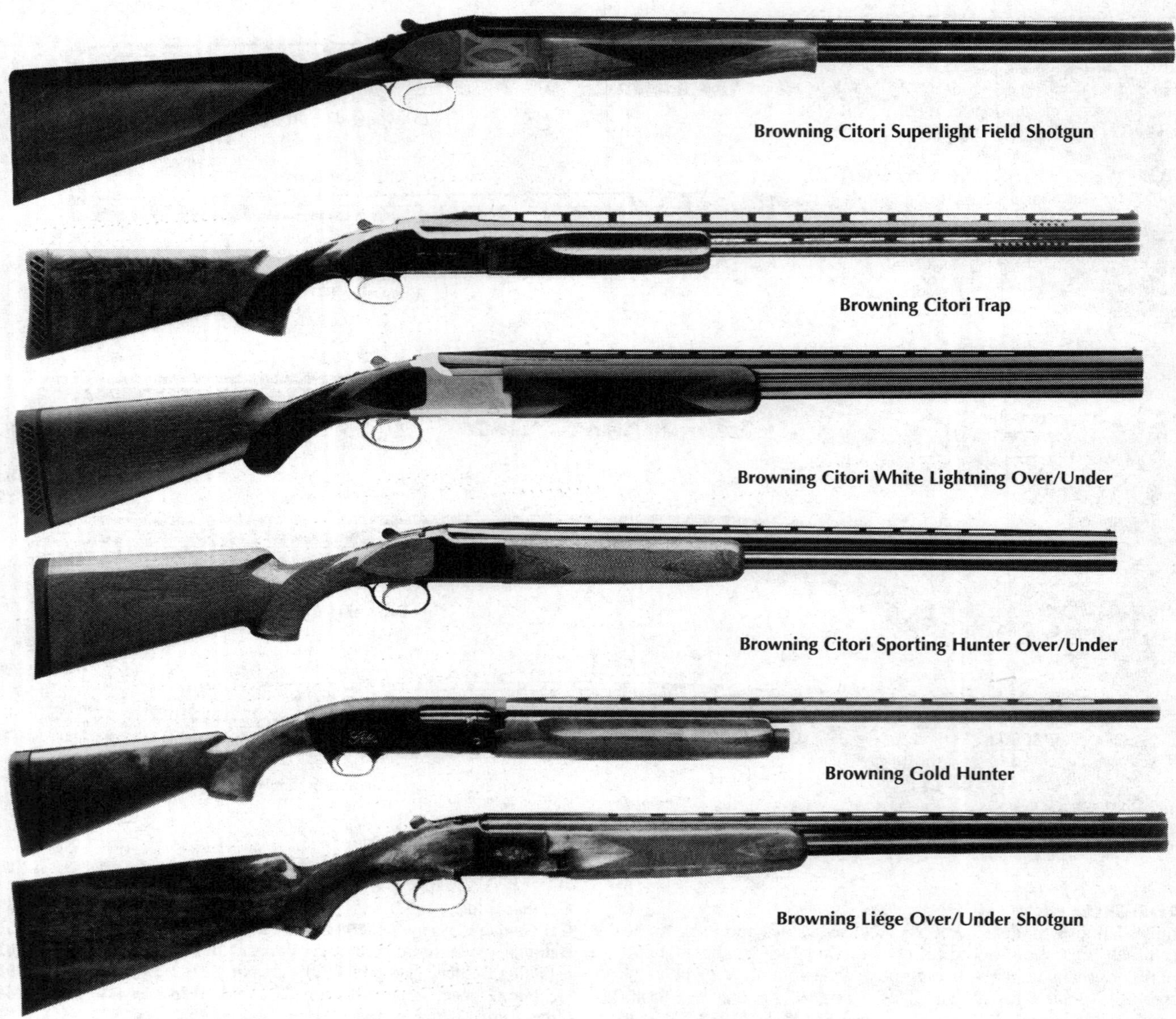
Browning Citori Superlight Field Shotgun

Browning Citori Trap

Browning Citori White Lightning Over/Under

Browning Citori Sporting Hunter Over/Under

Browning Gold Hunter

Browning Liége Over/Under Shotgun

CITORI SUPERLIGHT O/U FIELD SHOTGUNS
Similar to the Citori Hunting model except w/straight-grip stock and Schnabel forend tip. Made by Miroku 1982 to date.

Grade I . . . . NiB $1313 Ex $1061 Gd $740
Grade III . . . . NiB $1723 Ex $1389 Gd $968
Grade V (disc. 1985) . . . . NiB $2237 Ex $1803 Gd $1249
Grade VI . . . . NiB $2592 Ex $2091 Gd $1464
Models w/o Invector choke system, deduct $120
28 and .410 ga., add 15%

CITORI TRAP GUN
Same as Hunting model except 12 ga. only, has Monte Carlo or fully adjustable stock and beavertail forend, trap-style recoil pad; 20- or 32-inch bbls.; M/F, IM/F, or F/F. Available with either standard vent rib or special target-type, high-post, wide vent rib. Weight: 8 lbs. Made from 1974 to 2001 by Miroku.

Grade I Trap . . . . .NiB $1464 Ex $1188 Gd $835
Grade I Trap Pigeon grade
(disc. 1994). . . . . NiB $1750 Ex $1416 Gd $1049
Grade I Trap Signature grade (disc. 1994) . . . NiB $1716 Ex $1389 Gd $971
Grade I Plus Trap (disc. 1994) . . NiB $1799 Ex $1466 Gd $1017
Grade I Plus Trap
w/ported bbls. (disc. 1994) . . . . NiB $1916 Ex $1549 Gd $1081
Grade I Plus Trap
Combo (disc. 1994). . . . . NiB $4143 Ex $3358 Gd $2340
Grade I Plus Trap
Golden Clays (disc. 1994) . . . . NiB $1799 Ex $1456 Gd $1017
Grade II w/HP rib (disc. 1984) . . NiB $1582 Ex $1282 Gd $899
Grade III Trap . . . . NiB $1916 Ex $1555 Gd $1096
Grade V Trap (disc. 1984) . . . . . NiB $2112 Ex $1712 Gd $1200
Grade VI Trap (disc. 1994). . . . . NiB $2432 Ex $1964 Gd $1367
Grade VI Trap
Golden Clays (disc. 1994) . . . . NiB $2946 Ex $2378 Gd $1652

CITORI UPLAND SPECIAL O/U SHOTGUN
A shortened version of the Hunting model fitted with 24-inch bbls. and straight-grip stock.
Upland Special 12, 20 ga. models. . . . . . . NiB $1186 Ex $959 Gd $670
Upland Spec. 16 ga. mdl. (disc. 1989) . . NiB $1387 Ex $1120 Gd $780
Models w/o Inv. choke sys., deduct $120

CITORI WHITE LIGHTNING O/U SHOTGUN
Similar to the standard Citori Lightning model except w/silver nitride receiver w/scroll and rosette engraving. Satin wood finish w/round pistol grip. Made 1998-2001.
12, 20 ga. models. . . . . NiB $1391 Ex $1124 Gd $784
28, .410 ga. models (Intro. 2000) . . . . . . NiB $1507 Ex $1218 Gd $847

CITORI WHITE UPLAND SPECIAL . . . . . . NiB $1219 Ex $986 Gd $688
Similar to the standard Citori Upland model except w/silver nitride receiver w/scroll and rosette engraving. Satin wood finish w/round pistol grip. Made 2000-01.

DOUBLE AUTOMATIC (STEEL RECEIVER)
Short recoil system. Takedown. 12 ga. only. Two round capacity. Bbls.: 26-, 28-, 30-inches; any standard choke. Checkered pistol-grip stock and forend. Weight: About 7.75 lbs. Made 1955-1961.
With plain bbl. . . . . NiB $643 Ex $524 Gd $370
With recessed-rib bbl. . . . . NiB $805 Ex $653 Gd $458

GOLD DEER HUNTER AUTOLOADING SHOTGUN
Similar to the Standard Gold Hunter model except chambered 12 ga. only. 22-inch bbl. W/rifled bore or smooth bore w/5-inch rifled invector tube. Cantilevered scope mount. Made 1997 to date.
Gold Deer Hunter (w/standard finish) . . . . NiB $808 Ex $656 Gd $471
Field model (w/Mossy Oak finish) . . . . NiB $686 Ex $558 Gd $395

GOLD HUNTER SERIES
Self-cleaning, gas-operated, short-stroke action. Gauges: 10 or 12 (3.5-inch chamber); 12 or 20 (3-inch chamber). 26-, 28-, or 30-inch bbl. w/Invector or Invector Plus choke tubes. Checkered walnut stock. Polished or matte black metal finish. Made 1994 to date.
Gold Hunter (Light 10 ga. 3.5-inch w/wal. St.) . . . . NiB $884 Ex $733 Gd $514
Gold Hunter (12 ga. 3.5-inch) . . . . NiB $852 Ex $692 Gd $458
Gold Hunter (12 or 20 ga. 3-inch) . . . . NiB $560 Ex $457 Gd $325
Gld. Hunter Clas. Mdl. (12 or 20 Ga. 3-inch) . . . . . NiB $592 Ex $483 Gd $343
Gld. Hunter High Gr.
Classic (12 or 20 ga. 3-inch) . . . . NiB $1184 Ex $958 Gd $670
Gold Deer Hunter
(12 ga. w/22-inch bbl.) . . . . NiB $625 Ex $509 Gd $360
Gold Turkey Hunter Camo
(12 ga. w/24-inch bbl.) . . . . NiB $579 Ex $472 Gd $335
Gold Waterfowl Hunter
Camo (12 ga. w/24-inch bbl.) . . . . NiB $560 Ex $457 Gd $325

GOLD STALKER SERIES
Self-cleaning, gas-operated, short-stroke action. Gauges: 10 or 12 (3.5-inch chamber); 12 or 20 (3-inch chamber). 26-, 28-, or 30-inch bbl. w/Invector or Invector Plus choke tubes. Graphite/fiberglass composite stock. Polished or matte black metal finish. Made 1998 to date.
Gold Stalker (Light 10 ga.
3.5-inch w/composite stock) . . . . NiB $889 Ex $721 Gd $507
Gold Stalker (12 ga. 3.5-inch) . . . . NiB $818 Ex $665 Gd $469
Gold Stalker (12 or 20 ga. 3-inch) . . . . NiB $564 Ex $452 Gd $322
Gold Stalker Classic
Model (12 or 20 ga. 3-inch) . . . . NiB $560 Ex $457 Gd $325
Gold Deer Stalker
(12 ga. w/22-inch bbl.) . . . . NiB $625 Ex $509 Gd $360
Gold Turkey Stalker Camo
(12 ga. w/24-inch bbl.) . . . . NiB $579 Ex $462 Gd $335

Browning Over/Under Gold Classic

Gold Waterfowl Stalker
Camo (12 Ga. w/24-inch bbl.) . . . . NiB $953 Ex $536 Gd $464

GOLD SPORTING SERIES
Similar to Gold Hunter Series except w/2.75-inch chamber and 28- or 30-inch ported bbl. w/Invector Plus chokes. Made 1999 to date.
Gold Sporting Clays (standard) . . . . NiB $838 Ex $722 Gd $573
Gold Sporting Clays (youth or ladies) . . . . . NiB $856 Ex $737 Gd $583
Gold Sporting Clays w/Eng. nick. rec.. . . NiB $1292 Ex $1087 Gd $825

LIEGE O/U SHOTGUN (B26/27)
Boxlock. Automatic ejectors. Non-selective single trigger. 12 ga. only. Bbls.: 26.5-, 28-, or 30-inch; 2.75-inch chambers in 26.5- and 28-inch, 3-inch in 30-inch, IC/M, M/F, or F/F chokes; vent rib. Weight: 7 lbs., 4 oz.to 7 lbs., 14 oz., depending on bbls. Checkered pistol-grip stock and forearm. Made 1973-75 by FN.
Liège (B-26 BAC production) . . . . NiB $931 Ex $755 Gd $529
Liège (B-27 FN prod.) Stand. Game Mdl. . . NiB $901 Ex $731 Gd $512
Deluxe Game model. . . . . NiB $1012 Ex $819 Gd $573
Grand Delux Game model . . . . NiB $1231 Ex $995 Gd $695
Deluxe Skeet model . . . . NiB $1053 Ex $853 Gd $597
Deluxe Trap model . . . . NiB $1038 Ex $841 Gd $589
COL Commemorative model . . . . NiB $1469 Ex $1187 Gd $826

LIGHT SPORTING 802ES . . . . . . NiB $1343 Ex $1087 Gd $759
Over/under. Invector-plus choke tubes. 12 ga. only with 28-inch bbl. Weight: 7 lbs., 5 oz.

LIGHTNING SPORTING CLAYS
Similar to the standard Citori Lightning model except Classic-style stock with rounded pistol grip. 30-inch back-bored bbls. with Invector Plus tubes. Receiver with "Lightning Sporting Clays Edition" logo. Made 1989 to date.
Standard model . . . . NiB $1185 Ex $932 Gd $646
Pigeon grade . . . . NiB $1257 Ex $1009 Gd $704

O/U CLASSIC . . . . NiB $2210 Ex $1785 Gd $1241
Gauge: 20, 2.75-inch chambers. 26-inch blued bbls. choked IC/M. Gold-plated, single selective trigger. Manual, top-tang-mounted safety. Engraved receiver. High grade, select American walnut straight-grip stock with Schnabel forend. Fine-line checkering with pearl borders. High-gloss finish. 5,000 issued in 1986; made in Japan, engraved in Belgium.

O/U GOLD CLASSIC . . . . NiB $5349 Ex $4370 Gd $2974
Same general specifications as Over/Under Classic except more elaborate engravings, enhanced in gold, including profile of John M. Browning. Fine oil finish. 500 issued; made in 1986 in Belgium.

RECOILLESS TRAP SHOTGUN
The action and bbl. are driven forward when firing to achieve 72 percent less recoil. 12 ga, 2.75-inch chamber. 30-inch bbl. with Invector Plus tubes; adjustable vent rib. 51.63 inches overall. Weight: 9 lbs. Adj. checkered walnut buttstock and forend. Blued finish. Made from 1993-96.

Browning Superposed Broadway 12 Trap

Browning Superposed Grade I Lightning

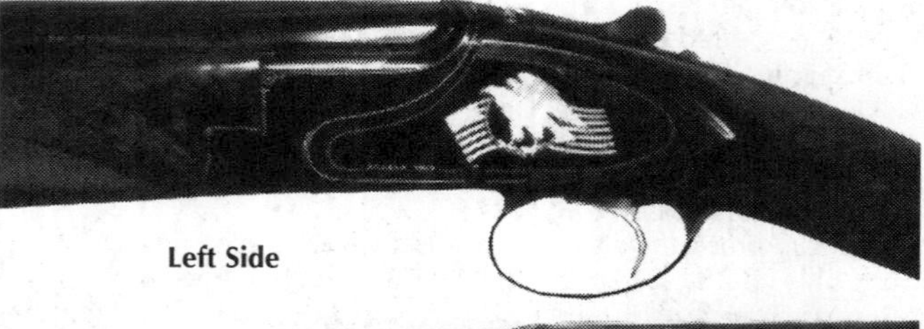

Left Side

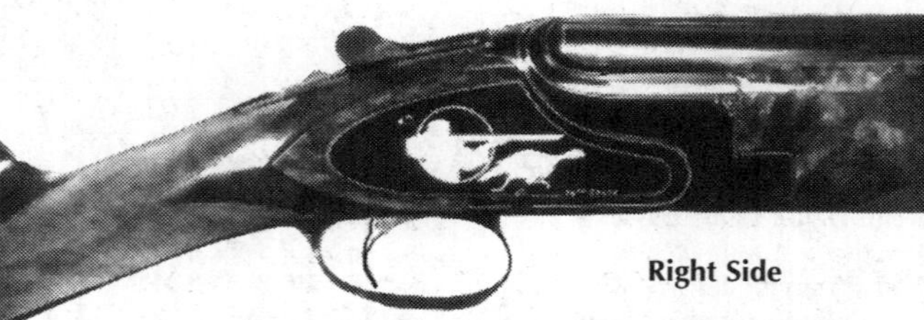

Right Side

Browning Superposed Bicentennial

Browning Superposed Grade IV Diana (Postwar)

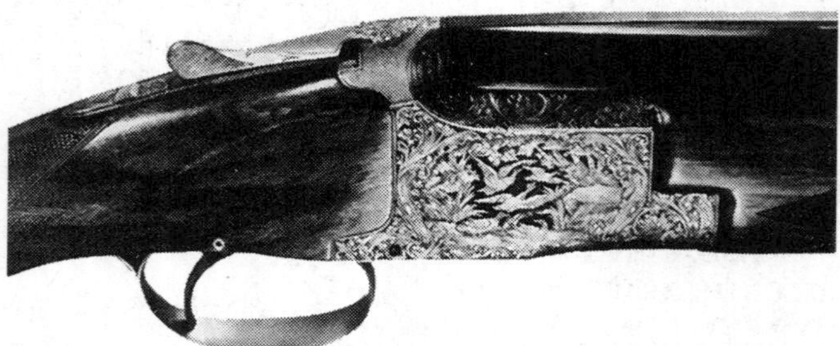

Browning Superposed Grade V Midas (Postwar)

Standard model. . . . . NiB $941 Ex $767 Gd $545
Micro model (27-inch bbl.) . . . . NiB $967 Ex $788 Gd $559
Signature model (27-inch bbl.) . . . . NiB $1387 Ex $1126 Gd $823

SUPERPOSED BICENTENNIAL
COMMEMORATIVE . . . . NiB $13,197 Ex $10,558 Gd $7180
Special limited edition issued to commemorate U.S. Bicentennial. 51 guns, one for each state in the Union plus one for Washington, D.C. Receiver with sideplates has engraved and gold-inlaid hunter and wild turkey on right side, U.S. flag and bald eagle on left side, together with state markings inlaid in gold, on blued background. Checkered straight-grip stock and Schnabel-style forearm of highly-figured American walnut. Velvet-lined wood presentation case. Made in 1976 by FN. Value shown is for gun in new, unfired condition. See illustration next page.

SUPERPOSED
BROADWAY 12 TRAP . . . . NiB $2052 Ex $1660 Gd $1146
Same as Standard Trap Gun except has 30- or 32-inch bbls. with wider Broadway rib. Disc. 1976.

SUPERPOSED SHOTGUNS, HUNTING MODELS
Over/under boxlock. Selective automatic ejectors. Selective single trigger; earlier models (worth 25% less) supplied w/double triggers, twin selective triggers or non-selective single trigger. Gauges: 12, 20 (intro. 1949, 3-inch chambers in later production), 28, .410 (latter two ga. intro. 1960). Bbls.: 26.5-, 28-, 30-, 32-inch, raised matted or vent rib, prewar Lightning Model made w/ribbed bbl., postwar version supplied only w/vent rib; any combination of standard chokes. Weight (w/26.5-inch vent-rib bbls.): Standard 12, 7 lbs., 11 oz., Lightning 12, 7 lbs., 6 oz.; Standard 20, 6 lbs., 8 oz.; Lightning 20, 6 lbs., 4 oz.; Lightning 28, 6 lbs., 7 oz.; Lightning .410, 6 lbs., 10 oz. Checkered pistol-grip stock/forearm.
Higher grades (Pigeon, Pointer, Diana, Midas, Grade VI) differ from standard Grade I models in overall quality, engraving, wood and checkering; otherwise, specifications are the same. Midas Grade and Grade VI guns are richly gold inlaid. Made by FN 1928-1976. Prewar models may be considered as disc. in 1940 when Belgium was occupied by Germany. Grade VI offered 1955-1960. Pointer Grade disc. in 1966, Grade I Standard in 1973, Pigeon Grade in 1974. Lightning Grade I, Diana and Midas Grades were not offered after 1976.
Grade I standard weight . . . . . . NiB $1778 Ex $1439 Gd $1007
Grade I Lightning . . . . NiB $2160 Ex $1749 Gd $1223
Grade I Lightning, prewar,
matted bbl., no rib . . . . NiB $3131 Ex $2508 Gd $1749
Grade II—Pigeon. . . . . NiB $3271 Ex $2628 Gd $1833

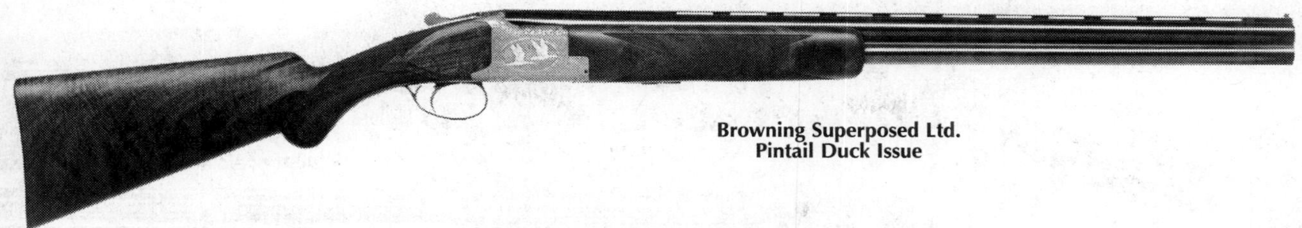
**Browning Superposed Ltd.
Pintail Duck Issue**

Grade III—Pointer. . . . . NiB $3166 Ex $2560 Gd $1786
Grade IV—Diana. . . . . NiB $3867 Ex $3122 Gd $2168
Grade V—Midas . . . . NiB $9550 Ex $7683 Gd $5293
Grade VI . . . . NiB $6483 Ex $5222 Gd $3599
Add for 20 ga. 20%
Add for 28 ga. 75%
Add for .410. . . . . 45%
Values shown are for models w/ventilated rib.
If gun has raised matted rib, deduct 10%

SUPERPOSED LIGHTNING AND SUPERLIGHT MODELS (REISSUE B-25)
Reissue of popular 12-and 20-ga. Superposed shotguns. Lightning models available in 26.5- and 28-inch bbl. lengths w/2.75- or 3-inch chambering, full pistol grip. Superlight models available in 26.5-inch bbl. lengths w/2.75-inch chambering only, and straight-grip stock w/Schnabel forend. Both have hand-engraved receivers, fine-line checkering, gold-plated single selective trigger, automatic selective ejectors, manual safety. Weight: 6 to 7.5 lbs. Reintroduced 1985.
Grade I, Standand . . . . NiB $1753 Ex $1499 Gd $1072
Grade II, Pigeon . . . . NiB $3219 Ex $2582 Gd $1813
Grade III, Pointer . . . . NiB $3991 Ex $3220 Gd $2233
Grade IV, Diana. . . . . NiB $4399 Ex $3540 Gd $2464
Grade V, Midas . . . . NiB $5709 Ex $4603 Gd $3187
W/extra bbls., add 45%

SUPERPOSED MAGNUM . . . . . . NiB $1688 Ex $1366 Gd $954
Same as Grade I except chambered for 12-ga. 3-inch shells, 30-inch vent-rib bbls., stock w/recoil pad. Weight: About 8.25 lbs. Disc. 1976.

**SUPERPOSED LTD.
BLACK DUCK ISSUE . . . . NiB $7416 Ex $5994 Gd $4128**
Gauge: 12. Superposed Lightning action. 28-inch vent-rib bbls. Choked M/F. 2.75-inch chambers. Weight: 7 lbs., 6 oz. Gold-inlaid receiver and trigger guard engraved w/black duck scenes. Gold-plated, single selective trigger. Top-tang mounted manual safety. Automatic, selective ejectors. Front and center ivory sights. High-grade, hand-checkered, hand-oiled select walnut stock and forend. 500 issued in 1983.

**SUPERPOSED LTD.
MALLARD DUCK ISSUE . . . . . . NiB $7610 Ex $6129 Gd $4235**
Same general specifications as Ltd. Black Duck issue except mallard duck scenes engraved on receiver and trigger guard, dark French walnut stock w/rounded pistol-grip. 500 issued in 1981.

**SUPERPOSED LTD.
PINTAIL DUCK ISSUE . . . . NiB $7796 Ex $6278 Gd $4335**
Same general specifications as Ltd. Black Duck issue except pintail duck scenes engraved on receiver and trigger guard. Stock is of dark French walnut w/rounded pistol-grip. 500 issued in 1982.

SUPERPOSED, PRESENTATION GRADES
Custom versions of Super-Light, Lightning Hunting, Trap and Skeet Models, w/same general specifications as those of standard guns, but of higher overall quality. The four Presentation grades differ in receiver finish (grayed or blued), engraving gold inlays, wood and checkering. Presentation 4 has sideplates. Made by FN, these models were Intro. in 1977.
Presentation 1 . . . . NiB $3205 Ex $2588 Gd $1799
Presentation 1, gold-inlaid. . . . . NiB $3663 Ex $2953 Gd $2047
Presentation 2 . . . . NiB $4113 Ex $3316 Gd $2316
Presentation 2, gold-inlaid. . . . . NiB $4841 Ex $3897 Gd $2697
Presentation 3, gold-inlaid. . . . . NiB $6257 Ex $5041 Gd $3483
Presentation 4 . . . . NiB $6994 Ex $5630 Gd $3885
Presentation 4, gold-inlaid. . . . . NiB $9041 Ex $7277 Gd $4719

SUPERPOSED SKEET GUNS, GRADE I
Same as standard Lightning 12, 20, 28 and .410 Hunting models, except has skeet-style stock and forearm, 26.5- or 28-inch vent-rib bbls. w/SK choke. Available also in All Gauge Skeet Set: Lightning 12 w/one removable forearm and three extra sets of bbls. in 20, 28 and .410 ga. in fitted luggage case. Disc. 1976. (For higher grades see listings for comparable Hunting models)
12 or 20 ga.. . . . . NiB $1926 Ex $1553 Gd $1075
28 or .410 ga. . . . . NiB $2387 Ex $1927 Gd $1336
All ga. skeet set . . . . NiB $6102 Ex $4918 Gd $3349

**SUPERPOSED SUPER
LIGHT MODEL . . . . NiB $1898 Ex $1532 Gd $1062**
Ultralight field gun version of Standard Lightning Model has classic straight-grip stock and slimmer forearm. Available only in 12 and 20 gauges (2.75-inch chambers), w/26.5-inch vent-rib bbls. Weight: 6.5 lbs., (12 ga.); 6 lbs., (20 ga.). Made 1967-76.

SUPERPOSED TRAP GUN . . . . . NiB $1963 Ex $1583 Gd $1097
Same as Grade I except has trap-style stock, beavertail forearm, 30-inch vent-rib bbls., 12 ga. only. Disc. 1976. (For higher grades see listings for comparable hunting models)

TWELVETTE DOUBLE AUTOMATIC
Lightweight version of Double Automatic w/same general specifications except aluminum receiver. Bbl. w/plain matted top or vent rib. Weight: 6.75 to 7 lbs., depending on bbl. Receiver is finished in black w/gold engraving; 1956-1961 receivers were also anodized in gray, brown and green w/silver engraving. Made 1955-71
W/plain bbl. . . . . NiB $583 Ex $474 Gd $334
W/vent rib bbl. . . . . NiB $712 Ex $577 Gd $405

CENTURY INTERNATIONAL ARMS INC. — St. Albans, VT

CENTURION . . . . NiB $371 Ex $303 Gd $217
O/U boxlock action with double triggers and extractors. 12 ga. w/2.75-inch chamber. Bbls: 28-inch choked modified/full with ventilated rib. Weight: 7-1/4 lbs. Checkered European walnut buttstock and forend. Polished blue finish. Imported 1993 to date.

SHOTGUNS

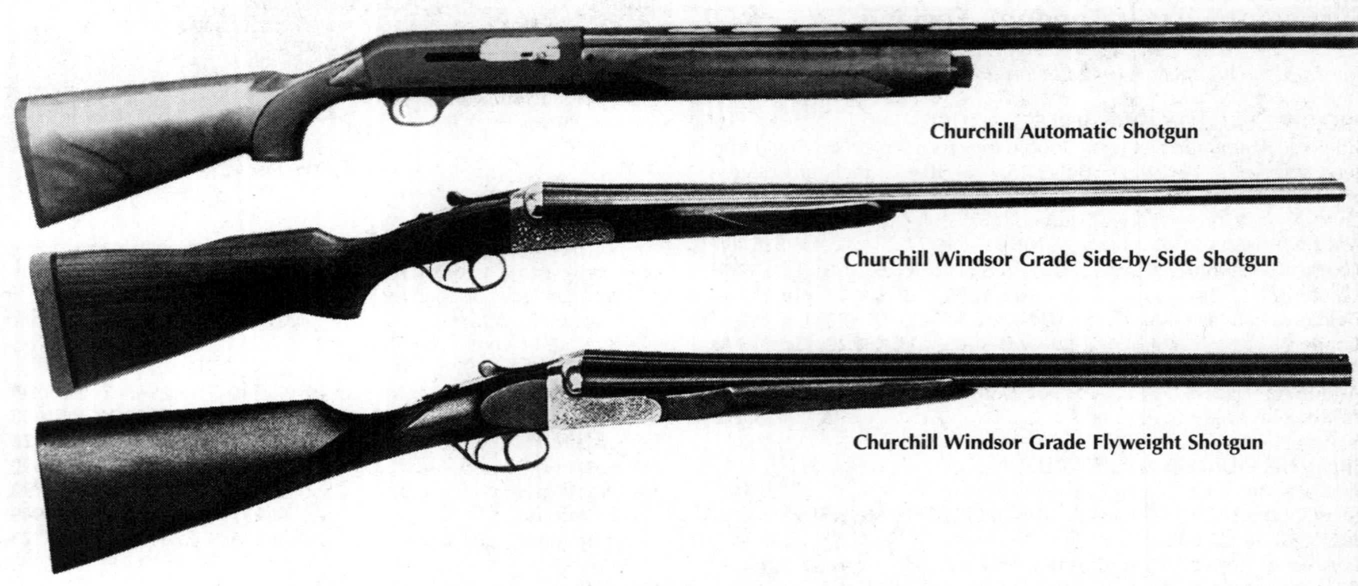

Churchill Automatic Shotgun

Churchill Windsor Grade Side-by-Side Shotgun

Churchill Windsor Grade Flyweight Shotgun

CHURCHILL SHOTGUNS — Italy and Spain Imported by Ellett Brothers, Inc., Chapin, SC; previously by Kassnar Imports, Inc., Harrisburg, PA

AUTOMATIC SHOTGUN
Gas-operated. Gauge: 12, 2.75- or 3-inch chambers. Five round magazine w/cutoff. Bbl.: 24-, 25-, 26-, 28-inch w/ICT choke tubes. Checkered walnut stock w/satin finish. Imported from Italy 1990-94.
Standard model . . . . NiB $554 Ex $451 Gd $320
Turkey model . . . . NiB $580 Ex $472 Gd $333

MONARCH O/U SHOTGUN
Hammerless, takedown w/engraved receiver. Selective single or double triggers. Gauges: 12, 20, 28, .410; 3-inch chambers. Bbls.: 25- or 26-inch (IC/M); 28-inch (M/F). Weight: 6.5-7.5 lbs. Checkered European walnut buttstock and forend. Made in Italy from 1986-93.
W/double triggers . . . . NiB $509 Ex $422 Gd $300
W/single trigger. . . . . NiB $576 Ex $468 Gd $331

REGENT O/U SHOTGUNS
Gauges: 12 or 20; 2.75-inch chambers. 27-inch bbls. w/interchangeable choke tubes and wide vent rib. Single selective trigger, selective automatic ejectors. Checkered pistol-grip stock in fancy walnut. Imported from Italy 1984-88 and 1990-94.
Regent V(disc. 1988). . . . . NiB $1044 Ex $838 Gd $588
Regent VII w/
sideplates (disc. 1994) . . . . NiB $1167 Ex $945 Gd $662

REGENT SKEET . . . . NiB $859 Ex $697 Gd $489
12 or 20 ga. w/2.75-inch chambers. Selective automatic ejectors, single-selective trigger. 26-inch over/under bbls. w/vent rib. Weight: 7 lbs. Made in Italy from 1984-88.

REGENT TRAP . . . . NiB $873 Ex $707 Gd $487
12-ga. competition shotgun w/2.75-inch chambers. 30-inch over/under bbls. choked IM/F, vent side ribs. Weight: 8 lbs. Selective automatic ejectors, single selective trigger. Checkered Monte Carlo stock w/Supercushion recoil pad. Made in Italy 1984-88.

SPORTING CLAYS O/U . . . . NiB $919 Ex $747 Gd $525
Same general specifications as Windsor IV except in 12 ga. only w/28-inch ported bbls. and choke tubes. Selective automatic ejectors. Weight: 7.5 lbs. Made from 1992-94.

WINDSOR O/U SHOTGUNS
Hammerless, boxlock w/engraved receiver, selective single trigger. Extractors or ejectors. Gauges: 12, 20, 28 or .410; 3-inch chambers. Bbls.: 24 to 30 inches w/fixed chokes or choke tubes. Weight: 6 lbs., 3 oz. (Flyweight) to 7 lbs., 10 oz. (12 ga.). Checkered straight (Flyweight) or pistol-grip stock and forend of European walnut. Imported from Italy 1984-93.
Windsor III w/fixed chokes. . . . . NiB $693 Ex $563 Gd $397
Windsor III w/choke tubes . . . . NiB $857 Ex $694 Gd $487
Windsor IV w/fixed
chokes (disc. 1993). . . . . NiB $804 Ex $652 Gd $458
Windsor IV w/choke tubes . . . . NiB $804 Ex $587 Gd $210

WINDSOR SIDE-BY-SIDE SHOTGUNS
Boxlock action w/double triggers, ejectors or extractors and automatic safety. Gauges: 10, (3.5-inch chambers); 12, 20, 28, .410 (3-inch chambers), 16 (2.75-inch chambers). Bbls.: 23 to 32 inches w/various fixed choke or choke tube combinations. Weight: 5 lbs., 12 oz. (Flyweight) to 11.5 lbs. (10 ga.). European walnut buttstock and forend. Imported from Spain 1984-90.
Windsor I 10 ga. . . . . NiB $777 Ex $631 Gd $445
Windsor I 12 thru .410 ga. . . . . NiB $600 Ex $479 Gd $347
Windsor II 12 or 20 ga. . . . . NiB $565 Ex $461 Gd $328
Windsor VI 12 or 20 ga. . . . . NiB $807 Ex $655 Gd $460

E.J. CHURCHILL, LTD. — Surrey (previously London), England

The E.J. Churchill shotguns listed below are no longer imported.

PREMIERE QUALITY HAMMERLESS DOUBLE
Sidelock. Automatic ejectors. Double triggers or selective single trigger. Gauges: 12, 16, 20, 28. Bbls.: 25-, 28- 30-, 32-inch; any degree of boring. Weight: 5-8 lbs. depending on ga. and bbl. length. Checkered stock and forend, straight or pistol-grip.
W/double triggers............... NiB $17,898 Ex $14,508 Gd $10,400
W/selective single trigger, add.................................10%

FIELD MODEL HAMMERLESS DOUBLE
Sidelock Hammerless ejector gun w/same general specifications as Premiere Model but of lower quality.
W/double triggers .... NiB $10,050 Ex $7970 Gd $6930
W/selective single trigger, add 10%

PREMIERE QUALITY O/U SHOTGUN
Sidelock. Automatic ejectors. Double triggers or selective single trigger. Gauges: 12, 16, 20, 28. Bbls.: 25-, 28-, 30-, 32-inch, any degree of boring. Weight: 5-8 lbs. depending on ga. and bbl. length. Checkered stock and forend, straight or pistol-grip.
W/double triggers............... NiB $20,150 Ex $16,120 Gd $10,961
W/selective single trigger, add.................................10%
Raised vent rib, add..15%

UTILITY MODEL HAMMERLESS DOUBLE-BARREL
Anson & Deeley boxlock action. Double triggers or single trigger. Gauges: 12, 16, 20, 28, .410. Bbls.: 25-, 28-, 30-, 32-inch, any degree of boring. Weight: 4.5-8 lbs. depending on ga. and bbl. length. Checkered stock and forend, straight or pistol-grip.
W/double triggers .... NiB $6750 Ex $4930 Gd $3630
W/selective single trigger, add 10%

XXV PREMIERE
HAMMERLESS DOUBLE ... NiB $17,226 Ex $13,780 Gd $9370
Sidelock. Assisted opening. Automatic ejectors. Double triggers. Gauges: 12, 20. 25-inch bbls. w/narrow, quick-sighting rib; any standard choke combination. English-style straight-grip stock and forearm, checkered.

XXV IMPERIAL .... NiB $14,332 Ex $11,466 Gd $7797
Similar to XXV Premiere but no assisted opening feature.

XXV HERCULES .... NiB $10,004 Ex $8002 Gd $5442
Boxlock, otherwise specifications same as for XXV Premiere.

XXV REGAL................ NiB $5661 Ex $4555 Gd $3141
Similar to XXV Hercules but w/o assisted opening feature. Gauges: 12, 20, 28, .410.

CLASSIC DOUBLES — Tochigi, Japan

Imported by Classic Doubles International, St. Louis, MO, and previously by Olin as Winchester Models 101 and 23.

MODEL 101 O/U SHOTGUN
Boxlock. Engraved receiver w/single selective trigger, auto ejectors and combination bbl. selector and safety. Gauges: 12, 20, 28 or .410, 2.75-, 3-inch chambers, 25.5- 28- or 30-inch vent-rib bbls. Weight: 6.25 – 7.75 lbs. Checkered French walnut stock. Imported from 1987-90.

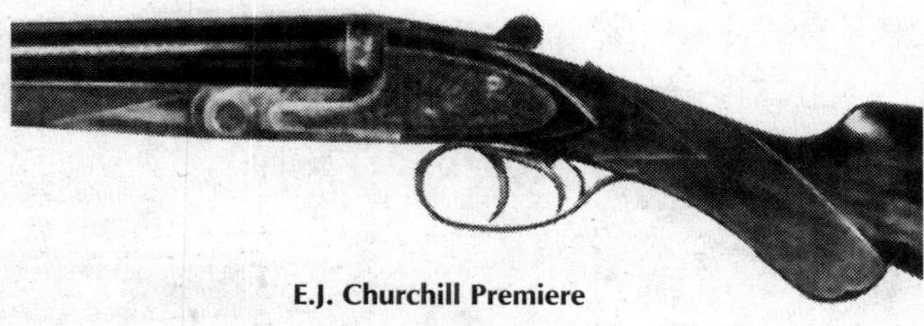
E.J. Churchill Premiere

Classic I Field .... NiB $1657 Ex $1345 Gd $949
Classic II Field.................... NiB $1859 Ex $1507 Gd $1058
Classic Sporter .... NiB $1989 Ex $1611 Gd $1128
Classic Sporter combo .... NiB $3204 Ex $2592 Gd $1810
Classic Trap........................ NiB $1631 Ex $1325 Gd $934
Classic Trap Single................ NiB $1657 Ex $1346 Gd $949
Classic Trap combo .... NiB $2409 Ex $1953 Gd $1371
Classic Skeet...................... NiB $1730 Ex $1404 Gd $988
Classic Skeet
2-bbl. set......................... NiB $2602 Ex $2109 Gd $1479
Classic Skeet
4-bbl. set......................... NiB $4416 Ex $3560 Gd $2488
ClassicWaterfowler................ NiB $1394 Ex $1135 Gd $804
For Grade II (28 ga.), add $750
For Grade II (.410 ga.), add $250

MODEL 201 SIDE-BY-SIDE SHOTGUN
Boxlock. Single selective trigger, automatic safety and selective ejectors. Gauges: 12 or 20; 3-inch chambers. 26- or 28-inch vent-rib bbl., fixed chokes or internal tubes. Weight: 6 to 7 lbs. Checkered French walnut stock and forearm. Imported 1987-90.
Field model....................... NiB $1653 Ex $1350 Gd $940
Skeet model .... NiB $1939 Ex $1569 Gd $1096
With internal choke tubes, add........................... $100

MODEL 201
SMALL BORE SET .... NiB $4892 Ex $3957 Gd $2761
Same general specifications as the Classic Model 201 except w/smaller frame, in 28 ga. (IC/M) and .410 (F/M). Weight: 6-6.5 lbs. Imported from 1987-90.

COGSWELL & HARRISON, LTD. — London, England

AMBASSADOR HAMMERLESS
DOUBLE-BARREL SHOTGUN .... NiB $6010 Ex $5412 Gd $3514
Boxlock. Sideplates w/game scene or rose scroll engraving. Automatic ejectors. Double triggers. Gauges: 12, 16, 20. Bbls.: 26-28-, 30-inch; any choke combination. Checkered straight-grip stock and forearm. Disc.

AVANT TOUT SERIES HAMMERLESS
DOUBLE-BARREL SHOTGUNS
Boxlock. Sideplates (except Avant Tout III Grade). Automatic ejectors. Double triggers or single trigger (selective or non-selective). Gauges: 12, 16, 20. Bbls.: 25-, 27.5-, 30-inch, any choke combination. Checkered stock and forend, straight grip standard. Made in three models (Avant Tout I or Konor, Avant Tout II or Sandhurst,

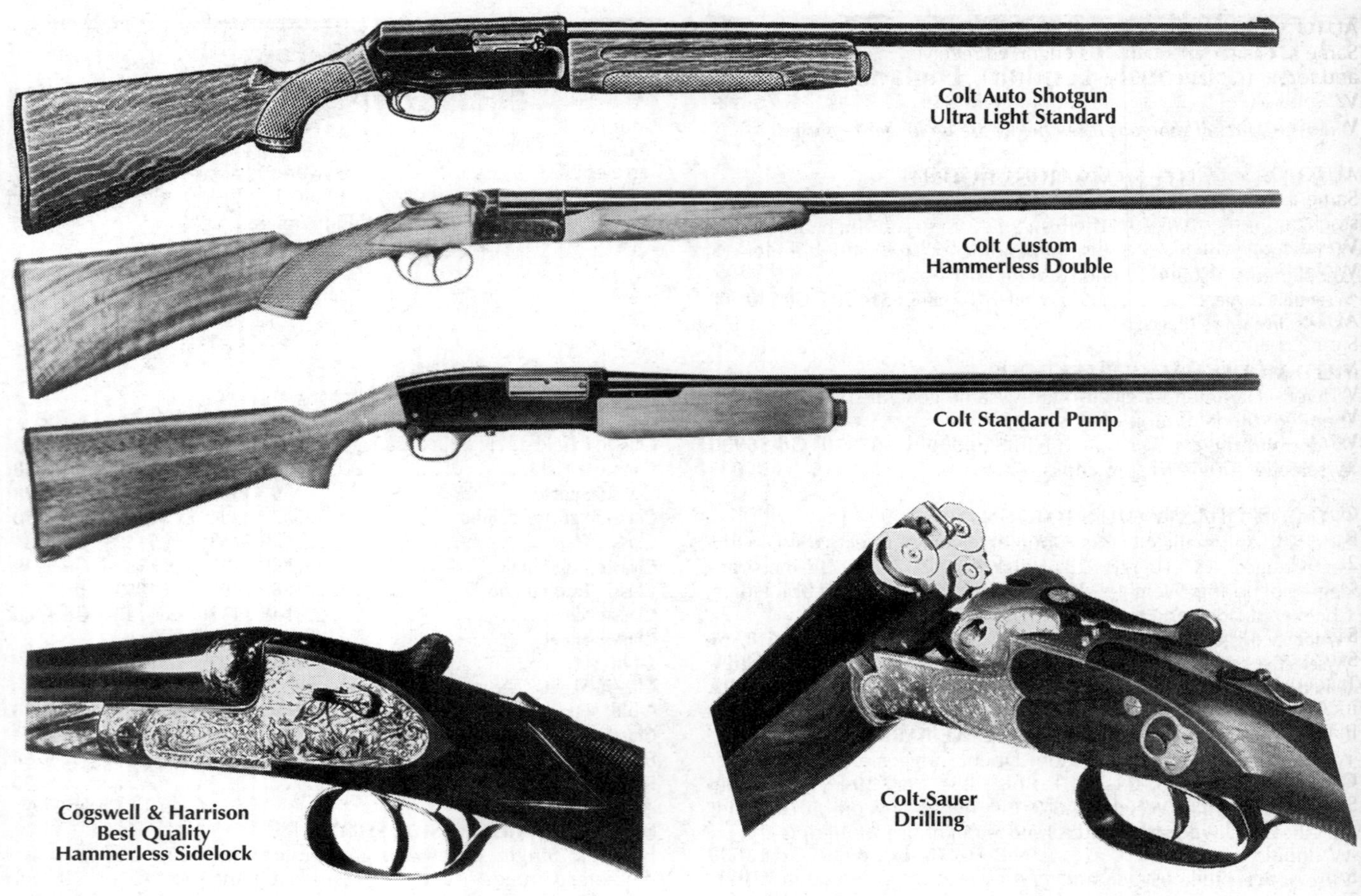

Colt Auto Shotgun Ultra Light Standard

Colt Custom Hammerless Double

Colt Standard Pump

Cogswell & Harrison Best Quality Hammerless Sidelock

Colt-Sauer Drilling

Avant Tout III or Rex) which differ chiefly in overall quality of engraving, grade of wood, checkering, etc. General specifications are the same. Disc.

Avant Tout I . . . . **NiB $3684 Ex $2963 Gd $2086**
Avant Tout II . . . . **NiB $3236 Ex $2624 Gd $1842**
Avant Tout III . . . . **NiB $2496 Ex $2029 Gd $1432**
Single trigger, non-selective, add **$225**
Single trigger, selective, add **$395**

BEST QUALITY HAMMERLESS SIDELOCK DOUBLE-BARREL SHOTGUN
Hand-detachable locks. Automatic ejectors. Double triggers or single trigger (selective or non-selective). Gauges: 12, 16, 20. Bbls.: 25-, 26-, 28-, 30-inch, any choke combination. Checkered stock and forend, straight grip standard.

Victor model . . . . **NiB $10,123 Ex $8141 Gd $5602**
Primic model (disc.) . . . . **NiB $7066 Ex $5695 Gd $3939**
Single trigger, non-selective, add **$225**
Single trigger, selective, add **$395**

HUNTIC MODEL HAMMERLESS DOUBLE
Sidelock. Automatic ejectors. Double triggers or single trigger (selective or non-selective). Gauges: 12, 16, 20. Bbls.: 25-, 27.5-, 30-inch; any choke combination. Checkered stock and forend, straight grip standard. Disc.

W/double triggers . . . . **NiB $4497 Ex $3655 Gd $2573**
Single trigger, non-selective, add **$225**
Single trigger, selective, add **$350**

MARKOR HAMMERLESS DOUBLE
Boxlock. Non-ejector or ejector. Double triggers. Gauges: 12, 16, 20. Bbls.: 27.5 or 30-inch; any choke combination. Checkered stock and forend, straight grip standard. Disc.

Non-ejector . . . . **NiB $1866 Ex $1514 Gd $1065**
Ejector model . . . . **NiB $2272 Ex $1842 Gd $1293**

REGENCY HAMMERLESS DOUBLE . . . . . **NiB $3139 Ex $2535 Gd $1770**
Anson & Deeley boxlock action. Automatic ejectors. Double triggers. Gauges: 12, 16, 20. Bbls.: 26-, 28-, 30-inch, any choke combination. Checkered straight-grip stock and forearm. Introduced in 1970 to commemorate the firm's bicentennial, this model has deep scroll engraving and the name "Regency" inlaid in gold on the rib. Disc.

COLT INDUSTRIES — Hartford, Connecticut
Auto Shotguns were made by Franchi and are similar to corresponding models of that manufacturer.

AUTO SHOTGUN — ULTRA LIGHT STANDARD
Recoil-operated. Takedown. Alloy receiver. Gauges: 12, 20. Mag. holds 4 rounds. Bbls.: plain, solid or vent rib, chrome-lined; 26-inch IC or M choke, 28-inch M or F choke, 30-inch F choke, 32-inch F choke. Weight: 12 ga., about 6.25 lbs. Checkered pistol-grip stock and forearm. Made 1964-66.

W/plain bbl. . . . . **NiB $525 Ex $427 Gd $302**
W/solid rib bbl. . . . . **NiB $395 Ex $323 Gd $231**
W/vent rib bbl. . . . . **NiB $421 Ex $344 Gd $246**

AUTO SHOTGUN — MAGNUM CUSTOM
Same as Magnum except has engraved receiver, select walnut stock and forearm. Made 1964-66.
W/Solid-rib bbl.. . . . . NiB $592 Ex $482 Gd $341
W/ventilated rib bbl. . . . . NiB $658 Ex $534 Gd $376

AUTO SHOTGUN — ULTRA LIGHT CUSTOM
Same as Standard Auto except has engraved receiver, select walnut stock and forearm. Made 1964-66.
W/solid-rib bbl. . . . . NiB $496 Ex $404 Gd $288
W/ventilated-rib bbl. . . . . NiB $528 Ex $430 Gd $305

AUTO SHOTGUN — MAGNUM
Same as Standard Auto except steel receiver,chambered for 3-inch Magnum shells, 30- and 32-inch bbls. in 12 ga., 28-inch in 20 ga. Weight: 12 ga., about 8.25 lbs. Made 1964-66.
W/plain bbl. . . . . NiB $476 Ex $388 Gd $277
W/solid-rib bbl. . . . . NiB $528 Ex $430 Gd $305
W/ventilated rib bbl. . . . . NiB $554 Ex $451 Gd $320

CUSTOM HAMMERLESS DOUBLE . . . . NiB $820 Ex $660 Gd $467
Boxlock. Double triggers. Auto ejectors. Gauges: 12 Mag., 16. Bbls.: 26-inch IC/M; 28-inch M/F; 30-inch F/F. Weight: 12 ga., about 7.5 lbs. Checkered pistol-grip stock and beavertail forearm. Made in 1961.

STANDARD PUMP
SHOTGUN . . . . NiB $382 Ex $313 Gd $224
Takedown. Gauges: 12, 16, 20. Magazine holds 4 rounds. Bbls.: 26-inch IC; 28-inch M or F choke; 30-inch F choke. Weight: About 6 lbs. Plain pistol-grip stock and forearm. Made 1961-65 by Manufrance.

CUSTOM PUMP . . . . NiB $417 Ex $341 Gd $243
Same as Standard Pump shotgun except has checkered stock, vent-rib bbl. Weight: About 6.5 lbs. Made 1961-63 by Manufrance.

SAUER DRILLING . . . . NiB $3191 Ex $2583 Gd $1807
Three-bbl. combination gun. Boxlock. Set rifle trigger. Tang bbl. selector, automatic rear sight positioner. 12 ga. over .30-06 or .243 rifle bbl. 25-inch bbls., F and M choke. Weight: About 8 lbs. Folding leaf rear sight, blade front w/brass bead. Checkered pistol-grip stock and beavertail forearm, recoil pad. Made 1974 to date by J. P. Sauer & Sohn, Eckernförde, Germany.

CONNECTICUT VALLEY CLASSICS — Westport, Connecticut

SPORTER 101 O/U
Gauge: 12; 3-inch chamber. Bbls.: 28-, 30- or 32-inch w/ screw-in tubes. Weight: 7.75 lbs. Engraved stainless or nitrided receiver; blued bbls. Checkered American black walnut buttstock and forend w/low-luster satin finish. Made from 1993 to date.
Classic Sporter. . . . . NiB $2212 Ex $1797 Gd $1266
Stainless Classic Sporter . . . . . . NiB $2602 Ex $2109 Gd $1479

FIELD O/U
Similar to the standard Classic Sporter over/under model except w/30-inch bbls. only and non-reflective matte blued finish on both bbls. and receiver for Waterfowler; other grades w/different degrees of embellishment; Grade I the lowest and Grade III the highest. Made 1993-1998.
Grade I . . . . NiB $2467 Ex $2168 Gd $1508
Grade II. . . . . NiB $2847 Ex $2305 Gd $1612
Grade III . . . . NiB $3207 Ex $2603 Gd $1815
Waterfowler . . . . NiB $2561 Ex $2077 Gd $1457

CONNENTO/VENTUR — Formerly imported by Ventura, Seal Beach, California

Model 51 . . . . NiB $545 Ex $345 Gd $270
Gauge: 12, 16, 20, 28 and .410. Double-barrel, box-lock action. Barrels: 26, 28, 30 and 32 inches; various chokes; extractors; and double triggers. Checkered walnut stock. Introduced in 1980, discontinued 1985.

Model 52 . . . . NiB $545 Ex $370 Gd $270
Same as Model 51 except in 10 gauge.

Model 53 . . . . NiB $585 Ex $395 Gd $295
Same as Model 51 except with scalloped receiver, automatic ejectors and optional single selective trigger. Discontinued in 1985.
W/single trigger, add 25%

Model 62 . . . . NiB $995 Ex $795 Gd $620
Holland & Holland-design sidelock shotgun with various barrel lengths and chokes; automatic ejectors; cocking indicators. Floral engraved receiver, checkered walnut stock. Discontinued in 1982.

Model 64 . . . . NiB $1240 Ex $925 Gd $755
Same as Model 62 except deluxe finish. Discontinued.

Grade I . . . . NiB $1180 Ex $855 Gd $730
Gauge: 12. Over/under shotgun. Barrels: 32 inches; screw-in choke tubes; high ventilated rib; automatic ejectors; single selective trigger standard. Checkered Monte Carlo walnut stock.

Mark II . . . . NiB $1430 Ex $1125 Gd $955
Same as Mark I model but with an extra single barrel and fitted leather case.
Mark III . . . . NiB $1680 Ex $1330 Gd $955
Same as Mark I model but with finely figured walnut stock and engraved metal.

Mark III Combo. . . . . NiB $3060 Ex $2510 Gd $1885
Same as Mark III model above but with extra single barrel and fitted leather case.

CHARLES DALY, INC. — New York, New York

The pre-WWII Charles Daly shotguns, w/the exception of the Commander, were manufactured by various firms in Suhl, Germany. The postwar guns, except for the Novamatic series, were produced by Miroku Firearms Mfg. Co., Tokyo. Miroku ceased production in 1976 and the Daly trademark was acquired by Outdoor Sports Headquarters, in Dayton, Ohio. OSHI continued to market O/U shotguns from both Italy and Spain under the Daly logo. Automatic models were produced in Japan for distribution in the USA. In 1996, KBI, Inc. in Harrisburg, PA acquired the Daly trademark and currently imports firearms under that logo.

COMMANDER O/U SHOTGUN
Daly-pattern Anson & Deeley system boxlock action. Automatic ejectors. Double triggers or Miller selective single trigger. Gauges: 12, 16,20, 28, .410. Bbls.: 26- to 30-inch, IC/M or M/F choke. Weight: 5.25 to 7.25 lbs. depending on ga. and bbl. length. Checkered stock and forend, straight or pistol grip. The two models, 100 and 200, differ in general quality, grade of wood, checkering, engraving, etc.; otherwise specs are the same. Made in Belgium c. 1939.

SHOTGUNS

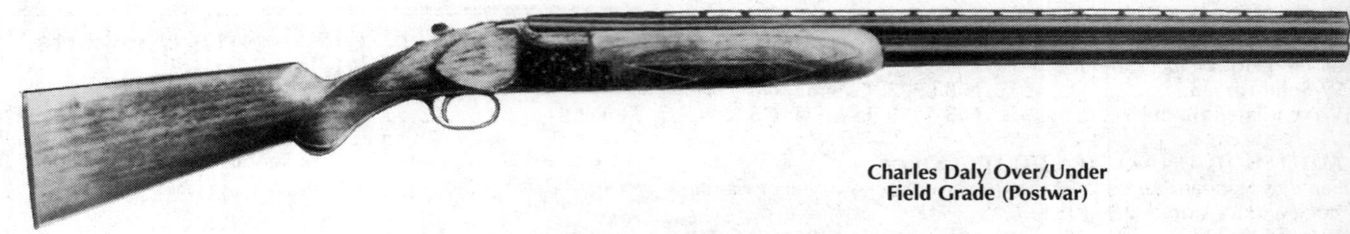
Charles Daly Over/Under Field Grade (Postwar)

Model 100 .... NiB $562 Ex $458 Gd $333
Model 200 .... NiB $729 Ex $593 Gd $418
Miller single trigger, add $100

HAMMERLESS DOUBLE-BARREL SHOTGUN
Daly-pattern Anson & Deeley system boxlock action. Automatic ejectors except "Superior Quality" is non-ejector. Double triggers. Gauges: 10, 12, 16, 20, 28, .410. Bbls.: 26- to 32-inch, any combination of chokes. Weight: from 4 to 8.5 lbs. depending on ga. and bbl. length. Checkered pistol-grip stock and forend. The four grades—Regent Diamond, Diamond, Empire, Superior—differ in general quality, grade of wood, checkering, engraving, etc.; otherwise specifications are the same. Disc. about 1933.
Diamond quality................ NiB $11,376 Ex $9100 Gd $6188
Empire quality.................... NiB $5526 Ex $4420 Gd $3006
Regent Diamond quality .... NiB $13,650 Ex $10,920 Gd $7426
Superior quality .... NiB $1281 Ex $1033 Gd $717

HAMMERLESS DRILLING
Daly pattern Anson & Deeley system boxlock action. Plain extractors. Double triggers, front single set for rifle bbl. Gauges: 12, 16, 20, .25-20, .25-35, .30-30 rifle bbl. Supplied in various bbl. lengths and weights. Checkered pistol-grip stock and forend. Auto rear sight operated by rifle bbl. selector. The three grades — Regent Diamond, Diamond, Superior—differ in general quality, grade of wood, checkering, engraving, etc.; otherwise, specifications are the same. Disc. 1933.
Diamond quality .... NiB $6386 Ex $5150 Gd $3539
Regent Diamond quality ... NiB $13,326 Ex $10,661 Gd $7249
Superior quality .... NiB $3489 Ex $2814 Gd $1951

HAMMERLESS DOUBLE
EMPIRE GRADE .... NiB $1035 Ex $890 Gd $701
Boxlock. Plain extractors. Non-selective single trigger. Gauges: 12, 16, 20; 3-inch chambers in 12 and 20, 2.75-inch in 16 ga. Bbls.: vent rib; 26-, 28-, 30-inch (latter in 12 ga. only); IC/M, M/F, F/F. Weight: 6 to 7.75 lbs., depending on ga. and bbls. Checkered pistol-grip stock and beavertail forearm. Made 1968-71.

1974 WILDLIFE COMMEMORATIVE .... NiB $2365 Ex $1924 Gd $1360
Limited issue of 500 guns. Similar to Diamond Grade over/under. 12-ga. trap and skeet models only. Duck scene engraved on right side of receiver, fine scroll on left side. Made in 1974.

NOVAMATIC LIGHTWEIGHT AUTOLOADER
Same as Breda. Recoil-operated. Takedown.12 ga., 2.75-inch chamber.

Four-round tubular magazine. Bbls.: Plain vent rib; 26-inch IC or Quick-Choke w/three interchangeable tubes, 28-inch M or F choke. Weight (w/26-inch vent-rib bbl.): 7 lbs., 6 oz. Checkered pistol-grip stock and forearm. Made 1968 by Ernesto Breda, Milan, Italy.
W/plain bbl. .... NiB $461 Ex $377 Gd $269
W/vent rib bbl. .... NiB $495 Ex $403 Gd $287
W/Quick-Choke, add $20

NOVAMATIC SUPER LIGHTWEIGHT
Lighter version of Novamatic Lightweight. Gauges: 12, 20. Weight (w/26-inch vent-rib bbl.): 12 ga., 6 lbs., 10 oz., 20 ga., 6 lbs. SK choke available in 26-inch vent-rib bbl. 28-inch bbls. in 12 ga. only. Quick-Choke in 20 ga. w/plain bbl. Made 1968 by Ernesto Breda, Milan, Italy.
12 ga., plain bbl. .... NiB $423 Ex $346 Gd $248
12 ga., vent rib bbl. .... NiB $461 Ex $377 Gd $269
20 ga., plain bbl. .... NiB $429 Ex $351 Gd $251
20 ga., plain bbl. w/Quick-Choke .... NiB $461 Ex $377 Gd $269
20 ga., vent rib bbl. .... NiB $487 Ex $398 Gd $284

NOVAMATIC SUPER LIGHTWEIGHT
20 GA. MAGNUM....................... NiB $487 Ex $398 Gd $283
Same as Novamatic Super Lightweight 2, except 3-inch chamber, has 3-round magazine, 28-inch vent-rib bbl., F choke.

NOVAMATIC
12 GA. MAGNUM...................... NiB $495 Ex $403 Gd $287
Same as Novamatic Lightweight, except chambered for 12-ga. Magnum 3-inch shell. Has 3-round magazine, 30-inch vent rib bbl., F choke, and stock w/recoil pad. Weight: 7.75 lbs.

Post-War Charles Daly shotguns were imported by Sloan's Sporting Goods trading as Charles Daly in New York. In 1976, Outdoor Sports Headquarters acquired the Daly trademark and continued to import European-made shotguns under that logo. In 1996, KBI, Inc., in Harrisburg, PA, acquired the Daly trademark and currently imports firearms under that logo.

NOVAMATIC TRAP GUN .... NiB $532 Ex $434 Gd $309
Same as Novamatic Lightweight except has 30-inch vent rib bbl., F choke and Monte Carlo stock w/recoil pad. Weight: 7.75 lbs.

O/U SHOTGUNS (PREWAR)
Daly-pattern Anson & Deeley-system boxlock action. Sideplates. Auto ejectors. Double triggers. Gauges: 12, 16, 20. Supplied in various bbl. lengths and weights. Checkered pistol-grip stock and forend. The two grades — Diamond and Empire — differ in general quality, grade of wood, checkering, engraving, etc.; otherwise specifications are the same. Disc. about 1933.
Diamond Quality............ NiB $5889 Ex $4746 Gd $3284
Empire Quality .... NiB $4531 Ex $3659 Gd $2544

O/U SHOTGUNS (POSTWAR)
Boxlock. Auto ejectors or selective auto/manual ejection. Selective single trigger. Gauges: 12, 12 Magnum (3-inch chambers), 20 (3-inch chambers), 28, .410. Bbls.: Vent rib; 26-, 28-, 30-inch; standard choke combinations. Weight: 6 to 8 lbs. depending on ga. and bbls. Select walnut stock w/pistol grip, fluted forearm checkered; Monte Carlo comb on trap guns; recoil pad on 12-ga. mag. and trap models. The various grades differ in quality of engraving and wood. Made from 1963-76.
Diamond grade .... NiB $1424 Ex $1165 Gd $834
Field grade .... NiB $838 Ex $694 Gd $511
Superior grade................. NiB $1064 Ex $876 Gd $635
Venture grade .... NiB $804 Ex $668 Gd $483

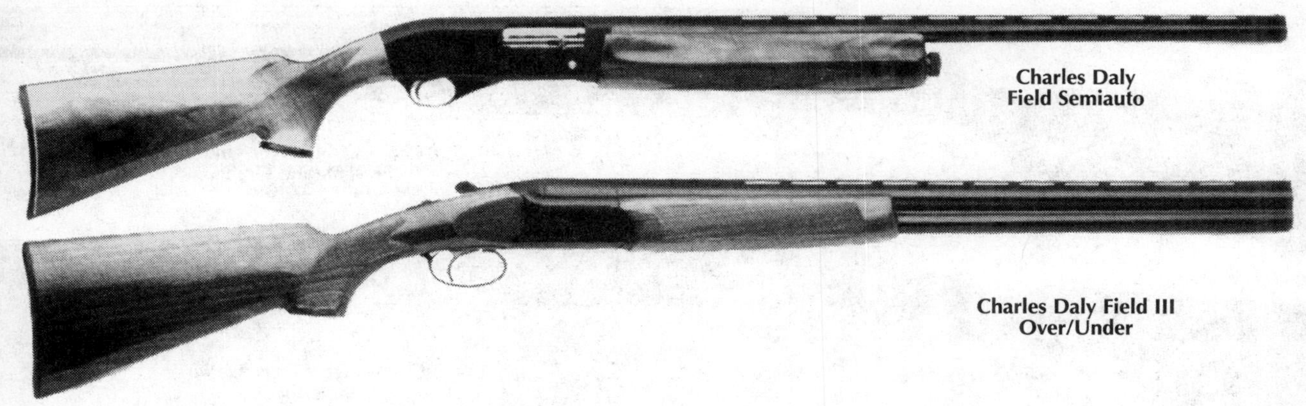
Charles Daly Field Semiauto

Charles Daly Field III Over/Under

SEXTUPLE MODEL SINGLE-BARREL TRAP GUN
Daly-pattern Anson & Deeley system boxlock action. Six locking bolts. Auto ejector. 12 ga. only. Bbls.: 30-, 32-, 34-inch, vent rib. Weight: 7.5 to 8.25 lbs. Checkered pistol-grip stock and forend. The two models made Empire and Regent Diamond differ in general quality, grade of wood, checkering, engraving, etc., otherwise specifications are the same. Disc. about 1933.
Regent Diamond quality (Linder) . . . . NiB $627 Ex $517 Gd $376
Empire quality (Linder) . . . . NiB $5132 Ex $4145 Gd $2882
Regent Diamond quality (Sauer) . . . . . . NiB $3677 Ex $2976 Gd $2079
Empire quality (Sauer) . . . . NiB $2747 Ex $2228 Gd $1564

SINGLE-SHOT TRAP GUN
Daly-pattern Anson & Deeley system boxlock action. Auto ejector. 12 ga. only. Bbls.: 30-, 32-, 34-inch, vent rib. Weight: 7.5 to 8.25 lbs. Checkered pistol-grip stock and forend. This model was made in Empire Quality only. Disc. about 1933.
Empire grade (Linder) . . . . NiB $4546 Ex $3674 Gd $2559
Empire grade (Sauer) . . . . NiB $2304 Ex $1874 Gd $1325

SUPERIOR GRADE SINGLE-SHOT TRAP . . NiB $876 Ex $731 Gd $523
Boxlock. Automatic ejector. 12 ga. only. 32- or 34-inch vent-rib bbl., F choke. Weight: About 8 lbs. Monte Carlo stock w/pistol grip and recoil pad, beavertail forearm, checkered. Made from 1968-76.

DIAMOND GRADE O/U
Boxlock. Single selective trigger. Selective automatic ejectors. Gauges: 12 and 20, 3-inch chambers (2.75 target grade). Bbls.: 26, 27- or 30-inch w/fixed chokes or screw-in tubes. Weight: 7 lbs. Checkered European walnut stock and forearm w/oil finish. Engraved antique silver receiver and blued bbls. Made from 1984-90.
Standard model . . . . NiB $910 Ex $747 Gd $540
Skeet model . . . . NiB $987 Ex $809 Gd $583
Trap model . . . . NiB $1050 Ex $860 Gd $618

DIAMOND GTX DL HUNTER O/U SERIES
Sidelock. Single selective trigger and selective auto ejectors. Gauges: 12, 20, 28 ga. or .410 bore. 26-, 28- and 30-inch bbls w/3-inch chambers (2.75-inch 28 ga.). Choke tubes (12 and 20 ga.), Fixed chokes (28 and 410). Weight: 5-8 lbs. Checkered European walnut stock w/hand-rubbed oil finish and recoil pad. Made from 1997-2001.
Diamond GTX DL Hunter . . . . NiB $9956 Ex $7992 Gd $5479
Diamond GTX EDL Hunter . . . . NiB $12,122 Ex $9698 Gd $6595
Diamond GTX Sporting (12 or 20 ga.) . . . . . NiB $5594 Ex $4503 Gd $3107
Diamond GTX Skeet (12 or 20 ga.) . . . . NiB $5204 Ex $4197 Gd $2895
Diamond GTX Trap (12 ga. only) . . . . . NiB $5906 Ex $4352 Gd $3040

EMPIRE DL HUNTER O/U . . . . . NiB $1293 Ex $1111 Gd $721
Boxlock. Ejectors. Single selective trigger. Gauges:12, 20, 28 ga. and .410 bore. 26- or 28- inch bbls. w/3-inch chambers (2.75-inch 28 ga.). Choke tubes (12 and 20 ga.), Fixed chokes (28 and .410). Engraved coin-silver receiver w/game scene. Imported from 1997-98.

EMPIRE EDL HUNTER SERIES
Similar to Empire DL Hunter except engraved sideplates. Made 1998 to date.
Empire EDL Hunter . . . . NiB $1302 Ex $1062 Gd $754
Empire Sporting . . . . NiB $1270 Ex $1036 Gd $736
Empire Skeet . . . . NiB $1238 Ex $1010 Gd $719
Empire Trap . . . . NiB $1302 Ex $1062 Gd $754
28 ga., add. $95
.410 ga, add. $120
Multi-chokes w/Monte
Carlo stock, add $125

DSS HAMMERLESS DOUBLE . . . . . NiB $746 Ex $610 Gd $435
Boxlock. Single selective trigger. Selective automatic ejectors. Gauges: 12 and 20; 3-inch chambers. 26-inch bbls. w/screw-in choke tubes. Weight: 6.75 lbs. Checkered walnut pistol-grip stock and semi-beavertail forearm w/recoil pad. Engraved antique silver receiver and blued bbls. Made from 1990. Disc.

FIELD GRADE O/U . . . . NiB $560 Ex $460 Gd $332
Boxlock. Single selective trigger. Extractors. Gauges: 12 and 20; 3-inch chambers. Bbls.: 26-inch, IC/M; 28-inch, M/F. Weight: 6.75 lbs. (12 ga.). Checkered walnut stock and forearm w/semi-gloss finish and recoil pad. Engraved color-casehardened receiver and blued bbls. Made from 1989. Disc.

FIELD SEMIAUTO SHOTGUN . . . . . NiB $444 Ex $367 Gd $269
Recoil-operated. Takedown. 12-ga. and 12-ga. Magnum. Bbls.: 27- and 30-inch; vent rib. Made from 1982-88.

FIELD III O/U SHOTGUN . . . . NiB $574 Ex $471 Gd $340
Boxlock. Plain extractors. Non-selective single trigger. Gauges: 12 or 20. Bbls.: vent rib; 26- and 28-inch; IC/M, M/F. Weight: 6 to 7.75 lbs. depending on ga. and bbls. Chrome-molybdenum steel bbls. Checkered pistol-grip stock and forearm. Made from 1982. Disc.

LUXIE O/U . . . . NiB $819 Ex $669 Gd $478
Similar to the Field Grade except w/selective automatic ejectors and choke tubes. Gauges: 12, 20, 28 and .410. Receiver w/antique silver finish and blued bbls. Made from 1989-1994.

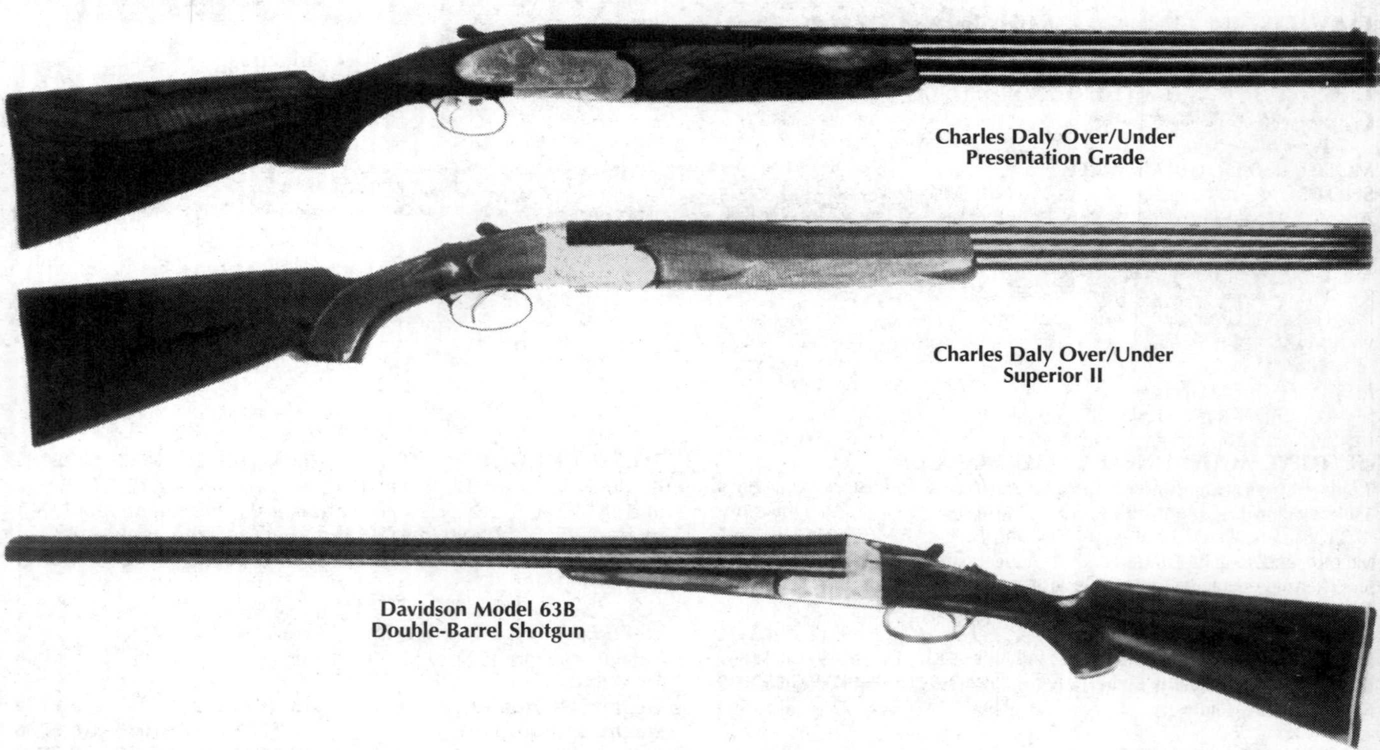

Charles Daly Over/Under
Presentation Grade

Charles Daly Over/Under
Superior II

Davidson Model 63B
Double-Barrel Shotgun

MULTI-XII SELF-LOADING SHOTGUN . . . . . . NiB $541 Ex $438 Gd $307
Similar to the gas-operated field semiauto except w/new Multi-Action gas system designed to shoot all loads w/o adjustment. 12 ga. w/3-inch chamber. 27-inch bbl. w/Invector choke tubes, vent rib. Made in Japan from 1987-1988.

O/U
PRESENTATION GRADE . . . . NiB $1149 Ex $930 Gd $646
Purdey boxlock w/double cross-bolt. Gauges: 12 or 20. Engraved receiver w/single selective trigger and auto-ejectors. 27-inch chrome-molybdenum steel, rectified, honed and internally chromed, vent-rib bbls. Hand-checkered deluxe European walnut stock. Made from 1982-86.

O/U
Superior II Shotgun . . . . NiB $981 Ex $794 Gd $555
Boxlock. Plain extractors. Non-selective single trigger. Gauges: 12 or 20. Bbls.: chrome-molybdenum vent rib 26-, 28-, 30-inch, latter in magnum only, assorted chokes. Silver engraved receiver. Checkered pistol-grip stock and forearm. Made from 1982-1988

SPORTING CLAYS O/U . . . . NiB $860 Ex $697 Gd $489
Similar to the Field Grade except in 12 ga. only w/ported bbls. and internal choke tubes. Made from 1990-1996.

DAKOTA ARMS, INC. — Sturgis, South Dakota

CLASSIC FIELD GRADE
S/S SHOTGUN . . . . NiB $8018 Ex $6381 Gd $4286
Boxlock. Gauge: 20 ga. 27-inch bbl. w/fixed chokes. Double triggers. Selective ejectors. Color-casehardened receiver. Weight: 6 lbs. Checkered English walnut stock and splinter forearm w/hand-rubbed oil finish. Made from 1996-1998.

PREMIUM GRADE
S/S SHOTGUN . . . . NiB $14,456 Ex $10,608 Gd $6760
Similar to Classic Field Grade model except w/50% engraving coverage. Exhibition grade English walnut stock. Made from 1996 to date.

AMERICAN LEGEND
S/S SHOTGUN . . . . NiB $17,290 Ex $14,040 Gd $9880
Limited edition built to customer's specifications. Gauge: 20 ga. 27-inch bbl. Double triggers. Selective ejectors. Fully engraved, coin-silver finished receiver w/gold inlays. Weight: 6 lbs. Hand checkered special-selection English walnut stock and forearm. Made from 1996 to date.

DARNE S.A. — Saint-Etienne, France

HAMMERLESS DOUBLE-BARREL SHOTGUNS
Sliding-breech action w/fixed bbls. Auto ejectors. Double triggers. Gauges: 12, 16, 20, 28; also 12 and 20 Magnum w/3-inch chambers. Bbls.: 27.5-inch standard, 25.5- to 31.5-inch lengths available; any standard choke combination. Weight: 5.5 to 7 lbs. depending on ga. and bbl. length. Checkered straight-grip or pistol-grip stock and forearm. The various models differ in grade of engraving and wood. Manufactured from 1881-1979.

Model R11
(Bird Hunter) . . . . NiB $1671 Ex $1515 Gd $839
Model R15
(Pheasant Hunter) . . . . NiB $2485 Ex $1986 Gd $1328
Model R16 (Magnum) . . . . NiB $3836 Ex $3312 Gd $2068
Model V19
(Quail Hunter) . . . . NiB $4920 Ex $4400 Gd $3880
Model V22 . . . . NiB $5526 Ex $4680 Gd $2662
Model V Hors Série No. 1 . . . . NiB $6930 Ex $6010 Gd $4855

DAVIDSON GUNS — Mfd. by Fabrica de Armas ILJA, Eibar, Spain; distributed by Davidson Firearms Co., Greensboro, North Carolina

MODEL 63B DOUBLE-BARREL SHOTGUN .... NiB $397 Ex $324 Gd $230
Anson & Deeley boxlock action. Frame engraved and nickel plated. Plain extractors. Auto safety. Double triggers. Gauges: 12, 16, 20, 28, .410. Bbl. lengths: 25 (.410 only), 26, 28, 30 inches (latter 12 ga. only). Chokes: IC/ M, M/F, F/F. Weight: 5 lbs., 11 oz. (.410) to 7 lbs. (12 ga.). Checkered pistol-grip stock and forearm of European walnut. Made in 1963. Disc.

MODEL 63B MAGNUM
Similar to standard Model 63B except chambered for 10 ga. 3.5-inch, 12 and 20 ga. 3-inch Magnum shells; 10 ga. has 32-inch bbls., choked F/F. Weight: 10 lb., 10 oz. Made from 1963. Disc.
12-and 20 ga. magnum .... NiB $462 Ex $377 Gd $268
10 ga. magnum................ NiB $539 Ex $438 Gd $309

MODEL 69SL DOUBLE-BARREL SHOTGUN............................ NiB $681 Ex $565 Gd $430
Sidelock action w/detachable sideplates, engraved and nickel plated. Plain extractors. Auto safety. Double triggers. 12 and 20 ga. Bbls.: 26-inch IC/M, 28-inch M/F. Weight: 12 ga., 7 lbs., 20 ga., 6.5 lbs. Pistol-grip stock and forearm of European walnut, checkered. Made from 1963-76.

MODEL 73 STAGECOACH HAMMER DOUBLE .... NiB $368 Ex $300 Gd $214
Sidelock action w/detachable sideplates and exposed hammers. Plain extractors. Double triggers. Gauges: 12, 20, 3-inch chambers. 20-inch bbls, M/F chokes. Weight: 7 lbs., 12 ga.; 6.5 lbs., 20 ga. Checkered pistol-grip stock and forearm. Made from 1976. Disc.

DIAMOND

Currently imported by ADCO Sales, Inc, Woburn, MA. Company established circa 1981, all guns manufactured in Turkey.

GOLD SERIES (SEMIAUTOMATIC) . NiB $610 Ex $435 Gd $310
12 gauge, 3-inch chamber. Gas operated. Bbl. 24 (slug) or 28 inches. Ventilated rib with three choke tubes. Semi-humpback design, anodized alloy frame, gold etching. Rotary bolt. Black synthetic or checkered Turkish walnut forearm and stock with recoil pad. Value $50 less for slug version.

IMPERIAL SERIES............... NiB $560 Ex $385 Gd $260
12 (3.5-inch) or 20 (3-inch); bbl. 24 (12 gauge slug), 26 (20 gauge) or 28 inches; ventilated rib, rotary bi-lateral bolt; deluxe checkered stock and forearm. Imported 2003.

ELITE SERIES .... NiB $510 Ex $385 Gd $300
12 gauge, 3-inch chamber. Bbl. 22 (slug), 24, 26 or 28 inches; ventilated rib, deluxe checkered walnut stock and forearm. Imported 2001. Value $20 less for slug version.

PANTHER SERIES............... NiB $460 Ex $310 Gd $205
12 gauge, 3-inch chamber. Gas-operated. Black synthetic stock and forearm. Bbl. 20 (slug or regular) or 28 inches. Imported 2002.

Walnut stock and forearm, add $50
Slug version .... deduct $25

MARINER .... NiB $560 Ex $335 Gd $210
12 gauge, 3-inch chamber. Gas-operated. Bbl. 20 (slug), or 22 inches; ventilated rib. Anodized alloy frame receiver, satin silver metal finish; checkered walnut stock and forearm. Imported 2002. Value $20 less for slug version.

GOLD ELITE SERIES (slide-action)... NiB $403 Ex $258 Gd $183
12 gauge, 3-inch chamber. Bbl. 24 (slug with open sights), or 28 inches; ventilated rib. Semi-humpback design. Anodized alloy frame, synthetic black or Turkish walnut stock and forearm. Weight: 7 lbs. Imported 2001. Value $40 less for synthetic stock.

IMPERIAL SERIES .... NiB $458 Ex $333 Gd $233
12 gauge, 3.5-inch chamber; slide-action. Bbl. 28 inches; ventilated rib, deluxe checkered wood stock and forearm. Imported 2003.

ELITE SERIES .... NiB $408 Ex $303 Gd $178
12 gauge, 3-inch chamber. Similar to Gold Elite Series except has engraved receiver. Bbl. 20 (slug or regular), 24, or 28 inches; ventilated rib, deluxe checkered walnut stock and forearm. Imported 2001. Value $25 less for slug version.

PANTHER SERIES.............. NiB $343 Ex $208 Gd $133
12 gauge, 3-inch chamber. Similar to Elite Series except with black synthetic stock and forearm. Bbl. 18.5 (slug) 20, 22 (slug) or 28 inches. Imported 2001.

MARINER MODEL .... NiB $473 Ex $318 Gd $233
12 gauge, 3-inch chamber. Bbl. 18.5-inch plain or 22 inches; ventilated rib. Five shell magazine. Black synthetic stock and forearm. Imported 2003. Value $20 less for 18.5 plain barrel version.

EXEL ARMS OF AMERICA — Gardner, Massachusetts

SERIES 100 O/U SHOTGUN
Gauge: 12. Single selective trigger. Selective auto ejectors. Hand-checkered European walnut stock w/full pistol grip, tulip forend. Black metal finish. Chambered for 2.75-inch shells (Model 103 for 3-inch). Weight: 6. 88 to 7.88 lbs. Disc 1988.
Model 101, 26-inch bbl., IC/M .... NiB $512 Ex $417 Gd $294
Model 102, 28-inch bbl., IC/IM .... NiB $518 Ex $422 Gd $297
Model 103, 30-inch bbl., M/F .... NiB $538 Ex $437 Gd $308
Model 104, 28-inch bbl., IC/IM .... NiB $589 Ex $478 Gd $336
Model 105, 28-inch bbl., 5 choke tubes...... NiB $748 Ex $607 Gd $427
Model 106, 28-inch bbl., 5 choke tubes...... NiB $894 Ex $719 Gd $505
Model 107 Trap, 30-inch bbl., Full or 5 tubes ..... NiB $963 Ex $760 Gd $631

SERIES 200 SIDE-BY-SIDE SHOTGUN .... NiB $544 Ex $443 Gd $314
Gauges: 12, 20, 28 and .410. Bbls.: 26-, 27- and 28-inch; various choke combinations. Weight: 7 lbs. average. American or European-style stock and forend. Made from 1985 to 87.

SERIES 300 O/U SHOTGUN .... NiB $614 Ex $499 Gd $352
Gauge: 12. Bbls.: 26-, 28- and 29-inch. Non-glare black-chrome matte finish. Weight: 7 lbs. average. Selective auto ejectors, engraved receiver. Hand-checkered European walnut stock and forend. Made from 1985-86.

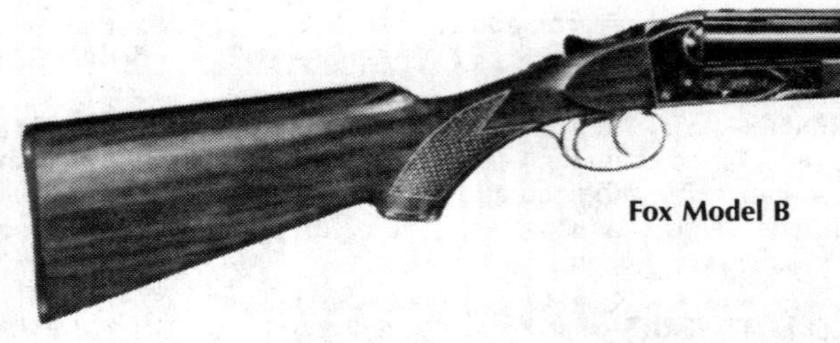
Fox Model B

FABARM SHOTGUNS — Brescia, Italy

Currently imported by Heckler & Koch, Inc., of Sterling, VA (previously by Ithaca Acquisition Corp., St. Lawrence Sales, Inc. and Beeman Precision Arms, Inc.)

See Current listings under "Heckler & Koch."

FIAS — Fabrica Italiana Armi Sabatti Gardone Val Trompia, Italy

GRADE I O/U
Boxlock. Single selective trigger. Gauges: 12, 20, 28, .410; 3-inch chambers. Bbls.: 26-inch IC/M; 28-inch M/F; screw-in choke tubes. Weight: 6.5 to 7.5 lbs. Checkered European walnut stock and forearm. Engraved receiver and blued finish.
12 ga. model.................. NiB $518 Ex $422 Gd $300
20 ga. model.................. NiB $582 Ex $473 Gd $335
28 and .410 ga. models.......... NiB $742 Ex $601 Gd $422

FOX SHOTGUNS — Made by A. H. Fox Gun Co., Philadelphia, PA, 1903 to 1930, and since then by Savage Arms, originally of Utica, NY, now of Westfield, MA. In 1993, Connecticut Manufacturing Co. of New Britain, CT, reintroduced selected models.

Values shown are for 12 and 16 ga. doubles made by A. H. Fox. Twenty gauge guns often are valued up to 75% higher. Savage-made Fox models generally bring prices 25% lower. With the exception of Model B, production of Fox shotguns was discontinued about 1942.

MODEL B HAMMERLESS DOUBLE...... NiB $333 Ex $273 Gd $196
Boxlock. Double triggers. Plain extractor. Gauges: 12, 16, 20, .410. 24- to 30-inch bbls., vent rib on current production; chokes: M/F, C/M, F/F (.410 only). Weight: About 7.5 lbs., 12 ga. Checkered pistol-grip stock and forend. Made about 1940-85.

MODEL B-ST .... NiB $516 Ex $420 Gd $298
Same as Model B except has non-selective single trigger. Made from 1955-66.

MODEL B-DE................. NiB $545 Ex $444 Gd $314
Same as Model B-ST except frame finished in satin chrome, select walnut buttstock w/checkered pistol grip and beavertail forearm. Made from 1965-66.

MODEL B-DL................. NiB $505 Ex $492 Gd $348
Same as Model B-ST except frame finished in satin chrome, select walnut buttstock w/checkered pistol grip side panels, beavertail forearm. Made from 1962-66.

MODEL B-SE.................. NiB $768 Ex $624 Gd $441
Same as Model B except has selective ejectors and single trigger. Made from 1966-89.

HAMMERLESS DOUBLE-BARREL SHOTGUNS
The higher grades have the same general specifications as the standard Sterlingworth model, w/differences chiefly in workmanship and materials. Higher grade models are stocked in fine select walnut; quantity and quality of engraving increases w/grade and price. Except for Grade A, all other grades have auto ejectors.
Grade A .... NiB $3044 Ex $2442 Gd $1710
Grade AE .... NiB $3448 Ex $2797 Gd $1951
Grade BE .... NiB $4750 Ex $3814 Gd $2660
Grade CE .... NiB $6005 Ex $4841 Gd $3351
Grade DE .... NiB $11,394 Ex $10,428 Gd $10,803
Grade FE .... NiB $21,357 Ex $17,085 Gd $11,618
Grade XE .... NiB $7582 Ex $6096 Gd $3920
Kautzky selective single trigger, add $350
Ventilated rib, add $450
Beavertail forearm, add.................................. $275
20 ga., add.. 60%

SINGLE-BARREL TRAP GUNS
Boxlock. Auto ejector.12 ga. only. 30- or 32-inch vent-rib bbl. Weight: 7.5 to 8 lbs. Trap-style stock and forearm of select walnut, checkered, recoil pad optional. The four grades differ chiefly in quality of wood and engraving; Grade M guns, built to order, have finest Circassian walnut. Stock and receiver are elaborately engraved and inlaid w/gold. Disc. 1942. Note: In 1932, the Fox Trap Gun was redesigned and those manufactured after that date have a stock w/full pistol grip and Monte Carlo comb; at the same time frame was changed to permit the rib line to extend across it to the rear.
Grade JE .... NiB $5212 Ex $4203 Gd $2913
Grade KE .... NiB $5907 Ex $4759 Gd $3290
Grade LE .... NiB $8243 Ex $6564 Gd $4529
Grade ME .... NiB $14,611 Ex $11,689 Gd $7948

"SKEETER" DOUBLE-BARREL SHOTGUN
.... NiB $4819 Ex $3902 Gd $2729
Boxlock. Gauge: 12 or 20. Bbls.: 28 inches w/full-length vent rib. Weight: Approx. 7 lbs. Buttstock and beavertail forend of select American walnut, finely checkered. Soft rubber recoil pad and ivory bead sights. Made in early 1930s.

STERLINGWORTH DELUXE
Same general specifications as Sterlingworth except 32-inch bbl. also available, recoil pad, ivory bead sights.
W/plain extractors.......... NiB $1776 Ex $1446 Gd $1024
W/automatic ejectors .... NiB $2241 Ex $1824 Gd $1314
20 ga., add.. 45%

STERLINGWORTH HAMMERLESS DOUBLE
Boxlock. Double triggers (Fox-Kautzky selective single trigger extra). Plain extractors (auto ejectors extra). Gauges: 12,16, 20. Bbl. lengths: 26-, 28-, 30-inch; chokes F/F, M/F, C/M (any combination of C to F choke borings was available at no extra cost). Weight: 12 ga., 6.88 to 8.25 lbs.; 16 ga., 6 to 7 lbs.; 20 ga., 5.75 to 6.75 lbs. Checkered pistol-grip stock and forearm.
W/plain extractors .... NiB $1608 Ex $1303 Gd $913
W/automatic ejectors .... NiB $2033 Ex $1644 Gd $1145
Selective single trigger, add 25%

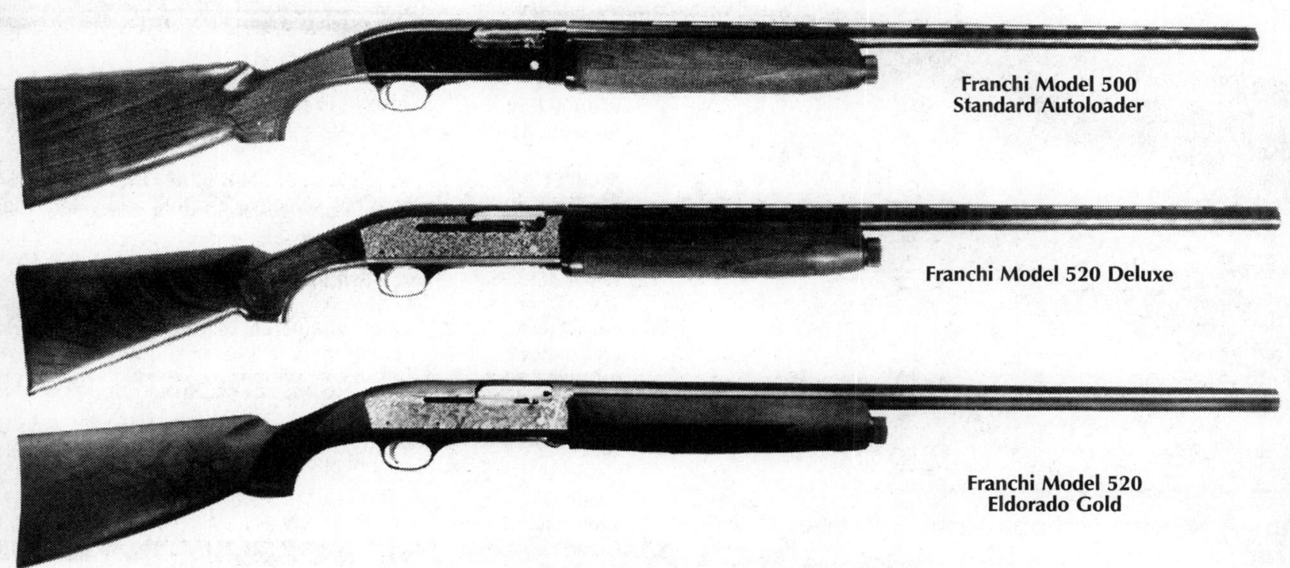

Franchi Model 500 Standard Autoloader

Franchi Model 520 Deluxe

Franchi Model 520 Eldorado Gold

STERLINGWORTH SKEET AND UPLAND GAME GUN
Same general specifications as the standard Sterlingworth except has 26- or 28-inch bbls. w/skeet boring only, straight-grip stock. Weight: 7 lbs. (12 ga.).
W/plain extractors. . . . . NiB $2413 Ex $1957 Gd $1373
W/automatic ejectors . . . . NiB $2869 Ex $2312 Gd $1621
20 ga., add 45%

SUPER HE GRADE. . . . . NiB $5643 Ex $4478 Gd $3117
Long-range gun made in 12 ga. only (chambered for 3-inch shells on order), 30- or 32-inch full choke bbls., auto ejectors standard. Weight: 8.75 to 9.75 lbs. General specifications same as standard Sterlingworth.

CMC HAMMERLESS DOUBLE-BARREL SHOTGUNS
High-grade doubles similar to the original Fox models. 20 ga. only. 26- 28- or 30-inch bbls. Double triggers automatic safety and ejectors. Weight: 5.5 to 7 lbs. Custom Circassian walnut stock w/hand-rubbed oil finish. Custom stock configuration: straight, semi- or full pistol-grip stock w/traditional pad, hard rubber plate checkered or skeleton butt; Schnabel, splinter or beavertail forend. Made 1993 to date.
CE grade . . . . NiB $8184 Ex $6585 Gd $4539
XE grade . . . . NiB $8648 Ex $6960 Gd $4800
DE grade . . . . NiB $12,344 Ex $9875 Gd $6715
FE grade . . . . NiB $16,563 Ex $13,250 Gd $9010
Exhibition grade . . . . NiB $23,744 Ex $18,995 Gd $12,917

LUIGI FRANCHI S.P.A. — Brescia, Italy

MODEL 48/AL ULTRA LIGHT SHOTGUN
Recoil-operated, takedown, hammerless shotgun w/tubular magazine. Gauges: 12 or 20 (2.75-inch); 12-ga. Magnum (3-inch chamber). Bbls.: 24- to 32-inch w/various choke combinations. Weight: 5 lbs., 2 oz. (20 ga.) to 6.25 lbs. (12 ga.). Checkered pistol-grip walnut stock and forend w/high-gloss finish.
Standard model. . . . . NiB $576 Ex $483 Gd $364
Hunter or magnum models . . . . . . NiB $614 Ex $513 Gd $385

MODEL 500 STANDARD AUTOLOADER . . . . NiB $482 Ex $401 Gd $298
Gas-operated. 12 gauge. Four round magazine. Bbls.: 26-, 28-inch; vent rib; IC, M, IM, F chokes. Weight: About 7 lbs. Checkered pistol-grip stock and forearm. Made from 1976-80.

MODEL 520 DELUXE . . . . NiB $527 Ex $437 Gd $323
Same as Model 500 except higher grade w/engraved receiver. Made from 1975-79.

MODEL 520 ELDORADO GOLD . . . . . . NiB $1046 Ex $853 Gd $608
Same as Model 520 except custom grade w/engraved and gold-inlaid receiver, finer quality wood. Intro. 1977.

MODEL 610VS SEMIAUTOMATIC SHOTGUN
Gas-operated Variopress system adjustable to function w/2.75- or 3-inch shells. 12 gauge. Four round magazine. 26- or 28-inch vent rib bbls. w/Franchoke tubes. Weight: 7 lbs., 2 oz. 47.5 inches overall. Alloy receiver w/four-lug rotating bolt and loaded chamber indicator. Checkered European walnut buttstock and forearm w/satin finish. Imported from 1997.
Standard SV model . . . . NiB $659 Ex $544 Gd $397
Engraved SVL model . . . . NiB $716 Ex $590 Gd $429

MODEL 612 VARIOPRESS AUTOLOADING SHOTGUN
Gauge: 12 ga. Only. 24- to 28-inch bbl. 45 to 49-inches overall. Weight: 6.8 to 7 lbs. Five round magazine. Bead type sights with C, IC, M chokes. Blued, matte or Advantage camo finish. Imported from 1999-2004. Disc.
Model 612 satin walnut
stock w/blued finish. . . . . NiB $504 Ex $414 Gd $300
Model 612 synthetic
stock w/matte finish. . . . . NiB $535 Ex $439 Gd $317
Model 612 Advantage stock and finish . . . . NiB $599 Ex $490 Gd $352
Model 612 Defense . . . . NiB $481 Ex $388 Gd $282
Model 612 Sporting . . . . NiB $830 Ex $641 Gd $484

MODEL 620 VARIOPRESS AUTOLOADING SHOTGUN
Gauge: 20 ga. Only. 24- 26- or 28-inch bbl. 45 to 49-inches overall. Weight: 5.9 to 6.1 lbs. Five round magazine. Bead type sights with C, IC, M chokes. Satin walnut or Advantage camo stock. Imported from 1999-2004. Disc.
Model 620 satin walnut
stock w/matte finish . . . . NiB $502 Ex $412 Gd $298
Model 620 Advantage
camo stock and finish . . . . NiB $597 Ex $488 Gd $350
Model 620 Youth (short stock). . . . . NiB $508 Ex $417 Gd $301

SHOTGUNS

Franchi 612 Variopress Advantage

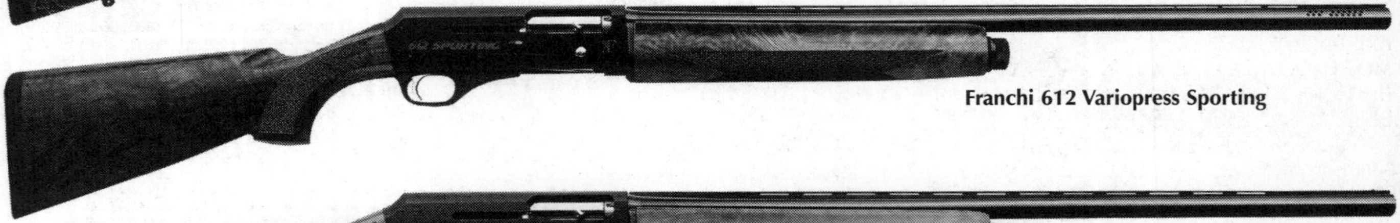

Franchi 612 Variopress Sporting

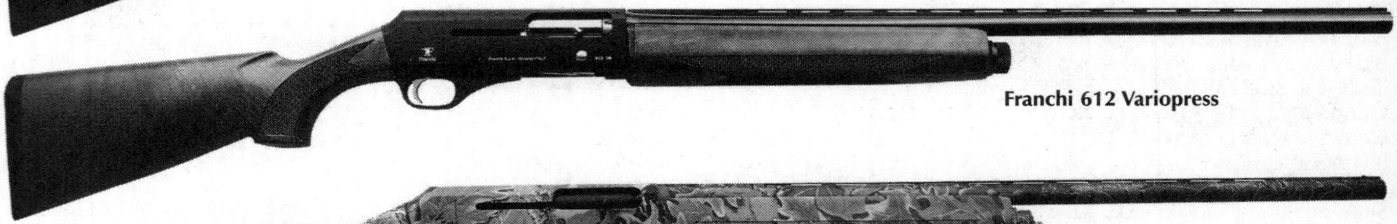

Franchi 612 Variopress

Franchi 620 Variopress Advantage

Franchi 620 Variopress

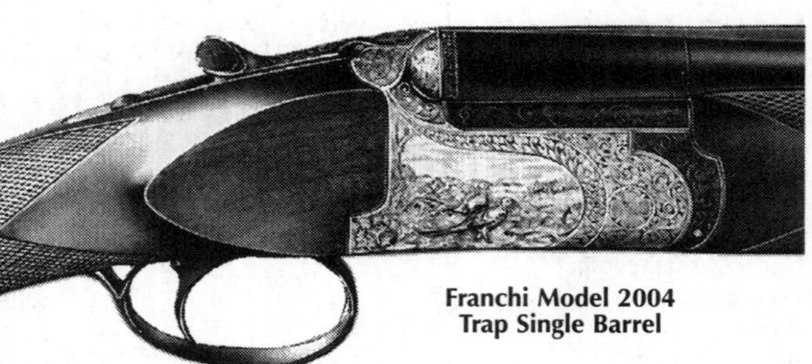

Franchi Model 2004 Trap Single Barrel

MODEL 2003 TRAP O/U . . . . NiB $1329 Ex $1221 Gd $920
Boxlock. Auto ejectors. Selective single trigger. 12 ga. Bbls.: 30-, 32-inch IM/F, F/F, high-vent rib. Weight (w/30-inch bbl.): 8.25 lbs. Checkered walnut beavertail forearm and stock w/straight or Monte Carlo comb, recoil pad. Luggage-type carrying case. Introduced 1976. Disc.

MODEL 2004 TRAP SINGLE BARREL . . . NiB $1361 Ex $1109 Gd $787
Same as Model 2003 except single bbl., 32- or 34-inch. Full choke. Weight (w/32-inch bbl.): 8.25 lbs. Introduced 1976. Disc.

MODEL 2005 COMBINATION TRAP . . NiB $1938 Ex $1576 Gd $1107
Model 2004/2005 type gun w/two sets of bbls., single and over/under. Introduced 1976. Disc.

MODEL 2005/3 COMBINATION TRAP. . . . . NiB $2722 Ex $2213 Gd $1562
Model 2004/2005 type gun w/three sets of bbls., any combination of single and over/under. Introduced 1976. Disc.

MODEL 3000/2 COMBINATION TRAP. . . . . NiB $3070 Ex $2497 Gd $1765
Boxlock. Automatic ejectors. Selective single trigger. 12 ga. only. Bbls.: 32-inch over/under choked F/IM, 34-inch underbarrel M choke; high vent rib. Weight (w/32-inch bbls.): 8 lbs., 6 oz. Choice of six different castoff buttstocks. Introduced 1979. Disc.

AIRONE HAMMERLESS DOUBLE . . . . . NiB $1279 Ex $1044 Gd $744
Boxlock. Anson & Deeley system action. Auto ejectors. Double triggers. 12 ga. Various bbl. lengths, chokes, weights. Checkered straight-grip stock and forearm. Made from 1940-50.

ALCIONE O/U SHOTGUN
Hammerless, takedown shotgun w/engraved receiver. Selective single trigger and ejectors. 12 ga. w/3-inch chambers. Bbls.: 26-inch (IC/M, 28-inch (M/F). Weight: 6.75 lbs. Checkered French walnut buttstock and forend. Imported from Italy. 1982-89.
Standard model . . . . NiB $717 Ex $583 Gd $411
SL model
(disc. 1986) . . . . NiB $1211 Ex $983 Gd $691

ALCIONE FIELD (97-12 IBS) O/U
Similar to the Standard Alcione model except w/nickel-finished receiver. 26- or 28-inch bbls. w/Franchoke tubes. Imported from 1998-2005 Disc.
Standard Field model . . . . NiB $921 Ex $748 Gd $528
SL Field model (w/sideplates, disc.) . . . . . NiB $1121 Ex $910 Gd $641

ALCIONE SPORT (SL IBS) O/U. . . . . NiB $1102 Ex $899 Gd $640
Similar to the Alcione Field model except chambered for 2.75 or 3-inch shells. Ported 29-inch bbls. w/target vent rib and Franchoke tubes.

ALCIONE 2000 SX O/U SHOTGUN. . . . NiB $1576 Ex $1278 Gd $898
Similar to the Standard Alcione model except w/silver finished receiver and gold inlays. 28-inch bbls. w/Franchoke tubes. Weight: 7.25 lbs. Imported from 1996-97.

ARISTOCRAT FIELD MODEL O/U . . . . NiB $671 Ex $512 Gd $360
Boxlock. Selective auto ejectors. Selective single trigger. 12 ga. Bbls.: 26-inch IC/M; 28- and 30-inch M/F choke, vent rib. Weight (w/26-inch bbls.): 7 lbs. Checkered pistol-grip stock and forearm. Made from 1960-69.

ARISTOCRAT DELUXE AND SUPREME GRADES
Available in Field, Skeet and Trap models w/the same general specifications as standard guns of these types. Deluxe and Supreme Grades are of higher quality, w/stock and forearm of select walnut, elaborate relief engraving on receiver, trigger guard, tang and top lever. Supreme game birds inlaid in gold. Made from 1960-66.
Deluxe grade . . . . NiB $1145 Ex $933 Gd $671
Supreme grade . . . . NiB $1609 Ex $1304 Gd $914

ARISTOCRAT IMPERIAL AND MONTE CARLO GRADES
Custom guns made in Field, Skeet and Trap models w/the same general specifications as standard for these types. Imperial and Monte Carlo grades are of highest quality w/stock and forearm of select walnut, fine engraving — elaborate on the latter grade. Made 1967-69.
Imperial grade . . . . NiB $2951 Ex $2391 Gd $1675
Monte Carlo grade . . . . NiB $4129 Ex $3340 Gd $2330

ARISTOCRAT MAGNUM MODEL. . . . . NiB $721 Ex $587 Gd $417
Same as Field Model except chambered for 3-inch shells, has 32-inch bbls. choked F/F; stock has recoil pad. Weight: About 8 lbs. Made from 1962-65.

ARISTOCRAT SILVER KING. . . . . . . NiB $824 Ex $670 Gd $473
Available in Field, Magnum, Meet and Trap models w/the same general specifications as standard guns of these types. Silver King has stock and forearm of select walnut more elaborately engraved silver-finished receiver. Made 1962-69.

ARISTOCRAT SKEET MODEL . . . . . NiB $784 Ex $638 Gd $452
Same general specifications as Field Model except made only w/26-inch vent-rib bbls. w/SK chokes No. 1 and No. 2, skeet-style stock and forearm. Weight: About 7.5 lbs. Later production had wider (10mm) rib. Made from 1960-69.

ARISTOCRAT TRAP MODEL . . . . . . NiB $791 Ex $643 Gd $455
Same general specifications as Field Model except made only w/30-inch vent-rib bbls., M/F choke, trap-style stock w/recoil pad, beavertail forearm. Later production had Monte Carlo comb, 10mm rib. Made from 1960-69.

ASTORE HAMMERLESS DOUBLE. . . . . . . NiB $1085 Ex $881 Gd $622
Boxlock. Anson & Deeley system action. Plain extractors. Double triggers. 12 ga. Various bbl. lengths, chokes, weights. Checkered straight-grip stock and forearm. Made 1937-60.

ASTORE II . . . . NiB $1341 Ex $1096 Gd $772
Similar to Astore S but not as high grade. Furnished w/either plain extractors or auto ejectors, double triggers, pistol-grip stock. Bbls.: 27-inch IC/IM; 28-inch M/F chokes. Currently manufactured for Franchi in Spain.

Franchi Astore 5

ASTORE 5 . . . . NiB $2234 Ex $1822 Gd $1295
Same as Astore except has higher grade wood, fine engraving. automatic ejectors, single trigger, 28-inch bbl. M/F or IM/F chokes are standard on current production. Disc.

STANDARD MODEL AUTOLOADER
Recoil operated. Light alloy receiver. Gauges: 12, 20. Four round magazine. Bbls.: 26-, 28-, 30-inch; plain, solid or vent rib, IC/ M, F chokes. Weight: 12 ga., about 6.25 lbs. 20 ga., 5.13 lbs. Checkered pistol-grip stock and forearm. Made from 1950. Disc.
W/plain bbl. . . . . NiB $533 Ex $376 Gd $306
W/solid rib . . . . NiB $482 Ex $399 Gd $288
W/vent rib. . . . . NiB $514 Ex $422 Gd $305

CROWN, DIAMOND AND IMPERIAL GRADE
Same general specifications as Standard Model except these are custom guns of the highest quality. Crown Grade has hunting scene engraving, Diamond Grade has silver-inlaid scroll engraving; Imperial Grade has elaborately engraved hunting scenes w/figures inlaid in gold. Stock and forearm of fancy walnut. Made from 1954-75.
Crown grade . . . . NiB $1751 Ex $1421 Gd $989
Diamond grade . . . . NiB $2271 Ex $1839 Gd $1286
Imperial grade . . . . NiB $2830 Ex $2281 Gd $1579

STANDARD MODEL MAGNUM
Same general specifications as Standard model except has 3-inch chamber, 32-inch (12 ga.) or 28-inch (20 ga.) F choke bbl., recoil pad. Weight: 12 ga., 8.25 lbs.; 20 ga., 6 lbs. Formerly designated "Superange Model." Made from 1954-88.
W/plain bbl. . . . . NiB $530 Ex $434 Gd $313
W/vent rib . . . . NiB $556 Ex $456 Gd $327

DYNAMIC-12
Same general specifications and appearance as Standard Model, except 12 ga. only, has heavier steel receiver. Weight: About 7.25 lbs. Made from 1965-72.
W/plain bbl. . . . . NiB $431 Ex $356 Gd $260
W/vent rib. . . . . NiB $469 Ex $386 Gd $280

DYNAMIC-12 SLUG GUN . . . . NiB $482 Ex $397 Gd $287
Same as standard gun except 12 ga. only, has heavier steel receiver. Made 1965-72.

DYNAMIC-12 SKEET GUN . . . . NiB $583 Ex $477 Gd $343
Same general specifications and appearance as Standard model except has heavier steel receiver, made only in 12 ga. w/26-inch vent-rib bbl., SK choke, stock and forearm of extra fancy walnut. Made from 1965-72.

ELDORADO MODEL . . . . NiB $616 Ex $505 Gd $363
Same general specifications as Standard model except highest grade w/gold-filled engraving, stock and forearm of select walnut, furnished w/vent-rib bbl. only. Made from 1954-75.

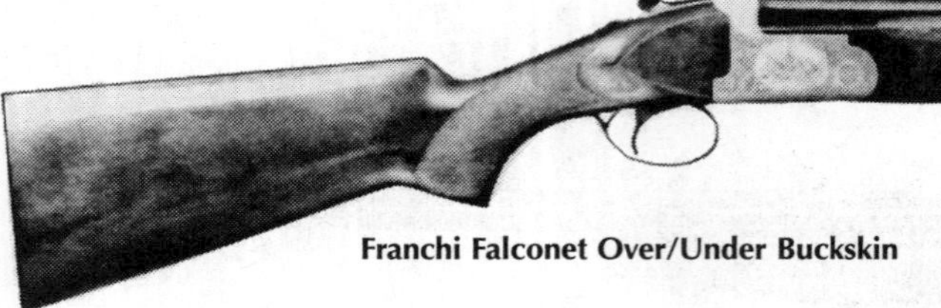
Franchi Falconet Over/Under Buckskin

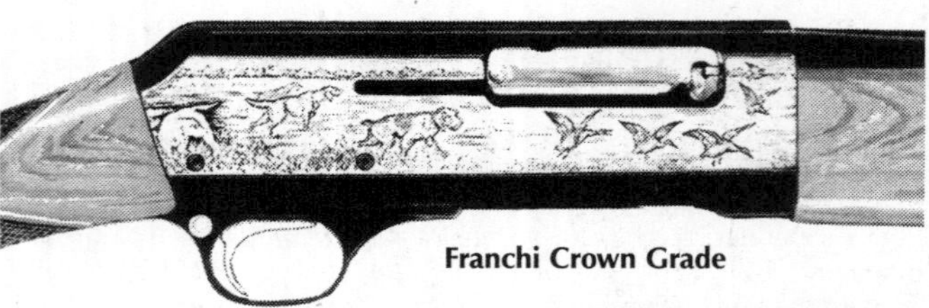
Franchi Crown Grade

Franchi Diamond Grade

Franchi Eldorado

FALCONET INTERNATIONAL SKEET MODEL... NiB $1213 Ex $989 Gd $702
Similar to Standard Skeet model but higher grade. Made from 1970-74.

FALCONET INTERNATIONAL TRAP MODEL .... NiB $1236 Ex $1008 Gd $715
Similar to Standard model but higher grade; w/straight or Monte Carlo comb stock. Made from 1970-74.

FALCONET O/U FIELD MODELS
Boxlock. Auto ejectors. Selective single trigger. Gauges: 12, 16, 20, 28, .410. Bbls.: 24-, 26-, 28-, 30-inch; vent rib. Chokes: C/IC, IC/M, M/F. Weight: from about 6 lbs. Engraved lightweight alloy receiver, light-colored in Buckskin model, blued in Ebony model, pickled silver in Silver model. Checkered walnut stock and forearm. Made from 1968-75.
Buckskin or Ebony model .... NiB $757 Ex $618 Gd $440
Silver model .... NiB $834 Ex $680 Gd $482

FALCONET STANDARD SKEET MODEL .... NiB $1039 Ex $855 Gd $597
Same general specifications as Field models except made only w/26-inch bbls. w/SK chokes No. 1 and No. 2, wide vent rib, color-casehardened receiver skeet-style stock and forearm. Weight: 12 ga., about 7.75 lbs. Made from 1970-74.

FALCONET STANDARD TRAP MODEL..... NiB $1050 Ex $858 Gd $613
Same general specifications as Field models except made only in 12 ga. w/30-inch bbls., choked M/F, wide vent rib, color-casehardened receiver, Monte Carlo trap style stock and forearm, recoil pad. Weight: About 8 lbs. Made from 1970-74.

GAS-OPERATED SEMIAUTOMATIC SHOTGUN
Gas-operated, takedown, hammerless shotgun w/tubular magazine. 12 ga. w/2.75-inch chamber. Five round magazine. Bbls.: 24 to 30 inches w/vent rib. Weight: 7.5 lbs. Gold-plated trigger. Checkered pistol-grip stock and forend of European walnut. Imported from Italy 1985-90.
Prestige model .... NiB $614 Ex $501 Gd $355
Elite model .... NiB $681 Ex $554 Gd $392

HAMMERLESS SIDELOCK DOUBLES
Hand-detachable locks. Self-opening action. Auto ejectors. Double triggers or single trigger. Gauges: 12,16, 20. Bbl. lengths, chokes, weights according to customer's specifications. Checkered stock and forend, straight or pistol grip. Made in six grades — Condor, Imperiale, Imperiale S, Imperiale Montecarlo No. 5, Imperiale Montecarlo No.11, Imperiale Montecarlo Extra — which differ chiefly in overall quality, engraving, grade of wood, checkering, etc.; general specifications are the same. Only the Imperial Montecarlo Extra Grade is currently manufactured.
Condor grade .... NiB $8559 Ex $6873 Gd $4717
Imperial, Imperial S grades.......... NiB $11,982 Ex $9585 Gd $6518
Imperial Monte Carlo grades No. 5, 11 .... NiB $16,862 Ex $13,489 Gd $9173
Imperial Monte Carlo Extra grade ...... NiB $19,613 Ex $15,690 Gd $10,669

HUNTER MODEL
Same general specifications as Standard Model except higher grade w/engraved receiver; w/ribbed bbl. only. Made from 1950-1990.
W/solid rib . ... NiB $469 Ex $382 Gd $271
W/vent rib .... NiB $502 Ex $408 Gd $288

HUNTER MODEL MAGNUM........... NiB $567 Ex $461 Gd $327
Same as Standard Model Magnum except higher grade w/engraved receiver, vent rib bbl. only. Formerly designated "Wildfowler Model." Made from 1954-73.

PEREGRINE MODEL 400......... NiB $775 Ex $631 Gd $447
Same general specifications as Model 451 except has steel receiver. Weight (w/26.5-inch bbl.): 6 lbs., 15 oz. Made from 1975-78.

PEREGRINE MODEL 451 O/U .... NiB $775 Ex $573 Gd $407
Boxlock. Lightweight alloy receiver. Automatic ejectors. Selective single trigger. 12 ga. Bbls.: 26.5-, 28-inch; choked C/IC, IC/M, M/F; vent rib. Weight (w/26.5-inch bbls.): 6 lbs., 1 oz. Checkered pistol-grip stock and forearm. Made from 1975-78.

SKEET GUN.................... NiB $557 Ex $455 Gd $323
Same general specifications and appearance as Standard Model except made only w/26-inch vent-rib bbl., SK choke. Stock and forearm of extra fancy walnut. Made from 1972-74.

SLUG GUN .... NiB $407 Ex $328 Gd $227
Same as Standard Model except has 22-inch plain bbl., Cyl. bore, folding leaf open rear sight, gold bead front sight. Made from 1960-90. Disc.

Franchi Hunter Model w/Ventilated Rib

Franchi Black Magic 48/AL Semiautomatic

Franchi LAW-12

Franchi SPAS-12

Franchi Sporting 2000

TURKEY GUN . . . . NiB $504 Ex $408 Gd $286
Same as Standard Model Magnum except higher grade w/turkey scene engraved receiver, 12 ga. only, 36-inch matted-rib bbl., Extra Full choke. Made from 1963-65.

BLACK MAGIC 48/AL SEMIAUTOMATIC
Similar to the Franchi Model 48/AL except w/Franchoke screw-in tubes and matte black receiver w/Black Magic logo. Gauge: 12 or 20, 2.75-inch chamber. Bbls.: 24-, 26-, 28-inch w/vent rib; 24-inch rifled slug w/sights. Weight: 5.2 lbs. (20 ga.). Checkered walnut buttstock and forend. Blued finish.
Standard model . . . . NiB $583 Ex $472 Gd $330
Slug bbl. model . . . . NiB $625 Ex $505 Gd $352

FALCONET 2000 O/U . . . . NiB $1348 Ex $1700 Gd $757
Boxlock. Single selective trigger. Selective automatic ejectors. Gauge: 12, 2.75-inch chambers. Bbls.: 26-inch w/Franchoke tubes; IC/M/F. Weight: 6 lbs. Checkered walnut stock and forearm. Engraved silver receiver w/gold-plated game scene. Imported from 1992-93.

LAW-12 SHOTGUN. . . . . NiB $611 Ex $496 Gd $348
Similar to the SPAS-12 Model except gas-operated semiautomatic action only, ambidextrous safety, decocking lever and adj. sights. Made from 1983-94.

SPAS-12 SHOTGUN
Selective operating system functions as a gas-operated semi-automatic or pump action. Gauge: 12, 2.75-inch chamber. Seven round magazine. Bbl.: 21.5 inches w/cylinder bore and muzzle protector or optional screw-in choke tubes, matte finish. 41 inches overall w/fixed stock. Weight: 8.75 lbs. Blade front sight, aperture rear sight. Folding or black nylon buttstock w/pistol grip and forend, non-reflective anodized finish. Made from 1983-94.
Fixed stock model . . . . NiB $941 Ex $764 Gd $537
Folding stock model . . . . NiB $1069 Ex $866 Gd $607
Optional choke tubes, add $125

SPORTING 2000 O/U. . . . . NiB $1434 Ex $1168 Gd $826
Similar to the Franchi Falconet 2000. Boxlock. Single selective trigger. Selective automatic ejectors. Gauge: 12; 2.75-inch chambers. Ported (1992-93) or unported 28-inch bbls., w/vent rib. Weight: 7.75 lbs. Blued receiver. Bead front sight. Checkered walnut stock and forearm; plastic composition buttplate. Imported from 1992-93 and 1997-98.

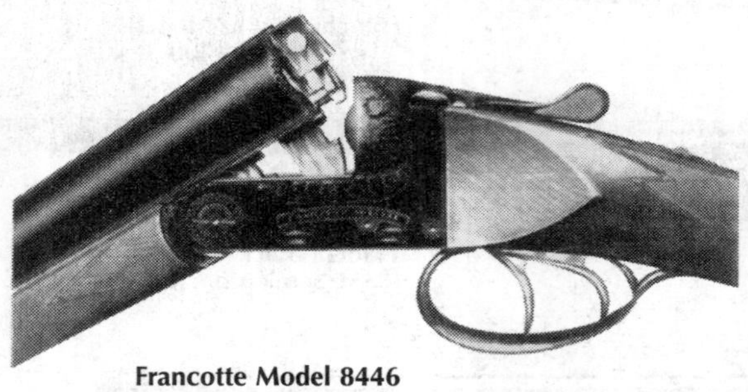
Francotte Model 8446

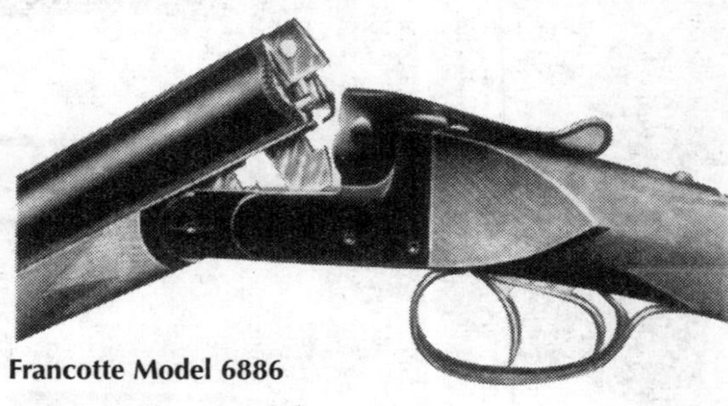
Francotte Model 6886

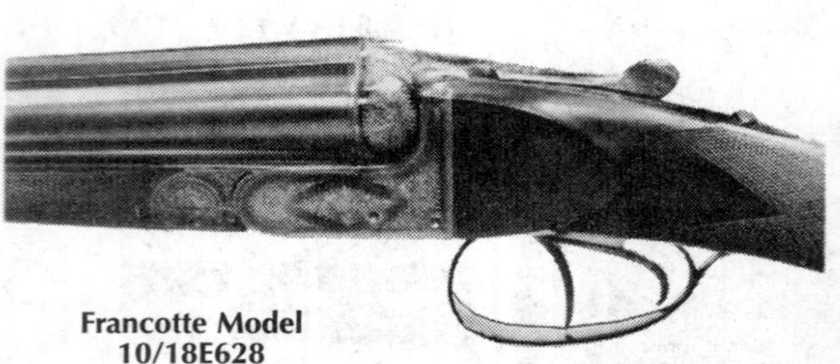
Francotte Model 10/18E628

Francotte Model 9261

AUGUSTE FRANCOTTE & CIE., S.A. — Liège, Belgium

Francotte shotguns for many years were distributed in the U.S. by Abercrombie & Fitch of New York City. This firm has used a series of model designations for Francotte guns which do not correspond to those of the manufacturer. Because so many Francotte owners refer to their guns by the A & F model names and numbers, the A & F series is included in a listing separate from that of the standard Francotte numbers.

BOXLOCK HAMMERLESS DOUBLES

Anson & Deeley system. Side clips. Greener crossbolt on models 6886, 8446, 4996 and 9261; square crossbolt on Model 6930, Greener-Scott crossbolt on Model 8457, Purdey bolt on Models 11/18E and 10/18E/628. Auto ejectors. Double triggers. Made in all standard gauges, barrel lengths, chokes, weights. Checkered stock and forend, straight or pistol-grip. The eight models listed vary chiefly in fastenings as described above, finish and engraving, etc.; general specifications are the same. Disc.

Model 6886 .... NiB $3595 Ex $2919 Gd $2054
Model 8446 (Francotte Special),
6930, 4996 .... NiB $4040 Ex $3276 Gd $2199
Model 8457,
9261 (Francotte Original), 11/18E .... NiB $5174 Ex $4215 Gd $2935
Model 10/18E/628 .... NiB $6523 Ex $5275 Gd $3678

BOXLOCK HAMMERLESS DOUBLES — A & F SERIES

Boxlock, Anson & Deeley type. Crossbolt. Sideplate on all except Knockabout Model. Side clips. Auto ejectors. Double triggers. Gauges: 12, 16, 20, 28, .410. Bbls.: 26- to 32-inch in 12 ga., 26- and 28-inch in other ga.; any boring. Weight: 4.75 to 8 lbs. depending on gauge and barrel length. Checkered stock and forend; straight, half or full pistol grip. The seven grades (No. 45 Eagle Grade, No. 30, No. 25, No. 20, No. 14, Jubilee Model, Knockabout Model) differ chiefly in overall quality, engraving, grade of wood, checkering, etc.; general specifications are the same. Disc.

Jubilee model
No. 14 .... NiB $2308 Ex $1890 Gd $1354
Jubilee model
No. 18 .... NiB $2970 Ex $2420 Gd $1717
Jubilee model
No. 20 .... NiB $3743 Ex $3041 Gd $2143
Jubilee model
No. 25 .... NiB $3433 Ex $3266 Gd $2298
Jubilee model
No. 30 .... NiB $6139 Ex $4887 Gd $3414
Eagle grade
No. 45 .... NiB $8348 Ex $6743 Gd $4689
Knockabout
model .... NiB $2691 Ex $2201 Gd $1573

BOXLOCK HAMMERLESS DOUBLES (SIDEPLATES)

Anson & Deeley system. Reinforced frame w/side clips. Purdey-type bolt except on Model 8455, which has Greener crossbolt. Auto ejectors. Double triggers. Made in all standard gauges, bbl. lengths, chokes, weights. Checkered stock and forend, straight or pistol grip. Models 10594, 8455 and 6982 are of equal quality, differing chiefly in style of engraving; Model 9/40E/38321 is a higher grade gun in all details and has fine English-style engraving. Built to customer specifications.

Models 10594, 8455, 6982 .... NiB $5241 Ex $4248 Gd $3017
Model 9/40E/38321 .... NiB $6337 Ex $5125 Gd $3575

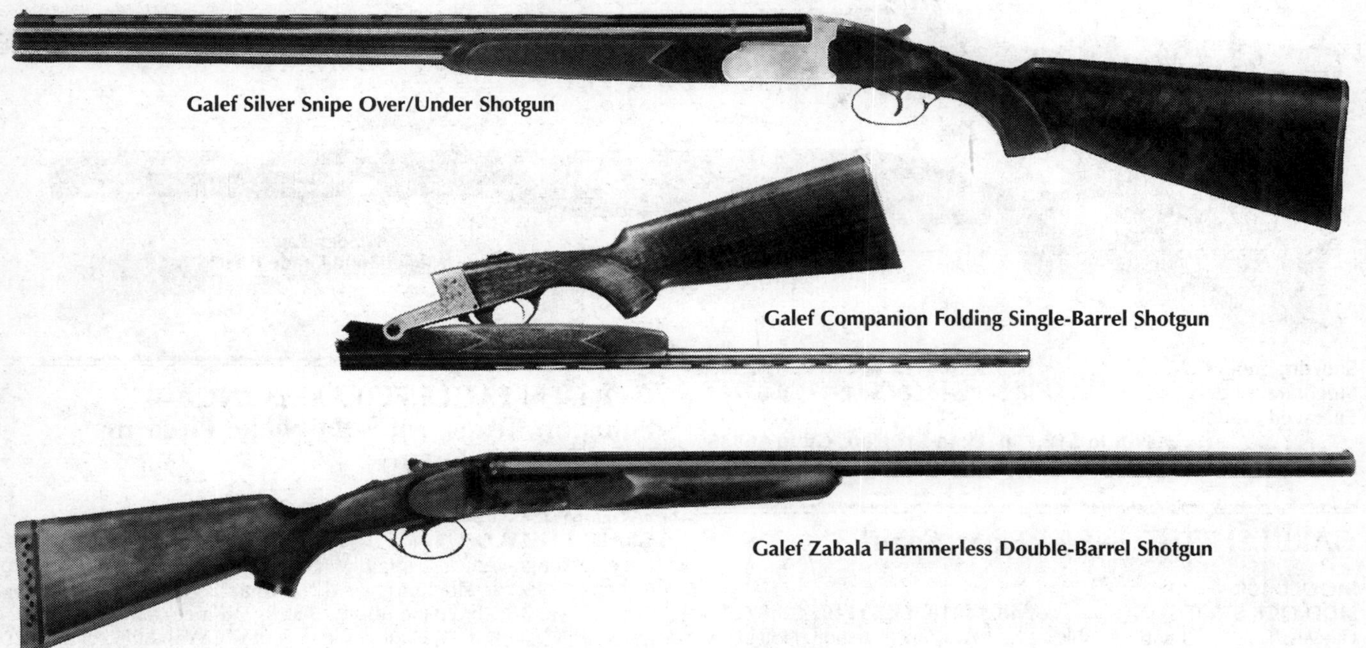

Galef Silver Snipe Over/Under Shotgun

Galef Companion Folding Single-Barrel Shotgun

Galef Zabala Hammerless Double-Barrel Shotgun

FINE O/U SHOTGUN $9356
Model 9/40.SE. Boxlock, Anson & Deeley system. Auto ejectors. Double triggers. Made in all standard gauges; bbl. length, boring to order. Weight: About 6.75 lbs. 12 ga. Checkered stock and forend, straight or pistol grip. Manufactured to customer specifications. Disc 1990.

FINE SIDELOCK
HAMMERLESS DOUBLE . . . . NiB $24,544 Ex $19,635 Gd $13,352
Model 120.HE/328. Automatic ejectors. Double triggers. Made in all standard ga.; bbl. length, boring, weight to order. Checkered stock and forend, straight or pistol-grip. Manufactured to customer specifications. Disc. 1990.

HALF-FINE O/U SHOTGUN . . . . NiB $10,104 Ex $8083 Gd $5447
Model SOB.E/11082. Boxlock, Anson & Deeley system. Auto ejectors. Double triggers. Made in all standard gauges; barrel length, boring to order. Checkered stock and forend, straight or pistol grip. Note: This model is similar to No. 9/40.SE except general quality lower. Disc. 1990.

GALEF SHOTGUNS — Manufactured for J. L. Galef & Son, Inc., New York, New York, by M. A. V. I., Gardone F. T., Italy, by Zabala Hermanos, Eiquetta, Spain, and by Antonio Zoli, Gardone V. T., Italy

SILVER SNIPE OVER/UNDER SHOTGUN . . . . NiB $572 Ex $444 Gd $326
Boxlock. Plain extractors. Single trigger. Gauges: 12, 20; 3-inch chambers. Bbls: 26-, 28-, 30-inch (latter in 12 ga. only); IC/M, M/F chokes; vent rib. Weight: 12 ga. w/28-inch bbls., 6.5 lbs. Checkered walnut pistol-grip stock and forearm. Introduced by Antonio Zoli in 1968. Disc. See illustration previous page.

GOLDEN SNIPE . . . . NiB $642 Ex $523 Gd $371
Same as Silver Snipe, except has selective automatic ejectors. Made by Antonio Zoli 1968 to date.

MONTE CARLO TRAP
SINGLE-BARREL SHOTGUN. . . . . NiB $273 Ex $224 Gd $160
Hammerless. Underlever. Plain extractor. 12 ga. 32-inch bbl., F choke, vent rib. Weight: About 8.25 lbs. Checkered pistol-grip stock w/Monte Carlo comb and recoil pad, beavertail forearm. Introduced by M. A. V. I. in 1968. Disc.

SILVER HAWK HAMMERLESS DOUBLE. . . . . NiB $545 Ex $444 Gd $315
Boxlock. Plain extractors. Double triggers. Gauges: 12, 20; 3-inch chambers. Bbls.: 26-, 28-, 30-inch (latter in 12 ga. only); IC/M, M/F chokes. Weight: 12 ga. w/26-inch bbls., 6 lbs. 6 oz. Checkered walnut pistol-grip stock and beavertail forearm. Made by Antonio Zoli 1968-72.

COMPANION FOLDING SINGLE-BARREL SHOTGUN
Hammerless. Underlever. Gauges: 12 Mag., 16, 20 Mag., 28, .410. Bbls.: 26-inch (.410 only), 28-inch (12, 16, 20, 28), 30-inch (12-ga. only); F choke; plain or vent rib. Weight: 4.5 lbs. for .410 to 5 lbs., 9 oz. for 12 ga. Checkered pistol-grip stock and forearm. Made by M. A. V. I. from 1968-83.
W/plain bbl. NiB $146 Ex $121 Gd $89
W/ventilated rib . . . . NiB $186 Ex $154 Gd $111

ZABALA HAMMERLESS DOUBLE-BARREL SHOTGUN
Boxlock. Plain extractors. Double triggers. Gauges: 10 Mag., 12 Mag., 16, 20 Mag., 28, .410. Bbls.: 22-, 26-, 28-, 30-, 32-inch; IC/IC, IC/M, M/F chokes. Weight: 12 ga. w/28-inch bbls., 7.75 lbs. Checkered walnut pistol-grip stock and beavertail forearm, recoil pad. Made by Zabala from 1972-83.
10 ga. . . . . NiB $309 Ex $251 Gd $178
Other ga. . . . . NiB $232 Ex $190 Gd $136

GAMBA — Gardone V. T. (Brescia), Italy

DAYTONA COMPETITION O/U
Boxlock w/Boss-style locking system. Anatomical single trigger; optional adj., single-selective release trigger. Selective automatic ejectors. Gauge: 12 or 20; 2.75- or 3-inch chambers. Bbls.: 26.75-, 28-, 30- or 32-inch choked SK/SK, IM/F or M/F. Weight: 7.5 to 8.5 lbs. Black or chrome receiver w/blued bbls. Checkered select walnut stock and forearm w/oil finish. Imported by Heckler & Koch until 1992.
American Trap model. . . . . NiB $5618 Ex $4534 Gd $3147
Pigeon, Skeet, Trap models . . . . NiB $6440 Ex $5192 Gd $3595

SHOTGUNS

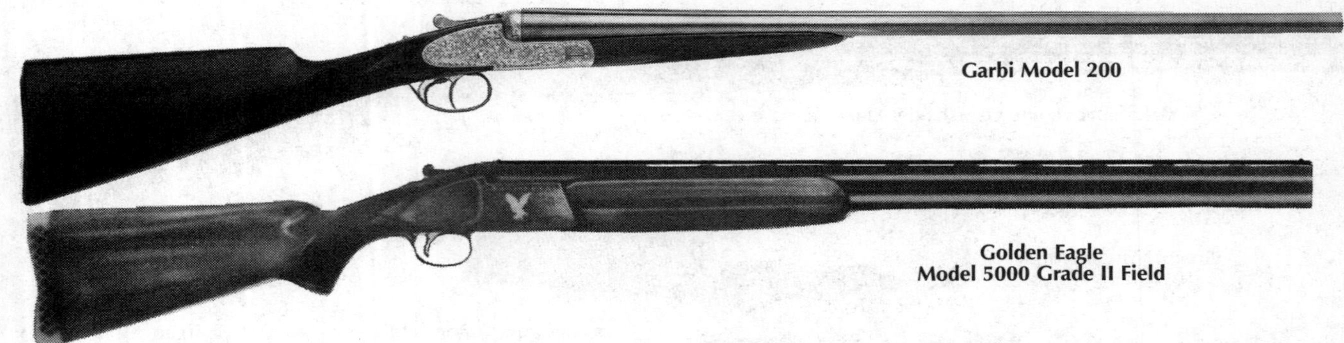
Garbi Model 200

Golden Eagle
Model 5000 Grade II Field

Sporting model . . . . NiB $5304 Ex $4270 Gd $2948
Sideplate model . . . . NiB $10,614 Ex $8491 Gd $5774
Engraved models
. . . . NiB to $12,750 Ex to $10,200 Gd to $6936
Sidelock model. . . . . NiB $27,412 Ex $21,930 Gd $14,912

GARBI SHOTGUNS — Eibar, Spain

MODEL 100
SIDELOCK SHOTGUN . . . . NiB $4010 Ex $3249 Gd $2275
Gauges: 12, 16, 20 and 28. Bbls.: 25-, 28-, 30-inch. Action: Holland & Holland pattern sidelock; automatic ejectors and double trigger. Weight: 5 lbs., 6 oz. to 7 lbs. 7 oz. English-style straight grip stock w/fine-line hand-checkered butt; classic forend. Made from 1985 to date.

MODEL 101
SIDELOCK SHOTGUN . . . . NiB $5049 Ex $4081 Gd $2842
Same general specifications as Model 100 above, except the sidelocks are handcrafted w/hand-engraved receiver; select walnut straight-grip stock.

MODEL 102
SIDELOCK SHOTGUN . . . . NiB $5392 Ex $4355 Gd $3029
Similar to the Model 101 except w/large scroll engraving. Made from 1985-93.

MODEL 103
HAMMERLESS DOUBLE
Similar to Model 100 except w/Purdey-type, higher grade engraving.
Model 103A Standard . . . . NiB $5469 Ex $4417 Gd $3071
Model 103A Royal Deluxe . . . NiB $10,005 Ex $8043 Gd $5532
Model 103B. . . . . NiB $8174 Ex $6589 Gd $4560
Model 103B Royal Deluxe . . . . NiB $14,018 Ex $11,214 Gd $7625

MODEL 200
HAMMERLESS DOUBLE . . . . . . NiB $8092 Ex $6521 Gd $4514
Similar to Model 100 except w/double heavy-duty locks. Continental-style floral and scroll engraving. Checkered deluxe walnut stock and forearm.

GARCIA CORPORATION — Teaneck, New Jersey

BRONCO 22/.410 O/U COMBO . . . NiB $143 Ex $119 Gd $88
Swing-out action. Takedown. 18.5-inch bbls.; .22 LR over, .410 ga. under. Weight: 4.5 lbs. One-piece stock and receiver, crackle finish. Intro. In 1976. Disc.

BRONCO .410 SINGLE SHOT. . . . . . . NiB $118 Ex $98 Gd $74
Swing-out action. Takedown. .410 ga. 18.5-inch bbl. Weight: 3.5 lbs. One-piece stock and receiver, crackle finish. Intro. In 1967. Disc.

GOLDEN EAGLE FIREARMS INC. — Houston, Texas, Mfd. By Nikko Firearms Ltd., Tochigi, Japan

EAGLE MODEL 5000
GRADE I FIELD O/U. . . . . NiB $931 Ex $845 Gd $584
Receiver engraved and inlaid w/gold eagle head. Boxlock. Auto ejectors. Selective single trigger. 12, 20 ga.; 2.75- or 3-inch chambers, 12 ga., 3-inch, 20 ga. Bbls.: 26-, 28-, 30-inch (latter only in 12-ga. 3-inch Mag.); IC/M, M/F chokes; vent rib. Weight: 6.25 lbs., 20 ga.; 7.25 lbs., 12 ga.; 8 lbs., 12-ga. Mag. Checkered pistol-grip stock and semi-beavertail forearm. Imported 1975-82. Note: Guns marketed 1975-76 under the Nikko brand name have white receivers; guns since 1976 are blued.

EAGLE MODEL 5000
GRADE I SKEET. . . . . NiB $1031 Ex $829 Gd $584
Same as Field model except has 26- or 28-inch bbls. w/wide (11 mm) vent rib, SK choked. Imported from 1975-82.

EAGLE MODEL 5000
GRADE I TRAP . . . . NiB $978 Ex $795 Gd $561
Same as Field model except has 30-, or 32-inch bbls. w/wide (11 mm) vent rib (M/F, IM/F, F/F chokes), trap-style stock w/recoil pad. Imported from 1975-82.

EAGLE MODEL 5000
GRADE II FIELD . . . . NiB $1065 Ex $865 Gd $609
Same as Grade I Field model except higher grade w/fancier wood, more elaborate engraving and "screaming eagle" inlaid in gold. Imported from 1975-82.

EAGLE MODEL 5000
GRADE II SKEET . . . . NiB $1101 Ex $895 Gd $632
Same as Grade I Skeet model except higher grade w/fancier wood, more elaborate engraving and "screaming eagle" inlaid in gold; inertia trigger, vent side ribs. Imported from 1975-82.

EAGLE MODEL 5000
GRADE II TRAP. . . . . NiB $1122 Ex $913 Gd $645
Same as Grade I Trap model except higher grade w/fancier wood, more elaborate engraving and "screaming eagle" inlaid in gold; inertia trigger, vent side ribs. Imported from 1975-82.

EAGLE MODEL 5000
GRADE III GRANDEE . . . . NiB $2903 Ex $2354 Gd $1652
Best grade, available in Field, Skeet and Trap models w/same general specifications as lower grades. Has sideplates w/game scene engraving, scroll on frame and bbls., fancy wood (Monte Carlo comb, full pistol-grip and recoil pad on Trap model). Made from 1976-82.

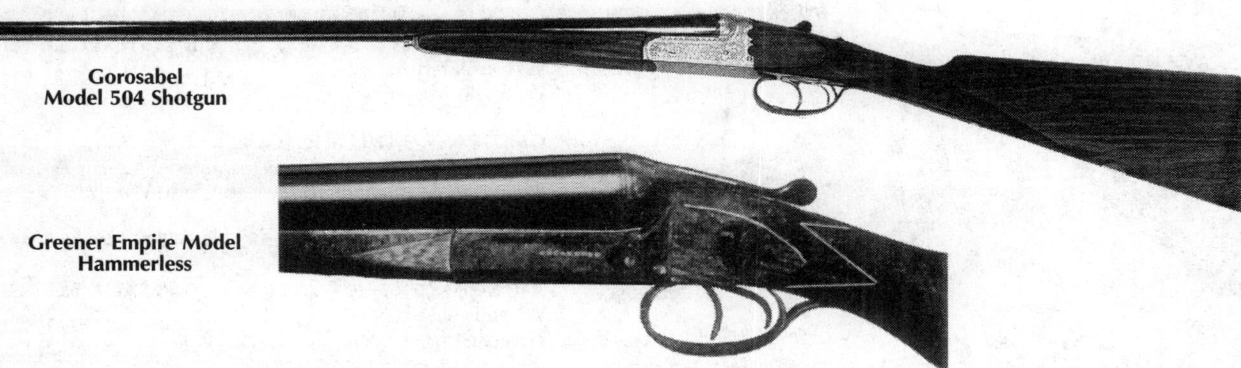

Gorosabel
Model 504 Shotgun

Greener Empire Model
Hammerless

GOROSABEL SHOTGUNS — Spain

MODEL 503 SHOTGUN . . . . NiB $955 Ex $778 Gd $551
Gauges: 12, 16, 20 and .410. Action: Anson & Deely-style boxlock. Bbls.: 26-, 27-, and 28-inch. Select European walnut, English or pistol grip, sliver or beavertail forend, hand-checkering. Scalloped frame and scroll engraving. Intro. 1985; disc.

MODEL 504 SHOTGUN . . . . NiB $1026 Ex $834 Gd $589
Gauge: 12 or 20. Action: Holland & Holland-style sidelock. Bbl.: 26-, 27-, or 28-inch. Select European walnut, English or pistol grip, sliver or beavertail forend, hand-checkering. Holland-style large scroll engraving. Inro. 1985; disc.

MODEL 505 SHOTGUN . . . . NiB $1401 Ex $1134 Gd $793
Gauge: 12 or 20. Action: Holland & Holland-style sidelock. Bbls.: 26-, 27-, or 28-inch. Select European walnut, English or pistol grip, silver or beavertail forend, hand-checkering. Purdey-style fine scroll and rose engraving. Intro. 1985; disc.

STEPHEN GRANT — London, England

BEST QUALITY SELF-OPENER DOUBLE-BARREL SHOTGUN . . . . NiB $15,313 Ex $12,250 Gd $8330
Sidelock, self-opener. Gauges: 12, 16 and 20. Bbls.: 25 to 30 inches standard. Highest-grade English or European walnut straight-grip buttstock and forearm w/Greener type lever. Imported by Stoeger in the 1950s.

BEST QUALITY SIDE-LEVER DOUBLE-BARREL SHOTGUN . . . . NiB $13,125 Ex $10,500 Gd $7140
Sidelock, self-lever. Gauges: 12, 16 and 20. Bbls.: 25 to 30 inches standard. Highest-grade English or European walnut straight-grip buttstock and forearm w/Greener type lever. Imported by Stoeger in the 1950s.

W. W. GREENER, LTD. — Birmingham, England

EMPIRE MODEL HAMMERLESS DOUBLES
Boxlock. Non-ejector or w/automatic ejectors. Double triggers. 12 ga. only (2.75-inch or 3-inch chamber). Bbls.: 28- to 32-inch; any choke combination. Weight: from 7.25 to 7.75 lbs. depending on bbl. length. Checkered stock and forend, straight- or half-pistol grip. Also furnished in "Empire Deluxe Grade," this model has same general specs, but deluxe finish.

Empire model, non-ejector . . . . NiB $2169 Ex $1769 Gd $1259
Empire model, ejector . . . . NiB $2356 Ex $1919 Gd $1361
Empire Deluxe model, non-ejector . . . NiB $2201 Ex $1796 Gd $1276
Empire Deluxe model, ejector . . . . NiB $2487 Ex $2025 Gd $1442

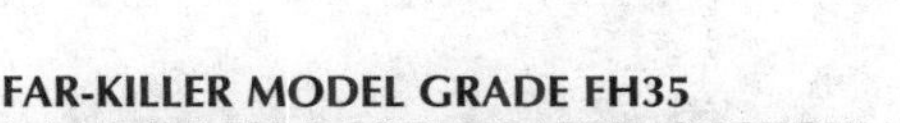

Greener
Far-Killer

FAR-KILLER MODEL GRADE FH35 HAMMERLESS DOUBLE-BARREL SHOTGUN
Boxlock. Non-ejector or w/automatic ejectors. Double triggers. Gauges: 12 (2.75-inch or 3-inch), 10, 8. Bbls.: 28-, 30- or 32-inch. Weight: 7.5 to 9 lbs. in 12 ga. Checkered stock, forend; straight or half-pistol grip.

Non-ejector, 12 ga. . . . . NiB $3074 Ex $2509 Gd $1806
Ejector, 12 ga. . . . . NiB $3687 Ex $3003 Gd $2127
Non-ejector, 10 or 8 ga. . . . . . NiB $3159 Ex $2580 Gd $1841
Ejector, 10 or 8 ga. . . . . NiB $4091 Ex $3337 Gd $2349

G. P. (GENERAL PURPOSE) SINGLE BARREL . . . . NiB $496 Ex $3405 Gd $290
Greener Improved Martini Lever Action. Takedown. Ejector. 12 ga. only. Bbl. lengths: 26-, 30-, 32-inch. M or F choke. Weight: 6.25 to 6.75 lbs. depending on bbl. length. Checkered straight-grip stock and forearm.

HAMMERLESS EJECTOR DOUBLE-BARREL SHOTGUNS
Boxlock. Auto ejectors. Double triggers, non-selective or selective single trigger. Gauges: 12, 16, 20, 28, .410 (two latter gauges not supplied in Grades DH40 and DH35). Bbls.: 26-, 28-, 30-inch; any choke combination. Weight: From 4.75 to 8 lbs. Depending on ga. and bbl. length. Checkered stock and forend, straight- or half-pistol grip. The Royal, Crown, Sovereign and Jubilee models differ in quality, engraving, grade of wood, checkering, etc. General specifications are the same.

Royal Model Grade DH75 . . . . . NiB $4898 Ex $3972 Gd $2787
Crown Model Grade DH55 . . . . NiB $3688 Ex $3004 Gd $2128
Sovereign Model Grade DH40 . . . . NiB $3276 Ex $2674 Gd $1905
Jubilee Model Grade DH35 . . . . NiB $2740 Ex $2241 Gd $1602
W/selective single trigger, add $330
W/non-selective single trigger, add $250
W/ventilated rib, add $395
W/single trigger, add $425

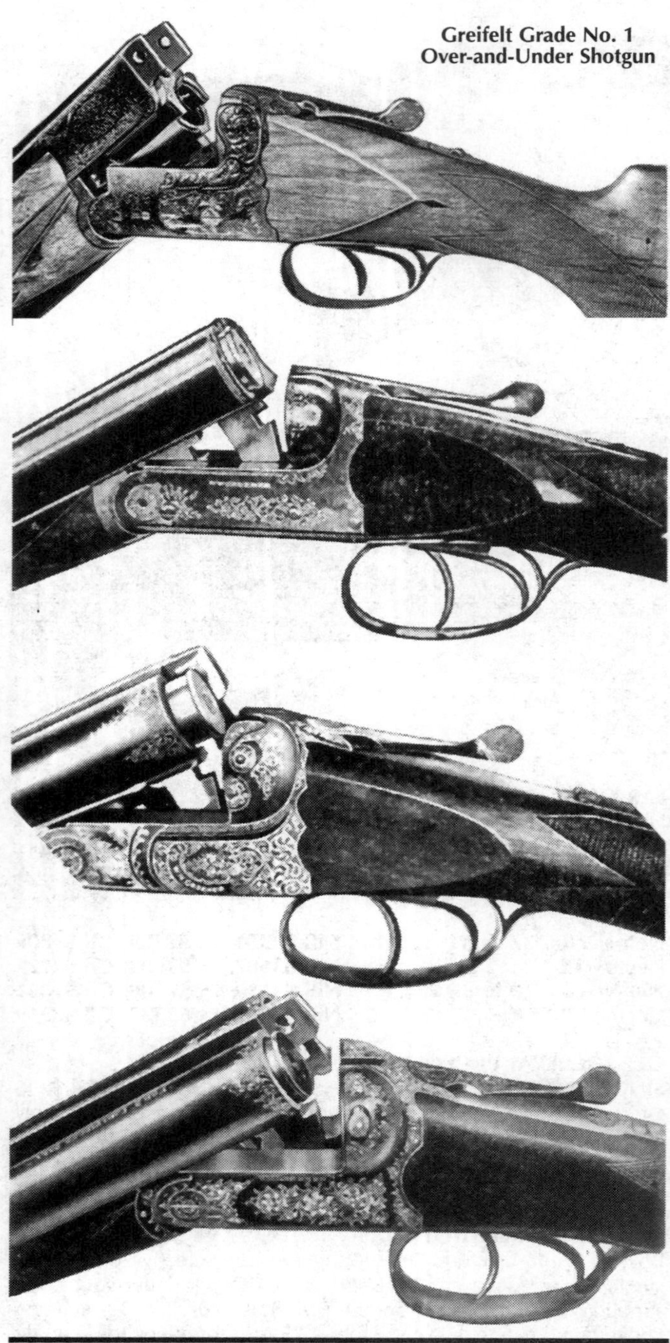
Greifelt Grade No. 1 Over-and-Under Shotgun

GREIFELT & COMPANY — Suhl, Germany

GRADE NO. 1 O/U SHOTGUN
Anson & Deeley boxlock, Kersten fastening. Auto ejectors. Double triggers or single trigger. Elaborately engraved. Gauges: 12, 16, 20, 28, .410. Bbls.: 26- to 32-inch, any combination of chokes, vent or solid matted rib. Weight: 4.25 to 8.25 lbs. depending on ga. and bbl. length. Straight- or pistol-grip stock, Purdey-type forend, both checkered. Manufactured prior to World War II.
W/solid matted-rib bbl.,
except .410 & 28 ga. . . . . NiB $3713 Ex $3019 Gd $2131
W/solid matted-rib bbl.,
.410 & 28 ga . . . . NiB $4616 Ex $3716 Gd $2634
W/ventilated rib, add $395
W/single trigger, add $425

GRADE NO. 3 O/U SHOTGUN
Same general specifications as Grade No. 1 except less fancy engraving. Manufactured prior to World War II.
W/solid matted-rib bbl.,
except .410 & 28 ga. . . . . NiB $3019 Ex $2464 Gd $1754
W/solid matted-rib bbl.,
.410 & 28 ga. . . . . NiB $3551 Ex $2891 Gd $2045
W/ventilated rib, add $395
W/single trigger, add. $425

MODEL 22
HAMMERLESS DOUBLE . . . . NiB $2049 Ex $1657 Gd $1176
Anson & Deeley boxlock. Plain extractors. Double triggers. Gauges: 12 and 16. Bbls.: 28- or 30-inch, M/F choke. Checkered stock and forend, pistol grip and cheekpiece standard, English-style stock also supplied. Manufactured since World War II.

MODEL 22E
HAMMERLESS DOUBLE . . . . . . NiB $2794 Ex $2275 Gd $1624
Same as Model 22 except has automatic ejectors.

MODEL 103
HAMMLERLESS DOUBLE . . . . . NiB $1982 Ex $1612 Gd $1139
Anson & Deeley boxlock. Plain extractors. Double triggers. Gauges: 12 and 16. Bbls.: 28- or 30-inch, M and F choke. Checkered stock and forend, pistol grip and cheekpiece standard, English-style stock also supplied. Manufactured since World War II.

MODEL 103E
HAMMERLESS DOUBLE . . . . . . NiB $2100 Ex $1707 Gd $1204
Same as Model 103 except has automatic ejectors.

MODEL 143E O/U SHOTGUN
General specifications same as pre-war Grade No. 1 Over-and-Under, except this model is not supplied in 28 and .410 ga. or w/32-inch bbls. Model 143E is not as high quality as the Grade No. 1 gun. Mfd. Since World War II.
W/raised matted rib,
double triggers . . . . NiB $2482 Ex $2031 Gd $1452
W/ventilated rib,
selective single trigger. . . . . NiB $2968 Ex $2453 Gd $1733

HAMMERLESS DRILLING (THREE-BARREL
COMBINATION GUN) . . . . NiB $3772 Ex $3050 Gd $2116
Boxlock. Plain extractors. Double triggers, front single set for rifle bbl. Gauges: 12, 16, 20; rifle bbl. in any caliber adapted to this type of gun. 26-inch bbls. Weight: About 7.5 lbs. Auto rear sight operated by rifle bbl. selector. Checkered stock and forearm, pistol-grip and cheekpiece standard. Manufactured prior to WW II. Note: Value shown is for guns chambered for cartridges readily obtainable. If rifle bbl. is an odd foreign caliber, value will be considerably less.

O/U COMBINATION GUN
Similar in design to this maker's over-and-under shotguns. Gauges: 12, 16, 20, 28, .410; rifle bbl. in any caliber adapted to this type of gun. Bbls.: 24- or 26-inch, solid matted rib. Weight: From 4.75 to 7.25 lbs. Folding rear sight. Manufactured prior to WWII. Note: Values shown are for gauges other than .410 w/rifle bbl. Chambered for a cartridge readily obtainable; if in an odd foreign caliber, value will be considerably less. .410 ga. increases in value by about 50%.
W/non-automatic ejector . . . . . NiB $6234 Ex $5051 Gd $3537
W/automatic ejector . . . . NiB $6988 Ex $5725 Gd $3795

HARRINGTON & RICHARDSON ARMS COMPANY — Gardner, Massachusetts, Now H&R 1871, Inc.

Formerly Harrington & Richardson Arms Co. of Worcester, Mass. One of the oldest and most distinguished manufacturers of handguns, rifles and shotguns, H&R suspended operations on January 24, 1986. In 1987, New England Firearms was established as an independent company producing selected H&R models under the NEF logo. In 1991, H&R 1871, Inc. was formed from the residual of the parent company and then took over the New England Firearms facility. H&R 1871 produced firearms under both their logo and the NEF brand name until 1999, when the Marlin Firearms Company acquired the assets of H&R 1871.

NO. 3 HAMMERLESS SINGLE-SHOT SHOTGUN . . . . NiB $135 Ex $99 Gd $74
Takedown. Automatic ejector. Gauges: 12, 16, 20, .410. Bbls.: plain, 26- to 32-inch, F choke. Weight: 6.5 to 7.25 lbs. depending on ga. and bbl. length. Plain pistol-grip stock and forend. Discontinued 1942.

NO. 5 STANDARD LIGHTWEIGHT HAMMER SINGLE . . . . NiB $156 Ex $105 Gd $79
Takedown. Auto ejector. Gauges: 24, 28, .410. Bbls.: 26- or 28-inch, F choke. Weight: About 4 to 4.75 lbs. Plain pistol-grip stock/forend. Discontinued 1942.

NO. 6 HEAVY BREECH SINGLE-SHOT HAMMER SHOTGUN . . . . NiB $156 Ex $105 Gd $79
Takedown. Automatic ejector. Gauges: 10, 12, 16, 20. Bbls.: Plain, 28- to 36-inch, F choke. Weight: About 7 to 7.25 lbs. Plain stock and forend. Discontinued 1942.

NO. 7 OR 9 BAY STATE SINGLE-SHOT HAMMER SHOTGUN . . . . NiB $156 Ex $105 Gd $79
Takedown. Automatic ejector. Gauges: 12, 16, 20, .410. Bbls.: Plain 26- to 32-inch, F choke. Weight: 5.5 to 6.5 lbs. depending on ga. and bbl. length. Plain pistol-grip stock and forend. Discontinued 1942.

NO. 8 STANDARD SINGLE-SHOT HAMMER SHOTGUN . . . . NiB $176 Ex $115 Gd $84
Takedown. Automatic ejector. Gauges: 12, 16, 20, 24, 28, .410. Bbl.: plain, 26- to 32-inch, F choke. Weight: 5.5 to 6.5 lbs. depending on ga. and bbl. length. Plain pistol-grip stock and forend. Made from 1908-42.

MODEL 348 GAMESTER BOLT-ACTION SHOTGUN . . . . NiB $135 Ex $99 Gd $74
Takedown. 12 and 16 ga. Two round tubular magazine, 28-inch bbl, F choke. Plain pistol-grip stock. Weight: About 7.5 lbs. Made from 1949-54.

MODEL 349 GAMESTER DELUXE . . . NiB $176 Ex $105 Gd $79
Same as Model 348 except has 26-inch bbl. W/adj. choke device, recoil pad. Made from 1953-55.

MODEL 351 HUNTSMAN BOLT-ACTION SHOTGUN . . . . . . NiB $182 Ex $150 Gd $110
Takedown. 12 and 16 ga. Two round tubular magazine. Pushbutton safety. 26-inch bbl. w/H&R variable choke. Weight: About 6.75 lbs. Monte Carlo stock w/recoil pad. Made from 1956-58.

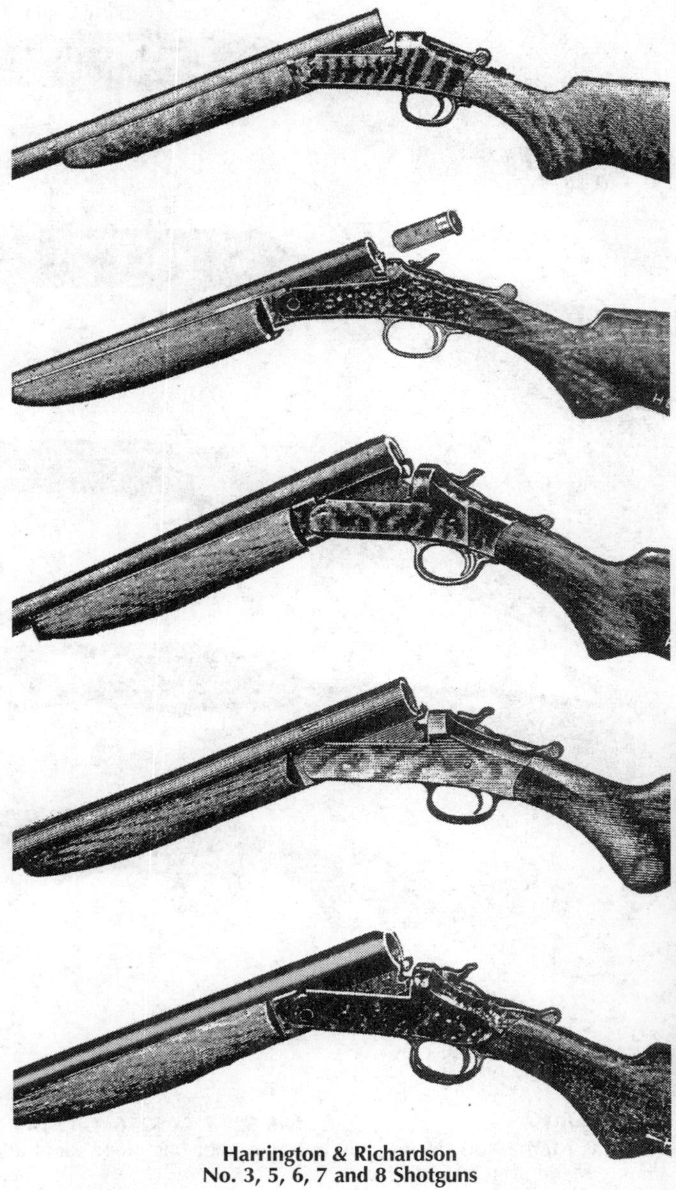

Harrington & Richardson No. 3, 5, 6, 7 and 8 Shotguns

SHOTGUNS

MODEL 400 PUMP . . . . NiB $248 Ex $203 Gd $146
Hammerless. Gauges: 12, 16, 20. Tubular magazine holds 4 shells. 28-inch bbl., F choke. Weight: About 7.25 lbs. Plain pistol-grip stock (recoil pad in 12 and 16 ga.), grooved slide handle. Made from 1955-67.

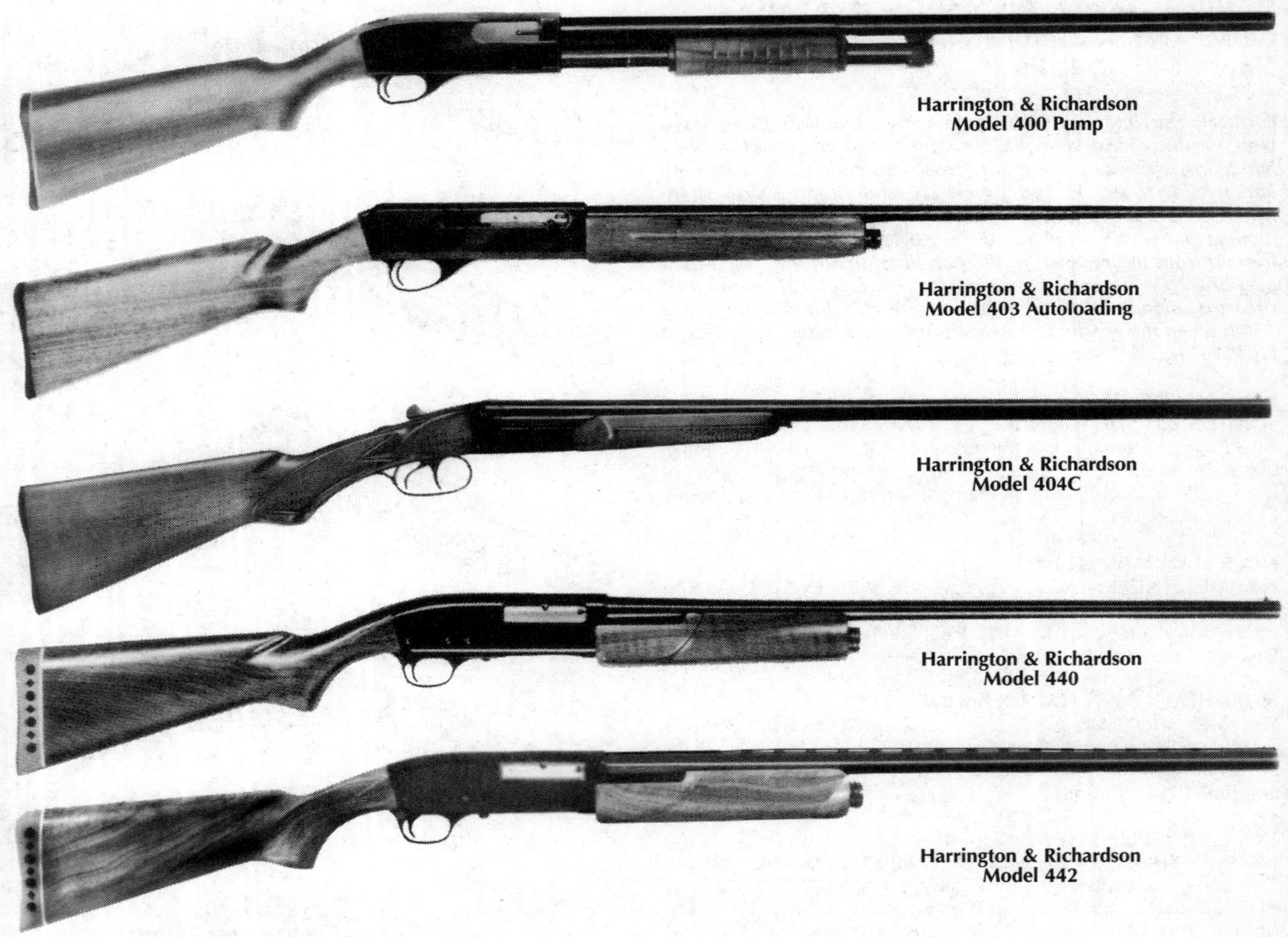

Harrington & Richardson
Model 400 Pump

Harrington & Richardson
Model 403 Autoloading

Harrington & Richardson
Model 404C

Harrington & Richardson
Model 440

Harrington & Richardson
Model 442

MODEL 401 .... NiB $246 Ex $256 Gd $149
Same as Model 400 on previous page, except has H&R variable choke. Made from 1956-63.

MODEL 402 .... NiB $254 Ex $217 Gd $157
Similar to Model 400 except .410 ga., weight: About 5.5 lbs. Made from 1959-67.

MODEL 403 AUTOLOADING
SHOTGUN .... NiB $267 Ex $222 Gd $160
Takedown. .410 ga. Tubular magazine holds four shells. 26-inch bbl., F choke. Weight: About 5.75 lbs. Plain pistol-grip stock and forearm. Made in 1964.

MODEL 404/404C.............. NiB $317 Ex $260 Gd $186
Boxlock. Plain extractors. Double triggers. Gauges: 12, 20, .410. Bbls.: 28-inch in 12 ga. (M/F choke), 26-inch in 20 ga. (IC/M and .410 (F/F). Weight: 5.5 to 7.25 lbs. Plain walnut-finished hardwood stock and forend on Model 404; 404C checkered. Made in Brazil by Amadeo Rossi from 1969-1972.

MODEL 440 PUMP............. NiB $213 Ex $176 Gd $129
Hammerless. Gauges: 12, 16, 20. 2.75-inch chamber in 16 ga., 3-inch in 12 and 20 ga. Three round magazine. Bbls.: 26-, 28-, 30-inch; IC, M, F choke. Weight: 6.25 lbs. Plain pistol-grip stock and slide handle, recoil pad. Made from 1968-73.

MODEL 442 .... NiB $264 Ex $217 Gd $157
Same as Model 440 except has vent rib bbl., checkered stock and forearm, weight: 6.75 lbs. Made from 1969-73.

ULTRA SLUG SERIES............ NiB $226 Ex $186 Gd $135
Singel shot 12 or 20 ga w/3-inch chamber w/heavy-wall 24-inch fully rifled bbl. w/scope . Weight: 9 lbs. Walnut-stained Monte Carlo stock, sling swivels, black nylon sling. Made from 1995 to date.

MODEL 1212 FIELD .... NiB $373 Ex $304 Gd $218
Boxlock. Plain extractors. Selective single trigger. 12 ga., 2.75-inch chambers. 28-inch bbls., IC/IM, vent rib. Weight: 7 lbs. Checkered walnut pistol-gip stock and fluted forearm. Made 1976-80 by Lanber Arms S. A., Zaldibar (Vizcaya), Spain.

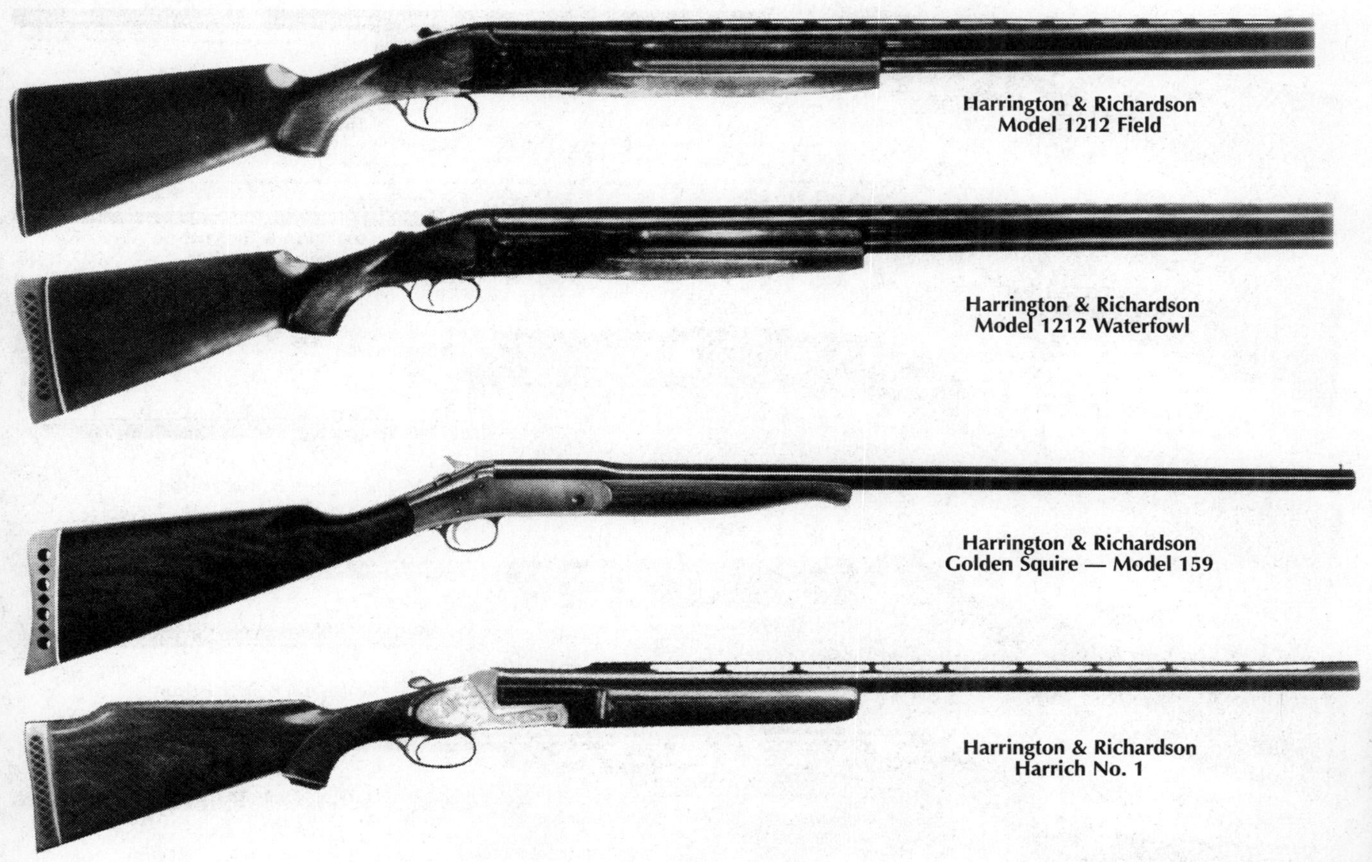

Harrington & Richardson
Model 1212 Field

Harrington & Richardson
Model 1212 Waterfowl

Harrington & Richardson
Golden Squire — Model 159

Harrington & Richardson
Harrich No. 1

MODEL 1212
WATERFOWL GUN. . . . . NiB $412 Ex $338 Gd $242
Same as Field Gun except chambered for 12-ga, 3-inch mag. shells, has 30-inch bbls., M/F chokes, stock and recoil pad, weight: 7.5 lbs. Made from 1976-1980.

MODEL 1908
SINGLE-SHOT SHOTGUN . . . . NiB $170 Ex $124 Gd $88
Takedown. Automatic ejector. Gauges: 12, 16, 24 and 28. Bbls.: 26- to 32-inch, F choke. Weight: 5.25 to 6.5 lbs. depending on ga. and bbl. length. Casehardened receiver. Plain pistol-grip stock. Bead front sight. Made from 1908-1934.

MODEL 1908 .410 (12MM)
SINGLE-SHOT SHOTGUN . . . . NiB $170 Ex $141 Gd $105
Same general specifications as standard Model 1908 except chambered for .410 or 12mm shot cartridge w/bbl. milled down at receiver to give a more pleasing contour.

MODEL 1915 SINGLE-SHOT SHOTGUN
Takedown. Both non-auto and auto-ejectors available. Gauges: 24, 28, .410, 14mm and 12mm. Bbls.: 26- or 28-inch, F choke. Weight: 4 to 4.75 lbs. depending on ga. and bbl. length. Plain black walnut stock w/semi pistol-grip.
24 ga. . . . . NiB $241 Ex $211 Gd $145
28, .410 ga. NiB $199 Ex $165 Gd $121

FOLDING GUN . . . . NiB $199 Ex $165 Gd $121
Single bbl. hammer shotgun hinged at the front of the frame, the bbl. folds down against the stock. Light Frame model: gauges — 28, 14mm, .410; 22-inch bbl.; weighs about 4.5 lbs. Heavy Frame model: gauges — 12, 16, 20, 28, .410; 26-inch bbl.; weighs from 5.75 to 6.5 lbs. Plain pistol-grip stock and forend. Disc. 1942.

GOLDEN SQUIRE MODEL 159
SINGLE-BARREL
HAMMER SHOTGUN . . . . NiB $154 Ex $129 Gd $96
Hammerless. Side lever. Automatic ejection. Gauges: 12, 20. Bbls: 30-inch in 12 ga., 28-inch in 20 ga., both F choke. Weight: About 6.5 lbs. Straight-grip stock w/recoil pad, forearm w/Schnabel. Made from 1964-66.

GOLDEN SQUIRE JR. MODEL 459 . NiB $164 Ex $144 Gd $107
Same as Model 159 except gauges 20 and .410, 26-inch bbl., youth stock. Made in 1964.

HARRICH NO. 1 SINGLE-BARREL
TRAP GUN . . . . NiB $1625 Ex $1320 Gd $829
Anson & Deeley-type locking system w/Kersten top locks and double underlocking lugs. Sideplates engraved w/hunting scenes. 12 ga. Bbls.: 32-, 34-inch; F choke; high vent rib. Weight: 8.5 lbs. Checkered Monte Carlo stock w/pistol-grip and recoil pad, beavertail forearm, of select walnut. Made in Ferlach, Austria, 1971-75.

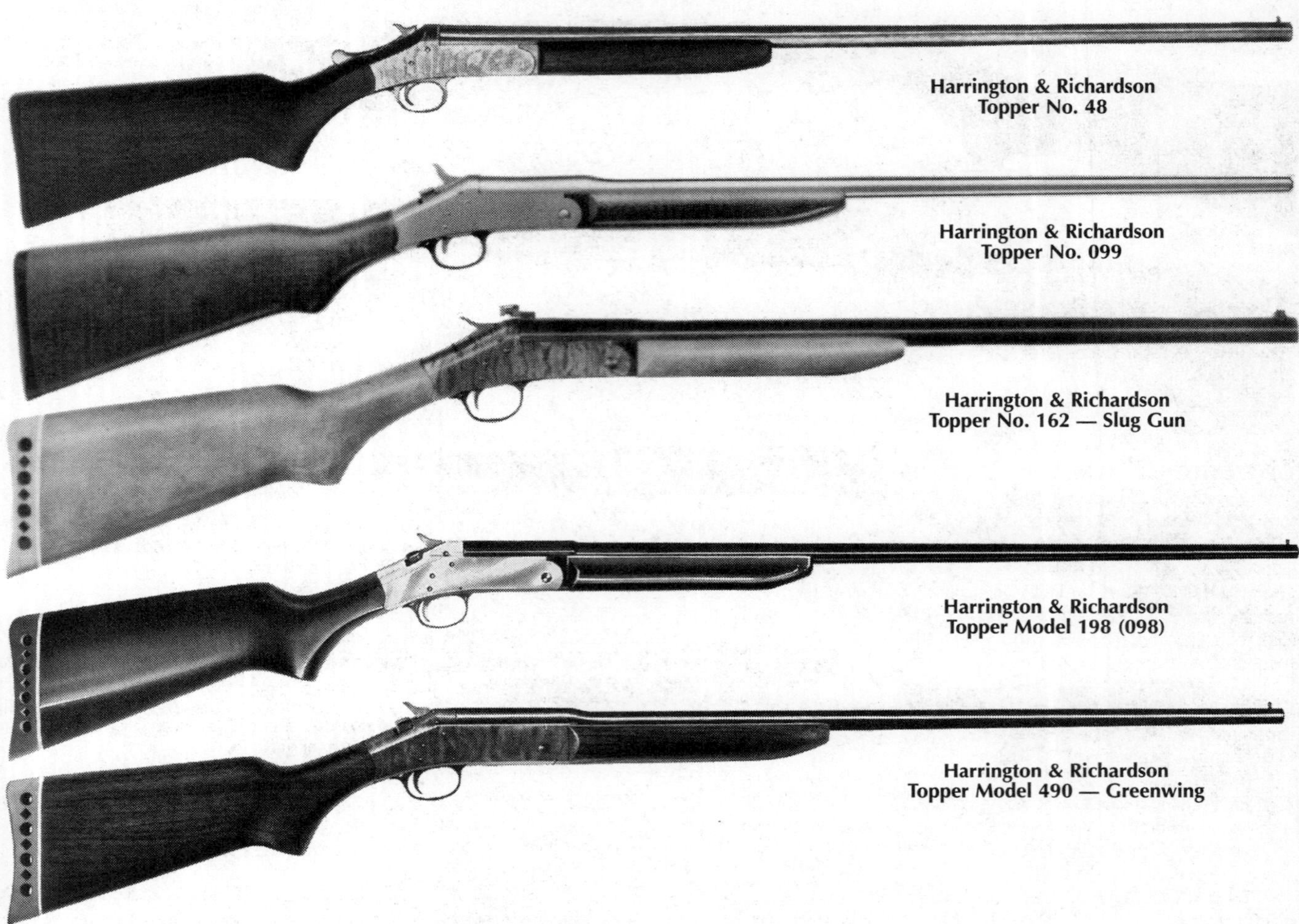

Harrington & Richardson
Topper No. 48

Harrington & Richardson
Topper No. 099

Harrington & Richardson
Topper No. 162 — Slug Gun

Harrington & Richardson
Topper Model 198 (098)

Harrington & Richardson
Topper Model 490 — Greenwing

"TOP RIB"
SINGLE-BARREL SHOTGUN . . . . NiB $244 Ex $208 Gd $163
Takedown. Auto ejector. Gauges: 12, 16 and 20. Bbls.: 28- to 30-inch, F choke w/full-length matted top rib. Weight: 6.5 to 7 lbs. depending on ga. and bbl. length. Black walnut pistol-grip stock (capped) and forend; both checkered. Flexible rubber buttplate. Made during 1930s.

TOPPER NO. 48 SINGLE-BARREL
HAMMER SHOTGUN . . . . NiB $198 Ex $166 Gd $123
Similar to old Model 8 Standard. Takedown. Top lever. Auto ejector. Gauges: 12, 16, 20, .410. Bbls.: plain; 26- to 30-inch; M or F choke. Weight: 5.5 to 6.5 lbs. depending on ga. and bbl. length. Plain pistol-grip stock and forend. Made from 1946-57.

TOPPER MODEL 099 DELUXE . . . . . NiB $157 Ex $130 Gd $95
Same as Model 158 except has matte nickel finish, semipistol grip walnut-finished American hardwood stock; semibeavertail forearm; 12, 16, 20, and .410 ga. Made from 1982-86.

TOPPER MODEL 148 SINGLE-SHOT
HAMMER SHOTGUN . . . . NiB $164 Ex $135 Gd $99
Takedown. Side lever. Auto-ejection. Gauges: 12, 16, 20, .410. Bbls.: 12 ga.,30-, 32- and 36-inch; 16 ga., 28- and 30-inch; 20 and .410 ga., 28-inch; F choke. Weight: 5 to 6.5 lbs. Plain pistol-grip stock and forend, recoil pad. Made from 1958-61.

TOPPER MODEL 158 (058) SINGLE-SHOT
HAMMER SHOTGUN . . . . NiB $170 Ex $140 Gd $103
Takedown. Side lever. Automatic ejection. Gauges: 12, 20, .410 (2.75-inch and 3-inch shells); 16 (2.75-inch). bbl. length and choke combinations: 12 ga., 36-inch/F, 32-inch/F, 30-inch/F, 28-inch/F or M; .410, 28-inch/F. Weight: about 5.5 lbs. Plain pistol-grip stock and forend, recoil pad. Made from 1962-81. Note: Designation changed to 058 in 1974.

TOPPER MODEL 162
SLUG GUN . . . . NiB $216 Ex $177 Gd $128
Same as Topper Model 158 except has 24-inch bbl., Cyl. bore, w/rifle sights. Made from 1968-86.

TOPPER MODEL 176 10 GA.
MAGNUM . . . . NiB $208 Ex $171 Gd $124
Similar to Model 158, but has 36-inch heavy bbl. chambered for 3.5-inch 10- ga. Mag. shells, weight: 10 lbs.; stock w/Monte Carlo comb and recoil pad, longer and fuller forearm. Made from 1977-86.

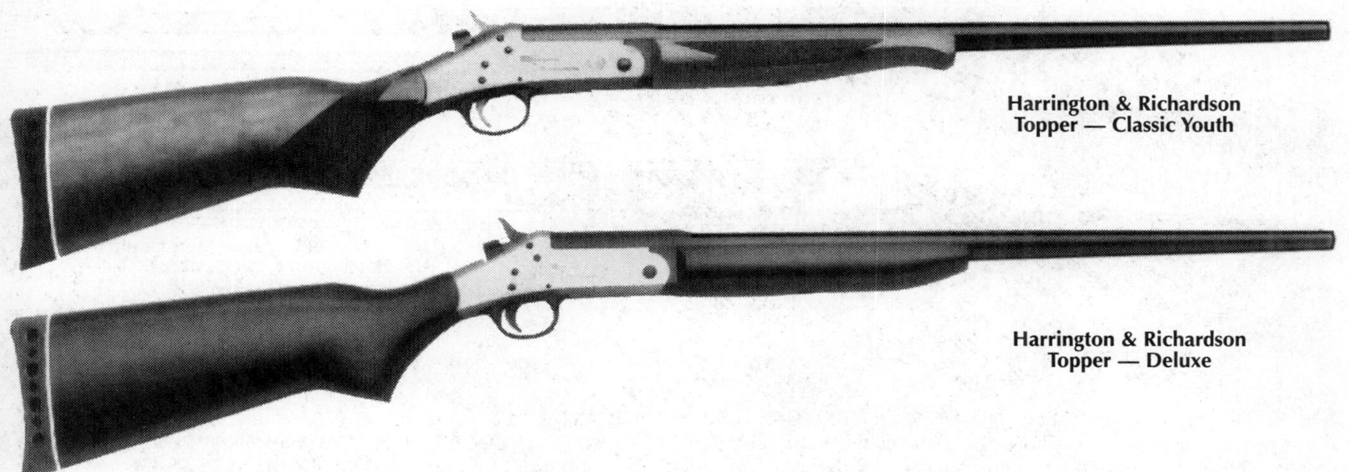

Harrington & Richardson
Topper — Classic Youth

Harrington & Richardson
Topper — Deluxe

TOPPER MODEL 188 DELUXE . . . . NiB $182 Ex $150 Gd $110
Same as standard Topper Model 148 except has chromed frame, stock and forend in black, red, yellow, blue, green, pink, or purple colored finish. .410 ga. only. Made from 1958-61.

TOPPER MODEL 198 (098) DELUXE . . . . . NiB $189 Ex $156 Gd $113
Same as Model 158 except has chrome-plated frame, black finished stock and forend; 12, 20 and .410 ga. Made 1962-81. Note: Designation changed to 098 in 1974.

TOPPER JR. MODEL 480 . . . . NiB $176 Ex $120 Gd $94
Similar to No. 48 Topper except has youth-size stock, 26-inch bbl, .410 ga. only. Made from 1958-61.

TOPPER NO. 488 DELUXE . . . . NiB $177 Ex $146 Gd $107
Same as standard No. 48 Topper except chrome-plated frame, black lacquered stock and forend, recoil pad. Disc. 1957.

TOPPER MODEL 490 . . . . NiB $170 Ex $140 Gd $103
Same as Model 158 except has youth-size stock (3 inches shorter), 26-inch bbl.; 20 and 28 ga. (M choke), .410 (F). Made 1962-86.

TOPPER MODEL 490 GREENWING. . . . . . NiB $189 Ex $156 Gd $113
Same as the Model 490 except has a special high-polished finish. Made from 1981-86.

TOPPER JR. MODEL 580. . . . . NiB $149 Ex $144 Gd $91
Same as Model 480 except has colored stocks as on Model 188. Made from 1958-61.

TOPPER MODEL 590 . . . . NiB $157 Ex $129 Gd $94
Same as Model 490 except has chrome-plated frame, black finished stock and forend. Made from 1962-63.

The following models are manufactured and distributed by the reorganized company of H&R 1871, Inc.

MODEL 098 TOPPER CLASSIC YOUTH . . . . NiB $143 Ex $119 Gd $88
Same as Topper Junior except also available in 28 ga. and has checkered American black walnut stock/forend w/satin finish and recoil pad. Made from 1991 to date.

MODEL 098 TOPPER DELUXE . . . . . NiB $143 Ex $119 Gd $88
Same as Model 098 Single Shot Hammer except in 12 ga., 3-inch chamber only. 28-inch bbl.; Mod. choke tube. Made from 1992 to date.

MODEL 098 TOPPER
DELUXE RIFLED SLUG GUN . . . . . NiB $175 Ex $144 Gd $105
Same as Topper Deluxe Shotgun except has compensated 24-inch rifled slug bbl. Nickel plated receiver and blued bbl. Black finished hardwood stock. Made from 1996 to date.

MODEL 098 TOPPER HAMMER
SINGLE-SHOT SHOTGUN . . . . NiB $124 Ex $104 Gd $77
Side lever. Automatic ejector. Gauges: 12, 20 and .410; 3-inch chamber. Bbls.: 28-inch, (12 ga./M); 26-inch, (20 ga./M); 26-inch (.410/F). Weight: 5 to 6 lbs. Satin nickel receiver, blued bbl. Plain pistol-grip stock and semibeavertail forend w/black finish. Re-Intro. 1992.

MODEL 098 TOPPER JUNIOR . . . . . NiB $130 Ex $109 Gd $81
Same as Model 098 except has youth-size stock and 22-inch bbl. 20 or .410 ga. only. Made 1991 to date.

MODEL .410 TAMER SHOTGUN . . . NiB $143 Ex $119 Gd $88
Takedown. Topper-style single-shot, side lever action w/auto ejector. Gauge: .410; 3-inch chamber. 19.5-inch bbl. 33 inches overall. Weight: 5.75 lbs. Black polymer thumbhole stock designed to hold 4 extra shotshells. Matte nickel finish. Made from 1994 to date.

MODEL N. W. T. F. TURKEY MAG
Same as Model 098 Single-Shot Hammer except has 24-inch bbl. chambered 10 or 12 ga. w/3.5-inch chamber w/screw-in choke tube. Weight: 6 lbs. American hardwood stock, Mossy Oak camo finish. Made from 1991-96.
NWTF 10 ga. Turkey Mag (Made 1996) . . . NiB $165 Ex $136 Gd $103
NWTF 12 ga. Turkey Mag (Made 1991-95). . NiB $148 Ex $123 Gd $90

MODEL N. W. T. F.
YOUTH TURKEY GUN. . . . . NiB $162 Ex $134 Gd $97
Same as Model N.W.T.F. Turkey Mag except has 22-inch bbl. chambered in 20 ga. w/3-inch chamber and fixed full choke. Realtree camo finish. Made from 1994-95.

MODEL SB1-920
ULTRA SLUG HUNTER . . . . NiB $213 Ex $175 Gd $127
Special 12 ga. action w/12 ga. bbl. blank underbored to 20 ga. to form a fully rifled slug bbl. Gauge: 20 w/3 inch chamber. 24-inch bbl. Weight: 8.5 lbs. Satin nickel receiver, blued bbl. Walnut finished hardwood Monte Carlo stock. Made from 1996-98.

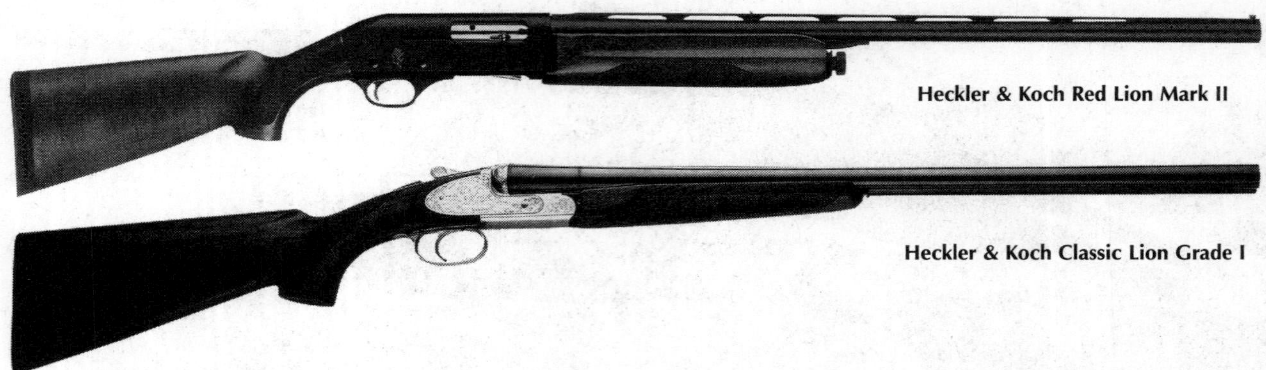

Heckler & Koch Red Lion Mark II

Heckler & Koch Classic Lion Grade I

MODEL ULTRA SLUG HUNTER . . . NiB $225 Ex $200 Gd $160
12 or 20 ga. w/3-inch chamber. 22- or 24-inch rifled bbl. Weight: 9 lbs. Matte black receiver and bbl. Walnut finished hardwood Monte Carlo stock. Made from 1997 to date.

MODEL ULTRA SLUG HUNTER DELUXE . . . . . NiB $220 Ex $180 Gd $129
Similar to Ultra Slug Hunter model except with compensated bbl. Made from 1997 to date.

HECKLER & KOCH FABARM SHOTGUNS — Oberndorf/Neckar, West Germany, and Sterling, Virginia

CLASSIC LION SIDE-BY-SIDE SHOTGUN
12 ga. only. 28- or 30-inch non-ported Tribor bbl. w/3-inch chamber. 46.5 to 48.5-inches overall. Weight: 7 to 7.2 lbs. Five choke tubes; C, IC, M, IM, F. Traditional boxlock design. Oil-finished walnut forearms and stocks w/diamond-cut checkering. Imported from 1999 to date.
Classic Lion Grade I . . . . NiB $1378 Ex $1116 Gd $780
Classic Lion Grade II. . . . . NiB $2060 Ex $1653 Gd $1146

CAMO LION SEMI-AUTO SHOTGUN . . . . NiB $907 Ex $779 Gd $499
12 ga. Only. 24 to 28-inches Tribor bbl. 44.25-48.25-inches overall. Weight: 7-7.2 lbs. 3 inch chamber w/5 choke tubes - C, IC, M, IM, F. Two round mag. Camo covered walnut stock w/rear front bar sights. Imp. 1999 to date.

MAX LION O/U SHOTGUN . . . . NiB $1797 Ex $1547 Gd $884
12 or 20 ga. 26- 28- or 30-inch TriBore system bbls. 42.5-47.25-inches overall. Weight: 6.8-7.8 lbs. 3-inch chamber w/5 choke tubes - C, IC, M, IM, F. Single selective adj. trigger and auto ejectors. Side plates w/high-grade stock and rubber recoil pad. Made from 1999 to date.

RED LION MARK II SEMI-AUTO SHOTGUN . . . . NiB $799 Ex $647 Gd $453
12 ga. Only. 24- 26- or 28-inch TriBore system bbls. 44.25 to 48.25-inches overall. Weight: 7 to 7.2 lbs. 3-inch chamber w/five choke tubes- C, IC, M, IM, F. Two round magazine. Matte finish w/walnut wood stock. Rubber vented recoil pad w/leather cover. Made from 1999 to date.

SILVER LION O/U SHOTGUN . . . . NiB $1209 Ex $977 Gd $685
12 or 20 ga. 26- 28- or 30-inch TriBore system bbls. 43.25-47.25 inchesoverall. 3-inch chamber w/5 choke tubes - C, IC, M, IM, F. Single selective trig. and auto ejectors. Wal. stock w/rubber recoil pad. Made from 1999 to date.

SPORTING CLAY LION SEMI-AUTO SHOTGUN . . . . NiB $925 Ex $748 Gd $521
12 ga. only. 28- or 30-inch bbl. w/3-inch chamber and ported Tribore system barrel. Matte finish w/gold plated trigger and carrier release button. Made from 1999 to date.

HERCULES SHOTGUNS

See Listings under "W" for Montgomery Ward.

HEYM SHOTGUNS — Münnerstadt, Germany

MODEL 22S "SAFETY" SHOTGUN/ RIFLE COMBINATION . . . . NiB $3401 Ex $2758 Gd $1923
16 and 20 ga. Cal: .22 Mag., .22 Hornet, .222 Rem., .222 Rem. Mag., 5.6x50R Mag., 6.5x57R, 7x57R, .243 Win. 24-inch bbls. 40 inches overall. Weight: About 5.5 lbs. Single-set trigger. Left-side bbl. selector. Integral dovetail base for scope mounting. Arabesque engraving. Walnut stock. Disc. 1993.

MODEL 55 BF SHOTGUN/ RIFLE COMBO . . . . NiB $7376 Ex $5958 Gd $4145
12, 16 and 20 ga. Calibers: 5.6x50R Mag., 6.5x57R, 7x57R, 7x65R, .243 Win., .308 Win., .30-06. 25-inch bbls., 42 inches overall. Weight: About 6.75 lbs. Black satin-finished, corrosion-resistant bbls. of Krupp special steel. Hand-checkered walnut stock w/long pistol-grip. Hand-engraved leaf scroll. German cheekpiece. Disc. 1988.

J. C. HIGGINS SHOTGUNS

See Sears, Roebuck & Company.

HUGLU HUNTING FIREARMS — Huglu, Turkey, Imported by Turkish Firearms Corp.

MODEL 101 B 12 AT-DT COMBO O/U TRAP . . . . NiB $2265 Ex $1758 Gd $1338
Over/Under boxlock. 12 ga. w/3-inch chambers. Combination 30- or 32-inch top single & O/U bbls. w/fixed chokes or choke tubes. Weight: 8 lbs. Automatic ejectors or extractors. Single selective trigger. Manual safety. Circassian walnut Monte Carlo trap stock w/palm-swell grip and recoil pad. Silvered frame w/engraving. Imported from 1993-97.

Heym Model 22S
"Safety" Shotgun/Rifle Combination Gun

Heym Model 55
BF Shotgun/Rifle

MODEL 101 B 12 ST O/U TRAP. . . . NiB $1468 Ex $1194 Gd $842
Same as Model 101 AT-DT except in 32-inch O/U configuration only. Imported from 1994-96.

MODEL 103 B 12 ST O/U
Boxlock. Gauges: 12, 16, 20, 28 or .410. 28-inch bbls. w/fixed chokes. Engraved action w/inlaid game scene and dummy sideplates. Double triggers, extractors and manual safety. Weight: 7.5 lbs. Circassian walnut stock. Imported 1995-96.
Model 103B w/extractors . . . . . . NiB $1098 Ex $897 Gd $640
28 and .410, add $100

MODEL 103 C 12 ST O/U
Same general specs as Model 103 B 12 S except w/extractors or ejectors. 12 or 20 ga. w/3-inch chambers. Black receiver w/50% engraving coverage. Imported from 1995-97.
Model 103C w/extractors . . . . . . NiB $1108 Ex $905 Gd $646
Model 103C w/ejectors. . . . . NiB $1369 Ex 1115 Gd $791

MODEL 103 D 12 ST O/U
Same gen. specs as Mdl. 103 B 12 ST except stand. boxlock. Ext. or eject. 12 or 20 ga. w/3-inch chambers. 80% engraving coverage. Imp. from 1995-97.
Model 103D w/extractors . . . . . . NiB $1064 Ex $866 Gd $614
Model 103D w/ejectors. . . . . NiB $1325 Ex $1076 Gd $758

MODEL 103 F 12 ST O/U
Same as Model 103 B except extractors or ejectors. 12 or 20 ga. only. 100% engraving coverage. Imported from 1996-97.
Model 103F w/extractors . . . . NiB $1180 Ex $963 Gd $686
Model 103F w/ejectors . . . . NiB $1445 Ex $1177 Gd $834

MODEL 104 A 12 ST O/U
Boxlock. Gauges: 12, 20, 28 or .410. 28-inch bbls. w/fixed chokes or choke tubes. Silvered, engraved receiver w/15% engraving coverage. Double triggers, manual safety and extractors or ejectors. Weight: 7.5 lbs. Circassian walnut stock w/field dimensions. Imported from 1995-97.
Model 104A w/extractors . . . . . .NiB $1047 Ex $855 Gd $610
Model 104A w/ejectors. . . . . NiB $1307 Ex $1064 Gd $754
28 and .410, add $100
W/Choke Tubes, add $50

MODEL 200 SERIES DOUBLE
Boxlock. Gauges: 12, 20, 28, or .410 w/3-inch chambers. 28-inch bbls. w/fixed chokes. Silvered, engraved receiver. Extractors, manual safety, single selective trigger or double triggers. Weight: 7.5 lbs. Circassion walnut stock. Imported from 1995-97.
Model 200 (w/15% engraving coverage, SST) . . . . NiB $1084 Ex $886 Gd $634
Model 201 (w/30% engraving coverage, SST). . . . . . . NiB $1375 Ex $1121 Gd $796
Model 202 (w/Greener cross bolt, DT). . . . . NiB $1158 Ex $947 Gd $678
28 and .410, add $100

HIGH STANDARD SPORTING ARMS — East Hartford, Connecticut, Formerly High Standard Mfg. Corp. of Hamden, Conn.

In 1966, High Standard introduced new series of Flite-King Pumps and Supermatic autoloaders, both readily identifiable by the damascened bolt and restyled checkering. To avoid confusion, these models are designated "Series II" in this text. This is not an official factory designation. Operation of this firm was discontinued in 1984.

FLITE-KING FIELD PUMP—12 GA. . . . . NiB $302 Ex $247 Gd $177
Hammerless. Magazine holds five rounds. Bbls.: 26-inch IC, 28-inch M or F, 30-inch F choke. Weight: 7.25 lbs. Plain pistol-grip stock and slide handle. Made from 1960-66.

FLITE-KING BRUSH—12 GA. . . . . . NiB $232 Ex $212 Gd $181
Same as Flite-King Field 2 except has 18- or 20-inch bbl. (cylinder bore) w/rifle sights. Made from 1962-64.

SHOTGUNS

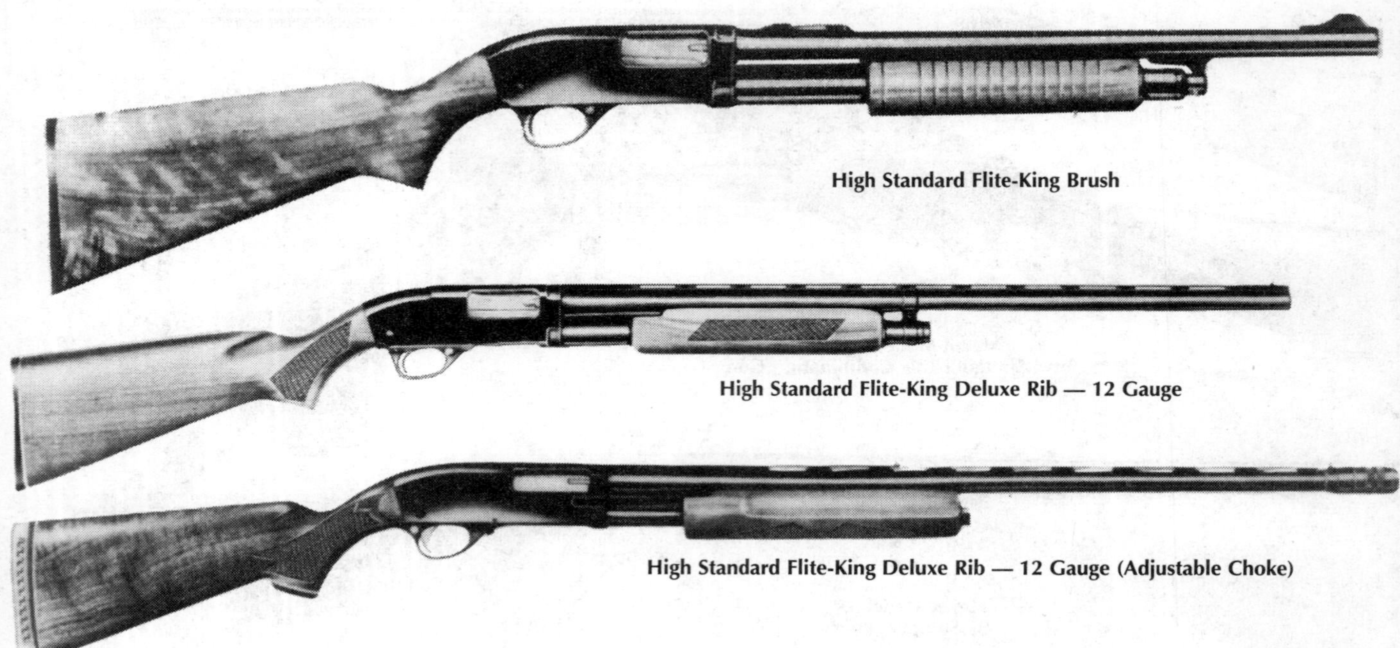

High Standard Flite-King Brush

High Standard Flite-King Deluxe Rib — 12 Gauge

High Standard Flite-King Deluxe Rib — 12 Gauge (Adjustable Choke)

FLITE-KING BRUSH DELUXE . . . . . NiB $297 Ex $262 Gd $180
Same as Flite-King Brush except has adj. peep rear sight, checkered pistol grip, recoil pad, fluted slide handle, swivels and sling. Not available w/18-inch bbl. Made from 1964-66.

FLITE-KING BRUSH (SERIES II) . . . . NiB $287 Ex $235 Gd $168
Same as Flite-King Deluxe 12 (II) except has 20-inch bbl., cylinder bore, w/rifle sights. Weight: 7 lbs. Made from 1966-75.

FLITE-KING BRUSH DELUXE (II) . . NiB $332 Ex $270 Gd $190
Same as Flite-King Brush (II) except has adj. peep rear sight, swivels and sling. Made from 1966-75.

FLITE-KING DELUXE 12 GA. (SERIES II)
Hammerless. Five round magazine. 27-inch plain bbls.w/adj. choke. 26-inch IC, 28-inch M or F. 30-inch F choke. Weight: About 7.25 lbs. Checkered pistol-grip stock and forearm, recoil pad. Made from 1966-75.
W/adj. choke . . . . NiB $332 Ex $272 Gd $194
W/O adj. choke . . . . NiB $304 Ex $249 Gd $178

FLITE-KING DELUXE
20, 28, .410 GA. (SERIES II) . . . . . . NiB $300 Ex $246 Gd $177
Same as Flite-King Deluxe 12 (II) except chambered for 20 and .410 ga. 3-inch shell, 28 ga. 2.75-inch shell w/20- or 28-inch plain bbl. Weight: About 6 lbs. Made from 1966-75.

FLITE-KING DELUXE RIB 12 GA. . . . . . NiB $363 Ex $296 Gd $210
Same as Flite-King Field 12 except vent rib bbl. (28-inch M or F. 30-inch F). Checkered stock and forearm. Made from 1961-66.

FLITE-KING DELUXE RIB 12 GA. (II)
Same as Flite-King Deluxe 12 (II) except has vent rib bbl., available in 27-inch w/adj. choke, 28-inch M or F, 30-inch F choke. Made from 1966-75.
W/adj. choke . . . . NiB $377 Ex $316 Gd $224
W/O adj. choke. . . . . NiB $363 Ex $296 Gd $211

FLITE-KING DELUXE RIB 20 GA. . . . . NiB $353 Ex $289 Gd $207
Same as Flite-King Field 20 except vent-rib bbl. (28 inch M or F), checkered stock and slide handle. Made from 1962-66.

FLITE-KING DELUXE RIB 20, 28, .410 GA. (SERIES II)
Same as Flite-King Deluxe 20, 28, .410 (II) except 20 ga. available w/27-inch adj. choke, 28-inch M or F choke. Weight: about 6.25 lbs. Made from 1966-75.
W/adj. choke. . . . . NiB $409 Ex $334 Gd $238
W/O adj. choke. . . . . NiB $384 Ex $314 Gd $224

FLITE-KING DELUXE SKEET GUN
12 GA. (SERIES II) . . . . NiB $358 Ex $293 Gd $209
Same as Flite-King Deluxe Rib 12 (II) except available only w/26-inch vent rib bbl., SK choke, recoil pad optional. Made from 1966-75.

FLITE-KING DELUXE SKEET GUN
20, 28, .410 GA. (SERIES II) . . . . . . NiB $409 Ex $334 Gd $238
Same as Flite-King Deluxe Rib 20, 28, .410 (II) except available only w/26-inch vent-rib bbl., SK choke. Made from 1966-75.

FLITE-KING DELUXE
TRAP GUN (II). . . . . NiB $342 Ex $280 Gd $200
Same as Flite-King Deluxe Rib 12 (II) except available only w/30-inch vent-rib bbl., F choke; trap-style stock. Made from 1966-75.

FLITE-KING FIELD PUMP 20 GA. . . . . NiB $277 Ex $227 Gd $164
Hammerless. Chambered for 3-inch Magnum shells, also handles 2.75-inch. Magazine holds four rounds. Bbls.: 26-inch IC, 28-inch M or F choke. Weight: About 6 lbs. Plain pistol-grip stock and slide handle. Made from 1961-66.

FLITE-KING PUMP SHOTGUNS 16 GA.
Same general specifications as Flite-King 12 except not available in Brush, Skeet and Trap Models or 30-inch bbl. Values same as for 12-ga. guns. Made from 1961-65.

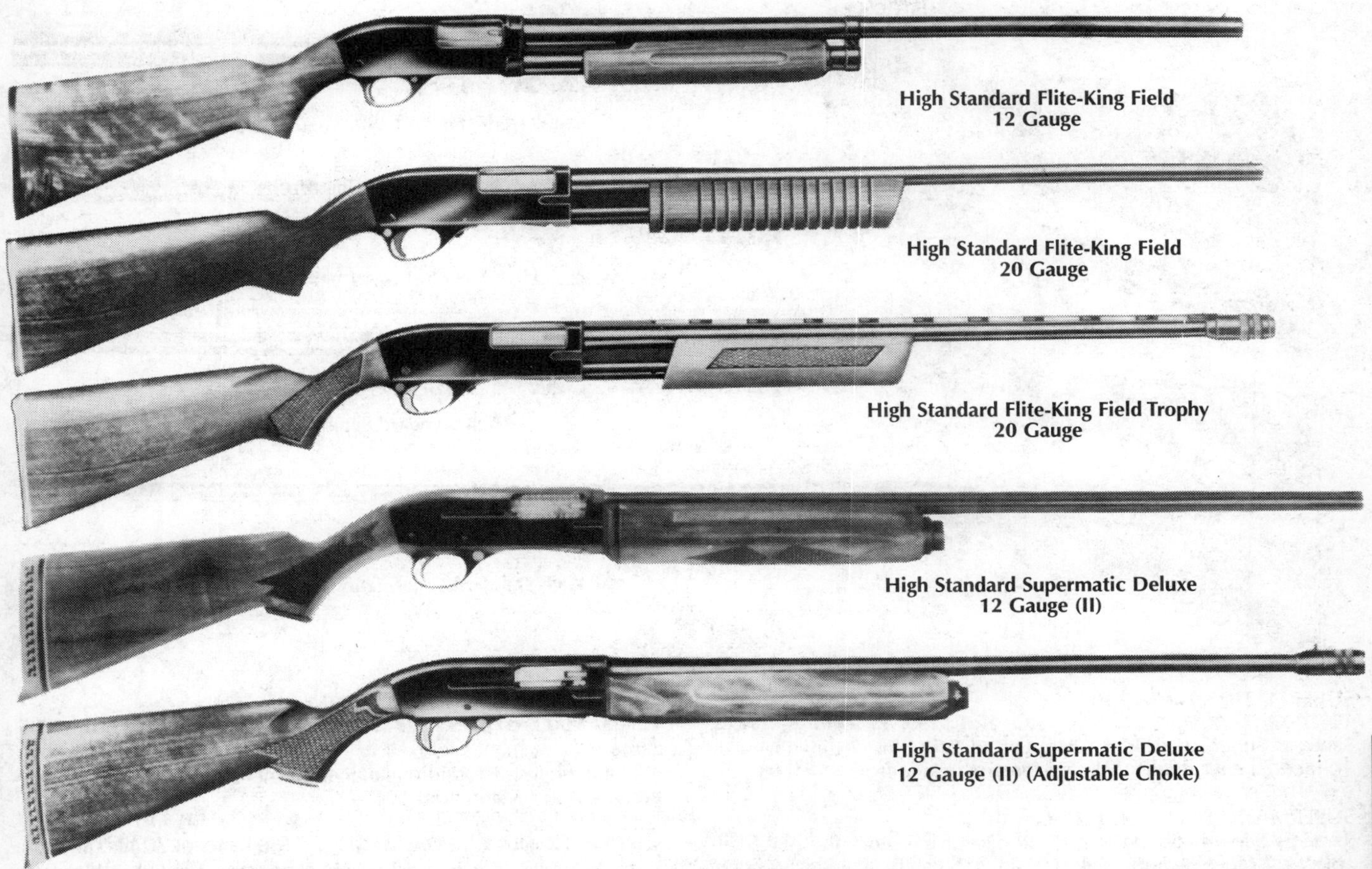

High Standard Flite-King Field
12 Gauge

High Standard Flite-King Field
20 Gauge

High Standard Flite-King Field Trophy
20 Gauge

High Standard Supermatic Deluxe
12 Gauge (II)

High Standard Supermatic Deluxe
12 Gauge (II) (Adjustable Choke)

FLITE-KING PUMP SHOTGUNS (.410 GA.)
Same general specifications as Flite-King 20 except not available in Special and Trophy Models, or w/other than 26-inch choke bbl. Values same as for 20 ga. guns. Made from 1962-66.

FLITE-KING SKEET
12 GA. . . . . NiB $395 Ex $324 Gd $232
Same as Flite-King Deluxe Rib except 26-inch vent rib bbl., w/SK choke. Made from 1962-66.

FLITE-KING SPECIAL 12 GA. . . . . . NiB $293 Ex $241 Gd $174
Same as Flite-King Field 12 except has 27-inch bbl. w/adj. choke. Made from 1960-66.

FLITE-KING SPECIAL 20 GA. . . . . . NiB $299 Ex $246 Gd $178
Same as Flite-King Field 20 except has 27-inch bbl. w/adj. choke. Made from 1961-66.

FLITE-KING TRAP 12 GA. . . . . NiB $393 Ex $322 Gd $280
Same as Flite-King Deluxe Rib 12 except 30-inch vent rib bbl., F choke, special trap stock w/recoil pad. Made from 1962-66.

FLITE-KING TROPHY 12 GA. . . . . . NiB $369 Ex $302 Gd $217
Same as Flite-King Deluxe Rib 12 except has 27-inch vent rib bbl. w/adj. choke. Made from 1960-66.

FLITE-KING TROPHY
20 GA. . . . . NiB $394 Ex $323 Gd $228
Same as Flite-King Deluxe Rib 20 except has 27-inch vent rib bbl. w/adj. choke. Made from 1962-66.

SUPERMATIC DEER GUN . . . . NiB $388 Ex $320 Gd $228
Same as Supermatic Field 12 except has 22-inch bbl. (cylinder bore) w/rifle sights, checkered stock and forearm, recoil pad. Weight: 7.75 lbs. Made in 1965.

SUPERMATIC DELUXE 12 GA. (SERIES II)
Gas-operated autoloader. Four round magazine. Bbls.: Plain; 27-inch w/adj. choke (disc. about 1970); 26-inch IC, 28-inch M or F. 30-inch F choke. Weight: About 7.5 lbs. Checkered pistol-grip stock and forearm, recoil pad. Made from 1966-75.
W/adj. choke . . . . NiB $415 Ex $340 Gd $244
W/O adj. choke . . . . NiB $342 Ex $287 Gd $217

SUPERMATIC DELUXE 20 GA. (SERIES II)
Same as Supermatic Deluxe 12 (II) except chambered for 20 ga. Three inch shell; bbls. available in 27-inch w/adj. choke (disc. about 1970), 26-inch IC, 28-inch M or F choke. Weight: About 7 lbs. Made from 1966-75.
W/adj. choke . . . . NiB $310 Ex $255 Gd $185
W/O adj. choke . . . . NiB $361 Ex $296 Gd $212

SUPERMATIC DELUXE DEER GUN (II) NiB $454 Ex $371 Gd $265
Same as Supermatic Deluxe 12 (II) except has 22-inch bbl., cylinder bore, w/rifle sights. Weight: 7.75 lbs. Made from 1966-74.

SUPERMATIC DELUXE DUCK
12 GA. MAGNUM (SERIES II) . . . . . NiB $321 Ex $265 Gd $195
Same as Supermatic Deluxe 12 (II) except chambered for 3-inch magnum shells, 3-round magazine, 30-inch plain bbl., F choke. Weight: 8 lbs. Made from 1966-74.

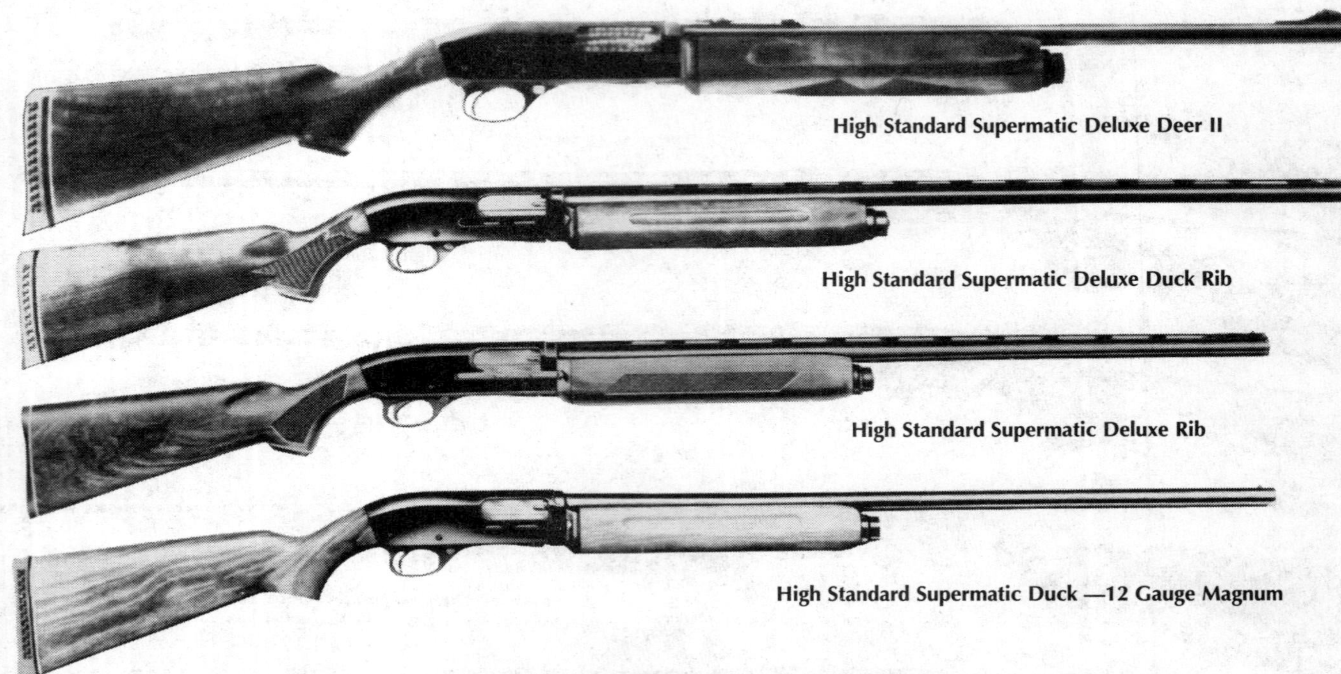

High Standard Supermatic Deluxe Deer II

High Standard Supermatic Deluxe Duck Rib

High Standard Supermatic Deluxe Rib

High Standard Supermatic Duck —12 Gauge Magnum

SUPERMATIC DELUXE RIB
12 GA.. . . . . NiB $299 Ex $245 Gd $176
Same as Supermatic Field 12 except vent rib bbl. (28-inch M or F, 30-inch F), checkered stock and forearm. Made from 1961-66.

SUPERMATIC DELUXE RIB 12 GA. (II)
Same as Supermatic Deluxe 12 (II) except has vent rib bbl.; available in 27-inch w/adj. choke, 28-inch M or F, 30-inch F choke. Made from 1966-75.
W/adj. choke . . . . NiB $374 Ex $306 Gd $220
W/O adj. choke . . . . NiB $342 Ex $281 Gd $202

SUPERMATIC DELUXE RIB
20 GA.. . . . . NiB $374 Ex $306 Gd $220
Same as Supermatic Field 20 except vent rib bbl. (28-inch M or F), checkered stock and forearm. Made from 1963-66.

SUPERMATIC DELUXE RIB 20 GA. (II)
Same as Supermatic Deluxe 20 (II) except has vent rib bbl. Made from 1966-75.
W/adj. choke . . . . NiB $345 Ex $283 Gd $203
W/O adj. choke . . . . NiB $321 Ex $263 Gd $201

SUPERMATIC DELUXE
SKEET GUN
12 GA. (SERIES II) . . . . NiB $345 Ex $283 Gd $203
Same as Supermatic Deluxe Rib 12 (II) except available only w/26-inch vent rib bbl., SK choke. Made from 1966-75.

SUPERMATIC DELUXE SKEET GUN
20 GA. (SERIES II) . . . . NiB $355 Ex $292 Gd $210
Same as Supermatic Deluxe Rib 20 (II) except available only w/26-inch vent rib bbl., SK choke. Made from 1966-75.

SUPERMATIC DELUXE
TRAP GUN (SERIES II) . . . . NiB $369 Ex $302 Gd $217
Same as Supermatic Deluxe Rib 12 (II) except available only w/30-inch vent rib bbl., full choke; trap-style stock. Made from 1966-75.

SUPERMATIC DELUXE DUCK RIB
12 GA. MAG. (SERIES II) . . . . NiB $346 Ex $284 Gd $204
Same as Supermatic Deluxe Rib 12 (II) except chambered for 3-inch magnum shells, 3-round magazine; 30-inch vent rib bbl., F choke. Weight: 8 lbs. Made from 1966-75.

SUPERMATIC DUCK 12 GA. MAG. . . . . NiB $346 Ex $284 Gd $204
Same as Supermatic Field 12 except chambered for 3-inch Magnum shell, 30-inch F choke bbl., recoil pad. Made from 1961-66.

SUPERMATIC TROPHY 12 GA.. . . . . NiB $296 Ex $244 Gd $177
Same as Supermatic Deluxe Rib 12 except has 27-inch vent-rib bbl. w/adj. choke. Made from 1961-66.

SUPERMATIC DUCK RIB 12 GA. MAG.. . . . . NiB $370 Ex $304 Gd $218
Same as Supermatic Duck 12 Magnum except has vent rib bbl., checkered stock and forearm. Made from 1961-66.

SUPERMATIC FIELD AUTOLOADING
SHOTGUN 12 GA. . . . . NiB $394 Ex $323 Gd $231
Gas-operated. Magazine holds four rounds. Bbls.: 26-inch IC, 28-inch M or F choke, 30-inch F choke. Weight: About 7.5 lbs. Plain pistol-grip stock and forearm. Made from 1960-66.

SUPERMATIC FIELD AUTOLOADING
SHOTGUN 20 GA.. . . . . NiB $310 Ex $255 Gd $185
Gas-operated. Chambered for 3-inch mag. shells, also handles 2.75-inch. Magazine holds three rounds. Bbls.: 26-inch IC, 28-inch M or F choke. Weight: About 7 lbs. Plain pistol-grip stock and forearm. Made from 1963-66.

SUPERMATIC SHADOW AUTOMATIC . . . NiB $440 Ex $359 Gd $256
Gas-operated. Ga.: 12, 20, 2.75- or 3-inch chamber in 12 ga., 3-inch in 20 ga. Mag. holds four 2.75-inch shells, three 3-inch. Bbls.: Full-size airflow rib; 26-inch (IC or SK choke), 28-inch (M, IM or F), 30-inch (trap or F choke), 12-ga. 3-inch Mag. available only in 30-inch F choke; 20 ga. not available in 30-inch. Weight: 12 ga., 7 lbs. Checkered walnut stock and forearm. Made from 1974-75 by Caspoll Int'l., Inc., Tokyo.

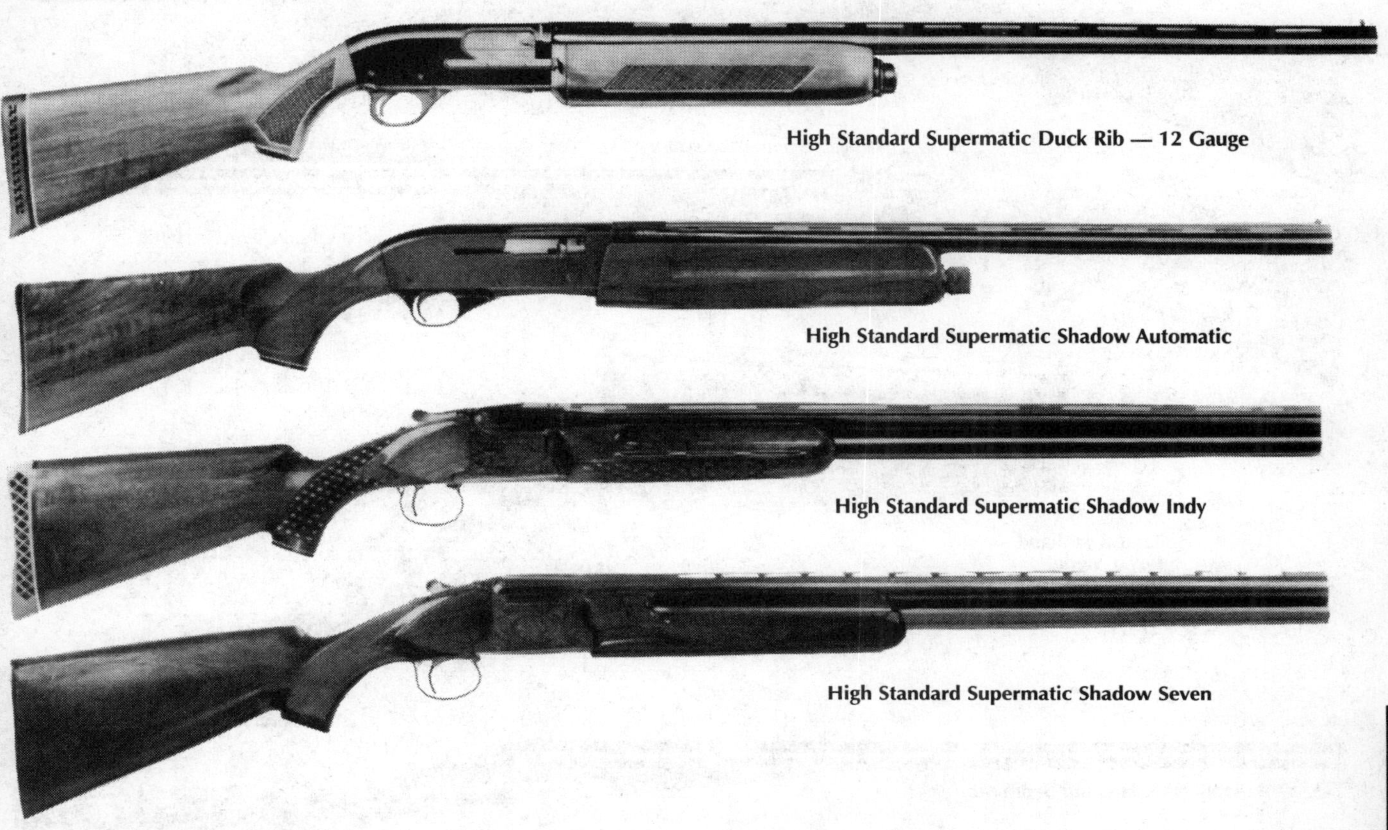

High Standard Supermatic Duck Rib — 12 Gauge

High Standard Supermatic Shadow Automatic

High Standard Supermatic Shadow Indy

High Standard Supermatic Shadow Seven

SUPERMATIC SHADOW INDY O/U . . . . NiB 1107 Ex $904 Gd $645
Boxlock. Fully engraved receiver. Selective auto ejectors. Selective single trigger. 12 ga. 2.75-inch chambers. Bbls.: Full-size airflow rib; 27.5 inch both SK choke, 29.75-inch IM/F or F/F. Weight: W/29.75-inch bbls., 8 lbs. 2 oz. Pistol-grip stock w/recoil pad, ventilated forearm, skip checkering. Made from 1974-75 by Caspoll Int'l., Inc., Tokyo.

SUPERMATIC SHADOW SEVEN . . . NiB $930 Ex $757 Gd $536
Same general specifications as Shadow Indy except has conventional vent rib, less elaborate engraving, standard checkering forearm is not vented, no recoil pad. 27.5-inch bbls.; also available in IC/M, M/F choke. Made from 1974-75.

SUPERMATIC SKEET 12 GA. . . . . . . NiB $303 Ex $248 Gd $178
Same as Supermatic Deluxe Rib 12 except 26-inch vent-rib bbl. w/SK choke. Made from 1962-66.

SUPERMATIC SKEET 20 GA. . . . . . . NiB $323 Ex $264 Gd $188
Same as Supermatic Deluxe Rib 20 except 26-inch vent-rib bbl. w/SK choke. Made from 1964-66.

SUPERMATIC SPECIAL 12 GA. . . . . NiB $272 Ex $223 Gd $161
Same as Supermatic Field 12 except has 27-inch bbl. w/adj. choke. Made from 1960-66.

SUPERMATIC SPECIAL 20 GA. . . . . NiB $297 Ex $243 Gd $175
Same as Supermatic Field 20 except has 27-inch bbl. w/adj. choke. Made from 1963-66.

SUPERMATIC TRAP 12 GA.. . . . . . . NiB $303 Ex $248 Gd $178
Same as Supermatic Deluxe Rib 12 except 30-inch vent rib bbl., F choke, special trap stock w/recoil pad. Made from 1962-66.

SUPERMATIC TROPHY 20 GA. . . . . NiB $316 Ex $258 Gd $185
Same as Supermatic Deluxe Rib 20 except has 27-inch vent rib bbl. w/adj. choke. Made from 1963-66.

HOLLAND & HOLLAND, LTD. — *London England*

BADMINTON MODEL HAMMERLESS DOUBLE-BARREL SHOTGUN. ORIGINALLY NO. 2 GRADE
General specifications same as Royal Model except without self-opening action. Made as a game gun or pigeon and wildfowl gun. Introduced in 1902. Disc.
W/double triggers . . . . NiB $10,856 Ex $8684 Gd $5905
W/single trigger . . . . NiB $12,416 Ex $9932 Gd $6754
20 ga., add 25%
28 ga., add 40%
.410, add 65%

CENTENARY MODEL HAMMERLESS DOUBLE-BARREL SHOTGUN
Lightweight (5.5 lbs.). 12 ga. game gun designed for 2-inch shell. Made in four grades — Model Deluxe, Royal, Badminton, Dominion. Values same as shown for standard guns in those grades. Disc. 1962.

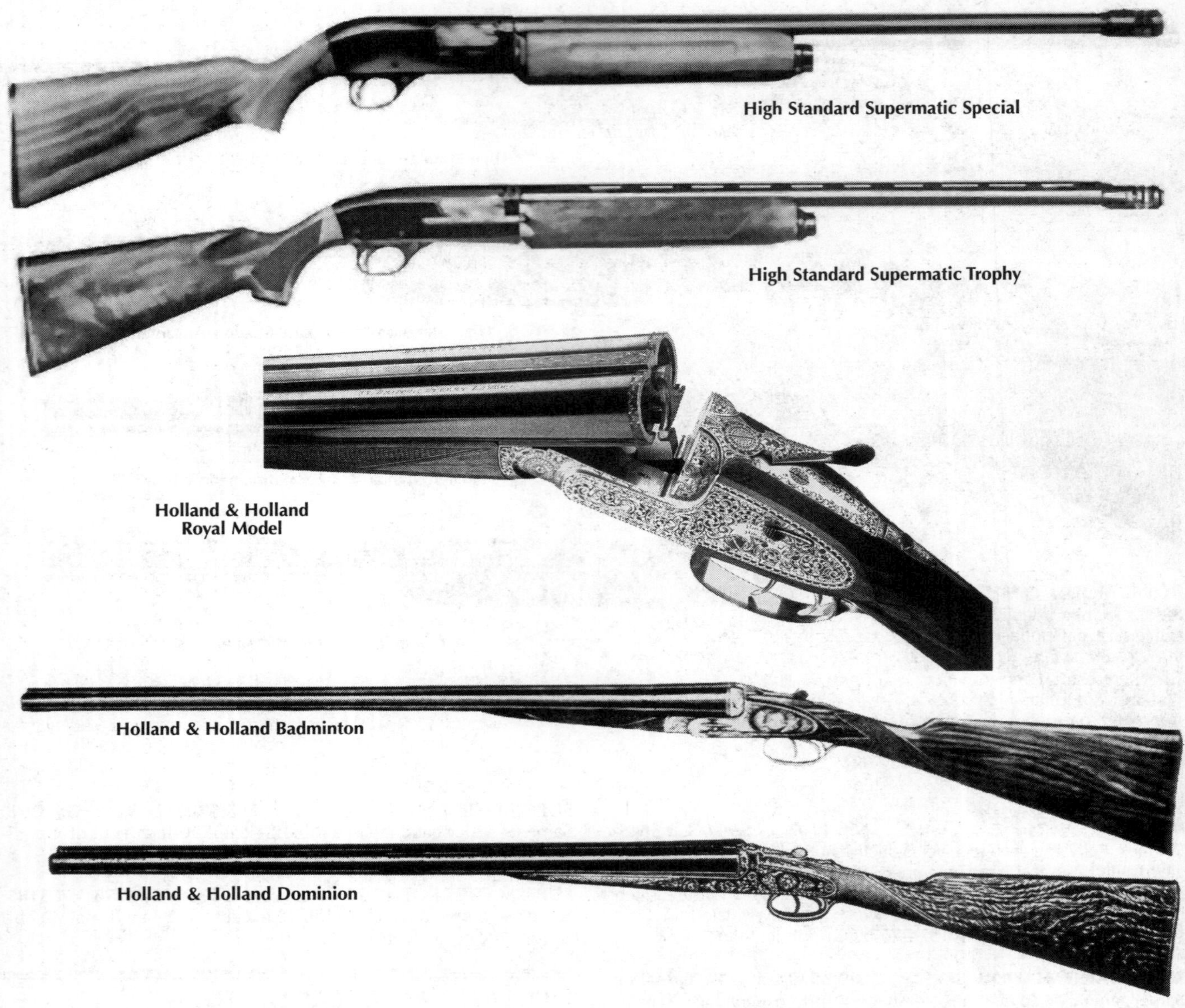
High Standard Supermatic Special

High Standard Supermatic Trophy

Holland & Holland Royal Model

Holland & Holland Badminton

Holland & Holland Dominion

DOMINION MODEL HAMMERLESS DOUBLE-BBL. SHOTGUN . . . . NiB $6650 Ex $5368 Gd $3728
Game Gun. Sidelock. Auto ejectors. Double triggers. Gauges: 12, 16, 20. bbls. 25- to 30-inch, any standard boring. Checkered stock and forend, straight grip standard. Disc. 1967.

MODEL DELUXE HAMMERLESS DOUBLE
Same as Royal Model except has special engraving and exhibition grade stock and forearm. Currently manufactured.
W/double triggers . . . . . . NiB $59,150 Ex $47,320 Gd $32,178
W/single trigger . . . . NiB $64,675 Ex $51,740 Gd $35,183

NORTHWOOD MODEL HAMMERLESS DOUBLE-BARREL SHOTGUN . . NiB $6884 Ex $5507 Gd $3745
Anson & Deeley system boxlock. Auto ejectors. Double triggers. Gauges: 12, 16, 20, 28 in Game Model; 28 ga. not offered in Pigeon Model; Wildfowl Model in 12 ga. only (3-inch chambers available). Bbls.: 28-inch standard in Game and Pigeon Models, 30-inch in Wildfowl Model; other lengths, any standard choke combination available. Weight: From 5 to 7.75 lbs. depending on ga. and bbls. Checkered straight-grip or pistol-grip stock and forearm. Disc.

RIVIERA MODEL PIGEON GUN . . . . NiB $15,014 Ex $12,012 Gd $8168
Same as Badminton Model but supplied w/two sets of bbls., double triggers. Disc. 1967.

ROYAL MODEL HAMMERLESS DOUBLE
Self-opening. Sidelocks hand-detachable. Auto ejectors. Double triggers or single trigger. Gauges: 12, 16, 20, 28 .410. Built to customer's specifications as to bbl. length, chokes, etc. Made as a Game Gun or Pigeon and Wildfowl Gun, the latter having treble-grip action and side clips. Checkered stock and forend, straight grip standard. Made from 1885 to date.
W/double triggers . . . . . NiB $58,826 Ex $47,060 Gd $32,000
W/single trigger . . . . NiB $63,376 Ex $50,700 Gd $34,476

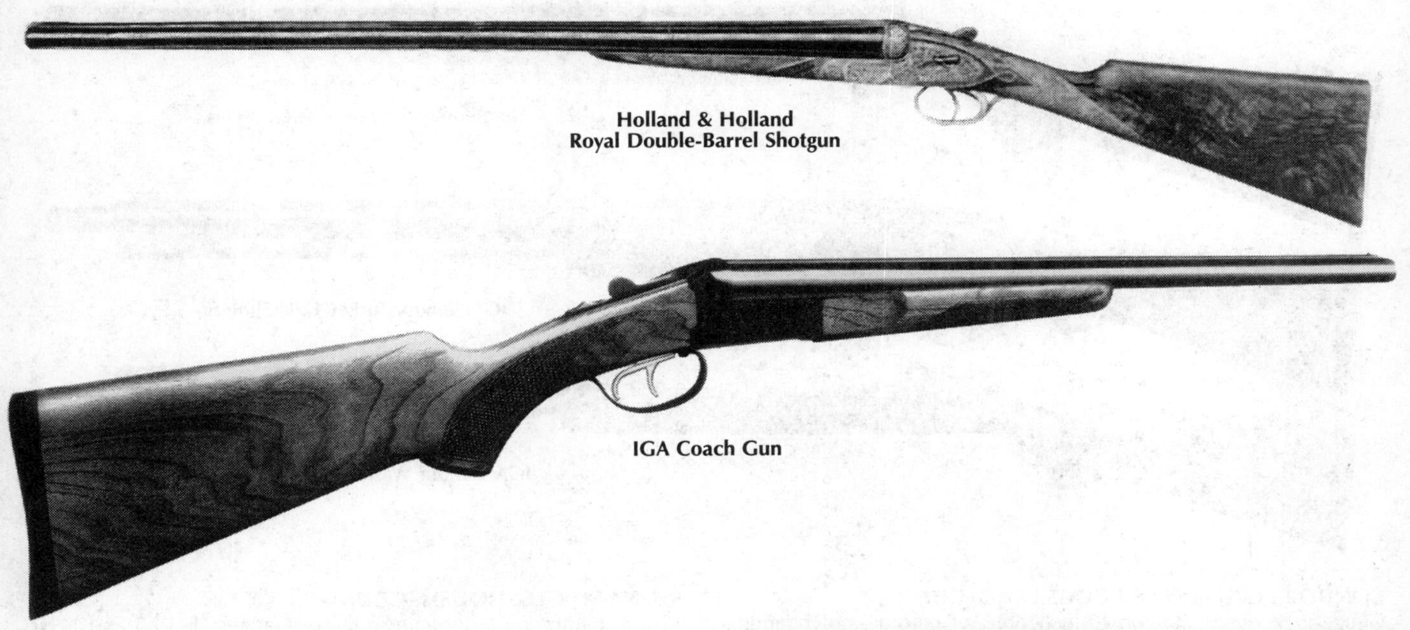
Holland & Holland
Royal Double-Barrel Shotgun

IGA Coach Gun

ROYAL MODEL O/U
Sidelocks, hand-detachable. Auto-ejectors. Double triggers or single trigger. 12 ga. Built to customer's specifications as to bbl. length, chokes, etc. Made as a Game Gun or Pigeon and Wildfowl Gun. Checkered stock and forend, straight grip standard. Note: In 1951 Holland & Holland introduced its New Model Under/Over w/an improved, narrower action body. Disc. 1960.
New model
(double triggers) .... NiB $38,026 Ex $30,420 Gd $20,686
New model
(single trigger) .... NiB $39,650 Ex $31,720 Gd $21,570
Old model
(double triggers) .... NiB $32,436 Ex $25,948 Gd $17,645
Old model
(single trigger) .... NiB $34,450 Ex $27,560 Gd $18,741

SINGLE-SHOT SUPER TRAP GUN
Anson & Deeley system boxlock. Auto-ejector. No safety. 12 ga. Bbls.: Wide vent rib, 30- or 32-inch, w/Extra Full choke. Weight: About 8.75 lbs. Monte Carlo stock w/pistol grip and recoil pad, full beavertail forearm. Models differ in grade of engraving and wood used. Disc.
Standard
grade .... NiB $5763 Ex $4657 Gd $3242
Deluxe
grade .... NiB $9020 Ex $7264 Gd $5018
Exhibition
grade .... NiB $10,791 Ex $8645 Gd $5899

SPORTING O/U .... NiB $27,950 Ex $22,360 Gd $15,205
Blitz action. Auto ejectors; single selective trigger. Gauges: 12 or 20 w/2.75-inch chambers. Barrels: 28- to 32-inch w/screw-in choke tubes. Hand-checkered European walnut straight-grip or pistol grip stock, forearm. Made from 1993 to date.

HOLLAND & HOLLAND SPORTING
O/U DELUXE .... NiB $36,336 Ex $29,068 Gd $19,766
Same general specs as Sporting O/U except better engraving and select wood. Made from 1993 to date.

HUNTER ARMS COMPANY — Fulton, New York

HUNFULTON HAMMERLESS DOUBLE-BARREL. SHOTGUN
Boxlock. Plain extractors. Double triggers or non-selective single trigger. Gauges: 12 16, 20. Bbls.: 26- to 32-inch various choke combinations. Weight: about 7 lbs. Checkered pistol-grip stock and forearm. Disc. 1948.
W/double triggers .... NiB $476 Ex $397 Gd $306
W/single trigger .... NiB $751 Ex $564 Gd $447

SPECIAL HAMMERLESS DOUBLE-BARREL. SHOTGUN
Boxlock. Plain extractors. Double triggers or non-selective single trigger. Gauges: 12,16, 20. Bbls.: 26- to 30-inch various choke combinations. Weight: 6.5 to 7.25 lbs. depending on bbl. length and ga. Checkered full pistol-grip stock and forearm. Disc. 1948.
W/double triggers .... NiB $687 Ex $566 Gd $412
W/single trigger .... NiB $836 Ex $687 Gd $495

IGA SHOTGUNS — Veranopolis, Brazil
Imported by Stoeger Industries, Inc. Accokeek, Maryland

COACH GUN
Side-by-side double. Gauges: 12, 20 and .410. 20-inch bbls. w/3-inch chambers. Fixed chokes (standard model) or screw-in tubes (deluxe model). Weight: 6.5 lbs. Double triggers. Ejector and automatic safety. Blued or nickel finish. Hand-rubbed oil-finished pistol grip stock and forend w/hand checkering (hardwood on standard model or Brazilian walnut (deluxe). Imported from 1983 to date.
Standard Coach Gun (blued finish).... NiB $302 Ex $248 Gd $179
Standard Coach Gun (nickel finish) ... NiB $364 Ex $297 Gd $212
Standard Coach Gun
(engraved stock) .... NiB $393 Ex $322 Gd $230
Deluxe Coach Gun (intro. 1997)... NiB $429 Ex $350 Gd $253
Choke tubes, add.. $20

SHOTGUNS

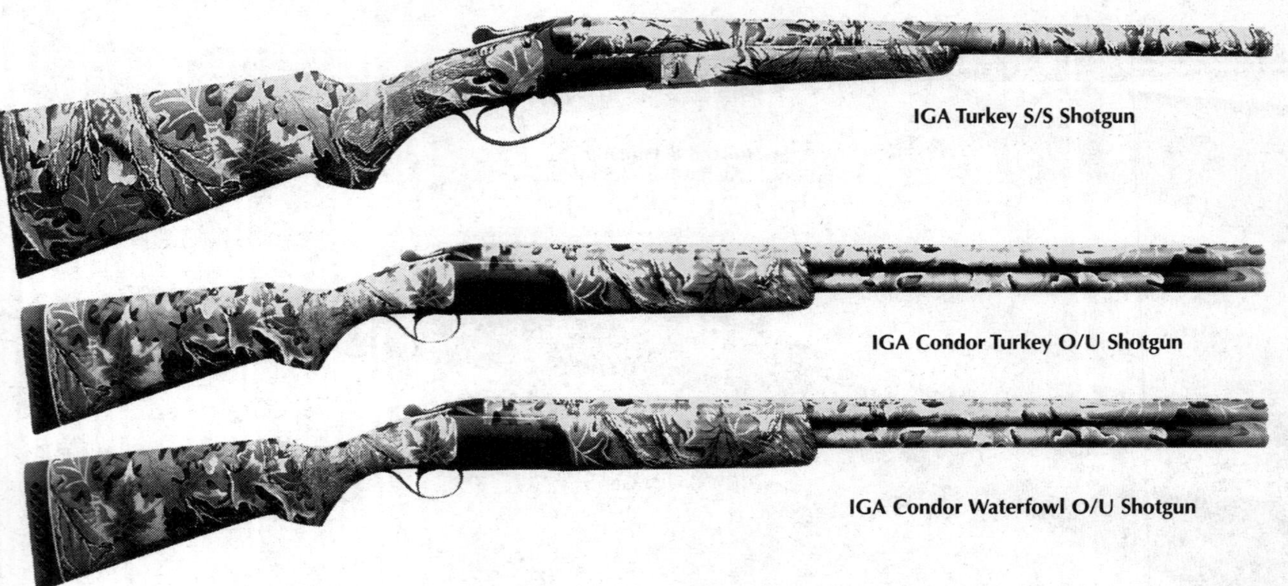

IGA Turkey S/S Shotgun

IGA Condor Turkey O/U Shotgun

IGA Condor Waterfowl O/U Shotgun

CONDOR I O/U SINGLE-TRIGGER SHOTGUN
Gauges: 12 or 20. 26- or 28-inch bbls. of chrome-molybdenum steel. Chokes: Fixed — M/F or IC/M; screw-in choke tubes (12 and 20 ga.). Three inch chambers. Weight: 6.75 to 7 lbs. Sighting rib w/anti-glare surface. Hand-checkered hardwood pistol-grip stock and forend. Imported from 1983 to date.
W/fixed chokes . . . . NiB $393 Ex $322 Gd $230
W/screw-in tubes . . . . NiB $442 Ex $360 Gd $256

CONDOR II O/U DOUBLE-TRIGGER SHOTGUN . . . . NiB $387 Ex $316 Gd $227
Same general specifications as the Condor I O/U except w/double triggers and fixed chokes only; 26-inch bbls., IC/M; 28-inch bbls., M/F.

CONDOR SUPREME . . . . NiB $585 Ex $476 Gd $337
Same general specifications as Condor I except upgraded w/fine-checkered Brazilian walnut buttstock and forend, a matte-laquered finish, and a massive monoblock that joins the bbls. in a solid one-piece assembly at the breech end. Bbls. w/recessed interchangeable choke tubes formulated for use w/steel shot. Automatic ejectors. Imported from 1996 to date.

CONDOR TURKEY MODEL O/U SHOTGUN . . . . NiB $677 Ex $550 Gd $388
12 gauge only. 26-inch vent-rib bbls. w/3-inch chambers fitted w/recessed interchangeable choke tubes. Weight: 8 lbs. Mechanical single trigger. Ejectors and automatic safety. Advantage camouflage on stock and bbls. Made from 1997 to date.

CONDOR WATERFOWL MODEL . . . . . NiB $691 Ex $561 Gd $395
Similar to Condor Turkey-Advantage camo model except w/30-inch bbls. Made from 1998 to date.

DELUXE HUNTER CLAY SHOTGUN
Same general specifications and values as IGA Condor Supreme. Imported from 1997-1999.

ERA 2000 O/U SHOTGUN . . . . NiB $508 Ex $414 Gd $294
Gauge: 12 w/3-inch chambers. 26- or 28-inch bbls. of chrome-molybdenum steel w/screw-in choke tubes. Extractors. Manual safety. (Mechanical triggers.) Weight: 7 lbs. Checkered Brazilian hardwood stock w/oil finish. Imported from 1992-95.

REUNA SINGLE-SHOT SHOTGUN
Visible hammer. Under-lever release. Gauges: 12, 20 and .410; 3-inch chambers. 26- or 28-inch bbls. w/fixed chokes or screw-in choke tubes (12 ga. only). Extractors. Weight: 5.25 to 6.5 lbs. Plain Brazilian hardwood stock and semi-beavertail forend. Imported from 1992-1998.
W/fixed choke . . . . NiB $129 Ex $108 Gd $68
W/choke tubes . . . . NiB $206 Ex $169 Gd $122

UPLANDER SIDE-BY-SIDE SHOTGUN
Gauges: 12, 20, 28 and .410. 26- or 28-inch bbls. of chrome-molybdenum steel. Various fixed-choke combinations; screw-in choke tubes (12 and 20 ga.). Three inch chambers (2.75-inch in 28 ga.). Weight: 6.25 to 7 lbs. Double triggers. Automatic safety. Matte-finished solid sighting rib. Hand checkered pistol-grip or straight stock and forend w/hand-rubbed, oil-finish. Imported from 1983 to date.
Upland w/fixed chokes . . . . NiB $328 Ex $269 Gd $193
Upland w/screw-in tubes . . . . NiB $387 Ex $319 Gd $226
English model (straight grip) . . . . . . NiB $377 Ex $307 Gd $220
Ladies model . . . . NiB $387 Ex $318 Gd $226
Supreme model . . . . NiB $510 Ex $412 Gd $292
Youth model . . . . NiB $350 Ex $288 Gd $206

UPLANDER TURKEY MODEL S/S DOUBLE . . . . NiB $505 Ex $411 Gd $291
12 gauge only. 24-inch solid rib bbls. w/3-inch chambers choked F&F. Weight: 6.75 lbs. Double triggers. Automatic safety. Advantage camouflage on stock and bbls. Made from 1997-2000.

ITHACA GUN COMPANY — King Ferry (formerly Ithaca), New York. Ithaca Acquisition Corp./Ithaca Gun Co.

MODEL 37 BICENTENNIAL COMMEMORATIVE. . . . . NiB $717 Ex $487 Gd $349
Limited to issue of 1976. Similar to Model 37 Supreme except has special Bicentennial design etched on receiver, fancy walnut stock and slide handle. Serial numbers U.S.A. 0001 to U.S.A. 1976. Originally issued w/presentation case w/cast-pewter belt buckle. Made in 1976. Best value is for gun in new, unfired condition.

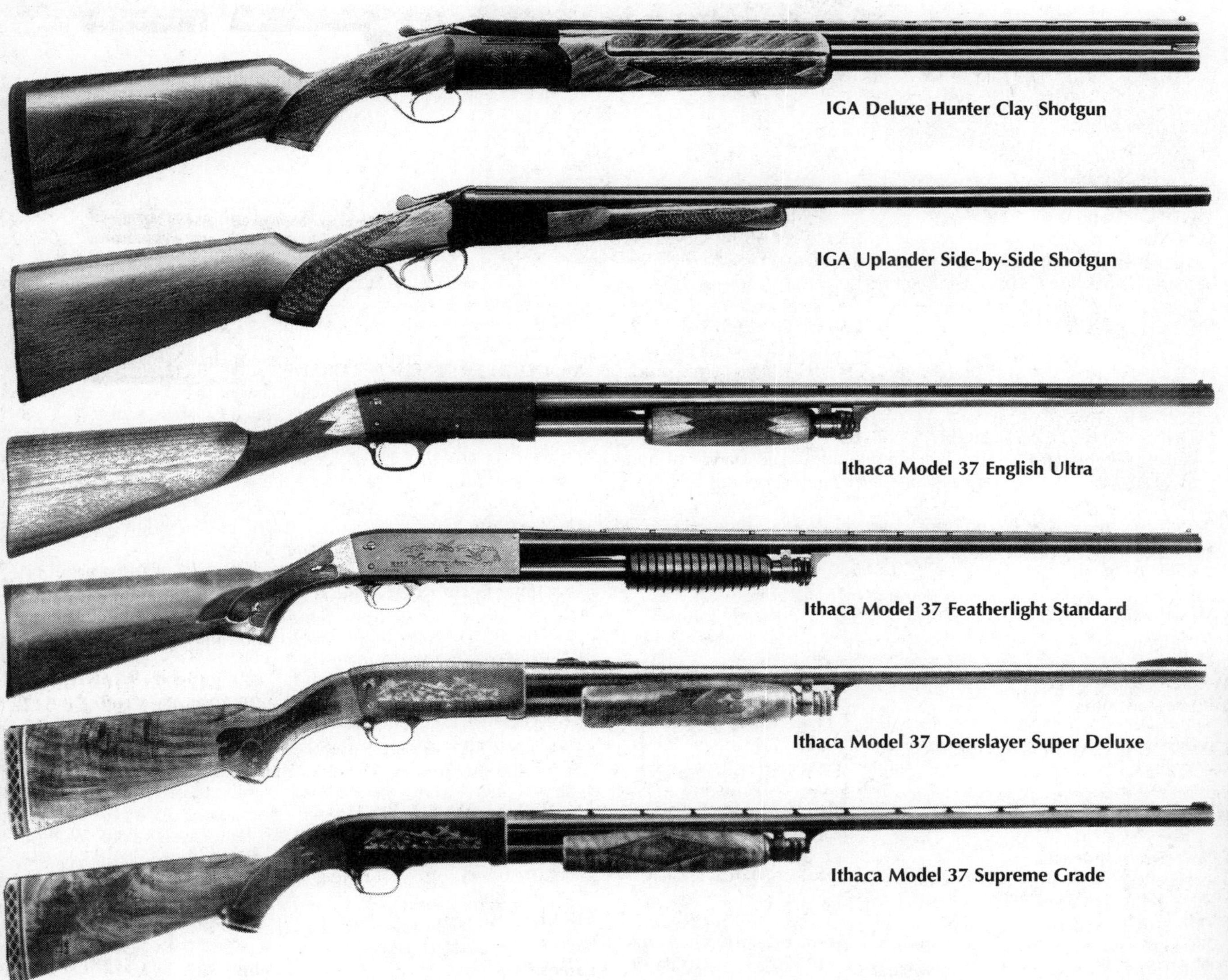

IGA Deluxe Hunter Clay Shotgun

IGA Uplander Side-by-Side Shotgun

Ithaca Model 37 English Ultra

Ithaca Model 37 Featherlight Standard

Ithaca Model 37 Deerslayer Super Deluxe

Ithaca Model 37 Supreme Grade

MODEL 37 DEERSLAYER DELUXE
Formerly "Model 87 Deerslayer Deluxe" reintroduced under the original Model 37 designation w/the same specifications. Available w/smooth bore or rifled bbl. Reintroduced 1996. Disc.
Deluxe model (smoothbore) . . . . . . NiB $488 Ex $398 Gd $284
Deluxe model (rifled bbl.) . . . . NiB $542 Ex $441 Gd $312

MODEL 37 DEERSLAYER II . . . . NiB $575 Ex $468 Gd $332
Gauges: 12 or 20 ga. Five round capacity. 20- or 25-inch rifled bbl. Weight: 7 lbs. Monte Carlo checkered walnut stock and forearm. Receiver drilled and tapped for scope mount. Made from 1996-2000.

MODEL 37 DEERSLAYER STANDARD . . . . NiB $355 Ex $291 Gd $209
Same as Model 37 Standard except has 20- or 26-inch bbl. bored for rifled slugs, rifle-type open rear sight and ramp front sight. Weight: 5.75 to 6.5 lbs. depending on ga. and bbl. length. Made from 1959-86.

MODEL 37 DEERSLAYER
SUPER DELUXE . . . . NiB $452 Ex $369 Gd $273
Formerly "Deluxe Deerslayer." Same as Model 37 Standard Deerslayer except has stock and slide handle of fancy walnut. Made from 1962-86.

MODEL 37 ENGLISH ULTRA . . . . . NiB $515 Ex $419 Gd $298
Same general specifications as Model 37 Ultralite except straight buttstock, 25-inch Hot Forged vent-rib bbl. Made from 1984-87.

MODEL 37 FEATHERLIGHT STANDARD GRADE
SLIDE-ACTION REPEATING SHOTGUN
Adaptation of the earlier Remington Model 17, a Browning design patented in 1915. Hammerless. Takedown. Gauges: 12, 16 (disc. 1973), 20. Four round magazine. Bbl. lengths: 26-, 28-, 30-inch (the latter in 12 ga. only); standard chokes. Weight: From 5.75 to 7.5 lbs. depending on ga. and bbl. length. Checkered pistol-grip stock and slide handle. Some guns made in the 1950s and 1960s have grooved slide handle; plain or checkered pistol-grip. Made from 1937-84.
Standard w/checkered pistol-grip . . NiB $319 Ex $261 Gd $188
W/plain stock . . . . NiB $287 Ex $236 Gd $171
Mdl 37D Deluxe (1954-77) . . . . NiB $397 Ex $324 Gd $232
Mdl 37DV Deluxe vent rib (1962-84) . . . NiB $454 Ex $371 Gd $265
Mdl 37R Deluxe
solid rib (1955-61). . . . . NiB $385 Ex $314 Gd $225
Mdl 37V Standard
vent rib (1962-84) . . . . NiB $3721 Ex $304 Gd $218

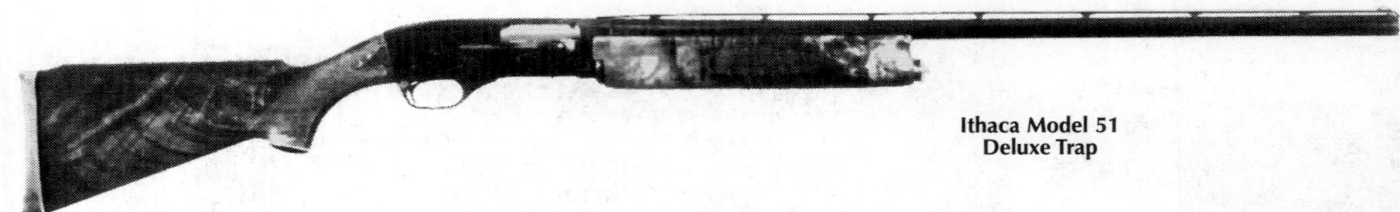
Ithaca Model 51
Deluxe Trap

MODEL 37 FIELD GRADE
MAG. W/TUBES . . . . NiB $374 Ex $306 Gd $221
Same general specifications as Model 37 Featherlight except 32-inch bbl. and detachable choke tubes. Vent rib bbl. Made from 1984-87.

MODEL 37 NEW CLASSIC . . . . NiB $685 Ex $563 Gd $409
Ggs: 12 or 20 ga. 20- or 28-inch vent rib bbl. w/choke tubes. Knuckle-cut receiver and orig. style "ring-tail" forend. Lim. prod. Made from 1998-2005.

MODEL 37 THOUSAND DOLLAR GRADE
Custom built, elaborately engraved and inlaid w/gold, hand-finished working parts, stock and forend of select figured walnut. General specifications same as standard Model 37. Note: The same gun was designated the $1000 Grade prior to World War II. Made 1937-67.
$1000 grade . . . . NiB $6866 Ex $5520 Gd $3819
$5000 grade . . . . NiB $6560 Ex $5285 Gd $3653

MODEL 37 SUPREME GRADE. . . . . NiB $719 Ex $585 Gd $414
Available in Skeet or Trap Gun, similar to Model 37T. Made 1967-86 and 1996-97.

MODEL 37 ULTRALITE
Same general specifications as Model 37 Featherlight except streamlined forend, gold trigger, Sid Bell grip cap and vent rib. Weight: 5 to 5.75 lbs. Made from 1984-87.
Standard . . . . NiB $504 Ex $411 Gd $292
W/choke tubes . . . . NiB $545 Ex $444 Gd $315

MODEL 37R SOLID RIB GRADE
Same general specifications as the Model 37 Featherlight except has a raised solid rib, adding about .25 pounds of weight. Made from 1937-67.
W/checkered grip
and slide handle . . . . NiB $416 Ex $340 Gd $242
W/plain stock . . . . NiB $410 Ex $437 Gd $239

MODEL 37S SKEET GRADE. . . . . . . NiB $579 Ex $470 Gd $332
Same general specifications as the Model 37 Featherlight except has vent rib and large extension-type forend; weight: About .5 lb. more. Made from 1937-55.

MODEL 37T TARGET GRADE . . . . . NiB $540 Ex $439 Gd $309
Same general specifications as Model 37 Featherlight except has vent-rib bbl., checkered stock and slide handle of fancy walnut (choice of skeet- or trap-style stock). Note: This model replaced Model 37S Skeet and Model 37T Trap. Made from 1955-61.

MODEL 37T TRAP GRADE . . . . NiB $581 Ex $472 Gd $334
Same gen. specs. as Mdl. 37S except has straighter trap-style stock of select walnut, recoil pad; weight: About .5 lb. more. Made from 1937-55.

MODEL 37 TURKEYSLAYER
Gauges: 12 ga. (Standard) or 20 ga. (youth). Slide action. 22-inch bbl. Extended choke tube. Weight: 7 lbs. Advantage camouflage or Realtree pattern. Made from 1996-2005.
Standard model . . . . NiB $506 Ex $412 Gd $292
Youth model(intro. 1998) . . . . NiB $540 Ex $439 Gd $310

MODEL 37 WATERFOWLER . . . . . . NiB $526 Ex $429 Gd $303
12 ga. only w/28-inch bbl. Wetlands camouflage. Made from 1998-2005.

MODEL 51 DEERSLAYER. . . . . NiB $404 Ex $330 Gd $236
Same as Model 51 Standard except has 24-inch plain bbl. w/slug boring, rifle sights, recoil pad. Weight: About 7.25 lbs. Made from 1972-84.

MODEL 51 DELUXE SKEET GRADE . . . NiB $542 Ex $441 Gd $312
Same as Model 51 Standard except 26-inch vent-rib bbl. only, SK choke, skeet-style stock, semi-fancy wood. Weight: About 8 lbs. Made from 1970-87.

MODEL 51 DELUXE TRAP GRADE
Same as Model 51 Standard except 12 ga. only, 30-inch bbl. w/broad floating rib, F choke, trap-style stock w/straight or Monte Carlo comb, semifancy wood, recoil pad. Weight: About 8 lbs. Made from 1970-87.
W/straight stock . . . . NiB $473 Ex $386 Gd $275
W/Monte Carlo stock . . . . NiB $499 Ex $407 Gd $289

MODEL 51 STANDARD AUTOMATIC SHOTGUN
Gas-operated. Gauges: 12, 20. Three round. Bbls.: Plain or vent rib, 30-inch F choke (12 ga. only), 28-inch F or M, 26-inch IC. Weight: 7.25-7.75 lbs. depending on ga. and bbl. Checkered pistol-grip stock, forearm. Made 1970-80. Still avail. in 12 and 20 ga., 28-inch M choke only.
W/plain barrel. . . . . NiB $328 Ex $269 Gd $193
W/ventilated rib . . . . NiB $385 Ex $314 Gd $225

MODEL 51 STANDARD MAGNUM
Same as Model 51 Standard except has 3-inch chamber, handles Magnum shells only; 30-inch bbl. in 12 ga., 28-inch in 20 ga., F or M choke, stock w/recoil pad. Weight: 7.75-8 lbs. Made from 1972-82.
W/plain bbl. (disc. 1976) . . . . NiB $299 Ex $241 Gd $187
W/ventilated rib . . . . NiB $365 Ex $298 Gd $213

MODEL 51A TURKEY GUN. . . . . . . NiB $389 Ex $318 Gd $226
Same general specifications as standard Model 51 Magnum except 26-inch bbl. and matte finish. Disc. 1986.

MODEL 66 LONG TOM . . . . NiB $147 Ex $122 Gd $89
Same as Model 66 Standard except has 36-inch F choke bbl., 12 ga. only, checkered stock and recoil pad standard. Made from 1969-74.

MODEL 66 STANDARD SUPER SINGLE LEVER
Single shot. Hand-cocked hammer. Gauges: 12 (disc. 1974), 20, .410, 3-inch chambers. Bbls.: 12 ga., 30-inch F choke, 28-inch F or M; 20 ga., 28-inch F or M; .410, 26-inch F. Weight: About 7 lbs. Plain or checkered straight-grip stock, plain forend. Made from 1963-78.
Standard model . . . . NiB $179 Ex $148 Gd $107
Vent rib model (20 ga., checkered
stock, recoil pad, 1969-74) . . . . . . NiB $205 Ex $168 Gd $121
Youth model (20 & .410 ga., 26-inch bbl.,
shorter stock, recoil pad, 1965-78). . . . NiB $179 Ex $147 Gd $107

MODEL 66RS BUCKBUSTER. . . . . . NiB $214 Ex $175 Gd $126
Same as Model 66 Standard except has 22-inch bbl. cylinder bore w/rifle sights, later version has recoil pad. Originally offered in 12 and 20 ga.; the former was disc. in 1970. Made from 1967-78.

Ithaca Model
66RS Buckbuster

Previously issued as the Ithaca Model 37, the Model 87 guns listed below were made available through the Ithaca Acquisition Corp. From 1986-95. Production of the Model 37 resumed under the original logo in 1996.

MODEL 87 DEERSLAYER SHOTGUN
Gauges: 12 or 20, 3-inch chamber. Bbls.: 18.5-, 20- or 25-inch (w/special or rifled bore). Weight: 6 to 6.75 lbs. Ramp blade front sight, adj. rear. Receiver grooved for scope. Checkered American walnut pistol-grip stock and forearm. Made from 1988-96.
Basic model .... NiB $387 Ex $317 Gd $227
Basic Field Combo (w/extra 28-inch bbl.)
.... NiB $438 Ex $357 Gd $253
Deluxe model .... NiB $412 Ex $337 Gd $241
Deluxe Combo (w/extra 28-inch bbl.)
.... NiB $516 Ex $420 Gd $298
DSPS (8-round model) .... NiB $393 Ex $322 Gd $230
Field model .... NiB $342 Ex $281 Gd $199
Monte Carlo model .... NiB $361 Ex $296 Gd $211
Ultra model (disc. 1991) .... NiB $485 Ex $395 Gd $281

MODEL 87 DEERSLAYER II
RIFLED SHOTGUN .... NiB $449 Ex $366 Gd $263
Similar to Standard Deerslayer except w/solid frame construction and 25-inch rifled bbl. Monte Carlo stock. Made from 1988-96.

MODEL 87 ULTRALITE
FIELD PUMP SHOTGUN......... NiB $433 Ex $353 Gd $253
Gauges: 12 and 20; 2.75-inch chambers. 25-inch bbl. w/choke tube. Weight: 5 to 6 lbs. Made from 1988-90.

MODEL 87 FIELD GRADE
Gauge: 12 or 20.; 3-inch chamber. Five round magazine. Fixed chokes or screw-in choke tubes (IC, M, F). Bbls.: 18.5-inch (M&P); 20- and 25-inch (Combo); 26-, 28-, 30-inch vent rib. Weight: 5 to 7 lbs. Made from 1988-96.
Basic field model (disc. 1993)..... NiB $408 Ex $334 Gd $239
Camo model .... NiB $440 Ex $359 Gd $256
Deluxe model .... NiB $471 Ex $385 Gd $274
Deluxe Combo model .... NiB $478 Ex $390 Gd $278
English model .... NiB $414 Ex $339 Gd $243
Hand grip model
(w/polymer pistol-grip) .... NiB $452 Ex $370 Gd $263
M&P model (disc. 1995) .... NiB $395 Ex $324 Gd $232
Supreme model .... NiB $614 Ex $499 Gd $352
Turkey model.................. NiB $414 Ex $339 Gd $243
Ultra Deluxe model (disc. 1992)... NiB $503 Ex $410 Gd $291

HAMMERLESS DOUBLE-BARREL SHOTGUNS
Boxlock. Plain extractors, auto ejectors standard on the "E" grades. Double triggers, non-selective or selective single trigger extra. Gauges: Magnum 10, 12; 12, 16, 20, 28, .410. Bbls.: 26- to 32-inch, any standard boring. Weight: 5.75 (.410) to 10.5 lbs. (Magnum 10). Checkered pistol-grip stock and forearm standard. Higher grades differ from Field Grade in quality of workmanship, grade of wood, checkering, engraving, etc.; general specifications are the same. Ithaca doubles made before 1925 (serial number 425,000) the rotary bolt and a stronger frame were adopted. Values shown are for this latter type; earlier models valued about 50% lower. Smaller gauge guns may command up to 75% higher. Disc. 1948.
Field grade.................... NiB $924 Ex $750 Gd $527
No. 1 grade .... NiB $984 Ex $798 Gd $662
No. 2 grade .... NiB $1477 Ex $1195 Gd $838
No. 3 grade .... NiB $1859 Ex $1503 Gd $1048
No. 4E grade (ejector)........ NiB $3296 Ex $2558 Gd $1846
No. 5E grade (ejector)........ NiB $7769 Ex $3599 Gd $4309
No. 7E grade (ejector) $12,825
$2000 (pre-war $1000) grade
ejector and selective single trigger standard $9329

Extras:
Magnum 10 or 12 ga.
(in other than the four highest grades), add............. 20%
Automatic ejectors (grades No. 1, 2, 3, w/ejectors designated No. 1E, 2E, 3E), add.................................. $300
Selective single trigger, add............................ $350
Non-selective single trigger, add $275
Beavertail forend (Field No. 1 or 2), add................ $250
Beavertail forend (No. 3 or 4), add $275
Beavertail forend (No. 5, 7 or $2000 grade), add $350
Ventilated rib (No. 4, 5, 7 or $2000 grade), add.......... $350
Ventilated rib (lower grades), add $275

LSA-55 TURKEY GUN .... NiB $804 Ex $671 Gd $499
Over/under shotgun/rifle combination. Boxlock. Exposed hammer. Plain extractor. Single trigger. 12 ga./222 Rem. 24.5-inch ribbed bbls. (rifle bbl. has muzzle brake). Weight: About 7 lbs. Folding leaf rear sight, bead front sight. Checkered Monte Carlo stock and forearm. Made 1970-77 by Oy Tikkakoski AB, Finland.

MAG-10 AUTOMATIC SHOTGUN
Gas-operated. 10 ga. 3.5-inch Magnum. Three round capacity. 32-inch plain (Standard Grade only) or vent-rib bbl. F choke. Weight: 11 lbs., plain bbl.; 11.5 lbs., vent rib. Standard grade has plain stock and forearm. Deluxe and Supreme Grades have checkering, semi-fancy and fancy wood respectively, and stud swivel. All have recoil pad. Deluxe and Supreme grades made 1974-1982. Standard Grade intro. in 1977. All grades disc. 1986.
Camo model .... NiB $767 Ex $623 Gd $439
Deluxe grade................. NiB $803 Ex $652 Gd $458
Roadblocker .... NiB $827 Ex $671 Gd $472
Standard grade, plain barrel ...... NiB $672 Ex $555 Gd $393
Standard grade,
ventilated rib................. NiB $713 Ex $579 Gd $409
Standard grade, w/tubes .... NiB $803 Ex $652 Gd $458
Supreme grade................ NiB $924 Ex $749 Gd $524

SHOTGUNS

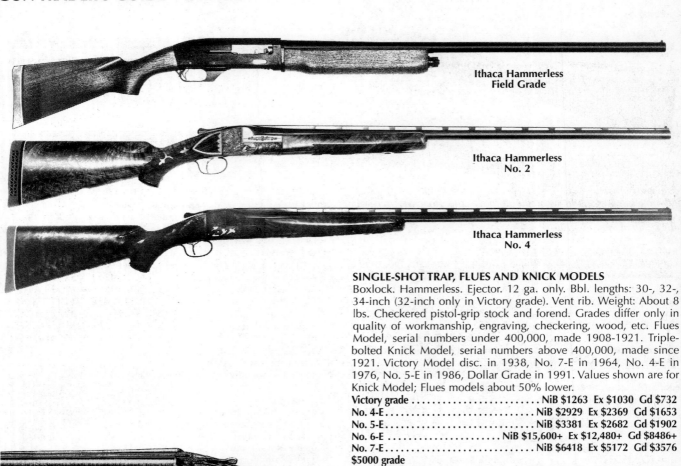

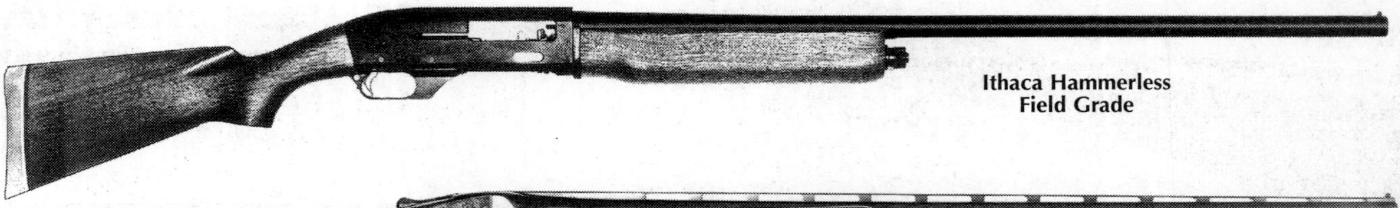

Ithaca Hammerless Field Grade

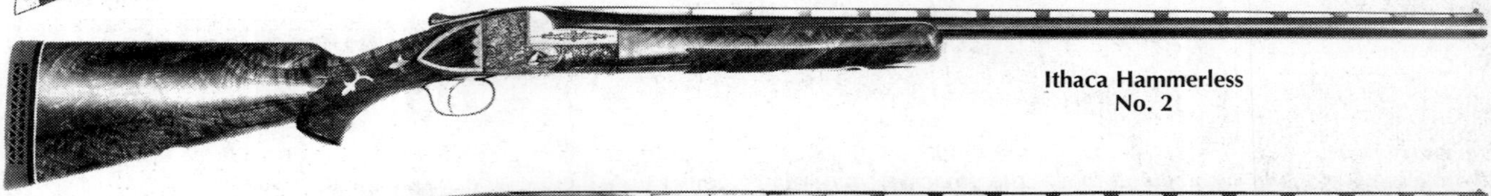

Ithaca Hammerless No. 2

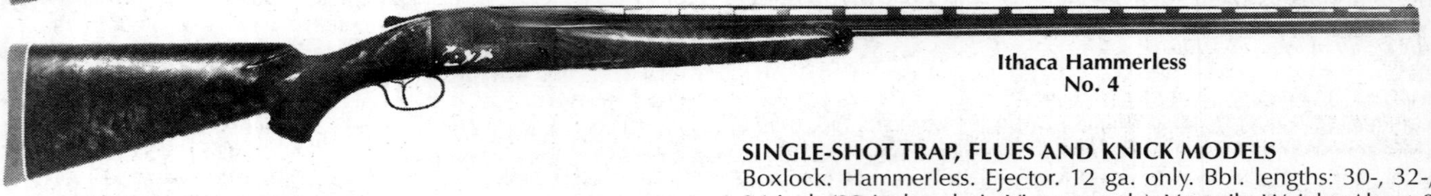

Ithaca Hammerless No. 4

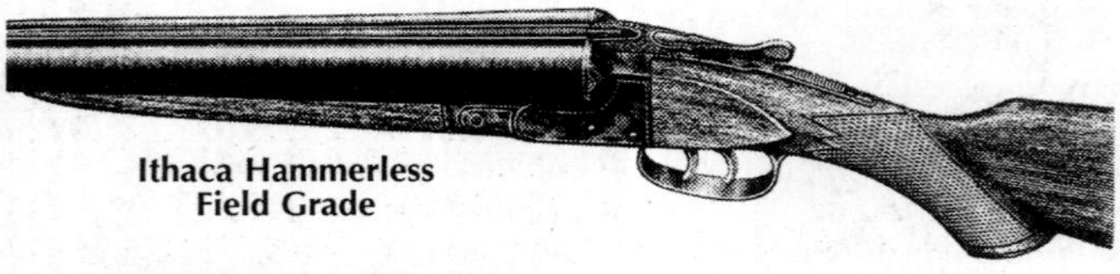

SINGLE-SHOT TRAP, FLUES AND KNICK MODELS
Boxlock. Hammerless. Ejector. 12 ga. only. Bbl. lengths: 30-, 32-, 34-inch (32-inch only in Victory grade). Vent rib. Weight: About 8 lbs. Checkered pistol-grip stock and forend. Grades differ only in quality of workmanship, engraving, checkering, wood, etc. Flues Model, serial numbers under 400,000, made 1908-1921. Triple-bolted Knick Model, serial numbers above 400,000, made since 1921. Victory Model disc. in 1938, No. 7-E in 1964, No. 4-E in 1976, No. 5-E in 1986, Dollar Grade in 1991. Values shown are for Knick Model; Flues models about 50% lower.
Victory grade .... NiB $1263 Ex $1030 Gd $732
No. 4-E .... NiB $2929 Ex $2369 Gd $1653
No. 5-E .... NiB $3381 Ex $2682 Gd $1902
No. 6-E .... NiB $15,600+ Ex $12,480+ Gd $8486+
No. 7-E .... NiB $6418 Ex $5172 Gd $3576
$5000 grade
(prewar $1000 grade) .... NiB $11,569 Ex $9269 Gd $6314
Sousa grade .... NiB $13,000+ Ex $10,400+ Gd $7072+

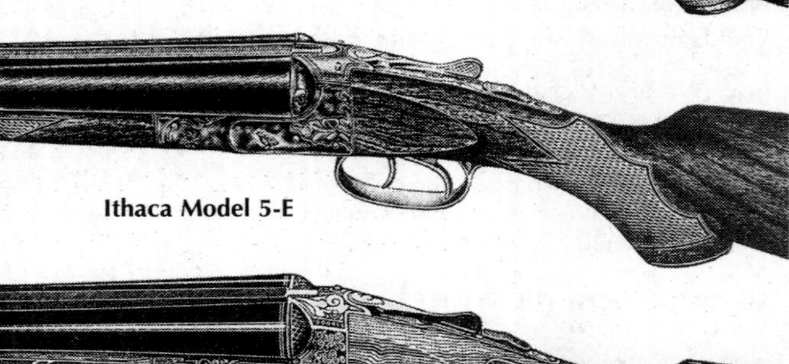

Ithaca Hammerless Field Grade

Ithaca Model 5-E

Ithaca Single-Shot Trap "Dollar Grade"

NOTE: *The following Ithaca-Perazzi shotguns were manufactured by Manifattura Armi Perazzi, Brescia, Italy. See also separate Perazzi listings.*

PERAZZI COMPETITION I SKEET........ NiB $3595 Ex $2905 Gd $2094
Boxlock. Auto ejectors. Single trigger. 12 ga. 26.75-inch vent-rib bbls. SK choke w/integral muzzle brake. Weight: About 7.75 lbs. Checkered skeet-style pistol-grip buttstock and forearm; recoil pad. Made from 1969-74.

PERAZZI COMPETITION TRAP I O/U .... NiB $3725 Ex $2905 Gd $2094
Boxlock. Auto ejectors. Single trigger. 12 ga. 30- or 32-inch vent-rib bbls. IM/F choke. Weight: About 8.5 lbs. Checkered pistol-grip stock, forearm; recoil pad. Made from 1969-74.

PERAZZI COMPETITION I
TRAP SINGLE BARREL................. NiB $2681 Ex $2173 Gd $1524
Boxlock. Auto ejection. 12 ga. 32- or 34-inch bbl., vent rib, F choke. Weight: 8.5 lbs. Checkered Monte Carlo stock and beavertail forearm, recoil pad. Made from 1973-78.

PERAZZI COMPETITION IV
TRAP GUN.......................... NiB $3263 Ex $2640 Gd $1843
Boxlock. Auto ejection. 12 ga. 32- or 34-inch bbl. With high, wide vent rib, four interchangeable choke tubes (Extra Full, F, IM, M). Weight: About 8.75 lbs. Checkered Monte Carlo stock and beavertail forearm, recoil pad. Fitted case. Made from 1977-78.

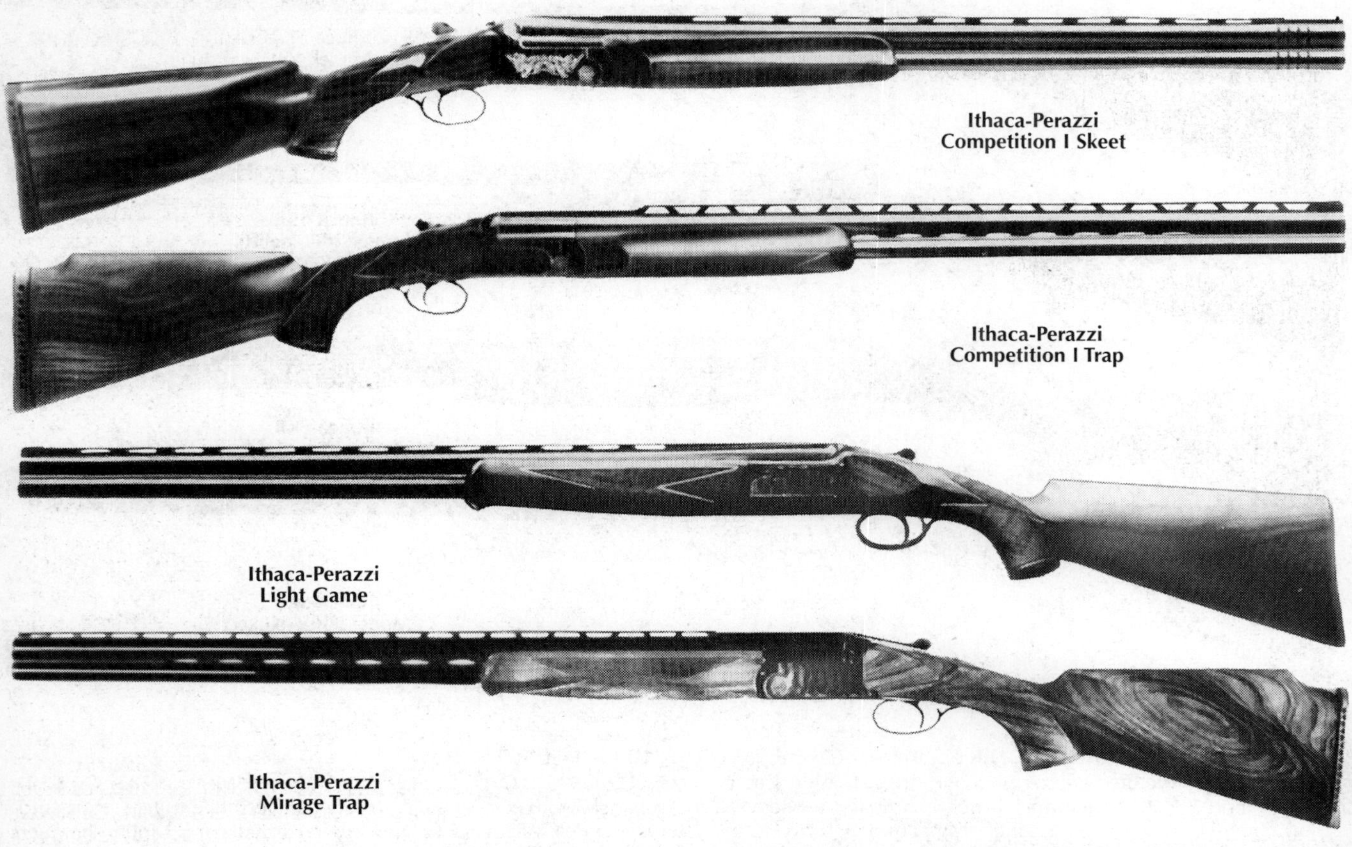

Ithaca-Perazzi Competition I Skeet

Ithaca-Perazzi Competition I Trap

Ithaca-Perazzi Light Game

Ithaca-Perazzi Mirage Trap

PERAZZI LIGHT GAME O/U FIELD .... NiB $4062 Ex $3272 Gd $2261
Boxlock. Auto ejectors. Single trigger. 12 ga. 27.5-inch vent rib bbls., M/F or IC/M choke. Weight: 6.75 lbs. Checkered field-style stock and forearm. Made from 1972-74.

PERAZZI MIRAGE LIVE BIRD . . NiB $4551 Ex $3662 Gd $2527
Same as Mirage Trap except has 28-inch bbls., M and Extra Full choke, special stock and forearm for live bird shooting. Weight: About 8 lbs. Made from 1973-78.

PERAZZI MIRAGE SKEET...... NiB $3857 Ex $3106 Gd $2146
Same as Mirage Trap except has 28-inch bbls. w/integral muzzle brakes, SK choke, skeet-stype stock and forearm. Weight: About 8 lbs. Made from 1973-78.

PERAZZI MIRAGE TRAP ...... NiB $3996 Ex $3158 Gd $2221
Same general specifications as MX-8 Trap except has tapered rib. Made from 1973-78.

PERAZZI MT-6 SKEET .... NiB $3996 Ex $3158 Gd $2182
Same as MT-6 Trap except has 28-inch bbls. w/two skeet choke tubes instead of Extra Full and F, skeet-style stock and forearm. Weight: About 8 lbs. Made from 1976-78.

PERAZZI MT-6 TRAP COMBO .... NiB $5031 Ex $4059 Gd $2794
MT-6 w/extra single under bbl. w/high-rise aluminum vent rib, 32- or 34-inch; seven interchanageable choke tubes (IC through Extra Full). Fitted case. Made from 1977-78.

PERAZZI MT-6 TRAP O/U .... NiB $3510 Ex $2829 Gd $1957
Boxlock. Auto selective ejectors. Non-selective single trigger. 12 ga. Barrels separated, wide vent rib, 30-or 32-inch, five interchangeable choke tubes (Extra full, F, IM, M, IC). Weight: About 8.5 lbs. Checkered pistol-grip stock/forearm, recoil pad. Fitted case. Made from 1976-78.

PERAZZI MX 8 TRAP COMBO .... NiB $5525 Ex $4447 Gd $3067
MX-8 w/extra single bbl., vent rib, 32- or 34-inch, F choke, forearm; two trigger groups included. Made from 1973-78.

PERAZZI MX-8 TRAP O/U .... NiB $4075 Ex $3284 Gd $2274
Boxlock. Auto selective ejectors. Non-selective single trigger. 12 ga. Bbls.: High vent rib; 30- or 32-inch, IM/F choke. Weight: 8.25 to 8.5 lbs. Checkered Monte Carlo stock and forearm, recoil pad. Made from 1969-78.

PERAZZI SINGLE-BARREL TRAP GUN .... NiB $2711 Ex $2185 Gd $1513
Boxlock. Auto ejection. 12 ga. 34-inch vent rib bbl., F choke. Weight: Abaout 8.5 lbs. Checkered pistol-grip stock, forearm; recoil pad. Made from 1971-72.

The following Ithaca-SKB shotguns, manufactured by SKB Arms Company, Tokyo, Japan, were distributed in the U.S. by Ithaca Gun Company from 1966-1976. See also listings under SKB.

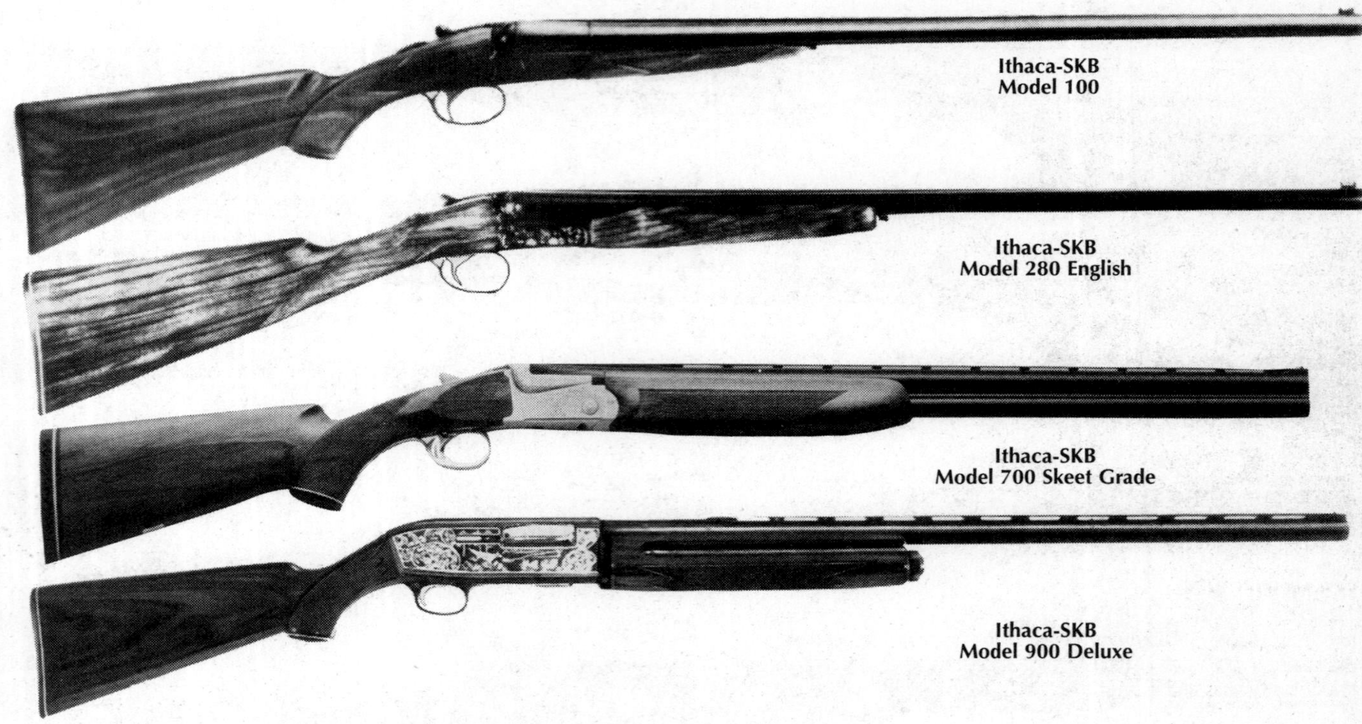

Ithaca-SKB Model 100

Ithaca-SKB Model 280 English

Ithaca-SKB Model 700 Skeet Grade

Ithaca-SKB Model 900 Deluxe

SKB MODEL 100 SIDE-BY-SIDE. . . . NiB $570 Ex $465 Gd $331
Boxlock. Plain extractors. Selective single trigger. Auto safety. Gauges: 12 and 20; 2.75-inch and 3-inch chambers respectively. Bbls.: 30-inch, F/F (12 ga. only); 28-inch, F/M; 26-inch, IC/M (12 ga. only); 25-inch, IC/M (20 ga. only). Weight: 12 ga., about 7 lbs.; 20 ga., about 6 lbs. Checkered stock and forend. Made from 1966-76.

SKB MODEL 150 FIELD GRADE . . . NiB $591 Ex $510 Gd $348
Same as Model 100 except has fancier scroll engraving, beavertail forearm. Made from 1972-74.

SKB 200E FIELD GRADE S/S . . . . . . NiB $834 Ex $677 Gd $475
Same as Model 100 except auto selective ejectors, engraved and silver-plated frame, gold-plated nameplate and trigger, beavertail forearm. Made from 1966-76.

SKB MODEL 200E SKEET GUN . . . . NiB $906 Ex $735 Gd $518
Same as Model 200E Field Grade except 26-inch (12 ga.) and 25-inch (20 ga./2.75-inch chambers) bbls., SK choke; nonautomatic safety and recoil pad. Made from 1966-76.

SKB MODEL 280 ENGLISH . . . . . . NiB $1063 Ex $865 Gd $611
Same as Model 200E except has scrolled game scene engraving on frame, English-style straight-grip stock; 30-inch bbls. not available; special quail gun in 20 ga. has 25-inch bbls., both bored IC. Made from 1971-76.

SKB MODEL 300 STANDARD AUTOMATIC SHOTGUN
Recoil-operated. Gauges: 12, 20 (3-inch). Five round capacity. Bbls.: plain or vent rib; 30-inch F choke (12 ga. only), 28-inch F or M, 26-inch IC. Weight: about 7 lbs. Checkered pistol-grip stock and forearm. Made from 1968-72.
W/plain barrel. . . . . NiB $337 Ex $275 Gd $197
W/ventilated rib . . . . NiB $375 Ex $307 Gd $218

SKB MODEL 500 FIELD GRADE O/U . . . . NiB $592 Ex $482 Gd $341
Boxlock. Auto selective ejectors. Selective single trigger. Non-automatic safety. Gauges: 12 and 20; 2.75-inch and 3-inch chambers respectively. Vent-rib bbls.: 30-inch M/F (12 ga. only); 28-inch M/F; 26-inch IC/M. Weight: 12 ga., about 7.5 lbs; 20 ga., about 6.5 lbs. Checkered stock and forearm. Made from 1966-76.

SKB MODEL 500 MAGNUM. . . . . . NiB $688 Ex $558 Gd $393
Same as Model 500 Field Grade except chambered for 3-inch 12 ga. shells, has 30-inch bbls., IM/F choke. Weight: About 8 lbs. Made from 1973-76.

SKB MODEL 600 DOUBLES GUN . . . . NiB $802 Ex $650 Gd $456
Same as Model 600 Trap Grade except specially choked for 21-yard first target, 30-yard second. Made from 1973-75.

SKB MODEL 600 FIELD GRADE . . . NiB $758 Ex $615 Gd $431
Same as Model 500 except has silver-plated frame, higher grade wood. Made from 1969-76.

SKB MODEL 600 MAGNUM. . . . . . NiB $786 Ex $637 Gd $447
Same as Model 600 Field Grade except chambered for 3-inch 12 ga. shells; has 30-inch bbls., IM/F choke. Weight: 8.5 lbs. Made from 1969-72.

SKB MODEL 600 SKEET GRADE
Same as Model 500 except also available in 28 and .410 ga., has silver-plated frame, higher grade wood, recoil pad, 26- or 28-inch bbls. (28-inch only in 28 and .410), SK choke. Weight: 7 to 7.75 lbs. depending on ga. and bbl. length. Made from 1966-76.
12 or 20 ga. NiB $926 Ex $792 Gd $599
28 or .410 ga. . . . . NiB $1022 Ex $860 Gd $652

SKB MODEL 600 SKEET SET . . . . NiB $2149 Ex $1734 Gd $1203
Model 600 Skeet Grade w/matched set of 20, 28 and .410 ga. bbls., 28-inch, fitted case. Made from 1970-76.

SKB MODEL 600
TRAP GRADE O/U . . . . NiB $738 Ex $598 Gd $420
Same as Model 500 except 12 ga. only, has silver-plated frame, 30- or 32-inch bbls. choked F/F or F/IM, choice of Monte Carlo or straight stock of higher grade wood, recoil pad. Weight: About 8 lbs. Made from 1966-76.

SKB MODEL 680 ENGLISH . . . . . . NiB $775 Ex $629 Gd $440
Same as Model 600 Field Grade except has intricate scroll engraving, English-style straight-grip stock and forearm of extra-fine walnut; 30-inch bbls. not available. Made from 1973-76.

SKB MODEL 700
SKEET COMBO SET . . . . NiB $3411 Ex $2751 Gd $1907
Model 700 Skeet Grade w/matched set of 20, 28 and .410 ga. bbls., 28-inch fitted case. Made from 1970-71.

SKB MODEL 700 SKEET GRADE . . NiB $1005 Ex $795 Gd $484
Same as Model 600 Skeet Grade except not available in 28 and .410 ga., has more elaborate scroll engraving, extra-wide rib, higher grade wood. Made from 1969-75.

SKB MODEL 700 TRAP GRADE. . . . NiB $968 Ex $785 Gd $550
Same as Model 600 Trap Grade except has more elaborate scroll engraving, extra-wide rib, higher grade wood. Made from 1969-75.

SKB MODEL 700
DOUBLES GUN . . . . NiB $1135 Ex $879 Gd $632
Same as Model 700 Trap Grade except choked for 21-yard first target, 30-yard second target. Made from 1973-75.

SKB MODEL 900
DELUXE AUTOMATIC . . . . NiB $450 Ex $368 Gd $263
Same as Model 30 except has game scene etched and gold-filled on receiver, vent rib standard. Made 1968-72.

SKB MODEL 900 SLUG GUN . . . . . NiB $410 Ex $336 Gd $242
Same as Model 900 Deluxe except has 24-inch plain bbl. w/slug boring, rifle sights. Weight: About 6.5 lbs. Made from 1970-72.

SKB CENTURY SINGLE-SHOT
TRAP GUN . . . . NiB $865 Ex $702 Gd $492
Boxlock. Auto ejector. 12 ga. Bbls.: 32- or 34-inch, vent rib, F choke. Weight: About 8 lbs. Checkered walnut stock w/pistol grip, straight or Monte Carlo comb, recoil pad, beavertail forearm. Made from 1973-74.

SKB CENTURY II . . . . NiB $793 Ex $643 Gd $452
Boxlock. Auto ejector. 12 ga. Bbls: 32- or 34-inch, vent rib, F choke. Weight: 8.25 lbs. Improved version of Century. Same general specifications except has higher comb on checkered stock stock, reverse-taper beavertail forearm w/redesigned locking iron. Made from 1975-76.

SKB MODEL XL300 STANDARD AUTOMATIC
Gas-operated. Gauges: 12, 20 (3-inch). Five round capacity. Bbls.: Plain or vent rib; 30-inch F choke (12 ga. only), 28-inch F or M, 26-inch IC. Weight: 6 to 7.5 lbs. depending on ga. and bbl. Checkered pistol-grip stock, forearm. Made from 1972-76.
W/plain barrel. . . . . NiB $314 Ex $258 Gd $185
W/ventilated rib . . . . NiB $340 Ex $278 Gd $200

SKB MODEL XL900
DELUXE AUTOMATIC . . . . NiB $392 Ex $320 Gd $228
Same as Model XL300 except has game scene finished in silver on receiver, vent rib standard. Made from 1972-76. See illustration previous page.

SKB MODEL XL
900 SKEET GRADE . . . . NiB $472 Ex $384 Gd $273
Gas-operated. Gauges: 12, 20 (3-inch). Five round tubular magazine. Same as Model XL900 Deluxe except has scrolled receiver finished in black chrome, 26-inch bbl. only, SK choke, skeet-style stock. Weight: 7 or 7.5 lbs. depending on ga. Made from 1972-76.

SKB MODEL XL
900 SLUG GUN . . . . NiB $420 Ex $343 Gd $245
Same as Model XL900 Deluxe except has 24-inch plain bbl. w/slug boring, rifle sights. Weight: 6.5 or 7 lbs. depending on ga. Made from 1972-76.

SKB MODEL
XL900 TRAP GRADE . . . . NiB $461 Ex $376 Gd $268
Same as Model XL900 Deluxe except 12 ga. only, has scrolled receiver finished in black chrome, 30-inch bbl. only, IM or F choke, trap style w/straight or Monte Carlo comb, recoil pad. Weight: About 7.75 lbs. Made from 1972-76.

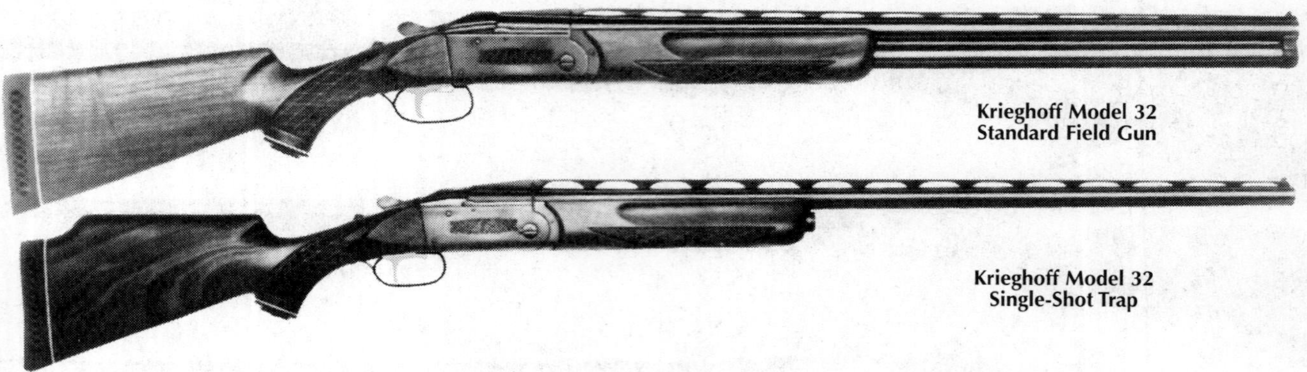

Krieghoff Model 32
Standard Field Gun

Krieghoff Model 32
Single-Shot Trap

IVER JOHNSON ARMS & CYCLE WORKS — Fitchburg, Massachusetts. Currently a division of the American Military Arms Corp., Jacksonville, Arkansas

CHAMPION GRADE SINGLE-SHOT HAMMER SHOTGUN

Auto ejector. Gauges: 12,16, 20, 28 and .410. Bbls.: 26- to 36-inch, F choke. Weight: 5.75 to 7.5 lbs. depending on ga. and bbl.length. Plain pistol-grip stock and forend. Extras include checkered stock and forend, pistol-grip cap and knob forend. Known as Model 36. Also made in a Semi-Octagon Breech, Top Matted and Jacketed Breech (extra heavy) models. Made in Champion Lightweight as Model 39 in gauges 24, 28, 32 and .410, .44 and .45 caliber, 12 and 14mm w/same extras. $200; add $100 in the smaller and obsolete gauges. Made from 1909-73.

Standard model . . . . NiB $206 Ex $169 Gd $121
Semi-octagon breech . . . . NiB $323 Ex $263 Gd $185
Top matted rib (disc. 1948) . . . . NiB $305 Ex $248 Gd $175

HERCULES GRADE HAMMERLESS DOUBLE

Boxlock. (Some made w/false sideplates.) Plain extractors and auto ejectors. Double or Miller single triggers (both selective or non-selective). Gauges: 12, 16, 20 and .410. Bbl. lengths: 26- to 32-inch, all chokes. Weight: 5.75 to 7.75 lbs. depending on ga. and bbl. length. Checkered stock and forend. Straight grip in .410 ga. w/both 2.5- and 3-inch chambers. Extras include Miller single trigger, Jostam Anti-Flinch recoil pad and Lyman ivory sights at extra cost. Disc. 1946.

W/double triggers, extractors . . . . . NiB $771 Ex $630 Gd $449
W/double triggers, auto. ejectors . . . . . NiB $915 Ex $744 Gd $527
W/non-selective single trigger, add $100
W/selective single trigger, add. $135
.410 ga., add $185

MATTED RIB SINGLE-SHOT HAMMER SHOTGUN IN SMALLER GAUGES. . . . . NiB $392 Ex $320 Gd $228

Same general specifications as Champion Grade except has solid matted top rib, checkered stock and forend. Weight: 6 to 6.75 lbs. Disc. 1948.

SILVER SHADOW O/U SHOTGUN

Boxlock. Plain extractors. Double triggers or non-selective single trigger. 12 ga., 3-inch chambers. Bbls.: 26-inch IC/M; 28-inch IC/M, 28-inch M/F; 30-inch both F choke; vent rib. Weight: w/28-inch bbls., 7.5 lbs. Checkered pistol-grip stock/forearm. Made by F. Marocchi, Brescia, Italy from 1973-78.

Model 412 w/double triggers . . . . . NiB $526 Ex $428 Gd $303
Model 422 w/single trigger . . . . . . NiB $650 Ex $527 Gd $371

SKEETER MODEL HAMMERLESS DOUBLE

Boxlock. Plain extractors or selective auto ejectors. Double triggers or Miller single trigger (selective or non-selective). Gauges: 12, 16, 20, 28 and .410. 26- or 28-inch bbls., skeet boring standard. Weight: About 7.5 lbs.; less in smaller gauges. Pistol- or straight-grip stock and beavertail forend, both checkered, of select fancy-figured black walnut. Extras include Miller single trigger, selective or non-selective, Jostam Anti-Flinch recoil pad and Lyman ivory rear sight at additional cost. Disc. 1942.

W/double triggers,
plain extractors . . . . NiB $1471 Ex $1192 Gd $834
W/double triggers,
automatic ejectors . . . . NiB $1785 Ex $1444 Gd $1007
W/non-selective
single trigger, add $150
W/selective single
trigger, add $200
20 ga., add 25%
28 ga., add 75%
.410 ga., add 90%

SPECIAL TRAP SINGLE-SHOT HAMMER SHOTGUN . . . . NiB $430 Ex $349 Gd $247

Auto ejector. 12 ga. only. 32-inch bbl. w/vent rib, F choke. Checkered pistol-grip stock and forend. Weight: about 7.5 lbs. Disc. 1942.

SUPER TRAP HAMMERLESS DOUBLE

Boxlock. Plain extractors. Double trigger or Miller single trigger (selective or non-selective), 12 ga. only, F choke 32-inch bbl., vent rib. Weight: 8.5 lbs. Checkered pistol-grip stock and beavertail forend, recoil pad, Disc. 1942.

W/double triggers . . . . NiB $1196 Ex $832 Gd $468
W/non-selective
single trigger, add $100
W/selective single trigger, add. $100

KBI INC. SHOTGUNS

See listings under Armscor, Baikal, Charles Daly, Fias, & Omega

KESSLER ARMS CORP. — Silver Creek, New York

LEVER-MATIC REPEATING SHOTGUN

. . . . . NiB $202 Ex $165 Gd $119

Lever action. Takedown. Gauges: 12, 16, 20; three-round magazine. Bbls.: 26-, 28-, 30-inch; F choke. Plain pistol-grip stock, recoil pad. Weight: 7 to 7.75 lbs. Disc. 1953.

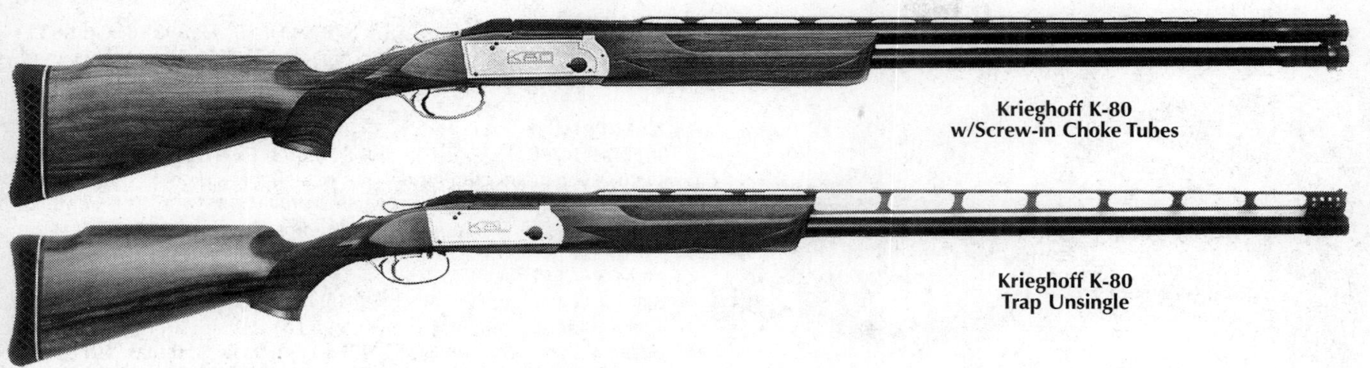

Krieghoff K-80
w/Screw-in Choke Tubes

Krieghoff K-80
Trap Unsingle

THREE SHOT BOLT-ACTION REPEATER . . NiB $117 Ex $97 Gd $73
Takedown. Gauges: 12, 16, 20. Two-round detachable box magazine. Bbls.: 28-inch in 12 and 16 ga.; 26-inch in 20 ga.; F choke. Weight: 6.25 to 7.25 lbs. depending on ga. and bbl. length. Plain one-piece pistol-grip stock recoil pad. Made from 1951-53.

H. KRIEGHOFF JAGD UND SPORTWAFFEN-FABRIK — Ulm (Donau), West Germany

MODEL 32 FOUR-BARREL SKEET SET
Over/under w/four sets of matched bbls.: 12, 20, 28 and .410 ga., in fitted case. Available in six grades that differ in quality of engraving and wood. Disc. 1979.
Standard grade . . . . NiB $11,524 Ex $9218 Gd $6269
München grade . . . . NiB $12,811 Ex $10,249 Gd $6969
San Remo grade. . . . . NiB $15,772 Ex $12,617 Gd $8580
Monte Carlo grade . . . . . . NiB $20,536 Ex $16,428 Gd $11,171
Crown grade. . . . . NiB $25,428 Ex $20,342 Gd $13,833
Super Crown grade. . . . . . NiB $27,681 Ex $22,145 Gd $15,059
Exhibition grade . . . . NiB $38,561 Ex $30,849 Gd $20,977

MODEL 32 STANDARD GRADE O/U
Similar to prewar Remington Model 23. Boxlock. Auto ejector. Single trigger. Gauges: 12, 20, 28, .410. Bbls.: Vent rib, 26.5- to 32-inch, any chokes. Weight: 12 ga. Field gun w/28-inch bbls., about 7.5 lbs. Checkered pistol-grip stock and forearm of select walnut; available in field, skeet and trap styles. Made from 1958-1981.
W/one set of bbls. . . . . NiB $3768 Ex $3043 Gd $2119
Low-rib two-bbl. trap combo . . NiB $4798 Ex $3870 Gd $2681
Vandalia (high-rib) two- bbl. trap combo . . NiB $5046 Ex $4079 Gd $2818

MODEL 32 STANDARD GRADE SINGLE-SHOT TRAP GUN . . . . NiB $1849 Ex $1490 Gd $1030
Same action as over/under. 12 ga. 32- or 34-inch bbl. w/high vent rib on bbl.; M, IM, or F choke. Checkered Monte Carlo buttstock w/thick cushioned recoil pad, beavertail forearm. Disc. 1979.

MODEL K-80
Refined and enhanced version of the Mdl. 32. Single selective mech. trig., adj. for position; release trigger optional. Fixed chokes or screw-in choke tubes. Interchangeable front bbl. Hangers to adjust point of impact. Quick-removable stock. Color casehardened or satin grey fin. rec.; alum. alloy rec. on lightweight models. Avail. in stand. plus 5 engraved grades. Made from 1980 to date. Standard grade shown except where noted.

SKEET MODELS
Skeet International . . . . NiB $6192 Ex $4981 Gd $3441
Skeet Special . . . . NiB $5300 Ex $4394 Gd $3031
Skeet standard model . . . . NiB $5220 Ex $4202 Gd $2901
Skeet w/choke tubes . . . . NiB $6252 Ex $5028 Gd $3464
SKEET SETS - Disc. 1999.
Standard grade 2-bbl. set. . . . . NiB $9731 Ex $7791 Gd $5309
Standard grade 4-bbl. set. . . NiB $13,279 Ex $10,623 Gd $7224
Bavaria grade 4-bbl. set . . NiB $18,926 Ex $15,141 Gd $10,296
Danube grade 4-bbl. set. . . . NiB $24,643 Ex $19,714 Gd $13,405
Gold Target grade 4-bbl. set. . . . NiB $28,969 Ex $23,175 Gd $15,759
SPORTING MODELS
Pigeon . . . . NiB $6811 Ex $5481 Gd $3779
Sporting Clays . . . . NiB $6854 Ex $5515 Gd $3802
TRAP MODELS
Trap Combo. . . . . NiB $9236 Ex $7435 Gd $5130
Trap Single. . . . . NiB $6535 Ex $5259 Gd $3628
Trap Standard . . . . NiB $6100 Ex $4917 Gd $3403
Trap Unsingle . . . . NiB $6810 Ex $5485 Gd $3790
RT models (removable trigger) add $1385

KRIEGHOFF MODEL KS-5 SINGLE-BARREL TRAP
Boxlock w/no sliding top-latch. Adjustable or optional release trigger. Gauge: 12; 2.75-inch chamber. Bbl.: 32-, 34-inch w/fixed choke or screw-in tubes. Weight: 8.5 lbs. Adjustable or Monte Carlo European walnut stock. Blued or nickel receiver. Made from 1980 to date. Redesigned and streamlined in 1993.
Standard model w/fixed chokes . . . NiB $3400 Ex $2742 Gd $1902
Standard model w/tubes . . . . . . NiB $3972 Ex $3200 Gd $2214
Special model w/adj. rib & stock
. . . . . NiB $4243 Ex $3420 Gd $2367
Special model w/adj. rib
& stock, choke tubes . . . . NiB $4840 Ex $3899 Gd $2696

TRUMPF DRILLING . . . . NiB $9502 Ex $8061 Gd $6217
Boxlock. Steel or Dural receiver. Split extractor or ejector for shotgun bbls. Double triggers. Gauges: 12, 16, 20; latter w/either 2.75- or 3-inch chambers. Calibers: .243, 6.5x57r5, 7x57r5, 7x65r5, .30-06; other calibers available. 25-inch bbls. w/solid rib, folding leaf rear sight, post or bead front sight; rifle bbl. soldered or free floating. Weight: 6.6 to 7.5 lbs. depending on type of receiver, ga. and caliber. Checkered pistol-grip stock w/cheekpiece and forearm of figured walnut, sling swivels. Made from 1953-2003.

NEPTUN DRILLING . . . . NiB $12,406 Ex $9946 Gd $6799
Same general specifications as Trumpf model except has sidelocks w/hunting scene engraving. Disc. 2003.

NEPTUN-PRIMUS DRILLING
. . . . . NiB $14,225 Ex $11,403 Gd $7794
Deluxe version of Neptun model; has detachable sidelocks, higher grade engraving and fancier wood. Disc. 2003.

SHOTGUNS

Krieghoff Neptun Drilling

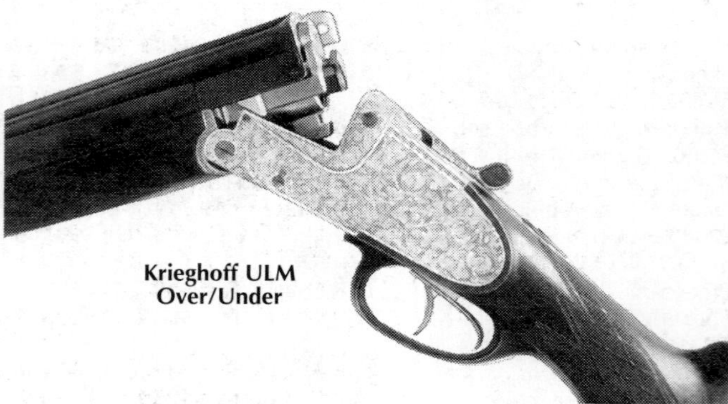
Krieghoff ULM Over/Under

TECK O/U RIFLE-SHOTGUN . . . . NiB $7049 Ex $5670 Gd $3907
Boxlock. Kersten dble. crossbolt system. Steel or Dural receiver. Split extractor or eject. for shotgun bbl. Single or double triggers. Gauges: 12, 16, 20; latter w/either 2.75- or 3-inch chamber. Cal: .22 Hornet, .222 Rem., .222 Rem. Mag., 7x57r5, 7x64, 7x65r5, .30-30, .300 Win. Mag., .30-06, .308, 9.3x74R. 25-inch bbls. With solid rib, folding leaf rear sight, post or bead front sight; over bbl. is shotgun, under bbl. rifle (later fixed or interchangeable; ext. rifle bbl., $175). Wt: 7.9-9.5 lbs. depending on type of rec. and caliber. Checkered pistol-grip stock w/cheekpiece and semi-beavertail forearm of fig. walnut, sling swivels. Made from 1967-2004. Note: This comb. gun is similar in appearance to the same model shotgun.

TECK O/U SHOTGUN . . . . NiB $6604 Ex $5315 Gd $3665
Boxlock. Kersten double crossbolt system. Auto ejector. Single or double triggers. Gauges: 12, 16, 20; latter w/either 2.75- or 3-inch chambers. 28-inch vent-rib bbl., M/F choke. Weight: About 7 lbs. Checkered walnut pistol-grip stock and forearm. Made from 1967-89.

ULM O/U RIFLE-SHOTGUN . . . . NiB $16,416 Ex $14,162 Gd $11,279
Same general specifications as Teck model except has sidelocks w/leaf Arabesque engraving. Made from 1963-2004. Note: This combination gun is similar in appearance to the same model shotgun.

ULM O/U SHOTGUN . . . . . NiB $12,225 Ex $10,192 Gd $7590
Same general specifications as Teck model except has sidelocks w/leaf Arabesque engraving. Made from 1958-2004.

ULM-P LIVE PIGEON GUN
Sidelock. Gauge: 12. 28- and 30-inch bbls. Chokes: F/IM. Weight: 8 lbs. Oil-finished, fancy English walnut stock w/semi-beavertail forearm. Light scrollwork engraving. Tapered, vent rib. Made from 1983-2004.
Bavaria . . . . NiB $18,154 Ex $14,935 Gd $10,815
Standard . . . . NiB $14,099 Ex $11,690 Gd $8609

ULM-PRIMUS O/U. . . . . NiB $11,619 Ex $9296 Gd $6321
Deluxe version of Ulm model; detachable sidelocks, higher grade engraving and fancier wood. Made from 1958-2004.

ULM-PRIMUS O/U RIFLE-SHOTGUN . . . . NiB $18,663 Ex $16,269 Gd $13,206
Deluxe version of Ulm model; has detachable sidelocks, higher grade engraving and fancier wood. Made 1963-2004. Note: This combination gun is similar in appearance to the same model shotgun.

ULM-S SKEET GUN
Sidelock. Gauge: 12. Bbl.: 28-inch. Chokes: Skeet/skeet. Other specifications similar to the Model ULM-P. Made from 1983-86.
Bavaria . . . . NiB $12,039 Ex $10,083 Gd $7780
Standard . . . . NiB $9979 Ex $8435 Gd $6459

ULM-P O/U LIVE TRAP GUN
Over/under sidelock. Gauge: 12. 30-inch bbl. Tapered vent rib. Chokes: IM/F; optional screw-in choke. Custom grade versions command a higher price. Disc. 1986.
Bavaria . . . . NiB $18,032 Ex $14,878 Gd $10,840
Standard . . . . NiB $14,299 Ex $11,890 Gd $8809

ULTRA O/U RIFLE-SHOTGUN
Deluxe Over/Under combination w/25-inch vent-rib bbls. Chambered 12 ga. only and various rifle calibers for lower bbl. Kickspanner design permits cocking w/thumb safety. Satin receiver. Weight: 6 lbs. Made from 1985-95 Disc.
Ultra O/U combination. . . . . . . NiB $5061 Ex $4393 Gd $3538
Ultra B w/selective front trigger . . . NiB $5319 Ex $4599 Gd $3677

LANBER SHOTGUNS — Spain

MODEL 82 O/U SHOTGUN . . . . . . NiB $570 Ex $467 Gd $335
Boxlock. Gauge: 12 or 20; 3-inch chambers. 26- or 28-inch vent-rib bbls. w/ejectors and fixed chokes. Weight: 7 lbs., 2 oz. Double or single-selective trigger. Engraved silvered receiver. Checkered European walnut stock and forearm. Imported 1994.

MODEL 87 DELUXE . . . . NiB $864 Ex $704 Gd $498
Over/Under; boxlock. Single selective trigger. 12 or 20 gauge w/3-inch chambers. Barrels: 26- or 28-inch w/choke tubes. Silvered engraved receiver. Imported 1994 only.

MODEL 97 SPORTING CLAYS . . . . NiB $897 Ex $729 Gd $515
Over/Under; boxlock. Single selective trigger. 12 ga. w/2.75-inch chambers. Bbls: 28-inch w/choke tubes. European walnut stock, forend. Engraved receiver. Imported 1994 only.

MODEL 844 MST MAGNUM O/U . . . . NiB $487 Ex $400 Gd $290
Field grade. Gauge: 12. 3-inch Mag. chambers. 30-inch flat vent-rib bbls. Chokes: M/F. Weight: 7 lbs., 7 oz. Single selective trigger. Blued bbls. and engraved receiver. European walnut stock w/hand-checkered pistol grip and forend. Imported from 1984-86.

MODEL 2004 LCH O/U . . . . NiB $657 Ex $534 Gd $378
Field grade. Gauge: 12. 2.75-inch chambers. 28-inch flat vent-rib bbls. 5 interchangeable choke tubes: Cyl, IC, M, IM, F. Weight: About 7 lbs. Single selective trigger. Engraved silver receiver w/fine-line scroll. Walnut stock w/checkered pistol-grip and forend. Rubber recoil pad. Imported from 1984-86.

MODEL 2004 LCH O/U SKEET . . . . NiB $814 Ex $661 Gd $465
Same as Model 2004 LCH except 28-inch bbls. w/5 interchangeable choke tubes. Imported from 1984-86.

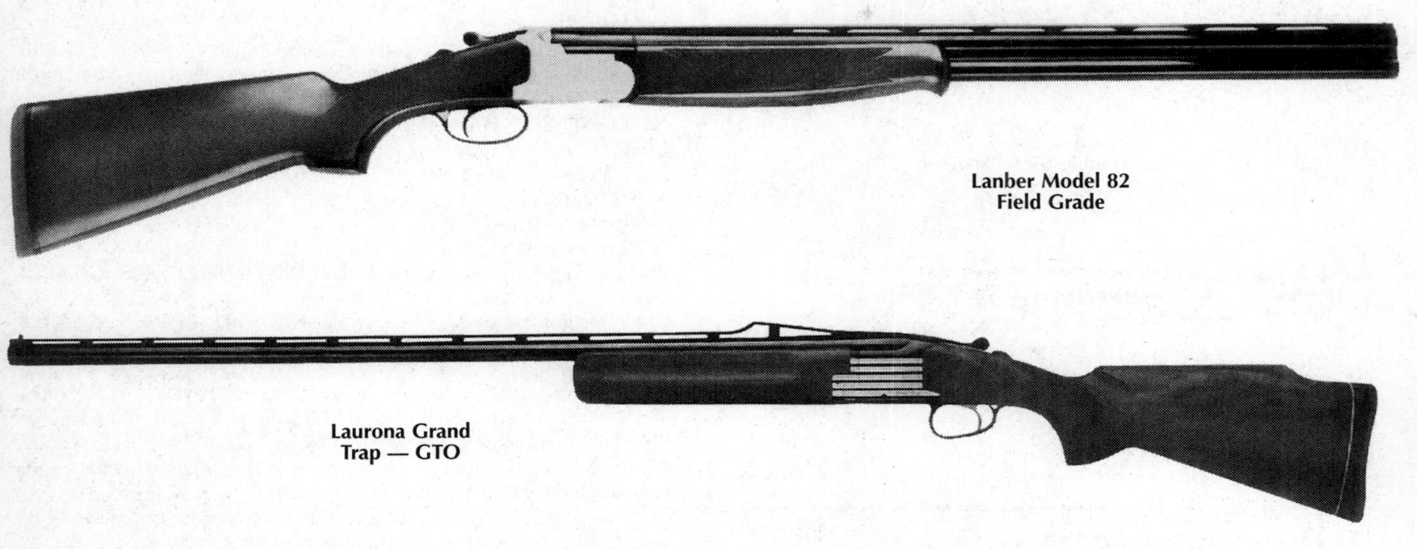

Lanber Model 82 Field Grade

Laurona Grand Trap — GTO

MODEL 2004
LCH O/U TRAP . . . . NiB $795 Ex $644 Gd $452
Gauge: 12. 30-inch vent-rib bbls. Three interchangeable choke tubes: M, IM, F. Manual safety. Other specifications same as Model 2004 LCH O/U. Imported from 1984-86.

CHARLES LANCASTER — London, England

"TWELVE-TWENTY" DOUBLE-BARREL
SHOTGUN . . . . NiB $15,313 Ex $12,250 Gd $8330
Sidelock, self-opener. Gauge: 12. Bbls.: 24 to 30 inches standard. Weight: About 5.75 lbs. Elaborate metal engraving. Highest quality English or French walnut buttstock and forearm. Imported by Stoeger in the 1950s.

JOSEPH LANG & SONS — London, England

HIGHEST QUALITY
O/U SHOTGUN. . . . . NiB $27,000 Ex $21,600 Gd $14,688
Sidelock. Gauges: 12, 16, 20, 28 and .410. Bbls.: 25 to 30 inches standard. Highest grade English or French walnut buttstock and forearm. Selective single trigger. Imported by Stoeger in 1950s.

LAURONA SHOTGUNS — Eibar, Spain

GRAND TRAP COMBO
Same general specifications as Model 300 except supplied w/29-inch over/under bbls., screw-in choke tubes and 34-inch single barrel. Disc. 1992.
Model GTO (top single). . . . . . . NiB $2380 Ex $1921 Gd $1335
Model GTU (bottom single) . . . NiB $2516 Ex $2030 Gd $1409
Extra Field O/U bbls.
(12 or 20 ga.), ... NiB $911 Ex $742 Gd $525

SILHOUETTE 300 O/U
Boxlock. Single selective trigger. Selective automatic ejectors. Gauge: 12; 2.75-, 3- or 3.5-inch chambers. 28- or 29-inch vent-rib bbls. w/flush or knurled choke tubes. Weight: 7.75 to 8 lbs. Checkered pistol-grip European walnut stock and beavertail forend. Engraved receiver w/silvered finish and black chrome bbls. Made from 1988-92.
Model 300 Sporting Clays . . . . . . NiB $1382 Ex $1099 Gd $765
Model 300 Trap . . . . NiB $1382 Ex $1099 Gd $765
Model 300 Trap, single . . . . NiB $1382 Ex $1099 Gd $765
Model 300 Ultra-Magnum. . . . . . NiB $1434 Ex $1151 Gd $865

SUPER MODEL O/U SHOTGUNS
Boxlock. Single selective or twin single triggers. Selective automatic ejectors. Gauges: 12 or 20; 2.75- or 3-inch chambers. 26-, 28- or 29-inch vent-rib bbls. w/fixed chokes or screw-in choke tubes. Weight: 7 to 7.25 lbs. Checkered pistol-grip European walnut stock. Engraved receiver w/silvered finish and black chrome bbls. Made from 1985-89.
Model 82 Super Game (disc.) . . . . . NiB $726 Ex $592 Gd $420
Model 83 MG Super Game . . . . . . NiB $1139 Ex $934 Gd $671
Model 84 S Super Trap . . . . NiB $1462 Ex $1193 Gd $848
Model 85 MG Super Game . . . . . . NiB $1153 Ex $945 Gd $679
Model 85 MG 2-bbl. set . . . . . . NiB $2036 Ex $1625 Gd $1154
Model 85 MS Special Sporting (disc.). . . NiB $1421 Ex $1159 Gd $823
Model 85 MS Super Trap . . . . NiB $1392 Ex $1165 Gd $830
Model 85 MS Pigeon . . . . NiB $1469 Ex $1171 Gd $814
Model 85 S Super Skeet. . . . . NiB $1469 Ex $1198 Gd $851

LEBEAU-COURALLY SHOTGUNS — Belgium

BOXLOCK SIDE
BY-SIDE SHOTGUNS. . . . . . NiB $17,438 Ex $13,950 Gd $9486
Gauges: 12, 16, 20 and 28. 26- to 30-inch bbls. Weight: 6.5 lbs. average. Checkered, hand-rubbed, oil-finished, straight-grip stock of French walnut. Classic forend. Made from 1986-1988, and 1993.

SHOTGUNS

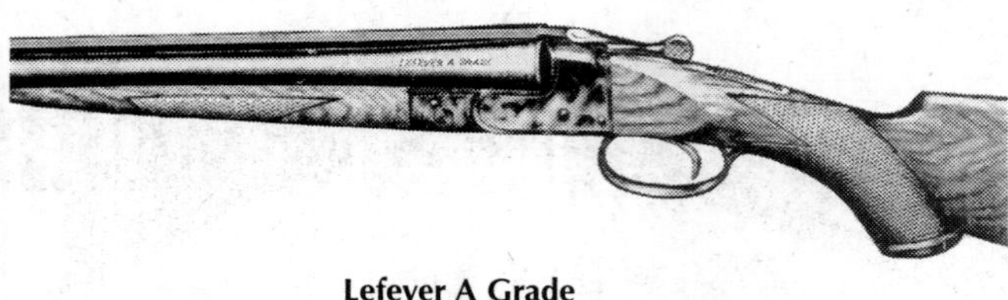

Lefever A Grade
Hammerless Double-Barrel Shotgun

LEFEVER ARMS COMPANY — Syracuse and Ithaca, N.Y.

Lefever sidelock hammerless double-barrel shotguns were made by Lefever Arms Company of Syracuse, New York from about 1885-1915 (serial numbers 1 to 70,000) when the firm was sold to Ithaca Gun Company of Ithaca, New York. Production of these models was continued at the Ithaca plant until 1919 (serial numbers 70,001 to 72,000). Grades listed are those that appear in the last catalog of the Lefever Gun Company, Syracuse. In 1921, Ithaca introduced the boxlock Lefever Nitro Special double, followed in 1934 by the Lefever Grade A; there also were two single-barrel Lefevers made from 1927-42. Manufacture of Lefever brand shotguns was disc. in 1948. Note: "New Lefever" boxlock shotguns made circa 1904-06 by D. M. Lefever Company, Bowling Green, Ohio, are included in a separate listing.

GRADE HAMMERLESS DOUBLE-BARREL SHOTGUN

Boxlock. Plain extractors or auto ejector. Single or double triggers. Gauges: 12, 16, 20, .410. Bbls.: 26-32 inches, standard chokes. Weight: About 7 lbs. in 12 ga. Checkered pistol-grip stock and forearm. Made from 1934-42.

W/plain extractors, double triggers. NiB $1072 Ex $870 Gd $612
W/automatic ejector, add $250
W/single trigger, add $100
W/Beavertail Forearm, add $75
16 ga., add 25%
20 ga., add 45%
.410 ga., add 200%

GRADE SKEET MODEL

Same as A Grade except standard features include auto ejector, single trigger, beavertail forearm; 26-inch bbls., skeet boring. Disc. 1942.

A Grade Skeet model, 12 ga. . . . . NiB $1284 Ex $1039 Gd $730
16 ga., add 45%
20 ga., add 90%
.410 ga., add 200%

HAMMERLESS SINGLE-SHOT TRAP GUN . . . . NiB $629 Ex $511 Gd $360

Boxlock. Ejector. 12 ga. only. 30- or 32-inch bbl.; vent rib. Weight: About 8 lbs. Checkered pistol-grip stock and forend, recoil pad. Made from 1927-42.

LONG RANGE HAMMERLESS SINGLE-BARREL FIELD GUN . . . . . NiB $349 Ex $317 Gd $225

Boxlock. Plain extractor. Gauges: 12, 16, 20, .410. Bbl. lengths: 26-32 inches. Weight: 5.5 to 7 lbs. depending on ga. and bbl. length. Checkered pistol-grip stock and forend. Made from 1927-42.

NITRO SPECIAL HAMMERLESS DOUBLE

Boxlock. Plain extractors. Single or double triggers. Gauges: 12, 16, 20, .410. Bbls.: 26- to 32-inch, standard chokes. Weight: about 7 lbs. in 12 ga. Checkered pistol-grip stock and forend. Made from 1921-48.

Nitro Special W/ double triggers . . . . NiB $578 Ex $449 Gd $284
Nitro Special W/ single trigger . . . . NiB $682 Ex $553 Gd $388
16 ga., add 25%
20 ga., add 50%
.410 ga., add 200%

SIDELOCK HAMMERLESS DOUBLES

Plain extractors or auto ejectors. Double triggers or selective single trigger. Gauges: 10, 12, 16, 20. Bbls.: 26-32 inches; standard choke combinations. Weight: 5.75 to 10.5 lbs. depending on ga. and bbl. length. Checkered walnut straight-grip or pistol-grip stock and forearm. Grades differ chiefly in quality of workmanship, engraving, wood, checkering, etc.; general specifications are the same. DS and DSE Grade guns lack the cocking indicators found on all other models. Suffix "E" means model has auto ejector; also standard on A, AA, Optimus, and Thousand Dollar Grade guns.

H grade . . . . NiB $1970 Ex $1592 Gd $1109
HE grade . . . . NiB $2593 Ex $2093 Gd $1452
G grade . . . . NiB $2295 Ex $1854 Gd $1290
GE grade . . . . NiB $3061 Ex $2469 Gd $1712
F grade. . . . . NiB $2060 Ex $1666 Gd $1161
FE grade. . . . . NiB $3116 Ex $2513 Gd $1741
E grade. . . . . NiB $2967 Ex $2394 Gd $1660
EE grade. . . . . NiB $4542 Ex $3659 Gd $2529
D grade . . . . NiB $3651 Ex $2942 Gd $2035
DE grade . . . . NiB $5666 Ex $4560 Gd $3146
DS grade . . . . NiB $1595 Ex $1288 Gd $895
DSE grade . . . . NiB $1964 Ex $1583 Gd $1096
C grade . . . . NiB $4994 Ex $4022 Gd $2779
CE grade . . . . NiB $9329 Ex $7510 Gd $5182
B grade . . . . NiB $5984 Ex $4815 Gd $3319
BE grade . . . . NiB $10,559 Ex $8447 Gd $5744
A grade. . . . . NiB $18,339 Ex $16,054 Gd $14,829
AA grade. . . . . NiB $27,170 Ex $21,736 Gd $14,780
Optimus grade . . . . NiB $37,050 Ex $29,640 Gd $20,155
Thousand Dollar grade . . . NiB $55,250 Ex $44,200 Gd $30,056
W/single trigger, add 10%
10 ga., add 15%
16 ga., add 45%
20 ga., add 90%

D. M. LEFEVER COMPANY — Bowling Green, Ohio

In 1901, D. M. "Uncle Dan" Lefever, founder of the Lefever Arms Company, withdrew from that firm to organize D. M. Lefever, Sons & Company (later D. M. Lefever Company) to manufacture the "New Lefever" boxlock double- and single-barrel shotguns. These were produced at Bowling Green, Ohio, from about 1904-1906, when Dan Lefever died and the factory closed permanently.

HAMMERLESS DOUBLE-BARREL SHOTGUNS
"New Lefever." Boxlock. Auto ejector standard on all grades except O Excelsior, which was regularly supplied w/plain extractors (auto ejector offered as an extra). Double triggers or selective single trigger (latter standard on Uncle Dan Grade, extra on all others). Gauges: 12, 16, 20. Bbls.: Any length and choke combination. Weight: 5.5 to 8 lbs. depending on ga. and bbl. length. Checkered walnut straight-grip or pistol-grip stock and forearm. Grades differ chiefly in quality of workmanship, engraving, wood, checkering, etc. General specifications are the same.

O Excelsior grade
w/plain extractors . . . . NiB $3449 Ex $2785 Gd $1936
O Excelsior grade
w/automatic ejectors. . . . . NiB $3897 Ex $3144 Gd $2181
No. 9, F grade . . . . NiB $4828 Ex $3893 Gd $2697
No. 8, E grade . . . . NiB $5703 Ex $4597 Gd $3183
No. 7, D grade. . . . . NiB $5725 Ex $4935 Gd $3412
No. 6, C grade . . . . NiB $6951 Ex $5600 Gd $3881
No. 5, B grade . . . . NiB $9100 Ex $7398 Gd $5104
No. 4, AA grade. . . . . NiB $13,000 Ex $10,400 Gd $7072
Uncle Dan grade . . . . NiB $19,500 Ex $15,600 Gd $10,608
W/single trigger, add 10%
16 ga., add 45%
20 ga., add 15%

D. M. LEFEVER SINGLE-BARREL
TRAP GUN. . . . . NiB $6604 Ex $5305 Gd $3643
Boxlock. Auto ejector. 12 ga. only. Bbls.: 26- to 32 inches, F choke. Weight: 6.5 to 8 lbs. depending on bbl. length. Checkered walnut pistol-grip stock and forearm.

MAGTECH SHOTGUNS — San Antonio, Texas Mfd. By CBC in Brazil

MODEL 586.2 SLIDE-ACTION SHOTGUN
Gauge: 12; 3-inch chamber. 19-, 26- or 28-inch bbl.; fixed chokes or integral tubes. 46.5 inches overall. Weight: 8.5 lbs. Double-action slide bars. Brazilian hardwood stock. Polished blued finish. Imported 1992-1995.

Model 586.2 F
(28-inch bbl., fixed choke) . . . . NiB $249 Ex $204 Gd $147
Model 586.2 P
(19-inch plain bbl., cyl. bore) . . . . . NiB $249 Ex $204 Gd $147
Model 586.2 S
(24-inch bbl., rifle sights, cyl. bore) . . . NiB $255 Ex $210 Gd $151
Model 586.2 VR
(vent rib w/tubes) . . . . NiB $249 Ex $204 Gd $147

MARLIN FIREARMS CO. — North Haven (formerly New Haven), Conn.

MODEL 16 VISIBLE HAMMER SLIDE-ACTION REPEATER
Takedown. 16 ga. Five round tubular magazine. Bbls.: 26- or 28-inch, standard chokes. Weight: About 6.25 lbs. Pistol-grip stock, grooved slide handle; checkering on higher grades. Difference among grades is in quality of wood, engraving on Grades C and D. Made from 1904-10.

Grade A . . . . NiB $449 Ex $366 Gd $260
Grade B . . . . NiB $609 Ex $494 Gd $347
Grade C . . . . NiB $746 Ex $605 Gd $425
Grade D. NiB $1508 Ex $1221 Gd $854

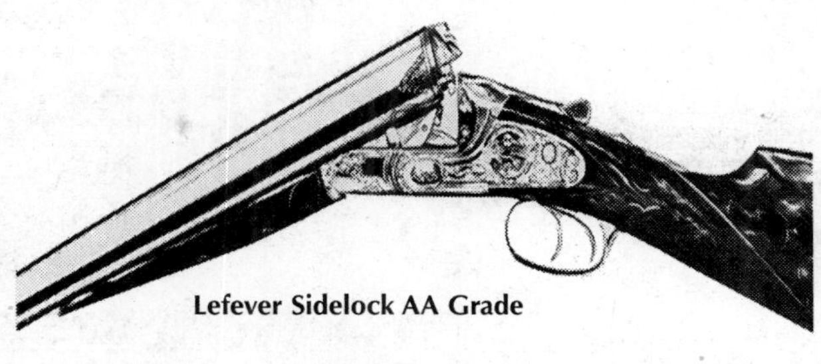
Lefever Sidelock AA Grade

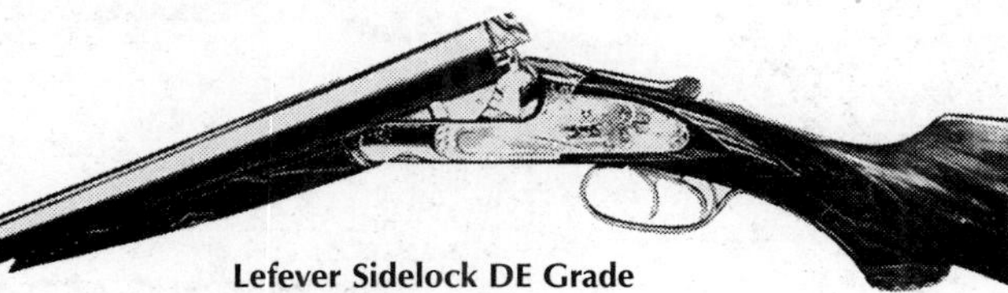
Lefever Sidelock DE Grade

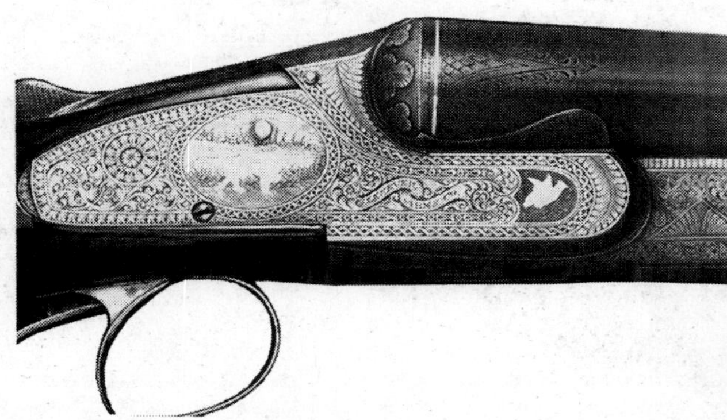

Lefever Sidelock Sideplate BE Grade

Lefever Sidelock Sideplate CE Grade

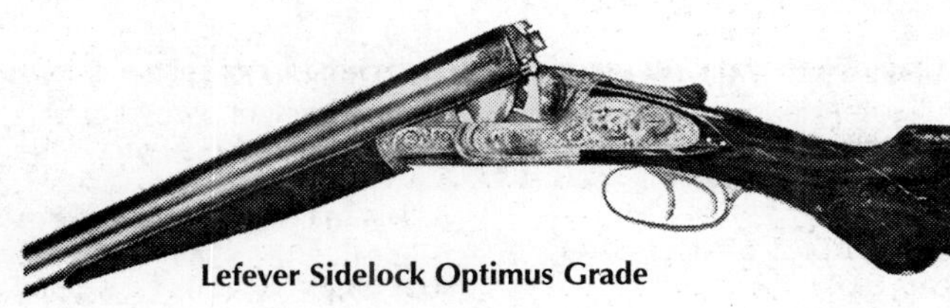
Lefever Sidelock Optimus Grade

SHOTGUNS

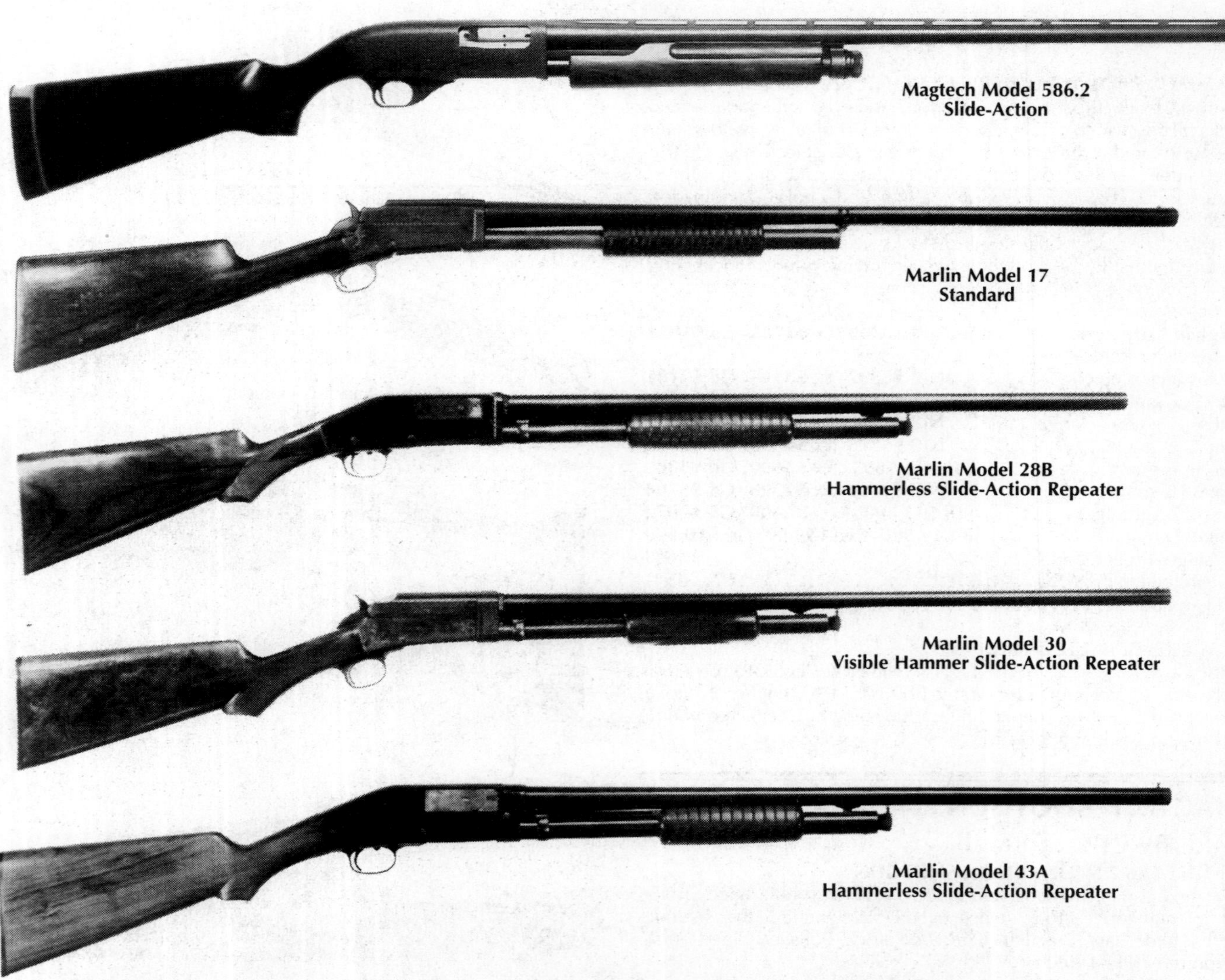

Magtech Model 586.2
Slide-Action

Marlin Model 17
Standard

Marlin Model 28B
Hammerless Slide-Action Repeater

Marlin Model 30
Visible Hammer Slide-Action Repeater

Marlin Model 43A
Hammerless Slide-Action Repeater

MODEL 17 BRUSH GUN . . . . NiB $408 Ex $327 Gd $235
Same as Model 17 Standard except has 26-inch bbl., cylinder bore. Weight: About 7 lbs. Made from 1906-08.

MODEL 17 RIOT GUN . . . . NiB $423 Ex $346 Gd $248
Same as Model 17 Standard except has 20-inch bbl., cylinder bore. Weight: About 6.88 lbs. Made from 1906-08.

MODEL 17 STANDARD VISIBLE HAMMER SLIDE-ACTION REPEATER . . . . NiB $408 Ex $327 Gd $235
Solid frame.12 ga. Five round tubular magazine. Bbls.: 30- or 32-inch, F choke. Weight: About 7.5 lbs. Straight-grip stock, grooved slide handle. Made from 1906-08.

MODEL 19 VISIBLE HAMMER SLIDE-ACTION REPEATER
Similar to Model 1898 but improved, lighter weight, w/two extractors, matted sighting groove on receiver top. Weight: About 7 lbs. Made from 1906-07.

Grade A . . . . NiB $404 Ex $332 Gd $239
Grade B . . . . NiB $677 Ex $551 Gd $391
Grade C . . . . NiB $742 Ex $594 Gd $419
Grade D . . . . NiB $1466 Ex $1187 Gd $830

MODEL 21 TRAP VISIBLE HAMMER SLIDE-ACTION REPEATER
Similar to Model 19 w/same general specifications except has straight-grip stock. Made from 1907-09.

Grade A . . . . NiB $410 Ex $329 Gd $237
Grade B . . . . NiB $569 Ex $464 Gd $330
Grade C . . . . NiB $712 Ex $578 Gd $408
Grade D . . . . NiB $1412 Ex $1146 Gd $803

MODEL 24 VISIBLE HAMMER SLIDE-ACTION REPEATER
Similar to Model 19 but has improved takedown system and auto recoil safety lock, solid matted rib on frame. Weight: About 7.5 lbs. Made from 1908-15.

Grade A . . . . NiB $377 Ex $311 Gd $226
Grade B . . . . NiB $596 Ex $486 Gd $344
Grade C . . . . NiB $742 Ex $602 Gd $423
Grade D. . . . . NiB $1527 Ex $1238 Gd $847

MODEL 26 BRUSH GUN . . . . NiB $336 Ex $275 Gd $197
Same as Model 26 Standard except has 26-inch bbl., cylinder bore. Weight: About 7 lbs. Made from 1909-15.

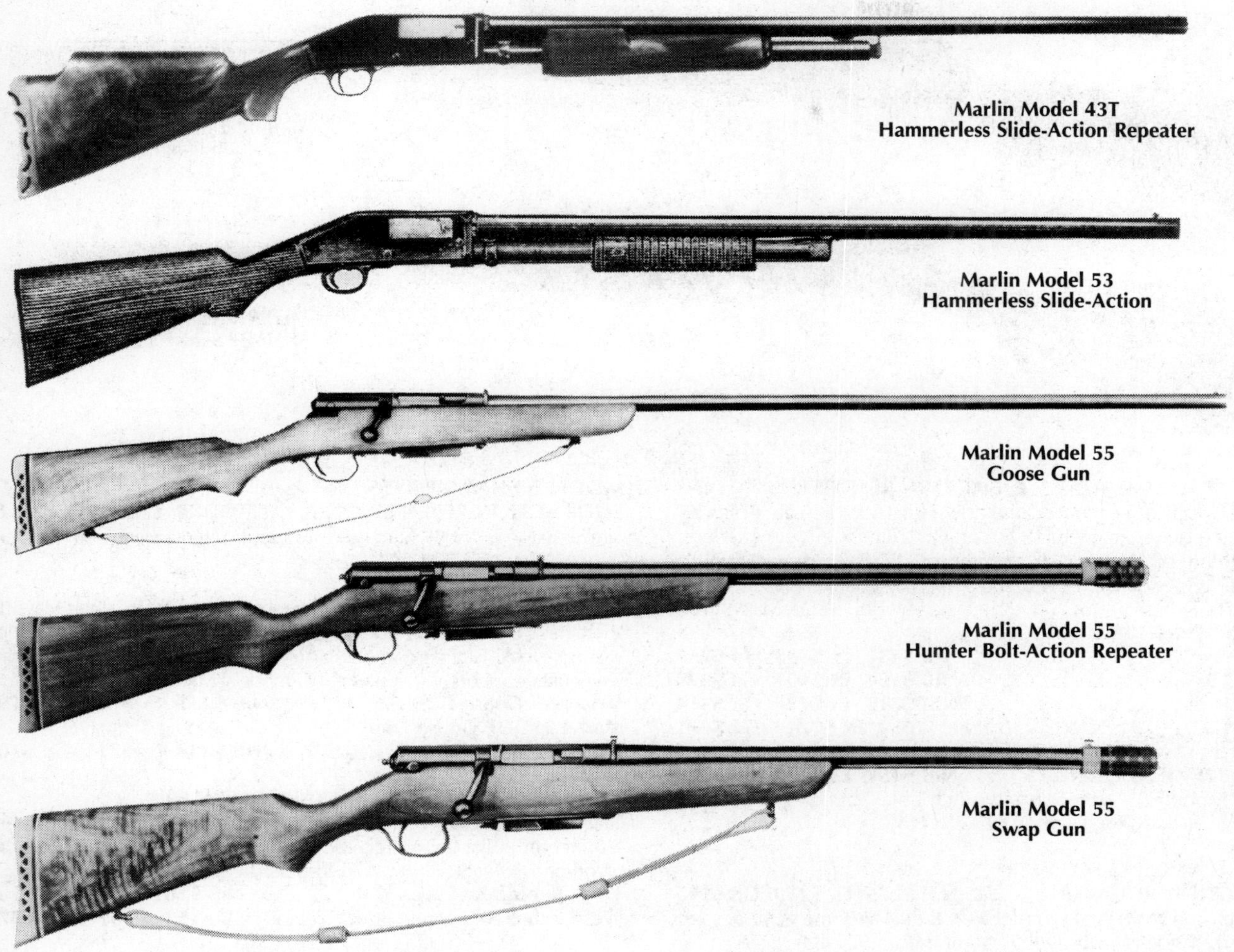

Marlin Model 43T
Hammerless Slide-Action Repeater

Marlin Model 53
Hammerless Slide-Action

Marlin Model 55
Goose Gun

Marlin Model 55
Humter Bolt-Action Repeater

Marlin Model 55
Swap Gun

MODEL 26 RIOT GUN . . . . NiB $302 Ex $248 Gd $179
Same as Model 26 Standard except has 20-inch bbl., cylinder bore. Weight: About 6.88 lbs. Made from 1909-15.

MODEL 26 STANDARD VISIBLE HAMMER SLIDE-ACTION REPEATER. . . . . NiB $316 Ex $258 Gd $186
Similar to Model 24 Grade A except solid frame and straight-grip stock. 30- or 32-inch full choke bbl. Weight: About 7.13 lbs. Made from 1909-15.

MODEL 28 HAMMERLESS SLIDE-ACTION REPEATER
Takedown. 12 ga. Five round tubular magazine. Bbls.: 26-, 28-, 30-, 32-inch, standard chokes; matted-top bbl. except on Model 28D, which has solid matted rib. Weight: About 8 lbs. Pistol-grip stock, grooved slide handle; checkering on higher grades. Grades differ in quality of wood, engraving on Models 28C and 28D. Made 1913-22; all but Model 28A disc. in 1915.

Model 28A . . . . NiB $370 Ex $301 Gd $215
Model 28B . . . . NiB $532 Ex $435 Gd $310
Model 28C . . . . NiB $684 Ex $558 Gd $396
Model 28D . . . . NiB $1406 Ex $1141 Gd $801

MODEL 28T TRAP GUN . . . . NiB $655 Ex $534 Gd $380
Same as Model 28 except has 30-inch matted-rib bbl., F choke, straight-grip stock w/high-fluted comb of fancy walnut, checkered. Made in 1915.

MODEL 28TS TRAP GUN . . . . NiB $480 Ex $393 Gd $282
Same as Model 28T except has matted-top bbl., plainer stock. Made in 1915.

MODEL 30 FIELD GUN . . . . NiB $373 Ex $305 Gd $220
Same as Model 30 Grade B except has 25-inch bbl., M choke, straight-grip stock. Made from 1913-14.

MODEL 30 VISIBLE HAMMER SLIDE-ACTION REPEATER
Similar to Model 16 but w/Model 24 improvements. Made from 1910-14. See illustration previous page.

Grade A . . . . NiB $406 Ex $332 Gd $238
Grade B . . . . NiB $608 Ex $495 Gd $349
Grade C . . . . NiB $776 Ex $630 Gd $444
Grade D . . . . NiB $1641 Ex $1329 Gd $929

MODELS 30A, 30B, 30C, 30D
Same as Model 30; designations were changed in 1915. Also available in 20 ga. w/25- or 28-inch bbl., matted-top bbl. on all grades. Suffixes "A," "B," "C" and "D" correspond to former grades. Made in 1915.

Model 30A . . . . NiB $479 Ex $394 Gd $284
Model 30B . . . . NiB $586 Ex $500 Gd $342
Model 30C . . . . NiB $850 Ex $689 Gd $486
Model 30D . . . . NiB $1452 Ex $1177 Gd $827

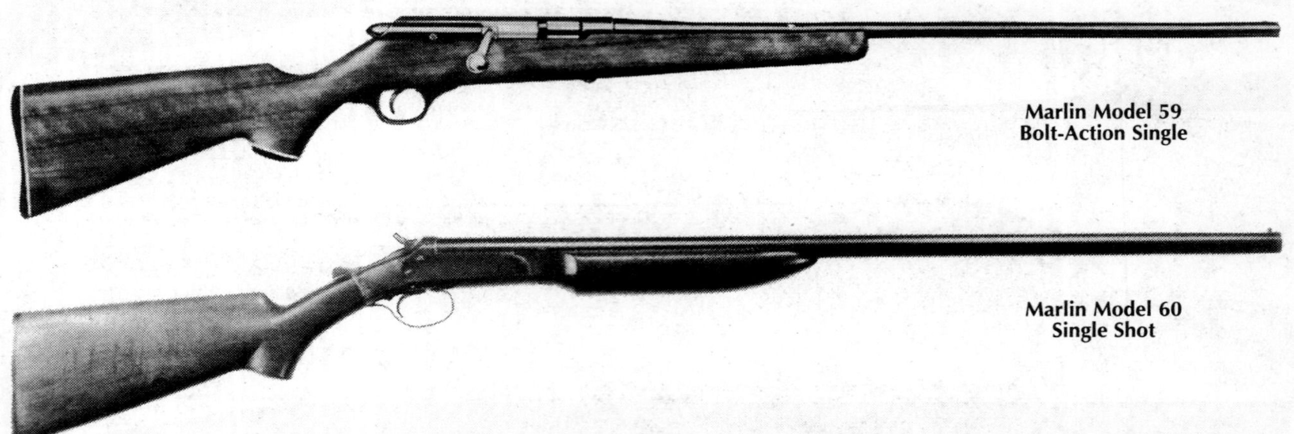

MODEL 31 HAMMERLESS SLIDE-ACTION REPEATER
Similar to Model 28 except scaled down for 16 and 20 ga. Bbls.: 25-inch (20 ga. only), 26-inch (16 ga. only), 28-inch, all w/matted top, standard chokes. Weight: 16 ga., about 6.75 lbs.; 20 ga., about 6 lbs. Pistol-grip stock, grooved slide handle; checkering on higher grades; straight-grip stock optional on Model 31D. Made from 1915-17; Model 31A until 1922.
Model 31A . . . . NiB $431 Ex $355 Gd $257
Model 31B . . . . NiB $564 Ex $461 Gd $329
Model 31C . . . . NiB $718 Ex $788 Gd $414
Model 31D . . . . NiB $1534 Ex $1244 Gd $871

MODEL 31F FIELD GUN. . . . . NiB $451 Ex $400 Gd $298
Same as Model 31B except has 25-inch bbl., M choke, straight- or pistol-grip stock. Made from 1915-17.

MODEL 42A VISIBLE HAMMER SLIDE-ACTION REPEATER. . . . . NiB $276 Ex $250 Gd $174
Similar to pre-World War I Model 24 Grade A w/same general specifications but not as high quality. Made from 1922-34.

MODEL 43 HAMMERLESS SLIDE-ACTION REPEATER
Similar to pre-World War I Models 28A, 28T and 28TS, w/same general specifications but not as high quality. Made from 1923-30.
Model 43A . . . . NiB $308 Ex $251 Gd $177
Model 43T . . . . NiB $613 Ex $499 Gd $354
Model 43TS . . . . NiB $647 Ex $526 Gd $372

MODEL 44 HAMMERLESS SLIDE-ACTION REPEATER
Similar to pre-World War I Model 31A w/same general specifications but not as high quality. 20 ga. only. Model 44A is a standard-grade field gun. Model 44S Special Grade has checkered stock and slide handle of fancy walnut. Made from 1923-35.
Model 44A . . . . NiB $417 Ex $343 Gd $247
Model 44S . . . . NiB $498 Ex $407 Gd $292

MODEL 49 VISIBLE HAMMER SLIDE-ACTION REPEATING SHOTGUN . . NiB $499 Ex $408 Gd $292
Economy version of Model 42A, offered as a bonus on the purchase of four shares of Marlin stock. About 3000 were made 1925-28.

MODEL 50DL BOLT ACTION SHOTGUN . . . . NiB $302 Ex $238 Gd $179
Gauge: 12 w/3-inch chamber. Two round magazine. 28-inch bbl. w/modified choke. 48.75 inches overall. Weight: 7.5 lbs. Checkered black synthetic stocks w/ventilated rubber recoil pad. Made 1997-99.

MODEL 53 HAMMERLESS SLIDE-ACTION REPEATER. . . . . . . NiB $388 Ex $317 Gd $225
Similar to Model 43A w/same general specifications. Made from 1929-30.

MODEL 55 GOOSE GUN
Same as Model 55 Hunter except chambered for 12-ga. 3-inch Magnum shell, has 36-inch bbl., F choke, swivels and sling. Weight: About 8 lbs. Walnut stock (standard model) or checkered black synthetic stock w/ventilated rubber recoil pad (GDL model). Made from 1962-96.
Model 55 Goose Gun . . . . NiB $251 Ex $207 Gd $150
Model 55GDL Goose Gun (intro. 1997) . . . . NiB $358 Ex $213 Gd $209

MODEL 55 HUNTER BOLT-ACTION REPEATER
Takedown. Gauges: 12, 16, 20. Two round clip magazine. 28-inch bbl. (26-inch in 20 ga.), F or adj. choke. Plain pistol-grip stock; 12 ga. has recoil pad. Weight: About 7.25 lbs.; 20 ga., 6.5 lbs. Made 1954-65.
W/plain bbl. NiB $101 Ex $84 Gd $63
W/adj. choke . . . . NiB $123 Ex $102 Gd $75

MODEL 55 SWAMP GUN. . . . . NiB $126 Ex $105 Gd $77
Same as Model 55 Hunter except chambered for 12-ga. 3-inch Magnum shell, has shorter 20.5-inch bbl. w/adj. choke, sling swivels and slightly better-quality stock. Weight: About 6.5 lbs. Made from 1963-65.

MODEL 55S SLUG GUN. . . . . NiB $168 Ex $138 Gd $101
Same as Model 55 Goose Gun except has 24-inch bbl., cylinder bore, rifle sights. Weight: About 7.5 lbs. Made from 1974-79.

MODEL 59 AUTO-SAFE BOLT-ACTION SINGLE . . . . NiB $129 Ex 108 Gd $80
Takedown. Auto thumb safety, .410 ga. 24-inch bbl., F choke. Weight: About 5 lbs. Plain pistol-grip stock. Made from 1959-61.

MODEL 60 SINGLE-SHOT SHOTGUN . . . . NiB $226 Ex $185 Gd $134
Visible hammer. Takedown. Boxlock. Automatic ejector. 12 ga. 30- or 32-inch bbl., F choke. Weight: About 6.5 lbs. Pistol-grip stock, beavertail forearm. Note: Only about 600 were produced in 1923.

MODEL 63 HAMMERLESS SLIDE-ACTION REPEATER
Similar to Models 43A and 43T w/same general specifications. Model 63TS Trap Special is same as Model 63T Trap Gun except stock style and dimensions to order. Made from 1931-35.
Model 63A . . . . NiB $365 Ex $299 Gd $213
Model 63T or 63TS . . . . NiB $459 Ex $374 Gd $265

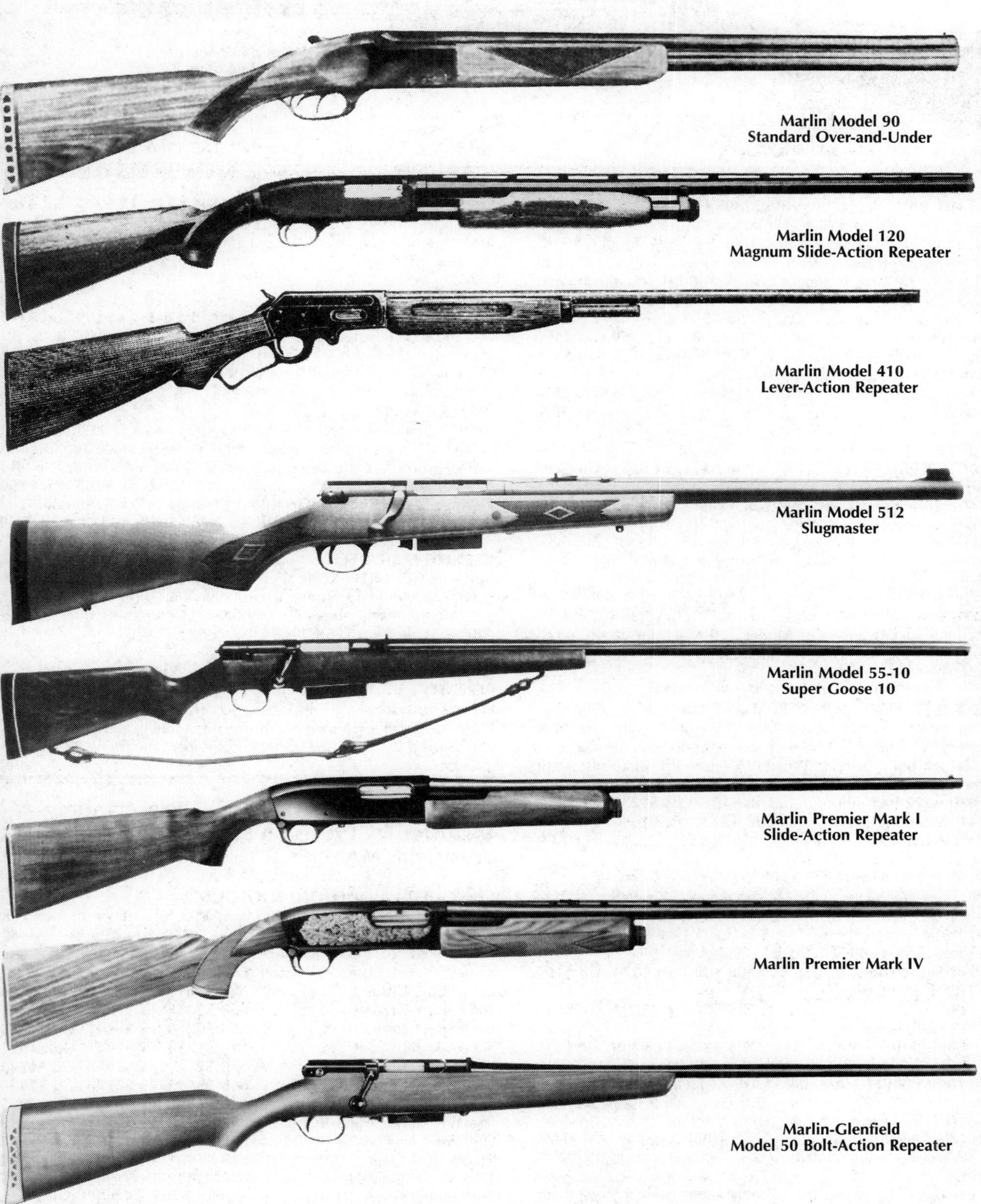

Marlin Model 90
Standard Over-and-Under

Marlin Model 120
Magnum Slide-Action Repeater

Marlin Model 410
Lever-Action Repeater

Marlin Model 512
Slugmaster

Marlin Model 55-10
Super Goose 10

Marlin Premier Mark I
Slide-Action Repeater

Marlin Premier Mark IV

Marlin-Glenfield
Model 50 Bolt-Action Repeater

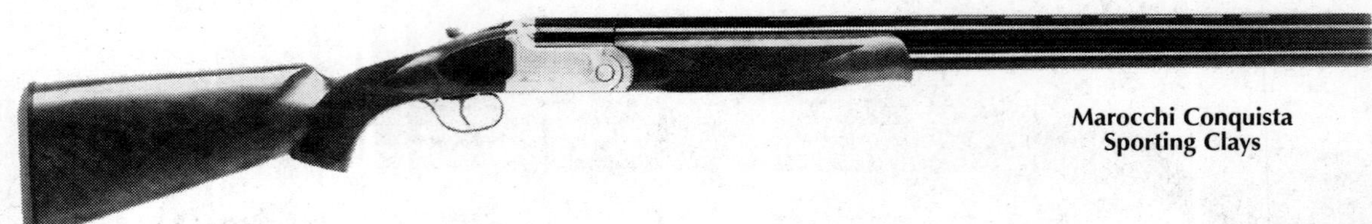

Marocchi Conquista
Sporting Clays

MODEL 90 STANDARD O/U SHOTGUN
Hammerless. Boxlock. Double triggers; non-selective single trigger was available as an extra on pre-war guns except .410. Gauges: 12, 16, 20, .410. Bbls.: Plain; 26-, 28- or 30-inch; chokes IC/M or M/F; bbl. design changed in 1949, eliminating full-length rib between bbls. Weight: 12 ga., about 7.5 lbs.; 16 and 20 ga., about 6.25 lbs. Checkered pistol-grip stock and forearm, recoil pad standard on prewar guns. Postwar production: Model 90-DT (double trigger), Model 90-ST (single trigger). Made from 1937-58.
W/double triggers .... NiB $558 Ex $462 Gd $340
W/single trigger .... NiB $680 Ex $559 Gd $406
Combination model............ NiB $803 Ex $659 Gd $475
16 ga., deduct 10%
20 ga., add 15%
.410, add 30%

MODEL 120 MAGNUM
SLIDE-ACTION REPEATER........ NiB $331 Ex $281 Gd $204
Hammerless. Takedown. 12 ga. (3-inch). Four round tubular magazine. Bbls.: 26-inch vent rib, IC; 28-inch vent rib M choke; 30-inch vent rib, F choke; 38-inch plain, F choke; 40-inch plain, F choke; 26-inch slug bbl. w/rifle sights, IC. Weight: About 7.75 lbs. Checkered pistol-grip stock and forearm, recoil pad. Made from 1971-85.

MODEL 120 SLUG GUN......... NiB $322 Ex $266 Gd $191
Same general specifications as Model 120 Magnum except w/20-inch bbl. and about .5 lb. lighter in weight. No vent rib. Adj. rear rifle sights; hooded front sight. Disc. 1990.

MODEL 410 LEVER-ACTION REPEATER
Action similar to that of Marlin Model 93 rifle. Visible hammer. Solid frame. .410 ga. (2.5-inch shell). Five round tubular magazine. 22- or 26-inch bbl., F choke. Weight: About 6 lbs. Plain pistol-grip stock and grooved beavertail forearm. Made from 1929-32.
Model 410 w/22-inch bbl...... NiB $1527 Ex $1238 Gd $857
Model 410 w/26-inch bbl...... NiB $2137 Ex $1050 Gd $742
Deluxe model, add................................ 30%

MODEL 512 SLUGMASTER SHOTGUN
Bolt-action repeater. Gauge: 12; 3-inch chamber, 2-round magazine. 21-inch rifled bbl. w/adj. open sight. Weight: 8 lbs. Walnut-finished birch stock (standard model) or checkered black synthetic stock w/ventilated rubber recoil pad (GDL model). Made from 1994-99.
Model 512 Slugmaster........... NiB $334 Ex $274 Gd $196
Model 512DL Slugmaster
(intro. 1998) .... NiB $360 Ex $295 Gd $211
Model 512P Slugmaster
w/ported bbl. (intro. 1999)....... NiB $368 Ex $300 Gd $215

MODEL 1898 VISIBLE HAMMER SLIDE-ACTION REPEATER
Takedown. 12 ga. Five shell tubular magazine. Bbls.: 26-, 28-, 30-, 32-inch; standard chokes. Weight: About 7.25 lbs. Pistol-grip stock, grooved slide handle; checkering on higher grades. Difference among grades is in quality of wood, engraving on Grades C and D. Made 1898-05. Note: This was the first Marlin shotgun.
Grade A (Field) .... NiB $390 Ex $313 Gd $237
Grade B .... NiB $624 Ex $543 Gd $344
Grade C .... NiB $966 Ex $795 Gd $589
Grade D..................... NiB $1915 Ex $1665 Gd $836

MODEL 55-10 SUPER GOOSE 10.. NiB $251 Ex $207 Gd $150
Similar to Model 55 Goose Gun except chambered for 10 ga. 3.5-inch Magnum shell, has 34-inch heavy bbl., F choke. Weight: About 10.5 lbs. Made from 1976-85.

PREMIER MARK I
SLIDE-ACTION REPEATER........ NiB $241 Ex $199 Gd $145
Hammerless. Takedown. 12 ga. Magazine holds 3 shells. Bbls.: 30-inch F choke, 28-inch M, 26-inch IC or SK choke. Weight: About 6 lbs. Plain pistol-grip stock and forearm. Made in France from 1960-63.

PREMIER MARK II AND IV
Same action and mechanism as Premier Mark except engraved receiver (Mark IV is more elaborate), checkered stock and forearm, fancier wood, vent rib and similar refinements. Made from 1960-63.
Premier Mark II .... NiB $321 Ex $263 Gd $190
Premier Mark IV (plain barrel) .... NiB $353 Ex $289 Gd $207
Premier Mark IV (vent rib barrel) .... NiB $410 Ex $335 Gd $239

GLENFIELD MODEL 50
BOLT-ACTION REPEATER .... NiB $97 Ex $80 Gd $59
Similar to Model 55 Hunter except chambered for 12-or 20-ga., 3-inch Magnum shell; has 28-inch bbl. in 12 ga., 26-inch in 20 ga., F choke. Made from 1966-74.

GLENFIELD 778 SLIDE-ACTION
REPEATER .... NiB $257 Ex $210 Gd $150
Hammerless. 12 ga. 2.75-inch or 3-inch. Four round tubular magazine. Bbls.: 26-inch IC, 28-inch M, 30-inch F, 38-inch MXR, 20-inch slug bbl. Weight: 7.75 lbs. Checkered pistol-grip. Made from 1979-84.

MAROCCHI SHOTGUNS — Brescia, Italy Imported by Precision Sales International of Westfield, MA

CONQUISTA MODEL O/U SHOTGUN
Boxlock. Gauge: 12; 2.75-inch chambers. 28-, 30- or 32-inch vent rib bbl. Fixed choke or internal tubes. 44.38 to 48 inches overall. Weight: 7.5 to 8.25 lbs. Adj. single-selective trigger. Checkered American walnut stock w/recoil pad. Imported since 1994.
Lady Sport Grade I .... NiB $2018 Ex $1635 Gd $1144
Lady Sport Grade II.......... NiB $2418 Ex $1948 Gd $1361
Lady Sport Grade III .... NiB $4270 Ex $3441 Gd $2385
Skeet Model Grade I .... NiB $1734 Ex $1421 Gd $1001
Skeet Model Grade II .... NiB $2169 Ex $1858 Gd $1233
Skeet Model Grade III........ NiB $3423 Ex $2770 Gd $1922
Sporting Clays Grade I .... NiB $1899 Ex $1557 Gd $1095
Sporting Clays Grade II....... NiB $2215 Ex $1591 Gd $1250
Sporting Clays Grade III ...... NiB $3383 Ex $2733 Gd $1892
Trap Model Grade I.......... NiB $1967 Ex $1592 Gd $1104
Trap Model Grade II .... NiB $2352 Ex $1906 Gd $1325
Trap Model Grade III......... NiB $3292 Ex $2907 Gd $2018
Left-handed model, add.................................. 10%

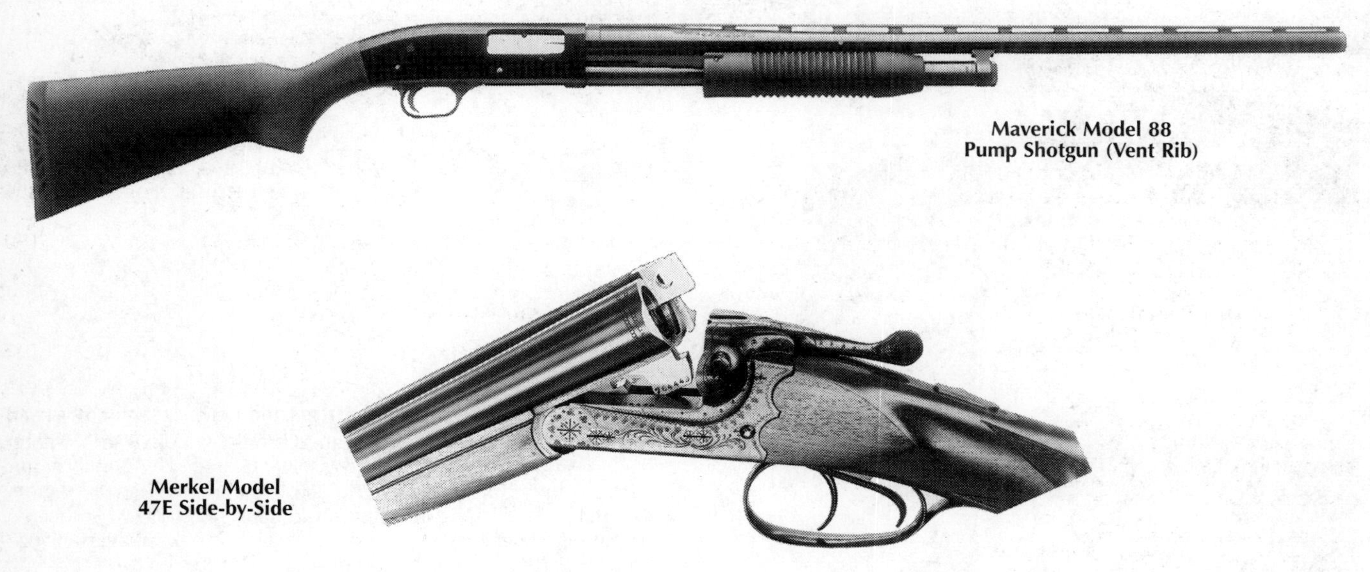

Maverick Model 88
Pump Shotgun (Vent Rib)

Merkel Model
47E Side-by-Side

MAVERICK ARMS, INC. — Eagle Pass, Texas

MODEL 88 BULLPUP . . . . NiB $325 Ex $267 Gd $194
Gauge: 12; 3-inch chamber. Bbl.: 18.5-inch w/fixed choke, blued. Weight: 9.5 lbs. Dual safeties: Grip style and crossbolt. Fixed sights in carrying handle. High-impact black synthetic stock; trigger-forward bullpup configuration w/twin pistol-grip design. Made from 1991-94.

MODEL 88 DEER GUN . . . . NiB $215 Ex $176 Gd $126
Crossbolt safety and dual slide bars. Cylinder bore choke. Gauge: 12 only w/3-inch chamber. Bbl.: 24-inch. Weight: 7 lbs. Synthetic stock and forearm.

MODEL 88 PUMP SHOTGUN
Gauge: 12; 2.75- or 3-inch chamber. Bbl.: 28 inches/M or 30 inches/F w/fixed choke or screw-in integral tubes; plain or vent rib, blued. Weight: 7.25 lbs. Bead front sight. Black synthetic or wood buttstock and forend; forend grooved. Made from 1989 to date.
Synthetic stock
w/plain bbl. NiB $193 Ex $159 Gd $115
Synthetic stock
w/vent-rib bbl.. . . . . NiB $213 Ex $174 Gd $125
Synthetic Combo
w/18.5 inch bbl. . . . . NiB $238 Ex $194 Gd $139
Wood stock
w/vent-rib bbl./tubes. . . . . NiB $231 Ex $189 Gd $135
Wood Combo w/vent-rib bbl./tubes . . . . NiB $270 Ex $220 Gd $157

MODEL 88 SECURITY . . . . NiB $202 Ex $165 Gd $119
Crossbolt safety and dual slide bars. Optional heat shield. Cylinder bore choke. Gauge: 12 only w/3-inch chamber. Bbl.: 18.5-inches. Weight: 6 lbs., 8 ozs. Synthetic stock and forearm. Made from 1993 to date.

MODEL 91 PUMP SHOTGUN
Same as Model 88, except w/2.75-, 3- or 3.5-inch chamber, 28-inch bbl. W/ACCU-F choke, crossbolt safety and synthetic stock only. Made from 1991-95.
Synthetic stock w/plain bbl. . . . . . . NiB $254 Ex $128 Gd $148
Synthetic stock w/vent-rib bbl. . . . . NiB $277 Ex $218 Gd $156

MODEL 95 BOLT-ACTION . . . . NiB $183 Ex $151 Gd $111
Modified, fixed choke. Built-in two round magazine. Gauge: 12 only. Bbl.: 25-inch. Weight: 6.75 lbs. Bead sight. Synthetic stock and rubber recoil pad. Made from 1995-1997.

GEBRÜDER MERKEL — Suhl, Germany Mfd. by Suhler Jagd-und Sportwaffen GmbH, *Imported by GSI, Inc., Trussville, AL, (Previously by Armes de Chasse)*

MODEL 8 HAMMERLESS DOUBLE. . NiB $1292 Ex $1051 Gd $742
Anson & Deeley boxlock action w/Greener double-bbl. hook lock. Double triggers. Extractors. Automatic safety. Gauges: 12, 16, 20; 2.75- or 3-inch chambers. 26-or 28-inch bbls. w/fixed standard chokes. Checkered European walnut stock, pistol-grip or English-style w/or w/o cheekpiece. Scroll-engraved receiver w/tinted marble finish.

SIDE-BY-SIDE MODEL 47E . . . . NiB $2483 Ex $2423 Gd $1678
Hammerless boxlock similar to Model 8 except w/automatic ejectors and cocking indicators. Double hook bolting. Single selective or double triggers. 12, 16 or 20 ga. w/2.75-inch chambers. Standard bbl lengths, choke combos. Hand-checkered European walnut stock, forearm; pistol-grip and cheekpiece or straight English style; sling swivels.

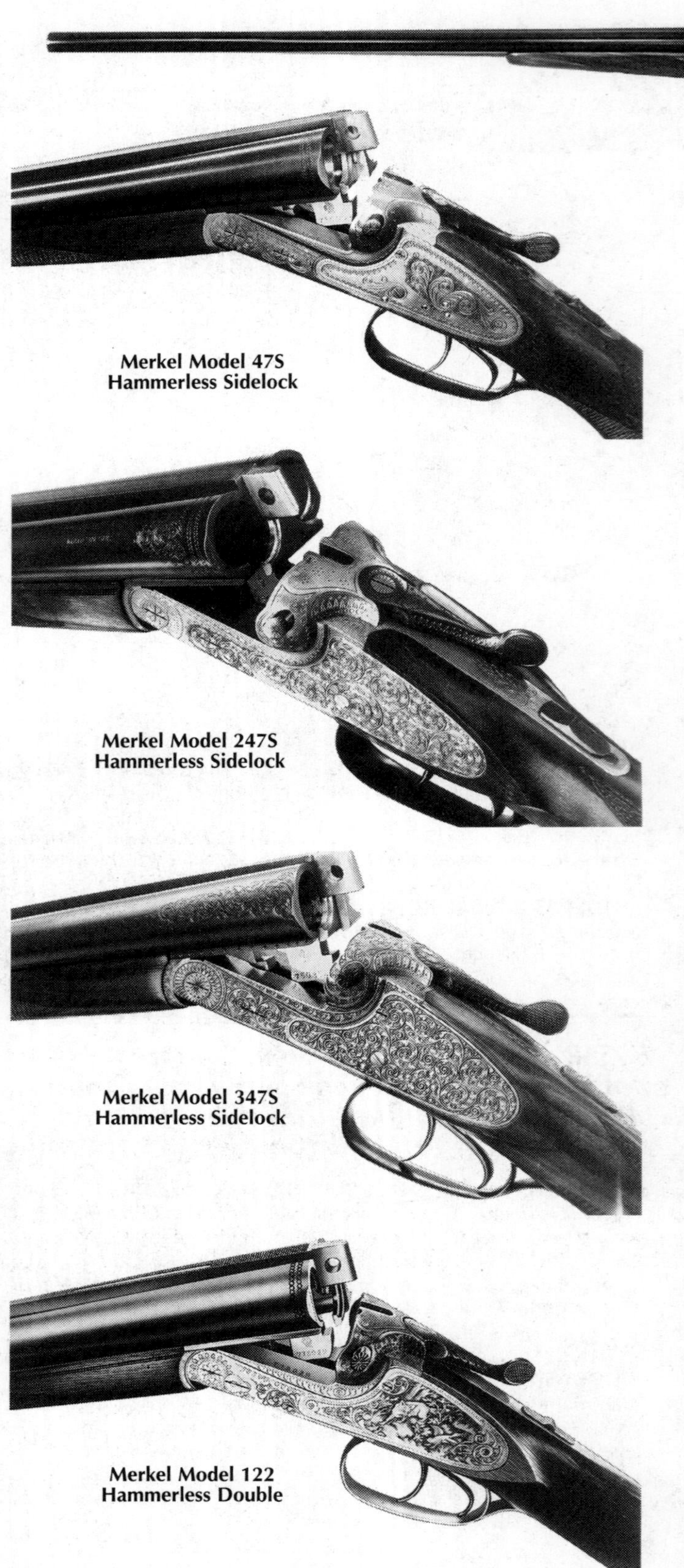

Merkel Model 47LSC
Sporting Clay

Merkel Model 47S
Hammerless Sidelock

Merkel Model 247S
Hammerless Sidelock

Merkel Model 347S
Hammerless Sidelock

Merkel Model 122
Hammerless Double

MODEL 47LSC
SPORTING CLAYS S/S . . . . . NiB $2952 Ex $2387 Gd $1664
Anson & Deeley boxlock action w/single-selective adj. trigger, cocking indicators and manual safety. Gauge: 12; 3-inch chambers. 28-inch bbls.w/Briley choke tubes and H&H-style ejectors. Weight: 7.25 lbs. Color case-hardened receiver w/Arabesque engraving. Checkered select-grade walnut stock, beavertail forearm. Imported from 1993-94.

MODELS 47SL, 147SL, 247SL, 347SL, 447SL
HAMMERLESS SIDELOCKS
Same general specifications as Model 147E except has sidelocks engraved w/Arabesques, borders, scrolls or game scenes in varying degrees of elaborateness.
Model 47SL . . . . NiB $5331 Ex $4263 Gd $2960
Model 147SL . . . . NiB $5834 Ex $4665 Gd $3233
Model 147SSL. . . . . NiB $6327 Ex $5111 Gd $3554
Model 247SL . . . . NiB $5795 Ex $4771 Gd $3323
Model 347SL . . . . NiB $6264 Ex $5060 Gd $3569
Model 447SL . . . . NiB $6753 Ex $5451 Gd $3785
28 ga. .410, add 20%

NOTE: Merkel over/under guns were often supplied with accessory barrels, interchangeable to convert the gun into an arm of another type; for example, a set might consist of one pair each of shotgun, rifle and combination gun barrels. Each pair of interchangeable barrels has a value of approximately one-third that of the gun with which they are supplied.

MODEL 100 O/U SHOTGUN
Hammerless. Boxlock. Greener crossbolt. Plain extractor. Double triggers. Gauges: 12, 16, 20. Made w/plain or ribbed bbls. in various lengths and chokes. Plain finish, no engraving. Checkered forend and stock w/pistol grip and cheekpiece or English-style. Made prior to WWII.
W/plain bbl. . . . . NiB $2018 Ex $1627 Gd $1128
W/ribbed bbl. . . . . NiB $2085 Ex $1681 Gd $1164

MODELS 101 AND 101E O/U
Same as Model 100 except ribbed bbl. standard, has separate extractors (ejectors on Model 101E), English engraving. Made prior to World War II.
Model 101 . . . . NiB $2145 Ex $1730 Gd $1210
Model 101E . . . . NiB $2303 Ex $1857 Gd $1285

MODEL 122
HAMMERLESS DOUBLE . . . . NiB $3916 Ex $3152 Gd $2174
Similar to the Model 147S except w/nonremovable sidelocks in gauges 12, 16 or 20. Imported since 1993.

MODEL 122E
HAMMERLESS SIDELOCK. . . . . NiB $4419 Ex $3570 Gd $2484
Similar to the Model 122 except w/removable sidelocks and cocking indicators. Importation disc. 1992.

MODEL 126E
HAMMERLESS SIDELOCK . . . . NiB $28,969 Ex $23,175 Gd $15,759
Holland & Holland system, hand-detachable locks. Auto ejectors. Double triggers. 12, 16 or 20 gauge w/standard bbl. lengths and chokes. Checkered forend and pistol-grip stock; available w/cheekpiece or English-style buttstock. Elaborate game scenes and engraving. Made prior to WW II.

MODEL 127E
HAMMERLESS SIDELOCK . . . . NiB $29,549 Ex $23,639 Gd $16,074
Similar to the Model 126E except w/elaborate scroll engraving on removable sidelocks w/cocking indicators. Made prior to WW II.

MODEL 128E
HAMMERLESS BOXLOCK DOUBLE. . . NiB $12,554 Ex $10,042 Gd $6829
Scalloped Anson & Deeley action w/hinged floorplate and removable sideplates. Auto-ejectors. Double triggers. Elaborate hunting scene or Arabesque engraving. 12, 16 or 20 gauge w/various bbl. lengths and chokes. Checkered forend and stock w/pistol grip and cheekpiece or English-style. Made prior to WW II.

MODEL 130
HAMMERLESS BOXLOCK DOUBLE. . . NiB $12,554 Ex $10,042 Gd $6829
Similar to Model 128E except w/fixed sideplates. Auto ejectors. Double triggers. Elaborate hunting scene or Arabesque engraving. Made prior to WW II.

MODESL 147 & 147E HAMMERLESS BOXLOCK DOUBLE-BARREL SHOTGUN
Anson & Deeley system w/extractors or auto ejectors. Single selective or double triggers. Gauges: 12, 16, 20 or 28 ga. (Three-inch chambers available in 12 and 20 ga.). Bbls.: 26-inch standard, other lengths available w/any standard choke combination. Weight: 6.5 lbs. Checkered straight-grip stock and forearm. Disc. 1998.
Model 147 w/extractors . . . . . . NiB $2731 Ex $2217 Gd $1560
Model 147E w/ejectors . . . . NiB $3188 Ex $2582 Gd $1808

MODELS 200, 200E, 201, 201E, 202 AND 202E O/U SHOTGUNS
Hammerless. Boxlock. Kersten double crossbolt. Scalloped frame. Sideplates on Models 202 and 202E. Arabesque or hunting engraving supplied on all except Models 200 and 200E. "E" models have ejectors, others have separate extractors, signal pins, double triggers. Gauges: 12, 16, 20, 24, 28, 32 (last three not available in postwar guns). Ribbed bbls. in various lengths and chokes. Weight: 5.75 to 7.5 lbs. depending on bbl. length and gauge. Checkered forend and stock w/pistol grip and cheekpiece or English-style. The 200, 201, and 202 differ in overall quality, engraving, wood, checkering, etc.; aside from the faux sideplates on Models 202 and 202E, general specifications are the same. Models 200, 201, 202, and 202E, all made before WW II, are disc. Models 201E &202E in production w/revised 2000 series nomenclature.
Model 200 . . . . NiB $2483 Ex $2034 Gd $1438
Model 200E . . . . NiB $3424 Ex $2781 Gd $1899
Model 200 ES Skeet . . . . NiB $4988 Ex $4036 Gd $2818
Model 200ET Trap . . . . NiB $4801 Ex $3886 Gd $2716
Model 200 SC Sporting Clays . . . . NiB $5381 Ex $4352 Gd $3035
Model 201 (disc.). NiB $2972 Ex $2417 Gd $1709
Model 201E (Pre-WW II) . . . . NiB $3393 Ex $2759 Gd $1946
Model 201E (Post-WW II) . . . . NiB $4754 Ex $3849 Gd $2693
Model 201 ES Skeet . . . . NiB $7474 Ex $6033 Gd $4189
Model 201 ET Trap. . . . . NiB $7416 Ex $5987 Gd $4157
Model 202 (disc.). NiB $3871 Ex $3138 Gd $2201
Model 202E (Pre-WW II) . . . . NiB $4534 Ex $3670 Gd $2566
Model 202 E (Post-WW II & 2002EL). . . . . NiB $7006 Ex $5732 Gd $3944

Merkel Model 147E
Hammerless Boxlock Double-Barrel Shotgun

Merkel Model 200E
O/U Shotgun

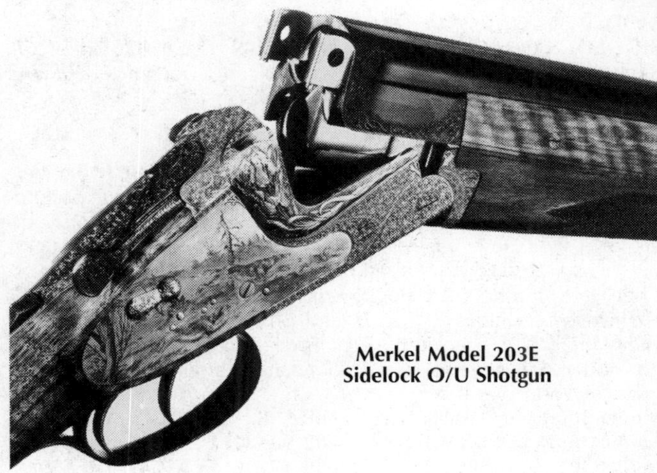

Merkel Model 203E
Sidelock O/U Shotgun

SHOTGUNS

Merkel Model 303E O/U Shotgun

MODEL 203E SIDELOCK O/U SHOTGUNS
Hammerless action w/hand-detachable sidelocks. Kersten double cross bolt, auto ejectors and double triggers. Gauges: 12 or 20 (16, 24, 28 and 32 disc.). 26.75- or 28-inch vent rib bbls. Arabesque engraving standard or hunting engraving optional on coin-finished receiver. Checkered English or pistol-grip stock and forend. See illustration previous page.
Model 203E sidelock (disc. 1998) . . NiB $6416 Ex $5188 Gd $3617
Model 203ES skeet
(imported 1993-97) . . . . NiB $9065 Ex $7285 Gd $4991
Model 203ET trap (disc. 1997) . . . . NiB $9116 Ex $7356 Gd $5103

MODEL 204E
O/U SHOTGUN . . . . NiB $7729 Ex $6247 Gd $4352
Similar to Model 203E; has Merkel sidelocks, fine English engraving. Made prior to World War II.

MODEL 210E
SIDE-LOCK O/U SHOTGUN. . . NiB $6165 Ex $5069 Gd $3539
Kersten double cross-bolt, scroll-engraved, casehardened receiver. 12, 16 or 20 ga. Double-triggers; pistol-grip stock w/cheekpiece.

MODEL 211E
SIDE-LOCK O/U SHOTGUN. . . NiB $7449 Ex $6102 Gd $4250
Same specifications as Model 210E except w/engraved hunting scenes on silver-gray receiver.

MODELS 300, 300E, 301, 301E AND 302 O/U
Merkel-Anson system boxlock. Kersten double crossbolt, two underlugs, scalloped frame, sideplates on Model 302. Arabesque or hunting engraving. "E" models and Model 302 have auto ejectors, others have separate extractors. Signal pins. Double triggers. Gauges: 12, 16, 20, 24, 28, 32. Ribbed bbls. in various lengths and chokes. Checkered forend and stock w/pistol grip and cheekpiece or English-style. Grades 300, 301 and 302 differ in overall quality, engraving, wood, checkering, etc.; aside from the dummy sideplates on Model 302, general specifications are the same. Manufactured prior to World War II.
Model 300 . . . . NiB $2821 Ex $2385 Gd $1598
Model 300E . . . . NiB $3421 Ex $2763 Gd $1923
Model 301 . . . . NiB $7136 Ex $5747 Gd $3969
Model 301E . . . . NiB $8515 Ex $6863 Gd $4728
Model 302 . . . . NiB $14,803 Ex $11,842 Gd $8052

MODEL 303EL O/U
SHOTGUN . . . . NiB $17,349 Ex $13,879 Gd $9438
Similar to Model 203E. Has Kersten crossbolt, double underlugs, Holland & Holland-type hand-detachable sidelocks, auto-ejectors. This is a finer gun than Model 203E. Currently manufactured. Special order items.

MODEL 304E O/U
SHOTGUN . . . . NiB $22,306 Ex $17,752 Gd $12,134
Special version of the Model 303E-type, but higher quality throughout. This is the top grade Merkel over/under. Currently manufactured. Special order items.

MODELS 400, 400E, 401, 401E O/U
Similar to Model 101 except have Kersten double crossbolt, Arabesque engraving on Models 400 and 400E, hunting engraving on Models 401 and 401E, finer general quality. "E" models have Merkel ejectors, others have separate extractors. Made prior to World War II.
Model 400 . . . . NiB $2347 Ex $1908 Gd $1346
Model 400E . . . . NiB $2958 Ex $2389 Gd $1673
Model 401 . . . . NiB $2489 Ex $2021 Gd $1423
Model 401E . . . . NiB $4033 Ex $3262 Gd $2274

O/U COMBINATION GUNS ("BOCKBÜCHSFLINTEN")
Shotgun bbl. over, rifle bbl. under. Gauges: 12, 16, 20; calibers: 5.6x35 Vierling, 7x57r5, 8x57JR, 8x60R Mag., 9.3x53r5, 9.3x72r5, 9.3x74R and others including domestic calibers from .22 Hornet to .375 H&H. Various bbl. lengths, chokes and weights. Other specifications and values correspond to those of Merkel over/under shotguns listed below. Currently manufactured. Model 210 & 211 series disc. 1992.
Models 410, 410E, 411E (see shotgun models 400, 400E, 401, 401E)
Models 210, 210E, 211, 211E, 212, 212E
(see shotgun models 200, 200E, 201, 201E, 202, 202E)

MODEL 2000EL O/U SHOTGUNS
Kersten double cross-bolt. Gauges: 12 and 20. 26.75- or 28-inch bbls. Weight: 6.4 to 7.28 lbs. Scroll engraved silver-gray receiver. Automatic ejectors and single selective or double triggers. Checkered forend and stock w/pistol grip and cheekpiece or English-style stock w/luxury grade wood. Imported from 1998 to date.
Model 2000EL Standard . . . . . NiB $5242 Ex $4280 Gd $2953
Model 2000EL Sporter . . . . NiB $5452 Ex $4404 Gd $3065

MODEL 2001EL O/U SHOTGUNS
Gauges: 12, 16, 20 and 28; Kersten double cross-bolt lock receiver. 26.75- or 28-inch IC/mod, mod/full bbls. Weight: 6.4 to 7.28 lbs. Three-piece forearm, automatic ejectors and single selective or double triggers. Imported from 1993 to date.
Model 2001EL 12 ga. . . . . NiB $6220 Ex $5025 Gd $3496
Model 2001EL 16 ga.
(disc. 1997) . . . . NiB $6220 Ex $5025 Gd $3496
Model 2001EL 20 ga. . . . . NiB $6220 Ex $5025 Gd $3496
Model 2001EL 28 ga.
(made 1995) . . . . NiB $6839 Ex $5521 Gd $3836

MODEL 2002EL . . . . NiB $6976 Ex $5632 Gd $3911
Same specifications as Model 2000EL except hunting scenes w/Arabesque engraving.

ANSON DRILLINGS
Three-bbl. combination guns; usually made w/double shotgun bbls., over rifle bbl., although "Doppelbüchsdrillingen" were made w/two rifle bbls. over and shotgun bbl. under. Hammerless.

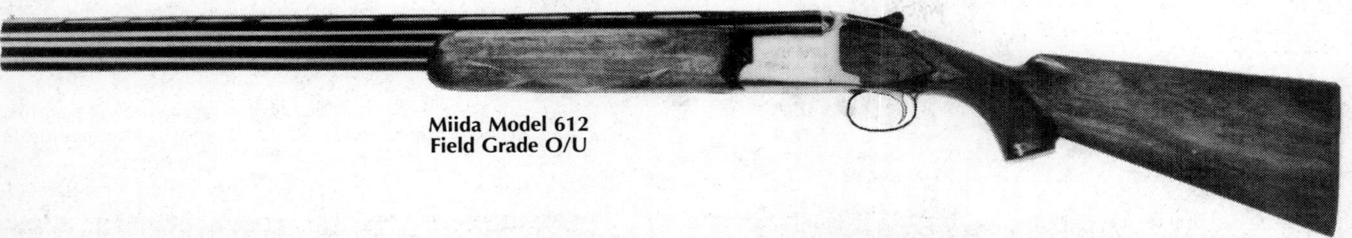
Miida Model 612
Field Grade O/U

Boxlock. Anson & Deeley system. Side clips. Plain extractors. Double triggers. Gauges: 12, 16, 20; rifle calibers: 7x57r5, 8x57JR and 9.3x74R are most common, but other calibers from 5.6mm to 10.75mm available. Bbls.: standard drilling 25.6 inches; short drilling, 21.6 inches. Checkered pistol-grip stock and forend. The three models listed differ chiefly in overall quality, grade of wood, etc.; general specifications are the same. Made prior to WW II.
Model 142 Engraved . . . . NiB $5541 Ex $4473 Gd $3107
Model 142 Standard . . . . NiB $4221 Ex $3414 Gd $2382
Model 145 Field . . . . NiB $3542 Ex $2868 Gd $2007

MIIDA SHOTGUNS — Manufactured for Marubeni America Corp., New York, N.Y., by Olin-Kodensha Co., Tochigi, Japan

MODEL 612 FIELD GRADE O/U. . . NiB $914 Ex $749 Gd $538
Boxlock. Auto ejectors. Selective single trigger. 12 ga. Bbls.: Vent rib; 26-inch, IC/M; 28-inch, M/F choke. Weight: W/26-inch bbl., 6 lbs., 11 oz. Checkered pistol-grip stock and forearm. Made from 1972-74.

MODEL 2100 SKEET GUN . . . . . . NiB $1027 Ex $841 Gd $602
Similar to Model 612 except has more elaborate engraving on frame (50 percent coverage), skeet-style stock and forearm of select grade wood; 27-inch vent-rib bbls., SK choke. Weight: 7 lbs., 11 oz. Made from 1972-74.

MODEL 2200T TRAP GUN,
MODEL 2200S SKEET GUN . . . . . NiB $1070 Ex $876 Gd $626
Similar to Model 612 except more elaborate engraving on frame (60 percent coverage), trap- or skeet-style stock and semi-beavertail forearm of fancy walnut, recoil pad on trap stock. Bbls.: Wide vent rib; 29.75-inch, IM/F choke on Trap Gun; 27-inch, SK choke on Skeet Gun. Weight: Trap, 7 lbs., 14 oz.; Skeet, 7 lbs., 11 oz. Made from 1972-74.

MODEL 2300T TRAP GUN,
MODEL 2300S SKEET GUN . . . . . NiB $1146 Ex $938 Gd $670
Same as models 2200T and 2200S except more elaborate engraving on frame (70% coverage). Made from 1972-74.

GRANDEE MODEL GRT/IRS
TRAP/SKEET GUN. . . . . NiB $2715 Ex $2203 Gd $1547
Boxlock w/sideplates. Frame, breech ends of bbls., trigger guard and locking lever fully engraved and gold inlaid. Auto ejectors. Selective single trigger. 12 ga. Bbls.: Wide vent rib; 29-inch, F choke on Trap Gun; 27-inch, SK choke on Skeet Gun. Weight: Trap, 7 lbs., 14 oz.; Skeet, 7 lbs., 11 oz. Trap- or skeet-style stock and semi-beavertail forearm of extra fancy wood, recoil pad on trap stock. Made from 1972-74.

MITCHELL ARMS — Santa Ana, California

MODEL 9104/9105 PUMP SHOTGUNS
Slide action in Field/Riot configuration. Gauge: 12; 5-round tubular magazine. 20-inch bbl.; fixed choke or screw-in tubes. Weight: 6.5 lbs. Plain walnut stock. Made from 1994-1996.
Model 9104 (w/plain bbl.) . . . . NiB $269 Ex $222 Gd $160
Model 9105 (w/rifle sight). . . . . NiB $539 Ex $234 Gd $987
W/choke tubes, add $20

MODEL 9108/9109 PUMP SHOTGUN
Slide action in Military/Police/Riot configuration. Gauge: 12, 7-round tubular magazine. 20-inch bbl.; fixed choke or screw-in tubes. Weight: 6.5 lbs. Plain walnut stock and grooved slide handle w/brown, green or black finish. Blued metal. Made from 1994-1996.
Model 9108 (w/plain bbl.) . . . . NiB $276 Ex $227 Gd $165
Model 9109 (w/rifle sights). . . . . . . NiB $297 Ex $242 Gd $175
W/choke tubes, add $20

MODEL 9111/9113 PUMP SHOTGUN
Slide action in Military/Police/Riot configuration. Gauge: 12; 6-round tubular magazine. 18.5-inch bbl.; fixed choke or screw-in tubes. Weight: 6.5 lbs. Synthetic or plain walnut stock and grooved slide handle w/brown, green or black finish. Blued metal. Made from 1994 to date.
Model 9111 (w/plain bbl.) . . . . NiB $269 Ex $222 Gd $162
Model 9113 (w/rifle sights). . . . . . . NiB $294 Ex $242 Gd $175
W/choke tubes, add $20

MODEL 9114/9114FS
Slide action in Military/Police/Riot configuration. Gauge: 12; 7-round tubular magazine. 20-inch bbl.; fixed choke or screw-in tubes. Weight: 6.5-7 lbs. Synthetic pistol-grip or folding stock. Blued metal. Made from 1994-1996.
Model 9114. . . . . NiB $322 Ex $263 Gd $190
Model 9114FS . . . . NiB $353 Ex $289 Gd $207

MODEL 9115/9115FS
PUMP SHOTGUN. . . . . NiB $353 Ex $289 Gd $207
Slide action in Military/Police/Riot configuration. Gauge: 12; 6-round tubular magazine. 18.5-inch bbl. w/heat-shield handguard. Weight: 7 lbs. Gray synthetic stock and slide handle. Parkerized metal. Made from 1994-1996.

MONTGOMERY WARD

See shotgun listings under "W"

MORRONE SHOTGUN — Manufactured by Rhode Island Arms Company, Hope Valley, RI

STANDARD MODEL 46 O/U . . . . NiB $1053 Ex $859 Gd $610
Boxlock. Plain extractors. Non-selective single trigger. Gauges: 12, 20. Bbls.: Plain, vent rib; 26-inch IC/M; 28-inch M/F choke. Weight: About 7 lbs., 12 ga.; 6 lbs., 20 ga. Checkered straight- or pistol-grip stock and forearm. Made 1949-53. Note: Fewer than 500 of these guns were produced, about 50 in 20 ga.. A few had vent-rib bbls. Value shown is for 12 ga. w/plain bbls.. The rare 20 ga. and vent-rib types should bring considerably more.

Mossberg Model 83D

Mossberg Model 85D
Bolt-Action Repeating Shotgun

Mossberg Model 183K

Mossberg Model 185K

Mossberg Model 200K
Slide-Action Repeater

Mossberg Model 395K
Bolt-Action Repeater

O. F. MOSSBERG & SONS, INC. — North Haven, Connecticut, Formerly New Haven, Conn.

MODEL 83D OR 183D . . . . NiB $155 Ex $129 Gd $94
3-round. Takedown. .410 ga. only. Two shell fixed top-loading magazine. 23-inch bbl. w/two interchangeable choke tubes (M/F). Later production had 24-inch bbl. Plain one-piece pistol-grip stock. Weight: about 5.5 lbs. Originally designated Model 83D, changed in 1947 to Model 183D. Made from 1940-71.

MODEL 85D OR 185D BOLT-ACTION REPEATING SHOTGUN . . . . NiB $135 Ex $113 Gd $82
Takedown. Three-round. 20 ga. only. Two-shell detachable box magazine. 25-inch bbl., three interchangeable choke tubes (F, M, IC). Later production had 26-inch bbl. w/F/IC choke tubes. Weight: About 6.25 lbs. Plain one-piece, pistol-grip stock. Originally designated Model 85D, changed in 1947 to Model 185D. Made from 1940-71.

MODEL 183K . . . . NiB $149 Ex $123 Gd $91
Same as Model 183D except has 25-inch bbl. w/variable C-Lect-Choke instead of interchangeable choke tubes. Made from 1953-86.

MODEL 185K . . . . NiB $156 Ex $129 Gd $91
Same as Model 185D except has variable C-Lect-Choke instead of interchangeable choke tubes. Made from 1950-63.

MODEL 190D . . . . NiB $149 Ex $123 Gd $91
Same as Model 185D except in 16 ga. Weight: About 6 lbs. Made from 1955-71.

Mossberg Mode 500
Accu-Choke

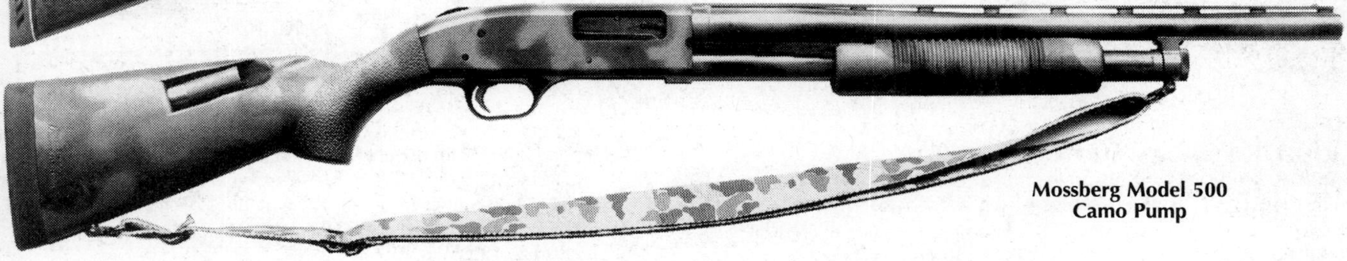

Mossberg Model 500
Camo Pump

Mossberg Model 500
Bullpup Shotgun

MODEL 190K .... NiB $156 Ex $129 Gd $94
Same as Model 185K except in 16 ga. Takedown. Three round capacity; 2-round magazine. Weight: About 6.75 lbs. Made from 1956-63.

MODEL 195D .... NiB $156 Ex $128 Gd $94
Same as Model 185D except in 12 ga. Takedown. Three round capacity; 2-round magazine. Weight: About 6.75 lbs. Made from 1955-71.

MODEL 195K .... NiB $156 Ex $128 Gd $94
Same as Model 185K except in 12 ga. Takedown. Three round capacity; 2-round magazine. Weight: About 7.5 lbs. Made from 1956-63.

MODEL 200D .... NiB $161 Ex $133 Gd $99
Same as Model 200K except w/two interchangeable choke tubes instead of C-Lect choke. Made from 1955-59.

MODEL 200K
SLIDE-ACTION REPEATER................ NiB $176 Ex $145 Gd $104
12 ga. 3-round detachable box magazine. 28-inch bbl. C-Lect choke. Plain pistol-grip stock. Black nylon slide handle. Weight: About 7.5 lbs. Made from 1955-59.

MODEL 395K BOLT-ACTION REPEATER ...... NiB $150 Ex $124 Gd $91
Takedown. Three round (detachable-clip magazine holds two rounds).12 ga. (3-inch chamber). 28-inch bbl. w/C-Lect-Choke. Weight: About 7.5 lbs. Monte Carlo stock w/recoil pad. Made from 1963-83.

MODEL 385K .... NiB $150 Ex $124 Gd $91
Same as Model 395K except 20 ga. (3-inch), 26-inch bbl. w/C-Lect-Choke. Weight: About 6.25 lbs.

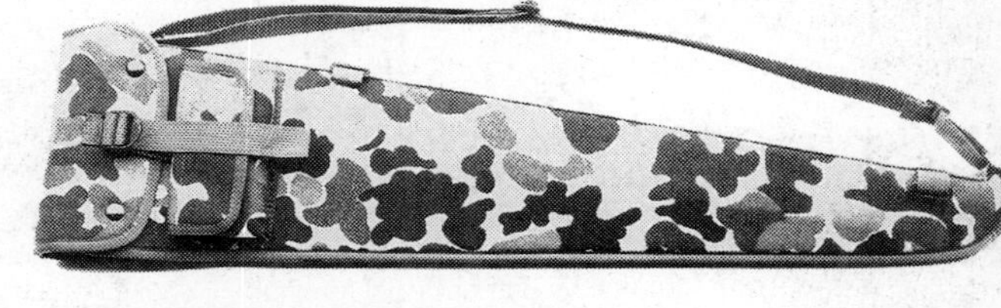

Mossberg Model 500
Camper

MODEL 390K .... NiB $161 Ex $133 Gd $99
Same as Model 395K except 16 ga. (2.75-inch). Made from 1963-74.

MODEL 395S SLUGSTER......... NiB $189 Ex $155 Gd $112
Same as Model 395K except has 24-inch bbl., cylinder bore, rifle sights, swivels and web sling. Weight: About 7 lbs. Made from 1968-81.

MODEL 500 ACCU-CHOKE SHOTGUN ..... NiB $295 Ex $240 Gd $170
Pump-action. Gauge: 12. 24- or 28-inch bbl. Weight: 7.25 lbs. Checkered walnut-finished wood stock w/ventilated recoil pad. Available w/synthetic field or Speed-Feed stocks. Drilled and tapped receivers, swivels and camo sling on camo models. Made from 1987 to date.

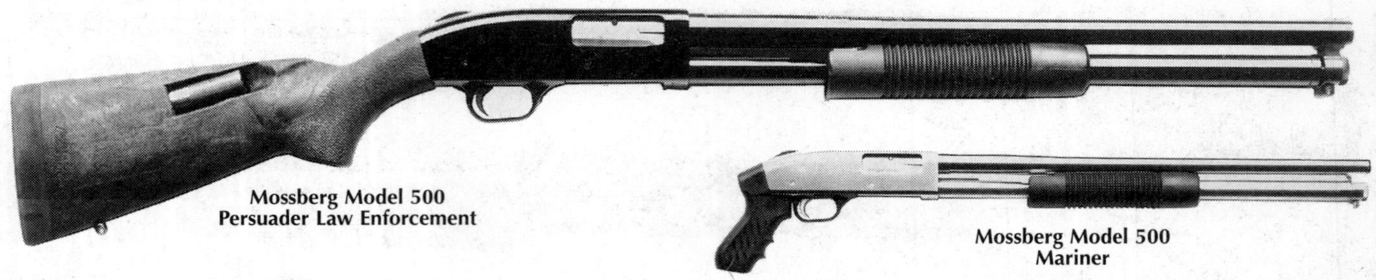

Mossberg Model 500
Persuader Law Enforcement

Mossberg Model 500
Mariner

MODEL 500 BANTAM SHOTGUN
Same as Model 500 Sporting Pump except 20 or .410 ga. only. 22-inch w/ACCU-Choke tubes or 24-inch w/F choke; vent rib. Scaled-down checkered hardwood or synthetic stock w/standard or Realtree camo finish. Made from 1990-96 and 1998-99.

Bantam Model (hardwood stock) . . . . NiB $257 Ex $209 Gd $149
Bantam Model (synthetic stock) . . . . NiB $253 Ex $199 Gd $141
Bantam Model (Realtree camo), add. $50

MODEL 500 BULLPUP SHOTGUN . . . . . . NiB $516 Ex $419 Gd $296
Pump. Gauge: 12. Six or 8-round capacity. Bbl.: 18.5 to 20 inches. 26.5 and 28.5 inches overall. Weight: About 9.5 lbs. Multiple independent safety systems. Dual pistol grips, rubber recoil pad. Fully enclosed rifle-type sights. Synthetic stock. Ventilated bbl. heat shield. Made from 1987-90.

MODEL 500 CAMO PUMP
Same as Model 500 Sporting Pump except 12 ga. only. Receiver drilled and tapped. QD swivels and camo sling. Special camouflage finish.

Standard model . . . . NiB $264 Ex $211 Gd $152
Combo model (w/ext. Slugster bbl.) . . . NiB $332 Ex $263 Gd $187

MODEL 500 CAMPER . . . . NiB $272 Ex $224 Gd $160
Same general specifications as Model 500 Field Grade except .410 bore, 6-round magazine, 18.5-inch plain cylinder bore bbl. Synthetic pistol grip and camo carrying case. Made from 1986-90.

MODEL 500 FIELD GRADE
HAMMERLESS SLIDE-ACTION REPEATER
Pre-1977 type. Takedown. Gauges: 12, 16, 20, .410. Three inch chamber (2.75-inch in 16 ga.). Tubular magazine holds five 2.75-inch rounds or four three-inch. Bbls.: Plain- 30-inch regular or heavy Magnum, F choke (12 ga. only); 28-inch, M or F; 26-inch, IC or adj. C-Lect-Choke; 24-inch Slugster, cylinder bore, w/rifle sights. Weight: 5.75 to lbs. Plain pistol-grip stock w/recoil pad, grooved slide handle. After 1973, these guns have checkered stock and slide handles; Models 500AM and 500AS have receivers etched w/game scenes. The latter has swivels and sling. Made from 1962-76.

Model 500A, 12 ga., ... NiB $280 Ex $231 Gd $167
Model 500AM, 12 ga., hvy. Mag. bbl. . . . . NiB $288 Ex $237 Gd $171
Model 500AK, 12 ga., C-Lect-Choke . . . . NiB $320 Ex $263 Gd $189
Model 500AS, 12 ga., Slugster . . . . NiB $318 Ex $269 Gd $193
Model 500B 16 ga., ... NiB $280 Ex $231 Gd $167
Model 500BK, 16 ga., C-Lect-Choke . . . . . NiB $332 Ex $273 Gd $196
Model 500BS, 16 ga., Slugster . . . . NiB $320 Ex $263 Gd $189
Model 500C 20 ga., ... NiB $282 Ex $232 Gd $168
Model 500CK, 20 ga., C-Lect-Choke . . . . . NiB $355 Ex $291 Gd $208
Model 500CS, 20 ga., Slugster . . . . NiB $322 Ex $265 Gd $191
Model 500E, .410 ga., ... NiB $348 Ex $285 Gd $205
Model 500EK, .410 ga., C-Lect-Choke . . . . NiB $387 Ex $316 Gd $226

MODEL 500 "L" SERIES
"L" in model designation. Same as pre-1977 Model 500 Field Grade except not available in 16 ga., has receiver etched w/different game scenes; Accu-Choke w/three interchangeable tubes (IC, M, F) standard, restyled stock and slide handle. Bbls.: plain or vent rib; 30- or 32-inch, heavy, F choke (12 ga. Magnum and vent rib only); 28-inch, Accu-Choke (12 and 20 ga.); 26-inch F choke (.410 bore only); 18.5-inch (12 ga. only), 24-inch (12 and 20 ga.) Slugster w/rifle sights, cylinder bore. Weight: 6 to 8.5 lbs. Intro. 1977.

Model 500ALD, 12 ga.,
plain bbl. (disc. 1980) . . . . NiB $312 Ex $258 Gd $189
Model 500ALDR, 12 ga., vent rib . . . . NiB $353 Ex $289 Gd $206
Model 500ALMR, 12 ga.,
Heavy Duck Gun (disc. 1980) . . . . NiB $353 Ex $289 Gd $206
Model 500CLD, 20 ga.,
plain bbl. (disc. 1980) . . . . NiB $282 Ex $232 Gd $168
Model 500CLDR, 20 ga., vent rib . . . . NiB $320 Ex $263 Gd $189
Model 500CLS, 20 ga.,
Slugster (disc. 1980) . . . . NiB $353 Ex $289 Gd $206
Model 500EL, .410 ga.,
plain bbl. (disc. 1980) . . . . NiB $308 Ex $252 Gd $181
Model 500ELR, .410 ga., vent rib . . . . NiB $353 Ex $289 Gd $206

MODEL 500 MARINER SHOTGUN . . . . . . NiB $450 Ex $347 Gd $192
Slide action. Gauge: 12. 18.5 or 20-inch bbl. Six round and 8-round respectively. Weight: 7.25 lbs. High-strength synthetic buttstock and forend. Available in extra round-carrying Speed Feed synthetic buttstock. All metal treated for protection against saltwater corrosion. Intro. 1987.

MODEL 500 MUZZLELOADER COMBO . . NiB $362 Ex $305 Gd $218
Same as Model 500 Sporting Pump except w/extra 24-inch rifled .50-caliber muzzleloading bbl. w/ramrod. Made from 1992 to date.

MODEL 500 PERSUADER LAW ENFORCEMENT
Similar to pre-1977 Model 500 Field Grade except 12 ga. only, 6- or 8-round capacity, has 18.5- or 20-inch plain bbl., cylinder bore, either shotgun or rifle sights, plain pistol-grip stock and grooved slide handle, sling swivels. Special Model 500ATP8-SP has bayonet lug, Parkerized finish. Currently manufactured.

Model 500ATP6, 6-round, 18.5-inch
bbl., shotgun sights . . . . NiB $280 Ex $231 Gd $167
Model 500ATP6CN, 6-round,
nickle finish "Cruiser" pistol-grip. . . . . NiB $295 Ex $241 Gd $184
Model 500ATP6N, 6-round, nickel
finish, 2.75- or 3-inch Mag. shells . . . . NiB $287 Ex $236 Gd $170
Model 500ATP6S, 6-round,
18.5-inch bbl., rifle sights . . . . NiB $280 Ex $231 Gd $177
Model 500ATP8, 8-round,
20-inch bbl., shotgun sights . . . . NiB $307 Ex $252 Gd $190
Model 500ATP8S, 8-round,
20-inch bbl., rifle sights . . . . NiB $323 Ex $265 Gd $201
Model 500ATP8-SP Spec. Enforcement . . . NiB $376 Ex $308 Gd $221
Model 500 Bullpup . . . . NiB $574 Ex $466 Gd $330
Model 500 Intimidator w/laser sight, blued . . . NiB $532 Ex $434 Gd $308
Model 500 Intimidator w/laser sight,
parkerized . . . . NiB $547 Ex $445 Gd $315
Model 500 Security combo pack . . . . NiB $239 Ex $198 Gd $146
Model 500 Cruiser w/pistol grip . . . . NiB $239 Ex $198 Gd $146

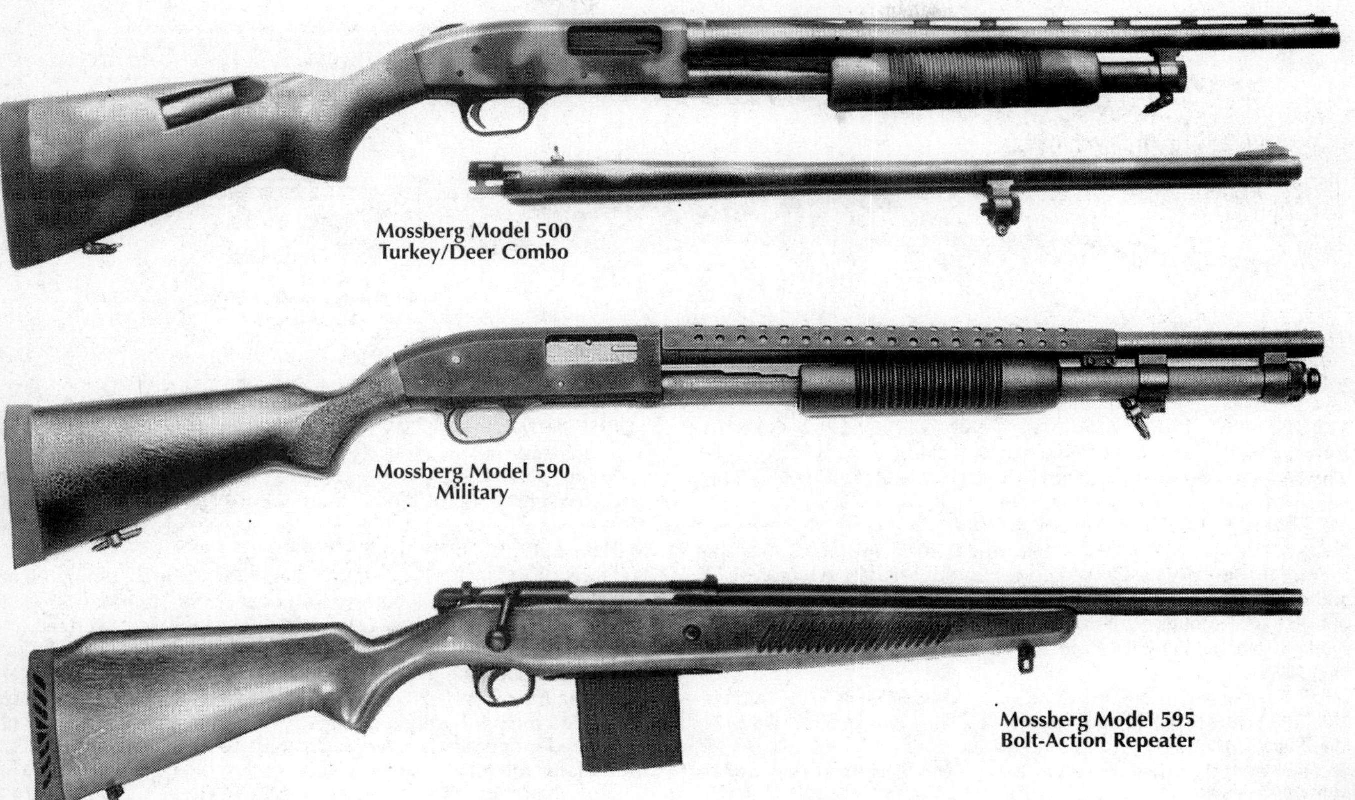

Mossberg Model 500 Turkey/Deer Combo

Mossberg Model 590 Military

Mossberg Model 595 Bolt-Action Repeater

MODEL 500 PIGEON GRADE

Same as Model 500 Super Grade except higher quality w/fancy wood, floating vent rib; field gun hunting dog etching, trap and skeet guns have scroll etching. Bbls.: 30-inch, F choke (12 ga. only); 28-inch, M choke; 26-inch, SK choke or C-Lect-Choke. Made from 1971-75.

Model 500APR, 12 ga., field, trap or skeet . . . NiB $496 Ex $405 Gd $290
Model 500APKR, 12 ga. field gun, C-Lect-Choke . . . NiB $508 Ex $416 Gd $297
Model 500 APTR, 12 ga., Trap gun, Monte Carlo stock . . . NiB $594 Ex $485 Gd $345
Model 500CPR, 20 ga., field or skeet gun . . . NiB $515 Ex $421 Gd $300
Model 500EPR, .410 ga. field or skeet gun . . . NiB $528 Ex $431 Gd $308

MODEL 500 PUMP COMBO SHOTGUN . . . . NiB $358 Ex $295 Gd $215

Gauges: 12 and 20. 24- and 28-inch bbl. w/adj. rifle sights. Weight: 7 to 7.25 lbs. Available w/blued or camo finish. Drilled and tapped receiver w/sling swivels and camo web sling. Made from 1987 to date.

MODEL 500 PUMP SLUGSTER SHOTGUN

Gauges: 12 or 20 w/3-inch chamber. 24-inch smoothbore or rifled bbl. w/adj. rifle sights or intregral scope mount and optional muzzle break (1997 porting became standard). Weight: 7 to 7.25 lbs. Wood or synthetic stock w/standard or Woodland Camo finish. Blued, matte black or Marinecote metal finish. Drilled and tapped receiver w/camo sling and swivels. Made 1987 to date.

Slugster (w/cyl. bore, rifle sights) . . . NiB $280 Ex $231 Gd $167
Slugster (w/rifled bore, ported) . . . NiB $344 Ex $282 Gd $203
Slugster (w/rifled bore, unported) . . . NiB $309 Ex $253 Gd $183
Slugster (w/rifled bore, ported, integral scope mount) . . . NiB $379 Ex $311 Gd $221
Slugster (w/Marinecote and synthetic stock), add . . . $60
Slugster (w/Truglo fiber optics), add . . . $30

MODEL 500 REGAL SLIDE-ACTION REPEATER

Similar to regular Model 500 except higher quality workmanship throughout. Gauges: 12 and 20. Bbls.: 26- and 28-inch w/various chokes, or Accu-Choke. Weight: 6.75 to 7.5 lbs. Checkered walnut stock and forearm. Made from 1985 to date.

Model 500 w/Accu-Choke . . . NiB $282 Ex $233 Gd $169
Model 500 w/fixed choke . . . NiB $263 Ex $216 Gd $158

MODEL 500 SPORTING PUMP

Gauges: 12, 20 or .410, 2.75- or 3-inch chamber. Bbls.: 22 to 28 inches w/fixed choke or screw-in tubes; plain or vent rib. Weight: 6.25 to 7.25 lbs. White bead front sight, brass mid-bead. Checkered hardwood buttstock and forend w/walnut finish.

Standard model . . . NiB $284 Ex $234 Gd $170
Field combo (w/extra Slugster bbl.) . . . NiB $350 Ex $287 Gd $207

MODEL 500 SUPER GRADE

Same as pre-1977 Model 500 Field Grade except not made in 16 ga., has vent rib bbl., checkered pistol grip and slide handle. Made from 1965-76.

Model 500AR, 12 ga. . . . NiB $297 Ex $243 Gd $176
Model 500AMR, 12 ga., heavy magnum bbl. . . . NiB $335 Ex $276 Gd $200
Model 500AKR, 12 ga., C-Lect-Choke . . . NiB $342 Ex $281 Gd $203
Model 500CR 20 ga. . . . NiB $322 Ex $265 Gd $192
Model 500CKk, 20 ga., C-Lect-Choke . . . NiB $410 Ex $356 Gd $289
Model 500ER, .410 ga. . . . NiB $294 Ex $243 Gd $177
Model 500EKR, .410 ga., C-Lect-Choke . . . NiB $362 Ex $298 Gd $214

MODEL 500 TURKEY/DEER COMBO . . . NiB $384 Ex $315 Gd $226

Pump (slide action). Gauge: 12. 20- and 24-inch bbls. Weight: 7.25 lbs. Drilled and tapped receiver, camo sling and swivels. Adj. rifle sights and camo finish. Vent rib. Made from 1987 to date.

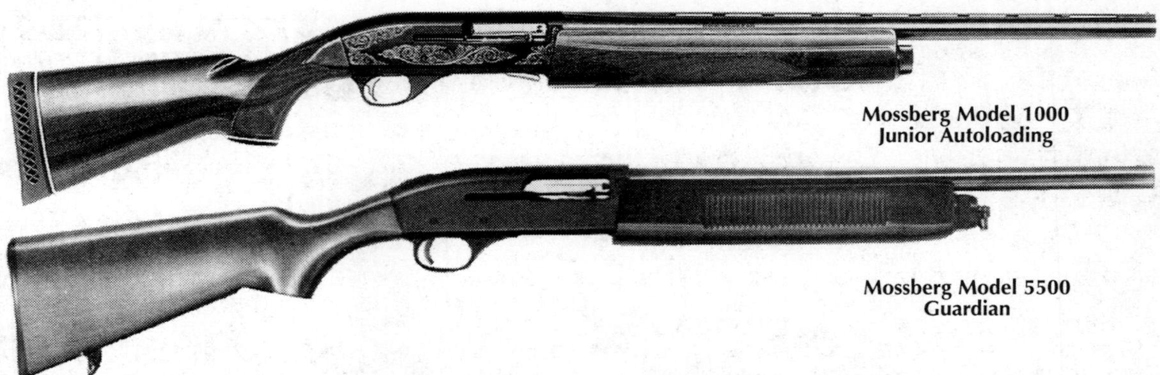

Mossberg Model 1000
Junior Autoloading

Mossberg Model 5500
Guardian

MODEL 500 TURKEY GUN....... NiB $345 Ex $282 Gd $201
Same as Model 500 Camo Pump except w/24-inch ACCU-Choke bbl. w/extra full choke tube and ghost ring sights. Made from 1992-97.

MODEL 500 VIKING PUMP SHOTGUN
Gauges: 12 or 20 w/3-inch chamber. 24-, 26- or 28-inch bbls. available in smoothbore w/Accu-Choke and vent rib or rifled bore w/iron sights and optional muzzle brake (1997 porting became standard). Optional optics: Slug Shooting System (SSS). Weight: 6.9 to 7.2 lbs. Moss-green synthetic stock. Matte black metal finish. Made from 1996-98.

Mdl. 500 Viking
(w/VR & choke tubes, unported)........... NiB $250 Ex $206 Gd $148
Mdl. 500 Viking (w/rifled bore, ported) ... NiB $304 Ex $239 Gd $171
Mdl. 500 Viking
(w/rifled bore, SSS & ported) .... NiB $382 Ex $311 Gd $221
Mdl. 500 Viking
(w/rifled bore, unported) .... NiB $279 Ex $229 Gd $168
Mdl. 500 Viking Turkey
(w/VR, tubes, ported) .... NiB $254 Ex $208 Gd $151

MODEL 500
WATERFOWL/DEER COMBO.......... NiB $369 Ex $301 Gd $213
Same general specifications as the Turkey/Deer combo except w/either 28- or 30-inch bbl. along w/the 24-inch bbl. Made from 1987 to date.

MODEL 500 ATR SUPER
GRADE TRAP .... NiB $467 Ex $381 Gd $271
Same as pre-1977 Model 500 Field Grade except 12 ga. only w/vent-rib bbl.; 30-inch F choke, checkered Monte Carlo stock w/recoil pad, beavertail slide handle. Made from 1968-71.

MODEL 500DSPR DUCK STAMP
COMMEMORATIVE .... NiB $736 Ex $598 Gd $422
Limited edition of 1000 to commemorate the Migratory Bird Hunting Stamp program. Same as Model 500DSPR Pigeon Grade 12-Gauge Magnum Heavy Duck Gun w/heavy 30-inch vent-rib bbl., F choke; receiver has special wood duck etching. Gun accompanied by a special wall plaque. Made in 1975.

MODEL 590 BULLPUP .... NiB $487 Ex $396 Gd $281
Same general specifications as the Model 500 Bullpup except 20-inch bbl. and 9-round magazine. Made from 1989-90.

MODEL 590 MARINER PUMP
Same general specifications as the Model 590 Military Security except has Marinecote metal finish and field configuration synthetic stock w/pistiol-grip conversion included. Made from 1989-99.

Model 590 Mariner (w/18.5-inch bbl.)....... NiB $348 Ex $284 Gd $202
Model 590 Mariner (w/20-inch bbl.) .... NiB $363 Ex $296 Gd $210
Model 590 Mariner (w/grip conversion), add $20
Model 590 Mariner (w/ghost ring sight), add $50

MODEL 590 MILITARY SECURITY......... NiB $427 Ex $349 Gd $249
Same general specifications as the Model 590 Military except there is no heat shield and gun has short pistol-grip style instead of butt-stock. Weight: About 6.75 lbs. Made from 1987-93.

MODEL 590 MILITARY SHOTGUN
Slide-action. Gauge: 12. 9-round capacity. 20-inch bbl. Weight: About 7 lbs. Synthetic or hardwood buttstock and forend. Ventilated bbl. heat shields. Equipped w/bayonet lug. Blued or Parkerized finish. Made from 1987 to date. See illustration Previous Page.

Synthetic model, blued .... NiB $377 Ex $309 Gd $221
Synthetic model Parkerized ...... NiB $403 Ex $330 Gd $236
Speedfeed model, blued .... NiB $396 Ex $324 Gd $232
Speedfeed model, Parkerized ..... NiB $396 Ex $324 Gd $232
Intimidator model
w/laser sight, blued .... NiB $510 Ex $416 Gd $295
Intimidator model
w/laser sight, Parkerized .... NiB $523 Ex $426 Gd $303
For ghost ring sight, add $75

MODEL 595/595K
BOLT-ACTION REPEATER .... NiB $201 Ex $164 Gd $118
12 ga. only. Four round detachable magazine. 18.5-inch bbl. Weight: About 7 lbs. Walnut finished stock w/recoil pad and sling swivels. Made from 1985-86.

MODEL 695 BOLT-ACTION SLUGSTER
Gauge: 12 w/3-inch chamber. Two round detachable magazine. 22-inch fully rifled and ported bbl. w/blade front and folding leaf rear sights. Receiver drilled and tapped for Weaver style scope bases. Also available w/1.5x-4.5x scope or fiber optics installed. Weight: 7.5 lbs. Black synthetic stock w/swivel studs and recoil pad. Made 1996-2002.

Model 695 (w/ACCU-choke bbl.) .. NiB $233 Ex $191 Gd $136
Model 695
(w/open sights) .... NiB $300 Ex $241 Gd $171
Model 695
(w/1.5x-4.5x Bushnell scope) ..... NiB $320 Ex $339 Gd $239
Model 695 (w/Truglo fiber optics) .... NiB $335 Ex $271 Gd $193
Model 695 OFM Camo .... NiB $285 Ex $232 Gd $165

MODEL 695 BOLT-ACTION TURKEY GUN NiB $287 Ex $233 Gd $166
Similar to 695 Slugster Model except has smoothbore 22-inch bbl. w/extra-full turkey Accu-choke tube. Bead front and U-notch rear sights. Full OFM camo finish. Made from 1996-2002.

MODEL 712 AUTOLOADING SHOTGUN
Gas-operated, takedown, hammerless shotgun w/5-round (4-round w/3-inch chamber) tubular magazine. 12 ga. Bbls.: 28-inch vent rib or 24-inch plain bbl. Slugster w/rifle sights. Fixed choke or ACCU-choke tube system. Weight: 7.5 lbs. Plain alloy receiver w/top-mounted ambidextrous safety. Checkered.

Mdl. 712 w/fixed chokes . . . . NiB $304 Ex $250 Gd $180
Mdl. 712 w/ACCU-Choke tube system . . . . . NiB $338 Ex $277 Gd $199
Mdl. 712 Regal w/ACCU-Choke tube system . NiB $372 Ex $304 Gd $217
Mdl. 712 Regal w/ACCU-Choke II tube sys. . . NiB $406 Ex $331 Gd $236

MODEL 835 FIELD PUMP SHOTGUN
Similar to the Model 9600 Regal except has walnut-stained hardwood stock and one ACCU-Choke tube only.
Standard model . . . . NiB $310 Ex $254 Gd $183
Turkey model . . . . NiB $322 Ex $265 Gd $191
Combo model (24- & 28-inch bbls.) NiB $348 Ex $285 Gd $205

MODEL 835 "NWTF" ULTI-MA SHOTGUN
National Wild Turkey Federation pump-action. Gauge: 12, 3.5-inch chamber. 24-inch vent-rib bbl. w/four ACCU-MAG chokes. Realtree camo finish. QD swivel and post. Made from 1989-93.
Limited Edition model . . . . NiB $491 Ex $400 Gd $285
Special Edition model . . . . NiB $420 Ex $344 Gd $247

MODEL 835 REGAL ULTI-MAG PUMP
Gauge: 12, 3.5-inch chamber. Bbls.: 24- or 28-inch vent-rib w/ACCU-Choke screw-in tubes. Weight: 7.75 lbs. White bead front, brass mid-bead. Checkered hardwood or synthetic stock w/camo finish. Made from 1991-96.
Special model . . . . NiB $327 Ex $270 Gd $196
Standard model . . . . NiB $398 Ex $326 Gd $234
Camo Synthetic model . . . . NiB $424 Ex $347 Gd $248
Combo model . . . . NiB $454 Ex $373 Gd $266

MODEL 835 VIKING PUMP SHOTGUN
Gauge: 12 w/3-inch chamber. 28-inch smoothbore bbl. w/Accu-Choke, vent rib and optional muzzle brake (in 1997 porting became standard). Weight: 7.7 lbs. Green synthetic stock. Matte black metal finish. Made from 1996-98.
Model 835 Viking (w/VR and choke tubes, ported) . . . . NiB $314 Ex $259 Gd $187
Model 835 Viking (w/VR and choke tubes, unported). . . . . . . NiB $302 Ex $248 Gd $181

MODEL 1000 AUTOLOADING SHOTGUN
Gas-operated, takedown, hammerless shotgun w/tubular magazine. Gauges: 12, 20; 2.75- or 3-inch chamber. Bbls.: 22- to 30-inch vent rib w/fixed choke or ACCU-Choke tubes; or 22-inch plain bbl, Slugster w/rifle sights. Weight: 6.5 to 7.5 lbs. Scroll-engraved alloy receiver, crossbolt-type safety. Checkered walnut buttstock and forend. Imported from Japan 1986-87.
Junior model, 20 ga., 22-inch bbl. . . NiB $466 Ex $382 Gd $275
Standard model w/fixed choke . . . . NiB $479 Ex $402 Gd $280
Standard model w/choke tubes . . . NiB $503 Ex $412 Gd $294

MODEL 1000 SUPER AUTOLOADING SHOTGUN
Similar to Model 1000, but in 12 ga. only w/3-inch chamber and new gas metering system. Bbls.: 26-, 28- or 30-inch vent rib w/ACCU-Choke tubes.
Standard model w/choke tubes . . . NiB $561 Ex $461 Gd $331
Waterfowler model (Parkerized) . . NiB $601 Ex $492 Gd $352

MODEL 1000S SUPER SKEET . . . . . NiB $664 Ex $542 Gd $388
Similar to Model 1000 in 12 or 20 ga., except w/all-steel receiver and vented jug-type choke for reduced muzzle jump. Bright-point front sight and brass mid-bead. 1 and 2 oz. forend cap weights.

MODEL 5500 AUTOLOADING SHOTGUN
Gas-operated. Takedown. 12 ga. only. Four round magazine (3-round w/3-inch shells). Bbls.: 18.5- to 30-inch; various chokes. Checkered walnut finished hardwood. Made from 1985-86.
Model 5500 w/ACCU-Choke . . . . . NiB $327 Ex $270 Gd $196
Model 5500 modified junior . . . . . NiB $334 Ex $274 Gd $198
Model 5500 Slugster . . . . NiB $344 Ex $283 Gd $205
Model 5500 12 ga. . . . . NiB $298 Ex $246 Gd $179
Model 5500 Guardian . . . . NiB $287 Ex $237 Gd $173

MODEL 5500 MKII AUTOLOADING SHOTGUN
Same as Model 5500 except equipped w/two Accu-Choke bbls.: 26-inch ported for non-Magnum 2.75-inch shells; 28-inch for magnum loads. Made from 1988-93.
Standard model . . . . NiB $312 Ex $257 Gd $187
Camo model . . . . NiB $344 Ex $282 Gd $204
NWTF Mossy Oak model . . . . NiB $374 Ex $307 Gd $220
USST model (Made 1991-92) . . . . . NiB $325 Ex $268 Gd $195

MODEL 6000 AUTO SHOTGUN. . . NiB $325 Ex $268 Gd $205
Similar to the Model 9200 Regal except has 28-inch vent-rib bbl. w/mod. ACCU-Choke tube only. Made 1993 only.

MODEL 9200 CAMO SHOTGUN
Similar to the Model 9200 Regal except has synthetic stock and forend and is completely finished in camouflage pattern (incl. bbl.). Made from 1993 to date.
Standard model (OFM camo) . . . . . NiB $448 Ex $367 Gd $264
Turkey model (Mossy Oak camo) . . . . . NiB $491 Ex $401 Gd $287
Turkey model (Shadow Branch camo) . . . NiB $575 Ex $460 Gd $333
Comb. model (24 & 28-inch bbls. w/OFM camo) . . . . NiB $540 Ex $432 Gd $314

MODEL 9200 CROWN (REGAL) AUTOLOADER
Gauge: 12; 3-inch chamber. Bbls.: 18.5- to 28-inch w/ACCU-Choke tubes; plain or vent rib. Weight: 7.25 to 7.5 lbs. Checkered hardwood buttstock and forend w/walnut finish. Made from 1992-2001.
Model 9200 Bantam (w/1-inch shorter stock) . . . . NiB $429 Ex $351 Gd $251
Model 9200 w/ACCU-Choke . . . . NiB $443 Ex $362 Gd $259
Model 9200 w/rifled bbl. . . . . NiB $447 Ex $374 Gd $268
Model 9200 Combo (w/extra Slugster bbl.). . . . NiB $508 Ex $414 Gd $293
Model 9200 SP (w/matte blue finish, 18.5-inch bbl.) . . . . NiB $354 Ex $292 Gd $211

MODEL 9200 PERSUADER . . . . NiB $379 Ex $311 Gd $223
Similar to the Model 9200 Regal except has 18.5-inch plain bbl. w/fixed mod. choke. Parkerized finish. Black synthetic stock w/sling swivels. Made from 1996-2001.

MODEL 9200 A1 JUNGLE GUN . . . NiB $673 Ex $570 Gd $287
Similar to the Model 9200 Persuader except has mil-spec heavy wall 18.5-inch plain bbl. w/cyl. bore designed for 00 Buck shot. 12 ga. w/2.75-inch chamber. Five round magazine. 38.5 inches overall. Weight: 7 lbs. Black synthetic stock. Parkerized finish. Made from 1998-2001.

MODEL 9200 SPECIAL HUNTER . . NiB $441 Ex $360 Gd $257
Similar to the Model 9200 Regal except has 28-inch vent-rib bbl. w/ACCU-Choke tubes. Parkerized finish. Black synthetic stock. Made from 1998-2001.

MODEL 9200 TROPHY
Similar to the Model 9200 Regal except w/24-inch rifled bbl. or 24- or 28-inch vent-rib bbl. w/ACCU-Choke tubes. Checkered walnut stock w/sling swivels. Made from 1992-98.
Trophy (w/vent rib bbl.) $335
Trophy (w/rifled bbl. & cantilever scope mount) $351
Trophy (w/rifled bbl. & rifle sights) $324

MODEL 9200 USST AUTOLOADER $349
Similar to the Model 9200 Regal except has 26-inch vent-rib bbl. w/ACCU-Choke tubes. "United States Shooting Team" engraved on receiver. Made from 1993 to date.

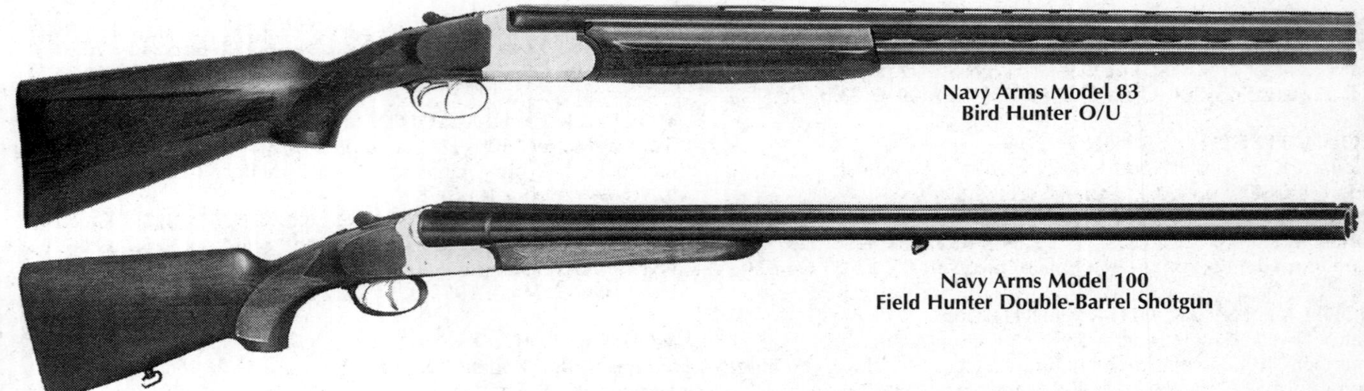

Navy Arms Model 83
Bird Hunter O/U

Navy Arms Model 100
Field Hunter Double-Barrel Shotgun

MODEL 9200
VIKING AUTOLOADER.......... NiB $405 Ex $330 Gd $235
Gauge: 12 w/3-inch chamber. 28-inch smoothbore bbl. W/Accu-Choke and vent rib. Weight: 7.7 lbs. Green synthetic stock. Matte black metal finish. Made from 1996-98.

MODEL HS410
HOME SECURITY PUMP SHOTGUN
Gauge: .410; 3-inch chamber. Bbl.: 18.5-inch w/muzzle brake; blued. Weight: 6.25 lbs. Synthetic stock and pistol-grip slide. Optional laser sight. Made from 1990 to date. A similar version of this gun is marketed by Maverick Arms under the same model designation.
Standard model .... NiB $266 Ex $219 Gd $162
Laser model .... NiB $446 Ex $363 Gd $256

LINE LAUNCHER............... NiB $929 Ex $755 Gd $533
Gauge: 12 w/blank cartridge. Projectile travels from 250 to 275 feet.

"NEW HAVEN BRAND" SHOTGUNS
Promotional models, similar to their standard guns but plainer in finish, are marketed by Mossberg under the "New Haven" brand name. Values generally are about 20 percent lower than for corresponding standard models.

NAVY ARMS SHOTGUNS — Ridgefield, New Jersey

MODEL 83/93 BIRD HUNTER O/U
Hammerless. Boxlock, engraved receiver. Gauges: 12 and 20; 3-inch chambers. Bbls.: 28-inch chrome lined w/double vent-rib construction. Checkered European walnut stock and forearm. Gold plated triggers. Imported 1984-90.
Model 83 w/extractors .... NiB $327 Ex $270 Gd $196
Model 93 w/ejectors .... NiB $379 Ex $311 Gd $223

MODEL 95/96 O/U SHOTGUN
Same as the Model 83/93 except w/five interchangeable choke tubes. Imported 1984-90.
Model 95 w/extractors .... NiB $425 Ex $349 Gd $242
Model 96 w/ejectors .... NiB $553 Ex $451 Gd $320

MODEL 100/150 FIELD HUNTER
DOUBLE-BARREL SHOTGUN
Boxlock. Gauges: 12 and 20. Bbls.: 28-inch chrome lined. Checkered European walnut stock and forearm. Imported 1984-90.
Model 100 .... NiB $401 Ex $330 Gd $238
Model 150 (auto ejectors) .... NiB $514 Ex $420 Gd $299

MODEL 100 O/U SHOTGUN..... NiB $273 Ex $226 Gd $165
Hammerless, takedown shotgun w/engraved chrome receiver. Single trigger. 12, 20, 28, or .410 ga. w/3-inch chambers. Bbls.: 26-inch (F/F or SK/SK); vent rib. Weight: 6.25 lbs. Checkered European walnut buttstock and forend. Imported 1986-90.

NEW ENGLAND FIREARMS — Gardner, Massachusetts

In 1987, New England Firearms was established as an independent company producing selected H&R models under the NEF logo after Harrington & Richardson suspended operations on January 24, 1986. In 1991, H&R 1871, Inc. was formed from the residual of the parent H&R company and then took over the New England Firearms facility. H&R 1871 produced firearms under both their logo and the NEF brand name until 1999, when the Marlin Firearms Company acquired the assets of H&R 1871.

NEW ENGLAND FIREARMS NWTF TURKEY SPECIAL
Similar to Turkey and Goose models except 10 or 20 gauge w/22- or 24-inch plain bbl. w/screw-in full-choke tube. Mossy Oak camo finish on entire gun. Made from 1992-96.
Turkey Special 10 ga. .... NiB $220 Ex $191 Gd $175
Turkey Special 20 ga. .... NiB $139 Ex $119 Gd $88

NRA FOUNDATION YOUTH ..... NiB $202 Ex $167 Gd $123
Smaller scale version of Pardner Model chambered for 20, 28 or .410 w/22- inch plain bbl. High luster blue finish. NRA Foundation logo laser etched on stock. Made from 1999-2002.

PARDNER SHOTGUN
Takedown. Side lever. Single bbl. Gauges: 12, 20 and .410 w/3-inch chamber; 16 and 28 w/2.75-inch chamber. 26-, 28- or 32-inch, plain bbl. w/fixed choke. Weight: 5-6 lbs. Bead front sight. Pistol grip-style hardwood stock w/walnut finish. Made from 1988 to date.
Standard model .... NiB $127 Ex $106 Gd $81
Youth model .... NiB $134 Ex $113 Gd $84
Youth Turkey model .... NiB $148 Ex $123 Gd $92
W/32-inch bbl., add $15

PARDNER SPECIAL PURPOSE 10 GA. SHOTGUN
Similar to the standard Pardner model except chambered 10 ga. only w/3.5-inch chamber. 24- or 28-inch, plain bbl. w/full choke tube or fixed choke. Weight: 9.5 lbs. Bead front sight. Pistol-grip-style hardwood stock w/camo or matte black finish. Made from 1989 to date.
Special Purpose model w/fixed choke .. NiB $154 Ex $128 Gd $96
W/camo finish, add $15
W/choke tube, add $20
W/24-inch bbl. turkey option, add $30

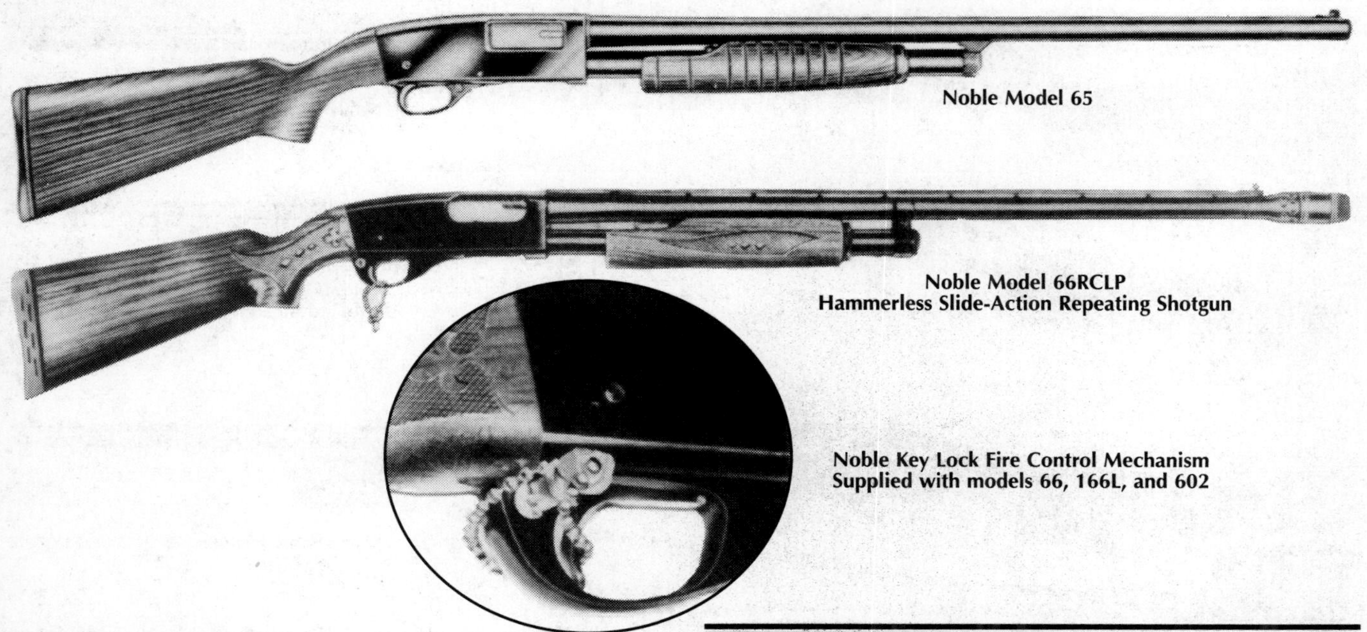

Noble Model 65

Noble Model 66RCLP
Hammerless Slide-Action Repeating Shotgun

Noble Key Lock Fire Control Mechanism
Supplied with models 66, 166L, and 602

PARDNER SPECIAL PURPOSE
WATERFOWL SINGLE-SHOT . . . . . NiB $180 Ex $148 Gd $107
Similar to Special Purpose 10 Ga. model except w/32-inch bbl. Mossy Oak camo stock w/swivel and sling. Made from 1988 to date.

PARDNER TURKEY GUN
Similar to Pardner model except chambered in 12 ga. w/3.0- or 3.5-inch chamber. 24-inch plain bbl. W/turkey full-choke tube or fixed choke. Weight: 9.5 lbs. American hardwood stock w/camo or matte black finish. Made from 1999 to date.
Standard Turkey model . . . . NiB $161 Ex $132 Gd $96
Camo Turkey model . . . . NiB $174 Ex $143 Gd $102

SURVIVOR SERIES
Takedown single bbl. shotgun w/side lever release, Automatic ejector and patented transfer-bar safety. Gauges: 12, 20, and .410/.45 ACP w/3-inch chamber. 22-inch bbl. w/modified choke and bead sight. Weight: 6 lbs. Polymer stock and forend w/hollow cavity for storage. Made 1992-93 and 1995 to date.
12 or 20 ga.
w/blued finish . . . . NiB $139 Ex $115 Gd $84
12 or 20 ga.
w/nickel finish . . . . NiB $171 Ex $141 Gd $102
.410/.45 ACP, add . . . . NiB $57 Ex $49 Gd $39

TRACKER SLUG GUN
Similar to Pardner model except in 10, 12 or 20 ga. w/24-inch w/cylinder choke or rifled slug bbl. (Tracker II). Weight: 6 lbs. American hardwood stock w/walnut or camo finish, Schnabel forend, sling swivel studs. Made from 1992-2001.
Tracker Slug
(10 ga.) . . . . NiB $142 Ex $117 Gd $86
Tracker Slug
(12 or 20 ga.) . . . . NiB $143 Ex $112 Gd $71
Tracker II (rifled bore) . . . . NiB $174 Ex $143 Gd $81

NIKKO FIREARMS LTD. — Tochigi, Japan

See listings under Golden Eagle Firearms, Inc.

NOBLE MANUFACTURING COMPANY — Haydenville, Massachusetts

Series 602 and 70 are similar in appearance to the corresponding Model 66 guns.

MODEL 40 HAMMERLESS SLIDE-ACTION
REPEATING SHOTGUN . . . . NiB $166 Ex $136 Gd $98
Solid frame. 12 ga. only. Five round tubular magazine. 28-inch bbl. w/ventilated Multi-Choke. Weight: About 7.5 lbs. Plain pistol-grip stock, grooved slide handle. Made from 1950-55.

MODEL 50
SLIDE-ACTION . . . . NiB $166 Ex $136 Gd $98
Same as Model 40 except w/o Multi-Choke. M or F choke bbl. Made from 1953-55.

MODEL 60 HAMMERLESS SLIDE-ACTION
REPEATING SHOTGUN . . . . NiB $229 Ex $187 Gd $133
Solid frame. 12 and 16 ga. Five round tubular magazine. 28-inch bbl. w/adj. choke. Plain pistol-grip stock w/recoil pad, grooved slide handle. Weight: About 7.5 lbs. Made from 1955-66.

MODEL 65 . . . . NiB $192 Ex $157 Gd $113
Same as Model 60 except without adj. choke and recoil pad. M or F choke bbl. Made from 1955-66.

MODEL 66CLP . . . . NiB $179 Ex $147 Gd $106
Same as Model 66RCLP except has plain bbl. Introduced in 1967. Disc.

MODEL 66RCLP HAMMERLESS SLIDE-ACTION
REPEATING SHOTGUN . . . . NiB $221 Ex $181 Gd $123
Solid frame. Key lock fire control mechanism. Gauges: 12, 16. 3-inch chamber in 12 ga. Five round tubular magazine. 28-inch bbl., vent rib, adj. choke. Weight: About 7.5 lbs. Checkered pistol-grip stock and slide handle, recoil pad. Made from 1967-70.

MODEL 66RLP . . . . NiB $204 Ex $167 Gd $120
Same as Model 66RCLP except w/F or M choke. Made from 1967-1970.

SHOTGUNS

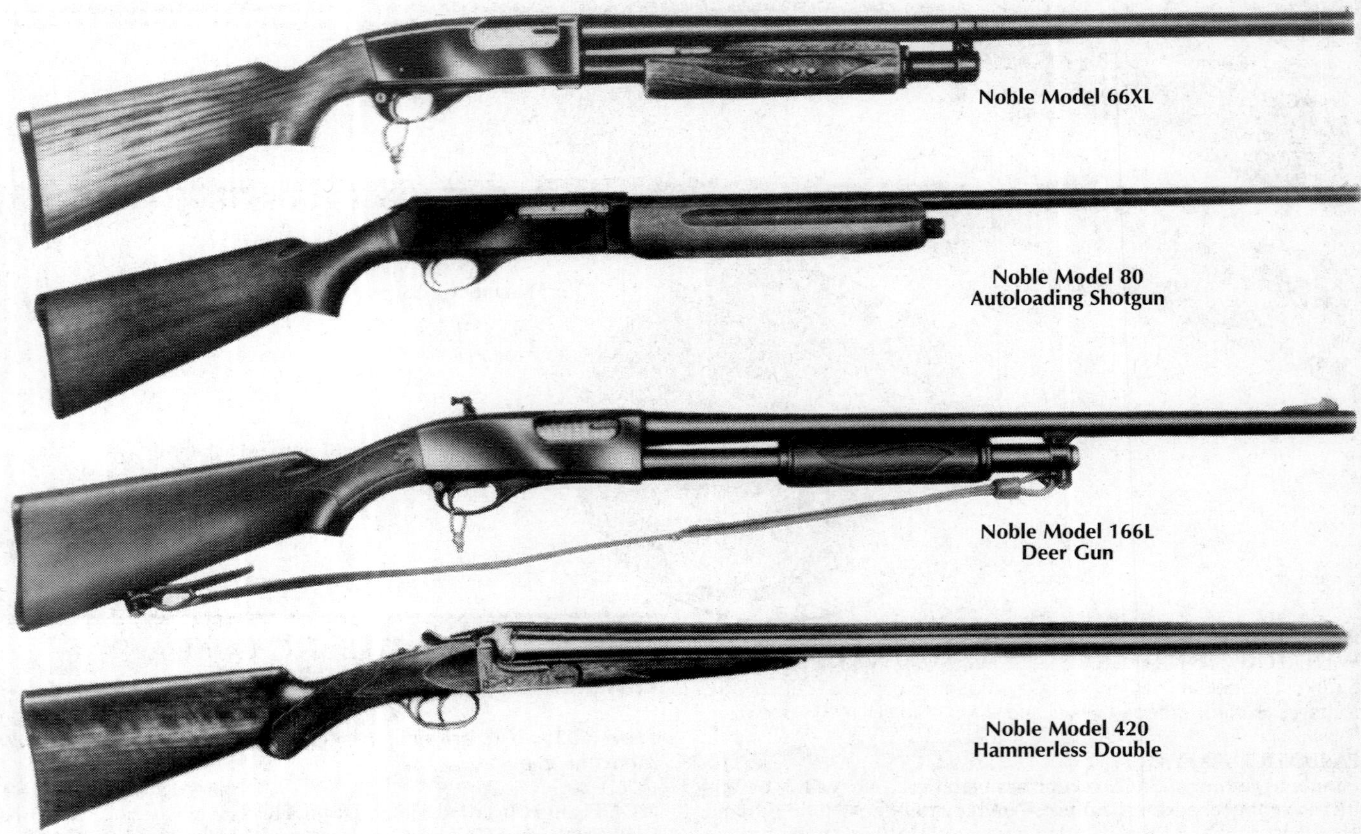

Noble Model 66XL

Noble Model 80 Autoloading Shotgun

Noble Model 166L Deer Gun

Noble Model 420 Hammerless Double

MODEL 66XL . . . . NiB $179 Ex $147 Gd $106
Same as Model 66RCL except has plain bbl., F or M choke, slide handle only checkered, no recoil pad. Made from 1967-70.

MODEL 70CLP HAMMERLESS SLIDE-ACTION REPEATING SHOTGUN . . . . NiB $204 Ex $167 Gd $120
Solid frame. .410 gauge. Magazine holds 5 rounds. 26-inch bbl. w/adj. choke. Weight: About 6 lbs. Checkered buttstock and forearm, recoil pad. Made from 1958-70.

MODEL 70RCLP . . . . NiB $212 Ex $172 Gd $123
Same as Model 70CLP except has vent rib. Made from 1967-70.

MODEL 70RLP . . . . NiB $198 Ex $162 Gd $116
Same as Model 70CLP except has vent rib and no adj. choke. Made from 1967-70.

MODEL 70XL . . . . NiB $154 Ex $126 Gd $91
Same as Model 70CLP except without adj. choke and checkering on buttstock. Made from 1958-70.

MODEL 80 AUTOLOADING SHOTGUN. . . . . . NiB $259 Ex $211 Gd $151
Recoil-operated. .410 ga. Magazine holds three 3-inch shells, four 2.5-inch shells. 26-inch bbl., full choke. Weight: About 6 lbs. Plain pistol-grip stock and fluted forearm. Made from 1964-66.

MODEL 166L DEER GUN . . . . NiB $287 Ex $233 Gd $166
Solid frame. Key lock fire control mechanism. 12 ga. 2.75-inch chamber. Five round tubular magazine. 24-inch plain bbl., specially bored for rifled slug. Lyman peep rear sight, post ramp front sight. Receiver dovetailed for scope mounting. Weight: About 7.25 lbs. Checkered pistol-grip stock and slide handle, swivels and carrying strap. Made from 1967-70.

MODEL 420 HAMMERLESS DOUBLE . . . . NiB $374 Ex $305 Gd $217
Boxlock. Plain extractors. Double triggers. Gauges: 12 ga. 3-inch mag.; 16 ga.; 20 ga. 3-inch mag.; .410 ga. Bbls.: 28-inch, except .410 in 26-inch, M/F choke. Weight: About 6.75 lbs. Engraved frame. Checkered walnut stock and forearm. Made from 1958-70.

MODEL 450E HAMMERLESS DOUBLE . . . . NiB $415 Ex $338 Gd $240
Boxlock. Engraved frame. Selective auto ejectors. Double triggers. Gauges: 12, 16, 20. 3-inch chambers in 12 and 20 ga. 28-inch bbls., M/F choke. Weight: About 6 lbs., 14 oz., 12 ga. Checkered pistol-grip stock and beavertail forearm, recoil pad. Made from 1967-70.

MODEL 602CLP . . . . NiB $225 Ex $185 Gd $185
Same as Model 602RCLP except has plain barrel. Made from 1958-70.

MODEL 602RCLP HAMMERLESS SLIDE-ACTION REPEATING SHOTGUN . . . . NiB $237 Ex $195 Gd $140
Solid frame. Key lock fire control mechanism. 20 ga. 3-inch chamber. Five round tubular magazine. 28-inch bbl., vent rib, adj. choke. Weight: About 6.5 lbs. Checkered pistol-grip stock/slide handle, recoil pad. Made from 1967-70.

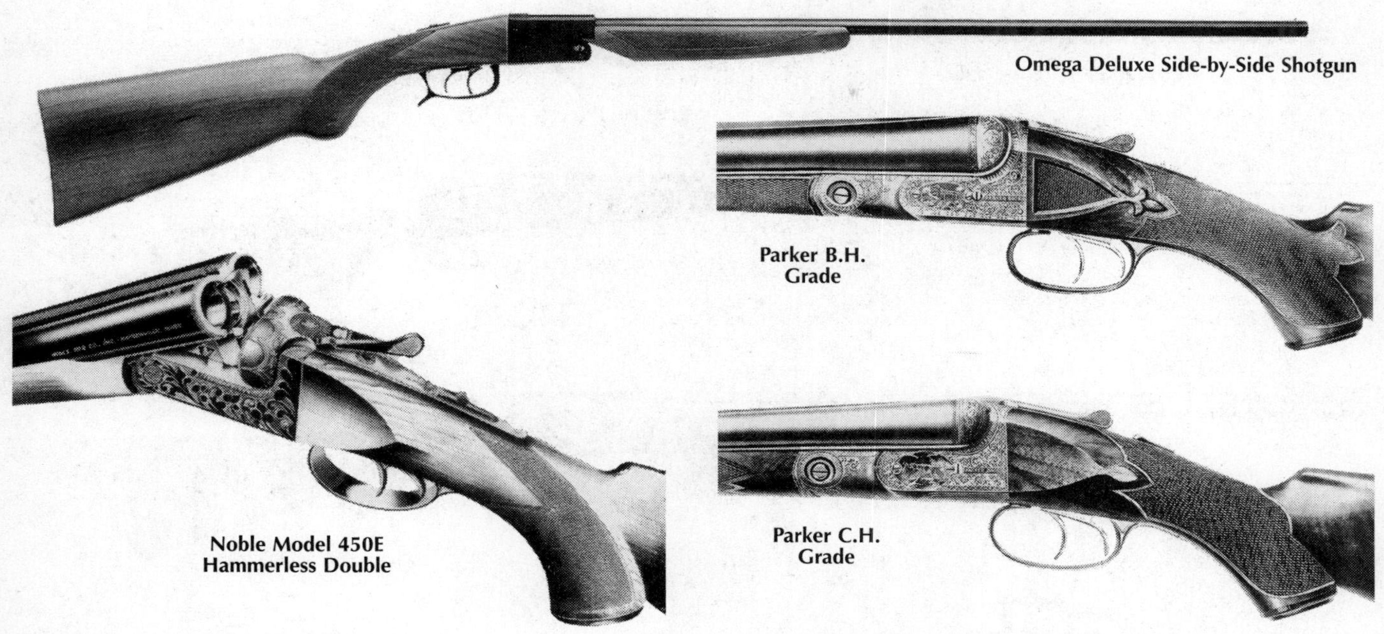
Omega Deluxe Side-by-Side Shotgun

Parker B.H. Grade

Noble Model 450E Hammerless Double

Parker C.H. Grade

MODEL 602RLP . . . . NiB $215 Ex $175 Gd $126
Same as Model 602RCLP except without adj. choke, bored F or M choke. Made from 1967-70.

MODEL 602XL . . . . NiB $182 Ex $150 Gd $109
Same as Model 602RCL except has plain bbl., F or M choke, slide handle only checkered, no recoil pad. Made from 1958-70.

MODEL 662 . . . . NiB $221 Ex $181 Gd $129
Same as Model 602CLP except has aluminum receiver and bbl. Weight: About 4.5 lbs. Made from 1966-70.

OMEGA SHOTGUNS — Brescia, Italy, and Korea

FOLDING OVER/UNDER SHOTGUN, STANDARD
Hammerless Boxlock. Gauges: 12, 20, 28 w/2.75-inch chambers or .410 w/3-inch chambers. Bbls.: 26- or 28-inch vent-rib w/fixed chokes (IC/M, M/F or F/F (.410). Automatic safety. Single trigger. 40.5 inches overall (42.5 inches, 20 ga., 28-inch bbl.). Weight: 6 to 7.5 lbs. Checkered European walnut stock and forearm. Imported from 1984-94.
Standard model (12 ga.) . . . . NiB $485 Ex $387 Gd $253
Standard model (20 ga.) . . . . NiB $485 Ex $387 Gd $253
Standard model (28 ga. & .410) . . . . NiB $560 Ex $458 Gd $328

O/U SHOTGUN, DELUXE . . . . NiB $477 Ex $389 Gd $280
Gauges: 20, 28 and .410. 26- or 28-inch vent-rib bbls. 40.5 inches overall (42.5 inches, 20 ga., 28-inch bbl.). Chokes: IC/M, M/F or F/F (.410). Weight: About 5.5-6 lbs. Single trigger. Automatic safety. European walnut stock w/checkered pistol grip and tulip forend. Imported from Italy 1984-90.

OMEGA DELUXE SIDE-BY-SIDE SHOTGUN . . . . NiB $236 Ex $194 Gd $139
Same general specifications as the Standard Side-by-Side except has checkered European walnut stock and low bbl. rib. Made in Italy from 1984-89.

STANDARD SIDE-BY-SIDE SHOTGUN, ...NiB $235 Ex $193 Gd $138
Gauge: .410. 26-inch bbl. 40.5 inches overall. Choked F/F. Weight: 5.5 lbs. Double trigger. Manual safety. Checkered beechwood stock and semi-pistol grip. Imported from Italy 1984-89.

DELUXE SINGLE-SHOT SHOTGUN . . . . . . NiB $129 Ex $107 Gd $81
Same general specifications as the Standard single bbl. except has checkered walnut stock, top lever break, fully-blued receiver, vent rib. Imported from Korea 1984-87.

STANDARD SINGLE-SHOT SHOTGUN
Gauges: 12, 16, 20, 28 and .410. Bbl. lengths: 26-, 28- or 30-inches. Weight: 5 lbs., 4 oz. to 5 lbs., 11 oz. Indonesian walnut stock. Matte-chromed receiver and top lever break. Imported from Korea 1984-87.
Standard fixed . . . . NiB $204 Ex $188 Gd $106
Standard folding . . . . NiB $176 Ex $150 Gd $109
Deluxe folding . . . . NiB $223 Ex $183 Gd $131

PARKER BROTHERS — Meriden, Connecticut

This firm was taken over by Remington Arms Company in 1934 and its production facilities moved to Remington's Ilion, New York, plant. In 1984, Winchester took over production until 1999.

HAMMERLESS DOUBLE-BARREL SHOTGUNS
Grades V.H. through A-1 Special. Boxlock. Auto ejectors. Double triggers or selective single trigger. Gauges: 10, 12, 16, 20, 28, .410. Bbls.: 26- to 32-inch, any standard boring. Weight: 6.88-8.5 lbs.,12 ga. Stock and forearm of select walnut, checkered; straight, half-or full-pistol grip. Grades differ only in quality of workmanship, grade of wood, engraving, checkering, etc. General specifications are the same for all. Disc. about 1940.
V.H. grade, 12 or 16 ga. . . . . NiB $3447 Ex $2805 Gd $1983
V.H. grade, 20 ga. . . . . NiB $4935 Ex $3994 Gd $2791
V.H. grade, 28 ga. . . . . NiB $7921 Ex $6388 Gd $4427
V.H. grade, .410 ga. . . . . NiB $19,249 Ex $15,398 Gd $10,471
G.H. grade, 12 ga. . . . . NiB $4611 Ex $3737 Gd $2618
G.H. grade, 16 ga. . . . . NiB $4811 Ex $3896 Gd $2726

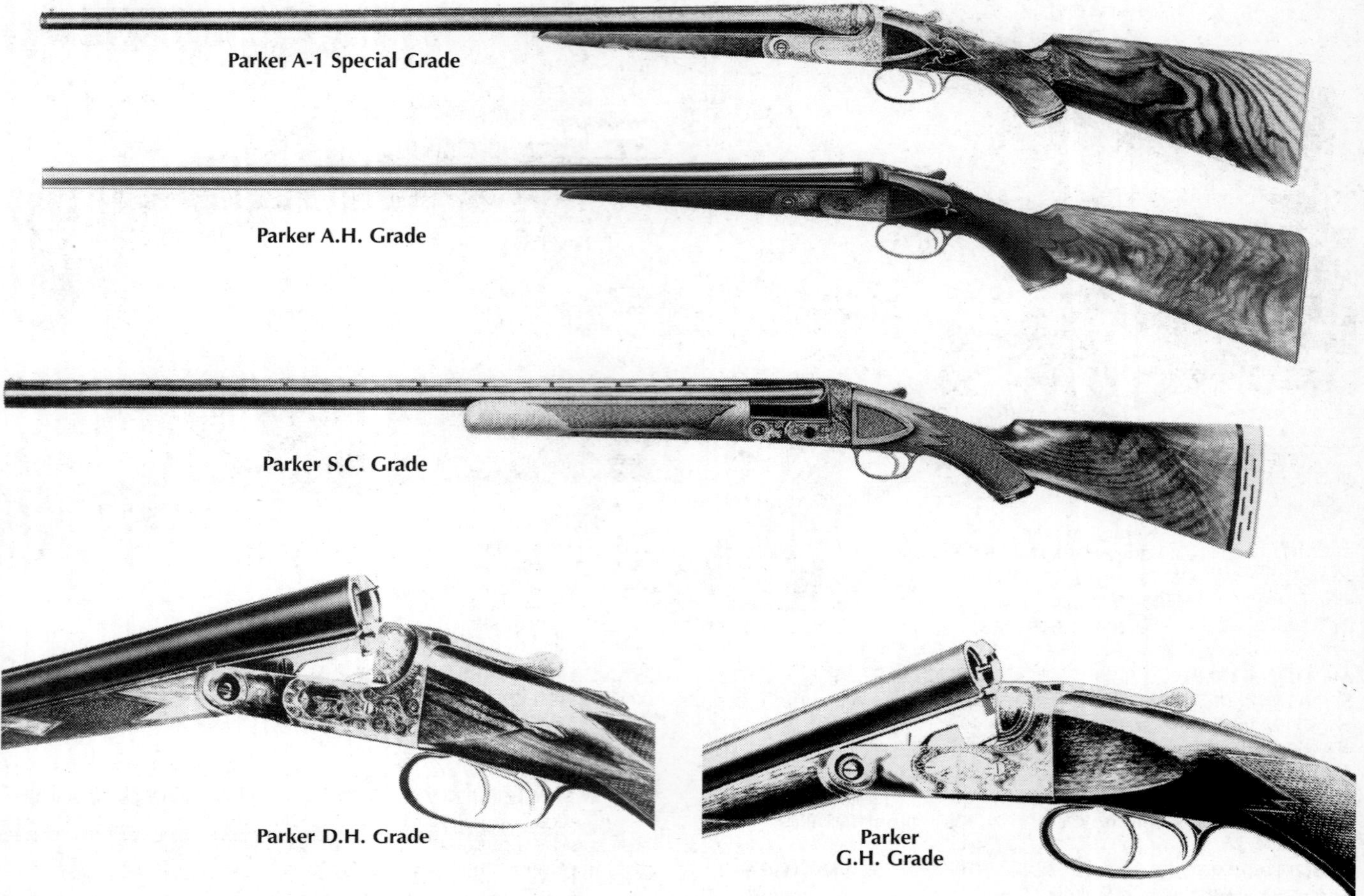
Parker A-1 Special Grade

Parker A.H. Grade

Parker S.C. Grade

Parker D.H. Grade

Parker G.H. Grade

G.H. grade, 20 ga. . . . . NiB $6732 Ex $5088 Gd $3500
G.H. grade, 28 ga. . . . . NiB $9821 Ex $7890 Gd $5400
G.H. grade, .410 ga. . . . . NiB $24,463 Ex $19,714 Gd $1400
D.H. grade, 12 or 16 ga. . . . . NiB $7105 Ex $5699 Gd $3898
D.H. grade, 20 ga. . . . . NiB $9113 Ex $7305 Gd $4991
D.H. grade, 28 ga. . . . . NiB $13,738 Ex $11,021 Gd $7542
D.H. grade, .410 ga. . . . . NiB $45,577 Ex $36,462 Gd $24,794
C.H. grade, 12 or 16 ga. . . . . NiB $7877 Ex $6317 Gd $4315
C.H. grade, 20 ga. . . . . NiB $10,289 Ex $8251 Gd $5643
C.H. grade, 28 ga. . . . . NiB $10,530 Ex $7900 Gd $5700
B.H. grade, 12 or 16 ga. . . . . NiB $11,765 Ex $9432 Gd $6445
B.H. grade, 20 ga. . . . . NiB $20,471 Ex $16,377 Gd $11,136
B.H. grade, 28 ga. . . . . NiB $38,239 Ex $30,591 Gd $20,802
A.H. grade, 12 or 16 ga. . . . . NiB $27,038 Ex $21,630 Gd $14,708
A.H. grade, 20 ga. . . . . NiB $33,604 Ex $26,883 Gd $18,280
A.H. grade, 28 ga. . . . . NiB $59,482 Ex $47,586 Gd $32,080
A.A.H. grade, 12 or 16 ga. . . . . NiB $61,723 Ex $49,378 Gd $33,577
A.A.H. grade, 12 or 16 ga. . . . . NiB $51,371 Ex $41,097 Gd $27,946
A.A.H. grade, 20 ga. . . . . NiB $74,932 Ex $59,946 Gd $40,763
A.A.H. grade, 28 ga. . . . . NiB $111,626 Ex $89,301 Gd $60,724
A-1 Special grade,
12 or 16 ga. NiB $96,562 Ex $77,250 Gd $52,530
A-1 Special grade, 20 ga. . . . . NiB $142,140 Ex $113,712 Gd $77,324
A-1 Special grade, 28 ga. . . . . NiB $190,035 Ex $152,028 Gd $103,379
W/selective-single trigger, add 20%
W/ventilated rib, add 35%
For non-ejector guns, deduct 30%

SINGLE-SHOT TRAP GUNS

Hammerless. Boxlock. Ejector. 12 ga. only. Bbl. lengths: 30-, 32-, 34-inch, any boring, vent rib. Weight: 7.5-8.5 lbs. Stock and forearm of select walnut, checkered; straight, half-or full-pistol grip. The five grades differ only in quality of workmanship, grade of wood, checkering, engraving, etc. General specifications same for all. Disc. about 1940.

S.C. grade . . . . NiB $5156 Ex $4152 Gd $2867
S.B. grade . . . . NiB $6276 Ex $5048 Gd $3474
S.A. grade . . . . NiB $7010 Ex $5635 Gd $3875
S.A.A. grade . . . . NiB $8948 Ex $7189 Gd $4936
S.A.1 Special . . . . NiB $27,038 Ex $21,630 Gd $14,708

SKEET GUN

Same as other Parker doubles from Grade V.H.E. up except selective single trigger and beavertail forearm are standard on this model, as are 26-inch bbls., SK choke. Discontinued about 1940. Values are 35 percent higher.

TROJAN HAMMERLESS DOUBLE-BARREL SHOTGUN

Boxlock. Plain extractors. Double trigger or single trigger. Gauges: 12, 16, 20. Bbls.: 30-inch both F choke (12 ga. only), 26- or 28-inch M and F choke. Weight: 6.25-7.75 lbs. Checkered pistol-grip stock and forearm. Disc. 1939.

12 ga. . . . . NiB $2433 Ex $1965 Gd $1367
16 ga. . . . . NiB $3209 Ex $2586 Gd $1811

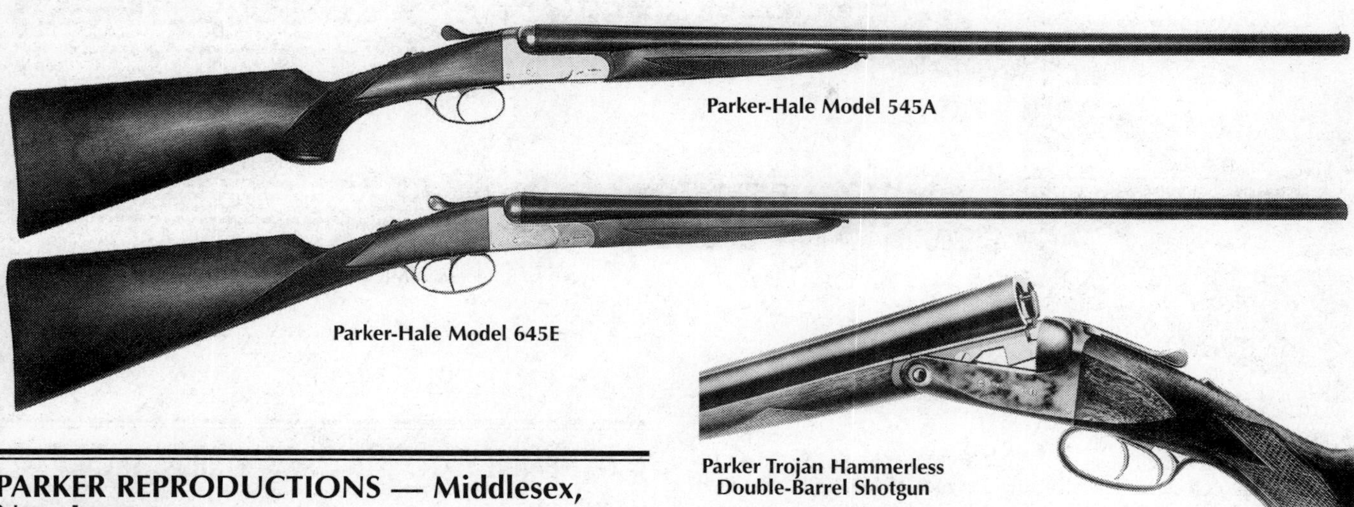

Parker-Hale Model 545A

Parker-Hale Model 645E

Parker Trojan Hammerless Double-Barrel Shotgun

PARKER REPRODUCTIONS — Middlesex, New Jersey

HAMMERLESS DOUBLE-BARREL SHOTGUNS

Reproduction of the original Parker boxlock. Single selective trigger or double triggers. Selective automatic ejectors. Automatic safety. Gauges: 12, 16, 20, 28 or .410 w/2.75- or 3-inch chambers. Bbls.: 26- or 28-inch w/fixed or internal screw choke tubes SK/SK, IC/M, M/F. Weight: 5.5-7 lbs. Checkered English-style or pistol-grip American walnut stock w/beavertail or splinter forend and checkered skeleton buttplate. Color casehardened receiver with game scenes and scroll engraving. Produced in Japan by Olin Kodensha from 1984-88.

DHE grade, 12 ga. NiB $3587 Ex $2904 Gd $1203
DHE grade, 12 ga Sporting Clays. . . . . NiB $4461 Ex $3605 Gd $2509
DHE grade, 20 ga. NiB $2989 Ex $2434 Gd $1701
DHE grade, 28 ga. NiB $3338 Ex $2686 Gd $1879
DHE grade 2-barrel set (16 & 20 ga.). . . . . NiB $5682 Ex $4587 Gd $3187
DHE grade 2-barrel set (28 & .410) . . . . . . NiB $6331 Ex $5107 Gd $3542
DHE grade 3-barrel set . . . . NiB $7830 Ex $6312 Gd $4369
B grade Bank Note Lim. Ed., 12 ga. . . . . . . NiB $5611 Ex $4531 Gd $3149
B grade Bank Note Lim. Ed., 20 ga. . . . . . . NiB $6980 Ex $5627 Gd $3897
B grade Bank Note Lim. Ed., 28 ga. . . . . . NiB $10,691 Ex $8581 Gd $5880
B grade Bank Note Lim. Ed., .410 ga. . . . NiB $10,069 Ex $8690 Gd $5872
A-1 Special grade, 12 ga. . . . . NiB $9869 Ex $7923 Gd $53410
A-1 Special grade, 16 ga. . . . . NiB $11,674 Ex $9368 Gd $6419
A-1 Special grade, 20 ga. . . . . NiB $9483 Ex $7604 Gd $5199
A-1 Special grade, 28 ga. . . . . NiB $14,099 Ex $11,278 Gd $7669
A-1 Special gr. 2-barrel set . . . . NiB $11,124 Ex $8921 Gd $6113
A-1 Special gr. 3-barrel set . . . . . NiB $26,394+ Ex $21,115+ Gd $14,358+
A-1 Special gr. custom engraved. . . . . . NiB $16,094 Ex $12,875 Gd $8955
A-1 Special gr. custom 2-barrel set . . . . . NiB $12,296 Ex $9836 Gd $6689
Extra barrel set, add $250

PARKER-HALE SHOTGUNS — Mfd. by Ignacio Ugartechea, Spain

MODEL 645A (AMERICAN)

SIDE-BY-SIDE SHOTGUN . . . . NiB $1195 Ex $983 Gd $711

Gauges: 12, 16 and 20. Boxlock action. 26- and 28-inch bbls. Chokes: IC/M, M/F. Weight: 6 lbs. average. Single non-selective trigger. Automatic safety. Hand-checkered pistol grip walnut stock w/beavertail forend. Raised matted rib. English scroll-design engraved receiver. Discontinued 1990.

MODEL 645E (ENGLISH) SIDE-BY-SIDE SHOTGUN

Same general specifications as the Model 645A except double triggers, straight grip, splinter forend, checkered butt and concave rib. Disc. 1990.

12, 16, 20 ga. with 26- or 28-inch bbl. . . . . . NiB $1240 Ex $1014 Gd $727
28, .410 ga. with 27-inch bbl. . . . . NiB $1653 Ex $1346 Gd $954

MODEL 645E-XXV

12, 16, 20 ga. with 25-inch bbl. . . . . NiB $1175 Ex $987 Gd $691
28, .410 ga. with 25-inch bbl. . . . . NiB $1553 Ex $1265 Gd $897

PEDERSEN CUSTOM GUNS — North Haven, Connecticut, Div. of O. F. Mossberg & Sons, Inc.

MODEL 1000 O/U HUNTING SHOTGUN

Boxlock. Auto ejectors. Selective single trigger. Gauges: 12, 20. 2.75-inch chambers in 12 ga., 3-inch in 20 ga. Bbls.: Vent rib; 30-inch M/F (12 ga. only); 28-inch IC/M (12 ga. only), M/F; 26-inch IC/M. Checkered pistol-grip stock and forearm. Grade I is the higher quality gun with custom stock dimensions, fancier wood, more elaborate engraving, silver inlays. Made from 1973-75.

Grade I . . . . NiB $2419 Ex $1956 Gd $1363
Grade II . . . . NiB $1959 Ex $1586 Gd $1110

MODEL 1000 MAGNUM

Same as Model 1000 Hunting Gun except chambered for 12-ga. Magnum 3-inch shells, 30-inch bbls., IM/F choke. Made from 1973-75.

Grade I . . . . NiB $2619 Ex $2116 Gd $1474
Grade II . . . . NiB $2162 Ex $1751 Gd $1226

MODEL 1000 SKEET GUN

Same as Model 1000 Hunting Gun except has skeet-style stock; 26- and 28-inch bbls. (12 ga. only), SK choke. Made from 1973-75.

Grade I . . . . NiB $2265 Ex $1833 Gd $1471
Grade II . . . . NiB $1838 Ex $1489 Gd $1042

MODEL 1000 TRAP GUN

Same as Model 1000 Hunting Gun except 12 ga. only, has Monte Carlo trap-style stock, 30- or 32-inch bbls., M/F or IM/F choke. Made from 1973-75.

Grade I . . . . NiB $2003 Ex $1632 Gd $1135
Grade II . . . . NiB $1635 Ex $1327 Gd $931

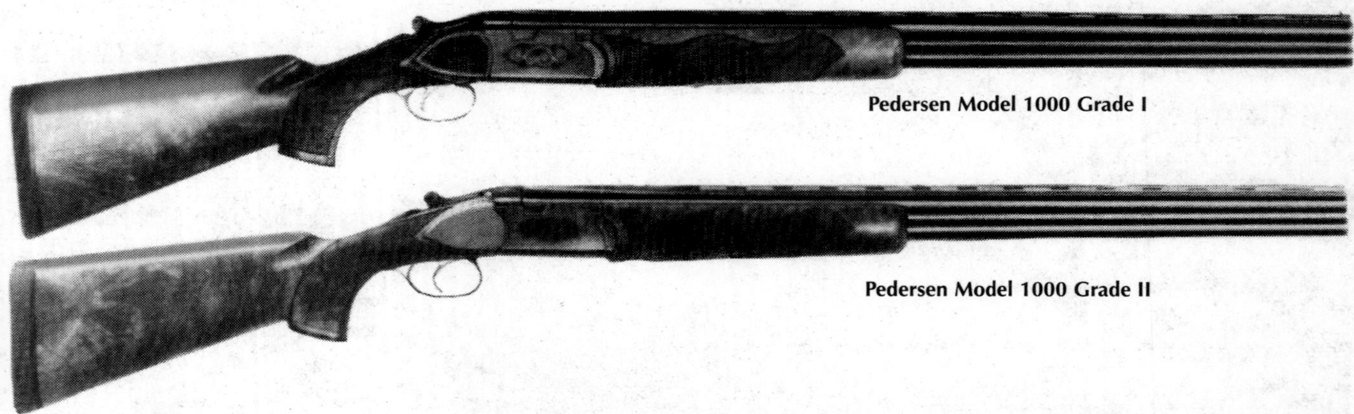

Pedersen Model 1000 Grade I

Pedersen Model 1000 Grade II

MODEL 1500 O/U
HUNTING SHOTGUN .... NiB $833 Ex $675 Gd $475
Boxlock. Auto ejectors. Selective single trigger. 12 ga. 2.75- or 3-inch chambers. Bbls.: vent rib; 26-inch IC/M; 28- and 30-inch M/F; Magnum has 30-inch, IM/F choke. Weight: 7-7.5 lbs., depending on bbl. length. Checkered pistol-grip stock and forearm. Made from 1973-75.

MODEL 1500 SKEET GUN .... NiB $856 Ex $695 Gd $490
Same as Model 1500 Hunting Gun except has skeet-style stock, 27-inch bbls., SK choke. Made from 1973-75.

MODEL 1500 TRAP GUN .... NiB $718 Ex $584 Gd $414
Same as Model 1500 Hunting Gun except has Monte Carlo trap-style stock, 30- or 32-inch bbls., M/F or IM/F chokes. Made from 1973-75.

MODEL 2000 HAMMERLESS DOUBLE
Boxlock. Auto ejectors. Selective single trigger. Gauges: 12, 20. 2.75-inch chambers in 12 ga., 3-inch in 20 ga. Bbls.: Vent rib; 30-inch M/F (12 ga. only); 28-inch M/F, 26-inch IC/M choke. Checkered pistol-grip stock and forearm. Grade I is the higher quality gun w/custom dimensions, fancier wood, more elaborate engraving, silver inlays. Made from 1973-74.
Grade I .... NiB $2643 Ex $2140 Gd $1498
Grade II .... NiB $2236 Ex $1974 Gd $1383

MODEL 2500
HAMMERLESS DOUBLE .... NiB $503 Ex $409 Gd $288
Boxlock. Auto ejectors. Selective single trigger. Gauges: 12, 20. 2.75-inch chambers in 12 ga., 3-inch in 20 ga. Bbls.: Vent rib; 28-inch M/F; 26-inch IC/M choke. Checkered pistol-grip stock and forearm. Made from 1973-74.

MODEL 4000 HAMMERLESS SLIDE-ACTION
REPEATING SHOTGUN .... NiB $516 Ex $419 Gd $296
Custom version of Mossberg Model 500. Full-coverage floral engraving on receiver. Gauges: 12, 20, .410. Three-inch chamber. Bbls.: Vent rib; 26-inch IC or SK choke; 28-inch F or M; 30-inch F. Weight: 6-8 lbs. depending on ga. and bbl. Checkered stock and slide handle of select wood. Made in 1975.

MODEL 4000 TRAP GUN .... NiB $527 Ex $429 Gd $303
Same as standard Model 4000 except 12 ga. only, has 30-inch F choke bbl., Monte Carlo trap-style stock w/recoil pad. Made in 1975.

MODEL 4500 .... NiB $472 Ex $384 Gd $272
Same as Model 4000 except has simpler scroll engraving. Made in 1975.

MODEL 4500 TRAP GUN .... NiB $484 Ex $393 Gd $278
Same as Model 4000 Trap Gun except has simpler scroll engraving. Made in 1975.

J. C. PENNEY CO., INC. — Dallas, Texas

MODEL 4011
AUTOLOADING SHOTGUN...... NiB $247 Ex $202 Gd $145
Hammerless. Five round magazine. Bbls.: 26-inch IC; 28-inch M or F; 30-inch F choke. Weight: 7.25 lbs. Plain pistol-grip stock and slide handle.

MODEL 6610
SINGLE-SHOT SHOTGUN .... NiB $122 Ex $102 Gd $75
Hammerless. Takedown. Auto ejector. Gauges: 12, 16, 20 and .410. Bbl. length: 28-36 inches. Weight: About 6 lbs. Plain pistol-grip stock and forearm.

MODEL 6630
BOLT-ACTION SHOTGUN .... NiB $160 Ex $132 Gd $96
Takedown. Gauges: 12, 16, 20. Two round clip magazine. 26- and 28-inch bbl. lengths; with or without adj. choke. Plain pistol-grip stock. Weight: About 7.25 lbs.

MODEL 6670
SLIDE-ACTION SHOTGUN ...... NiB $186 Ex $153 Gd $116
Hammerless. Gauges: 12, 16, 20, and .410. Three round tubular magazine. Bbls.: 26- to 30-inch; various chokes. Weight: 6.25-7.25 lbs. Walnut finished hardwood stock.

MODEL 6870 SLIDE-ACTION
SHOTGUN .... NiB $265 Ex $214 Gd $157
Hammerless. Gauges: 12, 16, 20, .410. Four round magazine. Bbls.: Vent rib; 26- to 30-inch, various chokes. Weight: Average 6.5 lbs. Plain pistol-grip stock.

PERAZZI SHOTGUNS — Manufactured by Manifattura Armi Perazzi, Brescia, Italy

See also listings under Ithaca-Perazzi.

DB81 O/U TRAP .... NiB $5114 Ex $4130 Gd $2869
Gauge: 12; 2.75-inch chambers. 29.5- or 31.5-inch bbls. w/wide vent rib; M/F chokes. Weight: 8 lbs., 6 oz. Detachable and interchangeable trigger with flat V-springs. Bead front sight. Interchangeable and custom-made checkered stock; beavertail forend. Imported 1988-94.

DB81 SINGLE-SHOT TRAP .... NiB $5114 Ex $4130 Gd $2869
Same general specifications as the DB81 over/under except in single bbl. version w/32- or 34-inch wide vent-rib bbl., F choke. Imported 1988-94.

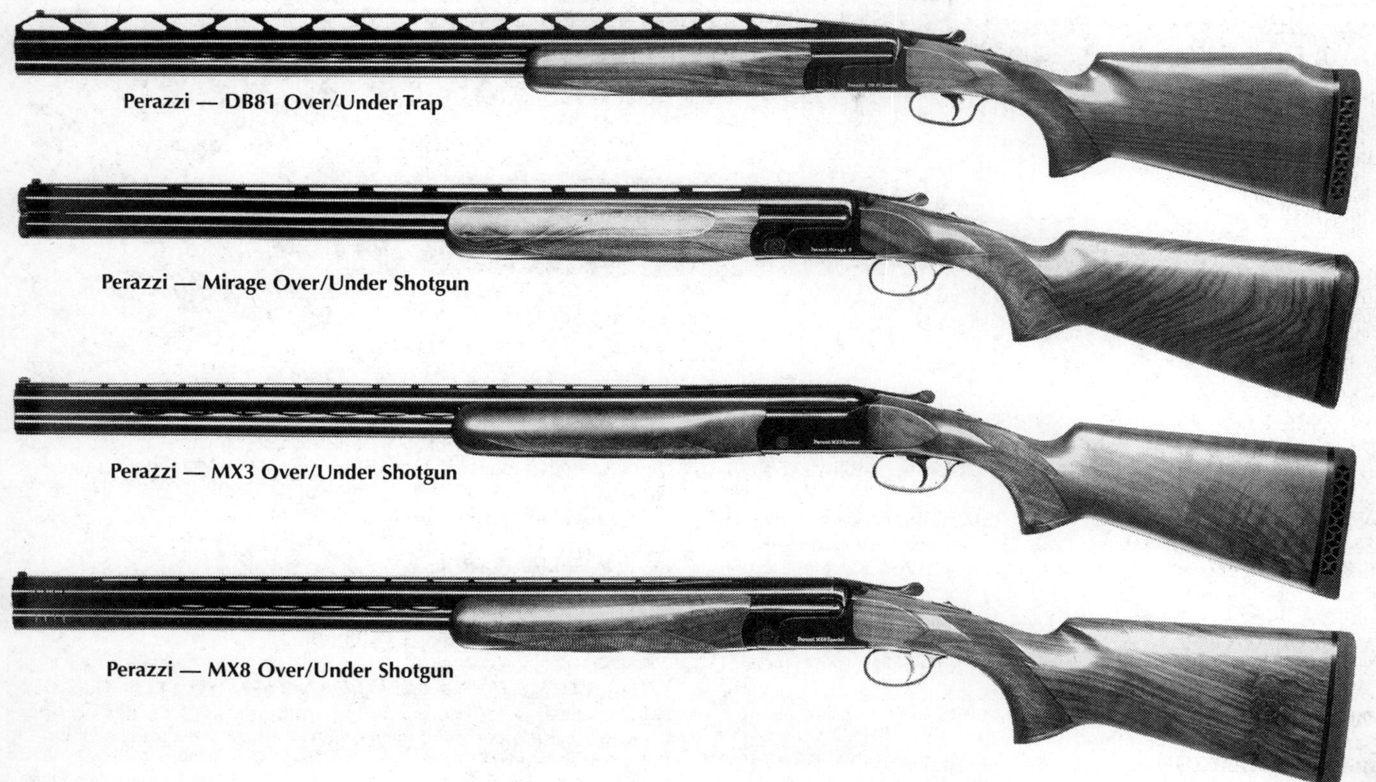

Perazzi — DB81 Over/Under Trap

Perazzi — Mirage Over/Under Shotgun

Perazzi — MX3 Over/Under Shotgun

Perazzi — MX8 Over/Under Shotgun

GRAND AMERICAN 88 SPECIAL SINGLE TRAP
Same general specifications as MX8 Special Single Trap except w/high ramped rib. Fixed choke or screw-in choke tubes.
Model 88 standard .... NiB $4500 Ex $3630 Gd $2518
Model 88 w/interchangeable
choke tubes .... NiB $4783 Ex $3857 Gd $2672

MIRAGE O/U SHOTGUN
Gauge: 12; 2.75-inch chambers. Bbls.: 27.63-, 29.5- or 31.5-inch vent-rib w/fixed chokes or screw-in choke tubes. Single selective trigger. Weight: 7 to 7.75 lbs. Interchangeable and custom-made checkered buttstock and forend.
Competition Trap,
Skeet, Pigeon, Sporting .... NiB $6308 Ex $5065 Gd $3473
Skeet 4-barrel sets .... NiB $13,197 Ex $10,557 Gd $7179
Competition Special (w/adj. 4-position trigger) add $350

MX1 O/U SHOTGUN
Similar to Model MX8 except w/ramp-style, tapered rib and modified stock configuration.
Competition Trap, Skeet,
Pigeon & Sporting .... NiB $3377 Ex $2729 Gd $1907
MXlC (w/choke tubes) .... NiB $3556 Ex $2873 Gd $1995
MXlB (w/flat low rib) .... NiB $3248 Ex $2626 Gd $1827

MX2 O/U SHOTGUN
Similar to Model MX8 except w/broad high-ramped competition rib.
Competition-Trap, Skeet,
Pigeon & Sporting .... NiB $4075 Ex $3289 Gd $2284
MX2C (w/choke tubes) .... NiB $4629 Ex $3734 Gd $2589

MX3 O/U SHOTGUN
Similar to Model MX8 except w/ramp-style, tapered rib and modified stock configuration.
Competition Trap, Skeet,
Pigeon & Sporting ...... NiB $46,289 Ex $37,032 Gd $25,181
Competition Special (w/adj. 4-position trigger) add $300
Game models .... NiB $4252 Ex $3429 Gd $2376
Combo O/U plus SB .... NiB $5246 Ex $4228 Gd $2927
SB Trap 32- or 34-inch .... NiB $3587 Ex $2893 Gd $2025
Skeet 4-bbl. sets .... NiB $11,009 Ex $8806 Gd $5988
Skeet Special 4-bbl. sets .... NiB $11,233 Ex $8987 Gd $6111

MX3 SPECIAL PIGEON SHOTGUN. . . NiB $5062 Ex $4087 Gd $2827
Gauge: 12; 2.75-inch chambers. 29.5- or 31.5-inch vent rib bbl.; IC/M and extra full chokes. Weight: 8 lbs., 6 oz. Detachable and interchangeable trigger group w/flat V-springs. Bead front sight. Interchangeable and custom-made checkered stock for live pigeon shoots; splinter forend. Imported 1991-92.

MX4 O/U SHOTGUN
Similar to Model MX3 in appearance and shares the MX8 locking system. Detachable, adj. 4-position trigger standard. Interchangeable choke tubes optional.
Competition Trap, Skeet, Pigeon & Sporting
.... NiB $4848 Ex $3907 Gd $2704
MX4C (w/choke tubes) .... NiB $5171 Ex $4168 Gd $3316

MX5 O/U GAME GUN
Similar to Model MX8 except in hunting configuration, chambered in 12 or 20 ga. Non-detachable single selective trigger.
MX5 Standard .... NiB $3309 Ex $2675 Gd $1853
MX5C (w/choke tubes) .... NiB $3654 Ex $2943 Gd $2027

MX6 AMER. TRAP SINGLE-BARREL . . NiB $3054 Ex $2462 Gd $1704
Single shot. Removable trigger group. 12 ga. Barrels: 32- or 34-inch with fixed or choke tubes. Raised vent rib. Checkered European walnut Monte Carlo stock, beavertail forend. Imported 1995-1998.

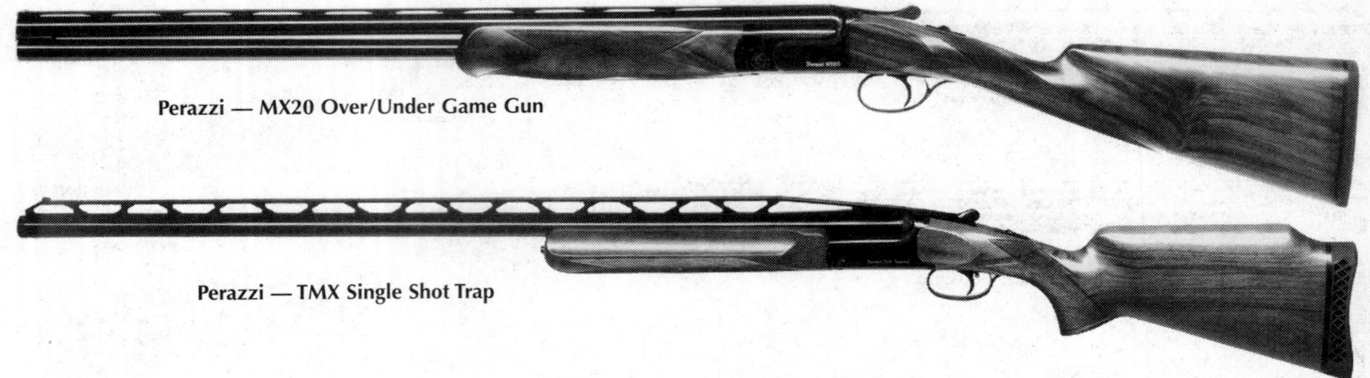

Perazzi — MX20 Over/Under Game Gun

Perazzi — TMX Single Shot Trap

MX6 SKEET O/U . . . . NiB $3440 Ex $2790 Gd $1933
Same general specs as MX6 American Trap single barrel except over/under; boxlock. Barrels: 26.75- or 27.50-inch. Imported 1995-1998.

MX6 SPORTING O/U . . . . NiB $3626 Ex $2924 Gd $2024
Same specs as MX6 American Trap single barrel except over/under; boxlock. Single selective trigger; external selector. Barrels: 28.38-, 29.50-, or 31.50-inch. Imported 1995-1998.

MX6 TRAP O/U . . . . NiB $3039 Ex $2449 Gd $1693
Same general specs as MX6 American Trap single barrel except over/under; boxlock. Barrels: 29.50-, 30.75-, or 31.50-inch. Imported 1995-1998.

MX7 O/U SHOTGUN . . . . NiB $4318 Ex $3490 Gd $2409
Similar to Model MX12 except w/MX3-style receiver and top-mounted trigger selector. Bbls.: 28.73-, 2.5-, 31.5-inch w/vent rib; screw-in choke tubes. Imported 1992-1998.

MX8 O/U SHOTGUN
Gauge: 12, 2.75-inch chambers. Bbls.: 27.63-, 29.5- or 31.5-inch vent-rib w/fixed chokes or screw-in choke tubes. Weight: 7 to 8.5 lbs. Interchangeable and custom-made checkered stock; beavertail forend. Special models have detachable and interchangeable 4-position trigger group w/flat V-springs. Imported 1988 to date.
MX8 Standard . . . . NiB $3929 Ex $3158 Gd $2183
MX8 Special (adj. 4-pos. trigger) . . . . . . NiB $4032 Ex $3240 Gd $2240
MX8 Special single
(32-or 34-inch bbl.) . . . . NiB $3816 Ex $3075 Gd $2135
MX8 Special combo . . . . NiB $7815 Ex $6192 Gd $4342

MX8/20 O/U SHOTGUN. . . . . NiB $3972 Ex $3200 Gd $2211
Similar to the Model MX8 except w/smaller frame and custom stock. Available in sporting or game configurations with fixed chokes or screw-in tubes. Imported 1993 to date.

MX9 O/U SHOTGUN . . . . NiB $7151 Ex $5762 Gd $3984
Gauge: 12; 2.75-inch chambers. Bbls.: 29.5- or 30.5-inch w/choke tubes and vent side rib. Selective trigger. Checkered walnut stock w/adj. cheekpiece. Available in single bbl., combo, O/U trap, skeet, pigeon and sporting models. Imported 1993-1994.

MX10 O/U SHOTGUN . . . . NiB $6989 Ex $5630 Gd $3892
Similar to the Model MX9 except w/fixed chokes and different rib configuration. Imported 1993.

MX10 PIGEON-ELECTROCIBLES O/U . . . . NiB $6815 Ex $5491 Gd $3798
Over/Under; boxlock. Removable trigger group; external selector. 12 gauge. Barrels: 27.50- or 29.50-inch. Checkered European walnut adjustable stock, beavertail forend. Imported 1995 to date.

MX11 AMERICAN TRAP COMBO . . NiB $5547 Ex $4474 Gd $3099
Over/Under; boxlock. External selector. Removable trigger group; single selective trigger. 12 ga. Bbls: 29-1/2- to 34-inch with fixed or choke tubes; vent rib. European walnut Monte Carlo adjustable stock, beavertail forend. Imported 1995 to date.

MX11 AMERICAN TRAP
SINGLE BARREL . . . . NiB $4922 Ex $3960 Gd $2742
Same general specs as MX11 American Trap combo except 32- or 34-inch single bbl. Imported 1995-96.

MX11 PIGEON-ELECTROCIBLES O/U . NiB $5122 Ex $4130 Gd $2862
Same specs as MX11 American Trap combo except 27.50 O/U bbls. Checkered European walnut pistol grip adjustable stock, beavertail forend. Imported 1995-96.

MX11 SKEET O/U . . . . NiB $5180 Ex $4177 Gd $2893
Same general specs as MX11 American Trap combo except 26.75 or 27.50-inch O/U bbls. Checkered European walnut pistol-grip adjustable stock, beavertail forend. Imported 1995-96.

MX11 SPORTING O/U . . . . NiB $5644 Ex $4549 Gd $3149
Same general specs as MX11 American Trap combo except 28.38, 29.50-, or 31.50-inch O/U bbls. Checkered European walnut pistol-grip adjustable stock, beavertail forend. Imported 1995-96.

MX11 TRAP O/U. . . . . NiB $5122 Ex $4130 Gd $2862
Same general specs as MX11 American Trap combo except 29.50,-30.75, or 31.50-inch O/U bbls. Checkered European walnut pistol-grip adjustable stock, beavertail forend. Imported 1995-96.

MX12 O/U GAME GUN
Gauge: 12, 2.75-inch chambers. Bbls.: 26-, 27.63-, 28.38- or 29.5-inch, vent rib, fixed chokes or screw-in choke tubes. Non-detachable single selective trigger group w/coil springs. Weight: 7.25 lbs. Interchangeable and custom-made checkered stock; Schnabel forend.
MX12 Standard . . . . NiB $5122 Ex $4130 Gd $2862
MX12C (w/choke tubes) . . . . . . NiB $5637 Ex $4542 Gd $3142

MX14 AMERICAN TRAP
SINGLE-BARREL . . . . NiB $4313 Ex $3480 Gd $2414
Single shot. Removable trigger group; unsingle configuration. 12 ga. Bbl: 34-inch with fixed or choke tubes; vent rib. Checkered European walnut Monte Carlo adjustable stock, beavertail forend. Imported 1995-1996.

MX15 AMERICAN TRAP
SINGLE-BARREL . . . . NiB $4791 Ex $3863 Gd $2675
Full choke. Detachable trigger group. Gauge: 12 only with 2.75-inch chamber. Bbls: 32 and 34-inch. Weight: 8 lbs., 6 oz.

Piotti
Piuma Boxlock Side-by-Side Shotgun

Powell No. 7
Aristocrat Grade Double

MX20 O/U GAME GUN
Gauges: 20, 28 and .410; 2.75- or 3-inch chambers. 26-inch vent-rib bbls., M/F chokes or screw-in chokes. Auto selective ejectors. Selective single trigger. Weight: 6 lbs., 6 oz. Non-detachable coil-spring trigger. Bead front sight. Interchangeable and custom-made checkered stock w/Schnabel forend. Imported from 1988 to date.
Standard grade . . . . NiB $5040 Ex $4043 Gd $2792
Standard grade
w/gold outline . . . . NiB $8666 Ex $6965 Gd $4889
MX20C w/choke tubes . . . . NiB $5388 Ex $4337 Gd $2992
SC3 grade . . . . NiB $9382 Ex $7548 Gd $5199
SCO grade . . . . NiB $12,785 Ex $10,252 Gd $7002

MX28 O/U GAME GUN . . . NiB $14,098 Ex $11,278 Gd $7669
Similar to the Model MX12 except chambered in 28 ga. w/26-inch bbls. fitted to smaller frame. Imported from 1993 to date.

MX410 O/U GAME GUN . . . . . NiB $14,098 Ex $11,278 Gd $7669
Similar to the Model MX12 except in .410 bore w/3-inch chambers, 26-inch bbls. fitted to smaller frame. Imported from 1993 to date.

TM1 SPECIAL
SINGLE-SHOT TRAP . . . . NiB $4406 Ex $3560 Gd $2478
Gauge: 12- 2.75-inch chambers. 32- or 34-inch bbl. w/wide vent rib; full choke. Weight: 8 lbs., 6 oz. Detachable and interchangeable trigger group with coil springs. Bead front sight. Interchangeable and custom-made stock w/checkered pistol grip and beavertail forend. Imported from 1988-1995.

TMX SPECIAL
SINGLE-SHOT TRAP . . . . NiB $4576 Ex $3697 Gd $2573
Same general specifications as Model TM1 Special except w/ultra-high rib. Interchangeable choke tubes optional.

PIOTTI SHOTGUNS — Italy

BOSS O/U . . . . NiB $34,000 Ex $28,000 Gd $13,000
Over/Under; sidelock. Gauges: 12 or 20. Barrels: 26- to 32-inch. Standard chokes. Best quality walnut. Custom-made to customer's specifications. Imported from 1993 to date.

KING NO. 1 SIDELOCK . . . NiB $20,900 Ex $17,000 Gd $7000
Gauges: 10, 12, 16, 20, 28 and .410. 25- to 30-inch bbls. (12 ga.), 25- to 28-inch (other ga.). Weight: About 5 lbs. (.410) to 8 lbs. (12 ga.) Holland & Holland pattern sidelock. Double triggers standard. Coin finish or color casehardened. Level file-cut rib. Full-coverage scroll engraving, gold inlays. Hand-rubbed, oil-finished, straight-grip stock with checkered butt, splinter forend.

KING EXTRA SIDE-BY-SIDE
SHOTGUN . . . . NiB $21,125 Ex $17,000 Gd $10,000
Same general specifications as the Piotti King No. 1 except has choice of engraving, gold inlays, plus stock is of exhibition-grade wood.

LUNIK SIDE-LOCK
SHOTGUN . . . . NiB $21,438 Ex $17,950 Gd $13,486
Same general specifications as the Monte Carlo model except has level, file-cut rib. Renaissance-style, large scroll engraving in relief, gold crown in top lever, gold name, and gold crest in forearm, finely figured wood.

MONTE CARLO
SIDE-LOCK SHOTGUN . . . . . NiB $10,938 Ex $8750 Gd $5950
Gauges: 10, 12, 16, 20, 28 or .410. Bbls.: 25- to 30-inch. Holland & Holland pattern sidelock. Weight: 5-8 lbs. Automatic ejectors. Double triggers. Hand-rubbed oil-finished straight-grip stock with checkered butt. Choice of Purdey-style scroll and rosette or Holland & Holland-style large scroll engraving.

PIUMA BOXLOCK
SIDE-BY-SIDE SHOTGUN. . . . NiB $10,494 Ex $8395 Gd $5709
Same general specifications as the Monte Carlo model except has Anson & Deeley boxlock action w/demi-bloc bbls., scalloped frame. Standard scroll and rosette engraving. Hand-rubbed, oil-finished straight-grip stock.

WILLIAM POWELL & SON LTD. — Birmingham, England

NO. 1 BEST GRADE
DOUBLE-BARREL
SHOTGUN . . . . NiB $50,112 Ex $39,000 Gd $18,000
Sidelock. Gauges: Made to order with 12, 16 and 20 the most common. Bbls.: Made to order in any length but 28 inches was recommended. Highest grade French walnut buttstock and forearm with fine checkering. Metal elaborately engraved. Imported by Stoeger from about 1938-51.

NO. 2 BEST GRADE
DOUBLE-BARREL . . . . . . NiB $27,500 Ex $22,000 Gd $14,960
Same general specifications as the Powell No. 1 except plain finish without engraving. Imported by Stoeger from about 1938-51.

NO. 6 CROWN GRADE
DOUBLE-BARREL . . . . NiB $13,950 Ex $11,200 Gd $7680
Boxlock. Gauges: Made to order with 12, 16 and 20 the most common. Bbls.: Made to order, but 28 inches was recommended. Highest grade French walnut buttstock and forearm with fine checkering. Metal elaborately engraved. Uses Anson & Deeley locks. Imported by Stoeger from about 1938-51.

NO. 7 ARISTOCRAT GRADE
DOUBLE-BARREL
SHOTGUN . . . . NiB $7160 Ex $5785 Gd $4025
Same general specifications as the Powell No. 6 Crown Grade Double-Barrel above, except with lower quality wood and metal engraving.

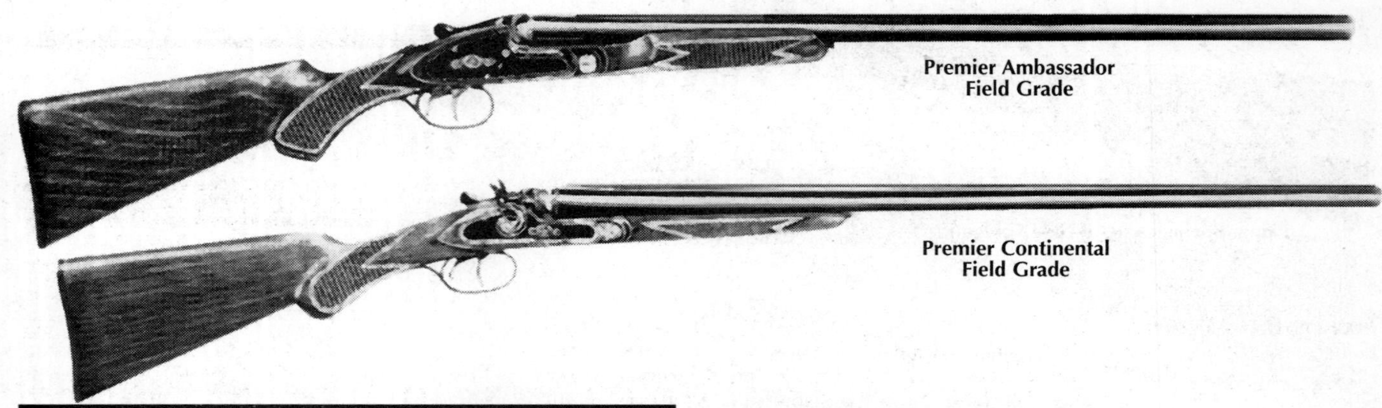

PRECISION SPORTS SHOTGUNS — Cortland, New York, Manufactured by Ignacio Ugartechea, Spain

600 SERIES AMERICAN HAMMERLESS DOUBLES
Boxlock. Single selective trigger. Selective automatic ejectors. Automatic safety. Gauges: 12, 16, 20, 28, .410; 2.75- or 3-inch chambers. Bbls.: 26-,27- or 28-inch w/raised matte rib; choked IC/M or M/F. Weight: 5.75-7 lbs. Checkered pistol-grip walnut buttstock with beavertail forend. Engraved silvered receiver with blued bbls. Imported from Spain 1986-94.
640A (12, 16, 20 ga. w/extractors) ..... NiB $1001 Ex $827 Gd $604
640A (28, .410 ga. w/extractors) .... NiB $1152 Ex $949 Gd $689
640 Slug Gun (12 ga. w/extractors) ..... NiB $1131 Ex $932 Gd $679
645A (12, 16, 20 ga. w/ejectors) .... NiB $1077 Ex $889 Gd $649
645A (28, .410 ga. w/ejectors) .... NiB $1309 Ex $1079 Gd $784
645A (20/28 ga. two-bbl. set) .... NiB $1525 Ex $1245 Gd $901
650A (12 ga. w/extractors, choke tubes) .. NiB $1035 Ex $838 Gd $611
655A (12 ga. w/ejectors, choke tubes) .. NiB $1110 Ex $914 Gd $663

600 SERIES ENGLISH HAMMERLESS DOUBLES
Boxlock. Same general specifications as American 600 series except w/double triggers and concave rib. Checkered English-style walnut stock w/splinter forend, straight grip and oil finish.
640E (12, 16, 20 ga. w/extractors) ...... NiB $855 Ex $704 Gd $512
640E (28, .410 ga. w/extractors) .... NiB $950 Ex $781 Gd $564
640 Slug Gun (12 ga. w/extractors) ..... NiB $1118 Ex $919 Gd $666
645E (12, 16, 20 ga. w/ejectors) .... NiB $1147 Ex $944 Gd $684
645E (28, .410 ga. w/ejectors) .... NiB $1099 Ex $905 Gd $658
645E (20/28 ga. two-bbl. set) .... NiB $1420 Ex $1173 Gd $838
650E (12 ga. w/extractors, choke tubes) .... NiB $994 Ex $817 Gd $593
655E (12 ga. w/ejectors, choke tubes) ... NiB $1054 Ex $866 Gd $626

MODEL 640M MAGNUM 10 HAMMERLESS DOUBLE
Similar to Model 640E except in 10 ga. w/3.5-inch Mag. chambers. Bbls.: 26-, 30-, 32-inch choked F/F.
Model 640M Big Ten, Turkey ..... NiB $984 Ex $810 Gd $588
Model 640M Goose Gun........ NiB $1010 Ex $831 Gd $603

MODEL 645E-XXV HAMMERLESS DOUBLE
Similar to Model 645E except w/25-inch bbl. and Churchill-style rib.
645E-XXV (12, 16, 20 ga. w/ejectors) ..... NiB $1054 Ex $866 Gd $626
645E-XXV (28, .410 ga. w/ejectors) ...... NiB $1194 Ex $979 Gd $705

PREMIER SHOTGUNS

Premier shotguns have been produced by various gunmakers in Europe.

AMBASSADOR MODEL FIELD GRADE HAMMERLESS DOUBLE-BARREL SHOTGUN..... NiB $467 Ex $382 Gd $274
Sidelock. Plain extractors. Double triggers. Gauges: 12, 16, 20, .410. 3-inch chambers in 20 and .410 ga., 2.75- inch in 12 and 16 ga. Bbls.: 26-inch in .410 ga., 28 inch in other ga.; choked M/F. Weight: 6 lbs., 3 oz.-7 lbs., 3 oz. depending on gauge. Checkered pistol-grip stock and beavertail forearm. Intro. in 1957; disc.

BRUSH KING .... NiB $344 Ex $285 Gd $207
Same as standard Regent model except chambered for 12 (2.75-inch) and 20 ga. (3-inch) only; has 22-inch bbls., IC/M choke, straight-grip stock. Weight: 6 lbs., 3 oz. in 12 ga.; 5 lbs., 12 oz. in 20 ga. Introduced in 1959; disc.

CONTINENTAL MODEL FIELD GRADE HAMMER DOUBLE-BARREL SHOTGUN..... NiB $467 Ex $382 Gd $274
Sidelock. Exposed hammers. Plain extractors. Double triggers. Gauges: 12, 16, 20, .410. Three inch chambers in 20 and .410 ga., 2.75-inch in 12 and 16 ga. Bbls.: 26-inch in .410 ga.; 28-inch in other ga.; choked M/F. Weight: 6 lbs., 3 oz.-7 lbs., 3 oz. depending on gauge. Checkered pistol-grip stock and English-style forearm. Introduced in 1957; disc.

MONARCH SUPREME GRADE HAMMERLESS DOUBLE-BARREL SHOTGUN..... NiB $497 Ex $406 Gd $292
Boxlock. Auto ejectors. Double triggers. Gauges: 12, 20. 2.75-inch chambers in 12 ga., 3-inch in 20 ga. Bbls.: 28-inch M/F; 26-inch IC/M choke. Weight: 6 lbs., 6 oz., 7 lbs., 2 oz. depending on gauge and bbl. Checkered pistol-grip stock and beavertail forearm of fancy walnut. Introduced in 1959; disc.

PRESENTATION CUSTOM GRADE .... NiB $1255 Ex $1024 Gd $729
Similar to Monarch model but made to order of higher quality with hunting scene engraving, gold and silver inlay, fancier wood. Introduced in 1959; disc.

REGENT 10 GA. MAGNUM EXPRESS .... NiB $396 Ex $325 Gd $233
Same as standard Regent model except chambered for 10-ga. Magnum 3.5-inch shells, has heavier construction, 32-inch bbls. choked F/F, stock with recoil pad. Weight: 11.25 lbs. Introduced in 1957; disc.

REGENT 12 GA. MAGNUM EXPRESS .... NiB $359 Ex $295 Gd $213
Same as standard Regent model except chambered for 12-ga. Magnum 3-inch shells, has 30-inch bbls. choked F and F, stock with recoil pad. Weight: 7.25 lbs. Introduced in 1957; disc.

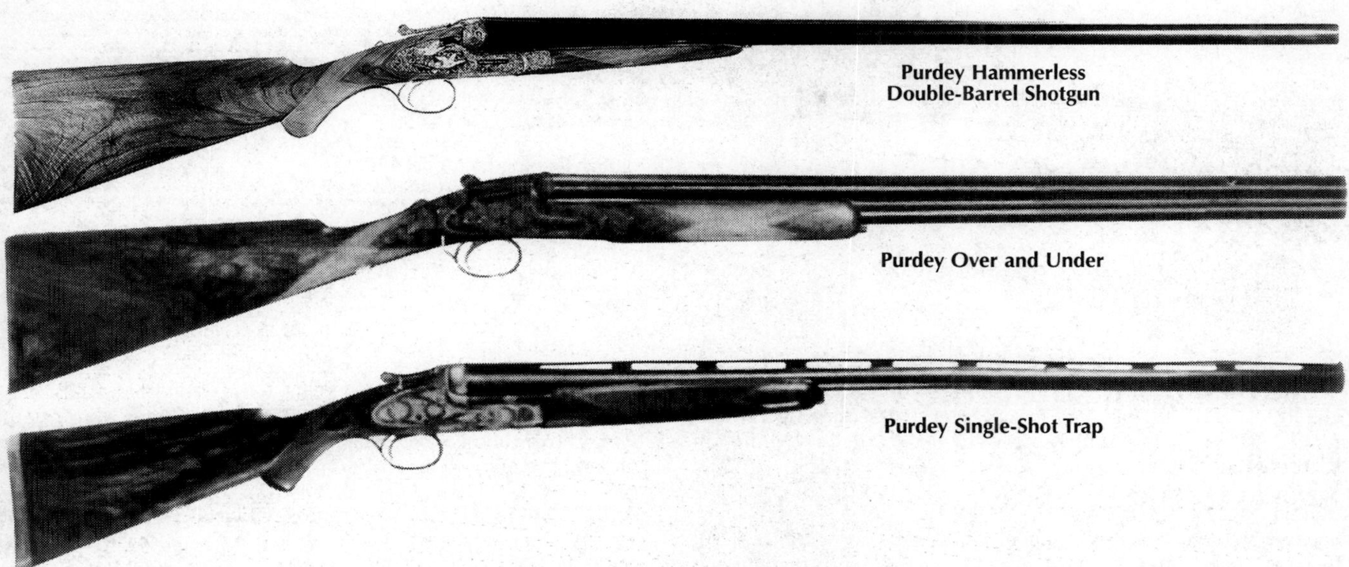

Purdey Hammerless Double-Barrel Shotgun

Purdey Over and Under

Purdey Single-Shot Trap

REGENT FIELD GRADE HAMMERLESS DOUBLE-BARREL SHOTGUN..... NiB $316 Ex $264 Gd $185
Boxlock. Plain extractors. Double triggers. Gauges: 12,16, 20, 28, .410. Three inch chambers in 20 and .410 ga., 2.75-inch in other gauges. Bbls.: 26-inch IC/M, M/F (28 and .410 ga. only); 28-inch M/F; 30-inch M/F (12 ga. only). Weight: 6 lbs., 2 oz.-7 lbs., 4 oz. depending on gauge and bbl. Checkered pistol-grip stock and beavertail forearm. Introduced in 1955; disc.

JAMES PURDEY & SONS, LTD. — London, England

HAMMERLESS DOUBLE-BARREL SHOTGUN
Sidelock. Auto ejectors. Single or double triggers. Gauges: 12, 16, 20. Bbls.: 26-, 27-, 28-, 30-inch (latter in 12 ga. only);any boring, any shape or style of rib. Weight: 5.25-5.5 lbs. depending on model, gauge and bbl length. Checkered stock and forearm, straight grip standard, pistol-grip also available. Purdey guns of this type have been made from about 1880 to date. Models include: Game Gun, Featherweight Game Gun, Two-Inch Gun (chambered for 12 ga. 2-inch shells), Pigeon Gun (w/3rd fastening and side clips), values of all models are the same.
With double triggers..... NiB $40,625 Ex $32,500 Gd $22,100
With single trigger ...... NiB $43,438 Ex $34,750 Gd $23,630

OVER/UNDER SHOTGUN
Sidelock. Auto ejectors. Single or double triggers. Gauges: 12 16, 20. Bbls.: 26-, 27-, 28-, 30-inch (latter in 12 ga. only); any boring, any style rib. Weight: 6-7.5 pounds depending on gauge and bbl. length. Checkered stock and forend, straight or pistol grip. Prior to WW II, the Purdey Over/Under Gun was made with a Purdey action; since the war James Purdey & Sons have acquired the business of James Woodward & Sons and all Purdey over/under guns are now built on the Woodward principle. General specifications of both types are the same.
With Purdey action, double triggers .... NiB $80,000 Ex $50,000 Gd $22,000
With Woodward action, double triggers .... NiB $55,750 Ex $45,000 Gd $31,240
W/single trigger, add .... NiB $1875 Ex $1500 Gd $1020

SINGLE-BARREL TRAP GUN................ NiB $11,800 Ex $9475 Gd $6499
Sidelock. Mechanical features similar to those of the over/under model with Purdey action. 12 ga. only. Built to customer's specifications. Made prior to World War II.

REMINGTON ARMS CO. — Ilion, New York

Eliphalet Remington Jr. began making long arms with his father in 1816. In 1828 they moved their facility to Ilion, N.Y., where it remained a family-run business for decades. As the family began to diminish, other people bought controlling interests and today, still a successful gunmaking company, it is a subsidiary of the DuPont Corporation.

MODEL 10A STANDARD GRADE SLIDE-ACTION REPEATING SHOTGUN .... NiB $410 Ex $335 Gd $240
Hammerless. Takedown. Six-round capacity. 12 ga. only. Five shell tubular magazine. Bbls.: Plain; 26- to 32-inch; choked F, M or Cyl. Weight: About 7.5 lbs. Plain pistol-grip stock, grooved slide handle. Made from 1907-29.

MODEL 11 SPECIAL, TOURNAMENT, EXPERT AND PREMIER GRADE GUNS
These higher grade models differ from the Model 11A in general quality, grade of wood, checkering, engraving, etc. General specifications are the same.
Model 11B Special grade ....NiB $624 Ex $509 Gd $362
Model 11D Tournament grade . . .NiB $1205 Ex $995 Gd $700
Model 11E Expert grade ...... NiB $1691 Ex $1368 Gd $955
Model 11F Premier grade .....NiB $2699 Ex $2179 Gd $1512

MODEL 11A STANDARD GRADE AUTOLOADER
Hammerless Browning type. Five round capacity. Takedown. Gauges: 12, 16, 20. Tubular magazine holds four rounds. Bbls.: Plain, solid or vent rib, lengths from 26-32 inches, F, M, IC, Cyl., SK chokes. Weight: About 8 lbs., 12 ga.; 7.5 lbs., 16 ga.; 7.25 lbs., 20 ga. Checkered pistol grip and forend. Made from 1905-49.
With plain barrel .... NiB $362 Ex $298 Gd $215
With solid-rib barrel ....NiB $458 Ex $375 Gd $268
With ventilated-rib barrel ....NiB $510 Ex $416 Gd $295

SHOTGUNS

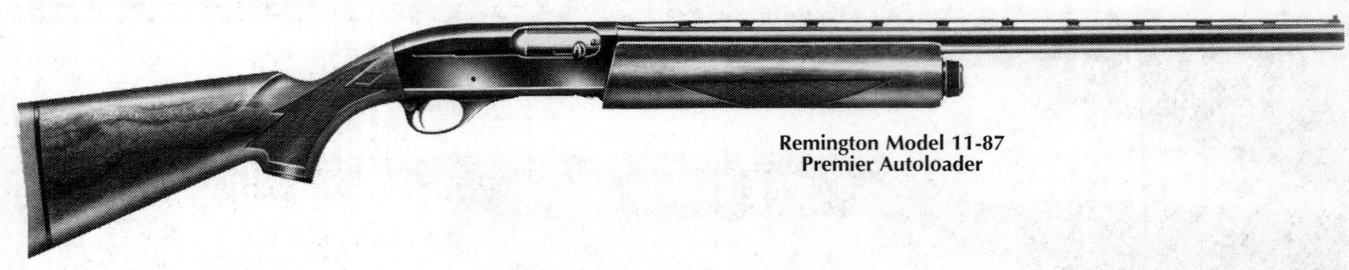

Remington Model 11-87
Premier Autoloader

MODEL 11R RIOT GUN .... NiB $410 Ex $335 Gd $240
Same as Model 11A Standard grade except has 20-inch plain barrel, 12 ga. only. Remington Model 11-48. (See Remington Sportsman-48 Series.)

MODEL 11-87 PREMIER AUTOLOADER
Gas-operated. Hammerless. Gauge: 12; 3-inch chamber. Bbl.: 26-, 28- or 30-inch with REMChoke. Weight: 8.13- 8.38 lbs., depending on bbl. length. Checkered walnut stock and forend in satin finish. Made from 1987 to date.
Premier Deer Gun .... NiB $600 Ex $491 Gd $352
Premier Deer Gun w/cantilever scope mount .... NiB $750 Ex $554 Gd $361
Premier Skeet .... NiB $619 Ex $507 Gd $364
Premier Sporting Clays .... NiB $738 Ex $604 Gd $433
Premier Sporting Clays SCNP (nickel plated)...... NiB $777 Ex $634 Gd $453
Premier Standard Autoloader .... NiB $619 Ex $507 Gd $364
Premier Trap........................... NiB $723 Ex $591 Gd $422
Left-hand models, add......................................$55

MODEL 11-87 SPECIAL PURPOSE MAGNUM
Same general specifications as Model 11-87 Premier except with non-reflective wood finish and Parkerized metal. 21-, 26- or 28-inch vent-rib bbl. with REMChoke tubes. Made from 1987-93.
Model 11-87 SP Field Magnum .... NiB $721 Ex $590 Gd $421
Model 11-87 SP Deer Gun (w/21-inch bbl.)... NiB $659 Ex $541 Gd $388
Model 11-87 SP Deer Gun w/cantilever scope mount............... NiB $709 Ex $580 Gd $415

MODEL 11-87 SPS MAGNUM
Same general specifications as Model 11-87 Special Purpose Magnum except with synthetic buttstock and forend. 21-, 26- or 28-inch vent-rib bbl. with REMChoke tubes. Matte black or Mossy Oak camo finish (except NWTF turkey gun). Made from 1990 to date.
Model 11-87 SPS Magnum (matte black)..... NiB $642 Ex $535 Gd $384
Model 11-87 SPS Camo (Mossy Oak camo) .. NiB $681 Ex $557 Gd $400
Model 11-87 SPS Deer Gun (w/21 inch bbl.).. NiB $590 Ex $484 Gd $348
Model 11-87 SPS Deer Gun w/cant. scope mt. .... NiB $667 Ex $546 Gd $392
Model 11-87 NWTF Turkey Gun (Brown Trebark) disc. 1993................ NiB $770 Ex $630 Gd $451
Model 11-87 NWTF Turkey Gun (Greenleaf) disc. 1996.................... NiB $743 Ex $608 Gd $436
Model 11-87 NWTF Turkey Gun (Mossy Oak) disc. 1996.............. NiB $756 Ex $619 Gd $444
Model 11-87 NWTF Turkey Gun (Mossy Oak Breakup) introduced 1999........ NiB $70 Ex $30 Gd $451
Model 11-87 NWTF 20 ga. Turkey Gun (Mossy Oak Breakup) Produced 1998 only ... NiB $723 Ex $591 Gd $422
Model 11-87 SPST Turkey Gun (matte bl.) ... NiB $667 Ex $546 Gd $391

MODEL 11-96 EURO LIGHTWEIGHT AUTOLOADING SHOTGUN .... NiB $719 Ex $588 Gd $420
Lightweight version of Model 11-87 w/reprofiled receiver. 12 ga. only w/3-inch chamber. 26- or 28-inch bbl. w/6mm vent rib and REM Choke tubes. Semi-fancy Monte Carlo walnut buttstock and forearm. Weight: 6.8 lbs. w/26-inch bbl. Made in 1996 only.

MODEL 17A STANDARD GRADE SLIDE-ACTION REPEATING SHOTGUN
Hammerless. Takedown. Five round capacity. 20 ga. only. Four round tubular magazine. Bbls.: plain; 26- to 32-inch; choked F, M or Cyl. Weight: About 5.75 lbs. Plain pistol-grip stock, grooved slide handle. Made 1921-33. Note: The present Ithaca Model 37 is an adaptation of this Browning design.
Plain barrel .... NiB $429 Ex $338 Gd $237
Solid rib...................... NiB $560 Ex $452 Gd $316

MODEL 29A STANDARD GRADE SLIDE-ACTION REPEATING SHOTGUN ..... NiB $479 Ex $392 Gd $283
Hammerless. Takedown. Six round capacity. 12 ga. only. Five round tubular magazine. Bbls.: plain- 26- to 32-inch, choked F, M or Cyl. Weight: About 7.5 lbs. Checkered pistol-grip stock and slide handle. Made from 1929-33.

MODEL 29T TARGET GRADE ..... NiB $542 Ex $444 Gd $318
Same general specifications as Model 29A except has trap-style stock with straight grip, extension slide handle, vent rib bbl. Disc. 1933.

MODEL 31 AND 31L SKEET GRADE
Same general specifications as Model 31A except has 26-inch bbl. with raised solid or vent rib, SK choke, checkered pistol-grip stock and beavertail forend. Weight: About 8 lbs., 12 ga. Made from 1932-1939.
Model 31 Standard w/raised solid rib .... NiB $835 Ex $683 Gd $487
Model 31 Standard w/ventilated rib ..... NiB $994 Ex $810 Gd $582
Model 31L Lightweight w/raised solid rib .... NiB $763 Ex $624 Gd $446
Model 31L Lightweight w/ventilated rib .. NiB $912 Ex $745 Gd $519

MODEL 31 SPECIAL, TOURNAMENT, EXPERT AND PREMIER GRADE GUNS
These higher grade models differ from the Model 31A in general quality, grade of wood, checkering, engraving, etc. General specifications are the same.
Model 31B Special grade .... NiB $730 Ex $595 Gd $423
Model 31D Tournament grade ... NiB $1038 Ex $844 Gd $594
Model 31E Expert grade .... NiB $1439 Ex $1171 Gd $828
Model 31F Premier grade ..... NiB $2307 Ex $1870 Gd $1312

MODEL 31S TRAP SPECIAL/31TC TRAP GRADE
Same general specifications as Model 31A except 12 ga. only, has 30- or 32-inch vent-rib bbl., F choke, checkered trap stock with full pistol grip and recoil pad, checkered extension beavertail forend. Weight: About 8 lbs. (Trap Special has solid-rib bbl., half pistol-grip stock with standard walnut forend).
Model 31S Trap Special .... NiB $569 Ex $465 Gd $332
Model 31TC Trap grade .... NiB $739 Ex $601 Gd $425

Remington Model 11-87 SPS

Remington Model 11-87 SPS Camo

Remington Model 11-87 SP Walnut Stock

Remington Model SP-10 Magnum Camo

MODEL 31A SLIDE-ACTION REPEATER
Hammerless. Takedown. 3- or 5-round capacity. Gauges: 12, 16, 20. Tubular magazine. Bbls.: Plain, solid or vent rib; lengths from 26 -32 inches; F, M, IC, C or SK choke. Weight: About 7.5 lbs., 12 ga.; 6.75 lbs., 16 ga.; 6.5 lbs., 20 ga. Earlier models have checkered pistol-grip stock and slide handle; later models have plain stock and grooved slide handle. Made from 1931-49.

Model 31A with plain barrel ..... NiB $442 Ex $362 Gd $260
Model 31A with solid rib barrel ... NiB $528 Ex $431 Gd $308
Model 31A with vent rib barrel ... NiB $564 Ex $460 Gd $327
Model 31H Hunters' Special w/sporting-style stock .... NiB $528 Ex $431 Gd $308
Model 31R Riot Gun w/20-inch plain bbl., 12 ga. .... NiB $381 Ex $313 Gd $226

MODEL 32A STANDARD GRADE O/U
Hammerless. Takedown. Auto ejectors. Early model had double triggers, later built with selective single trigger only. 12 ga. only. Bbls.: Plain, raised matted solid or vent rib; 26-, 28-, 30-, 32-inch; F/M choke standard, option of any combination of F, M, IC, C, SK choke. Weight: About 7.75 lbs. Checkered pistol-grip stock and forend. Made from 1932-42.

With double triggers .... NiB $2073 Ex $1673 Gd $1163
With selective single trigger ... NiB $2331 Ex $1879 Gd $1303
With raised solid rib, add $200
With ventilated rib, add $300

MODEL 32 TOURNAMENT, EXPERT AND PREMIER GRADE GUNS
These higher-grade models differ from the Model 32A in general quality, grade of wood, checkering, engraving, etc. General specifications are the same. Made from 1932-42.

Model 32D Tournament grade .... NiB $3998 Ex $3227 Gd $2240
Model 32E Expert grade ...... NiB $4987 Ex $4020 Gd $2783
Model 32F Premier grade .... NiB $6746 Ex $5443 Gd $3762

MODEL 32 SKEET GRADE
Same general specifications as Model 32A except 26- or 28-inch bbl., SK choke, beavertail forend, selective single trigger only. Weight: About 7.5 lbs. Made from 1932-42.

MODEL 32TC
TARGET (TRAP) GRADE ...... NiB $3245 Ex $2620 Gd $1820
Same general specifications as Model 32A except 30- or 32-inch vent-rib bbl., F choke, trap-style stock with checkered pistol-grip and beavertail forend. Weight: About 8 lbs. Made from l932-42.

MODEL 89 (1889)............ NiB $1283 Ex $1037 Gd $724
Hammers. Circular action. Gauges: 10, 12, 16, 28- to 32-inch bls.; steel or Damascus twist. Weight 7-10 lbs. Made from 1889-1908.

MODEL 90-T SINGLE-SHOT TRAP ..... NiB $2173 Ex $1752 Gd $1226
Gauge: 12; 2.75-inch chambers. 30-, 32- or 34-inch vent-rib bbl. with fixed chokes or screw-in REMChokes; ported or non-ported. Weight: 8.25 lbs. Checkered American walnut standard or Monte Carlo stock with low-luster finish. Engraved sideplates and drop-out trigger group optional. Made from 1990-97.

MODEL 396 O/U
Boxlock. 12 ga. only w/2.75-inch chamber. 28- and 30-inch blued bbls. w/Rem chokes. Weight: 7.50 lbs. Nitride-grayed, engraved receiver, trigger guard, tang, hinge pins and forend metal. Engraved sideplates. Checkered satin-finished American walnut stock w/target style forend. Made from 1996-98.

396 Sporting Clays .... NiB $2029 Ex $1643 Gd $1149
396 Skeet.................. NiB $2102 Ex $1702 Gd $1191

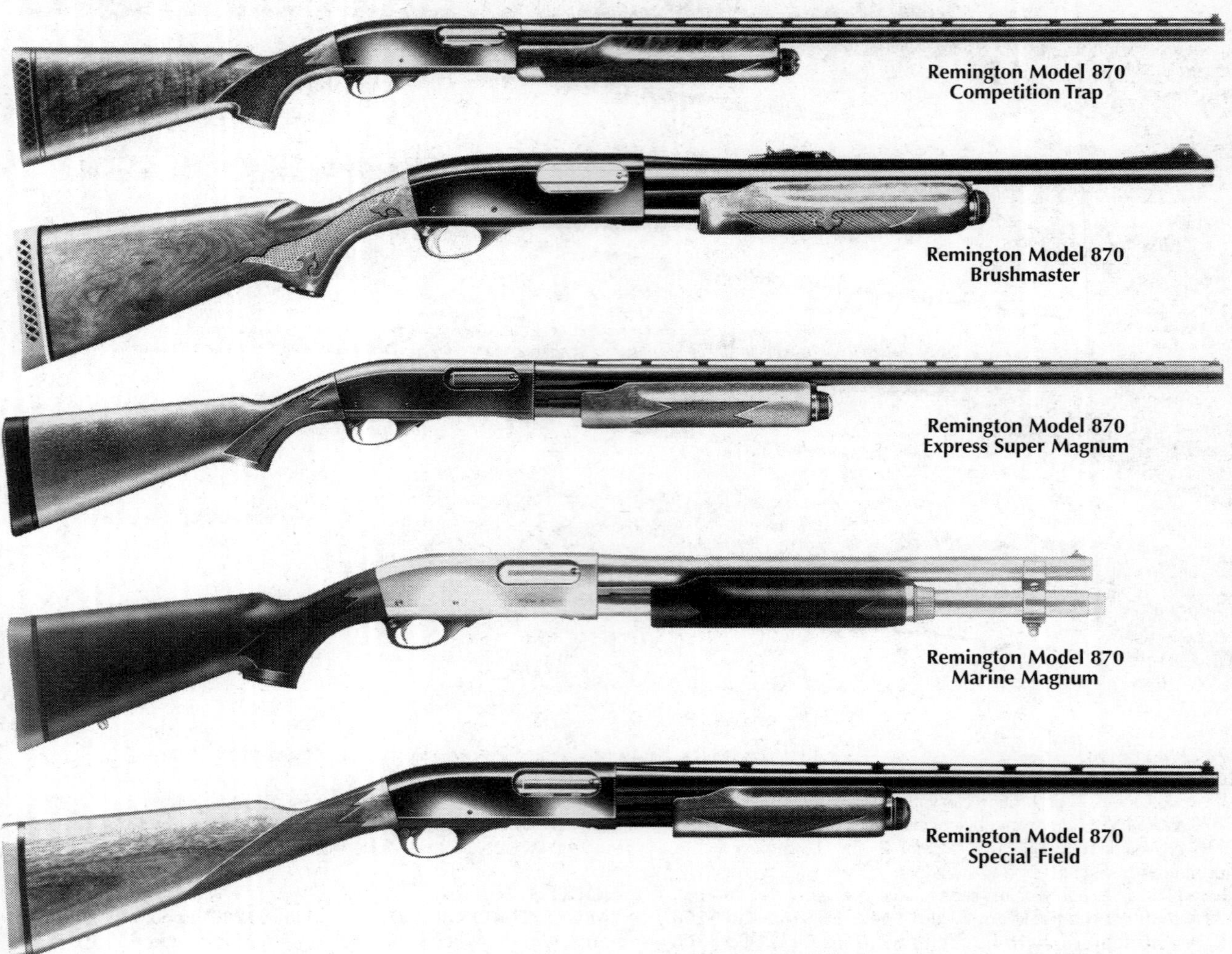

Remington Model 870
Competition Trap

Remington Model 870
Brushmaster

Remington Model 870
Express Super Magnum

Remington Model 870
Marine Magnum

Remington Model 870
Special Field

MODEL 870
"ALL AMERICAN" TRAP GUN . . . NiB $1117 Ex $912 Gd $649
Same as Model 870TB except custom grade with engraved receiver, trigger guard and bbl.; Monte Carlo or straight-comb stock and forend of fancy walnut; available only with 30-inch F choke bbl. Made from 1972-77.

MODEL 870 COMPETITION TRAP
. . . . . NiB $633 Ex $516 Gd $368
Based on standard Model 870 receiver except is single-shot with gas-assisted recoil-reducing system, new choke design, a high step-up vent rib and redesigned stock, forend with cut checkering and satin finish. Weight: 8.5 lbs. Made from 1981-87.

MODEL 870 STANDARD. . . . . NiB $426 Ex $350 Gd $253
Same as Model 870 Wingmaster Riot Gun, on page 524, except has rifle-type sights.

MODEL 870 BRUSHMASTER DELUXE
Same as Model 870 Standard except available in 20 ga. as well as 12, has cut-checkered, satin-finished American walnut stock and forend, recoil pad.
Right-hand model . . . . NiB $463 Ex $380 Gd $274
Left-hand model . . . . NiB $534 Ex $436 Gd $312

MODEL 870 EXPRESS
Same general specifications Model 870 Wingmaster except has low-luster walnut-finished hardwood stock with pressed checkering and black recoil pad. Gauges: 12, 20 or .410, 3-inch chambers. Bbls.: 26- or 28-inch vent-rib with REMChoke; 25-inch vent-rib with fixed choke (.410 only). Black oxide metal finish. Made from 1987 to date.
Model 870 Express
(12 or20 ga., REMChoke) . . . . NiB $285 Ex $235 Gd $171
Model 870 Express
(.410 w/fixed choke) . . . . NiB $318 Ex $261 Gd $189
Express Combo (w/extra
20-inch deer bbl.) . . . . NiB $375 Ex $307 Gd $219

MODEL 870
EXPRESS DEER GUN
Same general specifications as Model 870 Express except in 12 ga. only, 20-inch bbl. with fixed IC choke, adj. rifle sights and Monte Carlo stock. Made from 1991 to date.
Express Deer Gun
w/standard barrel . . . . NiB $310 Ex $255 Gd $183
Express Deer Gun
w/rifled barrel . . . . NiB $345 Ex $282 Gd $202

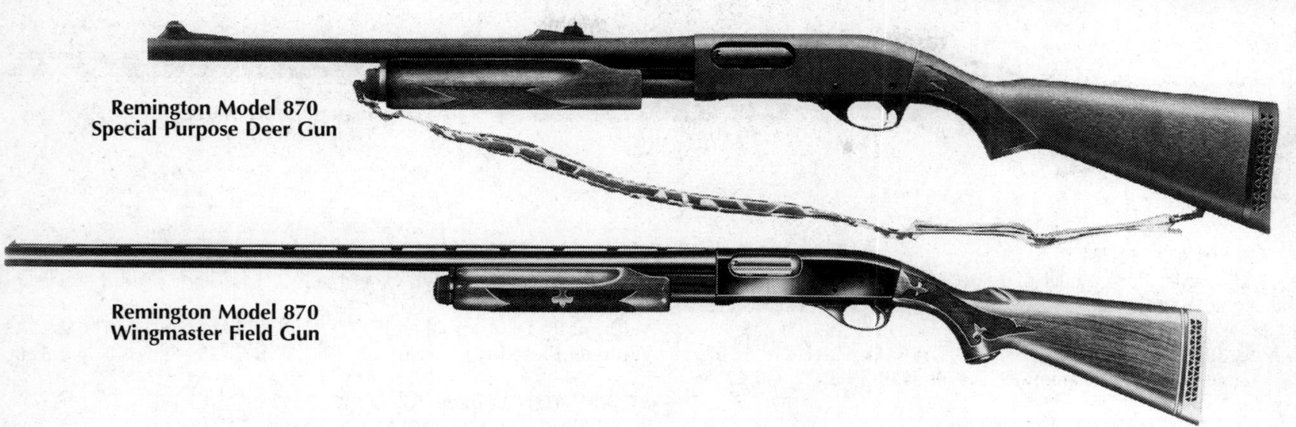

Remington Model 870
Special Purpose Deer Gun

Remington Model 870
Wingmaster Field Gun

MODEL 870 EXPRESS SUPER MAGNUM
Similar to Model 870 Express except chambered for 12 ga. mag. w/3.5-inch chamber. Bbls.: 23-, 26- or 28-inch vent rib w/REM Choke. Checkered low-luster walnut-finished hardwood, black synthetic or camo buttstock and forearm. Matte black oxide metal finish or full camo finish. Made from 1998 to date.

Model 870 ESM (w/hardwood stock) . . . . NiB $296 Ex $243 Gd $176
Model 870 ESM (w/black synthetic stock) . . . . NiB $310 Ex $254 Gd $184
Model 870 ESM (w/camo synthetic stock) . . . . NiB $417 Ex $342 Gd $246
Model 870 ESM Synthetic Turkey (w/synthetic stock) . . . . NiB $315 Ex $259 Gd $189
Model 870 ESM como Turkey (w/full camo) . . . . NiB $393 Ex $322 Gd $232
Model 870 ESM combo (w/full camo, extra bbl.) . . . . NiB $459 Ex $377 Gd $270

MODEL 870 EXPRESS SYNTHETIC HOME DEFENSE . . . . . NiB $283 Ex $234 Gd $170
Slide action, hammerless, takedown. 12 ga. only. 18-inch bbl. w/cylinder choke and bead front sight. Positive checkered synthetic stock and forend with non-reflective black finish. Made from 1995 to date.

MODEL 870 EXPRESS TURKEY GUN . . NiB $310 Ex $244 Gd $254
Same general specifications as Model 870 Express except has 21-inch vent-rib bbl. and Turkey Extra-Full REMChoke. Made from 1991 to date.

MODEL 870 EXPRESS YOUTH GUN . . NiB $296 Ex $243 Gd $176
Same general specifications as Model 870 Express except has scaled-down stock with 12.5-inch pull and 21-inch vent rib bbl. with REMChoke. Made from 1991 to date.

MODEL 870 LIGHTWEIGHT
Same as standard Model 870 but with scaled-down receiver and lightweight mahogany stock; 20 ga. only. 2.75-inch chamber. Bbls.: plain or vent rib; 26-inch, IC; 28-inch, M or F choke. REMChoke available from 1987. Weight 5.75 lbs. w/26-inch plain bbl. American walnut stock and forend with satin or Hi-gloss finish. Made from 1972-94.

With plain barrel . . . . NiB $325 Ex $268 Gd $195
With ventilated rib barrel . . . . NiB $355 Ex $292 Gd $211
With REMChoke barrel . . . . NiB $398 Ex $326 Gd $234

MODEL 870 LIGHTWEIGHT MAGNUM
Same as Model 870 Lightweight but chambered for 20 ga. Magnum 3-inch shell; 28-inch bbl., plain or vent rib, F choke. Weight: 6 lbs. with plain bbl. Made from 1972-94.

With plain barrel . . . . NiB $393 Ex $323 Gd $235
With ventilated rib barrel . . . . NiB $441 Ex $362 Gd $260

MODEL 870 MAGNUM DUCK GUN
Same as Model 870 Field Gun except has 3-inch chamber 12 and 20 gauge Magnum only. 28- or 30-inch bbl., plain or vent rib, M or F choke, recoil pad. Weight: About 7 or 6.75 lbs. Made from 1964 to date.

With plain barrel . . . . NiB $462 Ex $379 Gd $273
With ventilated rib barrel . . . . NiB $504 Ex $413 Gd $295

MODEL 870 MARINE MAGNUM . . . . NiB $482 Ex $394 Gd $304
Same general specifications as Model 870 Wingmaster except with 7-round magazine, 18-inch plain bbl. with fixed IC choke, bead front sight and nickel finish. Made from 1992 to date.

MODEL 870 SA SKEET GUN, SMALLBORE. . . . . NiB $463 Ex $380 Gd $273
Similar to Wingmaster Model 870SA except chambered for 28 and .410 ga. (2.5-inch chamber for latter); 25-inch vent rib bbl., SK choke. Weight: 6 lbs., 28 ga.; 6.5 lbs., .410. Made from 1969-82.

MODEL 870 MISSISSIPPI MAGNUM DUCK GUN . . . . NiB $473 Ex $387 Gd $278
Same as Remington Model 870 Magnum duck gun except has 32-inch bbl. "Ducks Unlimited" engraved receiver, Made in 1983.

MODEL 870 SPECIAL FIELD SHOTGUN . . . . NiB $463 Ex $379 Gd $273
Pump action. Hammerless. Gauge: 12 or 20. 21-inch vent-rib bbl. with REMChoke. 41.5 inches overall. Weight: 6-7 lbs. Straight-grip checkered walnut stock and forend. Made from 1987-95.

MODEL 870 SPECIAL PURPOSE DEER GUN
Similar to Special Purpose Magnum except with 20-inch IC choke, rifle sights. Matte black oxide and Parkerized finish. Oil-finished, checkered buttstock and forend with recoil pad. Made from 1986 to date.

Model 870 SP Deer Gun . . . . NiB $399 Ex $328 Gd $238
Model 870 SP Deer Gun, cant. scope mt. . . . . NiB $463 Ex $380 Gd $273

MODEL 870 SPECIAL PURPOSE MAGNUM . . . . NiB $463 Ex $379 Gd $273
Similar to the 870 Magnum duck gun except with 26-, 28- or 30-inch vent rib REMChoke bbl.12 ga. only; 3-inch chamber. Oil-finished field-grade stock with recoil pad, QD swivels and Cordura sling. Made from 1985 to date.

SHOTGUNS

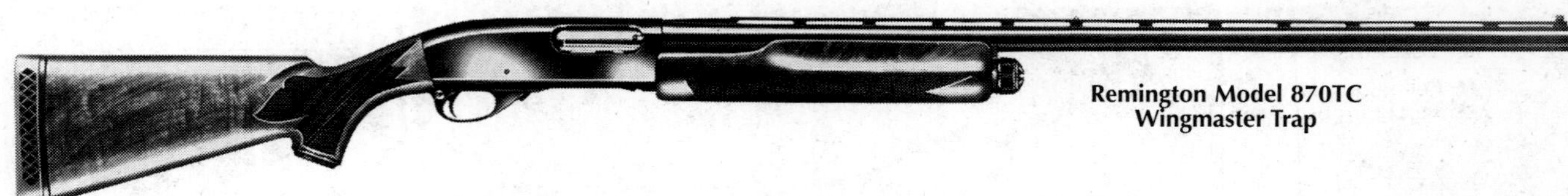

Remington Model 870TC Wingmaster Trap

MODEL 870SPS MAGNUM
Same general specifications Model 870 Special Purpose Magnum except with synthetic stock and forend. 26- or 28-inch vent-rib bbl. with REMChoke tubes. Matte black or Mossy Oak camo finish. Made from 1991 to date.
70 SPS Mag. (black syn. stock) . . . . NiB $445 Ex $364 Gd $262
870 SPS-T Camo (Mossy Oak camo). . . . . . NiB $459 Ex $377 Gd $270

MODEL 870 WINGMASTER FIELD GUN
Same general specifications as Model 870AP except checkered stock and forend. Later models have REMChoke systems in 12 ga. Made from 1964 to date.
With plain barrel . . . . NiB $315 Ex $259 Gd $179
With ventilated rib barrel . . . . NiB $363 Ex $298 Gd $216

MODEL 870 WINGMASTER FIELD GUN, SMALL BORE
Same as standard Model 870 except w/scaled-down lightweight receivers. Gauges: 28 and .410. Plain or vent rib 25-inch bbl. choked IC, M or F. Weight: 5.5-6.25 lbs. depending on gauge and bbl. Made from 1969-94.
With plain barrel . . . . NiB $568 Ex $464 Gd $331
With ventilated-rib barrel . . . . NiB $646 Ex $518 Gd $368

MODEL 870 WINGMASTER MAGNUM DELUXE GRADE . . . . . . NiB $572 Ex $468 Gd $334
Same as Model 870 Magnum standard grade except has checkered stock and extension beavertail forearm, bbl. with matted top surface. Disc. in 1963.

MODEL 870 WINGMASTER MAGNUM STANDARD GRADE . . . NiB $508 Ex $417 Gd $299
Same as Model 870AP except chambered for 12 ga. 3-inch Magnum, 30-inch F choke bbl., recoil pad. Weight: About 8.25 lbs. Made from 1955-63.

MODEL 870 WINGMASTER REMCHOKE SERIES
Slide action, hammerless, takedown with blued all-steel receiver. Gauges: 12, 20; 3-inch chamber. Tubular magazine. Bbls.: 21-, 26-, 28-inch vent-rib with REM Choke. Weight: 7.5 lbs. (12 ga.). Satin-finished, checkered walnut buttstock and forend with recoil pad. Right- or left-hand models. Made from 1986 to date.
Standard model, 12 ga. . . . . NiB $385 Ex $316 Gd $228
Standard model, 20 ga. . . . . NiB $408 Ex $334 Gd $241
Youth model, 21-inch barrel . . . . . . NiB $412 Ex $330 Gd $238

MODEL 870ADL WINGMASTER DELUXE GRADE
Same general specifications as Wingmaster Model 870AP except has pistol-grip stock and extension beavertail forend, both finely checkered; matted top surface or vent-rib bbl. Made from 1950-63.
With matted top-surface barrel. . . . NiB $391 Ex $321 Gd $233
With ventilated-rib barrel . . . . NiB $434 Ex $356 Gd $256

MODEL 870AP WINGMASTER STANDARD GRADE
Hammerless. Takedown. Gauges: 12, 16, 20. Tubular magazine holds four rounds. Bbls.: Plain, matted top surface or vent rib; 26-inch IC, 28-inch M or F choke, 30-inch F choke (12 ga. only). Weight: About 7 lbs., 12 ga.; 6.75 lbs., 16 ga.; 6.5 lbs., 20 ga. Plain pistol-grip stock, grooved forend. Made from 1950-63.
With plain barrel . . . . NiB $288 Ex $237 Gd $171
With matted surface barrel . . . . NiB $302 Ex $247 Gd $178
With ventilated rib barrel . . . . NiB $333 Ex $273 Gd $197
Left-hand model . . . . NiB $345 Ex $283 Gd $204

MODEL 870BDL WINGMASTER DELUXE SPECIAL
Same as Model 870ADL except select American walnut stock and forend. Made from 1950-63.
With matted surface barrel . . . . NiB $415 Ex $340 Gd $245
With ventilated-rib barrel . . . . NiB $455 Ex $373 Gd $266

REMINGTON MODEL 870D, 870F WINGMASTER TOURNAMENT AND PREMIER GRADE GUNS
These higher-grade models differ from the Model 870AP in general quality, grade of wood, checkering, engraving, etc. General operating specifications are essentially the same. Made from 1950 to date.
Model 870D Tournament grade . . . . . . NiB $2670 Ex $2161 Gd $1511
Model 870F Premier grade . . . . NiB $5754 Ex $4635 Gd $3203
Model 870F Premier gr. w/gold inlay . . . . . NiB $9122 Ex $7346 Gd $5074

REMINGTON MODEL 870R WINGMASTER RIOT GUN . . . . NiB $394 Ex $322 Gd $230
Same as Model 870AP except 20-inch bbl., IC choke, 12 ga. only.

REMINGTON MODEL 870SA WINGMASTER SKEET GUN
Same general specifications as Model 870AP except has 26-inch vent-rib bbl., SK choke, ivory bead front sight, metal bead rear sight, pistol-grip stock and extension beavertail forend. Weight: 6.75 to 7.5 lbs. depending on gauge. Made 1950-82.
Model 870SA Skeet grade (disc. 1982) . . . . . . NiB $406 Ex $331 Gd $236
Model 870SC Skeet Target grade (disc. 1980) . . . . NiB $577 Ex $469 Gd $333

REMINGTON MODEL 870TB WINGMASTER TRAP SPECIAL . . . . NiB $494 Ex $403 Gd $288
Same general specifications as Model 870AP Wingmaster except has 28- or 30-inch vent rib bbl., F choke, metal bead front sight, no rear sight. "Special" grade trap-style stock and forend, both checkered, recoil pad. Weight: About 8 lbs. Made from 1950-81.

REMINGTON MODEL 870TC TRAP GRADE. . . . . NiB $666 Ex $544 Gd $390
Same as Model 870 Wingmaster TC except has tournament-grade walnut in stock and forend w/satin finish. Over-bored 30-inch vent rib bbl. w/ 2.75-inch chamber and RemChoke tubes. Reissued in 1996. See separate listing for earlier model.

REMINGTON MODEL 870TC WINGMASTER TRAP GRADE
Same as Model 870TB except higher-grade walnut in stock and forend, has both front and rear sights. Made 1950-79. Model 870 TC reissued in 1996. See separate listing for later model.
Model 870 TC Trap (Standard). . . . . NiB $672 Ex $549 Gd $393
Model 870 TC Trap (Monte Carlo) . . NiB $698 Ex $570 Gd $407

REMINGTON MODEL 878A AUTOMASTER . . . . NiB $308 Ex $250 Gd $177
Gas-operated Autoloader. 12 ga., 3-round magazine. Bbls.: 26-inch IC, 28-inch M choke, 30-inch F choke. Weight: About 7 lbs. Plain pistol-grip stock and forearm. Made from 1959-62.

NOTE: *New stock checkering patterns and receiver scroll markings were incorporated on all standard Model 1100 field, magnum, skeet and trap models in 1979.*

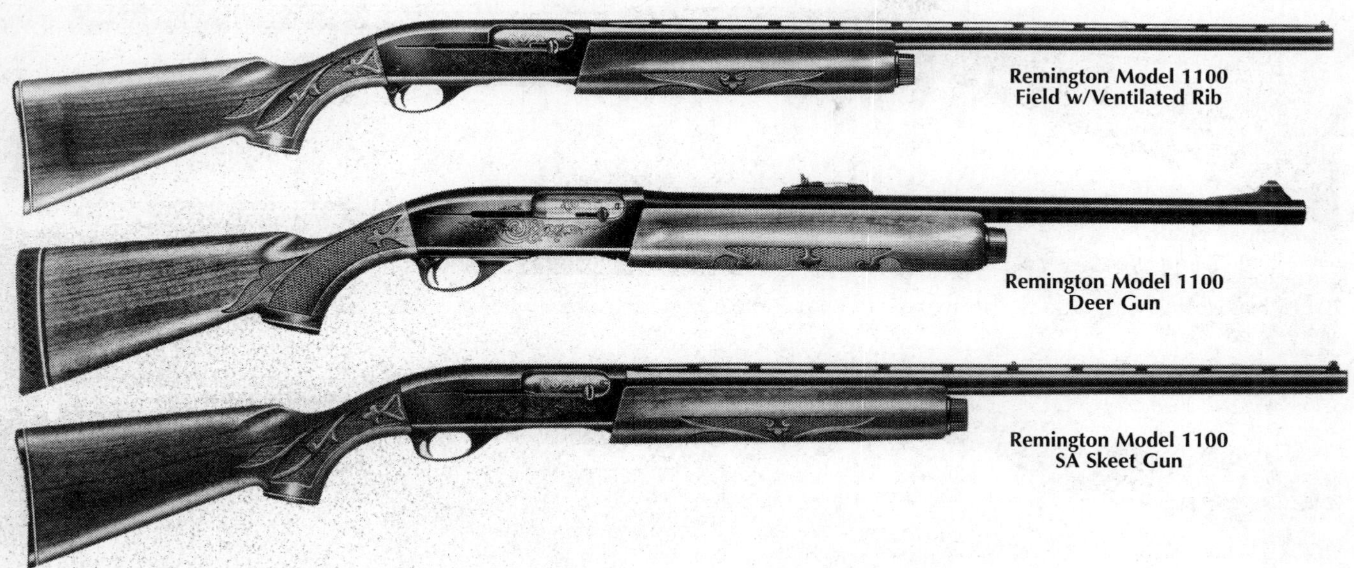

MODEL 1100 AUTOMATIC FIELD GUN
Gas-operated. Hammerless. Takedown. Gauges: 12, 16, 20. Bbls.: plain or vent. rib; 30-inch F, 28-inch M or F, 26-inch IC; or REMChoke tubes. Weight: Average 7.25-7.5 lbs. depending on ga. and bbl. length. Checkered walnut pistol-grip stock and forearm in high-gloss finish. Made from 1963 to date. 16 ga. discontinued.
With plain barrel .... NiB $387 Ex $319 Gd $231
With ventilated-rib barrel .... NiB $438 Ex $360 Gd $259
REMChoke model .... NiB $478 Ex $391 Gd $281
REMChoke, Left-hand action ..... NiB $515 Ex $422 Gd $301

MODEL 1100 DEER GUN .... NiB $485 Ex $397 Gd $285
Same as Model 1100 Field Gun except has 22-inch barrel, IC, with rifle-type sights; 12 and 20 ga. only; recoil pad. Weight: About 7.25 lbs. Made from 1963-96.

MODEL 1100 DUCKS UNLIMITED
ATLANTIC COMMEMORATIVE... NiB $1062 Ex $866 Gd $615
Limited production for one year. Similar specifications to Model 1100 Field except with 32-inch F choke, vent rib bbl. 12-ga. Magnum only. Made in 1982.

MODEL 1100 DUCKS UNLIMITED "THE CHESAPEAKE"
COMMEMORATIVE............. NiB $779 Ex $638 Gd $466
Limited edition 1 to 2400. Same general specifications as Model 1100 Field except sequentially numbered with markings "The Chesapeake." 12 ga. Magnum with 30-inch F choke, vent rib bbl. Made in 1981.

REMINGTON MODEL 1100 FIELD GRADE, SMALL BORE
Same as standard Model 1100 but scaled down. Gauges: 28, .410. 25-inch bbl., plain or vent rib; IC, M or F choke. Weight: 6.25-7 lbs. depending on gauge and bbl. Made from 1969-94.
With plain barrel .... NiB $563 Ex $454 Gd $360
With ventilated rib .... NiB $709 Ex $580 Gd $414

MODEL 1100 LIGHTWEIGHT
Same as standard Model 1100 but scaled-down receiver and lightweight mahogany stock; 20 ga. only, 2.75-inch chamber. Bbls.: Plain or vent rib; 26-inch IC; 28-inch M and F choke. Weight: 6.25 lbs. Made from 1970-76.
With plain barrel .... NiB $529 Ex $434 Gd $312
With ventilated rib .... NiB $590 Ex $482 Gd $346

MODEL 1100 LIGHTWEIGHT MAGNUM
Same as Model 1100 Lightweight but chambered for 20 gauge Magnum 3-inch shell; 28-inch bbl., plain or vent rib, F choke. Weight: 6.5 lbs. Made from 1977-98.
With plain barrel .... NiB $557 Ex $455 Gd $325
With ventilated rib .... NiB $617 Ex $504 Gd $359
With choke tubes .... NiB $659 Ex $536 Gd $381

MODEL 1100 LT-20
DUCKS UNLIMITED
SPECIAL COMMEMORATIVE ..... NiB $688 Ex $560 Gd $397
Limited edition 1 to 2400. Same general specifications as Model 1100 Field except sequentially numbered with markings, "The Chesapeake." 20 ga. only. 26-inch IC, vent-rib bbl. Made in 1981.

MODEL 1100 LT-20 SERIES
Same as Model 1100 Field Gun except in 20 ga. with shorter 23-inch vent rib bbl., straight-grip stock. REMChoke series has 21-inch vent rib bbl., choke tubes. Weight: 6.25 lbs. Checkered grip and forearm. Made from 1977-95.
Model 1100
LT-20 Special .... NiB $568 Ex $464 Gd $331
Model 1100
LT-20 Deer Gun................ NiB $540 Ex $442 Gd $316
Model 1100
LT-20 Youth .... NiB $555 Ex $454 Gd $323

REMINGTON MODEL
1100 MAGNUM .... NiB $499 Ex $408 Gd $293
Limited production. Similar to the Model 1100 Field except with 26-inch F choke, vent rib bbl. and 3-inch chamber. Made in 1981.

MODEL 1100
MAGNUM DUCK GUN
Same as Model 1100 Field Gun except has 3-inch chamber, 12 and 20 ga. Mag. only. 30-inch plain or vent rib bbl. in 12 ga., 28-inch in 20 ga.; M or F choke. Recoil pad. Weight: About 7.75 lbs. Made from 1963-88.
With plain barrel .... NiB $447 Ex $366 Gd $265
With ventilated
rib barrel..................... NiB $500 Ex $410 Gd $294

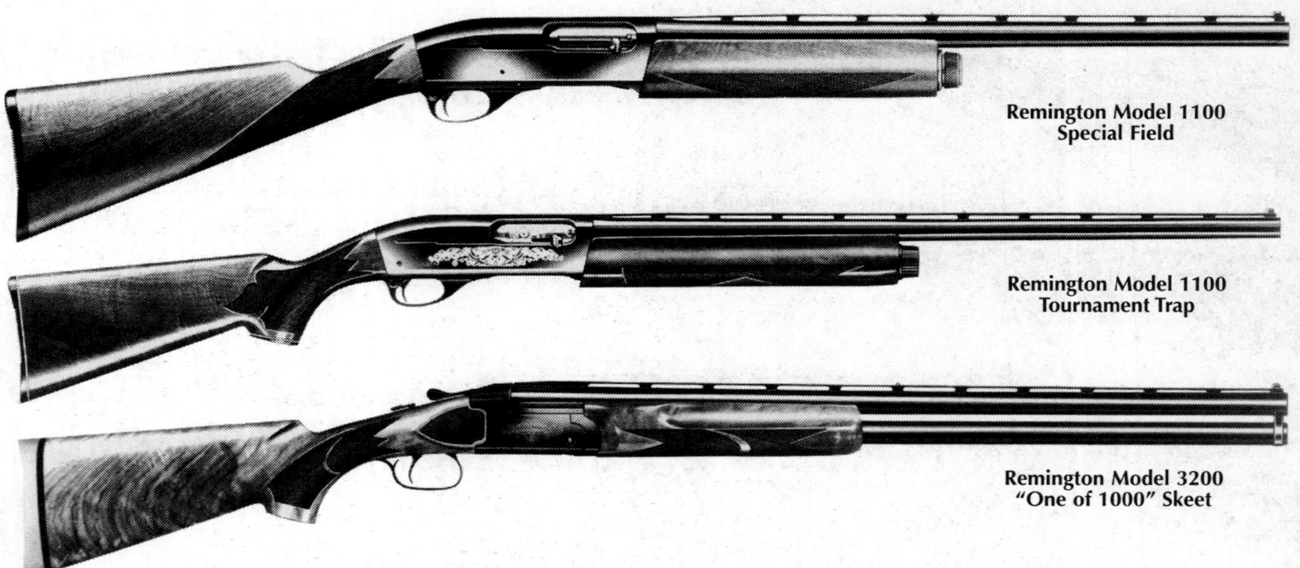

Remington Model 1100 Special Field

Remington Model 1100 Tournament Trap

Remington Model 3200 "One of 1000" Skeet

MODEL 1100
ONE OF 3000 FIELD. . . . . NiB $1309 Ex $1166 Gd $755
Limited edition, numbered 1 to 3000. Similar to Model 1100 Field except with fancy wood and gold-trimmed etched hunting scenes on receiver. 12 gauge with 28-inch Mod., vent rib bbl. Made in 1980.

MODEL 1100 SA SKEET GUN
Same as Model 1100 Field Gun, 12 and 20 ga. except has 26-inch vent-rib bbl., SK choke or with Cutts Compensator. Weight: 7.25-7.5 lbs. Made from 1963-94.
With skeet-
choked barrel . . . . NiB $563 Ex $461 Gd $331
With Cutts Comp. . . . . NiB $582 Ex $477 Gd $341
Left-hand action . . . . NiB $601 Ex $492 Gd $352

MODEL 1100 SA
LIGHTWEIGHT SKEET. . . . . NiB $533 Ex $436 Gd $313
Same as Model 1100 Lightweight except has skeet-style stock and forearm, 26-inch vent-rib bbl., SK choke. Made from 1971-97.

MODEL 1100 SA
SKEET SMALL BORE . . . . NiB $602 Ex $493 Gd $353
Similar to standard Model 1100SA except chambered for 28 and .410 ga. (2.5-inch chamber for latter); 25-inch vent-rib bbl., SK choke. Weight: 6.75 lbs., 28 ga.; 7.25 lbs., .410. Made from 1969-94.

MODEL 1100 SB
LIGHTWEIGHT SKEET. . . . . NiB $589 Ex $481 Gd $345
Same as Model 1100SA Lightweight except has select wood. Introduced in 1977.

MODEL 1100
SB SKEET GUN . . . . NiB $562 Ex $460 Gd $330
Same specifications as Model 1100SA except has select wood. Made from 1963-97.

MODEL 1100
SPECIAL FIELD SHOTGUN . . . . NiB $589 Ex $481 Gd $345
Gas-operated. Five round capacity. Hammerless. Gauges: 12 and 20. 21-inch vent-rib bbl. with REMChoke. Weight: 6.5-7.25 lbs. Straight-grip checkered walnut stock and forend. Made from 1983-99.

MODEL 1100 SP MAGNUM
Same as Model 1100 Field except 12 ga. only with 3-inch chambers. Bbls.: 26- or 30-inch F choke; or 26-inch with REM Choke tubes; vent rib. Non-reflective matte black, Parkerized bbl. and receiver. Satin-finished stock and forend. Made 1986.
With fixed choke . . . . NiB $466 Ex $383 Gd $276
With REMChoke . . . . NiB $518 Ex $424 Gd $303

MODEL 1100 TOURNAMENT
AND PREMIER
These higher grade guns differ from standard models in overall quality, grade of wood, checkering, engraving, gold inlays, etc. General specifications are the same. Made from 1963-94;1997-99; 2003.
Model 1100D
Tournament . . . . NiB $2799 Ex $2026 Gd $1460
Model 1100F
Premier . . . . NiB $6016 Ex $4471 Gd $2985
Model 1100F Premier
with gold inlay . . . . NiB $9156 Ex $5293 Gd $3620

MODEL 1100
TOURNAMENT SKEET. . . . . NiB $702 Ex $633 Gd $409
Similar to Model 1100 Field except with 26-inch bbl. SK choke. Gauges: 12, LT-20, 28, and .410. Features select walnut stocks and new cut-checkering patterns. Made from 1979-89.

MODEL 1100TA TRAP GUN . . . . . . NiB $505 Ex $404 Gd $292
Similar to Model 1100TB Trap Gun except with regular-grade stocks. Available in both left- and right-hand versions. Made from 1979-86.

MODEL 1100TB TRAP GUN
Same as Model 1100 Field Gun except has special trap stock, straight or Monte Carlo comb, recoil pad; 30-inch vent-rib bbl., F or M trap choke; 12 ga. only. Weight: 8.25 lbs. Made from 1963-79.
With straight stock . . . . NiB $536 Ex $439 Gd $285
With Monte Carlo stock . . . . NiB $561 Ex $459 Gd $328

MODEL 1900
HAMMERLESS DOUBLE . . . . NiB $1175 Ex $956 Gd $675
Improved version of Model 1894. Boxlock. Auto ejector. Double triggers. Gauges: 10, 12, 16. Bbls.: 28 to 32 inches. Value shown is for standard grade with ordnance steel bbls. Made from 1900-10.

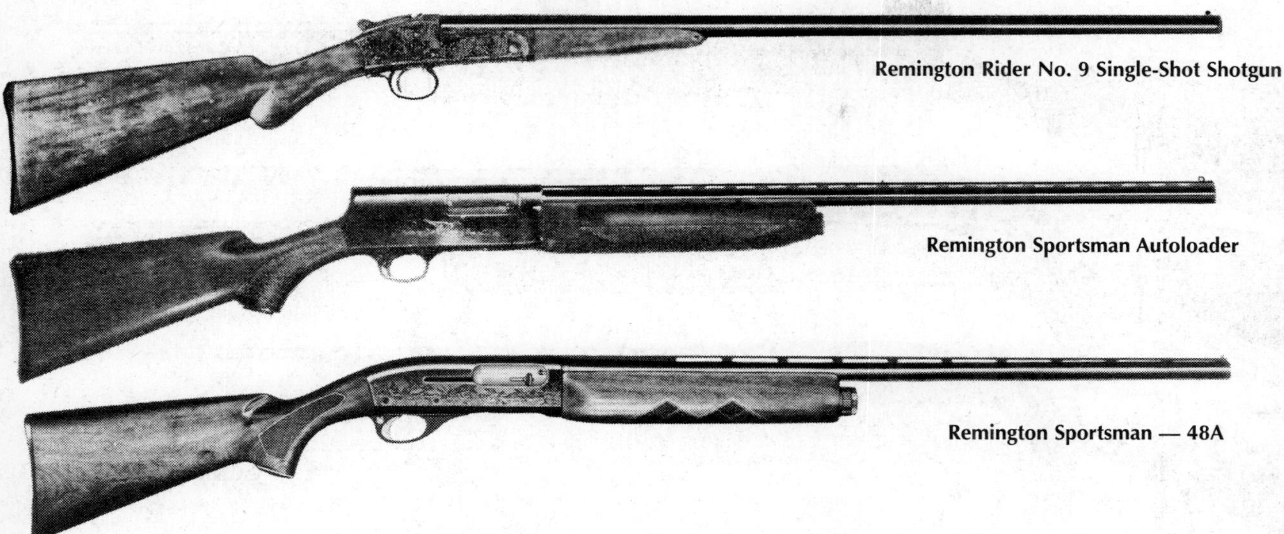

Remington Rider No. 9 Single-Shot Shotgun

Remington Sportsman Autoloader

Remington Sportsman — 48A

MODEL 3200
COMPETITION SKEET GUN . . . NiB $1795 Ex $1459 Gd $1029
Same as Model 3200 Skeet Gun except has gilded scrollwork on frame, engraved forend, latch plate and trigger guard, select fancy wood. Made from 1973-84.

MODEL 3200
COMPETITION SKEET SET . . . . NiB $5545 Ex $4466 Gd $3096
Similar specifications to Model 3200 Field. 12-ga. O/U with additional, interchangeable bbls. in 20, 28, and .410 ga. Cased. Made from 1980-84.

MODEL 3200
COMPETITION TRAP GUN. . . . NiB $2209 Ex $1796 Gd $1268
Same as Model 3200 Trap Gun except has gilded scrollwork on frame, engraved forend, latch plate and trigger guard, select fancy wood. Made from 1973-84.

MODEL 3200
FIELD GRADE MAGNUM . . . . . NiB $1855 Ex $1506 Gd $1060
Same as Model 3200 Field except chambered for 12 ga. mag. 3-inch shells 30-inch bbls., M and F or both F choke. Made from 1975-84.

MODEL 3200 FIELD GRADE O/U . . NiB $1253 Ex $1023 Gd $727
Boxlock. Auto ejectors. Selective single trigger. 12 ga. 2.75-inch chambers. Bbls.: Vent rib, 26- and 28-inch M/F; 30-inch IC/M. Weight: About 7.75 lbs. with 26-inch bbls. Checkered pistol-grip stock/forearm. Made from 1973-78.

MODEL 3200
"ONE OF 1000" SKEET . . . . NiB $2025 Ex $1642 Gd $1151
Same as Model 3200 "One of 1000" Trap except has 26- or 28-inch bbls., SK choke, skeet-style stock and forearm. Made in 1974.

MODEL 3200
"ONE OF 1000" TRAP . . . . NiB $2222 Ex $1805 Gd $1273
Limited edition numbered 1 to 1000. Same general specifications as Model 3200 Trap Gun but has frame, trigger guard and forend latch elaborately engraved (designation "One of 1,000" on frame side), stock and forearm of high grade walnut. Supplied in carrying case. Made in 1973.

MODEL 3200 SKEET GUN . . . . . NiB $1611 Ex $1307 Gd $919
Same as Model 3200 Field Grade except skeet-style stock and full beavertail forearm, 26- or 28-inch bbls., SK choke. Made from 1973-80.

MODEL 3200
SPECIAL TRAP GUN . . . . NiB $1482 Ex $1208 Gd $858
Same as Model 3200 Trap Gun except has select fancy-grade wood and other minor refinements. Made from 1973-84.

MODEL 3200 TRAP GUN . . . . . . NiB $1373 Ex $1120 Gd $798
Same as Model 3200 Field Grade except trap-style stock w/Monte Carlo or straight comb, select wood, beavertail forearm, 30- or 32-inch bbls. w/ventilated rib, IM/F or F/F chokes. Made from 1973-77.

RIDER NO. 9
SINGLE-SHOT SHOTGUN . . . . NiB $473 Ex $390 Gd $283
Improved version of No. 3 Single Barrel Shotgun made in the late 1800s. Semi-hammerless. Gauges 10, 12, 16, 20, 24, 28. 30- to 32-inch plain bbl. Weight: About 6 lbs. Plain pistol-grip stock and forearm. Auto ejector. Made from 1902-10.

SP-10
MAGNUM AUTOLOADER . . . . NiB 1105 Ex $900 Gd $634
Takedown. Gas-operated with stainless steel piston. 10 ga., 3.5-inch chamber. Bbls.: 26- or 30-inch vent-rib with REMChoke screw-in tubes. Weight: 11 to 11.25 lbs. Metal bead front. Checkered walnut stock with satin finish. Made from 1989 to date.

SP-10
MAGNUM TURKEY COMBO . . . . NiB $1116 Ex $908 Gd $643
Same general specifications as Model SP-10 Magnum except has extra 22-inch REMChoke bbl. with M, F and Turkey extra-full tubes. Rifle sights. QD swivels and camo sling. Made from 1991 to date.

PEERLESS O/U. . . . . NiB $1150 Ex $936 Gd $662
Boxlock action and removable, engraved sideplates. Gauge: 12 only with 3-inch chambers. Barrels: 26-, 28-, or 30-inch with vent rib and REMChoke system. Automatic safety and single selective trigger. Weight: 7.25 lbs. to 7.5 lbs. Blued receiver and bbls. Checkered American walnut stock. Made from 1993-98.

SPORTSMAN A STANDARD GRADE
AUTOLOADER
Same general specifications as Model 11A except magazine holds two shells. Also available in "B" Special Grade, "D" Tournament Grade, "E" Expert Grade, "F" Premier Grade. Made from 1931-48. Same values as for Model 11A.
48D . . . . NiB $1214 Ex $931 Gd $544

SHOTGUNS

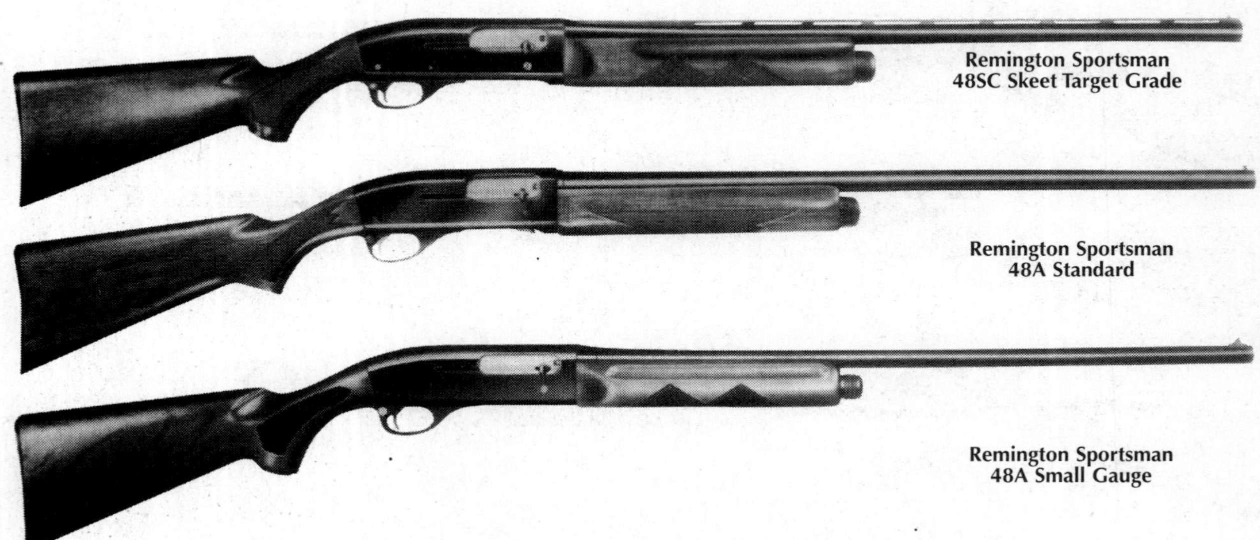

Remington Sportsman 48SC Skeet Target Grade

Remington Sportsman 48A Standard

Remington Sportsman 48A Small Gauge

SPORTSMAN SKEET GUN
Same general specifications as the Sportsman A except has 26-inch bbl. (plain, solid or vent rib), SK choke, beavertail forend. Disc. in 1949.
With plain barrel . . . . NiB $453 Ex $270 Gd $271
With solid-rib barrel . . . . NiB $539 Ex $442 Gd $319
With ventilated rib barrel . . . . NiB $587 Ex $481 Gd $345

SPORTSMAN-48A STANDARD GRADE AUTOLOADER
Streamlined receiver. Hammerless. Takedown. Gauges: 12, 16, 20. Tubular magazine holds two rounds. Bbls.: Plain, matted top surface or vent rib; 26-inch IC, 28-inch M or F choke, 30-inch F choke (12 ga. only). Weight: About 7.5 lbs., 12 ga.; 6.25 lbs., 16 ga.; 6.5 lbs., 20 ga. Pistol-grip stock, grooved forend, both checkered. Made from 1949-59.
With plain bbl. . . . . NiB $416 Ex $360 Gd $242
With matted top-surface bbl. . . . . . NiB $452 Ex $373 Gd $271
With ventilated rib bbl. . . . . NiB $477 Ex $393 Gd $286

SPORTSMAN-48 B, D, F SPECIAL, TOURNAMENT AND PREMIER GRADE GUNS
These higher grade models differ from the Sportsman-48A in general quality, grade of wood, checkering, engraving, etc. General specifications are the same. Made from 1949-59.
Sportsman-48B Special grade . . . . . NiB $490 Ex $403 Gd $291
Sportsman-48D Tournament grade . . NiB $1004 Ex $814 Gd $571
Sportsman-48F Premier grade . . . . NiB $2200 Ex $1785 Gd $1255

SPORTSMAN-48SA SKEET GUN
Same general specifications as Sportsman-48A except has 26-inch bbl. with matted top surface or vent rib, SK choke, ivory bead front sight, metal bead rear sight. Made from 1949-60.
With matted top-surface barrel . . . NiB $407 Ex $336 Gd $246
With ventilated rib barrel . . . . NiB $483 Ex $388 Gd $281
Sportsman-48SC Skeet Target grade . . . . NiB $570 Ex $467 Gd $335
Sportsman-48SD Skeet Tournament grade . . . . NiB $988 Ex $803 Gd $566
Sportsman-48SF Skeet Premier grade . . . . NiB $2342 Ex $1875 Gd $1317

MODEL 11-48A RIOT GUN . . . . . . NiB $279 Ex $286 Gd $206
Same as Model 11-48A except 20-inch plain barrel and 12 ga. only. Disc. in 1969.

MODEL 11-48A STANDARD GRADE 4-ROUND AUTOLOADER .410 & 28 GAUGE
Same general specifications as Sportsman-48A except gauge, 3-round magazine, 25-inch bbl. Weight: About 6.25 lbs. 28 ga. introduced 1952, .410 in 1954. Disc. in 1969. Values same as shown for Sportsman-48A.

MODEL 11-48A STANDARD GRADE AUTOLOADER
Same general specifications as Sportsman-48A except magazine holds four rounds, forend not grooved. Also available in Special Grade (11-48B), Tournament Grade (11-48D) and Premier Grade (11-48F). Made 1949-69. Values same as shown for Sportsman-48A.

MODEL 11-48SA
.410 AND 28 GA. SKEET . . . . NiB $436 Ex $355 Gd $253
Same general specifications as Model 11-48A 28 gauge except has 25-inch vent rib bbl., SK choke. 28 ga. introduced 1952, .410 in 1954.

SPORTSMAN-58 SKEET, TARGET, TOURNAMENT AND PREMIER GRADES
These higher grade models differ from the Sportsman-58SA in general quality, grade of wood, checkering, engraving, and other refinements. General operating and physical specifications are the same.
Sportsman-58C Skeet Target . . . . . . NiB $640 Ex $523 Gd $365
Sportsman-58D Skeet Tournament. . . . . NiB $922 Ex $752 Gd $544
Sportsman-58SF Skeet Premier . NiB $1770 Ex $1436 Gd $1009

SPORTSMAN-58 TOURNAMENT AND PREMIER
These higher grade models differ from the Sportsman-58ADL with vent-rib bbl. in general quality, grade of wood, checkering, engraving, etc. General specifications are the same.
Sportsman-58D Tournament . . . . . . NiB $999 Ex $814 Gd $580
Sportsman-58F Premier. . . . . . . NiB $1807 Ex $1466 Gd $1029

SPORTSMAN-58ADL AUTOLOADER
Deluxe grade. Gas-operated. 12 ga. Three round magazine. Bbls.: plain or vent rib, 26-, 28- or 30-inch; IC, M or F choke, or Remington Special Skeet choke. Weight: About 7 lbs. Checkered pistol-grip stock and forearm. Made from 1956-64.
With plain barrel . . . . NiB $381 Ex $312 Gd $224
With ventilated rib barrel . . . . NiB $435 Ex $356 Gd $254

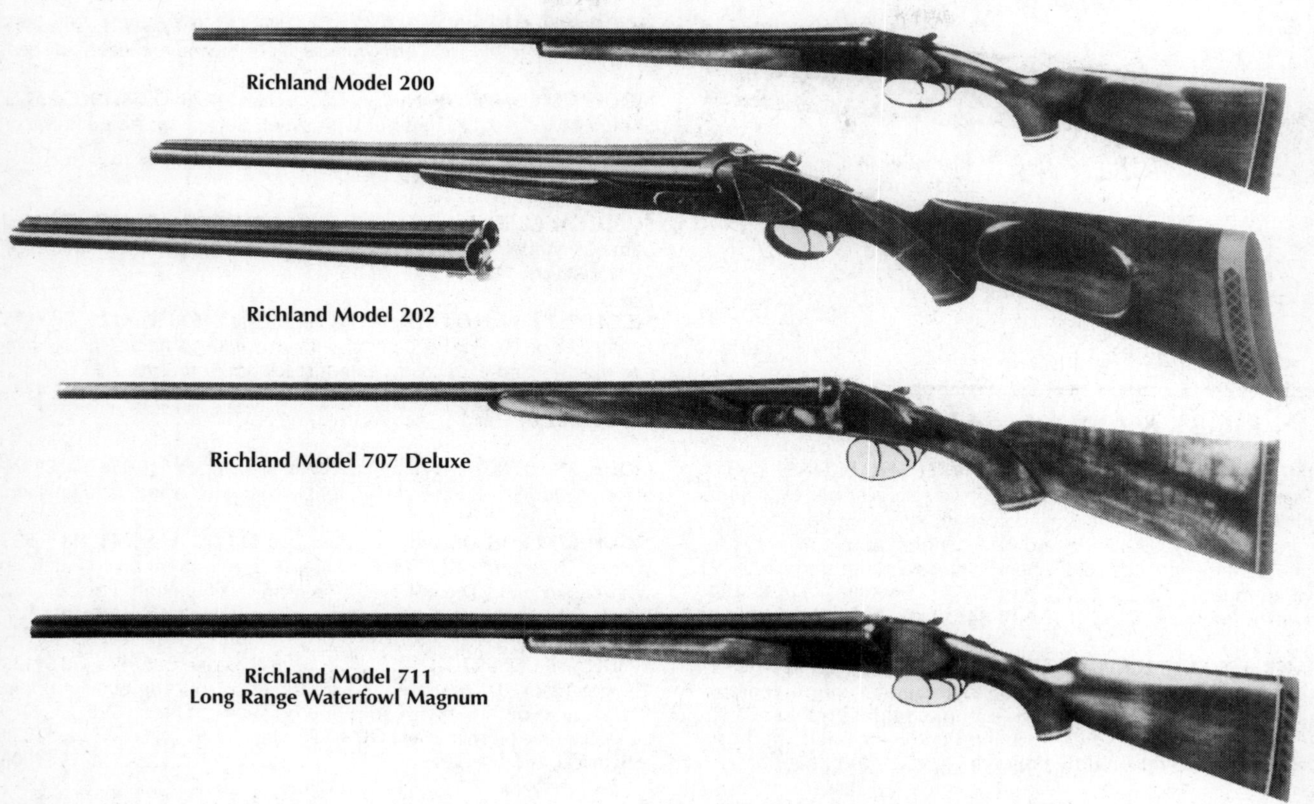

Richland Model 200

Richland Model 202

Richland Model 707 Deluxe

Richland Model 711
Long Range Waterfowl Magnum

SPORTSMAN-58BDL DELUXE SPECIAL GRADE
Same as Model 58ADL except select grade wood.
With plain barrel .... NiB $407 Ex $335 Gd $243
With ventilated rib barrel .... NiB $469 Ex $384 Gd $277

SPORTSMAN-58SA
SKEET GRADE................ NiB $457 Ex $375 Gd $269
Same general specifications as Model 58ADL with vent-rib bbl. except special skeet stock and forearm.

REVELATION SHOTGUNS

See Western Auto listings.

RICHLAND ARMS COMPANY — Blissfield, Michigan; Manufactured in Italy and Spain

MODEL 200
FIELD GRADE DOUBLE .... NiB $370 Ex $335 Gd $222
Hammerless, boxlock, Anson & Deeley-type. Plain extractors. Double triggers. Gauges: 12, 16, 20, 28, .410 (3-inch chambers in 20 and .410; others have 2.75-inch). Bbls.: 28-inch M/F choke, 26-inch IC/M; .410 with 26-inch M/F only; 22-inch IC/M in 20 ga. only. Weight: 6 lbs., 2 oz. to 7 lbs., 4 oz. Checkered walnut stock with cheekpiece, pistol grip, recoil pad; beavertail forend. Made in Spain from 1963-85.

MODEL 202
ALL PURPOSE FIELD GUN .... NiB $356 Ex $294 Gd $214
Hammerless, boxlock, Anson & Deeley-type. Same as Model 200 except has two sets of barrels same gauge. 12 ga.: 30-inch bbls. F/F, 3-inch chambers; 26-inch bbls. IC/M, 2.75-inch chambers. 20 gauge: 28-inch bbls. M/F; 22-inch bbls. IC/M, 3-inch chambers. Made from 1963 to date.

MODEL 707
DELUXE FIELD GUN........... NiB $388 Ex $319 Gd $231
Hammerless, boxlock, triple bolting system. Plain extractors. Double triggers. Gauges: 12, 2.75-inch chambers; 20, 3-inch chambers. Bbls.: 12 ga., 28-inch M/F, 26-inch IC/M; 20 ga., 30-inch F/F, 28-inch M/F, 26-inch IC/M. Weight: 6 lbs., 4 oz. to 6 lbs., 15 oz. Checkered walnut stock and forend, recoil pad. Made from 1963-72.

MODEL 711 LONG-RANGE
WATERFOWL MAGNUM
DOUBLE-BARREL SHOTGUN
Hammerless, boxlock, Anson & Deeley-type, Purdey triple lock. Plain extractors. Double triggers. Auto safety. Gauges: 10, 3.5-inch chambers; 12, 3-inch chambers. Bbls.: 10 ga., 32-inch; 12 ga., 30-inch; F/F. Weight: 10 ga., 11 pounds; 12 ga., 7.75 lbs. Checkered walnut stock and beavertail forend; recoil pad. Made in Spain from 1963-85.
10 ga. magnum .... NiB $465 Ex $347 Gd $241
12 ga. magnum .... NiB $402 Ex $296 Gd $207

MODEL 808
O/U SHOTGUN .... NiB $468 Ex $385 Gd $278
Boxlock. Plain extractors. Non-selective single trigger. 12 ga. only. Bbls. (Vickers steel): 30-inch F/F; 28-inch M/F; 26-inch IC/M. Weight: 6 lbs., 12 oz. to 7 lbs., 3 oz. Checkered walnut stock/forend. Made in Italy from 1963-68.

JOHN RIGBY & CO. — London, England

HAMMERLESS BOX LOCK DOUBLE-BARREL SHOTGUNS
Auto ejectors. Double triggers. Made in all gauges, barrel lengths and chokes. Checkered stock and forend, straight grip standard. Made in two grades: Sackville and Chatsworth. These guns differ in general quality, engraving, etc.; specifications are the same.
Sackville grade .... NiB $6173 Ex $4985 Gd $3465
Chatsworth grade .... NiB $4651 Ex $3759 Gd $2619

HAMMERLESS SIDE LOCK DOUBLE-BARREL SHOTGUNS
Auto ejectors. Double triggers. Made in all gauges, barrel lengths and chokes. Checkered stock and forend, straight grip standard. Made in two grades: Regal (best quality) and Sandringham; these guns differ in general quality, engraving, etc., specifications are the same.
Regal grade .... NiB $12,500 Ex $10,000 Gd $6000
Sandringham grade .... NiB $9650 Ex $7650 Gd $3925

RIZZINI, BATTISTA — Marcheno, Italy

Rizzini was purchased by San Swiss AG IN 2002. Imported in the U. S. by SIB Arms, Exeter, New Hampshire; William Larkin Moore & Co., Scottsdale, Arizona; and New England Arms Co., Kittery, Maine

AURUM O/U .... NiB $3750 Ex $2900 Gd $1995
Gauge: 12, 16 and 20. Boxlock action, light engraving. Case included. Introduced 1996.

AURUM LIGHT .... NiB $1850 Ex $1675 Gd $1225
Similaar to Aurum but 16 gauge only. Imported beginning in 2000.

ARTEMIS .... NiB $1925 Ex $1595 Gd $1195
Similarf to Aurum but with improved engraving and gold inlays.

ARTEMIS DELUXE .... NiB $4300 Ex $3675 Gd $2950
Similar to Artemis but with detailed game scene engraving. Available in all gauges

ARTEMIS EL .... NiB $13,000 Ex $10,000 Gd $8500
Same as Artemis Deluxe. Custom gun with superior quality wood and detailed hand engraving. Disc. 2000.

MODEL 780 FIELD .... NiB $1150 Ex $925 Gd $795
Gauge: 10, 12 or 16. Boxlock action, double triggers, extractors, walnut stock and forearm. Disc. 2000.
10 gauge, add $600
Ejector model (S780EL), add $200
Single selective trigger with ejectors, add $250
SST, ejectors and upgraded stock, add.................. $400

MODEL S780 EMEL .... NiB $6250 Ex $4974 Gd $3895
Same as Model 780 Field but with special engraving and hand finished.

MODEL 780 COMPETITION .... NiB $1425 Ex $1110 Gd $925
Same as Model 780 Field but with skeet, trap or sporting clays features. Disc.1998.

MODEL 780
SMALL GAUGE SERIES .... NiB $1375 Ex $995 Gd $775
Same as Model 780 Field but in 20, 28, or 36 gauge. Double triggers, ejectors. Disc. 1998.

MODEL 782 EM FIELD .... NiB $1625 Ex 1125 Gd $895
Gauge: 12 or 16. Boxlock action with sideplates, single selective trigger, ejectors and extractors, walnut stock and forearm. Disc. 1998.
MODEL 782 EM SLUG, add $525
MODEL 782 EML, add $400

MODEL S7820 EMEL .... NiB $12,995 Ex $10,850 Gd $9525
Same as Model 782 EM Field but specially engraved and hand finished.

MODEL S782 EMEL DELUXE .... NiB $10,125 Ex $8725 Gd $6995
Gauge: 10, 12, 16, 20, 28, 36 and .410. Barrel:28-inch ventilated rib with choke tubes (except .410); coin-finish engraving; gold inlaids; fine scroll borders; Deluxe English walnut stock. Imported 1994.

MODEL 790 COMPETITION .... NiB $2100 Ex $1495 Gd $1125
Gauge: 12 or 20. Available in trap, skeet or sporting clays models. Black frame outlined with gold line engraving. Disc. 1999.
20 ga. Sporting (sideplates and QD stock), add $1050
Trap model, add $4000

MODEL 790 SMALL GUAGE .... NiB $1595 Ex $1050 Gd $895
Similar to Model 790 Competition but in 20, 29, or 36 guages. Single selective trigger, ejectors. Disc. 2000.

MODEL 790 EMEL .... NiB $10,225 Ex $8750 Gd $7025
Same as Model 790 but hand finished with 18k gold inlays, hand engraving.

MODEL 790 EL .... NiB $6650 Ex $4150 Gd $3275
Same as Model 790 but with multiple chokes, fitted case. Disc. 2000.

MODEL S790 EMEL DELUXE .... NiB $8275 Ex $6550 Gd $4195
Guages: All. Custom gun with 27.5-inch ventilated-rib bbls. choke tubes (except .410); color case-hardened or coin-finished receiver; ornate engraving with Rizzini crest. Stock is deluxe English walnut; leather case included.

MODEL 792 SMALL GUAGE MAGNUM .. NiB $2150 Ex $1825 Gd $895
Gauge: 20, 28, or 36. Magnum chambers. Single selective trigger; ejectors; engraved sideplates. Disc. 1998.

MODEL 792 EMEL DELUXE .... NiB $8000 Ex $6950 Gd $4995
Same as Model 793 but hand finished with 18k gold inlays and hand engraving.

MODEL S792 EMEL DELUXE .... NiB $8500 Ex $7750 Gd $5595
Guages: All. Custom gun with 27.5-inch ventilated-rib bbls. choke tubes (except .410); coin-finished receiver; sideplates with fine game scene engraving and scroll borders; deluxe English walnut stock; leather case included. Imported 1994.

MODEL 2000 TRAP .... NiB $2100 Ex $1550 Gd $1295
Guage: 12 only. Nickel-finished receiver; sideplates; gold trigger; ventilated-rib bbls.. Disc 1998.

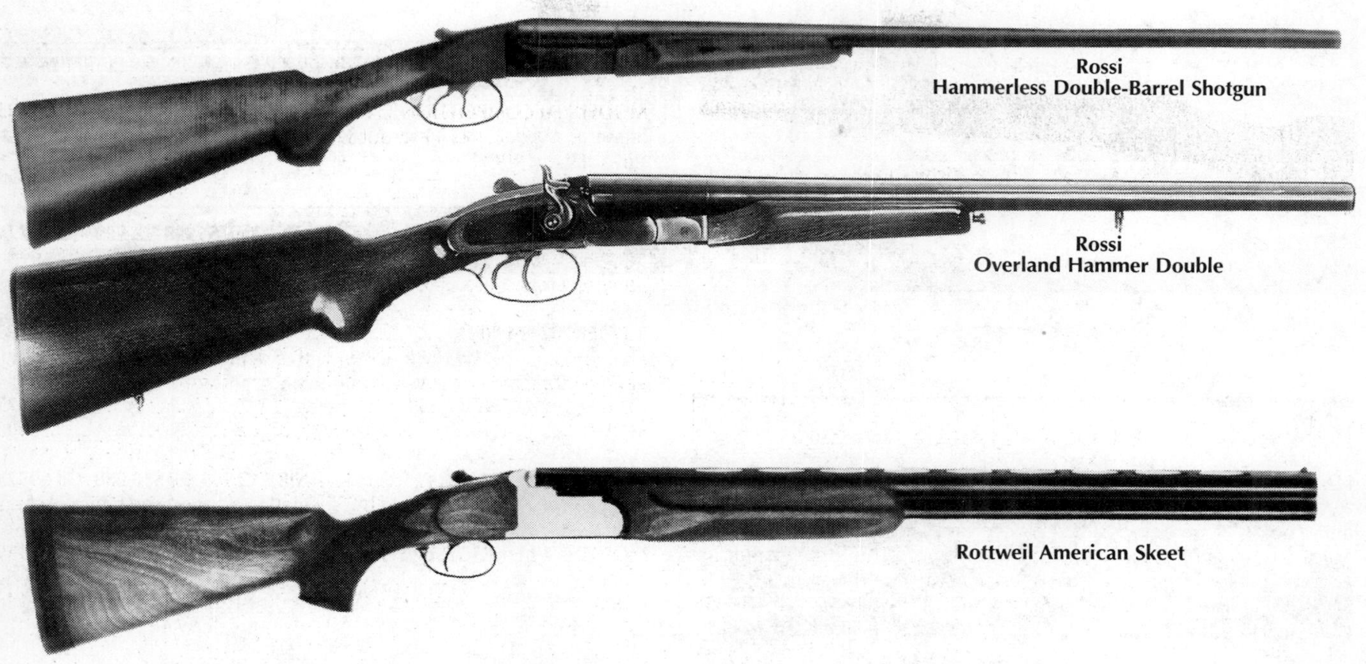
Rossi Hammerless Double-Barrel Shotgun

Rossi Overland Hammer Double

Rottweil American Skeet

MODEL 2000
TRAP EL............................NiB $5995 Ex $3890 Gd $2995
Same as Model 2000 Trap but hand finished with 18k gold inlays and ornate hand engraving.

MODEL 2000-SP....................NiB $3595 Ex $2825 Gd $2000
Guage: 12 only. Bbls.: 26, 29.5, or 32 inches. Over-bored barrels with choke tubes. Engraved sideplates, semi-fancy select QD stock. Case included. Imported 1994-98.

PREMIER SPORTING................NiB $2950 Ex $2125 Gd $1595
Guages: 12 or 20. Bbls.: 28, 29.5 or 32 inches five chokes per bbl.. Custom built on request. Imported 1994

SPORTING EL ....NiB $5995 Ex $3890 Gd $2995
Same as Premier model but includes multiple chokes and fitted case. Disc. 2000.

UPLAND EL ....NiB $5995 Ex $3890 Gd $2995
Guages: All. Custom gun with 27.5-inch ventilated-rib bbls. choke tubes (except .410); case-hardened receiver; deluxe walnut stock. Hard case included. Imported 1994.

AMADEO ROSSI, S.A. — Sao Leopoldo, Brazil

HAMMERLESS DOUBLE-
BARREL SHOTGUN.....................NiB $375 Ex $307 Gd $221
Boxlock. Plain extractors. Double triggers. 12 ga. Three-inch chambers. Bbls.: 26-inch IC/M; 28-inch M/F choke. Weight: 7 to 7.5 lbs. Pistol-grip stock and beavertail forearm, uncheckered. Made 1974 to date. Note: H&R Model 404 (1969-72) is same gun.

OVERLAND
HAMMER DOUBLE..................NiB $305 Ex $251 Gd $182
Sidelock. Plain extractors. Double triggers. Gauges: 12, .410; 3-inch chambers. Bbls.: 20-inch, IC/M in 12 g.; 26-inch, F/F choke in .410. Weight: 7 lbs. (12 ga.); 6 lbs. (.410). Pistol-grip stock and beavertail forearm, uncheckered. Note: Because of its resemblance to the short-barreled doubles carried by guards riding shotgun on 19th-century stagecoaches, the 12 ga. version originally was called the "Coach Gun." Made from 1968-89.

ROTTWEIL SHOTGUNS — West Germany

MODEL 72 O/U
SHOTGUN.........................NiB $2056 Ex $1665 Gd $1166
Hammerless, takedown with engraved receiver. 12 ga.; 2.75-inch chambers. 26.75-inch bbls. with SK/SK chokes. Weight: 7.5 lbs. Interchangeable trigger groups and buttstocks. Checkered French walnut buttstock and forend. Imported from Germany.

MODEL 650 FIELD
O/U SHOTGUN ....NiB $842 Ex $690 Gd $494
Breech action. Gauge: 12. 28-inch bbls. Six screw-in choke tubes. Automatic ejectors. Engraved receiver. Checkered pistol grip stock. Made from 1984-86.

AMERICAN SKEET.........NiB $1996 Ex $1616 Gd $1131
Boxlock action. Gauge: 12. 27-inch vent-rib bbls. 44.5 inches overall. SK chokes. Weight: 7.5 lbs. Designed for tube sets. Hand-checkered European walnut stock with modified forend. Made from 1984-87.

INTERNATIONAL
TRAP SHOTGUN ....NiB $2051 Ex $1660 Gd $1161
Box lock action. Gauge: 12. 30-inch bbls. 48.5 inches overall. Weight: 8 lbs. Choked IM/F. Selective single trigger. Metal bead front sight. Checkered European walnut stock w/pistol grip. Engraved action. Made from 1984-87.

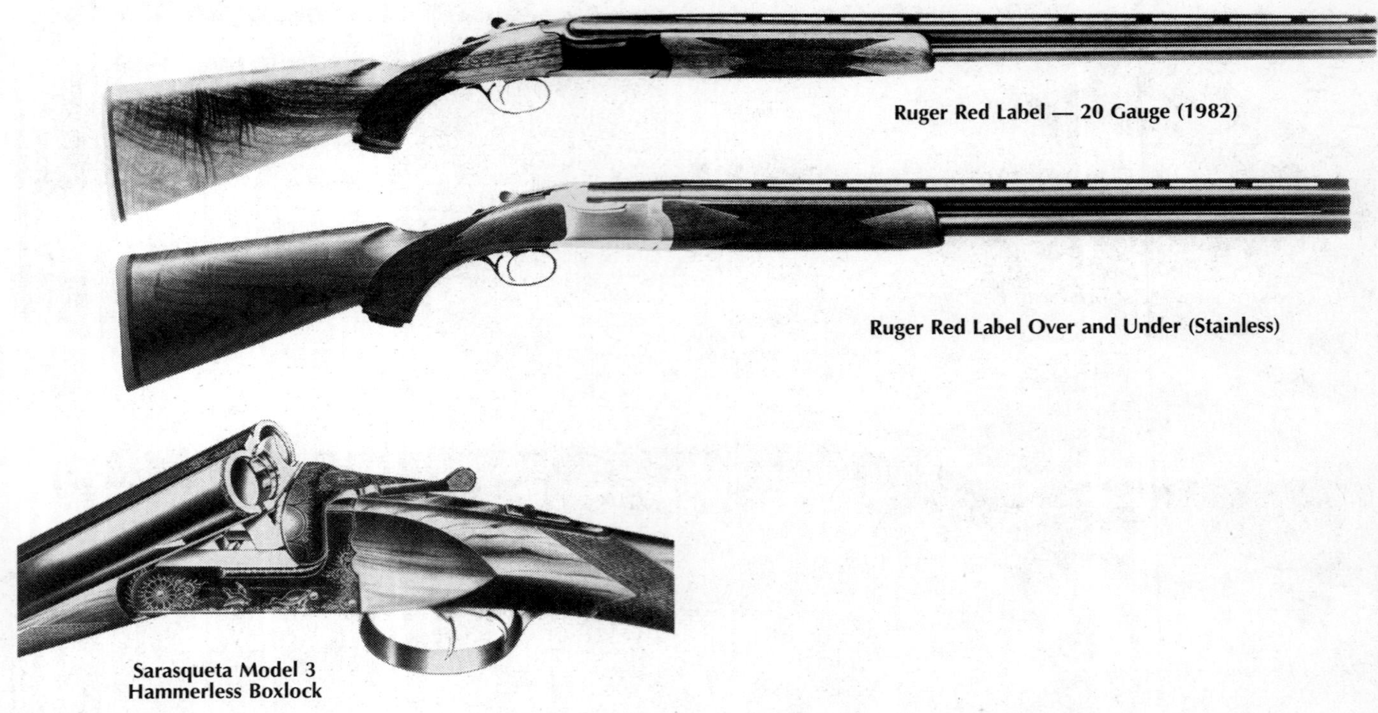

Ruger Red Label — 20 Gauge (1982)

Ruger Red Label Over and Under (Stainless)

Sarasqueta Model 3
Hammerless Boxlock

STURM, RUGER & COMPANY, INC. — Southport, Connecticut

PLAIN GRADE RED LABEL O/U

Boxlock. Auto ejectors. Selective single trigger. 12, 20 or 28 ga. w/2.75- or 3-inch chambers. 26-inch vent-rib bbl., IC/M or SK choke. Single selective trigger. Selective automatic ejectors. Automatic top safety. Standard gold bead front sight. Pistol-grip or English-style American walnut stock and forearm w/hand-cut checkering. The 20 ga. Model was introduced in 1977; 12 ga. version in 1982 and the stainless receiver became standard in 1985. Choke tubes were optional in 1988 and standard in 1990. Weight: 7.0 to 7.5 lbs.

Red Label w/fixed chokes .... NiB $897 Ex $729 Gd $515
Red Label w/screw-in tubes ..... NiB $1163 Ex $949 Gd $674
Red Label w/grade 1 engraving ... NiB $2303 Ex $1866 Gd $1308
Red Label w/grade 2 engraving ... NiB $2648 Ex $2144 Gd $1497
Red Label w/grade 3 engraving ... NiB $3009 Ex $2433 Gd $1696

RED LABEL O/U ALL-WEATHER STAINLESS

Gauges: 12 ga. Only. Bbls.: 26- 28- or 30-inch w/various chokes, fixed or screw-in tubes. Stainless receiver and barrel. Checkered black synthetic stock and forearm. Weight: 7.5 lbs. Made from 1999 to date.

All-weather stainless model .... NiB $1240 Ex $1008 Gd $711
W/30-inch bbl., add $100

RED LABEL "WOODSIDE" O/U

Similar to the Red Label O/U Stainless except in 12 ga. only with wood sideplate extensions. Made from 1995-97. Disc.

Standard Woodside .... NiB $1602 Ex $1298 Gd $910
Engraved Woodside .... NiB $2258 Ex $1830 Gd $1281

RED LABEL SPORTING CLAYS O/U

Similar to the standard Red Label model except chambered 12 or 20 ga. only w/30-inch vent-rib bbls., no side ribs; back-bored w/screw-in choke tubes (not interchangeable w/other Red Label O/U models). Brass front and mid-rib beads. Made from 1992 to date.

Standard Sporting Clays........ NiB $1410 Ex $1145 Gd $805
Engraved Sporting Clays ...... NiB $2478 Ex $2006 Gd $1404

RED LABEL SPECIAL EDITION - WILDLIFE FOREVER

Limited edition commemorating the 50th Wildlife Forever anniversary. Similar to the standard Red Label model except chambered 12 ga. only w/engraved receiver enhanced w/gold mallard and pheasant inlays. 300 produced in 1993.

Special edition.............. NiB $1804 Ex $1465 Gd $1029
Special edition w/hard case ... NiB $1959 Ex $1589 Gd $1115

VICTOR SARASQUETA, S. A. — Eibar, Spain

SARASQUETA MODEL 3 HAMMERLESS BOXLOCK DOUBLE-BARREL SHOTGUN

Plain extractors or auto ejectors. Double triggers. Gauges: 12, 16, 20. Made in various bbl. lengths, chokes and weights. Checkered stock and forend, straight grip standard. Imported from 1985-87.

Model 3, plain extractors .... NiB $507 Ex $416 Gd $299
Model 3E, automatic ejectors ..... NiB $624 Ex $508 Gd $362

HAMMERLESS SIDELOCK DOUBLES

Automatic ejectors (except on Models 4 and 203 which have plain extractors). Double triggers. Gauges: 12, 16, 20. Barrel lengths, chokes and weights made to order. Checkered stock and forend, straight grip standard. Models differ chiefly in overall quality, engraving, grade of wood, checkering, etc.; general specifications are the same. Imported from 1985-87.

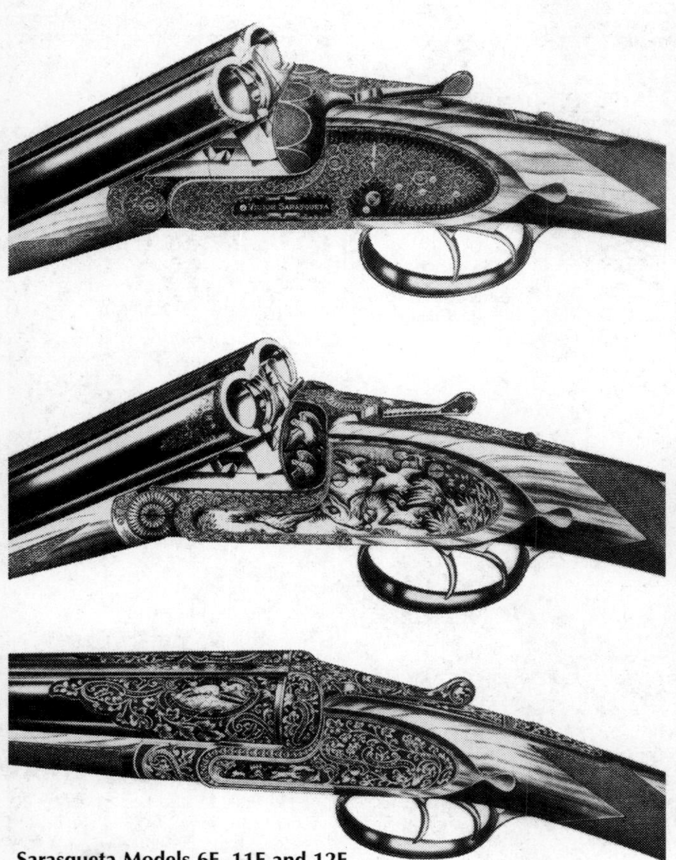

Sarasqueta Models 6E, 11E and 12E

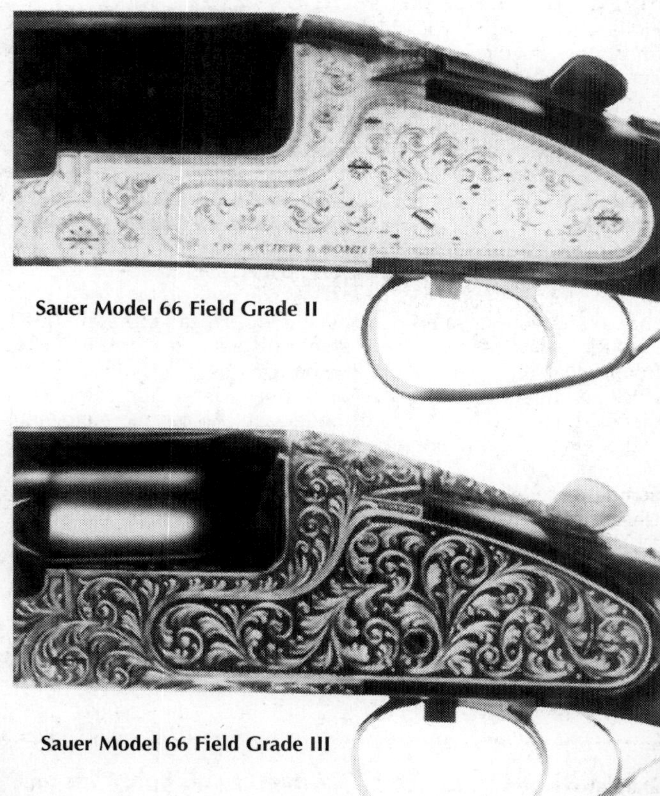

Sauer Model 66 Field Grade II

Sauer Model 66 Field Grade III

Model 4	**NiB $658**	**Ex $530**	**Gd $366**
Model 4E	**NiB $709**	**Ex $571**	**Gd $395**
Model 203	**NiB $686**	**Ex $553**	**Gd $382**
Model 203E	**NiB $743**	**Ex $599**	**Gd $413**
Model 6E	**NiB $872**	**Ex $705**	**Gd $489**
Model 7E	**NiB $933**	**Ex $753**	**Gd $523**
Model 10E	**NiB $1738**	**Ex $1409**	**Gd $989**
Model 11E	**NiB $1794**	**Ex $1455**	**Gd $1019**
Model 12E	**NiB $2057**	**Ex $1666**	**Gd $1169**

J. P. SAUER & SOHN — Eckernförde, Germany, Formerly located in Suhl, Germany

MODEL 66 O/U FIELD GUN

Purdey-system action with Holland & Holland-type sidelocks. Selective single trigger. Selective auto ejectors. Automatic safety. Available in three grades of engraving. 12 ga. only. Krupp special steel bbls. w/vent rib 28-inch, M/F choke. Weight: About 7.25 lbs. Checkered walnut stock and forend; recoil pad. Made from 1966-75.

Grade I	**NiB $2540**	**Ex $2060**	**Gd $1446**
Grade II	**NiB $3337**	**Ex $2699**	**Gd $1884**
Grade III	**NiB $4427**	**Ex $3578**	**Gd $2492**

MODEL 66 O/U SKEET GUN

Same as Model 66 Field Gun except 26-inch bbls. with wide vent rib, SK choked- skeet-style stock and ventilated beavertail forearm; non-automatic safety. Made from1966-75.

Grade I	**NiB $2466**	**Ex $2000**	**Gd $1403**
Grade II	**NiB $3340**	**Ex $2702**	**Gd $1886**
Grade III	**NiB $4715**	**Ex $3809**	**Gd $2652**

MODEL 66 O/U TRAP GUN

Same as Model 66 Skeet Gun except has 30-inch bbls. choked F/F or M/F; trap-style stock. Values same as for Skeet model. Made from1966-75.

MODEL 3000E DRILLING

Combination rifle and double barrel shotgun. Blitz action with Greener crossbolt, double underlugs, separate rifle cartridge extractor, front set trigger, firing pin indicators, Greener side safety, sear slide selector locks right shotgun bbl. for firing rifle bbl. Gauge/calibers12 ga. (2.75-inch chambers); .222, .243, .30-06, 7x65R. 25-inch Krupp-Special steel bbls.; M/F choke automatic folding leaf rear rifle sight. Weight: 6.5 to 7.25 lbs. depending on rifle caliber. Checkered walnut stock and forend; pistol grip, Monte Carlo comb and cheekpiece, sling swivels. Standard model with Arabesque engraving; Deluxe model with hunting scenes engraved on action. Currently manufactured. Note: Also see listing under Colt.

Standard model	**NiB $4589**	**Ex $3709**	**Gd $2585**
Deluxe model	**NiB $5524**	**Ex $4459**	**Gd $3196**

ARTEMIS DOUBLE-BARREL SHOTGUN
Holland & Holland-type sidelock with Greener crossbolt double underlugs, double sear safeties, selective single trigger, selective auto ejectors. Grade I with fine-line engraving, Grade II with full English Arabesque engraving. 12 ga. (2.75-inch chambers). Krupp special steel bbls., 28-inch, M/F choke. Weight: About 6.5 lbs. Checkered walnut pistol-grip stock and beavertail forend; recoil pad. Made from1966-77.
Grade I . . . . NiB $5858 Ex $4726 Gd $3278
Grade II . . . . NiB $7250 Ex $5848 Gd $4054

BBF 54 O/U COMBINATION RIFLE/SHOTGUN
Blitz action with Kersten lock, front set trigger fires rifle bbl., slide-operated sear safety. Gauge/calibers: 16 ga.; .30-30, .30-06, 7x65R, 25-inch Krupp special steel bbls.; shotgun bbl. F choke, folding-leaf rear sight. Weight: About 6 lbs. Checkered walnut stock and forend; pistol grip, mod. Monte Carlo comb and cheekpiece, sling swivels. Standard model with Arabesque engraving; Deluxe model with hunting scenes engraved on action. Currently manufactured.
Standard model . . . . NiB $2818 Ex $2282 Gd $1595
Deluxe model . . . . NiB $3248 Ex $2626 Gd $1831

ROYAL DOUBLE-BARREL SHOTGUNS
Anson & Deeley action (boxlock) with Greener crossbolt, double underlugs, signal pins, selective single trigger, selective auto ejectors, auto safety. Scalloped frame with Arabesque engraving. Krupp special steel bbls. Gauges: 12, 2.75-inch chambers, 20, 3-inch chambers. Bbls.: 30-inch (12 ga. only) and 28-inch, M/F- 26-inch (20 ga. only), IC/M. Weight: 12 ga., about 6.5 lbs.; 20 ga., 6 lbs. Checkered walnut pistol-grip stock and beavertail forend; recoil pad. Made from 1955-77.
Standard model . . . . NiB $1682 Ex $1365 Gd $969
20 ga. NiB $2205 Ex $1788 Gd $1256

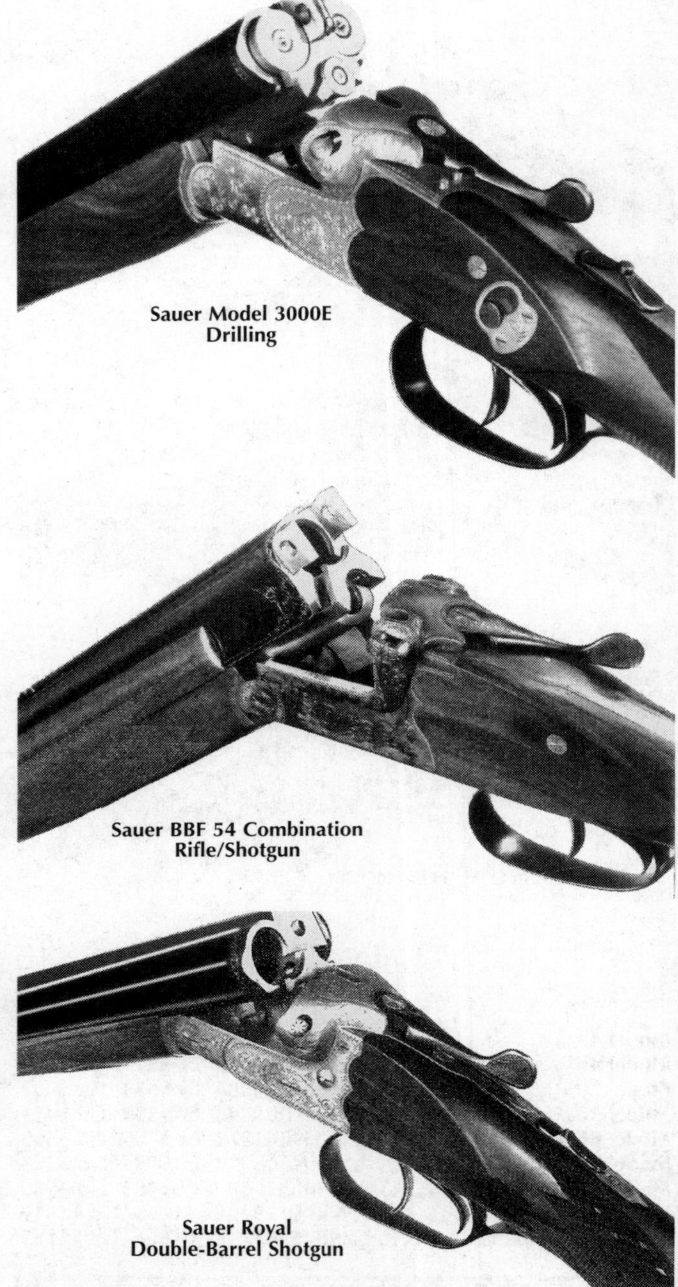
Sauer Model 3000E Drilling

Sauer BBF 54 Combination Rifle/Shotgun

Sauer Royal Double-Barrel Shotgun

SAVAGE ARMS — Westfield, Massachusetts Formerly located in Utica, New York

MODEL 24 22-.410
O/U COMBINATION . . . . NiB $189 Ex $156 Gd $113
Same as Stevens No. 22-.410 with walnut stock and forearm. Made from 1950-65.

MODEL 24C
CAMPER'S COMPANION . . . . NiB $218 Ex $159 Gd $116
Same as Model 24FG except made in .22 Magnum/20 ga. only; has 20-inch bbls., shotgun tube Cyl. bore. Weight: 5.75 lbs. Trap in butt provides ammunition storage; comes with carrying case. Made 1972-89.

MODEL 24 . . . . NiB $261 Ex $214 Gd $154
Same as Models 24DL and 24MDL except frame has black or case-hardened finish. Game scene decoration of frame eliminated in 1974; forearm uncheckered after 1976. Made from 1970-88.

MODEL 24DL . . . . NiB $197 Ex $163 Gd $119
Same general specifications as Model 24S except top-lever opening; satin-chrome-finished frame decorated with game scenes, checkered Monte Carlo stock and forearm. Made from 1962-69.

MODEL 24F-12T TURKEY GUN . . . NiB $486 Ex $396 Gd $281
12- or 20-ga. shotgun bbl./.22 Hornet, .223 or .30-30 caliber rifle. 24-inch blued bbls., 3-inch chambers, extra removable F choke tube. Hammer block safety. Color casehardened frame. DuPont Rynite camo stock. Swivel studs. Made from 1989 to date.

MODEL 24FG FIELD GRADE . . . . . NiB $197 Ex $165 Gd $122
Same general specifications as Model 24S except top lever opening. Made 1972. Disc.

MODEL 24MDL. . . . . NiB $209 Ex $174 Gd $128
Same as Model 24DL except rifle bbl. chambered for 22 WMR. Made from 1962-69.

MODEL 24MS . . . . NiB $197 Ex $165 Gd $122
Same as Model 24S except rifle bbl. chambered for 22 WMR. Made from 1964-71.

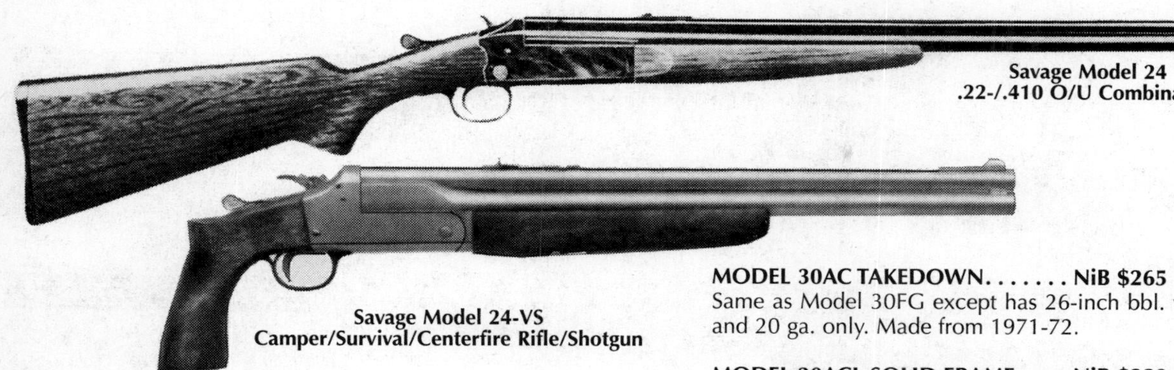

Savage Model 24
.22-/.410 O/U Combination

Savage Model 24-VS
Camper/Survival/Centerfire Rifle/Shotgun

MODEL 24S O/U COMBINATION . NiB $211 Ex $174 Gd $127
Boxlock. Visible hammer. Side lever opening. Plain extractors. Single trigger. 20 ga. or .410 bore shotgun bbl. under 22 LR bbl., 24-inch. Open rear sight, ramp front, dovetail for scope mounting. Weight: About 6.75 lbs. Plain pistol-grip stock and forearm. Made from 1965-71.

MODEL 24V . . . . NiB $338 Ex $276 Gd $196
Similar to Model 24D except 20 ga. under .222 Rem., .22 Rem., .357 Mag., .22 Hornet or .30-30 rifle bbl. Made from 1971-89.

MODEL 24-VS CAMPER/SURVIVAL/ CENTERFIRE RIFLE/SHOTGUN. . . . NiB $287 Ex $234 Gd $168
Similar to Model 24V except .357 Rem. Mag. over 20 ga. Nickel finish full-length stock and accessory pistol-grip stock. Overall length: 36 inches with full stock; 26 inches w/pistol grip. Weight: About 6.5 lbs. Made from 1983-88.

MODEL 28A STANDARD GRADE SLIDE-ACTION REPEATING SHOTGUN . . . . . NiB $355 Ex $291 Gd $209
Hammerless. Takedown. 12 ga. Five round tubular magazine. Plain bbl., lengths: 26-,28-, 30-, 32-inches, choked C/M/F. Weight: About 7.5 lbs. with 30-inch bbl. Plain pistol-grip stock, grooved slide handle. Made from 1928-31.

MODEL 28B . . . . NiB $374 Ex $306 Gd $220
Raised matted rib; otherwise the same as Model 28A.

MODEL 28D TRAP GRADE. . . . . . . NiB $399 Ex $327 Gd $234
Same general specifications as Model 28A except has 30-inch F choke bbl. w/matted rib, trap-style stock w/checkered pistol grip, checkered slide handle of select walnut.

MODEL 30 SOLID FRAME HAMMERLESS SLIDE-ACTION SHOTGUN. . . . . . . NiB $260 Ex $215 Gd $155
Gauges: 12, 16, 20, .410. 2.75-inch chamber in 16 ga., 3- inch in other ga. Magazine holds four 2.75-inch shells or three 3-inch shells. Bbls.: Vent rib; 26-, 28-, 30-inch; IC, M, F choke. Weight: Average 6.25 to 6.75 lbs. depending on ga. Plain pistol-grip stock (checkered on later production), grooved slide handle. Made from 1958-70.

MODEL 30 TAKEDOWN SLUG GUN . . NiB $243 Ex $200 Gd $146
Same as Model 30FG except 21-inch cyl. bore bbl. with rifle sights. Made from 1971-79.

MODEL 30AC SOLID FRAME . . . . . NiB $267 Ex $220 Gd $159
Same as Model 30 Solid Frame except has 26-inch bbl. with adj. choke; 12 ga. only. Made from 1959-70.

MODEL 30AC TAKEDOWN. . . . . . . NiB $265 Ex $218 Gd $157
Same as Model 30FG except has 26-inch bbl. with adj. choke; 12 and 20 ga. only. Made from 1971-72.

MODEL 30ACL SOLID FRAME . . . . NiB $280 Ex $230 Gd $167
Same as Model 30AC Solid Frame except left-hand model with ejection port and safety on left side; 12 ga. only. Made from 1960-64.

MODEL 30D TAKEDOWN. . . . . NiB $243 Ex $200 Gd $146
Deluxe Grade. Same as Model 30FG except has receiver engraved with game scene, vent rib bbl., recoil pad. Made from 1971 to date.

MODEL 30FG TAKEDOWN HAMMERLESS SLIDE-ACTION SHOTGUN. . . . . . . NiB $201 Ex $172 Gd $123
Field Grade. Gauges: 12, 20, .410. Three-inch chamber. Magazine holds four 2.75-inch shells or three 3-inch shells. Bbls.: plain; 26-inch F choke (.410 ga. only); 28-inch M/F choke; 30-inch F choke (12 ga. only). Weight: Average 7 to 7.75 lbs. depending on gauge. Checkered pistol-grip stock, fluted slide handle. Made from 1970-79.

MODEL 30L SOLID FRAME . . . . . . NiB $233 Ex $191 Gd $139
Same as Model 30 Solid Frame except left-handed model with ejection port and safety on left side; 12 ga. only. Made 1959-70.

MODEL 30T SOLID FRAME TRAP AND DUCK . . . . NiB $263 Ex $216 Gd $156
Same as Model 30 Solid Frame except only in 12 ga. w/30-inch F choke bbl.; has Monte Carlo stock with recoil pad, weight: About 8 lbs. Made from 1963-70.

MODEL 30T TAKE DOWN TRAP GUN . . . . NiB $241 Ex $196 Gd $142
Same as Model 30D except only in 12 ga. w/30-inch F choke bbl. Monte Carlo stock with recoil pad. Made from 1970-73.

MODEL 69-RXL SLIDE-ACTION SHOTGUN . . . . NiB $226 Ex $186 Gd $135
Similar to Model 67 (law enforcement configuration). Hammerless, side ejection top tang safe for left- or right-hand use. 12 ga. chambered for 2.75- and 3-inch magnum shells. 18.25-inch bbl. Tubular magazine holds 6 rounds (one less for 3-inch mag). Walnut finish hardwood stock with recoil pad and grooved operating handle. Weight: About 6.5 lbs. Made from 1982-89.

MODEL 210F BOLT-ACTION SLUG GUN . . . . NiB $387 Ex $317 Gd $227
Built on Savage 110 action. Gauge: 12 w/3-inch chamber. Two round detachable magazine. 24-inch fully rifled bbl. Receiver drilled and tapped for scope mounts w/no sights. Weight: 7.5 lbs. Checkered black synthetic stock w/swivel studs and recoil pad. Made from 1997-2000.

MODEL 210FT BOLT-ACTION SHOTGUN . . . NiB $457 Ex $373 Gd $264
Similar to Model 210F except has smoothbore 24-inch bbl. w/choke tubes. Bead front and U-notch rear sights. Advantage Camo finish. Made from 1997-2000.

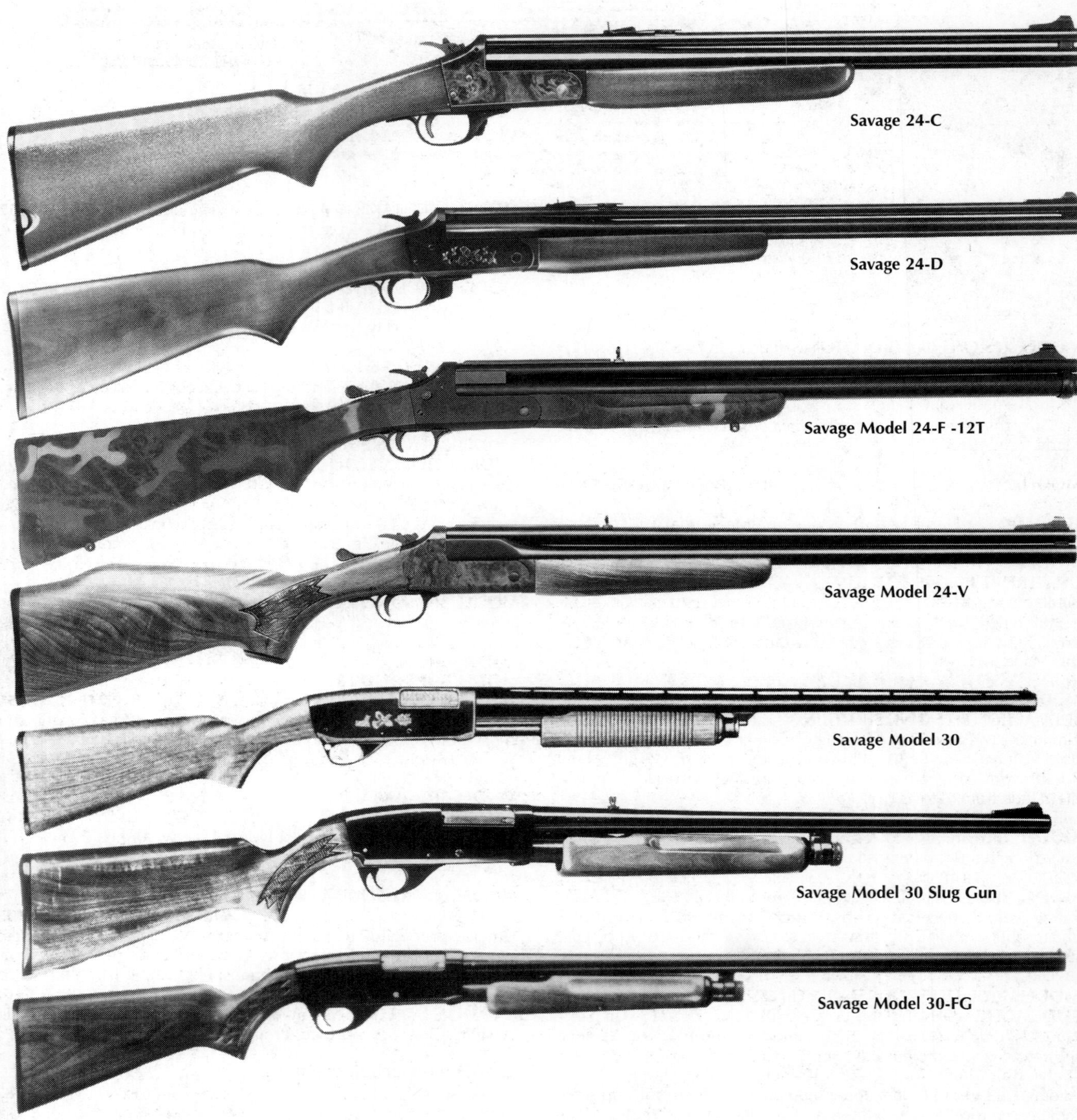

Savage 24-C

Savage 24-D

Savage Model 24-F -12T

Savage Model 24-V

Savage Model 30

Savage Model 30 Slug Gun

Savage Model 30-FG

MODEL 220 SINGLE-BARREL SHOTGUN. . NiB $149 Ex $124 Gd $92
Hammerless. Takedown. Auto ejector. Gauges: 12,16, 20 .410. Single shot. Bbl. lengths: 12 ga., 28- to 36-inch, 16 ga., 28- to 32-inch; 20 ga., 26- to 32-inch; .410 bore, 26-and 28-inch. F choke. Weight: about 6 lbs. Plain pistol-grip stock and wide forearm. Made from 1938-65.

MODEL 220AC . . . . NiB $174 Ex $143 Gd $105
Same as Model 220 except has Savage adj. choke.

MODEL 220L. . . . . NiB $131 Ex $110 Gd $82
Same general specifications as Model 220 except has side lever opening instead of top lever. Made from 1965-72.

MODEL 220P . . . . NiB $149 Ex $124 Gd $91
Same as Model 220 except has PolyChoke bbl., made in 12 ga. with 30-inch bbl., 16 and 20 ga. with 28-inch bbl., no .410 bore; recoil pad.

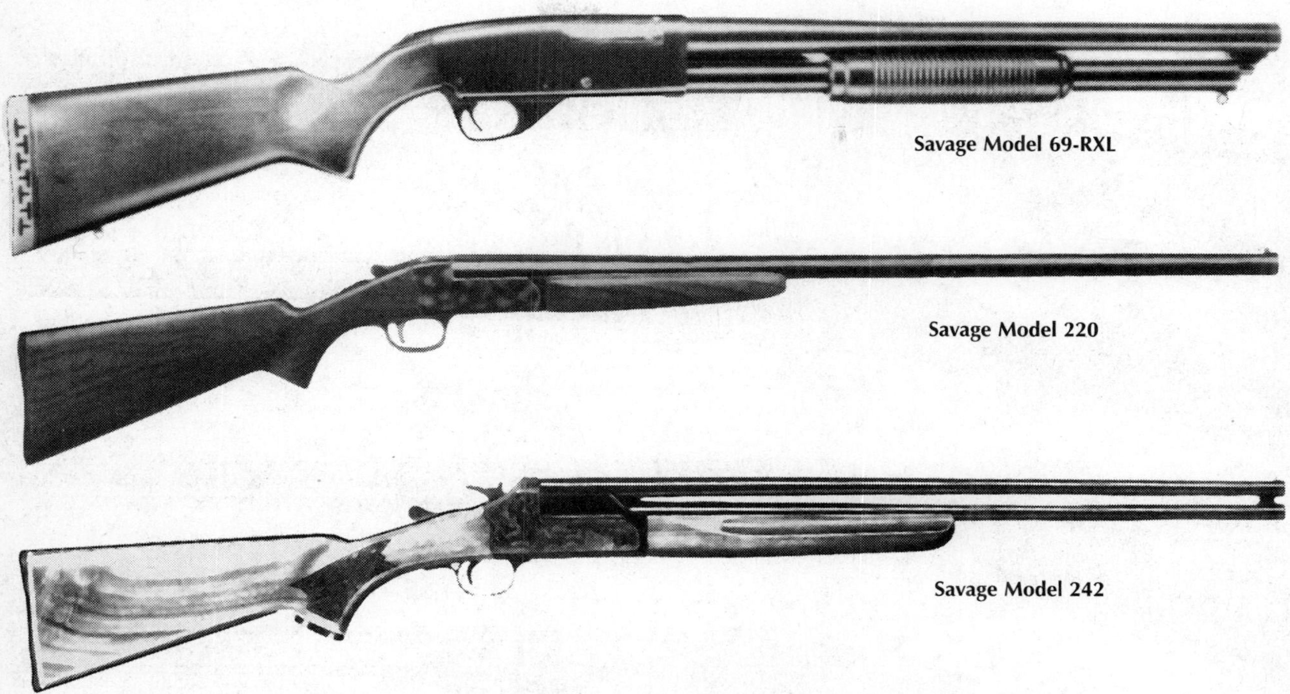
Savage Model 69-RXL

Savage Model 220

Savage Model 242

MODEL 242 O/U SHOTGUN. . . . . NiB $396 Ex $327 Gd $231
Similar to Model 24D except both bbls. .410 bore, F choke. Weight: About 7 lbs. Made from 1977-80.

MODEL 312 FIELD GRADE O/U. . . NiB $575 Ex $466 Gd $330
Gauge: 12; 2.75- or 3-inch chambers. 26- or 28-inch bbls. w/vent rib; F/M/IC chokes. 43 or 45 inches overall. Weight: 7 lbs. Internal hammers. Top tang safety. American walnut stock with checkered pistol grip and recoil pad. Made from 1990-93.

MODEL 312 SPORTING CLAYS O/U . . . . . NiB $613 Ex $500 Gd $354
Same as Model 312 Field Grade except furnished with number 1 and number 2 Skeet tubes and 28-inch bbls. only. Made from 1990-93.

MODEL 312 TRAP O/U. . . . . NiB $653 Ex $532 Gd $375
Same as Model 312 Field Grade except with 30-inch bbls. only, Monte Carlo buttstock, weight: 7.5 lbs. Made from 1990-93.

MODEL 330 O/U SHOTGUN. . . . . NiB $613 Ex $500 Gd $354
Boxlock. Plain extractors. Selective single trigger. Gauges: 12, 20. 2.75-inch chambers in 12 ga., 3-inch in 20 gauge. Bbls.: 26-inch IC/M; 28-inch M/F; 30-inch M/F choke (12 ga. only). Weight: 6.25 to 7.25 lbs., depending on gauge. Checkered pistol-grip stock and forearm. Made from 1969-78.

MODEL 333 O/U SHOTGUN
Boxlock. Auto ejectors. Selective single trigger. Gauges: 12, 20. 2.75-inch chambers in 12 ga., 3-inch in 20 ga. Bbls.: vent rib; 26-inch SK choke, IC/M; 28-inch M/F; 30-inch M/F choke (12 ga. only). Weight: Average 6.25 to 7.25 lbs. Checkered pistol-grip stock and forearm. Made from 1973-79.
Model 333 12 ga. . . . . NiB $693 Ex $563 Gd $397
Model 333 20 ga. . . . . NiB $834 Ex $676 Gd $474

MODEL 333T TRAP GUN . . . . NiB $619 Ex $504 Gd $357
Similar to Model 330 except only in 12 ga. with 30-inch vent-rib bbls., IM/F choke; Monte Carlo stock w/recoil pad. Weight: 7.75 lbs. Made from 1972-79.

MODEL 420 O/U SHOTGUN
Boxlock. Hammerless. Takedown. Automatic safety. Double triggers or non-selective single trigger. Gauges: 12, 16, 20. Bbls.: Plain, 26- to 30-inch (the latter in 12 ga. only); choked M/F, C/IC. Weight with 28-inch bbls.: 12 ga., 7.75 lbs.; 16 ga., 7.5 lbs.; 20 ga., 6.75 lbs. Plain pistol-grip stock and forearm. Made from 1938-42.
With double triggers . . . . NiB $467 Ex $382 Gd $273
With single trigger . . . . NiB $527 Ex $430 Gd $305

MODEL 430
Same as Model 420 except has matted top bbl., checkered stock of select walnut with recoil pad, checkered forearm. Made from 1938-42.
With double triggers . . . . NiB $528 Ex $430 Gd $305
With single trigger . . . . NiB $577 Ex $468 Gd $332

MODEL 440 O/U SHOTGUN . . . . . NiB $554 Ex $451 Gd $352
Boxlock. Plain extractors. Selective single trigger. Gauges: 12, 20. 2.75-inch chambers in 12 ga., 3-inch in 20 ga. Bbls.: Vent rib; 26-inch SK choke, IC/M; 28-inch M/F; 30-inch M/F choke (12 ga. only). Weight: Average 6 to 6.5 lbs. depending on ga. Made from 1968-72.

MODEL 440T TRAP GUN . . . . NiB $572 Ex $466 Gd $330
Similar to Model 440 except only in 12 ga. with 30-inch bbls., extra-wide vent rib, IM/F choke. Trap-style Monte Carlo stock and semibeavertail forearm of select walnut, recoil pad. Weight: 7.5 lbs. Made from 1969-72.

MODEL 444 DELUXE
O/U SHOTGUN . . . . NiB $577 Ex $468 Gd $332
Similar to Model 440 except has auto ejectors, select walnut stock and semi-beavertail forearm. Made from 1969-72.

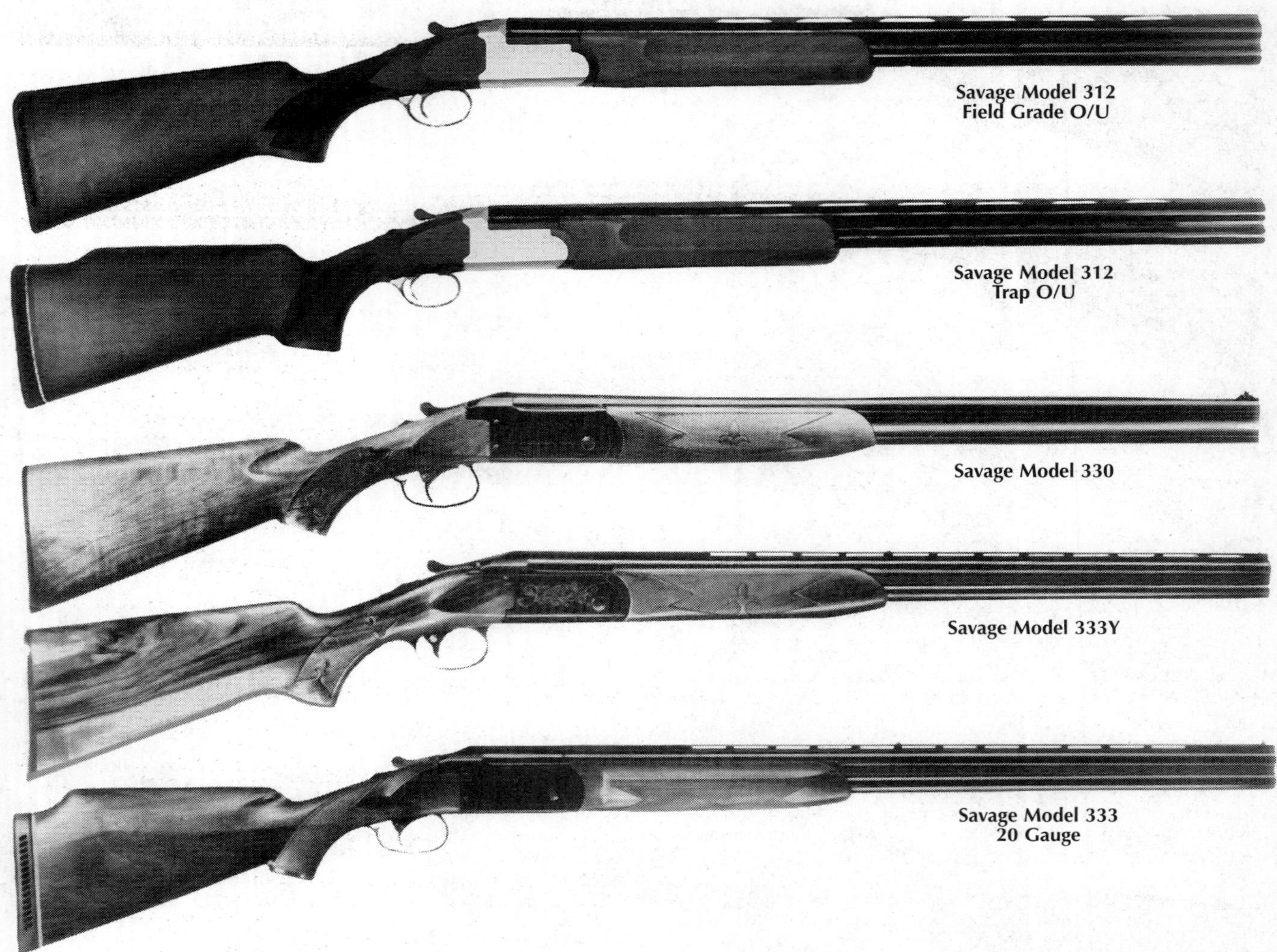

Savage Model 312
Field Grade O/U

Savage Model 312
Trap O/U

Savage Model 330

Savage Model 333Y

Savage Model 333
20 Gauge

MODEL 550
HAMMERLESS DOUBLE . . . . NiB $302 Ex $248 Gd $180
Boxlock. Auto ejectors. Non-selective single trigger. Gauges: 12, 20. 2.75-inch chamber in 12 ga., 3-inch in 20 ga. Bbls.: Vent rib; 26-inch IC/M; 28-inch M/F; 30-inch M/F choke (12 ga. only). Weight: 7 to 8 lbs. Checkered pistol-grip stock and semi-beavertail forearm. Made 1971-73. See illustration page 516.

MODEL 720 STANDARD GRADE
5 SHOT AUTOLOADING
SHOTGUN . . . . NiB $304 Ex $207 Gd $181
Browning type. Takedown. 12 and 16 ga. Four round tubular magazine. Bbl.: plain; 26- to 32-inch (the latter in 12 ga. only); choked IC, M, F. Weight: About 8.25 lbs., 12 ga. with 30-inch bbl.; 16 ga., about .5 lb. lighter. Checkered pistol-grip stock and forearm. Made from 1930-49.

MODEL 726 UPLAND SPORTER GRADE
3-SHOT AUTOLOADING
SHOTGUN . . . . NiB $308 Ex $253 Gd $182
Same as Model 720 except has 2-round magazine capacity. Made from 1931-49.

MODEL 740C
SKEET GUN. . . . . NiB $383 Ex $304 Gd $266
Same as Model 726 except has special skeet stock and full beavertail forearm, equipped with Cutts Compensator. Bbl. length overall with spreader tube is about 24.5 inches. Made from 1936-49.

MODEL 745LIGHT-WEIGHT
AUTOLOADER . . . . NiB $304 Ex $250 Gd $181
Three- or five-round models. Same general specifications as Model 720 except has lightweight alloy receiver, 12 ga.only, 28-inch plain bbl. Weight: About 6.75 lbs. Made from 1940-49.

MODEL 750
AUTOMATIC SHOTGUN . . . . NiB $313 Ex $257 Gd $186
Browning-type autoloader. Takedown. 12 ga. Four round tubular magazine. Bbls.: 28-inch F or M choke; 26-inch IC. Weight: About 7.25 lbs. Checkered walnut pistol-grip stock and grooved forearm. Made from 1960-67.

MODEL 750-AC. . . . . NiB $348 Ex $285 Gd $204
Same as Model 750 except has 26-inch bbl. with adj. choke. Made from 1964-67.

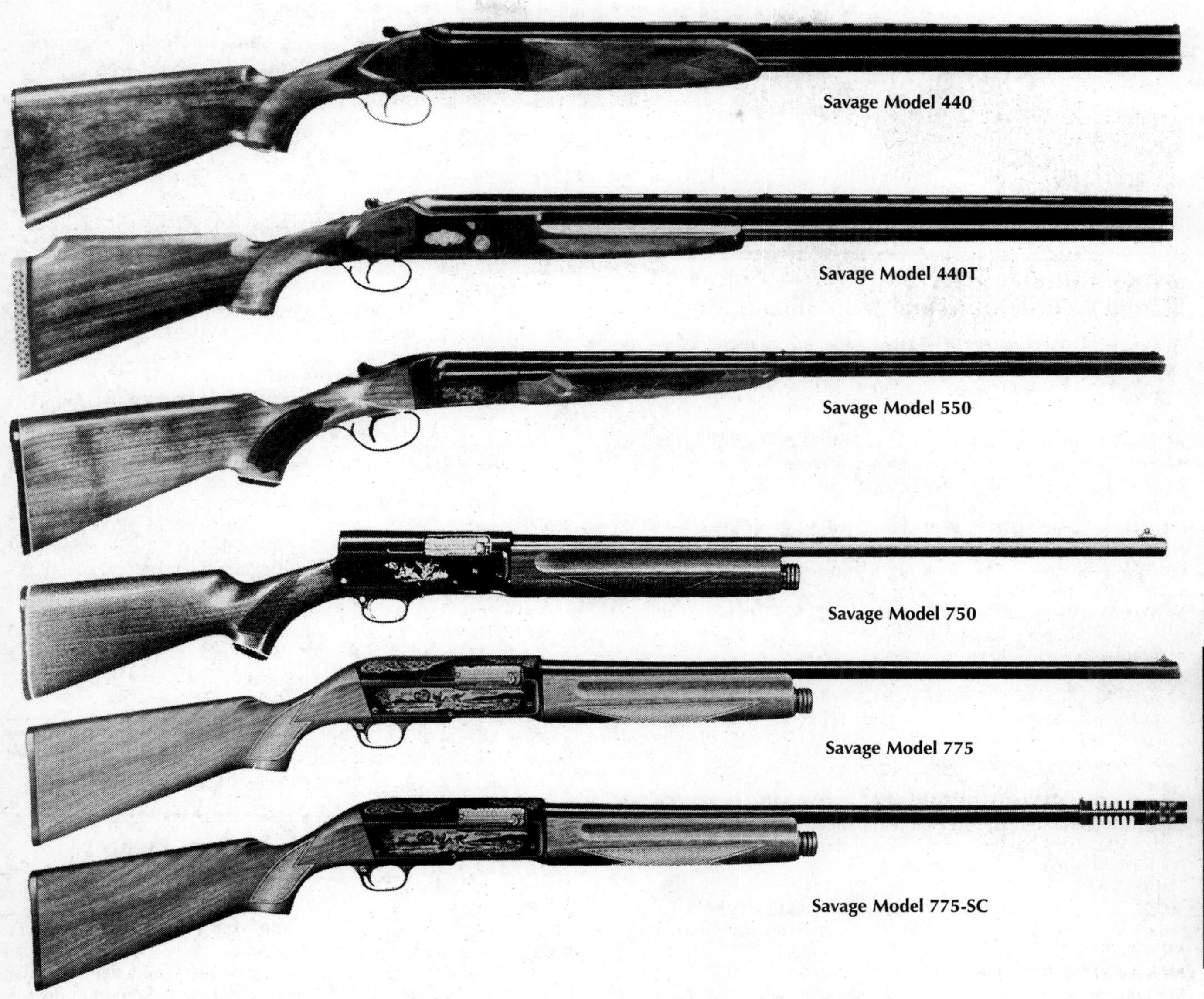

Savage Model 440

Savage Model 440T

Savage Model 550

Savage Model 750

Savage Model 775

Savage Model 775-SC

MODEL 750-SC . . . . NiB $321 Ex $263 Gd $190
Same as Model 750 except has 26-inch bbl. with Savage Super Choke. Made from 1962-63.

MODEL 755 STANDARD GRADE AUTOLOADER . . . . NiB $305 Ex $251 Gd $182
Streamlined receiver. Takedown.12 and 16 ga. Four round tubular magazine (a three-round model with magazine capacity of two rounds was also produced until 1951). Bbl.: Plain, 30-inch F choke (12 ga. only), 28-inch F or M, 26-inch IC. Weight: About 8.25 lbs., 12 ga. Checkered pistol-grip stock and forearm. Made from 1949-58.

MODEL 755-SC . . . . NiB $301 Ex $248 Gd $179
Same as Model 755 except has 26-inch bbl. w/recoil-reducing, adj. Savage Super Choke.

MODEL 775 LIGHTWEIGHT . . . . . . NiB $308 Ex $253 Gd $183
Same general specifications as Model 755 except has lightweight alloy receiver, weight: About 6.73 lbs. Made from 1950-65.

MODEL 775-SC . . . . NiB $321 Ex $263 Gd $190
Same as Model 775 except has 26-inch bbl. with Savage Super Choke.

MODEL 2400 O/U COMBINATION . . . . NiB $671 Ex $626 Gd $569
Boxlock action similar to that of Model 330. Plain extractors. Selective single trigger. 12-ga. (2.75-inch chamber) shotgun bbl., F choke over .308 Win. or .222 Rem. rifle bbl.; 23.5-inch; solid matted rib with blade front sight and folding leaf rear, dovetail for scope mounting. Weight: About 7.5 lbs. Monte Carlo stock w/pistol grip and recoil pad, semibeavertail forearm, checkered. Made from 1975-79 by Valmet.

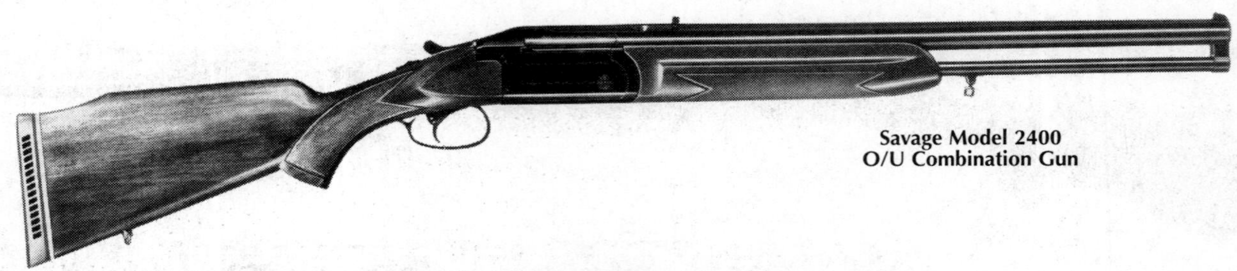
Savage Model 2400
O/U Combination Gun

SEARS, ROEBUCK & COMPANY — Chicago, Illinois. (J. C. Higgins and Ted Williams Models)

Although they do not correspond to specific models below, the names Ted Williams and J. C. Higgins have been used to designate various Sears shotguns at various times.

MODEL 18
BOLT-ACTION REPEATER . . . . NiB $129 Ex $108 Gd $80
Takedown. Three round top-loading magazine. Gauge: .410 only. Bbl.: 25-inch w/variable choke. Weight: About 5.75 lbs.

MODEL 20 SLIDE-ACTION REPEATER . . NiB $235 Ex $192 Gd $137
Hammerless. Five round magazine. Bbls.: 26- to 30-inch w/various chokes. Weight: 7.25 lbs. Plain pistol-grip stock and slide handle.

MODEL 21 SLIDE-ACTION REPEATER . . . . . NiB $257 Ex $212 Gd $152
Same general specifications as the Model 20 except vent rib and adustable choke.

MODEL 30 SLIDE-ACTION REPEATER . . . NiB $246 Ex $201 Gd $144
Hammerless. Gauges: 12, 16, 20 and .410. Four round magazine. Bbls.: 26- to 30-inch, various chokes. Weight: 6.5 lbs. Plain pistol-grip stock, grooved slide handle.

MODEL 97 SINGLE-SHOT SHOTGUN. . . . . . NiB $103 Ex $87 Gd $66
Takedown. Visible hammer. Automatic ejector. Gauges: 12, 16, 20 and .410. Bbls.: 26- to 36-inch, F choke. Weight: Average 6 lbs. Plain pistol-grip stock and forearm.

MODEL 97-AC SINGLE-SHOT SHOTGUN. . . . NiB $123 Ex $103 Gd $76
Same general specifications as Model 97 except fancier stock and forearm.

MODEL 101.7 DOUBLE-BARREL
SHOTGUN . . . . NiB $237 Ex $194 Gd $139
Boxlock. Double triggers. Gauges: 12, 16, 20, .410. Bbls.: 26- to 32-inch, choked M and F. Weight: From 6 to 7.5 lbs. Plain stock and forend.

MODEL 101.7C DOUBLE-BARREL
SHOTGUN . . . . NiB $252 Ex $196 Gd $115
Same general specifications as Model 101.7 except checkered stock and forearm.

MODEL 101.25 BOLT-ACTION SHOTGUN . . . NiB $125 Ex $105 Gd $78
Takedown. .410 gauge. Five round tubular magazine. 24-inch bbl., F choke. Weight: About 6 lbs. Plain, one-piece pistol-grip stock.

MODEL 101.40 SINGLE-SHOT SHOTGUN . NiB $108 Ex $90 Gd $68
Takedown. Visible hammer. Automatic ejector. Gauges: 12, 16, 20 and .410. Bbls.: 26- to 36-inch, F choke. Weight: Average 6 lbs. Plain pistol-grip stock and forearm.

MODEL 101.1120 BOLT-ACTION REPEATER . . . . NiB $123 Ex $103 Gd $76
Takedown. .410 ga. 24-inch bbl., F choke. Weight: About 5 lbs. Plain one-piece pistol-grip stock.

MODEL 101.1380
BOLT-ACTION REPEATER . . . . NiB $136 Ex $113 Gd $83
Takedown. Gauges: 12, 16, 20. Two round detachable box magazine. 26-inch bbl., F choke. Weight: About 7 lbs. Plain one-piece pistol-grip stock.

MODEL 101.1610 DOUBLE-BARREL
SHOTGUN . . . . NiB $449 Ex $281 Gd $201
Boxlock. Double triggers. Plain extractors. Gauges: 12, 16, 20 and .410. Bbls.: 24- to 30-inch. Various chokes, but mostly M and F. Weight: About 7.5 lbs, 12 ga. Checkered pistol-grip stock and forearm.

MODEL 101.1701 DOUBLE-BARREL
SHOTGUN . . . . NiB $342 Ex $280 Gd $200
Same general specifications as Model 101.1610 except satin chrome frame and select walnut stock and forearm.

MODEL 101.5350-D
BOLT-ACTION REPEATER . . . . NiB $142 Ex $99 Gd $73
Takedown. Gauges: 12, 16, 20. Two round detachable box magazine. 26-inch bbl., F choke. Weight: About 7.25 lbs. Plain one piece pistol-grip stock.

MODEL 101.5410
BOLT-ACTION REPEATER . . . . NiB $123 Ex $101 Gd $75
Same general specifications as Model 101.5350-D.

SKB ARMS COMPANY — Tokyo, Japan *Imported by G.U. Inc., Omaha, Nebraska*

MODEL 385
SIDE-BY-SIDE. . . . . NiB $1775 Ex $1441 Gd $1014
Boxlock action w/double locking lugs. Gauges: 12, 20 and 28 w/2.75- and 3-inch chambers. 26- or 28-inch bbls. w/Inter-Choke tube system. Single selective trigger. Selective automatic ejectors and automatic safety. Weight: 6 lbs., 10 oz. Silver nitride receiver w/engraved scroll and game scene. Solid rib w/flat matte finish and metal front bead sight. Checkered American walnut English or pistol-grip stock. Imported from 1992.

MODELS 300 AND 400
SIDE-BY-SIDE DOUBLES
Similar to Model 200E except higher grade. Models 300 and 400 differ in that the latter has more elaborate engraving and fancier wood.
Model 300 . . . . NiB $1002 Ex $817 Gd $580
Model 400 . . . . NiB $1206 Ex $980 Gd $693

MODEL 400 SKEET . . . . NiB $1151 Ex $931 Gd $659
Similar to Model 200E Skeet except higher grade with more elaborate engraving and full fancy wood.

MODEL 480 ENGLISH . . . . NiB $1465 Ex $1189 Gd $835
Similar to Model 280 English except higher grade with more elaborate engraving and full fancy wood.

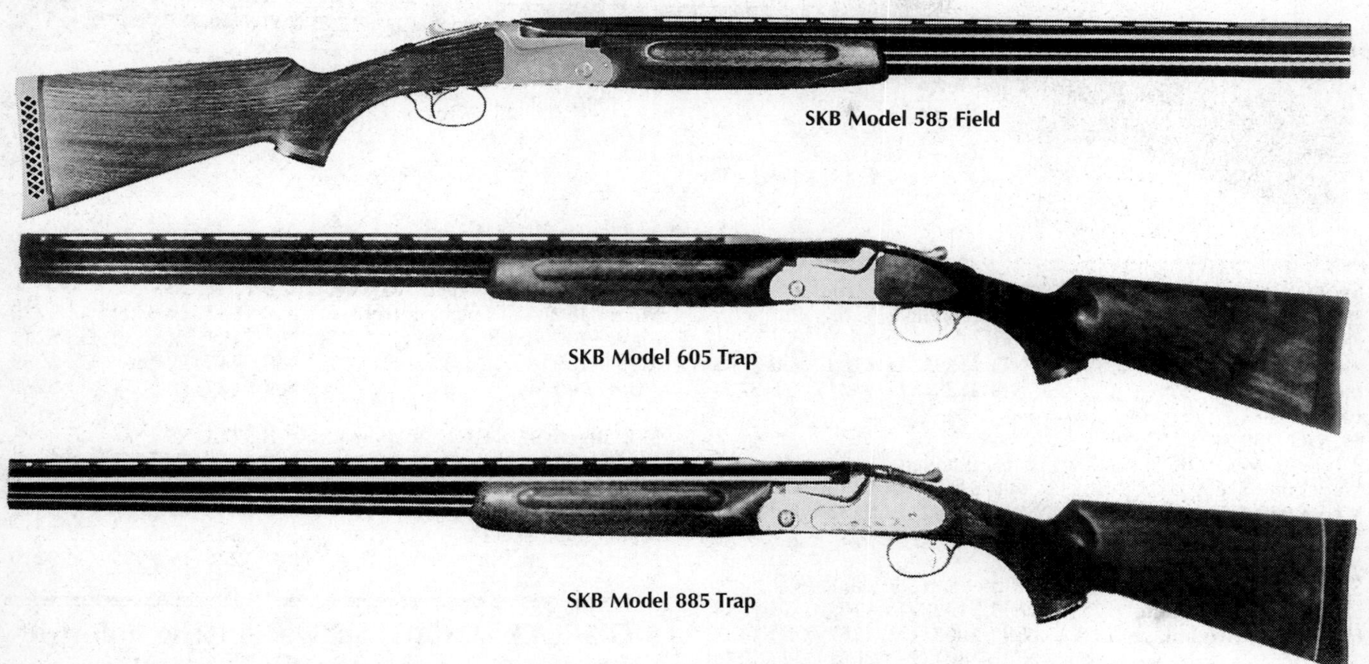

SKB Model 585 Field

SKB Model 605 Trap

SKB Model 885 Trap

MODEL 500 SERIES O/U SHOTGUN
Boxlock. Gauges: 12 and 20 w/2.75-or 3-inch chambers. Bbls.: 26-, 28- or 30-inch with vent rib; fixed chokes. Weight: 7.5 to 8.5 lbs. Single selective trigger. Selective automatic ejectors. Manual safety. Checkered walnut stock. Blue finish with scroll engraving. Imported from 1967-80.
500 Field, 12 ga. . . . . NiB $581 Ex $473 Gd $334
500 Field, 20 ga. . . . . NiB $682 Ex $553 Gd $389
500 Magnum, 12 ga.
3-inch chambers . . . . NiB $649 Ex $516 Gd $371

MODEL 500 SMALL GAUGE O/U SHOTGUN . . . . NiB $713 Ex $578 Gd $406
Similar to Model 500 except gauges 28 and .410; has 28-inch vent-rib bbls., M/F chokes. Weight: About 6.5 lbs.

MODEL 505 O/U SHOTGUN
Blued boxlock action. Gauge: 12, 20, 28 and .410. Bbls.: 26-, 28, 30-inch; IC/M, M/F or inner choke tubes. 45.19 inches overall. Weight: 6.6 to 7.4 lbs. Hand checkered walnut stock. Metal bead front sight, ejectors, single selective trigger and ejectors. Introduced 1988.
Standard Field, Skeet or Trap grade. . . . . . . NiB $949 Ex $769 Gd $559
Standard Two-bbl. Field set . . . . . NiB $1439 Ex $1165 Gd $815
Skeet grade, three-bbl. set . . . . NiB $2031 Ex $1640 Gd $1141
Sporting Clays . . . . NiB $1020 Ex $828 Gd $583
Trap grade two-bbl. set . . . . NiB $1729 Ex $1398 Gd $976

MODEL 585 DELUXE O/U SHOTGUN
Boxlock. Gauges: 12, 20, 28 and .410; 2.75-or 3-inch chambers. Bbls.: 26-, 28-, 30-, 32- or 34-inch with vent rib; fixed chokes or Inter-choke tubes. Weight: 6.5 to 8.5 lbs. Single selective trigger. Selective automatic ejectors. Manual safety. Checkered walnut stock in standard or Monte Carlo style. Silver nitride finish with engraved game scenes. Made from 1987 to date.
Field, Skeet, Trap grades . . . . . . NiB $1277 Ex $1042 Gd $729
Field grade, two-bbl. set . . . . . . NiB $2249 Ex $1818 Gd $1266
Skeet set (20, 28, .410 ga.) . . . . NiB $2716 Ex $2193 Gd $1522
Sporting Clays . . . . NiB $1549 Ex $1253 Gd $872
Trap Combo (two-bbl.) . . . . NiB $2244 Ex $1813 Gd $1261

MODEL 600 SERIES O/U SHOTGUN
Similar to 500 Series except w/silver nitride receiver. Checkered deluxe walnut stock in both Field and Target Grade configurations . Imported from 1969-80.
600 Field, 12 ga. . . . . NiB $730 Ex $595 Gd $423
600 Field, 20 ga. . . . . NiB $926 Ex $730 Gd $576
600 Magnum, 12 ga.
3-inch chambers . . . . NiB $799 Ex $576 Gd $396
600 Skeet or Trap grade . . . . NiB $778 Ex $623 Gd $473
600 Trap Doubles Gun. . . . . NiB $730 Ex $595 Gd $423

MODEL 600 SMALL GA. . . . . NiB $942 Ex $838 Gd $534
Same as Model 500 Small Gauge except higher grade with more elaborate engraving and fancier wood.

MODEL 605 SERIES O/U SHOTGUN
Similar to the Model 505 except w/engraved silver nitride receiver and deluxe wood. Introduced 1988.
Field, Skeet, Trap grade . . . . NiB $982 Ex $807 Gd $561
Skeet three-bbl. set . . . . NiB $2112 Ex $1703 Gd $1191
Sporting Clays . . . . NiB $993 Ex $807 Gd $568

MODEL 680 ENGLISH O/U SHOTGUN
Similar to 600 Series except w/English style select walnut stock and fine scroll engraving. Imported from 1973-77.
680 English, 12 ga. . . . . NiB $838 Ex $682 Gd $483
680 English, 20 ga. . . . . NiB $947 Ex $848 Gd $543

MODEL 685 DELUXE O/U
Similar to the 585 Deluxe except with semi-fancy American walnut stock. Gold trigger and jeweled barrel block. Silvered receiver with fine engraving.
Field, Skeet, Trap grade . . . . NiB $1360 Ex $1107 Gd $782
Field grade, two-bbl. set . . . . . . NiB $2078 Ex $1682 Gd $1176
Skeet set . . . . NiB $2834 Ex $2294 Gd $1604
Sporting Clays . . . . NiB $1407 Ex $1146 Gd $810
Trap Combo. two bbl. . . . . NiB $2063 Ex $1672 Gd $1173

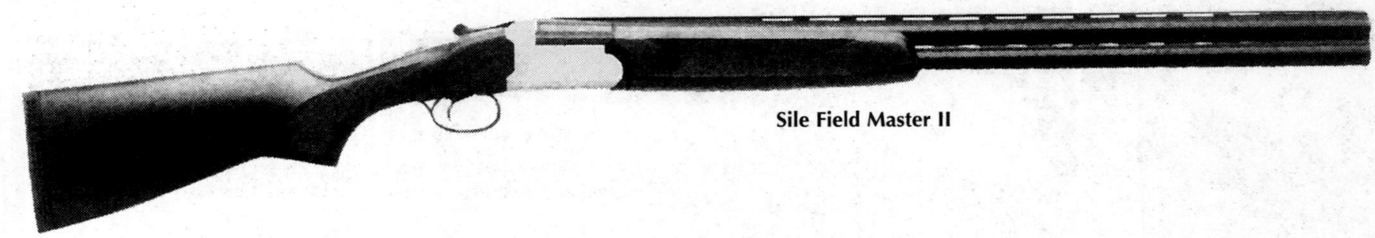

Sile Field Master II

MODEL 800 SKEET/TRAP O/U
Similar to Model 700 Skeet and Trap except higher grade with more elaborate engraving and fancier wood.

Model 800 Skeet .... **NiB $1391 Ex $1090 Gd $753**
Model 800 Trap .... **NiB $1257 Ex $1019 Gd $714**

MODEL 880 SKEET/TRAP
Similar to Model 800 Skeet except has sideplates.

Model 880 Skeet .... **NiB $1498 Ex $1290 Gd $912**
Model 880 Trap .... **NiB $1652 Ex $1337 Gd $933**

MODEL 885 DELUXE O/U
Similar to the 685 Deluxe except with engraved sideplates.

Field, Skeet, Trap grade .... **NiB $1323 Ex $1073 Gd $753**
Field grade, two-bbl. set ...... **NiB $2063 Ex $1667 Gd $1161**
Skeet Set .... **NiB $3321 Ex $2687 Gd $1874**
Sporting Clays .... **NiB $1685 Ex $1363 Gd $950**
Trap Combo .... **NiB $2753 Ex $2230 Gd $1559**

The following SKB shotguns were distributed by Ithaca Gun Co. from 1966-76. For specific data, see corresponding listings under Ithaca.

CENTURY SINGLE-BARREL TRAP GUN
The SKB catalog does not differentiate between Century and Century II; however, specifications of current Century are those of Ithaca-SKB Century II.

Century (505) .... **NiB $1007 Ex $822 Gd $585**
Century II (605) .... **NiB $1157 Ex $943 Gd $668**

GAS-OPERATED AUTOMATIC SHOTGUNS

Model XL300 with plain barrel .... **NiB $406 Ex $338 Gd $250**
Model XL300 with vent rib .... **NiB $445 Ex $369 Gd $278**
Model XL900 .... **NiB $401 Ex $334 Gd $247**
Model XL900 Trap .... **NiB $466 Ex $386 Gd $284**
Model XL900 Skeet .... **NiB $477 Ex $395 Gd $289**
Model XL900 Slug .... **NiB $427 Ex $355 Gd $266**
Model 1300 Upland, Slug .... **NiB $525 Ex $434 Gd $316**
Model 1900 Field, Trap, Slug ...... **NiB $582 Ex $479 Gd $347**

SKB OVER/UNDER SHOTGUNS

Model 500 Field .... **NiB $614 Ex $505 Gd $363**
Model 500 Magnum .... **NiB $714 Ex $583 Gd $421**
Model 600 Field .... **NiB $823 Ex $674 Gd $484**
Model 600 Magnum .... **NiB $851 Ex $697 Gd $500**
Model 600 Trap .... **NiB $820 Ex $637 Gd $460**
Model 600 Doubles .... **NiB $800 Ex $657 Gd $474**
Model 600 Skeet—12 or 20 ga. .... **NiB $864 Ex $708 Gd $508**
Model 600 Skeet—28 or .410 .... **NiB $934 Ex $765 Gd $548**
Model 600 Skeet Combo .... **NiB $2199 Ex $1788 Gd $1263**
Model 600 English .... **NiB $812 Ex $667 Gd $481**
Model 700 Trap .... **NiB $997 Ex $816 Gd $583**
Model 700 Doubles .... **NiB $887 Ex $728 Gd $523**
Model 700 Skeet .... **NiB $958 Ex $784 Gd $562**
Model 700 Skeet Combo .... **NiB $2390 Ex $1938 Gd $1359**

SKB RECOIL-OPERATED AUTOMATIC SHOTGUNS

Model 300—with plain barrel .... **NiB $363 Ex $302 Gd $225**
Model 300—with vent rib .... **NiB $401 Ex $333 Gd $245**
Model 900 .... **NiB $445 Ex $368 Gd $269**
Model 900 Slug .... **NiB $427 Ex $354 Gd $260**

SKB SIDE-BY-SIDE DOUBLE-BARREL SHOTGUNS

Model 100 .... **NiB $555 Ex $457 Gd $332**
Model 150 .... **NiB $614 Ex $504 Gd $363**
Model 200E .... **NiB $894 Ex $730 Gd $522**
Model 200E Skeet .... **NiB $883 Ex $722 Gd $517**
Model 280 English .... **NiB $1220 Ex $995 Gd $710**

SIG SAUER — (SIG) Schweizerische Industrie-Gesellschaft, Neuhausen, Switzerland

MODEL SA3 O/U SHOTGUN
Monobloc boxlock action. Single selective trigger. Automatic ejectors. Gauges: 12 or 20 w/3- inch chambers. 26-, 28- or 30-inch vent rib bbls. w/choke tubes. Weight: 6.8 to 7.1 lbs. Checkered select walnut stock and forearm. Satin nickel-finished receiver w/game scene and blued bbls. Imported from 1997-98.

Field model .... **NiB $1326 Ex $1071 Gd $759**
Sporting Clays model .... **NiB $1422 Ex $1157 Gd $818**

MODEL SA5 O/U SHOTGUN
Similar to SA3 Model except w/detachable sideplates. Gauges: 12 or 20 w/3- inch chambers. 26.5-, 28- or 30-inch vent rib bbls. w/choke tubes. Imported from 1997-99.

Field model .... **NiB $2399 Ex $1948 Gd $1370**
Sporting Clays model .... **NiB $2585 Ex $2096 Gd $1471**

SILE SHOTGUNS — Sile Distributors, New York, NY

FIELD MASTER II O/U SHOTGUN .... **NiB $627 Ex $510 Gd $362**
Gauge: 12, 3-inch chambers. 28-inch bbl., IC, M, IM, F choke tubes. 45.25 inches overall. Weight: 7.25 lbs. Satin-finished walnut, checkered stock and forend. Introduced 1989.

L. C. SMITH SHOTGUNS — Made 1890-1945 by Hunter Arms Company, Fulton, N.Y.; 1946-51 and 1968-73 by Marlin Firearms Company, New Haven, Conn.

L. C. SMITH DOUBLE-BARREL SHOTGUNS
Values shown are for L. C. Smith doubles made by Hunter. Those of 1946-51 Marlin manufacture generally bring prices about 1/3 lower. Smaller gauge models, especially in the higher grades, command premium prices: Up to 50 percent more for 20 gauge, up to 400 percent for .410 gauge.

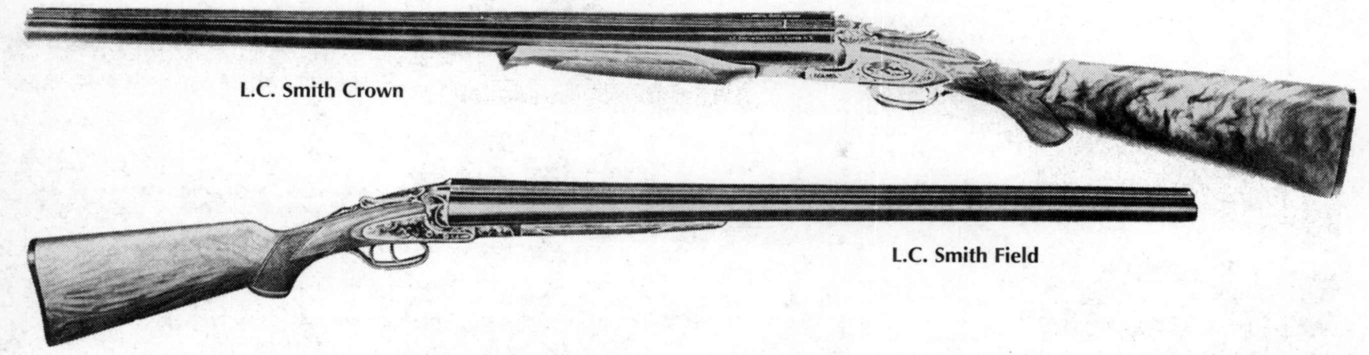
L.C. Smith Crown

L.C. Smith Field

Crown grade, double triggers, automatic ejectors .... NiB $6517 Ex $5247 Gd $3623
Crown grade, selective single trigger, automatic ejectors .... NiB $7598 Ex $5139 Gd $4211
Deluxe grade, selective single trigger, automatic ejectors . . . NiB $22,531+ Ex $18,025+ Gd $12,257+
Eagle grade, double triggers, automatic ejectors .... NiB $5340 Ex $4305 Gd $2982
Eagle grade, selective single trigger .... NiB $5686 Ex $4583 Gd $3170
Field grade, double trigger plain extractors .... NiB $1314 Ex $1072 Gd $763
Field grade, double triggers auto. ej..................... NiB $1720 Ex $1397 Gd $984
Field grade, non-selective single trigger, plain extractors .... NiB $1625 Ex $1321 Gd $912
Field grade, selective single trigger, automatic ejectors .... NiB $1720 Ex $1397 Gd $984
Ideal grade, double triggers, plain extractors .... NiB $1795 Ex $1456 Gd $1024
Ideal grade, double triggers, auto. ej.................... NiB $2425 Ex $1967 Gd $1381
Ideal grade, selective single trigger, automatic ejectors .... NiB $2786 Ex $2258 Gd $1584
Monogram grade, selective single trigger, automatic ejectors .... NiB $12,971 Ex $10,376 Gd $7057
Olympic grade, selective single trigger, automatic ejectors .... NiB $2564 Ex $2080 Gd $1460
Premier grade, selective single trigger automatic ejectors . . . NiB $17,703+ Ex $14,162+ Gd $9630+
Skeet Special, non-selective single trigger, automatic ejectors .... NiB $2476 Ex $2010 Gd $1413
Skeet Special, selective single trigger, auto ejectors .... NiB $3167 Ex $2558 Gd $1779
.410 ga. .... NiB $13,519 Ex $10,815 Gd $7354
Specialty grade, double triggers, auto ejectors .... NiB $4098 Ex $3315 Gd $2314
Specialty grade, selective single trigger, automatic ejectors........... NiB $4369 Ex $3531 Gd $2414
Trap grade, sel. single trigger, auto ej. .... NiB $1838 Ex $1488 Gd $1041

L C. SMITH HAMMERLESS DOUBLE-BARREL SHOTGUNS
Sidelock. Auto ejectors standard on higher grades, extra on Field and Ideal Grades. Double triggers or Hunter single trigger (non-selective or selective). Gauges: 12, 16, 20, .410. Bbls.: 26- to 32-inch, any standard boring. Weight: 6.5 to 8.25 lbs., 12 ga. Checkered stock and forend; choice of straight, half or full pistol grip, beavertail or standard-type forend. Grades differ only in quality of workmanship, wood, checkering, engraving, etc. Same general specifications apply to all. Manufacture of these L. C. Smith guns was discontinued in 1951. Production of Field Grade 12 ga. was resumed 1968-73. Note: L. C. Smith Shotguns manufactured by the Hunter Arms Co. 1890-13 were designated by numerals to indicate grade with the exception of Pigeon and Monogram.

00 grade .... NiB $1597 Ex $1293 Gd $905
0 grade .... NiB $1931 Ex $1560 Gd $1086
1 grade .... NiB $2163 Ex $1752 Gd $1259
2 grade .... NiB $2372 Ex $1919 Gd $1340
3 grade .... NiB $3344 Ex $2700 Gd $1876
Pigeon .... NiB $4177 Ex $3369 Gd $2335
4 grade .... NiB $8687 Ex $6988 Gd $4849
5 grade .... NiB $9436 Ex $7597 Gd $5244
Monogram .... NiB $11,413 Ex $9199 Gd $3427
A1 .... NiB $7009 Ex $4035 Gd $2824
A2..................... NiB $11,711 Ex $9413 Gd $6471
A3 .... NiB $25,750+ Ex $20,600+ Gd $14,008+

L. C. SMITH HAMMERLESS DOUBLE MODEL 1968 FIELD GRADE...... NiB $807 Ex $662 Gd $476
Re-creation of the original L. C. Smith double. Sidelock. Plain extractors. Double triggers. 12 ga. 28-inch vent-rib bbls., M/F choke. Weight: About 6.75 lbs. Checkered pistol-grip stock and forearm. Made from 1968-73.

L. C. SMITH HAMMERLESS DOUBLE MODEL 1968 DELUXE .... NiB $1178 Ex $967 Gd $699
Same as 1968 Field Grade except has Simmons floating vent rib, beavertail forearm. Made from 1971-73.

L. C. SMITH SINGLE-SHOT TRAP GUNS
Boxlock. Hammerless. Auto ejector.12 gauge only. Bbl. lengths: 32- or 34-inch. Vent rib. Weight: 8 to 8.25 lbs. Checkered pistol-grip stock and forend, recoil pad. Grades vary in quality of workmanship, wood, engraving, etc.; general specifications are the same. Disc. 1951. Note: Values shown are for L. C. Smith single-barrel trap guns made by Hunter. Those of Marlin manufacture generally bring prices about one-third lower.

Olympic grade.............. NiB $1920 Ex $1555 Gd $1087
Specialty grade .... NiB $2410 Ex $1951 Gd $1365
Crown grade .... NiB $4138 Ex $3340 Gd $2319
Monogram grade............ NiB $6141 Ex $4952 Gd $3432
Premier grade .... NiB $9461 Ex $7623 Gd $5273
Deluxe grade........... NiB $14,319 Ex $11,481 Gd $7847

SMITH & WESSON SHOTGUNS — Springfield, Massachusetts, Mfd. by Howa Machinery, Ltd., Nagoya, Japan

In 1985, Smith and Wesson sold its shotgun operation to O. F. Mossberg & Sons, Inc.

SHOTGUNS

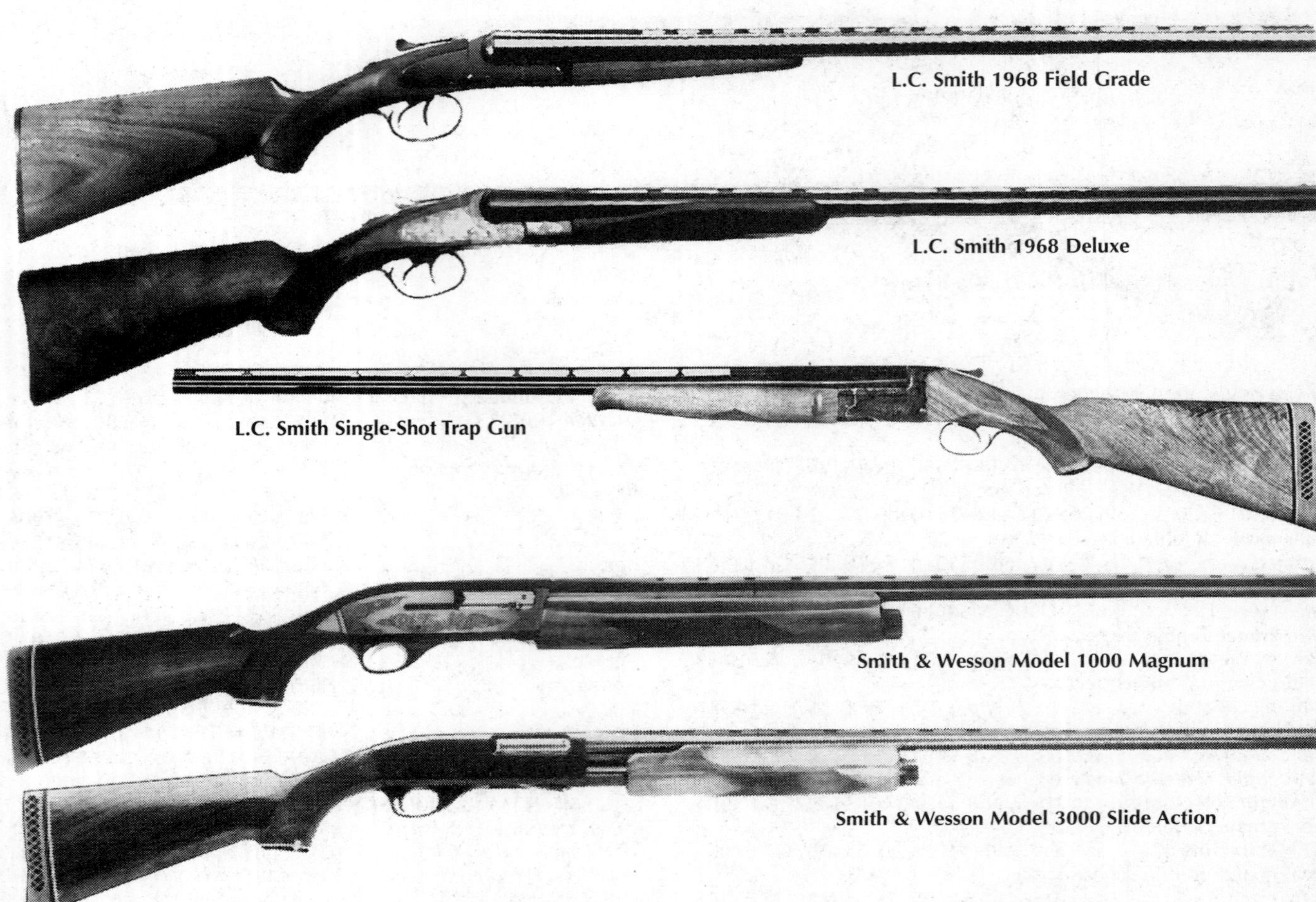

L.C. Smith 1968 Field Grade

L.C. Smith 1968 Deluxe

L.C. Smith Single-Shot Trap Gun

Smith & Wesson Model 1000 Magnum

Smith & Wesson Model 3000 Slide Action

MODEL 916 SLIDE-ACTION REPEATER
Hammerless. Solid frame. Gauges: 12, 16, 20. Three inch chamber in 12 and 20 ga. Five round tubular magazine. Bbls.: plain or vent rib; 20-inch C (12 ga., plain only); 26-inch IC- 28-inch M or F; 30-inch F choke (12 ga. only). Weight: With 28-inch plain bbl., 7.25 lbs. Plain pistol-grip stock, fluted slide handle. Made from 1972-81.
With plain bbl. . . . . NiB $204 Ex $170 Gd $126
With ventilated rib bbl. . . . . NiB $253 Ex $208 Gd $151

MODEL 916T
Same as Model 916 except takedown, 12 ga. only. Not available with 20-inch bbl. Made from 1976-81.
With plain bbl. . . . . NiB $219 Ex $181 Gd $132
With ventilated rib bbl. . . . . NiB $253 Ex $208 Gd $151

MODEL 1000 AUTOLOADER . . . . . NiB $373 Ex $308 Gd $223
Gas-operated. Takedown. Gauges: 12, 20. 2.75-inch chamber in 12 ga., 3-inch in 20 ga. Four round magazine. Bbls.: Vent rib, 26-inch SK choke, IC; 28-inch M or F; 30-inch F choke (12 ga. only). Weight: With 28-inch bbl., 6.5 lbs. in 20 ga.,7.5 lbs. in 12 ga. Checkered pistol-grip stock and forearm. Made from 1972. Disc.

MODEL 1000 MAGNUM . . . . NiB $449 Ex $367 Gd $263
Same as standard Model 1000 except chambered for 12 ga. magnum, 3-inch shells; 30-inch bbl. only, M or F choke; stock with recoil pad. Weight: About 8 lbs. Introduced in 1977.

MODEL 1000P . . . . NiB $392 Ex $322 Gd $231
Same general specifications as Model C 3000 Slide Action, but an earlier version.

MODEL 3000
SLIDE ACTION . . . . NiB $397 Ex $426 Gd $234
Hammerless. 20-ga. Bbls.: 26-inch IC; 28-inch M or F. Chambered for 3-inch magnum and 2.75-inch loads. American walnut stock and forearm. Checkered pistol grip and forearm. Introduced 1982.

SPRINGFIELD ARMS — Built by Savage Arms Company, Utica, New York

SPRINGFIELD DOUBLE-BARREL
HAMMER SHOTGUN . . . . NiB $454 Ex $371 Gd $265
Gauges: 12 and 16. Bbls.: 28 to 32 inches. In 12 ga., 32-inch model, both bbls. have F choke. All other gauges and barrel lengths are left barrel, Full; right barrel, Mod. Weight: 7.25 to 8.25 lbs., depending on gauge and barrel length. Black walnut checkered buttstock and forend. Disc. 1934.

SQUIRES BINGHAM CO., INC. — Makati, Rizal, Philippines

MODEL 30
PUMP SHOTGUN. . . . . NiB $225 Ex $184 Gd $132
Hammerless. 12 ga. Five round magazine. Bbl.: 20-inch Cyl.; 28-inch M; 30-inch F choke. Weight: About 7 lbs. Pulong Dalaga stock and slide handle. Currently manufactured.

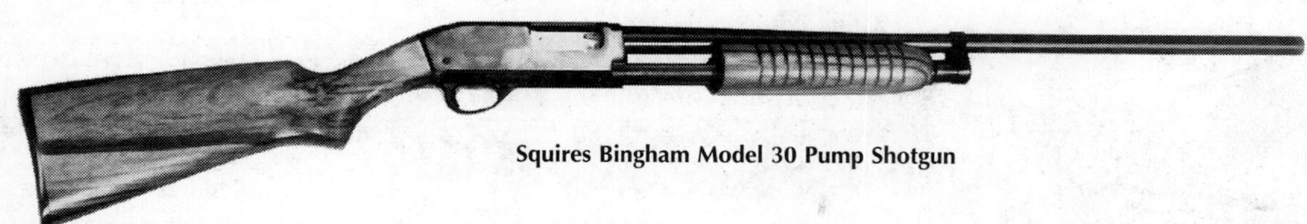
Squires Bingham Model 30 Pump Shotgun

J. STEVENS ARMS COMPANY — Chicopee Falls, Massachusetts, Division of Savage Arms Corporation

NO. 20 "FAVORITE" SHOTGUN . . NiB $368 Ex $300 Gd $215
Calibers: .22 and .32 shot. Smoothbore bbl. Blade front sight; no rear. Made from 1893-1939.

NO. 39 NEW MODEL POCKET SHOTGUN . . . . NiB $693 Ex $563 Gd $399
Gauge: .410. Calibers: .38-40 shot, .44-40 shot. Bbls.: 10, 12, 15 or 18 inches, half-octagonal smoothbore. Shotgun sights. Made from 1895-1906.

NO. 22-.410 O/U COMBINATION GUN
.22 caliber rifle barrel over .410 ga. shotgun barrel. Visible hammer. Takedown. Single trigger. 24-inch bbls., shotgun bbl. F choke. Weight: About 6 lbs. Open rear sight and ramp front sight of sporting rifle type. Plain pistol-grip stock and forearm; originally supplied with walnut stock and forearm. "Tenite" (plastic) was used in later production. Made 1938-50. Note: This gun is now manufactured as the Savage Model 24.
With wood stock and forearm . . . . NiB $254 Ex $210 Gd $152
With Tenite stock and forearm . . . . NiB $196 Ex $164 Gd $122

MODEL 51 BOLT-ACTION SHOTGUN . . . . NiB $131 Ex $110 Gd $82
Single shot. Takedown. .410 ga. 24-inch bbl., F choke. Weight: About 4.75 lbs. Plain one-piece pistol-grip stock. checkered on later models. Made from 1962-71.

MODEL 58 BOLT-ACTION REPEATER . . . . NiB $156 Ex $130 Gd $95
Takedown. Gauges: 12, 16, 20. Two round detachable box magazine. 26-inch bbl., F choke. Weight: About 7.25 lbs. Plain one piece pistol-grip stock on early models w/takedown screw on bottom of forend. Made 1933-81. Note: Later production models have 3-inch chamber in 20 ga., checkered stock with recoil pad.

MODEL 58-.410 BOLT-ACTION REPEATER. . . . . NiB $149 Ex $124 Gd $92
Takedown. .410 ga. Three round detachable box magazine. 24-inch bbl., F choke. Weight: About 5.5 lbs. Plain one piece pistol-grip stock, checkered on later production. Made from 1937-81.

MODEL 59 BOLT-ACTION REPEATER . . . . NiB $195 Ex $161 Gd $117
Takedown. .410 ga. Five round tubular magazine. 24-inch bbl., F choke. Weight: About 6 lbs. Plain, one piece pistol-grip stock, checkered on later production. Made from 1934-73.

MODEL 67 PUMP SHOTGUN
Hammerless, side-ejection solid-steel receiver. Gauges: 12, 20 and .410, 2.75- or 3-inch shells. Bbls.: 21-, 26-, 28- 30-inch with fixed chokes or interchangeable choke tubes, plain or vent rib. Weight: 6.25 to 7.5 lbs. Optional rifle sights. Walnut-finished hardwood stock with corncob-style forend.
Standard model, plain bbl. . . . . NiB $254 Ex $211 Gd $154
Standard model, vent rib . . . . NiB $269 Ex $222 Gd $162
Standard model, w/choke tubes . . . NiB $282 Ex $232 Gd $169
Slug model w/rifle sights . . . . NiB $243 Ex $201 Gd $147
Lobo model, matte finish . . . . NiB $297 Ex $252 Gd $182
Youth model, 20 ga. . . . . NiB $269 Ex $222 Gd $162
Camo model. w/choke tubes . . . . . NiB $320 Ex $262 Gd $189

MODEL 67 WATERFOWL SHOTGUN . . . . NiB $294 Ex $241 Gd $175
Hammerless. Gauge: 12. Three round tubular magazine. Walnut finished hardwood stock. Weight: About 7.5 lbs. Made from 1972-89.

MODEL 77 SLIDE-ACTION REPEATER . . . . NiB $234 Ex $193 Gd $142
Solid frame. Gauges: 12, 16, 20. Five round tubular magazine. Bbls.: 26-inch IC, 28-inch M or F choke. Weight: About 7.5 lbs. Plain pistol-grip stock with recoil pad, grooved slide handle. Made from 1954-71.

MODEL 77-AC. . . . . NiB $269 Ex $222 Gd $152
Same as Model 77 except has Savage Super Choke.

MODEL 79-VR SUPER VALUE . . . . . NiB $254 Ex $211 Gd $153
Hammerless, side ejection. Bbl.: Chambered for 2.75-inch and 3-inch mag. shells. 12, 20, and .410 ga. vent rib. Walnut finished hardwood stock with checkering on grip. Weight: 6.75-7 lbs. Made 1979-90.

MODEL 94 SINGLE-SHOT SHOTGUN. . NiB $140 Ex $117 Gd $87
Takedown. Visible hammer. Auto ejector. Gauges: 12, 16, 20, 28, .410. Bbls.: 26-, 28-, 30-, 32-, 36-inch, F choke. Weight: About 6 lbs. depending on gauge and barrel. Plain pistol-grip stock and forearm. Made from 1939-61.

MODEL 94C . . . . NiB $185 Ex $142 Gd $112
Same as Model 94 except has checkered stock, fluted forearm on late production. Made from 1965-90.

MODEL 94Y YOUTH GUN . . . . NiB $182 Ex $150 Gd $110
Same as Model 94 except made in 20 and .410 ga. only; has 26-inch F choke bbl., 12.5-inch buttstock with recoil pad; checkered pistol grip and fluted forend on late production. Made from 1959-90.

MODEL 95 SINGLE-SHOT SHOTGUN. . NiB $140 Ex $117 Gd $87
Solid frame. Visible hammer. Plain extractor. 12 ga. Three-inch chamber. Bbls.: 28-inch M- 30-inch F choke. Weight: About 7.25 lbs. Plain pistol-grip stock, grooved forearm. Made from 1965-69.

MODEL 107 SINGLE-SHOT HAMMER SHOTGUN . . . . NiB $133 Ex $112 Gd $84
Takedown. Auto ejector. Gauges: 12, 16, 20, .410. Bbl. lengths: 28- and 30-inch (12 and 16 ga.), 28-inch (20 ga.), 26-inch (.410); F choke only. Weight: About 6 lbs., 12 bore ga. Plain pistol-grip stock and forearm. Made from about 1937-53.

MODEL 124 CROSS-BOLT REPEATER . . . . NiB $194 Ex $161 Gd $117
Hammerless. Solid frame. 12 ga. only. Two round tubular magazine. 28-inch bbl.; IC, M or F choke. Weight: About 7 lbs. Tenite stock and forearm. Made from 1947-52.

SHOTGUNS

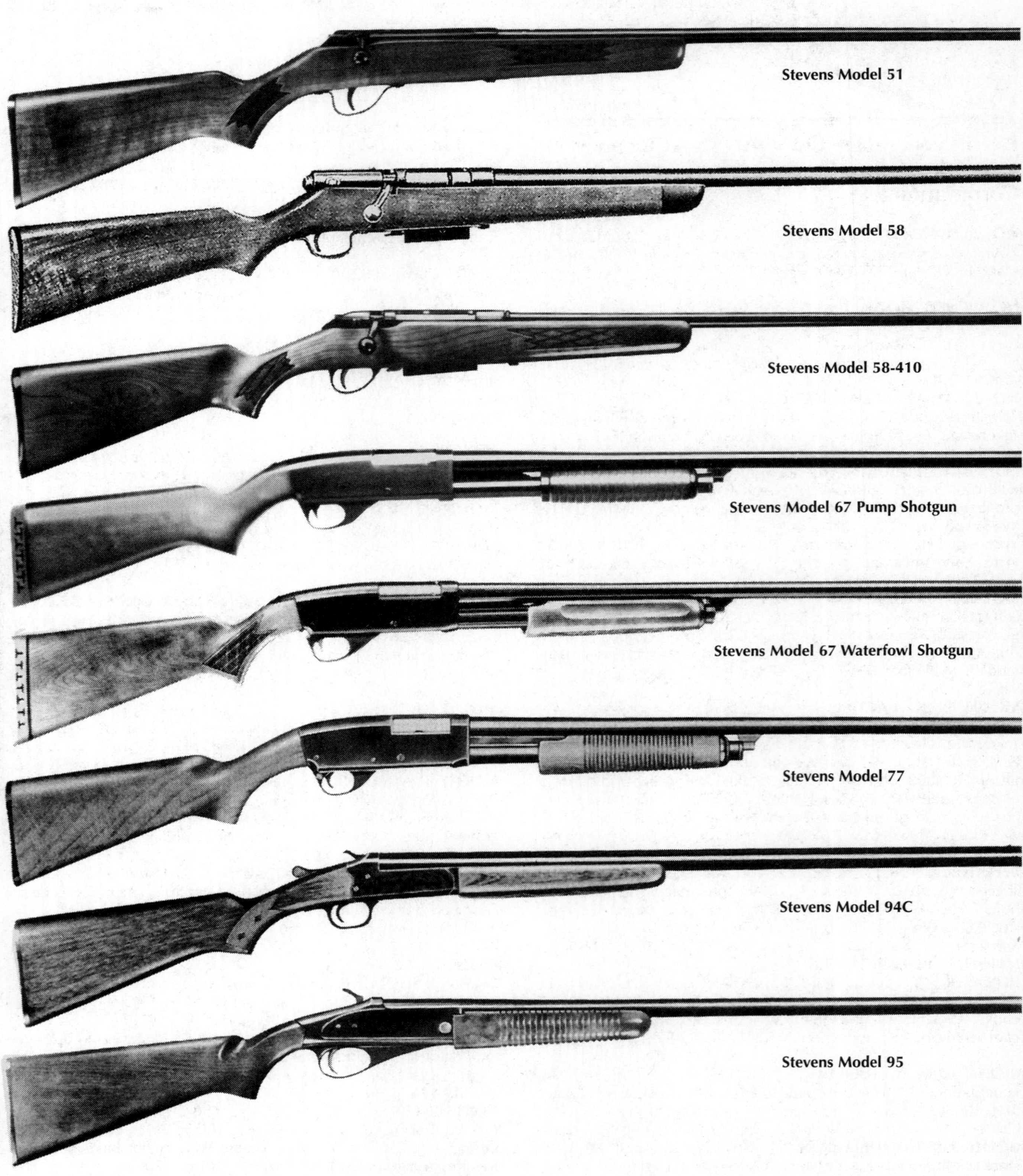

Stevens Model 51

Stevens Model 58

Stevens Model 58-410

Stevens Model 67 Pump Shotgun

Stevens Model 67 Waterfowl Shotgun

Stevens Model 77

Stevens Model 94C

Stevens Model 95

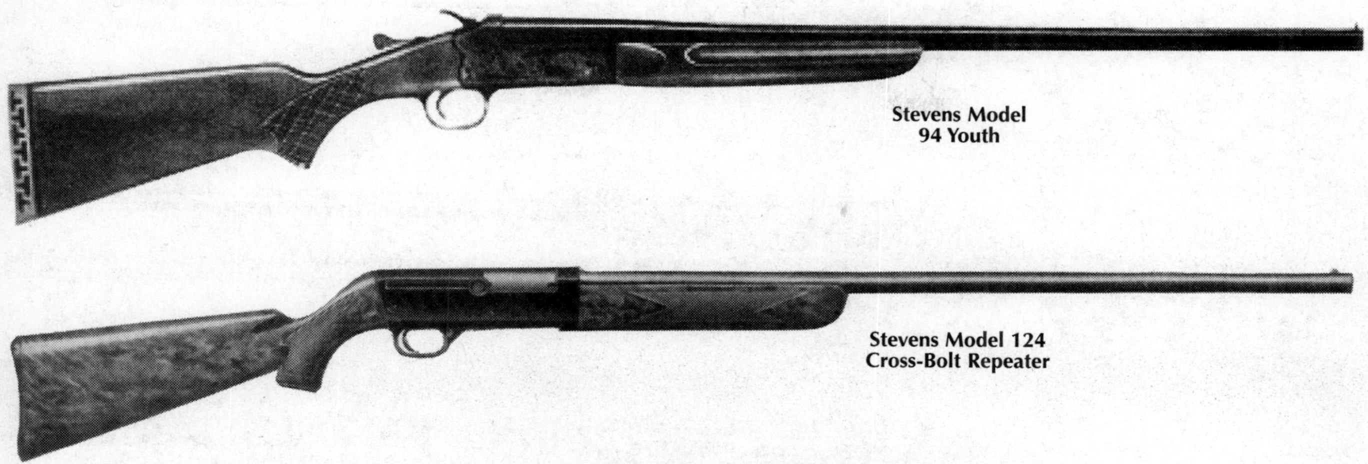

Stevens Model 94 Youth

Stevens Model 124 Cross-Bolt Repeater

MODEL 240 O/U SHOTGUN . . . . . NiB $348 Ex $285 Gd $204
Visible hammer. Takedown. Double triggers. .410 ga. 26-inch bbls., F choke. Weight: 6 lbs. Tenite (plastic) pistol-grip stock and forearm. Made from 1940-49.

MODEL 258 BOLT-ACTION REPEATER . . . . NiB $134 Ex $120 Gd $89
Takedown. 20-gauge. Two round detachable box magazine. 26-inch barrel, Full choke. Weight: About 6.25 lbs. Plain, one piece pistol-grip stock. Made from 1937-65.

MODEL 311 SPRINGFIELD HAMMERLESS DOUBLE
Same general specifications as Stevens Model 530 except earlier production has plain stock and forearm; checkered on current guns. Originally produced as a "Springfield" gun, this model became a part of the Stevens line in 1948 when the Springfield brand name was discontinued. Made from 1931-89.
Pre-WW II . . . . NiB $420 Ex $342 Gd $244
Post-WW II . . . . NiB $374 Ex $305 Gd $219

MODEL 311-R HAMMERLESS DOUBLE . . . . NiB $309 Ex $253 Gd $183
Same general specifications as Stevens Model 311 except compact design for law enforcement use. Bbls.: 18.25-inch 12 gauge with solid rib, chambered for 2.75 and 3-inch Mag. shells. Double triggers and auto top tang safety. Walnut finished hardwood stock with recoil pad and semi-beavertail forend. Weight: About 6.75 lbs. Made from 1982-89.

MODEL 530 HAMMERLESS DOUBLE . . . . NiB $371 Ex $303 Gd $217
Boxlock. Double triggers. Gauges: 12, 16, 20, .410. Bbl. lengths: 26- to 32-inch; choked M/F, C/M, F/F. Weight: 6 to 7.5 pounds depending on gauge and barrel length. Checkered pistol-grip stock and forearm; some early models with recoil pad. Made from 1936-54.

MODEL 530M . . . . NiB $278 Ex $229 Gd $166
Same as Model 530 except has Tenite (plastic) stock and forearm. Disc. about 1947.

MODEL 530ST DOUBLE GUN . . . . NiB $342 Ex $282 Gd $200
Same as Model 530 except has non-selective single trigger. Disc.

MODEL 620 HAMMERLESS SLIDE-ACTION REPEATING SHOTGUN . . . . NiB $348 Ex $285 Gd $204
Takedown. Gauges: 12, 16, 20. Five round tubular magazine. Bbl. lengths: 26-, 28-, 30-, 32-inch; choked F, M IC, C. Weight: About 7.75 lbs., 12 ga.; 7.25 lbs., 16 ga.- 6 lbs., 20 ga. Checkered pistol-grip stock and slide handle. Made from 1927-53.

MODEL 620-C. . . . . NiB $348 Ex $285 Gd $204
Same specifications as Model 620 except equipped with Cutts Compensator and two choke tubes.

MODEL 620-P . . . . NiB $362 Ex $296 Gd $213
Same specifications as Model 620 equipped with Aero-Dyne PolyChoke and 27-inch bbl.

MODEL 620-PV. . . . . NiB $362 Ex $296 Gd $213
Same specifications as Model 620 except equipped with ventilated PolyChoke and 27-inch bbl.

MODEL 621 . . . . NiB $421 Ex $343 Gd $244
Same as Model 620 except has raised solid matted-rib barrel. Disc.

MODEL 820 HAMMERLESS SLIDE-ACTION REPEATING SHOTGUN . . . . NiB $282 Ex $232 Gd $169
Solid frame. 12 gauge only. Five round tubular magazine. 28-inch barrel; IC, M or F choke. Weight: About 7.5 lbs. Plain pistol-grip stock, grooved slide handle. Early models furnished w/Tenite buttstock and forend. Made from 1949-54.

MODEL 820-SC. . . . . NiB $307 Ex $252 Gd $182
Same as Model 820 except has Savage Super Choke.

MODEL 940 SINGLE-SHOT SHOTGUN . . . . NiB $134 Ex $114 Gd $86
Same general specifications as Model 94 except has side lever opening instead of top lever. Made from 1961-70.

MODEL 940Y YOUTH GUN . . . . NiB $157 Ex $132 Gd $99
Same general specifications as Model 94Y except has side lever opening instead of top lever. Made from 1961-70.

MODEL 9478 .... NiB $130 Ex $108 Gd $80
Takedown. Visible hammer. Automatic ejector. Gauges: 12, 20, .410. Bbls.: 26-, 28-, 30-, 36-inch; Full choke. Weight: Average 6 pounds depending on gauge and barrel. Plain pistol-grip stock and forearm. Made from 1978-85.

MODEL 5151 SPRINGFIELD...... NiB $428 Ex $349 Gd $248
Same specifications as the Stevens Model 311 except with checkered grip and forend; equipped with recoil pad and two ivory sights.

STOEGER SHOTGUNS

See IGA and Tikka Shotguns

TAR-HUNT CUSTOM RIFLES, INC. — Bloomsburg, PA

MODEL RSG-12 MATCHLESS
BOLT-ACTION SLUG GUN.... NiB $1847 Ex $1497 Gd $1050
Similar to Professional model except has McMillan Fibergrain stock and deluxe blue finish. Made from 1995 to date.

MODEL RSG-12 PEERLESS
BOLT-ACTION SLUG GUN.... NiB $1925 Ex $1560 Gd $1092
Similar to Professional model except has McMillan Fibergrain stock and deluxe NP-3 (Nickel/Teflon) metal finish. Made from 1995 to date.

MODEL RSG-12 PROFESSIONAL BOLT-ACTION SLUG GUN
Bolt action 12 ga. w/2.75-inch chamber, 2-round detachable magazine, 21.5-inch fully rifled bbl. w/ or w/o muzzle brake. Receiver drilled and tapped for scope mounts w/no sights. Weight: 7.75 lbs. 41.5 inches overall. Checkered black McMillan fiberglass stock w/swivel studs and Pachmayr Deacelerator pad. Made from 1991 to date.
RSG-12 model
W/O muzzle brake (disc. 1993) . . . . NiB $1517 Ex $1235 Gd $874
RSG-12 model
W/muzzle brake . . . . NiB $1658 Ex $1348 Gd $952

MODEL RSG-20 MOUNTAINEER BOLT ACTION SLUG GUN . . . . . NiB $1375 Ex $1122 Gd $797
Similar to Professional model except 20 ga. w/2.75 inch chamber. Black McMillan synthetic stock w/blind magazine. Weight: 6.5 lbs. Made from 1997 to date.

TECNI-MEC SHOTGUNS — Italy, Imported by RAHN Gun Work, Inc., Hastings, MI

MODEL SPL 640 FOLDING SHOTGUN
Gauges: 12, 16, 20, 24, 28, 32 and .410 bore. 26-inch bbl. Chokes: IC/IM. Weight: 6.5 lbs. Checkered walnut pistol-grip stock and forend. Engraved receiver. Available with single or double triggers. Imported from 1988-94.
640 w/single trigger . . . . NiB $506 Ex $416 Gd $300
640 w/double trigger. . . . . NiB $564 Ex $462 Gd $332

THOMPSON/CENTER ARMS — Rochester, New Hampshire. *Purchased by Smith & Wesson in 2006.*

CONTENDER .410 GA. CARBINE . . . . NiB $410 Ex $338 Gd $246
Gauge: .410 smoothbore. 21-inch vent rib bbl. 34.75 inches overall. Weight: About 5.25 lbs. Bead front sight. Rynite stock and forend. Made 1991 to date.

ENCORE 20 GA. SHOTGUN
Gauge: 20 smoothbore w/rifled slug bbl. or 26-inch vent-rib bbl. w/three internal screw choke tubes, 38 to 40.5 inches overall. Weight: About 5.25 to 6 lbs. Bead or fiber optic sights. Walnut stock and forend. Made from 2000 to date.
Encore 20 ga.
W/vent rib. . . . . NiB $584 Ex $476 Gd $340
Encore 20 ga.
w/rifled slug bbl. . . . . NiB $542 Ex $444 Gd $318
W/extra
bbl., add $262

MODEL '87 HUNTER SHOTGUN. . . . . NiB $520 Ex $426 Gd $305
Single shot. Gauge: 10 or 12, 3.5-inch chamber, 25-inch field bbl. with F choke. Weight: 8 lbs. Bead front sight. American black walnut stock with recoil pad. Made from 1987 to 1992.

MODEL '87 HUNTER SLUG . . . . NiB $533 Ex $436 Gd $313
Gauge: 10 (3.5-inch chamber) or 12 (3-inch chamber). Same general specifications as Model '87 Hunter Shotgun except with 22-inch slug (rifled) bbl. and rifle sights. Made from 1987 to 1992.

TIKKA SHOTGUNS — Manufactured by: Armi Marocchi, Italy, (formerly by Valmet), Riihimaki, Finland

M 07 SHOTGUN/ RIFLE COMBINATION . . . . NiB $1130 Ex $925 Gd $663
Gauge/caliber: 12/.222 Rem. Shotgun bbl.: About 25 inches; rifled bbl.: About 22.75 inches. 40.66 inches overall. Weight: About 7 lbs. Dovetailed for telescopic sight mounts Single trigger with selector between the bbls. Vent rib. Monte Carlo-style walnut stock with checkered pistol grip and forend. Made from 1965-87.

M 77 O/U SHOTGUN. . . . . NiB $1229 Ex $1185 Gd $781
Gauge: 12. 27-inch vent-rib bbls., approx. 44 inches overall, weight: About 7.25 lbs. Bbl. selector. Ejectors. Monte Carlo-style walnut stock with checkered pistol grip and forend; rollover cheekpiece. Made from 1977-87.

M 77K SHOTGUN/ RIFLE COMBINATION . . . . NiB $1467 Ex $1196 Gd $850
Gauge: 12/70. Calibers: .222 Rem., 5.6x52r5, 6.5x55, 7x57r5, 7x65r5, .308 Win. Vent-rib bbls.: About 25 inches (shotgun); 23 inches (rifle), 42.3 inches overall. Weight: About 7.5 lbs. Double triggers. Monte Carlo-style walnut stock with checkered pistol grip and forend; rollover cheekpiece. Made from 1977-86.

412S/512S SHOOTING SYSTEM
Boxlock action with both under lug and sliding top latch locking mechanism designed to accept interchangeable monobloc barrels, including O/U shotgun, combination and double rifle configurations. Blued or satin nickel receiver w/cocking indicators. Selective single trigger design w/barrel selector incorporated into the trigger (double triggers available). Blued barrels assemblies w/extractors or auto ejectors as required. Select American walnut stock with checkered pistol grip and forend. Previously produced in Finland (same as the former Valmet Model 412) but currently manufactured in Italy by joint venture arrangement with Armi Marocchi. From 1990-93, Stoeger Industries imported this model as the 412/S. In 1993 the nomenclature of this shooting system was changed to 512/S. Disc. 1997. Note: For double rifle values, see Tikka Rifles.

MODEL 412S/512S O/U SHOTGUN
Gauge: 12 w/3-inch chambers. 24-, 26-, 28- or 30-inch chrome-lined bbls. w/blued finish and integral stainless steel choke tubes. Weight: 7.25 to 7.5 lbs. Blue or matte nickel receiver. Select American walnut from stock with checkered pistol grip and forend. Imported 1990-97.
Standard Field model . . . . NiB $859 Ex $699 Gd $483
Standard Trap model . . . . NiB $1019 Ex $827 Gd $582
Premium Field model . . . . NiB $914 Ex $750 Gd $528
Premium Trap model . . . . NiB $1218 Ex $987 Gd $692
Sporting Clays model . . . . NiB $1037 Ex $843 Gd $593
Standard Trap model . . . . NiB $1218 Ex $987 Gd $692
W/Extra O/U shotgun bbl., add $575
W/Extra O/U combination bbl., add $695
W/Extra O/U rifle bbl., add $995

MODEL 412S/512S OVER/UNDER COMBINATION
Gauge: 12 w/3-inch chamber. Calibers: .222 Rem., .30-06 or .308 Win. Blue or matte nickel receiver, 24-inch chrome-lined bbls. w/extractors and blued finish. Weight: 7.25 to 7.5 lbs. Select American walnut stock with checkered pistol grip and forend. Imported from 1990-97.
Standard Combination model . . . . NiB $1091 Ex $897 Gd $650
Premium Combination model . . . . NiB $1149 Ex $944 Gd $682
Extra barrel options. . . . . NiB $1149 Ex $944 Gd $682

SHOTGUNS

TRADITIONS PERFORMANCE FIREARMS — Importers of shotguns produced by Fausti Stefano of Brescia, Italy and ATA Firearms, Turkey.

CLASSIC SERIES, FIELD I O/U
Available in 12, 20, 28 (2 3/4-inch chamber) and .410 gauge, 26- or 28-inch vent rib bbls. W/fixed chokes and extractors. Weight: 6 3/4 to 7 1/4 lbs. Blued finish, silver receiver engraved with game birds. Single, selective trigger. Brass bead front sight. European walnut stock. Overall length 43 to 45 inches. Intro. 2000. .... **$657**

FIELD HUNTER MODEL
Same as Field I except 12 and 20 gauge, 3-inch chambers, screw-in chokes and extractors. **$709**

FIELD II MODEL
Same as Field I except with screw-in chokes and automatic ejectors. **$838**

FIELD III GOLD MODEL
Same as Field I model except 12 gauge only, high-grade, oil-finish walnut, coin-finish receiver with engraved pheasants and woodcock, deep blue finish on barrels, automatic ejectors and non-slip recoil pad. **$1079**

CLASSIC SERIES O/U SPORTING CLAY III
Available in 12 and 20 gauge, 3-inch chambers, high grade walnut stock, oil-satin finish, palm swell Schnabel forend. 28- and 30-inch bbls. with 3/8-inch top and middle vent rib, red target front bead sight. Automatic ejectors, extended choke tubes. Weight: 8 1/4 lbs. Intro. 2000. .... **$1275**

SPORTING CLAY II MODEL
Same as Sporting Clay III model but with European walnut stocks, cut checkering and extended choke tubes. Overall length: 47 inches. Weight: 7 3/4 lbs. **$1020**

UPLAND III MODEL
Same as Sporting Clay III model but round pistol grip and Schnabel forend, blued receiver with engraved upland scene, weight: 7 1/2 lbs. **$1141**

UPLAND II MODEL
Same as Upland III model except with English walnut straight-grip stock and Schnabel forend, 24- and 26-inch vent rib bbls., floral engraving on blued receiver, automatic ejectors. **$894**

MAG 350 SERIES
TURKEY II O/U
Magnum 3 1/2-inch chambers in 12 gauge only, 24- and 26-inch bbls., screw-in flush fitting chokes: F and XF. Matte finish, engraved receiver, Mossy Oak or Realtree camo. Intro. 2000. .... **$946**

WATERFOWL II MODEL
Same as Turkey II model except with Advantage Wetlands camo stock and barrels, weight: 8 lbs., overall length 45 inches. Waterfowl model has 28-inch bbls. **$946**

MAG HUNTER II
Same as Turkey II model except blued engraved receiver and matte finish walnut stocks, 3 1/2-inch chambers, 28-inch bbls. with screw-in chokes. **$853**

ELITE SERIES
DOUBLE-BARREL SHOTGUNS
ELITE FIELD III ST
Checkered English walnut straight stock, splinter forend, fixed chokes. Available in 28 and .410 gauge, 26-inch chrome-lined bbls., Cylinder and Modified chokes. Silver trigger guard and receiver with hand-finished engraving of upland game scenes with gold inlays. Automatic ejectors. Brass front sight bead. Weight: About 6 1/2 lbs. Intro. 2000 .... **$2227**

ELITE HUNTER ST
Same as Elite Field model except 12 and 20 gauge, European walnut stock, beavertail forend, screw-in choke tubes, extractors, three-inch chambers. Blued finish. Vent-rib, tang safety.
Weight: 6 1/2 pounds **$1064**

ELITE FIELD I ST
Same as Elite Field III except single trigger, fixed chokes, extractors; European walnut stock. Available in 12, 20, 28 (2 3/4-inch chambers) and .410 gauge; fixed IC/M chokes. Weight: 5 3/4 to 6 1/2 lbs. **$982**

ELITE FIELD I DT
Same as Elite Field I except with double triggers, fixed chokes, extractors. Available in 12, 20, 28 (2 3/4-inch chambers) and .410. Bbls: 26 inches, fixed IC/M chokes. Weight: 5 1/2 to 6 1/4 lbs **$930**

ALS 2100 SEMI-AUTOMATIC SHOTGUNS
FIELD SERIES, WALNUT MODEL
Gas-operated, 12 and 20 gauge, 3-inch chambers, cut-checkered Turkish walnut stock and forend, blued 26- and 28-inch vent rib bbls., multi-choke system, chrome bore lining. Weight: About 6 lbs. Rifled barrel with cantilever mount available Intro. 2001.... **$519**

SYNTHETIC STOCK MODEL
Same as the ALS 2100 Walnut model except with synthetic stock, matted finish on receiver and bbl., weight: About 6 lbs **$498**

YOUTH MODEL
Same as ALS 2100 Walnut model except with a shorter walnut stock (length of pull: 13 1/2 inches). Available in 12 or 20 gauge with 24-inch vent rib barrel, weight: 5 1/2 to 6 lbs **$519**

HUNTER COMBO MODEL
Same as ALS 2100 Walnut model except comes with two bbls. (28-inch vent rib and 24-inch slug), TruGlo adjustable sights and cantilever mount. Available with Turkish walnut or synthetic stock with matte barrel finish. Weight: 6 1/2 lbs.
(Walnut) **$674**
(Synthetic) **$621**

SLUG HUNTER MODEL
Same as ALS 2100 Walnut except with fully-rifled barrel, choice of walnut or synthetic stocks, matte or blue finish; rifle or TruGlo adjustable sights. Weight: About 6 1/4 lbs. **$590**

TURKEY HUNTER/WATERFOWL MODEL
Same as ALS 2100 Walnut except with synthetic stock, 3-inch chambers, 26-inch vent rib bbl., screw-in chokes, Mossy Oak or Realtree camo stocks. **$560**

HOME SECURITY MODEL
Same as ALS 2100 Walnut but with 20-inch cylinder-bore bbl., synthetic stock, 3-inch chambers, six-round capacity with 2 3/4-inch shells. Weight: About 6 lbs. **$431**

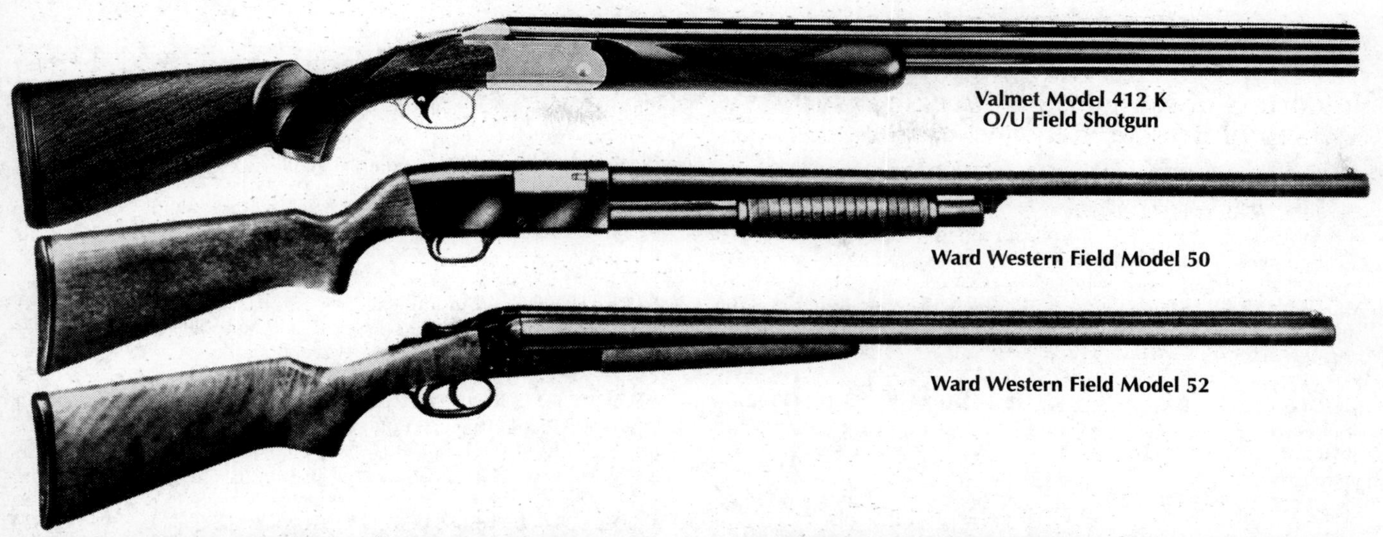

Valmet Model 412 K O/U Field Shotgun

Ward Western Field Model 50

Ward Western Field Model 52

TRISTAR SPORTING ARMS — North Kansas City, MO

MODEL 1887 LEVER-ACTION REPEATER . . . . NiB $630 Ex $514 Gd $365
Copy of John Browning's Winchester Model 1887 lever-action shotgun. 12 ga. only. 30-inch bbl. which may be cut down to any desired length of 18 inches or more. Version shown has 20-inch bbl. Imported from 1997-99.

MODEL 300 O/U SHOTGUN . . . . . NiB $468 Ex $385 Gd $278
Similar to the Model 333 except 12 ga. only w/3-inch chambers, 26- or 28-inch vent rib bbls. w/extractors and fixed chokes. Etched receiver w/double triggers and standard walnut stock. Imported from 1994-98.

MODEL 311 SIDE-BY-SIDE SHOTGUN
Boxlock action w/underlug and Greener cross bolt. 12 or 20 ga. w/3-inch chambers, 20, 28- or 30-inch bbls. w/choke tubes or fixed chokes (311R). Double triggers. Extractors. Black chrome finish. Checkered Turkish walnut buttstock and forend. Weight: 6.9 to 7.2 lbs. Imported from 1994-97.
311 Model (w/extractors and choke tubes) . . . NiB $630 Ex $513 Gd $355
311R Model
(w/20-inch bbls. and fixed chokes) . . . . NiB $468 Ex $385 Gd $278

MODEL 330 O/U SHOTGUN
Similar to the Model 333 except 12 ga. only w/3-inch chambers. 26-, 28- or 30-inch vent rib bbls w/extractors or ejectors and fixed chokes or choke tubes. Etched receiver and standard walnut stock. Imported from 1994-99.
330 model (w/ extractor and fixed chokes) . . . NiB $559 Ex $457 Gd $327
330 D model (w/ejectors and choke tubes) . . . NiB $731 Ex $596 Gd $423

MODEL 333 O/U SHOTGUN
Boxlock action. 12 or 20 ga. w/3-inch chambers. 26-, 28- or 30-inch vent rib bbls. w/choke tubes. Single selective trigger. Selective automatic ejectors. Engraved receiver w/satin nickel finish. Checkered Turkish fancy walnut buttstock and forend. Weight: 7.5 to 7.75 lbs. Imported from 1994-98.
333 Field model . . . . NiB $842 Ex $686 Gd $487
333 Sporting Clays model (1994-97) . . . . . NiB $944 Ex $767 Gd $543
333 TRL Ladies Field model . . . . NiB $855 Ex $697 Gd $495
333 SCL Ladies Sporting Clays model
(1994-97) . . . . NiB $963 Ex $784 Gd $553

SHOTGUNS OF ULM — Ulm, West Germany

See listings under Krieghoff.

U.S. REPEATING ARMS CO. — New Haven, Connecticut

See Winchester Shotgun listings.

VALMET OY — Jyväskylä, Finland

NOTE: In 1987, Valmet and Sako merged and the Valmet production facilities were moved to Riihimaki, Finland. In 1989 a joint venture agreement was made with Armi Marocchi, and when production began in Italy, the Valmet name was changed to Tikka (Oy Tikkakoski Ab).

See also Savage Models 330, 333T, 333 and 2400, which were produced by Valmet.

VALMET LION O/U SHOTGUN . . . NiB $537 Ex $439 Gd $313
Boxlock. Selective single trigger. Plain extractors. 12 ga. only. Bbls.: 26-inch IC/M; 28-inch M/F, 30-inch M/F, F/F. Weight: About 7 lbs. Checkered pistol-grip stock and forearm. Imported from 1947-68.

MODEL 412 K O/U FIELD SHOTGUN. . . . NiB $894 Ex $728 Gd $516
Hammerless. 12-ga., 3-inch chamber, 36-inch bbl., F/F chokes. American walnut Monte Carlo stock. Made from 1982-87.

MODEL 412 K SHOTGUN RIFLE
COMBINATION . . . . NiB $1086 Ex $886 Gd $631
Similar to model 412 K except bottom bbl. chambered for .222 Rem., .223 Rem., .243 Win., .308 Win. or .30-06. 12-ga. shotgun bbl. with IM choke. Monte Carlo American walnut stock, recoil pad.

MODEL 412 KE O/U
FIELD SHOTGUN . . . . NiB $868 Ex $708 Gd $522
12-ga. chambered for 2.75-inch shells. 26-inch bbl., IC/M chokes; 28-inch bbl., M/F chokes; 12-ga. chambered for 3-inch shells, 30-inch bbl., M/F chokes. 20-ga. (3-inch shells); 26-inch bbl., IC/M chokes; 28-inch bbl., M/ F chokes. American walnut Monte Carlo stock.

SHOTGUNS

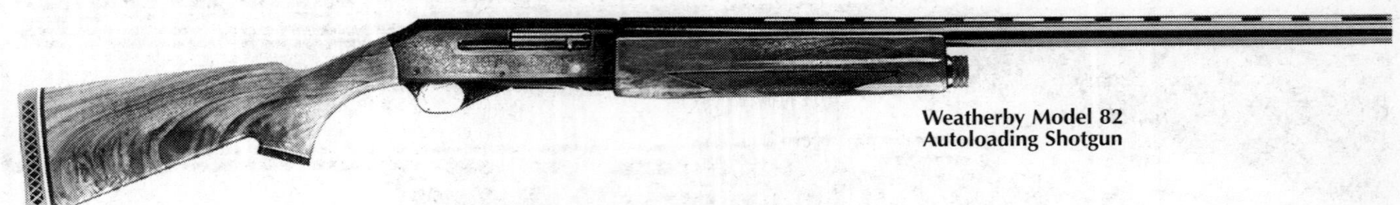
Weatherby Model 82
Autoloading Shotgun

MODEL 412 KE SKEET. . . . . NiB $994 Ex $806 Gd $566
Similar to Model 412 K except skeet stock and chokes. 12 and 20 ga. Disc. 1989.

MODEL 412 KE TRAP . . . . NiB $1035 Ex $839 Gd $608
Similar to Model 412 K Field except trap stock, recoil pad. 30-inch bbls., IM/F chokes. Disc.1989.

MODEL 412 3-BARREL SET . . . . .NiB $2704 Ex $2190 Gd $1533

MONTGOMERY WARD — Chicago, Illinois Western Field and Hercules Models

Although they do not correspond to specific models below, the names Western Field and Hercules have been used to designate various Montgomery Ward shotguns at various times.

MODEL 25 SLIDE-ACTION REPEATER . . . . . . NiB $235 Ex $194 Gd $142
Solid frame. 12 ga. only. Two- or 5-round tubular magazine. 28-inch bbl., various chokes. Weight: About 7.5 lbs. Plain pistol-grip stock, grooved slide handle.

MODEL 40 O/U SHOTGUN . . . . . . NiB $760 Ex $620 Gd $439
Hammerless. Boxlock. Double triggers. Gauges: 12, l6, 20, .410. Bbls.: Plain; 26- to 30-inch, various chokes. Checkered pistol-grip stock and forearm.

MODEL 40N
SLIDE-ACTION REPEATER. . . . . NiB $241 Ex $199 Gd $145
Same general specifications as Model 25.

(WESTERN FIELD) MODEL 50 PUMPGUN . . . NiB $250 Ex $206 Gd $151
Solid frame. Gauges: 12 and 16. Two- and 5-round magazine. 26-, 28- or 30-inch bbl., 48 inches overall w/28-inch bbl. Weight: 7.25 - 7.75 lbs. Metal bead front sight. Walnut stock and grooved forend.

(WESTERN FIELD) MODEL 52
DOUBLE-BARREL SHOTGUN. . . . . NiB $280 Ex $231 Gd $168
Hammerless coil-spring action. Gauges: 12, 16, 20 and .410. 26-, 28-, or 30-inch bbls., 42 to 46 inches overall, depending upon bbl. length. Weight: 6 (.410 ga. w/26-inch bbl.) to 7.25 lbs. (12 ga. w/30-inch bbls.), depending upon gauge and bbl. length. Casehardened receiver; blued bbls. Plain buttstock and forend. Made circa 1954.

MODEL 172 BOLT-ACTION SHOTGUN . . . . . . NiB $129 Ex $108 Gd $83
Takedown. Two-round detachable clip magazine.12 ga. 28-inch bbl. with variable choke. Weight: About 7.5 lbs. Monte Carlo stock with recoil pad.

MODEL 550A SLIDE-ACTION REPEATER . . . . NiB $278 Ex $228 Gd $165
Takedown. Gauges: 12, 16, 20, .410. Five-round tubular magazine. Bbls.: Plain, 26- to 30-inch, various chokes. Weight: 6 (.410 ga. w/26-inch bbl.) to 8 lbs. (12 ga. w/30-inch bbls.). Plain pistol-grip stock and grooved slide handle.

MODEL SB300 DOUBLE-BARREL
SHOTGUN. . . . . NiB $298 Ex $245 Gd $176
Same general specifications as Model SD52A.

MODEL SB312 DOUBLE-BARREL SHOTGUN. . . NiB $336 Ex $276 Gd $198
Boxlock. Double triggers. Plain extractors. Gauges: 12, 16, 20, .410. Bbls.: 24- to 30-inch. Various chokes. Weight: About 7.5 lbs. in 12 ga.; 6.5 lbs in .410 ga. Checkered pistol-grip stock and forearm.

MODEL SD52A DOUBLE-BARREL SHOTGUN. . . . NiB $256 Ex $211 Gd $154
Boxlock. Double triggers. Plain extractors. Gauges: 12, 16, 20, .410. Bbls.: 26- to 32-inch, various chokes. Plain forend and pistol-grip buttstock. Weight: 6 (.410 ga., 26-inch bbls.) to 7.5 lbs. (12 ga., 32-inch bbls.).

WEATHERBY, INC. — Atascadero, California (previously South Gate, California)

MODEL 82 AUTOLOADING SHOTGUN
Hammerless, gas-operated. 12 ga. only. Bbls.: 22- to 30-inch, various integral or fixed chokes. Weight: 7.5 lbs. Checkered walnut stock and forearm. Imported from 1982-89.
Standard Autoloading Shotgun . . . . NiB $467 Ex $384 Gd $277
BuckMaster Auto Slug
w/rifle sights (1986-90) . . . . NiB $474 Ex $389 Gd $281
W/fixed chokes, deduct. $40

MODEL 92 SLIDE-ACTION SHOTGUN
Hammerless, short-stroke action. 12 ga.; 3-inch chamber. Tubular magazine. Bbls.: 22-, 26-, 28-, 30-inch with fixed choke or IMC choke tubes; plain or vent rib with rifle sights. Weight: 7.5 lbs. Engraved, matte black receiver and blued barrel. Checkered high-gloss buttstock and forend. Imported from Japan since 1982.
Standard Model 92 . . . . NiB $378 Ex $311 Gd $225
BuckMaster Pump Slug
w/rifle sights (intro. 1986). . . . . NiB $402 Ex $331 Gd $239
W/fixed chokes, deduct. $25

ATHENA O/U SHOTGUN
Engraved boxlock action with Greener crossbolt and sideplates. Gauges: 12, 20, 28 and .410; 2.75- or 3.5-inch chambers. Bbls.: 26-, 28-, 30- or 32-inch with fixed or IMC Multi-choke tubes. Weight: 6.75 to 7.38 lbs. Single selective trigger. Selective auto ejectors. Top tang safety. Checkered Claro walnut stock and forearm with high-luster finish. Imported from 1982-2002.
Field Model w/IMC multi-choke
(12 or 20 ga.). . . . . NiB $2310 Ex $1879 Gd $1327
Field Model w/fixed chokes (28 or .410 ga.) . . . NiB $2255 Ex $1715 Gd $1244
Skeet Model w/fixed chokes (12 or 20 ga.) . . . . NiB $1951 Ex $1589 Gd $1127
Skeet Model w/fixed chokes
(28 or .410 ga.) . . . . NiB $2173 Ex $1769 Gd $1252
Master skeet tube set . . . . NiB $3639 Ex $2943 Gd $2052
Trap Model w/IC tubes . . . . NiB $1991 Ex $1622 Gd $1149
Grade V (1993 to date) . . . . NiB $2414 Ex $1962 Gd $1384

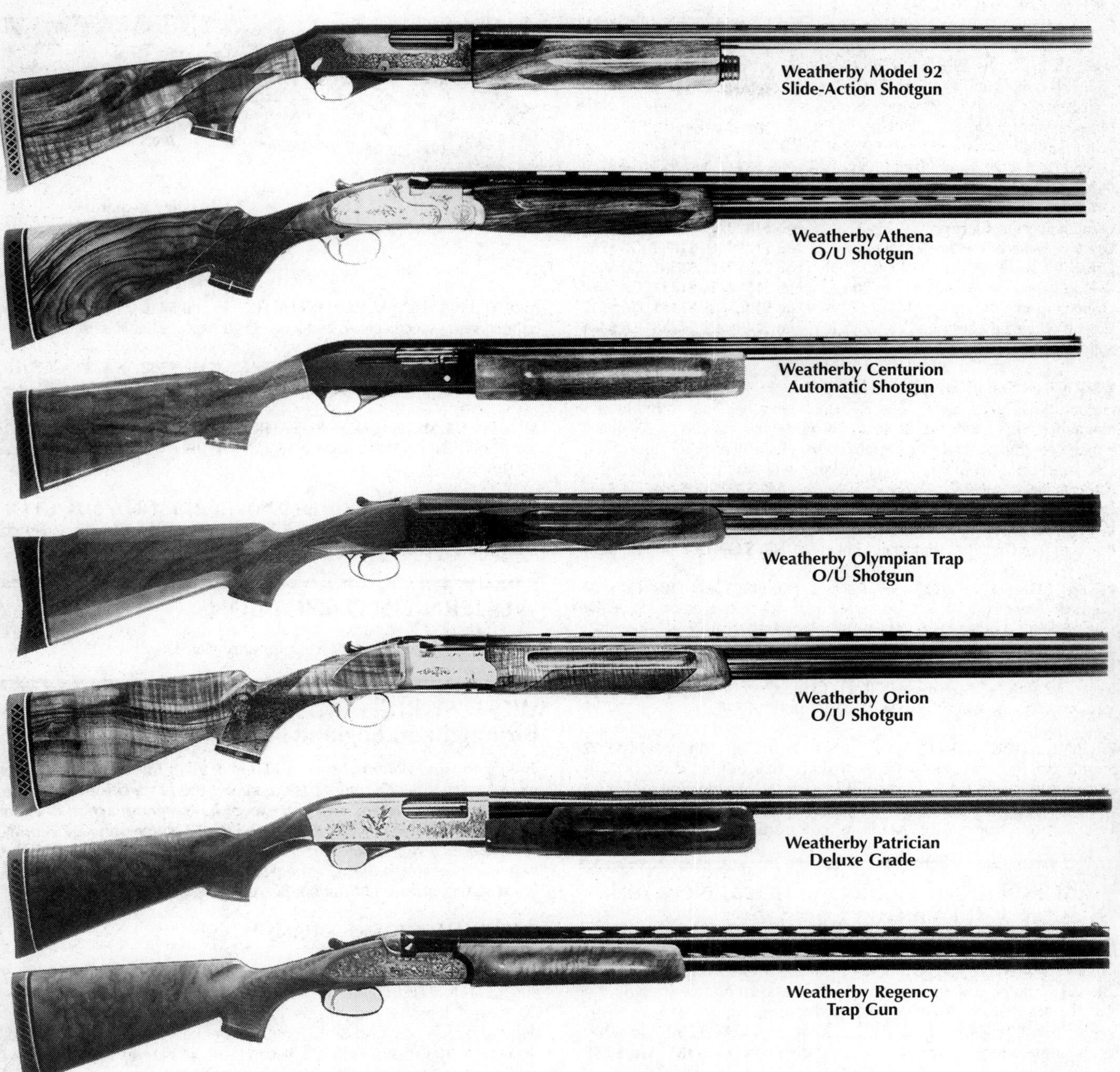

Weatherby Model 92
Slide-Action Shotgun

Weatherby Athena
O/U Shotgun

Weatherby Centurion
Automatic Shotgun

Weatherby Olympian Trap
O/U Shotgun

Weatherby Orion
O/U Shotgun

Weatherby Patrician
Deluxe Grade

Weatherby Regency
Trap Gun

CENTURION AUTOMATIC SHOTGUN

Gas-operated. Takedown. 12 ga. 2.75-inch chamber. Three round magazine. Bbls.: Vent ribs; 26-inch SK, IC or M 28-inch M or F; 30-inch Full choke. Weight: With 28-inch bbl., 7 lbs. 10.5 oz. Checkered pistol-grip stock and forearm, recoil pad. Made in Japan from 1972-81.

Centurion Field grade . . . . NiB $387 Ex $328 Gd $230
Centurion Trap Gun
(30-inch full choke bbl.) . . . . NiB $442 Ex $362 Gd $260
Centurion Deluxe (etched
receiver, fancy wood) . . . . NiB $568 Ex $464 Gd $331

OLYMPIAN O/U SHOTGUN

Gauges: 12 and 20. 2.75- (12 ga.) and 3-inch (20 ga.) chambers. Bbls.: 26-, 28-, 30, and 32-inch. Weight: 6.75 - 8.75 lbs. American walnut stock and forend.

Field
Model . . . . NiB $1006 Ex $823 Gd $590
Skeet
Model . . . . NiB $1030 Ex $843 Gd $604
Trap
Model . . . . NiB $1013 Ex $828 Gd $594

ORION O/U SHOTGUN
Boxlock with Greener crossbolt. Gauges: 12, 20, 28 and .410; 2.75- or 3-inch chambers. Bbls.: 26-, 28, 30-, 32- or 34-inch with fixed or IMC Multi-Choke tubes. Weight: 6.5 to 9 lbs. Single selective trigger. Selective auto ejectors. Top tang safety. Checkered, high-gloss pistol-grip Claro walnut stock and forearm. Finish: Grade I, plain blued receive; Grade II, engraved blued receiver; Grade III, silver gray receiver. Imported from 1982 and 2002.
Orion I Field w/IC (12 or 20 ga.) . . . . NiB $1211 Ex $992 Gd $710
Orion II Field w/IC (12 or 20 ga.) . . . . NiB $1255 Ex $1028 Gd $735
Orion II Classic w/IC (12, 20 or 28 ga.) . . . . NiB $1240 Ex $1011 Gd $727
Orion II Sporting Clays w/IC (12 ga.) . . . . . . NiB $1430 Ex $1168 Gd $831
Orion III Field w/IC (12 or 20 ga.) . . . . NiB $1299 Ex $1062 Gd $760
Orion III Classic w/IC (12 or 20 ga.) . . . . . . NiB $1549 Ex $1264 Gd $901
Orion III English Field w/IC (12 or 20 ga.) . . NiB $1508 Ex $1232 Gd $878
Orion Upland w/IC (12 or 20 ga.) . . . . NiB $1388 Ex $1133 Gd $817
Skeet II w/fixed chokes . . . . NiB $1496 Ex $1220 Gd $866
Super Sporting Clays . . . . NiB $1824 Ex $1486 Gd $1054

PATRICIAN SLIDE-ACTION SHOTGUN
Hammerless. Takedown. 12 ga. 2.75-inch chamber. Four round tubular magazine. Bbls.: Vent rib; 26-inch, SK, IC M; 28-inch, M F; 30-inch, F choke. Weight: With 28-inch bbl., 7 lbs., 7 oz. Checkered pistol-grip stock and slide handle, recoil pad. Made in Japan from 1972-82.
Patrician Field grade . . . . NiB $322 Ex $264 Gd $192
Patrician Deluxe (etched receiver,
fancy grade wood) . . . . NiB $340 Ex $303 Gd $218
Patrician Trap Gun (30-inch F choke bbl.) . . . . NiB $339 Ex $279 Gd $211

REGENCY FIELD GRADE O/U SHOTGUN . . NiB $1353 Ex $1103 Gd $784
Boxlock with sideplates, elaborately engraved. Auto ejectors. Selective single trigger. Gauges: 12, 20. 2.75-inch chamber in 12 ga., 3-inch in 20 ga. Bbls.: Vent rib; 26-inch SK, IC/M, M/F (20 ga. only); 28-inch SK, IC/M, M/F; 30-inch M/F (12 ga only). Weight with 28-inch bbls.: 7 lbs., 6 oz., 12 ga.; 6 lbs., 14 oz., 20 ga. Checkered pistol-grip stock and forearm of fancy walnut. Made in Italy from 1965-82.

REGENCY TRAP GUN . . . . NiB $1385 Ex $1129 Gd $802
Similar to Regency Field Grade except has trap-style stock with straight or Monte Carlo comb. Bbls. have vent side ribs and high, wide vent top rib; 30- or 32-inch, M/F, IM/F or F/F chokes. Weight: With 32-inch bbls., 8 lbs. Made in Italy from 1965-1982.

WESTERN ARMS CORP. — Ithaca, New York Division of Ithaca Gun Company

LONG RANGE HAMMERLESS DOUBLE
Boxlock. Plain extractors. Single or double triggers. Gauges: 12, 16, 20, .410. Bbls.: 26- to 32-inch, M/F choke standard. Weight: 7.5 lbs., 12 ga. Plain pistol-grip stock and forend. Made from 1929-46.
With double triggers . . . . NiB $353 Ex $290 Gd $209
With single trigger . . . . NiB $442 Ex $361 Gd $258

WESTERN AUTO SHOTGUNS — Kansas City, Missouri

MODEL 300H SLIDE-ACTION REPEATER . . . . NiB $287 Ex $237 Gd $174
Gauges: 12,16, 20, .410. Four round tubular magazine. Bbls.: 26- to 30-inch, various chokes. Weight: About 7 lbs. Plain pistol-grip stock, grooved slide handle.

MODEL 310A SLIDE-ACTION REPEATER . . . . NiB $274 Ex $227 Gd $168
Takedown. 12 ga. Five round tubular magazine. Bbls.: 28- and 30-inch. Weight: About 7.5 lbs. Plain pistol-grip stock.

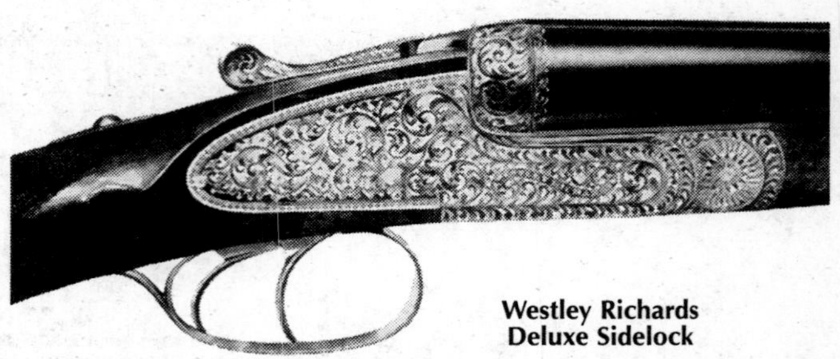
Westley Richards
Deluxe Sidelock

MODEL 310B SLIDE-ACTION REPEATER . . . . . NiB $256 Ex $211 Gd $154
Same general specifications as Model 310A except chambered for 16 ga.

MODEL 310C SLIDE-ACTION REPEATER . . . . NiB $282 Ex $232 Gd $170
Same general specifications as Model 310A except chambered for 20 ga.

MODEL 310E SLIDE-ACTION REPEATER . . . . . NiB $320 Ex $262 Gd $189
Same general specifications as Model 310A except chambered for .410 bore.

MODEL 325BK BOLT-ACTION REPEATER . . . . . NiB $146 Ex $124 Gd $94
Takedown. Two round detachable clip magazine. 20 ga. 26-inch bbl. with variable choke. Weight: 6.25 lbs.

WESTERN FIELD SHOTGUNS

See "W" for listings under Montgomery Ward.

WESTLEY RICHARDS & CO., LTD. — Birmingham, England

The Pigeon and Wildfowl gun, available in all of the Westley Richards models except the Ovundo, has the same general specifications as the corresponding standard field gun except has magnum action of extra strength and treble bolting, chambered for 12 gauge only (2.75- or 3-inch); 30-inch full choke barrels standard. Weight: About 8 lbs. The manufacturer warns that 12-gauge magnum shells should not be used in their standard weight double-barrel shotguns.

BEST QUALITY BOXLOCK HAMMERLESS DOUBLE-BARREL SHOTGUN
Boxlock. Hand-detachable locks and hinged cover plate. Selective ejectors. Double triggers or selective single trigger. Gauges: 12, 16, 20. Barrel lengths and boring to order. Weight: 5.5 to 6.25 lbs. depending on ga. and bbl. length. Checkered stock and forend, straight or half-pistol grip. Also supplied in Pigeon and Wildfowl models with same values. Made from 1899 to date.
With double triggers . . . . NiB $21,312 Ex $17,050 Gd $11,594
With selective single trigger . . . . NiB $24,062 Ex $19,250 Gd $13,090

BEST QUALITY SIDELOCK HAMMERLESS DOUBLE-BARREL SHOTGUN
Hand-detachable sidelocks. Selective ejectors. Double triggers or selective single trigger. Gauges: 12, 16, 20, 28, .410. Bbl. lengths and boring to order. Weight: 4.75 to 6.75 lbs., depending on ga. and bbl. length. Checkered stock and forend, straight or half-pistol grip. Also supplied in Pigeon and Wildfowl models with same values. Currently manufactured.
With double triggers. . . . . NiB $25,031 Ex $20,225 Gd $14,073
With selective single trigger . . . . NiB $27,250 Ex $22,000 Gd $15,280

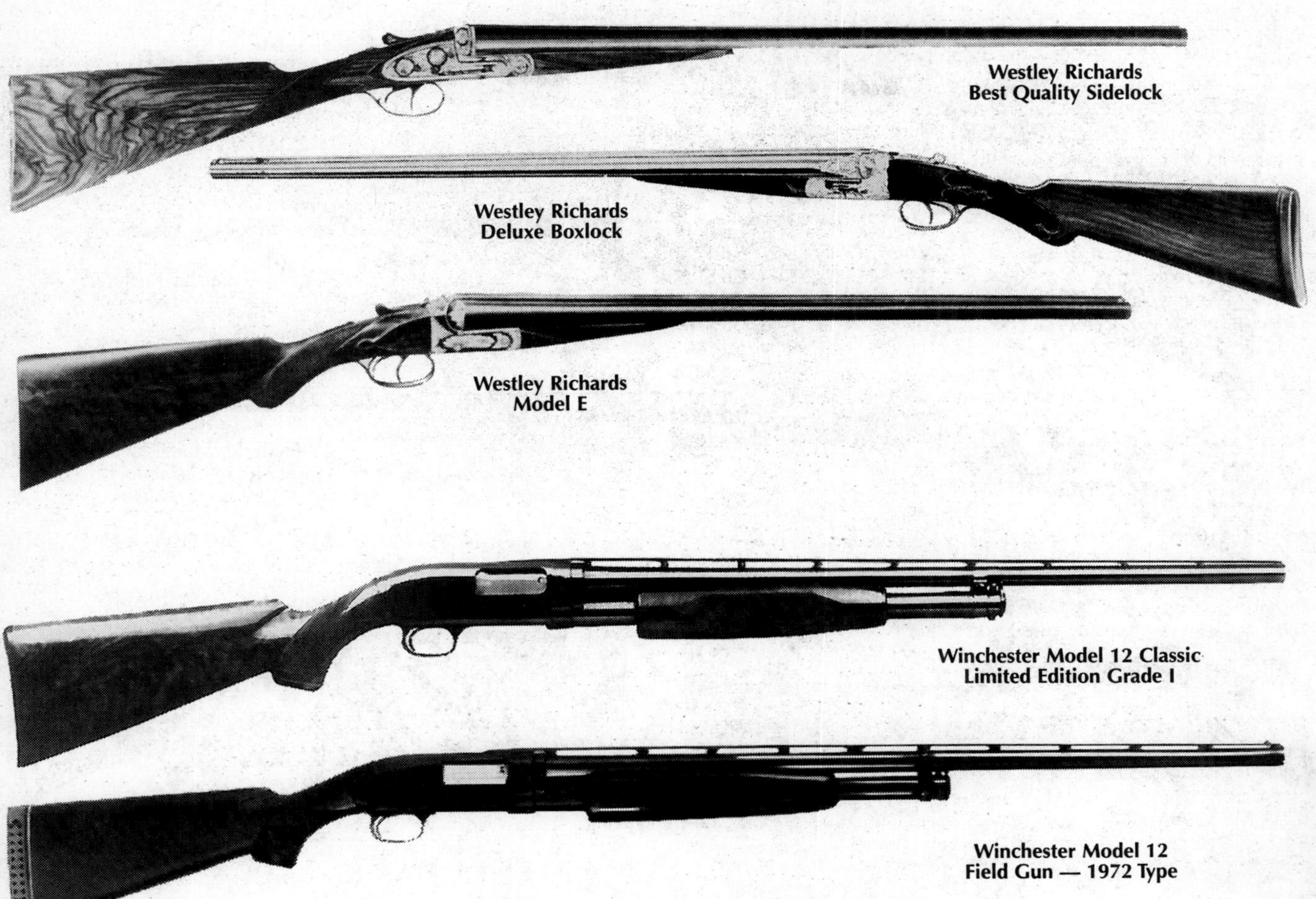

Westley Richards
Best Quality Sidelock

Westley Richards
Deluxe Boxlock

Westley Richards
Model E

Winchester Model 12 Classic
Limited Edition Grade I

Winchester Model 12
Field Gun — 1972 Type

MODEL DELUXE BOX LOCK HAMMERLESS DOUBLE-BARREL SHOTGUN

Same general specifications as standard Best Quality gun except higher quality throughout. Has Westley Richards top-projection and treble-bite lever-work, hand-detachable locks. Also supplied in Pigeon and Wildfowl models with same values. Currently manufactured.

With double triggers .... NiB $11,388 Ex $9150 Gd $6286
With selective single trigger .... NiB $30,000 Ex $28,000 Gd $12,000

MODEL DELUXE SIDELOCK

Same as Best Quality Sidelock except higher grade engraving and wood. Currently manufactured.

With double triggers .... NiB $25,000 Ex $20,000 Gd $13,600
With single trigger ...... NiB $30,000 Ex $24,000 Gd $16,320

MODEL E HAMMERLESS DOUBLE

Anson & Deeley-type boxlock action. Selective ejector or non-ejector. Double triggers. Gauges: 12, 16, 20. Barrel lengths and boring to order. Weight: 5.5 to 7.25 lbs. depending on type, ga. and bbl. length. Checkered stock and forend, straight or half-pistol grip. Also supplied in Pigeon and Wildfowl models with same values. Currently manufactured.

Ejector model .... NiB $4989 Ex $4040 Gd $2816
Non-ejector model .... NiB $4370 Ex $3545 Gd $2989

OVUNDO (O/U) .... NiB $18,744 Ex $14,995 Gd $10,197
Hammerless. Boxlock. Hand-detachable locks. Dummy sideplates. Selective ejectors. Selective single trigger. 12 ga. Barrel lengths and boring to order. Checkered stock/forend, straight or half-pistol grip. Mfd. before WW II.

TED WILLIAMS SHOTGUNS

See Sears shotguns.

WINCHESTER SHOTGUNS — New Haven, Connecticut

Formerly Winchester Repeating Arms Co., and then mfd. by Winchester-Western Div., Olin Corp., later by U.S. Repeating Arms Company. In 1999, production rights were acquired by Browning Arms Company.

MODEL 12 CLASSIC LIMITED EDITION

Gauge: 20; 2.75-inch chamber. Bbl.: 26-inch vent rib; IC. Weight: 7 lbs. Checkered walnut buttstock and forend. Polished blue finish (Grade I) or engraved with gold inlays (Grade IV). Made from 1993 to 1995.

Grade I (4000) .... NiB $950 Ex $771 Gd $542
Grade IV (1000) .... NiB $1465 Ex $1183 Gd $822

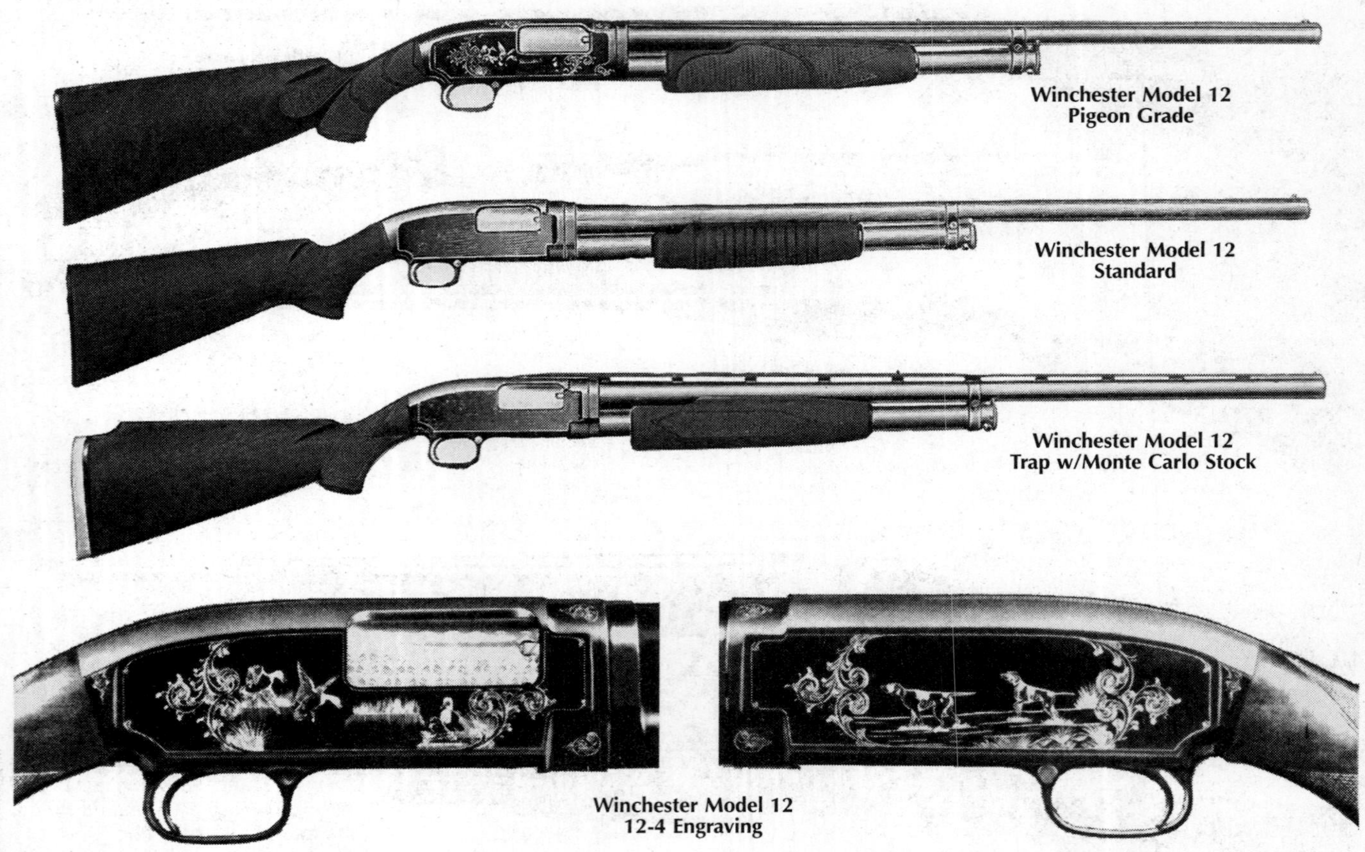

Winchester Model 12
Pigeon Grade

Winchester Model 12
Standard

Winchester Model 12
Trap w/Monte Carlo Stock

Winchester Model 12
12-4 Engraving

MODEL 12
FEATHERWEIGHT . . . . NiB $571 Ex $467 Gd $333
Same as Model 12 Standard w/plain barrel except has alloy trigger guard. Modified takedown w/redesigned magazine tube, cap and slide handle. 12 ga. only. Bbls.: 26-inch IC; 28-inch M or F; 30-inch F choke. Serial numbers with "F" prefix. Weight: About 6.75 lbs. Made from 1959-62.

MODEL 12 FIELD GUN, 1972 TYPE . . . . . . NiB $688 Ex $560 Gd $396
Same general specifications as Standard Model 12 but 12 ga. only, 26- 28- or 30-inch vent rib bbl., standard chokes. Engine-turned bolt and carrier. Hand-checkered stock/slide handle of semifancy walnut. Made from 1972-75.

MODEL 12 HEAVY DUCK GUN
Same general specifications as Standard Grade except 12 ga. only chambered for 3-inch shells. 30- or 32-inch plain, solid or vent rib bbl. w/full choke only. Three round magazine. Checkered slide handle and pistol-grip walnut buttstock w/recoil pad. Weight: 8.5 to 8.75 lbs. Made from 1935-63.
Heavy Duck Gun, plain bbl. . . . . NiB $8915 Ex $745 Gd $527
Heavy Duck Gun, solid rib (disc. 1959) . . . . NiB $1393 Ex $1137 Gd $809
Heavy Duck Gun, vent rib (Special order only) . . . . NiB $1785 Ex $1451 Gd $1024

MODEL 12 PIGEON GRADE
Deluxe versions of the regular Model 12 Standard or Field Gun, Duck Gun, Skeet Gun and Trap Gun made on special order. This grade has finer finish throughout, hand-smoothed action, engine-turned breech bolt and carrier, stock and extension slide handle of high grade walnut, fancy checkering, stock dimensions to individual specifications. Engraving and carving available at extra cost ranging from about $135 to over $1000. Disc. 1965.
Field Gun, plain bbl. . . . . NiB $1891 Ex $1536 Gd $1083
Field Gun, vent rib . . . . NiB $2299 Ex $1867 Gd $1314
Skeet Gun, matted rib . . . . NiB $2111 Ex $1715 Gd $1209
Skeet Gun, vent rib . . . . NiB $2615 Ex $2120 Gd $1485
Skeet Gun, Cutts Compensator . . . . NiB $1556 Ex $1266 Gd $894
Trap Gun, matted rib . . . . NiB $2231 Ex $1805 Gd $1267
Trap Gun, vent rib . . . . NiB $2457 Ex $1989 Gd $1391
16 ga. (Field), add 20%
16 ga. (Skeet), add 90%
20 ga. (Field), add 25%
20 ga. (Skeet), add 45%
28 ga. (Skeet), add 350%

MODEL 12 RIOT GUN . . . . NiB $874 Ex $714 Gd $508
Same general specifications as plain barrel Model 12 Standard except has 20-inch cylinder bore bbl.,12 gauge only. Made from 1918-1963.

MODEL 12 SKEET GUN . . . . NiB $1193 Ex $973 Gd $693
Gauges: 12, 16, 20, 28. Five round tubular magazine. 26-inch matted rib bbl., SK choke. Weight: About 7.75 lbs., 12 ga.; 6.75 lbs., other gauges. Bradley red or ivory bead front sight. Winchester 94B middle sight. Checkered pistol-grip stock and extension slide handle. Disc. after WWII.

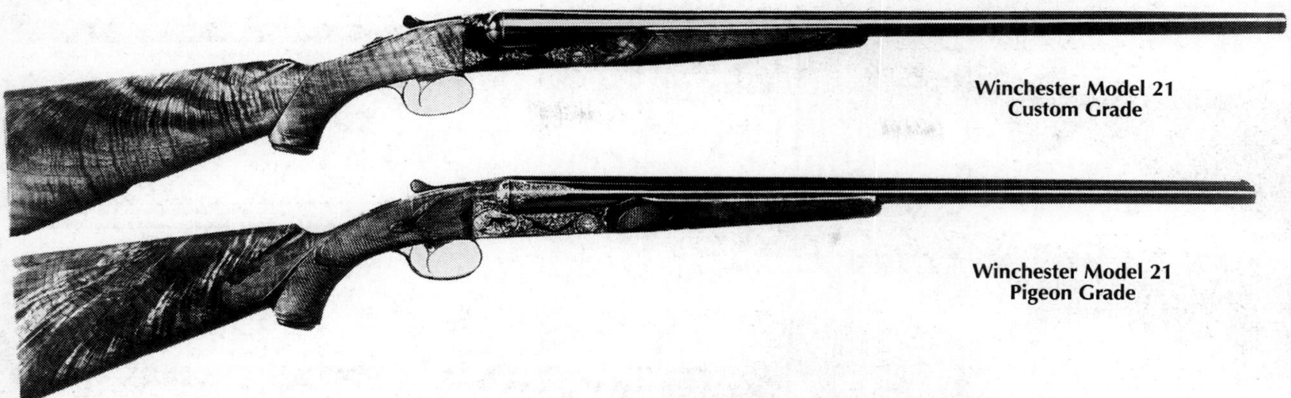

Winchester Model 21
Custom Grade

Winchester Model 21
Pigeon Grade

MODEL 12 SKEET GUN, CUTTS COMPENSATOR . . . . NiB $1006 Ex $821 Gd $586
Same general specifications as standard Model 12 Skeet Gun except has plain bbl. fitted with Cutts Compensator, 26 inches overall. Disc. 1954.

MODEL 12 SKEET GUN, PLAIN-BARREL . . . . . NiB $938 Ex $768 Gd $550
Same general specifications as standard Model 12 Skeet except w/no rib.

MODEL 12 SKEET GUN, VENT RIB . . . . NiB $1596 Ex $1299 Gd $920
Same general specifications as standard Model 12 Skeet Gun except has 26-inch bbl. with vent rib, 12 and 20 ga. Disc. in 1965.

MODEL 12 SKEET GUN, 1972 TYPE. . . . . NiB $1021 Ex $835 Gd $596
Same gen. specifications as Standard Model 12 but 12 ga. only. 26-inch vent rib bbl., SK choke. Engine-turned bolt and carrier. Hand-checkered skeet-style stock and slide handle of choice walnut, recoil pad. Made from 1972-75.

MODEL 12 STANDARD GR., MATTED RIB. . . . . NiB $1277 Ex $1032 Gd $749
Same general specifications as plain bbl. Model 12 Standard except has solid raised matted rib. Disc. after World War II.

MODEL 12 STANDARD GR., VENT RIB. . . . NiB $1430 Ex $1165 Gd $827
Same general specifications as plain barrel Model 12 Standard except has vent rib. 26.75- or 30-inch bbl.,12 ga. only. Disc. after World War II.

MODEL 12 STANDARD SLIDE-ACTION REPEATER
Hammerless. Takedown. Gauges: 12, 16, 20, 28. Six round tubular magazine. Plain bbl. Lengths: 26- to 32-inches; choked F to Cyl. Weight: About 7.5 lbs., 12 ga. 30-inch, 6.5 lbs. in other ga. with 28-inch bbl. Plain pistol-grip stock, grooved slide handle. Made from 1912-64.
12 ga., 28-inch bbl. (full choke) . . . . NiB $836 Ex $683 Gd $487
16 ga. . . . . NiB $846 Ex $611 Gd $438
20 ga. . . . . NiB $965 Ex $786 Gd $557
28 ga. . . . . NiB $4069 Ex $3298 Gd $2321

MODEL 12 SUPER PIGEON GRADE . NiB $3274 Ex $2657 Gd $1868
Custom version of Model 12 with same general specifications as standard models. 12 ga. only. 26-, 28- or 30-inch vent-rib bbl., any standard choke. Engraved receiver. Hand-smoothed and fitted action. Full fancy walnut stock and forearm made to individual order. Made from 1965-72.

MODEL 12 TRAP GUN
Same general specifications as Standard Model 12 except has straighter stock, checkered pistol grip and extension slide handle, recoil pad, 30-inch matted-rib bbl., F choke, 12 ga. only. Disc. after World War II; vent rib model disc. 1965.
Matted rib bbl. . . . . NiB $1095 Ex $898 Gd $646
With straight stock, vent rib . . . . . NiB $1088 Ex $892 Gd $641
With Monte Carlo stock, vent rib . . . . NiB $1411 Ex $1155 Gd $827

MODEL 12 TRAP GUN, 1972 TYPE . . . . NiB $1025 Ex $846 Gd $557
Same general specifications as Standard Model 12 but 12 gauge only. 30-inch vent-rib bbl., F choke. Engine-turned bolt and carrier. Hand-checkered trap-style stock (straight or Monte Carlo comb) and slide handle of select walnut, recoil pad. Intro. in 1972. Disc.

MODEL 20 SINGLE-SHOT HAMMER GUN . . . . NiB $783 Ex $639 Gd $453
Takedown. .410 bore. 2.5-inch chamber. 26-inch bbl., F choke. Checkered pistol-grip stock and forearm. Weight: About 6 lbs. Made from 1919-24.

ORIGINAL MODEL 21 DOUBLE-BARREL SHOTGUNS (ORIGINAL PRODUCTION SERIES - 1930 to 1959)
Hammerless. Boxlock. Automatic safety. Double triggers or selective single trigger, selective or non-selective ejection (all postwar Model 21 shotguns have selective single trigger and selective ejection). Gauges: 12, 16, 20, 28 and .410 bore. Bbls.: Raised matted rib or vent rib; 26-, 28-, 30-, 32-inch, the latter in 12 ga. only; F, IM, M, IC, SK chokes. Weight: 7.5 lbs., 12 ga. w/30-inch bbl.; about 6.5 lbs. 16 or 20 ga. w/28-inch bbl. Checkered pistol- or straight-grip stock, regular or beavertail forend. Made from 1930-59.
Standard grade, 12 ga. . . . . NiB $5176 Ex $4199 Gd $2948
Standard grade, 16 ga. . . . . NiB $6441 Ex $5210 Gd $3635
Standard grade, 20 ga. . . . . NiB $6657 Ex $5383 Gd $3754
Tournament grade, 12 ga. (1933-34) . . . . NiB $5434 Ex $4405 Gd $3089
Tournament grade, 16 ga. (1933-34) . . . . NiB $6664 Ex $5378 Gd $3757
Tournament grade, 20 ga. (1933-34) . . . . NiB $7965 Ex $6447 Gd $4504
Trap grade, 12 ga. (1940-59) . . . . . NiB $5247 Ex $4255 Gd $2987
Trap grade, 16 ga. (1940-59) . . . . . NiB $5846 Ex $4734 Gd $3312
Trap grade, 20 ga. (1940-59) . . . . . NiB $7245 Ex $5866 Gd $4100
Skeet grade, 12 ga. (1936-59). . . . . NiB $5171 Ex $4194 Gd $2943
Skeet grade, 16 ga. (1936-59). . . . . NiB $5905 Ex $4781 Gd $3342
Skeet grade, 20 ga. (1936-59). . . . . NiB $6887 Ex $5578 Gd $3991
Duck Gun, 12 ga. 3-inch (1940-52) . . . NiB $5686 Ex $4606 Gd $3224
Magnum, 12 ga. 3-inch (1953-59) . . . NiB $5500 Ex $4456 Gd $3122
Magnum, 20 ga. 3-inch (1953-59) . . . NiB $6724 Ex $5448 Gd $3817
Cust. built/deluxe gr., 12 ga.(1933-59). . . . . NiB $8134 Ex $6590 Gd $4614
Cust. built/deluxe gr., 16 ga. (1933-59) . . . . NiB $9429 Ex $7638 Gd $5348
Cust. built/deluxe gr., 20 ga. (1933-59). . . . . NiB $10,180 Ex $8209 Gd $5688
Custom built/deluxe grade, 28 ga.(1933-59) . . . . Very Rare*
Custom built/deluxe grade, .410 1933-59) . . . . Very Rare*
*Fewer than 100 sm. bore models (28 ga. and .410) were built, which precludes accurate pricing, but projected values could exceed $30,000. Such rare specimens should be authenticated by factory letter and/or independent appraisals.

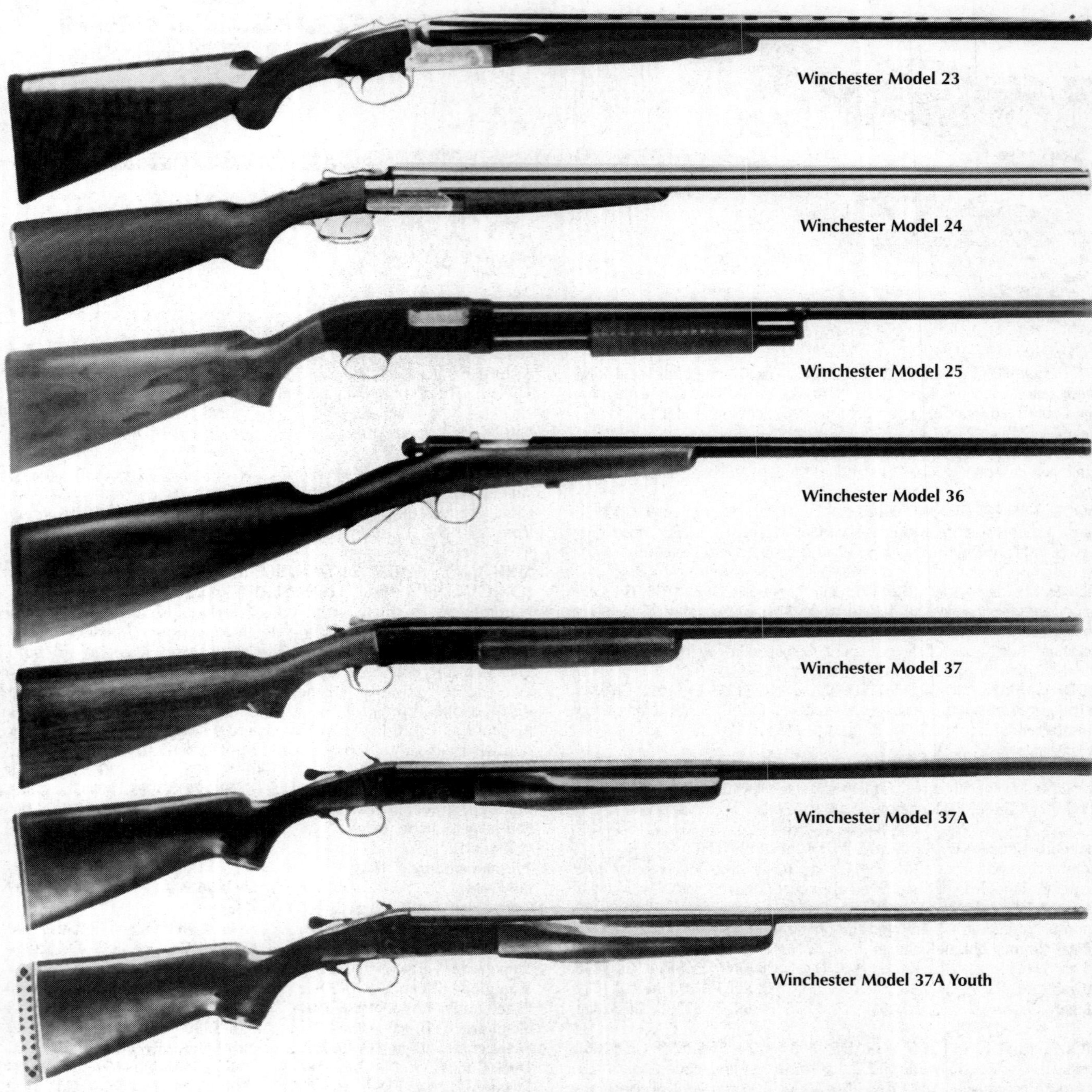
Winchester Model 23

Winchester Model 24

Winchester Model 25

Winchester Model 36

Winchester Model 37

Winchester Model 37A

Winchester Model 37A Youth

W/vent rib on 12 ga. models, add $710
W/vent rib on 16 ga. models, add $1650
W/vent rib on 20 ga. models, add $1125
W/double triggers ans extractors, deduct 30%
W/double trigger, selective ejection, deduct 20%
For Custom Engraving from this period:
No. 1 Pattern, add 25%
No. 2 Pattern, add 35%
No. 3 Pattern, add 50%
No. 4 Pattern, add 35%
No. 5 Pattern, add 65%
No. 6 Pattern, add 75%

MODEL 21 CUSTOM, PIGEON, GRAND AMERICAN (CUSTOM SHOP SERIES - PRODUCTION 1959 TO 1981)

Since 1959 the Model 21 has been offered through the Custom Shop in deluxe models. (Custom, Pigeon, Grand American) on special order. General specifications same as for Model 21 standard models except these custom guns have full fancy American walnut stock and forearm with fancy checkering, finely polished and hand-smoothed working parts, etc.; engraving inlays, carved stocks and other extras are available at additional cost. Made from 1959-81.

Custom grade, 12 ga.................. NiB $9971 Ex $8026 Gd $5538
Custom grade, 16 ga.............. NiB $15,006 Ex $12,045 Gd $8255
Custom grade, 20 ga.............. NiB $13,398 Ex $10,757 Gd $7379

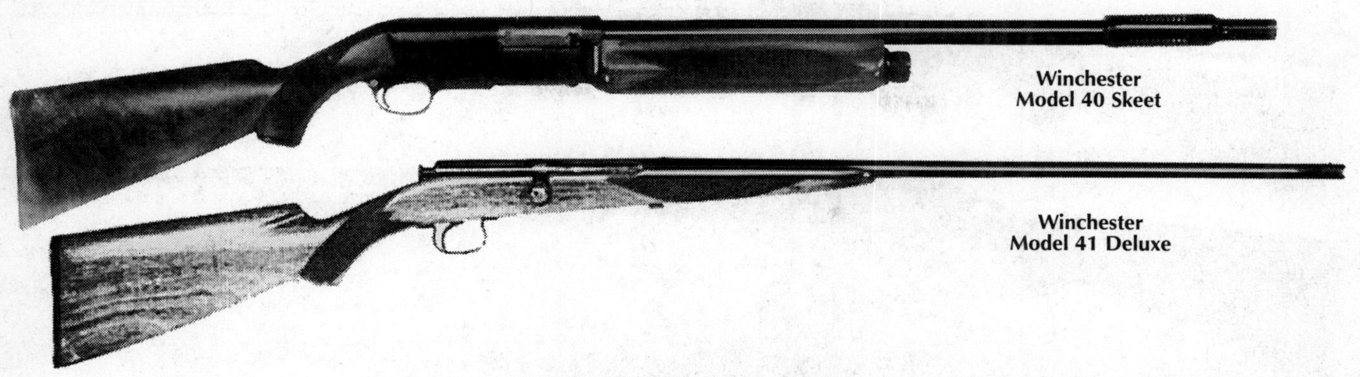

Pigeon grade, 12 ga. .... **NiB $15,329 Ex $12,302 Gd $8430**
Pigeon grade, 16 ga. .... **NiB $21,244 Ex $16,995 Gd $11,557**
Pigeon grade, 20 ga. .... **NiB $19,635 Ex $15,707 Gd $10,681**
Grand American, 12 ga. .... **NiB $23,111 Ex $18,488 Gd $12,572**
Grand American, 16 ga. .... **NiB $36,694 Ex $29,355 Gd $19,961**
Grand American, 20 ga. .... **NiB $27,360 Ex $29,355 Gd $14,883**
Grand American 3-barrel Set .... **$23,175 to $39,140**
Small Bore Models
(28 ga. And .410) .... **Very Rare***
*Fewer than 20 Small Bore models (28 ga. and .410) were built during this period, which precludes accurate pricing, but projected values could exceed $35,000. Such rare specimens should be authenticated by factory letter and/or independent appraisals.
For Custom Shop Engraving from this period:
#1 Pattern, add **10%**
#2 Pattern, add **15%**
#3 Pattern, add **25%**
#4 Pattern, add **35%**
#5 Pattern, add **45%**
#6 Pattern, add **50%**

MODEL 21 - U.S.R.A. CUSTOM-BUILT SERIES (CUSTOM SHOP PRODUCTION 1982 TO DATE)

In 1982, the individual model designations for the Model 21 were changed again when U. S. Repeating Arms Company assumed production. The new model nomenclature for the Custom/Built catagory, includes: Standard Custom, Special Custom and Grand American — all of which are available on special order through the Custom Shop. General specifications remained the same on these consolidated model variations and included the addition of a Small Bore 2-Barrel Set (28/.410) and a 3-Barrel Set (20/28/.410). Made from 1982 to date.
Custom Built -
Standard Custom.. .... **NiB $6570 Ex $5320 Gd $3722**
Custom Built -
Special Custom .... **NiB $7804 Ex $6322 Gd $4407**
Custom Built - Grand American ...... **NiB $13,694 Ex $10,990 Gd $7529**
Custom Built - Grand
American 2-barrel set............ **NiB $44,999 Ex $35,998 Gd $24,479**
Custom Built - Grand
American 3-barrel set............ **NiB $67,594 Ex $54,075 Gd $36,771**
The values shown above represent the basic model in each catagory. Since many customers took advantage of the custom built options, individual gun appointments vary and values will need to be adjusted accordingly. For this reason, individual appraisals should be obtained on all subject firearms.

MODEL 23 SIDE-BY-SIDE SHOTGUN

Boxlock. Single trigger. Automatic safety. Gauges: 12, 20, 28, .410. Bbls.: 25.5-, 26-, 28-inch with fixed chokes or Winchoke tubes. Weight: 5.88 to 7 lbs. Checkered American walnut buttstock and forend. Made in 1979 for Olin at its Olin-Kodensha facility, Japan.
Classic 23 — Gold inlay, engraved ...... **NiB $2111 Ex $1675 Gd $1190**
Custom 23 — Plain receiver,
Winchoke system .... **NiB $1306 Ex $1075 Gd $780**
Heavy Duck 23 — Standard .... **NiB $2040 Ex $1604 Gd $1182**
Lightweight 23 — Classic .... **NiB $2020 Ex $1645 Gd $1163**
Light Duck 23 — Standard .... **NiB $1920 Ex $1561 Gd $1109**
Light Duck 23 — 12 ga. Golden Quail ... **NiB $2269 Ex $1852 Gd $1317**
Light Duck 23 — .410 Golden Quail ..... **NiB $3831 Ex $3105 Gd $2175**
Custom Set 23 — 20 & 28 ga.. .... **NiB $5958 Ex $4817 Gd $3355**

MODEL 24 HAMMERLESS DOUBLE

Boxlock. Double triggers. Plain extractors. Auto safety. Gauges: 12, 16, 20. Bbls.: 26-inch IC/M; 28-inch M/F (also IC/M in 12 ga. only); 30-inch M and F in 12 ga. only. Weight: About 7.5 lbs., 12 ga. Metal bead front sight. Plain pistol-grip stock, semi-beavertail forearm. Made from 1939-57.
Model 24, 12 ga. .... **NiB $773 Ex $640 Gd $469**
Model 24, 16 ga. .... **NiB $849 Ex $699 Gd $509**
Model 24, 20 ga. .... **NiB $1196 Ex $759 Gd $553**

MODEL 25 RIOT GUN .... NiB $600 Ex $494 Gd $358

Same as Model 25 Standard except has 20-inch cylinder bore bbl., 12 ga. only. Made from 1949-55.

MODEL 25 SLIDE-ACTION REPEATER .... NiB $543 Ex $446 Gd $323

Hammerless. Solid frame. 12 ga. only. Four round tubular magazine. 28-in. Plain bbl.; IC, M or F choke. Weight: About 7.5 lbs. Metal bead front sight. Plain pistol-grip stock, grooved slide handle. Made from 1949-55.

MODEL 36 SINGLE-SHOT BOLT ACTION.... NiB $650 Ex $533 Gd $385

Takedown. Uses 9mm Short or Long shot or ball cartridges interchangeably. 18-inch bbl. Plain stock. Weight: About 3 lbs. Made from 1920-27.

MODEL 37 SINGLE-SHOT SHOTGUN

Semi-hammerless. Auto ejection. Takedown. Gauges: 12, 16, 20, 28, .410. Bbl. lengths: 28-, 30-, 32-inch in all gauges except .410; 26- or 28-inch in .410; all barrels plain with F choke. Weight: About 6.5 pounds, 12 ga. Made from 1937-63.
12 ga. .... **NiB $358 Ex $295 Gd $215**
16 ga. .... **NiB $296 Ex $246 Gd $182**
20 ga. .... **NiB $405 Ex $333 Gd $241**
20 ga. (Youth w/red dot indicator) .... **NiB $490 Ex $422 Gd $304**
28 ga. (red letter only) .... **NiB $1602 Ex $1333 Gd $920**
410 ga. .... **NiB $483 Ex $397 Gd $288**
Other "Red Letter" models, add **20%**
W/32-inch bbl., add **15%**

SHOTGUNS

Winchester Model 42
Classic Limited Edition

Winchester Model 42
Standard

MODEL 37A SINGLE SHOT SHOTGUN
Similar to Model 370 except has engraved receiver and gold trigger, checkered pistol-grip stock, fluted forearm; 16 ga. available with 30-inch bbl. only. Made from 1973-80.
Model 37A, 12, 16, or 20 ga. . . . . . NiB $188 Ex $156 Gd $115
Model 37A, 28 ga. . . . . NiB $273 Ex $226 Gd $165
Model 37A, .410 . . . . NiB $324 Ex $267 Gd $193
W/32-inch bbl., add $20

MODEL 37A YOUTH. . . . . NiB $201 Ex $166 Gd $122
Similar to Model 370 Youth except has engraved receiver and gold trigger, checkered pistol-grip stock, fluted forearm. Made from 1973-80.

MODEL 40 STANDARD AUTOLOADER. . NiB $788 Ex $639 Gd $449
Streamlined receiver. Hammerless. Takedown. 12 ga. only. Four round tubular magazine. 28- or 30-inch bbl.; M or F choke. Weight: About 8 lbs. Bead sight on ramp. Plain pistol-grip stock, semi-beavertail forearm. Made from 1940-41.

MODEL 40 SKEET GUN . . . . NiB $1071 Ex $877 Gd $630
Same general specifications as Model 40 Standard except has 24-inch plain bbl. w/Cutts Compensator and screw-in choke tube, checkered forearm and pistol grip, grip cap. Made from 1940-1941.

MODEL 41 SINGLE-SHOT BOLT ACTION
Takedown. .410 bore. 2.5-inch chamber (chambered for 3-inch shells after 1932). 24-inch bbl., F choke. Plain straight stock standard. Also made in deluxe version. Made from 1920-34.
Standard model . . . . NiB $712 Ex $583 Gd $419
Deluxe model. . . . . NiB $842 Ex $688 Gd $490

MODEL 42 CLASSIC LTD. EDITION. NiB $1710 Ex $1387 Gd $975
Gauge: .410 with 2.75-inch chamber. Bbl.: 26-inch vent rib; F choke. Weight: 7 lbs. Checkered walnut buttstock and forend. Engraved blue with gold inlays. Limited production of 850. Made from 1993.

MODEL 42 DELUXE . . . . NiB $5977 Ex $4813 Gd $3337
Same general specifications as the Model 42 Trap Grade except available w/vent rib after 1955. Finer finish throughout w/hand-smoothed action, engine-turned breech bolt and carrier, stock and extension slide handle of high grade walnut, fancy checkering, stock dimensions to individual specifications. Engraving and carving were offered at extra cost. Made 1940-63. Note: Exercise caution on VR models not marked "DELUXE" on the bottom of the receiver. A factory letter will insure that the rib was installed during the initial manufacturing process. Unfortunately, factory authentication is not always possible due to missing or destroyed records. To further complicate this matter, not all VR ribs were installed by Winchester. From 1955-63, both Deluxe and Skeet Grade models were available with Simmons style ribs. After-market rib installations are common.

MODEL 42 PIGEON GRADE
This higher-grade designation is similar to the Deluxe grade and is available in all configurations. May be identified by engraved Pigeon located at the base of the magazine tube. Most production occurred in the late 1940's. *NOTE: To determine the value of any Model 42 Pigeon Grade, add 50 % to value listed under the specified Model 42 configuration.*

MODEL 42 SKEET GUN
Same general specifications as Model 42 Standard except has checkered straight or pistol-grip stock and extension slide handle, 26- or 28-inch plain, solid-rib or vent-rib bbl. May be choked F., Mod., Imp. Cyl. or Skeet. Note: Some Model 42 Skeet Guns are chambered for 2.5-inch shells only. Made from 1933-63.
Model 42 Skeet
w/plain bbl. . . . . NiB $2635 Ex $2147 Gd $1522
Model 42 Skeet
w/solid rib . . . . NiB $3412 Ex $2770 Gd $1947
Model 42 Skeet
w/vent rib . . . . NiB $4573 Ex $3710 Gd $2606
W/2.5-inch
chamber, add 35%

MODEL 42 TRAP GRADE
This higher grade designation was available in both field and skeet configurations and is fitted w/deluxe wood w/trap grade checkering pattern and marked "TRAP" on bottom of receiver. Made 1934-39. Superseded by the Deluxe model in 1940.
Model 42 Trap grade
w/plain bbl. . . . . NiB $9000 Ex $7455 Gd $3850
Model 42 Trap grade
w/solid rib . . . . NiB $5895 Ex $4865 Gd $2290
Model 42 Trap grain
w/vent rib . . . . NiB $6940 Ex $5395 Gd $2562

MODEL 42 STANDARD GRADE
Hammerless. Takedown. .410 bore (3- or 2.5-inch shell). Tubular magazine holds five 3-inch or six 2.5-inch shells. 26- or 28-inch plain or solid-rib bbl.; cylinder bore, M or F choke. Weight: 5.8 to 6.5 lbs. Plain pistol-grip stock; grooved slide handle. Made from 1933-63.
Model 42 Standard w/plain bbl. . NiB $1366 Ex $1120 Gd $782
Model 42 Standard w/solid rib . . . . NiB $2148 Ex $1974 Gd $1562

MODEL 50 FIELD GUN, VENT RIB . . . NiB $557 Ex $455 Gd $325
Same as Model 50 Standard except has vent rib.

MODEL 50 SKEET GUN . . . . NiB $629 Ex $513 Gd $363
Same as Model 50 Standard except has 26-inch vent-rib bbl. with SK choke, skeet-style stock of select walnut.

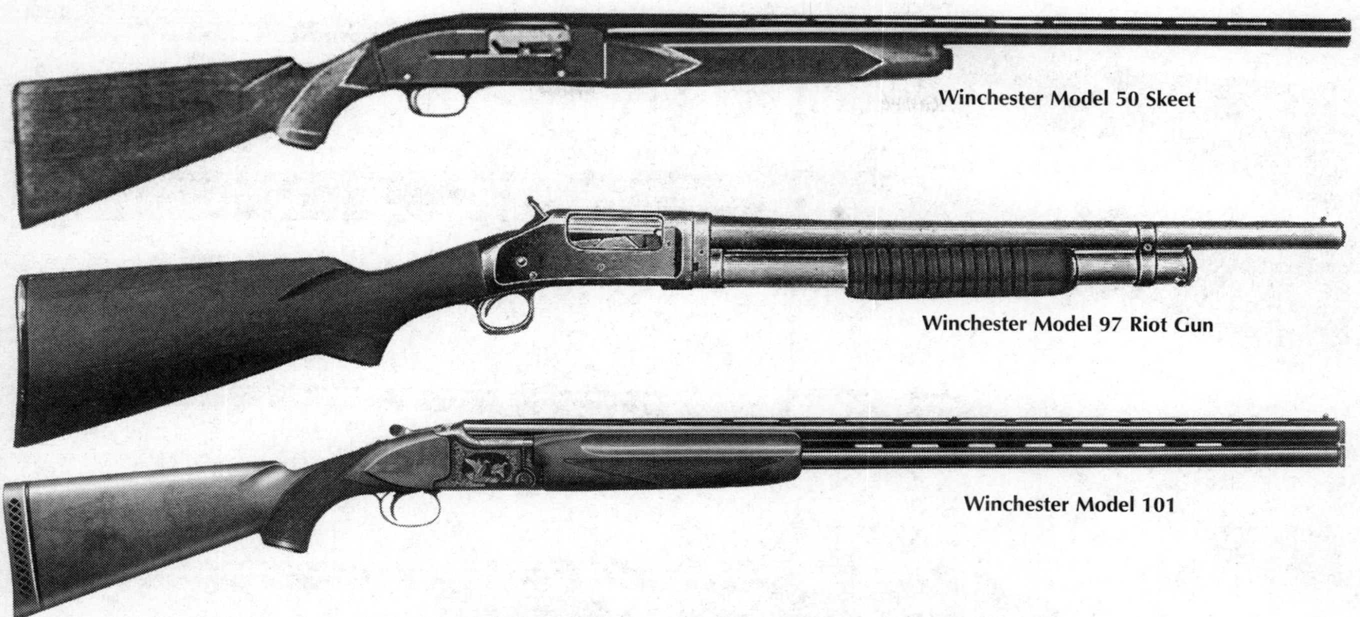

Winchester Model 50 Skeet

Winchester Model 97 Riot Gun

Winchester Model 101

MODEL 50 STANDARD GRADE . . . NiB $497 Ex $407 Gd $291
Non-recoiling bbl. and independent chamber. Gauges: 12 and 20. Two round tubular magazine. Bbl.: 12 ga. — 26-, 28-, 30-inch; 20 ga. — 26-, 28-inch; IC, SK, M, F choke. Checkered pistol-grip stock and forearm. Weight: About 7.75 lbs. Made from 1954-61.

MODEL 50 TRAP GUN . . . . NiB $857 Ex $677 Gd $445
Same as Model 50 Standard except 12 ga. only, has 30-inch vent-rib bbl. with F choke, Monte Carlo stock of select walnut.

MODEL 59 AUTO-LOADING SHOTGUN . . . NiB $694 Ex $571 Gd $416
Gauge: 12. Magazine holds two rounds. Alloy receiver. Win-Lite steel and fiberglass bbl.: 26-inch IC, 28-inch M or F choke, 30-inch F choke; also furnished with 26-inch bbl. with Versalite choke (interchangeable F, M, IC tubes; one supplied with gun). Weight: About 6.5 lbs. Checkered pistol-grip stock and forearm. Made from 1959-65.

MODEL 97 BUSH GUN
Takedown or solid frame. Same general specifications as standard Model 97 except w/26-inch cylinder bore bbl. Made from 1897-1931.
Model 97 Bush Gun w/solid frame . NiB $852 Ex $592 Gd $467
Model 97 Bush Gun takedown . . . . NiB $1114 Ex $902 Gd $630

MODEL 97 RIOT GUN
Takedown or solid frame. Same general specifications as standard Model 97 except 12 ga. only, 20-inch cylinder bore bbl. Made from 1898-1935.
Model 97 Riot Gun w/solid frame . . NiB $1304 Ex $1058 Gd $745
Model 97 Riot Gun takedown . . . . NiB $1142 Ex $930 Gd $658

MODEL 97 TRAP, TOURNAMENT AND PIGEON
These higher grade models offer higher overall quality than the standard grade. Made from 1897-39.
Standard Trap grade . . . . NiB $1534 Ex $1244 Gd $873
Special Trap grade . . . . NiB $1649 Ex $1398 Gd $978
Tournament grade (Black Diamond) . . . . NiB $2694 Ex $2182 Gd $1525
Pigeon grade . . . . NiB $5142 Ex $4150 Gd $2881

MODEL 97 TRENCH GUN . . . . NiB $2133 Ex $1722 Gd $1197
Solid frame. Same as Model 97 Riot Gun except has handguard and is equipped with a bayonet. World War I government issue, from 1917-18.
Model 97 Trench Gun w/solid frame . . . . NiB $3113 Ex $2510 Gd $1739
Model 97 Trench Gun takedown. . . . NiB $1323 Ex $1085 Gd $758

MODEL 97 SLIDE-ACTION REPEATER
Standard Grade. Takedown or solid frame. Gauges: 12 and 16. Five-round tubular magazine. Bbl.: Plain; 26 to 32 inches, the latter in 12 ga. only; choked F to Cyl. Weight: About 7.75 lbs. (12 ga. w/28-inch barrel). Plain pistol-grip stock, grooved slide handle. Made from 1897-1957.
Model 97, 12 ga. w/solid frame . . . NiB $926 Ex $756 Gd $537
Model 97, 16 ga. w/solid frame . . NiB $1190 Ex $968 Gd $684
Model 97, 12 ga. takedown. . . . . . . NiB $956 Ex $780 Gd $554
Model 97, 16 ga. takedown. . . . . . NiB $1227 Ex $998 Gd $704

NOTE: All Winchester Model 101s are mfd. for Olin Corp. at its Olin-Kodensha facility in Tochigi, Japan. Production for Olin Corp. stopped in Nov. 1987. Importation of Model 101s was continued by Classic Doubles under that logo until 1990. See separate heading for additional data.

MODEL 101 DIAMOND GRADE TARGET . . . . NiB $1831 Ex $1480 Gd $1053
Similar to Model 101 Standard except silvered frame and Winchoke interchangeable choke tubes. Made from 1981-90.

MODEL 101 FIELD GUN O/U
Boxlock. Engraved receiver. Auto ejectors. Single selective trigger. Combination bbl. selector and safety. Gauges: 12 and 28, 2.75-inch chambers; 20 and .410, 3-inch chambers. Vent rib bbls.: 30- (12 ga. only) and 26.5-inch, IC/M. Weight: 6.25 to 7.75 lbs. depending on gauge and bbl. length. Hand-checkered French walnut and forearm. Made from 1963-81. Gauges other than 12 introduced 1966.
12 and 20 ga. . . . . NiB $1051 Ex $847 Gd $600
28 and .410 ga. . . . . NiB $1276 Ex $1027 Gd $723
12 and 20 ga. mag. . . . . NiB $1109 Ex $904 Gd $642

SHOTGUNS

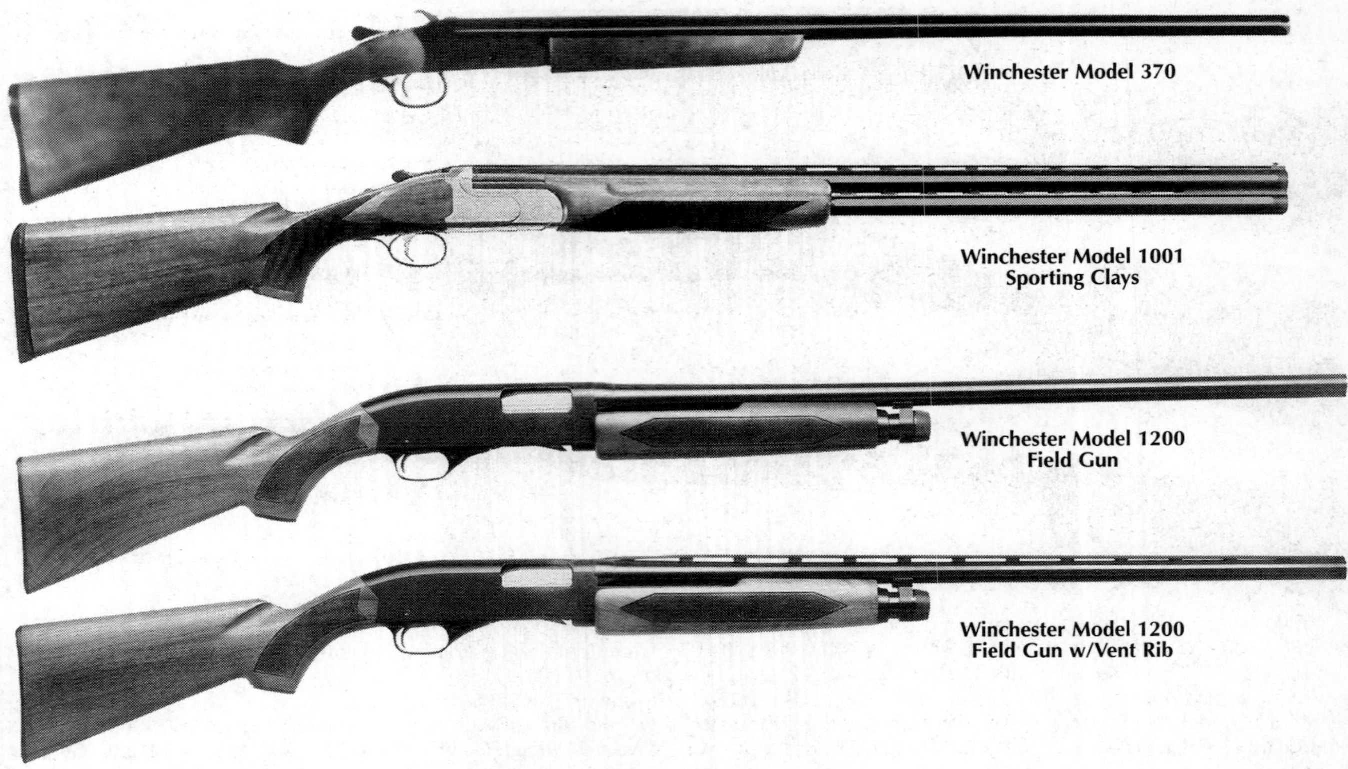

Winchester Model 370

Winchester Model 1001 Sporting Clays

Winchester Model 1200 Field Gun

Winchester Model 1200 Field Gun w/Vent Rib

MODEL 101 QUAIL SPECIAL O/U

Same specifications as small-frame Model 101 except in 28 and .410 ga. with 3-inch chambers. 25.5-inch bbls. with choke tubes (28 ga.) or M/F chokes (.410). Imported from Japan in 1984-87.

12 ga. NiB $2286 Ex $1854 Gd $1303
20 ga. NiB $2693 Ex $2179 Gd $1524
28 ga. NiB $3337 Ex $2701 Gd $1938
.410 ga. . . . . NiB $2361 Ex $1914 Gd $1343

MODEL 101 SHOTGUN/RIFLE
COMBINATION GUN. . . . . NiB $2425 Ex $1967 Gd $1381

12-ga. Winchoke bbl. on top and rifle bbl. chambered for .30-06 on bottom (over/under). 25-inch bbls. Engraved receiver. Hand checkered walnut stock and forend. Weight: 8.5 lbs. Mfd. for Olin Corp. in Japan.

MODEL 370
SINGLE-SHOT SHOTGUN . . . . NiB $148 Ex $124 Gd $93

Visible hammer. Auto ejector. Takedown. Gauges: 12, 16, 20, 28, .410. 2.75-inch chambers in 16 and 28 ga., 3-inch in other ga. Bbls.: 12 ga., 30-, 32- or 36-inch,16 ga; 30- or 32-inch; 20 and 28 ga., 28-inch; .410 bore, 26-inch, all F choke. Weight: 5.5-6.25 lbs. Plain pistol-grip stock and forearm. Made from 1968-73.

MODEL 370 YOUTH

Same as standard Model 370 except has 26-inch bbl. and 12.5-inch stock with recoil pad; 20 gauge with IM choke, .410 bore with F choke. Made from 1968-73.

Model 370, 12,
16, or 20 ga. . . . . NiB $167 Ex $139 Gd $102
Model 37A, 28 ga.. . . . . NiB $228 Ex $187 Gd $136
Model 37A, .410 ga. . . . . NiB $193 Ex $161 Gd $118

MODEL 1001 O/U SHOTGUN

Boxlock. 12 ga., 2.75- or 3-inch chambers. Bbls.: 28- or 30-inch vent rib; WinPlus choke tubes. Weight: 7-7.75 lbs. Checkered walnut buttstock and forend. Blued finish with scroll engraved receiver. Made from 1993-98.

Field model
(28-inch bbl., 3-inch) . . . . NiB $1067 Ex $873 Gd $623
Sporting
Clays . . . . NiB $1190 Ex $970 Gd $690
Sporting
Clays Lite. NiB $1103 Ex $901 Gd $643

MODEL 1200
DEER GUN . . . . NiB $282 Ex $232 Gd $131

Same as standard Model 1200, except has special 22-inch bbl. with rifle-type sights, for rifled slug or buckshot; 12 ga. only. Weight: 6.5 lbs. Made from 1965-74.

MODEL 1200 DEFENDER SERIES
SLIDE-ACTION SECURITY SHOTGUNS

Hammerless. 12 ga. w/3-inch chamber. 18-inch bbl. w/cylinder bore and metal front bead or rifle sights. Four- or 7-round magazine. Weight: 5.5 to 6.75 lbs. 25.6 inches (PG Model) or 38.6 inches overall. Matte blue finish. Synthetic pistol grip or walnut finished hardwood buttstock w/grooved synthetic or hardwood slide handle. NOTE: Even though the 1200 series was introduced in 1964 and was supplanted by the Model 1300 in 1978, the Security series (including the Defender model) was marketed under 1200 series alpha-numeric product codes (G1200DM2R) until 1989. In 1990, the same Defender model was marketed under a 4-digit code (7715) and was then advertised in the 1300 series.

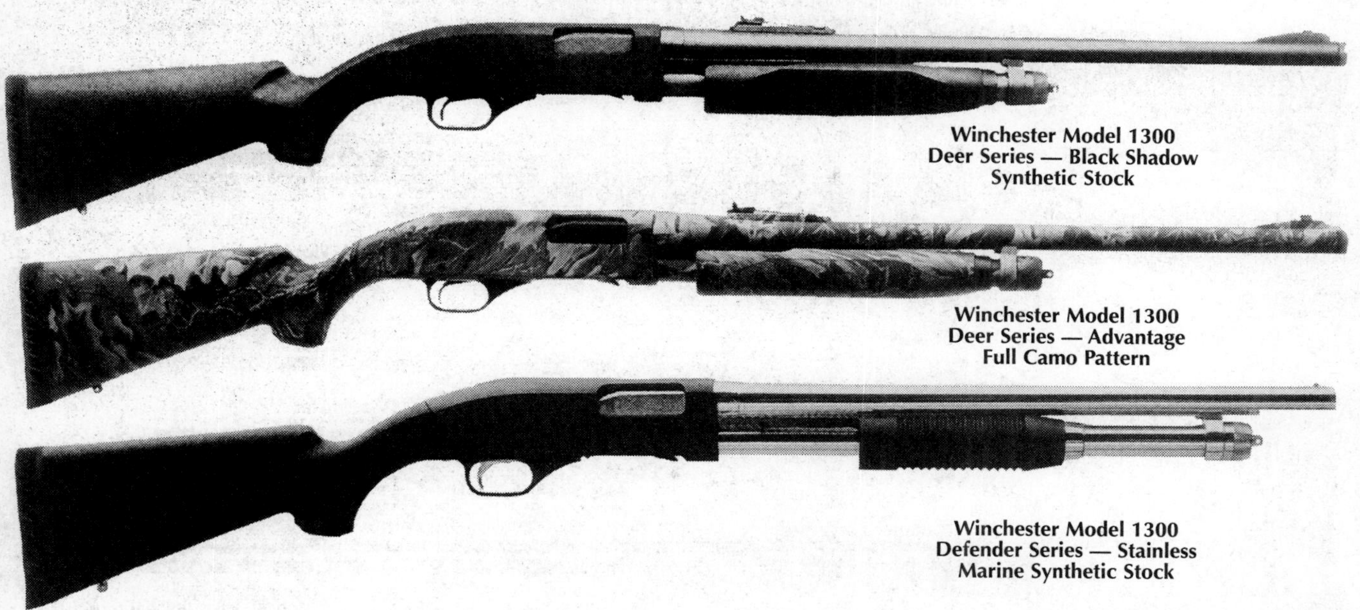

Winchester Model 1300
Deer Series — Black Shadow
Synthetic Stock

Winchester Model 1300
Deer Series — Advantage
Full Camo Pattern

Winchester Model 1300
Defender Series — Stainless
Marine Synthetic Stock

Defender
w/hardwood stock,bead sight . . . . . NiB $241 Ex $199 Gd $145
Defender
W/hardwood stock, rifle sights . . . . NiB $254 Ex $210 Gd $152
Defender model w/pistol-grip stock . . . NiB $261 Ex $215 Gd $155
Defender Combo model
W/extra 28-inch plain bbl. . . . . NiB $292 Ex $240 Gd $173
Defender Combo model
W/extra 28-inch vent rib bbl. . . . . . NiB $312 Ex $255 Gd $184

MODEL 1200 FIELD GUN — MAGNUM
Same as standard Model 1200 except chambered for 3-inch 12 and 20 ga. magnum shells; plain or vent-rib bbl., 28- or 30-inch, F choke. Weight: 7.38 to 7.88 lbs. Made from 1964-83.
With plain bbl. . . . . NiB $273 Ex $215 Gd $155
With vent rib bbl. . . . . NiB $288 Ex $237 Gd $171
Add for Winchester recoil reduction system $65

MODEL 1200 RANGER
SLIDE-ACTION SHOTGUN. . . . . NiB $260 Ex $215 Gd $155
Hammerless. 12 and 20 ga.; 3-inch chambers. Walnut finished hardwood stock, ribbed forearm. 28-inch vent-rib bbl.; Winchoke system. Weight: 7.25 lbs. Made from 1982 to 1990 by U. S. Repeating Arms.

MODEL 1200 RANGER YOUTH
SLIDE-ACTION SHOTGUN. . . . . NiB $254 Ex $210 Gd $152
Same general specifications as standard Ranger Slide-Action except chambered for 20 ga. only, has Four round magazine, recoil pad on buttstock, weight: 6.5 lbs. Mfd. by U. S. Repeating Arms.

MODEL 1200 SLIDE-ACTION FIELD GUN
Front-locking rotary bolt. Takedown. Four round magazine. Gauges: 12, 16, 20 (2.75-inch chamber). Bbl.: Plain or vent rib; 26-, 28-, 30-inch; IC, M, F choke or with Winchoke (interchangeable tubes IC-M-F). Weight: 6.5 to 7.25 lbs. Checkered pistol-grip stock and fore arm (slide handle), recoil pad; also avail. 1966-70 w/Winchester recoil reduction system (Cycolac stock). Made from 1964-83.
With plain bbl. . . . . NiB $256 Ex $212 Gd $154
With vent rib bbl. . . . . NiB $269 Ex $221 Gd $161
Add for Winchester recoil reduction system $65
Add for Winchoke $25

MODEL 1200 STAINLESS
MARINE SERIES SLIDE-ACTION
SECURITY SHOTGUN
Similar to Model 1200 Defender except w/6-round magazine. 18-inch bbl. of ordnance stainless steel w/cylinder bore and rifle sights. Weight: 7 lbs. Bright chrome finish. Synthetic pistol grip or walnut finished hardwood buttstock w/grooved synthetic or hardwood slide handle.Made from 1984-90.
Marine model w/hardwood stock . . NiB $288 Ex $227 Gd $120
Marine model w/pistol-grip stock . NiB $288 Ex $227 Gd $120

MODEL 1200 STAINLESS
POLICE SERIES SLIDE-ACTION
SECURITY SHOTGUN
Similar to Model 1200 Defender except w/6-round magazine. 18-inch bbl. of ordnance stainless steel w/cylinder bore and rifle sights. Weight: 7 lbs. Matte chrome finish. Synthetic pistol grip or walnut-finished hardwood buttstock w/grooved synthetic or hardwood slide handle.Made from 1984-90.
Police model w/hardwood stock . . . NiB $309 Ex $253 Gd $186
Police model w/pistol grip stock . . . NiB $369 Ex $404 Gd $219

MODEL 1200 TRAP GUN
Same as standard Model 1200 except 12 gauge only. Has 2-round magazine, 30-inch vent-rib bbl., Full choke or 28-inch with Winchoke. Semi-fancy walnut stock, straight Made from 1965-73. Also available 1966-70 with Winchester recoil reduction system.
With straight-trap stock. . . . . NiB $368 Ex $303 Gd $221
With Monte Carlo stock . . . . NiB $447 Ex $366 Gd $263
Add for Winchester recoil reduction system $75
Add for Winchoke $30

Winchester Model 1300
Lady Defender — Synthetic Full Stock

Winchester Model 1300
Lady Defender — Synthetic Pistol Grip Stock

Winchester Model 1300
Defender 5-Shot Combo

Winchester Model 1300
Turkey Gun

Winchester Model 1300
XTR w/Winchoke

Winchester Model 1300
Magnum Waterfowl

MODEL 1200 RANGER COMBINATION SHOTGUN...... NiB $309 Ex $255 Gd $186
Same as Ranger Deer combination except has one 28-inch vent-rib bbl. with M choke and one 18-inch Police Cyl. bore bbl. Made from 1987-90.

MODEL 1200 SKEET GUN .... NiB $379 Ex $310 Gd $223
Same as standard Model 1200 except 12 and 20 ga. only; has 2-round magazine, specially tuned trigger, 26-inch vent-rib bbl. SK choke, semi-fancy walnut stock and forearm. Weight: 7.25 to 7.5 lbs. Made 1965-73. Also avail. 1966-70 with Winchester recoil reduction system (add $50 to value).

MODEL 1300 CAMOPACK .... NiB $421 Ex $345 Gd $247
Gauge: 12.3-inch Magnum. Four round magazine. Bbls.: 30-and 22-inch with Winchoke system. Weight: 7 lbs. Laminated stock with Win-Cam camouflage green, cut checkering, recoil pad, swivels and sling. Made from 1987-88.

MODEL 1300 DEER SERIES
Similar to standard Model 1300 except 12 or 20 ga. only w/special 22-inch cyl. bore or rifled bbl. and rifle-type sights. Weight: 6.5 lbs. Checkered walnut or synthetic stock w/satin walnut, black or Advantage Full Camo Pattern finish. Matte blue or full-camo metal finish. Made from 1994 to 2006.
Deer model w/walnut stock (intro. 1994)...... NiB $394 Ex $324 Gd $233
Black Shadow Deer w/synthetic stock (intro. 1994).... NiB $281 Ex $233 Gd $171
Advantage Full Camo Pattern (1995-98) .... NiB $381 Ex $312 Gd $225
Deer Combo w/22- and 28-inch bbls. (1994-98).... NiB $341 Ex $281 Gd $170
W/rifled bbl. (intro. 1996), add....................... $25

MODEL 1300 DEFENDER SERIES
Gauges: 12 or 20 ga. 18- 24- 28-inch vent rib bbl. w/3-inch chamber. Four-, 7- or 8- round magazine. Weight: 5.6 to 7.4 lbs. Blued, chrome or matte stainless finish. Wood or synthetic stock. Made from 1985 to 2006.
Combo model .... NiB $475 Ex $388 Gd $278
Hardwood stock model.......... NiB $285 Ex $236 Gd $173
Synthetic pistol-grip model .... NiB $312 Ex $257 Gd $186
Synthetic stock .... NiB $299 Ex $246 Gd $180
Lady Defender synthetic Stock (made 1996) .... NiB $319 Ex $272 Gd $190
Lady Defender synthetic Pistol-grip (made 1996).......... NiB $287 Ex $237 Gd $174
Stainless marine synthetic stock ... NiB $454 Ex $372 Gd $265

MODEL 1300 DELUXE SLIDE-ACTION
Gauges: 12 and 20 w/3-inch chamber. Four round magazine. Bbl.:22, 26 or 28 inch vent rib bbl. w/Winchoke tubes. Weight: 6.5 lbs. Checkered walnut buttstock and forend w/high luster finish. Polished blue metal finish with roll-engraved receiver. Made from 1984 to 2006.
Model 1300 Deluxe w/high gloss finish.............. NiB $395 Ex $324 Gd $232
Model 1300 Ladies/Youth w/22-inch bbl.(disc. 1992) .... NiB $352 Ex $289 Gd $209

MODEL 1300 FEATHERWEIGHT SLIDE-ACTION SHOTGUN
Hammerless. Takedown. Four round magazine. Gauges: 12 and 20 (3-inch chambers). Bbls.: 22, 26 or 28 inches w/plain or vent rib w/Winchoke tubes. Weight: 6.38 to 7 lbs. Checkered walnut buttstock, grooved slide handle. Made from 1978-94.
Model 1300 FW (plain bbl.) ...... NiB $319 Ex $262 Gd $190
Model 1300 FW (vent rib) .... NiB $367 Ex $301 Gd $218
Model 1300 FW XTR .... NiB $381 Ex $312 Gd $225

MODEL 1300 RANGER SERIES
Gauges: 12 or 20 ga. w/3-inch chamber. Five round magazine. 22-(Rifled), 26- or 28-inch vent-rib bbl. w/Winchoke tubes. Weight: 7.25 lbs. Blued finish. Walnut-finished hardwood buttstock and forend. Made from 1984 to 2006.
Standard model .... NiB $325 Ex $268 Gd $194
Combo model .... NiB $389 Ex $319 Gd $229
Ranger Deer combo (D&T w/rings & bases) .... NiB $408 Ex $334 Gd $239
Ranger Ladies/Youth .... NiB $332 Ex $273 Gd $197

MODEL 1300 SLIDE-ACTION FIELD GUN
Takedown w/front-locking rotary bolt. Gauges: •12, 20 w/3-inch chamber. Four round magazine. Bbl.: Vent rib; 26-, 28-, 30-inch w/ Win-choke tubes IC-M-F). Weight: 7.25 lbs. Checkered walnut or synthetic stock w/standard, black or Advantage Full Camo Pattern finish. Matte blue or full-camo metal finish. Made from 1994 to 2006.
Model 1300 Standard Field (w/walnut stock) .... NiB $297 Ex $245 Gd $179
Model 1300 Black Shadow (w/black synthetic stock)......... NiB $258 Ex $215 Gd $157
Model 1300 Advantage Camo ..... NiB $359 Ex $296 Gd $212

MODEL 1300 SLUG HUNTER SERIES
Similar to standard Model 1300 except chambered 12 ga. only w/special 22-inch smoothbore w/sabot-rifled choke tube or fully rifled bbl. w/rifle-type sights. Weight: 6.5 lbs. Checkered walnut, hardwood or laminated stock w/satin walnut or WinTuff finish. Matte blue metal finish. Made from 1988-94.
Slug Hunter w/hardwood stock ... NiB $339 Ex $279 Gd $201
Slug Hunter w/laminated stock.... NiB $392 Ex $321 Gd $231
Slug Hunter w/walnut stock ...... NiB $365 Ex $300 Gd $217
Whitetails Unlimited w/beavertail forend .... NiB $373 Ex $305 Gd $220
W/sabot-rifled choke tubes, add $15

MODEL 1300 TURKEY SERIES
Gauges: 12 or 20 ga. 22-inch bbl. w/3-inch chamber. Four round magazine. 43 inches overall. Weight: 6.4 to 6.75 lbs. Buttstock and magazine cap, sling studs w/Cordura sling. Drilled and tapped to accept scope base. Checkered walnut, synthetic or laminated wood stock w/low luster finish. Matte blue or full camo finish. Made from 1985 to 2006.
Turkey Advantage Full Camo......... NiB $353 Ex $290 Gd $208
Turkey Realtree All-Purpose Full Camo.... NiB $383 Ex $313 Gd $226
Turkey Realtree Gray All-Purpose Full Camo .... NiB $395 Ex $324 Gd $232
Turkey Realtree All-Purpose Camo (matte metal) .... NiB $339 Ex $279 Gd $201
Turkey Black Shadow (black synthetic stock) .... NiB $245 Ex $203 Gd $150
Turkey Win-Cam (green laminated wood) ... NiB $358 Ex $294 Gd $212
Turkey Win-Cam Combo (22- and 30-inch bbls.) .... NiB $393 Ex $324 Gd $232
Turkey Win-Cam NWTF (22- and 30-inch bbls.) .... NiB $373 Ex $305 Gd $220
Turkey Win-Cam Youth/ Ladies model (20 ga.) .... NiB $437 Ex $357 Gd $575
Turkey Win-Tuf (br. laminated wood) .. NiB $367 Ex $302 Gd $219

MODEL 1300 WATERFOWL SLIDE-ACTION SHOTGUN
Similar to 1300 Standard model except has 28- or 30-inch vent rib bbl. w/Winchoke tubes. Weight: 7 lbs. Matte blue metal finish. Checkered walnut finished hardwood or brown laminated Win-Tuffwood stock w/camo sling, swivels and recoil pad. Made from 1984-92.
Model 1300 Waterfowl w/hardwood stock ... NiB $339 Ex $279 Gd $201
Model 1300 Waterfowl w/laminated stock.... NiB $365 Ex $300 Gd $217

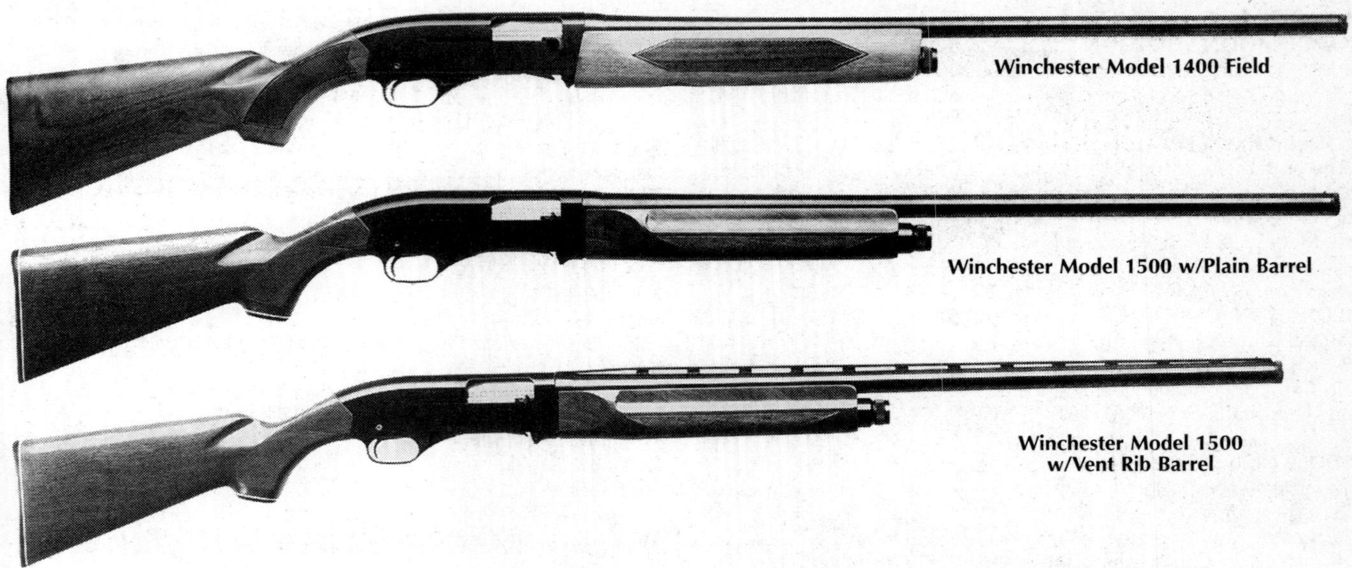

Winchester Model 1400 Field

Winchester Model 1500 w/Plain Barrel

Winchester Model 1500 w/Vent Rib Barrel

MODEL 1300 XTR SLIDE-ACTION . NiB $435 Ex $355 Gd $255
Hammerless. Takedown. Four shot magazine. Gauges: 12 and 20 (3-inch chambers). Bbl.: Plain or vent rib; 28-inch bbls.; Winchoke (interchangeable tubes IC-M-F). Weight: About 7 lbs. Disc. 2006.

MODEL 1400 AUTOMATIC FIELD GUN
Gas-operated. Front-locking rotary bolt. Takedown. Two round magazine. Gauges: 12, 16, 20 (2.75-inch chamber). Bbl.: Plain or vent rib; 26-, 28-, 30-inch; IC, M, F choke, or with Winchoke (interchangeable tubes IC-M-F). Weight: 6.5 to 7.25 lbs. Checkered pistol-grip stock and forearm, recoil pad, also available with Winchester recoil reduction system (Cycolac stock). Made from 1964-68.
With plain bbl. . . . . NiB $341 Ex $280 Gd $202
With vent rib bbl. . . . . NiB $371 Ex $304 Gd $219
Add for Winchester recoil reduction system $100
Add for Winchoke $25

MODEL 1400 DEER GUN . . . . NiB $339 Ex $279 Gd $211
Same as standard Model 1400 except has special 22-inch bbl. with rifle-type sights, for rifle slug or buckshot; 12 ga. only. Weight: 6.25 lbs. Made from 1965-68.

MODEL 1400 MARK II DEER GUN. NiB $389 Ex $319 Gd $229
Same general specifications as Model 1400 Deer Gun. Made from 1968-73.

MODEL 1400 MARK II FIELD GUN
Same general specifications as Model 1400 Field Gun, except not chambered for 16 gauge; Winchester Recoil Reduction System not available after 1970- only 28-inch barrels w/Winchoke offered after 1973. Made from 1968-78.
With plain bbl. . . . . NiB $359 Ex $295 Gd $212
With plain bbl. and Winchoke. . . . . NiB $386 Ex $316 Gd $230
With vent-rib bbl. . . . . NiB $406 Ex $332 Gd $238
With vent-rib bbl. and Winchoke . . NiB $435 Ex $355 Gd $255
Add for Winchester recoil reduction system $100

MODEL 1400 MARK II SKEET GUN. NiB $454 Ex $355 Gd $265
Same general specifications as Model 1400 Skeet Gun. Made from 1968-73.

MODEL 1400 MARK II TRAP GUN
Same general specifications as Model 1400 Trap Gun except also furnished with 28-inch bbl. and Winchoke. Winchester recoil reduction system not available after 1970. Made from 1968-73.
With straight stock . . . . NiB $499 Ex $409 Gd $294
With Monte Carlo stock . . . . NiB $546 Ex $447 Gd $321
With Winchester recoil reduction system, add $100
With Winchoke, add $25

MODEL 1400 MARK II UTILITY SKEET NiB $386 Ex $319 Gd $233
Same general specifications as Model 1400 Mark II Skeet Gun except has stock and forearm of field grade walnut. Made from 1970-73.

MODEL 1400 MARK II UTILITY TRAP . NiB $421 Ex $347 Gd $252
Same as Model 1400 Mark II Trap Gun except has Monte Carlo stock/forearm of field grade walnut. Made from 1970-73.

MODEL 1400 RANGER SEMIAUTOMATIC SHOTGUN . . . . NiB $299 Ex $246 Gd $180
Gauges: 12, 20. Two round magazine. 28-inch vent rib bbl. with F choke. Overall length: 48.63 inches. Weight: 7 to 7.25 lbs. Walnut finish, hardwood stock and forearm with cut checkering. Made from 1984 to 1990 by U. S. Repeating Arms.

MODEL 1400 RANGER SEMIAUTOMATIC DEER SHOTGUN. . . . . NiB $312 Ex $257 Gd $187
Same general specifications as Ranger Semiautomatic except 24.13-inch plain bbl. with rifle sights. Mfd. by U.S. Repeating Arms.

MODEL 1400 SKEET GUN . . . . NiB $426 Ex $348 Gd $249
Same as standard Model 1400 except 12 and 20 ga. only, 26-inch vent-rib bbl., SK choke, semi-fancy walnut stock and forearm. Weight: 7.25 to 7.5 lbs. Made from 1965-68. Also available with Winchester recoil reduction system (add $50 to value).

MODEL 1400 TRAP GUN
Same as standard Model 1400 except 12 ga. only with 30-inch vent-rib bbl., F choke. Semi-fancy walnut stock, straight or Monte Carlo trap style. Also available with Winchester recoil reduction system. Weight: About 8.25 lbs. Made from 1965-68.
With straight stock . . . . NiB $489 Ex $403 Gd $292
With Monte Carlo stock . . . . NiB $523 Ex $429 Gd $309

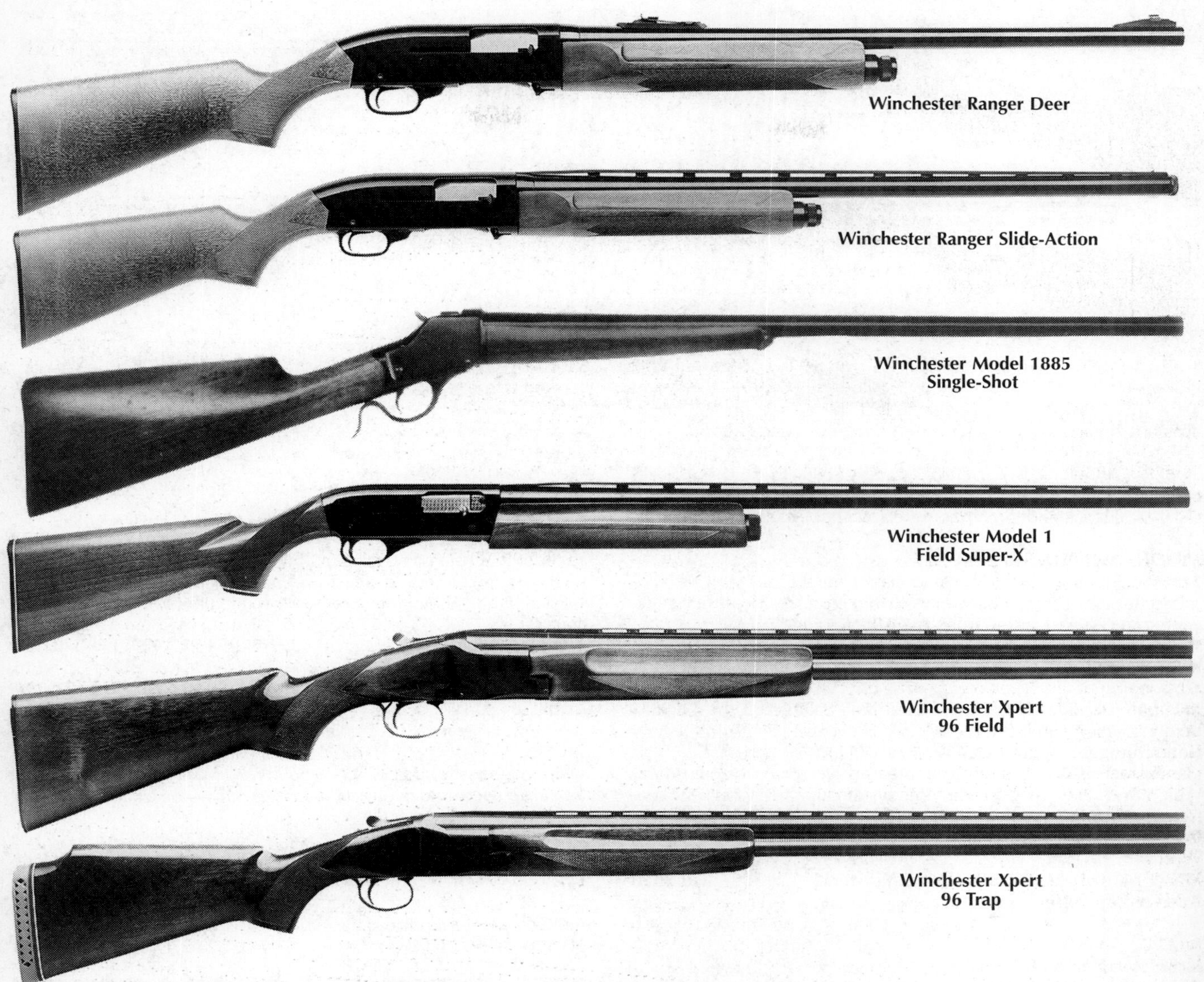

Winchester Ranger Deer

Winchester Ranger Slide-Action

Winchester Model 1885 Single-Shot

Winchester Model 1 Field Super-X

Winchester Xpert 96 Field

Winchester Xpert 96 Trap

MODEL 1500 XTR SEMIAUTOMATIC . . NiB $360 Ex $296 Gd $214
Gas-operated. Gauges: 12 and 20 (2.75-inch chambers). Bbl.: Plain or vent rib; 28-inch; WinChoke (interchangeable tubes IC-M-F). American walnut stock and forend; checkered grip and forend. Weight: 7.25 lbs. Made from 1978-82.

MODEL 1885
SINGLE-SHOT SHOTGUN . . . . NiB $3974 Ex $3240 Gd $2253
Falling-block action, same as Model 1885 Rifle. Highwall receiver. Solid frame or takedown. 20 ga. 3-inch chamber. 26-inch bbl.; plain, matted or matted rib; Cyl. bore, M or F choke. Weight: About 5.5 lbs. Straight-grip stock and forearm. Made from 1914-16.

MODEL 1887 LEVER-ACTION SHOTGUN
First of John Browning's patent shotgun designs produced by Winchester. 10 or 12 ga. on casehardened frame fitted w/20-inch blued, cylinder bore or full choke 30- or 32-inch bbl. Plain or checkered walnut stock and forend. Made from 1887 to 1901.
Model 1887 10 or 12 ga. standard . . . . NiB $2549 Ex $2070 Gd $1456
Model 1887 10 or 12 ga. deluxe. . . NiB $5296 Ex $4292 Gd $3007
Model 1887 10 or 12 ga. riot gun . . . . NiB $2435 Ex $1978 Gd $1393
W/.70-150 Ratchet rifled bbl.
.70 cal. rifle/87 produced) . . . . NiB $3474 Ex $2805 Gd $1976
W/3 or 4 blade Del. Damascus bbl., add. 20%

MODEL 1901 LEVER-ACTION SHOTGUN
Same general specifications as Model 1887, of which this is a redesigned version. 10 ga. only. Made from 1901-20.
Model 1901 Standard. . . . . NiB $2160 Ex $1761 Gd $1249
Model 1901 Deluxe . . . . NiB $2709 Ex $2199 Gd $1546

MODEL 1911 AUTO-
LOADING SHOTGUN. . . . . NiB $692 Ex $569 Gd $413
Hammerless. Takedown. 12 gauge only. Four round tubular magazine. Bbl.: plain, 26- to 32-inch, standard borings. Weight: About 8.5 lbs. Plain or checkered pistol-grip stock and forearm. Made from 1911-25.

RANGER DEER COMBINATION . . . NiB $322 Ex $263 Gd $188
Gauge: 12, 3-inch Magnum. Three round magazine. Bbl.: 24-inch Cyl. bore deer bbl. and 28-inch vent rib bbl. with WinChoke system. Weight: 7.25 lbs. Made from 1987-90.

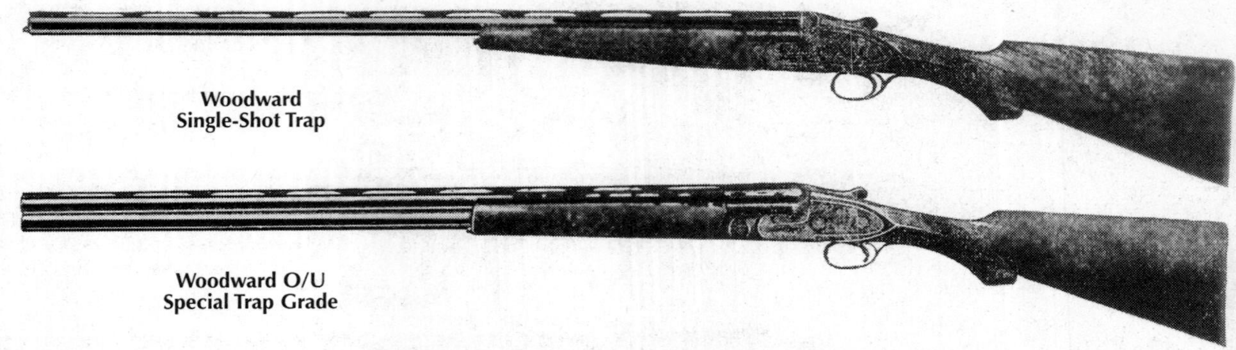

Woodward
Single-Shot Trap

Woodward O/U
Special Trap Grade

SUPER-X MODEL I AUTO FIELD GUN. . . . NiB $470 Ex $426 Gd $302
Gas-operated. Takedown.12 ga. 2.75-inch chamber Four round magazine. Bbl.: Vent rib 26-inch IC; 28-inch M or F; 30-inch F choke. Weight: About 7 lbs. Checkered pistol-grip stock. Made from 1974-84.

SUPER-X MODEL I SKEET GUN . . . NiB $790 Ex $635 Gd $449
Same as Super-X Field Gun except has 26-inch bbl., SK choke, skeet-style stock and forearm of select walnut. Made from 1974-84.

SUPER-X MODEL I TRAP GUN
Same as Super-X Field Gun except has 30-inch bbl., IM or F choke, trap-style stock (straight or Monte Carlo comb) and forearm of select walnut, recoil pad. Made from 1974-84.
With straight stock . . . . NiB $619 Ex $504 Gd $357
With Monte Carlo stock . . . . NiB $713 Ex $580 Gd $409

XPERT MODEL 96 O/U FIELD GUN . . . . NiB $1003 Ex $819 Gd $585
Boxlock action similar to Model 101. Plain receiver. Auto ejectors. Selective single trigger. Gauges: 12, 20. 3-inch chambers. Bbl.: Vent rib; 26-inch IC/M; 28-inch M/F, 30-inch F/F choke (12 ga. only). Weight: 6.25 to 8.25 lbs. depending on ga. and bbls. Checkered pistol-grip stock and forearm. Made from 1976-81 for Olin Corp. at its Olin-Kodensha facility in Japan.

XPERT MODEL 96 SKEET GUN. . . NiB $1061 Ex $887 Gd $620
Same as Xpert Field Gun except has 2.75-inch chambers, 27-inch bbls., SK choke, skeet-style stock and forearm. Made from 1976-1981.

XPERT MODEL 96 TRAP GUN
Same as Xpert Field Gun except 12 ga. only, 2.75-inch chambers, has 30-inch bbls., IM/F or F/F choke, trap-style stock (straight or Monte Carlo comb) with recoil pad. Made from 1976-81.
With straight stock . . . . NiB $975 Ex $799 Gd $572
With Monte Carlo stock . . . . NiB $1000 Ex $818 Gd $585

JAMES WOODWARD & SONS — London, England

James Woodward & Sons was acquired by James Purdey & Sons after World War II.

BEST QUALITY HAMMERLESS DOUBLE
Sidelock. Automatic ejectors. Double triggers or single trigger. Built to order in all standard gauges, bbl. lengths, boring and other specifications. Made as a field gun, pigeon and wildfowl gun, skeet gun or trap gun. Manufactured prior to World War II.
12 ga.
w/double triggers . . . . . . NiB $26,906 Ex $21,525 Gd $14,637
20 ga.
w/double triggers . . . . . . NiB $30,516 Ex $24,412 Gd $16,600
28 ga.
w/double triggers . . . . . . NiB $37,731 Ex $30,187 Gd $20,527
.410 ga.
w/double triggers . . . . . . NiB $42,656 Ex $34,125 Gd $23,205
W/selective single trigger, add 5%

BEST QUALITY
O/U SHOTGUN
Sidelock. Automatic ejectors. Double triggers or single trigger. Built to order in all standard gauges, bbl. lengths, boring and other specifications, including Special Trap Grade with vent rib. Woodward introduced this type of gun in 1908. Made until World War II.
12 ga.
w/double triggers . . . . . . NiB $29,531 Ex $23,425 Gd $16,065
20 ga.
w/double triggers . . . . . . NiB $39,703 Ex $31,762 Gd $21,598
28 ga.
w/double triggers . . . . . . NiB $52,172 Ex $41,737 Gd $28,381
.410 ga.
w/double triggers . . . . NiB $59,062 Ex $47,250+ Gd $32,130
W/single trigger, add 5%

BEST QUALITY
SINGLE-SHOT TRAP . . . . . . NiB $12,581 Ex $10,000 Gd $6924
Sidelock. Mechanical features of the O/U gun. Vent rib bbl. 12 ga. only. Built to customer's specifications and measurements, including type and amount of checkering, carving and engraving. Made prior to World War II.

ZEPHYR SHOTGUNS — Manufactured by Victor Sarasqueta Company, Eibar, Spain

MODEL 1
O/U SHOTGUN . . . . NiB $1311 Ex $1073 Gd $768
Same general specifications as Field Model O/U except with more elaborate engraving, finer wood and checkering. Imported by Stoeger 1930s-51.

MODEL 2
O/U SHOTGUN . . . . NiB $1688 Ex $1375 Gd $976
Sidelock. Auto ejectors. Gauges: 12, 16, 20, 28 and .410. Bbls.: 25 to 30 inches most common. Modest scroll engraving on receiver and sideplates. Checkered, straight-grain select walnut buttstock and forend. Imported by Stoeger 1930s-51.

MODEL 3
O/U SHOTGUN . . . . NiB $2296 Ex $1865 Gd $1314
Same general specifications as Zephyr Model 2 O/U except with more elaborate engraving, finer wood and checkering. Imported by Stoeger 1930s-51.

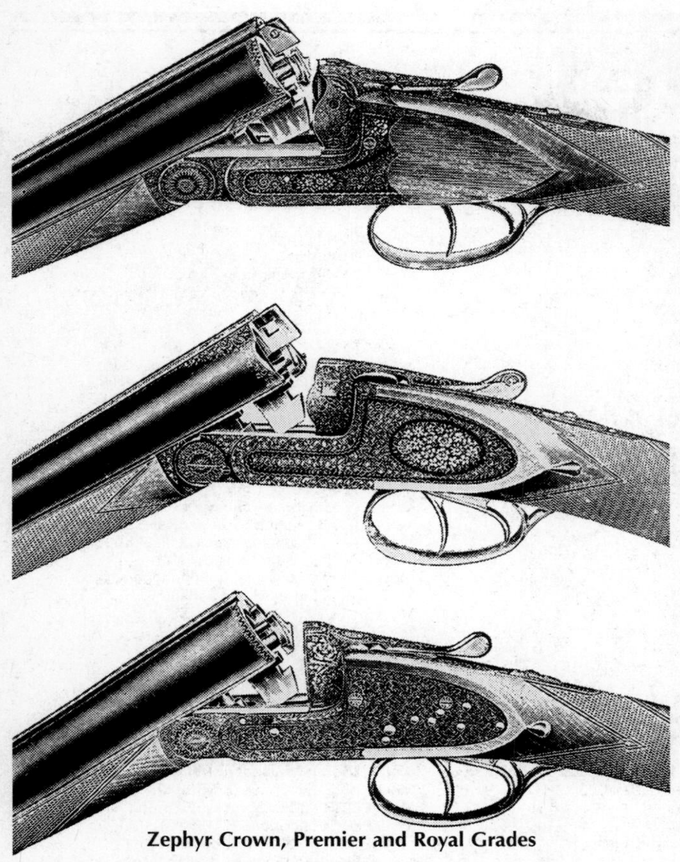

Zephyr Crown, Premier and Royal Grades

MODEL 400E FIELD GRADE DOUBLE-BARREL SHOTGUN
Anson & Deeley boxlock system. Gauges: 12 16, 20, 28 and .410. Bbls.: 25 to 30 inches. Weight: 4.5 lbs. (.410) to 6.25 lbs. (12 ga.). Checkered French walnut buttstock and forearm. Modest scroll engraving on bbls., receiver and trigger guard. Imported by Stoeger 1930s-50s.
12, 16 or 20 ga. . . . . NiB $1997 Ex $1235 Gd $874
28 or .410 ga. . . . . NiB $1692 Ex $1375 Gd $869
W/selective single trigger, add $200

MODEL 401 E SKEET GRADE DOUBLE-BARREL SHOTGUN
Same general specifications as Field Grade except with beavertail forearm. Bbls.: 25 to 28 inches. Imported by Stoeger 1930s-50s.
12, 16 or 20 ga. . . . . NiB $1788 Ex $1452 Gd $1022
28 or .410 ga. . . . . NiB $1963 Ex $1563 Gd $1120
W/selective single trigger, add $350
W/nonselective single trigger, add $250

MODEL 402E DELUXE
DOUBLE-BARREL SHOTGUN . . NiB $2263 Ex $1835 Gd $1287
Same general specifications as Model 400E Field Grade except for custom refinements. The action was carefully hand-honed for smoother operation; finer, elaborate engraving throughout, plus higher quality wood in stock and forearm. Imported by Stoeger 1930s-50s.

CROWN GRADE . . . . NiB $1634 Ex $1332 Gd $936
Boxlock. Gauges: 12, 16, 20, 28 and .410. Bbls.: 25 to 30 inches standard but any lengths could be ordered. Weight: 6 lbs., 4 oz. (.410) to 7 lbs., 4 oz. (12 ga.). Checkered Spanish walnut stock and beavertail forearm. Receiver engraved with scroll patterns. Imported by Stoeger 1938-51.

FIELD MODEL
O/U SHOTGUN . . . . NiB $802 Ex $652 Gd $462
Anson & Deeley boxlock. Auto ejectors. Gauges: 12, 16 and 20. Bbls.: 25 to 30 inches standard- full-length matt rib. Double triggers. Checkered buttstock and forend. Light scroll engraving on receiver. Imported by Stoeger 1930s-51.

HONKER SINGLE-SHOT SHOTGUN . . . . . NiB $560 Ex $458 Gd $327
Sidelock. Gauge: 10; 3.5-inch magnum. 36-inch vent rib barrel w/F choke. Weight: 10.5 lbs. Checkered select Spanish walnut buttstock and beavertail forend; recoil pad. Imported by Stoeger 1950s-72.

PINEHURST
DOUBLE-BARREL SHOTGUN . . . . NiB $1158 Ex $939 Gd $658
Boxlock. Gauges: 12, 16, 20, 28 and .410. Bbls.: 25 to 28 inches most common. Checkered, select walnut buttstock and forend. Selective single trigger and auto ejectors. Imported by Stoeger 1950s-72.

PREMIER GRADE
DOUBLE-BARREL SHOTGUN . . . . NiB $2492 Ex $2017 Gd $1409
Sidelock. Gauges: 12, 16, 20, 28 and .410. Bbls.: Any length, but 25 to 30 inches most popular. Weight: 4.5 lbs. (.410) to 7 lbs. (12 ga.). Checkered high-grade French walnut buttstock and forend. Imported by Stoeger 1930s-51.

ROYAL GRADE
DOUBLE-BARREL SHOTGUN . . . . NiB $3811 Ex $1078 Gd $2141
Same general specifications as the Premier Grade except with more elaborate engraving, finer checkering and wood. Imported by Stoeger 1930s-51.

STERLINGWORTH II
DOUBLE-BARREL SHOTGUN . . . . NiB $1011 Ex $826 Gd $591
Genuine sidelocks with color-casehardened sideplates. Gauges: 12, 16, 20 and .410. Bbls.: 25 to 30 inches. Weight: 6 lbs., 4 oz. (.410) to 7 lbs., 4 oz. (12 ga.). Select Spanish walnut buttstock and beavertail forearm. Light scroll engraving on receiver and sideplates. Automatic, sliding-tang safety. Imported by Stoeger 1950s-72.

THUNDERBIRD
DOUBLE-BARREL SHOTGUN . . . NiB $1012 Ex $827 Gd $592
Sidelock. Gauges: 12 and 10 Magnum. Bbls.: 32-inch, both F choke. Weight: 8 lbs., 8 oz. (12 ga.), 12 lbs. (10 ga.). Receiver elaborately engraved with waterfowl scenes. Checkered select Spanish walnut buttstock and beavertail forend. Plain extractors, double triggers. Imported by Stoeger 1950-72.

UPLAND KING
DOUBLE-BARREL SHOTGUN . . . NiB $1166 Ex $952 Gd $678
Sidelock. Gauges: 12, 16, 20, 28 and .410. Bbls.: 25 to 28 inches most popular. Checkered buttstock and forend of select walnut. Selective single trigger and auto ejectors. Imported by Stoeger 1950-72.

UPLANDER 4E
DOUBLE-BARREL SHOTGUN . . . . NiB $959 Ex $785 Gd $563
Same general specifications as the Zephyr Sterlingworth II except with selective auto ejectors and highly polished sideplates. Imported by Stoeger 1951-72.

WOODLANDER II
DOUBLE-BARREL SHOTGUN . . . . NiB $677 Ex $554 Gd $399
Boxlock. Gauges: 12, 20 and .410. Bbls.: 25 to 30 inches. Weight: 6 lbs., 4 oz. (.410) to 7 lbs., 4 oz. (12 ga.). Checkered Spanish walnut stock and beavertail forearm. Engraved receiver. Imported by Stoeger 1950-72.

Index

INDEX

INDEX

INDEX

INDEX

INDEX

INDEX

INDEX